THE ALASKA
WILDERNESS
GUIDE

Vernon Publications Inc.
3000 Northup Way, Suite 200, Box 96043
Bellevue, WA 98009-9643

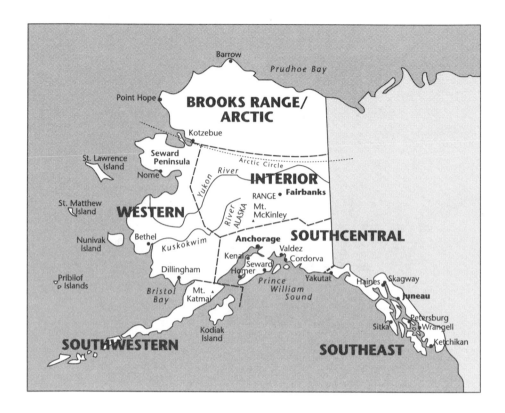

COVER—Photo by © Karen Jettmar.

MILEPOST Publications Editor, Kris Valencia Graef.
Associate Editor, Abigail Reid Francis.

Production Manager, Jon Flies.
Publication Artists: David Ranta, Chris Knox.
Illustrations, Carol Haffar.
Cartography: David Berger, David A. Shott.

Fulfillment Manager, Jessica Raefsky.

Associate Publisher, Michele Andrus Dill.
Publisher, Geoffrey P. Vernon.

ISBN 1-878425-50-1   ISSN 1070-003X
Key title: The Alaska Wilderness Guide
Printed on recyclable, acid-free paper.
Printed in U.S.A.

Vernon Publications Inc.
3000 Northup Way, Suite 200, Box 96043
Bellevue, WA 98009-9643
(206) 827-9900, 1-800-726-4707

Publishers of:
The MILEPOST®
The ALASKA WILDERNESS GUIDE
NORTHWEST MILEPOSTS®
ALASKA A-Z

CONTENTS

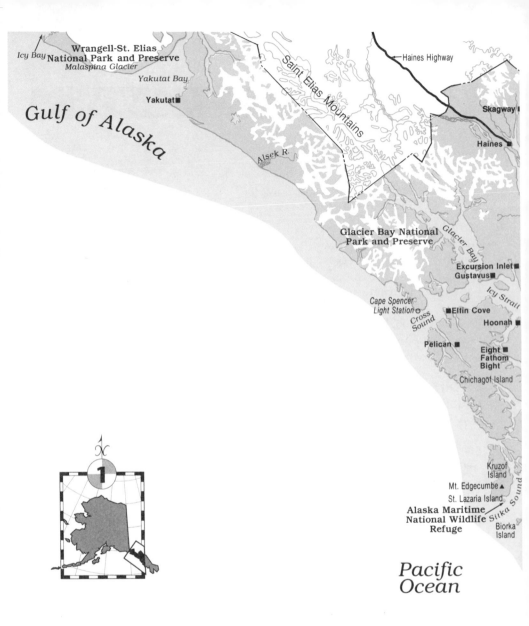

Wrangell-St. Elias
Icy Bay **National Park and Preserve**
Malaspina Glacier

Yakutat Bay

Yakutat■

Saint Elias Mountains

←Haines Highway

Skagway

Haines■

Gulf of Alaska

Alsek R.

**Glacier Bay National
Park and Preserve**

Glacier Bay

Excursion Inlet
Gustavus■

Icy Strait

*Cape Spencer
Light Station*○

*Cross
Sound*

■**Elfin Cove**

Hoonah ■

Pelican ■

Eight ■
**Fathom
Bight**

Chichagof Island

N
①

Kruzof
Island

Mt. Edgecumbe ▲

St. Lazaria Island

**Alaska Maritime
National Wildlife
Refuge**

Sitka Sound

Biorka
Island

Pacific
Ocean

Wilderness Areas of
Tongass National Forest

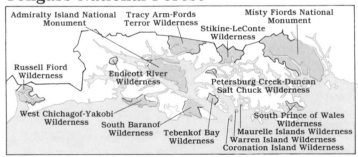

Admiralty Island National
Monument

Tracy Arm-Fords
Terror Wilderness

Misty Fiords National
Monument

Stikine-LeConte
Wilderness

Russell Fiord
Wilderness

Endicott River
Wilderness

Petersburg Creek-Duncan
Salt Chuck Wilderness

West Chichagof-Yakobi
Wilderness

South Baranof
Wilderness

Tebenkof Bay
Wilderness

South Prince of Wales
Wilderness
Maurelle Islands Wilderness
Warren Island Wilderness
Coronation Island Wilderness

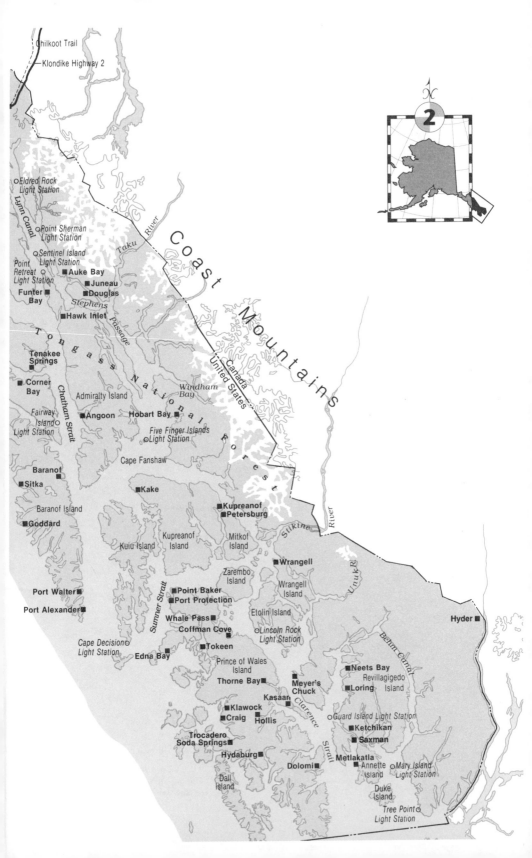

Chilkoot Trail

Klondike Highway 2

Coast Mountains

Taku River

Canada
United States

○ Eldred Rock
Light Station

Lynn Canal

○ Point Sherman
Light Station

○ Sentinel Island
Light Station

Point
Retreat ○
Light Station

■ Auke Bay

■ Juneau

■ Douglas

Funter ■
Bay

■ Hawk Inlet

Stephens

Passage

Tongass National Forest

Windham
Bay

■ Tenakee
Springs

■ Corner
Bay

Admiralty Island

Chatham Strait

Fairway
Island ○
Light Station

■ Angoon

■ Hobart Bay

Five Finger Islands
○ Light Station

Cape Fanshaw

■ Baranof

■ Sitka

■ Kake

Baranof Island

■ Kupreanof

■ Goddard

Kupreanof
Island

Kuiu Island

Mitkof
Island

■ Petersburg

Stikine River

■ Wrangell

Port Walter ■

Port Alexander ■

Sumner Strait

■ Point Baker

■ Port Protection

Whale Pass ■

Coffman Cove ■

Zarembo
Island

Wrangell
Island

Etolin Island

○ Lincoln Rock
Light Station

Unuk R.

■ Hyder

Cape Decision ○
Light Station

■ Edna Bay

■ Tokeen

Prince of Wales
Island

■ Thorne Bay

■ Meyer's
Chuck

■ Neets Bay

■ Loring

Revillagigedo
Island

Behm Canal

■ Kasaan

Clarence

■ Klawock

■ Craig

Hollis

○ Guard Island Light Station

■ Ketchikan

Trocadero ■
Soda Springs

■ Hydaburg

■ Dolomi

Strait

■ Saxman

Metlakatla ■
■ Annette
Island

○ Mary Island
Light Station

Dall
Island

Duke
Island

Tree Point ○
Light Station

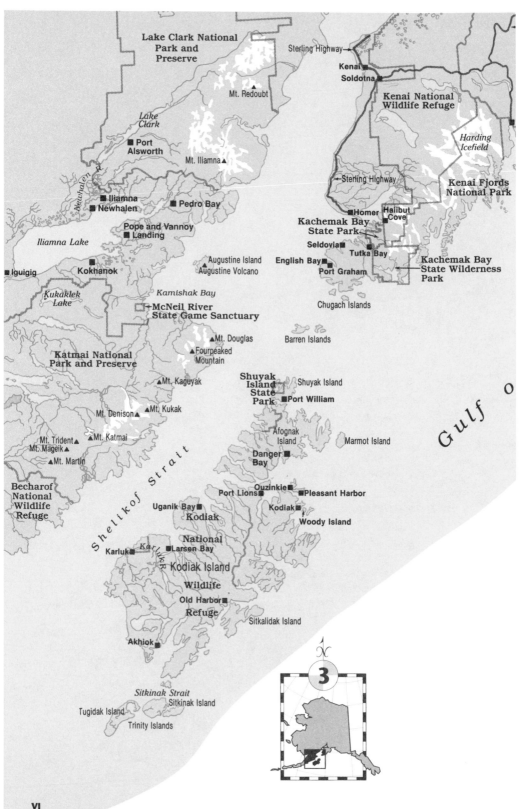

Lake Clark National Park and Preserve

Sterling Highway→

Kenai
Soldotna

Kenai National
Wildlife Refuge

Mt. Redoubt

Lake
Clark

Harding
Icefield

Port
Alsworth

Mt. Iliamna▲

←Sterling Highway

Kenai Fjords
National Park

Iliamna
Newhalen

Pedro Bay

←Homer
Halibut
Cove

Kachemak Bay
State Park

Pope and Vannoy
Landing

Seldovia

Kachemak Bay
State Wilderness
Park

Iliamna Lake

English Bay
Tutka Bay

Port Graham

■Iguigig

Kokhanok

Augustine Island
Augustine Volcano

Chugach Islands

Kukaklek
Lake

Kamishak Bay

McNeil River
State Game Sanctuary

▲Mt. Douglas

Barren Islands

Katmai National
Park and Preserve

▲Fourpeaked
Mountain

▲Mt. Kaguyak

Shuyak
Island
State
Park

Shuyak Island

■Port William

Mt. Denison▲ ▲Mt. Kukak

Afognak
Island

Marmot Island

Mt. Trident▲
Mt. Mageik▲

▲Mt. Katmai

Danger
Bay

▲Mt. Martin

Becharof
National
Wildlife
Refuge

Ouzinkie■
Port Lions■

■Pleasant Harbor

Uganik Bay■

Kodiak■

Shelikof Strait

Kodiak

Woody Island

National

Karluk■ *Karluk R.*

■Larsen Bay

Kodiak Island

Wildlife

Old Harbor■

Refuge

Sitkalidak Island

Akhiok■

Sitkinak Strait
Sitkinak Island

Tugidak Island

Trinity Islands

Gulf o

3

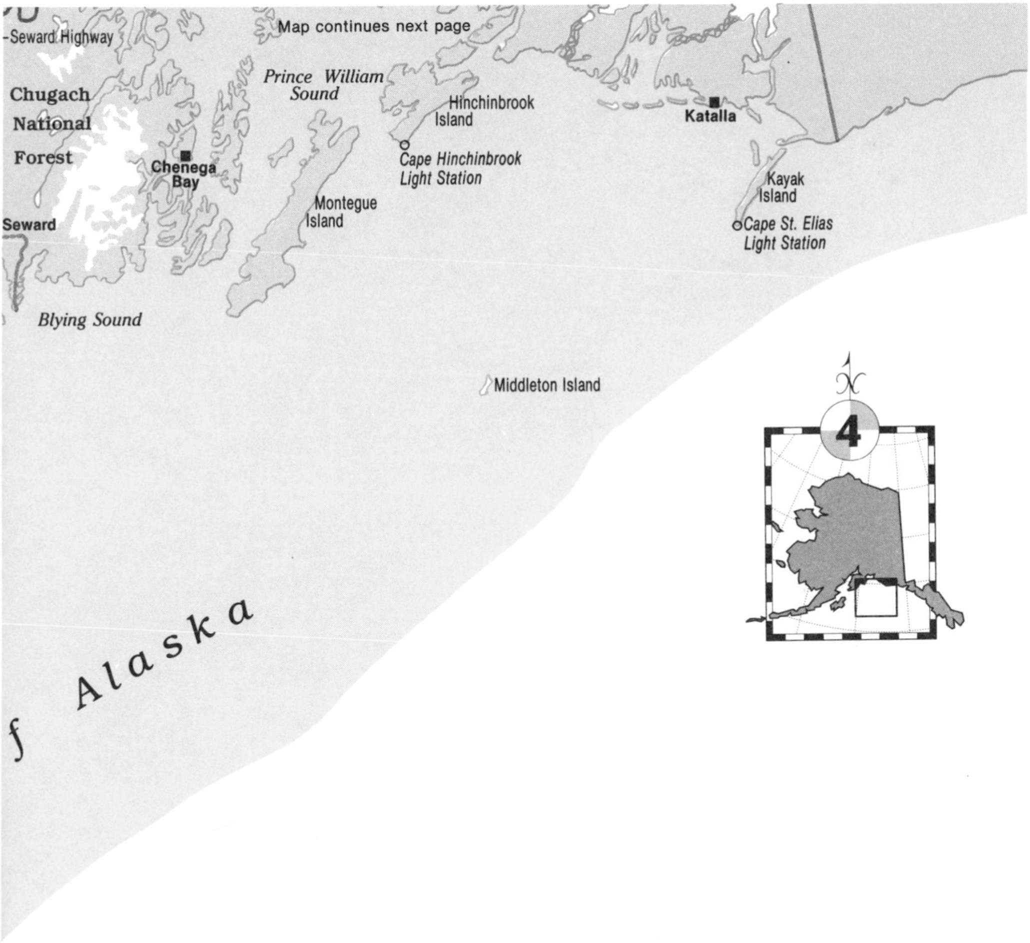

-Seward Highway

Map continues next page

Chugach
National
Forest

Prince William
Sound

Hinchinbrook
Island

Katalla

Chenega
Bay

Cape Hinchinbrook
Light Station

Kayak
Island

Seward

Montegue
Island

○Cape St. Elias
Light Station

Blying Sound

Middleton Island

f *A l a s k a*

4

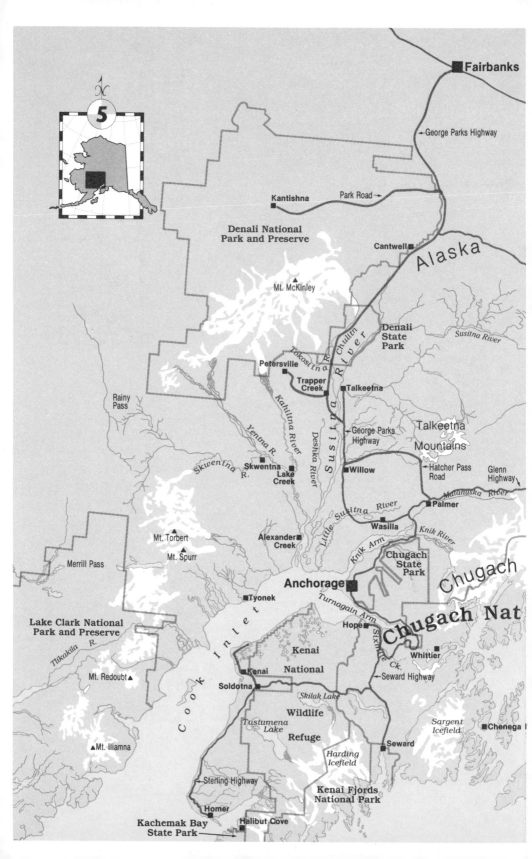

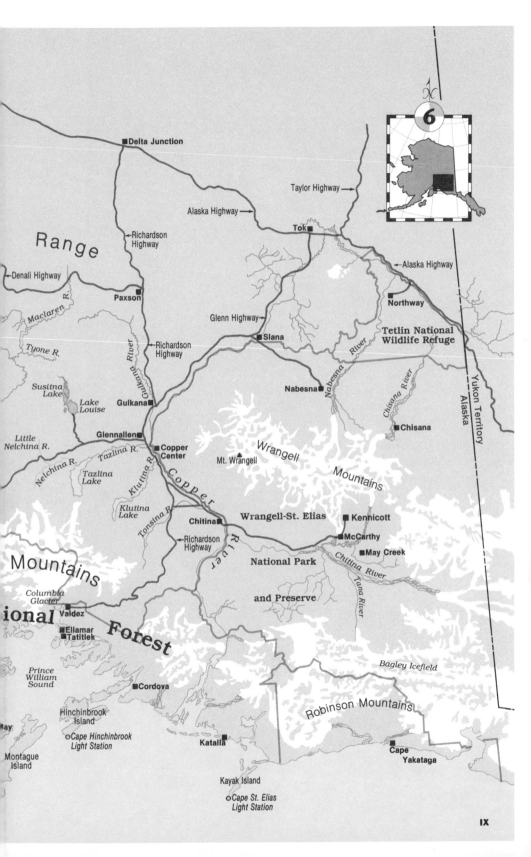

Delta Junction

Taylor Highway →

Alaska Highway →

← Richardson
Highway

Range

← Denali Highway

Tok

← Alaska Highway

Northway

Paxson

Glenn Highway →

Maclaren R.

Tetlin National
Wildlife Refuge

Tyone R.

← Richardson
Highway

Slana

Susitna
Lake

Lake
Louise

Gulkana

Nabesna

Nabesna River

Chisana River

Chisana

Little
Nelchina R.

Glennallen

Copper
Center

Mt. Wrangell

Wrangell

Mountains

Yukon Territory

Alaska

Nelchina R.

Tazlina R.

Klutina R.

Tazlina
Lake

Klutina
Lake

Tonsina R.

Copper River

Chitina

Wrangell-St. Elias

Kennicott

McCarthy

May Creek

← Richardson
Highway

National Park

Chitina River

Tana River

Mountains

and Preserve

Columbia
Glacier

Valdez

Forest

Ellamar
Tatitlek

Bagley Icefield

ional

Prince
William
Sound

Cordova

Robinson Mountains

Hinchinbrook
Island

ay

○ Cape Hinchinbrook
Light Station

Montague
Island

Katalla

Cape
Yakataga

Kayak Island

○ Cape St. Elias
Light Station

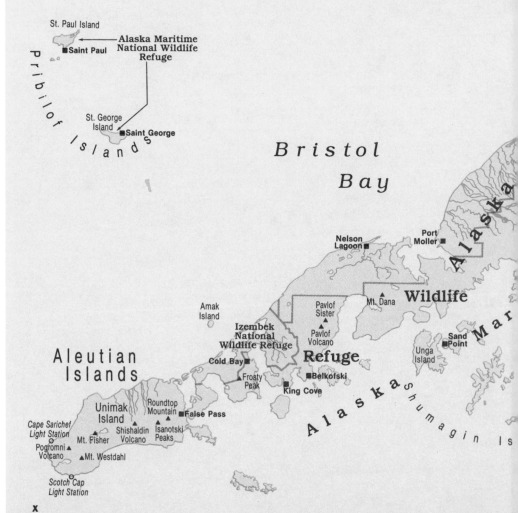

St. Paul Island

Alaska Maritime
National Wildlife
Refuge

■Saint Paul

P r i b i l o f   I s l a n d s

St. George
Island

■Saint George

B r i s t o l

B a y

Nelson
Lagoon ■

Port
Moller ■

A l a s k a

Mt. Dana ▲

Wildlife

Pavlof
Sister ▲

M a r

Amak
Island

Izembek
National
Wildlife Refuge

Pavlof
Volcano ▲

Refuge

Sand
Point ■

Unga
Island

Aleutian
Islands

Cold Bay ■

Belkofski ■

A l a s k a

S h u m a g i n   I s

Frosty
Peak ▲

King Cove ■

Roundtop
Mountain ▲

■False Pass

Unimak
Island

Cape Sarichef
Light Station

Shishaldin
Volcano ▲

Isanotski
Peaks ▲

Mt. Fisher ▲

Pogromni ▲
Volcano

▲ Mt. Westdahl

Scotch Cap
Light Station

Mt. Douglas▲

▲ Fourpeaked Mountain

Katmai National Park and Preserve

Grosvenor Lake

Mt. Kaguyak▲

Naknek ■ King Salmon ■

Naknek Lake

Kvichak Bay

South Naknek ■

Lake Camp ■

Brooks Camp ■

Mt. Denison ▲ ▲Mt. Kukak

Mt. Griggs ▲
Mt. Novarupta ▲ ▲Mt. Katmai
Mt. Trident ▲

King

Salmon River

Egegik R.

Mt. Mageik ▲

Egegik ■

Mt. Martin ▲

Shelikof Strait

Becharof National Wildlife Refuge

Becharof Lake

Mt. Peulik ▲

Kodiak Island

Pilot Point ■

Ugashik Lakes

Ugashik ■

Alaska

N a t i o n a l   W i l d l i f e   R e f u g e

Mt. Chiginagak ▲

Peninsula

Port Heiden ■

Mt. Aniakchak ▲

Aniakchak R.

Peninsula

Aniakchak National Monument and Preserve

Aniakchak Bay

National

Chignik Bay

Chignik Lagoon ■ ■Chignik

■ Chignik Lake

Mt. Veniaminof ▲

vanof 3ay

■ Perryville

itime

N a t i o n a l

Pacific Ocean

l a n d s

8

XI

9

Bering Sea

Aleutian
Islands

Chagulak
Island   Mt. Yunaska
▲

Mt. Korovin ▲ ▲ Mt. Sarichef   Mt. Amukta   Yunaska
Mt. Kliuchef ▲   ▲   Island

Mt. Koniuji   Mt. Seguam   Amukta
▲   ▲   Island

Great   ■ Atka
Sitkin Island   Atka Island   Seguam
▲   Island
Great Sitkin   Seguam Pass
Volcano   Amlia Island

A l a s k a   M a r i t i m e   N

Map continues below

B e r i n g

Attu
Attu
Island   Shemya   A l e u t i a
              Island
              ■ Shemya
Semichi Islands
Near Islands   Buldir
                                Volcano   Kiska
Agattu   ▲   Volcano
Island   Buldir Island   Kiska   ▲
                                               Kiska   Island

10   A l a s k a   R a t

A l a s k a   M a r i t i m e   N a   I s l

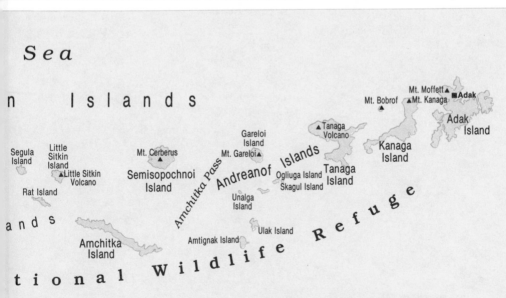

Akutan
Island

Akun
Island

Mt. Akutan▲ ■Akutan

Krenitzin Islands

Mt. Bogoslof ▲

Makushin ▲ ■Dutch Harbor
Volcano ■Unalaska

Islands

Unalaska
Island

Mt. Okmok ▲
Umnak
Island

Fox

Islands

of Four Mountains Pass ▲Mt. Vsevidof

Mt. Kagamil▲ Kagamil
Island
Anangula
Island

■Nikolski

Refuge

▲Mt. Carlisle
▲Mt. Cleveland

Samalga

Herbert
Island

ational Wildlife

Pacific Ocean

Sea

n Islands

Mt. Moffett▲
Mt. Bobrof ▲Mt. Kanaga ■Adak
▲

Adak
Island

Tanaga ▲
Volcano

Segula
Island

Little
Sitkin
Island

Gareloi
Island

Mt. Cerberus ▲Mt. Gareloi▲
▲

Islands

Kanaga
Island

▲Little Sitkin
Volcano

Semisopochnoi
Island

Amchitka Pass

Andreanof

Ogliuga Island
Skagul Island

Tanaga
Island

Rat Island

Unalga
Island

nds

Amchitka
Island

Ulak Island
Amtignak Island

tional Wildlife Refuge

Pacific Ocean

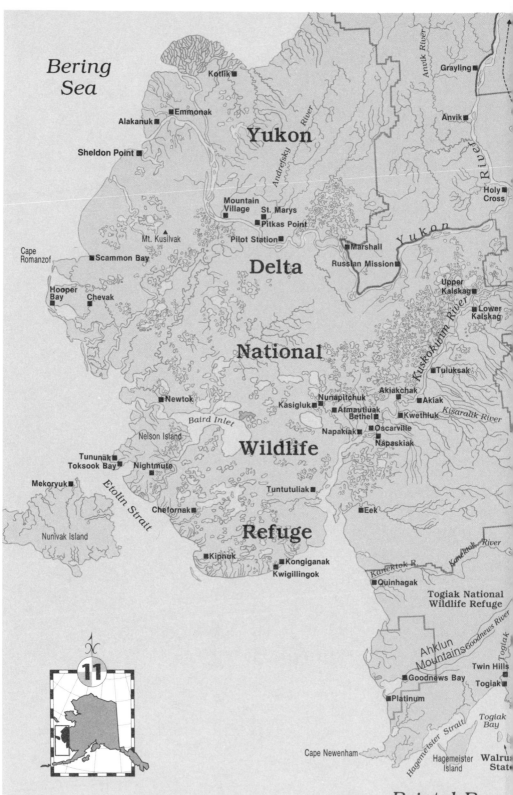

Bering
Sea

Kotlik

Emmonak

Alakanuk

Sheldon Point

Yukon

Anaktvik River

Grayling

Anvik

Holy
Cross

Mountain
Village
St. Marys
Pitkas Point
Pilot Station

Mt. Kusilvak

Marshall

Russian Mission

Yukon

Cape
Romanzof
Scammon Bay

Delta

Upper
Kalskag

Hooper
Bay
Chevak

Lower
Kalskag

Kuskokwim River

National

Tuluksak

Newtok

Baird Inlet

Nelson Island

Kasigluk

Nunapitchuk
Atmautluak
Bethel
Napakiak

Akiakchak
Akiak
Kwethluk

Oscarville
Napaskiak

Kisaralik River

Wildlife

Tununak
Toksook Bay

Nightmute

Tuntutuliak

Mekoryuk

Etolin Strait

Chefornak

Eek

Refuge

Nunivak Island

Kipnuk

Kongiganak
Kwigillingok

Kanektok R.

Kanektok River

Quinhagak

Togiak National
Wildlife Refuge

Ahklun
Mountains

Goodnews River

Togiak River

Twin Hills

Goodnews Bay
Togiak

Platinum

Togiak
Bay

Cape Newenham

Hagemeister Strait

Hagemeister
Island

Walrus
State

Bristol Bay

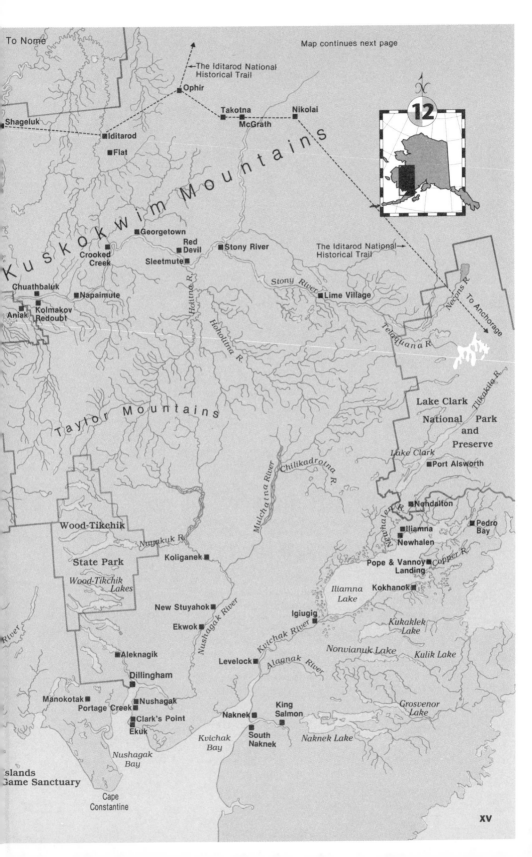

Map continues next page

The Iditarod National
Historical Trail

Ophir

Takotna   Nikolai
     McGrath

Shageluk

Iditarod

Flat

K u s k o k w i m   M o u n t a i n s

Georgetown

Red
Devil   Stony River

Crooked
Creek

Sleetmute

The Iditarod National →
Historical Trail

Chuathbaluk

Napaimute

Stony River

Lime Village

Aniak

Kolmakov
Redoubt

Holitna R.

Hoholitna R.

Negons R.   To Anchorage

Telaquana R.

Tlikakila R.

T a y l o r   M o u n t a i n s

Lake Clark

National   Park

and

Preserve

Chilikadrotna R.

Lake Clark

Port Alsworth

Mulchatna River

Nondalton

Newhalen R.

Pedro
Bay

Iliamna

Copper R.

Newhalen

Wood-Tikchik

Nuyakuk R.

State Park

Koliganek

Pope & Vannoy
Landing

Kokhanok

Wood-Tikchik
Lakes

Iliamna
Lake

Kukaklek
Lake

New Stuyahok

Nushagak River

Igiugig

Ekwok

Kvichak River

Nonvianuk Lake

Kulik Lake

River

Aleknagik

Levelock

Alagnak River

Dillingham

Grosvenor
Lake

Manokotak

Nushagak

Naknek

King
Salmon

Portage Creek

Clark's Point

Ekuk

Kvichak
Bay

South
Naknek

Naknek Lake

Nushagak
Bay

slands
Game Sanctuary

Cape
Constantine

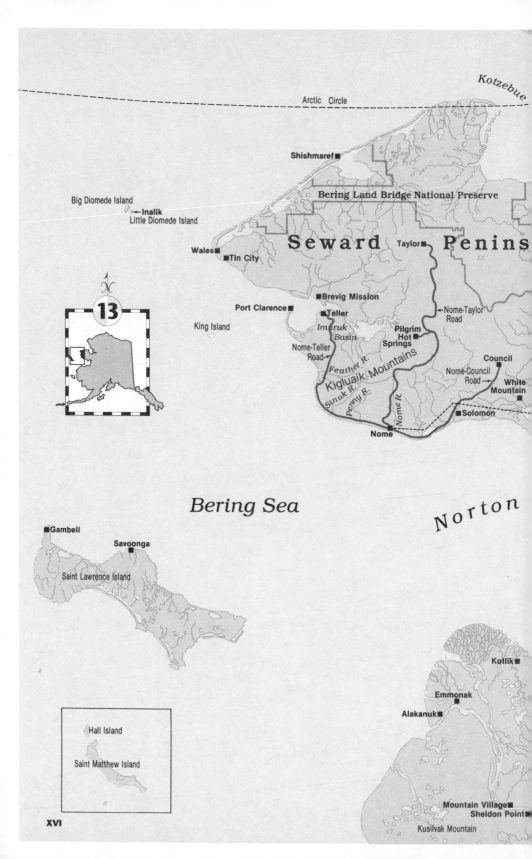

Kotzebue

Arctic Circle

Shishmaref ■

Bering Land Bridge National Preserve

Big Diomede Island
■ ←Inalik
Little Diomede Island

Se w a r d   Taylor ■   P e n i n s

Wales ■ ■ Tin City

■ Brevig Mission

Port Clarence ■   ■ Teller   Nome-Taylor Road →

Imuruk Basin   Pilgrim Hot ■ Springs

King Island

Nome-Teller Road →   *Feather R.*   Kigluaik Mountains   Council
Sinuk R.   Nome-Council Road →   White Mountain
Penny R.   *Nome R.*   ■ Solomon

Nome

Bering Sea   N o r t o n

■ Gambell

Savoonga ■

Saint Lawrence Island

Kotlik ■

Emmonak ■

Alakanuk ■

Hall Island

Saint Matthew Island

Mountain Village ■
Sheldon Point ■
Kusilvak Mountain

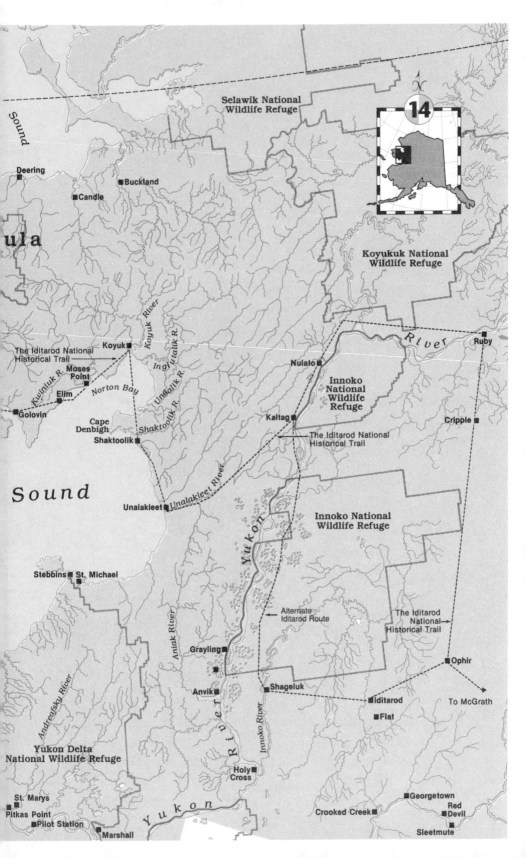

Selawik National
Wildlife Refuge

Koyukuk National
Wildlife Refuge

Deering

Buckland

Candle

ula

Koyuk River

River

Ruby

Koyuk

The Iditarod National
Historical Trail

Nulato

Ing*Yutalik R.

Moses
Point

Kwintuk R.

Innoko
National
Wildlife
Refuge

Cripple

Elim

Ungalik R.

Norton Bay

Kaltag

Golovin

Cape
Denbigh

Shaktoolik R.

The Iditarod National
Historical Trail

Shaktoolik

Sound

Yukon

Innoko National
Wildlife Refuge

Unalakleet

Unalakleet River

Stebbins St. Michael

Aniak River

Alternate
Iditarod Route

The Iditarod
National
Historical Trail

Grayling

Ophir

Andreafsky River

Anvik

Shageluk

Iditarod

To McGrath

Innoko River

Flat

Yukon Delta
National Wildlife Refuge

River

St. Marys

Holy
Cross

Pitkas Point

Georgetown

Pilot Station

Crooked Creek

Red
Devil

Marshall

Yukon

Sleetmute

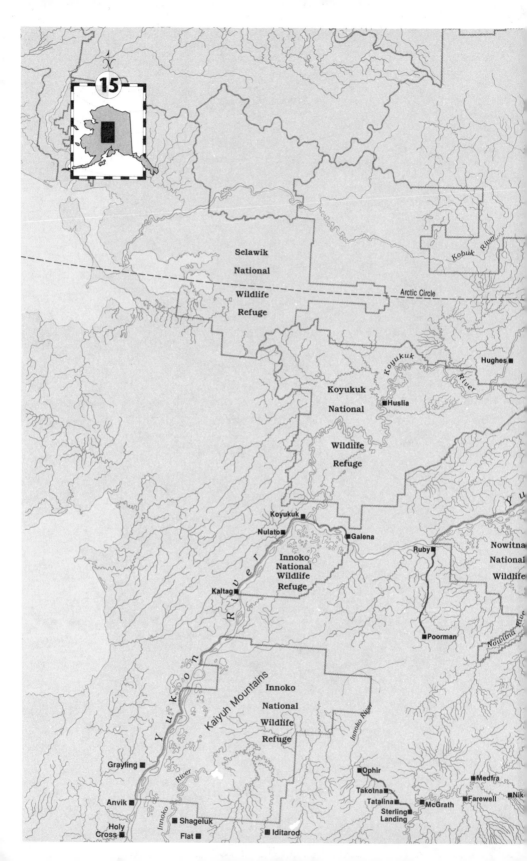

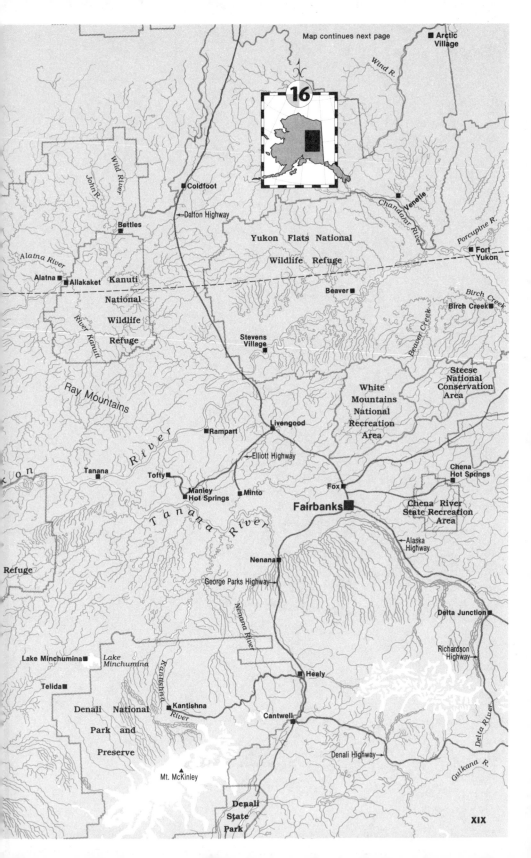

Map continues next page

■ Arctic
Village

16

Wind R.

Chandalar River

Venetie ■

■ Coldfoot

Porcupine R.

←Dalton Highway

Yukon Flats National

■ Fort
Yukon

■ Bettles

Wildlife Refuge

Alatna River

Beaver ■

Birch Creek

Alatna ■ ■Allakaket   Kanuti

Birch Creek■

National

River Kanuti

Wildlife

Stevens
Village

Beaver Creek

Steese
National
Conservation
Area

Refuge

Ray Mountains

White
Mountains
National
Recreation
Area

■Rampart   Livengood■

River

←Elliott Highway

Chena
Hot Springs■

Tanana ■

Tofty■

Fox ■

Chena River
State Recreation
Area

Manley
Hot Springs   ■Minto

Fairbanks ■

Tanana   River

Refuge

←Alaska
Highway

Nenana ■

George Parks Highway→

Nenana River

Delta Junction ■

Lake Minchumina■   Lake
Minchumina

Kantishna River

Richardson
Highway→

Telida■

Denali National

■Healy

Park   and

Kantishna ■

Cantwell ■

Preserve

Denali Highway→

Gulkana R.

Delta River

▲
Mt. McKinley

Denali
State
Park

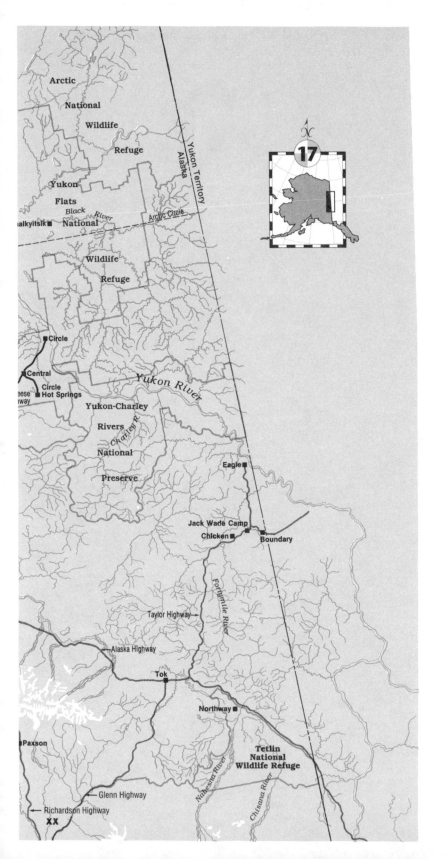

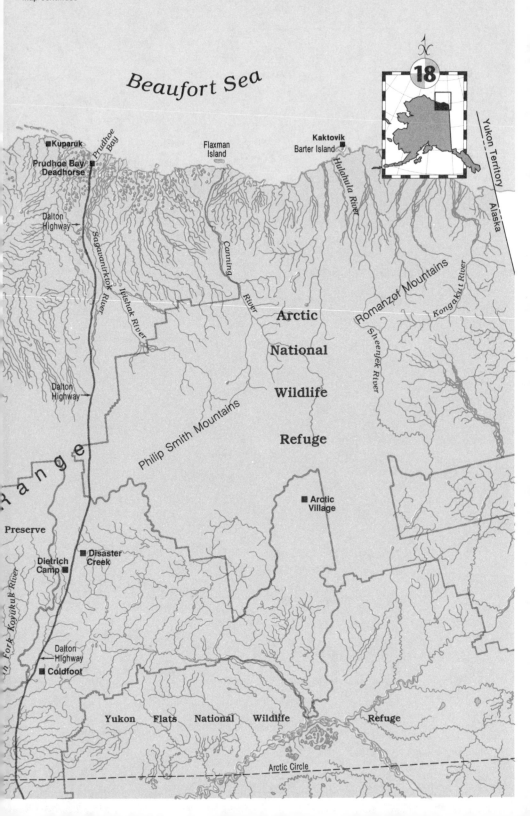

Beaufort Sea

■Kuparuk

Prudhoe
Bay

Flaxman
Island

Kaktovik
Barter Island■

■
Prudhoe Bay
Deadhorse

Hulahula River

Yukon Territory

Dalton
Highway

Alaska

Sagavanirktok River

Iqigak River

Canning
River

Arctic

National

Wildlife

Refuge

Romanzof Mountains

Kongakut River

Sheenjek River

Dalton
Highway

Philip Smith Mountains

ange

■Arctic
Village

Preserve

■Disaster
Creek

Dietrich
Camp ■

South Fork Koyukuk River

Dalton
Highway

■Coldfoot

Yukon   Flats   National   Wildlife   Refuge

Arctic Circle

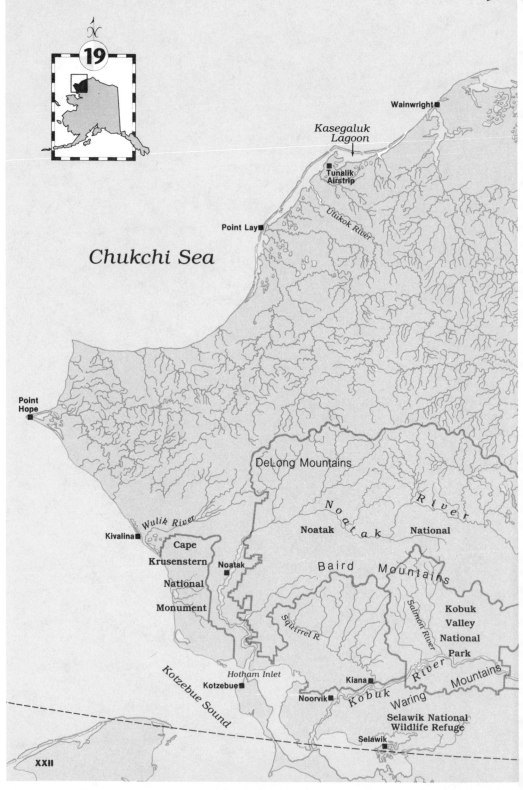

19

Wainwright ■

Kasegaluk Lagoon

Tunalik Airstrip ■

Utukok River

Point Lay ■

Chukchi Sea

Point Hope ■

DeLong Mountains

Noatak *River* National

Noatak

Baird Mountains

Wulik River

Kivalina ■

Cape Krusenstern National Monument

Noatak ■

Squirrel R.

Salmon River

Kobuk Valley National Park

Kotzebue Sound

Hotham Inlet

Kotzebue ■

Kiana ■

Kobuk River Waring Mountains

Noorvik ■

Selawik National Wildlife Refuge

Selawik ■

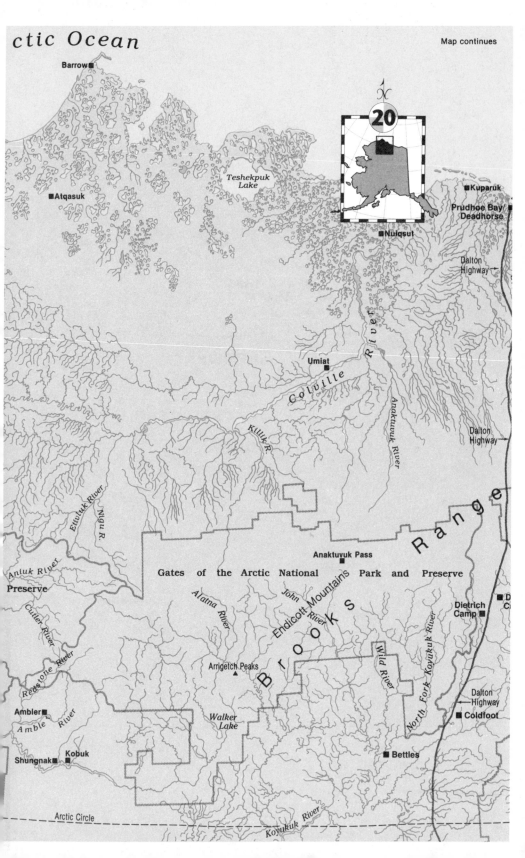

20

Barrow■

■Atqasuk

Teshekpuk Lake

■Kuparuk

Prudhoe Bay/ Deadhorse■

■Nuiqsut

Dalton Highway→

Colville River

Umiat■

Anaktuvuk River

Dalton Highway→

Killik R.

Etivluk River

Nigu R.

Aniuk River

Preserve

Anaktuvuk Pass■

Gates   of   the   Arctic   National   Park   and   Preserve

Alatna River

John River

Endicott Mountains

B r o o k s

R a n g e

Dietrich Camp■

■D Cl

North Fork Koyukuk River

Cutler River

Redstone River

Wild River

▲ Arrigetch Peaks

Ambler■

Amble River

Walker Lake

Dalton Highway

■Coldfoot

Shungnak■

Kobuk■

■Bettles

— — — Arctic Circle

Koyukuk River

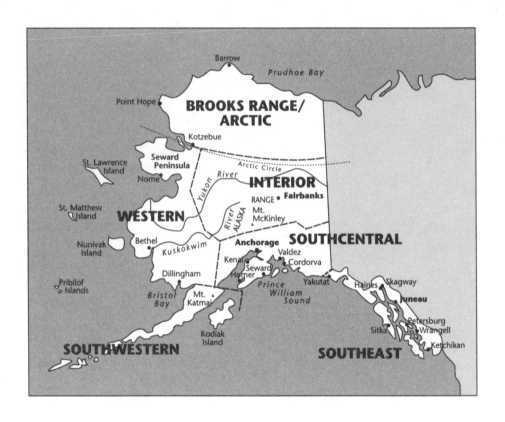

INTRODUCTION

THE ALASKA WILDERNESS GUIDE is for the traveler visiting Alaska's backcountry. (For information on communities and attractions along Alaska's road system, refer to *The MILEPOST®*.) It has been designed to help you get the most out of your travels in the North. Questions about Alaska and traveling in Alaska are answered in the General Information section, which covers everything from Air Travel to Wildlife Watching. Also use the Index in the back of the book to find specific subjects or place-names. Another good way to find out about travel in the Bush is to ask people who provide these services. The Adventure Travel Directory in the back of the book lists everything from fishing charter operators to wilderness lodges. Reading through this section will give you a good idea of what is available.

Information throughout *The Alaska Wilderness Guide* is organized by geographic region (see map on opposite page), beginning with the most southerly region, Southeast, and moving north around Southcentral to Southwestern, then Western, Brooks Range/Arctic, and, finally, the Interior. (Additionally, Western is broken down into 3 subregions: Bristol Bay, Yukon-Kuskokwim Delta and Seward Peninsula/Norton Sound.)

Each of the 6 regional sections begins with an introduction to the region. The introduction is followed by a section on the region's communities, listed alphabetically and keyed to the maps in the front of the book. Community descriptions include information on transportation, climate, airstrips, visitor facilities and population, along with details on history, geography and lifestyle.

The Communities section is followed by a section on the attractions of the region. The Attractions section covers national and state parks, national forests and wildlife refuges, state game refuges, river running, sportfishing, recreation cabins and hiking trails. A Special Features section at the end of the Attractions section covers those unique attractions that don't fit our other categories, such as lighthouses, hot springs and unusual landforms.

Note that icons for parks, cabins, river running, sea kayaking, hiking trails and sportfishing appear at the top of each page in the Attractions sections. (See the icon key this page.)

And finally, a note of caution to travelers. Some facilities you may encounter on your trip to the Bush may be considerably more rustic than what you're used to. This is frontier country. You'll get lots of smiles, but not many of the frills of city travel.

Between the time our questionnaires were returned to us and the time of your trip, changes may have taken place. Costs may be higher hours of operation may change; and businesses may close. In all such cases the publisher will not be held responsible.

Readers are requested to inform us of any changes they encounter in their travels. Write to: *The Alaska Wilderness Guide*, Vernon Publications Inc., 3000 Northup Way, Suite 200, Bellevue, WA 98004.

A sincere effort has been made to give

⊥	Parks and other public lands
⊤	Wildlife refuges
🏠	Cabins
⛰	River running
✕	Sea kayaking
🏃	Hiking trails
✦	Fishing

you a complete, accurate and up-to-date guidebook for this immense state. Your understanding of the reasons for the unavoidable exceptions is appreciated.

Thanks

The Alaska Wilderness Guide appreciates the assistance of the following government agencies in compiling the information in this guide:

The U.S. National Park Service; U.S. Postal Service; U.S. Forest Service; U.S. Bureau of Land Management; U.S. Bureau of Customs; U.S. Coast Guard, 17th District; U.S. Fish and Wildlife Service; U.S. Geological Survey; U.S. Bureau of Indian Affairs; U.S. National Oceanic and Atmospheric Administration.

State of Alaska Division of Tourism; Dept. of Community and Regional Affairs; Office of Enterprise; Division of Marine Highway Systems; Dept. of Transportation and Public Facilities; Dept. of Fish and Game; Division of Forestry; Division of Mining; Division of Parks and Outdoor Recreation; Office of History and Archaeology; Alaska State Troopers; Dept. of Education; Division of Occupational Licensing; Dept. of Health and Social Services; Dept. of Revenue, Division of Public Services and Alcoholic Beverage Control Board; Alaska State Museum; University of Alaska Museum; Dept. of Environmental Conservation; Dept. of Labor, Division of Research and Analysis; Division of State Libraries; University of Alaska, Arctic Environmental Information and Data Center, Cooperative Extension Service and the Alaska Wilderness Studies program.

We would also like to thank the chambers of commerce, visitors bureaus, the Native corporations, postmasters, teachers, park rangers and hundreds of other individuals who provided information on questionnaires, including:

Melanie Otte, Mary Jo Lord-Wild, Rita Wilson, Sandy Schroth, Frank S. Alby, Beatrice Franklin, Marvin Yoder, Helen Gray, Darcy M. Neal, Lisa Stevens, Elizabeth Clauson, Betty Adams, Sheri Paddock, Tami Lyon, Becky Bryant, Joe Giefer, Laurie Sica, Ginny Tierney, Jim Baker, Sharon Hillis, Beth McKibben, Sylvia Geraghty, Virginia Copsey, Kathie Wasserman, Ken Morris, Laura Law, Connie Sackett, Don and Lahoma Leishman, Lavon Branshaw, Mary L. Shannon, Shan Johnson, Larry and Fedora Hedrick, Cyndy Dickson, Nancy P. Radtke, Nelda Osgood, Sandy Frost, Celeste Fenger, Ivan Widom, Willy Dunne, Tara Nielsen, Doug Welch, Lila Dogracia, Zenia Borenin, Debbie Rippey, Elizabeth Kalmakoff, Marcella Dalke, Scott Janke, Elizabeth Manfred, Mark Massion, Zack Chichenoff, Janice Ball, Peggy Osterback, Brian Spetz, Steve Sipper, Pauline Kohler, Alice Ruby, John Nelson, Dolly Olympic, Debi Wilson-Jacko, Willie Kasayulie, Jane Elam, C.L. Williams, Dave Martin, Mira Ericksen, Frieda Costley, Jeanie Smith, Willie Fitka, Daniel Nelson, Karen Maxie, James Chase, Walter Seetot, Avis Hadley, Philip Ahkinga, Luther Nagaruk, Linda Conley, Dora M. Rivera, Morris Kiyutelluk, Allan J. Okpealuk, Sheila Taranto, Rich Thorne, Margaret Shugasvk, Selina Hamilton, Mary Ann Custer, Linda Kush, Arlene Pitka, James Nathaniel, Carole R. Lay, Sheryl Kepler, David C. Smith, Carl A. Walker, Bessie Titus, Emma Hildebrand, Peter L. Platten, Katy White, Bill Garry, Bill Zack, Marianne Mills, Geoff Gross, Nathan Borson, Alroy DeAngelis, Dan Hollenkamp, Jacob Cebula, Dean Stewart, Terry Sanders, David Rak, Mary Lou King, Willy Dunne, Lynn Wallen, Tina Cyr, Gary Lidholm, Marilyn Sigman, Art Schmidt, Jeff Mow, Dan Verhhalle, Jack Sinclair, Maria Gillett, Margie Steigerwold, Herman Griese, Lori Zatz, Susan Savage, Kevin Murphy, Angie Terrell-Wagner, Paul Taylor, Dan Hourihan, Larry Kajdan, C. Fred Zeillemaker, Heather Johnson, Glenn Sherrill, Kimberly Valentino, Michael Rearden, Lorrie Beck, Kim Francisco, Bill Arvey, Fred DeCicco, Wayne Biessel, Jan B. Dick, Lester Fortune, Ed Merritt, Dave Stearns, Barry Whitehill, Dave Dapkus, Anne Jeffrey, Kathryn Reid, Laura Law, Faith Guthert, J.D. Swed, Janet Swanson, Don Pegues.

GENERAL INFORMATION

Air Travel

Alaska is the "flyingest" state in the Union; the only practical way to reach many parts of rural Alaska is by airplane. According to the Federal Aviation Administration, in 1993 there were 9,391 registered pilots (1 out of every 61 Alaskans) and 9,408 registered aircraft (1 for every 61 Alaskans). This figure is approximately 6 times as many pilots per capita and 16 times as many airplanes per capita as in the other states.

Alaska has 583 airports, ranking it sixth in the U.S. Information on some of these airfields is included in the community listings of *The Alaska Wilderness Guide*. These brief descriptions are not intended as a guide for pilots flying in the North. Pilots planning to fly their own planes to Alaska should have the latest U.S. government flight information publication *Alaska Supplement,* available from NOAA, 222 W. 7th, #38, Anchorage, AK 99513-7587; phone 271-5040. For the free booklet, *Flight Tips for Pilots Flying to Alaska,* write FAA, 222 W. 7th Ave., #14, Anchorage, AK 99513-7587; or phone 271-5296. Pilots may also get in touch with the Alaska Airmen's Assoc., Inc., (272-1251) for a copy of the *Alaska Airmen's Logbook for Alaska, Northwest Canada and Russia.*

There are at least 17 national and international airlines serving Alaska's major cities. At least 32 others provide scheduled service to other communities within Alaska. Consult a travel agent for current schedules and fares.

Air taxi operators are found in most Alaskan communities and aircraft can be chartered to fly you to a wilderness spot and pick you up later at a prearranged time and location. (Many charter services charge an hourly standby fee if the customer is not on time at the pickup point.) Most charter operators charge an hourly rate either per plane load or per passenger (sometimes with a minimum passenger requirement); others may charge on a per mile basis. Flightseeing trips to area attractions often are available at a fixed price per passenger. Multiengine planes are generally more expensive to charter than single-engine planes.

The cheapest way to get to an out-of-the-way location is to take a commercial flight or scheduled mail plane to the closest community that has an air taxi service, then charter a flight to your destination.

Alcoholic Beverages

The legal drinking age in Alaska is 21. Children may enter licensed premises, but only with a parent or guardian. There are several types of licensed premises in Alaska, including bars, restaurants, roadhouses and clubs. Consumption regulations are generally very broad, except that in some restaurants you may not be able to purchase beer or wine without also purchasing food. Closing hours are 5 A.M. at the latest; opening hours are 8 A.M. at the earliest. However, some cities have imposed tighter regulations. Packaged liquor, beer and wine are sold by licensed retailers rather than in state liquor stores.

Some villages are "dry" to varying degrees, and visitors should know this in advance to avoid breaking the law inadvertently. Bethel, Barrow and Kotzebue, among others, ban the *sale* of liquor, though impor-

3

tation for personal consumption is permitted. Other villages ban both *sale and importation*. And 18 villages have an even stricter law which bans *possession* of an alcoholic beverage. Do not bring even a hip flask into a village which bans importation or possession.

Information on whether a village prohibits the sale, sale and importation, or possession of liquor is included in the community listings.

Antiquities Laws

State and federal laws prohibit excavation or removal of historic and prehistoric cultural materials without a permit. Nearly all 50 states have historic preservation laws; Alaska's extends even to tidal lands, thereby making it illegal to pick up artifacts on the beach. Penalties range from a $1,000 fine to 6 months in jail, or both. On federal lands, second-offense penalties can range as high as 10 years in jail and $100,000 in fines; additionally, materials used in commission of the act (e.g., airplanes, boats) can be seized, and civil penalties for restoration can be assessed.

It sometimes is difficult to distinguish between historic sites and abandoned property. Old gold mining towns and cabins, plus areas such as the Chilkoot and Iditarod trails, should always be considered historic sites or private property. Also, cabins that appear to be abandoned may in fact be seasonally used trapping cabins where the structure and possessions are vital to the survival of the owner.

Alaska law also prohibits the disturbance of fossils, including prehistoric animals such as mammoths.

Arctic Circle

This is an imaginary line that lies in an arc across the upper third of Alaska at approximately 66°33' north from the equator. (We say "approximately" because the Arctic Circle varies a few seconds in latitude from year to year.)

During the summer solstice, June 20 or 21, the sun does not set at the Arctic Circle (it appears not to set for 4 days because of refraction). Farther north, at Barrow, the sun does not set from May 10 to Aug. 2. At winter solstice, Dec. 21 or 22, the sun does not rise for 1 day at the Arctic Circle. At Barrow, the sun does not rise above the horizon for 67 days — daytime is more like twilight during that time.

You can cross the Arctic Circle with any of several airline- and air taxi-operated arctic tours to such places as Fort Yukon, Prudhoe Bay, Barrow and Kotzebue. These firms may give you a certificate commemorating your crossing.

Aurora Borealis

The aurora borealis, or northern lights, is produced by charged electrons and protons striking gas particles in the earth's upper atmosphere. The electrons and protons are released through sun spot activity and emanate into space. A few drift the 1- to 2-day course to Earth where they are pulled to the most northern and southern latitudes by the planet's magnetic forces.

Auroras can range from simple arcs to draperylike forms in green, red, blue and purple. The color depends on how hard the gas particles are being struck.

In northern latitudes auroras most often occur in the spring and fall months because of the tilt of the planet in relationship to the sun's plane. But displays may occur on dark nights throughout the winter.

Some observers claim the northern lights make a noise similar to the rustle of taffeta, but scientists say the displays cannot be heard in the audible frequency range.

Bears

Most of Alaska qualifies as bear country. Although bears may be more abundant in some places like Katmai National Park and Preserve, Kodiak Island or Admiralty Island National Monument, you're likely to encounter a black bear or brown bear on a hike just about anywhere.

The Alaska Dept. of Fish and Game publishes *The Bears and You,* recommended reading for hikers in bear country. The pamphlet is available from ADF&G offices and government information centers.

To minimize confrontations with bears:

Be aware when you are in prime bear habitat, such as near salmon streams, in willow or berry thickets, or areas with lots of bear trails, prints or droppings. If you do spot a bear, travel in a direction that will avoid it.

Feeding bears is illegal, dangerous and encourages them to hang around campgrounds. Don't do it.

Keep a clean camp. Cook and eat well away from your tent and do not keep food

4

in your tent. Wash dishes immediately. Set up a "food cache" out of reach of bears, such as in a tree, or well away from your camp if there are no trees. Pack out all garbage that is not burnable to avoid attracting bears. Clean all fish into the stream or river, being sure the current carries away the offal.

Travel with others and make noise. Do not let children travel separately from the group. Whistle, sing, ring a bell or shake a can with a few pebbles in it. Around streams, a whistle is most effective in penetrating water noise. Most bears would just as soon not run into you either; let them know you are coming and they will get out of the way.

Do not camp on a bear trail. This is asking for trouble. Bear trails often are located along salmon streams, near berry patches and in saddles on ridgetops. Trails may have staggered oval depressions because bears commonly step in the same places.

Never approach a bear cub or get between a sow and her cubs. Cubs are curious and may approach you. Back away; the sow will defend them ferociously from any perceived threat.

Use a telephoto lens. Do not approach a bear for a close-up shot.

Avoid game carcasses. If it is partially concealed with branches and leaves, this may be a bear's food cache. The bear may be nearby and will defend its food.

Leave your dog at home. When hard pressed, your dog may run to you and bring a bear along, too.

Berry Picking

Alaska has been blessed with an abundance of wild berries. You may want to browse on red currants as you hike along, or steer your kayak toward the bank and grab a handful of highbush cranberries. Or you may set out with containers and won't come home until you have your quota of blueberries or lowbush cranberries or beach strawberries. Berries and other edible plants have long been an important source of roughage and vitamins for Alaska Natives and homesteaders. Whichever category of berry-picker you fall into, Alaska has the berries for you.

A couple of important cautions: Alaska does have poisonous plants, including one berry, the baneberry. Others are: narcissus-flowered anemone, poison water hemlock (very similar to wild celery), wild sweetpea, Nootka lupine, vetch, false hellebore, and death camas, a lily. Be sure you can identify these and know exactly what you are putting into your mouth.

The second danger: bears also like berries. Remember, there are no undiscovered berry patches in Alaska. The bears know them all.

Bird Watching

Alaska's varied habitats offer unparalleled opportunities to view North American and Asian bird species, some of which are found only in remote corners of Alaska's Bush. Some 424 species of birds have been recorded in Alaska.

You'll find birds in every region of Alaska, and in every section of *The Alaska Wilderness Guide*, where species present are listed under the wildlife descriptions for both attractions and communities. However, there are several areas of special interest to bird-watchers in Alaska. Following is a summary of some of the more significant bird-watching spots; refer to regional sections for a more complete description of the park or refuge.

Millions of shorebirds and waterfowl gather on the Yukon-Kuskokwim Delta (see Attractions in the WESTERN/YUKON-KUSKOKWIM section). A bush flight out from Bethel, headquarters for Yukon Delta National Wildlife Refuge, offers views of swans, brant, cackling Canada geese, emperor geese and numerous other species. Boaters and hikers are likely to flush lesser golden plovers, snipe, jaegers, godwits, sandpipers and sandhill cranes.

Offshore, in the Pribilof Islands, and to the south in the Aleutian Islands, seabirds mass in great colonies, their cries penetrating the fog. Red- and black-legged kittiwakes; horned and tufted puffins; crested, least, parakeet and whiskered auklets; northern fulmars; common and thick-billed murres; and pigeon guillemots. Just as the daytime feeders return to their island burrows or ledges, the nighttime feeders take to the skies. Tours are offered to St. Paul and St. George islands. Individual bird-watchers are also welcome. (See Special Features in the SOUTHWESTERN section.)

Fall visitors to Izembek National Wildlife Refuge can view virtually the world's population of brant geese as they feed on eelgrass prior to their flight to wintering grounds farther south on the continent. (See Attractions in the SOUTHWESTERN section.)

Islands just off the rugged outer coast of the Kenai Peninsula shelter puffins, black-legged kittiwakes, cormorants, murres and numerous other species. These areas, partly

5

within Alaska Maritime National Wildlife Refuge or Kenai Fjords National Park, are easily reached from Seward or by a more strenuous trip from Homer. Bird watching is also popular on the Kenai Peninsula, where dozens of species of birds are found on Kenai National Wildlife Refuge. (See Attractions in the SOUTHCENTRAL section.)

Bald eagles top the bird watching attractions of Southeast. Each fall, bald eagles gather along the banks of the Chilkat River near Haines, fishing on a late run of salmon. The Alaska Chilkat Bald Eagle Preserve has been established in recognition of this habitat's critical importance to the country's national symbol. (See Attractions in the SOUTHEAST section.)

Alaska's Interior and Arctic offer abundant habitat for waterfowl and shorebirds. Sandhill cranes and numerous duck and geese species gather at Minto Flats, north of the Tanana River. The watery maze of Yukon Flats, along the Yukon River, nourishes some of the largest concentrations of waterfowl in the country. (See Wildlife Refuges under Attractions in both the BROOKS RANGE/ARCTIC and INTERIOR sections.)

Check with one of the state's 5 chapters of the National Audubon Society for the latest information on bird sightings: Anchorage Audubon Society, Inc., P.O. Box 101161, Anchorage 99510; Juneau Audubon Society, P.O. Box 021725, Juneau 99802; Arctic Audubon Society, P.O. Box 82098, Fairbanks 99708; Kenai Peninsula Audubon Society, P.O. Box 114, Kasilof 99610; and Kodiak Audubon Society, Box 1756, Kodiak 99615. Call Anchorage Audubon Society's hotline, 248-2473, for updates on birding in Southcentral.

Boating, Canoeing and Kayaking

Whether traveling by sailboat, cruiser, rowboat, canoe, inflatable raft or kayak, Alaska offers thousands of miles of challenging and scenic waterways. Coastal waters provide miles and miles of spectacular recreational boating opportunities. Inland it is possible to travel great distances on a number of river and lake systems.

For marine sailors, southeastern Alaska's Inside Passage and southcentral Alaska's Prince William Sound provide a sheltered

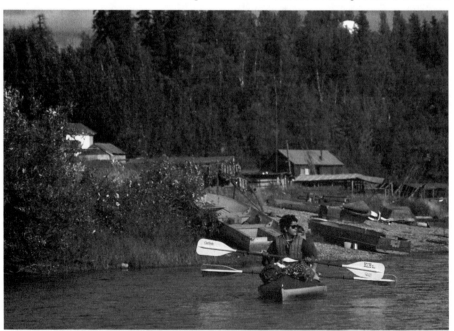

Kayakers at Ambler on the Kobuk River. Informal camping is permitted at many villages, but river runners should ask permission before camping on community lands. (Karen Jettmar)

transportation route and scenic recreational boating opportunities. There are numerous marine charter services throughout Southeast and in Southcentral, most offering sportfishing or sightseeing tours, others with marine craft for charter (most skippered, some bare-boat). Marine facilities and transient moorage are noted in the descriptions of communities in *The Alaska Wilderness Guide*. See also Marine Parks under Attractions in the SOUTHEAST and SOUTHCENTRAL sections for details on state campgrounds for boaters.

Boaters should have appropriate nautical charts and pilot guides. Coastal travelers should have current NOAA (National Oceanic and Atmospheric Administration) Tidal Current Tables. For U.S. waters, check locally for authorized nautical chart dealers or contact NOAA. Local offices should be listed in the phone book under United States Government, Dept. of Commerce, or write the National Ocean Survey Distribution Division (C44), 5601 Lafayette Ave., Riverdale, MD 20840. (To order nautical charts by mail see Maps this section.) For Washington and Alaska waters you need the *United States Coast Pilot* (Books 8 and 9). For British Columbia waters, see the *British Columbia Coast Pilot* (Volumes I and II), available from authorized dealers or the Government of Canada Fisheries & Oceans Scientific Information and Publications Branch, Ottawa. Charts of Canadian coastal waters are available from authorized dealers or from Chart Distribution Office, Dept. of the Environment, Box 8080, 1675 Russel Road, Ottawa, ON, Canada K1G 3H6.

Remember that U.S. visitors entering Canada by private boat must report to Canadian customs on arrival.

Marine travelers should check local bookstores for boating guides to Alaska. The State of Alaska publishes the *Southeast Alaska Harbor and Boating Facilities Directory*, available for $5 from Alaska Dept. of Transportation and Public Facilities, Administration Section, 6860 Glacier Hwy., Juneau, AK 99801-7999; phone 465-1754.

Inland boaters will find hundreds of river and lake systems suitable for traveling by boat, raft, kayak or canoe. For details on Alaska's navigable rivers, consult River Running under Attractions in each of the regional sections.

Rivers included in *The Alaska Wilderness Guide* are rated according to the International Scale of River Difficulty, obtained from the Bureau of Land Management,

which administers some of Alaska's wild and scenic rivers.

Class I: Moving water with a few riffles and small waves. Few or no obstructions.

Class II: Easy rapids with waves up to 3 feet and wide, clear channels that are obvious without scouting. Some maneuvering required.

Class III: Rapids with high, irregular waves often capable of swamping an open canoe. Narrow passages that often require complex maneuvering. May require scouting from shore.

Class IV: Long, difficult rapids with constricted passages that often require precise maneuvering in turbulent waters. Scouting from shore is often necessary and conditions make rescue difficult. Generally not possible for open canoes. Boaters in covered canoes and kayaks should be able to Eskimo roll.

Class V: Extremely difficult, long and very violent rapids with highly congested routes which nearly always must be scouted from the shore. Rescue conditions are difficult and there is significant hazard to life in the event of an accident. Ability to Eskimo roll is essential for kayakers.

Class VI: Difficulties of Class V carried to the extreme of navigability. Nearly impossible and very dangerous. For teams of experts only after close study and with all precautions taken.

Alaska's rivers pass through wild country for the most part. Be extremely careful because help is often far away. BLM cautions that anyone planning a river trip in Alaska should prepare a "float plan" telling the number and ages of those in your party, number and type of craft you are using, what route you are taking and approximately how long the trip should take. Leave the plan with friends or relatives who will contact authorities after a specific time. Be sure to inform them of your safe arrival to avoid unnecessary searches.

BLM further advises the following:

Every member of your party should wear a U.S. Coast Guard-approved "white-water" life jacket. Alaskan waters are extremely cold and safe immersion time is short. Even the best swimmers should wear life vests at all times because the cold quickly saps strength, along with the will and ability to save yourself. Dress to protect yourself from the cold water and weather extremes. If you overturn, stay with your craft.

Never travel alone; a minimum of 2 to 3 craft is recommended. Have honest knowledge of your boating abilities. Be in good physical condition and equipped with adequate clothing. Be practiced in escape from an overturned craft, self-rescue and artificial respiration. Know first aid. At least 1 member of your party should be trained in cardio-pulmonary resuscitation.

River difficulty ratings may change drastically during high water or low water. Use good judgment. Have reasonable knowledge of the difficult parts of the trip. Equipment should be in good repair. Never get broadside of the current in fast water. Keep weight low in the craft. Overloading can be dangerous. Be careful of trees hanging in the water: go around, not under.

Sea kayakers from around the world are drawn to Alaska to paddle its sheltered waterways and challenge its open coast. Kayakers in Alaska can visit tidewater glaciers and natural hot springs, meeting whales and sea otters along the way. Finding a campsite is generally no problem in the popular kayaking regions of Southeast and Prince William Sound, because so much of the land is managed by the U.S. Forest Service or the State of Alaska. See Marine Parks and Sea Kayaking under Attractions in the SOUTHEAST and SOUTHCENTRAL sections for more information.

The sea kayak with a spray cover (or the closed-deck canoe) is well-suited to exploring the labyrinth of channels and fjords found along much of Alaska's coast. Kayaks can slip through channels where the water is just inches deep at high tide. They can take refuge on tiny islands when the weather kicks up, or tie up to public docks in town.

The boats can be carried aboard Alaska ferries. Arrangements should be made in advance. Operators of key sightseeing vessels and many small-boat operators offer drop-off service for kayakers, and folding boats can be flown into remote spots.

June, July and August are prime months for kayaking, as shirtsleeve weather alternates with rain. Knee-high rubber boots and foul-weather gear (including a sou'wester) are essential on the water, in camp and in town. A good-sized tarp and tent with plenty of headroom makes life in camp much more pleasant on rainy days.

Fast-drying polypropylene and pile clothing serve Alaska kayakers better than cotton or wool outdoor wear. Gore-tex is not the fabric of choice for kayak touring and camping in this environment; salt water and soil clog the pores and Alaska generates more than its share of reports of problems with leaking seams.

The newer compressible synthetic sleeping bags are gaining favor for their space-saving advantages over down insulation and their added performance when wet. A bag designed for use at 20°F and above is an appropriate choice.

Tides and tidal currents are forces to be reckoned with. A campsite close to the water may be under it or a mile away on the opposite tide. Tidal currents limit the times that ferries can reach their docks. Currents can give a kayaker a welcome lift, an upstream struggle, or a real white-knuckle trip.

The water is cold between 50°F and 60°F. Capsizing can quickly lead to hypothermia, which can cause death in just over an hour. Rescue and self-rescue skills are critical. Many kayakers wear wetsuits, or lightweight dry suits designed for water sports use, when making long crossings. Others simply choose protected routes and stay ashore when paddling conditions are hazardous.

Kayakers and other boaters are advised to maintain safe distances from tidewater glaciers. Calving glaciers can send ice and debris crashing down. There is also danger from waves caused by falling ice. Small craft should not approach closer than a half-mile from tidewater glacier fronts.

The other major hazard is Alaska's bears, found on the mainland in Southeast and Southcentral regions as well as on Admiralty, Baranof, Chichagof and Kodiak islands, and on most of the islands in Prince William Sound. Campers in bear country should try to avoid encounters, making plenty of noise so bears know they are there, and be especially careful not to attract them with food.

The wildness of Alaska's environment sets it apart from other places popular for sea kayaking. That same wildness (and distance from help in case of trouble) makes it important to go equipped with all of the standard safety gear recommended for outdoor recreationists and kayakers. It would be foolhardy not to take the appropriate nautical charts and tide and current tables. USGS Topographic maps are useful for scouting the shoreline and possible campsites. All marine travelers should leave a copy of a planned itinerary with a responsible person. Marine VHF radios are extremely useful tools and highly recommended. One can receive weather forecasts and in an emergency communicate with passing vessels or call the authorities for assistance. It is possible to call via a telephone connection if one is delayed by poor weather, thus eliminating undue concern.

The Bush

Originally used to describe large expanses of wilderness beyond the fringes of civilization inhabited by trappers and miners, "the Bush" has come to stand for any part of Alaska not accessible by road. Now a community accessed only by air, water, sled or snow machine transportation is considered a bush village, and anyone living there is someone from the Bush.

The Bush is home to most of Alaska's Native people and to individualists who live on homesteads, operate mines or work as guides, pilots, trappers or fishermen.

The term Bush has been adapted to the small planes and their pilots who service areas that lack roads or elaborately developed airports. Bush planes are commonly equipped with floats or skis, depending on the terrain and season. Because of their oftentimes courageous air service, bush pilots have become the modern frontier hero.

Cabins

The U.S. Forest Service, the Bureau of Land Management, the Fish and Wildlife Service and Alaska State Parks offer nearly 200 wilderness cabins for rent. Following is a summary of what's available from these different agencies. For detailed information, see Cabins under Attractions in SOUTHEAST, SOUTHCENTRAL, SOUTHWESTERN and INTERIOR sections.

Forest Service public-use recreational cabins are available in both Chugach and Tongass national forests. Cost is $20 per party per night. A computer cabin reservation system enables any Forest Service office to process a cabin reservation for any cabin the Forest Service manages.

Anyone who is at least 18 years old may apply for a cabin permit for noncommercial use. Applications may be made in writing up to 179 days in advance of required times. *Payment must accompany the cabin application.* If there is more than 1 applicant for a specific cabin and time, a drawing will determine the permittee. Special drawings are held for certain cabins during high-use periods; drawing times and rules

are available from the Forest Service office. Fees will be refunded to unsuccessful applicants; refunds also are made upon written notice and return of permit at least 10 days prior to intended use. Only 1 change in reservations will be granted. Carry permits along to the cabin.

Cabins have tables, benches, bunks (without mattresses), wood or oil heating stoves, brooms and pit toilets. You must bring your own bedding and cooking utensils. An ax or maul is provided at cabins with wood stoves, but bring a small ax or hatchet in case the tools are not there. Be sure to check which kind of stove is provided. The Forest Service does not provide stove oil; only #1 diesel oil will work properly and 5 to 10 gallons per week are required, depending on weather conditions. Almost all cabins located on lakes have skiffs (bring your own life preservers and motor). Bring extra supplies in case bad weather prolongs your stay.

For information contact: Alaska Public Lands Information Center, 605 W. Fourth, Suite 105, Anchorage, AK 99501; phone 271-2599. Or, one of the Tongass National Forest offices: Federal Building, Ketchikan, AK 99901, phone 225-3101; 204 Siginaka Way, Sitka, AK 99835, phone 747-6671; or P.O. Box 309, Petersburg, AK 99833, phone 772-3871.

BLM has 5 recreational cabins within 100 miles of Fairbanks, available by advance reservation for $10 per night. For reservations or information contact the BLM Fairbanks Support Center, 1541 Gaffney Road, Fairbanks, AK 99703-1399; phone 356-5345.

The Fish and Wildlife Service maintains 9 public-use recreational cabins on Kodiak National Wildlife Refuge available by advance reservation for $15 per night. For information or a reservation application contact: Refuge Manager, Kodiak National Wildlife Refuge, 1390 Buskin River Road, Kodiak, AK 99615; phone 487-2600.

Alaska State Parks has both remote and road accessible public-use cabins for rent. Nightly fees start at $25. Stay limits vary from 3 to 7 nights. The cabins sleep 3 to 10 people. Reservations are confirmed when the full amont is paid in person or by mail (credit cards are not accepted). Reservations can by made up to 180 days in advance. For available dates or more information, contact DNR Public Information Center, P.O. Box 107001, Anchorage, AK 99510-7005; phone 762-2617.

Camping

Almost all private and government developed campgrounds in Alaska are located on the road system. Off the road there is usually wilderness camping only available on state and federal lands. (Some exceptions include established campgrounds at Katmai National Park and Preserve and at Katchemak Bay State Park.)

Bush villages may allow campers to set up tents in their community, but always ask permission. Village land is generally either private or owned by the Native corporation. Some communities have had problems (mainly sewage) with groups of outdoor recreationists setting up camp in town. This may put a strain on already limited community resources. While some villages have unofficial camping areas, particularly those located along popular river running routes, it is a good idea to call or write ahead about permission to camp. (See also Visiting Native Villages this section.)

For information on roadside campgrounds, consult *The MILEPOST®*, a complete guide to Alaska's road and marine highway systems.

For information on wilderness camping opportunties, contact the state or federal agency responsible for the recreation lands you are visiting. Addresses and phone numbers for more information are included in descriptions of all national and state parks, forests, wildlife refuges, etc., listed in *The Alaska Wilderness Guide.*

Wilderness campers should keep in mind that Alaska's tree line is erratic: all of the Aleutians, the greater part of the Alaska Peninsula, the Bering Sea coastal plain, as well as the north slope of the Brooks Range are devoid of trees. Timberline ranges from 1,500 to 2,500 feet in the Interior; above that altitude is tundra. In Southeast and Southcentral, tree line varies from about 3,000 feet near Ketchikan to about 1,500 feet along Prince William Sound near Valdez. Beyond tree line, firewood is limited to clumps of willows and alders, which cannot sustain heavy backcountry use. Primus stoves using white gasoline or kerosene (not butane or propane because the empty containers must be packed out) are a necessity. *NOTE: Primus fuel is not allowed on scheduled airlines, so make arrangements with your bush pilot, who can transport*

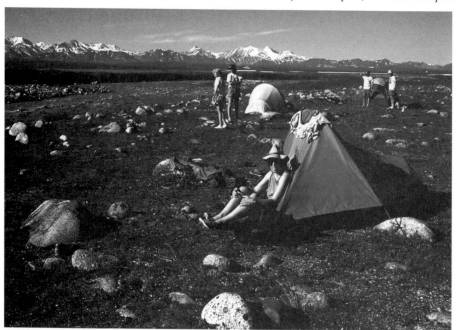

A backpackers' camp on the Arctic coastal plain in Arctic National Wildlife Refuge. Most of the refuge is above tree line. (Karen Jettmar)

it, to have a supply available when you are flown in.

Tents should be of good quality with a mosquito netting and able to withstand strong winds, especially above tree line. As frozen ground is quite often found a few feet below the surface, especially in the Interior and the Arctic, take a foam pad for insulation under a sleeping bag.

Be prepared to wait out the weather when depending on small bush planes for transportation. The terrain is rugged and there are no navigational aids to facilitate landing in remote areas. Take extra food, fuel and other necessary supplies and keep your schedule flexible. In Interior and northern Alaska, a flashlight is unnecessary from May to mid-August.

Further information and details about routes, plane charters, outfitters and guides in any particular area can be obtained by contacting offices of the Alaska Public Lands Information Centers, National Park Service, Bureau of Land Management, U.S. Fish and Wildlife Service, the U.S. Forest Service, and the Alaska Division of Parks; see Information Sources this section for addresses. Addresses for particular units are included with the descriptions of those units (see INDEX).

State and federal agencies that manage Alaska's public lands request that campers exercise minimum impact camping and hiking techniques to reduce damage to fragile wilderness areas. These techniques include the following:

Plan ahead to avoid impact: Travel and camp in small groups. Repackage food to reduce containers. Take a litterbag to carry out trash. Carry a stove and foods that require little cooking. Check with national forest and refuge offices for low-use areas.

Travel to avoid impact: Walk single file in the center of the trail. Stay on the main trail even if it is wet or snow-covered. Never short-cut switchbacks. Travel cross-country only on rocky or timbered areas, not on fragile vegetation. Look at and photograph, never pick or collect. In many areas no man-made trails exist. To minimize impact when in these areas, groups should travel in a fan pattern whenever possible. Use game trails, but be aware that you may surprise wildlife when hiking in brushy areas.

Make no-trace camps: Seek ridgetop, beach or timbered campsites. Camp away from the main trail, lakeshores and fragile plant communities. Choose well-drained, rocky or sandy campsites. Never cut standing trees, use only fallen dead wood. Avoid leveling or digging hip holes and drainage trenches. Make only small campfires in safe areas. Carry small firewood from timbered areas outside camp. Take lightweight, soft shoes for around camp. Avoid trampling vegetation. Use biodegradable soaps and wash well away from water sources (at least 100 feet). Bury human waste 6 to 8 inches deep and at least 150 feet from all potential water sources. On tundra, remove a fist-full of vegetation, scoop out a depression and replace the tundra when finished. Mosses, leaves and snow are natural toilet paper. If you do use paper, burn it or pack it out. Don't bury other waste or trash (pack it out). Stay as quiet as possible and enjoy the stillness. Leave radios and tape players at home.

Leave a no-trace campsite: Pick up and pack out every trace of litter (including cigarette filters). Erase all signs of a fire. Replace rocks and logs where they were.

Daylight Hours

SUMMER MAXIMUM			
	Sunrise	Sunset	Hrs. of daylight
Barrow	May 10	Aug. 2	84 days continuous
Fairbanks	2:59 A.M.	12:48 P.M.	21:49 hours
Anchorage	4:21 A.M.	11:42 P.M.	19:21 hours
Juneau	3:51 A.M.	10:09 P.M.	18:18 hours
Ketchikan	4:04 A.M.	9:32 P.M.	17:28 hours
Adak	6:27 A.M.	11:10 P.M.	16:43 hours

WINTER MAXIMUM			
	Sunrise	Sunset	Hrs. of daylight
Barrow	Jan. 24 noon	Nov. 18 noon	none
Fairbanks	10:59 A.M.	2:41 P.M.	3:42 hours
Anchorage	10:14 A.M.	3:42 P.M.	5:28 hours
Juneau	8:46 A.M.	3:07 P.M.	6:21 hours
Ketchikan	8:12 A.M.	3:18 P.M.	7:05 hours
Adak	9:52 A.M.	5:38 P.M.	7:46 hours

Disabled Visitor Services

Disabled visitors are going to have to do some homework before traveling to the Bush. Challenge Alaska (P.O. Box 110065, Anchorage, AK 99511; phone 563-1658) may be able to offer some help. Phone ahead about wheelchair-accessible lodging and transportation. At least 1 Forest Service public-use cabin is designed for wheelchair access. Some guides and outfitters can accommodate disabled visitors. King of the Rivers charter on the Kenai Peninsula, for example, has wheelchair-accessible boats and the only deaf fishing guides in the area.

Dog Mushing

Some years back, snow machines had virtually replaced the working dog team, but the sled dog has made a comeback due in part to the resurgence of interest in racing, and a rekindled appreciation of the reliability of nonmechanical transportation. More than one bush traveler has survived an unexpected winter storm by curling up with several of the team dogs for warmth.

In addition to working and racing dog teams, many Alaskans keep 2 to 10 sled dogs for recreational mushing. And more winter visitors are experiencing the unique thrill of riding (or driving!) behind a team of dogs over a beautiful snow landscape.

Sled dog racing is Alaska's official state sport. It represents the state's rich history and frontier tradition. Races ranging from local club meets to world-class championships are held throughout the winter. (See The Iditarod this section.)

Emergency Medical Services

Phone numbers of emergency medical services (if available) such as ambulance, clinic or hospital, are listed along with police and fire departments at the beginning of each community description. CB Channels 9 and 11 are monitored for emergencies in many areas; Channels 14 and 19 in some areas.

Employment

A popular misconception about Alaska is that high-paying jobs go begging. Alaska's unemployment rate is above the national average. It is characterized by a very seasonal labor market. Increased activity of all types in the summer makes unemployment fairly low, while a lack of activity pushes up the unemployment rate in the winter months.

Unemployment figures vary dramatically not only from winter to summer, but also from one region to another. High unemployment rates in Alaska's rural areas are common. In the Interior, for example, the unemployment rate approaches 20 percent in the winter months. On the other hand, bustling seaports such as Kodiak in Southwestern experience unemployment rates below 3 percent during the summer.

For information on jobs in Alaska, write: Alaska Dept. of Labor, Alaska State Employment Service, P.O. Box 3-7000, Juneau, AK 99802.

Ferries

Vessels of the Alaska Marine Highway System carry vehicles as well as passengers. There are 2 different systems serving 2 different areas: Southeast and Southcentral/Southwest. These 2 systems DO NOT connect with each other.

The Southeastern system connects Bellingham, WA, and Prince Rupert, BC, with southeastern Alaska cities from Ketchikan to Skagway. Its vessels include the *Columbia, Matanuska, Malaspina* and *Taku,* and the smaller *Aurora* and *LeConte.* Only 3 southeastern cities are connected to the Alaska Highway: Haines, via the Haines Highway, Hyder, via the Cassiar Highway, and Skagway, via Klondike Highway 2. All other communities in southeastern Alaska are accessible only by ferry or by air. In Southeast, mainline ferries call at Ketchikan, Wrangell, Petersburg, Sitka, Juneau, Haines and Skagway. (Feeder vessels serve the smaller communities of Kake, Angoon, Tenakee, Hoonah, Pelican, Hollis, Metlakatla and Hyder/Stewart, BC.) The summer schedule is in effect from May 1 to late September.

In southcentral Alaska, the *Tustumena* travels to Kodiak, Port Lions, Homer, Seldovia and Seward. The *Bartlett* operates between Valdez and Cordova throughout the winter, then in summer extends its run to Whittier. There also is limited service during the summer to Chignik, Sand Point, King Cove and Cold Bay on the Alaska Peninsula and Unalaska/Dutch Harbor in the Aleutians.

Travel on the Alaska ferries is at a leisurely pace, with observation decks, food service and vehicle decks on all ferries. Cabins are available only on the 4 larger Southeast ferries and 1 Southcentral/Southwest ferry. Travelers may schedule stopovers at any port on either route. Short local tours are available in many communities to coincide with ferry stopovers.

Keep in mind that the state ferries are not cruise ships: They do not have beauty salons, deck games and the like. The small stores on the larger ferries are open limited hours and sell a limited selection of items. The cafeteria-style food service is open only for meals. Cocktail lounges on board the larger vessels are open from late morning to midnight. It's a good idea to bring your own snacks, books, games and toiletries, since these are not always available on board.

The state ferries are popular in summer, so make reservations as far in advance as possible to get the sailing dates you want; cabin space is often sold out by mid-December on the Bellingham sailings. (Fares are normally reduced during the winter months and crowds are virtually nonexistent.) Cabin and/or vehicle reservations are required on all vessels. Passenger reservations are required on all sailings.

If cabin space is filled, you may go deck passage with reservations. This means you'll be sleeping on lounge chairs or on the deck itself. A limited number of lockers are available for passengers.

If you do not have reservations, or wish to sail on a different date, check with the Marine Highway office for space. Generally, walk-on passenger space is available except for Bellingham sailings, and cabin and vehicle space is at a premium all year. You may go standby, which is literally standing by in the ferry traffic lanes until all reserved passengers and vehicles are on board: If there is space, standbys may board. However, as a standby you may not get guaranteed through-passage to your destination as standby passengers are subject to off-loading at each port of call! Make sure you understand how standby works before giving up your reservation.

Passenger fares are charged as follows: Adults and children 12 and over, full fare; children 6 to 11, half fare; children under 6, free. Passenger fares do not include cabins or meals. Senior citizens (over 65) may travel at the reduced rate of $5 within Alaska on a space-available basis on all vessels between Oct. 1 and April 30. Between May 1 and Sept. 30, senior citizens may travel at the reduced rate of $5 on all vessels except the *Columbia, Malaspina, Matanuska* and *Taku,* and sailings via Columbia Glacier or the Aleutian Chain sailings. Cabins and vehicle space are charged as usual. Cabin and vehicle space reservations are allowed 30 days prior to sailing if you are traveling on a senior citizen pass. Unless other arrangements are made and noted in your reservation itinerary, full payment is required as follows: If you are booking 55 or more days prior to the departure date payment is due 30 days after the date you book the reservation; if you are booking less than 55 days prior to the departure date payment is due within 10 days after the date you book the

reservation; reservations that are booked 10 days or less prior to departure require payment at time of booking. Failure to meet this requirement may result in the cancellation of reservations. Payment may be made by mail with a certified or cashier's check, or money order. VISA, MasterCard, American Express, Discover and Diners Club credit cards are accepted at all terminals (some restrictions may apply) and by phone. Personal checks will not be accepted unless written on an Alaskan bank. Cancellation charges will be applied to any cancellation or change made within 14 days of sailing, that results in a reduction in the amount paid. The penalty is $15 or 15 percent of the unused portion, whichever is greater. You can pick up prepaid tickets at your departure point, but you must pay for the tickets in advance and arrange with the Alaska Marine Highway office to hold your tickets at your departure point.

From June 1 through Labor Day each year, U.S. Forest Service interpreters staff the *Columbia, Malaspina, Matanuska* and *Taku* ferries through waters bordering the Tongass National Forest in Southeast Alaska, and they also serve on portions of the trips by the *Bartlett* and *Tustumena* in Prince William Sound near Chugach National Forest in Southcentral. Programs vary according to each ship's activities and include: narrative talks, films, slides, children's activities and brochures about the natural and cultural resources of Alaska's national forests.

For additional information, schedules, fares and reservations, write the Alaska Marine Highway, Box R, Juneau, AK 99811-2505, or phone toll free 1-800-642-0066, fax (907) 277-4829; from Washington state phone toll-free 1-800-585-8445, from Canada 1-800-665-6414.

Fishing

In describing fishing opportunities in the Southeast region of Alaska, the Dept. of Fish and Game stated: "The wide range of species and availability is overwhelming and beyond the capability of most anglers to visit and test the waters." This could be said for most regions of Alaska: the choices are many. A roundup of fishing spots is included under Sportfishing in each regional Attractions section in *The Alaska Wilderness Guide,* but it is by no means exhaustive.

For detailed information on specific sportfishing opportunities in a region, contact the regional office of the Alaska Dept. of

Fish and Game (addresses follow). These offices have literally hundreds of pamphlets on fishing regional waters, with details on species and peak availability times. You may also be referred to an area office of the Alaska Dept. of Fish and Game. Area offices offer sportfishing guides to waters in their area.

Regional offices of the Alaska Dept. of Fish and Game are: Southeast, Division of Sport Fish, P.O. Box 240020, Douglas, AK 99824; Southcentral, Division of Sport Fish, 333 Raspberry Rd., Anchorage, AK 99518; and Interior Division of Sport Fish, 1300 College Rd., Fairbanks, AK 99701.

For the free annual *Alaska Sport Fishing Regulations Summary* booklet or general information, phone 465-6186 or write the Alaska Dept. of Fish and Game, P.O. Box 25526, Juneau, AK 99802. Be sure you have the most recent information on bag limits and special permits for the year you are fishing.

A nonresident fishing license, valid for the calendar year issued, costs $50. A special 3-day nonresident license costs $15, or $30 for 14 days. Nonresidents under age 16 do not need a fishing license.

Resident sportfishing licenses cost $10. A resident is a person who has maintained a permanent place of abode within the state for 12 consecutive months and has continuously maintained his or her voting residence in the state, and any member of the military service who is on active duty and is permanently stationed in Alaska.

Nearly all sporting goods stores in Alaska sell fishing licenses. But because of irregular hours of operation sometimes found in the Bush and the possibility of unexpected fishing opportunities, it is advisable to buy your license in one of the larger communities before you head for the backcountry.

Alaska Fish Species

King salmon — Also called the chinook, tyee or spring salmon, this is the largest and longest lived of the Pacific salmon. They commonly range along the coastline from southeastern Alaska through the Bering Sea, choosing wide, deep rivers for spawning.

Silver salmon — Also called coho or silver sides, this is the most popular game fish of the Pacific salmon. Silvers are found along the Alaska coastline as far north as Kotzebue Sound and commonly spawn in smaller streams than do kings.

Sea-run coho are the most voracious of the salmon and will readily attack almost

any spoon or streamer fly. Heavy line is recommended as the coho is an extremely difficult fish to land in fast water.

Many lakes planted with rainbow trout also contain coho. Most of the 12- to 18-inch fish are caught through the ice in winter, however, excellent summer fishing can be had by using dry or wet flies and by trolling small diving plugs. Corn and natural baits are also productive.

Red salmon — Also called sockeye and blueback. Landlocked red salmon are called kokanee. Fishing is spotty as the species is moody and characteristics for hitting lures vary from river to river. Found in streams and lakes along the Alaska coast as far north as the Seward Peninsula. Saltwater fishing for sockeye has not developed in Alaska.

Pink salmon — Also called humpback, this species is the smaller of the Pacific salmon. Good fishing in both fresh and salt water from southeastern Alaska up the coastline; in Cook Inlet from the lower Kenai Peninsula into Susitna drainage; the Kodiak-Afognak area; and throughout the Bristol Bay area.

Chum salmon — Also called dog salmon, range the farthest north of the Pacific salmon. It is common to Kotzebue Sound.

Rainbow trout — The sea-run of the species is known as the steelhead. Rainbow are found naturally as far north as Stony River, a tributary of the Kuskokwim, and have been transplanted to the Interior, mostly around Fairbanks.

Cutthroat trout — The common trout of southeastern Alaska ranges as far north as Montague Island in Prince William Sound.

Eastern brook trout — Has been introduced to southeastern Alaska waters.

Dolly Varden trout — A member of the char family with the widest distribution of any trout in Alaska. It is primarily an anadromous trout in Alaska, but freshwater forms are known.

Arctic char — Found from Kodiak Island, the Alaska Peninsula and the Aleutian Islands along the coast of Alaska north and east to the Mackenzie River and in scattered locations in Interior Alaska.

Lake trout — Found in suitable lakes from the Alaska Peninsula northward and in the Copper River drainage near Cordova.

Arctic grayling — The major game fish in many parts of central and northern Alaska. Fly-fishing for grayling is considered to be an ultimate sport by many.

Sheefish — Sometimes called the "Northern tarpon", this is the largest member of the whitefish family. Found in the drainages of the Kuskokwim, Selawik and Kobuk rivers and the Yukon and its tributaries.

Northern pike — Found in Alaska Peninsula streams that feed into Bristol Bay and north to the Arctic coast and throughout the Interior. Also in the Ahrnklin River, 10 miles/16 km southeast of Yakutat.

Halibut — Found in all waters in Alaska, both inshore and offshore grounds, extending as far north as Norton Sound and south to Dixon Entrance. A considerable sport fishery for halibut has developed in the Cook Inlet area (in the Homer area in particular) and in some other regions of Alaska.

Rockfish — There are at least 34 species, but anglers commonly catch the yelloweye rockfish (also called "red snapper"), the black rockfish (or "black bass") and quillback rockfish. Tasty and relatively easy to catch, this saltwater fish is susceptible to overfishing.

Other species — These include humpback whitefish, kokanee salmon, lingcod or burbot, and inconnu.

Giardiasis

Alaska's many crystal-clear rivers and streams give the false impression that the water is pure and safe to drink. However, that pristine-looking water may contain a hidden hazard — a microscopic organism called *Giardia lamblia*, which causes an intestinal disorder called giardiasis. *Giardia* are carried in the intestinal waste of humans and some domestic and wild animals. The cysts of *Giardia* may contaminate surface water supplies such as lakes, streams and rivers. The organisms can survive in water for at least 2 months, so the problem is not limited to a particular time of year or sections of streams.

Giardiasis can cause severe discomfort. After ingestion by humans *Giardia* attach themselves to the walls of the small intestine. Disease symptoms usually include diarrhea, increased gas, loss of appetite, abdominal cramps and bloating. Weight loss may occur from nausea and loss of appetite. These discomforts may first appear a few days to a few weeks after ingestion of *Giardia*, and may last up to 6 weeks. Most people are unaware they have been infected and often have returned home from vacations before the onset of symptoms. The symptoms may disappear on their own, only to recur intermittently during a period of many months. Other diseases can have similar symptoms, but if you have drunk untreated water you should suspect giardiasis and so inform your doctor. The disease is curable when treated with a prescribed medication.

To avoid this problem altogether, purify all surface water that is to be used for drinking or cooking.

The most certain method to destroy *Giardia* is to boil water (bring it to a full rolling boil, not simply steaming) for at least 1 minute. Boiling also will destroy other organisms that cause waterborne diseases. At high altitudes, you should boil the water for 3 to 5 minutes for an added margin of safety. If the water has a flat taste, pour it back and forth between clean containers 2 or 3 times.

Chemical disinfectants such as iodine or chlorine tablets work well against most waterborne bacteria and viruses that can cause disease, but they may not be totally reliable against *Giardia*, according to the U.S. Forest Service. The amount of iodine or chlorine necessary to kill *Giardia* depends on water temperature, pH, turbidity and contact time between the chemical and parasite. Research to determine the amount of chemical and duration of contact time is under way. In an emergency, it is recommended that you use an iodine-based water purification product, since iodine is often more effective than chlorine. If possible, filter or strain the water first, then allow the iodine to work at least 30 minutes before you drink the water. If the water is cold or cloudy, wait at least an hour, or use more iodine.

Gold Panning

If you are interested in gold panning, sluicing or suction dredging in Alaska — whether for fun or profit — you'll have to know whose land you are on and familiarize yourself with current regulations. Recreational gold panning is allowed on some state and federal lands. Regulations on use of gold pans and hand shovels, nonmechanized sluice boxes and suction dredges vary depending on where you are.

Throughout Alaska, there are two sets of mining regulations to be familiar with — state and federal. Free pamphlets describing the respective requiremens of each can be obtained from mining information offices of the State Division of Mining or Bureau of Land Management. Contact them at: State

Division of Mining, P.O. Box 107016, Anchorage 99510-7016, phone 762-2518; Bureau of Land Management, 222 W. 7th Ave. #13, Anchorage 99513-7599, phone 271-5960; State Division of Mining, 3700 Airport Way, Fairbanks 99709, phone 451-2788; Bureau of Land Management, 1150 University Ave., Fairbanks 99709-3844, phone 474-2200.

Panning, sluicing and suction dredging on private property, established mining claims and Native lands is considered trespassing unless you have the consent of the owner.

Guides

Choosing the right guide for a hunting or fishing trip, rafting or climbing trip, calls for research and planning.

If you don't know anyone who has taken a trip similar to the one you're planning and can personally recommend a guide, several resources can help you pull together a list of prospective guides to interview. Check the Adventure Travel Directory in the back of *The Alaska Wilderness Guide.* Also check the advertisements Alaskan guides place in national magazines and *The MILEPOST®.* Write for the current *Official State Vacation Planner* (Alaska Division of Tourism, P.O. Box 110801, Juneau, AK 99811; phone 465-2012). Also many state and national parks and refuges in Alaska provide lists of approved guides and concessionaires. Another source: the Alaska Professional Hunters Association. This organization publishes a quarterly magazine and furnishes a list of guides who make up their membership. For details, contact APHA, P.O. Box 91932, Anchorage, AK 99509; phone 522-3221, fax 349-9645.

Individuals providing guided hunts, tent camps or outfitted hunts are required to have a Guide-Outfitter license and employ licensed assistants. Guide-outfitters (registered guides) serve a 3-year apprenticeship as assistant guide, along with completing oral and written exams and demonstrating a knowledge of first aid and CPR. Individuals providing transportation must have a Transporter license unless it is part of a guide-outfitted hunt. A Commercial Use Permit is required of individuals providing accommodations in the field at lodges or cabins.

Freshwater sportfishing guides in certain areas (including Southeast, Yakutat, Susitna-West Cook Inlet and the Kenai River) must be registered. Freshwater guide requirements may vary according to area.

A complete list of registered guide-outfitters for hunting and freshwater fishing is available for $5 from the Dept. of Commerce, Division of Occupational Licensing, Box D-Lic, Juneau, AK 99811-0800, or from the same office at 3601 C St., Anchorage, AK 99503. The Juneau office, phone 465-2543, can also provide information on how long a hunting guide has been in business and whether any complaints have been lodged against the guide.

Some guides, particularly the fishing and hunting guides, set up information booths at travel and sporting shows held in the Lower 48. If you can get to one of these shows, you may have the opportunity to interview your prospective guide in person.

In lieu of a personal interview, once you have a list of prospective guides, write for information and after you have received the brochures, call each guide. Ask how long the guide has been in business and ask for the names and addresses of 2 or 3 clients from the previous year. Then contact those clients and get a report.

Also find out the details about the trip you have chosen, advises Bob Jacobs of St. Elias Alpine Guides in McCarthy. What will be the maximum number of people allowed in the group? The minimum? Who will be your guide(s), and what are their age(s), experience, and number of years with the guide service? Do they guide as a full-time occupation, or only as a sideline?

Prices of big game guiding services as well as other adventure trips vary greatly depending on the services offered and the logistics involved. With big game guides, the species hunted also influences the price.

Hiking

The majority of backcountry regions have no established trails. Wilderness hiking only is available in most national and state parks and refuges. Established hiking trails on public lands are included under Hiking Trails in the Attractions section of the SOUTHEAST, SOUTHCENTRAL and INTERIOR regions in *The Alaska Wilderness Guide.*

Knowledge of the use of topographical maps and a compass is essential. No footbridges or cable cars exist to carry travelers over the many streams and rivers that crisscross the country. A heavy downpour of rain or glacial runoff from high summer temperatures can cause a stream that is ankle deep in the early morning to be a hip-deep torrent in the afternoon. Streams will be the most shallow and have less current where they are the broadest or most braided. Always wear shoes when fording streams as waters are excruciatingly cold and a rock rolled on a bare foot can result in a bruise or fracture.

Always expect the unexpected, as far as weather is concerned. Be equipped with good lightweight rain gear and hope that it won't be needed too often. Hypothermia can strike even in temperatures above freezing, when combined with wind, exhaustion and damp clothing. Don't forget sunglasses and sunscreen lotion.

Practice minimum-impact hiking techniques. All campfires should be scattered so that no evidence remains. Don't build firerings out of rocks. It blackens the rocks and has no essential use.

Where dead wood is plentiful (never cut a slow-growing tree in this country), campfires should be restricted to gravel bars or mineral soil. Even though the tundra is damp to the touch, it is a veritable peat bog and once ignited it can burn underground, even under the snow, for several years.

The northern environment is fragile. Trampled tundra plants take much longer to recover than flora found in more temperate climates. Lichens, essential for caribou sustenance, can take up to 100 years to regrow. Tin cans, plastics and aluminum foil become embalmed rather than decaying. Frost will heave up any refuse that is buried, so pack out anything except paper, which can be burned. Plan menus accordingly; think about what you'll have to carry back out. Fishing can vary from mediocre to fantastic; don't plan to live off the land.

Plan a strategy for dealing with human waste prior to going. Pack out all disposables connected with human waste, and bury the waste deeply.

Never wash your dishes or dispose of food in any clear water streams. There are no fish or organisms that will eat this garbage and it will remain forever.

Never build cairns to mark the trail; follow the game trails.

The USDA Forest Service has developed Recreational Opportunity Guides for most of the trails in the Tongass and Chugach National Forests. Copies of the Forest Service publications may be obtained from the Forest Service field office near the trails you plan to hike.

The Bureau of Land Management office in Fairbanks has prepared brochures on the 26-mile-long Pinnell Mountain National Recreational Trail in the Steese National Conservation Area, and other handout material for trails in the nearby White Mountains National Recreational Area. A network of trails on BLM lands in the Tangle Lakes area west of Paxson are open to hiking and off-road vehicle use. Contact the BLM office in Glennallen for information on hiking in east-central Alaska, phone 822-3217.

Holidays

The following list of observed holidays in Alaska can help you plan your trip. Keep in mind that banks and other agencies may be closed on these holidays.

New Year's Day	Jan. 1
Martin Luther King Day	3rd Mon. in Jan.
Presidents Day	3rd Mon. in Feb.
Seward's Day*	Last Mon. in March
Memorial Day	Last Mon. in May
Independence Day	July 4
Labor Day	1st Mon. in Sept.
Columbus Day	2nd Mon. in Oct.
Alaska Day*	Oct. 18
Veterans Day	Nov. 11
Thanksgiving Day	4th Thurs. in Nov.
Christmas Day	Dec. 25

*Seward's Day commemorates the signing of the treaty by which the United States bought Alaska from Russia, signed on March 30, 1867. Alaska Day is the anniversary of the formal transfer of the territory and the raising of the U.S. flag at Sitka on Oct. 18, 1867.

Homesteading

There is no "free" land in Alaska. The state's 365 million acres are owned by the federal government (Bureau of Land Management, National Park Service, etc.), the state, Native claims and private individuals. The easiest and fastest way to acquire land for private use is by purchase from the private sector, through real estate agencies or directly from individuals. Federal homesteading laws were repealed in 1986. Although there is no longer a federal homesteading program, the state of Alaska administers some land disposal. The state Dept. of Natural Resources controls these programs.

Under the state homestead program, residents have a chance to receive up to 40 acres of nonagricultural land or up to 160 acres of agricultural land without paying for the acreage itself. The homesteader, however, must survey, occupy and improve the land in certain ways, and within specific time frames to receive title.

The homestead act also allows homesteaders to purchase parcels at fair market value without occupying or improving the land. This option requires only that non-agricultural land be staked, brushed and surveyed, and that parcels designed for agricultural use also meet clearing requirements.

Other state programs available for acquiring land and homesites include lottery sales (1-year residency required; participants must be 18 years or older), and public auction.

Details on these programs are available from the Dept. of Natural Resources, Division of Lands, 400 Willoughby Ave., Suite 400, Juneau, AK 99801; phone 465-3400.

Hot Springs

The U.S. Geological Survey identifies 79 thermal springs in Alaska. Almost half of these hot springs occur along the volcanic Alaska Peninsula and Aleutian chain. The second greatest regional concentration of springs is in southeastern Alaska. Hot springs are scattered throughout the Interior and western Alaska as far north as the Brooks Range and as far west as the Seward Peninsula.

Early miners and trappers were quick to use the naturally occurring warm waters for baths. Today approximately 25 percent of the recorded thermal springs are used for bathing, irrigation or domestic use. Only a handful of the known hot springs can be considered developed and these are found in Southeast, Interior and the Western Alaska regions. Facilities can range from full resorts to simple changing shacks at crude dams to create sitting pools. (See Hot Springs under Special Features in SOUTHEAST, WESTERN and INTERIOR regions.)

Hunting

Hunting is a popular sport in Alaska and a way of life for many residents. While there is no specific hunting section in *The Alaska Wilderness Guide*, species present on public lands are noted under the wildlife description throughout the Attractions section for each region. In addition, if hunting is allowed it is included in the description of activities for that area.

Hunters in Alaska must be aware of the rules and regulations BEFORE entering the field. The intricacies of licenses, tags, reports, stamps, seals, permits, tickets and guiding contracts should be worked out in advance.

Be sure your guide explains pertinent rules to you (see Guides this section). Failure to comply can result in substantial monetary fines, loss of trophies and property and even imprisonment. Several undercover "sting" operations in recent years have resulted in convictions of both guides and clients.

In general, the rules of common sense and fair chase apply: no shooting from or across a highway; no use of a helicopter (except for emergency rescue); no shooting from a moving motorboat; no driving or herding game with a plane, boat, or ATV; no fully automated weapons (machine guns); no hunting during the same day airborne (except for 1 or 2 species in certain areas); no radio communications or artificial lights.

The Alaska Dept. of Fish and Game has a small, no-nonsense brochure titled *Help for the Nonresident Hunter,* which lays out what hunters must do before, during, and after their hunt. Acquiring one could prove advantageous. Copies of *Help for the Nonresident Hunter* are available from the Alaska Dept. of Fish and Game, P.O. Box 25526, Juneau, AK 99802. That office can also supply copies of the complete hunting regulations, which may be obtained from any of the many department offices throughout the state as well.

One other note from ADF&G: Hunters who kill game, and who may not use all the meat legally required to be salvaged, are urged to contact the village council of the nearest town or village to offer the meat for their use. Wild game is important to many rural Alaskans. When giving game meat away, be sure to get a written receipt of it.

There are 26 game management units in Alaska and a wide variation in both seasons and bag limits for various species. Check for special regulations in each unit.

Licenses are available from any designated licensing agent. (It's a good idea to get your license before you head into the backcountry.) Licenses may be obtained by mail from ADF&G, Licensing Section, P.O. Box 2-5525, Juneau, AK 99802-5525; phone 465-2376. They are also available at the major Dept. of Fish and Game offices in Anchorage, Fairbanks and Juneau.

A complete list of registered Alaskan guides is available for $5 from the Dept. of Commerce and Economic Development, Big Game Commercial Services Board, P.O. Box D, Juneau, AK 99811.

Licenses and Tag Fees: Residents and nonresidents must submit a $5 fee with each application for a game species involved in a limited drawing. The musk-ox drawing requires a $10 fee.

Big game tags are required for residents hunting musk-ox and brown/grizzly bear and for nonresidents hunting any big game animal. These nonrefundable, nontransferable metal locking tags (valid for the calendar year) must be purchased prior to the taking of the animal. A tag may be used for any species for which the tag fee is of equal or less value.

Resident License Fees: No hunting or trapping licenses are required of residents of Alaska under age 16 or residents age 60 or older who have resided in the state for 1 year. A special identification card is issued for the senior citizen exemption.

Trapping license, $10; hunting license, $12; hunting and trapping license, $22; hunting and sportfishing license, $22; hunting, trapping and sportfishing license, $32.

Resident Tag Fees: Brown/grizzly bear, $25; musk-ox (bull), $500 on Nunivak Island and in Arctic National Wildlife Refuge, $25 from Nelson Island, and musk-ox (cow), $25.

Nonresident License Fees: Hunting license, $85; hunting and sportfishing license, $135; hunting and trapping license, $250.

Nonresident Tag Fees: Brown/grizzly bear, $500; black bear, $225; bison, $450; moose or caribou, $325; sheep, $425; elk or goat, $300; deer, $150; wolf, $175; wolverine, $175; musk-ox, $1,100.

Nonresident Alien Tag Fees: Brown/grizzly bear, $650; black bear, $300; bison, $650; moose, $500; caribou, $425; sheep, $550; elk or goat, $400; deer, $200; wolf, $250; wolverine, $250; musk-ox, $1,500.

Nonresident hunters must be accompanied by a registered guide (or a close relative over 19 who is an Alaska resident) when hunting brown bear, Dall sheep or mountain goats.

Following is a roundup of big game species and their ranges in Alaska:

Brown bear *(Ursus arctos)* are found throughout the state, though they are commonly called grizzlies when they live inland, away from coastal areas. Kodiak and Admiralty islands and the Alaska Peninsula are traditionally prime areas for hunting these large, dangerous omnivores, but other parts of the state also boast excellent sport.

Black bear *(Ursus americanus)* occur over most of the forested areas of the state excluding Kodiak and major islands in Southeast and Prince William Sound. In

many areas they are less common than browns. The best hunting is probably from the tidal areas in Prince William Sound, the Kenai Peninsula, the Susitna River drainages, and throughout Southeast, in late May, early June, and September.

Caribou *(Rangifer tarandus)*, the most nomadic of Alaska's mammals, range throughout the state except for Southeast and most offshore islands. The adult bull is one of the most impressive trophy animals in the North, and the hunt for them attracts several thousand nonresident sportsmen a year. Caribou also serve as a major food source for Alaska Natives and other rural Alaskans.

Dall sheep *(Ovis dalli dalli)* are the only sheep native to Alaska and are found in the Brooks, Alaska, Chugach and Kenai ranges, the Talkeetnas, and the Wrangells. Stalking one of these proud white rams with the massive curling horns requires stamina and skill.

Mountain goat *(Oreamnos americanus)* hunting can be even tougher. It should be attempted only by properly equipped hunters in good physical condition. Goats occur from Southeast north and west along the coastal mountains in Cook Inlet and north into the Talkeetnas and the southern drainages of the Wrangells. They have also been transplanted to Kodiak and Baranof islands.

Moose *(Alces alces)*, the world's largest member of the deer family, occur throughout most of Alaska, except for the major islands of Southeast. They are most abundant in second-growth birch forests, timberline plateaus, and along the major rivers of Southcentral and the Interior. Trophy-class bulls are found throughout the state, but the largest come from the Alaska Peninsula, the Susitna Valley, and Westcentral Alaska.

Sitka black-tailed deer *(Odocoileus hemionus sitkensis)* inhabit the wet, coastal rainforests of Southeast and Prince William Sound, and also occur on Kodiak and Afognak islands. Populations fluctuate with the severity of the winters. Because most winters in their range are mild and deer have a high reproductive potential, bag limits are generous, with the season open from August through December. Early season hunters climb to alpine areas, where they enjoy not only the hunt but unsurpassed scenery as well. Most deer, however, are taken in November, when the blacktails are on lower ranges.

Other big game species include the wolf,

19

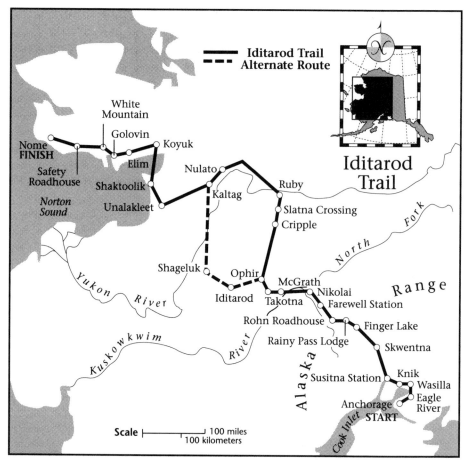

bison, elk, musk-ox and wolverine, while small game animals include grouse, ptarmigan and hares. Fur animals that might be hunted are the coyote, fox and lynx. At present there is no recreational hunting of polar bear, walrus or other marine animals.

Waterfowl are also abundant and the bag limits usually generous in seasons that often begin on Sept. 1. Taking of brant, geese, cranes, ducks, snipe and swans (the latter with only 300 permits issued and only for the Bering Sea region) requires both a state and federal duck stamp.

Hypothermia

Exposure to wet, cold and windy conditions can lead to hypothermia, the number one killer of outdoor recreationists. Hypothermia is the body's reaction when it is exposed to cold and cannot maintain normal temperatures. In an automatic survival reaction, blood flow to the extremities is shut down in favor of preserving warmth in the vital organs. As internal temperature drops, judgment and coordination become impaired. Allowed to continue, hypothermia leads to stupor, collapse and possibly death. Most hypothermia cases develop in air temperatures between 30°F and 50°F.

Any of the following are symptoms of hypothermia: severe shivering; vague, slow, slurred speech; memory lapses; incoherence; clumsiness, lack of control of hands and feet; drowsiness, exhaustion.

The victim may deny any problem. Believe the symptoms, not the victim. Even mild symptoms require immediate treatment. Get the victim out of the wind and rain and into a shelter, if possible. Remove all wet clothes. If the victim is only mildly impaired, give him warm drinks (nonalcoholic) to raise his body temperature. Get the person into dry clothes and a warm sleeping bag. Well-wrapped, warm (not hot) rocks or canteens will help.

Put the victim in a sleeping bag with another person—both stripped. If you have a double bag, put the victim between 2 warm people. Build a fire to warm the camp.

To prevent hypothermia, the U.S. Forest Service advises the following: stay dry. When clothes get wet, they lose about 90 percent of their insulating value. If dry clothes are available, cover high heat-loss areas — head, neck, groin and sides. Wool loses less heat than cotton, down and some synthetics. Choose clothing that covers the head, neck, body and legs, and provides good protection against wind-driven rain. Polyurethane-coated nylon is best.

The Iditarod

The Iditarod Trail Sled Dog Race is a major annual sporting event in Alaska. The first race, conceived and organized by musher Joe Redington, Sr., of Knik, and historian Dorothy Page of Wasilla, was run in 1967 and covered only 56 miles. The race was lengthened in 1973, and the first-ever 1,100-mile sled dog race began in Anchorage on March 3, 1973, and ended April 3 in Nome. Of the 34 who started the race, 22 finished. The Iditarod has been run every year since its inception, and in 1976 Congress designated the Iditarod as a National Historic Trail.

Following the old dog team mail route blazed in 1910 from Knik to Nome, the trail crosses 2 mountain ranges, follows the Yukon River for about 150 miles, runs through several bush villages and crosses the pack ice of Norton Sound. It is strictly a winter trail because the ground is mostly spongy muskeg swamp.

The route attracted national attention in 1925, when sled dog mushers, including the famous Leonhard Seppala, relayed 300,000 units of life-saving diphtheria serum to epidemic-threatened Nome. In later years, as the airplane and snowmobile replaced the dog team, the trail fell into disuse. Through Redington's efforts, the trail has been assured a place in Alaska history.

From the starting line on Fourth Avenue in Anchorage, mushers race their teams to Eagle River, where they load the dogs onto trucks to Settler's Bay in Wasilla, where the race officially begins. It heads out into the Bush, then, 1,000 miles later, to the finish line at Nome. In odd-numbered years, the race takes an alternate route south. While the route is traditionally described as 1,049 miles long (a figure that was selected because Alaska is the 49th state), actual distance is close to 1,100 miles. (See map.)

For more information contact the Iditarod Trail Committee, Pouch X, Wasilla, AK 99687; phone 376-5155, fax 373-6998.

Information Sources

Agriculture
State Division of Agriculture
P.O. Box 949
Palmer 99645
Phone 745-7200

USDA Cooperative Extension Service
University of Alaska
Fairbanks 99775-5200
Phone 474-7246

Employment
Alaska Dept. of Labor
P.O. Box 25509
Juneau 99802-5509
Phone 465-2712

Ferries
Alaska Dept. of Transportation
Division of Marine Highways
P.O. Box 25535
Juneau 99802-5535
Phone 465-3940

Fishing and Hunting
Alaska Dept. of Fish and Game
P.O. Box 25526
Juneau 99802-5526
Phone 465-4112

Mining
U.S. Dept. of the Interior
Bureau of Mines
P.O. Box 20550
Juneau 99802-0550
Phone 364-2111

National Forests
Chugach National Forest
201 E. 9th Ave., Suite 206
Anchorage 99501-3698
Phone 271-2599

Tongass National Forest
USDA Public Affairs Office
P.O. Box 21628
Juneau 99802-1628
Phone 586-8806

21

Public Lands
Alaska Public Lands Information Center
605 W. 4th Ave., Suite 105
Anchorage 99501
Phone 271-2737

Bureau of Land Management
701 C St., Box 13
Anchorage 99513
Phone 271-5076

U.S. Fish & Wildlife Service
1101 E. Tudor Rd.
Anchorage 99503
Phone 786-3486

Tourism
Alaska State Division of Tourism
P.O. Box 11081
Juneau 99811-0801
Phone 465-2010

Insect Pests

An often asked question about travel to Alaska is "When's the best time to avoid mosquitoes?" The answer is probably midwinter. Summer is bug season and you will run into mosquitoes, black flies (also called whitesox, simulids and buffalo gnats), no-see-ums (also called punkies) and snipe flies.

Mosquitoes emerge from hibernation before the snow has entirely disappeared. They peak in about June, but continue to harass humans through the fall. Mosquitoes are especially active in the early morning and at dusk. Mosquito eggs hatch in water, so Alaska with its many square miles of marshy tundra and lakes is prime breeding ground.

The female mosquito penetrates the skin with a hollow snout to draw blood to nourish her eggs. Mosquito saliva, injected into the wound, is what causes the itch, redness and swelling. Mosquitoes are attracted to warmth, moisture, carbon dioxide and dark colors, among other things. Mosquitoes fly into the wind, relying on their antennae to sense a potential meal. They then home in to within a few inches to determine if it is a good meal. Insect repellents work by jamming mosquitoes' sensors so they can't tell if you are a meal. Government sources recommend that you wear a lightweight hooded parka, tight fitting at the wrists, with a drawstring hood so it fits snugly around the face, and trousers tucked securely into socks, to reduce your chances of getting bitten. Mosquitoes can bite through thin material (such as a cotton shirt), so wear some heavier protection

where mosquitoes are active. You may also want to wear a head net when mosquitoes are numerous. Choose a campsite away from mosquito-breeding areas. A 5-mph wind velocity grounds most mosquitoes, so locating your campsite where you'll catch a breeze also helps. Tents should be well-screened against bugs. Cooking outdoors also attracts mosquitoes, so keep food covered.

Many Alaska hikers minimize the mosquito problem by selecting alpine hikes well above tree line in June and early July, when these pests are at their worst. They use the woodsy trails in May, August or even after the first frost in the fall.

The **black fly** biting season starts in May and lasts until freezeup. Activity may be quite localized, depending on your proximity to streams from which the adults are emerging. The reaction to a black fly bite is usually pronounced, and the swelling and itching may last a week or more. Unlike mosquitoes, black flies crawl on the skin under loose clothing and into the hair and ears to bite. The lightweight parka with drawstring hood and trousers tucked into socks will reduce black fly biting.

In some locations along the coast, **no-see-ums** are the major biting insect pest. The swarms of this tiny, gray-black, silver-winged gnat can be extremely bothersome. The no-see-um season extends from June through August. Their bite is a most annoying prolonged prick, after which the surrounding skin becomes inflamed, producing a small red spot that itches intermittently. No-see-ums bite exposed parts of the body. Clothing that covers as much of the body as possible gives the best protection.

Snipe flies are a troublesome pest in certain mountainous localities as far north as the Alaska Range. The pest season extends from late June to early August. The bite stings and is decidedly painful, but shortly afterward there may be little, if any, trace of the bite. These insects retire at sunset. Snipe flies can bite through thin clothing. Tightly woven outer garments that do not directly contact the body help to prevent biting.

According to government sources, mosquito repellents containing diethylmeta-toluamide (DEET) are most effective. Folk wisdom has it that moisturizer made by a cosmetics firm (Avon's Skin-So-Soft) does the best job. It needs to be applied more frequently, but it does not melt plastics and fishing lines as the repellents high in DEET will. Make sure you apply repellent to all exposed skin, including hands, ears and feet.

Repellent is less effective for black flies, no-see-ums and snipe flies. However, these pests are deterred by low humidity and wind.

Language

English is the primary language in Alaska. Many Native languages are still spoken, however, and the majority of Native people are bilingual in English and their own tongue.

Alaskans use several terms that visitors will hear constantly. "Outside" refers to anywhere outside of Alaska, most commonly the contiguous 48 states, which are also called the "Lower 48." "Cheechakos" (*chee-CHAH-koes*) are newcomers, while "sourdoughs" have lived in the North Country for a long time. "Freezeup" comes in the fall, when the rivers and lakes freeze for the winter. This is followed in the spring by "breakup," when the ice breaks up.

Maps

The best source for maps is the U.S. Geological Survey. USGS topographic maps are available in scales from 1:24,000 to 1:250,000. Maps of Alaska are available by mail from the USGS Distribution Branch, Federal Center, Bldg. 810, Box 25286, Denver, CO 80225. Write for an index of maps for Alaska; the index shows published topographic maps available, quadrangle location, name and survey date. (The index and a booklet describing topographic maps are free.)

Sales counters are maintained at USGS offices throughout the country; check the phone book to see if there's an office near you. In Alaska, USGS maps may be purchased over the counter (no mail order) at USGS offices located at 4230 University Dr., Room 101, Anchorage, AK 99508; 605 W. 4th Ave., Room G-84, Anchorage, AK 99501; and Room 126, Federal Bldg., 101 12th Ave., Fairbanks, AK 99701. Residents of Alaska may order maps by mail from the Alaska Distribution Section, Federal Bldg., Box 12, Room 126, 101 12th Ave., Fairbanks, AK 99701. Many commercial dealers also sell USGS maps.

An excellent reference to use along with *The Alaska Wilderness Guide* is the *Alaska Atlas & Gazetteer* published by DeLoreme Mapping, P.O. Box 379-1141, Thomaston, Maine 04861; phone 1-800-225-5669, ext. 1141. The atlas has topo maps of the entire state. Most of the maps are at a scale of 1:300,000 (1 inch represents 4.8 miles). All maps show public-use cabins, trails, park boundaries, and other useful features.

Alaska forest maps may be obtained by sending a check to Tongass National Forest, Forest Service Information Center, 101 Egan Dr., Juneau, 99801. Map prices are: $2 for the Tongass Forest Visitor Map or the Chugach Forest Visitor Map; and $3 each for Road Guide Maps (Prince of Wales, Mitkof Island, Wrangell Island and Hoonah area), Canoe/ Kayak Route Maps (Cross Admiralty, Kuiu Island, Stikine River), or Wilderness/ Monument Maps (Misty Fiords, Admiralty).

Much of the travel in Southeast and Southcentral is by boat, and nautical charts are required for safe navigation. Contact local sporting goods or boat supply stores for charts of your route. For nautical charts through the mail, write: National Ocean Survey, Chart Sales and Control Data, 632 6th Ave., Room 405, Anchorage, AK 99501. Ask for a copy of Nautical Chart Catalog 3 for Alaska.

Money/Credit Cards

Alaska uses American currency. Major bank and credit cards are widely accepted in the larger communities. The larger communities also have at least 1 bank (hours are generally from 10 A.M. to 3 P.M. weekdays; until 6 P.M. Friday). However, the majority of small communities have no banking facilities. Availability of cash may be limited, so even cashing a traveler's check may be difficult. It's a good idea to carry cash with you when traveling to remote areas.

Mountain Climbing

Seeking the heights in Alaska can take you anywhere from the 20,320-foot summit of Mount McKinley to the 3,000-foot peak of an unnamed mountain in the Chugach Range. If there's one thing Alaska has plenty of, it's mountains. And the climbing is superb.

McKinley, North America's tallest peak, attracts some 1,000 climbers a year, with about half that number actually making the summit. The climb requires preparation, planning, and training, with time on the mountain averaging 21 days. Only the strongest and most experienced climbers should attempt McKinley, and even then tragedies occur. Each year the mountain claims an average of 2 climbers. In 1992, 11 climbers died. District Ranger J.D. Swed commented that these deaths could be attributed to "a combination of bad weather, bad judgment and bad luck." That same year, 512 climbers reached the summit out of the 1,070 climbers who made the attempt.

The West Buttress route is the most popular way to the summit and usually takes 18 to 20 days. In 1992, 77 percent of all climbers used this route. Each year a few groups, taking about 4 weeks, tackle traverse expeditions that approximate the route of the sourdoughs on Muldrow Glacier and Karstens Ridge. Other summit routes include the West Rib, Cassin Ridge, South Buttress, South Face, Northwest Buttress and East Buttress.

Because of Mount McKinley's popularity and the brief climbing season (April to July), trash and sanitation problems have developed along the heavily traveled West Buttress. Expeditions have been mounted for the sole purpose of cleanup, and National Park Service regulations require that all trash be packed out, though human wastes may be collected and disposed of into a deep crevasse.

Seven authorized guide services offer climbs up McKinley. Four air services based in Talkeetna specialize in the glacier landings necessary to ferry climbers and their equipment to and from the mountain. An information packet available from the Park Service lists the guides, plus air taxis and dog teams for shuttling climbers' gear. The packet also contains information for foreign climbers, a bibliography, tips on radio, photography, equipment and the like.

The National Park Service rangers based in Talkeetna are experienced climbers and take turns patrolling the mountain to help collect trash, provide emergency rescues, and assist at the 14,000-foot ranger station. Rangers estimate a McKinley climb to cost between $2,000 and $5,000, depending on whether the climb is guided. The estimates do not include the cost of transportation to Alaska.

Many serious climbers head for Alaska's lesser known but more difficult peaks. For ice climbs there is Mount Hunter or Mount Huntington (14,573 feet and 12,240 feet, respectively, both in the Alaska Range). Those interested in steep rock faces might choose peaks near Ruth Glacier, also in the Alaska Range. The Mooses Tooth, a 10,335-foot mountain 15 miles southeast of McKinley, offers steep rock and is itself a prominent peak. The Ruth Gorge is said to closely resemble Yosemite Valley.

To receive an information packet on climbs in Denali National Park, contact the Talkeetna Ranger Station, P.O. Box 588, Talkeetna, AK 99676; phone 733-2231.

Those wishing to escape the crowds on McKinley might opt for 18,008-foot Mount St. Elias, Alaska's second highest peak. (Mount Logan, second tallest mountain in North America, lies across the border in Canada's Kluane National Park and is usually accessed through the Yukon.) The Wrangell and St. Elias mountain peaks have been attracting climbers for more than a century, and each year about a dozen international expeditions head into this mountain wilderness.

The Wrangell-St. Elias National Park and Preserve rangers are headquartered at Glennallen, and like the rangers at Talkeetna will send out information packets upon request. But unlike the McKinley rangers, those at Glennallen are just building their mountaineering program. They ask that climbers who have attempted one of the park's mountains stop into their office and report on the climb, the route used, the difficulties encountered, etc. This information, in spiral notebooks, is available in the office and is a rich source of last-minute advice for expeditions heading out. That address is: Superintendent, Wrangell-St. Elias National Park and Preserve, P.O. Box 29, Glennallen, AK 99588; phone 822-5235.

Climbs in the Brooks Range, on sedimentary rock, are less technically difficult and without so much ice and snow. These appeal to climbers seeking real solitude in high tundra country with the opportunity for considerable wildlife viewing. Technical climbs on granite abound in the Arrigetch Peaks in Gates of the Arctic National Park. Check with guides and air taxi operators in Bettles for specific climbs and logistical support. Check too with park officials: Superintendent, Gates of the Arctic National Park and Preserve, P.O. Box 74680, Fairbanks, AK 99707; phone 456-0281.

Paralytic Shellfish Poisoning

Alaska has a significant problem with poisonous shellfish. This problem is commonly referred to as Paralytic Shellfish Poisoning or PSP, a serious illness caused by poisons concentrated in tiny organisms called *dinoflagellates*. Clams, mussels, geoducks, oysters, snails and scallops filter these food organisms from the water, then absorb and store the toxin. Razor clams appear to accumulate toxin less readily than do hardshell clams; in Cook Inlet there has never been a documented case of PSP from properly cleaned razor clams. However, in southeastern Alaska there have been numerous poisonings from other types of clams. Toxin levels may be extremely high — death has occurred after ingestion of only 1 mussel. You cannot use the presence or absence of a red tide (caused by the rapid growth of certain kinds of planktons which may or may not produce toxins) to determine whether a beach is safe for clamming. In the case of butter clams and mussels, it does not matter whether there has been a red tide within the past 2 weeks or the past 2 years; there is no guarantee that they will be free of PSP. The organisms that cause PSP may be present at any time during the year. Neither cooking nor freezing eliminates the toxin.

Alaska clams may be poisonous unless they have been harvested from an approved beach. Commercial harvesting areas are tested for this poisoning and require approval from the Dept. of Environmental Conservation. Visitors to most beaches cannot be assured that the shellfish is safe; therefore it is wise to use caution when collecting shellfish for consumption. In general, avoid eating shellfish from recreational beaches and areas where shellfish could be infected by sewage from homes or campgrounds. All clams should be eviscerated (the gut and dark-colored parts removed) before eating. Discard clams with cracked shells, if the animal is discolored or if it appears to be dead.

When toxin is present, symptoms usually occur within 10 to 30 minutes of eating a clam or its broth. The first sign is tingling or burning of the lips, gums, tongue and face, gradually progressing to the neck, arms, fingertips, legs and toes. If a lot of toxin has been ingested, symptoms may extend to dryness of the mouth, nausea and vomiting, shortness of breath, loss of coordination, a choking sensation in the throat, dizziness, weakness and confused or slurred speech.

While death seldom occurs, it can result from respiratory muscle paralysis within 3 to 12 hours after the clams are eaten. Anyone who has eaten clams and has begun to experience symptoms like those above should promptly get medical care. An emetic to empty the stomach and a rapid-acting laxative are current treatment. Leftover clams should be saved for laboratory tests.

The latest information on which beaches are approved is available through the Alaska Dept. of Environmental Conservation, P.O. Box 1088, Palmer, AK 99645; phone 745-3236.

Poisonous Plants

There are poisonous plants in Alaska, but not many considering the total number of plant species growing in the state. Baneberry *(Actaea rubra)*, water hemlock *(Cicuta douglasii* and *C. mackenzieana)* and fly agaric mushroom *(Amanita muscaria)* are the most dangerous. Be sure you have properly identified plants before harvesting for food. Alaska has no plants that are poisonous to the touch such as poison ivy or poison oak, although some people develop allergic reactions from coming in contact with such plants as Indian rhubarb and nettles.

For more information on plants, read *Wild Edible and Poisonous Plants of Alaska,* available for $2 from Alaska bookstores or from the Cooperative Extension Service, University of Alaska, Fairbanks, AK 99775-5200.

Radio

Alaska's radio stations broadcast a wide variety of music, talk shows, religious and educational programs. Several stations also broadcast personal messages, long a popular and necessary form of communication in bush Alaska. These programs bring news of weddings, births and deaths, but also provide a quick way of telling Auntie at Brevig Mission, for instance, that her groceries will be on the next mailplane.

Stations with personal message programs include the following:

Anchorage, KYAK 650 kHz; 2800 Dowling, 99507. "Bush Pipeline," 8 P.M., transmitting within a 300-mile radius of Anchorage.

Barrow, KBRW-AM 680 kHz; P.O. Box 109, 99723. "Tundra Drums," ongoing 6 A.M. to midnight.

Bethel, KYUK 640 kHz; Pouch 468, 99559. "Tundra Drums," 8:30 and 11:30 A.M., 3:30 and 8:30 P.M.

Dillingham, KDLG 670 kHz; P.O. Box 670, 99576. "Bay Messenger," 10:25 A.M., 12:25, 2:25, 4:25 and 8:25 P.M.

Fairbanks, KIAK 970 kHz; P.O. Box 73410, 99707. "Pipeline of the North," 6:45 and 8:45 P.M. Monday through Saturday.

Galena, KIYU-AM 910 kHz; P.O. Box 165, 99741. "Yukon Wireless," 8 and 11:45 A.M. and 7:00 P.M.

Glennallen, KCAM 790 kHz; P.O. Box 249, 99588. "Caribou Clatter," 7:20 A.M. and 12:20, 5:50 and 9:20 P.M.

Haines, KHNS-FM 102.3 MHz; P.O. Box 1109, 99827. "Listener Personals," 8:40 and 11:40 A.M., 1:40, 4:40 and 10:40 P.M.

Homer, KBBI-AM 890 kHz; 3913 Kachemak Way, 99603. "The Bay Bush Lines," 7:20 and 9:55 A.M., and 2, 6 and 9 P.M.

Ketchikan, KRBD-FM 105.9 MHz; 716 Totem Way, 99901. Also received in Metlakatla, Hollis and Thorne Bay. Translator service to Klawock and Hydaburg, 90.1 MHz; Craig, 101.7 MHz. "Muskeg Messenger," 8:30 A.M., 1:30 and 7:30 P.M.

Kodiak, KVOK-AM 560 kHz and KJJZ-FM 101.1 MHz; P.O. Box 708, 99615. "Highliner Crabbers," 6:15 and 9:15 A.M., 12:25, 7:10 and 11:50 P.M. daily.

McGrath, KSKO 870 kHz; P.O. Box 70, 99627. "KSKO Messages," 58 minutes past the hour.

Nome, KICY 850 kHz; P.O. Box 820, 99762. "Ptarmigan Telegraph," 12:25 and 6:25 P.M.

Nome, KNOM 780 kHz; P.O. Box 988, 99762. "Hot Lines," 12:15 and 5:15 P.M. daily.

North Pole, KJNP 1170 kHz; P.O. Box 0, 99705. "Trapline Chatter," 9:20 P.M. Monday through Friday, 9:30 P.M. Saturday, 9:35 P.M. Sunday. Emergency messages any time.

Petersburg, KFSK-FM 100.9 MHz; P.O. Box 149, 99833. "Muskeg Messages," 5:19, 6:19, 7:19, 8 A.M., noon, 5:45 and 10 P.M.

Petersburg, KRSA 580 kHz; P.O. Box 650, 99833. "Channel Chatters," 6:20 and 7:20 A.M., 12:35, 5:45 and 9:10 P.M.

Sitka, KCAW-FM 104.7 MHz; 102 B. Lincoln St., 99835. Translator service to Angoon, 105.5 MHz; Kake, 107.1 MHz; Pelican, 91.7 MHz; Port Alexander and Tenakee Springs, 91.9 MHz. "Muskeg Messages," 6:55, 7:55 and 8:55 A.M., 1 and 6:15 P.M. weekdays; 6:59 and 7:59 A.M., 1 and 5 P.M. on weekends.

Soldotna, KSRM 920 kHz; SR2, Box 852, 99669. "Tundra Tom Tom," 6:30 P.M. daily.

Wrangell, KSTK-FM 101.7 MHz; P.O. Box 1141, 99929. Radiograms, 7:30 and 11:30 A.M., 5:30 and 9:30 P.M.

Railroads

The Alaska Railroad offers service between Fairbanks, Anchorage, Whittier and Seward. The railroad provides express service between Anchorage and Denali National Park from May to September. Local service stops anywhere along the line between Anchorage and Hurricane Gulch. Schedules vary depending on the season. For information contact the Alaska Railroad, P.O. Box 107500, Anchorage, AK 99510; phone 265-2494 or 800-544-0552.

The White Pass & Yukon Route, the historic railroad between Skagway and Whitehorse, offers daily summer service from Skagway. Operating 40 miles of the original 110 mile narrow-gauge line, the WP&YR offers 3 excursions: the 3-hour, 40-mile, round trip to White Pass Summit; the 6-hour, 80-mile, round trip to Lake Bennett; and the combination train and connecting bus service between Skagway and Whitehorse. Passenger train service also hauls hikers from the end of the Chilkoot Trail at Lake Bennett. Contact the railroad for current information at White Pass Depot, P.O. Box 435, Skagway, AK 99840; phone 983-2217 or toll free in the United States 1-800-343-7373, fax 983-2734.

Snow Machining

In bush villages, which have few if any roads and cars, snow machines provide winter transportation and freight hauling as well as winter fun. Many trappers use snow machines on their traplines, and homesteaders rely on them as well.

Recreational snow machining by both bush and urban Alaskans has grown into one of Alaska's most popular wintertime activities, though backcountry travelers must take special precautions. Each spring more than one snowmobiler is lost when rider and machine break through ice that is too thin to support their almost 600-pound combined weight. Monty Alford in his *Wilderness Survival Guide* advises that for safety you need a bare minimum of 3 inches of ice on a lake — provided that it is black ice totally supported by water and that the snow machine speed is kept below 10 mph. River ice, he advises, is 15 percent weaker than lake ice; and sea ice, 50 percent weaker. Temperatures should be no higher than 20°F/-7°C.

Public lands have varying rules about where snow machines are allowed, so before you head out, check with local land managers to make sure you will be riding legally. Historic conflicts between cross-country skiers and snowmobilers have resulted in strict divisions of popular trails and areas between mechanized and nonmechanized use. Alaska has no publicly developed trail system specifically for snowmobilers.

Snow machine races are scattered throughout the state from November into April.

Special Events

Here are some special events happening in communities around the state. For a more extensive calendar of events, contact the Division of Tourism.

January
Kuskokwim 300 Sled Dog Race (Bethel)

February
Fur Rendezvous (Anchorage)
Gold Rush Classic Snowmachine Race
    (Nome)
Yukon Quest International Sled Dog Race
    (Fairbanks)

March
Beaver Roundup Festival (Dillingham)
Bering Sea Ice Gold Classic (Nome)
Iditarod Sled Dog Race (Anchorage to Nome)
Nome to Golovin Snow Machine Race
    (Nome)
Open North American Championship Sled
    Dog Race (Fairbanks)

April
Archie Ferguson-Willy Goodwin Memorial
    Snow Machine Race (Kotzebue)
Piuraagiaqta/Spring Festival (Barrow)

May
Walrus Festival (Savoonga)
Little Norway Festival (Petersburg)
Miners Day (Talkeetna)

June
Nalukatag/Whaling Festival (Barrow)
Yukon 800 Marathon Boat Race (Fairbanks)

July
Moose Dropping Festival (Talkeetna)
World Eskimo-Indian Olympics (Fairbanks)

August
Alaska State Fair (Palmer)
Southeast Alaska State Fair (Haines)
Tanana Valley Fair (Fairbanks)

Telephone, Telegraph, Money Orders

All of Alaska uses the 907 telephone area code.

Telegrams, cablegrams, mailgrams, telex and FAX can be sent by telephone from anywhere in Alaska through Western Union. Major credit cards are accepted. Money orders by wire can also be arranged through Western Union, which is located at 3605 Arctic Blvd., Anchorage, AK 99503; phone 563-3131. (Banks can also wire money, but bank wires take considerably longer.) The Western Union office in Anchorage is open Monday through Saturday from 8 A.M. to 8 P.M. and Sunday from 10 A.M. to 4 P.M. except on national holidays. Western Union branch offices are located throughout the state. Information about branch offices may be obtained by calling 1-800-325-6000.

Television

Television in Alaska's larger communities, such as Anchorage and Fairbanks, was available years before satellites. Television reached the Bush in the late 1970s with the construction of telephone earth stations which could receive television programming via satellite transmissions. Same day broadcasts to the Bush, arriving via satellite, of news and sports events are subsidized in part by state revenues. The state also funds the rural Alaska television network, bringing general and education programming to nearly 250 communities.

Time Zones

At Alaska's request, the federal government reduced the state's time zones from 4 to 2, effective Oct. 30, 1983. The state now is operating on Alaska time, or 1 hour earlier than Pacific time. The only residents of the state not setting their clocks on Alaska time are in the 4 small western Aleutian communities of Atka, Adak, Shemya and Attu and on St. Lawrence Island, which moved to Aleutian-Hawaii time, 1 hour earlier than Alaska time.

Tours

Tours have become so popular in recent years that tour companies have designed packages to meet the requirements of almost anyone, including those who wish to experience Alaska's wilderness areas. A packaged tour does not mean that you are bound by an itinerary that includes areas of little interest to you, nor by a time schedule that does not allow you to see and do the things of greatest interest to you.

There is such a wide variety of tours offered that chances are you can find one that includes areas you wish to see, your preference for mode of travel and one that will fit your pocketbook and calendar. The trip may be a complete air-travel tour, a cruise through the Inside Passage, a motorcoach tour from Seattle to Fairbanks, or a combination of air, sea and land travel. Tour companies offer escorted tours, independent

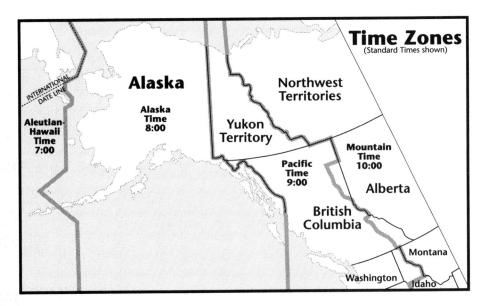

Time Zones
(Standard Times shown)

Alaska

Alaska
Time
8:00

Northwest Territories

Aleutian-
Hawaii
Time
7:00

INTERNATIONAL DATE LINE

Yukon Territory

Mountain
Time
10:00

Pacific
Time
9:00

Alberta

British Columbia

Montana

Washington   Idaho

tours or a combination.

You may select an escorted tour which is overseen by a competent director who accompanies the group on the entire trip, takes care of all luggage, tickets, hotel check-ins and alleviates all cares and anxieties, leaving the traveler free to enjoy the trip.

You may select an independent tour where you are completely by yourself, although there may be others traveling on the same itinerary. You would handle your own tickets, luggage, hotel check-ins and personal activities. The service companies are alerted to your arrival and arrangements are prepaid so you merely present a voucher for each requirement. At the larger transfer points, a company representative is available to answer questions and make possible changes so you are not left completely on your own; assistance is always nearby.

For more information about tours to Alaska, contact your travel agent. Also see the Adventure Travel Directory in the back of this book for listings of businesses offering services for wilderness travelers.

Trichinosis

Trichinosis is a serious disease commonly associated with eating improperly cooked pork. The same parasite infects Alaska's bears, foxes, wolves, mink, walrus and seals; therefore, thorough cooking is necessary for the safe preparation of these meats.

Tularemia

The Dept. of Environmental Conservation advises visitors to Alaska to exercise caution in handling the snowshoe hare, which is often infected with tularemia, a disease transmissable to humans. The bacteria causing the disease are present in the blood and body fluids of infected hares. Humans usually acquire the disease during skinning and cleaning of the animals. The bacteria enter through cuts and breaks in a person's skin. Normal cooking kills the bacteria. Ticks transmit the disease from animal to animal and could expose humans to the disease if crushed while handling the hare, although these ticks do not feed on humans. Greatest risk is from May through September when ticks are present; the disease falls to low levels after freezing weather. Another, less virulent, variety of tularemia occurs in rodents and can be contracted by drinking improperly disinfected surface water.

Visiting Native Villages

If you're going to the Bush you probably will be visiting at least 1 village. You will encounter different languages and customs and a different, more leisurely sense of time. You may see racks of salmon drying during the summer season, or a whale being butchered in the spring. You will meet some wonderful people. The village phone may not work and you may not have a flush toilet. If you are flexible and can cope without all the amenities you may be accustomed to, you can have a memorable trip.

Accommodations may be scarce. Hotels are available in larger communities such as Bethel, Kotzebue or Barrow. Smaller villages may have a community-operated lodge, but then again they may not. Most villages have general stores, but their stocks can be limited and many do not have regular hours. It's best to be prepared to be self-sufficient. Bring a sleeping bag (a tent may be a good idea, too) and your own groceries. Also, camera film may not be available, so bring your own. Laundromats and showers are available in some, but not all, communities.

Following are a few guidelines for visiting a village from the Tanana Chiefs Conference, Fairbanks, and the National Park Service.

Visitors should treat the village as they would a private home, where people respect local lifestyles, customs and the privacy of others. The village or city chief or the community council office is the best place to get general information. Information about accommodations and other conditions in villages also may be available from the bush airlines that serve them. *The Alaska Wilderness Guide* includes information on accommodations in the community listings, but it is a good idea to write to a village leader before your trip for permission and/or to make arrangements for accommodations. (Some villages do not encourage visitors, while others do.) Advance reservations are recommended, particularly during the summer construction season. During winter months it is wise to call ahead to be sure lodges and facilities are open. Many operate only seasonally. If there is no lodge, visitors may be able to pay a local family or the school teachers for room and board. Be sure to ask permission before setting up a tent in or near a village; a few villages have campgrounds, but most do not. Visitors should always be courteous and never impose on the residents. Again, it's best to be prepared to be self-sufficient.

Visitors to bush villages should be aware of local ordinances concerning firearms, importation and use of alcoholic beverages, vehicles and pets. Photography is generally acceptable if done with consideration for the local residents; ask permission.

English is spoken in villages throughout the Bush. Translation should not be required except with elderly people. Sensitivity is the key to communicating in a cross-cultural setting. Visitors should avoid asking too many questions and making comparisons with "how we do it back home." It is important to speak slowly, listen intently and avoid intensely serious tones.

Local transportation is usually by snow machine, boat or 3-wheeler, but larger communities have a few cars and trucks. Visitors should be willing to pay local people for rides to and from the airport or for other transportation. Informal guiding for fishing is generally available; make arrangements in advance or ask around.

Gasoline is available from local vendors in nearly all communities. Special camp fuels may not be available. Travelers should expect irregular hours at all service facilities.

Be aware that much of the land around bush communities is owned by Native corporations and you may need their permission to camp, hike, fish or hunt. Some village corporations are now charging user fees. Addresses of village corporations are included in the community listings in *The Alaska Wilderness Guide*. Also, there may be public easements across Native lands to provide access to national parks or wildlife refuges. Contact the park or refuge office for information concerning your planned route.

Wilderness travelers may encounter local residents engaged in hunting, trapping or other subsistence activities. These activities are permitted on national park and refuge lands, and can include free-ranging activities, as well as stationary fishing and hunting camps or traplines. Your presence can influence game movements and thus disrupt subsistence uses. You may need to change your trip route to avoid interfering with subsistence activities. While a camp may look abandoned, chances are it is used periodically and should not be disturbed. Also, never touch fish nets, traps or other subsistence gear. This equipment is crucial to the livelihood of local residents.

When to Go/What to Wear

One of the most often asked questions is "When is the best time to travel?" The high season is June through August, which are generally the sunniest months in Alaska, although July is often one of the wettest months in some regions.

In general, dress is casual. Comfortable shoes and easy-care clothes are best, dressy clothes are certainly appropriate for a night out in the larger cities. If you forget something, there are stores in the larger communities where you can buy what you need.

In southeastern Alaska, summers average nearly 60°F in July, with an occasional heat wave pushing temperatures into the 70s and 80s. Winters mean snow, more rain and sunshine, with a relatively warm January average in Juneau of about 29°F.

In Southeast, dressing in layers is the best plan throughout the year. Spring through fall, start with short sleeves, add a sweater or wool shirt and top it off with a light, waterproof jacket. When you're out in misty weather on the water, or near a glacier, gloves and hat are useful. In winter, just add another sweater or fiberfill jacket, plus light long underwear. Walking shoes like the moccasin style with rubber bottoms and low leather tops work well all year in Southeast.

Southcentral has a mixture of weather patterns. Prince William Sound has a mild, maritime climate, while Anchorage and inland areas have less precipitation and greater temperature ranges. Temperatures in July in Anchorage average nearly 60°F, with highs in the 70s. Snow stays on the ground generally from late October through mid-April.

To dress for a Southcentral summer of 50°F to 70°F with low humidity, bring light clothing with a sweater or light jacket for cooler days. Light rain gear is advisable. For fall or spring, add a layer of wool or down, plus a light hat and gloves. For winter, wear a down jacket, wool hat and gloves, warm slacks and lined boots.

On the Alaska Peninsula and Kodiak and Aleutian islands of Southwestern, arctic weather clashes with the more temperate climate of the North Pacific. The weather can change hourly. The Aleutians have an annual temperature variation of only 25 degrees, from 30°F to 55°F. Clothing in several light layers, topped by water- and windproof outer layers works best. In mainland areas, dress warmly for winter with fiberfill and wool, with windproof outer garments. Wool hat and gloves, plus lined boots, are essential for snowy months.

The same type of clothing will suffice throughout Western Alaska: several light layers in summer, and warmer layers in winter. Waterproof boots are advisable during breakup season when the ground is soggy.

The arctic region gets little precipitation; its humidity is comparable to the world's deserts. Light, dry snow stays on the ground from September to May. Ice masses remain in the ocean through the summer. Only the top several inches of earth thaw for a few months.

The year-round rule for clothing is warm and windproof. In summer, wear a windproof jacket with a warm shirt or sweater underneath for the 40°F days. Layers allow for the most flexibility if the temperature changes. Rubber-soled footwear is useful. For fall, winter and spring, bring long underwear, warm slacks and shirt, wool sweater and thick down jacket. Warm, windproof covering for head and hands is essential.

The Interior has the greatest temperature variations in the state. You may see clear summer days in the 90s, and winter nights in the -50s. Total annual precipitation is low, but there are occasional thunderstorms in summer. Snow is on the ground from October through April. Winds are light.

Summer clothing means light slacks or shorts, light blouses or shirts, and a sweater for cloudy days. Add a couple of layers for spring and fall. The extremely low winter temperatures require layers of wool and down clothing, with warm hats, mittens and lined boots.

Wilderness Classes

Imagine getting college credits for a course titled "Wilderness Adventures and Natural History of Alaska." Or one called "Backpacking"; or "Ski Mountaineering: Ruth Glacier"; or "Tracking," "Canoeing," or "Family Camping." This is not a fantasy curriculum dreamed up by some desperate city-bound worker longing for the beauty and freedom of Alaska. It is a sampling of the courses offered for credit by the Alaska Wilderness Studies program within the College of Community and Continuing Education, University of Alaska Anchorage, 3211 Providence Dr., Anchorage, AK 99508; phone 786-1468, fax 786-1563.

The Alaska Wilderness Studies program teaches outdoor skills to almost a thousand people a year in its summer, fall and winter classes. Winter classes include skiing, telemarking, ice climbing, winter survival, map and compass reading, wilderness emergency care, dog mushing (the Anchorage Sled Dog Assoc. supplies the dogs and sleds), and ski joring (you bring the family mutt).

Winter classes usually cost less than $100; summer courses (including travel) can be more expensive. "Advanced Backpacking: Wrangell-St. Elias National Park," for example, costs $711. In the past only a few non-Alaskans have taken these courses, but

Alaska Wilderness School Director Todd Miner is hoping to attract out-of-state visitors. All classes include weekend field days; and group, safety, and camping equipment are provided. Anyone interested in learning a new skill and experiencing Alaska on an intimate level is encouraged to apply. The program's noncredit courses offer an even wider variety of topics: fly-fishing, rock climbing, ocean kayaking, expedition rafting, wildflowers, glacier travel and crevasses rescue, mountaineering for hunters, and others.

The wilderness school curriculum is not, unfortunately, duplicated throughout the state, though university branches elsewhere offer a few similar courses from time to time. But the university system is only one option for those seeking to acquire or improve on wilderness skills.

Wildlife Watching

Alaska has a well-deserved reputation for abundant wildlife. Observing and photographing birds and mammals in their natural habitat can add immensely to your visit.

For an overview of wildlife viewing opportunities in Alaska, request a copy of the brochure on wildlife viewing from the Alaska Public Lands Information Center, (605 W. 4th Ave., Suite 105, Anchorage, AK 99501; phone 271-2737). The Bureau of Land Management also offers a publication on wildlife viewing, *Watchable Wildlife Guide.*

Following are some guidelines from the Alaska Dept. of Fish and Game for observing or photographing wildlife.

Observe animals from a distance. Use binoculars, spotting scopes or telephoto lenses to get a closer look. If an animal shows signs of being crowded or disturbed, sit quietly or move slowly away. Signs you are too close include the following:

From a mammal: Raises head high with ears pointed in your direction; is skittish, jumps at sounds or movements; moves away or lowers head, ears back in preparation for a charge, has erect hairs on neck and shoulders; displays aggressive/nervous behavior.

From a bird: Raises head, looks at you; is skittish; preens excessively or pecks at dirt or food; wipes bill; makes alarm calls, repeatedly chirps or chips; performs tail spread or distraction display—broken wing.

Move slowly. Let the animal keep you in view. Avoid sneaking up on animals.

Limit the time you spend at or near a nest to 5 or 10 minutes. Do not disturb the plants around the nest or handle the eggs or young. Keep far enough away from nesting colonies that you don't flush the birds.

Never chase, flush or harass animals on foot, in an auto, boat, plane, ATV, snow machine or any other vehicle. Harassing animals is against state law and punishable by a $1,000 fine and up to 6 months in jail. Never allow your pets to harass wildlife.

Do not use tape recorded calls or other attraction devices except in areas people visit infrequently and then use them only sparingly. Bears attracted by predator calls can be extremely dangerous.

Never approach an animal when other people are observing it. Inconsiderate observers who approach too closely ruin their own wildlife photos and those of others. Frightened or nervous animals are less interesting to watch, and experienced wildlife observers can easily tell if the animal in a photo was alarmed or harassed.

Stop on roadsides to view wildlife only if a safe pullout area is available. Remain quiet and in your car. If you frighten the animal, you deny others the chance to see it.

Always obtain permission from landowners before traveling on private property, even if you just want to look at the plants or wildlife. (Thousands of acres of land in the state have become the private property of Alaska Native corporations under the Alaska Native Claims Settlement Act.)

Never litter or deface property or the natural environment. Trespassing and littering soon lead to No Trespassing signs and regulations that limit everyone's opportunities to enjoy wildlife.

Always keep a good distance between you and a cow moose with calves. A cow may charge on little provocation, and her flying hooves can seriously injure a person.

Totem parks are found throughout Southeast, with major collections at Ketchikan, Klawock, Wrangell, Sitka and Haines. (Lee Foster)

SOUTHEAST

A lush northern rain forest of incom-par-able beauty, Alaska's Southeast is a land where eagles soar, whales frolic and brown bear roam at will. Dramatic tidewater glaciers, spectacular fjords, massive ice fields and rugged mountains bear the imprint of the last ice age. A rich cultural mix of Indians, Russians and gold prospectors enlivens the more recent history of the communities.

Southeast's mighty Indian cultures ruled the region when the first white men, the Russians, came to the area. After several skirmishes, the Russians won a foothold in the area and made Sitka, known as *Nova Arkhangelsk* or New Archangel, the capital of Russian America for the Russia–American Co. After the Americans took over in 1867, mining, fishing and timber provided the economic base.

Southeast remained Alaska's dominant region until WWII, when military activity and construction of the Alaska Highway shifted the emphasis to Anchorage and Fairbanks.

Today fishing, government, tourism and timber fuel Southeast's economy. Seven population centers and hundreds of little settlements dot the region's shoreline. About 20 percent of the region's population is Native, predominantly Tlingit, Haida and Tsimshian. Most of the Haidas live near Hydaburg and the Tsimshians make their home at Metlakatla.

Amid the breathtaking beauty and the rich history of Southeast, opportunities for outdoor adventure abound. The protected waterways offer a lifetime of bays, fjords and channels to explore and some of the finest fishing in Alaska. Watching whales, rafting rivers, hiking and hunting, skiing the ice fields or retreating to a snug lodge in a secluded cove are other popular pursuits.

Location: Southeast stretches 560 miles from Dixon Entrance at the U.S.–Canada border south of Ketchikan to Icy Bay northwest of Yakutat.

Geography: Geological activity has sculpted more than a thousand islands in Southeast, including Prince of Wales, third largest in the country at 2,231 square miles. The region's narrow strip of mainland is isolated from the rest of North America by the St. Elias and Coast mountains. The St. Elias, topping out at 18,008 feet at the summit of Mount St. Elias, is the highest coastal range in the world. Numerous rivers drain this wet, steep land. Among the more important are the Stikine and Taku, which breach the mountain barrier and provide some access into the Interior.

Heavy rainfall and a mild climate encourage timber growth. Three-quarters of Southeast is covered with dense forests, primarily western hemlock and Sitka spruce, interspersed with red cedar and Alaska yellow cedar. Ground cover is luxuriant and includes devil's club, blueberries, huckleberries, mosses and ferns.

Climate: Warmed by ocean currents, Southeast enjoys mild, warm temperatures averaging around 60°F in the summer. Winters are cool, alternating snow, rain and sunshine; January temperatures average 20°F to 40°F. Subzero winter temperatures are uncommon.

The region experiences considerable annual rainfall, from 80 to more than 200 inches, with the heaviest rains in late fall and the lightest in summer. Populated areas receive from 30 to 200 inches of snow annually; the high mountains get more than 400 inches a year.

Wildlife: Southeast has prime habitat for Sitka black-tailed deer, bears and wolves. Brown bears inhabit Admiralty, Baranof and Chichagof islands, and portions of the mainland. Black bears occur on other forested islands and the mainland. Moose browse in scattered populations and mountain goats stick to steep cliffs in Glacier Bay and other mountainous areas.

Furbearers and nongame species in Southeast include lynx, wolverines, foxes, mink, river otters, marten, porcupines and an assortment of small mammals.

Marine mammals abound in the region. Humpback and killer whales, sea lions and seals are easily seen in season in many waterways.

Southeast boasts the largest bald eagle population in the world. Thousands congregate each fall at the Alaska Chilkat Bald Eagle Preserve near Haines. Waterfowl pass through the area during migration, with huge flocks staging on the Stikine Flats and near other estuaries.

Salmon, halibut, black cod, shellfish, herring, steelhead, trout, grayling — Southeast has some of the finest fishing, both sport and commercial, in the world.

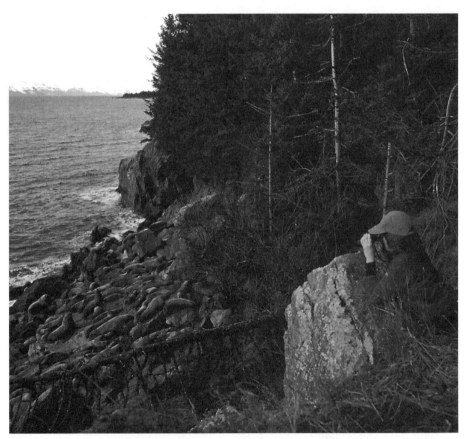

Southeast offers many opportunities for observing marine mammals. These sea lions are hauled out along Lynn Canal. (David Job)

Angoon

[MAP 2] Located on the west coast of Admiralty Island on Chatham Strait, at the mouth of Kootznahoo Inlet, 55 miles southwest of Juneau, 41 miles northeast of Sitka. **Transportation:** Scheduled ferry service via Alaska Marine Highway; scheduled seaplane service from Juneau. **Population:** 708. **Zip code:** 99820. **Emergency Services:** Police, Volunteer Fire Department, phone 788-3631; Clinic, phone 788-3633.

Elevation: Sea level. **Climate:** Moderate maritime weather, with monthly mean temperatures of 28°F in January and 55°F in July. Annual rainfall is 40 inches.

Private Aircraft: Angoon seaplane base; 0.9 mile southeast.

Visitor Facilities: Accommodations are available at Favorite Bay Inn/Whalers Cove Sports Fishing Lodge (788-3125) and Kootznahoo Inlet Lodge (788-3501). Groceries and supplies are available at Angoon Trading Co. (788-3111). Angoon Community Assoc. operates a laundry. No banking services. Fishing/hunting licenses may be purchased locally. Charter fishing boats and canoes are available; no other rental transportation. Fuel service (gas and diesel) and transient moorage are available at boat harbor.

Angoon is a long-established Tlingit Indian settlement at the entrance to Kootznahoo Inlet. It is the only permanent community on Admiralty Island. On Killisnoo Island, across the harbor from the state ferry landing at Angoon, a community of summer homes has grown along the island beaches. The lifestyle of this primarily Tlingit town is heavily subsistence: fish, clams, seaweed, berries and venison. Fishing, mostly hand trolling for king and coho salmon, is the principal industry. Unemployment in Angoon is high throughout the year.

The scenery of Admiralty Island draws many visitors to Angoon. The island boasts the largest nesting population of eagles anywhere. Angoon and vicinity offer exceptional feeding areas for killer and humpback whales and excellent saltwater and freshwater fishing. All but the northern portion of the island was declared a national monument and is managed by the U.S. Forest Service.

Kootznahoo Inlet and Mitchell Bay near Angoon offer a network of small wooded islands, reefs and channels for kayaking. Wildlife includes many brown bears (Admiralty Island's Indian name *Kootznoowoo* means "Fortress of Bears"), Sitka black-tailed deer and bald eagles.

Local residents can provide directions to the interesting old Killisnoo graveyards, located both on Killisnoo Island and on the Angoon shore of the old Killisnoo settlement, which once was one of the larger communities in southeastern Alaska.

Communications include phones in most households (and CB radios for local communication), daily mail service by plane, good radio reception and TV via satellite and cable. There are churches and a school with grades kindergarten through 12. Angoon prohibits the possession of alcoholic beverages. Community electric power, water and sewage systems are available. Freight comes in by barge and ferry. Government address: City of Angoon, P.O. Box 189, Angoon, AK 99820; phone 788-3653, fax 788-3821. Village corporation address: Kootznoowoo Inc., P.O. Box 116, Angoon, AK 99820.

Coffman Cove

[MAP 2] Located on the northeast coast of Prince of Wales Island, 53 miles north of Klawock, 42 miles southeast of Wrangell, and 73 miles northeast of Ketchikan. **Transportation:** Accessible via Prince of Wales Island road system and by boat; weekly floatplane service from Ketchikan. **Population:** 272. **Zip code:** 99918. **Emergency Services:** Alaska State Troopers in Klawock, phone 755-2955; Craig Medical Clinic, Wrangell and Ketchikan hospitals.

Edna Bay

[MAP 2] Located on Edna Bay at the southeast end of Kosciusko Island off the northwest coast of Prince of Wales Island, 45 miles north of Craig, 90 miles northwest of Ketchikan. **Transportation:** By boat or floatplane. **Population:** 80. **Zip code:** 99917. **Emergency Services:** For medical emergencies contact the U.S. Coast Guard, VHF radio channel 16; Alaska State Troopers in Ketchikan, contact by VHF radio.

Elevation: Sea level. **Climate:** Cool and wet. Private Aircraft: Floatplane landings only.

Visitor Facilities: Edna Bay is primarily a fishing community with no visitor facilities or services. (A fish buyer is located in the bay in the summer.) Supplies are brought in by cargo plane or boat from Craig, Ketchikan or Petersburg, and supplies and groceries are available at the Cedar Bite Trading Post. Many logging roads can be used for hunting. Communications are by mail plane, radio and community phone (594-9001). There is a post office. The Edna Bay school has grades 1 through 12.

Eight Fathom Bight

(See **Cube Cove**)

Elfin Cove

[MAP 1] Located at the northern tip of Chichagof Island, 70 miles west of Juneau, 33 miles northwest of Hoonah. **Transportation:** By seaplane or boat. **Population:** 47. **Zip code:** 99825. **Emergency Services:** EMT in Elfin Cove, physician's assistant in Pelican, hospital in Juneau; Alaska State Troopers in Juneau, phone 789-2161, and Hoonah, phone 945-3655. Village Public Safety Officer in Pelican, phone 735-2212.

Elevation: 20 feet. **Climate:** Cool and wet in summer, with a mean monthly temperature in July of 54°F and 4.98 inches of precipitation. Precipitation averages 9.54 inches in January, with low temperatures to 28°F.

Private Aircraft: Floatplane dock; emergency fuel (100) available. *CAUTION: Westerly swells.*

Visitor Facilities: Elfin Cove is primarily a fish-buying and supply center for fishermen. Services are seasonal. The Elf Inn & Cafe (phone 239-2204) rents 2 rooms. Piedra's (239-2208) is a bed and breakfast. Pelican Seafoods–Elfin Cove (239-2232) offers showers, laundry, and hostel-style accommodations

on a limited basis aboard their fish-buying scow. Groceries are available at Elfin General Supply (239-2211) and Pelican Seafoods (239-2208). Fishing gear, public laundry, showers, sauna, liquor, gifts, stationery, boat electronics and marine hardware are available. Marine repair available in Pelican. No banking services. Marine gas, diesel and propane are available at the fuel dock. Fishing/hunting licenses are available. Transient moorage available at Elfin Cove dock.

Paul Johnson, a professional guide (239-2211 summer, 463-5374 winter), offers custom bear-photography tours. Sandy Craig (P.O. Box 13, Elfin Cove, AK 99825 summer, phone 364-2181 winter) and Sandy Darnell (239-2206) offer day sightseeing and wildlife viewing charters. Sportfishing packages are available at Cross Sound Lodge (239-2210 summer, 206-256-1337 winter), Elfin Cove Sportfishing Lodge (239-2212 summer, 206-228-7092 winter), and Tanaku Lodge (239-2205). Elfin Cove Travel (239-2202) is the local agent for most air taxi services and can help locate rental cabins and charter boats.

This protected, flask-shaped harbor was originally called "Gunkhole" by fishermen anchoring here. Its safe anchorage and proximity to the Fairweather fishing grounds made this a natural spot for fish buyers and a supply point for fishermen. Ernie Swanson built a store, restaurant and dock here in the late 1920s. When his wife, Ruth, applied for a post office in 1936, she gave it the new name of Elfin Cove. John Lowell, another fish buyer, arrived in the 1940s and built a second dock, a warehouse, store and restaurant. According to locals, the Tlingits who visited the harbor would not overwinter because of "evil spirits" there.

Everything at Elfin Cove is connected by boardwalks and most structures are built over the water on pilings. It is still a mostly seasonal community, active during the fishing season when local businesses serve the commercial fishing fleet. Many people migrate south or to Juneau for the winter. But, says resident Mary Jo Lord-Wild, "There are (also) many of us who live here, raise our children here, shovel snow and call it home." While most local people are fishermen or depend on the commercial fishing industry for a living, the area's scenery, sportfishing and other recreation are drawing an increasing number of tourists, and 3 lodges have been established in recent years. There is year-round bottom fish and halibut fishing. Clamming has declined due to competition from sea otters, which returned to the area in the mid-1980s. There is also salmon fishing in season. Local activities include berry picking, mushrooming, hiking and cross-country skiing. Several attractions are within an hour's boat ride. Glacier Bay National Park is an hour's skiff ride; Port Althorp Bear Preserve is 40 minutes away by boat; and the abandoned Port Althorp cannery is a 20-minute skiff ride, as is the WWII George Island Coastal Gun Emplacement.

Communications at Elfin Cove, which is unincorporated, include phones, mail plane and VHF radio. Messages may be phoned in to Elfin Cove Travel at 239-2202. There is community water and power, but there is no public sewer system. Freight comes in by plane or by boat.

Excursion Inlet

[MAP 1] Located 38 miles northwest of Juneau, due east of Gustavus, at the mouth of Excursion Inlet off Icy Strait. **Transportation:** By boat or plane. **Population:** 350 in summer, 3 or 4 in winter. **Zip code:** 99850. **Emergency Services:** Hospital and Alaska State Troopers in Juneau.

Elevation: Sea level. **Climate:** Cool and wet.

Private Aircraft: Seaplane base. Dirt road near cannery serves as airstrip.

Visitor Facilities: Excursion Inlet Packing

Co. camp (945-3203) operates here in summer, and the company store (also known as Coho Mercantile) stocks clothing, first-aid supplies, hardware, camera film and sporting goods. Fishing/hunting licenses may be purchased. No overnight accommodations or food service for visitors. Marine gas, diesel, propane and regular gasoline are available in summer. Transient moorage available at Excursion Inlet Dock; fuel available at Excursion Inlet Cannery dock. Communications in summer include phones, mail plane, radio and TV. Freight comes in by barge and ship.

Funter Bay

[MAP 2] Located 19 miles southwest of Juneau at the north end of Admiralty Island. **Transportation:** By boat or plane. **Population:** 10 to 20. **Zip code:** 99850. **Emergency Services:** Hospital and Alaska State Troopers in Juneau.

Elevation: Sea level. **Climate:** Cool and wet.

Private Aircraft: Floatplane landings only with dock.

Visitor Facilities: Joe and Karey Giefer (4 Crab Cove, Funter Bay, AK 99850, phone 789-4786) rent their guest house with meals or on a housekeeping basis. Boat charters are available with an emphasis on whales, eagles and brown bears. Ford and Susan Horst (780-

Fishing and fish processing support the community of Elfin Cove. (David Job)

5181) offer food, lodging and fishing charters for up to 6 guests. Advance reservations are required at both places. Fishing licenses may be purchased in Funter Bay. Service is seasonal. There are 2 public dock facilities and 2 coves in the bay for anchoring small boats.

Funter Bay is an important anchorage and the site of an abandoned cannery, gold mine and World War II Aleut relocation camp. The cemetery provides interesting glimpses of the lives and deaths of some of those Aleuts. This area is the site of a state marine park. There are some summer cabins at Funter Bay. Most of the permanent residents are commercial fishermen. Funter Bay is not just a remarkable place to visit; it's a wonderful place to live and raise a family, says Joe Giefer. Excellent area fishing for salmon and halibut. There is a 3-mile trail to Bear Creek and about a 7-mile trail to Mount Robert Barron; both are unmaintained. Residents provide their own power, water and sewage disposal. Communications include radio and a weekly mail plane. Freight comes in by cargo plane and private boat.

Gustavus

[MAP 1] Located at the mouth of the Salmon River on the north shore of Icy Passage off Icy Strait, near the entrance to Glacier Bay, 48 miles northwest of Juneau and 10 miles from Bartlett Cove, headquarters of Glacier Bay National Park. **Transportation:** Year-round charter air service from Juneau, scheduled boat and jet service in summer; private boat. **Population:** 250 in winter, and up to 500 in summer. **Zip code:** 99826. **Emergency Services:** Volunteer Emergency Response, phone 911; Alaska State Troopers in Hoonah.

Elevation: 20 feet and rising as the land rebounds $1^{1}/_{2}$ inches per year due to the retreat of the adjacent glaciers. **Climate:** Cool and rainy with average temperatures in January of 27°F and in July of 55°F. Mean precipitation ranges from 7.66 inches in October to 2.40 inches in June.

Private Aircraft: Gustavus airport 0.5 mile northeast; elev. 36 feet; length 6,800 feet; asphalt. Year-round public phone, air taxi offices, transient tie-downs, travel center and taxi; summer additions of passenger terminal, ticket counter, arts and crafts shop, fish products shop and bus service.

Visitor Facilities: As the gateway to Glacier Bay National Park and Preserve, Gustavus offers most visitor services, including several lodges, inns, cabin rentals and bed and breakfasts. Meals available at Open Gate Cafe (697-2227), Annie Mae Lodge (697-2346), Glacier Bay Puffin Lodge (697-2260), Glacier Bay Country Inn and Whalesong Lodge (697-2288) and Gustavus Inn (697-2254). One lodge and a campground are located within the park at Bartlett Cove, approximately 12 sea miles from Gustavus. There is a restaurant with bakery goods. There is a lumber yard. Groceries, hardware, fishing licenses and some fishing supplies may be purchased at Bear Track Mercantile (697-2358) and Gusto Building Supply (697-2297). Gift shops and art galleries are located in Gustavus and Bartlett Cove. Travel services are available at Puffin Travel (697-2260), and a few rental cars are available at BW Auto Rental (697-2245). For TLC Taxi Service, call 697-2239. Gustavus-based air taxis and flightseeing are available from Air Excursions (697-2375) and Glacier Bay Airways (697-2249). Boats and planes may be chartered for sightseeing, photography or fishing trips. Kayak rentals and guided trips may be arranged. Spirit Walker Expeditions (P.O. Box 240, Gustavus, AK 99826; phone 697-2266, in Alaska, 800-478-9255) offers day and overnight kayak trips from the Gustavus dock. Alaska Discovery Expeditions (697-2411) offers day kayak trips from Bartlett Cove. Propane and white gas for camping are available. Gustavus Dray sells avgas and Jet A fuel at the airport (697-2299). Marine fuel can be purchased at Bartlett Cove. Public moorage at the state-operated dock and float; phone near the dock; no facilities.

Surrounded on three sides by the snow-covered peaks of the Chilkat Range and the Fairweather Mountains, Gustavus offers miles of level land with expansive sandy beaches, farmland and forest. Homesteaded in 1914 as a small agricultural community, the area was once named Strawberry Point because it produced abundant wild strawberries along the beach and in the meadows. Today, local residents and visitors still enjoy huckleberries, blueberries, nagoonberries, strawberries and other berries and flowers and a variety of animals and birds. Most residents maintain gardens and make their living by fishing, processing fish, supplying services, creating arts and crafts and working for the Gustavus School or the National Park Service. Gustavus caters to fishermen, sightseers and park visitors. Local residents recommend fishing for salmon, halibut and trout as well as beachcombing, hiking, kayaking, bird watching and photography.

The Gustavus Arts Council and National Park Service sponsor activities including folk dancing and concerts throughout the summer. The community enjoys an old-fashioned Fourth of July celebration with a parade, art auction, community events and annual 3-mile run. Says one longtime resident, "Gustavus still feels like a return to my impression of 1930s-style country life: dirt roads, bicycles and horses. Everybody drives slow, and everybody waves."

The Dude Creek Critical Habitat Area, adjacent to Gustavus and Glacier Bay National Park, offers the awesome sight of thousands of lesser sandhill cranes as they stop briefly in the wet meadows during the spring and especially in September during their fall migration. The open wet meadow bisected by forest-fringed Dude Creek is the largest such complex of its kind in the region and is enjoyed by local residents for recreation year-round. Primary access is gained via a section line extension of the Good River Road to the west of town. There are no public-use facilities.

Communications include phones, mail plane, radio and TV. The community has a church, fire station, library, community park and a school for grades kindergarten through 12. Heavy freight arrives by barge. For more information write, Gustavus Visitors Assoc., Box 167, Gustavus, AK 99826.

Haines

[MAP 1] Located on Portage Cove, Chilkoot Inlet, on the upper arm of Lynn Canal, 80 air miles northwest of Juneau, 13 nautical miles southwest of Skagway, 155 road miles south of Haines Junction, YT. **Transportation:** Scheduled air service from Juneau; mainline port on the Alaska Marine Highway's Southeast ferry system; connected to the Alaska Highway by the Haines Highway. **Population:** 1,238. **Zip code:** 99827. **Emergency Services:** City Police, phone 766-2121; Alaska State Troopers, Fire Department and Ambulance, emergency only phone 911; Doctor, phone 766-2521.

Elevation: Sea level. **Climate:** Average daily maximum temperature in July, 66°F; average daily minimum in January, 17°F. Average annual precipitation 61 inches. Snow on ground usually from October through April.

Private Aircraft: Haines airport, 3.5 miles west, elev. 16 feet; length 4,600 feet; asphalt/gravel; unattended; fuel 100. Passenger terminal with restroom and pay phone.

Commercial airlines provide transportation to and from motels and some motels offer courtesy car pickup.

Visitor Facilities: Haines has all visitor facilities. There are 6 hotels/motels, 5 bed-and-breakfast accommodations, a lodge and 4 public campgrounds, 5 private camper parks and bunk-style accommodations. All supplies are available from local hardware and grocery stores, including Howsers Supermarket (766-2040), Food Center (766-2181) and Mountain Market (766-3340). Fishing/ hunting licenses may be purchased in Haines; there are 2 registered hunting guides and local charter boat operators offer fishing trips. There are 11 restaurants and cafes, several taverns, a laundromat, bank, car rentals, automotive and marine repair, and gas stations. Propane, diesel, regular gasoline and marine gas are available. Transient moorage at the city small-boat harbor 1 block from city center.

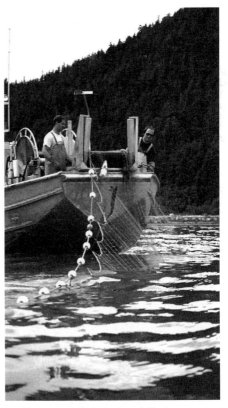

A gill-netter works Lynn Canal. Trollers, purse seiners and gill-netters all work Southeast's waters. (David Job)

"Haines is a small, idyllic Alaska community where there's a little bit of something for everyone," says Mira Ericksen of the Haines Visitor Bureau. "Surrounded by magnificent snow-capped mountains and pristine waters, Haines offers Tlingit Indian culture, pioneer and natural history, abundant wildlife viewing, sportfishing, outdoor adventure of all kinds and beautiful local artwork."

The Chilkat Valley was first inhabited by Tlingit Indians, who jealously guarded fur trading routes from the coast into the Interior. A Presbyterian missionary named S. Hall Young established a mission at the present site of Haines in 1881. By 1884 there was a post office here, and as placer gold mining began in the Porcupine District, about 36 miles upriver from Haines, the town became an important outlet. The Klondike gold rush of 1898 brought an influx of gold seekers, who opened up the Chilkat mountain pass to the Interior. In 1904, the U.S. government established Fort William H. Seward, which was renamed Chilkoot Barracks in 1922 and deactivated in 1946. The fort is a popular tourist attraction today. Haines was incorporated in 1910.

As a mainline port on the state ferry system and 1 of 3 Southeast communities connected to the Alaska Highway (the others are Hyder and Skagway), Haines remains an important route to the Interior for today's travelers. The Haines Highway, which connects the port of Haines with the Alaska Highway at Haines Junction, YT, is open year-round. The majority of employment in Haines is in service trades, including tourism, followed by fishing, timber, government and construction. Fishing was one of the initial industries in Haines' early days, and remains a commercial industry and a visitor attraction. A sawmill owned by Chilkoot Lumber Co. began operation in November 1987, at the site of the former, idle sawmill along Lutak Inlet.

Along with sportfishing, visitors may explore the town's early history at Fort Seward, where the Chilkat Dancers interpret ancient Tlingit Indian legends and a local melodrama is performed. The Southeast Alaska State Fair is held in Haines in August. From October through December, the world's greatest concentration of American bald eagles comes together on the Chilkat River near Haines. The Chilkat Valley is the annual home of more than 4,000 bald eagles, which gather to feed on the late run of chum salmon in the Chilkat River. The 48,000-acre Alaska Chilkat Bald Eagle Preserve was established in 1982. Several custom and group tour operators offer trips to the preserve, including trips on snow machines, snowshoes, cross-country skis and jet boats, and photographic blinds for serious wildlife photographers. There are also opportunities to bike, hike, flightsee and take a sled-dog ride. A water taxi cruises to and from Skagway. Raft trips are available in summer.

Other attractions include Sheldon Museum and Cultural Center, located at the corner of Front and Main streets. The museum features the art, history, ethnology and geology of the Haines area. The museum has special exhibits, guided tours, workshops and films, including the Audubon Society's *Last Stronghold of the Eagles* about the annual congregation of bald eagles near Haines. Summer hours are 1–4 P.M. daily; morning hours are posted. Winter hours are 1–4 P.M. on days the state ferry arrives; open by appointment at other times. Another attraction is Alaska Indian Arts Inc., an arts center and gallery located in Building 23 on Fort Seward Drive, featuring the arts and crafts of southeastern Alaska's Tlingit and Haida Indians; the museum has guided tours, workshops and demonstrations. Year-round hours are 9 A.M. to 5 P.M. Monday through Friday. One local business offers glacier walks. Dalton City, Haines' newest visitor attraction, is an 1890s style gold-rush town recreated from the movie set of *White Fang.*

Communications include phones (most households have phones), a local newspaper (*Chilkat Valley News*), radio (local FM) and numerous TV channels provided by satellite and cable. There are churches and kindergarten, elementary, junior and senior high schools. The city operates water and sewage systems, and a private utility supplies electricity. Freight arrives by ship, barge, plane or truck. Government address: City of Haines, P.O. Box 1049, Haines, AK 99827; phone 766-2231. Visitor Bureau, Box 530, Haines, AK 99827; phone 766-2234, fax 766-3155.

Hobart Bay

[MAP 2] Located 70 miles south of Juneau and 40 miles north of Petersburg on the east shore of Stephens Passage. **Transportation:** Boat or seaplane. **Population:** approximately 40. **Zip code:** 99850. **Emergency Services:** None available.
Elevation: Sea level.

Private Aircraft: No facilities.
Visitor Facilities: Lodging is available at Goldbelt Guest House (673-2247 or 673-2282), and food is available at the bunkhouse. No supplies are available. There is a public dock.

Hobart Bay is a logging camp owned by Goldbelt, Inc., the Juneau-based Native corporation which owns nearly 23,000 acres in the area. Ninety percent of the logging is done by helicopter. Hobart Bay is a beautiful spot with great fishing.

Hollis

[MAP 2] Located on the east coast of Prince of Wales Island on Twelvemile Arm, 25 road miles east of Klawock, 35 miles west of Ketchikan. **Transportation:** By ferry from Ketchikan; on the Prince of Wales Island road system. **Population:** est. 125. **Zip code:** 99950. **Emergency Services:** Alaska State Troopers in Klawock; Hospital in Ketchikan. Emergency medical service can be contacted by using CB Channel 14 or "phone through just about anyone who lives here," says Johnnie Laird.

Elevation: 20 feet. **Climate:** Mean monthly temperature in January is 32°F and in July, 58°F. Mean monthly precipitation ranges from 3.28 inches in July to 18.14 inches in October.

Private Aircraft: Seaplane base with aircraft float and sheltered anchorage.

Visitor Facilities: There are no stores, restaurants, gas stations or other visitor facilities here. The ferry from Ketchikan that serves Prince of Wales Island docks at Hollis. Ferry terminal 530-7115; public phones are located at the ferry terminal, floatplane dock and harbor (which has a boat ramp, docks and floats for moorage).

Hollis was a mining town with a population of 1,000 from about 1900 to 1915. In the 1950s, Hollis became the site of Ketchikan Pulp Co.'s logging camp, and served as the base for timber operations on Prince of Wales Island until 1962, when the camp was moved to Thorne Bay. Recent state land sales have spurred the growth of a small residential community here, the subdivisions built in thick second-growth timber with trees 40 to 60 feet tall. A school with grades 1 through 12, the ferry terminal, and U.S. Forest Service buildings are located here.

Hollis has public utilities, including electricity and phone service. There is a community phone (530-7112) and a public library

in the school. Local government consists of a nonprofit community council. A letter addressed to the Hollis Community Council, Hollis, AK 99950, will eventually find its way there after going through Ketchikan then coming over by pouch. Hollis itself has no post office.

Hoonah

[MAP 1] Located on the northeast shore of Chichagof Island, about 40 miles west of Juneau and 20 miles south across Icy Strait from the entrance to Glacier Bay. **Transportation:** Scheduled and charter air service from Juneau; twice weekly state ferry service in summer. **Population:** 895. **Zip code:** 99829. **Emergency Services:** Alaska State Troopers and city police, phone 945-3655; Volunteer Fire Department; Clinic, phone 945-3235 or 945-3386; emergencies, phone 911.

Elevation: 30 feet. **Climate:** Typical southeastern Alaska climate, with considerable rainfall (100 inches annually). Summer temperatures in the 50s; winter lows to 14°F in February.

Private Aircraft: Hoonah airport, adjacent southeast; elev. 30 feet; length 3,100 feet; gravel; unattended, prior visual inspection recommended. Seaplane base with sheltered anchorage and dock.

Visitor Facilities: Food and lodging are available at Hoonah Lodge (945-3663) and Mary's Inn (945-3228; for room reservation, call Hoonah Cold Storage at 945-3264). Lodging is also available at Tina's Room Rental (945-3442) and Hubbard's Bed and Breakfast (945-3414), and food at Spanky's Pizza & Deli (945-3453). For groceries and supplies, contact Hoonah Seafoods (945-3211), L. Kane Store (945-3311) or Harbor Lights Mini Mart (945-3200).

Hoonah has a gift shop and a bank. Fishing/hunting licenses may be purchased here. Guided hunting and fishing trips may be arranged locally. Major marine repair and marine gas, diesel and regular gasoline are available. Transient moorage available at the city harbor; the marina, which has showers and a laundromat, is a popular layover for boaters awaiting permits to enter Glacier Bay.

Hoonah is a small coastal community with a quiet harbor for the seining and trolling fleets. The most prominent structures are a cold storage facility, the lodge, bank, post office and public school. The village has been occupied since prehistory by the Tlingit people. In the late 1800s, missionaries settled here. Canneries established in the area in the early 1900s spurred the growth of commercial fishing, which remains the mainstay of Hoonah's economy. During the summer fishing season, residents work for nearby Excursion Inlet Packing Co. or Hoonah Cold Storage in town. Halibut season begins in May and salmon season opens in midsummer and runs through September. Some logging also contributes to the economy. Subsistence hunting and fishing remain an important lifestyle here, and many families gather food in the traditional way: catching salmon and halibut in summer, shellfish and bottom fish year-round; hunting deer, geese and ducks; and berry-picking in late summer and fall.

Communications include phones in most households (residents also use CB radios for local communication), mail plane, radio and TV via satellite and cable. There are several churches and both an elementary school and high school. There are community water and sewage systems, and electricity is provided by a public utility. Freight arrives by plane or barge. Government address: City of Hoonah, P.O. Box 360, Hoonah, AK 99829; phone 945-3663, fax 945-3445. Village corporation address: Huna Totem Corp., 9309 Glacier Highway, Suite A-103, Juneau, AK 99801.

Hydaburg

[MAP 2] Located on the southwest coast of Prince of Wales Island, 36 road miles from Hollis, 45 road miles from Craig, 50 air miles west of Ketchikan. **Transportation:** Scheduled air service from Ketchikan; state ferry service to Hollis; private boat. **Population:** 475. **Zip code:** 99922. **Emergency Services:** State Troopers in Klawock, phone 755-2918; Village Public Safety Officer, phone 285-3321; Clinic, phone 285-3462; Volunteer Fire Department, phone 285-3333.

Elevation: 30 feet. **Climate:** Cool, moist maritime climate with complete cloud cover about 60 percent of the time. Summer temperatures from 46°F to 70°F. June and July are the driest months with an average of 5 inches of precipitation. Mild winter temperatures, range from 32°F to the low 40s. October and November are the wettest months with up to 18 inches of precipitation. Annual average precipitation is 160 inches.

Private Aircraft: Seaplane base with sheltered anchorage and dock; watch for boat traffic.

Visitor Facilities: Bed-and-breakfast accommodations are available at Fran Sanderson's (285-3139) and at Marlene Edenshaw's (285-3254). Food is available at TJ's Cafe (285-3920), open regular hours during the summer and rather irregular hours in winter. Do Drop In Grocery (285-3311) offers foodstuffs, and Dot's Dry Goods and Hardware (285-3375) has household items for sale. Crafts, such as Haida Indian carvings and baskets, may be purchased from residents. There are no public laundry facilities, banking services or rental transportation. Fishing/hunting licenses and guide services are available at the local hardware store. Marine machine shop and fuel available at harbor. Diesel and regular gasoline are available in town. Moorage at city of Hydaburg floats, 0.5 mile north of town.

Hydaburg was founded in 1911 and combined the populations of 3 Haida villages: Sukkwan, Howkan and Klinkwan. President William Howard Taft established an Indian reservation on the surrounding land in 1912, but, at the residents' request, most of the land was restored to its former status as part of Tongass National Forest in 1926. Hydaburg was incorporated in 1927, 3 years after its people had become citizens of the United States.

Most of the residents are commercial fishermen, although there are some jobs in construction and the timber industry. Subsistence is also a traditional and necessary part of life here. Hydaburg has an excellent collection of restored Haida totems. The totem park was developed in the 1930s by the Civilian Conservation Corps. There is also good salmon fishing here in the fall. According to Frank Alby, "Hydaburg retains its small-town quality — lots of fishing, shrimping, hunting, hiking ... things to do that don't take money."

Communications include phones and cable TV. There are Assembly of God and Presbyterian churches here. Hydaburg has both elementary and high schools. There are community water, sewage and electrical power systems. No alcoholic beverages are sold in Hydaburg. Freight arrives by plane, barge and truck. Government address: City of Hydaburg, P.O. Box 49, Hydaburg, AK 99922; phone 285-3761, fax 285-3760. Village corporation address: Haida Corp., P.O. Box 89, Hydaburg, AK 99922.

Hyder

[MAP 2] Located at the head of Portland Canal, 2 miles west of Stewart, BC. **Transportation:** By road via a spur of the Cassiar Highway; once-a-week state ferry service from Ketchikan in summer; charter air service and mail plane. **Population:** 95. **Zip code:** 99923. **Emergency Services:** Hospital and RCMP in Stewart, BC.

Elevation: Sea level. **Climate:** Maritime, with warm winters and cool, rainy summers. Slightly less summer rain than other southeastern communities, but heavy snowfall in winter. Summer temperatures range from 57°F to 80°F; winter temperatures range from 25°F to 43°F.

Private Aircraft: Seaplane base at Hyder; airstrip at Stewart.

Visitor Facilities: Lodging is available at Sealaska (604-636-9001) and Grand View (604-636-9174) in Hyder, and at King Edward Hotel (604-636-2244) in nearby Stewart. Food is available at Sealaska and the Border Cafe (604-636-2379) in Hyder, and at King Edward Hotel and Fong's Garden (604-636-9074) in Stewart. Groceries are available at Dean's Grocery (604-636-2422) in Hyder.

Hyder has gift shops, a post office, 3 cafes, 3 bars, and 2 inns which offers rooms, cocktail lounge and restaurant. A small-boat harbor operated by the state offers open moorage and a launching ramp. Hardware and sporting goods available. Stewart has 3 hotels/motels, 3 restaurants, 2 grocery stores, service stations, a bank, liquor store and other shops, a deep draft dock and marine fuel. There are no repair facilities in Hyder, but Stewart has shops and a repair service.

Hyder and Stewart, on either side of the U.S.-Canada border, share commerce and history. Captain D.D. Gaillard explored Portland Canal in 1896 for the U.S. Army Corps of Engineers. In the late 1890s, gold and silver were discovered in the hills near Hyder, attracting some prospectors. With the discovery in 1917 and 1918 of rich silver veins in the upper Salmon River basin, Hyder boomed. Few of the structures from this boom period survive, although many of the pilings which supported the buildings are still visible on the tidal flats. Hyder became an access and supply point for the mines, while Stewart served as the center for Canadian mining activity. Mining ceased in 1956, with the exception of the Granduc copper mine, which operated until 1984.

Today's economy is based on local trade and tourism. Some Hyder residents supplement their incomes by fishing, hunting and gardening.

Attractions in the Hyder/Stewart area include the stone storehouse built by Capt. D.D. Gaillard in 1896; it is the oldest masonry building in Alaska. Sightseeing tours of Salmon Glacier are available out of Stewart, and charter small-boat trips on Portland Canal are available at the Hyder marina. Five species of Pacific salmon are found in waters near Hyder, with Salmon River and Fish Creek supporting one of Southeast's largest chum salmon runs. A new viewing platform on Fish Creek provides safe views of the chum salmon spawning area and the many black bears that come to feed each summer.

The U.S. Forest Service operates a visitor information center for Misty Fiords National Monument during the summer months (June to Labor Day). The office is located in the Hyder post office and fire hall.

Communications include phones, mail plane, radio and TV. Hyder has no public schools; students attend school in Stewart. The community has electricity provided by a public utility. Wood and diesel are used to heat most homes. Residents rely on individual wells for water and septic tanks for sewage waste disposal. Freight arrives by barge, plane or truck. Government address: Hyder Community Assoc. Inc., Box 149, Hyder, AK 99923; phone (604) 636-9148, fax (604) 636-2714.

Icy Bay

[MAP 1] Located 66 miles northwest of Yakutat, 150 miles southeast of Cordova, at the terminus of Guyot and Malaspina glaciers on the Gulf of Alaska coast. **Transportation:** Charter plane. **Population:** Varies. **Zip code:** 99850. **Emergency Services:** Alaska State Troopers in Cordova; medical facilities in Cordova and Yakutat.

Elevation: 50 feet. **Climate:** Cool and rainy in summer, with rain and snow in winter. Some below-zero days in winter.

Private Aircraft: Icy Bay airstrip, 0.3 mile from camp; elev. 50 feet; length 4,000 feet; gravel; unattended and unmaintained.

Visitor Facilities: This is a privately operated logging camp; there are no visitor facilities or services here. The camp obtains supplies from Cordova and freight arrives by cargo plane or barge. Communications include mail plane, radio and TV. Icy Bay school has grades kindergarten through 12.

Juneau

[MAP 2] Located on Gastineau Channel opposite Douglas Island, 91 nautical miles south of Haines, 577 air miles southeast of Anchorage, 900 air miles north of Seattle, WA. **Transportation:** Daily scheduled jet service from Seattle and from Alaska communities; commuter air service from Haines, Skagway and other Southeast points; year-round state ferry service. **Population:** 29,251. **Zip code:** 99801, 99802, 99803, 99811. **Emergency Services:** Alaska State Troopers, Police, Fire Department and Ambulance, phone 911; Bartlett Memorial Hospital, phone 586-2611.

Elevation: Sea level. **Climate:** Mild and wet. Average daily maximum temperature in July is 64°F; daily minimum in January is 16.1°F. Record high was 90°F in July of 1975; record low, -22°F in January 1972. Average annual precipitation 91.98 inches downtown and 53.15 inches at the airport. Snow on ground intermittently from mid-November to mid-April.

Private Aircraft: Juneau International Airport, 9 miles northwest of downtown; elev. 24 feet; length 8,456 feet; asphalt; fuel 100, Jet A. Full-service passenger terminal. Bus service to downtown. Juneau International Seaplane Basin, 9 miles northwest of downtown, dock and ramp available for public use. Juneau Harbor Seaplane, adjacent north; unattended; watch for harbor boat traffic; fuel 80, 100 and A1. Juneau AFSS (789-7351).

Visitor Facilities: As capital of Alaska and the largest city in Southeast, Juneau has all services. This includes 12 hotels/motels, approximately 20 bed and breakfasts and a youth hostel, dozens of restaurants and gift shops, a few major shopping centers, laundries, banks, major repair service and rental transportation. Many fishing charter services operate out of Juneau and hunting/fishing licenses may be purchased at numerous outlets, including the main visitor center. All types of fuel are available. The City and Borough of Juneau operates harbors. Transient moorage is available at Harris Harbor, 1 mile from city center; at the Douglas Boat Harbor, across the channel from Juneau; and at the Auke Bay float facilities, 12 miles north of Juneau. Harbormaster, phone 586-5255. Juneau is a gateway for fly/boat tours to Glacier Bay. For information on the Pack Creek Bear Preserve on Admiralty Island, contact the U.S. Forest Service at 586-8751.

The area was originally the home of the Alaska Native Tlingit people. When gold was discovered in 1880 by Joe Juneau and Dick Harris, the gold rush boomtown of Juneau came to be and prospered due to its location on the water route to Skagway and the Klondike. By 1900, after the Russians left Sitka and Sitka's whaling and fur trade fell off, it was decided to move Alaska's capital to Juneau. Transfer of government functions occurred in 1906. Today, government (federal, state and local) comprises an estimated half of the total basic industry, with tourism, construction, mining, retail trade and services making up the total. Despite being a regional supply and service center for Southeast Alaska, Juneau has been able to preserve its special character and charm because it is not connected by road to anywhere else.

Dubbed "a little San Francisco," Juneau is a picturesque city, backed by the steep slopes of Mount Juneau (elev. 3,819 feet) and looking out over Gastineau Channel. The city has an attractive waterfront park, a good spot to watch the floatplanes and ships in the channel. Juneau's skyline is dominated by several government buildings, including the Federal Building, the massive State Office Building, and the older brick and marble-columned Capitol Building.

The city and surrounding area offer a number of attractions. Boat, plane and helicopter operators offer charter sightseeing and fishing. A rustic 9-hole par 3 golf course puts golfers amid fields of wildflowers in full view of the Mendenhall Glacier. There is downtown shopping and self-guided walking tours to see the government buildings and Governor's Mansion. The Alaska State Museum, located just off Egan Drive at 395 Whittier St., features the archaeology, art, botany, history, ethnology, geology and paleontology of the state. The museum offers special exhibits, guided tours, workshops, lectures, film presentations and demonstrations. More than 150 exhibits depict wildlife and habitats, Native culture, Russian America, pioneer days and industrial history. Hours from mid-May to mid-September are 9 A.M. to 6 P.M. Monday through Friday and 10 A.M. to 6 P.M. Saturday and Sunday. Hours from October through mid-May are 10 A.M. to 4 P.M. Tuesday through Saturday. Admission is $2. A $5 pass, good for the calendar year, can also be purchased. Another popular attraction is the Juneau Douglas City Museum, 114 W. 4th. It features Juneau's mining history from a personal viewpoint. Persons visiting the museum receive specialized historical walking tour maps. Summer hours are 9 A.M. to 5 P.M. Monday through Friday and 11 A.M. to 5 P.M. Saturday and Sunday. Open winters at reduced hours. Donations are requested. Gastineau Salmon Hatchery, 3 miles from downtown, offers tours for a small charge (daily tours in summer, reduced hours in winter).

There are several hiking trails accessible from downtown: Perseverance trail, 3.5 miles, begins at the end of Basin Road and leads to the old Perseverance Mine; Mount Juneau trail, steep and rugged, begins 0.5 mile up Perseverance trail; Granite Creek Basin trail begins about 1.8 miles up Perseverance trail and leads 1.5 miles along Granite Creek to a scenic basin; Mount Roberts trail begins at the top of Starr Hill (the east end of 6th Street) and leads 3.7 miles to Mount Roberts.

For bicyclists there are intermittent bike paths to Douglas and to Mendenhall Glacier. The glacier bike path begins at the intersection of 12th Street and Glacier Avenue and leads 13 miles north to Mendenhall Glacier. This magnificent glacier is about 13 miles by car from downtown Juneau. The U.S. Forest Service visitor center at the glacier has audiovisual displays, daily slide and film programs and guided hikes from early June through Labor Day and on weekends during the winter months. In the other direction from Juneau, on Douglas Island, is Eaglecrest ski area. Eaglecrest has downhill and cross-country skiing in winter.

Juneau has all the amenities of city life. There are many churches, ranging from Russian Orthodox to Apostolic to nondenominational. Juneau Borough Schools enroll more than 5,000 students in 5 elementary schools, 2 middle schools and 1 high school. The University of Alaska Southeast, Juneau branch, enrolls 2,000 students. Four Native corporations have offices in Juneau. Freight arrives by cargo plane or water. Government address: City and Borough of Juneau, City and Borough Manager, 155 S. Seward St., Juneau, AK 99801; phone 586-5240. Visitor Information Center, 134 3rd St., Juneau, AK 99801; phone 586-2201.

Kake

[MAP 2] Located on the northwest coast of Kupreanof Island, 40 air miles and 65 nautical miles northwest of Petersburg, 95 air miles southwest of Juneau. **Transportation:** Scheduled airline from Petersburg or Juneau; state ferry from Petersburg and Sitka. **Popu-** lation: 700. **Zip code:** 99830. **Emergency Services:** Police, phone 785-3393; Health Center, phone 785-3333; Volunteer Fire Department, phone 785-3464.

Elevation: 10 feet. **Climate:** Temperate, with summer temperatures in the 50s, occasional highs in the 80s. Moderate rainfall most months, very little snow in winter.

Private Aircraft: Seaplane base southwest of town with dock. Airstrip 1 mile west of town; elev. 148 feet; length 4,000 feet; paved; unattended, prior visual inspection recommended.

Visitor Facilities: Accommodations and meals available. There is also a coffee shop. Some hardware, clothing and other supplies available at the 3 local grocery stores. Fishing/hunting licenses are sold locally. No banking services. Laundromat available. There is a car mechanic and all types of fuel are available (marine, diesel, propane, unleaded and regular). Public moorage at City of Kake floats.

The town is a permanent village of the Kake tribe of the Tlingit Indians. The Tlingits from Kake had a well-earned reputation for aggression in the 18th and 19th centuries. In 1869, the Kakes murdered 2 Sitka traders in revenge for the shooting of a Native by a Sitka sentry. Reprisals taken by the United States resulted in the shelling and destruction of 3 Kake villages. The tribe eventually settled at the present-day site of Kake, where the government established a school in 1891. Presently, Kake is noted for its friendliness and is very hospitable to visitors.

Residents have historically drawn ample subsistence from the sea. However, with the advent of a cash economy, the community has come to depend on commercial fishing, fish processing (there is a cannery) and logging. The post office was established in 1904 and the city was incorporated in 1952. The city's claim to fame is its totem, reputedly the world's tallest, at 132 feet, 6 inches. It was carved for the 1967 Alaska Purchase Centennial Celebration.

Kake has phones, radio, TV and mail plane service. Church groups include Baptist, Salvation Army, Presbyterian, Assembly of God and Kake Evangelistic Outreach. Schools include an elementary school and a high school. Community electrical power, water and sewage systems are available. Freight comes in on the airlines or by barge. Government address: City of Kake, P.O. Box 500, Kake, AK 99830; phone 785-3804. Village corporation address: Kake Tribal Corp., P.O. Box 263, Kake, AK 99830.

Kasaan

[MAP 2] Located on the east side of Prince of Wales Island, southeast of Thorne Bay, on Kasaan Bay on the Kasaan Peninsula. **Transportation:** Charter plane or private boat. **Population:** 75. **Zip code:** 99950-0340. **Emergency Services:** Alaska State Troopers and hospital in Ketchikan; Village Public Safety Officer, Certified Health Aide, Health Clinic and Volunteer Fire Department.

Elevation: Sea level. **Climate:** Typical Southeast, cool and rainy, with average temperatures of 55°F in summer. Precipitation ranges from 3.89 inches in June to 11.30 inches in November.

Private Aircraft: Seaplane base, dock.

Visitor Facilities: Overnight accommodations with cooking and laundry facilities are maintained by Kavilco Inc., the local Native corporation, in remodeled buildings that were originally used as bunkhouses by the salmon cannery until 1953. Groceries and supplies are available from Capella's General Store; other supplies are flown in from Ketchikan or Craig. There is a post office. Propane, diesel and regular gasoline are available at the public floats and dock.

Kasaan is a beautiful, secluded village situated along the beachfront in Kasaan Bay. Nestled against the forest, Kasaan is one of the few places in Southeast Alaska that still reflects an older, simple, yet fulfilling lifestyle.

Kasaan was founded by a group of businessmen from Outside as a copper mine site. A sawmill and general store were established around 1900 and a salmon cannery was built in 1902. Members of the tribe of Haidas living at Old Kasaan, located south of Kasaan on Skowl Arm, eventually relocated at New Kasaan, site of the mine and cannery. The copper mining company went bankrupt after 4 years, but the cannery continued to operate sporadically with a half-dozen different owners until 1953. Kasaan incorporated in 1976 under the Alaska Native Claims Settlement Act.

The community has revitalized somewhat in recent years with the incorporation, but jobs are still scarce. Residents depend heavily on a subsistence lifestyle: fishing for salmon, halibut and bottom fish (in July, the whole village goes up to Karta Bay for subsistence fishing); hunting for deer; trapping for mink and marten; going out for black seaweed in April and May; and gathering clams (which are plentiful), some shrimp and Dungeness crab. The valuable timberland owned by Kavilco holds promise for economic improvement, and the community is hoping for a connecting road system to the rest of the island. There are a few jobs with the city and the power plant, but as one resident puts it, "most people fish or are retired."

A 1,300-foot boardwalk leads from the harbor to a gravel footpath, which leads another half-mile through the village to a totem park. The Kasaan Totem Park, part of a government-sponsored totem restoration program begun in 1937, contains a number of totems from Old Kasaan. Kasaan is only a few miles away from the Karta River, a favorite of sportsmen. The village corporation, however, does not allow camping on its land for fear of forest fires. Residents also fish in front of the village; watch for killer whales going up the bay; and watch the great numbers of eagles that soar overhead. The village has a community house and hosts a number of community dinners.

Communications include phones, mail plane, radio and TV. Kasaan's one-room schoolhouse has an enrollment of 12 students and a kindergarten through grade 12 curriculum. The community has electric power and water systems; sewage system is individual septic tanks. Freight is brought in by barge or cargo plane. Government address: City of Kasaan, P.O. Box KXA-Kasaan, Ketchikan, AK 99950-0340; phone 542-2212. Village corporation address: Kavilco Inc., P.O. Box KXA-Kasaan, Ketchikan, AK 99950-0340.

Ketchikan

[MAP 2] Located on the southwest side of Revillagigedo Island on Tongass Narrows opposite Gravina Island, 235 miles south of Juneau, 90 miles north of Prince Rupert, BC. **Transportation:** Scheduled jet service, commuter and charter flights; state ferry service. **Population:** 14,800 (Borough). **Zip code:** 99901. **Emergency Services:** Alaska State Troopers, phone 225-5118; Police, phone 225-6631; Hospital, phone 225-5171; Fire Department/Ambulance, phone 225-9611 or 225-9616. Emergency only for police, fire or ambulance, phone 911.

Elevation: Sea level. **Climate:** Rainy. Average yearly rainfall 162 inches and snowfall of 32 inches, with June the driest month and October the wettest. July high temperatures average 65°F, minimum 51°F. Daily maximum in January 39°F; minimum 29°F.

Private Aircraft: Ketchikan International

Airport on Gravina Island; elev. 88 feet; length 7,500 feet; asphalt; fuel 80, 100, Jet A. All facilities at airport. Ketchikan Harbor seaplane base downtown; fuel 80, 100.

Visitor Facilities: Ketchikan has 8 hotels/motels. There are numerous bed-and-breakfast accommodations and a youth hostel (open Memorial Day through Labor Day). There are 5 area lodges, 4 resorts and 3 marinas. A full-service community, Ketchikan offers all the amenities of a medium-sized city: restaurants, laundromats, banks, 2 shopping centers, gift shops and all types of fuel. Fishing/hunting licenses are available. There are 2 registered hunting guides (deer and bear hunting season begin in August), and more than 80 charter boat operators offer fishing and sightseeing trips. Rental cars are available at the airport and downtown. Rental boats are also available. Transient moorage is available at Thomas Basin, Ryus Float and the City Float downtown, and at Bar Harbor north of downtown. Contact the City Port and Harbors Department in advance for moorage.

Ketchikan's colorful history is highlighted in several local attractions, including Creek Street, a former red-light district; Dolly's House, which was the brothel of the street's most famous madam; First City Players' weekly performance of *The Fish Pirate's Daughter;* Totem Heritage Center; Tongass Historical Museum; and Totem Bight State Park, 10 miles north of town; and Saxman Totem Park, 2.5 miles south of town.

Ketchikan hosts a Mayfest celebration, several summer fishing derbies and a Blueberry Festival in August. The July 4 celebration includes Ketchikan's famous Logging Carnival. The Festival of the North in February includes music, Native arts and culture.

Ketchikan is the gateway to Misty Fiords National Monument located 30 miles east of town and accessible only by boat or floatplane. A number of tour operators in Ketchikan offer a variety of trips into this scenic area.

The area supports 4 public elementary schools, a junior high school, 2 high schools, a branch campus of the University of Alaska, and several churches. Freight arrives by cargo plane and barge. Government addresses: Ketchikan Gateway Borough, 344 Front St., Ketchikan, AK 99901; Borough Manager, phone 228-6625; City of Ketchikan, 334 Front St., Ketchikan, AK 99901; phone 225-3111. Parks and Recreation, phone 228-5608. Visitor's Bureau, phone 225-6166 or 800-770-2200 for a free visitors packet.

For more information see *The MILE-POST®,* a complete guide to communities on Alaska's road and ferry systems.

Klawock

[MAP 2] Located on the west coast of Prince of Wales Island on Klawock Inlet, 24 road miles west of Hollis, 7 road miles north of Craig, 55 air miles west of Ketchikan. **Transportation:** Scheduled air service from Ketchikan; private boat; state ferry to Hollis. **Population:** 897. **Zip code:** 99925. **Emergency Services:** Alaska State Troopers, phone 755-2918; Police, phone 755-2261; Clinic, phone 755-2900; Fire and Rescue, phone 755-2222.

Elevation: Sea level. **Climate:** Maritime with cool, moist, cloudy weather; mild winters. Average temperature in January is 34°F, in July it is 56°F. Mean monthly precipitation ranges from 3.62 inches in June to 14.88 inches in October. Annual precipitation is 120 inches, including 40 inches of snow.

Private Aircraft: Klawock airstrip, 2 miles northeast; elev. 50 feet; length 5,000 feet; paved; fuel 80; unattended; air service provides courtesy bus to town. Klawock seaplane base, sheltered anchorage, dock, fuel 80.

Visitor Facilities: Food and lodging are available at Fireweed Lodge (755-2930); lodging is also available at Prince of Wales Lodge (755-2227) and Log Cabin Sports (755-2205). Food is also available at Dave's Diner (755-2986) and Sugar Shack (755-2905). Groceries and supplies are available at Island Foods (755-2931), Black Bear (755-2292) and Isaac's Sentry Hardware (755-2912). Rental cabins and RV spaces are available. Gas, banking services, laundromat, camera film and first-aid supplies, sporting goods, clothing and some Native arts and crafts are available. Fishing/hunting licenses may be purchased locally. Guided hunting and fishing trips and equipment available. Major repair services include cars; marine engines and boats may be repaired in nearby Craig. Automobiles and boats may be rented in Klawock. All types of fuel are available. Transient moorage available at public floats and public dock.

Klawock originally was a Tlingit Indian summer fishing village; a trading post and salmon saltery were established here in 1868. Ten years later a salmon cannery was built—the first cannery in Alaska and the first of several cannery operations in the area. Over the years the population of Klawock, like other Southeast communities, grew and then declined with the salmon harvest. The local economy is still dependent on fishing and cannery operations, along with timber cutting and sawmilling. A state fish hatchery is located on Klawock Lake, very near the site of a salmon hatchery that operated from 1897 until 1917. Klawock Lake offers good canoeing and boating.

Recreation here includes good fishing for trout, salmon and steelhead in Klawock River, salmon and halibut fishing in Big Salt Lake and surrounding salt water, and deer and bear hunting. Klawock's totem park contains 21 totems (both replicas and originals) from the abandoned Indian village of Tuxekan.

Klawock is a first-class city, incorporated in 1929. Communications include phones, mail plane, radio and cable TV. Churches include Catholic, Baha'i and Assembly of God. Schools include an elementary school, junior high school and high school. Public electric power, water and sewage systems are available. No alcoholic beverages are sold in Klawock. (An ordinance which goes back to the Wheeler Howard Act of 1934 required, among other things, that Klawock be kept free of liquor before receiving federal funding for cannery operations.) Freight arrives by cargo plane, barge and truck. Government address: City of Klawock, P.O. Box 113, Klawock, AK 99925; phone 755-2261. Village corporation address: Klawock Heenya Corp., P.O. Box 25, Klawock, AK 99925.

Klukwan

[MAP 1] Located along the Haines Highway, 21 miles north of Haines, on the north shore of the Chilkat River and near the junction of Klehini and Tsirku rivers, 22 miles west of Skagway and 100 miles northeast of Juneau. **Transportation:** Road from Haines. **Population:** 110. **Zip code:** 99827. **Emergency Services:** Alaska State Troppers and Clinic in Haines; Fire Department, phone 767-5555; Klukwan Village Safety Officer, phone 767-5588; Klukwan Health Aide, phone 767-5505.

Elevation: Less than 500 feet above sea level.

Private Aircraft: No facilities. See Haines, this section.

Visitor Facilities: No visitor accommodations or services. Virtually all facilities are available in nearby Haines.

Klukwan is the only surviving village of 4 Tlingit villages in the Chilkat Valley. A survey in the late 1800s showed a population of more than 500 persons in Klukwan. It is the only inland settlement in southeastern Alaska. Klukwan has a strong sense of identity. Although the town has electricity, phone service and a modern school with grades kindergarten through 12, many residents continue a lifestyle based, in part, on subsistence activities. They fish for salmon and eulachon in the Chilkat River and use berries, trees and animals of the Tongass National Forest. The area also borders the Alaska Chilkat Bald Eagle Preserve.

Kupreanof

[MAP 2] Located on Lindenberg Peninsula, on the northeast shore of Kupreanof Island, across from Petersburg. **Transportation:** Primarily by small boat from Petersburg. **Population:** "30 people, about 40 cats, 20 dogs, 1 goat, 1 pig, 2 geese and 1 ferret." **Zip code:** 99833. **Emergency Services:** Alaska State Troopers and hospital in Petersburg; Volunteer Fire Department.

Elevation: Sea level. **Climate:** Summer temperatures range from 40°F to 76°F, winter temperatures from 0°F to 43°F. Average annual precipitation 105 inches, with mean monthly snowfall in winter from 0.9 to 29.2 inches.

Private Aircraft: Floatplane landings only, public dock.

Visitor Facilities: There are no facilities or services here for visitors. Residents obtain services and supplies in Petersburg, which is accessible by skiff and kayak.

Formerly known as West Petersburg, Kupreanof incorporated as a second-class city in 1975, mostly to avoid annexation by the City of Petersburg and preserve its independent and rustic lifestyle.

A small sawmill was started here in 1911 by the Knudsen brothers, and in the 1920s the Yukon Fur Farm began raising foxes, then mink; both the mill and fur farm operated into the 1960s. Today, Kupreanof has no industrial base or commercial activities. Most residents are self-employed or work outside the community. Subsistence activities also contribute to each household.

Boardwalks and trails connect some of Kupreanof, although locals use skiffs to travel around the community. Kupreanof is adjacent to Petersburg Creek–Duncan Salt Chuck Wilderness Area. A planked trail runs behind private property toward the Petersburg Mountain Trail and another trail which leads 1 mile to Petersburg Creek.

Communications include radio and 3 households have phones. Mail is received in Petersburg, as Kupreanof has no post office. Children also attend school in Petersburg. Less than half the residents have electricity, supplied by individual diesel or gasoline-powered generators. Most homes use wood stoves for heating. Residents also provide their own water (from wells or creeks) and sewage systems (septic tanks or privies). Freight is transported by private skiff from Petersburg to Kupreanof. Government address: City of Kupreanof, P.O. Box 50, Petersburg, AK 99833; phone 772-3660 or 772-4548.

Labouchere Bay

[MAP 2] Located on the northwest tip of Prince of Wales Island, 2 miles south of Point Baker, 50 air miles west of Wrangell, 121 road miles from Hollis ferry terminal. **Transportation:** Private boat, floatplane or by road.

Elevation: Sea level.

This is a logging camp operated by Louisiana-Pacific Corp. No accommodations or gas are available, so begin your drive with enough fuel to return. A small store provides limited groceries and logging clothing. There are public phones available. There are private floats available with permission, and one of them contains a floatplane ramp. There is a small boat launching ramp.

Long Island

[MAP 2] Located 50 miles southwest of Ketchikan and 42 miles south of Craig. **Transportation:** Boat or floatplane; mail plane. **Population:** 150. **Zip code:** NA.

Elevation: Sea level.

Private Aircraft: Floatplane landings only.

Visitor Facilities: This is a logging camp operated by Klukwan Inc. No visitor services or supplies available.

Loring

[MAP 2] Located on Revillagigedo Island, 20 miles north of Ketchikan, at the northeast corner of Naha Bay on the east side of Behm Canal. **Transportation:** Accessible by boat or floatplane only.

Visitor Facilities: Open moorage available at state float; no other services or facili-

ties here. There is a village phone, reached through the Ratz Mountain marine operator.

A small group of residents lives at this former cannery site. Established in 1885, the cannery closed in 1930 and the post office was discontinued in 1936.

In 1889, the side-paddle steamer *Ancon*, which carried mail, freight and passengers between the U.S. West Coast and southeastern Alaska, was wrecked at Loring. A cannery hand had cast off the lines as the ship prepared to depart, when no one was in control of the vessel. The ship drifted onto a reef, a rock punctured the hull and the ship sank (no lives were lost). Today, pieces of the *Ancon*'s rusted boiler can be seen at Loring at low tide.

Metlakatla

[MAP 2] Located on the west coast of Annette Island, 15 miles south of Ketchikan. **Transportation:** Charter air service; state ferry from Ketchikan. **Population:** 1,736. **Zip code:** 99926. **Emergency Services:** Police, phone 886-4011; Clinic, phone 886-4741; Fire Department, phone 886-7922. Police, Fire and Ambulance, emergency only, phone 911.

Elevation: Sea level. **Climate:** Mild and moist. Summer temperatures range from 36°F to 65°F, winter temperatures from 28°F to 44°F. Average annual precipitation is 115 inches; October is the wettest month with a maximum of 35 inches of rainfall. Annual snowfall averages 61 inches.

Private Aircraft: Floatplane landings only at seaplane base. Annette Island airstrip, length 7,500 feet, asphalt. Request permission to land from Metlakatla Indian Community.

Visitor Facilities: Permit required for long-term visits to Metlakatla; contact the tourism department, phone 886-4441. Overnight accommodations, including several bed and breakfasts, and restaurant service are available; phone 886-4441 for information. Groceries and other supplies and banking services are available. Transient moorage available at Metlakatla boat harbor; marine gas at Union fuel dock, marine repairs available at cannery in season. An enclosed bay is popular with kayakers.

Metlakatla was founded in 1887 by William Duncan, a Scottish-born lay minister, who moved here with several hundred Tsimshian Indians from a settlement in British Columbia after a falling out with church authorities. Congress granted reservation status and title to the entire island in 1891 and the new settlement prospered under Duncan, who built a salmon cannery and sawmill. Today, fishing and lumber continue to be the main economic base of Metlakatla. The community and island also retain the status of a federal Indian reservation, which is why Metlakatla is allowed to have fish traps.

This well-planned community has a town hall, a recreation center with an Olympic-size swimming pool, well-maintained wood-frame homes, a post office, the mill and cannery. The Metlakatla Indian Community is the largest employer in town, with retail and service trades the second largest. Many residents also are commercial fishermen. Subsistence activities remain an important source of food for residents, who harvest seaweed, salmon, halibut, cod, clams and waterfowl.

Attractions include the Duncan Museum, the original cottage occupied by Father William Duncan until his death in 1918. A replica of the turn-of-the-century William Duncan Memorial Church, built after the original was destroyed by fire in 1948, is also open to the public. The JOM Dancers perform at the community Long House; phone 886-4441 for schedule.

Communications include phones, daily mail plane from Ketchikan, radio and TV. There are several churches, and both elementary and high schools. The City of Metlakatla provides electric power, water and sewage systems. Freight arrives by barge. Government address: City of Metlakatla, P.O. Box 8, Metlakatla, AK 99926; phone 886-4868 or 886-4441.

Meyers Chuck

[MAP 2] Located on the northwest tip of Cleveland Peninsula off Clarence Strait, 40 miles northwest of Ketchikan. **Transportation:** Floatplane or private boat. **Population:** 19 year-round. **Zip code:** 99903. **Emergency Services:** Police and Hospital in Ketchikan and the Coast Guard.

Elevation: Sea level. **Climate:** No official records exist for Meyers Chuck. Residents say it's cool and rainy, with temperatures usually ranging from 20°F to 40°F, with a few weeks of 0°F to 20°F weather in winter.

Private Aircraft: Seaplane base with sheltered anchorage and dock.

Visitor Facilities: Accommodations at local lodge, or visitors may arrange for food and lodging in private homes. Fishing/hunting licenses may be purchased at the post office. Fuel, groceries, banking services, laundromat and rental transportation are not available. Open moorage available at the community dock. The harbor offers excellent shelter from storms. There is a state boat grid available for repairs.

The early history of Meyers Chuck is a bit hazy, although records suggest that white settlers began living here in the late 1800s, and the community was probably named after one of these early residents. (The name, too, is a bit hazy; there has been some argument whether it was Meyer, Myer, Myers or Meyers. Longtime resident Leo C. "Lone Wolf" Smith favored Myers Chuck. "Chuck" is a Chinook jargon word, usually applied to a saltwater body that fills at high tide.)

The natural harbor and the large Union Bay cannery nearby (which operated from 1916 to 1945) attracted fishermen to the townsite in the 1920s and postal service began in 1922. Today, most residents make their living fishing and supplement their income by working outside the community or depend on subsistence. Several retired people also make their homes here. There is not much in the way of traditional tourist attractions. The chief attractions, according to Robert Meyer, are "the lovely sunsets and scenery."

Communications include phones, mail plane, radio and TV (via satellite dish). The Meyers Chuck School, which also serves as a community center, has approximately 9 students enrolled in kindergarten through grade 12. Most households have their own electrical generators and heat with wood. There is a community water system but no public sewage disposal; households are either on septic tanks or pipe sewage into the bay. Freight comes in by ship or plane. The village phone (946-1234) is situated outdoors on a community pathway, where it is answered by postmaster Mary Ann Glenz or anyone who happens by.

Pelican

[MAP 1] Located on Lisianski Inlet on the northwest coast of Chichagof Island, 70 miles west of Juneau, 80 miles north of Sitka. **Transportation:** Scheduled air service from Juneau; charter air service available from other points; state ferry service monthly in winter, bimonthly in summer. **Population:** 265. **Zip code:** 99832. **Emergency Services:** Fire or health emergencies, phone 911; Public Safety Officer, phone 735-2213; Clinic, phone 735-2250; Fire Department, phone 735-2312.

Elevation: Sea level. Climate: Winter temperatures range from 21°F to 39°F, summer temperatures from 51°F to 62°F. Total average annual precipitation is 127 inches, with 120 inches of snow.

Private Aircraft: Seaplane base with sheltered anchorage and dock; fuel 80, 100.

Visitor Facilities: Food is served at Pelican Bar & Grill (735-2294), Rose's Bar & Grill (735-9909) and Lisianski Inlet Cafe (735-2282; breakfast and lunch). Rooms are available at Rose's "Plaza," Harbor Bed & Breakfast (735-2310) and Lisianski Lodge (735-2266). Harbor Bed & Breakfast also has a public laundromat. Pelican Wet Goods provides a steambath and showers for public use. Fishing charters are available through Lisianski Lodge, Howard Brothers Charters (735-2207), Terry's Marine Repair (735-2233) and Paul Corbin. Pelican Seafoods Inc. (735-2204) provides groceries, hardware, first-aid supplies, camera film and fishing gear at the General Store; also marine gas, diesel, propane, and regular gasoline. Transient moorage is available at the Pelican City Harbor, and repairs at Terry's Marine Repair.

Established in 1938 by Kalle (Charley) Raataikainen, and named for his fish packer, *The Pelican,* Pelican relies on commercial fishing and seafood processing for its economic base. The cold storage plant processes salmon, halibut, crab, herring and black cod, and is the primary year-round employer. Pelican has dubbed itself "closest to the fish," a reference to its proximity to the rich Fairweather salmon grounds. Nonresident fishermen swell the population during the fishing season, from about May to mid-October. Pelican was incorporated in 1943. Most of Pelican is built on pilings over tidelands. A wooden boardwalk extends the length of the community, and there are about 2 miles of gravel road.

Local recreation includes kayaking, hiking, fishing and watching birds and marine mammals. According to a local wag, special events here include the arrival and departure of the state ferry, the tide change, sunny days and a woman in a dress.

Chichagof Island boasts several attractions, such as abandoned mines and White Sulphur Hot Springs, where there is a Forest Service cabin. Across Lisianski Inlet from Pelican is the West Chichagof–Yakobi Wilderness of Tongass National Forest, a 265,000-acre area encompassing a 65-mile stretch of rugged Pacific Ocean coastline, a paradise for powerboat, sailboat and kayak enthusiasts. Gail Corbin from Lizianski Lodge (735-2266)

guides hikers up game trails to spectacular alpine lakes and scenic viewpoints.

Communications include phones, mail plane, radio courtesy of Raven Radio, Sitka 91-AM and TV. There is one church and a public school system serving kindergarten through 12th grade. Public electric power and water and sewage systems are available. Freight arrives by barge or on the state ferry. Government address: City of Pelican, P.O. Box 737, Pelican, AK 99832; phone 735-2202, fax 735-2258.

Petersburg

[MAP 2] Located on the northwest tip of Mitkof Island at the northern end of Wrangell Narrows, midway between Juneau and Ketchikan. Transportation: Daily scheduled jet service from major Southeast cities: Juneau, Ketchikan and Wrangell; local flights and charter air service; scheduled state ferry service. Population: 3,680. Zip code: 99833. Emergency Services: Alaska State Troopers, phone 772-3100; City Police, Ambulance and Fire Department, phone 772-3838; Hospital, phone 722-4291.

Elevation: Sea level. Climate: Maritime, wet and cool.

Private Aircraft: Petersburg airport, 1 mile southeast; elev. 107 feet; length 6,000 feet; asphalt; fuel 100, Jet A; ticket counter and waiting room. Petersburg seaplane base has sheltered anchorage, dock, and fuel 80, 100.

Visitor Facilities: Accommodations are available at Scandia House (772-4281), Tides Inn (772-4288), Beachcomber Inn (772-3888), Jewels by the Sea (772-4820). Petersburg restaurants include Beachcomber Inn (772-3888), Harbor Lights Pizza (772-3424) and the Homestead Cafe (772-3900). Groceries, hardware and fishing supplies are available at The Trading Union, Inc. (772-3881) and Hammer & Wikan, Inc. (772-4246). Petersburg also has a bakery, a public bathhouse, 2 banks, drugstores, gas stations and gift shops. Fishing/hunting licenses are sold at several outlets and charter fishing trips are available locally. Major engine repair and all types of fuel are also available. There are 3 car rental agencies, 4 air charters, and several outfits offering boat rentals. Transient moorage available at city harbor.

Petersburg's attractions include the Sons of Norway Hall, built in 1912 and on the National Register of Historic Places; Clausen Memorial Museum, with its collection of local historical items; its busy waterfront, Scandinavian decorations, neatly laid-out streets and spectacular scenery. The big event of the year is the Little Norway Festival, held usually on the weekend closest to Norwegian Independence Day (May 17), when residents and visitors celebrate the community's heritage with costumes, dancing, contests and a big fish bake.

The community has all communications and public utilities. There are more than a dozen churches in Petersburg and both elementary and high schools. Freight arrives by barge, ferry or cargo plane. Government address: City of Petersburg, P.O. Box 329, Petersburg, AK 99833; phone 772-4511.

For more information see *The MILE-POST®*, a complete guide to communities on Alaska's road and marine highway systems.

Point Baker

[MAP 2] Located at the northwest tip of Prince of Wales Island, 50 miles west of Wrangell. **Transportation:** Private boat or charter plane. **Population:** 30. **Zip code:** 99927. **Emergency Services:** Alaska State Troopers in Petersburg; Hospital in Wrangell; trained emergency technicians in Point Baker. **Elevation:** Sea level. **Climate:** Like other Prince of Wales Island communities, a maritime climate with cool, wet, cloudy weather.

Private Aircraft: Seaplane float in harbor.

Visitor Facilities: No accommodations and limited services for visitors. There are a bar, restaurant, showers and laundry. Groceries, liquor, ice, gas, diesel, propane and aviation fuel, fishing/hunting licenses and bait are available at the trading post (559-2204). Transient moorage with power is available at the state-operated floats. The community building on the dock contains the post office, and there are pay phones at both dock ends.

Point Baker was named by Capt. George Vancouver in 1793 for the second lieutenant on his ship *Discovery*. Fish buyers operated here from about 1919 through the 1930s. The Forest Service opened the area for homesites, then in 1955 withdrew the townsite from Tongass National Forest. Most of Point Baker's year-round residents are fishermen, and the population increases in summer with visiting fishermen. Halibut and salmon fishing is excellent in the area and residents also hunt for deer. Humpback whales pass by Point Baker and the bird life here includes eagles and blue herons.

Communications include mail plane, radio and TV. Residents take care of their own electric power and sewage, and get their water either from collecting rain water or from streams, although there is a freshwater hose at the dock. Freight arrives by plane or barge.

Port Alexander

[MAP 2] Located on the south end of Baranof Island, 5 miles northeast of Cape Ommaney on the west side of Chatham Strait, 65 miles south of Sitka, 90 miles west of Wrangell. **Transportation:** Private boat or charter plane and scheduled air taxi service from Sitka. **Population:** 120. **Zip code:** 99836. **Emergency Services:** Alaska State Troopers and Hospital in Sitka; emergency technicians in Port Alexander.

Elevation: 20 feet. **Climate:** Average summer temperatures range from 41°F to 55°F; winter temperatures from 32°F to 45°F. Record high was 80°F in June 1958; record low 4°F in January 1953. Average annual precipitation is 172 inches, with October the wettest month.

Private Aircraft: Seaplane base. Sheltered anchorage and dock.

Visitor Facilities: Limited groceries are available at Puget Sound Fisherman's Service (locals call it "Bud's Store"), phone 568-2206. Rainforest Retreat bed and breakfast offers lodging and macrobiotic meals. Public moorage at state floats (inner and outer harbors).

Port Alexander evolved into a year-round fishing community in the 1920s, settled by fishermen who trolled the Chatham Strait fishing grounds. In its heyday, Port Alexander's protected harbor was filled with up to 1,000 fishing boats at a time. The community prospered until the late 1930s, when the decline in salmon and herring stocks and the outbreak of WWII knocked the bottom out of fish buying, packing and processing at Port Alexander. Today, the majority of residents are commercial fishermen who choose to live here for the independent and subsistence lifestyle the area offers. Port Alexander was incorporated in 1974.

Communications include phones, a mail plane twice a week and radio. Port Alexander has a community water system, but electrical power and sewage systems are provided by individual households. The school, located next to Bear Hall community center, has grades kindergarten through 12. Port Alexander prohibits the sale of alcoholic beverages. Freight arrives by plane or barge. Government address: City of Port Alexander, P.O. Box 8068, Port Alexander, AK 99836; phone 568-2211.

Port Protection

[MAP 2] Located at the northwest tip of Prince of Wales Island near Point Baker, 50 miles west of Wrangell and southwest of Petersburg. **Transportation:** Private boat or charter plane. **Population:** 74. **Zip code:** 99950. **Emergency Services:** Alaska State Troopers in Petersburg; Hospital in Wrangell; emergency technicians in Port Protection. **Elevation:** Sea level. **Climate:** Like other Prince of Wales Island communities, a maritime climate with cool, wet, cloudy weather. According to one resident, "the summers are nice and the winters are not."

Private Aircraft: Floatplane landings only.

Visitor Facilities: Food and lodging available in a private home, phone 489-2212. Groceries, hardware, film, bait, ice, gas and diesel are available. Aviation fuel is available upon request, for emergency purposes only. No propane is available. No banking services. Laundromat, public showers are available. Limited boat repair and state-owned grid are available. Fishing/hunting licenses are available. Guide service may be arranged. Transient moorage at public float.

Like its neighbor Point Baker, Port Protection was used as a fish-buying station and later settled by fishermen who had long used the cove for shelter from southeast storms. Credit for its "discovery" is given to a man named Johnson, who came ashore in the early 1900s to replace a wooden wheel lost off his boat and gave the spot its first name—Wooden Wheel Cove. In the late 1940s, Laurel "Buckshot" Woolery established a trading post and fish-buying station. Although the original trading post burned several years ago, a new store was erected, and the post still functions as a fish-buying station. The residents are either fishermen or retirees. Each household has at least one small boat, in addition to fishing vessels, to travel between homes in Port Protection and to Point Baker to pick up mail.

Excellent fishing in the immediate area in summer for salmon, halibut and rockfish. Boaters, kayakers and canoeists can make Port Protection their starting point for circumnavigating Prince of Wales Island. The trading post sponsors an end-of-fishing-season barbecue.

Communications include phones; CB radios are used by most households. A public phone for collect or credit card calls is availble at the trading post. Port Protection also has radio and TV reception. A school housed in the community building offers grades kindergarten through 12 for about 9 students. Residents have their own generators for power or use kerosene for lighting. Wood-burning stoves provide heat. A community water system provides fresh water to all homes, the trading post float and for fire hydrants. No water is available at the state float. Sewage system is outdoor privies or outfall pipes into the cove. Freight comes in by chartered boat or floatplane.

Saxman

[MAP 2] Located 2 miles south of Ketchikan. **Transportation:** Road from Ketchikan. **Population:** 309. **Zip code:** 99901. **Emergency Services:** Alaska State Troopers and hospital in Ketchikan; Fire Department, phone 225-1981.

Elevation: Sea level.

Visitor Facilities: Virtually all facilities are available in nearby Ketchikan. Saxman has a restaurant, gas station and seasonal gift shop. There is no public boat dock or boat gas; no seaplane dock. There is a city-owned seaport.

The town's major attraction is Saxman Totem Park, which contains the largest collection of totem poles in the world. Saxman is also home to the Beaver Clan House, which is the only clan house built in Alaska in the last 50 years. Constructed of hand-adzed cedar, it features artwork by Tlingit artist Nathan Jackson. The local gift store specializes in Native and Alaskan handmade goods. The park is open year-round. Admission is charged. Also in summer, Native artists can usually be seen in various parts of Saxman, carving totems, weaving spruce baskets or doing beadwork. Government address: City of Saxman, Route 2, Box 1, Saxman, AK 99901; phone 225-4166, fax 225-6450.

Sitka

[MAP 2] Located on the west side of Baranof Island, 95 miles southwest of Juneau. Unlike many Southeast Alaska towns, Sitka faces the open ocean. **Transportation:** Scheduled jet service, commuter and charter flights; state ferry service. **Population:** 8,588. **Zip code:** 99835. **Emergency Services:** Alaska State Troopers, Police, Ambulance and Fire Department, phone 911; Hospital, phone 747-3241.

Elevation: Sea level. **Climate:** Maritime, with cool summers (55°F daily temperature in July) and mild winters (33°F in January). Annual precipitation, 96 inches.

Private Aircraft: Sitka airport on Japonski Island; elev. 21 feet; length 6,500 feet; asphalt; fuel 80, 100, Jet A-50. Sitka seaplane base adjacent; fuel 80, 100. Passenger terminal at airport.

Visitor Facilities: Overnight accommodations available at 4 hotels, 2 lodges, 9 bed and breakfasts, a youth hostel in town and a U.S. Forest Service campground 8 miles north of town. The downtown area has an array of businesses, including restaurants, bookstore, biking/camping store, library, laundromats, banks, drugstore, clothing and grocery stores and gift shops. Fishing/hunting licenses are sold at several outlets. Local charter operators offer sportfishing trips and there are 2 registered hunting guides. Major engine repair, rental transportation and all types of fuel available. Transient moorage available at the city float.

Sitka National Historical Park preserves the community's Tlingit and Russian heritage. Here a fine collection of totem poles is set among majestic spruce and hemlocks on a trail to the Russian fort site. In mid- and late summer blueberries and huckleberries ripen along this trail. One visitor reflected, "The Native presence in the stand of totems adds such a powerful reminder of the history of the area." Sitka's Tlingit and Russian past is the major attraction for visitors. Replicas of the old Russian Blockhouse and St. Michael's Cathedral (rebuilt from original plans after a fire in 1966), and the original Russian Bishop's House (built in 1842), are open to the public. Museums in town include the Sheldon Jackson Museum on the campus of Sheldon Jackson College and the Isabel Miller Museum located in the Centennial Building.

The city has all communications and public utilities. There are more than a dozen churches, 3 elementary schools, a junior high school, 2 high schools (including a boarding school) and 2 colleges: Sheldon Jackson College and University of Alaska Southeast, Sitka branch. Freight comes in by barge and cargo plane. For visitor information contact: Sitka Convention and Visitors Bureau, P.O. Box 1226, Sitka, AK 99835; phone 747-5940, fax 747-3739. Government address: City and Borough of Sitka, 304 Lake St., Room 104, Sitka, AK 99835; phone 747-3294. Native corporation address: Shee-Atika, Inc., P.O. Box 1949, Sitka, AK 99835; phone 747-3534.

For more information see *The MILE-POST®*, a complete guide to communities on Alaska's road and marine highway systems.

Skagway

[MAP 1] Located at the north end of Taiya Inlet on Lynn Canal, 90 air miles northwest of Juneau, 13 nautical miles from Haines, 100 road miles from the Alaska Highway. **Transportation:** Daily scheduled flights from Juneau and Haines via local commuter services; charter air service; scheduled state ferry service; connected to the Alaska Highway by Klondike Highway 2. **Population:** 701. **Zip code:** 99840. **Emergency Services:** Police, phone 983-2301; Clinic, phone 983-2255; Fire Department and Ambulance, phone 983-2300, or 911.

Elevation: Sea level.

Private Aircraft: Skagway airport adjacent west; elev. 44 feet; length 3,500 feet; asphalt, fuel 80, 100. Due to downdrafts and winds in the area, landing a small plane can be tricky. Also, the airport approach is different from the norm.

Visitor Facilities: There are 7 hotels/motels; 2 hostels; 2 bed and breakfasts; a dozen or so restaurants, cafes and bars; grocery, hardware and clothing stores; a laundromat; a bank; and many gift and novelty shops. City-owned RV park on waterfront. Rental cars are available. Propane, marine and automobile gas are available, as are major repair services. Transient boat moorage available at the city harbor.

A 6-block area of downtown Skagway is included in Klondike Gold Rush National Historical Park. The main street, Broadway, is lined with false-fronted buildings and boardwalks. The city is easy to get around by foot, and Park Service rangers lead walks through downtown. Films and slide shows are offered at the visitor center. The Trail of '98 Museum, owned and operated by the citizens of Skagway, has an interesting collection of gold rush memorabilia. Also included in the historical park is the 33-mile-long Chilkoot Trail, the old gold rush route over the mountains to Lake Bennett, where early gold seekers built boats to take them down the Yukon River to the Klondike. The Chilkoot Trail attracts more than 2,000 hardy souls each summer.

The historic White Pass & Yukon Route railroad provided train service between Skagway and Whitehorse until 1982, when it shut down operations. In the spring of 1988 it renewed operation as an excursion train to the summit of White Pass and back. The 3-hour trip departs daily from Skagway May to September. There is a scheduled switch-thru service from Skagway to Whitehorse,

YT, with a bus shuttling passengers between the border and Whitehorse. There is a hikers' service into Lake Bennett (see Chilkoot Trail under Special Features in Attractions section).

Special events in the community include the annual Windfest held the third weekend in March; the Buckwheat Ski Classic, cross-country skiing on a groomed trail in scenic White Pass; a large Fourth of July celebration; the Dyea Dash, a 3.5-mile race held the last Saturday in August; and the Klondike Trail of '98 Road Relay from Skagway to Whitehorse held the third weekend in September.

Communications include phones, mail plane, radio and TV. There are 4 churches, an elementary school and a high school. There are community electric power, water and sewage systems. Freight arrives by ferry or barge and by road. Government address: City of Skagway, P.O. Box 415, Skagway, AK 99840; phone 983-2297.

For more information, see *The MILE-POST®*, a complete guide to communities on Alaska's road and marine highway systems.

Tenakee Springs

[MAP 2] Located on the north shore of Tenakee Inlet on the east side of Chichagof Island, 50 miles northeast of Sitka. **Transportation:** Scheduled and charter air service; state ferry service. **Population:** 108. **Zip code:** 99841. **Emergency Services:** Alaska State Troopers in Juneau; Volunteer Fire Department; Village Public Safety Officer, phone 736-2211.

Elevation: Sea level. **Climate:** Maritime, with cool summers (45°F to 65°F) and mild winters (24°F to 39°F). Total precipitation averages 69 inches a year.

Private Aircraft: Seaplane base with dock.

Visitor Facilities: Lodging is available at Snyder's Mercantile (736-2205) and Tenakee Hot Springs Lodge (736-2400), which also supplies custom sportfishing packages. Lodging, laundromat, bar and snacks at Tenakee Inn and Tavern (736-2241). Meals at Blue Moon Cafe. Groceries, first-aid supplies, hardware, camera film, sporting goods and fishing/hunting licenses available. No banking services. Fuel available includes marine gas, diesel and propane. There is a boat mechanic in town. Supplies, charter boat information and rental cabins available through Snyder's Mercantile. Tenakee Springs has one street — Tenakee

Avenue — which is about 2 miles long and 4 to 12 feet wide. There are only 2 vehicles in town. Residents walk or use bicycles or 3-wheel motorbikes for transportation. Public moorage available at city-operated floats.

Tenakee's natural hot springs first drew early prospectors and miners, and by 1895 the springs were enlarged to accommodate the increasing number of visitors. Ed Snyder built a general store here in 1899 and a post office was established in 1903. Three canneries operated at various times at Tenakee from 1916 to the 1960s. Some residents still make their living fishing commercially, although most year-round residents are retirees. The community also sees an influx of summer visitors: tourists, commercial fishermen and pleasure boaters, and Juneau and Sitka residents who have summer homes here. Tenakee Springs was incorporated as a second-class city in 1971.

Tenakee's major attractions are its quiet isolation and its hot springs. The bathhouse is located on the waterfront and has posted times of use by men and women. There is a U.S. Forest Service trail that runs east 7.8

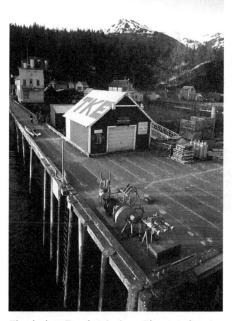

The dock at Tenakee Springs. The state ferry Le Conte *serves Tenakee several times a week. (David Job)*

miles from Tenakee Springs along the shoreline of Tenakee Inlet to Coffee Cove. The area also offers beachcombing and hunting and fishing.

Communications include phones, daily mail plane, radio and TV. A new school offers grades kindergarten through 12. A large generator plant provides electrical service to most households. There are no water or sewage systems. Residents haul water from streams, and households have their own privies. Freight comes in by seaplane, ferry and barge. Government address: City of Tenakee Springs, P.O. Box 52, Tenakee Springs, AK 99841; phone 736-2221.

Thorne Bay

[MAP 2] Located on the east coast of Prince of Wales Island, in the heart of the scenic Tongass National Forest, 47 air miles northwest of Ketchikan, 42 road miles east of Craig. **Transportation:** Scheduled air service from Ketchikan; 60 road miles from Hollis (ferry port); private boat. **Population:** 614. **Zip code:** 99919. **Emergency Services:** Village Public Safety Officer, phone 828-3905; Alaska State Troopers in Klawock; Clinic, phone 828-3906; doctor in Craig; Volunteer Fire Department, phone 911.

Elevation: Sea level. **Climate:** Maritime, with cool, moist weather and mild temperatures.

Private Aircraft: Seaplane base with sheltered anchorage and dock.

Visitor Facilities: Accommodations available at Thorne Bay Inn (828-3400), McFarland's Floatel (828-3335) and Boardwalk Wilderness Lodge (828-3918). Stores and services include a restaurant; auto and boat repair; grocery, liquor, sporting goods, gift and hardware stores; and fuel supply outlets (marine gas, diesel, propane, unleaded and regular gasoline available). Gifts include pine needle raffia baskets made locally. No banking services. Fishing/hunting licenses and charter trips available.

Thorne Bay was incorporated in 1982, making it one of Alaska's newest cities. The settlement began as a logging camp in 1962, when Ketchikan Pulp Co. (now Louisiana-Pacific) moved its operations from Hollis. Thorne Bay was connected to the island road system in 1974. Camp residents created the community—and gained city status from the state as private ownership of the land was made possible under the Alaska Statehood Act. Employment here depends mainly on the lumber company and the U.S. Forest Service, with assorted jobs in local trades and services. Thorne Bay is home to one of the area's largest log sort yards. The area has good access to hunting, camping and saltwater and freshwater sport-fishing.

Communications include phones, regular mail service, radio and cable TV. A dock serves private boats and commercial fishing vessels, and a concrete boat launch ramp and fish cleaning station are available. There is 1 church and a school with grades kindergarten through 12. The community has electric power, water and sewage systems. Freight comes in by plane, barge, ship and truck. Government address: City of Thorne Bay, P.O. Box 19110, Thorne Bay, AK 99919.

Tokeen

[MAP 2] Located on the west coast of El Capitan Island off Sea Otter Sound, 60 miles southwest of Wrangell, 30 miles northwest of Craig, 80 miles northwest of Ketchikan. **Transportation:** Charter air service or private boat. Ketchikan Air Service provides daily mail flights. **Population:** 3. **Zip code:** 99950. **Emergency Services:** Alaska State Troopers in Klawock; hospital in Ketchikan.

Private Aircraft: Seaplane base, unattended.

Visitor Facilities: A store here carries some groceries, first-aid supplies, hardware, camera film, sporting goods and liquor. Limited emergency fuel available includes marine gas, diesel and regular gasoline. Tokeen Lodge (P.O. Box TKI, Ketchikan, AK 99950-0230) provides rental camping units, skiffs, kayaks and canoes. Contact the lodge through the marine operator (Tokeen 1, WYW8107). Public moorage at float.

Tokeen once had a mink farm and a cold storage plant. Tokeen is now privately owned and operated. It is a store and commercial fishermen's stop. The settlement likely was established by the former residents of Old Tokeen in the late 1930s or early 1940s.

Old Tokeen, located on the northwest end of Marble Island, 7 miles to the northwest, once had Alaska's largest marble quarry. Nearly $2 million worth of marble was taken out between 1905 and 1932. Tokeen marble was used in the Federal Building in Fairbanks, the Capitol Building in Juneau, Washington's state capitol in Olympia, WA, and in various other buildings around the country. Little remains of the mining operation except piles of waste marble.

Whale Pass

[MAP 2] Located on the northeast coast of Prince of Wales Island on Whale Passage, 64 road miles north of Klawock. **Transportation:** By road from other Prince of Wales Island communities; floatplane or private boat. **Population:** 93. **Zip code:** 99950. **Emergency Services:** 911.

Elevation: Sea level. **Climate:** Maritime, with cool, moist weather and mild temperatures.

Private Aircraft: Floatplane landings only.

Visitor Facilities: Lodging is available at Northend Cabin (846-5315). Snacks, fuel, propane, showers and laundromat are available at Whale Pass Gas and Grocery (846-5205). There are 2 pay phones.

Whale Pass was the site of a floating logging camp. The camp moved out in the early 1980s, but new residents moved in after a state land sale. The community was connected to the Prince of Wales Island road system in 1981, and private phones were installed in 1992.

Whale Pass is nestled in the scenic Tongass National Forest along the inside coastline. Many birds rest here on their migrations. It is not uncommon to see wolves, otter, martin and mink. There are many natural caves and pits in the surrounding area. Sitka blacktail deer and black bear hunting are popular, as well as fishing for salmon, halibut, steelhead, trout, etc. Whale Pass has retained its rustic, rural atmosphere, and the people are friendly and helpful.

Wrangell

[MAP 2] Located at the northwest tip of Wrangell Island on Zimovia Strait near the Stikine River delta, 154 miles south of Juneau and 90 miles north of Ketchikan. **Transportation:** Daily scheduled jet service from major Southeast cities and Seattle; daily commuter service to Ketchikan and Petersburg; air charter services; state ferry service. **Population:** 3,112. **Zip code:** 99929. **Emergency Services:** Alaska State Trooper, phone 874-3215; Police, phone 874-3304; Hospital, phone 874-3356; Ambulance, Rescue Squad and Fire Department, phone 874-2000.

Elevation: Sea level. **Climate:** Mild and moist with slightly less rain than other Southeast communities. Mean annual precipitation is 79.16 inches, with 63.9 inches of snow. Average daily maximum temperature in July is 61°F; daily minimum in January is 21°F.

Private Aircraft: Wrangell airport adjacent northeast; elev. 44 feet; length 6,000 feet; lighted asphalt runway; fuel 80, 100, A. Seaplane base adjacent south.

Visitor Facilities: There are 4 hotels/motels, 4 bed and breakfasts, a municipal campground and RV park; 7 restaurants, 2 fast-food outlets, gas stations, hardware, drugstore, grocery, clothing and sporting goods stores, gift shops, banks and a laundromat. Car rental, major repair service and all types of fuel are available. Fishing/hunting licenses may be purchased locally and there are several charter operations for fishing, hunting, Stikine River trips and glacier flightseeing. Transient moorage is available at the city harbor downtown and at Shoemaker Bay, 4.5 miles south of the city. A visitor information center, located in the A-frame building next to city hall, is open during the summer. Visitor information is also available from Wrangell Museum (874-3770). The museum also has information on digging for garnets at Garnet Ledge, a garnet schist ledge located 8 miles from Wrangell by boat.

Wrangell's history is featured at 3 local museums: Our Collections, Tribal House of the Bear on Chief Shakes Island, and Wrangell Museum. The Wrangell Museum is housed in the oldest building in Wrangell and, according to a local source, its collection is second only to the state museum in Juneau for its age and quality.

Wrangell is home of Wrangell Forest Products, and the mill is open for tours each Friday during the summer season.

Celebrations and events include a salmon derby, held mid-May to early June; a big Fourth of July celebration; annual Coho and Halibut Derby on Labor Day weekend, and Tent City Days, the first weekend in February, which commemorates Wrangell's 3 gold rushes.

A variety of U.S. Forest Service roads (excellent for mountain biking) lead to hiking trails, trout and steelhead streams and scenic overlooks. There are 12 Forest Service cabins available for public use by reservation in the Wrangell area. The most popular, the Anan cabin has plank trails to excellent black and brown bear observation posts during the pink salmon run from July through August.

See Tongass National Forest Cabins this section or contact the Wrangell District Rangers office for information on Forest Service lands. The Forest Service has a courtesy phone at the Alaska Marine Highway ferry terminal to help facilitate visitor inquiries. The entire area has excellent salmon and halibut fishing, a large bald eagle population and outstanding scenery.

Wrangell has all communications and public utilities. There are a dozen churches, an elementary school and a high school. Freight arrives by ship, barge, ferry and cargo plane. Government address: City of Wrangell, P.O. Box 531, Wrangell, AK 99929; phone 874-2381.

For more information, see *The MILEPOST®*, a complete guide to communities on Alaska's road and marine highway systems.

Yakutat

[MAP 1] Located on Yakutat Bay on the Gulf of Alaska coast, where southeastern Alaska joins the major body of Alaska to the west; 225 miles northwest of Juneau, 220 miles southeast of Cordova. **Transportation:** Daily scheduled jet service; air charter; private boat. **Population:** 729. **Zip code:** 99689. **Emergency Services:** Police or Fire Department, phone 911; Clinic, phone 784-3391.

Elevation: Sea level. **Climate:** Maritime, with mild rainy weather. Average summer temperatures 42°F to 60°F, with a record high of 86°F. Average winter temperatures 17°F to 39°F, with a record low of -24°F. "Cloudiness is abundant," says one resident.

Private Aircraft: Yakutat airport, 3 miles southeast; elev. 33 feet; length 7,800 feet; asphalt; fuel 80, 100, A1+. Passenger and freight terminals; transportation to town available. Seaplane base 1 mile northwest; sheltered anchorage and dock.

Visitor Facilities: Meals and lodging available at Glacier Bear Lodge (784-3202), Harlequin Lodge (784-3341) and Yakutat Lodge (784-3232). Lodging is available at the Silvertip Guest House (784-3533) and the Blue Heron Inn (784-3287). Cabins with kitchens for rent at Leonard's Landing Lodge (784-3245). The Light House Cafe (784-3238) serves meals, and there are 3 bars in town. All supplies are available at local businesses. There is a bank, but no public laundry. Fishing/hunting licenses may be purchased locally. Fishing guide services are available through local lodges and there are 5 registered hunting guides. Rental cars and charter aircraft are available. Marine gas, diesel, unleaded and regular gasoline are sold locally. Transient moorage at borough harbor.

Yakutat Bay is one of the few refuges for vessels along this long stretch of coast in the Gulf of Alaska. The site was originally the principal winter village of the local Tlingit Indian tribe. Sea otter pelts brought Russians to the area in the 19th century. Fur traders were followed by gold seekers, who came to work the black sand beaches. Commercial salmon fishing developed in this century and the first cannery was built here in 1904. Today's economy is based primarily on fishing and fish processing. Salmon, black cod, halibut and crab make up the fishery. Government and local businesses employ most people. Subsistence activities are primarily fishing (salmon and shellfish), hunting (moose, bear, goats, ducks and small game) and gathering seaweed and berries. The soil is not suitable for agriculture and a vegetable garden requires a great deal of preparation to produce even small quantities.

The Yakutat School District's information sheet for teacher applicants describes Yakutat's primary attraction as outdoor recreation: "If you enjoy the outdoors, there is plenty for you to do, including cross-country skiing, snowmobiling, hunting, fishing, hiking, biking and berry-picking in the late summer and early fall." Hunting and fishing in particular draw visitors. Steelhead fishing is considered among the finest anywhere, and king and silver salmon run in abundance in Yakutat area salt water, rivers and streams May through September. The Situk River, 12 miles south of Yakutat by road, is one of Alaska's top fishing spots.

The surrounding scenery is also spectacular. Some Lower 48 travelers flying to Anchorage pick a flight with a Yakutat stop, hoping for a clear day and a clear view from the air of Malaspina Glacier northwest of town. Some cruise ships include Hubbard Glacier and Yakutat Bay in their itineraries. Nearer to town, Cannon Beach has good beachcombing and a picnic area. Surfing fanatics from as far away as Fairbanks and Sitka make an annual pilgrimage to ride the waves which pound Yakutat's beaches.

Communications include phones in most households, a local radio station and 1 TV channel via satellite. Mail and newspapers are delivered daily by plane. There are 4 churches, an elementary school and a high school. Freight comes in by cargo plane or barge. Government address: City and Borough of Yakutat, P.O. Box 160, Yakutat, AK 99689; phone 784-3323, fax 784-3281. Native corporation address: Yaktat Kwaan, Inc., P.O. Box 416, Yakutat, AK 99689.

National and State Parks, Forests, Etc.

Admiralty Island National Monument (Kootznoowoo Wilderness)

Located about 15 miles west of Juneau, this monument encompasses 955,567 acres, or over 90 percent of Admiralty Island. The island is bounded on the east and north by Stephens Passage, on the west by Chatham Strait and on the south by Frederick Sound.

The predominantly Tlingit Indian village of Angoon lies at the mouth of Mitchell Bay on the west side of Admiralty Island, adjacent to the wilderness. Excluded from the monument are mining interests at the north end of the island. The terrain of most of the island is gentle and rolling, with spruce-hemlock forest interspersed with small areas of muskeg. Tree line generally is at 1,500 to 2,000 feet. Above timberline the forest changes to alpine-tundra with rock outcrops and ice fields. Annual precipitation is 100 inches over most of the island, although Angoon, in the rain shadow of Baranof Island, is drier.

Wildlife on the island includes the densest population of brown bears in the world, averaging 1 per square mile. (The Indians referred to the area as the "Fortress of Bears.") Other wildlife includes Sitka black-tailed deer, bald eagles, harbor seals, whales and sea lions. Because it is isolated from the mainland, some species occurring elsewhere in Southeast are not found on the island.

Outstanding areas are the numerous bays and inlets. Seymour Canal, the major inlet on the east side of the island supports one of the largest concentrations of bald eagles in southeastern Alaska. Mitchell Bay and Admiralty Lakes Recreational Area are the 2 major recreational attractions within the monument. A 25-mile trail system links the 8 major lakes on the island and is part of the Cross-Admiralty canoe trail, which consists of a series of lakes, streams and portages across the island from Mole Harbor on the east to Mitchell Bay. Kayaking and canoeing around the island is popular, as is hunting, fishing, bird watching, nature study and photography.

Primary access to the monument is by boat from Juneau or Angoon or floatplane from Juneau. There are overnight accommodations at Angoon. Facilities in the monument include 1 commercial lodge on Thayer Lake, and scattered shelters and 18 recreation cabins maintained by the Forest Service. (See Tongass National Forest Cabins in this section.) Alaska Discovery (369 S. Franklin, Juneau, AK 99801; phone 586-1911) offers guided trips and canoe rentals on the Cross-Admiralty trail. The trail is a popular winter traverse when the lakes are frozen.

For additional information: Contact Admiralty Island National Monument, P.O. Box 2097, Juneau, AK 99803; phone 586-8790. Related USGS Topographic maps: Juneau, Sitka, Sumdum.

Chilkat State Park

Located south of Haines on the Chilkat Peninsula, Chilkat State Park offers spectacular views and excellent recreational opportunities. The 6,045-acre park consists of 2 sections. The northern unit, about 3,000 acres, includes Battery Point which was known as the Battery Point State Recreation Area until 1975 when the legislature added the 3,090-acre southern part and changed the name to Chilkat State Park.

Climate: In general, area weather is clearer and drier than in other areas of Southeast with warmer summers and colder winters. Average annual precipitation at Haines is 53 inches compared to 91 inches in downtown Juneau. In winter, the coldest temperature recorded in Haines was -17°F, but on sunny summer days it is not uncommon for temperatures to rise to 80°F.

Wildlife: Within the park boundaries, animal populations include black bear, brown/grizzly bear, moose, eagles, grouse, coyotes and wolverine. Sitka black-tailed deer have also been spotted. In the waters surrounding the park, visitors are likely to see humpback whale, seals, sea lions, porpoises, and occasionally killer whales. There is also an abundance of waterfowl, and anglers will find 5 species of salmon and Dolly Varden, char and cutthroat trout.

Activities: The park offers camping, beachcombing, fishing, boating and hiking. (See description of Seduction Point Trail in Hiking Trails, Haines Area, this section.) Cross-country skiing and snowshoeing are popular in winter. Chilkat State Park is particularly well-situated for beach and mountain scenic views.

Hikers and campers are cautioned to be prepared for changes in weather, especially if hiking above tree line. Take extra food, warm clothing, map, compass, first-aid kit, knife, matches and sunglasses even on day hikes.

Accommodations: The park offers both developed and undeveloped campsites. Facilities include 32 units for RV or tent campers with a 15-day camping limit. A $6 fee per night is charged for overnight camping. Annual decals may be purchased from the Alaska Division of Parks for $75. Picnic sites, toilets with handicap access, water and a shelter are also found in the park. Near the launch ramp are 3 waterfront tent sites. Deeper into the park, one will find remote camping sites.

Access: Chilkat State Park is one of the few road-accessible parks in Southeast, located 7 miles south of Haines on the Mud Bay Road. A small dock and concrete boat launch provide boat access to the ocean.

For more information: Contact Alaska Division of Parks and Outdoor Recreation, Southeast Region, 400 Willoughby, Juneau, AK 99801; phone 465-4563 or fax 586-3113; or Haines District Office, Box 430, Haines, AK 99827; phone 766-2292.

Chuck River Wilderness Area

The 72,503-acre Chuck River area was designated a Wilderness Area in 1990. The area is adjacent to the Tracy Arm-Fords Terror Wilderness on the east, and abuts areas of logging activity on the south and southeast.

Fishing and hunting are popular activities in this wilderness area, which is accessible by boat or floatplane from Juneau. The Chuck River boasts the largest pink salmon run in Southeast. All 5 species of salmon are found in Windham Bay. According to rangers, much of the trail system shown on topographic maps is overgrown. There is a trail from Windham Bay to Taylor Lake. Watch for private land holdings at the head of Windham Bay.

For more information: Contact Tongass National Forest, P.O. Box 2097, Juneau, AK 99803; phone 586-8800.

Coronation Island, Warren Island, Maurelle Islands Wilderness Areas

All 3 of these island wilderness areas are located off the northwest coast of Prince of Wales Island, south of Kuiu Island and north of Noyes Island. By air from Ketchikan it is 73 miles to the Maurelle Islands, 75 miles to Warren Island, and 110 miles to Coronation Island.

The Coronation Island Wilderness encompasses 19,232 acres; the Maurelle Islands Wilderness, 4,937 acres; and the Warren Island Wilderness, 11,181 acres. Warren Peak is a prominent feature of the Warren Island Wilderness, rising abruptly from sea level to 2,329 feet. The Coronation Island Wilderness includes the Spanish Island group as well as Coronation Island, which has numerous peaks rising sharply to nearly 2,000 feet. Maurelle Islands Wilderness is a group of nearly 30 small islands rising less than 400 feet above sea level. A number of islets, pinnacles and rocky shoals are found in surrounding waters. These island wildernesses have rocky, windswept beaches with steep cliffs. Trees near the shoreline are often wind sculpted. Tall stands of spruce are found in more sheltered portions of the islands.

Wildlife includes wolves, black bears, Sitka black-tailed deer, bald eagles, whales, seals, sea lions and sea otters. The cliffs and rocks are important seabird nesting and perching areas. Some streams contain trout and salmon.

Kayaking among the Maurelle Islands is possible, although rugged. On the 2 larger islands, principal activities are beachcombing, wildlife observation and photography. There is a protected harbor at Hole-in-the-wall in the San Lorenzo Islands, which form the southern point of the Maurelle group. Access to these islands is by boat or floatplane from Ketchikan, Craig or Klawock.

Access to many of the islands is difficult as there is a lack of boat anchorage and plane landing sites and the islands are exposed to the winds and surf of the Pacific Ocean. Warren Island is so exposed to the prevailing southeast winds that it is inaccessible much of the year. The leeward sides of some of the islands do have some protected coves and beaches. There are no facilities on any of these islands.

For additional information: Contact Tongass National Forest, Thorne Bay Ranger District, Recreation and Lands Dept., P.O. Box 1, Thorne Bay, AK 99919; phone 828-3304. Related USGS Topographic map: Craig.

Endicott River Wilderness Area

Located on the Chilkat Peninsula, on the west side of Lynn Canal, 45 miles northwest of Juneau and 30 miles south of Haines. The western alpine portion of this 98,729-acre Wilderness Area abuts Glacier Bay National Park for about 40 miles. This area is rugged, extending from sea level to elevations up to 5,280 feet. The Endicott River is the central feature of this wilderness area. It heads in broad, brush-covered flats within the Chilkat Mountains and flows easterly through a deep, glacially carved canyon. Glaciers cover the highlands of the upper valley. The vegetation is typical southeastern Alaska spruce and hemlock rain forest at lower elevations, and brush, small trees and alpine plants higher up. Average annual precipitation is 92 inches, highest in the fall and lowest April through June.

Wildlife includes black and brown bears, mountain goats and a limited number of moose. Hundreds of bald eagles may be seen along the river during salmon runs; a high number of eagles nest here also. Some deer may be present. Fish in the Endicott River include chum, coho and pink salmon.

Access is primarily by boat from Juneau or Haines to the confluence of the Endicott River and Lynn Canal, then by foot 2.5 miles through dense alder and thick brush to the eastern boundary of the wilderness. According to the Forest Service, it is another 2- to 3-day hike through extremely difficult terrain to reach the plateau. The plateau can be reached from Adams Inlet on the Glacier Bay National Park side, but this route is also

considered extremely difficult as it crosses many glacier fed streams and there is heavy brush.

Boat access is best in spring and summer. There is limited wheel plane access near the headwaters of the Endicott River. There are no facilities in this wilderness.

For more information contact: Tongass National Forest, 204 Siginaka Way, Sitka, AK 99835; phone 747-6671. Related USGS Topographic maps: Juneau.

Glacier Bay National Park and Preserve

This 3.3-million-acre park is located 50 air miles west of Juneau near the northern end of the Alaska Panhandle. It is bordered by Icy Strait and Cross Sound on the south, the Pacific Ocean on the west and Canada on the north. The park contains some of the world's most impressive examples of tide water glaciers. Other major attractions are the bay itself, whales and other wildlife, the massive Fairweather Range and the vast, unspoiled outer coast.

Glacier Bay is the ancestral home of the Chookenaidi and Wukitan clans of the Native Tlingit people, whose descendants now reside primarily in Hoonah. The clans hunted and fished, gathered berries, eggs

Glacier travel requires a rope and ice axe. (Karen Jettmar)

and intertidal food along the shores of Glacier Bay before the glaciers advanced. Captain James Cook sighted and named 15,300-foot Mount Fairweather in 1778. A French explorer, Jean Francois de la Perouse, made the first recorded landing in what is now the park at Lituya Bay on the outer coast in 1786.

Russians and Aleuts pursuing sea otters and prospectors looking for gold were the only visitors to the vast wilderness until the late 19th century. In 1879 naturalist John Muir, with a group of Indian guides and interpreters, paddled a canoe into Glacier Bay from Wrangell. Muir returned in 1880 and again in 1890 when he built a cabin at what is now called Muir Point. Other scientists followed, and a few settlers homesteaded on the expanse of the glacial alluvial outwash at nearby Gustavus.

In 1794, when Capt. George Vancouver sailed through Icy Strait, he charted but did not enter Glacier Bay. The bay then was just a slight indentation in a 4,000-foot-thick wall of ice which marked the terminus of a massive glacier flowing down 100 miles from the St. Elias Range. Almost 100 years later, when Muir built his cabin at Muir Point just north of Mount Wright, the terminus of Muir Glacier was just to the north, 35 miles from where Vancouver had seen it.

In what is the most rapid retreat of glaciers documented since the Ice Age, the Muir Glacier terminus has retreated more than 25 additional miles, leaving a broad bay and a long, narrow inlet.

Glacier Bay is an invaluable outdoor laboratory for scientists seeking to understand the dynamics of glaciers. It is possible to travel from the "little ice age" across 2 centuries of plant succession, seeing how ice-scoured land evolves by stages into mature coastal forest.

For summer visitors the boat excursion from park headquarters at Bartlett Cove up Glacier Bay to calving Margerie Glacier is like watching a time-lapse movie which condenses the centuries of glaciation and plant succession into a day. Leaving the dock, passengers watch vegetation along the shoreline change from moss-laden coastal hemlock forests to spruce forests as the boat chugs along. Spruce trees, in turn, give way to thickets of willow and alder in Muir Inlet, which is often full of floating pan ice and icebergs. Here and there the stumps of huge trees, buried by moraines centuries ago then exposed by erosion, stick out along a barren beach.

Glacier Bay National Park and Preserve encompasses 16 active tidewater glaciers, including several on the remote and seldom-visited western edge of the park along the Gulf of Alaska and Lituya Bay. Icebergs calved off the glaciers float in the waters of the bay.

Climate: The Glacier Bay visitor season runs from mid-May through mid-September. (The park is not closed the remainder of the year, but most visitor facilities and transportation are closed.) Gray and rainy days are typical. May and June usually have the most sunshine. Rainfall generally increases as the summer progresses. Summer temperatures average 50°F, but can vary to extremes. Visitors should bring clothing for possible below-freezing temperatures no matter what the month. Also bring full rain gear from head to foot. Layer clothing, with shirts and sweaters worn under a windproof, rainproof parka or jacket, so you can withstand a range of temperatures when outdoors. Alaska's infamous biting insects are very much in evidence at Glacier Bay; gnats and flies are generally worse than mosquitoes. Bring plenty of insect repellent.

Wildlife: A trip by water into the park's many fjords offers sightings of humpback, minke and killer whales cutting the water with their tall dorsal fins, or hair seals poking their heads up to stare at passing boats. During late spring hundreds of seals haul out on floating ice to give birth to their pups.

A decline in the number of humpback whales using Glacier Bay for feeding and calf-rearing led the National Park Service to limit the number of boats visiting the bay between June and September. These regulations apply to all commercial fishing boats, private craft, cruise ships and excursion boats. Check with the National Park Service office for current regulations. *NOTE: The whales come to Glacier Bay for only one reason: to eat enough to store the fat needed to see them through the winter. They do not feed year-round. Do not disturb them.*

Along gravel beaches, brown/grizzly, black and occasionally rare glacier bears (the bluish color phase of the black bear) forage for food. On high rocky ledges mountain goats are often sighted. *CAUTION: Wildlife in the park is protected and hunting is not allowed. Firearms are prohibited within the park.* Backcountry users should be careful to avoid encounters with bears.

More than 225 bird species have been reported in the park. Among the more common are black oystercatchers, cormorants, guillemots, puffins, gulls and terns. Fishing for silver and king salmon, Dolly Varden, cutthroat trout and halibut is excellent in the bay. An Alaska fishing license is required; charter fishing trips are available in Gustavus.

Activities: Glacier Bay offers many opportunities for exploration by kayak, canoe or motorboat (caution is advised because storms are sudden and floating ice can overturn or fracture off without warning). Kayaks may be rented and guided kayak trips are available at Gustavus. Certain areas of the park offer excellent cross-country hiking and backpacking possibilities. Many peaks more than 10,000 feet high challenge the experienced mountaineer. There are no established trails, but camping and hiking are generally permitted throughout the park. (Some areas may have camping restrictions because of bear, bird and seal activity. Be sure to check for safe areas with park service personnel.)

Campers and kayakers can arrange to be dropped off by concession vessels originating in Bartlett Cove or Juneau. All campers arriving at Bartlett Cove are provided with an orientation on safety and camping procedures by a park naturalist. A campground with 35 sites is located near the lodge and park headquarters at Bartlett Cove. The campground has a 2-week limit; it is free and no reservations are required. Two nature trails radiate from Bartlett Cove. One section of trail is handicap accessible, leading 0.2 mile through the rain forest to Blackwater Pond.

Park naturalists lead hikes daily and board cruise ships and tour boats to answer questions and interpret the scenery and wildlife. There are exhibits at the lodge, the dock and the Gustavus airfield; films and slide-illustrated talks are scheduled daily. In the summer rangers are stationed up the bay and elsewhere in the park.

Accommodations: Meals and lodging are available by advance reservation at Glacier Bay Lodge. The concessionaire operates a tour boat; a list of other charter operators can be obtained from the Park Service. Accommodations and meals also are available in Gustavus. Gasoline and diesel fuel may be purchased at Bartlett Cove, where a good anchorage is available for boats. There are no other public facilities for boats within the park; Gustavus has a dock and a high tide small-boat harbor. *CAUTION: Do not attempt to navigate Glacier Bay without appropriate charts, tide tables and local knowledge.*

Access: No roads lead to Glacier Bay. Access is by scheduled airline or air charter to Gustavus, cruise ships and charter boats, private boats and kayak tours. Packaged tours to the park also are available.

For more information: Selected books, maps, charts, guides and other publications are offered for sale at the park or through the mail by the Alaska Natural History Assoc., Glacier Bay National Park and Preserve, Gustavus, AK 99826. Write for a free price list. For additional information contact: Superintendent, Glacier Bay National Park and Preserve, Box 140, Gustavus, AK 99826; phone 697-2230.

Related USGS Topographic Series maps: Mount Fairweather, Skagway and Yakutat.

Karta River Wilderness Area

This 39,889-acre area is located on Prince of Wales Island, about 5 miles from Hollis. The main attraction of the wilderness area is the Karta River.

A 5-mile trail runs the length of the river system, offering good hiking and access to excellent stream fishing for steelhead and trout. The Karta River area contains high value habitat for coho salmon. The 2 major lakes, Salmon Lake and Karta Lake, are important spawning sites for sockeye salmon. Wildlife in the area includes black bears, Sitka black-tailed deer and wolves. There are no brown bears on Prince of Wales Island.

Karta Lake is a popular site for photographers who fly in to capture mirror images on the lake. The 4 Forest Service cabins in the wilderness area are in such high demand that reservations are managed using a lottery system (see Tongass National Forest Cabins this section for details).

For additional information contact: Tongass National Forest, Thorne Bay Ranger District, Recreation and Lands Dept., P.O. Box 1, Thorne Bay, AK 99919; phone 828-3304, fax 828-3309. Related USGS Topographic maps: Craig.

Klondike Gold Rush National Historical Park

This park was authorized in 1976 by the United States to commemorate the Klondike Gold Rush of 1897-98. Highlight of this park is the 33-mile-long Chilkoot Trail, over which 20,000 to 30,000 hopeful gold seekers struggled during the gold rush. Canadian Parks Service is creating a Chilkoot Trail

National Historic Park. The park also includes a visitors' center in Seattle (jumping-off point for the gold rush throngs), the 6-block historic district in Skagway, the townsite of Dyea (dai-YEE) and the White Pass trail.

The Chilkoot Trail had long been used by Indians as a trading route, then by explorers, prospectors and surveyors. (For details on the Chilkoot Trail, see the description under Special Features at the end of this Attractions section.) By the time of the major Klondike gold strike, nearly 2,000 prospectors had already crossed into the Yukon River drainage.

In August 1896, George Washington Carmack and 2 Indian companions, Skookum Jim and Tagish Charlie, found gold in a tributary of the Klondike River, setting off one of the greatest gold rushes in history. Although most of the good claims were already staked by the time the rush got under way, that didn't stop a horde of gold seekers, disheartened and out of work because of a severe, nationwide economic depression, from streaming to Seattle and other West Coast ports to book passage North.

In July 1897, the first boatloads of stampeders landed at Skagway and nearby Dyea. One year later, the population of Skagway had ballooned from a handful of homesteaders to approximately 15,000. The stampeders each spent an average of 3 months hauling their year's supply of goods over either the Chilkoot Trail or the longer White Pass trail to Lake Bennett, where they built boats to float the remaining 560 miles downriver to Dawson, the Klondike and (they hoped) their fortunes. The frenzied parade lasted until the newly built White Pass & Yukon Route reached Lake Bennett in the summer of 1899, supplanting the Chilkoot Trail. Then, it was over. The Chilkoot Trail was all but abandoned. Dyea became a ghost town; its post office closed in 1902 and its population in 1903 consisted of 1 settler. Skagway's population plummeted to 1,000 by 1905. But the memories, the relics and the historic buildings of those exciting days still remain.

Many buildings in Skagway have been restored. Boardwalks and false-fronted buildings help evoke the atmosphere of the town during the gold rush. The Skagway Convention and Visitors Bureau (P.O. Box 415, Skagway, AK 99840; phone 983-2854, fax 983-2151) operates an information center in the historic Arctic Brotherhood Hall. The park's visitor center is located in the refurbished railroad depot on 2nd Avenue and Broadway. It opens at 8 A.M. in the summer, when park rangers are on duty to provide information about the park. Closing times vary. Try to check in before 5 P.M. Anyone intending to hike the Chilkoot Trail should stop at this center to find out about such things as current trail conditions and customs requirements. Walking tours and other programs are presented by the center from mid-May through mid-September.

In Seattle, an interpretive center (117 S. Main St., Seattle, WA 98104) has been established in Pioneer Square. This unit of the park explains the role of Seattle in the Klondike gold rush, and has exhibits of supplies sold to stampeders and newspaper stories of the day. A mannequin surrounded by food and equipment depicts the "ton of goods" each stampeder was required to have before he was allowed to enter Canada. (The so-called "ton of goods" actually amounted to roughly 1,150 pounds of food and about 400 pounds of other necessities for survival.) This center also has information to help in planning a trip on the Chilkoot Trail, including lists of recommended equipment and maps. For more about the Chilkoot Trail, see Chilkoot Trail in Special Features, this section.

Marine Parks

The state of Alaska has established 34 marine parks as part of an international system of shoreline parks and recreation areas stretching from near Olympia, WA, up through British Columbia, Canada, and as far north as Prince William Sound. Eventually there may be more than 150 of these parks, most a 1-day boat trip from each other. The majority of these parks have no developed facilities. Following is a list of the 15 marine parks located in southeastern Alaska, listed from south to north. For more information contact Alaska Division of Parks, Southeast Region, 400 Willoughby Ave., Juneau, AK 99801; phone 465-4563.

Dall Bay. Located 12 miles south of Ketchikan. The 850-acre marine park provides boaters a protected anchorage before venturing out of Nichols Passage into Clarence Strait.

Grindall Island. Located 18 miles northwest of Ketchikan. This is a protected holdover spot for small boats venturing across Clarence Strait in stormy weather. Mooring buoy. State public-use cabin available (see Cabins this section).

Thoms Place. Located in a cove 22 miles south of Wrangell, off Zimovia Strait. A trail leads from the 1,400-acre marine park to Thoms Lake.

Beecher Pass. Located 15 miles south of Petersburg at the junction of Duncan Canal and Wrangell Narrows. The 740-acre marine park is filled with inlets and reefs.

Joe Mace Island. Located near the community of Point Baker on the northern tip of Prince of Wales Island. Activities at the 62-acre marine park (surrounded by old-growth forest) include boating and fishing.

Security Bay. Located on Kuiu Island, 20 miles southwest of Kake, near the junction of Chatham Strait and Frederick Sound. This is an island-filled bay which offers protected anchorage.

Magoun Islands. This small group of islands 10 miles north of Sitka in Krestof Sound offers protected anchorage for through boaters as well as day use for nearby residents.

Big Bear/Baby Bear. These 2 bays in the middle of Peril Straits offer the only protected anchorage for boaters traveling this waterway. About 25 miles north of Sitka on Baranof Island, this is a well-used anchorage for both recreational and commercial fishing vessels.

Taku Harbor. Located 19 miles south of Juneau. The 700-acre park provides a well-protected anchorage and is a popular weekend boating destination.

Oliver Inlet. Located 12 miles south of Juneau on Admiralty Island between Seymour Canal and Stephens Passage. Good protected moorages are available in both Oliver Inlet and Seymour Canal. Oliver Inlet is one end of an overland portage route for boaters entering Seymour Canal from Juneau and provides access to Admiralty Island National Monument. The area has a State Parks Division recreation cabin (see State Park Cabins this section for details), a 1-mile narrow gauge tramway and a registration/information station for the monument. Recreational activities include hunting, fishing, boating, kayaking, beachcombing and wildlife viewing and photography. Humpback and killer whales, seals, sea lions, porpoise, salmon, halibut, rock fish, Sitka black-tailed deer and brown bear inhabit this area.

Funter Bay. Located 30 miles from Juneau on the west side of Admiralty Island. The park offers one of the best protected anchorages in the area and is popular for hunting and fishing.

Shelter Island. Located 6 miles west of Tee Harbor and approximately 20 miles northwest of downtown Juneau. The park, located on the northcentral portion of the island, offers kayaking, boating, fishing, diving, beachcombing, picnicking, hiking and fall hunting for Sitka black-tailed deer.

St. James Bay. Located on the west side of Lynn Canal, 12 miles northwest of Tee Harbor (Juneau) and approximately 42 miles south of Haines. This bay is a recreational destination as well as an overnight stop for boaters traveling between Haines and Juneau. There are many protected beaches and tidal flats. Activities include boating, kayaking, fishing, beachcombing, hiking, camping and picnicking. The Alaska Dept. of Fish and Game has identified this bay as the best waterfowl habitat and hunting area on Lynn Canal. Black and brown bear and mountain goats occur in the area.

Sullivan Island. Located in Lynn Canal approximately 19 miles south of Haines and 6 miles south of the Chilkat Islands. The park is on a 3-mile-long peninsula at the southern tip of the island. There is protected moorage within the area. Recreational activities include salmon and halibut fishing, picnicking, beachcombing and camping. The area also is popular for deer hunting.

Chilkat Islands. Located 13 miles south of Haines, directly off the tip of the Chilkat Peninsula, which is part of Chilkat State Park. This 503-acre marine park includes 4 small, forested islands with several reasonably well-protected anchorages. The islands offer excellent kayaking, boating, fishing, beachcombing and camping.

Misty Fiords National Monument

Located at the southern end of the national forest adjacent to the Canadian border on the east and south, extending northward from Dixon Entrance to beyond the Unuk River. Its western boundary is about 22 air miles east of Ketchikan.

Misty Fiords National Monument encompasses 2.3 million acres (of which only 142,757 acres is nonwilderness), making it the largest wilderness in Alaska's national forests and the second largest in the nation. In the nonwilderness portion at Quartz Hill, U.S. Borax and Chemical Corp. has so far unsuccessfully attempted to acquire permits to develop and mine a deposit of molybdenum estimated to be one of the largest in the world. Fort Tongass, occupied from 1868 to 1870 as Alaska's first U.S. Army post, was located within this monument.

Taking its name from the almost constant precipitation characteristic of the area, Misty Fiords is covered with thick forests which grow on nearly vertical slopes from sea level to mountaintops. Dramatic waterfalls plunge into the salt water through narrow clefts or course over great rounded granite shoulders, fed by lakes and streams which absorb the annual rainfall of more than 14 feet. The major waterway cutting through the monument, Behm Canal, is more than 100 miles long and extraordinary among natural canals for its length and depth. Active glaciers along the Canadian border are remnants of massive ice sheets that covered the region as recently as 10,000 years ago. Periodic lava flows have occurred for the last several thousand years in an area near the Blue River in the eastern portion of the wilderness. The latest of these flows was in the early 1900s and is an attractive and unusual geologic feature.

Forested areas consist of Sitka spruce, western hemlock and cedar. Some Pacific silver fir, subalpine and black cottonwood are found. Beneath these trees grow huckleberry, alder, willow and other brush creating impenetrable thickets.

Few areas of the United States contain as many unusual wildlife species: mountain goats, brown bears, black bears, moose, martens, wolves, wolverines, river otters, sea lions, harbor seals, killer whales and Dall porpoises. A large number of birds, ranging from hummingbirds and trumpeter swans to herons and bald eagles, are found in the area. Misty Fiords is a major producer of coho, sockeye, pink and chum salmon and is especially important for king salmon. Numerous other saltwater and freshwater fish and shellfish also occur.

This monument offers magnificent scenery. Inlets, bays, arms and coves — some long and narrow, some short and broad — are variations on the fjords for which the area is named. The highlands are dotted with thousands of lakes, large and small, and innumerable streams. The Walker Cove-Rudyerd Bay Scenic Area, with its vertical granite cliffs topped by snowy peaks, has been protected for many years and is now part of the monument.

Kayak trips are popular, despite the rainy weather. Campsites, however, are difficult. Tides of up to 18 feet may be encountered; often the only safe campsite is up among the trees above high tide line. Firewood is plentiful, but usually wet. Forest Service wilderness rangers patrol Misty Fiords by kayak. Two rangers are stationed in the Rudyerd Bay area. A sea kayakers brochure, with paddling and camping information, is available from the Forest Service. Guided kayak trips and kayak drop-off and pick-up service are available in Ketchikan.

The most comfortable way to visit Misty Fiords is by cabin cruiser or some other sleep-aboard boat. Good moorages can be found; fresh water is plentiful ashore. The monument also is readily accessible by floatplane from Ketchikan or any other Southeast community. Tours are available on charter boats out of Ketchikan and large cruise ships often sail the deep waters of Behm Canal and Rudyerd Bay. There are 3 wilderness lodges in or near the monument: Yes Bay Lodge, Salmon Falls Resort and Mink Bay Lodge. The Forest Service maintains 14 recreational cabins in the Misty Fiords area, both on freshwater lakes and on salt water, as well as several saltwater mooring buoys and some 20 miles of trails. (See Tongass National Forest Cabins this section.)

For additional information contact: Misty Fiords National Monument, 3031 Tongass Ave., Ketchikan, AK 99901; phone 225-2148. Related USGS Topographic maps: Prince Rupert, Ketchikan, Bradfield Canal.

Petersburg Creek-Duncan Salt Chuck Wilderness Area

This 46,777-acre area is located on the northeast portion of Kupreanof Island. The eastern boundary is near the unincorporated community of Kupreanof, directly across Wrangell Narrows from the city of Petersburg. The area continues west through the Petersburg Creek drainage to the salt chuck at the north end of Duncan Canal.

The Petersburg Creek drainage is a typical U-shaped glacier-carved valley. Its walls are steep in some areas, with visible rock out-croppings. The valley sides are forested with spruce and hemlock; muskeg bogs are common below.

Wildlife includes black bears, Sitka black-tailed deer, wolves, numerous furbearers and a variety of waterfowl. All species of salmon (except kings), Dolly Varden and cutthroat trout are found in Petersburg Creek and Petersburg Lake and its tributaries.

Recreational activities include hiking, backpacking, kayaking, fishing, wildlife observation and photography, as well as hunting in season. The wilderness area is reached primarily by boat at high tide from Petersburg to Petersburg Creek or to Duncan Canal and Duncan Salt Chuck. Floatplanes can land in Duncan Canal, on the Salt Chuck at high tide, and on Petersburg Lake. Petersburg Lake National Recreation Trail leads from salt water to Petersburg Lake. The Forest Service maintains 3 recreation cabins in the area, located at Petersburg Lake, and in the vicinity of Duncan Canal and Salt Chuck. (See Tongass National Forest Cabins in this section.)

For additional information contact: Tongass National Forest, Stikine Area, P.O. Box 309, Petersburg, AK 99833; phone 772-3841. Related USGS Topographic map: Petersburg.

Pleasant-Lemesurier-Inian Islands Wilderness Area

This 23,154-acre area consists of islands located in Icy Strait between Chichagof Island and Glacier Bay National Park. Pleasant Island is just offshore of the community of Gustavus. The Inian Islands are close to Elfin Cove. This area was designated wilderness in 1990.

Wildlife on Pleasant Island includes Sitka black-tailed deer and black bears. On Lemesurier and Inian islands are deer and brown bears which may have swum from the mainland to the islands. Cliffy areas of the Inian Islands provide opportunities for observing cliff-nesting shorebirds. Sea otters, porpoise, seals, sea lions and whales inhabit the waters of Icy Strait.

There are no facilities within the wilderness area. Guided sea kayaking trips to Pleasant Island are available out of Gustavus. Charter boats may be hired in Elfin Cove for sightseeing the Inian Islands. Currents in the Inian Islands area are treacherous and boaters should exercise extreme caution and consult with locals before navigating the area.

For more information contact: Tongass National Forest, Hoonah Ranger District, Resource Officer, P.O. Box 135, Hoonah, AK 99829; phone 945-3631. Related USGS Topographic maps: Mount Fairweather and Juneau.

Point Bridget State Park

Located 38 miles north of Juneau, this 2,850-acre park stretches from Juneau Veterans' Memorial Highway west to Lynn Canal and Berners Bay. The park encompasses meadowland, open forest, rocky beaches and ocean cliffs. Point Bridget State Park was created in 1988, largely through local efforts to get a state park for the state capital.

The major activity in the park is hiking. In summer, be ready for rain and wet ground; carry extra dry clothes. The park is open for skiing and showshoeing in winter.

The main trail is the 3.5-mile-long Point Bridget Trail, which leads from the trailhead at Milepost 39 on the highway (watch for turnout 1 mile north of North Bridget Cove sign) to Point Bridget. The panoramic view of Lynn Canal and the Chilkat Mountains from the point is highly recommended. Hiking time is 7 hours round-trip. Meadowlands along the trail support wildflowers (mid- and late May through June) and a variety of birdlife. The rocky beaches at Point Bridget offer prime viewing of sea lions and humpback whales (April through September). In the spring, thousands of white-winged and surf scoters feed on blue mussels in Lynn Canal. Tidepooling is possible with minus 1-foot tides (check local tide tables). See Hiking Trails this section for information on other trails. There are no established campgrounds in the park, but wilderness camping is allowed. A public-use cabin is available for rent at Cowee Meadow; see Cabins this section for details.

For additional information on the park contact: Alaska Division of Parks and Outdoor Recreation, 400 Willoughby Ave., Juneau, AK 99801; phone 465-4563.

Russell Fiord Wilderness Area

Located 25 miles northeast of Yakutat between the rugged Fairweather Range and the Brabazon Range. The most dramatic features of this 348,701-acre area are the heavily glaciated Russell Fiord, which extends more than 35 miles inland from Disenchantment Bay, and Nunatak Fjord, a narrow, 15-mile channel off Russell Fiord to the southeast.

Russell Fiord made headlines in 1986 when it was dammed by advancing Hubbard Glacier. The ice dam eventually weakened and broke, but scientists predict the glacier will close off the fjord again. There are numerous active glaciers above the fjords and the area is scientifically important for its record of recent geological events, post-glacial ecological succession and the effects of frequent earthquakes. Vegetation ranges from heavily forested river channels to alpine meadows. Situk Lake and the headwaters of the Situk Wild and Scenic River Study Area are within the wilderness area.

Wildlife includes mountain goats, wolves, brown and black bear, numerous furbearers, harbor seals, sea lions, shorebirds, songbirds, waterfowl and bald eagles. Fisheries are fairly limited, with the exception of lower Russell Fiord and the headwaters of the Ahrnklin River.

Access is by floatplane from Juneau, 200 miles to the southeast, or by plane or boat from Yakutat, which has overnight accommodations and scheduled commercial air service.

Sea kayakers fly in to Yakutat, then paddle up Yakutat Bay to Disenchantment Bay and enter Russell Fiord at the neck of the fiord (a long paddle; inquire about hazardous sections). There is also logging road access from Yakutat to a 3/4-mile portage to the head of Russell Fiord. Guided sea kayaking trips of Russell Fiord are available.

There is 1 Forest Service cabin within the wilderness area at Situk Lake. A second cabin is located just outside the park boundary at Harlequin Lake. (See Tongass National Forest Cabins under Cabins this section.)

For information: Contact Tongass National Forest, Box 327, Yakutat, AK 99689; phone 784-3359. Related USGS Topographic maps: Yakutat, Mount St. Elias.

South Baranof Wilderness Area

This 319,568-acre wilderness is located on the southern portion of Baranof Island, bounded by the open Gulf of Alaska on the west and Chatham Strait on the east. It is 50 miles south of Sitka and 20 miles north of Port Alexander.

High mountains rise sharply from sea level to more than 4,000 feet in less than 2 miles from the beach. Much of the higher areas have permanent ice fields and numerous active glaciers. Many valleys are U-shaped, carved by recent glacial activity with amphitheaterlike cirques at their sources, hanging valleys along their walls and dramatic waterfalls. Most of the valleys empty into long, deep fjords. Rainfall in portions of this area is among the highest in Southeast; recording up to 200 inches a year at Little Port Walter, just south of the wilderness. Storms from September through December can generate winds exceeding 100 mph.

Wildlife in the area includes Sitka black-tailed deer, brown bears, hair seals, mink, marten, land otters, bald eagles and a variety of other birds. There are major steelhead producing lakes and streams in this wilder-

Kayakers on Russell Fiord rig a sail. The fiord extends more than 35 miles. (Karen Jettmar)

ness; other fish available include coho, red, pink and chum salmon, cutthroat and rainbow trout and Dolly Varden. Marine species include Dungeness and tanner crab, shrimp, herring and halibut.

Recreational activities include boating, kayaking, fishing and hunting. Access is primarily by floatplane or boat from Sitka, which has commercial air service and is on the Alaska Marine Highway System route. Many sheltered bays and fjords provide safe anchorage and sheltered floatplane landings. The Forest Service maintains 3 recreation cabins, located at Avoss, Davidof and Plotnikof lakes. (See Tongass National Forest Cabins in this section.)

For additional information contact: Tongass National Forest, Chatham Area, 204 Siginaka Way, Sitka, AK 99835; phone 747-6671. Related USGS Topographic map: Port Alexander.

South Etolin Island Wilderness Area

Located about midway between Ketchikan and Wrangell, and about 15 miles north of Thorne Bay, this wilderness area comprises 83,642 acres on the south end of Etolin Island.

Elk were introduced on the island in 1987, prior to its designation as wilderness. The state traded 15 mountain goats for 33 elk from Oregon, then obtained 17 more elk in exchange for some river otters, for a total transplant of 50 elk. Other wildlife include wolves, black bears, brown bears, Sitka black-tailed deer and bald eagles.

The multitude of small islands and passages provide numerous anchorages for recreational activities and opportunities for small-boat travel. The area has also been studied for potential sites for mariculture activities. Wrangell residents use this area for subsistence harvests.

For additional information contact: Tongass National Forest, Wrangell Ranger District, P.O. Box 51, Wrangell, AK 99929; phone 874-2323, fax 874-2095. Related USGS Topographic maps: Craig.

South Prince of Wales Wilderness Area

This 90,996-acre wilderness is located at the southern tip of Prince of Wales Island, about 40 miles southwest of Ketchikan and approximately 15 miles south of Hydaburg. The area fronts on Dixon Entrance and on Cordova Bay, extending north to take in all of Klakas Inlet.

One of the first Haida Indian villages in southeastern Alaska, Klinkwan, is within the South Prince of Wales Wilderness. This historic village site was established in the 19th century and abandoned in 1911.

The coast of Prince of Wales Island is deeply indented with numerous bays and inlets. The Barrier Islands, a collection of more than 75 islets ranging in size from a few acres up to 500 acres, jut out into Cordova Bay. They are exposed to fierce ocean storms and their trees are stunted and sculpted by the wind. Topography on Prince of Wales Island ranges from lowlands containing many streams, lakes and wetlands to the sheer, 2,000-foot rock walls of Klakas Inlet, which extends 12 miles inland from Cordova Bay.

Precipitation usually exceeds 100 inches per year and vegetation includes dense stands of large old-growth Sitka spruce, western hemlock, Alaska cedar and western red cedar, as well as numerous shrubs, wildflowers and grasses.

Wildlife includes black bears, wolves, Sitka black-tailed deer, small furbearers, land and shorebirds and bald eagles. This is one of the better sea otter habitats in southeastern Alaska. Many species of waterfowl migrate along the coastline. Coho, red, pink and chum salmon, cutthroat and rainbow trout and Dolly Varden occur in waters of this area. Also, Dungeness and tanner crab, shrimp, herring, halibut, abalone, giant barnacles, clams, mussels, octopus, sea urchins, sea anemones and starfish.

Access to this area is by floatplane or boat. Small boats can negotiate the area during the summer; however, Dixon Entrance is exposed to the ocean and can be extremely stormy and rough during other seasons. There are no facilities in this wilderness area.

For more information contact: Tongass National Forest, Craig Ranger District, P.O. Box 500, Craig, AK 99921; phone 826-3271, fax 826-2972. Related USGS Topographic maps: Dixon Entrance, Craig.

Stikine-LeConte Wilderness Area

Located on the mainland of southeastern Alaska, 6 miles east of Petersburg and 7 miles north of Wrangell, this wilderness area extends from Frederick Sound on the west to the Alaska-Canada border on the east.

The most prominent feature of this 448,841-acre wilderness area is the powerful

Stikine River. The river valley is narrow, surrounded by steep, rugged peaks, many of them glaciated. The river is heavily laden with silt from the numerous glaciers. The delta at the mouth of the river is 17 miles wide, formed from numerous slow-moving braided channels (3 of which are navigable). One hot and 2 warm springs are found along the river. The vicinity of LeConte Glacier—southernmost glacier in North America to empty directly into salt water—is mountainous, with numerous ice fields that extend into Canada. Alpine vegetation, including mosses, lichens and other small plants, grows above 2,000 feet. The lower slopes near salt water support typical Southeast spruce-hemlock rain forest. In the east, rainfall decreases and cottonwoods appear.

This is an important fish and wildlife area. Moose, mountain goats, brown and black bears, Sitka black-tailed deer and wolves inhabit the area. The delta of the Stikine is a major resting area for migratory birds. The lower Stikine has the second largest seasonal concentration of bald eagles in southeastern Alaska when the birds gather to feed on hooligan (also called eulachon or smelt) runs in April. Several varieties of salmon, including kings, are found in the area.

Recreational activities include fishing and hunting in season, as well as kayak, canoe and raft trips down the Stikine. Thick brush along the river makes hiking difficult. Access is primarily by small boat from Wrangell. Charter boat tours to the Stikine River and LeConte Bay are available from Wrangell and Petersburg. Air taxis in both communities also offer flightseeing trips. There is limited access to the wilderness by floatplane. There are no commercial lodges. The Forest Service maintains a number of recreational cabins in the area and 2 bathhouses at Chief Shakes Hot Springs. (See Tongass National Forest Cabins under Cabins, and Hot Springs under Special Features, this section.)

For additional information contact: Tongass National Forest, Wrangell Ranger District, P.O. Box 51, Wrangell, AK 99929; phone 874-2323, fax 874-2095. Related USGS Topographic maps: Petersburg, Bradfield Canal, Sumdum.

Tebenkof Bay and Kuiu Wilderness Areas

Both of these wilderness areas are located on Kuiu (pronounced CUE-you) Island, 50 miles southwest of Petersburg and 35 miles south of Kake. Tebenkof Bay Wilderness Area includes 66,839 acres on the west side of Kuiu Island. Kuiu Wilderness Area, designated in 1990, spans Kuiu south of Tebenkof Bay.

This expansive and complex system of bays includes many small islands, islets and coves. Kayaking is excellent in the protected waters of Tebenkof Bay. The area has spruce-hemlock forest up to about the 2,000-foot elevation, where alpine plants take over. There is some muskeg and many small lakes and creeks.

Wildlife includes black bears, wolves and some smaller furbearers. Marine mammals are abundant. The area is on the migration route of many waterfowl. Trumpeter swans and bald eagles also occur here. The area is rich in fish and shellfish, including coho, red, pink and chum salmon, rainbow and steelhead trout, Dolly Varden, Dungeness and tanner crab, shrimp and halibut. The remains of Tlingit villages and camps as well as fur farms may be seen.

Recreational activities include kayaking and exploring the many streams, bays and coves. Access is by boat or floatplane from Petersburg or Wrangell. Many coves provide good anchorage. Chatham Strait can be hazardous at times because of swells and strong winds from the Pacific Ocean. There are 4 kayak portage trails (descriptions follow) which provide access to Tebenkof Bay Wilderness Area. The trailheads, marked by large red-and-white portage diamonds, are reached by water from the town of Kake, a ferry stop on the Alaska Marine Highway System. Portage trails are marked with blue diamond markers. Canoers and kayakers are advised to pay attention to changing weather and water conditions for their safety.

Affleck Canal Portage Trail. Trail begins on the beach at the north end of Affleck Canal and extends 1.5 miles to the beach at Petrof Bay. Usable June to September. Rated difficult due to blown down trees along trail. Elevation gain 50 feet. Estimated time across 1 1/2 hours. Trail offers spectacular views and access to beachcombing. Shore and land birds, wolves and black bear may be seen. Bears are especially common in summer along the creek that parallels the trail as they feed on spawning salmon. Make plenty of noise to avoid an encounter with a bear and hang food in a tree at night. Related USGS Topographic map: Port Alexander B-1.

Alecks Creek Portage Trail. Trail begins on the beach at the very head of No Name Bay and extends 4 miles to the mouth of Alecks Creek in Elena Bay. Usable June to

September. Rated difficult due to blown down trees along trail. Elevation gain 45 feet. Estimated time across 2¹/₂ hours. Portagers on this trail can put in at a small lake just to the south of Alecks Lake, then paddle across Alecks Lake and through the narrow finger lakes that are the headwaters of Alecks Creek. Once the shallower waters of the creek are reached, it is best to line the kayak down the stream to avoid grounding or running into downed logs. The easiest trail through the braided channel of Alecks Creek is marked. This trail offers spectacular views, as well as excellent fishing in Alecks Creek for steelhead in April to May, red salmon in July and silver, pink, and chum salmon mid-August to October. During the summer the tide flat at the mouth of Alecks Creek is often covered with black bears, which also range upstream in search of fish. Make plenty of noise to avoid any unexpected encounters; always hang food in a tree at night. Related USGS Topographic maps: Petersburg B-6, C-6; Port Alexander B-1, C-1.

Bay of Pillars Portage Trail. Trail begins on the beach at the east end of Bay of Pillars on Kuiu Island and extends 1.2 miles to the beach at Port Camden. Usable June to September. Rated moderate. Elevation gain 100 feet. Estimated time across 1¹/₂ hours. This portage passes through a beaver pond and follows a Forest Road for a short distance. During the summer black bears will be on or near the portage trail; make plenty of noise to let them know you're coming. Always hang food in a tree at night. Related USGS Topographic map: Port Alexander C-1.

Threemile Arm Portage Trail. Trail begins on the beach at the northwest end of Threemile Arm on Kuiu Island and extends 1.1 miles to the beach at the southeast end of Port Camden. Usable June to September. Rated difficult; elevation gain 100 feet. Estimated time across 1 hour. This trail follows a creek for the first 1,500 feet; the portager can put in and paddle the deeper sections and line the shallower areas. A beaver pond also can be paddled for about 1,300 feet. This trail offers spectacular views and fishing. During the summer there are plenty of black bears on or near the trail; make noise to let them know you are there. Always hang food in a tree at night. Related USGS Topographic map: Petersburg C-6.

For additional information contact: Tongass National Forest, Stikine Area, P.O. Box 309, Petersburg, AK 99833; phone 772-3841. Related USGS Topographic maps: Port Alexander.

Tongass National Forest

This national forest encompasses 16.9 million acres, or more than 73 percent of all the land in southeastern Alaska. Created in 1907 by President Theodore Roosevelt to protect the timber resources, wildlife and fisheries of Southeast, this is the largest national forest in the United States. Its name comes from the Tongass clan of Tlingit Indians, who lived on an island at the southern end of the forest.

The forest lies west of the U.S.-Canada border and stretches from Ketchikan north to Cross Sound and up the eastern side of Lynn Canal. Excluded from the forest are Glacier Bay National Park and the general area around Haines and Skagway. Another section of the forest surrounds Yakutat. Like all national forests, this is managed as a working forest, with logging and mining activities taking place along with recreational pursuits and fishery management.

Tree line usually extends from sea level to about 3,000 feet in the southern part of the forest and to 1,800 feet farther north around Icy Strait. In the south, the forests are primarily western hemlock and Sitka spruce, with scattered red cedar and Alaska yellow cedar. In the north the percentage of spruce increases and mountain hemlock becomes more abundant. Red cedar extends only to the northern shore of Frederick Sound and Alaska yellow cedar often is found only as a small tree in swamps or muskeg. Other common species are red alder, black cottonwood and lodgepole pine.

Beneath the towering conifers are young evergreens and shrubs such as devil's club, blueberry and huckleberry. Moss and ferns cover the ground, and lichens drape many trees. The dense forest is broken by muskeg bogs, glacial outwash plains and marshlands in river valleys and deltas. Wildflowers splash color against a variegated green background.

Wildlife: Sitka black-tailed deer and its 2 main predators, the wolf and the bear are found in the forest. Wolves and black bears range throughout the mainland and most islands, except Baranof, Chichagof and Admiralty. These 3 islands, plus the mainland, are home for enormous brown/grizzly bears. The blue, or glacier, bear (a color phase of the black bear) is seen occasionally near Yakutat. Mountain goats have been transplanted to Baranof and Revillagigedo islands, but their natural range is the alpine area of the mainland. Some moose inhabit the larger river drainages and the Yakutat area. A limited number of lynx, wolverines, foxes, mink and land otters range widely through the area. The forest also is home for smaller mammals, including shrews, red squirrels, brown bats, flying squirrels, deer mice, red-backed voles, porcupines and pine marten.

Blue grouse, great horned owls, woodpeckers, Steller's jays and thrushes are some of the common birds in the forests. Robins, fox sparrows, hummingbirds and swallows can be seen along the forest edge. More bald eagles live in this region than in any other place in the world. Large numbers of waterfowl, such as diving ducks, mallards, mergansers and Canada geese, and more than 50 species of seabirds, including terns, gulls, kittiwakes, auklets and murres can be seen here.

Marine mammals found along the shores of the forest include Dall and harbor porpoises, hair seals and humpback, minke, sei and Pacific killer whales. Gray whales and northern fur seals pass by during migrations and an occasional elephant seal has been spotted. Sea otters have been successfully reintroduced and are expanding their range in western Southeast Alaska. Waters of the region teem with fish, including halibut and 5 species of salmon. Also present are Dungeness, tanner and king crab, shrimp and butter clams.

Activities and Accommodations: Camping is permitted anywhere in the national forest unless it is a day-use area or there is a sign specifically prohibiting it, such as at an archaeological site. No permits or fees are required for wilderness camping. Fees are charged for some developed campgrounds. Contact any Forest Service field office for information. Practice minimum impact camping techniques. Because of the wet climate, backpacking stoves are recommended. If campfires are made, use only dead or down wood and make sure that any campfires are extinguished; forest fires can occur even in this rainy region. Pack out all unburnable trash. Much of the forest is bear country. Be alert and cautious. Do not camp on bear trails or near salmon streams; wear a bell or make noise when hiking. Cook and store food well away from your tent. Bells and other noises are not guarantees against encounters. Avoid salmon streams during spawning and do not approach such areas from downwind. It is legal to carry firearms in the national forest for bear protection. Rifles with a caliber larger than .30-06 are recommended.

Gathering forest resources was once a necessity. Today it is enjoyed as a recreational activity and can lead to understanding the forest ecosystem, as well as the region's pioneer heritage.

Opportunities for obtaining berries, firewood, Christmas trees, and other forest resources are found throughout Tongass National Forest and local communities. Some resources are best captured through photography, and plant and wildflowers throughout Southeast offer excellent opportunities for the photographer.

Visitors should exercise discretion in gathering plants, the Forest Service advises. Fragile alpine and meadow areas may harbor rare and possibly endangered species, and plant regeneraton may be very slow, if not impossible once the plants are gathered. A general rule of thumb is to leave 6 plants for every 1 plant picked and pick plants 100 feet or more from all roadways or trails.

The local Forest Service office should be contacted prior to cutting live trees to learn the areas where this activity is permitted.

You should know edible plants well before picking. There are at least 2 poisonous plants in Southeast (baneberry and poison hemlock) and visitors gather wild plants at their own risk. Permits are not required for Forest Service managed lands.

The U.S. Forest Service maintains some 150 cabins (see charts, page 79–83) in Southeast which are available by advance reservation. The current fee is $20 per party per night. Many Southeast communities have Forest Service offices which will provide information on local places to camp and hike (see Cabins and Hiking Trails this section). The Forest Service operates road-accessible campgrounds for tents and trailers at Juneau, Ketchikan, Sitka and Petersburg. For additional information contact: Tongass National Forest, Regional Office, P.O. Box 21628, PAO, Juneau, AK 99802; phone 586-8806. A Tongass National Forest map detailing cabins and campgrounds is available for $2.

Timber harvest has taken place in this region since before the Tongass National Forest was established. All but a small percentage has occurred since 1950. Out of the 16.9 million acres encompassed by the national forest, about 5 million acres have been identified as commercial forest, with about 2 million acres of that considered available for harvesting. Another 5.6 million acres has been set aside as wilderness in 2 national monuments and 17 designated wilderness areas, most of which are remote and accessible only by boat or aircraft.

Wilderness areas within Tongass National Forest were established by President Jimmy Carter on Dec. 2, 1980, under the Alaska National Interest Lands Conservation Act, which set aside nearly 103 million acres throughout the state as national parks, wildlife refuges, wilderness areas, wild and scenic rivers and other conservation areas. Additional wilderness was added in 1990 by the Tongass Timber Reform Act.

Wilderness classification directs that these areas be managed to retain their natural qualities, unmarked by works of man. However, there are some exceptions because of Alaska's terrain: Motorized vehicles such as airplanes, boats and snow machines may be used for access to and within some of the wilderness areas. Also, because of the climate, existing shelter cabins were allowed to remain and others may be built for public safety. Fishing, hunting and trapping are allowed, subject to state regulations. Check with the local Forest Service office for the most up-to-date regulations.

The 19 wilderness areas within the Tongass National Forest, from south to north, are: South Prince of Wales Wilderness Area; Misty Fiords National Monument; Karta River Wilderness Area; South Eotlin Island Wilderness Area; Coronation Island, Warren Island and Maurelle Islands Wilderness Areas; Tebenkof Bay and Kuiu Wilderness Areas; Stikine-LeConte Wilderness Area; Petersburg Creek-Duncan Salt Chuck Wilderness Area; South Baranof Wilderness Area; Chuck River Wilderness Area; Tracy Arm-Fords Terror Wilderness Area; Admiralty Island National Monument (Kootznoowoo Wilderness Area); Pleasant-Lemesurier-Inian Islands Wilderness Area; West Chichagof-Yakobi Wilderness Area; Endicott River Wilderness Area; and Russell Fiord Wilderness Area. See descriptions of each in this section.

Tracy Arm-Fords Terror Wilderness Area

Located 50 miles southeast of Juneau and 70 miles north of Petersburg adjacent to Stephens Passage and bordered on the east by Canada.

Tracy and Endicott arms are the major features of this 653,179-acre wilderness area. Both are long, deep and narrow fjords that extend more than 30 miles into the heavily glaciated Coast Mountain Range. At the head of these fjords are active tidewater glaciers, which continually calve icebergs into the fjords. During the summer, both fjords have quantities of floating ice ranging from the size of a 3-story building to hand-sized chunks, often obstructing small-boat travel. Fords Terror, off of Endicott Arm, is an area of sheer rock walls enclosing a narrow entrance into a small fjord. The fjord was named for a crew member of a naval vessel who rowed into the narrow canyon at slack tide in 1889 and was caught in turbulent, iceberg-laden currents for 6 "terrifying" hours when the tide changed. Most of the area is rugged snow- and glacier-covered mountains with steeply walled valleys dotted with high, cascading waterfalls. The lower slopes are covered with typical southeastern Alaska spruce-hemlock rain forest; tree line is about 1,500 feet elevation. There are a few muskeg bogs with sedges, grass and sphagnum moss.

Wildlife includes mountain goats, wolverines, brown and black bears, numerous furbearers, a few Sitka black-tailed deer, bald eagles, shorebirds, sea lions, whales and harbor seals.

Access to this wilderness area is primarily by boat or floatplane from Juneau. These fjords are increasingly popular destinations for sea kayakers. Large cruise ships and small charter boats include Tracy Arm and Endicott Arm on their itineraries. There are no facilities available in these areas. Camping is limited due to the steep terrain; beware of areas with rockfall. A boat with sleeping accommodations is a comfortable means of visiting this wilderness.

For additional information contact: Tongass National Forest, P.O. Box 2097, Juneau, AK 99803; phone 586-8800.

West Chichagof-Yakobi Wilderness Area

This 264,747-acre wilderness occupies the western portions of Chichagof and Yakobi islands in the extreme northwest portion of the Alexander Archipelago of southeastern Alaska. It is a few miles west of Pelican and 30 miles north of Sitka.

The most dramatic feature of this wilderness area is the 65-mile-long stretch of rugged Pacific coastline, with exposed offshore islands and rocky highlands. Behind the barrier islands, rocks and reefs of the outer coast lie the quiet waters of a scenic inside passage, honeycombed with bays, inlets and lagoons. There are quiet tidal meadows and estuaries and steep mountains with peaks to 3,600 feet that rise out of the ocean. Western hemlock and Sitka spruce forests cover about one-third of the area and there are scattered lodgepole pines and cedar. Offshore islands support glades under open spruce cover, and there is scattered alpine terrain, muskeg and estuaries. Hiking can be difficult in upland meadows because of downed logs, holes and hidden streams.

Wildlife includes Sitka black-tailed deer, brown bear, numerous furbearers, sea otters, sea lions and seals. The area is wonderful for boaters and kayakers. Strong winds off the Pacific Ocean can be dangerous in exposed stretches.

Access is by charter boat from Pelican or Sitka or chartered floatplane from Sitka or Juneau. The coastal area has excellent moorage and landing sites for boats and planes. There are Forest Service cabins on west Chichagof at Goulding Lake, Lake Suloia and White Sulphur Springs, which also has a bathhouse overlooking Bertha Bay, and at Greentop Harbor on Yakobi Island. (See Tongass National Forest Cabins in this section.)

For additional information contact: Tongass National Forest, Chatham Area, 204 Siginaka Way, Sitka, AK 99835; phone 747-6671. Related USGS Topographic maps: Sitka, Mount Fairweather.

Wildlife Refuges

Alaska Chilkat Bald Eagle Preserve

This 48,000-acre state park located in the Chilkat River valley northwest of Haines was created in 1982 to protect the largest known congregation of bald eagles in North America. Each year, thousands of bald eagles come to this 5-mile stretch of the Chilkat River from October through January to feed on spawned-out chum salmon. Alaska has more bald eagles than all the other states combined.

An upwelling of warm water usually prevents the Chilkat River from freezing over at its confluence with the Tsirku River near the village of Klukwan. The open water and the late salmon run draw eagles from throughout southeastern Alaska, and provide abundant food when other sources are low. As many as 3,900 eagles have

gathered here during peak times in November and hundreds stay into January. Extremely cold weather, which will freeze the open water, may force the eagles to leave at any time.

Bald eagles develop their characteristic white head and tail between 4 and 6 years of age. Immature bald eagles are mottled brown and white and sometimes are confused with golden eagles. Wingspan of these birds is 5½ to 8 feet; average weight is 12½ pounds, with females slightly larger than the males.

Bald eagles can fly at 30 mph and dive at 100 mph. They can see fish in the water at a distance of more than half a mile. Their basic diet consists of fish, although they do feed on waterfowl, small mammals and carrion when food is in short supply. Preferred habitat for these birds is in old-growth stands of timber along coastal shorelines. It is easy to spot their white heads as they perch high in trees, sit on rocks on beaches or soar on the winds.

The gathering of eagles takes place within sight of the Haines Highway, which parallels the river. The heaviest concentration of eagles occurs between Milepost 17 from Haines and Milepost 22. This core area was set aside in 1972 as the Chilkat River Critical Habitat Area, 10 years before the protective area was enlarged and the larger area designated a preserve. Activities permitted within the preserve include hunting, fishing, trapping, berry picking and picnicking as long as the eagles are not disturbed. The eagles have adjusted to the noise along the highway, but they become greatly agitated and will take flight if approached too closely. State land surrounding the preserve is part of the Haines State Forest Resource Management Area, in which logging, mining and other development is permitted. In the vicinity of Klukwan, much of the easily accessible land is Native-owned and should be treated as private property.

There are no visitor facilities in the preserve. The park office provides a list of commercial guides for permitted activities in the area, including river raft trips, photography and natural history tours. Rental cars and bus transportation, all other visitor facilities and guide services are available in Haines. There are pullouts along the highway from which to view and photograph eagles (telephoto lenses are recommended; best light is between 10 A.M. and 2 P.M.); heavy truck traffic makes it unsafe to park or walk along the roadway. Visitors should also avoid walking out on the mud flats for their own safety and to avoid disturbing the eagles. Visitors should note that weather during the peak gathering times can be rainy, windy and/or snowy. Permits are required to build temporary blinds and for certain other activities in the preserve.

Haines is accessible via the Haines Highway from the north, the Alaska Marine Highway System from the south, and scheduled airlines from Juneau. For additional information on the park contact: Alaska State Parks, 400 Willoughby Ave., Juneau, AK 99801; phone 465-4563.

Alaska Maritime National Wildlife Refuge

This wildlife refuge includes more than 2,400 parcels of land on islands, islets, rocks, spires, reefs and headlands of Alaska coastal waters from Point Franklin in the Arctic Ocean to Forrester Island in southern Southeast Alaska. The refuge totals about 3.5 million acres and is divided into 5 management units.

Most of this refuge is managed to protect wildlife and the coastal ecosystem. The refuge has the most diverse wildlife species of all the refuges in Alaska, including thousands of sea lions, seals, walrus and sea otters. Alaska Maritime is synonymous with seabirds — millions of them. They congregate in colonies along the coast. Each species has a specialized nesting site, be it rock ledge, crevice, boulder rubble, pinnacle or burrow. (This adaptation allows many birds to use a small area of land.) Of the 50 million seabirds which nest in Alaska, 80 percent of them nest on the refuge.

Most refuge lands are wild and lonely, extremely rugged and virtually inaccessible. Some portions are classified as wilderness. Swift tides, rough seas, high winds, rocky shorelines and poor anchorages hamper efforts to view wildlife.

Southeast Alaska islands included in the Gulf of Alaska Unit are: 5-mile-long Forrester Island, located 10 miles west of Dall Island; the Hazy Islands, a group of small islands extending 2.7 miles in Christian Sound, 9 miles west of Coronation Island; and St. Lazaria Island, located at the entrance to Sitka Sound, approximately 15 miles southwest of Sitka.

St. Lazaria Island is host to one of the largest seabird colonies in Southeast. This 65-acre, volcanic island has been set aside as a wildlife refuge since 1909. A half million seabirds of 11 different species breed here. Burrowing seabirds include tufted puffins; rhinoceros auklets; ancient murrelets; and storm-petrels, both Leach's and fork-tailed. Common and thick-billed murres, pelagic cormorants, glaucous-winged gulls, pigeon guillemots and others inhabit the sea cliffs, while song and fox sparrows and hermit thrushes flit through the lush growth. A nearly impenetrable mass of salmonberry bushes, growing up to 6 feet high, hinders foot travel on the island. St. Lazaria was uninhabited and apparently seldom visited until a military outpost was established there during WWII. Remains of the outpost are overgrown and difficult to find; the metal is corroding and the wood is rotting rapidly in the mild, wet climate.

Since seabirds are sensitive to disturbance and the closely spaced burrows of ground nesting birds are crushed by foot traffic, one should not land on the island. Small boats can land on the island only at high tide and then only with great difficulty because of constant swells from the open ocean. The seabirds can be seen easily from boats which can circle the island. Binoculars and spotting scopes are recommended to view wildlife from a distance. The best time to visit is May through June. Visitors should be prepared for wet and windy weather. Charter boats, lodging and campgrounds are available in Sitka.

For more information contact: Refuge Manager, Alaska Maritime National Wildlife Refuge, 509 Sterling Hwy., Homer, AK 99603; phone 235-6961, fax 235-7469.

Mendenhall Wetlands State Game Refuge

This 3,800-acre refuge located along the coastline adjacent to the Juneau road system provides excellent opportunities to view a variety of migrating birds, including geese, ducks, swans, shorebirds and a variety of overwintering birds. The refuge encompasses estuaries created by numerous streams which flow into Gastineau Channel from the surrounding mountains. As the tides ebb and flow, much of the refuge becomes alternately a pasture, then a shallow sea. During the year the wetlands host about 200 species of birds, 18 species of mammals, over 40 fish species and a variety of other marine life.

Spring bird migrations peak in April and May and by June most of the waterfowl and shorebirds have moved on to breeding grounds farther north. Relatively few species of birds nest in the Mendenhall Refuge, but it remains important through the summer as a feeding station. After the breeding season, birds traveling south to wintering grounds stop at the refuge. Shorebirds arrive first, feeding on mollusks and other invertebrates in late July. Waterfowl begin arriving in late August and September, feeding on the seeds of sedges, grasses and other plants. Species of waterfowl and shorebirds found along the edge of the sedge meadow include mallards, pintails, green-winged teals, northern shovelers, American wigeons and several species of sandpipers.

A number of waterfowl species winter in the ice-free marine waters of the refuge. Species include mallards, goldeneyes, scaup, scoters, bufflehead and harlequin ducks.

Beach ryegrass, which grows in sandy soils beyond the reach of most high tides, provides shelter for American kestrels, marsh hawks, semipalmated sandpipers, western sandpipers, least sandpipers, arctic terns, short-eared owls and savannah sparrows. A spruce-hemlock forest rims most of the refuge, providing a year-round home for bald eagles, common ravens and northwestern crows, as well as habitat for migratory songbirds, including American robins, hermit thrush, ruby-crowned kinglet and warblers.

In the tidal mudflats and open salt water of the channel may be found goldeneye, bufflehead, scoters, pigeon guillemots, loons, grebes, scaup, mergansers and marbled murrelets.

The most visible waterfowl in the refuge are Vancouver Canada geese, 400 to 600 of whom form a resident population that overwinters on open water near the mouth of the Mendenhall River and some creeks. Other geese found in the refuge include cackling Canada geese, lesser Canada geese, white-fronted geese and snow geese.

Mammals found in the refuge include harbor seals, Sitka black-tailed deer, black bears, muskrats, land otter, mink, short-tailed weasels, snowshoe hares, porcupines, little brown bats and long-tailed voles.

Recreational activities allowed in the refuge include hiking, wildlife viewing and photography, boating, fishing, sightseeing and waterfowl hunting in season. Boats are the only motorized vehicles permitted. Visitors walking in the refuge should wear waterproof footwear. Always consult a tide book; much of the land is submerged at high tide.

The refuge is accessible by road from several points along Egan Drive or off Berners Avenue, just west of the airport. A raised dike trail, accessible from the Berners Avenue access point, has been developed as an interpretive trail with educational signs to aid visitors.

For more information or a list of birds that occur in the refuge contact: Alaska Dept. of Fish and Game, Wildlife Division, P.O. Box 240020, Douglas, AK 99824; phone 465-4265, fax 465-2034. Or, the Juneau Audubon Society, P.O. Box 1725, Juneau, AK 99802.

Cabins

State Park Cabins

Alaska State Parks maintains 3 public-use cabins in Southeast. The state public-use cabins may be rented for $25 per night. Maximum stay is 3 nights. Reservations are required. Reservations are confirmed when the full amount is paid. This can be done in person or by mail. Credit cards are not accepted. Reservations can be made up to 180 days in advance.

State park public-use cabins in Southeast are located at: Oliver Inlet State Marine Park near Juneau (Seymour Canal cabin, sleeps 6); Point Bridget State Park near Juneau (Cowee Meadow cabin, sleeps 9); and Grindall Island State Marine Park near Ketchikan (Grindall Island cabin, sleeps 6).

Contact Alaska State Parks office in Juneau (400 Willoughby Ave., 99801; phone 465-4563) or in Ketchikan (9883 North Tongass Highway, 99901; phone 247-8574).

Tongass National Forest Cabins

The more than 150 Tongass National Forest recreational cabins are among the best lodging bargains in the state. Current cost is $20 per night for these rustic, but comfortable cabins which are accessible only by boat, floatplane, helicopter or hiking trail. Use is limited to 7 consecutive days between April 1 and Oct. 31 and 10 consecutive days between Nov. 1 and March 31. A few cabins in the Chatham area have a 2-night limit. Permit days begin and end at noon.

Permits for the use of recreation cabins are issued on a first-come, first-served basis. Permits may be obtained in person or by mail. Applications are accepted up to 190 days in advance of intended use. Fee must be included with application. The Application for Recreation Cabin Permit form has

TONGASS NATIONAL FOREST CABINS

	SLEEPS	AIR ACCESS	BOAT ACCESS	TRAIL ACCESS	HUNTING	FISHING	BEACHCOMB	SKIFF	STOVE
YAKUTAT AREA (Phone 784-3359)									
Alsek River *(Landing strip)*	4	•			•	•			O
East Alsek River *(National Park Service, landing strip)*	4	•				•			O
Harlequin Lake duplex *(Landing strip, adjacent Wilderness Area)*	8	•		•	•				OH
Italio River *(Near salt water)*	4	•			•	•	•		O
Lower Dangerous River *(Landing strip)*	4	•			•		•		O
Middle Dangerous River *(Trail can be flooded; bring water)*	4			•	•				O
Middle Situk River duplex	12	•	•	•	•	•			OH
Situk Lake *(In Russell Fiord Wilderness Area)*	6	•		•	•	•		•	W
Situk River *(Available after July 15)*	4	•		•	•	•		•	W
Situk River Weir *(Trail can be muddy)*	6	•	•	•	•	•			W
Square Lake *(Northwest of Dry Bay)*	4	•			•	•		•	O
Tanis Mesa duplex *(North of Dry Bay, landing strip)*	8	•			•				O
ADMIRALTY ISLAND (Phone 586-8800)									
Admiralty Cove *(10 miles south of Juneau)*	6	•	•		•	•			W
Big Shaheen *(Hasselborg Lake, on Canoe Route)*	8	•	•		•	•		•	W
Church Bight *(Gambier Bay, east coast of island)*	8	•	•		•	•			W
Distin Lake *(On Canoe Route)*	4	•	•		•	•		•	W
East Florence Lake *(Near west coast of island)*	8	•			•	•		•	W
Hasselborg Creek *(On Canoe Route)*	2	•	•			•			W
Jim's Lake *(On Canoe Route)*	6	•			•	•			W
Lake Alexander *(On Canoe Route)*	6	•		•	•	•		•	W
Lake Kathleen *(Near west coast of island)*	5	•			•	•		•	W
Little Shaheen *(100 yards from Big Shaheen, on Canoe Route)*	8	•	•		•	•		•	W
North Young Lake *(North end of island)*	6	•	•	•	•	•		•	W
Pybus Bay *(Southeast coast of island)*	10	•	•		•				W
South Young Lake *(North end of island)*	6	•			•			•	W
Sportsmen *(Distin Lake, on Canoe Route)*	4	•			•	•			W
West Florence Lake *(Near west coast of island)*	4	•			•	•		•	W
JUNEAU AREA (Phone 586-8800)									
Dan Moller *(On Dan Moller Trail, Douglas Island; 2-night limit)*	12			•					W
East Turner *(20 miles east of Juneau)*	6	•				•		•	W
John Muir *(On Spaulding Trail; 2-night limit)*	16			•					W

Type of stove provided is indicated as follows: O=oil stove, W=wood stove, G=outdoor grill, OH=oil heater.

TONGASS NATIONAL FOREST CABINS *continued*

	SLEEPS	AIR ACCESS	BOAT ACCESS	TRAIL ACCESS	HUNTING	FISHING	BEACHCOMB	SKIFF	STOVE
Katzehin *(East side Chilkoot Inlet near Haines; airstrip)*	8	•	•		•	•			W
Laughton Glacier *(Near Skagway, access trail by train)*				•					W
Peterson Lake *(On Peterson Lake Trail; 2-night limit)*	6		•			•		•	W
Spruce *(On Taku River, 55 miles by boat from Juneau)*	6	•	•		•	•			W
West Turner *(18 miles east Juneau near Turner River)*	8	•	•	•		•		•	W
SITKA AREA (Phone 747-6671)									
Avoss Lake *(South Baranof Wilderness Area)*	10	•			•	•		•	OH
Baranof Lake *(20 miles east Sitka)*	6	•			•	•		•	W
Brents Beach *(15 miles northwest Sitka on Kruzof Island)*	6	•	•		•	•	•	•	W
Davidof Lake *(South Baranof Wilderness Area)*	10	•				•		•	W
East Sitkoh Lake *(30 miles northwest Sitka)*	6	•	•			•		•	W
Fred's Creek *(10 miles west Sitka on Kruzof Island)*	6	•	•				•		W
Goulding Lake *(West Chichagof-Yakobi Wilderness Area)*	8	•				•		•	W
Kook Lake *(45 miles northwest Sitka)*	10	•				•		•	W
Lake Eva *(Handicap access; 27 miles northeast Sitka)*	6	•				•		•	W
Moser Island *(48 miles north Sitka)*	6					•			W
Plotnikof Lake *(South Baranof Wilderness Area)*	6	•			•	•		•	O
Redoubt Lake *(10 miles south Sitka, hike in from Silver Bay)*	10	•	•	•	•	•		•	W
Salmon Lake *(12 miles south Sitka)*	6	•	•	•		•		•	W
Samsing Cove *(5.5 miles south Sitka)*	10+		•		•	•			W
Seven Fathom Bay *(22 miles south Sitka)*	8		•		•	•	•		W
Shelikof *(20 miles northwest Sitka on Kruzof Island)*	8	•		•	•	•			W
Sulola Lake *(West Chichagof-Yakobi Wilderness Area)*	6	•			•	•		•	W
West Sitkoh Lake *(30 miles northwest Sitka)*	6	•	•			•		•	W
White Sulphur Springs *(West Chichagof-Yakobi Wilderness Area)*	4	•	•		•	•	•		W
PETERSBURG AREA (Phone 772-3841)									
Beecher Pass *(Salmon fishing; need boat)*	4	•	•		•	•			O&W
Bit John Bay *(Road access from Kake to 1.5-mile trail in)*	4	•		•	•	•			O
Brelland Slough	7	•	•		•	•			O
Cascade Creek *(Salmon and halibut fishing; need boat)*	6	•	•		•	•			O&W
Castle Flats *(On mudflats; 13- to 15-foot tide needed for access)*	5	•	•		•	•		•	O&W
Castle River *(16-foot tide needed for access)*	7	•	•	•	•	•		•	W

Type of stove provided is indicated as follows: O=oil stove, W=wood stove, G=outdoor grill, OH=oil heater.

TONGASS NATIONAL FOREST CABINS *continued*

	SLEEPS	AIR ACCESS	BOAT ACCESS	TRAIL ACCESS	HUNTING	FISHING	BEACHCOMB	SKIFF	STOVE
DeBoer Lake *(Carry extra supplies; may weather in)*	6	•			•	•		•	O
Devil's Elbow *(16-foot tide needed for plane access)*	7	•	•		•	•			O
Harvey Lake *(Easy 1-mile trail from salt water)*	7	•	•		•	•		•	W
Kadake Bay *(18-foot tide needed for boat access)*	6	•	•		•	•			O&W
Kah Sheets Bay *(14-foot tide needed for access)*	4	•	•		•	•			O&W
Kah Sheets Lake *(2.7-mile hike from bay to cabin; renovated to access wheelchairs)*	4	•	•		•	•		•	O
Petersburg Lake *(Petersburg Creek-Duncan Salt Chuck Wilderness Area)*	4	•	•	•	•	•		•	O&W
Portage Bay	6	•	•		•	•			O
Ravens Roost *(Bring dry kindling)*	8	•		•	•				W
Salt Chuck East *(Petersburg Creek-Duncan Salt Chuck Wilderness Area)*	7	•	•		•	•		•	W
Salt Chuck West *(Petersburg Creek-Duncan Salt Chuck Wilderness Area)*	4	•	•		•	•			O&W
Spurt Cove *(Boat needed for fishing)*	4	•	•		•	•		•	O
Swan Lake *(Carry extra supplies; may weather in)*	7	•			•	•		•	O
WRANGELL AREA (Phone 874-2323)									
Anan Bay *(No black or brown bear hunting; trail to bear observation point)*	7	•	•			•			O
Berg Bay *(Mooring buoy provided)*	7	•	•		•	•			O
Binkley Slough *(No access at low tide; bring water)*	6	•			•				O
Eagle Lake	4	•	•		•	•		•	W
East Florence	4	•			•	•		•	W
Garnet Ledge *(15-foot tide needed for access; rock hounding)*	7		•						W
Gut Island #1 *(15- to 17-foot tide needed for access; bring water)*	6	•	•		•				O
Gut Island #2 *(15- to 17-foot tide needed for access; bring water)*	4	•	•		•				O
Harding River	6	•	•		•	•			O
Koknuk *(16-foot tide needed for access; carry water)*	4		•		•				O
Little Dry Island *(15- to 17-foot tide needed for access; carry water)*	7	•	•		•				W
Mallard Slough *(14- to 16-foot tide needed for access; bring water)*	7	•	•		•				W
Marten Lake	4	•			•	•		•	W

Type of stove provided is indicated as follows: O=oil stove, W=wood stove, G=outdoor grill, OH=oil heater.

TONGASS NATIONAL FOREST CABINS *continued*

	SLEEPS	AIR ACCESS	BOAT ACCESS	TRAIL ACCESS	HUNTING	FISHING	BEACHCOMB	SKIFF	STOVE
Mount Flemer *(Boat needed for hunting)*	7	•	•		•				O
Mount Rynda *(High river needed for plane or boat access)*	7	•	•		•	•			O
Sergief Island *(15- to 17-foot tide needed for access; carry water)*	4	•	•		•				O
Shakes Slough #1 *(Boat needed for fishing; bring water)*	4	•	•		•	•			O
Shakes Slough #2 *(Bring water)*	7	•	•		•	•			O
Steamer Bay *(Carry water)*	5	•	•		•	•	•		O
Twin Lakes *(Bring water)*	7	•	•		•	•			O
Virginia Lake	4	•			•	•		•	O
PRINCE OF WALES ISLAND (Phone 828-3309)									
Barnes Lake	6	•	•		•	•		•	W
Black Bear Lake *(Good weather required for access)*	6	•			•	•		•	W
Control Lake	8	•	•		•	•		•	W
Essowah	6	•			•	•		•	W
Grindall Island *(Good salmon fishing)*	6	•	•				•		W
Honker Lake	6	•		•	•	•		•	W
Josephine Lake	6	•			•			•	OH
Karta Lake *(Karta River Wilderness Area)*	6	•	•	•	•	•			W
Karta River *(Karta River Wilderness Area)*	6	•	•		•	•			O
Kegan Cove	6	•	•		•	•			W
Kegan Creek *(Boat and trail access from Kegan Cove)*	6	•	•	•	•	•		•	W
McGilvery Creek	6	•			•	•		•	W
Point Amargura	6	•	•		•	•			W
Red Bay Lake *(1-mile hike from salt water, road access)*	2-3	•		•	•	•		•	W
Salmon Bay Lake *(Karta River Wilderness Area)*	6	•	•	•	•	•		•	W
Salmon Lake *(Karta River Wilderness Area)*	6	•		•	•	•		•	W
Sarkar Lake	6	•	•		•	•		•	W
Shipley Bay *(Skiff 0.8 mile from cabin at Shipley Lake outlet)*	6	•	•		•	•		•	W
Staney Creek *(Road access to trail)*	6	•	•	•	•	•			W
Sweetwater Lake *(Road access)*	4	•	•		•	•		•	W
Trollers Cove	6	•	•		•	•			W

Type of stove provided is indicated as follows: O=oil stove, W=wood stove, G=outdoor grill, OH=oil heater.

TONGASS NATIONAL FOREST CABINS *continued*

	SLEEPS	AIR ACCESS	BOAT ACCESS	TRAIL ACCESS	HUNTING	FISHING	BEACHCOMB	SKIFF	STOVE
KETCHIKAN AREA (Phone 225-2148)									
Anchor Pass	6	•	•		•	•	•		W
Blind Pass	6	•	•		•	•	•		W
Deer Mountain	6			•	•				—
Fish Creek	6	•	•		•	•			OH
Fisheries	6	•			•	•		•	W
Heckman Lake *(Boat to Naha Bay, 6.3-mile trail to cabin)*	6	•		•	•	•		•	W
Helm Bay	8	•	•		•	•	•		O&W
Helm Creek	6	•	•		•	•	•		W
Jordan Lake *(Hike from Heckman Lake or Naha Bay)*	6		•	•	•	•		•	W
McDonald Lake *(Boat to Yes Bay, 1.5-mile trail to cabin)*	6	•	•	•	•	•		•	W
Orchard Lake	6	•			•	•		•	OH
Patching Lake	6	•			•	•		•	W
Phocena Bay	6	•	•		•	•	•		W
Plenty Cutthroat *(Boat to Shrimp Bay, 1-mile trail to cabin)*	6	•	•	•	•	•		•	OH
Rainbow Lake	6	•			•	•			W
Reflection Lake *(Boat to Short Bay, 2-mile trail to cabin)*	6	•	•	•	•	•		•	OH
MISTY FIORDS AREA (Phone 225-2148)									
Alava Bay	6	•	•		•	•	•		W
Bakewell Lake	6	•			•	•		•	W
Beaver Camp	6	•			•	•		•	W
Big Goat Lake	6	•			•	•		•	OH
Checats Lake	6	•			•	•		•	W
Ella Narrows	6	•			•	•		•	W
Hugh Smith Lake	6	•			•	•		•	W
Humpback Lake	6	•			•	•		•	W
Manzanita Lake	6	•			•	•		•	OH
Red Alders	6	•			•	•		•	W
Wilson Narrows	6	•			•	•		•	W
Wilson View	6	•			•	•		•	W
Winstanley Island	6	•	•		•	•			W
Winstanley Lakes	6	•			•	•		•	W
HOONAH AREA (PHONE 945-3631)									
Greentop Harbor *(On Yakobi Island in Wilderness Area)*		•	•		•	•			W
Salt Lake Bay *(10 miles southwest Hoonah)*		•	•		•	•			W

Type of stove provided is indicated as follows: O=oil stove, W=wood stove, G=outdoor grill, OH=oil heater.

first, second and third choice cabin selections. If a specific cabin is not available, and you have not agreed to a substitute selection, your money will be returned to you. (Advance payment is also refundable upon written notice and return of the original cabin permit at least 10 days prior to intended use.) If more than one application is received for a cabin for the same starting date, a drawing will be held to determine the permittee.

Scheduled drawings are held for some popular cabins during peak use periods. The 14 public recreation cabins in the Yakutat area, for example, are reserved by lottery in the spring for use during the popular fall moose season.

Anyone who is at least 18 years of age may apply for a cabin permit. Permits are not issued to guides or outfitters for commercial purposes.

Cabins have tables, benches, bunks (without mattresses), wood or oil stoves, brooms and pit toilets. You must bring your own bedding and cooking utensils. An ax or maul is provided at cabins with wood stoves, but bring a small ax or hatchet in case the tools are not there. Be sure to check which kind of stove is provided. The Forest Service does not provide stove oil. Only #1 diesel oil will work properly and 5 to 10 gallons per week are required, depending on weather conditions. It is advisable to bring a gas camp stove for cooking. Most cabins located on lakes have skiffs with oars. You must bring your own life preservers and motor. Be sure to pull the boat above the high-water mark and tie it. Also, turn it over so it does not fill with rain water. Bring good rain gear, waterproof boots and plenty of warm clothing. Also bring extra food and other supplies in case bad weather prolongs your stay. Insect repellent is a must during the summer. Those traveling in bear country may want to carry a .30-06 or larger caliber rifle as a safety precaution if you know how to use the weapon. Burn all combustible trash and pack out all other garbage to avoid attracting bears. Resist the temptation to leave unused food for the next campers. The Forest Service cautions that you are "on your own" at these remote cabins. Be prepared to be self-sufficient and bring emergency equipment such as maps, compass, waterproof matches, a strong knife, first-aid kit and a space blanket. A detailed list of suggested items to take along is available from the Forest Service on request.

The charts beginning on page 79 provide basic information on each cabin within Tongass National Forest. Obtain additional information or make reservations through any ranger district office: **Hoonah area**: Tongass National Forest, Hoonah Ranger District, P.O. Box 135, Hoonah, AK 99829; phone 945-3631. **Juneau area** (including Admiralty Island): Tongass National Forest, Juneau Ranger District, 8465 Old Dairy Road, Juneau, AK 99801; phone 586-8800. Or Centennial Hall Visitors Information Center, 101 Egan Dr., Juneau, AK 99801; phone 586-8751. **Ketchikan area** (including Misty Fiords): Tongass National Forest, Ketchikan Ranger District, Ketchikan, AK 99901; phone 225-2148. **Petersburg area:** Tongass National Forest, Petersburg Ranger District, P.O. Box 1328, Petersburg, AK 99833; phone 772-3841. **Prince of Wales Island area**: Tongass National Forest, Thorne Bay Ranger District, P.O. Box 1, Thorne Bay, AK 99919; phone 828-3304, fax 828-3309. **Sitka area:** Tongass National Forest, Sitka Ranger District, 204 Siginaka Way, Sitka, AK 99835; phone 747-6671. **Wrangell area:** Tongass National Forest, Wrangell Ranger District, P.O. Box 51, Wrangell, AK 99929; phone 874-2323. **Yakutat area**: Tongass National Forest, Yakutat Ranger District, Box 327, Yakutat, AK 99689; phone 784-3359.

The charts on pages 79 through 83 list cabins alphabetically within each of the 10 major areas of Tongass National Forest. The charts show how many people the cabin sleeps; if the cabin is accessible by air, boat or trail; if hunting, fishing or beachcombing are available; and if the cabin has a skiff or stove. Location, special features or restrictions may also be noted. Keep in mind that trail access is often required in addition to plane or boat access. (Check Hiking Trails this section for details on trails to cabins.) Check with the nearest ranger district for current information on individual cabins.

Hiking Trails

Following is a partial list of trails in Southeast, most maintained by the U.S. Forest Service. For more information on U.S. Forest Service trails, contact the Forest Service, P.O. Box 21628-PAO, Juneau, AK 99802-1628.

Most trails in Southeast are more difficult than trails with similar ratings in the Lower 48. This is because oversteepened slopes caused by glacial action, and high seasonal and daily variations in rainfall, can drastically alter trail conditions. Waterproof footwear such as knee-high rubber boots with good traction soles are often the best choice. Trail crews may be working on some trails; check with the local Forest Service or Alaska State Parks office for current trail conditions. Space limitations prohibit listing all of Southeast's fine hiking trails, so check locally for others.

Craig Area Trails

Kegan Lake Trail. This easy 0.5-mile trail begins at Kegan Cove cabin and ends at the lake, where steelhead, sockeye and coho runs are internationally acclaimed. The lake has a native rainbow population and excellent fishing, which has been featured in fishing magazines. Recommended season, July to September. The Kegan Cove and Kegan Creek Forest Service cabins are so popular that they are on a lottery system and must be reserved well in advance. The trail is an easy, pleasant walk through an old-growth forest with very little undergrowth. Related USGS Topographic map: Craig A-1.

One Duck Trail. This more difficult 1-mile trail begins 1.5 miles south of Harris River bridge on Hydaburg Road and climbs 700 feet to a large alpine area with easy walking, good hunting for deer and bear and good cross-country skiing in winter and spring. Although the trail is unfinished, it is passable and easy to find. It has been brushed and basic treadwork has been done. Related USGS Topographic map: Craig B-3.

Haines Area Trails

Trails here are found on USGS Topographic maps Skagway A-1, A-2 and B-2. Only the Mount Riley, Seduction Point and Battery Point trails are maintained by state parks on a regular basis. The others receive periodic volunteer maintenance, so check at the Haines Visitor Center before you hike.

Battery Point Trail. The trail starts 2 miles east of Port Chilkoot and 1 mile beyond Portage Cove at the end of the road. This is a fairly level walk of about 2 miles with a primitive campsite behind Kelgaya Point. The last 0.75 mile of the trail is along pebble beaches and across Kelgaya Point with excellent views of Lynn Canal. Allow 2 hours for a round-trip.

Mount Riley Trails. There are 3 routes to the 1,760-foot summit of Mount Riley: Mud Bay Road, via Port Chilkoot and from Portage Cove.

Mud Bay Road: This route is the steepest and most direct. Take the Mud Bay Road from Port Chilkoot, heading southward on the west side of the Chilkat Peninsula, to the top of the second steep hill a few yards short of the Mile 3 marker. The marked path starts on the left side of the road and heads for the ridge in a southeasterly direction. Distance to the summit is 2.1 miles. Estimated round-trip time is 3.5 hours.

Via Port Chilkoot: This route connects with the Mud Bay Road trail. Take the FAA Road behind Officers Row in Port Chilkoot and follow it to its end, about 1 mile. Walk along the city of Haines water supply access route about 2 miles then take the spur trail which branches to the right to connect with the route from Mud Bay Road. Estimated round-trip time, 4.5 hours.

From Portage Cove: This route is recommended for snowshoe travel in winter. Follow the Battery Point trail almost 2 miles to a junction then take the right fork which climbs steeply at first through thick undergrowth and tall spruce forests. The trail becomes less steep and continues through small muskeg meadows over Half Dome before the final climb to the summit.

It is also possible to traverse Mount Riley from Portage Cove to the Mud Bay Road. This trip is about 7.6 miles and takes about 4 hours.

Mount Ripinsky Summit. The trail starts north of Haines toward Lutak Inlet at the top of Young Road and along the pipeline right-of-way. The pipeline road rises gradually through wooded hillside, then descends steeply after about a mile. At this point, the tank farm is visible. The trail takes off to the left a few yards down the hill and ascends through hemlock and spruce forest to alpine meadows above Johnson Creek, elevation 2,500 feet. From the ridge on clear days, you can see snow-capped mountain peaks from Haines all the way to Admiralty Island. At the summit there are views of Lutak Inlet, Taiya Inlet and a panorama of peaks and ice fields. This is a strenuous, all-day hike or overnight camp. It is possible to descend the summit and continue west-northwest along a ridge to Peak 3,920 and down to 7 Mile Saddle to the Haines Highway. This traverse is about 10 miles and overall elevation gain is about 5,100 feet. The trail is steep in places and easily lost. Until late June, water or snowmelt is found on the ridge. After that it is necessary to carry water beyond Johnson Creek where the last water is found. Related USGS Topographic maps: Skagway A-2, B-2.

Seduction Point. Drive the Mud Bay Road to the Chilkat State Park and park at the bend of the steep hill at the cul-de-sac. The trail alternates between inland forest trail and beach walking with excellent views of the Davidson Glacier. Estimated round-trip time for the 13.5-mile hike is 9 to 10 hours. Seasonal water supplies at Twin and David's coves. Campsites along the way and at the cove east of Seduction Point. Hikers should check the tides before leaving and plan to do the last long beach stretch after David's Cove at low or mid-tide.

7 Mile Saddle. The trailhead is located 0.2 mile east of Milepost 7. The trail climbs steeply at first through small pine forest then more gradually through spruce and hemlock until open slopes are reached at about 2,000 feet. Water is available all year in streams found in the forested sections but water should be carried after passing through those areas. It is possible to continue east toward Mount Ripinsky and reverse the traverse described above.

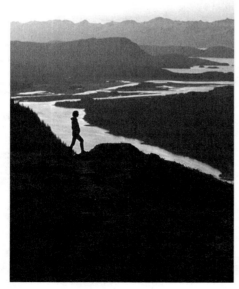

A hiker on Mount Roberts is silhouetted by the setting sun. (David Job)

Juneau Area Trails

Hikers in the Juneau area rely on 2 excellent trail guides, *Juneau Trails* and *90 Short Walks in Juneau*. Both are available from Alaska Natural History Assoc., Forest Service Visitor Center, 101 Eagan Dr., Juneau, AK 99801, and from Juneau bookstores.

Amalga (Eagle Glacier) Trail. Trailhead is in the parking lot on the left at Mile 28.4 from Juneau on the Juneau Veterans' Memorial Highway. Trail extends 4 miles to the old Amalga mine site and another 3.5 miles to the front of Eagle Glacier. Usable spring, summer and fall. First 5.5 miles rated more difficult, last 2 miles most difficult. Elevation gain 500 feet. Estimated round-trip time 10 to 12 hours. Rubber boots recommended. Bring mosquito repellent in summer. Amalga was a settlement between 1902 and 1927; the mine site is now difficult to find. Wildlife includes bears and beavers. Black and brown bears use this trail intensely. Impressive views of Eagle Glacier. This trail was extended in 1990 to provide access to the Juneau Icefield via the Eagle Glacier. Related USGS Topographic map: Juneau C-3.

Auke Nu Trail. This Forest Service trail is reached from the Spaulding trail, which begins at a parking area just off the Juneau Veterans' Memorial Highway at Mile 12.3 (just past the post office.) The Auke Nu trailhead is 0.5 mile up the Spaulding trail, on the left. Trail then extends 2.5 miles to the John Muir Cabin. Usable all year; cross-country skiing in winter. Rated moderate. Elevation gain 1,552 feet. Estimated round-trip time 5 to 6 hours.

First part of trail runs through forested area and contains some sections of an old corduroy road. Middle part also is forested. The last section of trail goes through muskeg meadows. The majority of the trail is planked to protect the fragile plants. Rubber boots are recommended. Blueberries and huckleberries are found in season. Be alert for bears. This trail features views of the Chilkat Mountains, Admiralty Island, Gastineau Channel and Mounts Stroller White and McGinnis. An unmarked cross-country route leads to Peterson Lake. Map, compass and a good sense of direction are essential. Related USGS Topographic map: Juneau B-3.

Blackerby Ridge Trail. From Egan Drive, take the Salmon Creek exit and drive about 0.1 mile. Walk up short road to the right. Trail begins to the left just before the end of the road and extends 3.6 miles to Cairn

Peak. Trail crosses state, private and Forest Service lands. Usable summer and fall. Rated most difficult; it's steep and strenuous. The trail is not maintained and reportedly in poor condition. Elevation gain 4,505 feet. No switchbacks. Estimated round-trip time 8 to 10 hours. Waterproof hiking boots recommended; carry your own water. Above timberline carpets of alpine flowers bloom in season. Salmonberries and blueberries are found in season. Views of Salmon Creek Reservoir and Stephens Passage from the ridge; views of Lemon and Ptarmigan glaciers from Cairn Peak. Related USGS Topographic map: Juneau B-2.

Dan Moller Trail. Located on Douglas Island. Cross Juneau-Douglas bridge, turn left on Douglas Highway and take first right on Cordova Street. Turn left on Pioneer Avenue, and the trail starts past the fifth or sixth house on the right. Trailhead is marked and there is a small parking area. This Forest Service trail extends 3 miles to the Dan Moller cabin in an alpine meadow. (This is a public warming cabin from 10 A.M. to 5 P.M., but can be rented for overnight use through the Forest Service; see Cabins this section.) Usable all year. Open to snowmobiles (12 inches of snow required) and cross-country skiing in winter. Rated easy. Boardwalk section over muskeg may be slippery when wet or frosty. Elevation gain 1,800 feet. Waterproof hiking boots recommended. Sneakers are fine on the boardwalks. Estimated round-trip time 5 to 6 hours. Trail offers excellent wildflowers in season, wildlife and scenery. Climb from bowl to ridge for view of Stephens Passage and Admiralty Island. This area is avalanche prone; cross snowslide paths quickly. Contact the Weather Service at 586-SNOW for avalanche conditions before skiing or hiking this trail. Related USGS Topographic map: Juneau B-2.

Heintzleman Ridge Route. Trailheads off Mendenhall Loop Road behind Glacier Valley Elementary School at the end of Jennifer Drive or at Mile 7 Old Glacier Highway just past Dept. of Transportation maintenance facility. This undeveloped Forest Service trail extends 9.5 miles to the top of Heintzleman Ridge. Usable in summer only. Extreme avalanche danger in winter or early spring. Rated most difficult. Should be attempted only by those in excellent physical condition. Estimated round-trip time 10 to 12 hours, so start early in the morning or plan to camp overnight. Trail is sparsely marked and extremely steep with no switchbacks and many false side trails. Elevation gain 3,000 to 4,000 feet. Mountain goats may be seen; many alpine wildflowers in season. The top of Steep Creek Bowl offers an excellent view of Mendenhall Glacier. Ridge continues toward Nugget Glacier and Nugget Mountain. It is possible to hike to the Mendenhall Glacier visitor center on the Nugget Creek trail from the ridge. Related USGS Topographic map: Juneau B-2.

Herbert Glacier Trail. Trailhead is just past the Herbert River bridge, 28 miles from Juneau on the Juneau Veterans' Memorial Highway. A small gravel parking lot is located to the right of the trailhead. Trail extends 4.6 miles to the moraine about 0.5 mile from Herbert Glacier. Usable all year. Rated easy. Elevation gain 300 feet. Estimated round-trip time is 5 to 6 hours. Trail relatively flat, but wet in places. Trail offers opportunity to view wildflowers in season, wildlife and a good view of the glacier. Notice the plant succession as you hike up the valley through large Sitka spruce to pioneering alder and bare rock. Cross-country skiing possible in winter. Do not cross the branching streams to approach the glacier. It is possible to climb over the rocks to the left of the glacier for a good view of the glacier and a spectacular waterfall. *CAUTION: Do not approach the face of the glacier. Ice falls are dangerous. Also, this is bear country; keep a clean camp and make noise while hiking.* Related USGS Topographic map: Juneau C-3.

Montana Creek Trail. From Mendenhall Loop Road, take the Montana Creek Road about 3 miles to the end at the rifle range. Forest Service trail leads northwest 9.5 miles to Windfall Lake, where it connects with the Windfall Lake trail. This is part of a trail system established in 1907-09 by the Territory of Alaska to serve mining sites. Trail usable for hiking from late spring through fall and for cross-country skiing in winter. Rated moderate. Elevation gain 800 feet. Estimated 8 to 10 hours ending at Windfall Lake trailhead (where you should leave a car). There are high concentrations of bears on this trail, especially during late summer when salmon are spawning. This trail is scheduled for improvement in 1993. Related USGS Topographic maps: Juneau B-2 and B-3.

Mount Bradley (Mount Jumbo) Trail. Trail begins in Douglas at a vacant lot behind the 300 section of 5th Street. The trail extends 2.6 miles to the summit of Mount Bradley and crosses state and private lands. Usable spring, summer and fall. Rated most difficult. Elevation gain 3,337 feet. Estimated round-trip time 10 to 12 hours. Both rubber boots and hiking boots recommended. Mountain was originally named after the Jumbo Mine at its base, but was renamed in 1939 to honor a former president of the American Mining Institute. Trail is muddy with windblown trees and is not maintained. Trail crosses Paris Creek, then the Treadwell Ditch. The muskeg meadows are boardwalked. In the alpine the trail is difficult to follow so observe your route to the summit carefully. There are dangerous dropoffs near the top and the trail becomes quite slippery when wet. An ice ax will be helpful during ascents in late spring. The trail offers scenery, wildflowers in season and spectacular views of Gastineau Channel and Juneau from the summit. Related USGS Topographic maps: Juneau A-2 and B-2.

Mount McGinnis Trail. Trailhead is at the end of the West Glacier trail, but is difficult to find. Look for survey flagging and rock cairns. This unmaintained Forest Service trail extends 2 miles to the summit of Mount McGinnis. Usable in summer and fall. Rated most difficult. Elevation gain 4,228 feet. Estimated round-trip time 8 hours. Trail steep and sparsely marked. It should be attempted only by those in excellent physical condition who have a good sense of direction and are carrying a map and compass. Lower section of trail passes through thick brush and hikers should watch for markers. Trail ascends through dense forest then continues to the top above timberline. The top part is generally covered with snow and an ice ax should be carried. Exercise extreme care in sliding on snow patches. The trail is best hiked from mid-July on. Avalanche danger may continue until late spring. From the summit there is a remarkable view of Auke Bay and Mendenhall Valley. Wildlife that may be seen includes bears and mountain goats. Alpine wildflowers in season. Related USGS Topographic map: Juneau B-2.

Perserverance Trail. This easy, 3-mile trail to the ruins of the old Perserverance Mine is the most popular in the Juneau area. The mine, located in Silverbow Basin, operated between 1885 and 1895, when a snowslide destroyed the mill and camp buildings. From downtown Juneau take Gold Street to Basin Road past the slide on the left above the city's main water supply lines. After crossing Gold Creek, take the lefthand fork. The trail follows a gentle grade around the horn of Mount Juneau. There is extreme danger of snowslide during winter and early spring. Old mining ruins are scattered throughout the area so use caution while exploring. Athletic shoes or light boots are recommended. Estimated round-trip time is 4 to 5 hours; elevation gain 1,000 feet. Related USGS Topographic maps: Juneau B-2.

Peterson Lake Trail. Trailhead is at Mile 24.5 on the Juneau Veterans' Memorial Highway. Parking is limited; be sure not to park on private property. Forest Service trail extends 4.3 miles to Peterson Lake cabin. (This is a public warming cabin from 10 A.M. to 5 P.M., but can be rented for overnight use through the Forest Service; see Cabins this section.) Trail usable all year. Rated more difficult, but it is muddy in some places. Waterproof footwear recommended. Elevation gain 700 feet. Estimated round-trip time 5 to 7 hours. Trail named for John Peterson, a prospector who had a claim in the area during 1899. Trail starts out on steps but soon joins an old tramway. Narrow rails are still in place in some sections; planks have been placed alongside the old rails. About 0.7 mile from the trailhead, a spur trail to the left leads to a good fishing spot below some steep waterfalls. Keep right on this spur to avoid a portion of the lower trail that is subject to landslides. Main trail continues through forest and muskeg areas. (All of the muskeg areas have been planked.) Trail turns right in the last muskeg and continues through dense forest to Peterson Lake, which has Dolly Varden fishing. Related USGS Topographic map: Juneau B-3.

Point Bishop/Dupont Trail. Trailhead is at the end of Thane Road, 5.5 miles south of downtown Juneau. This is a Forest Service trail except for the start, which passes over state and private lands; some of which are scheduled for clear-cutting. It's 1.5 miles to the Dupont dock and 8 miles to Point Bishop. Usable spring, summer and fall. Rated easy, but tiring due to many roots, windfalls and other obstacles. Elevation gain 200 feet. Estimated round-trip time to Dupont is 2 hours; 12 hours to Point Bishop, longer if heavy windfalls from 1991 have not been cleared. Point Bishop was named in 1794 by Capt. George Vancouver for the Bishop of Salisbury. Dupont was named after the Dupont Powder Co., which built the powder magazine there in 1914 to supply local mines. Trail is fairly level, but quite muddy. Waterproof boots recommended. About 1 mile from the trailhead a branch to the right leads to Dupont, where there is good saltwater Dolly Varden fishing in the spring. Main trail runs above Dupont to Point Salisbury then to Point Bishop. Related USGS Topographic maps: Juneau A-1 and B-1.

Point Bridget State Park Trails. Trailhead for the main Point Bridget Trail is at Milepost 39 Juneau Veterans' Memorial Highway, on the left side of the road 1 mile north of the North Bridget Cove sign. The 3.5-mile-long trail (7 hours round-trip) leads northwest through meadows to Point Bridget and a panoramic view of Lynn Canal and the Chilkat Mountains. At Upper Cowee Meadow, 0.5 mile from the trailhead, watch for black bear feeding in the meadows or fishing in Cowee Creek. Make a lot of noise; it is important not to surprise bears. Also, please respect private property boundaries of Echo Bible Camp to the northeast across Cowee Creek. The Point Bridget Trail junctions with the Cedar Lake Trail approximately 2.5 miles from the Glacier Highway trailhead. Cedar Lake Trail begins about 500 feet east of Echoeing Creek just above the Intertidal Meadow and leads 2.1 miles southwest to Camping Cove on Lynn Canal. Cedar Lake itself lies at about 400 feet elevation, 1.5 miles from Camping Cove. From the Camping Cove trailhead, a popular

picnic site for hikers and boaters, it is 1.5 miles to Akiyama Bight to the east, and 1 mile out Trappers Trail to the west. Trappers Trail goes up and down along the outer coast; it is difficult to get to the water along much of this trail. From Akiyama Bight, the McMurchie Cat Road leads 1.2 miles north to Upper Cowee Meadow on the Point Bridget Trail. The Raleigh Trailhead at Milepost 38.6 Juneau Veterans' Memorial Highway connects with the McMurchie Cat Road (0.5 mile). The North Bridget Cove beach access trail, just before Milepost 38 on Juneau Veterans' Memorial Highway, is a Juneau City/Borough trail that leads to Akiyama Bight. (See also Point Bridget State Park this section.) Related USGS Topographic map: Juneau C-3.

Salmon Creek Trail. Drive north from Juneau, then turn right just past the cement abutment at mile 2.5 of Egan Drive. Turnoff is located just before the Salmon Creek exit. Trail begins behind the new Salmon Creek powerhouse. It extends 3.5 miles to Salmon Creek dam. Usable spring, summer and early fall. Rated moderate. Condition good; trail was replaced with a road in 1984. Elevation gain 1,100 feet. Estimated round-trip time 5 to 6 hours. Hiking boots recommended. The

Spaulding Meadows, accessible via Spaulding Trail from Juneau Veterans' Memorial Highway, is a popular cross-country skiing area. (David Job)

first part of the trail follows the route of the old tramline and consists of a roadbed up a long, steep slope. (Many berries along the road in season.) At the top, the trail continues to the right and eventually branches. The right branch leads to a dam (a sign marks the intersection). The dam was built in 1914 by the Alaska-Gastineau Mining Co. It is the world's first true constant-angle arch dam and still is the largest of its kind. Just before the dam, the trail goes up a steep slope to the reservoir. There is fishing for eastern brook trout in the reservoir. The trail is on BLM lands and is maintained by Alaska Electric Light & Power Co.; watch for occasional company vehicles using the road. Related USGS Topographic map: Juneau B-2.

Sheep Creek Trail. Trailhead is located on Thane Road, 4 miles south of downtown Juneau. Trail extends 3 miles to alpine ridge. Usable late spring, summer and fall. Winter travel not recommended due to avalanche danger. Rated moderate. Elevation gain 700 in valley, 3,500 feet to ridge. Estimated round-trip time 2 hours to valley, 5 to 8 hours to ridge. Waterproof hiking or rubber boots recommended. Joe Juneau and Richard Harris named Sheep Creek in 1880 after mistaking mountain goats for sheep. Gold mining in the valley began in 1881. This is a scenic trail with historical mining ruins. Slope is switch-backed and brushy. Trail begins through moss-covered forest with dense brush, then rises abruptly and drops into Sheep Creek valley. A profusion of songbirds make this the ultimate early morning bird walk. Marmot, porcupine and black bear are frequently encountered. Old mining buildings are barely standing and should not be disturbed. Trail is relatively level through the valley, then scrambles up a forested hillside until it reaches the alpine zone. If trail is hard to find above timberline, follow the power line, but stay a safe distance from the lines. Carry an ice ax; snow sometimes persists on the ridge through the summer. A Canadian company is attempting to reopen the A-J gold mine and proposes to use Sheep Camp valley as a tailings disposal site. Check with Alaska State Parks for trail status. Active exploration is ongoing in the Portal Camp area and a dirt road leads into the valley. Related USGS Topographic map: Juneau B-1.

Spaulding Trail. Trailhead located at Milepost 12.6 from Juneau on the Juneau Veterans' Memorial Highway, just past the Auke Bay post office. Trail extends 3 miles to Spaulding Meadows. Usable all year though largely unmaintained above the Auke Nu turnoff. Rated moderate. Elevation gain 1,800 feet. Estimated round-trip time 5 to 6 hours. This trail is extremely muddy during the warm seasons (waterproof footwear is a must), but is an important cross-country ski route in winter. Trail starts on an old road that leads to the first muskeg meadow, then continues about 1 mile through a wooded area to a second meadow. After another stand of trees, the trail ends in the last muskeg meadow. Provides access via Auke Nu Trail to John Muir cabin, a public-use cabin available for rent through the Forest Service; see Cabins this section. In winter, the rolling hills of Auke Mountain and Spaulding Meadows offer excellent cross-country skiing, with views of the Chilkat Mountains, upper Mendenhall Glacier, Lynn Canal and Auke Bay. Related USGS Topographic maps: Juneau B-2 and B-3.

Treadwell Ditch Trail. Trail may be reached by hiking about 1 mile from the beginning of the Dan Moller trail, or from the Eaglecrest ski area on North Douglas Island. Trail extends 12 miles from Eaglecrest to the Dan Moller trail. Usable all year. Rated easy. Elevation gain/drop 700 feet. Estimated time 10 hours one way. The 18-mile-long Treadwell Ditch once carried water from Cropley Lake and Fish Creek to the Treadwell Mine and other mines at the south end of Douglas. The ditch was built between 1882 and 1889. Remains of the ditch project are historic artifacts and should not be disturbed. Trail features porcupines, deer, muskeg meadows and a view of Gastineau Channel. The trail was developed as a hiking and cross-country ski trail, but skiing is often marginal because heavy forest prevents sufficient snow cover in some areas. This is a good sheltered hike for dreary days. The trail was brushed from Eaglecrest all the way to Douglas in 1981; the section between the Dan Moller trail and downtown Douglas (accessible just above D Street in Douglas) is on City and Borough of Juneau land and is not maintained. Trail is flat and wide, but slopes in some places. Stay on the trail during the warmer months; delicate muskeg vegetation deteriorates rapidly with constant foot traffic. Be prepared to encounter windfalls and bridges out. Related USGS Topographic map: Juneau B-2.

West Glacier Trail. Turn off the Mendenhall Loop Road onto Montana Creek Road and take the first right. Follow this road past the campground entrance and the remains of Skaters Cabin to the parking area at the end of the road. This Forest Service trail begins on the north side of the parking lot. It extends 3.4 miles to a rock outcrop above Mendenhall Glacier. Usable in spring and summer. Rated moderate. Elevation gain 1,300 feet. Estimated round-trip time 5 to 6 hours. Athletic shoes or waterproof hiking boots recommended, depending on the weather. Most of this trail is below the glacier trimline and passes through willow and alder trees. In a few places the trail skirts spruce and hemlock forest which the glacier did not reach on its most recent advances. The trail seems to end at a scenic overlook and then curves back toward the glacier; be alert for cairns that mark the route. The trail ends at the top of a rock outcrop and offers spectacular views of Mendenhall Glacier, ice falls and other glacial features. This trail also is used for access onto the glacier by experienced and properly equipped climbers; this is not recommended for inexperienced hikers. On most summer days there is significant tour-related helicopter and small plane traffic overhead. Related USGS Topographic map: Juneau B-2.

Windfall Lake Trail. Turn right off the Juneau Veterans' Memorial Highway at Milepost 27 from Juneau, just before the Herbert River. This 0.2-mile road ends in a parking lot; trailhead is to the right. Forest Service trail extends 3.5 miles to Windfall Lake. Usable all year. Rated easy. Elevation gain 100 feet. Estimated round-trip time 4 hours. Waterproof boots recommended in summer. Used for cross-country skiing in winter. Trail follows the Herbert River through Sitka spruce and western hemlock forest. Trail muddy in summer, but some of the worst spots have been planked over. A spur trail once led to Herbert Glacier, but flooding from beaver dams has made this impassable. When the river is safely frozen, many people ski 5 miles from the parking lot to the glacier. The Windfall Lake trail connects with the Montana Creek trail at Windfall Lake. There is a small rowboat for fishing at the lake; fishing is good for searun cutthroat trout and Dolly Varden. Pink, chum, red and silver salmon spawn in the area. Other features are highbush cranberries, blue heron, swans and geese and a healthy mosquito population. Bears frequent the area. Related USGS Topographic map: Juneau C-3.

Ketchikan Area Trails

Bakewell Lake Trail. Trailhead located on the east side of Bakewell Creek, south side of Bakewell Arm about 40 miles east of Ketchikan in Misty Fiords National Monument. This Forest Service trail extends 1 mile to Bakewell Lake; does not provide access to Bakewell Lake Forest Service recreation cabin. Accessible by boat or floatplane. Rated moderate. Elevation gain 200 feet. Estimated round-trip time 2 hours. Rubber boots recommended. The first half mile of this trail follows an overgrown, abandoned road. At the midpoint there is a waterfall and fish ladder overlook. The remaining half mile leads through timber, wet muskeg. Fishing in Bakewell Lake for Dolly Varden, cutthroat trout; fishing near the lake outlet for red, pink, chum and silver salmon and some steelhead. (See Sportfishing, Ketchikan Area, in this section.) Related USGS Topographic map: Ketchikan B-2.

Black Mountain Trail. Trailhead is in Ice House Cove off Carroll Point 7 miles southeast of Ketchikan. Forest Service trail extends 2.5 miles to Snag and Hidden lakes. Accessible by boat, but watch for submerged rocks. The first 0.5-mile traverses moderate slopes with grades of more than 20 percent. The rest of the trail is on rolling muskeg and scrub timberland. The tread is in poor shape with many wet spots and rough stretches. Primarily used for hiking and fishing access to the lakes. No developed facilities on this trail system. Related USGS Topographic map: Ketchikan B-5.

Checats Cove Trail. Trailhead is on the east side of Checats Creek in Checats Cove, about 35 miles northeast of Ketchikan in Misty Fiords National Monument. Forest Service trail extends 1.1 miles to Lower Checats Lake. Does not provide access to Forest Service recreation cabin on Upper Checats Lake. Trail accessible by boat or floatplane; cove large enough for safe anchorage. Trail usable late spring through early fall. Rated moderate; elevation gain 100 feet. Estimated round-trip time is 2½ hours. The trail begins in spruce-hemlock forest; tread is level but low boggy areas will be encountered. At the 0.5-mile mark the trail enters a large blowdown area. The point where the lake becomes visible is a good camping spot. After this point, the trail has a steep incline then levels off when it returns to the creek's edge. At the logjam there is another good camping spot. The trail continues along the lake for another quarter mile, then ends by a small rock island. No developed facilities. Brown bears frequent this area. Good fishing in the lake. Related USGS Topographic map: Ketchikan B-3.

Deer Mountain/John Mountain Trail. This most difficult 9.9-mile trails begins at the junction of Granite Basin and Ketchikan Dump roads and gains 3,000 feet before ending at Lower Silvis Lake. Spectacular views of Ketchikan and Tongass Narrows make the long climb worthwhile. Experienced hikers can continue past the summit. There is a Forest Service recreation cabin just below and north of the summit and a remote shelter 2.3 miles farther above timberline at Blue Lake. The shelter is not maintained and may be in poor repair. Related USGS Topographic map: Ketchikan B-5.

Ella Lake Trail. Trailhead is at the mouth of Ella Creek on Ella Bay on East Behm Canal, 24 miles northeast of Ketchikan in Misty Fiords National Monument. Access is by boat or floatplane. Forest Service trail extends 2.5 miles to Lower Ella Lake. Trail does not reach Forest Service recreation cabin at Ella Narrows. Trail usable spring to fall. Rated moderate. Elevation gain 250 feet. Estimated round-trip time 5 1/2 hours. Rubber boots recommended. There is a beach marker sign at the trailhead which is visible from Ella Bay. The first 0.25 mile runs through old second-growth timber. The next 1.5 miles cross wet muskeg and marsh with tall grass. The last 0.8 mile leads through timber with a slight incline that levels off at the lake outlet. There is excellent trout and salmon fishing in Ella Creek. The area also features beaver, wildflowers and berries. Near the trailhead are soda springs ringed with concrete foundations built by the Civilian Conservation Corps in the 1930s. Related USGS Topographic maps: Ketchikan B-3, B-4 and C-4.

Humpback Lake Trail. Trailhead at the mouth of Humpback Creek in Mink Bay off Boca de Quadra, about 60 miles southeast of Ketchikan. Forest Service trail extends 3 miles to Humpback Lake. Accessible by boat or floatplane; Forest Service buoy in Mink Bay. Usable late spring through fall. Rated moderate. Elevation gain 270 feet. Rubber boots recommended. Trail is in fair condition. Fairly level for the first 2 miles. After passing small waterfall on the right, the trail begins a steep climb for approximately 500 feet with a grade increase of 50 to 70 percent. At the top of the ridge the trail levels off and leads through muskeg for 0.5 mile. No boardwalk. Trail is hard to follow. After the muskeg, the trail enters timber area where recent slides have buried the trail. Trail ends where a 3-sided shelter stood until it was demolished by a landslide. Excellent trout fishing at the outlet of Humpback Lake. Brown bear very abundant on this

trail. Related USGS Topographic maps: Ketchikan A-2 and A-3, Prince Rupert D-2 and D-3.

Low Lake Trail. Trailhead located at mouth of Fish Creek in the northeast corner of Thorne Arm on Revillagigedo Island, in Misty Fiords National Monument. Accessible by floatplane or boat; Forest Service buoy in Fish Creek Cove for small boat moorage. Forest Service trail extends 2.1 miles to Big Lake. Usable late spring through fall. Rated moderate. Elevation gain 290 feet. Estimated round-trip time 3 1/2 hours. The first 0.5 mile of the trail is partly boardwalk with split log and drainage structures in wet areas. The trail proceeds without tread improvement to the lake. Short stretches traverse sections of steep, rocky ground, some with a 20 percent grade. Fish Creek supports a run of steelhead, Dolly Varden, salmon and cutthroat trout. (See Sportfishing, Ketchikan Area, in this section.) Also, black bears, wildflowers and berries in the area. Related USGS Topographic map: Ketchikan A-4.

Manzanita Lake Trail. Trailhead located on the west side of Manzanita Bay on East Behm Canal about 28 miles northeast of Ketchikan in Misty Fiords National Monument. Forest Service trail extends 3.5 miles to Manzanita Lake; does not provide access to the 2 Forest Service recreation cabins on the lake. Accessible by floatplane or boat. Usable late spring through fall. Rated moderate. Elevation gain 250 feet. Estimated round-trip time 9 hours. There is a floating dock and mooring buoy within sight of the trailhead sign. The first mile of trail is largely muskeg, after which it closely parallels the creek, eventually climbing away from the creek. The trail crosses the creek on a puncheon bridge in the last half mile and ends at the lake. There are no developed facilities on the trail. The tread is mostly natural, with wet and muddy footing in places. Large rocks and steep dropoffs along the last third of the trail may be hazardous. Trail's primary use is hiking, sightseeing and access to fishing in Manzanita Lake. (See Sportfishing, Ketchikan Area, in this section.) Related USGS Topographic maps: Ketchikan C-3 and C-4.

Naha River Trail. From Naha Bay (accessible by boat or floatplane) this 5.4-mile trail ends at Heckman Lake. The trail features excellent salmon and trout fishing, one of the best steelhead runs in Southeast, and the scenic, interesting salt chuck at the outlet of Roosevelt Lagoon. Jordan Lake and Heckman Lake cabins are located on this trail. Small boat tram at outlet to Roosevelt

Lagoon. Picnic shelters at outlet of Roosevelt Lagoon and on Naha River. Beginning on boardwalk, the trail does have some wet and muddy spots farther in, but is generally in good condition. Allow 5 hours one-way walking time. Related USGS Topographic map: Ketchikan C-5.

Nooya Lake Trail. Trailhead located in a small bight on the west shore of the North Arm of Rudyerd Bay, in Misty Fiords National Monument. Forest Service trail extends 1.1 miles to Nooya Lake. Access is by boat or floatplane. Usable late spring through fall. Rated moderate. Elevation gain 400 feet. Estimated round-trip time 2 to 3 hours. Access to the trail is fair; anchorage at the mouth of Nooya Creek is poor. The first quarter-mile leads through wet, boggy areas, the next half-mile gently increases in grade and wet areas are less common. At the 0.8-mile point, the trail turns left away from the creek and starts a steep, 35 to 45 percent grade. The trail is wet but solid. There is a 3-sided Civilian Conservation Corps shelter at the outlet of Nooya Lake. Black and brown bears are common along this trail. Related USGS Topographic map: Ketchikan C-3.

Punchbowl Lake Trail. Trailhead located at the south end of Punchbowl Cove in the Rudyerd Bay area of Misty Fiords National Monument. Forest Service trail extends 0.7 mile to Punchbowl Lake. Accessible by floatplane or boat; moorage buoy in cove. Trail usable late spring through fall. Rated moderate. Elevation gain 600 feet. Estimated round-trip time 3½ hours. This is a fairly steep trail with switchbacks, but its condition is good. Trail is very scenic. At the 0.5-mile point there is an overlook of Punchbowl Creek waterfall. Within 500 feet of this point is another vista overlooking Punchbowl Cove. Here the trail runs along a 2-foot-wide rock ledge with a 300-foot drop. Near the lake, the trail runs along Punchbowl Creek where rock walls rise approximately 250 feet. Trail ends at a new 3-sided shelter on Punchbowl Lake. Activities include fishing in the lake. (See Sportfishing, Ketchikan Area, in this section.) Related USGS Topographic map: Ketchikan C-3.

Shelokum Lake Trail. Trailhead is approximately 90 miles north of Ketchikan on Bailey Bay, 0.5 mile south of Shelokum Creek. The trail climbs 2.2 miles to Shelokum Lake at an elevation of 348 feet. Rated most difficult. Estimated round-trip hiking time 4 hours. This trail is perhaps the most scenic trail in the Ketchikan area. Special features include the largest waterfall in the area, an undeveloped hot springs, views of extremely scenic mountains and cliffs and developed boat access. Hikers must ford Maude Creek before reaching Shelokum Lake. It is impassable during high water. A 3-sided shelter is located at the inlet of Lake Shelokum, near Shelokum Hot Springs. Related USGS Topographic map: Ketchikan D-5.

Winstanley Lake Trail. Trailhead located in Misty Fiords National Monument on the south side of Winstanley Creek, across from the southern tip of Winstanley Island in East Behm Canal. Forest Service trail extends 2.3 miles to Winstanley Lake. Accessible by floatplane or boat. Usable late spring through fall. Rated moderate. Elevation gain 400 feet. Estimated round-trip time 4 to 5 hours.

The trail begins 30 feet to the right of the south bank of Winstanley Creek. There is a beach marker and mooring buoy. The first mile of trail leads through dense spruce and hemlock forest. The trail crosses over a handmade bridge to the north side of the creek at the 1-mile marker. There is a scenic view of Winstanley Creek and falls. The trail continues on the north side of Lower Winstanley Lake, crossing over to the south side of Winstanley Creek at the lake's inlet. The remaining 0.5-mile of trail goes through 2 small muskegs before it ends at a 3-sided Civilian Conservation Corps shelter on Winstanley Lake. There are no other facilities on the trail. Related USGS Topographic map: Ketchikan B-3.

Wolf Lake Trail. This more difficult 2.6-mile trail leads from salt water in Moser Bay, 19 miles from Ketchikan, through muskegs and river bottomland and past 2 small unnamed ponds and Lower Wolf Lake, terminating at the Upper Wolf Lake shelter. Rubber boots are a must because of the wet tread. There are deer, black bears, and a large population of wolves, especially evident in winter. Cutthroats can be caught in Upper Wolf Lake. This is a year-round trail, good for skiing or snowshoeing in winter. Related USGS Topographic map: Ketchikan C-5.

Petersburg Area Trails

Big John Bay Trail. Trail extends 2.2 miles from Forest Road 6314, 16 miles from Kake, to the Big John Bay recreation cabin. Trailhead accessible by auto from Kake. No access to cabin by trail at high tide. Rated moderate. Elevation gain 100 feet. Estimated round-trip time 2 hours. Usable spring, summer and fall. Trail marked with blue diamonds with blazes, and pink flagging. Provides access to excellent waterfowl, grouse and black bear hunting. Related USGS Topographic maps: Petersburg D-5, D-6.

Cascade Creek Trail. Trail extends 4.5 miles to Swan Lake from the Forest Service recreation cabin at Cascade Creek, 14 air miles northeast of Petersburg on Thomas Bay. Accessible by floatplane or boat. Rated most difficult. The upper portion of the trail is currently closed due to safety hazards. Requires good hiking skills; use caution. Elevation gain 1,514 feet. Provides access to mouth of Cascade Creek at 1 mile, Falls Lake at 3 miles and Swan Lake at 5 miles. Follows edge of Thomas Bay and north side of creek. There is fishing in Falls Lake and outstanding scenery and photo opportunities. There is exit from Swan Lake to salt water. Hikers cannot reach the Swan Lake Forest Service cabin by this trail. Related USGS Topographic maps: Petersburg D-3, Sumdum A-3.

Cathedral Falls Trail. Trail extends 0.3 mile to Cathedral Falls from Forest Road 6312, about 9 miles from Kake. Usable spring, summer and fall. Rated moderate. Elevation loss 100 feet. Estimated round-trip time 30 minutes. Provides access to trout and salmon fishing and photo opportunities at the falls. Related USGS Topographic maps: Petersburg D-5, D-6.

Colp Lake Trail. Trail extends 2.3 miles from the mouth of Five Mile Creek on Frederick Sound to Colp Lake, 5 miles northwest of Petersburg. Accessible by boat or floatplane. Usable spring, summer and fall. Rated moderate. Elevation gain 588 feet. Estimated round-trip time 2¹/₂ hours. Provides access to fishing, hiking, swimming and cross-country skiing. Excellent view of Del Monte Peak and surrounding alpine terrain.

Petersburg Lake Trail. This trail extends 6.8 miles from Petersburg Creek to Petersburg Lake cabin, 9 miles northwest of Petersburg. Rated easy. Tide of 15 feet is best for reaching trailhead, which is approximately 3 miles up Petersburg Creek from Wrangell Narrows. (Or hikers can walk 10 miles on a partial boardwalk from the public dock just across Wrangell Narrows from Petersburg.) The trail follows Petersburg Creek most of the way. There is fishing for salmon and trout, wildflower meadows and photo opportunities. Related USGS Topographic maps: Petersburg D-3 and D-4.

Petersburg Mountain Trail. Trail extends 2.5 miles from Wrangell Narrows to the top of Petersburg Mountain. Located within Petersburg Creek-Duncan Salt Chuck Wilderness. Primarily accessible by boat. Trail rated

difficult. High tide access is behind Sasby Island. Low tide access is from the Kupreanof public dock. Trail offers outstanding views and photo opportunities of Petersburg, coastal mountains and glaciers, Wrangell Narrows and part of the wilderness area. Related USGS Topographic map: Petersburg D-3.

Portage Mountain Loop Trail. Trail begins at the junction of the Petersburg Creek trail and the spur trail to Petersburg Lake recreation cabin and extends 10.5 miles to the Salt Chuck East recreation cabin. Usable summer and fall for hiking; winter for cross-country skiing and snowshoeing. Rated moderately difficult. Elevation gain 150 feet. Round-trip hiking time 12 hours. Trailhead accessible by floatplane via the Petersburg Lake cabin drop-off point, or by boat and foot to the Petersburg Creek trail. Portions of this trail were blazed by the Civilian Conservation Corps in the 1930s. Efforts to reestablish the trail began in 1978. When completed, the trail will extend from near the Petersburg Lake cabin to Goose Cove, to Salt Chuck East cabin, loop around the base of Portage Mountain and then connect back to the existing trail at Petersburg Lake. Trail passes through areas of muskeg and heavy timber and crosses numerous streams. Trail offers spectacular views of Portage Mountain and the Duncan Canal Salt Chuck. Moose, deer, black bear, waterfowl and other birds may be seen. Related USGS Topographic map: Petersburg D-4.

Raven Trail. Trail extends 3.9 miles from behind the Petersburg airport to Ravens Roost Forest Service recreational cabin. Drive to end of the airport road past the red-and-white water tower and watch for trail marker. Trail rated moderate. About half the trail is boardwalk, but some very steep (70 percent slope) sections require good hiking skills. Trail offers outstanding views of Petersburg, Frederick Sound and Wrangell Narrows, as well as access to upland bird hunting and winter cross-country skiing and snowshoeing. Related USGS Topographic map: Petersburg D-3.

Spurt Lake Trail. Trail extends 1.1 miles from Thomas Bay to Spurt Lake. Trailhead on bay south of Wind Point. Accessible by boat or floatplane. Trail usable spring, summer and fall. Rated easy, elevation gain 450 feet. Estimated round-trip time 1¹/₂ hours. This trail provides access to Spurt Lake, which was the original location of the Spurt Cove cabin. Lake has fair fishing for cutthroat trout; small boat provided. Related USGS Topographic map: Sumdum A-3.

Twin Ridge Ski Trail. Trail begins at Milepost 3.4 on Twin Creeks Road and extends 4.9 miles to Ravens Roost cabin. Usable October to June for cross-country skiing; June to October for hiking. Rated moderately difficult. Elevation gain 1,200 feet. Estimated round-trip time 8 hours. Trailhead at Raven's Roost cabin can be reached via the 3.8-mile Raven Trail from town. Intermediate skiing skills required at this end. Trailhead on Twin Creeks Road can be reached by driving or skiing 3.4 miles up the road, which is very steep and narrow. Road is dangerous when it is covered with snow; at those times, park at beginning of road and ski to trailhead in a small muskeg clearing on the left-hand side of the road. Trail marked with pink flagging and blue diamond markers, which may become covered with snow at times. Trail follows ridge. Advanced skiing skills or snowshoes required to traverse the steeper slopes. Trail offers spectacular views of Wrangell Narrows, LeConte Bay and the mainland. Moose, deer and black bear may be seen. Related USGS Topographic maps: Petersburg C-3, D-3.

Upper Twin Ski Trail. This 3.2-mile loop trail connects to Twin Creeks Road at Miles 3.3 and 4. Usable October to June for intermediate and advanced cross-country skiing; June to October for hiking. Rated moderately difficult. Elevation gain 600 feet. Estimated loop time 3 hours. Trailhead on Twin Creeks Road can be reached by driving or skiing up the road, which is very steep and narrow. Road is very dangerous when it is covered with snow; at those times, park at beginning of road and ski to trailheads on the right-hand side of the road. Trail marked with pink flagging and blue diamond markers, which may become covered with snow at times. Entire length of trail is good for intermediate skiers, except for one steep 0.3-mile slope about 0.5 mile in from the western trailhead. Skiers of intermediate skill may want to start from the eastern trailhead, then walk down the steep slope. Advanced skiers should have no trouble. This trail offers spectacular views of the mainland. Moose, deer and black bear may be seen. Related USGS Topographic map: Petersburg C-3.

Sitka Area Trails

Contact the Public Affairs Office, Tongass National Forest, Chatham Area, 204 Siginaka Way, Sitka, AK 99835, for an up-to-date guide to Sitka trails. There will be a small fee.

Beaver Lake Trail. Begins at Sawmill Creek Recreation area about 5 air miles east of Sitka. Trail extends 0.8 mile to Beaver Lake. From Sawmill Creek Road, then turn left onto the uphill dirt road which leads 1.5 miles to the Sawmill Creek Recreation area. Usable all year. Rated moderate. Elevation gain, 250 feet. Round-trip hiking time between 1 and 2 hours. This is a popular maintained trail suited to family outings. It offers good views of nearby mountains and a nice walk over muskeges, along marshes and through stunted forests. The trail begins across the bridge over Sawmill Creek on the south side of a small clearing. At the beginning, a series of switchbacks and stairs lead through forest of hemlock, Sitka spruce and yellow cedar up 200 feet. After the climb, the planked boardwalk portion of the trail begins as it breaks out onto sloping stunted forests. The trail ends with a dilapidated pier in a small muskeg at the western edge of Beaver Lake which was stocked with grayling in 1986, 1987 and 1988. Bears may be present; use caution. Related USGS Topographic map: Sitka A-4.

Blue Lake River Trail. Trailhead is 9 miles east of Sitka at the inlet stream on the east end of Blue Lake. Access by floatplane, canoe or kayak or car via Sawmill Creek Road and Blue Lake. This unmaintained Forest Service trail extends 2.5 miles to the south end of Glacier Lake. Usable spring through fall. Rated difficult. Elevation gain 1,200 feet. Estimated round-trip time 4 to 6 hours. Rubber boots recommended. This trail was built in 1898 as a mining road. Trail begins on the north side of Blue Lake's inlet stream, runs through forest on the north side of the stream for about 0.5 mile, then crosses a stretch of open brushy areas. About a mile from the trailhead it begins to climb through spruce-hemlock forest and gains 700 feet in 0.3 mile. The last half mile to Glacier Lake is a difficult up-and-down scramble through rocky, brushy and finally subalpine terrain. Wildlife includes deer around Blue Lake and mountain goats higher up. Rainbow trout are found in Blue Lake. Related USGS Topographic map: Sitka A-4.

Gavan Hill Trail. Trail starts just past the house at 508 Baranof Street, within walking distance of downtown Sitka. Trail extends 3 miles to the 2,505-foot summit of Gavan Hill and connects with the Harbor Mountain Ridge Trail. Rated moderate. Elevation gain 2,500 feet. Estimated round-trip time 6 to 8 hours. Trail usable midspring to late fall. First built in 1937 to provide access to recreationists and hunters, this maintained trail continues to offer access to alpine country for exploring and camping. The first 0.5 mile of the trail follows the path of an old pipeline and heads northeast across gently sloping muskegs and scrubby forests before entering the forests and beginning the climb up Gavan Hill. About 0.75 mile up the hill the Cross Trail, which skirts Sitka, branches off to the left while the Gavan Hill Trail continues looping up east and north along a low ridge. Once on the Gavan Hill Ridge, about elevation 500 feet, the trail runs through a forest of stunted trees which gives way to subalpine meadows after a 0.25 mile. The first peak at 2,100 feet is reached after 0.5 mile and includes a steep 200-foot climb. The trail continues another 0.25 mile northwest along the ridge to the second, higher peak. Bears may be present. Related USGS Topographic map: Sitka A-4.

Goulding Lake Trail. Trailhead is located at the head of Goulding Harbor on West Chichagof Island about 65 miles northwest of Sitka. Accessible by floatplane. Trail extends 1 mile to the outlet of the lowest Goulding Lake. Trail is located within West Chichagof-Yakobi Wilderness Area; it does not extend to the Forest Service's Goulding Lakes recreation cabin. Trail usable all year. Rated moderate. Elevation gain 200 feet. This trail is wet and muddy; rubber boots highly recommended. Estimated round-trip time 2 hours. Trail generally follows the lower part of an abandoned mining tramway. Some of the old mining machinery, structures and a railroad engine remain. Do not disturb them. The trail begins on the north side of the inlet stream at the head of the harbor. Sections of the trail pass through spruce-hemlock forest, muskeg and marsh. At the point where the trail meets the Goulding River is a good viewpoint for a large waterfall just upstream. Above the viewpoint, the trail crosses a tributary and continues a short distance to the lowest Goulding Lake. Fishing is good for steelhead and small cutthroat trout. Related USGS Topographic map: Sitka D-7.

Harbor Mountain Ridge Trail. Trailhead is 9 miles from Sitka at the end of the Harbor Mountain Road. The trail extends 2 miles where it joins the Gavan Hill Trail at a peak with an elevation of 2,505 feet. Usable spring through fall. Rated moderate. Elevation gain 500 feet. This is the only subalpine area in southeastern Alaska that is accessible by road. It offers wonderful views of Sitka Sound, Sitka Mount Edgecombe and numerous other mountains and islands. The trailhead is marked by a bulletin board and

handrailings. It proceeds 300 feet up the hillside in a series of switchbacks. At the ridge, a short spur trail leads to the left to an overlook. The main trail turns to the right and follows the ridge toward the summit of a knob where WWII lookout ruins are located. As the trail continues along the ridge toward the peaks, it forks to the right and skirts the hillside, circling around to join the Gavin Hill Trail. The last section of the trail is little more than a deer path and is difficult to locate at times. The other fork of the trail continues up the steep shoulder slope of the peaks and ends as it reaches the steep rocky alpine at about 2,500 feet. Related USGS Topographic maps: Sitka A-4, A-5.

Indian River Trail. Trailhead is located within walking distance from Sitka. Trail extends 4.3 miles to the base of Indian River Falls, usable year-round. Rated easy. Elevation gain 700 feet. Estimated round-trip time 8 hours. The trail offers views of the Sisters Mountains and is a relaxing walk through northwest coastal rain forest. To find the trailhead, follow Sawmill Creek road a short distance to Indian River Road, an unmarked road east of the Troopers Academy driveway. Walk around the gate and follow the road east about 0.5 mile to the pumphouse. The trail follows Indian River up a wide valley, meandering from the trailhead. Good picnic spots can be found in numerous places along the trail. Birds and animals are common in the forest and along the river. Deer are seen frequently and bears may be present. Related USGS Topographic map: Sitka A-4.

Lake Eva-Hanus Bay Trail. Trailhead is at Hanus Bay on the northeast coast of Baranof Island about 27 miles northeast of Sitka. Accessible by floatplane or boat. Trail extends 2.9 miles to an old Civilian Conservation Corps shelter on the southwest shore of Lake Eva. Usable all year. Rated moderate. Elevation gain 50 feet. Estimated round-trip time 4 to 8 hours. Rubber boots recommended. Trail begins on the west side of the bay, on the east side of the Lake Eva outlet stream. Trail heads west along the south side of the estuary, then winds along the south side of the Lake Eva outlet stream through dense spruce-hemlock forest that offers fine vistas and good fishing for spring-run steelhead, fall coho salmon and year-round cutthroat trout and Dolly Varden. (See Sportfishing, Sitka Area, in this section.) Lake is accessed at Mile 1.1 from salt water. The trail follows the south shore of Lake Eva through old-growth forest and ends at the shelter, which is in poor condition. The last

0.5 mile of the trail is difficult due to wind-fall and landslides. The trail does not lead to the Forest Service Lake Eva recreation cabin, which is on the northwest side of the lake. Related USGS Topographic map: Sitka B-4.

Mount Edgecumbe Trail. Trailhead is behind the Freds Creek recreation cabin on the southeast shore of Kruzof Island about 10 miles west of Sitka. Accessible by float-plane or half-hour boat ride from Sitka. Trail extends 6.4 miles to the summit crater of Mount Edgecumbe, an inactive volcano. Usable spring through late fall. Rated moderate. Elevation gain 3,000 feet. Estimated round-trip time 8 to 12 hours. Rubber boots recommended. The trail starts on flat, forested land then gradually rises while running through several miles of muskeg alternating with forest. About 3 miles up the trail at an elevation of 700 feet, a spur leads to a trail shelter. About 1 mile beyond the shelter turnoff, the trail steepens considerably. Timberline is at about 2,000 feet, where the trail ends. Above this the ground is covered with red volcanic ash. To reach the crater rim, continue straight up the mountain. The summit offers spectacular views on clear days. If you use any flagging or marking, be sure to remove it all. Also, pack out all garbage. Related USGS Topographic maps: Sitka A-5 and A-6.

Mount Verstovia Trail. Trail begins a mile east of Sitka along Sawmill Creek Road, near the Kiksadi Club and extends 2.5 miles to the summit of Mount Verstovia. Usable mid-spring to mid-fall. Rated difficult. Elevation gain 2,550 feet to Verstovia and 3,300 feet to Arrowhead. Estimated round-trip hiking time 6 hours. The lower hillside was logged by the Russians in 1860 and charcoal pits are still somewhat visible about 0.25 mile up the trail. The trail was built in the 1930s for recreational purposes. The view from Verstovia is spectacular and the trail progresses through thickets of salmonberry and alder to western hemlock-spruce forest into brushy meadows, across snowfields, through grassy meadows and finally into a rocky alpine area with stunted, twisted plants. The trail is not well maintained and it is possible to lose track of the switchbacks which begin about 0.35 mile up the trail. At about 2,000 feet the trail reaches a gentle ridge which it follows east to the summit of Verstovia. Arrowhead Peak can be climbed by heading northeast along the rocky alpine ridge. The last part of the climb is quite steep and exposed. Bears may be present. Related USGS Topographic map: Sitka A-4.

Salmon Lake-Redoubt Lake Trail. Trailhead located at the southwest end of Silver Bay about 10 miles southeast of Sitka. Accessible by boat or floatplane. Trail extends 5.9 miles to the Forest Service's recreation cabin on Redoubt Lake. Usable all year. Rated moderate. Elevation gain 600 feet. Estimated round-trip time 8 to 10 hours. Rubber boots recommended. Trail begins on the east side of the mouth of the Salmon Lake stream, which is the westernmost inlet stream at the head of Silver Bay. Trail passes through Sitka spruce, hemlock and cedar forest for the first 3 miles and follows the eastern shore of Salmon Lake for about a mile. The trail crosses several creeks and streams that must be forded. At about 3 miles, the trail travels through muskegs and meadows. There are trail forks in this area; stay on the main (southwestern) trail as the forks are unmaintained trails leading up to the Lucky Chance Mountain mining areas. The trail then reenters the forest and climbs 500 feet up a narrow saddle to the pass that separates the Salmon Lake and Redoubt Lake drainages. The tread is rough in areas, planking is often slick and there are muddy areas. The pass is about 1 mile from Redoubt Lake; the downhill slope can be slippery and muddy. The trail follows the lakeshore for about half a mile, then turns southwest a short distance to the cabin. Along this trail there is fishing for cutthroat and rainbow trout and Dolly Varden. Related USGS Topographic map: Port Alexander D-4.

Sashin Lake Trail. Trailhead is at the head of Little Port Walter on the eastern side of Baranof Island about 55 miles southeast of Sitka. Accessible by boat or floatplane. Trail extends 1.7 miles to Sashin Lake. Usable all year. Rated moderate. Elevation gain 400 feet. Rubber boots recommended. Trail was built and planked by the Civilian Conservation Corps in the 1930s. Go ashore at the dock in front of the fisheries research station (a large white brick house) in Little Port Walter. The trail heads southwest along the western shore of Little Port Walter for a quarter-mile, past various research station buildings and then past the king salmon holding pens, which are quite interesting. The bridge is out above the fish weir and the Forest Service recommends using hip-boots to make the crossing. The trail then meanders southwest up Sashin Creek through open forests and meadows. Just northeast of Sashin Lake, the trail goes over a low shoulder and enters a heavy forest; stay on the north side of the lake. The trail ends at a

Civilian Conservation Corps shelter. About 1.3 miles from the trailhead another branch leads north to Round Lake. Round Lake trail is not maintained and difficult to follow. There is good trout fishing in Sashin Lake. This is bear country, so exercise caution. Related USGS Topographic maps: Port Alexander B-2, B-3 and B-4.

Sea Lion Cove Trail. Trailhead at Kalinin Bay on the north side of Kruzof Island, about 25 miles northwest of Sitka. Access is by boat or floatplane. Trail extends 2.5 miles to Sea Lion Cove, a beautiful mile-long white sand beach. Usable all year. Rated moderate. Elevation gain 250 feet. Estimated round-trip time 4 hours. Rubber boots recommended; trail is muddy and rough in places. Some sections are planked. Hikers should be aware that bears frequent this area. Trail begins at the southern end of Kalinin Bay on the upper beach just west of the high-water island where there is a red, diamond-shaped trail marker on a tree. The trail runs south along the western side of the estuary for about half a mile. This stretch is inundated during high tides. The trail then turns west up into the forest at the next trail sign. At the top of the hill it cuts through muskeg, reenters the forest and follows the north shore of an unnamed lake. The trail becomes rougher and begins to drop into the Sea Lion Cove drainage just past the lake. For the last mile it winds west on low flat ground through forest and muskeg. The trail breaks out on the northern end of Sea Lion Cove. This beach is wonderful for beachcombing, exploring, camping, watching sea lions and viewing surf and the open Pacific Ocean. Camping also is possible at Kalinin Bay. During the summer, there usually is a fish-buying scow anchored in the bay from which groceries and showers may be purchased. Related USGS Topographic map: Sitka B-6.

Sitkoh Lake Trail. Trailhead at Sitkoh Bay on the southeast part of Chichagof Island about 35 miles northeast of Sitka. Accessible by floatplane and boat. Trail extends 4.3 miles to the Forest Service recreation cabin on Sitkoh Lake. Trail usable spring through fall. Rated moderate. Elevation gain 200 feet. Estimated round-trip time 6 to 8 hours. Rubber boots recommended. Trail begins on the north side of the mouth of Sitkoh Creek (about 0.5 mile northwest of the abandoned Chatham Cannery, which is on the western shore of Sitkoh Bay). The trail marker is just above the beach. The trail

is easy to follow. Some sections are planked and some have stairs. Near the lake the trail crosses some muskeg and in some areas it is muddy and/or under water. At the cabin a spur trail leads northwest about 0.5 mile to an old logging road. Bears are numerous in the area. There is good fishing in Sitkoh Creek and Lake. The creek has a good run of pink salmon from July to mid-August; red salmon from mid-July to mid-August; and silver salmon from late August through September. The creek reportedly has the best spring steelhead run in the Sitka Ranger District, generally starting in late April. The lake has an over-wintering population of cutthroat trout and Dolly Varden. (See Sportfishing, Sitka Area, in this section.) Deer hunting is good in the area. Related USGS Topographic maps: Sitka C-3 and C-4.

Warm Springs Bay Trail. Located 20 miles east of Sitka on the east shore of Baranof Island. Accessible by boat or floatplane. Trail extends 0.5 mile from Baranof Warm Springs to Baranof Lake where a Forest Service cabin is located (see Cabins this section). Rated easy with no elevation gain. Round-trip hiking time 1 hour. Usable all year. A private hot spring bath (status unknown) is located at the Warm Springs end of the trail, which is on salt water. Hot springs, pools and streamlets are common interruption of the mossy forest floor. Generally the trail is on boardwalk over areas with hot springs. The trail terminates by fading out near the north side of the lake's outlet. Several short, unmaintained spur trails radiate from this area; these go along the lakeshore, along the river, into the muskeg and one leads to Sadie Lake. Related USGS Topographic map: Sitka A-3.

Skagway Area Trails

For information on hiking in the Skagway area, write the Skagway Convention and Visitors Bureau for a free brochure: P.O. Box 415, Skagway, AK 99840; phone 983-2854.

Chilkoot Trail. This 33-mile-long trail begins on Dyea Road about 8 miles from Skagway. The trail is part of Kondike Gold Rush National Historical Park and is managed by the National Park Service and Canadian Parks Service. See the description of the Chilkoot Trail in Special Features at the end of the Attractions section.

Dewey Lakes Trail. This steep trail takes off from near the east end of 4th Avenue. Lower Dewey Lake is a ½- to 1-hour hike. Upper Dewey Lake is a steep, 2½- to 4-hour hike to above tree line. Both lakes were stocked with Colorado brook trout in the 1920s.

Wrangell Area Trails

Aaron Creek Trail. Trail extends 4 miles from the Berg Bay recreation cabin, located 15 miles southeast of Wrangell, to the mouth of Berg Creek. Accessible by float-plane or boat. Rated easy. The Berg Creek trail continues 5 miles up Berg Creek into the mountains. Former mining activity in this area. Trail provides access to waterfowl, moose and bear hunting on tideflats; goat hunting in the mountains.

Anan Creek Trail. Trail extends 1 mile from the mouth of Anan Creek to Anan Fish-pass and Bear Observatory, a wood-frame shelter. Accessible by floatplane or boat 34 miles south of Wrangell on the mainland. Rated easy; elevation gain 100 feet. Estimated round-trip time 1½ hours. Trail begins at marker just above beach adjacent to Anan Bay cabin. Most of trail follows easy grade through spruce-hemlock forest. Trail is unsurfaced except for occasional staircases and bridges used for abrupt elevation changes or wet spots. Provides access to fishpass and bear viewing station at falls. Wildlife viewing/photography and pink salmon fishing available. Bears also use this trail heavily, so make your presence known. Related USGS Topographic map: Bradfield A-6.

Kunk Lake Trail. Trail extends 1.3 miles from Zimovia Strait to Kunk Lake on the northeast coast of Etolin Island about 13 miles south of Wrangell. Accessible by boat or floatplane. Rated difficult, estimated round-trip time about 2 hours. Trail covers varied terrain with grades ranging from easy to steep and with much wet ground. Waterproof boots highly recommended. Provides access to trout fishing and picnicking areas. Related USGS Topographic map: Petersburg B-2.

Mill Creek Trail. Trail extends 0.8 mile from Eastern Passage to the Virginia Lake outlet about 10 miles east of Wrangell. Accessible by boat or floatplane. Rated easy. Elevation gain 100 feet. Estimated round-trip time 1½ hours. Provides portage from salt water to the lake. Abandoned sawmill site at the head of the trail. A portion of the trail lies atop an old corduroy truck road. Evidence of old mining activity in the area. Activities include trout fishing and picnicking. The trail also provides snowmobile access to ice fishing in winter. Related USGS Topographic map: Petersburg B-1.

Rainbow Falls and Institute Creek

trails. Rainbow Falls Trail begins at Mile 4.6 Zimovia Highway directly across from the Shoemaker Bay Recreation Area and Boat Harbor. It extends 0.8 mile to Rainbow Falls and leads to picnicking and scenic views at 2 modest observation sites. Midway between the 2 sites is the junction with Institute Creek Trail, which leads 3.5 miles (1,100-foot elevation gain) to Shoemaker Overlook Recreation Site. Here are excellent vistas and cross-country skiing opportunities, also access to grouse and deer hunting in season. At trail's end are a 3-sided shelter, picnic table, fire grill and outdoor privy. Although trail was recently surfaced, conditions can range from excellent to poor. Allow 1½ hours round-trip hiking time for the Rainbow Falls portion and 6 hours (round-trip) for the Institute Creek hike. These 2 trails are the most popular on Wrangell Island. Related Topographic map: Petersburg B-2.

River Running

Alsek-Tatshenshini rivers. These 2 spectacular rivers join together in Canada and flow (as the Alsek) to the Gulf of Alaska at

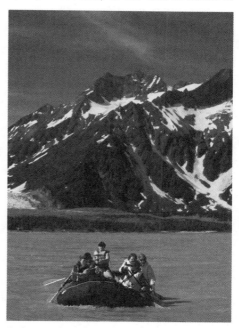

Rafters make their way down the spectacular Alsek-Tatshenshini rivers. (Karen Jettmar)

RIVER OF ICE: THE TATSHENSHINI-ALSEK

In early July, seven of us rendezvoused at Dalton Post on the Haines Highway. We were going to follow the Tatshenshini, or Tat, as river runners refer to it, from the mountains of Yukon Territory to the Gulf of Alaska.

We pulled my two 16-foot Avon rafts from the truck and, with everyone's help, had the boats blown up and rigged in less than an hour. Three boatloads of paddle rafters from Whitehorse pulled in along the riverbank, having just run the upper Tat from Bear Flats, a popular day trip with an exciting whitewater canyon. "River's really high," one of the guides told us. "It's really churning through the canyon."

We ate dinner on the riverbank and watched the current race by. I felt excited but a bit anxious, as I always do before I wet the paddle or oar in a river. Within an hour of putting in on the Tat you enter an 8-mile-long whitewater canyon. From where we sat, the river didn't look very formidable, but I knew better. Every year people are stranded or die on the river because of poor planning, lack of experience or bad luck.

We began our trip after breakfast the next day, pushing out from the cottonwoods along the bank into the swift current. After a warm-up on the oars, we paused at Village Creek to zip up our rain gear, then pushed off again, entering the canyon.

We dropped into the boiling and churning river canyon. Whooping and hollering, we maneuvered around sharp turns and big rocks in boats that felt like bucking broncos. My hands never loosened their grip on the oars, and Denny bailed furiously. In what simultaneously felt like an eternity and a millisecond, we punched through the canyon, laughing, yelping, and high-fiving, having produced enough adrenaline to power a rocket launch.

We pulled out at Silver Creek to dry out our rain gear and soak up some sun. An emerald green river corridor enclosed us. Cottonwoods, aspen and willow grew along the riverbank, horsetail and cottongrass filled wetland meadows, and a field of dwarf fireweed bloomed before us.

After lunch, we continued downriver, stopping at a log cabin with beautiful dovetail joinery. This kind of craftsmanship is rarely found in the North Country anymore. A note posted on the door implored: "Do not break into this cabin unless you are in dire straits." We climbed back into our boats and drifted out of Yukon Territory and into British Columbia.

We camped that night on a sandy beach a hundred yards down from a tiny clearwater creek. The Tat is fed mostly by glacial streams and the water is milky gray, so a clear creek is a lucky find. (The best way to treat silty river water is to let it settle in a bucket overnight. By morning the water is clear and sweet.)

The third day, upriver winds hindered our progress, even though the river current clipped along at 7 to 10 mph. High water on the river was subsiding, leaving floating tangles of logs and trees. We set up camp below Sediments Creek. This is a prime camping spot on the river because of a nearby game trail which has become a major natural history interpretive trail. The trail leads through cottonwood and aspen forest, up through meadows of waist-high wildflowers to an open talus slope, and finally to a mosaic of green alpine meadows, stone outcrops and snow patches. The steep hike rewarded us with views down the broad, U-shaped valley and of the surrounding peaks of the Alsek Range.

We spent two days at our camp, watching golden eagles and kingfishers and exploring the upper reaches of the creek. I baked cornbread and chicken in a dutch oven in a small firepan-contained fire. A National Park Service regulation requires that fires only be built in firepans to prevent black fire rings scarring the land.

Below Sediments Creek, the river entered another canyon of stratified rock, where we counted a dozen eagles perched on sweepers and logjams. As we passed O'Connor River, where the river begins to braid, we came within a dozen feet of a cow moose standing on a gravel bar midstream. Suddenly, she leaped into the river and in a matter of seconds swam to the opposite shore. She emerged from the frigid water with legs lifted high and ears laid back, then trotted up the creek.

A day hike up Tat Creek reminded us that as you draw nearer the coast, travel off the river grows more difficult. Three experienced Southeast Alaska hikers in our group took off to climb through the narrow band of alder above the rocky creek bank to alpine terraces. First back was Tom, who emerged from the brush with tales of horror: 12-foot-high alders mixed with devil's club and head-high larkspur, and bear beds every 50 feet. Dave and Rick appeared minutes later with similar stories: bear signs everywhere in a near-impenetrable quagmire of vegetation.

As the Alsek poured into the Tatshenshini, we entered an amphitheatre of mountains with hanging glaciers draped over every peak. The river picked up volume, and silt sang on the bottoms of the boats as we rode through haystacks and chutes and over riffles, determined to stay in the deepest channel in the now very wide, very braided river. Jaegers, arctic terns and gulls wheeled overhead. Grizzly, wolf and moose tracks covered every beach we landed on. Soon, the river was more than two miles wide and felt more like the ocean, with its huge rolling swells.

Each day we devoured mounds of food and reluctantly moved into the tents at night, even though it never got dark. In Alsek Bay, we paddled among house-sized icebergs past Gateway Knob and camped near the face of the 5-mile-wide glacier, falling asleep to the rumble of calving ice. During the day we hiked glaciers, jumping over small crevasses and stepping around sinkholes, as we crisscrossed our way up the rivers of ice. Up the valley and off the ice we found meadows still emerging from winter's snow.

On our last day we rowed out into Alsek Lake for a view of the Fairweather Range. Then, dodging the icebergs headed downriver, we moved into the strong current, bucked through a couple of rapids, and before the afternoon was over reached Dry Bay. The river was about to enter the ocean, and we were back in civilization, so to speak—a rough airstrip and a small fish-processing plant. Soon our bush plane would carry us to Yakutat. We'd traversed 120 miles of Alaska and Canada, from the mountains to the sea.

—*Karen Jettmar, who lives in Anchorage, is a writer/photographer and a guide for Equinox wilderness trips. She is also author of* The Alaska River Guide: Canoeing, Kayaking and Rafting in the Last Frontier *(Alaska Northwest Books, 1993)*

Dry Bay, about 50 miles east of Yakutat and 110 miles northwest of Gustavus. Part of the river flows through Glacier Bay National Park and is under the jurisdiction of the National Park Service.

Due to a dramatic increase in river traffic, the Park Service is enforcing permit requirements on both the Alsek and Tatshenshini. Check with the National Park Service for details on permits for commercially guided trips and private tour groups.

Portions of the upper Alsek are considered dangerous, even for seasoned river runners. The entire Alsek River has been traveled by only a few parties. There is a 10-mile portage of Tweedsmuir Glacier, which crosses the river, approximately 140 miles downstream from the access point on the Dezedeash River near Haines Junction, YT. The entire Alsek River is 230 miles in length.

The section above Tweedsmuir Glacier is difficult Class IV white water, with high water volume and velocity. High winds and brown bears are other hazards. After the long, difficult portage the river still demands respect, but becomes broader and moves more slowly. This trip is a major undertaking not to be embarked upon lightly.

The Tatshenshini is floated each year by numerous raft and kayak parties, including many commercial groups. (See *River of Ice: The Tatshenshini-Alsek* this section for a description of one trip.) The best months are July and August. Access to the Tatshenshini is at the abandoned Dalton Post (turnoff at Milepost 104.2 from Haines on the Haines Highway), which once served as a way point on the famed Dalton Trail. Those running the river should have advanced to expert river skills and also be well versed in wilderness and survival skills, as the distances from the nearest communities are considerable. For pickup, arrangements should be made in advance with charter plane operators from Yakutat, Gustavus or Juneau, since communication from Dry Bay is limited.

The Tatshenshini route winds through 120 miles of rugged wilderness, judged by many to be some of the best in Alaska. The trip can take 11 to 12 days. Allow time for exploring the river-level glaciers and pristine country. Use caution as this is bear country.

Below Dalton Cache, there are several rapids rated Class III and IV. From there to near the confluence with the Alsek, the Tat-shenshini winds through numerous valleys where high winds can sometimes stall boat movement. There are some Class IV rapids in the lower reaches and a section near Tree Ash Corner that may need to be portaged. In the lower river, standing waves of 4 to 12 feet may be encountered. *CAUTION: At Gateway Knob, boaters should scout downriver for icebergs floating at the entrance of Alsek Lake. The bergs can prohibit boat passage.* The Tatshenshini joins the Alsek below Tweedsmuir Glacier. This area is used by many river runners in the summer and campers should be courteous. Leave campsites in their primitive state.

Chickamin-LeDuc-South Fork rivers. This river system, which offers excellent scenery, is located 45 miles northeast of Ketchikan within Misty Fiords National Monument. The Chickamin River heads at Chickamin Glacier and flows southwest 40 miles to Behm Canal. The LeDuc heads at a glacier in British Columbia and flows southwest 30 miles to the Chickamin. The South Fork Chickamin River heads at a glacier and flows west 18 miles to the Chickamin. Since these rivers are fed by alpine glaciers they are silty. Boaters should be alert for sweepers, logs and high water.

Brown bears inhabit this drainage. Fish include rainbow trout and several species of salmon.

Access is by riverboat, floatplane or helicopter from Ketchikan.

Chilkat-Klehini-Tsirku rivers. The 42-mile-long Klehini and the 25-mile-long Tsirku are tributaries to the Chilkat River, which enters salt water near Haines. These are swift rivers, but have no white water. Season of use is June to September. Rafts are recommended. The trip down the Klehini-Chilkat takes 4 to 6 hours. The trip down the Tsirku-Chilkat takes 1 to 2 days, allowing time to explore glaciers.

The Chilkat and Tsirku rivers flow through the Chilkat Bald Eagle Preserve. Many Haines residents use airboats on the rivers in summer.

Access to the Chilkat River is by car to Milepost 19 from Haines on the Haines Highway. Access to the Klehini River is by car to Milepost 26 on the Haines Highway. Access to the lower Tsirku is from a turnoff at Milepost 25 on the Haines Highway. Access to the Tsirku headwaters is by plane to LeBlondeau Glacier.

Stikine River. The Stikine, a National Wild and Scenic River, has headwaters in British Columbia and flows 400 miles through 2 Provincial parks and the Coast Range to salt water near Wrangell. The lower 130 miles of the river, from Telegraph Creek, BC, to Alaska tidewater, are used by many canoeists, kayakers and rafters. A 60-mile section above Telegraph Creek flows through the Grand Canyon of the Stikine and is considered unnavigable and dangerous.

The Stikine is multichanneled in the lower reaches and is heavily laden with silt throughout. Glaciers cover the mountains along the route and descend down to river level in some points along the side channels. Fish available in the Stikine include several species of trout and salmon.

The river's name is derived from a Tlingit name meaning "Great River." For centuries the river has been a highway for the coastal Indians to travel inland to fish or trade. Stern-wheel steamers ferried gold seekers to and from Alaska and Canada until 1916 along this route. Only one town, Telegraph Creek, is found along the entire river.

Access is from Wrangell, Petersburg or Telegraph Creek. Boaters can drive to Telegraph Creek via the all-weather Cassiar Highway, then the 75-mile Telegraph Creek Road. (The latter is not designed for large vehicles, has many hairpin turns and steep slopes, but offers spectacular scenery.) Other boaters use air charter services from Wrangell, Petersburg or Telegraph Creek for transportation to upstream put in sites. Charter boats from Wrangell also deliver some river runners. The river also can be accessed from Petersburg (Mile 35.5 of the Mitkof Highway) or from the Wrangell waterfront. Many rafters arrange for pickup from the Stikine flats by boat or plane.

The water level can change considerably in the Stikine, varying from 10 to 25 feet. The river can rise several feet in 1 day, so camping areas should be planned carefully. The river is runnable from May through October. Usually snow is off the ground by mid-May. The mosquitoes do not usually become bothersome until mid-June.

From Telegraph Creek the river can be floated or paddled in a few days. However, a trip of 7 to 10 days will allow river enthusiasts time to explore the sloughs, many of which lead to glaciers or fine fishing areas, and to soak in Chief Shakes Hot Springs. Several Forest Service recreation cabins along the river are available on a reservation basis (see Tongass National Forest Cabins in this section). No public-use cabins are located on the Canadian side.

Although the river flow is swift at various points, it is considered easy Class I or II. The Stikine drops 8 feet per mile. Boaters should, however, be alert for logjams along some of the side routes and sweepers and floating logs throughout. The water is extremely cold. Black and brown bears are common along the river. Deer, moose, wolves, beavers, mountain goats and bald eagles also may be seen.

The U.S. Forest Service has a $1 booklet, *Stikine River Canoe-Kayak Trails,* which shows the main and secondary river routes in the lower river where it divides into numerous channels. It shows tent spots, logjams and which routes are best at the varying water stages. The guide shows 3 routes for canoers and kayakers who wish to go upstream following eddies, tides and side sloughs to the Canadian border, about 35 miles from tidewater. But the guide also points out that lining will be necessary (for those going upriver) in several places where the water is too shallow or too swift. The booklet is available from the Forest Service in Wrangell (P.O. Box 51, Wrangell, AK 99929) or Petersburg (P.O. Box 1328, Petersburg, AK 99833).

Taku River. This river heads in Canada and flows southwest 54 miles into Taku Inlet, 20 miles northeast of Juneau. This silty river is rated moderately difficult. Usable in summer. Rafts and canoes used most often. Access is by boat or small plane from Juneau. Most float trips start at Canoe Corner in Canada.

Floaters should be alert for numerous jet and motorboats and numerous sweepers. This river offers excellent wildlife viewing, fishing, hunting and climbing areas.

Unuk River. This silty river heads in Canada on the east side of Mount Stoeckl and flows southwest 28 miles to the head of Burroughs Bay, 50 miles northeast of Ketchikan. The river is located within Misty Fiords National Monument. It can be floated in 1 to 2 days. Many old mining claims line the river and its small tributaries.

Access is by riverboat upriver or by floatplane to Border Lake in Canada or to other points on the river itself. One turn about one-third of the way down the river from the Canadian border may need to be portaged. The Unuk becomes braided near its outlet. Floaters should be alert for sweepers and logs. Huge and numerous brown bears inhabit this area. Fish in the river include rainbow, cutthroat and steelhead trout and pink, king, silver and chum salmon.

Sea Kayaking

The hundreds of miles of sheltered waterways in Southeast are ideal for sea kayaking. There are endless choices of routes for paddling, places to camp and wildly beautiful country to explore, all without encountering very many other humans. It is hard to paddle in Southeast without seeing whales, porpoises, eagles and ravens.

The solitude, rich wildlife and breathtaking scenery help compensate for the discomfort and inconvenience of wet, rainy weather that is as characteristic of the area as the solitude and beauty. The kayak's covered deck makes it the paddlecraft of choice here.

Boats can be carried aboard ferries of the Alaska State Ferry System which serves Southeast's communities. Tour operators offer drop-off services for kayakers and charter boats are also available for drop-offs and pickups. Flying in to remote spots by charter aircraft is suitable for folding boats only.

Hypothermia is the resident hazard to be reckoned with—more of a threat than the local bears. Water temperatures in the 40s

A kayaker takes in the view from Gull Island in Favorite Channel northwest of Juneau. (David Job)

quickly sap the energy of anyone who goes for a swim. It's important to have a reliable self-rescue system that works *fast*, and an extra set of dry clothes that mean comfort anywhere may mean survival here. Stormy weather combined with the remoteness of the area demand that kayakers be skilled, well equipped and prepared to wait out hazardous conditions. (See Boating in the GENERAL INFORMATION section for more about safety in the Alaskan environment.)

Locals and visitors alike go kayaking. Among the favorite put-in places are the following:

Gastineau Channel. Day-trippers enjoy paddling the northern portion of this channel from Auke Bay to downtown Juneau, with glaciers and mountains as a backdrop to the Mendenhall Wetlands State Game Refuge and the busy harbor scene. (The 19-mile-long water passage extends from Auke Bay south to Stephens Passage.) Kayak rentals and drop-off service are available locally. State ferries dock at Auke Bay, so if you have brought your own kayak, you can put in at the terminal and head down the channel for town. Remember that much of the shallow channel goes dry at low tide; it's easy to find yourself high and dry—and red-faced. North of Auke Bay you'll find a series of beautiful coves, popular with local kayakers for day trips and weekend outings. Berner's Bay, 34 miles northwest of Juneau on the east shore of Lynn Canal, is the northernmost of them. Easy paddling. Juneau is accessible by air and via the Alaska state ferry.

Glacier Bay. Unless you're into marathon paddling, plan to stay at least a week in Glacier Bay National Park and Preserve. Drop-off and pickup service can be arranged with tour boats based at Bartlett Cove. Rental kayaks available in Gustavus. First-time visitors often are surprised to find that upper reaches of the bay are not forested (because they so recently lay under glacial ice). Most motorized vessels head up the bay's longer west arm to Tarr and John Hopkins inlets. Guided kayak trips that concentrate on the east arm, Muir Inlet, are available. Easy to moderate difficulty. There is no state ferry service to Glacier Bay. There is ferry service to Hoonah, a small community on the northeast shore of Chichagof Island. From Hoonah it is a 20-mile paddle across Icy Strait to the entrance of Glacier Bay. Planes land at Gustavus, 9 miles away from the park; bus and taxi service to Glacier Bay. (See Glacier Bay National Park and Preserve for more information.)

Misty Fiords. A sheltered circle route out of Ketchikan makes this national monument popular with kayakers. A natural hot spring makes an appealing stop amid the scenic fjords. Kayak rentals, drop-offs, pickups and support services for kayakers available in Ketchikan. Easy to moderate difficulty. Access via Alaska Airlines, small air services and Alaska state ferry. (See Misty Fiords National Monument this section for more information.)

Outer Chichagof Island. Spectacular sunsets, beaches open to the ocean swells, and protected paddling in beautiful coves make this one of Southeast's great places for kayaking. At White Sulphur Springs you'll find a natural hot spring (attractively roofed by the Forest Service) where you can soak as the sun sinks into the open Pacific. Kayak rentals available in Sitka. This trip is not for novices, as exposed stretches of water can challenge the best. Access via Alaska Airlines, smaller air services and Alaska state ferry to Sitka; via smaller air services and Alaska state ferry (twice monthly in summer) to Pelican.

Point Adolphus. A point of land at the north end of Chichagof Island, in Icy Strait, this is the premier place for whale-watching at any time during the summer. It's not uncommon to see humpbacks feeding cooperatively with their unique bubble-net technique. Orcas and minke whales also frequent the rich feeding grounds. Easy paddling along the north shore of Chichagof Island. Access via Alaska state ferry to Hoonah.

Russell Fiord. Located 25 miles northeast of Yakutat, this estuary extends 25 miles to Disenchantment Bay at the head of Yakutat Bay. Kayakers fly in to Yakutat, then paddle up Yakutat Bay to Disenchantment Bay and enter Russell Fiord at the neck of the fiord. It is a long paddle. There is road access from Yakutat to a 3/4-mile portage to the head of Russell Fiord. (See Russell Fiord Wilderness Area this section for more information.)

Seymour Canal. An estuary on the east coast of Admiralty Island, this 40-mile-long canal offers fishing and wildlife viewing within Admiralty Island National Monument. Supervised brown bear viewing at Pack Creek. North end of the canal is a day's paddle south of Juneau via Oliver Inlet and a manually operated tram that makes for an easy portage of less than a mile. Easy paddling except for one exposed crossing between Juneau and Oliver Inlet. Drop-off and pickup service available in Juneau. (See Admiralty Island National Monument this section.)

Sitka Sound. A beautiful scattering of islands and semi-protected water draws daytrippers and overnighters from Sitka. Goddard Hot Springs to the south is a popular destination, as is Brent's Beach on the sound's western shore. Other attractions include beachcombing and bird refuge (San Lazario Island). Kayak rentals available in Sitka. Easy to moderate difficulty, depending on wind and ocean swells. Access via Alaska Airlines, smaller air services and Alaska state ferry to Sitka.

Tebenkof Bay and Kuiu Island. This major wilderness area draws kayakers with its wildlife, islands, and well-marked network of portages among the coves and bays. Easy paddling. Access via Alaska state ferry to Kake. (See Tebenkof Bay and Kuiu Island Wilderness Areas this section.)

Tracy Arm and Fords Terror. Located 50 miles south of Juneau, this dramatic wilderness area long has lured kayakers with its cascading waterfalls, steep-sided glacial fjords, glaciers, icebergs, abundant wildlife and the wild tidal exchange that frightened Ford out of his name. Moderate to easy paddling; main hazards are wind and limited haul-out sites. Drop-off and pickup service available in Juneau. (For more information, see Tracy Arm-Fords Terror Wilderness Area this section.)

Yakutat Bay. Wildlife abounds in this beautiful bay ringed with islands. Yakutat Bay is 18 miles across, extending southwest from Disenchantment Bay to the Gulf of Alaska, southeast of Malaspina Glacier. It is one of the few refuges for vessels along this stretch of coast. At its upper reaches it accesses Russell Fiord and Nunatak Fiord. The community of Yakutat is situated on Monti Bay on the southeast shore of Yakutat Bay. Yakutat Bay offers easy to moderate difficulty. Access via Alaska Airlines and smaller air carriers.

Sportfishing

About fishing in Southeast Alaska, the Dept. of Fish and Game has stated: "The wide range of species and availability is overwhelming and beyond the capability of most anglers to visit and test the waters." Fishermen are advised to identify whether they wish to fish freshwater or saltwater and their desired species.

A variety of species are available in Southeast. Salmon are the most popular sport fish; during the summer several communities sponsor derbies that offer prizes for the largest salmon caught.

The sheltered marine waters of Southeast are perhaps the best place in Alaska to fish for king salmon. These fish range from 10 to 50 pounds, which is trophy size, and can reach 90 to 100 pounds. Kings are present in southeastern Alaska marine waters all year. The best period for big fish, however, is from mid-April to mid-June when mature fish are moving through. "Feeders" or smaller kings up to 25 pounds are available throughout the remainder of the year. Preferred bait is trolled or drifted herring. Try the edges of reefs where they drop off into deep water.

Silver (coho) salmon are available from July through September; best month is August. Herring or large spoons are used for bait and flashers often are used for attraction. These flashy fighters usually run shallow, but do not necessarily follow shorelines. Silvers average 12 pounds, but can exceed 20 pounds.

Fishing for pink salmon is good during July and August. Pinks often follow the beach in schools as they swim toward their spawning streams. These fish are best if caught fresh from the sea. Use small, bright spoons (most fishermen use spinning gear) and keep the spoon or spinner moving and lively. These salmon average 3 or 4 pounds, but occasionally reach 10 pounds.

Chum and red (sockeye) salmon do not take bait in salt water nearly as well as other species of salmon. In freshwater streams, reds can be taken on small flies drifted slowly or on small spinning lures. Chum salmon are available in Southeast waters from July to September. They range from 2 to 15 pounds, but commercially caught chums have weighed in at 35 pounds. Red salmon are available in June and July. These are small salmon, commonly weighing 2 to 7 pounds (trophy size is anything over 10 pounds).

Other fish found in Southeast include halibut, which can weigh more than 300 pounds; rainbow trout and steelhead, which may tip the scales at 10 pounds and occasionally reach 20 pounds; Dolly Varden, which usually weigh 1 to 3 pounds (world's record is 8.07 pounds); cutthroat trout from 1 to 3 pounds, may reach 7 pounds; arctic grayling up to 2 pounds; and brook trout from 1 to 5 pounds. An isolated population of northern pike is found in the Pike Lakes system near Yakutat.

Since the majority of southeastern Alaska's best fish locations are accessible only by plane or boat, the availability and cost of a charter must also be considered. A charter flight can range in cost from $180 to $450 an hour, depending on the size of the plane. Charter planes are available in the larger communites, such as Ketchikan, Juneau, Sitka, etc. (See *Flying For Fish* this section for a description of one charter air trip experience.) Bare-boat charters are generally not available, but there are dozens of skippered boat fish charters to choose from in most Southeast communities.

In narrowing down their choices, fishermen might also consider whether or not a public-use cabin is available. Many of the Tongass National Forest cabins are located on fishing lakes. (See Cabins this section.)

For more information about fishing in Southeast consult the current sportfishing regulations or contact Alaska Dept. of Fish and Game, Sport Fish Division, P.O. Box 240020, Douglas, AK 99824; phone 465-4270.

For Juneau-Yakutat area (including Admiralty Island, Haines and Skagway): Area Management Biologist, Sport Fish Division, P.O. Box 240020, Douglas, AK 99824; phone 465-4270.

For Ketchikan-Petersburg-Wrangell area: Area Management Biologist, Sport Fish Division, 2030 Sea Level Dr., Suite 205, Ketchikan, AK 99901; phone 225-2859.

For Sitka area: Area Management Biologist, Sport Fish Division, 304 Lake St., Room 103, Sitka, AK 99835-0510; phone 747-5355.

Admiralty Island Fishing

Barlow Cove. A 4-mile-long cove located on the north end of the Mansfield Peninsula, 19 miles northwest of Juneau. Accessible by boat. Fish available: king salmon available all year but best for large fish May to June, use herring or spoons; silver salmon best in August, use herring or spoons; pink salmon July to August, use small spoons; chum salmon July to September, use spoons; Dolly Varden May to October, use bait, spinners, flies; cutthroat trout best mid- to late summer, use bait, spinners, flies; halibut available all year but season closed in January, best in summer, use bait or jigs; rockfish all year, best May to September, use smaller bait or jigs.

Chatham Strait. Located on the west side of Admiralty Island. Accessible by boat. Fish available: king salmon available all year but best for large fish May to June, use herring or spoons; silver salmon best in August, use herring or spoons; pink salmon July to August, use small spoons; Dolly Varden May to October, use bait, spinners, flies; cutthroat trout best mid- to late summer, use bait, spinners or flies; halibut available all year, season closed in January, best in summer, use bait; rockfish all year, best May to September, use smaller baits or jigs.

Doty Cove. Located on the northeast coast of the Glass Peninsula on the east side of Admiralty Island, 16 miles southeast of Juneau. Accessible by boat. Fish available: king salmon available all year but best for large fish May to June, use herring or spoons; silver salmon best in August, use herring or spoons; pink salmon July to August, use small spoons; chum salmon July to September, use spoons; Dolly Varden May to October, use bait, spinners, flies; halibut available all year but season closed in January, best in summer, use bait; rockfish all year, best May to September, use smaller baits or jigs.

Gambier Bay. Located on the southeast coast of Admiralty Island, 70 boat miles south of Juneau, 57 miles east of Sitka. Forest Service cabin available. Fish available: king salmon available all year but best for large fish May to June, use herring or spoons; silver salmon best in August, use herring or spoons; pink salmon July to August, use small spoons; Dolly Varden May to October, use bait, spinners, flies; halibut all year, season closed in January, best in summer, use bait.

Hasselborg Lake. An 8.5-mile-long lake located on central Admiralty Island, 17 miles northeast of Angoon, 37 air miles south of Juneau. Forest Service cabin and boat available. Accessible by floatplane. Fish available: cutthroat trout best May to September, use bait, spinners, flies; Dolly Varden best May to October, use bait, spinners, flies; kokanee best May to September, use spinners, eggs.

Jims, Davidson, Distin and Guerin lakes. Group of small lakes located on central Admiralty Island, 45 air miles south of Juneau. Forest Service cabins and boats available. Accessible by floatplane. Fish available: cutthroat trout best May to September, use bait, spinners, flies; Dolly Varden best May to October, use bait, spinners, flies; kokanee best May to September, use spinners, eggs.

Lake Florence. A 4-mile-long lake located on the west coast of Admiralty Island, 21 miles north of Angoon, 33 air miles southwest of Juneau. Forest Service cabin and boat available. Accessible by floatplane. Fish available: cutthroat trout best May to September, use bait, spinners, flies; Dolly Varden best May to October, use bait, spinners, flies.

Lake Kathleen. A 1.7-mile-long lake located on the west coast of Admiralty Island, 28 miles north of Angoon, 28 air miles southwest of Juneau. Forest Service cabin and boat available. Accessible by floatplane. Fish available: cutthroat trout best May to September, use bait, spinners, flies; Dolly Varden best May to October, use bait, spinners, flies.

Mitchell Bay. A 3.5-mile-wide bay located on west central Admiralty Island, 7 miles northeast of Angoon, 49 air miles south of Juneau. Accessible by floatplane from Juneau or boat from Angoon. Excellent spring sea-run cutthroat trout fishing, use bait, spinners, flies. Other fish: Dolly Varden May to October, use bait, spinners; king salmon available all year but best for large fish May to June, use herring or spoons; silver salmon best in August, use herring or spoons; pink salmon July to August, use small spoons.

Mole Harbor. A 1.3-mile-wide bay located on Seymour Canal on the southeast side of Admiralty Island, 24 air miles northeast of Angoon, and 45 air miles or 70 boat miles south of Juneau. Accessible by floatplane or boat. Fish available: king salmon available all year but best for large fish May to June, use herring or spoons; silver salmon best in August, use herring or spoons; pink salmon July to August, use small spoons; chum salmon July to September, use spoons; Dolly Varden May to October, use bait, spinners, flies; cutthroat trout best mid- to late summer, use bait, spinners or flies; steelhead April to June, use spoons, eggs.

Piling Point. Located on Stephens Passage on the northeast coast of the Mansfield Peninsula on Admiralty Island, 14 miles west of Juneau. Accessible by boat. Fish available: king salmon available all year but best for large fish May to June, use herring or spoons; silver salmon best in August, use herring or spoons; pink salmon July to August, use small spoons; chum salmon July to September, use spoons; red salmon best in June, use spoons; Dolly Varden May to October, use bait, spinners, flies; halibut all year, season closed in January, best in summer, use bait or jigs; rockfish all year, best May to September, use smaller baits or jigs.

Pleasant Bay Creek. Located on Admiralty Island on the west shore of Seymour Canal, 2 miles southeast of Mole Harbor, 50 air miles and 65 boat miles south of Juneau. Popular for steelhead, April to June, use spoons, eggs. Other fish: silver salmon best in August, use herring or spoons; pink salmon July to August, use small spoons;

Dolly Varden May to October, use bait, spinners, flies; cutthroat trout best mid- to late summer, use bait, spinners or flies.

Point Arden. Located on Admiralty Island in Stephens Passage on the north coast of Glass Peninsula, 13 miles southeast of Juneau. Accessible by boat. Fish available: king salmon available all year but best for large fish May to June, use herring or spoons; silver salmon best in August, use herring or spoons; pink salmon July to August, use small spoons; chum salmon July to September, use spoons; Dolly Varden May to October, use bait, spinners, flies; halibut all year, season closed in January, best in summer, use bait or jigs; rockfish all year, best May to September, use smaller baits or jigs.

Point Retreat. Located on the north tip of the Mansfield Peninsula on Admiralty Island, 20 miles northwest of Juneau. Accessible by boat. Lighthouse on point. Fish available: king salmon available all year but best for large fish May to June, use herring or spoons; silver salmon best in August, use herring or spoons; pink salmon July to August, use small spoons; chum salmon July to September, use spoons; red salmon best in June, use spoons; Dolly Varden May to October, use bait, spinners, flies; halibut all year, season closed in January, best in summer, use bait; rockfish all year, best May to September, use smaller baits or jigs.

Pybus Bay. A 4-mile-wide bay located on the east coast of Admiralty Island, 53 miles east of Sitka, 80 boat miles south of Juneau. Accessible by boat. Good summer fishing for large king salmon (smaller kings available all year), use herring or spoons. Other fish: silver salmon best in August, use herring or spoons; pink salmon July to August, use small spoons; Dolly Varden May to October, use bait, spinners, flies; halibut all year, season closed in January, best in summer, use bait.

Thayer Lake. A 7-mile-long lake located on west central Admiralty Island, 10 miles northeast of Angoon, 42 air miles south of Juneau. Lodge with all facilities on lake. Fish available: cutthroat trout and kokanee best May to September, use bait, spinners, flies; Dolly Varden best May to October, use bait, spinners, flies.

Youngs Lake. A 6-mile-long lake located on the northeast end of Admiralty Island, 15 miles south of Juneau by boat or plane. Forest Service cabins with boats available. Fish available: rainbow trout all year, best May to September, use flies, lures, bait; steelhead April to June, use spoons, eggs; cut-throat trout best May to September, use bait, spinners, flies; Dolly Varden best May to October, use bait, spinners, flies; silver salmon use spoons.

Haines-Skagway Area Fishing

Chilkat Inlet. Inlet extends 16 miles south from the mouth of the Chilkat River, 1 mile southwest of Haines, to Lynn Canal. Accessible by boat; beach access from Mud Bay Road (get directions locally.) Chilkat State Park provides camping sites, picnic areas, boat launch, small dock and trails and is a good access point for the inlet. Fish available: king salmon best early summer, use herring or spoons; silver salmon September to October, use herring or spoons; pink salmon July to August, use small spoons; Dolly Varden May to October, use bait, spinners, flies; cutthroat trout best mid- to late summer, use bait, spinners, flies; halibut all year, season closed in January, best in summer particularly between Kochu Island and Lehunua Island, use bait; rockfish all year, best May to September, use smaller baits or jigs. Also shrimp and crab (July through November; 2 to 5 pounds) in Kalhagu Cove.

Chilkat Lake. A 6-mile-long lake located 3 miles south of Klukwan and about 15 miles northwest of Haines. Accessible by boat or air from Haines or Skagway. Fish available: cutthroat trout best May to September, use flies; Dolly Varden May to October, use bait, spinners, flies; silver salmon September to October, use spoons; red salmon June, use spoons or flies.

Chilkat River. Flows into Chilkat Inlet 1 mile southwest of Haines. Accessible by boat from Haines or from the Haines Highway, which parallels the river at intervals. Fish available: king salmon best in the inlet in June, use herring or spoons; silver salmon September to October, use herring or spoons; chum salmon September to October, use spoons; red salmon best in June, use spoons or flies; Dolly Varden May to October, use bait, spinners, flies; cutthroat trout best mid- to late summer, use bait, spinners, flies.

Chilkoot Inlet. Extends 20 miles to Lynn Canal about 5 miles north of Haines, 32 miles south of Skagway. Accessible by boat from Haines or Skagway; beach access from Lutak Road from Haines. Fish available: king salmon best early summer; use herring or spoons; silver salmon September to October, use herring or spoons; pink salmon July to

August, use small spoons; Dolly Varden May to October, use bait, spinners, flies; cutthroat trout best mid- to late summer, use bait, spinners, flies; halibut all year, season closed in January, best in summer, use bait; rockfish all year, best May to September, use smaller baits or jigs.

Chilkoot Lake. A 3.6-mile-long lake near the mouth of the Chilkoot River, 12 miles southwest of Skagway. Accessible by boat or from the end of Lutak Road north of Haines. Fish available: silver salmon September to October, use spoons or flies; pink salmon best July to August, use small spoons; chum salmon September to October, use spoons; red salmon best in June, use spoons or flies; Dolly Varden May to October, use bait, spinners, flies; cutthroat trout best mid- to late summer, use bait, spinners, flies. A 32-unit camping site, located on the southern shore of the lake, is part of the Chilkoot Lake State Recreation Area.

Chilkoot River. Flows into Lutak Inlet at the head of Chilkoot Inlet, 12 miles southwest of Skagway. Accessible by boat from Haines or Skagway or from the end of Lutak Road from Haines. Fish available: silver salmon September to October, spoons or flies; pink salmon best July to August, use small spoons; chum salmon September to October, use spoons; red salmon best in June, use spoons or flies; Dolly Varden May to October, use bait, spinners, flies; cutthroat trout best mid- to late summer, use bait, spinners, flies.

Dewey Lakes. Lower Dewey Lake, 0.8 mile long, located 2 miles southeast of Skagway. Upper Dewey Lake, 0.4 mile long, located 1.4 miles east of Lower Dewey Lake. Lower lake accessible by 0.8-mile trail from the end of 4th Street in Skagway; trail continues to upper lake. Fish available: brook trout 8 to 14 inches, June to September, use salmon eggs, small spinners and flies; Dolly Varden May to October, use bait, spinners, flies.

Herman Lake. A 0.3-mile-long lake located on Herman Creek, southwest of Haines. Accessible via trail from Porcupine Road (get directions locally.) Fish available: grayling best July to September, use flies.

Letnikof Cove. Located on the southwest coast of the Chilkat Peninsula in Chilkat Inlet south of Haines. Accessible by boat or from Mile 5 Mud Bay Road (get directions locally). Fish available: king salmon best early summer, use herring or spoons; silver salmon September to October, use herring or spoons; pink salmon July to

August, use small spoons; chum salmon 8 to 17 pounds, September to early November, fish from banks with flashing lures; Dolly Varden May to October, use bait, spinners, flies; cutthroat trout best mid- to late summer, use bait, spinners, flies; halibut all year, season closed in January, best in summer, use bait; rockfish all year, best May to September, use smaller baits or jigs.

Lost Lake. Located 10 miles from Skagway by road at head of Taiya Inlet, then a strenuous 2-mile hike westerly to lake. Rainbow trout present, use flies, lures, bait. Use of guide recommended; information available locally.

Lutak Inlet. Located north of Haines on Lutak Road. Chilkoot River empties into head of Lutak Inlet. Accessible by boat or from Lutak Road, which parallels the inlet. Fish available: pink salmon July and early August, use small spoons; red salmon June to August, use spoons or flies; ocean run Dolly Varden June through November, use bait, spinners, flies; king salmon best early summer, use herring or spoons; silver salmon September to October, use herring or spoons; cutthroat trout best mid- to late summer, use bait, spinners, flies; halibut all year, season closed in January, best in summer, use bait; rockfish all year, best May to September, use smaller baits or jigs.

Lynn Canal. A 60-mile-long channel that extends south from Chilkat Island near Haines to Chatham Strait, 22 miles west of Juneau. Accessible by boat. Weather and water conditions should be watched closely in this large open waterway. Fish available: king salmon best early summer, use herring or spoons; silver salmon September to October, use herring or spoons; pink salmon July to August, use small spoons; Dolly Varden June to November, use bait, spinners; cutthroat trout best mid- to late summer, use bait, spinners or flies; halibut all year, season closed in January, best in summer, use bait or jigs; rockfish all year, best May to September, use smaller baits or jigs.

Skagway Harbor. Located in front of the city of Skagway. Accessible from shore or by boat. Fish available: Dolly Varden 18 to 20 inches, May to June, use spoons, good fishing from shore; king salmon 8 to 30 pounds all summer, use herring. Windy weather often dangerous for small boats.

Taiya Inlet. Extends 13 miles south from the mouth of the Taiya River to Chilkoot Inlet, 12 miles south of Skagway. Accessible by boat or from shore in Skagway. Fish available: king salmon best early summer, use herring or spoons; silver salmon September to October, use herring or spoons; pink salmon July to August, use small spoons; Dolly Varden 18 to 20 inches, May to June, use Dardevles and other spoons, good fishing from shore; cutthroat trout best mid- to late summer, use bait, spinners, flies; halibut all year, season closed in January, best in summer, use bait; rockfish all year, best May to September, use smaller baits or jigs.

Taiya River. Enters Taiya Inlet 1 mile north of Dyea Point, 2 miles northwest of Skagway. Accessible by boat or from the bridge on Dyea Road. Fish available: silver salmon September to October, use spoons; pink salmon July to August, use small spoons; chum salmon September to October, use spoons; Dolly Varden 18 to 20 inches, May to June, use Dardevles and other spoons.

Walker Lake. A 1-mile-long lake located southwest of Haines. Accessible by floatplane or by trail off Porcupine River Road (ask directions locally). Fish available: grayling best July to September, use flies.

Juneau Area Fishing

Aaron Island. A 0.4-mile-long island located in Favorite Channel, 17 miles northwest of Juneau. Accessible by boat. Fish available: king salmon best May to June, use herring or spoons; silver salmon best in August, use herring or spoons; pink salmon July to August, use small spoons; chum salmon July to September, use spoons; Dolly Varden May to October, use bait, spinners; halibut all year, season closed in January, best in summer, use bait or jigs; rockfish all year, best May to September, use smaller baits or jigs.

Antler Lake. Located on the mainland 11 miles east of Berners Bay and 39 air miles northwest of Juneau. Accessible by floatplane. No facilities. Grayling to 18 inches, best July to September, use flies.

Auke Bay. Located 11.8 miles north of Juneau on the Glacier Highway. Fishing primarily accessible by boat. Fish available: king salmon available all year but best for large fish May to June, use herring or spoons; silver salmon best in August, use herring or spoons; pink salmon July to August, use small spoons; chum salmon July to September, use spoons; Dolly Varden May to October, use bait, spinners, flies; halibut available all year, season closed in January, best in summer, use bait or jigs; rockfish all year, best May to September, use smaller baits or jigs.

Benjamin Island. A 1.5-mile-long island located on the east shore of Favorite Channel, 25 miles northwest of Juneau. Accessible by boat. Fish available: king salmon available all year but best for large fish May to June, use herring or spoons; silver salmon best in August, use herring or spoons; pink salmon July to August, use small spoons; Dolly Varden May to October, use bait, spinners, flies; halibut available all year, season closed in January, best in summer, use bait or jigs; rockfish all year, best May to September, use smaller baits or jigs.

Berners Bay. A 3-mile-wide bay located on the east shore of Lynn Canal, 34 miles northwest of Juneau. Accessible by boat or from the end of the Glacier Highway (39.6 miles north of Juneau). Fish available: king salmon available all year but best for large fish May to June, use herring or spoons; silver salmon best in August, use herring or spoons; pink salmon July to August, use small spoons; chum salmon July to September, use spoons; Dolly Varden May to October, use bait, spinners, flies; cutthroat trout best mid- to late summer, use bait, spinners or flies; halibut available all year, season closed in January, best in summer, use bait; rockfish all year, best May to September, use smaller baits or jigs.

The Breadline. A 1.2-mile-long stretch of cliffs on the east shore of Favorite Channel, just north of Tee Harbor, 17 miles northwest of Juneau. Accessible by boat. Fish available: king salmon available all year but best for large fish May to June, use herring or spoons; silver salmon best in August, use herring or spoons; pink salmon July to August, use small spoons; chum salmon July to September, use spoons; Dolly Varden May to October, use bait, spinners, flies; cutthroat trout best mid- to late summer, use bait, spinners or flies; halibut available all year, season closed in January, best in summer, use bait; rockfish all year, best May to September, use smaller baits or jigs.

Dupont. Located on the northeast shore of Gastineau Channel, 7.5 miles southeast of Juneau. Accessible by boat or by trail 1.5 miles from the end of Thane Road. Fish available: king salmon available all year but best for large fish May to June, use herring or spoons; silver salmon best in August, use herring or spoons; pink salmon July to August, use small spoons; chum salmon July to September, use spoons; Dolly Varden May to October, use bait, spinners, flies; halibut available all year, season closed in January, best in summer, use bait or jigs; rockfish all year, best May to September, use smaller baits or jigs.

Echo Cove. A 1.8-mile-long cove located on the south shore of Berners Bay, 34 miles northwest of Juneau. Accessible by boat or from the end of the Glacier Highway (39.6 miles north of Juneau). Fish available: king salmon available all year but best for large fish May to June, use herring or spoons; silver salmon best in August, use herring or spoons; pink salmon July to August, use small spoons; chum salmon July to September, use spoons; Dolly Varden May to October, use bait, spinners, flies; cutthroat trout best mid- to late summer, use bait, spinners or flies; halibut available all year, season closed in January, best in summer, use bait or jigs; rockfish all year, best May to September, use smaller baits or jigs.

Favorite Reef. Located off the southwest coast of Shelter Island, about 28 miles north of Juneau. Accessible by boat. Fish available: king salmon available all year but best for large fish May to June, use herring or spoons; silver salmon best in August, use herring or spoons; pink salmon July to August, use small spoons; chum salmon July to September, use spoons; Dolly Varden May to October, use bait, spinners, flies; halibut available all year, season closed in January, best in summer, use bait or jigs; rockfish all year, best May to September, use smaller baits or jigs.

Gastineau Channel. A 19-mile-long channel that lies between Juneau on the mainland and Douglas Island. Accessible by boat from Juneau or Douglas or from access points along area roads to shorelines. Fish available: king salmon available all year but best for large fish May to June, use herring or spoons; silver salmon best in August, use herring or spoons; pink salmon July to August, use small spoons; chum salmon July to September, use spoons; Dolly Varden May to October, use bait, spinners, flies; halibut available all year, season closed in January, best in summer, use bait or jigs; rockfish all year, best May to September, use smaller baits or jigs.

Hand Trollers Cove. Located on the northeast side of Shelter Island north of Juneau. Accessible by boat. Fish available: king salmon available all year but best for large fish May to June, use herring or spoons; silver salmon best in August, use herring or spoons; pink salmon July to August, use small spoons; Dolly Varden May to October, use bait, spinners, flies; cutthroat trout best mid- to late summer, use bait,

spinners, flies; halibut available all year, season closed in January, best in summer, use bait or jigs; rockfish all year, best May to September, use smaller baits or jigs.

Icy Point. Located on the south shore of Douglas Island, 9 miles south-southwest of Juneau. Accessible by boat. Fish available: king salmon available all year but best for large fish May to June, use herring or spoons; silver salmon best in August, use herring or spoons; pink salmon July to August, use small spoons; chum salmon July to September, use spoons; Dolly Varden May to October, use bait, spinners, flies; halibut available all year, season closed in January, best in summer, use bait; rockfish all year, best May to September, use smaller baits or jigs.

Lena Point. Located at the south entrance to Lena Cove on Favorite Channel, 14 miles northwest of Juneau. Accessible by boat. Wreck of *Princess Kathleen* down below. Fish available: king salmon available all year but best for large fish May to June, use herring or spoons; silver salmon best in August, use herring or spoons; pink salmon July to August, use small spoons; chum salmon July to September, use spoons; Dolly Varden May to October, use bait, spinners, flies; halibut available all year, season closed in January, best in summer, use bait or jigs; rockfish all year, best May to September, use smaller baits or jigs.

Lincoln Island. A 4.7-mile-long island located in Lynn Canal, 24 miles northwest of Juneau. Accessible by boat. Fish available: king salmon available all year but best for large fish May to June, use herring or spoons; silver salmon best in August, use herring or spoons; pink salmon July to August, use small spoons; Dolly Varden May to October, use bait, spinners, flies; cutthroat trout best mid- to late summer, use bait, spinners or flies; halibut available all year, season closed in January, best in summer, use bait or jigs; rockfish all year, best May to September, use smaller baits or jigs.

Marmion Island. A 0.2-mile-wide island located southeast of Douglas Island at the south end of Gastineau Channel, 9 miles southeast of Juneau. Accessible by boat. Fish available: king salmon available all year but best for large fish May to June, use herring or spoons; silver salmon best in August, use herring or spoons; pink salmon July to August, use small spoons; chum salmon July to September, use spoons; Dolly Varden May to October, use bait, spinners, flies; halibut available all year, season closed in January, best in summer, use bait or jigs; rockfish all year, best May to September, use smaller baits or jigs.

Middle Point. Located in Stephens Passage on the west coast of Douglas Island, 9 miles southwest of Juneau. Accessible by boat. Fish available: king salmon available all year but best for large fish May to June, use herring or spoons; silver salmon best in August, use herring or spoons; pink salmon July to August, use small spoons; chum salmon July to September, use spoons; Dolly Varden May to October, use bait, spinners, flies; halibut available all year, season closed in January, best in summer, use bait or jigs; rockfish all year, best May to September, use smaller baits or jigs.

North Pass. A passage between Lincoln Island and the north end of Shelter Island, 22 miles northwest of Juneau. Accessible by boat. Fish available: king salmon available all year but best for large fish May to June, use herring or spoons; silver salmon best in August, use herring or spoons; pink salmon July to August, use small spoons; chum salmon July to September, use spoons; Dolly Varden May to October, use bait, spinners, flies; halibut available all year, season closed in January, best in summer, use bait or jigs; rockfish all year, best May to September, use smaller baits or jigs.

Outer Point. Located on the west tip of Douglas Island in Stephens Passage, 4 miles northwest of Middle Point and 10 miles west of Juneau. Accessible by boat or by trail from end of North Douglas Highway. Fish available: king salmon available all year but best for large fish May to June, use herring or spoons; silver salmon best in August, use herring or spoons; pink salmon July to August, use small spoons; chum salmon July to September, use spoons; Dolly Varden May to October, use bait, spinners, flies; halibut available all year, season closed in January, best in summer, use bait or jigs; rockfish all year, best May to September, use smaller baits or jigs.

Peterson Lake. A 0.9-mile-long lake located 17 miles northwest of Juneau. Accessible by 4.5-mile trail beginning at Mile 24.4 on the Glacier Highway north of Juneau. Fish available: Dolly Varden best May to October, use bait, spinners, flies; rainbow trout, best May to September, use flies, lures, bait.

Point Bishop. Located at the south end of Taku Inlet on Stephens Passage, 4.8 miles southeast of Dupont and 12 miles southeast of Juneau. Accessible by boat or by trail 8 miles from the end of Thane Road. Fish available: king salmon available all year but

best for large fish May to June, use herring or spoons; silver salmon best in August, use herring or spoons; pink salmon July to August, use small spoons; chum salmon July to September, use spoons; Dolly Varden May to October, use bait, spinners, flies; halibut available all year, season closed in January, best in summer, use bait or jigs; rockfish all year, best May to September, use smaller baits or jigs.

Point Hilda. Located in Stephens Passage on the south shore of Douglas Island, 7 miles southwest of Juneau. Accessible by boat. Fish available: king salmon available all year but best for large fish May to June, use herring or spoons; silver salmon best in August, use herring or spoons; pink salmon July to August, use small spoons; chum salmon July to September, use spoons; Dolly Varden May to October, use bait, spinners, flies; halibut available all year, season closed in January, best in summer, use bait or jigs; rockfish all year, best May to September, use smaller baits or jigs.

Point Louisa. Located on the east shore of Stephens Passage, west of Auke Bay, 12 miles northwest of Juneau. Accessible by boat or short trail from Forest Service campground. This is a favorite spot to fish from shore. Fish available: king salmon available all year but best for large fish May to June, use herring or spoons; silver salmon best in August, use herring or spoons; pink salmon July to August, use small spoons; chum salmon July to September, use spoons; Dolly Varden May to October, use bait, spinners, flies; halibut available all year, season closed in January, best in summer, use bait; rockfish all year, best May to September.

Point Salisbury. Located on Stephens Passage at the south end of Gastineau Channel, 2.5 miles west of Point Bishop, 10 miles southwest of Juneau. Accessible by boat or the Dupont-Point Bishop trail from the end of Thane Road. Fish available: king salmon available all year but best for large fish May to June, use herring or spoons; silver salmon best in August, use herring or spoons; pink salmon July to August, use small spoons; chum salmon July to September, use spoons; Dolly Varden May to October, use bait, spinners, flies; halibut available all year, season closed in January, best in summer, use bait or jigs; rockfish all year, best May to September, use smaller baits or jigs.

Salmon Creek and Reservoir. Reservoir located 3 miles up trail beginning at Mile 2.3 on the Old Glacier Highway north of Juneau. Trail follows creek. Fish available in creek: pink and chum salmon July to August, use small spoons; Dolly Varden May to October, use bait, spinners, flies. Fish available in reservoir: eastern brook trout May to September, use eggs, spinners or flies.

Shrine of St. Therese. Located on Favorite Channel, 18 miles north of Juneau. Accessible by boat or from Mile 23.3 on the Glacier Highway. This is a favorite spot to fish from shore. Fish available: king salmon available all year but best for large fish May to June, use herring or spoons; silver salmon best in August, use herring or spoons; pink salmon July to August, use small spoons; Dolly Varden May to October, use bait, spinners, flies; cutthroat trout best mid- to late summer, use bait, spinners or flies.

South Shelter Island. South end of 9-mile-long island located between Favorite and Saginaw Channels, 15 miles northwest of Juneau. Accessible by boat. Fish available: king salmon available all year but best for large fish May to June, use herring or spoons; silver salmon best in August, use herring or spoons; pink salmon July to August, use small spoons; chum salmon July to September, use spoons; Dolly Varden May to October, use bait, spinners, flies; halibut available all year, season closed in January, best in summer, use bait or jigs; rockfish all year, best May to September, use smaller baits or jigs.

Stephens Passage. Located along the west side of Douglas Island, about 11 miles west of Juneau. Accessible by boat. Fish available: king salmon available all year but season is closed April 15 through June 14 in Stephens Passage and Taku Inlet, use herring or spoons; silver salmon best in August, use herring or spoons; pink salmon July to August, use small spoons; Dolly Varden May to October, use bait, spinners, flies; halibut available all year, season closed in January, best in summer, use bait or jigs; rockfish all year, best May to September, use smaller baits or jigs.

Tee Harbor. A 1.5-mile-long T-shaped bay on the east shore of Favorite Channel, 0.4 mile north of Lena Cove and 15 miles northwest of Juneau. Accessible by boat or from 18.5 Mile Glacier Highway north of Juneau. Fish available: king salmon available all year but best for large fish May to June, use herring or spoons; silver salmon best in August, use herring or spoons; pink salmon July to August, use small spoons; Dolly Varden May to October, use bait, spinners, flies; cutthroat trout best mid- to late summer, use bait, spinners or flies; halibut

available all year, season closed in January, best in summer, use bait or jigs.

Turner Lake. A 9-mile-long lake located 1 mile east of Taku Inlet, 25 air miles east of Juneau. Accessible by boat and trail from salt water or by floatplane. Two Forest Service cabins and boats available. Fish available: cutthroat trout May to September, use bait, spinners, flies; Dolly Varden May to October, use bait, spinners, flies; kokanee, May to September, use spinners, eggs.

White Marker. Located on the west coast of Douglas Island, south of Middle Point. Accessible by boat. Fish available: king salmon available all year but best for large fish May to June, use herring or spoons; silver salmon best in August, use herring or spoons; pink salmon July to August, use spoons; chum salmon July to September, use spoons; Dolly Varden May to October, use bait, spinners, flies; halibut available all year, season closed in January, best in summer, use bait or jigs; rockfish all year, best May to September, use smaller baits or jigs.

Windfall Lake. A 0.8-mile-long lake located south of the terminus of Herbert Glacier, 18 miles northwest of Juneau. Accessible by 4-mile trail from the end of Windfall Lake Road (no sign) at Mile 27.4 of the Glacier Highway north of Juneau. No facilities. Fish available: silver salmon September to October, use spoons; red salmon June to July, use flies; Dolly Varden May to October, use bait, spinners, flies; cutthroat trout May to September, use bait, spinners, flies.

Ketchikan Area Fishing

Bakewell Lake. A 4.3-mile-long lake located on the mainland east of East Behm Canal, 39 air miles southeast of Ketchikan. Accessible by floatplane or by boat to Smeaton Bay, then a 0.8-mile hike to the lake. Fish available: silver salmon late August to early September, use flies, spoons or spinners; cutthroat trout best May to September, use bait, spinners, flies; Dolly Varden best May to October, use bait, spinners, flies.

Bell Island. An 8.7-mile-long island located north of Revillagigedo Island in North Behm Canal, 45 miles north of Ketchikan. Accessible by boat or floatplane. Private resort (not open to the public) at hot springs on southwest end of island. Area considered a "hot spot" for king salmon, best mid-May to mid-June, use herring or spoons. Other fish: silver salmon best in August, use herring or spoons; pink salmon July to August, use small spoons; chum salmon July to September, use spoons; Dolly Varden May to October, use bait, spinners, flies; cutthroat trout best mid- to late summer, use bait, spinners, flies; steelhead April to June and October to November, use spoons, eggs; halibut available all year, season closed in January, best in summer, use bait; rockfish all year, best May to September, use smaller baits or jigs.

Big Goat Lake. A 2.4-mile-long lake located 38 air miles northeast of Ketchikan. Accessible by floatplane. Recreation cabin and skiff available. Fish available: grayling up to 2 pounds, use small flies, shrimp or spinners.

Blank Inlet. Extends northwest 3.3 miles off Nichols Passage on the east coast of Gravina Island, 7 miles south of Ketchikan by boat. Fish available: king salmon best May to June, use herring or spoons; silver salmon best in August, use herring or spoons; pink salmon July to August, use small spoons; chum salmon July to September, use spoons; halibut available all year, season closed in January, best in summer, use bait; rockfish all year, best May to September, use smaller baits or jigs; lingcod all year, best in summer, use herring.

Caamano Point. Located at the south tip of the Cleveland Peninsula between Behm Canal and Clarence Strait, 18 miles northwest of Ketchikan by boat. Use of guide recommended. Fish available: king salmon best May to June, use herring or spoons; silver salmon best in August, use herring or spoons; pink salmon July to August, use small spoons; chum salmon July to September, use spoons; halibut available all year, season closed in January, best in summer, use bait; rockfish all year, best May to September, use smaller baits or jigs; lingcod all year, best in summer, use herring.

Chasina Point. Located on the east coast of Prince of Wales Island between Cholmondeley Sound and Clarence Strait, 22 miles southwest of Ketchikan by boat. Use of guide recommended. Fish available: king salmon best May to June, use herring or spoons; silver salmon best in August, use herring or spoons; pink salmon July to August, use small spoons; chum salmon July to September, use spoons; halibut available all year, season closed in January, best in summer, use bait; rockfish all year, best May to September, use smaller baits or

jigs; lingcod all year, best in summer, use herring.

Clover Pass. Located at Potter Point on Revillagigedo Island, 11 miles northwest of Ketchikan by road or boat. Commercial lodges and marina available. Fish available: king salmon best May to June, use herring or spoons; silver salmon best in August, use herring or spoons; pink salmon July to August, use small spoons; chum salmon July to September, use spoons; halibut available all year, season closed in January, best in summer, use bait; rockfish all year, best May to September, use smaller baits or jigs; lingcod all year, best in summer, use herring.

Ella Lake. A 5-mile-long lake located on Revillagigedo Island, 24 air miles northeast of Ketchikan. Floatplane access. Forest Service cabin and skiff on lake. Fishing for cutthroat trout May to September and Dolly Varden May to October, use bait, spinners, flies.

Fish Creek. Located at the head of Thorne Arm, 21 miles east of Ketchikan by boat, or 18 miles by floatplane. Forest Service cabin available. Fish available: silver salmon best in August, use herring or spoons; pink salmon July to August, use small spoons; red salmon June, use spoons; Dolly Varden May to October, use bait, spinners, flies; cutthroat trout best mid- to late summer, use bait, spinners, flies; steelhead April to June and October to November, use spoons, eggs; rainbow trout May to September, use flies, lures, bait.

Grace Lake. Located inland from the east coast of Revillagigedo Island, 30 air miles from Ketchikan. Accessible by floatplane. Fishing for eastern brook trout, May to September, use eggs, spinners.

Grindall Island. A 1.5-mile-long island located between Clarence Strait and Kasaan Bay on the east coast of Prince of Wales Island, 20 miles northwest of Ketchikan by boat. Use of guide recommended. Fish available: king salmon best May to June, use herring or spoons; silver salmon best in August, use herring or spoons; pink salmon July to August, use small spoons; chum salmon July to September, use spoons; halibut available all year, season closed in January, best in summer, use bait; rockfish all year, best May to September, use smaller baits or jigs; lingcod all year, best in summer, use herring.

Humpback Lake. A 6.3-mile long lake located above Mink Bay in Boca de Quadra, 48 miles southeast of Ketchikan. Forest Service cabin and skiff and commercial lodge available. Fish available: cutthroat trout best May to September, use bait, spinners, flies; Dolly Varden best May to October, use bait, spinners, flies; grayling use small flies, shrimp or spinners.

Karta River. Located above Karta Bay on Prince of Wales Island, 42 air miles northwest of Ketchikan. Accessible by boat or floatplane. Forest Service cabins available. Fish available: silver salmon best in July and August, use flies or spoons; pink salmon July to August, use small spoons; red salmon in June and July, use spoons; chum salmon July to September, use spoons; Dolly Varden May to October, use bait, spinners, flies; cutthroat trout best mid- to late summer, use bait, spinners, flies; excellent for steelhead April to June, use spoons, eggs; rainbow trout May to September, use flies, lures, bait.

Klawock Creek. Heads in Klawock Lake on the west coast of Prince of Wales Island. Accessible by boat, state ferry or floatplane. Excellent spring run of steelhead, use spoons or eggs, also good October to November. Excellent silver salmon late August to September, use flies, spinners or spoons. Closed to red salmon fishing.

LeDuc Lake. A 2.5-mile-long lake located above the Chickamin River, 49 air miles northeast of Ketchikan. Accessible by float-plane. Fishing for rainbow trout May to September, use flies, lures, bait.

Manzanita Lake. Located above Manzanita Bay, 28 air miles northeast of Ketchikan. Forest Service cabin and skiff available. Fish available: cutthroat trout best May to September, use bait, spinners, flies; Dolly Varden best May to October, use bait, spinners, flies; kokanee best May to September, use spinners or eggs.

Manzoni Lake. A 2.4-mile-long lake located on the mainland, south of Walker Cove at the head of Granite Creek. Accessible by floatplane. Fishing for grayling up to 2 pounds, use small flies, shrimp or spinners.

McDonald Lake. Located 45 air miles north of Ketchikan above Yes Bay. Accessible by floatplane or boat and trail. Forest Service cabin and skiff available. Fish available: silver salmon best in September, use flies or spoons; red salmon August, use flies or spoons; Dolly Varden May to October, use bait, spinners, flies; cutthroat trout best mid- to late summer, use bait, spinners, flies; excellent for steelhead April to June, use spoons, eggs; rainbow trout May to September, use flies, lures, bait.

Naha River. Located on Revillagigedo

Island, 21 miles north of Ketchikan by boat. Also accessible by floatplane. Forest Service cabins and skiffs available; trail follows river. Fish available: silver salmon best in September, use flies or spoons; pink salmon July to August, use small spoons; red salmon June, use flies or spoons; chum salmon July to September, use spoons; Dolly Varden May to October, use bait, spinners, flies; cutthroat trout best mid- to late summer, use bait, spinners, flies; steelhead April to June and October to November, use spoons, eggs; rainbow trout May to September, use flies, lures, bait.

Orchard Lake. A 3.5-mile-long lake located on the northwest coast of Revillagigedo Island above Shrimp Bay, 32 air miles north of Ketchikan. Forest Service cabin available. Fish available: cutthroat trout best May to September, use bait, spinners, flies; Dolly Varden best May to October, use bait, spinners, flies.

Patching Lake. A 3.3-mile-long lake located in the course of the Naha River, 6 miles east of Loring, 19 air miles north of Ketchikan. Accessible by floatplane. Forest Service cabin available. Fish available: cutthroat trout best May to September, use bait, spinners, flies; Dolly Varden best May to October, use bait, spinners, flies.

Point Alava. Located on the south tip of Revillagigedo Island, 20 miles southeast of Ketchikan. Accessible by boat. Fish available: king salmon best May to June, use herring or spoons; silver salmon best in August, use herring or spoons; pink salmon July to August, use small spoons; chum salmon July to September, use spoons; halibut season closed in January, best in summer, use bait; rockfish all year, best May to September, use smaller baits or jigs; lingcod all year, best in summer, use herring.

Point Sykes. Located at the east point of the entrance to Behm Canal, 25 miles southeast of Ketchikan. Accessible by boat. Use of a guide is recommended. Fish available: king salmon best May to June, use herring or spoons; silver salmon best in August, use herring or spoons; pink salmon July to August, use small spoons; chum salmon July to September, use spoons; halibut season closed in January, best in summer, use bait; rockfish all year, best May to September, use smaller baits or jigs; lingcod all year, best in summer, use herring.

Reflection Lake. A 4.5-mile-long lake located above Short Bay on the Cleveland Peninsula, 46 air miles north of Ketchikan. Forest Service cabin and skiff available. Fish available: silver salmon best in July and August, use flies or spoons; cutthroat trout best mid- to late summer, use bait, spinners, flies.

Salt Lagoon Creek. Located at the head of George Inlet, 22 miles north of Ketchikan. Accessible by boat. Fish available: silver salmon best in July and August, use flies or spoons; pink salmon July to August, use small spoons; Dolly Varden May to October, use bait, spinners, flies; cutthroat trout best mid- to late summer, use bait, spinners, flies.

Silvis Lake. Located 1.5 miles from the end of the Tongass Highway, north of Ketchikan. Accessible by trail. Fish available: rainbow trout May to September, use flies, lures, bait.

Snow Lake. A 0.9-mile-long lake located on Revillagigedo Island near the head of the Naha River, 7 miles northeast of Loring. Accessible by floatplane. Fish available: grayling up to 2 pounds, use small flies, shrimp or spinners.

Unuk River. Located at the head of Burroughs Bay, 50 miles north of Ketchikan. Accessible by floatplane or boat. Fish available: silver salmon best in August and September, use flies or spoons; pink salmon July to August, use small spoons; chum salmon July to September, use spoons; Dolly Varden May to October, use bait, spinners, flies; cutthroat trout best mid- to late summer, use bait, spinners, flies.

Vallenar Point. Located at the north tip of Gravina Island, 11 miles northwest of Ketchikan. Accessible by boat. Fish available: king salmon best May to June, use herring or spoons; silver salmon best in August, use herring or spoons; pink salmon July to August, use small spoons; chum salmon July to September, use spoons; halibut season closed in January, best in summer, use bait; rockfish all year, best May to September, use smaller baits or jigs; lingcod all year, best in summer, use herring.

Walker Lake. Located on the mainland 3.5 miles east of Walker Cove in Misty Fiords National Monument; drains southwest into Rudyerd Bay. Accessible by floatplane. Fishing for rainbow trout May to September, use flies, lures, bait.

Wilson Lake. A 5-mile-long lake located on the mainland; drained by the Wilson River into Wilson Arm. Accessible by floatplane. Has 2 Forest Service cabins and skiffs. Fishing for Dolly Varden May to October, use bait, spinners, flies; cutthroat trout best mid- to late summer, use bait, spinners, flies.

Yes Bay. Located in North Behm Canal, 44 miles north of Ketchikan by boat. Also accessible by floatplane. Commercial resort available. Fish available: king salmon best May to June, use herring or spoons; silver salmon best in August and September, use herring or spoons; pink salmon July to August, use small spoons; chum salmon July to September, use spoons; halibut season closed in January, best in summer, use bait; rockfish all year, best May to September, use smaller baits or jigs; lingcod all year, best in summer, use herring.

Petersburg Area Fishing

Alecks Creek. Located on Kuiu Island on the east side of Elena Bay in Tebenkof Bay Wilderness Area. Accessible by boat or floatplane. The creek is part of the Alecks Creek Portage Trail. Fish available: steelhead April to May; red salmon July; silver, pink and chum salmon mid-August to October.

Cape Strait. Located off the Kupreanof Island shoreline, 12 miles north of Petersburg. Accessible by boat. Fish available: king salmon best May to June, use herring or spoons; silver salmon best in August, use herring or spoons; halibut season closed in January, best in summer, use bait; rockfish all year, best May to September, use smaller baits or jigs.

Castle River. Located on the west shore of Duncan Canal, 22 miles southwest of Petersburg. Accessible by floatplane or boat. Fish available: silver salmon best in August, use flies, bait or spoons; pink salmon July to August, use small spoons; chum salmon July to September, use spoons; Dolly Varden May to October, use bait, spinners, flies; cutthroat trout best mid- to late summer, use bait, spinners, flies; steelhead April to June and October to November, use spoons, eggs; rainbow trout May to September, use flies, lures, bait.

DeBoer Lake. A 1.5-mile-long lake located 20 air miles north of Petersburg. Accessible by floatplane. Fishing for rainbow trout midsummer to September, use flies, lures, bait.

Duncan Salt Chuck. Located at the head of Duncan Canal, 28 miles by boat west of Petersburg. Fish available: silver salmon best in August, use bait, flies or spoons; Dolly Varden May to October, use bait, spinners, flies; cutthroat trout best mid- to late summer, use bait, spinners, flies; steelhead April to June and October to

November, use spoons, eggs; rainbow trout May to September, use flies, lures, bait.

Frederick Sound. Located northeast of Petersburg. Accessible by boat. Fish available: king salmon best May to June, use herring or spoons; silver salmon best in August, use herring or spoons; halibut season closed in January, use bait; rockfish all year.

Kadake Creek. Located on Kuiu Island, 60 miles by boat or 20 minutes by floatplane west of Petersburg. Forest Service cabin available. Excellent spring cutthroat trout fishery. Other fish: silver salmon best in August, use bait, flies or spoons; pink salmon July to August, use small spoons; chum salmon July to September, use spoons; Dolly Varden May to October, use bait, spinners, flies; steelhead April to June and October to November, use spoons, eggs; rainbow trout May to September, use flies, lures, bait.

Kah Sheets Creek. Located on Kupreanof Island 21 miles southwest of Petersburg by boat. Also accessible by floatplane. Forest Service cabin on Kah Sheets Lake and on the bay. Fish available: silver salmon best in August, use bait, flies or spoons; pink salmon July to August, use small spoons; chum salmon July to September, use spoons; red salmon best in July, use flies and small spoons; Dolly Varden May to October, use bait, spinners, flies; steelhead April to June, use spoons, eggs; cutthroat trout best mid- to late summer, use bait, spinners, flies.

Petersburg Creek. Located across Wrangell Narrows from Petersburg by boat. Boats and accommodations available in Petersburg. Fish available: silver salmon best in August, use bait, flies or spoons; pink salmon July to August, use small spoons; chum salmon July to September, use spoons; red salmon best in June and July, use flies and small spoons; Dolly Varden May to October, use bait, spinners, flies; steelhead April to June and October to November, use spoons, eggs; cutthroat trout best mid- to late summer, use bait, spinners, flies; rainbow trout May to September, use flies, lures, bait.

Petersburg Lake. Located 4.5 miles by trail up Petersburg Creek (see above). Forest Service cabin and boat available. Fish available: silver salmon best in August, use bait, flies or spoons; Dolly Varden May to October, use bait, spinners, flies; cutthroat trout best mid- to late summer, use bait, spinners, flies.

Security Bay. Located on the north coast of Kuiu Island, 60 miles west of Petersburg by boat. Fish available: king salmon best May to June, use herring or spoons; silver salmon best in August, use herring or spoons; halibut season closed in January, best in summer, use bait; rockfish all year, best May to September, use smaller baits or jigs; lingcod all year, best in summer, use herring.

Swan Lake. Located on the mainland above Thomas Bay, 18 air miles north of Petersburg. Forest Service cabin and boat available. Excellent fall fishery for rainbow trout use flies, lures, bait.

Thomas Bay. Located 15 miles north of Petersburg on mainland. Two Forest Service cabins. Accessible by boat or plane. Fish available: king salmon best May to June, use herring or spoons; halibut season closed in January, best in summer, use bait.

Towers Lake. Located on Kupreanof Island 20 air miles west of Petersburg. Accessible by floatplane. Fish available: Dolly Varden May to October, use bait, spinners, flies; cutthroat trout best mid- to late summer, use bait, spinners, flies.

Sitka Area Fishing

Avoss Lake. A 1.7-mile-long lake located on central Baranof Island 29 air miles southeast of Sitka. Accessible by floatplane. Forest Service cabin available. Good fishery for rainbow trout May to September, use flies, lures, bait.

Baranof Lake. A 2.5-mile-long lake located on the east coast of Baranof Island, 18 miles west of Sitka. Accessible by floatplane and road. Forest Service cabin available. Fishing for cutthroat trout best mid- to late summer, use spinners, flies.

Davidof Lake. A 1.7-mile-long lake located on southcentral Baranof Island, 35 air miles southeast of Sitka. Accessible by floatplane. Forest Service cabin available. Good fishery for rainbow trout May to September, use flies, lures, bait.

Gar Lake. Located on Baranof Island, 39 air miles southeast of Sitka. Accessible by floatplane. Good fishing for rainbow trout May to September, use flies, lures, bait.

Goulding Lakes. Located on Chichagof Island, 61.3 air miles north of Sitka. Accessible by floatplane. Forest Service cabin available. Fish available: Dolly Varden May to October, use bait, spinners, flies; cutthroat trout best mid- to late summer, use spinners, flies.

Green Lake. A 2-mile-long lake located near the head of Silver Bay, 10 miles southeast of Sitka. Accessible by floatplane or boat and short hike. Fish available: brook trout best May to September, use eggs or spinners.

Heart Lake. A 0.1-mile-wide lake located 3.5 miles east of Sitka. Accessible by trail from Blue Lake Road. Fishing for brook trout best May to September, use eggs or spinners.

Katlian River. Located on the west coast of Baranof Island, 11 miles northeast of Sitka. Accessible by boat. Fish available: silver salmon best in August, use herring or spoons; pink salmon July to August, use small spoons; chum salmon July to September, use spoons; Dolly Varden May to October, use bait, spinners, flies.

Khvostof Lake. A 1.4-mile-long lake located on southcentral Baranof Island, 39 air miles southeast of Sitka. Accessible by floatplane. Fishing for rainbow trout May to September, use flies, lures, bait.

Lake Eva. A 1.7-mile-long lake located on the north coast of Baranof Island, 20 air miles northeast of Sitka. Forest Service cabin and boat available; cabin equipped for the handicapped. Accessible by floatplane. Excellent fishing for Dolly Varden May to October, use spinners, flies; cutthroat trout best mid- to late summer, use spinners, flies. Lake also has silver and red salmon and steelhead.

Lake Plotnikof. A 4-mile-long lake located on southcentral Baranof Island, 38 air miles southeast of Sitka. Accessible by floatplane. Forest Service cabin and boat available. Good fishing for rainbow trout May to September, use flies, lures, bait.

Little Lake Eva. Located on the north coast of Baranof Island, 20 air miles northeast of Sitka. Accessible by trail from Lake Eva. Excellent fishing for cutthroat trout best mid- to late summer, use spinners, flies.

Nakwasina River. Located 15 miles north of Sitka. Accessible by boat. Excellent sea-run Dolly Varden fishing in July and August. Other fish: silver salmon best in August, use herring or spoons; pink salmon July to August, use small spoons; chum salmon July to September, use spoons.

Pass Lake. Located on southeastern Baranof Island, 33 air miles southeast of Sitka. Accessible by floatplane. Fishing for rainbow trout May to September, use flies, lures, bait.

Port Banks. Located on the west coast of Baranof Island, 35 air miles southeast of Sitka. Accessible by boat or floatplane. No facilities. Excellent fishery for silver salmon late July and August, use herring or spoons.

Redoubt Lake. A 9.5-mile-long lake located at the head of Redoubt Bay on the west coast of Baranof Island, 12 miles south of Sitka. Accessible by floatplane or boat. Forest Service cabin available. Fish available: silver salmon best in August, use herring or spoons; pink salmon July to August, use small spoons; chum salmon July to September, use spoons; red salmon best in June, use spoons; Dolly Varden May to October, use bait, spinners, flies.

Rezanof Lake. A 3-mile-long lake located on southcentral Baranof Island, 40 air miles southeast of Sitka. Accessible by floatplane. Forest Service cabins and skiff available. Fishing for rainbow trout May to September, use flies, lures, bait.

Salmon Lake. A 1-mile-long lake located at the southeast end of Silver Bay, 11 miles by boat south of Sitka. Accessible by boat and 1-mile hike to lake. Skiff available. Fish available: silver salmon best in August, use herring or spoons; pink salmon July to August, use small spoons; chum salmon July to September, use spoons; red salmon best in June, use spoons; Dolly Varden May to October, use spinners, flies; steelhead April to June, use spoons; cutthroat trout best mid- to late summer, use spinners, flies.

Sitka Sound. Located in front of the city of Sitka. Accessible by boat. Boats, tackle and guides available in Sitka. Good fishing for king salmon best May to June, use herring or spoons; silver salmon best in September, use herring or spoons; pink salmon July to August, use small spoons; Dolly Varden May to October, use bait, spinners, flies; halibut all year except January when the fishery is closed, best in summer, use bait; rockfish all year, best May to September, use smaller baits or jigs; lingcod all year, best in summer, use herring.

Sitkoh Lake Creek. Located on the southeast end of Chichagof Island. Accessible by floatplane to lake (see below). Good steelhead fishing in April and May. Other fish: silver salmon best in August, use herring or spoons; Dolly Varden May to October, use spinners, flies; cutthroat trout best mid- to late summer, use spinners, flies.

Sitkoh Lake. A 2.5-mile-long lake located on the southeast tip of Chichagof Island, 30 air miles northeast of Sitka. Forest Service cabin and boat available. Excellent fishery for silver salmon best in August, use spoons;

cutthroat trout best mid- to late summer, use spinners, flies; cutthroat trout and Dolly Varden year-round.

Thimbleberry Lake. A 0.2-mile-wide lake located 3 miles east of Sitka. Accessible by trail from Blue Lake Road. Fishing for brook trout best May to September, use eggs or spinners.

Wrangell Area Fishing

Anan Creek. Located 40 miles south of Wrangell by boat or floatplane. Forest Service cabin available. Fish available: silver salmon best in August, use bait, flies or spoons; pink salmon July to August, use small spoons; chum salmon July to September, use spoons; Dolly Varden May to October, use bait, spinners, flies; steelhead April to June, use spoons, eggs; cutthroat trout best mid- to late summer, use bait, spinners, flies; rainbow trout May to September, use flies, lures, bait.

Anan Lake. A 2.5-mile-long lake located 30 air miles southeast of Wrangell. Accessible by floatplane. Forest Service cabin available. Fishing for silver and pink salmon, rainbow trout and Dolly Varden.

Greys Pass. Located 8 miles northwest of Wrangell by boat. Fish available: king salmon best before April 15, use herring or spoons, closed to salmon fishing from April 16 to June 15; halibut available all year but season closed in January, best in summer, use bait.

Harding River. Located in Bradfield Canal 35 air miles southeast of Wrangell. Accessible by boat or plane. Forest Service cabin available. Fish available: silver salmon best in August; chum salmon (possible record-size chum in this system) best in late June and July; Dolly Varden May to October; steelhead trout in spring; cutthroat trout mid- to late summer.

Kunk Lake. A 1.5-mile-long lake located on the northeast coast of Etolin Island, 14 miles south of Wrangell. Accessible by boat and short hike or by floatplane. Forest Service cabin and boat available. Fish available: silver salmon best in August, use bait, flies or spoons; Dolly Varden May to October, use bait, spinners, flies; steelhead April to June, use spoons, eggs; cutthroat trout best mid- to late summer, use bait, spinners, flies.

Luck Lake. Located inland from Luck Point on Prince of Wales Island, 35 miles southwest of Wrangell. Accessible by floatplane or road from Coffman Cove. Fish

available: silver salmon best in August, use bait, flies or spoons; pink salmon July to August, use small spoons; chum salmon July to September, use spoons; red salmon best in June and July, use flies and small spoons; Dolly Varden May to October, use bait, spinners, flies; steelhead April to June and October to November, use spoons, eggs; cutthroat trout best mid- to late summer, use bait, spinners, flies; rainbow trout May to September, use flies, lures, bait.

Marten Lake. Located 2 miles north of Bradfield Canal, 25 air miles southeast of Wrangell. Accessible by floatplane. Forest Service cabin and boat available. Fish available: Dolly Varden May to October, use bait, spinners, flies; cutthroat trout best mid- to late summer, use bait, spinners, flies; kokanee May to September, use spinners, eggs; steelhead available below lake toward mouth of Martin River, April to late May; coho available below lake toward mouth of Martin River, August and September.

Salmon Bay Lake. A 3-mile-long lake located on the north coast of Prince of Wales Island, 40 miles west of Wrangell. Accessible by floatplane. Forest Service cabin available. Fish available: silver salmon best in August, use bait, flies or spoons; pink salmon July to August, use small spoons; chum salmon July to September, use spoons; red salmon best in June, use spoons and flies; Dolly Varden May to October, use bait, spinners, flies; steelhead April to June and October to November, use spoons, eggs; cutthroat trout best mid- to late summer, use bait, spinners, flies; rainbow trout May to September, use flies, lures, bait.

Stikine River. Located north of Wrangell. Accessible by boat or floatplane. Guide recommended. Forest Service cabins available. Excellent fishery. Fish available: silver salmon best in August, use bait, flies or spoons; pink salmon July to August, use small spoons; chum salmon July to September, use spoons; Dolly Varden May to October, use bait, spinners, flies; steelhead April to June and October to November, use spoons, eggs; cutthroat trout best mid- to late summer, use bait, spinners, flies; whitefish all year, use flies or eggs. Fishery is closed to king salmon all year.

Thoms Lake. A 1.5-mile-long lake located on the southwest coast of Wrangell Island, 18 miles south-southeast of Wrangell. Accessible by boat and 2-mile hike, road and 0.5-mile hike, or by floatplane. Forest Service cabin available. Fish available: silver salmon best in August, use bait, flies or spoons; red salmon best in June, use flies or spoons; steelhead April to June, use spoons, eggs; cutthroat trout best mid- to late summer, use bait, spinners, flies.

Virginia Lake. A 2-mile-long lake located 8 miles east of Wrangell. Accessible by boat and short hike or floatplane. Forest Service cabin and boat available. Fish available: red salmon best in June, use spoons or flies; Dolly Varden May to October, use bait, spinners, flies; cutthroat trout best mid- to late summer, use bait, spinners, flies.

Wrangell Harbor. Located in front of the city of Wrangell. Accessible by skiff. Fish available: king salmon best April to June, use herring or spoons; silver salmon best in August, use herring or spoons; halibut available all year but season closed in January, best in summer, use bait; rockfish all year, best May to September, use smaller baits or jigs.

Zimovia Strait. Located west of Wrangell; separates Wrangell Island from Etolin and Woronkofski islands. A "hot spot" for king salmon best mid-May to mid-June, use trolled or drifted herring or spoons.

King salmon are one of the most popular sportfish in Alaska. (David Job)

Yakutat Area Fishing

Akwe River. Heads at Akwe Lake and flows southwest 20 miles to the Gulf of Alaska, 32 air miles southeast of Yakutat. Private airstrip. Excellent fishing at fork with Ustay River in fall. Fish available: king salmon best early summer, use spoons or flies; silver salmon mid-August, use spoons; red salmon best in June, use small spoons; Dolly Varden May to October, use bait, spinners, flies; cutthroat trout best mid- to late summer, use bait, spinners, flies.

Ankau Lagoon. An estuary system located 2.6 miles west of Yakutat. Accessible by boat or from bridge at Mile 4 White Alice Road. Fish available: silver salmon September to October, use spoons; red salmon best in June, use small spoons; Dolly Varden May to October, use bait, spinners, flies; cutthroat trout best mid- to late summer, use bait, spinners, flies.

Coast Guard Lake. Located about 4 miles southwest of Yakutat. Accessible from Beach Road or by canoe or trail from Kardy Lake (see Kardy Lake entry). Fish available: silver salmon September to October, use spoons; pink salmon July to August, use small spoons; red salmon best in June, use small spoons; Dolly Varden May to October, use bait, spinners, flies; cutthroat trout best mid- to late summer, use bait, spinners, flies.

Gulf of Alaska. Coastline located southeast of Yakutat. Accessible by boat, plane to beaches or via White Alice, Cannon Beach and Lost River roads. Fish available: king salmon available all year but best for large fish in early summer, use herring or spoons; silver salmon best August to September, use herring or spoons; pink salmon July to August, use small spoons; Dolly Varden May to October, use bait, spinners, flies; cutthroat trout best mid- to late summer, use bait, spinners, flies; halibut available all year, season closed in January, best in summer, use bait or jigs; rockfish all year, best May to September, use smaller baits or jigs.

Italio River. Heads 3 miles southeast of Harlequin Lake and flows west 20 miles to the Gulf of Alaska, 28 miles southeast of Yakutat. Accessible by boat or floatplane. Fish available: silver salmon September to October, use lures; Dolly Varden May to October, use bait, spinners, flies; cutthroat trout best mid- to late summer, use bait, spinners, flies. Smelt run in this river.

Kardy Lake. A 1-mile-long lake located on the Phipps Peninsula, 1.1 miles southeast of Ocean Cape and 3.4 miles southwest of Yakutat. Accessible by boat through the Ankau Lagoon system. Fish available: silver salmon September to October, use spoons; red salmon best in June, use small spoons; Dolly Varden May to October, use bait, spinners, flies; cutthroat trout best mid- to late summer, use bait, spinners, flies.

Monti Bay. A 3.5-mile-long bay located on the southeast shore of Yakutat Bay west of Yakutat. Accessible primarily by boat or from shorelines. Fish available: king salmon available all year but best for large fish in early summer, use herring or spoons; silver salmon best September to October, use herring or spoons; pink salmon July to August, use small spoons; Dolly Varden May to October, use bait, spinners, flies; cutthroat trout best mid- to late summer, use bait, spinners, flies; halibut available all year, season closed in January, best in summer, use bait or jigs; rockfish all year, best May to September, use smaller baits or jigs.

Ocean Cape. Located on the Gulf of Alaska at the west end of Phipps Peninsula, 4.6 miles west of Yakutat. Accessible by boat or White Alice Road. Fish available: king salmon available all year but best for large fish in early summer, use herring or spoons; silver salmon best September to October, use herring or spoons; pink salmon July to August, use small spoons; Dolly Varden May to October, use bait, spinners, flies; cutthroat trout best mid- to late summer, use bait, spinners, flies; halibut available all year, season closed in January, best in summer, use bait; rockfish all year, best May to September, use smaller baits or jigs.

Situk River. Heads at Situk Lake and flows southwest 18 miles to the Gulf of Alaska, 11 miles southeast of Yakutat. Accessible by boat, floatplane or Situk Road. One of the top fishing spots in Alaska, spring and fall. Fish available: king salmon best early summer, use spoons; outstanding for silver salmon mid-August to October, use spoons; pink salmon July to August, use small spoons; red salmon late June through August, use spoons or flies; Dolly Varden May to October, use bait, spinners, flies; cutthroat trout best mid- to late summer, use bait, spinners, flies; excellent runs of steelhead April to May and October to November, use spoons, eggs. Smelt run in this river.

Summit Lake. A 0.8-mile-long lake located on the Phipps Peninsula, 2.8 miles southwest of Yakutat. Accessible by canoe or trail from Kardy Lake (see above). Fish available: silver salmon September to October, use spoons; red salmon best in June, use small spoons; pink salmon July to August, use small spoons; Dolly Varden May to October, use bait, spinners, flies; cutthroat trout best mid- to late summer, use bait, spinners, flies.

Yakutat Bay. Located west of Yakutat. Accessible primarily by boat. Fish available: king salmon available all year but best for large fish in early summer, use herring or spoons; silver salmon late August through September, use herring or spoons; pink salmon August, use small spoons; Dolly Varden May to October, use bait, spinners, flies; cutthroat trout best mid- to late summer, use bait, spinners, flies; halibut available all year, season closed in January, best in summer, use bait or jigs; rockfish all year, best May to September, use smaller baits or jigs.

SPECIAL FEATURES

Anan Bear Observatory

Managed by the U.S. Forest Service, Anan (pronounced an-an) Bear Observatory is located 35 miles southeast of Wrangell. It is accessible by boat or plane only. During July, August and early September, visitors can watch bears catch pink salmon headed for the salmon spawning grounds. Bald eagles and seals also may be seen feeding on the fish.

The only facilities at the observatory are a concrete observation building and a public-use recreation cabin nearby. A ranger is on duty in the summer. Check with the Wrangell Visitors Bureau about local tours to Anan Bear Observatory available from Wrangell. Charter service to the observatory may be arranged, but there is no scheduled tour boat service. For more information, contact the Wrangell ranger district office, phone 874-2323.

Basket Bay

Located on Chichagof Island on the west side of Chatham Strait northwest of Angoon, 8 miles south of the mouth of Tenakee Inlet. The bay is exposed to the southeast, has a rocky bottom and depths of 12 to 40 fathoms. According to the *United States Coast Pilot*, it is not recommended as an anchorage. The midchannel course up the bay is clear. This is a scenic spot for

sightseeing or fishing. Lots of silver salmon enter this bay in August; use herring or spoons. A flat extends about 400 yards into the head of the bay from the mouth of Kook Creek, a large stream that enters the bay through a limestone cliff. The stream goes underground 3 times between the bay and Kook Lake, which has fishing for cutthroat and Dolly Varden trout. There is an old, unmaintained trail between Basket Bay and Kook Lake; the trail does not extend to the Forest Service cabin at the west end of the lake. Related USGS Topographic map: Sitka C-4.

Chilkoot Trail

This 33-mile-long trail climbs Chilkoot Pass (elev. 3,739 feet) to Lake Bennett, following the historic route of the gold seekers of 1898. The trail is jointly managed by the Canadian Parks Service and the U.S. National Park Service.

Permits are required for hiking the Chilkoot Trail. Permits are free and there are currently no daily use limits. Hiking parties are limited to groups of 12 to prevent overcrowding at campsites. Groups should contact the Park Service ahead of time to schedule a departure date.

To reach the trailhead, drive out Dyea Road 6.7 miles. The trail begins at a bridge over the Taiya River across from the Dyea townsite. Little is left of Dyea, which once rivaled Skagway as the largest town in Alaska, except some foundation ruins and several rows of piling stubs, remains of a nearly 2-mile-long wharf that once extended to salt water. Most of the buildings were torn down and the lumber used elsewhere. Of interest is the Slide Cemetery where some 60 victims of an avalanche in April 1898 lie buried, poignant reminders of the hardships and tragedies of the gold rush. Cab service is available in Skagway to and from the trailhead.

The 33-mile trail is marked and has designated campsites and several day-use shelters. The hike is arduous, usually taking 3 to 5 days. There are many opportunities for exploring which will be missed if the trip is rushed. This is not a trail that offers wilderness solitude. More than 2,600 hikers make the trip each year. Peak season is mid-July to mid-August. Detailed information and maps of the trail are included in *A Hiker's Guide to the Chilkoot Trail*, available from the National Park Service visitor center in Skagway. Information and trail registration are also available from the ranger station on Dyea Road near the trailhead.

The Chilkoot Trail is managed as a historic backcountry trail and follows the original trail where feasible. It is an outdoor museum. Do not disturb or remove any historical artifacts. All artifacts are protected under state, federal and provincial laws. The National Park Service requests you "leave nothing but footprints and take nothing but photographs."

The Park Service cautions that hikers must be properly equipped and prepared to be self-sufficient on this trail. Weather conditions can change rapidly from hour to hour, especially in the summit area. You must be prepared for cold temperatures, snow, rain, fog and wind. An inch of rain in 24 hours is not uncommon. Trail conditions below tree line are often rough, with deep mud, standing water, slick rocks and roots making footing tricky. Conditions along the 8 miles of trail above tree line are even more severe. High winds, driving rain, low temperatures, heavy fog and rocky terrain may make hiking this section extremely difficult. The Park Service recommends that hiking gear include a tent with waterproof rain fly, sturdy hiking boots, rain gear, wool or pile clothing, sunglasses, glacier cream and a small stove with adequate fuel (there is no wood in the summit area and campfires are not allowed on the Canadian portion). Camping gear and supplies are available in Skagway (Skagway Sports Emporium). Camping is permitted only in the 9 designated areas. If you bring a dog, it must be on a leash. If there are bears in any of the areas you travel, you do not want your dog chasing them—or bringing them back to you. Bear sightings should be reported to rangers at Sheep Camp or Lindeman (on the trail), or at Dyea or Skagway.

Current trail conditions are available from the ranger stations in Skagway, Dyea or Sheep Camp. Canadian Parks Service wardens are available for assistance at Lindeman. Northbound hikers must clear Canadian customs, (403) 821-4111, at Fraser. Southbound hikers must be sure to check in with U.S. customs in Skagway. Contact the Park Service for more information.

The White Pass & Yukon Route railroad offers daily service for Chilkoot Trail hikers from Lake Bennett to the customs office at Fraser. From Fraser hikers can travel the 28 miles back to Skagway on the regular train. For information on the White Pass & Yukon

Route, contact the White Pass Depot, P.O. Box 435, Skagway, AK 99840; phone 983-2217 in Skagway, or toll-free in the United States (800) 343-7373.

The Park Service is preparing a new General Management Plan for the park, which could result in fairly significant changes for Chilkoot hikers. They are considering moving some campgrounds, limiting the number of hikers, and dealing with the deteriorating day-use shelters. Input from the public is welcomed.

The Chilkoot Trail has been called "the longest museum in the world." Along the way you'll see historic ruins and artifacts from the gold rush. Highlights include the following:

Mile 4.9 Finnegan's Point. This is reputed to be the site of a bridge across a creek built by Pat Finnegan and his 2 sons. The Finnegans charged a toll for use of the bridge until they were overwhelmed by the hordes of gold seekers. A restaurant operated intermittently at the site.

Mile 7.8 Canyon City. In 1897 and 1898 this was the fourth largest settlement along the trail after Dyea, Lindeman and Sheep Camp. A year later it was gone.

Mile 10.5 Pleasant Camp. Site of a toll bridge (long since washed out) and a restaurant in 1897. As the best level spot north of Canyon City, it was a popular campsite.

Mile 13 Sheep Camp. In the summer and fall of 1897 some stampeders cached their goods here before ascending the final leg over the pass. A half-dozen businesses served the transient population.

Mile 16 The Scales. This was a weighing place for goods hoisted or packed over the pass. It is said that packers reweighed their loads here and charged a higher rate for the steep climb over the summit. Restaurants, saloons and bunkhouses served the stampeders, who cached or discarded their goods here for the final push across the pass.

Mile 16 to 16.5 The "Golden Stairs." This was the name by which the 45-degree climb from The Scales to the 3,739-foot summit became known. In the winter, steps were chopped into the snow; in late summer the snow melted and the route crossed large boulders. It took the stampeders approximately an hour per trip; some took as many as 30 trips to get their outfits across the pass.

At Chilkoot Summit (Mile 16.5), hikers cross the border into Canada. In February 1898 the Royal Northwest Mounted Police established a customs station near here.

Chilkoot Trail
33 miles
Dyea to Bennett

Bennett
33 miles
campsites, outhouse
Lake Bennett

Lake Lindeman

Bare Loon Lake
29 miles
campsites, outhouse

Lindeman City
26 miles
ranger station, campsites, outhouse

Log Cabin

Deep Lake
23 miles
campsites, outhouse
Long Lake

Happy Camp
20.5 miles
campsites, outhouse

Crater Lake

Chilkoot Pass
16.5 miles
warden station

Fraser
(Canada Customs)

Sheep Camp
13 miles
ranger station, campsites, outhouse

Pleasant Camp
10.5 miles
campsites, outhouse

White Pass

BRITISH COLUMBIA
ALASKA

Highway

Canyon City
7.8 miles
campsites, outhouse

Klondike

(2)

Finnegan's Point
4.9 miles
campsites, outhouse

White Pass &
Yukon Route

Taiya River

Trail head and
ranger station,
campsites,
outhouse

Dyea

SKAGWAY

◆	Trail Head
▲	Stopping Point
⌒‿⌒	Trail
+++	Railroad
▬▬	Gravel Road

They levied a duty on goods going into Canada and enforced a new rule requiring each person to carry a year's supply of food and equipment into the Yukon. The rule later prevented many stampeders from starving once they reached Dawson.

Mile 17 Stone Crib. Just above the shores of Crater Lake are the remains of the northern terminus of the Chilkoot Railroad and Transportation Co.'s aerial tramway. When it was completed in May 1898 this tramway looped 45 miles of metal cables along the 9 miles between Canyon City and Crater Lake, enabling stampeders to have their goods hauled for 7¢ per pound from Dyea to Lindeman City via wagon road and tramway. Within a year after its completion the tram system was purchased by the White Pass & Yukon Route and dismantled to avoid competition with the new railroad. The tramway towers have collapsed and their remains can be seen along the trail. The stone crib that anchored the end of the cable continues to crumble. Sections of the wagon road are followed by today's hikers.

Mile 23 Deep Lake. This was the site of a major freight transfer point. Goods were ferried across Long Lake in the summer, then transferred to horses at Deep Lake for the trip to Lindeman City.

Mile 26 Lindeman City. By the spring of 1898, this was a tent town of 10,000. Here stampeders built boats and prepared for their water journey across Lake Lindeman and Lake Bennett and down to Dawson. In a cemetery on a hillside, 11 stampeders are buried.

Mile 33 Bennett. Stampeders from both the White Pass and Chilkoot trails gathered here during the gold rush. The town's population swelled to 20,000 as they built boats along the shore of Lake Bennett and waited for the ice to leave the lake. There isn't much left at Bennett except some cabin sites and the shell of St. Andrews Presbyterian Church on the hill. The church was built during the winter and spring of 1899. Boat service is available between Bennett and Carcross.

For additional information contact: Superintendent, Klondike Gold Rush National Historical Park, P.O. Box 517, Skagway, AK 99840; phone 983-2921. Also, Superintendent, Yukon National Historic Sites, Canadian Parks Service, 205-300 Main St., Whitehorse, YT, Y1A 2B5; phone (403) 667-3910.

Related USGS Topographic maps for Dyea to Chilkoot Pass: Skagway B-1 and C-1. Related Canadian topographic maps for Chilkoot Pass to Lake Bennett: White Pass 104M/11 East and Homan Lake 104M/14 East (for sale from Canada Map Office, Dept. of Energy, Mines and Resources, 615 Booth St., Ottawa, ON, Canada K1A 0E9).

Hot Springs

Hot springs are scattered throughout Southeast Alaska. The soothing springs often are a destination for wilderness travelers but in many cases, they are simply an added treat. The town of Tenakee Springs actually grew up around the hot springs which are still a major attraction for this community. (See Communities this section.) Following are a few of the springs found in Southeast Alaska.

Baranof Warm Springs. Located 20 miles east of Sitka on the east shore of Baranof Island. A private hot springs bath is located on Warm Springs Bay (status unknown). Accessible by boat or floatplane. A Forest Service trail extends a half mile from the hot springs to Baranof Lake where a cabin is located. Cabin access is by floatplane. It is not possible to hike from the springs to the cabin.

Chief Shakes Hot Springs. Located off Ketili River, a slough of the Stikine River, approximately 12 miles upriver. The Hot Springs Slough Route is one of several established Canoe/Kayak Routes along the Stikine. Two hot tubs, 1 enclosed in a screened structure, provide a good place to soak. The open-air tub has a wooden deck around it, and both tubs have changing areas. There are also a picnic table, fire ring, benches, and an outdoor privy. The area is used heavily during evenings and weekends, according to the Forest Service. Paddlers should also be aware that use of the Stikine and the slough by powerboats is especially high during evenings and weekends. The Forest Service maintains 2 cabins just upriver.

Goddard Hot Springs. Located on the outer coast of Baranof Island on Hot Springs Bay off of Sitka Sound, 16 miles south of Sitka. This may have been the earliest Alaska mineral springs known to the Europeans, and before their arrival Indians came from many miles away to benefit from the healing waters. In the mid-1800s there were 3 cottages at Goddard that were used to house invalids from Sitka. In the late 1880s, a Sitka company erected frame buildings for the use of people seeking the water's benefits. By the 1920s a 3-story hotel was built to provide more sophisticated accommodations. The building was purchased in 1939 by the Territorial Legislature as an overflow home for the Sitka Pioneers' Home. After 1946 the building fell into disuse and was torn down. Today, the city of Sitka owns the property and maintains 2 modern cedar bathhouses for recreational use. A few people live year-round on nearby private land.

There are open shelters over the hot tubs, which feature natural hot springs water and cold water. The springs are very popular with area residents. The area has outhouses. Boardwalks provide easy walking. Boaters can anchor in the bay and go ashore in skiffs. This is not a place to take a boat without a chart; there are lots of rocks and shoals, especially around the hot springs. There are protected routes to Sitka and a fascinating series of coves and channels just north of the hot springs. At the springs there are campsites in a grassy meadowlike area and on higher ground. Biting black flies (whitesox) are plentiful in the summer months.

Shelokum Hot Springs. Located approximately 90 miles north of Ketchikan in the Tongass National Forest on the Cleveland Peninsula. A 2.2-mile trail begins at Bailey Bay just south of Shelokum Creek and leads to Lake Shelokum. At the inlet to the lake is a 3-sided shelter. The hot springs are completely undisturbed and support a healthy population of unique algal plant life.

Trocadero Soda Springs. This seldom-visited carbonated "soda" springs is located on the west coast of Prince of Wales Island about 12 miles southeast of Craig. Access is by boat. Rubber boots are advised for this hike. This is bear country; exercise caution, particularly when salmon are spawning. The springs are reached by walking up a nameless creek that has its outlet in a small inlet on the south shore of the bay. The springs flow into the creek about a mile upstream. The first sign of the springs are 2 giant golden steps. These are banks of yellow tufa formed by the constant runoff from the springs. Tufa is a geological term referring to a concretionary sediment of silica or calcium carbonate deposited near the mouth of a mineral spring or geyser. The 4- to 5-acre area around the bubbling, hissing springs features lunarlike mounds and craters, splashed with colors ranging from subtle yellow to iron red. The springs originate in muskeg, then the mineralized water

meanders about 100 feet, forming a deep crust of tufa in which there are hundreds of small vents with escaping gas and bubbling water. The highly carbonated water is described as having "a sharp, pleasant taste" and has no unpleasant odors. Although water from other carbonated springs in Southeast has been bottled and sold in the past, Trocadero water has never been commercially marketed.

White Sulphur Hot Springs. Located within the West Chichagof-Yakobi Wilderness area, some 65 miles northwest of Sitka. Many visitors fly in to a small lake nearby and hike to the cabin or boat to Mirror Harbor and walk the easy, year-round 0.8-mile trail to the hot springs. Various log bathhouses have been built over the principal springs and in earlier years occasional hunters and trappers camped here. At that time the pools were called Hoonah Warm Springs, but years ago they were renamed for a dentist, Dr. White. In 1916 the U.S. Forest Service built its first cabin and bathhouse here. This cabin has been modernized in recent years so bathers can pull back a translucent fiberglass screen and admire the view of the often turbulent Pacific Ocean while soaking in the hot water. This is a popular bathing spot for commercial fishing and charter boat guests, and a destination for kayakers (primarily paddling from Pelican).

Juneau Icefield

This is the world's largest glacial accumulation outside of Greenland and Antarctica. The ice cap is 15 miles wide and 70 miles long and covers 1,500 square miles. Located in the Coast Mountains 25 miles north of Juneau, it extends over the border into Canada and north nearly to Skagway. The glaciers of southeastern Alaska are born in the high mountains that rise out of the sea and tower more than 13,000 feet within a few miles of the coast. The Juneau Icefield's annual snowfall of more than 100 feet does not melt during the summer and thus accumulates over the years until the weight of the snow compacts it into ice which then deforms and begins to flow down the valleys and into the sea. When the rate of ice buildup is greater than the amount lost annually to melting or calving of icebergs at the terminus, the glacier will gain ground or advance. If the reverse happens and the ice melts faster than new ice accumulates, the glacier will lose ground or retreat.

More than 30 glaciers, including the most visited glacier in Alaska—Mendenhall—begin in this ice field. Mendenhall Glacier is about 12 miles long and 1.5 miles across at its face. It is retreating slowly, fewer than 100 feet per year. The glacier has melted back more than 2 miles in the last 200 years. The Mendenhall is only 13 miles from downtown Juneau by road and there's an excellent view of it even from the parking lot. The Forest Service maintains a visitor center and several trails in the area.

CAUTION: Do not approach the face of this or any glacier. The glacier can "calve" (break off) at any time and crush anyone too close under tons of ice.

Other glaciers emanating from the Juneau Icefield that can be seen from the highway north of Juneau or from the water include Lemon Creek Glacier, Herbert Glacier and Eagle Glacier. None of these descends to tidewater; all are retreating. One glacier that is definitely advancing at a steady rate is the Taku Glacier on the north side of Taku Inlet, 13 miles southeast of Juneau. Extending about 30 miles, this glacier is the largest from the Juneau Icefield. If it keeps advancing, perhaps one day ice bergs will float again in Juneau Harbor as they did in the 1890s. Today, the bergs melt before they reach Juneau. Taku Glacier can be accessed by charter boat and plane.

Since 1946, scientists have been studying the ice field each summer, searching for secrets about weather patterns, the ice age and about the plants and wildlife that survive some of the world's worst weather. The Coast Range is located in the path of storms that sweep eastward from the Pacific Ocean. Studying dust and other deposits laid down by storms going back hundreds of years can help scientists predict weather patterns of the future as well as the behavior of glaciers. There are at least 6 main research camps and 20 or so lesser camps on the ice field, where winds frequently reach 80 mph and the summer temperature drops into the 20s.

Several companies in Juneau and Skagway offer tours to the ice cap by small plane or helicopter that may include the opportunity to walk on the ice field.

Lighthouses

Southeastern Alaska is the location of 12 historic lighthouses that are part of a chain of navigational beacons operated by the U.S. Coast Guard. Nearly all aides to naviga-

tion in Alaska are being modified to add solar-powered battery assists. Within the next year, all Alaskan lighthouses will include solar-assist panels. Many are visible from the waterways near the lighthouses. Familiar sights to those who navigate the Inside Passage, no lighthouses are staffed today and some no longer operate. From south to north, they are:

Tree Point Light Station. This is the first light seafarers sight when traveling to Alaska from the south. It is located on a point extending to the southwest from the east shore of Revillagigedo Channel and marks the entrance to the channel near the U.S.-Canada border. It was built on a 1,207-acre lighthouse reservation. The light began operation April 30, 1904, and was disestablished in 1969.

Mary Island Light Station. This is the second lighthouse encountered by mariners entering Alaska's Inside Passage from the south. It is located on a 198-acre lighthouse reservation on a 5-mile-long island located between Felice Strait and Revillagigedo Channel, 30 miles southeast of Ketchikan. The light began service July 15, 1903. It was reduced to a minor light and unmanned in 1968.

*More than 30 glaciers begin in Juneau Icefield.
(David Job)*

Guard Island Light Station. Located about 8 miles from downtown Ketchikan, this light marks the easterly entrance to Tongass Narrows. It went into service in September 1904. The early station also featured a fog bell. In 1969, because of rising costs of maintenance and new technology, the Coast Guard automated the station.

Lincoln Rock Light Station. Located on the westerly end of Clarence Strait adjacent to Etolin Island, this lighthouse proved to be one of the most difficult to build. The only bidder on the project began work in May 1902 after losing a load of lumber, his small steamer and a barge en route to the job. Storms halted construction in August that year. The Lighthouse Board hired its own laborers and completed the project in December 1903. The station was disestablished and unmanned in 1968.

Cape Decision Light Station. Located at the south tip of Kuiu Island between Sumner and Chatham straits, 26 miles southeast of Port Alexander. This was the last lighthouse to be completed in Alaska, constructed at a cost of $158,000. It began operation March 15, 1932, and was automated in 1974.

Five Finger Islands Light Station. Located in the south entrance to Stephens Passage, 5 miles northwest of Whitney Island, 67 miles east of Sitka and 45 miles northwest of Petersburg. This light shares importance with Sentinel Island as one of the earliest lighthouses in Alaska, beginning operation March 1, 1902. It also was the last manned lighthouse in Alaska, being automated in 1984.

Fairway Island Light Station. Located just inside the easterly entrance to Peril Strait, 15 miles west of Angoon. This lighthouse was constructed during the summer of 1904 as a minor light marking a turning point for boats in Peril Strait. It was disestablished by 1925 after an effective system of unmanned stake lights was erected.

Cape Spencer Light Station. Located at the north side of the entrance to Cross Sound, 30 miles west of Gustavus, 45 miles northwest of Hoonah. It was first lighted in 1913 with a small, unwatched acetylene beacon placed 90 feet above the water. Federal funds allowed construction of the light station, which began service Dec. 11, 1925, with a 200-mile range radio beacon, the first in Alaska. Unmanned since 1974, it is now on the National Register of Historic Places.

Point Retreat Light Station. Located on the northerly tip of the Mansfield Peninsula on Admiralty Island, 20 miles northwest of Juneau. This was one of 4 minor light stations constructed in 1904. It was unmanned in 1917, upgraded and remanned in 1924, and again unmanned in 1973. The station now contains a foghorn that requires only periodic service.

Sentinel Island Light Station. Located on a small island in the center of the northerly end of Favorite Channel, 25 miles northwest of Juneau. It marks the entrance to Lynn Canal. This is one of the earliest lighthouses in Alaska. Constructed by George James of Juneau at a cost of $21,000, the station began operation on March 1, 1902. The station was unmanned and automated in 1966.

Point Sherman Light Station. Located on the east shore of Lynn Canal, 46 miles northwest of Juneau. Constructed during the summer of 1904, this station began service on Oct. 18, 1904. The station was disestablished and reduced to a minor light sometime before 1917. The light itself was abandoned by 1932.

Eldred Rock Light Station. Located in Lynn Canal, 55 miles northwest of Juneau and 20 miles southeast of Haines. This was the last major station commissioned in Alaska during the surge of lighthouse construction from 1902-06. Contractors completed construction June 1, 1906. The Coast Guard unmanned the station in 1973.

New Eddystone Rock

A spectacular, picturesque landmark located east of Revillgigedo Island in East Behm Canal, 35 miles northeast of Ketchikan and 3 miles north of Winstanley Island. It is within Misty Fiords National Monument. This 234-foot shaft of rock, called a "stack" by geologists, was named in 1793 by Capt. George Vancouver of the Royal Navy because of its resemblance to the lighthouse rock off Plymouth, England. A popular subject for photographers, the rock rises from a low, sandy island in the middle of the canal, with deep water surrounding it. It may be passed on either side, keeping at least 0.5-mile away to avoid the sand shoal.

Pack Creek

This excellent location for viewing and photographing brown bears is on the east side of Admiralty Island within Admiralty Island National Monument. Pack Creek flows east 8 miles to Seymour Canal at the mouth of Windfall Harbor, 28 air miles south of Juneau. Visitors may see brown bears fishing for spawning pink, chum and silver salmon. The photography is especially good during the summer and fall salmon runs. The best time for bear viewing is mid-July to late August. Seymour Canal is also known for its numerous humpback whales. Bald eagles, deer, and gulls also are numerous in the area. Best access is by charter floatplane or boat from Sitka or Juneau. Check locally for guided tours to Pack Creek.

Visitors must obtain a permit from the U.S. Forest Service or the Alaska Dept. of Fish and Game in Juneau before departing for Pack Creek. Regulations restrict access to limited portions of the area, when visitors may go and prohibit possession of food in the area. Camping is not allowed within the bear viewing area but is allowed on nearby islands. Camping is not recommended on Admiralty Island within 2 miles of Pack Creek. Hunting of brown bears is not allowed. For additional information: Contact U.S. Forest Service, Admiralty Island National Monument, 8465 Old Dairy Road, Juneau, AK 99801; phone 586-8790; or the Alaska Dept. of Fish and Game, Wildlife Division, P.O. Box 240020, Douglas, AK 99824; phone 465-4265.

Stikine Icefield

Naturalist-explorer John Muir ventured up one of the glaciers of the Stikine Icefield in 1879 and wrote with awe about what he saw. Adventurers today ski and climb and hike this icy wilderness, braving crevasses, avalanches, rock slides and the notoriously harsh weather.

The Stikine Icefield lies in Southeast's Coast Range along the British Columbia border. It covers 2,900 square miles and encompasses at least 4 peaks reaching higher than 10,000 feet — this is quite spectacular with sea level being only a few miles away. Much of the ice field lies within the Stikine-LeConte Wilderness. Mountain climbers are attracted by the 9,077-foot Devil's Thumb, and glacier ski touring and hiking parties are drawn by the area's spectacular scenery.

The weather does its best to keep human incursions mimimal. Wet and windy, it can pin parties in their tents for days. The unprepared or inexperienced had best stay home.

Petersburg or Wrangell serve as staging areas for ice field trips. Generally, Wrangell is used to enter the ice field via the Stikine River drainage. Petersburg is the better choice for access via the Thomas Bay drainages. If you plan to hire a helicopter, you'll have to be dropped off outside the wilderness boundaries, for no helicopters are allowed to operate within, except under emergency circumstances.

Good cross-country skiing opportunities abound for either day touring or extended excursions into the heart of the ice field. The most popular practice for day skiers is to wait for good weather then helicopter onto the Horn Mountain-Thunder Mountain ridgeline. A variety of terrain for touring and telemarking awaits skiers there. Day touring season lasts from January into June. Even on short outings, the party should carry safety and survival equipment in case the weather makes a return pickup impossible.

Extended ski touring is best between April and late June. Dozens of sites are suitable for base camps. Waxless skis best suit the variable snow conditions. Absolute necessities include *very* good rain gear and a completely waterproof domed tent. Plan to pack out everything you pack in, and bring plenty of extra food in case you get weathered in for several days.

Bear viewing towers at Pack Creek. (David Job)

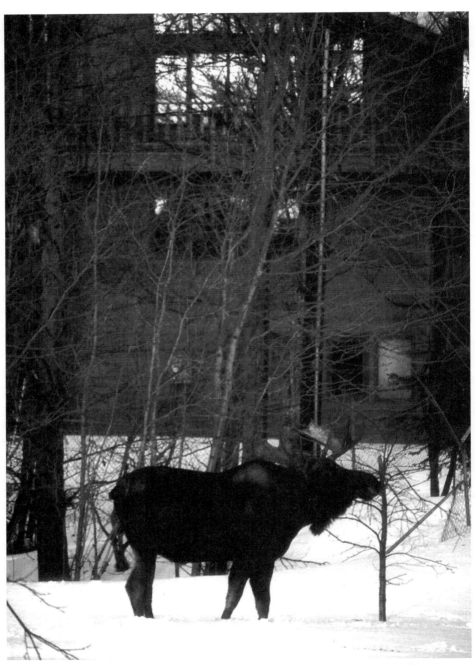

Moose frequent Anchorage city parks and trails, and even backyards, in search of food in winter. (Karen Jettmar)

SOUTHCENTRAL

Sooner or later, every visitor hears the old saying that Alaska is just 20 minutes from Anchorage. But as with most proverbs, there is some truth to that statement, both about Anchorage and about Southcentral.

Southcentral is Alaska's most populated region with Anchorage accounting for a huge chunk of the state's populace. Anchorage has skyscrapers, business suits, modern airports and freeways. But drive north or south from the city for 20 minutes and you can hike off the road into the kind of wild country and solitude that is truly Alaska. Fly a small plane 20 minutes in any direction and you'll be over roadless wilderness. You can't even entirely dismiss Anchorage as an urban area: moose wander through backyards and parking lots; sled dog races are held downtown in winter; and occasionally a bicyclist runs into a grizzly bear.

Southcentral is an incredibly diverse region, both geographically and historically. History and geography help to define it more closely into 4 distinct subregions: Copper River/Wrangell-St. Elias; Prince William Sound; Anchorage/Mat-Su Valley; and the Kenai Peninsula. (West Cook Inlet, a popular destination for bush planes from Anchorage, is included in the WESTERN section; the Kodiak archipelago, which extends southwest from the Kenai Peninsula, is included in the SOUTHWESTERN section.)

Location: The Southcentral region curves north and west from Yakutat in southeastern Alaska around the Gulf Coast to the Kenai Peninsula. It extends inland to the south flank of the Alaska Range, encompassing the Chugach and Wrangell-St. Elias mountains.

Geography: Southcentral's mainland has a roller coaster topography of high mountains and broad river valleys. At the eastern edge of the region lies 13.2-million-acre Wrangell-St. Elias National Park and Preserve, largest unit in the national park system. The area is famous for trophy Dall sheep hunting. The coast from Icy Bay to the Copper River Delta is primarily flatlands flanked by the Robinson Mountains and the large glaciers that flow from the Bagley Icefield in the Chugach Mountains.

The Copper River, historic gateway to rich copper deposits in the Wrangell Mountains, drains into the Gulf of Alaska east of Cordova. The mud flats of the Copper River Delta are a major landfall for migrating shorebirds and waterfowl. River rafting, bird watching (trumpeter swans nest here) and watching icebergs calve from Childs Glacier are favored activities.

At Hinchinbrook Entrance, the Gulf of Alaska merges with Prince William Sound, a 15,000-square-mile maze of water, ice and islands. The Sound is the site of important salmon, crab and shrimp fisheries. Columbia Glacier is a major visitor attraction. Tour boats and charter flightseeing services from Valdez and Whittier take visitors to view the glacier. Sportfishing, boating and blue water kayaking rate the top Prince William Sound recreation choices.

The Susitna River, flowing from the south slopes of the Alaska Range, and the Matanuska River, which heads in the

Chugach Mountains, make up the Mat-Su Valley area located north of Anchorage and bounded by the Talkeetna Mountains. The Matanuska River flows through Alaska's agricultural heartland. A 120-day growing season, with up to 19 hours of summer sunlight, nourishes the giant vegetables for which the Matanuska Valley is noted. River rafting, hunting, fishing, hiking and winter sports are popular activities.

The Susitna River winds through prime moose habitat into the silty upper reaches of Cook Inlet. The Iditarod Trail follows portions of an old mail and freight route from the Cook Inlet area to Nome on the Bering Sea coast of Western Alaska. The state's major long-distance sled dog race, the Iditarod Trail Sled Dog Race from Anchorage to Nome, runs along much of the trail. Anchorage, home to nearly half of Alaska's population, stands at the head of 220-mile-long Cook Inlet, which extends between the Kenai Peninsula and the Aleutian Range. Sportfishing, jet boating, flightseeing and hunting are popular here.

The Kenai Peninsula, famous for its sportfishing, is heavily used along portions of its road system, but sees little visitation in more remote areas. Kenai Fjords National Park, Chugach National Forest, Kenai National Wildlife Refuge, Kachemak Bay State Park and Kachemak Bay State Wilderness Park offer a wide range of recreational opportunities. The Kenai Peninsula and Resurrection Pass trail systems and the Swan Lake and Swanson River canoe trails should not be overlooked. Major access points include Seward, Kenai, Soldotna, Homer and Seldovia. Offshore, halibut fishing is particularly attractive. Homer and Kenai are major access points for flights across Cook Inlet, especially to McNeil River State Game Sanctuary.

Variable terrain and climate provide suitable habitat for an assortment of plants. The moisture-demanding vegetation of Southeast continues along the coast to the Kenai Peninsula. Sitka spruce and western hemlock dominate coastal forests. Inland, birch, alder and aspen are the primary species. At higher elevations, forests give way to subalpine brush thickets, fields of wildflowers, berries and alpine meadows. Major river valleys have stands of black cottonwood. Chugach National Forest (the nation's second largest) encompasses 5.8 million acres of Southcentral.

Climate: Southcentral's climate is primarily maritime, with rain and fog and mild temperature fluctuations. Nearer the mountains, the climate becomes transitional; temperature changes are greater and the climate is generally harsher. In Anchorage, January temperatures average 13°F and July temperatures average 57°F. Protected by the Chugach and Kenai mountains from the moisture-laden clouds from the gulf, Anchorage averages only about 15 inches of precipitation annually. However, at Whittier, on the coast side, average annual precipitation is 174 inches.

Wildlife: Brown bears and grizzly bears are found in the coastal forests of Prince William Sound and portions of the Matanuska and Susitna valleys. Mountain goats roam the sheer cliffs of the Chugach and Wrangell mountains. Moose thrive on the Kenai Peninsula, where the nearly 2-million-acre Kenai National Wildlife Refuge provides habitat for these giants. Moose occur throughout the rest of Southcentral, except on the islands of Prince William Sound. Dall sheep are found in the Talkeetna, Wrangell and Chugach mountains, on the slopes of the Alaska Range and on inland peaks of the Kenai Mountains. Sitka black-tailed deer inhabit the coastal forests of Prince William Sound. Wolves live on the Kenai Peninsula, in the Nelchina basin, the Copper River valley, the Eagle River valley near Anchorage and in the rolling country northwest of Cook Inlet.

Smaller nongame and fur-bearing mammals include lynx, martens, weasels, beavers, muskrats, minks, red foxes, land otters, porcupines, wolverines, snowshoe hares, shrews, voles and lemmings.

Southcentral has congregations of bald and golden eagles, hawks and falcons and an overwhelming number of shorebirds and waterfowl. The world's population of dusky Canada geese summers on the Copper River flats, and rare trumpeter swans nest on the Kenai Peninsula and near the Copper River. The mud flats of the river's delta are a major landfall for migrating shorebirds and waterfowl.

Rich Gulf Coast waters support crab, shrimp and clams. Salmon, herring, cod, Dolly Varden and cutthroat trout abound and nourish, in turn, harbor and Dall porpoises, sea lions, sea otters and killer whales. Largest marine mammals in the area are the baleen whales (humpbacks, fins and minkes) that feed on the krill and other marine invertebrates that thrive in the nutrient-rich waters.

Alexander Creek

[MAP 5] Located in the Mat-Su Valley area near the mouth of Alexander Creek in the Susitna River delta 27 miles northwest of Anchorage. **Transportation:** Boats; charter floatplane service from Anchorage. **Population:** 17. **Zip code:** 99695. **Emergency Services:** Alaska State Troopers, Anchorage; hospitals and clinics in Anchorage.

Visitor Facilities: Accommodations and meals available. No public laundry facilities. No stores; supplies are obtained from Anchorage. Marine engine and boat repair available. Boats and motors available for rent, and river-taxi service available. Guide services available. Hunting/fishing licenses and public moorage facilities available. Fuel available: regular gasoline.

Alexander Creek is a scattered, unincorporated community located on or near the former site of a small Indian village reported by U.S. Geological Survey geologist George Homans Eldridge in 1898.

Some residents of the area are commercial fishermen; others are retired.

Sportfishing is excellent for king salmon from May 20 to July 6; silver, pink, red and chum salmon from July 16 to September; rainbow trout in May and September; and grayling from July to September.

Hunting in the area is for moose, black bear and ducks.

Communications include mail plane, commercial radio and TV. There are no schools or churches. Electricity is from individual generators; water is from wells. Sewage system is flush toilets. Freight arrives by charter plane. Village corporation address: Alexander Creek Inc., 8126 Wisteria, Anchorage, AK 99502.

Anchorage

[MAP 5] Located on Knik Arm, Cook Inlet, 1,445 air miles north of Seattle, 578 miles northwest of Juneau, 263 miles south of Fairbanks. **Transportation:** Daily jet service by domestic and international airlines; automobile and scheduled bus service via the state highway system; Alaska Railroad from Fairbanks, Whittier or Seward. **Population:** 230,000. **Emergency Services:** Police, Fire Department, Ambulance and Search & Rescue, emergencies only, phone 911. Police, nonemergency, phone 786-8900. Alaska State Troopers, phone 269-5511. Hospitals: Alaska Regional Hospital, phone 276-1131; Alaska Native Medical Center, phone 279-6661; Providence Hospital, phone 562-2211; Elmendorf Air Force, phone 331-4544.

Elevation: 38 to 120 feet.

Private Aircraft: Anchorage airports provide facilities and services to accommodate all types of aircraft. See the *Alaska Supplement,* the U.S. government's flight information publication, for the following airports: Anchorage International, Merrill Field, Birchwood, Campbell airstrip, Providence Hospital heliport; Elmendorf Hospital heliport; Elmendorf AFB, Bryant Field (Fort Richardson) and Lake Hood seaplane base.

Visitor Facilities: Anchorage is the staging and supply point for travel to wilderness areas throughout Alaska, and offers a variety of visitor attractions and special events year-round. All services are available, including more than 60 hotels and motels, nearly as many bed and breakfasts and more than 300 restaurants. Clothing, food and other supplies for backcountry travel are available in local stores. There are 3 public campgrounds (open from May to October). Chugach State Park also has public campgrounds located near Anchorage, and there are several private campgrounds in the area.

Today, Anchorage is the main center of commerce and distribution for the rest of Alaska. Mainstays of the economy are federal, state and local government agencies, the oil industry, military bases (Fort Richardson, Elmendorf AFB) and transportation facilities, including an expanding port and international airport.

Attractions readily accessible from Anchorage include Chugach State Park, Prince William Sound and Portage Glacier. There are many air taxi operators based in Anchorage who can take you flightseeing or out on hunting, fishing, backpacking and photography excursions.

Winter offers miles of skiing, as well as plenty of opportunities for snowmobiling, snowshoeing and dogsledding.

Anchorage is home to 2 of the busiest small plane bases in the nation and half of the licensed pilots in the state. Merrill Field has ranked among the busiest airports in the nation for several years with more than 230,000 take-offs and landings a year, almost 25 percent of the total aircraft activity in Alaska. Located just 1 mile east of downtown Anchorage on 415 acres, Merrill Field has tiedowns for 1,422 planes. The number of planes leasing space runs about 1,000 planes, nearly one-half of the 2,400 small aircraft in Anchorage. Merrill Field was named in honor of pioneer commercial pilot Russell Hyde Merrill who completed a number of firsts in Alaska aviation, such as the first to fly a single-engine plane across the Gulf of Alaska, first to fly a commercial flight west of Juneau and first to attempt a night landing in Anchorage.

Most of the rest of the planes in Anchorage are based at Lake Hood, the busiest and largest seaplane base in the nation with more than 800 planes taking off or landing each day in the summer. Located just north of the Anchorage International Airport, the Lake Hood Seaplane Facility has seen the number of planes using its facilities double in the last 10 years. The growth is due, in large part, to the fact that more and more people want to visit Alaska's backcountry, and lakes and rivers provide the only landing sites in many of these areas.

Wilderness experiences are available for all visitors with or without their own equipment. There are many guide services specializing in hiking, mountaineering, ski touring, float trips, and backpacking. Equipment can be rented, and food and supplies can be shipped to wilderness areas by local expediting companies.

A good first stop for visitors planning to head into the backcountry is the Alaska Public Lands Information Center, 605 W. 4th Ave., Anchorage, AK 99501; phone 271-2737. Films, brochures and knowledgeable staffers provide information on every kind

of outdoor activity and will help you plan your trip. The center is open 7 days a week in summer. Adventurers can also phone 762-2261 for information on backcountry travel throughout Alaska.

Backcountry travel information for Chugach State Park is available at park headquarters, Frontier Bldg., 3601 C St., phone 561-2020. (Phone 694-6391 for a recorded message on current conditions.) The park also offers a trip planning service for overnight backpackers.

For information on backcountry travel in Chugach National Forest, contact the U.S. Forest Service, 201 E. 9th Ave., Suite 206, Anchorage, AK 99501; phone 271-2500. For information on specific areas, contact the district rangers: for Girdwood to Summit Lake and Hope area, phone the Girdwood ranger district at 783-3242; for Seward to the Russian River area, phone the Seward district at 224-3374; for Prince William Sound and the Copper River area, phone the Cordova district, 424-7661.

For Denali National Park and for areas in other regions of Alaska, such as Katmai and Glacier Bay national parks and the Chilkoot Trail in Klondike Gold Rush National Historic Park, contact the Alaska Public Lands Information Center (address above). The Bureau of Land Management, 701 C St. (P.O. Box 13, Anchorage, AK 99513), phone 271-5555, has information on hiking trails and canoe trails in many areas of Alaska. Other information may be obtained from the Anchorage Convention and Visitors Bureau, 1600 A St., Suite 200, Anchorage, AK 99501; phone 276-4118.

Anchorage, a unified home-rule municipality first incorporated in 1920, has all the amenities of big-city life, a daily newspaper, and several radio and TV stations. Government address: Municipality of Anchorage, Pouch 6-650, Anchorage, AK 99502-0650; phone 264-4431 or 4432.

For more information see *The MILE-POST®*, a complete guide to communities on Alaska's road and marine highway systems.

Cape Yakataga

[MAP 6] Located on the Gulf of Alaska, 35 miles west of Icy Bay, 106 miles west of Yakutat, 109 miles east of Cordova, 265 miles southeast of Anchorage. **Transportation:** Scheduled or charter air service. Gulf Air Taxi flies 3 scheduled flights a week from Yakutat to Cape Yakataga and Icy Bay; Fishing & Flying flies in mail once a week from

Cordova. **Population:** 4 to 8. **Emergency Services:** Alaska State Troopers, Cordova.

Elevation: 12 feet at airport. **Climate:** Mild in the summer with temperatures in the 60s and rainy in the winter, with temperatures dropping to the middle teens to 35°F, according to one resident. Mean annual precipitation is 102 inches.

Private Aircraft: Airstrip 2 miles from homes; elev. 12 feet; length 4,900 feet; gravel; no fuel; unattended. Mountains north through northeast to east; 2,258-foot hill 3 nautical miles east. Runway not maintained. Contact Cordova radio for latest field conditions. Water stands on runway; soft spots rutted when dry.

Visitor Facilities: Don and Lahoma Leishman (Box CYT, Cordova 99574-8998) run a bunkhouse-type lodge and provide meals. There are no other services available.

The Indian name Yakataga is said to mean "canoe road," referring to 2 reefs that form a canoe passage to the village. The name was reported in 1904 by C.G. Martin of the U.S. Geological Survey. At that time there was placer mining in the area. Cape Yakataga is the site of a Federal Aviation Administration aero-beacon. Some residents mine and also trap.

Activities in the area include beachcombing and hunting for moose, mountain goat, black bear and brown bear, according to one resident. Also, a large number of birds pass through the area during migrations.

Chenega Bay

[MAP 5] Located at Crab Bay on Evans Island in Prince William Sound, 50 miles east of Seward. **Transportation:** Boat or charter floatplane from Anchorage, Cordova, Seward or Valdez. **Population:** 70. **Zip code:** 99574. **Emergency Services:** Village Public Safety Officer; Alaska State Troopers, Seward, phone 224-3346; Clinic, phone 573-5129.

Climate: Moderately rainy, with daytime temperatures in the mid-50s, according to one resident. Winters mild with average snowfall accumulation of 4 to 5 feet. Daytime winter temperatures from the mid-20s to the 30s.

Private Aircraft: No airstrip. Floatplane landings only.

Visitor Facilities: Room with cooking facilities available in the community building. Laundry facilities available; no banking services. Limited supplies available. No arts and crafts available for purchase at present. Fishing/hunting licenses available; no guide

services. Fuel is not available. The community has a dock and a floatplane landing area.

The original community of Chenega, located on the south tip of Chenega Island north of Evans Island, was destroyed by the tidal wave that followed the 1964 Good Friday earthquake. Chenega Bay was dedicated on the 20th anniversary of that quake, the culmination of years of effort to provide a new village for former residents of Chenega.

Most of the buildings were constructed in the summer of 1984. The new village consists of 21 homes, an office building, school and community store, a church, community hall and 2 school faculty houses.

The primary occupations in Chenega Bay are subsistence and commercial fishing and other seasonal employment.

Chenega Bay is built on the site of the former Crab Bay herring saltery. At nearby Sawmill Bay between Chenega Bay and Port San Juan are the ruins of Port Ashton, another abandoned herring saltery, which is accessible by boat, floatplane or by foot along the beach at low tide.

The Port San Juan Hatchery, operated by the Prince William Sound Aquaculture Assoc., is located about 2 miles across Sawmill Bay by boat from Chenega Bay. The hatchery, which is open to visitors, grows pink and chum salmon and reportedly is one of the largest of its kind in the world in terms of number of fry released.

Latouche Island, site of an abandoned copper mining community, is located about 4 miles from Chenega Bay across Elrington Passage. Today there is a private airstrip on the island and a few homes.

The historic site of old Chenega is accessible by private air or boat charter.

Recreational activities at Chenega Bay include bottle collecting, rockhounding, beachcombing, hiking or backpacking. Cross-country skiing is good in winter. Whales and sea lions may be seen nearby. bird watching is possible year-round. Fishing in nearby waters is good in season for salmon, trout, halibut and rockfish. Hunting is primarily for deer and black bear on Evans and neighboring islands.

NOTE: Some lands near Chenega Bay are owned by the local village corporation, which should be contacted regarding the location of its lands and authorization for use.

Communications at Chenega Bay, which is unincorporated, include phones, twice-weekly mail plane, radio and TV. There are community electricity, water and sewer systems. Freight arrives by barge or mail plane. Government address: Chenega Bay I.R.A. Council, P.O. Box 8079, Chenega Bay, AK 99574; phone 573-5132. Village corporation address: Chenega Corp., P.O. Box 8060, Chenega Bay, AK 99574.

Chisana

[MAP 6] *(shoe-SHAN-na)* Located in the Wrangell Mountains on the Chisana River near its headwaters, 30 miles southeast of Nabesna and about 60 miles south of Northway. **Transportation:** Charter air service from Northway, Glennallen or Tok. **Population:** 6 to 20, depending on the season. **Zip code:** 99780. **Emergency Services:** Alaska State Troopers, Glennallen, phone 822-3263; Tok Clinic or Faith Hospital, Glennallen.

Elevation: 3,170 feet. **Climate:** Mean temperature in July 51°F; mean temperature in January -14°F, with lows to -30°F. According to resident Ray McNutt, 1991 saw the thermometer dip to -50°F twice in January. Mean annual precipitation 11.4 inches, with 61 inches of snow.

Private Aircraft: Airstrip adjacent north; elev. 3,318 feet; length 4,200 feet; turf and gravel; unattended. Runway has loose rocks up to 3 inches. Airport active for hunting from the end of August to mid-September.

Visitor Facilities: Accommodations and meals available by advance reservation at 2 local lodges, Wrangell R Ranch (radiophone 345-1160, call sign WHV 34) and Pioneer Outfitters. There are no other facilities. Guide services are available locally.

This community, located within Wrangell-St. Elias National Park and Preserve, was settled during the Chisana gold rush of 1913. At one time the area had a population of more than 1,000. The gold rush was short-lived and Chisana quickly became a ghost town. It now serves as the base of operations for a few hunting guides and recreationists.

Anthony Dimond, Alaska's territorial delegate to Congress from 1932-45, was the town's U.S. Commissioner. His courtroom, cabin, women's jail and several other historic structures, built of logs during the town's peak years (1913 to 1920), were restored by the National Park Service in 1988.

Hunting, horseback trips, hiking and history are the primary visitor attractions.

A regular mail plane serves Chisana, which is unincorporated. There are no phones, schools or churches. Electricity is from individual generators, water is from wells or the river. There is no community sewage system. Freight arrives by plane.

Chitina

[MAP 6] *(CHIT-na)* Located in the Copper River/Wrangell-St. Elias area on the Edgerton Highway at the confluence of the Copper and Chitina rivers, 116 miles northeast of Valdez. **Transportation:** Edgerton Highway, 33 miles from its junction with the Richardson Highway; air charter service from Gulkana. **Population:** 40. **Zip code:** 99566. **Emergency Services:** Copper River EMS, phone 822-3203; Alaska State Troopers at Glennallen, phone 822-3263.

Elevation: 556 feet. **Climate:** Summers warm (by Alaska standards) and sunny; winters cold, dark and snowy.

Private Aircraft: Airstrip adjacent; elev. 556 feet; length 3,000 feet; gravel; unattended. Runway conditions not monitored; visual inspection recommended prior to use. Aircraft at one end cannot see aircraft at other end because of downward slopes. Brush first 1,000 feet.

Visitor Facilities: Chitina has a post office, general store, gas station, bar, restaurant, tire repair service, public phone and National Park Service ranger station. Local artist Art Koeninger has a shop in Chitina. A big attraction in Chitina is the seasonal run of Copper River salmon, which draws hundreds of dip-netters and spectators. The fishery is open June through September (depending on harvest levels), and it's a fine opportunity to see fish wheels and dip nets in action. (The fishery is open only to Alaska residents with personal use and subsistence permits.)

A bridge crossing the Copper River at Chitina gives access to the 58-mile McCarthy Road, which leads deep into the Wrangell-St. Elias National Park and Preserve. Chitina, as one of the gateway communities to the Wrangell-St. Elias, serves as jumping-off point for a number of wilderness trips that originate along the McCarthy Road. For more about Chitina, see *The MILEPOST*®, a complete guide to communities on Alaska's road and marine highway systems.

Copper Center

[MAP 6] Located in the Copper River/Wrangell-St. Elias area on the Klutina River, 1 mile west of its junction with the Copper

River, 100 miles northeast of Valdez. **Transportation:** Via Richardson Highway, 100 miles from Valdez, about 15 miles south of Glennallen; charter air service. **Population:** 229. **Zip code:** 99573. **Emergency Services:** State Troopers and hospital in Glennallen.

Elevation: 1,000 feet.

Private Aircraft: Airstrip NR 1 adjacent west; elev. 1,033 feet; length 1,800 feet; turf; unattended. Ball field in summer; snowmobiles in winter. Airstrip NR 2, 0.9 mile south; elev. 1,150 feet; length 2,600 feet; gravel; unattended. Runway also used as a road.

Visitor Facilities: Meals, lodging, groceries, gas, general merchandise and other supplies available. A museum operated by the Copper Valley Historical Society is open June through September and features early mining, church and Native artifacts.

For more information see *The MILEPOST®*, a complete guide to communities on Alaska's road and marine highway systems.

Cordova

[MAP 6] Located on Orca Inlet on the southeast shore of Prince William Sound at the entrance to the Copper River valley, 147 miles southeast of Anchorage. **Transportation:** Daily jet service from Anchorage; Alaska Marine Highway System from Valdez, Whittier and Seward. **Population:** 2,585. **Zip code:** 99574. **Emergency Services:** Alaska State Troopers, phone 424-6100, emergency phone 911; Police, Fire Department, Ambulance, phone 424-6100, emergency phone 911; Hospital, phone 424-8000.

Elevation: Sea level to 400 feet. **Climate:** Average temperature in July 54°F, in January 21°F. Average annual precipitation 167 inches. Prevailing winds easterly at about 5 mph.

Private Aircraft: Two state-owned airports; Cordova Municipal, 0.9 mile east; elev. 12 feet; length 1,900 feet; gravel; unattended. Cordova, Mile 13, 11.3 miles east-southeast; elev. 42 feet; length 7,500 feet; asphalt. Eyak Lake seaplane base, 0.9 mile east.

Visitor Facilities: Cordova has 2 hotels, 2 motels, 9 restaurants, 2 laundromats and a variety of shopping facilities. Banking and all major repair services are available. The town has several air taxi operators. Boats also may be chartered. Cordova has a large small-boat harbor with facilities for transient boats. For additional information contact Cordova Chamber of Commerce, P.O. Box 99, Cordova, AK 99574, phone 424-7260.

Aerial view of the Prince William Sound community of Cordova. (Lee Foster)

The name Cordova probably is derived from the original Spanish name Puerto Cordova (Port Cordova), given to the area by the Spanish naval explorer Fidalgo, who sailed into Orca Inlet in 1790. Modern-day Cordova owes its origins to Michael J. Heney, builder of the Copper River & Northwestern Railway. The town was the railroad terminus and ocean shipping port for copper ore from the Kennecott mines near Kennicott and McCarthy, 112 air miles northeast of Cordova in the Wrangell Mountains. The railroad and the town prospered until 1938 when the mine was closed. Following the end of copper mining, fishing became the area's major economic base. One of the first producing oil fields in Alaska was located in Katalla, some 47 miles southeast of Cordova on the Gulf of Alaska. The discovery was made in 1902, and the field produced small amounts of oil until 1933 when part of the plant burned. (For more about McCarthy, Kennicott, Katalla and the Copper River Delta, see the Copper River/Wrangell-St. Elias subregion.)

As a result of the 1964 Good Friday earthquake, Cordova's land mass rose 6 to 7 feet, leaving part of its harbor high and dry. In the process of deepening the harbor, the Army Corps of Engineers reclaimed 15 acres of tideland by building a bulkhead, which served to corral the sand and mud dredged from the harbor basin. The earthquake also damaged the bridge over the Copper River known as the Million Dollar Bridge, but it has been repaired and motorists can drive 2 miles beyond the bridge. There is a covered viewing platform near Childs Glacier. The drive from Cordova to the bridge is 52 miles of beautiful scenery and excellent opportunities to view wildlife.

Supporting the area's economy are the Prince William Sound fishery and fish processing plants. The fishing and canning season for salmon runs from about May to September, with red, king and silver salmon taken from the Copper River area, and chum, king and pink salmon from Prince William Sound. The season for Dungeness crab is March to June and August to December; tanner crab is caught in January; king crab opens in October and continues until the quota is caught.

Government services for the surrounding area also contribute significantly to the job base. The Coast Guard cutter *Sweetbriar* is based at Cordova.

Surrounded by Chugach National Forest and the waters of Prince William Sound,

Cordova is a prime staging area for wilderness adventures such as ocean kayaking, hiking, fishing, canoeing, rafting, bird watching and sightseeing. Numerous guides and outfitters operate from Cordova.

Wildlife watchers can observe moose, bears, waterfowl, sea otters and shorebirds in and around Cordova. Each year, more than 5 million shorebirds pass through the Copper River Delta during their spring migration, and thousands of sandpipers may be observed on the tidal mudflats.

The Forest Service maintains 40 miles of hiking trails in the Cordova area, including trails to Sheridan Glacier, McKinley Lake and Crater Lake. It also maintains 17 recreational cabins in the Copper River Delta and eastern Prince William Sound. Visitors can rent these cabins for $20 a night. For more information on the hiking trails and other Forest Service facilities, contact the U.S. Forest Service, P.O. Box 280, Cordova, AK 99574, phone 424-7661.

Cordova Historical Society and City of Cordova operate Cordova Museum featuring art, history, geology and marine exhibits. Write Box 391, Cordova, AK 99574; phone 424-6665. In addition to its museum, Cordova has a library and Olympic-sized public swimming pool. There also is skiing from December to May on 3,500-foot Eyak Mountain, which has a chair lift and 2 rope tows.

Celebrations during the year include the Copper River Delta Shorebird Festival, a 10-day extravaganza celebrating the birds' annual migration. Participants enjoy field trips and workshops, as well as a dance, an auction and a dinner cruise. Also a hit is the Silver Salmon Derby from mid-August to the first of September, which offers a $5,000 prize for the heaviest sport-caught silver salmon, and the Iceworm Festival in February, with a parade, arts and crafts shows, dances, ski events and more. Highlight is the 100-foot-long "iceworm" that winds its way through the streets of Cordova.

Cordova, a home-rule city, has all the amenities of a medium-sized city, including a radio station (KLAM-AM), cable TV and a weekly newspaper, the *Cordova Times*. City government address: City of Cordova, P.O. Box 1210, Cordova, AK 99574; phone 424-6200.

For additional information see *The MILEPOST®*, a complete guide to communities on Alaska's road and marine highway system.

Ellamar

[MAP 6] Located on the east shore of Virgin Bay in Tatitlek Narrows on Prince William Sound, 180 miles east-southeast of Anchorage, 40 miles northwest of Cordova, 24 miles southwest of Valdez, 2 miles northeast of Tatitlek. **Transportation:** Boat; charter air service from Anchorage or Valdez direct or via Tatitlek. **Population:** About 10 year-round. **Zip code:** 99695. **Emergency Services:** Alaska State Troopers, Valdez; Health Aide, Tatitlek; Valdez Hospital.

Private Aircraft: Floatplane landings only at Ellamar. Airstrip located at Tatitlek.

Visitor Facilities: Arrangements for cabin rental may be made through Ellamar Properties based in Anchorage (Ellamar Properties, Inc., P.O. Box 203113, Anchorage, AK 99520; phone 278-1311). No laundromat. No stores or supplies available. Boat, aircraft may be chartered. Guide services available. No major repair services or fuel. Fishing/hunting licenses not available. Roads and dock facilities have been developed for those who purchase lots. Load and off-load dock was completed in 1988. Anchorage and moorings available.

Ellamar, a historic copper mining town, is in the process of being redeveloped as a summer and weekend recreational community by Ellamar Properties Inc. in Anchorage.

Copper was discovered at Ellamar in 1897. By 1902 Ellamar was a bustling town of 700 residents, complete with stores, shops, 3 bars and an opera house. Mines throughout Prince William Sound started closing in 1919 and by the end of the 1920s Ellamar Mining was closed.

The economy was revitalized for a time when 2 cannery operations, attracted by the dock and labor force from Tatitlek, opened at Ellamar. The first cannery burned down in the 1940s; the second quit operating in the 1950s.

Recreational activities in the area include fishing for salmon and halibut, boating, hunting, cross-country skiing and photography. Whales, sea otters and sea lions frequent the area. Behind Ellamar, 3,051-foot Ellamar Mountain offers good views of waterfalls. Columbia Glacier is 12 miles to the northwest.

Communications at Ellamar include a weekly mail plane and a public phone located at Tatitlek. There are no community electricity, sewer or water systems. Water is available from 3 creeks. The nearest church and school are at Tatitlek. Freight arrives at Ellamar by barge or floatplane.

English Bay

(See *Nanwalek*)

Glennallen

[MAP 6] Located in the Copper River/Wrangell-St. Elias area, on the Glenn Highway, near the junction of the Glenn and Richardson highways. **Transportation:** Via the Glenn and Richardson highways. **Population:** 928. **Zip code:** 99588. **Emergency Services:** Alaska State Troopers, phone 822-3263; Fire Department emergency, phone 911; Hospital, phone 822-3203.

Elevation: 1,460 feet.

Private Aircraft: Gulkana Airstrip, 4.3 miles northeast of Glennallen; elev. 1,579 feet; length 5,000 feet; asphalt; fuel 100LL, Jet B.

Visitor Facilities: Accommodations and meals are available, as are automobile parts, groceries, gifts, clothing, sporting goods and other supplies. Hunting/fishing licenses and guides available. Fuel and major car repairs are available.

Glennallen is a convenient staging area for trips into the Wrangell-St. Elias Park and for trips into the Copper River Valley. Several air taxis and guides and outfitters for wilderness trips are based here.

For more information see *The MILE-POST®*, a complete guide to communities on Alaska's road and marine highway systems.

Halibut Cove

[MAP 3] Located on the Kenai Peninsula on Halibut Cove on the south shore of Kachemak Bay, 6 miles southeast of Homer, 125 miles south of Anchorage. **Transportation:** Boat; Kachemak Bay Ferry service from Homer (235-7847). **Population:** 52. **Zip code:** 99603. **Emergency Services:** Alaska State Troopers, Homer, phone 235-8209; South Peninsula Hospital, Homer, phone 235-8101.

Elevation: 10 feet. **Climate:** Average daily temperature in July, the warmest month, is 54°F; average daily temperature in January, the coldest month, is 19°F. Mean annual precipitation is 18 inches, including 26 inches of snow.

Private Aircraft: No airstrip.

Visitor Facilities: Accommodations are available at Halibut Cove Cabins (296-2214) and Quiet Place Lodge Bed and Breakfast (296-2212). Meals are served at The Saltry restaurant (235-7847). Banking, laundromat and groceries not available. Supplies are obtained from Homer. Arts and crafts available for purchase at several galleries include octopus-ink paintings, oil paintings, fish prints, pottery, batiks and silkscreen prints. Fishing/hunting licenses not available. Guide service available. Boats available for charter; public moorage available. No major repair services or fuel available.

Between 1911 and 1928, Halibut Cove had 42 herring salteries and a population of about 1,000, according to one resident. From 1928 to 1975 the population stayed around 40, mostly fishermen. Since 1975 the community has steadily grown and now has a summer population of about 160, including several artists and many fishermen.

Bird watching in the area is excellent and there are good hiking trails. Kachemak Bay is one of Alaska's most popular spots for halibut fishing, with catches often weighing 100 to 200 pounds. Halibut up to 350 pounds are fished from June through September. Inquire locally or in Homer about fishing guides.

Communications in unincorporated Halibut Cove include phones, mail plane, radio

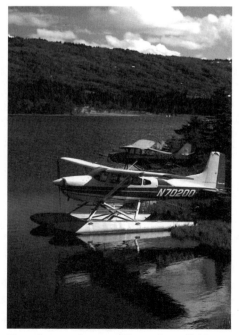

Floatplane service out of Homer is available at Beluga Lake. (Jerrianne Lowther)

and TV. There is a community electricity system; water is from creeks or wells. Sewage system is septic tanks or honey buckets. Freight arrives by charter or private boat.

Homer

[MAP 3] Located on the southwestern edge of the Kenai Peninsula on the north shore of Kachemak Bay at the easterly side of the mouth of Cook Inlet, about 173 road miles southwest of Seward and 225 miles via the Sterling Highway from Anchorage (40 minutes by jet aircraft). **Transportation:** By road via the Seward and Sterling highways from Anchorage; scheduled air service from Anchorage; Alaska State Ferry System connecting Seldovia, Kodiak, Seward, Port Lions, Valdez and Cordova, phone 800-382-9229. **Population:** 3,937. **Zip code:** 99603. **Emergency Services:** Phone 911 for all emergency services. City Police, phone 235-3150; Alaska State Troopers, phone 235-8239; Fire Department and Ambulance, phone 235-3155; Coast Guard, phone Zenith 5555; South Peninsula Hospital, phone 235-8101; Veterinary Clinic, phone 235-8960.

Private Aircraft: Airport 1.7 miles east; elev. 78 feet; length 7,400 feet; asphalt; fuel 80, 100, Jet A, B. Attended irregularly. Prior visual inspection recommended. A new airport terminal is being built.

Visitor Facilities: Homer has 8 hotels and motels, more than a dozen bed and breakfasts, almost 50 restaurants, a post office, library, museum, laundromats, gas stations with propane and dump stations, many churches, 2 banks and a hospital. There are many boat and aircraft charter operators, boat repair and storage facilities, marine fuel at Homer marina, bait, tackle and sporting goods stores, and grocery stores.

Several art galleries and gift shops are found in Homer, as well as a summer theater located on the Homer Spit. For visitor information contact the Homer Chamber of Commerce, P.O. Box 541, Homer, AK 99603. Visitor information is also available at the visitor center on Homer Spit. The Pratt Museum, 3779 Bartlett St., is open daily during the summer from 10 A.M. to 5 P.M. Winter hours are noon to 5 P.M., Saturday and Sunday. Admission is $3 for adults, children under 18 free. The museum is closed in January. The U.S. Fish and Wildlife Alaska Maritime National Wildlife Refuge, 509 Sterling Hwy., is open 8 A.M. to 5 P.M. Monday through Friday.

Homer's picturesque setting, mild climate and great fishing (especially for halibut) attract thousands of visitors each year. The more adventurous of these make Homer their jumping-off point for excursions onto beautiful Kachemak Bay or across the bay to Kachemak Bay State Park and State Wilderness Park. There is access to Fox River Flats Critical Habitat Area via a steep switchback trail that leads down to the flats from East End Road. Ocean kayaking, beachcombing, nature study, hiking, camping, clamming, fishing and mountain climbing are among the Homer area's activities. Several wilderness guides operate out of Homer.

Several booking agencies for guides, accommodations and charters operate in Homer. These include: Central Charters Booking Agency (235-7847), Homer Referral Agency (235-8996), and Homer Vacations and Conventions (235-2575).

Homer is a first-class city (incorporated in 1964) with a mayor, city manager and city council. It has all modern amenities. Communications include radio stations, TV and a weekly newspaper, the *Homer News*. City government address: City of Homer, 491 E. Pioneer Ave., Homer, AK 99603; phone 235-8121.

For more information see *The MILE-POST®*, a complete guide to communities on Alaska's road and marine highway systems.

Lake Creek

[MAP 5] Located in the Mat-Su Valley area on the Yentna River at Lake Creek, 70 miles northwest of Anchorage, 18 miles east of Skwentna. **Transportation:** Boat; charter air service or private plane. **Population:** 41 year-round. **Zip code:** 99667 (Skwentna). **Emergency Services:** Alaska State Troopers, Anchorage; Anchorage clinics and hospitals; Riversong Lodge is the first EMS responder station. Several local residents are trained as emergency medical technicians.

Climate: Summer temperatures can reach as high as 70°F to 80°F, according to one resident, while -50°F for periods of time during the winter is not uncommon.

Private Aircraft: No airstrip. Planes' land on the river or on a gravel bar. A winter ski plane landing strip is maintained by 2 local lodges, including Cottonwood Lodge, phone 733-2716.

Visitor Facilities: Accommodations at King Point Lodge (248-7447), Lake Creek Lodge (248-3530), Northwoods Lodge (694-1951), Riversong Lodge (696-2290) and

Wilderness Place Lodge (248-4337). No stores; most supplies are obtained from Anchorage, although a few grocery items, film and sporting goods may be purchased at the lodges. Raw furs may be purchased from local trappers. Native furs and crafts from the Kuskokwim Delta area are available at Riversong Lodge. Local residents' crafts are available at Northwoods Lodge. Fishing/hunting licenses are available at lodges. Boats may be rented. Guide services can be arranged, as well as natural history tours.

At the turn of the century a trading post was established on the Yentna River near Lake Creek to serve the trappers and gold miners in the area, writes one resident. Ruined cabins remain, as does the hulk of a paddle-wheeled steamboat once used for transportation.

Today, 11 families live year-round in the area. Residents guide fishermen and hunters, and provide lodging for recreationists. Residents travel 18 miles to Skwentna to pick up mail and some children attend school there, traveling by snow machine in winter.

There are cross-country ski trails in winter. Lake Creek is a checkpoint for the 200-mile Iditasport. The Iditarod Trail Sled Dog Race also passes by Lake Creek. Northwoods Lodge at Fish Lakes Creek, 3 miles above Lake Creek, welcomes winter guests.

Locally there is excellent fishing for 5 species of salmon, some up to 65 pounds, as well as for trout, northern pike and grayling. Wildlife that may be seen in the area includes eagles, ducks, moose, bears and beavers.

Lake Creek is a clear stream that flows about 50 miles south from near Mount McKinley through scenic countryside. (Both Mount McKinley and Mount Foraker can be seen from Lake Creek.) It provides white-water excitement for river floaters, as well as good fishing. Guided raft trips are also available.

Radio is the main form of communications at unincorporated Lake Creek, which does have private telephones. There is no church or school. Electricity is from individual generators; water is from private wells. Sewage is managed by septic tanks and outhouses. Freight arrives by barge or charter plane.

May Creek

[MAP 6] Located in the Copper River/Wrangell-St. Elias area on the Nizina River, 12 miles from McCarthy, 65 miles from

Chitina. **Transportation:** Mail plane on Wednesdays from Gulkana; charter air service from Gulkana, McCarthy. **Population:** Less than 12. **Zip code:** 99588. **Emergency Services:** Alaska State Troopers, Glennallen; Cross Road Medical Center, Glennallen.

Private Aircraft: Airstrip 1 mile south; elev. 1,650 feet; length 4,000 feet; gravel and dirt; no fuel; unattended. Runway condition not monitored; visual inspection recommended prior to using. Wind cone in 30-foot trees. Road adjacent to east side of runway.

Visitor Facilities: No hotel, restaurant, store or other facilities.

The May Creek area had a roadhouse during the early 1900s gold rush when the Nizina District was booming, according to one resident. Mining was the main reason for development in the area, and likewise its decline spelled the decline of the entire area. The May Creek airstrip was developed by the Alaska Road Commission in territorial days and was used by the entire region from McCarthy to Dan Creek before local strips were built. May Creek is located within Wrangell-St. Elias National Park and Preserve. A National Park Service Operations Center in May Creek is staffed only during the summer.

Area residents rely primarily on subsistence hunting, fishing and gathering, although there is some gold panning.

The biggest attraction in the area is superb hiking and beautiful scenery. Hiking opportunities range from easy rambles in meadows to more strenuous mountain and glacier treks. Roads and trails remaining from the early mining days make it fairly easy to get around, although many areas are wet. There are many beaver dams and swampy areas across or near the roads.

The area is rich in wildlife, particularly black and grizzly bears, beavers and other water mammals. Trumpeter swans migrate to this area in summer and nest in the lakes.

May Creek, which is unincorporated, has no phones or TV; KCAM radio from Glennallen is received. There are no churches, schools or community electricity, water or sewer systems. Freight arrives on the weekly mail plane.

McCarthy/Kennicott

[MAP 6] Located in the Copper River/ Wrangell-St. Elias area on the east side of the Kennicott River, 61 miles east of Chitina via the Edgerton Highway and McCarthy Road.

Transportation: Via the McCarthy Road to road end, then across the Kennicott River via hand-pulled cable trams; air service from Gulkana, Chitina and Anchorage; bus service from Valdez and Glennallen. **Population:** 25. **Zip code:** 99588. **Emergency Services:** Copper River EMS at Glennallen, phone 822-3203; Alaska State Troopers at Glennallen, phone 822-3263. *(WARNING: Do not attempt to wade across this glacial river; strong currents and cold water make it extremely treacherous. The trams are small open platforms and should be attempted only by travelers strong enough to pull themselves across several hundred feet, part of the distance is uphill. It is easier if a friend pulls on the return cable from the riverbank. Wear gloves.)* **Elevation:** 1,531 feet at McCarthy; Kennicott considerably higher. **Climate:** Summers bring cool, cloudy, often rainy weather, though hot, sunny days are not uncommon. Winters are cold, dark and usually clear, with temperatures dropping well below zero for long periods.

Private Aircraft: Airstrip adjacent; elev. 1,531 feet; length 3,500 feet; turf and gravel; no fuel; unattended. Runway conditions not monitored; visual inspection recommended prior to using.

Shuttle service is available between McCarthy and Kennicott.

Visitor Facilities: Accommodations and meals at McCarthy Lodge (333-5402) and Kennicott Glacier Lodge in Kennicott (258-2350); both have indoor plumbing and electricity. Gift shop in McCarthy offers candy, T-shirts, minimal first-aid supplies, and film. McCarthy has a package liquor store and a full-service bar. No other supplies or services available.

McCarthy and neighboring Kennicott lie in a beautiful area of glaciers and mountains in the heart of the Wrangell-St. Elias Park and Preserve. The Kennicott River flows by the west side of town and joins the Nizina River that flows into the Chitina River.

McCarthy's museum, located in the railway depot, has historical photos and artifacts from the early mining days. Kennicott, which lies 4.5 miles up the mountain from McCarthy, is itself a museum. The town was built by Kennecott Copper Corp. between 1910 and 1920 at the site of the richest copper mine in the world. (An early-day misspelling made the mining company Kennecott, while the region, river and settlement are Kennicott.) When economic conditions forced the mine to shut down abruptly in 1938, the town was left virtually intact: eating utensils still in kitchen drawers; maps, charts and records still in offices; surgical instruments in the infirmary. The distinctive red buildings perched on the side of the mountain were locked up and left as they were. And to a large extent they remain just as the workers left them, bar the toll taken by weather, aging and a small amount of vandalism. Kennicott is no longer owned by the copper company, but it remains in private hands, and property rights should be respected.

Besides poking around these historic communities (with or without a knowledgeable local guide), visitors to Kennicott and McCarthy have their choice of river rafting, mountaineering, glacier travel, backpacking, day hiking, bicycling, flightseeing, horseback riding, grayling fishing, taking nature walks, or simply relaxing in the rustic, historic accommodations. Cross-country skiing here in spring is becoming increasingly popular.

McCarthy and Kennicott have no phones, radio, TV or school. A mail plane comes in twice a week. The communities are unincorporated.

For more information see *The MILEPOST®*, a complete guide to communites on Alaska's road and marine highway system.

Nanwalek

[MAP 3] Located at the south entrance to Port Graham on the Kenai Peninsula, 10 miles southwest of Seldovia, 3 miles from Port Graham. **Transportation:** Boat; scheduled and charter air service from Homer. **Population:** 172. **Zip code:** 99603. **Emergency Services:** Village Public Safety Officer, phone 281-2218; Alaska State Troopers, Homer, phone 235-8573; Clinic, phone 281-2227.

Private Aircraft: Airstrip adjacent southwest; elev. 27 feet; length 1,800 feet; fuel Jet A-1; unattended. Runway not regularly maintained, visual inspection recommended prior to using. Approach to one end of runway restricted by village on hillside; approach to other end restricted by abrupt mountain face.

Visitor Facilities: Visitors with official business may be able to sleep on the floor of the school (281-2210) or in private homes. Village leaders ask that other visitors request permission from the village council before coming to Nanwalek. Store (281-2228) sells

limited groceries; no fuel, no hunting/fishing licenses. No bank or laundromat.

The Russians applied the name *Bukhta Anglitskaya* (English Bay) to what is now called Port Graham, probably because the area was mapped by the English explorer Nathaniel Portlock in 1789. Portlock, however, called the bay "Grahams Harbour," or Port Graham, and English Bay later was reapplied to a small cove in the bay. In 1991, English Bay was renamed Nanwalek, allegedly its original name meaning "place by lagoon."

This Native community is unincorporated. Its Russian Orthodox church, built about 1930 to replace the original 1870 structure, is a national historic site.

Nanwalek has community electricity, water and sewer systems. Communications include phones, TV and CB radios. The village has a school with grades kindergarten through 12. Freight arrives by commercial air service and barge. Government address: Nanwalek Traditional Council, General Delivery, Nanwalek, AK 99603; home phone of village leader 281-2226. Village corporation address: English Bay Corp., General Delivery, Nanwalek, AK 99603.

Port Graham

[MAP 3] Located on the south side of Port Graham Bay at the southern end of the Kenai Peninsula, 4 miles from Nanwalek and 28 air miles from Homer. **Transportation:** Boat, and air charter service from Homer and Anchorage; 4-mile trail from Nanwalek. **Population:** 199. **Zip code:** 99603 (via Homer). **Emergency Services:** Village Public Safety Officer, phone 284-2234; Alaska State Troopers, Homer, phone 235-8573; Clinic, phone 284-2241; Ambulance, phone 284-2227; Fire Department, phone 284-2224.

Private Aircraft: Airstrip adjacent west; elev. 93 feet; length 2,245 feet; gravel; maintained. Visual inspection recommended before landing. Orange highway cones mark the runway.

Visitor Facilities: Accommodations and meals by advance reservation at Fedora's Bed-N-Breakfast-N-Skiffs (284-2239). Accommodations may also be available in private homes, on the school floor and at the cannery. Supplies available at 2 stores, 1 operates a snack bar. Gas and diesel fuel available. Visitors may anchor boats (under 25 feet) in Port Graham Bay for short periods of time. A limited number of skiffs available for use by visitors.

The sport fisherman will find waters teaming with salmon, halibut, rock bass and cod. Wildlife enthusiasts can watch eagles, sea otters, land otters, bears and goats, even the occasional whale and sea lion.

The earliest known settlers in Port Graham were Russians who had established a trading post at Nanwalek. In 1850 the Russian-American Co. established a coal mine at Port Graham but this operation only lasted a few years because it was not economic.

The Aleuts who make up the majority of the current population came from Nanwalek and settled in Port Graham in 1911. The Fidalgo Island Packing Co. established a cannery in 1911 that provided the economic base of the community until it burned in 1960. Whitney/Fidalgo rebuilt the cannery in 1968 and sold it to the village corporation in 1983. The cannery continues to be the main economic force in the community. Most of the workers in the cannery are from Port Graham and Nanwalek. Residents also rely on local fish and game for food.

Communications in Port Graham include phones, radio and TV. The community is served by 2 churches, a school with grades kindergarten through 12 and a preschool. There are community electricity, water and sewage systems. Government address: Port Graham Traditional Village Council, General Delivery, Port Graham, AK 99603; phone 284-2227.

Seldovia

[MAP 3] Located on the east shore of Seldovia Bay on the Kenai Peninsula across Kachemak Bay 20 miles south of Homer, 130 miles south of Anchorage. **Transportation:** Boat; scheduled and charter air service from Homer; Alaska Marine Highway System from Homer or Kodiak. **Population:** 302. **Zip code:** 99663. **Emergency Services:** Police, phone 234-7640; Alaska State Troopers, Homer, phone 235-8239; Clinic, phone 234-7825; Fire Department and Ambulance, phone 234-7812 or 911 for emergencies.

Elevation: Sea level to 300 feet. **Climate:** Average daytime temperatures from 21°F in January to 57°F in July. Average annual precipitation 34.5 inches. Prevailing wind is from the north at 10 to 15 mph.

Private Aircraft: Airport 1 mile east; elev. 29 feet; length 2,145 feet; gravel; no fuel; unattended. Runway condition not monitored, visual inspection recommended prior to using. Turbulence southeast and southwest due to winds. Wind shear on approach to runway 16. Taxi service into town available. Seldovia seaplane base, adjacent south in boat harbor; unattended.

Visitor Facilities: Accommodations at Annie McKenzie's Boardwalk Hotel (234-7816), Seldovia Rowing Club Inn (234-7614), Crow Hill Bed & Breakfast (234-7410), Gerry's Place (234-7471), Harmony Pt.

Seldovia is a 1½-hour ferry ride from Homer. (Jerrianne Lowther)

Wilderness Lodge (234-7858) and Stamper's Bayview Lodge (234-7633). There are 3 restaurants, a general store, sports shop and gift shop.

Arts and crafts available for purchase include grass and pine-needle baskets, sculpture, batik and other handcrafted items, oil paintings, watercolors, and octopus ink drawings. Fishing guide services available. Fishing/hunting licenses available. Fuel available: marine gas, diesel, propane, unleaded and regular gasoline. Public moorage.

Because Seldovia is not connected to the road system, it has retained much of its old Alaska charm. Among activities enjoyed by residents and visitors are halibut, trout and salmon fishing, clam digging at low tides, kayaking and kayaking lessons, picnicking, hiking, cross-country skiing, bicycling (rentals available) and berry picking. These attractions, along with the town's proximity to population centers, make Seldovia a convenient, relaxing getaway destination.

Local special events include the Fourth of July celebration, Fishing Derby, Blueberry Festival and Winter Carnival.

Seldovia has phones, regular mail service, commercial radio reception from Anchorage and Homer, and TV. The community is served by 5 churches and a school with grades kindergarten through 12. There are community electricity, water and sewer systems. Freight arrives by barge, airlines and ferry. Government address: City of Seldovia, P.O. Drawer B, Seldovia, AK 99663; phone 234-7643. Chamber of Commerce, P.O. Drawer F, Seldovia, AK 99663. Village corporation address: Seldovia Native Assoc., P.O. Drawer L, Seldovia, AK 99663; phone 234-7625 or 7890.

For more information see *The MILE-POST®*, a complete guide to communities on Alaska's road and marine highway systems.

Seward

[MAP 3] Located on Resurrection Bay on the east coast of the Kenai Peninsula, 127 miles south of Anchorage by road. **Transportation:** Auto or bus via the Seward Highway from Anchorage; scheduled or charter air service; Alaska Marine Highway System from Kodiak, Homer, Cordova or Valdez; Alaska Railroad from Anchorage. **Population:** 3,000. **Zip code:** 99664. **Emergency Services:** Police, Fire Department and Ambulance, emergency only, phone 911; Seward General Hospital, phone 224-

5205; Coast Guard Search and Rescue, dial operator and ask for Zenith 5555.

Elevation: Sea level. **Climate:** Average daily maximum temperature in July 63°F; average daily minimum in January 18°F. Average annual precipitation 60 inches; average snowfall 80 inches.

Private Aircraft: Seward airport 2 miles northeast; elev. 22 feet; length 4,500 feet; asphalt; fuel 80, 100, Jet A, B. Taxi service available.

Visitor Facilities: Seward has all visitor facilities, including 3 hotels, 2 motels, 30 bed and breakfasts, 4 inns, many cafes and restaurants, post office, grocery stores, drugstores, travel agencies, gift shops, gas stations, bars, laundromats, churches, bowling alley and theater. Space for transients at the small-boat harbor. Several charter boat operators, who offer fishing trips, drop-off service and tours of Resurrection Bay, are based at the harbor. Air taxi operators offer flightseeing tours of the area.

Resurrection Bay is a year-round ice-free harbor, making Seward an important cargo and fishing port. Seward's economic base includes shipping, fisheries and government offices; the U.S. Coast Guard cutter *Mustang* is stationed here.

Seward is the gateway to Kenai Fjords National Park, which includes coastal mountains on the southeastern side of the Kenai Peninsula, the 300-square-mile Harding Icefield, Exit Glacier, fjords and substantial populations of marine mammals and seabirds.

Caines Head State Recreation Area, 6 miles south of Seward, is accessible by boat. An undeveloped parkland, it has several WWII bunkers and gun emplacements that once guarded the entrance to Resurrection Bay. (See Attractions this section.)

The annual Fourth of July celebration draws 15,000 people. The event includes a parade and the Mount Marathon Race. Winter activities such as skiing, skating and snowmobiling keep Seward bustling in the snowy, short winter days.

Seward, a home-rule city, has all the amenities of a medium-sized city, including radio stations, TV and a weekly newspaper, the *Seward Phoenix Log*. City government address: City of Seward, P.O. Box 167, Seward, AK 99664-0167; phone 224-3331.

For additional information see *The MILEPOST®*, a complete guide to communities on Alaska's road and marine highway systems.

Skwentna

[MAP 5] Located in the Mat-Su Valley area in the Yentna River valley on the Skwentna River at its junction with Eightmile Creek, 62 miles north of Tyonek, 70 miles northwest of Anchorage. **Transportation:** Riverboat; daily commuter service or air charter service from Anchorage. **Population:** About 20 locally; 200 more in the surrounding area. **Zip code:** 99667. **Emergency Services:** Alaska State Troopers, Talkeetna; Anchorage clinics and hospitals. Riversong Lodge at Lake Creek is the first responder EMS station. Several local residents have been trained as emergency medical technicians.

Climate: Mean temperature for July, the warmest month, is 58°F; mean temperature for January, the coldest month, is 5°F. Mean annual precipitation is 28 inches, including 119 inches of snow.

Private Aircraft: Airstrip adjacent northwest; elev. 148 feet; length 2,900 feet; gravel; fuel 80, 100 (available from Skwentna Roadhouse in 5-gallon cans only); unattended. Runway condition not monitored, visual inspection recommended prior to using. Runway soft during spring thaw. Ski strip west of west threshold.

Visitor Facilities: Accommodations and meals at area lodges, including those at nearby Lake Creek. Lodging at Skwentna includes Barony Lodge (345-7291), Shell Lake Lodge (733-2817) and Skwentna Roadhouse (733-2722). Groceries and laundry facilities available. Snow machines, boats, outboard motors, all-terrain vehicles, generators and parts are available locally. Arts and crafts available for purchase include carved wood burl spoons, fur mitts and hats, raw furs. Fishing/hunting licenses, guided and unguided fishing and hunting trips available locally. Snow machines, off-road vehicles and boats may be rented. Snow machine, marine engine, boat and aircraft repair services available. Fuel available: marine gas, diesel, unleaded and regular gasoline. Moorage facilities available.

Skwentna was founded in 1923 when Max and Belle Shellabarger homesteaded and started a guide service, and later a flying service and weather station. After WWII Morrison-Knudson built an airstrip and in 1950 the Army established a radar station at Skwentna and a recreation camp at Shell Lake, 15 air miles from Skwentna. The Shell Lake area remains a popular year-round outdoor recreation site. The airfield was turned over to the Federal Aviation Administration, who maintained it until the early 1970s when it was abandoned. The community grew up around the airstrip, which the state started maintaining in 1981.

Only a few families live in this unincorporated community; many more people receive their mail at the post office, but live up to 30 miles away. There are several fishing lodges in the area, most located on the Talachulitna River, Lake Creek and Fish Creek.

Most area residents make their living in Anchorage, on the North Slope or through their own fishing lodges. According to one resident, "There is no work and not everybody can live off of trapping as people will think they can when they show up."

Skwentna is an official checkpoint on the annual Iditarod Trail Sled Dog Race from Anchorage to Nome each March, as well as a gas stop for the Anchorage-to-Nome Gold Rush Classic snow machine race in February. It also is the turnaround point for the 200-mile Iditasport (combines skiing, mountain biking and snowshoes). The area is a popular spot for weekend snowmobilers and cross-country skiers.

Hunting is good along area rivers for moose and grizzly and black bear. Fly-out hunts for Dall sheep and caribou are available. There also is hunting in the area for grouse and ptarmigan.

The area drained by the Skwentna and Yentna rivers has many lakes and small streams. Five species of salmon are found here in season, as well as rainbow trout, Dolly Varden, grayling, whitefish and pike.

Communications in Skwentna include bush phone service, twice-weekly mail plane, radio and satellite TV. The community has a school with grades 1 through 12 depending on demand, but no church. Electricity is from private generators; water from the river or wells. Sewage systems vary from flush toilets to outhouses. Freight arrives via periodic barge service or plane.

Talkeetna

[MAP 5] Located in the Mat-Su Valley area, 14 miles out on a paved spur road that turns off the George Parks Highway 98 miles north of Anchorage. Also accessible by boat, plane or the Alaska Railroad.

While not technically in the Bush, Talkeetna is the jumping-off point for air travel into roadless areas of Southcentral and is the staging area for climbing assaults on Mount McKinley and other peaks of the central Alaska

Range. Numerous air taxis take visitors to Kahiltna Glacier Base Camp. Local flying services include Hudson Air Service (733-2321), K2 Aviation (733-2291), Mt. McKinley Flight Tours (733-2366) and Talkeetna Air Taxi (733-2218). All climbers must register for climbs of Mount McKinley and Mount Foraker. Mountaineering information may be obtained from Talkeetna Ranger Station, P.O. Box 588, Talkeetna, AK 99676; phone 733-2231.

As in the early years, Talkeetna's location near the junction of the Talkeetna, Chulitna and Susitna rivers acts as a magnet for adventurers.

Several river-running services operate out of Talkeetna for the Chulitna, Tokositna and other rivers flowing from the southern slopes of the Alaska Range. Riverboat service is available from Mahay's Riverboat Service (733-2223), Talkeetna Riverboat Service (733-2281) and Tri-River Charters (733-2400).

Talkeetna has all visitor facilities. For more information see *The MILEPOST®*, a complete guide to communities on Alaska's road and marine highways systems.

Tatitlek

[MAP 6] Located on the northeast shore of Tatitlek Narrows on Prince William Sound, 2 miles southeast of Ellamar, 25 miles southwest of Valdez, 40 miles northwest of Cordova. **Transportation:** Boat; scheduled and charter air service from Valdez. **Population:** 108. **Zip code:** 99677. **Emergency Services:** Village Public Safety Officer, phone 325-2248; Health Clinic, phone 325-2235; Fire Department, phone 325-2248 or 325-2311.

Climate: Rain frequent summer and winter. High winds possible in fall. January temperatures in Prince William Sound average 16°F to 30°F; July temperatures range from 48°F to 62°F. Temperatures are seldom below zero or above 75°F.

Private Aircraft: Airstrip adjacent northwest; elev. 25 feet; length approximately 2,500 feet; gravel; no fuel. Runway condition monitored daily, phone 325-2311. Visual inspection recommended prior to using. Use caution, dogs and children on runway at times.

Visitor Facilities: Accommodations at apartment operated by Tatitlek Village Council, or arrangements may be made to stay at private homes. Laundry facilities available. No banking services or hunting/fishing licenses. Some groceries may be available at private stores. One charter boat service may be available (Old Mid's Charters, 325-2310).

No major repair services available. Air charter services available through Cordova or Valdez; boats may be available locally for rent. Fuel available: diesel. Moorage facilities available.

An Indian village in Gladhaugh Bay was reported as "Tatikhlek" by Ivan Petroff in the 1880 census. Around the turn of the century the village was moved to its present location in the shadow of 3,858-foot Copper Mountain.

Many residents of the ruined village of Chenega moved to Tatitlek following the 1964 Good Friday earthquake and tsunami.

The dominant feature in Tatitlek is the blue-domed Russian Orthodox church.

Residents of this Native village make their living primarily by fishing. Tatitlek's traditional subsistence lifestyle was severely disrupted by the oil spill in Prince William Sound in the spring of 1989. In response to Tatitlek's plight, several Native villages on the shores of nearby Cook Inlet shared their own catch, which volunteers airlifted into Tatitlek.

Bird watching and wildlife viewing opportunities in the area are good. Seabirds, bald eagles, sea otters, bears and mountain goats are seen frequently.

Tatitlek's landmark Russian Orthodox church. (George Wuerthner)

Communications in unincorporated Tatitlek include phones, mail plane, radio and TV. The community is served by 3 churches and a school with grades kindergarten through 12, depending on demand, as well as a community college extension program. There are community electricity, water and sewer systems. The village prohibits the sale and importation of alcoholic beverages. Freight arrives by boat and cargo plane. Government address: Tatitlek Village IRA Council, P.O. Box 171, Tatitlek, AK 99677; phone 325-2311. Village corporation address: The Tatitlek Corporation, P.O. Box 650, Cordova, AK 99574.

Tutka Bay

[MAP 3] Located on the Kenai Peninsula on Tutka Bay 9 miles across Kachemak Bay south of Homer. **Transportation:** 45-minute boat ride or 10-minute floatplane or helicopter trip from Homer; water taxi service available from Homer. **Population:** About 30 year-round. **Zip code:** 99603 (via Homer). **Emergency Services:** Alaska State Troopers, Homer; South Peninsula Hospital, Homer.

Climate: Weather similar to Homer's. Winter temperatures occasionally fall below zero, but seldom colder. Highest temperature recorded in the area 81°F; average annual precipitation 28 inches.

Private Aircraft: No airstrip; helicopter or floatplane landings only.

Visitor Facilities: Accommodations and meals by advance reservation at Tutka Bay Lodge (235-3905). Water taxi service and fishing and hunting licenses are available at the lodge. There are no stores or other visitor facilities.

Residents of this tiny community are scattered about the coves, bights and lagoons of Tutka Bay, the largest bay adjoining Kachemak Bay. Much of the bay is within Kachemak Bay State Park, and there is a state fish hatchery in Tutka Lagoon.

Residents earn their livings by boat building, fishing, working for the Alaska Dept. of Fish and Game, and producing cottage crafts. One resident reports that what she likes best about Tutka Bay is living close to nature, scheduling activities according to the tides, weather and seasonal abundance of fish, crab, clams, berries and mushrooms.

Tutka Bay has secluded bays, virgin forests and tidepools teeming with marine life. Wildlife that may be seen includes orca and minke whales, sea lions, sea otters, land otters, black bear, seals, porpoises, bald eagles and a wide variety of birds including puffins, cormorants, mallards, oldsquaws, pintails, mergansers, buffleheads, goldeneyes, loons and common murres.

Recreational activities include fishing for salmon, halibut and Dolly Varden, harvesting shrimp and crab, clam digging, photography, berry picking, beachcombing, sea kayaking, hiking and hunting for bear and ducks.

Communications is by VHF Channel 16, CB Channel 13 or Tutka Bay Lodge, phone 235-3905.

For more information see *The MILEPOST®*, a complete guide to communities on Alaska's road and marine highway system.

Tyonek

[MAP 5] Located on the northwest shore of Cook Inlet on the Cook Inlet Lowland, 43 miles southwest of Anchorage. **Transportation:** Boat; scheduled and charter air service from Anchorage. **Population:** 280. **Zip code:** 99682. **Emergency Services:** Village Public Safety Officer; Clinic, phone 583-2461; Volunteer Fire Department; Rescue Squad.

Elevation: 80 feet. **Climate:** Maritime climate characterized by moderate precipitation, generally cool summers and warm winters. Lowest recorded temperature -27°F; recorded high 91°F. Average annual precipitation 23 inches.

Private Aircraft: Airstrip 0.3 mile northeast; elev. 110 feet; length 3,350 feet; gravel; no fuel. Pilots must obtain prior permission from the village before landing. Unicom radio is manned from 8 A.M. to 5 P.M. Monday through Friday. Pilots report turbulence when the wind blows from the east.

Visitor Facilities: Accommodations at guest house. No laundry facilities. Groceries available. No major repair services or rental transportation. Fuel available: regular gasoline. No public moorage facilities. Fishing/hunting licenses and fishing guide service available. Alaska Village Tours, Inc., offers day tours of Tyonek from Anchorage (1577 C St., Suite 304, Anchorage, AK 99501). *NOTE: Much of the land along the Chuitna River is owned by the Tyonek Native Corp., and fishermen must have a guide from Tyonek. Land on the north side of the Chuitna River mouth is public land.*

Prehistory of the upper Cook Inlet region is practically unknown. Earliest written descriptions of the Cook Inlet Athabascans are found in Captain Cook's journal. Cook explored the inlet that bears his name some 37 years after Vitus Bering discovered Alaska in 1741. Cook found that the Natives had iron knives and glass beads, which led him to conclude they were trading indirectly with the Russians. Russian fur-trading posts proliferated in Alaska, and trading settlements were established at Tuiunuk (one of the various past spellings of Tyonek) and Iliamna. These 2 outposts were destroyed in the 1790s due to dissension between the Natives and Russians. After the sale of Alaska to the United States in 1867, the American Alaska Commercial Co. (ACC) replaced the Russian-American Co. as the dominant trading company in Alaska.

ACC's major outpost in upper Cook Inlet was Tyonek. Records show that this post operated from at least 1875. Following the discovery of gold at Resurrection Creek near Turnagain Arm in the 1880s, Tyonek became a major disembarking point for goods and people. The population of Tyonek decreased when Anchorage was founded, but it still is the main settlement on the western shore of Cook Inlet.

In 1965 the Tyonek Indians won a landmark decision when the federal court ruled that the Bureau of Indian Affairs had no right to lease Tyonek Reservation land for oil development without permission of the Indians themselves. The tribe subsequently sold rights to drill for oil and gas beneath the reservation to a group of oil companies for $12.9 million, which has been invested for the benefit of Tyonek residents.

Employment opportunities at Tyonek are limited. Many residents are commercial fishermen or have jobs with the school, store, post office, village administration and other government agencies.

Tyonek residents continue to follow a subsistence lifestyle resembling that of their ancestors. They fish for king, pink and red salmon, hooligan, rainbow trout, Dolly Varden and whitefish. Hunting is for moose, ducks, geese, spruce hens, porcupines, beluga whales and seals. There is some trapping for marten, mink, red fox and beaver. Blueberries, raspberries, highbush and lowbush cranberries, and salmonberries are gathered in late summer and early fall.

Accessible by road from Tyonek is Trading Bay State Game Refuge, established to protect waterfowl nesting, feeding and migration wetlands; moose calving areas; and salmon spawning and rearing habitats. Tyonek residents hunt, fish, trap and gather plants and berries on the refuge. A number of commercial set-net fishing sites are operated along the coast of Trading Bay in the summer. Trapping is done in winter.

Communications at Tyonek include phones, daily mail service, radio and TV. The community is served by a Russian Orthodox church and a school with grades kindergarten through 12. There are community electricity and water systems. Sewage is managed by septic tanks. Freight arrives by cargo plane and barge. Government address: Native Village of Tyonek, P.O. Box 82009, Tyonek, AK 99682; phone 583-2201. Village corporation address: Tyonek Native Corp., 4433 Lake Otis Parkway, Anchorage, AK 99507; phone 563-0707.

Valdez

[MAP 6] *(val-DEEZ)* Located in southcentral Alaska near the east end of Port Valdez on Valdez Arm in Prince William Sound. **Transportation:** Daily scheduled jet service; Alaska Marine Highway Service to Cordova, Whittier and Seward; the Richardson Highway. **Population:** 3,686. **Zip code:** 99686. **Emergency Services:** Alaska State Troopers, phone 835-4359 or 835-4350; City Police, Fire Department and Ambulance, emergency only, phone 911; Valdez Community Hospital, phone 835-2249. To report oil spills to Dept. of Environmental Conservation, dial operator and ask for Zenith 9300, toll free. For Coast Guard Search and Rescue, dial operator and ask for Zenith 5555, toll free.

Elevation: Sea level. **Climate:** Normal daily maximum in January 30°F; daily minimum 21°F. Normal daily maximum in July 61°F; daily minimum 46°F. Snow from October to April. Winds up to 40 mph common in late fall.

Private Aircraft: Valdez, 3 miles east; elev. 120 feet; length 6,500 feet; asphalt; fuel 80, 100, Jet B.

Visitor Facilities: Valdez has 7 hotel/motel facilities and numerous bed and breakfasts. Other services include several restaurants and bars, grocery stores, sporting goods stores, drugstore, gift shops, hardware store, hair stylists, public library, museum, post office, and numerous churches. There are several charter boat operators at the small-boat harbor that offer tours to Columbia Glacier and Prince William Sound as well as fishing trips for pink, silver and king salmon and halibut. Several air charter operators offer flightseeing tours.

With its port the most northerly ice-free port in the Western Hemisphere and the Richardson Highway connecting it to the Alaska highway system, Valdez has evolved into a shipping center. This was one reason the city was chosen as the terminus of the trans-Alaska oil pipeline, which stretches 800 miles from Prudhoe Bay on the Arctic Ocean to Valdez.

Valdez's economy depends on the oil industry, the Prince William Sound fishery and tourism.

Raft and kayak trips of Prince William Sound, Keystone Canyon and surrounding rivers are available from local outfitters.

Valdez, a home-rule city incorporated in 1901, has all the amenities of a medium-sized city, including 2 radio stations, TV and a weekly newspaper, the *Valdez Vanguard*. City government address: City of Valdez, P.O. Box 307, Valdez, AK 99686; phone 835-4313. For visitor information: Valdez Convention and Visitors Bureau, Box 1603, Valdez, AK 99686; phone 835-2984.

For more information see *The MILEPOST®*, a complete guide to communities on Alaska's road and marine highway systems.

Whittier

[MAP 5] Located on the Kenai Peninsula at the head of Passage Canal on Prince William Sound, 75 miles southeast of Anchorage.

Transportation: Chartered air service from Anchorage; Alaska Railroad shuttle from Portage and Anchorage; Alaska Marine Highway System from Valdez and Cordova. **Population:** 300. **Zip code:** 99693. **Emergency Services:** Police, Fire and Medical emergencies, phone 472-2340; Clinic, phone 472-2303; Fire Department, phone 472-2560.

Elevation: 30 feet. **Climate:** Moderate; normal daily temperature for July 56°F; for January, 25°F. Recorded maximum 88°F; minimum -29°F. Mean annual precipitation 174 inches, with 263.5 inches of snow. Winter winds can reach 85 mph.

Private Aircraft: Airstrip adjacent northwest; elev. 30 feet; length 1,500 feet; gravel; no fuel; unattended. Birds in airport area. Runway condition not monitored, visual inspection recommended prior to landing. No winter maintenance; closed from first snowfall until after breakup.

Visitor Facilities: Accommodations available at the Anchor Inn (472-2354), the Sportsman's Inn (472-2352) and Whittier Bed & Breakfast (472-2396). A camping area is also available on a first-come basis. Groceries and supplies at the Country Store (472-2319), Anchor Store (472-2354), and the Harbor

An oil tanker docks at the Alyeska marine terminal on Valdez Arm to take on oil. (Jerrianne Lowther)

Store. The Anchor Inn and Sportsman's Inn serve meals. Food is also available from several vendors operating seasonally. Laundry facilities available. No banking services. As the gateway to western Prince William Sound, the 332-slip small-boat harbor is a busy place; marine supplies, charter boats, boat rentals and tours are available. Marine engine, boat and auto repair services available. Hunting/fishing licenses available. A list of guides, outfitters and charter services is available from the Chamber of Commerce (address follows). Fuel available: diesel, unleaded, regular and supreme gasoline and marine gas.

Whittier, named after the poet John Greenleaf Whittier, is nestled at the base of mountains that line Passage Canal, a fjord that extends eastward into Prince William Sound. The passage was, at one time, the quickest route from the sound to the Cook Inlet and interior regions. Originally it was used as part of a portage route for the Chugach Indians traveling the Turnagain Arm in search of fish. The surrounding peaks are snowcapped much of the year and a glacier hangs above the town to the west.

Whittier was created by the U.S. government during WWII as a port and petroleum delivery center tied to bases farther north by the Alaska Railroad and later a pipeline. Between 1942 and 1943 two railroad tunnels were constructed — one a mile in length, the other 3 miles. The tunnels remain Whittier's only land link with the rest of Alaska. The railroad spur from Portage was completed in 1943, and Whittier became the primary debarkation point for cargo, troops and dependents of the Alaska Command. No roads lead to this community; however, plans for completing a road by 1998 are under way. Construction of the huge buildings that dominate Whittier began in 1948 and the Port of Whittier, strategically valuable for its ice-free deep-water port, remained activated until 1960, at which time the population was 1,200. The government tank farm is still located here.

The 14-story Begich Towers, formerly the Hodge Building, contains 198 apartments and houses more than half Whittier's population. Now a condominium, the building was used by the U.S. Army for family housing and civilian bachelor quarters. The local museum is located on the first floor of the Begich Towers. Also in the building are a post office, library and video-rental store. The building was renamed in honor of U.S. Rep. Nick Begich of Alaska who, along with Rep. Hale Boggs of

Louisiana, disappeared in a small plane near here in 1972 while on a campaign tour.

The Buckner Building, completed in 1953, was once the largest building in Alaska and was called a "city under one roof." It contained 1,000 apartments, a hospital, bowling alley, theater, library, shops, gymnasium and swimming pool for the use of Army personnel serving at this isolated post. The 1964 earthquake damaged the building, and it is now a vacant ruin. The city owns it and has put it up for sale.

Whittier Manor was built in the early 1950s by private developers as rental units for civilian employees and soldiers who were ineligible for family housing elsewhere. In early 1964, the building was bought by another group of developers and became a condominium, which now houses the remainder of Whittier's population.

Since military and government activities ceased, the economy of Whittier rests largely on the fishing industry, charter boat and rental operations, guiding, tourism and the port.

Recreational activities at Whittier include hiking Shotgun Cove trail; climbing the path to Whittier Glacier; berry picking; scuba diving; fishing for silver, pink, chum and king salmon, halibut, red snapper, cutthroat trout, Dolly Varden, crab or shrimp; boating, sailing, sea kayaking and other water sports; photography; snowshoeing; cross-country skiing; snowmobiling; and snowboarding.

Wildlife in the area includes whales, porpoises, sea lions, bears, goats, eagles, puffins and sea otters. One of the otters that frequents the town is known affectionately as Oscar. Within Whittier, 2 reindeer are kept as livestock by a local merchant. Just across Passage Canal is Kittiwake Rookery, largest of its kind in the world. Whittier is also a berrypicker's paradise: blueberries and salmonberries grow in abundance at the edge of town.

Communications at Whittier, a secondclass city incorporated in 1969, include phones, radio (CB Channel 11 and Channel 16 VHF) and TV. The community has a school with grades preschool through 12. There are no churches, but services are held locally. There are community electricity, water and sewer systems. Freight arrives by barge or rail. Greater Whittier Chamber of Commerce, P.O. Box 607, Whittier, AK 99693. Government address: City of Whittier, P.O. Box 608, Whittier, AK 99693; phone 472-2327.

For more information see *The MILEPOST®*, a complete guide to communities on Alaska's road and marine highway systems.

National and State Parks, Forests, Etc.

Anchor River State Recreation Area

Located on the Kenai Peninsula approximately 15 miles north of Homer, Anchor River is known for its popular fishing holes.

According to tradition, Anchor River was named when Captain James Cook lost an anchor near the mouth of the river while on his British-sponsored expedition in 1778. At that time, the area was inhabited by the Kanaitze tribe of the Athabascan Indians. These people enjoyed a quiet lifestyle of hunting and gathering in a region with a mild climate and an abundant food supply. In 1785, the Russians arrived. These immigrants, unrelenting in their quest for pelts, put Natives to work hunting. Women and children were taken hostage to ensure that fur quotas were met, and Natives were forced to abandon their original villages and move closer to trading posts. The Anchor River area was not inhabited again until the early 1900s, when white settlers began homesteading.

Activities: The main attraction at Anchor River is fishing. Favorite fishing holes are located all along a two-mile segment of the river, which stretches from the Sterling Highway to Cook Inlet. Closer to the inlet are Boat Launch Hole and Chinaman Hole. A little farther upstream, with easy access to campsites, are Dudas, Grass, Slide Picnic, Campground and Cottonwood holes, Willow Run, and Bridge Hole. Farthest inland is the Forks, a fishing site on the north fork of the river, east of Old Sterling Road. The dedicated sportsman will be rewarded with king, pink and silver salmon, steelhead, and Dolly Varden. The Silver King Tackle Shop keeps visiting fishermen fully equipped.

Accommodations: There are 5 campgrounds along Beach Access Road, which runs parallel to Anchor River. Halibut Campsite is closest to the beach, and offers 6 sites for campers and picnickers. Slidehole Campsite has 13 sites, Steelhead Campsite has 12 sites, Cohoe Campsite has 8 sites, and Silverking Campsite has 9.

Nearby, Anchor River Inn (235-8531) offers 20 modern motel rooms and a restaurant. Wallin's Hilltop Bed & Breakfast (235-8354) overlooks the river, and Kyllonen's RV Park (235-7541) has water, electricity, sewer, showers and restrooms.

Access: Turn off Sterling Highway at Milepost 156.9 onto Old Sterling Highway and continue over the Anchor River Bridge, also known as the Erector Set Bridge. Take the first right onto a road, known alternately as Anchor River Road or Beach Access Road. Anchor River Visitor Information Center is located on Old Sterling Highway, 0.1 mile from the highway's junction with Sterling Highway.

Across from the visitors center is a plaque marking the westernmost point on the contiguous North American highway system.

For more information: Contact Kenai Area State Parks, South District Office, P.O. Box 321, Homer, AK 99603; 235-7024.

Caines Head State Recreation Area

This 5,961-acre park is located on Caines Head, a headland that juts into the west side of Resurrection Bay 8 miles south of Seward. To the west the terrain rises sharply to an elevation of 3,200 feet, from which Harding Icefield in Kenai Fjords National Park can be seen to the west and Bear Glacier is visible to the south. To the southeast, across Resurrection Bay, lie Renard (Fox) Island and others that form the gateway to Blying Sound and the Pacific Ocean.

This area has the abandoned Fort McGilvray and several WWII ammunition storage bunkers and gun emplacements that were used to guard the entrance to Resurrection Bay and the Port of Seward when the territory of Alaska was attacked and occupied by imperial Japanese ground forces.

Facilities include a latrine, fireplaces, campsites and a picnic shelter at North Beach. Campsites and a latrine are also located at South Beach. Approximately 4.5 miles of trail allow hikers to explore the WWII fort and the area's natural attractions, including scenic views of the mountains, glaciers and the bay. A ranger is on duty seasonally.

North Beach is marked by the remains of an Army dock built in 1941. The land on which the dock was built dropped 5 feet after the 1964 earthquake, and waves eventually destroyed the dock, leaving the pier to stand alone. The pier is no longer safe. Visitors are advised to stay away from the pier and not to attempt to tie up to its pilings.

Fort McGilvray is perched on a 650-foot rocky cliff with beautiful views of Resurrection Bay. Its two firing platforms are intact. The fort is open to explore, but visitors are advised to carry a flashlight as they explore the maze of underground passages and rooms, and to stay away from the cliffs, which are dangerous.

South Beach is a garrison ghost town with remains of the utility buildings and barracks that were home for the 500 soldiers stationed here from July 1941 to May 1943. Visitors are advised not to disturb the remaining structures, as they are unsafe.

Access is primarily by boat from Seward, which has all visitor facilities and is served by the Alaska Marine Highway System and a state highway. Adventurous hikers may hike the 4.5 miles from Lowell Point near Seward to Caines Head during periods of low tide.

A public cabin is available at Derby Cove. Call 762-2261 or 262-5581 for cost and availability. Open fires are permitted only on ocean beaches. Drinking water is scarce; all water must be boiled at least 5 minutes.

For more information: Contact Alaska Division of Parks and Outdoor Recreation, P.O. Box 107001, Anchorage, AK 99510; phone 762-2616. Or, Kenai Area, Division of Parks and Outdoor Recreation, P.O. Box 1247, Soldotna, AK 99669; phone 262-5581.

Captain Cook State Recreation Area

Virtually undiscovered by most visitors to the Kenai Peninsula, Captain Cook State Recreation Area offers a peaceful setting of forests, lakes, streams and saltwater beaches.

The recreation area is named for Captain James Cook, the English mariner, who in 1778 explored what is now known as Cook Inlet. At that time, the area was occupied by Taniana Indians, who harvested seasonal runs of salmon and other wild foods. Remains of Taniana barabaras, or housepits, are evidence of the Indians' earlier presence. In recent years, this area has been used for commercial fishing with beach set-nets.

Wildlife: Animals you may see during your visit include moose, bears, coyotes, wolves, beavers and muskrats. In the waters of the inlet are beluga whales and harbor seals, and in the salt-free waters of Swanson River and Stormy Lake, sportsmen will find rainbow trout, silver salmon and arctic char. Birds include bald eagles, sandhill cranes, trumpeter swans, arctic and common loons, golden-eye ducks, mergansers, thrushes, warblers and jays.

Activities: Visitors to the recreation area enjoy canoeing and boating on Stormy Lake, beachcombing the inlet's tide-swept shores, birdwatching, berry picking, riding ATVs (in restricted areas only), bow hunting, hiking nature trails, swimming and searching for agate along the beaches. Visitors are warned to be careful while exploring the mud flats, because the tide comes in quickly — it can move in 4 times faster than you can run. In winter, ice fishing, riding snow machines and cross-country skiing are popular.

Accommodations: Discovery Campground has 53 campsites, which cost $8 per night.

Access: From Kenai, drive north 25 miles on the North Kenai Road to Milepost 36.

For more information: Contact Alaska State Parks, Kenai Area Office, Box 1247, Soldotna, AK 99669; 262-5581.

Chugach National Forest

This national forest ranks second in size only to Tongass National Forest in southeastern Alaska. Chugach totals 5.8 million acres—about the size of the state of New Hampshire. It stretches from the Kenai Peninsula east across Prince William Sound to encompass the Gulf Coast surrounding the Copper River Delta then east from there as far as Bering Glacier. Special features of Chugach National Forest are Kayak Island, site of the first documented landing of Europeans in Alaska; Columbia Glacier, one of the largest tidewater glaciers in the world; the wetlands of the Copper River Delta, which serve as nesting, staging and feeding habitat for millions of birds each year; and Portage Glacier and the Begich, Boggs Visitor Center, one of the most visited recreational facilities in Alaska.

The Begich, Boggs Visitor Center at Portage Glacier offers sightseeing, photography and nature studies. The center contains an orientation area, enclosed observatory, exhibit room and a 196-seat theater with spaces for wheelchairs. The center is open 7 days a week during the summer; winter hours vary. A 200-seat tour boat operating under a Forest Service Special Use Permit offers close-up views of the face of the glacier. For further information, call the center at 783-2326. Portage Glacier is accessible via the Seward Highway south from Anchorage 79 miles then east 5 miles by access road.

The 127-mile Seward Highway connecting Anchorage and Seward was designated a National Forest Scenic Byway in 1990. The scenic byways program is designed to alert motorists to areas of unique interest, and inform them of the history, geology and biology of national forest lands along our nation's highways.

Summer visitors to Chugach National Forest should bring warm clothing, rain gear, adequate footwear and insect repellent. Much of the area is remote and emergency assistance may be far away. The Forest Service cautions that proper equipment and knowledge are essential for safe hiking and boating. Avoid traveling alone; always inform a responsible person of your itinerary and check in with them on your return. In the winter, when temperatures may fall below zero, visitors should wear layered clothing topped by goosedown, fiberfill or wool garments. Always carry emergency equipment. Unless you are experienced, stay away from glaciers. Also avoid avalanche hazard areas such as gullies or open slopes, particularly after a fresh snowfall. Travel in wide flat valleys or on ridges.

Wildlife. Chugach National Forest is home to a wide variety of birds, mammals and fish. Black and brown bear inhabit most of the forest, foraging on open tundra slopes and in intertidal zones. In late summer bears may be seen feeding on spawned-out salmon along streams and rivers. Black bear occur in most areas, with the exception of some of the islands. Brown bears are found along the eastern shore of Prince William Sound, on the Copper River Delta and occasionally on the Kenai Peninsula.

Record-size moose (some with antler spreads of more than 6 feet) inhabit the Kenai Peninsula; moose have been transplanted to the Copper River Delta. Sitka black-tailed deer have been transplanted to many islands in Prince William Sound and caribou have been transplanted to the Kenai Peninsula. Dall sheep can be seen on Kenai Peninsula mountainsides; mountain goats are found on steep hillsides along Prince William Sound, the Copper River Delta and occasionally above Portage Valley. Smaller mammals found within the Chugach include coyotes, lynx, red foxes, wolverines, wolves, porcupines, red squirrels, beavers, land otters, parka squirrels, pikas and hoary marmots.

Boaters in Prince William Sound may see Dall porpoises, harbor seals, sea otters, sea lions and killer and humpback whales.

More than 214 species of resident and migratory birds occur in Chugach. Seabirds, such as black-legged kittiwakes, nest in seacliff colonies by the thousands. Ptarmigan scurry over alpine tundra, bald eagles perch on shoreline snags and tangled rain forest undergrowth hosts Steller's jays, named in 1741 by naturalist Georg Wilhelm Steller, the first European to set foot on Alaskan soil. The Copper River Delta protects one of the larger known concentrations of nesting trumpeter swans in North America. The total population of dusky Canada geese on the delta ranges from 7,500 to 13,500; the delta is the only nesting area of this subspecies. Nesting waterfowl are joined in spring and fall by thousands of migrating shorebirds. Checklists of the birds found in the Chugach are available from Forest Service offices.

Saltwater fish available include halibut, red snapper and 5 species of salmon. Razor clams can be dug near Cordova and shrimp and 3 species of crab may be harvested. Lakes on the Kenai Peninsula contain landlocked Dolly Varden and many larger lakes and streams are migratory routes for Dolly Varden, rainbow trout and salmon. Other freshwater fish include arctic grayling, hooligan, burbot, lake trout and cutthroat trout.

Activities: Water recreational opportunities abound in the Chugach National Forest. Boating, fishing and kayaking are popular. Parts of streams on the Kenai Peninsula that are suitable for kayaking and canoeing include Kenai, Portage, Quartz and Sixmile creeks. Part of Sixmile is not suitable for canoeing and should be considered only by experienced boaters. Outfitters under permit from the Forest Service offer river-running trips on several rivers and creeks within the national forest.

Hunting is permitted within Chugach National Forest, subject to Alaska Dept. of Fish and Game regulations. Recreational gold panning also is permitted in several areas. *NOTE: Be sure to avoid trespassing on private mining claims. A leaflet containing open locations and guidelines is available from Forest Service offices.*

The Summit Lake/Manitoba Mountain area offers cross-country skiing, alpine mountaineering, snowshoeing and snow machine recreational opportunities. Accessible from Milepost 48 on the Seward Highway.

Turnagain Pass, 60 miles southeast of Anchorage, is open for winter use from Dec. 1 to Feb. 15 and later if snow cover is adequate. There is a snow machine area on the west side of the highway and snowshoeing and cross-country skiing on the east side of the highway. There are summer and winter rest areas with restrooms.

Some 200 miles of hiking trails lead to backcountry cabins, ski areas and popular fishing spots within the Chugach National Forest. For details on Resurrection Pass, Johnson Pass, and Russian Lakes, Resurrection River, Lost Lake, Primrose, Ptarmigan Creek, Crescent Lake and Carter Lake trails, see Hiking Trails this section.

Accommodations: Chugach National Forest has 16 campgrounds that are generally open from Memorial Day through Labor Day on a first-come basis (some campground gates remain open until the first snow, but water and trash services are discontinued after Labor Day). Facilities include restrooms, picnic tables, fire grates, garbage cans and water. No RV hookups; 14-day limit. A camping fee is charged.

There are 41 Chugach National Forest recreational cabins available to rent. Cost is $20 per night per party for these rustic but comfortable cabins, which are accessible by foot, boat or small plane. Local Forest Service offices can provide information about fees and can reserve any cabin managed by the Forest Service in Alaska. There is a 3-day limit for hike-in cabins from May 15 through Aug. 31; for other cabins the limit is 7 nights year-round. (See the chart under Cabins in this section.)

For more information: Contact one of the following Chugach National Forest offices: Cordova Ranger District, P.O. Box 280, Cordova, AK 99574-0280, phone 424-7661 (Cordova); Seward Ranger District, P.O. Box 390, Seward, AK 99664-0390, phone 224-3374 (Seward); Glacier Ranger District, Monarch Mine Road, P.O. Box 129, Girdwood, AK 99587, phone 783-3242 (Glacier); or, 201 E. 9th Ave., Anchorage, AK 99501; phone 271-2500.

Chugach State Park

Although located on the doorstep of Anchorage, Alaska's largest city, this moun-

Dall sheep roam the Chugach Mountains. (Bill Sherwonit)

tainous park offers excellent wilderness experiences, summer or winter. Chugach State Park is one of the nation's largest state parks, with nearly 495,000 acres.

Several thousand years ago massive glaciers covered this area. This park's beautiful mountain lakes, sharp ridges and broad U-shaped valleys all were glacially carved. Ice fields and glaciers still remain in the park, and a few such as Eklutna Glacier can be viewed on a day's hike.

Although the spectacular alpine scenery is the park's predominant feature, it offers other natural phenomena such as the bore tide in Turnagain Arm. Twice each day, a wall of water up to 6 feet high races up the channel as the tide comes in. Spectators say the bore tides come in at a speed of 10 to 15 mph, and larger ones sound like trains. A good place to watch the event is Beluga Point, which is located about halfway along the 9.4-mile Turnagain Arm Trail. (See Hiking Trails in this section.)

Wildlife: Chugach State Park's abundant wildlife ranges from the popular bald eagles and whales to the less popular mosquitoes (27 varieties inhabit the park). Viewing areas at Eklutna Lake and Eagle River valley afford excellent opportunities to see Dall sheep and moose. The adventurous can see more elusive species that live in remote areas of the park, such as mountain goats, wolves and sharp-shinned hawks. Brown/grizzly and black bears roam throughout the park. Do not leave open food around campsites, and make noise while hiking through the bush to avoid an encounter with one of these large beasts.

The elevation change in the park, from sea level to 8,000 feet, supports a variety of vegetation, from dense forests to alpine tundra. Warm summer months provide a wealth of wildflowers (ranging from common fireweed to orchids), mosses, mushrooms, trees, berries and lichens.

Activities: Chugach State Park provides a variety of recreational opportunities for all seasons. Hiking (either day hikes or backcountry hiking), wildlife viewing, camping, berry picking, skiing and snowmobiling are among the many wilderness activities available.

Between June and September, park staff offer guided nature walks and more strenuous hikes on the weekends to various points of interest in the park. The nature walks, which last about 2 hours, focus on some aspect of natural history, such as wildflower identification or bird watching. The more

strenuous hikes last approximately 4 hours. Phone 694-6391 for a recorded message on current programs.

There are several access points by highway to centers of activity in Chugach State Park, since the park flanks Anchorage to the north, east and south. North from Anchorage on the Glenn Highway take the Eklutna Road exit (Milepost A 26.3) and drive in 10 miles to reach Eklutna Lake Recreation Area. Eklutna Lake is 7 miles long, the largest lake in Chugach State Park. It is open to watercraft although there is no boat ramp. Watersports enjoyed by lake visitors include windsurfing, canoeing, kayaking, fishing, sailing and motorboating. The recreation area has a 50-site campground, picnic area, telescope and hiking trails. Good mountain biking, horseback riding and climbing area. Cross-country skiing and snowmobiling in winter.

Three free remote campsites are located in the backcountry along the Lakeside Trail at 8, 11 and 12 miles.

You may also reach the park's Eagle River Visitor Center by driving north on the Glenn Highway and taking the Eagle River exit (Milepost A 13.4). Follow Eagle River Road 12.7 miles to reach this beautifully situated visitor center, with its views of the Chugach Mountains. Excellent wildlife displays, a nature trail, Dall sheep viewing and other summer activities make this a worthwhile stop. Cross-country skiing and snowmobiling in winter. Phone 694-2108 for visitor center hours.

Kayaks, rafts and canoes can put in at Mile 7.5 Eagle River Road at the North Fork Eagle River access/day-use area. Additional river access at Mile 9 Eagle River Road for nonmotorized craft. The Eagle River offers Class II, III and IV float trips. Be sure to read the information posted at the trailhead before heading downriver.

Another easily accessible park area from Anchorage is Arctic Valley. Turn off the Glenn Highway at Arctic Valley Road, Milepost A 6.1, and drive in 7.5 miles. Arctic Valley offers spectacular views of Anchorage and Cook Inlet, and has good berry picking and hiking in summer, and downhill and cross-country skiing in winter.

The park's hillside trailheads may be reached by driving south from Anchorage to the O'Malley Road exit at Milepost 120.8 on the Seward Highway. Follow O'Malley Road east for 4 miles until Hillside Drive enters from the right; turn on Hillside and proceed about 1.5 miles to the intersection of Upper

Huffman Road and Hillside Drive. Turn left on Upper Huffman Road and continue 4 miles to the trailhead. Hiking is popular here in summer, as are cross-country skiing and snowmobiling in winter.

Thunderbird Creek, well known for its spectacular river canyon, is a haven for non-motorized-winter-sports enthusiasts. Cross-country skiing is popular here, as it is in other areas of Chugach State Park, including Indian Creek Valley, Campbell Creek and Bird Creek Valley.

The Seward Highway south from Anchorage gives access to several Chugach State Park hiking trails. See Hiking Trails this section for a list of Chugach State Park trails.

For more information: Contact Chugach State Park Rangers at 345-5014, or write Chugach State Park, HC 52, Box 8999, Indian, AK 99540. A 24-hour recorded message is available by calling 694-6391.

Denali State Park

Located adjacent to the southern border of Denali National Park, this 324,420-acre park offers a spectacular view of nearby Mount McKinley and surrounding peaks and glaciers. The park is located between the Talkeetna Mountains and the Alaska Range and straddles the George Parks Highway, the main route between Anchorage and Fairbanks. Denali State Park's landscape is dominated by Curry and Kesugi ridges, which form a rugged 30-mile spine down the length of the park. Small lakes dot these rock- and tundra-covered ridges; high points up to 3,500 feet overlook the heart of the Alaska Range. Mount McKinley's 20,320-foot summit, highest in North America, rises just 40 miles from Curry Ridge. The mountain and its companions, known as the McKinley Group, are accented by a year-round mantle of snow above 8,000 feet, spectacular glaciers and deep gorges. Other prominent peaks seen from Denali State Park viewpoints are Mounts Hunter and Silverthrone, the Moose's Tooth and the spires of the Tokosha Mountains. Valley glaciers, including Ruth, Buckskin and Eldridge, flow from these high peaks and feed the wide, braided Chulitna River.

The park is a relatively untouched wilderness: wildlife undisturbed by contact with man; a summer explosion of tundra plantlife; and constantly shifting channels of wide, glacier-fed streams.

The landscape is dominated by upland spruce-hardwood forests, especially along the highway, and by fragile alpine tundra above tree line at about 2,000 feet. Moist tundra occurs in some poorly drained areas and patches of dense birch, alder and willow thickets grow on hillsides. Black spruce grows in muskeg areas and large black cottonwoods inhabit riverbanks, particularly west of the Chulitna River. In late summer and early fall, berry pickers are rewarded with blueberries, highbush and lowbush cranberries, currants, watermelon berries, crowberries and cloud-berries.

This park is large and mostly undeveloped. Accidents are infrequent, but dangers do exist, cautions the Alaska State Parks Division. Proper equipment and experience are essential for safe backcountry travel. Emergency aid is often far away. The parks division recommends that USGS topographic maps be used; but travelers can avoid getting lost by remembering that all drainages in the park and surrounding areas lead to the Chulitna River near the Parks Highway or the Susitna River along the Alaska Railroad.

Travelers should use caution when crossing rivers; glacial and snowmelt streams rise drastically between morning and midday. Glaciers and avalanche terrain should be avoided unless you are experienced and properly equipped. Do not travel alone in the backcountry, especially in winter. Leave an itinerary with a friend or at the visitor information log cabin at the Byers Lake Campground and notify that person or office on your return.

Climate: Weather in the park is moderated by coastal waters 100 miles to the south near Anchorage. The Alaska Range shields the park from the extreme cold of the Interior to the north. Snow accumulations, beginning in October, build to 5 or 6 feet by March. Snow usually melts during April and May, although snow patches above 2,500 feet often last into July. Summer temperatures average 44°F to 68°F, with occasional highs above 80°F. Midsummer brings more than 20 hours of daylight. In winter, average temperatures range from 0°F to 40°F, although extreme lows can drop to -40°F and lower.

Summer visitors should bring warm clothing for cool evenings, rain gear, adequate footwear and insect repellent. Winter visitors should have warm clothing and carry emergency food and equipment, particularly on long trips. Hikers should plan for a variety of conditions, including gravel bars, woodland, heavy brush and soggy tundra.

Wildlife: Brown/grizzly and black bears are common throughout the park above and below tree line. Other large mammals found in the park are moose, wolf and occasionally caribou in the northern section. Smaller mammals include red fox, wolverine, lynx, marten, mink, weasel, beaver, snowshoe hare and red squirrel. A large number of resident and migratory birds, including ravens, ptarmigan, golden and bald eagles, peregrine falcons and many songbirds can be seen in the throughout the park.

The state parks office further cautions that wildlife, particularly bears, can be dangerous. Never approach wild animals, especially their young. To avoid surprises, warn animals of your presence by making noise, whistling or carrying bells.

Fish in the Susitna and Chulitna rivers include Dolly Varden, arctic grayling, rainbow trout and chum, king, red and silver salmon. Small numbers of lake trout occur in Byers, Spink and Lucy lakes and rainbow trout, grayling and Dolly Varden are found in Byers Lake and Troublesome and Little Coal creeks.

Activities: One of the focuses of Denali State Park is to provide hiking opportunities. There is access to the park's alpine areas and spectacular views from the Troublesome Creek and Little Coal Creek trailheads, and an easy hike around Byers Lake via Byers Lake Loop trail from the campground; see Hiking Trails this section.

Cross-country skiing is outstanding during March, April and often into May. No trails are maintained in the park in winter. Snow depths may reach 6 feet, covering most brush and rocks. Skiers who travel up Curry or Indian ridges should take care to avoid potential avalanche slopes, especially above timberline. Snow machines and other off-road vehicles are permitted in the park only when the snow is deep enough to protect vegetation (about 16 inches).

Accommodations: The main recreational development at the park is Byers Lake Campground at Milepost 147 from Anchorage on the Parks Highway. (The grizzlies seem fond of this campground too, and it is occasionally shut down because of a troublesome bear.) Overnight camping fee

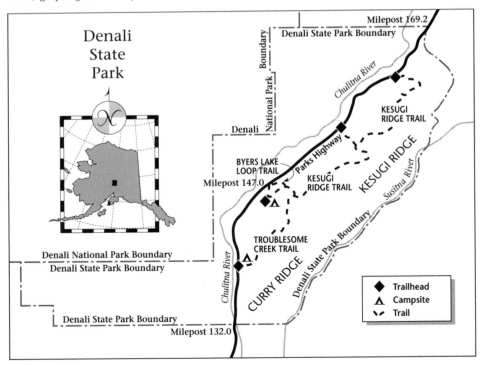

is $6. Byers Lake has 66 campsites, picnic areas, boating and fishing; gas-powered motors are not allowed on the lake. Fires must be confined to developed fireplaces or camp stoves. No fires are permitted in the backcountry, except in camp stoves. Minimum impact camping is encouraged; all trash should be hauled out of backcountry areas.

Access: Denali State Park is accessible from the George Parks Highway or the Alaska Railroad, which forms the eastern boundary of the park. The seldom-used east side of the park offers excellent wilderness recreation opportunities. The best place to get off the train is just after the railroad crosses the Susitna River past Gold Creek. The railroad offers regular local rural service from May to September between Anchorage and Denali National Park. Check with the Alaska Railroad for current schedules.

For more information: Contact Alaska State Parks, Mat-Su Area Office, HC32, Box 6706, Wasilla, AK 99687; phone 745-3975.

Hatcher Pass/Independence Mine State Historical Park

Located in the Talkeetna Mountains, Hatcher Pass has been a popular recreation area for many years and was the site of the Alaska Pacific Consolidated Mine Co.'s Independence Mine.

The 760-acre Independence Mine State Historical Park was established in 1980, 6 years after Independence Mine was added to the National Register of Historic Places. The park includes 2 former lode gold mining sites, which were active from 1909 to 1924 and again from about 1937 to 1941. Activity peaked in 1941 when 48,194 ounces of gold worth $1,686,790 were produced. But WWII put a stop to gold mining and efforts to restart mining after the war were short-lived. By 1951 the mines were closed and by 1958 the owners had sold the equip-ment and machinery. Only the buildings remained.

Since establishing the park, the state has restored the manager's house, which now serves as a visitor center and features interpretive exhibits and displays. Other buildings in the complex, including bunkhouses, timber shed, warehouse, mess halls and collapsed mill, have been preserved, though not totally restored. The assay office has been restored and contains a hard rock mining museum.

Today, the historical park preserves evidence of the once-booming mining operations while much of the surrounding area has been set aside to protect its value as a public recreation area and important wildlife habitat.

Climate: Elevations in the area range from less than 1,200 feet to more than 6,000 feet. Generally it is warmer and drier at lower elevations. The average maximum accumulation of snow at Independence Mine (3,300 feet) is 55 inches while along the Little Susitna River, at 1,700 feet, it is 42 inches. The average temperature in January ranges from 11.5°F to 24.7°F. Temperatures rise above 50°F only during the summer months. Temperature inversions are common on calm clear nights, and as the cold air drains down valley floors it can create winds up to 15 mph.

Wildlife: Moose populations in the forested western and southern portions of the Hatcher Pass area are said to be among the largest in Southcentral. Other wildlife present include occasional caribou, black and brown bears, wolves, wolverines, coyotes, beavers, foxes, martens, minks, weasels, lynx, hares, marmots and other small animals.

Nesting tundra birds occur within the area as well as bald and golden eagles, sharp-shinned hawks, red-tailed hawks, merlins, kestrels, gyrfalcons, peregrine falcons, boreal owls and great horned owls. Three resident ptarmigan species are found in the area as well as spruce grouse and a variety of songbirds.

Activities: Independence Mine State Historical Park includes several buildings and old mining machinery. The park visitor center is housed in a red-roofed building built in 1939 to house the mine manager. Guided tours of the bunkhouse, mess hall, warehouse and apartment complex are given from June to Labor Day; phone 745-2827 or 745-3975 for current information.

The area surrounding Independence Mine State Historical Park is a favorite for winter recreation. While other places in Southcentral may suffer from lack of snow, winter recreation enthusiasts usually can count on good snow conditions at Hatcher Pass. Several telemarking classes are held here as well as avalanche training. Other winter activities include dog mushing, sledding and riding snow machines.

During the summer and fall, visitors can enjoy photography, hiking, camping, mountaineering, fishing, horseback riding, picnicking, wildflower and wildlife viewing, moose hunting, berry picking and a number of other activities.

While the area is road accessible, it is still relatively remote, and visitors should take standard precautions for backcountry travel. Winter visitors should dress in warm layers and bring additional dry clothing. Sunglasses are essential on sunny days to block ultra-violet rays and protect against snow-blindness. Visitors planning travel away from the more accessible areas should be self-sufficient and knowledgeable in winter survival techniques. Summer visitors should be prepared for cool weather, also dressing in layers with a layer to protect against wind and rain. Insect repellent will be useful at lower elevations and in river valleys. Also be aware that pockets of private land and active mining claims are located within the area and should be respected.

Accommodations: Hatcher Pass Lodge (745-5897) at Independence Mine State Historical Park offers meals and lodging year-round and maintains several miles of groomed cross-country ski trails in the winter. There are no developed campgrounds in the area. Public restrooms are located at the park visitors center. Addi-

tional lodging and services available in Palmer and at Mile 6.5 Hatcher Pass Road.

Access: Located 68 miles from Anchorage via the Glenn Highway and Hatcher Pass Road. The 49-mile Hatcher Pass Road, a narrow, steep, rough and winding road, provides access to the area from Palmer. The mostly gravel road leads north, then west over 3,886-foot Hatcher Pass from Milepost 49.5 on the Glenn Highway. The road is open year-round from the Glenn Highway to the park visitor center at Mile 18, but it is closed over the pass and 14 miles up from the George Parks Highway from the first snow in late September until late June.

Hikers, skiers and snow machine users also take advantage of a number of former mining roads and trails to reach the more remote recreation areas.

For more information: Contact Alaska Division of Parks and Outdoor Recreation, Southcentral Region, P.O. Box 107001, Anchorage, AK 99510; phone 762-2616 or, the Mat-Su Area Office, HC32, Box 6706, Wasilla, AK 99687; phone 745-3975. Related USGS Topographic maps: Anchorage C-6, C-7, D-6, D-7 and D-8.

Cross-country skiers approach Independence Mine State Historical Park. Hatcher Pass is a popular winter recreation area. (Karen Jettmar)

Kachemak Bay State Park and State Wilderness Park

Located across Kachemak Bay from Homer, this is one of the largest and most scenic parks in the state system. It is also Alaska's first state park and its only wilderness state park. The state park encompasses 120,000 acres; the adjoining wilderness park 280,000 acres. This largely undeveloped park offers wilderness experiences combining ocean, forest, mountains, glaciers and a variety of wildlife. The waters of Kachemak Bay, reputedly among the most productive in the world, teem with marine life. Shifting weather patterns highlight the spectacular landscape. Twisted rock formations attest to the powerful forces produced by movement of the earth's crust. Scenic highlights and other attractions include Grewingk Glacier, Poot Peak, Gull Island, China Poot Bay, Humpy Creek, Halibut Cove Lagoon, Tutka Bay and Sadic Cove.

Climate: Kachemak Bay is an arm of the north Pacific Ocean and is subject to severe and unpredictable weather. On clear summer days, seas are usually calm until midmorning, when breezes begin, bringing southwest winds of 15 to 20 knots and seas of 3 to 6 feet. Conditions are often calm again in the evening.

Kachemak Bay's tides, among the largest in the world, are a primary factor affecting boating in the area. The average vertical difference between high and low tides is about 15 feet; the extreme, on large tide cycles, is 28 feet. Tidal currents are substantial and white-water rapids are frequently created in narrow passages. A tide book, available at local sporting goods stores, is essential. Use the tables for Seldovia and be aware of local variations. For weather and tide information, contact the Homer harbormaster, phone 235-8959.

Since the bay can be extremely rough, visitors should know the capabilities of their boats and themselves. Do not rush; wait for poor boating conditions to improve as they often do in the evenings. Fjords, bays and coves of Kachemak Bay contain navigational hazards; marine charts are available at sporting goods stores in Homer. Also, boaters should stay away from fishermen's buoys as their lines can damage outboard motors and propellers if run over, or the line may be cut. In July and August commercial salmon seiners operate in the area, particularly at Tutka Bay. Seine nets often stretch long distances across the water and recreational boaters must carefully maneuver around them.

Wildlife: This park offers excellent opportunities for observation and study of wildlife, including seabirds, seals, sea otters, whales, eagles and bears. Field guides to the bay's animals and plant life are available in Homer.

Activities: Park visitors have many opportunities for boating, beachcombing, camping, hiking and mountain climbing. Protected waters of the park can be visited by large and small craft. Intertidal zones provide an excellent setting for marine studies. Above tree line, climbers and skiers will find glaciers and snowfields stretching for miles. The park is open to hunting and fishing in accordance with state regulations.

Twenty-five miles of hiking trails, most of them accessible from Halibut Cove, wind through the park. These include Alpine Ridge, China Poot Lake, Goat Rope Spur, Grewingk Glacier, Lagoon, Poot Peak, Saddle and Wosnesenski trails. The state Division of Parks and Outdoor Recreation cautions that these trails receive little maintenance and often climb over steep, rugged terrain. Routes may be difficult to find and difficult to hike. Glacial streams cut across several trails and can be dangerous to cross. See map opposite page, see trail description under Hiking Trails this section. For the trails listed, the hiking times given are the minimum needed by a person in good physical condition without a pack to hike the trail one way. For more information, contact a state park ranger in Homer or Halibut Cove Lagoon.

Accommodations: While there are few visitor facilities, rough trails lead to various points of interest. A map is available from the park office. There are a few campsites in the Halibut Cove area. Campgrounds are located north of Rusty's Lagoon and on the south portion of Glacier Spit; restrooms, picnic tables and firepits are available. Fresh water is available from streams or springs; all drinking water obtained in the park should be boiled or treated. Open campfires are permitted only on beaches or gravel bars; portable stoves must be used elsewhere. Trash containers are not provided in the park; all litter must be packed out and human waste buried well away from sources of drinking water or trails. A public use cabin is available for rent in Halibut Cove Lagoon from May through September. Call 762-2261 for cost and availability information.

It is recommended that visitors to the park be equipped with high quality outdoor

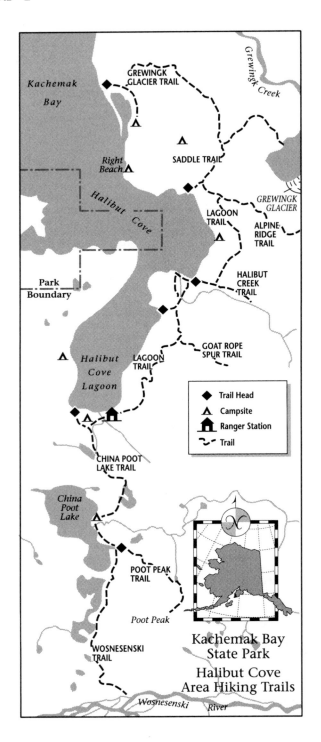

Kachemak Bay

GREWINGK GLACIER TRAIL

Grewingk Creek

SADDLE TRAIL

Right Beach

Halibut Cove

GREWINGK GLACIER

LAGOON TRAIL

ALPINE RIDGE TRAIL

Park Boundary

HALIBUT CREEK TRAIL

GOAT ROPE SPUR TRAIL

Halibut Cove Lagoon

LAGOON TRAIL

◆ Trail Head
⛺ Campsite
🏠 Ranger Station
〜 Trail

CHINA POOT LAKE TRAIL

China Poot Lake

POOT PEAK TRAIL

Poot Peak

Kachemak Bay State Park

Halibut Cove Area Hiking Trails

WOSNESENSKI TRAIL

Wosnesenski River

clothing and equipment including rain gear, waterproof boots, gloves and hats, extra clothing, matches, maps, tide book, compass, tent or tarp, sleeping bag, camp stove and extra food. Boaters should be equipped with life jackets, flares, extra line, anchor gear, nautical charts, oars, fire extinguishers and adequate fuel since none is available in the park or at Halibut Cove.

A ranger station is located at the end of Halibut Cove Lagoon, but it is staffed seasonally and the ranger is not always available for assistance. Park visitors should be self-sufficient. Emergency assistance can be obtained through the U.S. Coast Guard Auxiliary (CB Channel 9, VHF Channel 16); Homer harbormaster (CB Channel 17 call number KCN 7188 Base 3, VHF Channel 16 call number WAB 958); or Alaska State Troopers, phone 235-8239.

Access: This park is reached only by plane or boat. Air and water taxi services are available in Homer. Charter boats are available in Halibut Cove. Accommodations and meals are available at Homer, Seldovia and Halibut Cove.

Many of the most attractive beaches and camping sites in the park are privately owned. Respect No Trespassing signs. Much of China Poot Bay is owned by the Seldovia Native Assoc., although in May 1993 the state legislature approved spending to buy the Native-owned lands and timber rights inside the park, in an effort to block logging plans. Until the transaction takes place, visitors should contact the association, phone 234-7625, if they wish to use Seldovia land. The location of private lands can be obtained from the park office.

For more information: Contact Alaska State Parks, P.O. Box 321, Homer, AK 99603; phone 235-7024, fax 235-8386.

Kenai Fjords National Park

This park of approximately 580,000 acres encompasses a coastal mountain-fjord system on the southeastern side of the Kenai Peninsula. The park is capped by the 300-square-mile Harding Icefield almost a mile above the Gulf of Alaska. It is believed to be a remnant of the last ice age, when ice masses covered half of the state of Alaska. The ice field's skyline is marked by nunataks, the tips of mountains whose lower slopes are submerged in ice.

Moist marine air from the Gulf of Alaska dumps 700 to 1,000 inches of snow on the ice field each year. The pull of gravity and weight of the overlying new snow causes the ice to spread until it is shaped into glaciers that flow downward, carving the landscape into spectacular shapes. There are 33 named glaciers that radiate from the ice field; along the coast, tidewater glaciers calve directly into salt water.

The park was named after the long valleys once filled with glacial ice that are now deep, ocean-filled fjords. The seaward ends of mountain ridges are dipping into the water, being dragged under by the collision of 2 tectonic plates. As the land sinks into the sea, mountain peaks become wave-beaten islands, sea stacks and jagged shorelines. Glacier-carved cirques become half-moon bays.

Climate: A subarctic maritime climate prevails in Kenai Fjords. Spring is usually the driest time of the year; fall and early winter are wettest. Storms are most common in winter, when waves up to 30 feet have been reported. Mean annual rainfall for nearby Seward is 67 inches. June normally begins the travel season, as spring storms cease and daytime temperatures climb into the 50s and 60s. Mean winter low temperatures range from 0°F to 20°F. Warm, sunny days do occur, but they are the exception rather than the rule. Visitors should be prepared for the usual overcast and/or cool days by bringing comfortable wool clothing and good rain gear.

The Park Service cautions that the coastal fjords are rugged, remote and exposed to the stormy Gulf of Alaska. Strong currents flow past them and few landing sites exist. Those entering the fjords without a guide should seek information from the National Park Service headquarters or the U.S. Coast Guard in Seward on mooring areas, navigational hazards and weather. Also, crevasses and foul weather pose hazards on the Harding Icefield and its glaciers. The Park Service says anyone venturing to that area should have experience, good equipment and stamina. It also is recommended that you leave an itinerary with a friend, and contact that person upon completion of your trip.

Wildlife: Bald eagles nest in spruce and hemlock treetops along the shoreline, and mountain goats inhabit rocky slopes. Moose, black and brown bears, wolves and Dall sheep are found in the park. Raucous Steller sea lions live on rocky islands at the entrance to Aialik and Nuka bays; centuries of hauling out have worn the granite rocks smooth. Harbor seals can be seen resting on icebergs. Killer whales, Dall porpoise and sea otters, as well as minke, gray, fin and humpback whales also are found. Thousands of seabirds, including horned and tufted puffins, auklets, petrels, common murres and black-legged kittiwakes rear their young on steep cliffs.

Dolly Varden and 5 species of salmon spawn in clear-water drainages within the park. Shrimp, crabs and other shellfish are found off the coast. Sportfishing for salmon and bottom fish is popular in Resurrection and Aialik bays.

Activities and Access: Several charter boat operators in Seward, gateway to Kenai Fjords National Park, offer all-day tours to view the park's tidewater glaciers and abundant marine life. Tours are offered from mid-May to mid-September and some include lunch and beverages; check at the Seward Small Boat Harbor. Kenai Fjords is also a popular destination for experienced kayakers. Kayak rentals and guided kayak trips may be arranged in Seward. Seward is located 127 miles south of Anchorage via the Seward Highway.

Exit Glacier is the most accessible of the park's glaciers and a center of activity. Turn off at Milepost 3.7 Seward Highway and follow the 9-mile dirt and gravel Exit Glacier Road to its end at a parking lot with toilets and picnic area next to Exit Glacier ranger station. A flat and easy 0.8-mile Lower Loop trail (and steeper 0.5-mile Upper Loop trail) leads to the base of the glacier; the first 0.3 mile of the trail is paved and wheelchair accessible. There is also a nature trail. A strenuous 3.5-mile trail leads to Harding Icefield from the parking lot. Summer activities at Exit Glacier include daily ranger-led walks and hikes.

The Exit Glacier area is open in winter for skiing, snowshoeing, snowmobiling and dog mushing.

The visitor center in Seward features exhibits, a slide show and a wide selection of books. The center also offers daily interpretive programs.

Accommodations: There are overnight accommodations in Seward. For summer visitors, public-use cabins are located in Aialik Bay, Holgate Arm, Delight Spit and North Arm. The cabins have no conveniences. Fee for use is $20 per party per night, with a limit of 3 nights per party per year. In the winter, visitors may use a cabin at Exit Glacier for $25 per night. The cabin is open only when the road is closed to vehicle use. Reservations may be made up to 180 days in advance and will be confirmed upon receipt of fee. For information or to reserve the cabins, contact the park headquarters. Back-

country camping is permitted in the park; no fees or permits are required. There is a 10-site walk-in campground at Exit Glacier; no fee, water available. The park visitor center is located at 1212 4th Ave. in Seward next to the small-boat harbor.

For more information: Contact Superintendent, Kenai Fjords National Park, P.O. Box 1727, Seward, AK 99664; phone 224-3175. Related USGS Topographic maps: Seward, Blying Sound, Seldovia.

Marine Parks

The state of Alaska has established 33 marine parks, of which 14 are located in Southeast Alaska, 14 in Prince William Sound, and 5 in and around Resurrection Bay. These parks are part of an international system of shoreline parks and recreation areas stretching from near Olympia, WA, up through British Columbia, and as far north as Prince William Sound. Eventually there may be more than 150 of these parks, most a 1-day boat trip from each other. Following is a list of the 19 marine parks located in Prince William Sound and Resurrection Bay.

For more information: Contact the Alaska Division of Parks, P.O. Box 107001, Anchorage, AK 99510; phone 762-2617.

Western Prince William Sound

Surprise Cove. Located at the entrance to Cochrane Bay approximately 15 miles east of Whittier along a major route for pleasure boats between Whittier and western Prince William Sound. The park includes 2 small embayments off Cochrane Bay and 2 freshwater lakes, and offers a well-protected anchorage. A short trail with a rope-assisted climb begins at the cove to North Lake. Mountain goats are found on nearby peaks; porpoises often are observed at Point Cochrane. A small beach near the entrance to the cove is used as a campsite by kayakers. Other sites are available on the exposed beach north of Point Cochrane and by the northern bend in the coast.

Surprise Cove is one of the most popular anchorages in the area, and on weekends 8 or more boats may be anchored in the cove.

Zeigler Cove. Located on the northern shore of the entrance to Pigot Bay on the west side of Port Wells, approximately 14 miles east of Whittier. The cove is on a low, forested point extending into both Pigot Bay and Port Wells. It offers a small, but very well-protected anchorage suitable for 4 boats. There is good hiking in the uplands, and good fishing nearby for red snapper, halibut, pink, chum and king salmon, as well as Dungeness crab. A campsite is located on the east corner of the cove above the shale pebble beach.

Bettles Bay. Located on the western shore of Port Wells, approximately 20 miles from Whittier. This large, well-protected bay is a favorite of boaters exploring the Port Wells area, as it is considered one of the most scenic on the west shore. Wildlife in the area includes black bears, sea lions, whales, seals and waterfowl. Fish include halibut, pink and chum salmon and Dungeness crab. An abandoned mine is located approximately 0.5 mile southwest of the park.

South Esther Island. Located at the confluence of Wells Passage and Port Wells in upper Prince William Sound, approximately 20 miles due east of Whittier. This is a popular base of operations for excursions in the Port Wells, Port Nellie Juan and Culross Passage areas. Anchorages are found in both Lake and Quillian bays. Lake Bay is the home of one of the world's largest fish hatcheries. The Wally H. Noerenberg Fish Hatchery offers free tours of the facility. Esther Island is very scenic, with a number of 2,000-foot granite peaks. Whales may be observed in Port Wells; sea lions frequently haul out on nearby islands and rocks. Seabirds nest in the area and seals and sea otters also may be seen.

Horseshoe Bay. Located on Latouche Island in southwestern Prince William Sound, approximately halfway between Seward and Whittier. Although somewhat exposed to southwesterly winds, Horseshoe Bay offers the most protected anchorage along the island's shoreline. The bay and island are very scenic, with nearby peaks rising to 2,000 feet. The old gold mining town of Latouche is located 2 miles to the northeast. There is excellent hiking and climbing at nearby Broon Buttes. Whales, seals and sea lions frequent Latouche Passage. Except for recreational lots at the old town of Latouche and an area south of the park, Chugach Natives Ltd. owns most of the island. Private property should be respected; observe any No Trespassing signs.

Decision Point. Located at the eastern end of Passage Canal approximately 8 miles from Whittier. The park is generally used by kayakers and small boat users, as there is no adequate anchorage. Along with forested uplands of spruce and hemlock, there are two excellent camping beaches. At the head of Squirrel Cove, a small pebble and sand beach provides room for 2 tents during all but the highest tide cycles. Drinking water is not available at this site. Just south of Decision Point is an east-facing, medium-pebble beach that provides dry, flat camping for up to 10 tents between the dead trees. The camp areas are above high tide and have 2 fire rings. This is one of the sites most used by kayakers. Water is available in the bight, or bend, in the coast behind the small peninsula. Bountiful intertidal life on the rocks at Decision Point may be viewed during minus tides.

Entry Cove. Located 2 miles directly east of Decision Point on the northeast corner where Passage Canal and Port Wells meet. Forested uplands of spruce and hemlock, interspersed with muskeg, surround a small cove and lagoon. Near the cove entrance is good anchorage on northwind days, but it is generally not used overnight because of variable winds out of Blackstone Bay. The lagoon is a good site for clamming, but the entrance is shallow and can only be accessed by small boats during full high tide. Just east of the entrance to the lagoon, above the gravel beach, are sites for about 10 tents on beach gravel between the trees. A natural arch located on the east shore of the cove and a beautiful view of Tebenkof Glacier can be seen from the camp area. During moderate and low tide cycles, some people camp on the sand spit that attaches the Pigot Point Island.

Granite Bay. Located on the northwest corner of Esther Island about 25 miles from Whittier. The park includes 2 bays, protective islands, muskeg and old-growth forest uplands. Most of the shoreline has steep granite cliffs, boulders and slabs. The surrounding hills provide excellent hiking and climbing with views in all directions. Many lakes and ponds dot the uplands. Tange Lake drains into the head of the northern arm and has been stocked with rainbow trout.

Anchorage is excellent in both bays. A mooring buoy is located between the bays, behind the islands. A tent platform is located on the northernmost island at the mouth of the north bay. There are other tent sites on heather or in beach grass. Boaters should be aware of a reef that extends nearly a mile off shore, just south of the mouth of the southern bay.

Eastern Prince William Sound

Sawmill Bay. Located on the north shore of Port Valdez, approximately 14

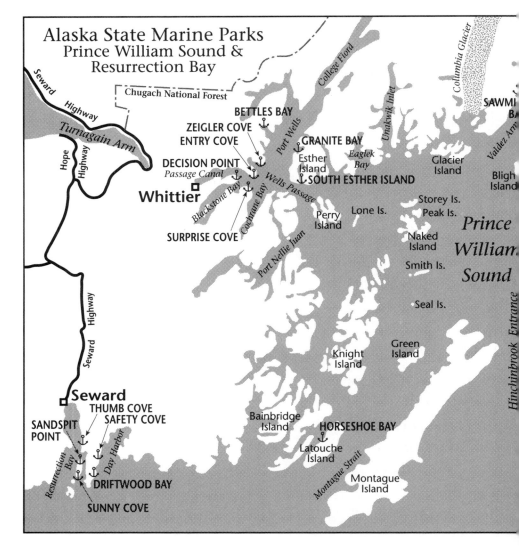

Alaska State Marine Parks
Prince William Sound &
Resurrection Bay

Chugach National Forest

Seward Highway
Turnagain Arm
Hope Highway

Whittier
Passage Canal
Blackstone Bay
Cochrane Bay
Wells Passage

DECISION POINT
ENTRY COVE
ZEIGLER COVE
BETTLES BAY
SURPRISE COVE

GRANITE BAY
Esther Island
Eaglek Bay
SOUTH ESTHER ISLAND

College Fiord
Port Wells
Unakwik Inlet

Columbia Glacier
SAWMI
B.
Glacier Island
Valdez Arm
Bligh Island

Storey Is.
Peak Is.
Lone Is.
Perry Island
Naked Island
Smith Is.

Prince William Sound

Seal Is.

Seward Highway

Port Nellie Juan

Knight Island
Green Island

Seward
THUMB COVE
SAFETY COVE
SANDSPIT POINT
Resurrection Bay
Day Harbor
DRIFTWOOD BAY
SUNNY COVE

Bainbridge Island
Latouche Island
HORSESHOE BAY
Montague Strait
Montague Island

Hinchinbrook Entrance

miles west and south of Valdez. This large, well-protected bay is surrounded by 4,000-foot peaks; it offers several good anchorages for pleasure boaters and receives considerable use by boaters from Valdez. There is fishing for silver salmon and halibut; crab and clams are also available. The boreal forest consists of spruce, hemlock and muskeg. There is good hiking along Twin Falls Creek and near Devish Lake. The entire western shore and uplands are privately owned by the Tatitlek Corp. Private-property rights should be respected.

Shoup Bay. Located on the north shore of Port Valdez, 7.5 miles west of Valdez. A well-protected anchorage does not exist in the bay, but short-term or fair-weather anchorages can be found in several areas depending on wind direction. Shoup Bay is very scenic; 17-mile-long Shoup Glacier extends almost to the bay from the northwest and a large sand spit extends across the mouth of the bay. Mountain goats can be seen on the slopes above the bay, and ducks feed on the tidal flats. A black-legged kittiwake rookery can be found in the

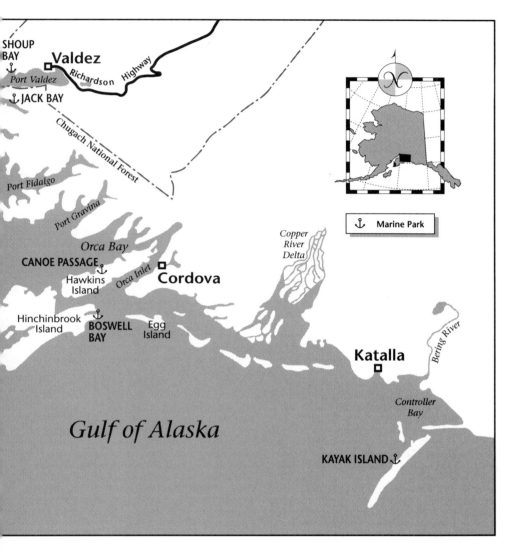

SHOUP BAY
⚓
Valdez
□
Port Valdez
Richardson Highway
⚓ JACK BAY
Chugach National Forest
Port Fidalgo
Port Gravina
Orca Bay
CANOE PASSAGE ⚓
Hawkins Island
Orca Inlet
Cordova □
Hinchinbrook Island
⚓ BOSWELL BAY
Egg Island
Copper River Delta
⚓ Marine Park
Katalla □
Bering River
Controller Bay
Gulf of Alaska
KAYAK ISLAND ⚓

lagoon. Bald eagles, arctic terns and various waterfowl are frequently seen there. Shoup Glacier is the main tributary of the huge glacier that carved Valdez Arm thousands of years ago. During the 1964 earthquake, an undersea slide from its submerged moraine created a 170-foot-high wave (listed in the *Guinness Book of World Records*); reportedly the bay emptied and refilled 3 times.

Campsites are available at the eastern end of the lagoon, around the perimeter of the bay and at the base of the spit at the eastern edge of the bay.

Jack Bay. Located 15 miles from Valdez, southeast of Valdez Narrows. The uplands of the park consist of alder, muskeg, salt-marsh and old-growth forest of spruce and hemlock. The northern arm of Jack Bay within the marine park becomes shallow one-quarter mile out and caution is recommended. Although the bay can be used as a fairweather anchorage, it is not protected. The best campsite is located on the island in the middle of the bay. On the southeast end of the island is a protected bight, or bend in the coast, with four campsites. The main one is immediately above the beach on beach gravel, while the others are behind in the forest and on the peninsula just north of the beach. Another site exists near the tip of the peninsula on the mainland just east of the island in a wet and boggy area. None of these campsites have water nearby. Water can be obtained on the northern shore of the bay.

Canoe Passage. Located on Hawkins Island 8 miles west of Cordova. This park encompasses the natural low pass on the island. Forested uplands and considerable wetlands line Canoe Passage. The seas are shallow to the south. The rest of Hawkins Island is private land.

Boswell Bay. Located on the eastern tip of Hinchinbrook Island. Evidence of a geologic land lift can be seen here. In 30 years, the shoreline has expanded toward the sea by more than 1 mile. This southern edge of the park is a high-energy beach exposed to the Gulf of Alaska. Beachcombing and hunting are popular. Areas of the park are adjacent to the Copper River Delta State Critical Habitat.

Kayak Island. Located 200 miles east-southeast of Anchorage and 62 miles southeast of Cordova in the Gulf of Alaska, this remote, narrow island is the location of the first documented landing by Europeans on North America's northwest coast. Naturalist George Wilhelm Steller and other members of an expedition led by Captain Commander Vitus Bering landed near the mouth of a creek on the leeward (west) shore of Kayak Island on July 20, 1741. They were the first Europeans to set foot on the island. Although the party was ashore just a few hours to replenish water supplies, Steller sketched and named many plants and animals in the area, including the Steller's jay. Reportedly, Stellar found an empty Native camp on the island and took some goods from its absent inhabitants, leaving European goods in their place. No trace of their landing remains today, and it is theorized that the landing site became submerged in the gulf during the 1964 earthquake. The Bering Expedition Landing Site is a National Historic Landmark. The state marine park is located at the site. The 22-mile-long, 1.5-mile-wide island also is the location of another historic site, the Cape St. Elias Light Station.

This wild, uninhabited island offers excellent opportunities for beachcombing, hiking, camping, photography, berry picking, fishing, hunting and exploring.

The U.S. Forest Service recommends that visitors bring extra food and other supplies since bad weather can prolong your stay for days at a time. Also, take a tide table with the Sitka-area tide data; some beaches are impassable at higher tides. Pinnacle Rock, 494 feet high, is connected to the southern-most tip of the island (Cape St. Elias) by a low, 0.2-mile ribbon of land and may not be accessible at higher tides. It's not a pleasant place to be stranded.

Kayak Island is not easy to get to because of its remoteness and frequent rainy, windy weather. A boat trip from Cordova usually takes 12 to 16 hours, one way, depending on conditions, which in this area are often extremely rough.

For additional information on Kayak Island contact Chugach National Forest, Cordova Ranger District, P.O. Box 280, Cordova, AK 99574; phone 424-7661.

Resurrection Bay

Thumb Cove. Located approximately 9 miles south of Seward on the east side of Resurrection Bay. The park's 720 acres include the southeast shoreline of the cove; a long beach of fine to medium sand and beach gravel; forested uplands of spruce, hemlock and alder; and most of the waters of Thumb Cove. Perhaps the most striking geologic feature in the area is Porcupine Glacier, towering above the park and providing a dramatic backdrop to this popular marine destination.

Thumb Cove is a favorite stop for Seward's recreational boaters, and camping is popular along the beaches. Fishing for salmon is a favorite activity during the various runs, and Thumb Cove offers good protection from the often unstable weather of Resurrection Bay. Fresh water is available from a stream flowing from Porcupine Glacier.

Sandspit Point. Located at the northeast tip of Fox Island (Renard Island) in Resurrection Bay, 12 miles southeast of Seward. The park includes steep, inaccessible uplands to the west and a half-mile-long spit to the east, for a total of 560 acres. The north beach of the spit is fine sand, while the south beach is medium to large cobbles. Marine tide pools abound near the west end of the spit, and a low spruce forest dominates the higher east end.

Sandspit Point offers spectactular panoramic views of Resurrection Bay to the north and Eldorado Narrows to the south. The variety of marine life found in tide pools, the ease of launching and landing on the sandy northern beach, and suitability for beach camping make this a popular destination for kayakers. The southern beach is not recommended for landings due to its rocky nature and the often heavy surf. There is no fresh water available in the park.

Sunny Cove. Located 14 miles south of Seward at the south end of Fox Island (Renard Island) in Resurrection Bay. The cove faces west, providing a good view of Callisto Head, Bear Glacier and Kenai Fjords National Park. The park provides a good camping beach along the south shore of the cove with fine to medium beach gravel. The park's 960 acres encompass the entire south portion of Fox Island, including an unnamed peak of 1,362 feet. With the exception of the south beach of Sunny Cove, the park's coastline is characterized by vertical rock cliffs.

Sunny Cove is popular as an anchorage for sailboats and power boats. Excellent wildlife viewing exists around the vertical cliffs, especially along the eastern shore. Numerous seabird species and marine mammals can be easily viewed from skiff or kayak. Fresh water is available seasonally in the park; during wet weather, water is generally available from small waterfalls south along the shore from the cove, but these can only be reached at low tide.

Driftwood Bay. Located along the southwest coast of Day Harbor to the east of Resurrection Bay, a 23-mile boat ride from Seward. The park's shoreline includes medium to coarse gravel beaches interspersed with steep rock cliffs. Driftwood Bay, the largest of the area's marine parks at 1,480 acres, offers excellent mountain views and wildlife viewing opportunities.

The bay is a popular anchorage for recreational boaters and offers good protection from Day Harbor's often rough seas. Fishing for saltwater fish species is popular in Driftwood Bay and Day Harbor. Fresh water is limited to runoff during wet weather.

Safety Cove. Located along the western side of Day Harbor to the east of Resurrection Bay, a 28-mile boat ride from Seward. The park's 960 acres include the cove's marine environment and an upland spruce, hemlock and alder forest. An attractive geologic feature of this park is a 3-acre freshwater lake just above a gravel storm berm at the head of the cove.

Safety Cove offers excellent beach camping as well as safe anchorage for recreational boats. Upland exploration is also an appealing activity in the park, and there are excellent views of Ellsworth Glacier, an arm of the Sargent Icefield near the cove's entrance. Fresh water can be taken from the lake at the head of the cove.

Nancy Lake State Recreation Area

Located just 67 miles north of Anchorage via the Glenn and Parks highways between the Susitna River and the Talkeetna Mountains, this 22,685-acre state recreation area provides easily accessible wilderness experiences all year.

The area is dominated by lakes, streams, and swamps which drain into the Susitna River or Cook Inlet. Mature spruce, birch and poplar forests surround the lake. Blueberry, raspberry and crowberry plants are plentiful and provide good berry picking in late summer and early fall. Pickers should learn to identify baneberry, which looks edible but is poisonous.

Once covered by huge glaciers, the area has been free of ice for at least 9,000 years and state archaeologists believe that the area was heavily used by early Natives. Nancy Lake's Indian Bay is the site of an Indian village that was established near the turn of the century and a few descendants of the village residents still live in the area. In 1917 the Alaska Railroad was built on the east side of the lower Susitna Valley bringing with it homesteaders and fueling the growth of the towns of Wasilla, Houston and Willow. The Nancy Lake area was avoided by settlers because it was too wet.

Climate: Summer temperatures range from lows between 40°F and 50°F and highs in the 70s and 80s reflecting the warmer and sunnier weather patterns of interior Alaska. Winter temperatures can fall to -40°F or colder and rarely rise above freezing before mid-March. The lakes freeze in late October, about the same time as the first snow falls, and are free of ice by late May. Average snow accumulation is about 48 inches.

Wildlife: Beavers are found on numerous lakes thoughout and are important in maintaining water levels in the area. Moose and black bears are common. Lynx, coyote, wolves and brown bears may be seen in more remote areas.

Grebes, ducks, geese and shorebirds use the lakes and ponds in the area during their migrations and many stay to nest in the area. Green-headed loons, with their eerie laughing call, are one of the trademarks of the area. Loons seen ashore are frequently nesting and easily spooked, often deserting their nests. Visitors should leave them alone. Arctic terns are also summer residents. The hiker unlucky enough to stumble into a nest is likely to be repeatedly dive-bombed by screeching terns. Sandhill cranes may be seen exhibiting their courtship dance along the Nancy Lake Parkway during their spring migration. Hawks, owls, kingfishers, woodpeckers and numerous songbirds are also seen in the area.

Lake trout, rainbow trout, whitefish and Dolly Varden are found in Red Shirt, Butterfly, Lynx and Nancy lakes. Big and Little Noluck lakes were restocked with trout and silver salmon in 1975 by the Alaska Dept. of Fish and Game. Northern pike are found in Red Shirt, Lynx and Tanaina lakes.

Vegetation within the recreation area is dominated in drier areas by white spruce and paper birch, with some aspen interspersed. Wetter forests support stands of smaller black spruce, which give way to low-brush bogs and muskeg swamps highlighted by cotton grass plumes. Violets, bluebells, fireweed, bog rosemary and wild iris add color. Large parts of the Nancy Lake area have been burned by forest fires in the past 100 years, resulting in thick stands of birch.

Activities: The area's summertime attraction is its canoe trail system. Visitors can spend an afternoon or a long weekend canoeing through the various chains of lakes and streams that dot the area. Two favorites are the 8-mile Lynx Lake Loop and the Little Susitna River. Canoes can be rented at a local marina and at South Rolly Campground. Other summer activities include hiking, camping and fishing.

The summer canoe and hiking trails are transformed in winter to 40 miles of trails for cross-country skiing, dog mushing, snowshoeing and snowmobiling. Most of the 40 miles of trails are open for motorized snow vehicles. Ten miles of trails are set aside for cross-country skiers only. Ice fishing is also a popular winter activity. Nancy Lake, Lynx Lake and Red Shirt offer the best opportunities for catching winter rainbow trout. Burbot and pike are found in Red Shirt.

Accommodations: Camping at South Rolly Lake Campground (106 sites, $6 fee), located at Mile 6.6 on the Nancy Lake Parkway. Nancy Lake State Recreation Site on the northeast shore of Nancy Lake has more than 30 sites and is reached from mile 66.5

of the Parks Highway. Rustic cabins are also available for rent. The cabins are insulated and equipped with bunks, shelves and a woodburning stove. All have outdoor fireplaces and a latrine. Call Mat-Su Area office in Wasilla, 745-3975, for reservations.

Access: Located 67 miles north of Anchorage via the George Parks Highway. The park's hiking trails, picnic area, campground and canoe launch are found along the gravel access (Nancy Lake Parkway).

For more information: Detailed maps of the canoe and hiking trails, and information on established campgrounds can be obtained from the Division of Parks and Outdoor Recreation, Southcentral Region, P.O. Box 107001, Anchorage, AK 99510; phone 561-2020. Or, the Mat-Su Area Office, HC32, Box 6706, Wasilla, AK 99687; phone 745-3975.

Wrangell-St. Elias National Park and Preserve

Located northwest of Yakutat and northeast of Cordova and Valdez, Wrangell-St. Elias is the largest unit in the national park system, encompassing 13.2 million acres of superlative scenery, abundant wildlife and fascinating history. In conjunction with adjacent Kluane National Park in Canada, the 2 areas make up the largest parkland in North America. Here the Wrangell, St. Elias and Chugach mountain ranges converge, forming a mountain wilderness unsurpassed in North America and comparable to all other major mountain groups in the world. The region contains the largest concentration of peaks exceeding 14,500 feet in North America; Wrangell-St. Elias park contains 9 of the 16 highest peaks in the United States. Mount St. Elias, at 18,008 feet, is the second tallest peak in the United States; Mount Logan, across the border in Kluane park, soars to a height of 19,850 feet, second only to Mount McKinley in North American summits.

This park has been shaped by both volcanoes and ice. Mount Wrangell (14,163 feet) experienced a phreatic eruption (like a geyser) as recently as 1924. Dormant volcanoes include Mount Blackburn (16,390 feet), Mount Sanford (16,237 feet) and Mount Drum (12,010 feet). On the western flank of Mount Drum are 3 large thermal springs known as mud volcanoes.

The area also contains the largest concentration of glaciers on the continent. One of these, Malaspina Glacier, is North America's largest piedmont glacier, a type formed when 2 or more glaciers flow from confined valleys to form a broad fan- or lobe-shaped ice mass. Malaspina Glacier covers an area of about 1,500 square miles—larger than the state of Rhode Island. It has been designated a national natural landmark. Hubbard Glacier, which flows out of the St. Elias Mountains into Disenchantment Bay, is one of the largest and most active glaciers in North America. In 1986, the glacier made national headlines when it surged forward, sealing off adjacent Russell Fiord. Within 2 months, the ice dam had broken, but Hubbard Glacier continues to advance and scientists agree the glacier will eventually close off the fjord permanently.

The Park Service says Chitistone and Nizina canyons "far exceed the scale of Yosemite Valley in California" and include an even greater variety of geological wonders. There is a spectacular 300-foot waterfall in upper Chitistone Canyon and the lower canyon has sheer walls rising 4,000 feet above the river.

Wrangell-St. Elias contains many prehistoric and historic sites, including ancient Eskimo and Indian villages and camps, sites of Russian fur-trading posts, gold rush relics and industrial complexes of the early 20th century—such as the Kennecott mine, the most famous and richest copper mine in Alaska until market conditions led to its abandonment in 1938. *NOTE: The Kennecott mine buildings are private property.*

Tree line in the park's interior is about 3,000 to 4,000 feet. Below this the forest cover is composed of white and black spruce and balsam poplar at lower elevations, and a mixture of aspen, birch and balsam poplar where fires have transformed the forest. Streambeds contain thick underbrush, usually alder, which also grows well on steep south-facing hillsides. Labrador tea and dwarf birch are major shrubs. Above 3,000 feet, moist sedges and grasses form open tundra meadows interlaced with blueberries and Labrador tea. The Bremner and Copper river valleys have typical coastal vegetation near their mouths: western and mountain hemlock and Sitka spruce rain forest with devil's club, blueberries and salmonberries.

Climate: Weather in most of the area is typical of interior Alaska. Summer brings cool, often cloudy and rainy weather, which can interfere with scheduled air pickups and prolong trips. Clear, hot days are not uncommon, particularly in July, which has the warmest weather. August is cooler and

wetter, but generally has less mosquitoes. Fall is excellent, but doesn't last long. Winters are cold and dark, with temperatures dropping to -50°F, but clear weather is common. Average snow cover is about 2 feet. In coastal areas precipitation is higher (130 inches in some areas) and temperatures are relatively moderate with winter lows around 0°F and summer highs in the 70s.

The Park Service cautions that visitors to the Wrangell-St. Elias backcountry must be self-sufficient, carry enough food to cover unexpected delays and be prepared for the Alaskan wilderness. Rain gear and synthetic pile or wool clothing are essential. Animals are wild and should be respected. Travelers should know their gear and have wilderness travel and survival skills; sources of assistance are frequently many miles away. Always leave an itinerary with the Park Service or with a friend and contact that person after returning. A Park Service ranger station is open year-round in Glennallen and during the summers at Slana, Chitina and Yakutat. Also, some of the land within the park/preserve is privately owned and local residents carry on subsistence lifestyles; respect their property and privacy.

Kennecott Copper Mine employed some 800 workers in its heyday. (Bill Sherwonit)

Wildlife: These diverse habitats support varied wildlife. On higher slopes range Dall sheep and mountain goats—sheep in the Wrangell Mountains and northern slopes of the Chugach Range, goats in the coastal mountains. Caribou from 3 herds forage on parklands. Moose browse throughout the lowlands and river bottoms and 2 herds of introduced bison range along the Copper and Chitina rivers. Brown/grizzly and black bears share lower elevations with wolves, wolverines, coyotes, red foxes and a variety of small furbearers.

Marine mammals which can be observed in Yakutat Bay, where the park touches the sea, include seals, sea lions, sea otters, 2 species of dolphin and killer whales.

Sport fish, such as arctic grayling, burbot and trout thrive in lakes adjacent to the Chitina River valley and on the northern slopes of the Wrangells, while the Copper River supports a major salmon run utilized by both commercial and subsistence fishermen.

Bird life is not outstanding within the park/preserve, although trumpeter swans, bald and golden eagles, 3 species of ptarmigan and ruffed and spruce grouse can be seen. Just to the south of the park the Copper River Delta is a major nesting area.

Activities: Recreational opportunities in Wrangell-St. Elias include hunting, fishing, expedition mountaineering, backpacking, photography, cross-country skiing, rafting/kayaking and wildlife observation. The Park Service offers a trip synopsis list to help in trip planning. None of the hikes listed are on marked or maintained trails; rather, they follow unimproved "backcountry" routes consisting of mining trails, historic routes, streambeds, shorelines, game trails, and open country.

Navigable rivers in the park include the Copper River and Chitina River. It is possible to float several other streams in the park, such as the Nabesna and Kennicott rivers. See River Running this section and check with the National Park Service for more information on rafting and kayaking rivers. Icy Bay is a popular sea kayaking destination.

The old mine buildings of the Kennecott Copper Corp. are located 4.5 miles from McCarthy on private land. The richest copper mine in the world until its closure in 1938, Kennicott's mill processed more than 591,535 tons of copper ore.

Accommodations: Privately operated lodges, cabins and camps are scattered throughout the park and preserve, in nearby McCarthy/Kennicott area and along the Nabesna and McCarthy roads. These include fishing camps, guide cabins, full-service lodges, commercial campgrounds and air taxi services. A list of these facilities and services is available from park headquarters. Several campgrounds are operated by the Bureau of Land Management and the state of Alaska along the Richardson Highway, Tok Cutoff and Edgerton Highway. There are no designated campgrounds within the park/preserve; wilderness camping only. No permits are necessary for camping or backpacking although voluntary registration is requested. All water obtained from streams or lakes should be boiled or treated. The park's visitor center is located at Milepost V 105.1, just north of Copper Center, on the Richardson Highway; rangers there provide briefings on the park and trip planning assistance. The center is open 8 A.M. to 6 P.M. daily, Memorial Day through Labor Day. There are also ranger stations at Slana, Mile 0.2 Nabesna Road, open 8 A.M. to 5 P.M. daily, June 1 through September; Chitina, Mile 33 Edgerton Highway, open 8 A.M. to 5 P.M. daily Memorial Day through Labor Day; and Yakutat.

Access: Wrangell-St. Elias is one of the more accessible national parks in Alaska; 2 roads lead into the area. Major access is by road along the Richardson Highway and Edgerton Highway from Glennallen to Chitina. The gravel McCarthy Road extends some 59 miles up the Chitina River valley from Chitina to the Kennicott River just west of McCarthy. The road follows the abandoned railroad bed of the Copper River and Northwestern Railway. During the summer it is generally passable by 2-wheel-drive vehicles. Inquire in Chitina about road conditions before proceeding to McCarthy. The trip to the Kennicott River can easily take 3 to 4 hours. The road ends about 1 mile west of McCarthy at the 2 forks of the Kennicott River. Crossing the river to reach McCarthy currently is by 9 hand-pulled cable trams and a footbridge. (DO NOT attempt to wade across this glacial river except at very low water.) The trams are small open platforms and should be attempted only by travelers strong enough to pull themselves across several hundred feet; part of the distance is uphill. Wear gloves. Crossing is easier if someone standing on the bank does the pulling. Once across the river, follow the road to the McCarthy Museum then take the right fork of the road to McCarthy. The abandoned Kennecott Copper Mine is 4 miles beyond the McCarthy Museum. Regularly scheduled van service is available from Glennallen, Valdez and Denali to McCarthy. Call Backcountry Connection for information, 822-5292.

Road access to the northern section of the park/preserve is from Slana (on the Tok Cutoff) along a 43-mile unpaved state-maintained road to the privately owned mining community of Nabesna. This road is plowed intermittently in winter. All other access to the park/preserve is by boat or air. There are 4,000-foot gravel airstrips at Chisana, McCarthy and May Creek. Floatplanes can land on lakes within the park/preserve. Charter air service is available in Anchorage, Fairbanks, Northway, Glennallen, McCarthy, Cordova, Valdez and Yakutat. Several guides and outfitters offer a variety of trips in the park and preserve.

For more information: Contact Superintendent, Wrangell-St. Elias National Park and Preserve, P.O. Box 29, Glennallen, AK 99588; phone 822-5235. Related USGS Topographic maps: Mount St. Elias, Yakutat, Icy Bay, Bering Glacier, McCarthy, Nabesna, Gulkana and Valdez.

Wildlife Refuges

Alaska Maritime National Wildlife Refuge

This wildlife refuge includes more than 2,400 parcels of land on islands, islets, rocks, spires, reefs and headlands of Alaska coastal waters from Point Franklin in the Arctic Ocean to Forrester Island in southeastern Alaska. The refuge totals about 3.5 million acres. In Southcentral, the Duck and Chisik islands in Cook Inlet, and the Barren, Pye and Chiswell islands off the Kenai Peninsula, are part of this refuge.

Most of this refuge is managed to protect wildlife and the coastal ecosystem. The refuge has the most diverse wildlife species of all the refuges in Alaska, and includes thousands of sea lions, seals, walrus and sea otters, and millions of seabirds. About 75 percent of Alaska's marine birds (40 million to 60 million birds among 38 species) use the refuge and congregate in colonies along the coast. Each species has a specialized nesting site, be it rock ledge, crevice, boulder rubble, pinnacle or burrow. This adaptation allows many birds to use a small area of land.

Wildlife: It is estimated that nearly 60 percent of the 105,000 nesting seabirds on

the south side of the Kenai Peninsula use the dozen islands of the Chiswell group. Reportedly the largest seabird colony in Cook Inlet, some 80,000 birds, mostly black-legged kittiwakes and common murres, is on 5,700-acre Chisik Island and tiny nearby Duck Island. Other birds that may be seen throughout this area include cormorants, puffins, parakeet and rhinoceros auklets, pigeon guillemots, gulls, kittiwakes and fork-tailed storm petrels. The arrival of an occasional bald eagle or peregrine falcon will send an explosion of smaller birds from the cliffs in a chorus of cries.

The Chiswells and the Pye Island group harbor Steller sea lion rookeries. Other marine mammals that may be seen in this area are sea otters, seals, porpoises and several species of whales. Land mammals in some areas include black bears and land otters.

The Barren Islands, so named by Capt. James Cook in May 1778 because of "their very naked appearance," are anything but barren when seabirds and sea mammals by the thousands arrive annually to give birth and rear their young. The 7 named islands, totaling more than 10,000 acres, are geologic remnants of the Kenai Mountains on the Kenai Peninsula. Some 18 bird species with an estimated population of 500,000 feed in the productive waters around the islands, as do sea lions, harbor seals and whales.

Most lands of the refuge are wild and lonely, extremely rugged and virtually inaccessible. Some portions are classified as wilderness. Swift tides, rough seas, high winds, rocky shorelines and poor anchorages hamper efforts to view wildlife.

Activities and Access: Accessible by charter boat from Seward are the Chiswell Islands, 35 miles southwest of Seward, and the Pye Islands, 30 miles west of the Chiswells. On the west side of Cook Inlet, Chisik and Duck islands, 55 miles southwest of Kenai, can be reached by charter boat from Kenai or Homer. The Barren Islands, located between the Kenai Peninsula and the Kodiak Island group, are accessible by boat or air charter from Homer.

Visitors who boat near most of the islands may view seabirds and marine mammals. Although permits for landing on the islands are required only for commercial activities, visitors are urged to view wildlife from boats whenever possible to reduce disturbance. Regulations are in effect at sea lion rookeries, where boats are restricted to a 3-nautical-mile limit. Similarly, no person will be allowed to approach on land closer than one-half mile or within sight of a listed Steller sea lion rookery. Binoculars and spotting scopes are recommended to view wildlife from a distance. Visitors should be prepared for wet and windy weather.

The refuge operates a visitor center, located on the Sterling Highway in Homer, which offers wildlife exhibits, films and information. The center is open daily from 10 A.M. to 6 P.M., Memorial Day to Labor Day.

For more information: Contact Refuge Manager, Alaska Maritime National Wildlife Refuge, 509 Sterling Hwy., Homer, AK 99603; phone 235-6961, fax 235-7469.

Anchorage Coastal Wildlife Refuge (Potter Marsh)

This refuge extends 16 miles south along the coast from Point Woronzof at Anchorage to Potter Creek. The 32,476-acre refuge, established in 1988, includes extensive tidal flats, marsh and alder-bog forest.

Wildlife: Peak concentrations of waterfowl during spring migration, including Canada geese, arctic terns, trumpeter swans and many species of ducks and shorebirds.

Activities: Bird-watching at Potter Marsh is the most popular activity in the refuge. There is a large parking area and an extensive elevated boardwalk with interpretive signs at Potter Marsh. Check with the Alaska Dept. of Fish and Game on location of waterfowl hunting areas on the refuge.

Accommodations: All visitor facilities are available in Anchorage.

Access: Highway access from Anchorage via the Seward Highway. Potter Marsh, the best known and most accessible portion of the Anchorage Coastal Wildlife Refuge, is at Mile S 117.4, about 10 miles south of Anchorage. Watch for sign reading Boardwalk Wildlife Viewing; exit east. For bicyclists, joggers and walkers, there is also the 11-mile Coastal Trail from Elderberry Park in Anchorage around Point Woronzof to Point Campbell. *CAUTION: The tidal flats in the refuge are extremely dangerous.*

Goose Bay State Game Refuge

Located on the west side of Knik Arm, this 10,880-acre refuge encompasses the Goose Bay wetlands complex drained by Goose Creek. It was established in 1975. The inland boundary is shrub habitat. The shoreline is subject to the extreme tides of Knik Arm and safety precautions are advised as

"essential" by the Alaska Dept. of Fish and Game.

Wildlife: The wetlands are a spring and fall stopover for migrating waterfowl. More than 20,000 geese stop at the refuge between mid-April and mid-May, and again in the fall on their way south. Canada geese are most numerous, followed by snow geese. Trumpeter and tundra swans may also be observed in the area in spring and fall. Other species observed include bald eagles, sandhill cranes, mallards, green-winged teal, pintails, northern shovelers, snipe and yellowlegs.

Activities: Good waterfowl hunting in the fall. Offroad use of motorized vehicles is restricted. Excellent spring bird-watching opportunities, with waterfowl and raptor numbers peaking between April 25 and May 5.

Accommodations: There are no developed public access points or public-use facilities in the refuge. Nearby Knik has a liquor store, gas station and private campground.

Access: From Wasilla, follow Knik-Goose Bay Road south approximately 18.5 miles. Point Mackenzie Road intersects with the Knik-Goose Bay Road and provides access to the refuge at several points. Also accessible from Big Lake Road via the Burma Road.

For more information: Contact the Alaska Dept. of Fish and Game, 1800 Glenn Highway, Suite 4, Palmer, AK 99645-6736; phone 745-5015, fax 745-7362.

Kenai National Wildlife Refuge

This refuge was originally established in 1941 as the Kenai National Moose Range to protect habitat of these huge animals. In 1980 the refuge was renamed and expanded to encompass 2 million acres — 1.35 million of which are wilderness lands. Kenai Refuge is bounded to the northeast by Chugach National Forest, to the southeast by Kenai Fjords National Park and to the south by Kachemak Bay State Park.

The refuge encompasses much of the total land area of the Kenai Peninsula. It includes the western slopes of the Kenai Mountains and forested lowlands along Cook Inlet. These lowlands feature spruce and birch forests intermingled with hundreds of lakes. The Kenai Mountains with their glaciers rise more than 6,000 feet to the southeast. The refuge includes a variety of Alaskan habitats: tundra, mountains, wetlands and forests.

Special features of the refuge include a portion of the Harding Icefield to the southeast — 1 of 4 major ice caps in the United States. Numerous lakes in the northern lowland region combine to form the only nationally designated canoe trails in the Alaska refuge system: the Swanson River and Swan Lake canoe trails, enjoyed annually by thousands of visitors.

Other special features are the Tustumena-Skilak benchlands, a unique ecological area of mountain and glacial formations; Dall sheep and mountain goat ranges, and brown bear and timberline moose habitat; the Kenai River Special Management Area which includes the Kenai River, its tributaries and several lakes which provide vital spawning and rearing habitat for millions of salmon; the Chickaloon watershed and estuary, the major waterfowl and shorebird staging area on the peninsula; and the Skilak Lake area, a road-accessible region with abundant wildlife and scenic vistas.

Climate: Summer temperatures on the Kenai Peninsula generally range in the 60s and 70s, and rarely rise above 80°F. The region receives up to 19 hours of daylight in the summer. Winter's extreme low is about -30°F, but extended periods of below 0°F are rare. Late summer and fall weather is wet; rain gear is recommended for hiking and hunting. Annual precipitation on the western side of the peninsula ranges from 19 inches at Kenai to 23 inches at Homer. On the mountainous eastern section, precipitation exceeds 40 inches annually. The first snow normally falls in October; by November the ground is usually snow-covered. Spring breakup on low lakes occurs in April, on high lakes in May.

Wildlife: Nearly 200 species of birds and mammals live in or seasonally use the refuge. Mammals include moose, brown and black bear, caribou, Dall sheep, mountain goat, wolverine, wolf, coyote, river otter, beaver, muskrat, lemming, marten, red squirrel, shrew, lynx, porcupine, snowshoe hare, weasel, red fox and hoary marmot.

Birds found on the refuge include trumpeter swan, bald and golden eagles, peregrine falcon, northern pintail, sandhill crane, arctic tern, gull, lesser Canada goose, mallard, green-winged teal, woodpecker, ptarmigan, spruce grouse, cormorant, great horned owl, snow geese, junco, Swainson's thrush, common redpoll and many more.

The Kenai River king salmon fishery is world renowned. The river is reputed to support the largest genetic strain of king salmon anywhere. The world's record sport-caught king salmon, weighing 97¼ pounds, was caught here in 1985. Other fish occurring in refuge waters include red, pink and silver salmon, lake trout, Dolly Varden, rainbow trout, steelhead, kokanee, grayling and arctic char.

Activities: Camping, fishing, hiking, hunting and canoeing are all popular activities in the refuge. There are more than 200 miles of trails in the refuge. Most trailheads — and campgrounds — are found along the Sterling Highway and Skilak Lake Loop Road. All of the established trails get a lot of use in the summer, but most of the refuge is undeveloped, with no roads or trails. The more adventurous can travel on foot through undeveloped areas. The winter is a good time to visit, as skiing and snowshoeing are excellent ways to explore the refuge. See Hiking Trails, Kenai Peninsula Area, this section for details.

The popular Swanson River and Swan Lake canoe trails provide excellent opportunities to see many kinds of wildlife in their natural habitat. Cow moose visit this area to give birth in late May or early June. Many species of songbirds, shorebirds and waterfowl nest along the lakeshores, marshlands and surrounding forests. Beaver inhabit many lakes and streams. Keep your distance from wildlife. Remember that cow moose and sow bears are very protective of their young and it is dangerous to approach them, especially in spring and summer. Also, do not disturb nesting birds by approaching their nests.

Canoe or kayak parties are limited to 15 people or less; register at the entrance to each trail. All trails and portages are well marked. Minimum-impact camping is expected of all visitors. A camp stove is recommended; if you must build a fire, use established fire rings. Use only dead or downed wood, do not cut living trees or brush for bedding or any other purpose. Wash dishes away from lakes or streams; boil or treat all drinking water. Bury human waste 100 yards from campsites and water sources, and pack out all trash. Life preservers must be carried; rain gear and waterproof footwear are recommended. *NOTE: Lakes can become dangerous during high winds. Stay close to shore and watch the weather.* Canoe rentals available in Sterling and Soldotna. (See River Running this section.)

Accommodations: The refuge has 15 road-accessible public campgrounds with tables, fireplaces, parking spurs, boat ramps, water and restrooms. Camping is restricted to 3 consecutive days at Kenai-Russian River

Campground, 7 days at Hidden Lake Campground and 14 days elsewhere. Camping along refuge roads is permitted only at improved sites. Backcountry camping opportunities vary from fly-in and boat-in locations to sites accessible only by trail. There are also a few unmaintained primitive cabins available. Use minimum-impact techniques in all backcountry areas. Build fires in established fire rings if possible; use only dead and downed timber and camp stoves where firewood is scarce. Pack out all trash.

Access: The Kenai Refuge is bisected by the Sterling Highway which enters the refuge westbound at Milepost 55. Secondary access roads are Skilak Lake Loop Road, Swanson River and Swan Lake roads and Funny River Road. The northern refuge boundary is 20 air miles from Anchorage. Airports are located at Kenai, Soldotna and Homer. The refuge also is accessible along river trails and by float- and skiplane to many lakes. However, some lakes are closed to aircraft to protect wildlife. Be sure to check with the refuge office regarding which lakes are open to aircraft landings. To reach refuge headquarters, drive south on the Sterling Highway to Soldotna and turn left after crossing the Kenai River bridge. Follow the signs to the office.

For more information: There is a U.S. Fish and Wildlife Service information cabin at the junction of Skilak Lake Loop Road, Milepost 58 on the Sterling Highway. The Kenai National Wildlife Refuge Visitor Center is located at the top of Ski Hill Road in Soldotna; turn off the Sterling Highway just south of the Kenai River Bridge.The modern center has dioramas containing lifelike mounts of area wildlife. A free video on the refuge is shown weekdays in summer, and free wildlife films are shown all day Saturday and Sunday. Information is available on canoeing, backcountry hiking and camping. Open weekdays, 8 A.M. to 4:30 P.M., and weekends 10 A.M. to 6 P.M. Mailing address: Refuge Manager, Kenai National Wildlife Refuge, P.O. Box 2139, Soldotna, AK 99669-2139; phone 262-7021.

Mile-by-mile logs of the Sterling Highway and other roads within the refuge are included in *The MILEPOST®*.

Palmer Hay Flats State Game Refuge

This 45-square-mile refuge encompasses the forest, wetlands and tideflats at the head of Knik Arm. The 26,048-acre refuge, established in 1975 and expanded in 1985, includes the mouths of the Knik and Matanuska rivers.

Wildlife: A major waterfowl stop during spring and fall migrations.

Activities: Palmer Hay Flats is one of the most heavily utilized waterfowl hunting areas in Alaska, according to the ADF&G. The refuge also offers salmon fishing in Rabbit Slough and Cottonwood Creek. Moose hunters and trappers also use Palmer Hay Flats Refuge.

Accommodations: Developed access point at Mile A 34 Glenn Highway. There are no campgrounds within the refuge, but camping, lodging and other services are readily available along the highways which form the eastern boundary of the refuge.

Access: Motorboat and foot access at Rabbit Slough. Park at turnout at Milepost A 34 on the Glenn Highway. When Glenn Highway is completed, boats will be launched at the Knik River Bridge. Cottonwood Creek off Knik Goose Bay Road offers foot and canoe access to the marsh. Aircraft landings on the refuge prohibited from April 1 to Nov. 9. Off-road vehicle use restricted to specified corridors and seasons.

For more information: Contact the Alaska Dept. of Fish and Game, 333 Raspberry Road, Anchorage, AK 99518-1599; phone 344-0541.

Susitna Flats State Game Refuge

An expansive lowlands area along upper Cook Inlet, the east side of Susitna Flats is bisected by the Little Susitna River. The Ivan, Lewis, Theodore and Beluga rivers cross the west side of the refuge. The 300,800-acre refuge encompasses salt marsh, meadow, numerous lakes and bogs.

Wildlife: An extremely high concentration of migrating waterfowl use the refuge during spring and fall. Large numbers of mallards, pintails and Canada geese are present by mid-April. As many as 100,000 waterfowl are present in early May when peak densities are reached. About 10,000 mallards, pintails and green-winged teal remain to nest in the refuge. Other birds using the refuge include lesser sand-hill cranes, swans, northern phalaropes, dowitchers, godwits, whimbrels, snipe, yellowlegs, sandpipers, plovers and dunlin.

Activities: Approximately 10 percent of the state's waterfowl harvest occurs on Susitna Flats, according to the ADF&G, with about 15,000 ducks and 500 geese taken.

The Little Susitna, Theodore and Lewis rivers are popular salmon fishing streams.

Accommodations: Little Susitna River public-use facility has 83 parking spaces, 65 campsites, boat ramps, dump station, water, tables and toilets.

Access: By road from Wasilla. Follow Knik-Goose Bay Road 17.2 miles south, then Goose Bay-Point Mackenzie Road (4-wheel drive recommended) 12 miles west to reach public-use facility at Little Susitna River. Boats may be launched at the Little Susitna facility. Many hunters reach the refuge by floatplane, using one of the area lakes. Extreme tides, winds and dangerous mudflats make boat access from Cook Inlet hazardous.

For more information: Contact the Alaska Dept. of Fish and Game, 333 Raspberry Road, Anchorage, AK 99518-1599; phone 344-0541.

Trading Bay State Game Refuge

Located on the west side of Cook Inlet, this 160,960-acre refuge encompasses a large coastal marsh fed by the Kustatan, McArthur, Chakachatna and Middle rivers, and Chuitkilnachna and Nikolai creeks. It was established in 1976.

Wildlife: The wetlands provide critical spring feeding, summer nesting and fall staging habitat for ducks, geese, swans and cranes. Nesting ducks include mallard, pintail, green-winged teal, widgeon, shoveler, common eider, mergansers, scoters, scaup and goldeneye. Healthy populations of moose, bear and other mammals use the refuge.

Activities: A popular waterfowl and moose hunting area in the fall. Summer sportfishing for salmon. The refuge is also used for subsistence hunting and fishing by residents of Tyonek.

Accommodations: There are no developed facilities within the refuge. Limited visitor facilities at Tyonek.

Access: By road from the community of Tyonek; also by small plane or boat.

For more information: Contact the Alaska Dept. of Fish and Game regional office at 333 Raspberry Road, Anchorage, AK 99518-1599; phone 344-0541.

Cabins

Chugach National Forest Cabins

There are 41 Chugach National Forest recreation cabins available to rent. Cost is $20 per night per party for these rustic but comfortable cabins which are accessible by foot, boat or small plane. Local Forest Service offices can provide information about fees and can reserve any cabin managed by the Forest Service in Alaska. There is a 3-day limit for hike-in cabins from May 15 through August 31; for other cabins the limit is 7 nights year-round.

Charts on the following pages list cabins alphabetically by name in 4 different areas of Southcentral: the Cordova area, West Prince William Sound, South Kenai Peninsula and North Kenai Peninsula. The chart shows how many people each cabin sleeps; if the cabin is accessible by air, boat or trail; if hunting, fishing or beachcombing are available; and if the cabin has a skiff or stove. Type of stove provided is indicated as follows: O=oil stove, W=wood stove, G=outdoor grill, OH=oil heater. (The Forest Service does not provide fuel.) Special features or restrictions are also noted.

For more information contact one of the following Chugach National Forest offices: Cordova Ranger District, P.O. Box 280, Cordova, AK 99574-0280, phone 424-7661; Seward Ranger District, P.O. Box 390, Seward, AK 99664-0390, phone 224-3374; Glacier Ranger District, Monarch Mine Road, P.O. Box 129, Girdwood, AK 99587; phone 783-3242; or 201 E. 9th Ave., Anchorage, AK 99501, phone 271-2500.

Nancy Lake State Recreation Area Cabins

There are 12 public-use cabins available for rent at Nancy Lake State Recreation Area. Cabins may be rented for up to 3 nights. Rates are $25 per night for the first 4 persons over 5 years of age; $5 each additional person. Most cabins accommodate 6, while a few larger cabins can sleep 10. Cabins may be reserved up to 180 days in advance and fees must be paid when the reservation is submitted. If more than one request is received for the same days, a lottery is held.

Cabins are furnished with plywood sleeping platforms, wood stove, window screens, kitchen counter, table and chairs or benches and an outdoor firepit and grill. A pit latrine is nearby. Bring sleeping pad and bag, food, cooking stove, fuel and personal items. Firewood can be hard to find in winter so bring firewood or presto logs for the first night.

Four cabins are located on Nancy Lake. Three are accessible by trail from the Nancy Lake Parkway. The fourth is surrounded by private property and is accessible only by

CHUGACH NATIONAL FOREST CABINS

	SLEEPS	AIR ACCESS	BOAT ACCESS	TRAIL ACCESS	HUNTING	FISHING	BEACHCOMB	SKIFF	STOVE
CORDOVA AREA									
Beach River (Wheelplane access only at low tide)	6	•			•	•	•		O&W
Double Bay (Boat approach difficult at low tide)	6	•	•		•	•			O
Green Island (Boaters use caution; uncharted rocks in area)	6	•	•		•	•			OH
Hook Point (Salmon stream 1 mile east of cabin)	10	•			•	•			O&W
Jack Bay	6	•	•		•	•			O
Log Jam Bay	4	•			•	•	•		O&W
Martin Lake	4	•			•	•			O
McKinley Lake (Boat access limited to high water periods)	6	•	•	•	•	•			W
McKinley Trail (Road access at Mile 22, Copper River Highway)	6		•	•	•	•			G
Nellie Martin River	6	•	•		•	•	•		O&W
Peter Dahl	6	•	•						O
Port Chalmers (Carry water)	6	•	•			•			O&W
San Juan Bay	4	•	•		•	•	•		O&W
Softuk Bay (Wheelplane access only at low tide)	6	•					•		O&W
Stump Lake (Wheelplane access only at low tide)	6	•			•	•	•		O&W
Tiedeman Slough	6	•	•						O
WEST PRINCE WILLIAM SOUND									
Coghill Lake (Fishermen bring inflatable boat)	10	•			•				W
Harrison Lagoon (No drinking water on site)	5		•		•				W
Paulson Bay	6	•	•		•				W
Pigot Bay	10	•	•		•				W
Shrode Lake (Bring stove; wood scarce)	10	•	•	•	•			•	OH
South Culross Pass (Anchor in outer bay)	6	•	•		•				W

Type of stove provided is indicated as follows: O=oil stove, W=wood stove, G=outdoor grill, OH=oil heater.

boat via Nancy Lake or by foot or snow-mobile when the lake is frozen.

Four cabins are located on Red Shirt Lake, 3 on Lynx Lake and 1 on James Lake. To reach the cabins on Red Shirt Lake it is necessary to hike 3 miles and canoe a short distance in the summer. Canoe rentals are available. The cabins on Lynx and James lakes are on the canoe trail system. All cabins are accessible in winter by snow machine or dog team. It is also possible to ski to most of the cabins but most access requires a full-day ski.

To reserve a cabin or obtain more information contact the Division of Parks and Outdoor Recreation, P.O. Box 107001, Anchorage, AK 99510; phone 762-2616 or the Mat-Su Area Office, HC32, Box 6706, Wasilla, AK 99687; phone 745-3975.

Hiking Trails

Anchorage/Mat-Su Area Trails

Bold Ridge Trail. To reach Bold Ridge Trail, hike Lakeside Trail (see write-up, this section) to mile 5. Here, the Bold Ridge Trail begins and climbs steeply to the alpine tundra. Hikers in good condition need about one hour, 45 minutes to ascend the trail, which is 3.5 miles long. The return trip takes about an hour.

CHUGACH NATIONAL FOREST CABINS *continued*

	SLEEPS	AIR ACCESS	BOAT ACCESS	TRAIL ACCESS	HUNTING	FISHING	BEACHCOMB	SKIFF	STOVE
SOUTH KENAI PENINSULA									
Aspen Flats *(On Russian Lakes Trail)*	6		•	•	•				W
Barber *(Handicap access at Lower Russian Lake)*	5	•		•	•	•		•	W
Crescent Lake	6	•		•	•	•			W
Devils Pass *(On Resurrection Pass Trail)*	10			•	•	•			O
Juneau Lake *(Snowmobile access)*	6	•		•	•	•		•	W
Lower Paradise Lake	6	•			•			•	W
Resurrection River *(On Resurrection River Trail)*	6			•	•	•			W
Romig *(On Resurrection Pass Trail)*	6	•		•	•	•		•	W
Saddle *(On Crescent Lake Trail)*	6	•		•	•	•		•	O
Swan Lake *(On Resurrection Pass Trail)*	6	•		•	•	•		•	W
Trout Lake *(On Resurrection Pass Trail)*	6	•		•	•	•		•	W
Upper Paradise Lake	6	•			•	•		•	W
Upper Russian Lake *(On Russian Lakes Trail)*	4	•		•	•	•		•	W
West Swan Lake	6	•			•	•		•	W
NORTH KENAI PENINSULA									
Caribou *(Snowmobile access)*	6			•	•				W
Crow Pass *(Bring stove; no firewood)*	10			•					
East Creek *(Snowmobile access)*	6			•	•				W
Fox Creek *(On Resurrection Pass Trail)*	6			•	•				W

Type of stove provided is indicated as follows: O=oil stove, W=wood stove, G=outdoor grill, OH=oil heater.

The soft, moss-covered tundra supports an abundance of hardy wildflowers and berries. Listen for the warning whistle of the marmot and watch for ground squirrels scampering across the tundra in search of food. Occasionally bears or wolves are seen on surrounding mountainsides.

This trail provides excellent views of the Eklutna Valley and Glacier, and the Knik Arm of Cook Inlet. The maintained trail ends at the base of the snowcapped Bold Peak. Experienced climbers may continue on to the summit of this 7,552-foot mountain. Hunters and other hikers use the Bold Ridge Trail to reach the Hunter Creek drainage.

This trail is considered moderate to difficult.

Byers Lake Trail. Trailhead at Byers Lake Campground in Denali State Park at Milepost A 147 George Parks Highway. This 4.8-mile trail offers an easy hike around Byers Lake. The trail connects with the 7-mile Cascade route at the northeast end of the lake and climbs Curry Ridge to Tarn Point, a 1,900-foot elevation change. Byers Lake Loop trail also accesses the longer Troublesome Creek and Little Coal Creek trails. Trail is regularly maintained. Related USGS Topographic maps: Talkeetna C-1, C-2 and D-1; Talkeetna Mountains C-6 and D-6.

Crow Pass (Old Iditarod) Trail. This trail is about 27 miles long—4 miles are within Chugach National Forest, the rest of the trail is in Chugach State Park. The trailhead is 7 miles up Crow Creek Road. Take the Seward Highway south from Anchorage 37 miles to Alyeska Access Road; drive up Alyeska Access Road 1.9 miles to junction with Crow Creek Road. The Crow Pass Trail climbs steeply to ruins of an old gold mine and a public-use cabin; 2,000 feet in altitude is gained between trailhead and the cabin at Mile 3 at

Crow Pass near Raven Glacier. Hiking time to the pass is approximately 2¹/₂ hours. Trail offers outstanding alpine scenery and access to several glaciers and peaks. From Crow Pass, the Old Iditarod trail extends 22.5 miles down Raven Creek drainage to the Chugach State Park Visitor Center on Eagle River Road. All of the hiking trail, from Crow Creek trailhead to the visitor center, is part of the Iditarod National Historic Trail. Trail closed to motorized vehicles; horses prohibited during April, May and June due to soft trail conditions. Winter travel not recommended due to extreme avalanche danger. Trail usually free of snow by mid-June. Cabin located in alpine area without firewood; camp stove recommended. Water available from glacial stream. Related USGS Topographic map: Anchorage A-6.

East Fork Trail. To reach East Fork Trail, hike Lakeside Trail (see write-up, this section) to mile 10.5. Here, this follow-the-leader trail begins, paralleling the East Fork of Eklutna River to a glacial lake that reflects the surrounding peaks and glacier. Bashful, the tallest peak in Chugach State Park, at 8,005 feet, and its neighbors, Bold and Baleful, tower above the river to the northeast, while the Mitre forms the west wall of the valley.

Colorful wildflowers line the trail, changing with the different ecosystems you pass through. Keep your binoculars handy, as Dall sheep, mountain goats and moose inhabit the mountain slopes. Watch for the ouzel, a small water bird that bobs in the water and feeds along the river bottom. Tulchina Falls at mile 2 is a pretty spot for a rest stop. Pack a pail in the fall for the many berries in this valley.

This trail is considered easy to moderate in difficulty.

Eklutna Glacier Trail. This trail begins 0.75 miles from mile 13 of the Lakeside Trail, and is considered easy to moderate in difficulty.

It begins where the Lakeside Trail ends and leads to an interpretive display and a view of the Eklutna Glacier. Notice the change in vegetation as you hike along. The glacier has quickly retreated in the last few years and you can witness the birth of a new landscape here.

The trail is well marked, but sections bordering the swiftly flowing Eklutna River require care. Rocks falling from the steep canyon walls present a hazard to hikers. For your safety, remain on the trail and do not approach the glacier. Because it is rapidly

receding, the glacier's snout is unstable and dangerous.

Glaciers and peaks in this area are popular with climbers. A traverse beginning at the end of this trail crosses the Eklutna, Whiteout, Eagle and Raven Glaciers, and ends 31 miles away at Crow Pass near Girdwood. Three huts along the route are maintained by the Mountaineering Club of Alaska. Only those who are trained and properly equipped should venture onto the glacier.

Hillside Trail System. There are several popular hikes in Chugach State Park's Hillside Trail System. From the Glen Alps Access there are Flattop Mountain, Powerline and Williwaw lakes. To reach the Glen Alps Access from downtown Anchorage, take the Seward Highway south to O'Malley exit, turn right on Hillside Drive, then take a left to the trailhead sign. The popular hike up Flattop Mountain begins here. Total elevation gain is 1,550 feet in 3.5 miles; hiking time is estimated at 3 to 5 hours. The trail is well-marked and well-traveled with stunning views of Anchorage and the Alaska Range on clear days. Snow is usually gone by early July.

The Glen Alps Access is also the trailhead for the Powerline Trail. Short easy walk to alpine terrain; berry picking in summer. Bicycles are allowed on the trail in summer, snow machine use on part of trail in winter. Total length of trail is 11 miles with an elevation gain of 1,300 feet. Trail ends at Indian near Milepost 103 Seward Highway.

Williwaw Lakes trail branches off Powerline Trail to several small alpine lakes beneath Mount Williwaw. Round-trip is 13 miles with a 742-foot elevation gain. Berry picking in season.

Lakeside Trail. Located in Eklutna Lake Valley in Chugach State Park. To reach the trailhead, take Glenn Highway to Milepost 26 and follow park signs 10 miles to Eklutna Lake. Begin at the trailhead parking lot, cross the Twin Peaks Creek bridge and take a right onto the Lakeside Trail. This scenic trail is an old roadbed that follows the north edge of the lake for 8 miles and then extends into the backcountry. In the summer the trail is bordered by colorful wildflowers, and in the fall currants, cranberries and raspberries provide a special treat.

The road was open to passenger vehicles until 1977 when sections washed out, making it unsafe for such vehicles. Today it is popular with hikers, skiers, joggers, bikers, ATVers and horseback riders. Each mile is marked for easy reference. It is considered a relatively easy trail, and typical travel time for the 13-mile trail, one-way is 6 hours. The trail is usually open to ATVs Sunday through Wednesday. For information call the ranger station or Chugach State Park Headquarters.

Little Coal Creek Trail. This Denali State Park trailhead is located at Milepost A 163.8 George Parks Highway. According to park rangers, this trailhead offers easy access to alpine country (1¹/₂-hour hike) and to Indian Mountain (a day-long hike of 9 miles round-trip, elevation gain 3,300 feet, outstanding view). It is 27.4 miles from the Little Coal Creek trailhead to Byers Lake Campground via the Kesugi Ridge route. It is 36.2 miles from Little Coal Creek trailhead to the Troublesome Creek trailhead via the Kesugi Ridge route. Marked by rock cairns, the Kesugi Ridge route is rated difficult. Related USGS Topographic maps: Talkeetna C-1, C-2 and D-1; Talkeetna Mountains C-6 and D-6.

Red Shirt Lake Trail. Located in the Nancy Lake Recreation Area, this 3-mile (one-way) route bridges the gap between the Nancy Lake Parkway and Red Shirt Lake. To find the trailhead, turn west onto the Nancy Lake Parkway at mile 67.3 of the Parks Highway. The trail leaves the parkway at mile 5.7. The route stays primarily on high ground and occasionally affords a view of the area's lakes with the Chugach Mountains on the distant horizon. There are lakeshore campsites at the end of the trail. Just 1¹/₂ miles south of the parkway there is a 2¹/₂-mile one-way trail that winds its way eastward between Big Noluck Lake and Chicken Lake, and Frazer and Little Frazer lakes.

Troublesome Creek Trail. This Denali State Park trail has 2 trailheads: the upper trailhead is at Milepost A 137.6 George Parks Highway; the lower trailhead is at Lower Troublesome Creek Campground at Milepost A 137.3 Parks Highway. It is a 15.2-mile hike from the Upper Troublesome Creek trailhead to Byers Lake. Rated moderate. The trailhead and trail to Mile 5.5 may be closed from mid-July through the end of season due to the high concentration of bears feeding on spawning salmon. Exercise extreme caution from the Chulitna River upstream to Ultima Poole. (Ultima Poole is reached via a 500-yard-long side trial at Mile 4.5 of Troublesome Creek trail; it is a deep pool at the base of a small falls on the creek and a pleasant place for a rest or a bracing swim.) Salmon cannot get beyond the falls and the bear danger beyond Ultima Poole is not as great. Park managers may reroute a portion of the trail to minimize bear encounters.

From Troublesome Creek trailhead to the Little Coal Creek trailhead via the Kesugi Ridge route it is 36.2 miles and rated difficult. The trail is marked by rock cairns. Related USGS Topographic maps: Talkeetna C-1, C-2 and D-1; Talkeetna Mountains C-6 and D-6.

Tulik Trail. Located in the Nancy Lake Recreation Area, this 1-mile, self-guided nature trail can be reached by turning west onto Nancy Lake Parkway at mile 67.3 of the Parks Highway. The trailhead is located at mile 2.5 on the parkway.

The trail leads hikers beyond the forest screen, alongside ponds and across bogs. Boardwalks and viewing platforms ease the way over wet areas and exposed roots. Using the brochure available at the trailhead and walking leisurely, most hikers take about an hour to complete the loop.

Twin Peaks Trail. Located in Eklutna Lake Valley in Chugach State Park. To reach the trailhead, take Glenn Highway to milepost 26 and follow park signs 10 miles to Eklutna Lake. The 3.5-mile trail begins at the parking lot, crosses the Twin Peaks Creek bridge and continues to the alpine tundra. It is rated moderate to difficult due to its steepness in places. Hiking time for those in good condition is about two hours going up and one hour down. It is well maintained, and offers good views of the valley.

About halfway up, there is a good spot to rest, have a picnic and enjoy views of the valley and lake. The trail continues around the west side of the mountain, where dozens of sheep are often seen grazing in the Goat Mountain bowl. Careful observers may spot ptarmigan roosting in the vegetation or a golden eagle in flight.

Hikers who reach the end of the maintained trail are rewarded with a panoramic view of the Eklutna Valley and Knik Arm. From here hikers may choose their own route across the tundra. Berry picking is very good along the upper part of the trail and beyond. Climbers use this trail to reach East and West Twin Peaks and Goat Mountain.

Kenai Peninsula Area Trails

For additional information on Chugach National Forest hiking trails, contact one of the following offices: Cordova Ranger District, P.O. Box 280, Cordova, AK 99574-0280, phone 424-7661; Seward Ranger District, P.O. Box 390, Seward, AK 99664-0390, phone 224-3374; Glacier Ranger District, Monarch Mine Road, P.O. Box 129, Girdwood, AK 99587, phone 783-3242; or

201 E. 9th Ave., Anchorage, AK 99501, phone 271-2500.

Alpine Ridge Trail. This steep 2-mile hike in Kachemak Bay State Park, rated moderate to difficult, begins at the high point on the Saddle Trail (see write-up, this section) and follows a ridge up through spruce and alder to alpine tundra and its many wildflowers. Views of Grewingk Glacier on one side and a deep glacial valley on the other are spectacular. Pick out some landmarks to help find the end of the trail for the trip back down. Hiking time is 1 hour, 40 minues to get above timberline.

Bear Creek Trail. Trailhead on north shore Tustumena Lake in Kenai National Wildlife Refuge; no road access. Length 16.5 miles; elevation range 100 to 3,200 feet; rated moderate; minimum maintenance.

Bear Mountain Trail. Trailhead at Mile 6.2 Skilak Lake Loop Road off the Sterling Highway in Kenai National Wildlife Refuge. Length 1 mile; elevation range 900 to 1,400 feet; rated moderate.

Carter Lake Trail. This fairly short Chugach National Forest trail with a 986-foot elevation gain provides access to alpine country. Dall sheep and goats may be seen. Trail steep in places. Rainbow trout fishing at Carter Lake at Mile 2; grayling in Crescent Lake at Mile 3. Trail closed to motorized vehicles May 1 to Nov. 30 and to horses April, May and June. Trail leads to excellent winter recreational area. Access from trailhead on Seward Highway at Milepost 33.1 from Seward. Related USGS Topographic maps: Seward B7, C7.

China Poot Lake Trail. This 2.5-mile trail, rated easy to moderate, begins at Halibut Cove Lagoon and passes 3 lakes beneath China Poot Peak in Kachemak Bay State Park. About 15 minutes of hiking uphill brings you to the first lake. The trail crosses the lake outlet stream and continues through forest and bog for 30 minutes to Two Loon Lake. China Poot Lake is another 30 minutes away through more spruce and muskeg. Hiking time is 1 hour, 15 minutes.

Coastal Trail. Located at Caines Head State Recreation Area near Seward on the eastern edge of the Kenai Peninsula, this 7-mile trail leads to the abandoned Fort McGilvray and garrison ghost town. To reach the trail, take Lowell Point Road south 2 miles from Seward. Park here, at Lowell Point, and begin the hike south. After 1¹/₂ miles, the trail reaches Tonsina Point. The 3-mile stretch of beach between this point and the next area of interest, North Beach, can only be hiked during very low tide. Leave Seward at least 2 hours before low tide to avoid being stranded. The trip takes the average hiker 2 to 3 hours. Most hikers stay overnight at North Beach.

North Beach is marked by the remains of an army dock built in 1941. A ranger station, anchorage, camping shelter, latrine and picnic area are located near the beach. Two miles further south is the abandoned Fort McGilvray. To reach the fort and sweeping vistas of the bay, hike the old roadbed until it forks, one mile south of the North Beach trailhead. Follow the left fork another 1¹/₄ miles to the fort. Along the way, explore the remains of old ammunition magazines and bog meadows.

In WWII, Fort McGilvray was the strategic command center for protecting the port of Seward from imperial Japanese forces. It is perched on a 650-foot rocky cliff. The fort is open to explore, but take a flashlight to find your way through the maze of underground passages and rooms.

To reach South Beach, travel back up the old road to the fork, this time choosing the southwestern branch. Follow this branch of the road 1¹/₂ miles to the South Beach ghost town. The town includes the remains of utility buildings and barracks that were home to the 500 soldiers stationed here from July 1941 to May 1943. These structures are not safe to enter or walk on.

Cottonwood Creek Trail. Length 3.1 miles; elevation range 200 to 2,200 feet; steep, rated strenuous; minimum maintenance. Trailhead on the south side of Skilak Lake in Kenai National Wildlife Refuge. No road access to trail; boat ramps at campgrounds on lake.

Crescent Lake Trail. This 6.4-mile Chugach National Forest trail ends at Crescent Lake; public-use cabin at lake outlet. Lake has grayling. The trail, which has a gain of 864 feet, is in excellent condition. Trail closed to motorized vehicles April 1 to Nov. 30; closed to horses April, May and June. Winter use hazardous because of avalanche danger. Access from parking area at Mile 3.5 Quartz Creek Road, off the Sterling Highway at Milepost 45 from Seward. Trailhead about 2.5 miles beyond Quartz Creek Campground. Related USGS Topographic maps: Seward B7, B8, C7, C8.

A low-maintenance connecting trail begins at Crescent Lake outlet and goes around the lake to Carter Lake. It is 4.5 miles from the outlet to Saddle cabin, and another 4 miles to junction with the Carter Lake

Trail. Creek on trail has no bridge; may be hazardous during heavy rain. Avalanche chutes may be unsafe to travel across during summer due to unstable slope conditions. Mud and snow avalanches possible at higher elevations into early July. Total distance combining Crescent Lake, Carter Lake and connecting trails is 17.9 miles.

Drake and Skookum Lakes Trail. Trailhead at Mile 13.3 Swanson River Road in Kenai National Wildlife Refuge. Length 2 miles; rainbow trout and arctic char fishing.

Finger Lake Trail. Trailhead at Mile 9.8 Swanson River Road in Kenai National Wildlife Refuge. Length 2.3 miles; good arctic char fishing.

Fuller Lakes Trail. Trailhead at Milepost S 57.1 Sterling Highway in Kenai National Wildlife Refuge. It is 4.8 miles to the lakes; elevation range 300 to 2,000 feet; rated strenuous. Grayling in South Fuller Lake. This is bear country.

Funny River Horse Trail. Access is reached via the Funny River Road, which branches off the Soldotna Airport Road near the airport. Also for hiking. Trail is 20.8 miles long; elevation range 250 to 2,200 feet; rated moderate. Provides access to alpine benchlands. Minimum maintenance.

Goat Rope Spur Trail. This short, steep trail, extending 0.5 mile and rated difficult, begins at the highest point on Lagoon Trail (see write-up, this section) in Kachemak Bay State Park. It leads hikers up through a "notch" to alpine areas, where the trail ends. Be sure to bring along your camera to record the views. Hiking time is 1 hour.

Grewingk Glacier Trail. This 3.5-mile trail, rated easy, covers flat terrain through stands of spruce and cottonwood and across the outwash of Grewingk Glacier in Kachemak Bay State Park. It offers superb views of the glacier and surrounding area. There is a small campground about 10 minutes from the trailhead and another at Right Beach, a favorite water taxi drop-off point. Rock cairns mark the trail across the outwash of the glacier. Access to the glacial ice is difficult and hazardous. There is a stream near the junction of this trail and the Saddle Trail. Hiking time is 1 hour, 20 minutes.

Hidden Creek Trail. Trailhead at Mile 4.7 Skilak Lake Loop Road off the Sterling Highway in Kenai National Wildlife Refuge. It is 1.5 miles to Skilak Lake; elevation range 450 to 200 feet; rated easy. Large driftwood on shore make for interesting photos.

Iditarod Trail. This National Historic Trail is actually a network of more than 2,300 miles of trails that at one time or another linked Seward, Anchorage, the Indian village of Iditarod, Nome and various historic mining claims. The trail was officially surveyed in 1910 as the Seward to Nome Mail Trail, and was used as a major route until 1924, when the airplane came into use. It is best known today for the Iditarod Trail Sled Dog Race (see GENERAL INFORMATION section). Only a small part of the trail is suitable for summer hiking. From Seward, the trail begins at the ferry terminal and follows a marked course through town, then north on the Seward Highway. At Mile 2.1 Nash Road (turn off at Milepost 3.2 Seward Highway) the trail continues from a gravel parking area on the east side of Sawmill Creek north to Bear Lake. The trail eventually rejoins the Seward Highway at Milepost 12 from Seward. A longer hike on the Iditarod Trail is possible from the Crow Pass trailhead on Crow Creek Road south of Anchorage; see Crow Pass Trail on page 179.

Johnson Pass Trail. This 23-mile Chugach National Forest trail follows a portion of the Iditarod National Historic Trail, which once extended from Seward to Nome. The trail was an important route for supplies and mail to gold mining camps in the area. Trail is fairly level. It offers spectacular views and emerges in alpine country. Black bears may be encountered along this trail. Fishing for grayling in Bench Lake and rainbow trout in Johnson Lake. Johnson Pass trail has 2 trailheads on the Seward Highway. North trailhead is at Milepost 63.8 from Anchorage; look for Forest Service trail sign on the highway. Turn on a gravel road and drive about 0.3 mile to the trailhead. South trailhead at Milepost 32.6 from Seward in a turnout area marked with a Forest Service sign. This trail is closed to motorized vehicles May 1 to Nov. 30 and is closed to horses during April, May and June. Avalanche danger high in winter, travel not recommended between Mile 2 from the north trailhead and Mile 10.6 at Johnson Lake. No cabins along this trail. Bench and Johnson lakes are above tree line; some dead wood may be found for campfires, but a portable stove is recommended. Related USGS Topographic maps: Seward C-6 and C-7.

Kenai River Trail. Trailheads at Mile 9.6 and 2.4 Skilak Lake Loop Road off the Sterling Highway in Kenai National Wildlife Refuge. It is 6.3 miles to Skilak Lake and beyond; elevation range 400 to 1,000 feet; rated moderate.

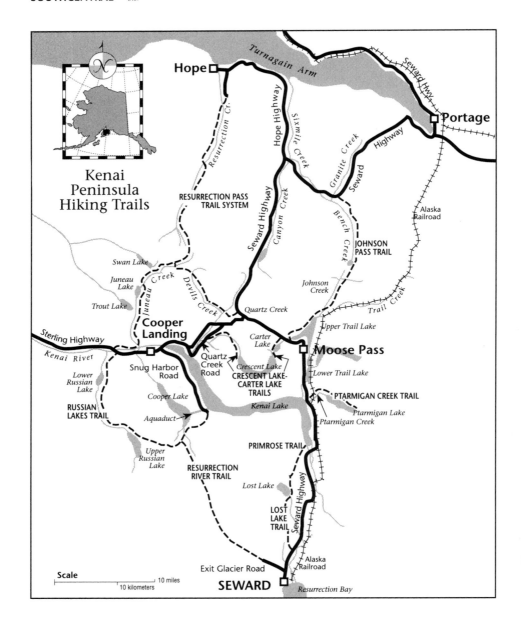

Kenai
Peninsula
Hiking Trails

Hope

Portage

Turnagain Arm

Seward Hwy

Resurrection Cr.

Hope Highway

Sixmile Creek

Granite Creek

Seward Highway

Alaska Railroad

RESURRECTION PASS
TRAIL SYSTEM

Seward Highway

Canyon Creek

Bench Creek

JOHNSON
PASS TRAIL

Swan Lake

Juneau
Lake

Juneau Creek

Devils Creek

Johnson
Creek

Trout Lake

Cooper
Landing

Quartz Creek

Upper Trail Lake

Trail Creek

Sterling Highway

Kenai River

Snug Harbor
Road

Quartz
Creek
Road

Carter
Lake

Moose Pass

Crescent Lake

Lower
Russian
Lake

CRESCENT LAKE-
CARTER LAKE
TRAILS

Lower Trail Lake

Cooper Lake

Kenai Lake

PTARMIGAN CREEK TRAIL

RUSSIAN
LAKES TRAIL

Aquaduct

Ptarmigan Lake

Ptarmigan Creek

Upper
Russian
Lake

PRIMROSE TRAIL

RESURRECTION
RIVER TRAIL

Lost Lake

Seward Highway

LOST
LAKE
TRAIL

Scale

10 miles

10 kilometers

Exit Glacier Road

Alaska
Railroad

SEWARD

Resurrection Bay

Lagoon Trail. This 5.5-mile trail, rated moderate to difficult, winds along Halibut Cove and passes through a boggy area to Halibut Creek Trailhead and delta in Kachemak Bay State Park. Continue on by walking upstream on the south side about 200 yards or walk around the delta on the tide flats. A series of steep switchbacks then leads through a spruce forest up to where the trail intersects Goat Rope Spur Trail at 1,200 feet. The trail continues downhill and south, across Falls Creek and on to the end of the lagoon and the ranger station. Here you may take the stairs down to the stream where a sign directs hikers to the China Poot Lake Trail. Hiking time for Lagoon Trail is 5 hours.

Lake Emma Trail. Trailhead on north shore Tustumena Lake in Kenai National Wildlife Refuge; no road access. Length 4.6 miles; elevation range 100 to 2,500 feet; rated strenuous; minimum maintenance.

Lost Lake Trail. Anyone who wishes to use this trail must contact Harbor View Partnership, 1343 G St., Suite #1, Anchorage, AK 99501; phone 274-2634, for permission. This 7-mile Chugach National Forest trail offers spectacular views and access to alpine country with an elevation gain of 1,800 feet. This trail connects with the Primrose Trail at Lost Lake. The upper trail is not free of snow until mid-July. Brown and black bear in the spring. Salmonberries near Miles 4 and 5 in August. Fishing for rainbow trout at Lost Lake at the end of the trail. Lake is above tree line; no wood for fires, so campers should carry a stove and tent. This is an excellent area for snowmobiling in winter. A snow machine trail leaves the summer trail at Mile 1.5. Access is from a parking area at Milepost 5.2 from Seward on the Seward Highway.

Moose Creek Trail. Trailhead on north shore Tustumena Lake in Kenai National Wildlife Refuge; no road access. Length 7.7 miles; elevation range 100 to 3,200 feet; rated moderate; minimum maintenance.

Poot Peak Trail. This steep, slick, unmaintained 2-mile route, rated difficult, begins across the China Poot Lake inlet stream bridge and heads up to timberline in Kachemak Bay State Park. Climbing the 2,100-foot peak is hazardous because of shifting scree and rotten rock. The trail affords superb views of Wosnesenski Glacier and Kachemak Bay. Hiking time is 1 hour, 30 minutes to 2 hours.

Primrose Trail. This 7.5-mile Chugach National Forest trail is accessible from Prim-

rose Campground, 1 mile north off the Seward Highway at Milepost 17.2. The Primrose Trail is closed to all motorized vehicles except for miners with active claims between May 1 to Nov. 30. Closed to horses April through June.

This trail now provides the only public access to Lost Lake, which was formerly reached from a 7-mile trail that started at Mile 5 of the Seward Highway. The Forest Service was unable to obtain a right-of-way for the Lost Lake trailhead and the first 2/3-mile of the trail in 1988. Until the right-of-way is obtained, access to Lost Lake is limited to the Primrose Trail. Related USGS Topographic maps: Seward A7, B7.

Ptarmigan Creek Trail. This 3.5-mile Chugach National Forest trail offers a good chance of seeing sheep and goats on mountain slopes. The lake outlet is at Mile 3.5 but the trail continues along the shore for another 3 miles. Popular summer and fall fisheries in the outlet of Ptarmigan Lake and a stream about 1 mile below the outlet. Insect repellent a must in summer. Trail closed to motorized vehicles May 1 to Nov. 30; closed to horses April, May and June. Winter use not recommended due to avalanche hazard. Access from Ptarmigan Creek Campground on the Seward Highway at Milepost 23.1 from Seward. Related USGS Topographic maps: Seward B6, B7.

Resurrection Pass Trail System. This popular National Recreation Trail follows a route originally established in the late 1800s by miners along gold-bearing Resurrection Creek. Eight public-use cabins are located along the 39-mile-long Chugach National Forest trail, which offers beautiful scenery, fairly easy backpacking and good fishing. The trail follows Resurrection Creek from Hope (on the Hope Highway, which joins the Seward Highway at Milepost 56.7 from Seward) to 2,600-foot-high Resurrection Pass, then down Juneau Creek to the Sterling Highway near Cooper Landing at Milepost 53.1 from Seward. To reach the north trailhead, turn left at the Resurrection Pass trail sign at Milepost 16.2 on the Hope Highway and follow Resurrection Creek Road about 4 miles to the beginning of the trail. Road not maintained in winter. The south trailhead (near Cooper Landing) is marked with a large sign at a parking area. Devils Pass trail is a 10-mile trail connecting a trailhead at Milepost 39.4 on the Seward Highway with the Resurrection Pass trail at the Devils Pass cabin at the 2,400-foot elevation. Hiking time for this trail is about 5¹/₂ hours. These trails are closed to motorized vehicles Feb. 15 to Nov. 30; and closed to horses during April, May and June due to soft trail conditions. Winter travel is not recommended on the Devils Pass Trail due to extreme avalanche danger. Dead and down wood may be scarce; carry a camp stove. No wood at Devils Pass cabin, which is above tree line. Related USGS Topographic maps: Seward D-7, D-8, C-8 and B-8.

Resurrection River Trail. This 17.8-mile Chugach National Forest trail connects with the Russian Lakes and Resurrection Pass trails to allow hikers to complete a 72-mile trek from Seward to Hope. The trail parallels the Resurrection River through spruce and hardwood forests. Black and brown bear may be encountered. This trail is not recommended for horses. The trail gets extremely muddy during rainstorms. During heavy rains, the south trailhead may flood; do not park your car at south trailhead. Recommended for snowshoeing only in winter. A public-use cabin is located 6.5 miles from the trailhead. (See Chugach National Forest Cabins under Cabins this section.) Trail is closed to motorized vehicles May 1 to Nov. 30 and is closed to horses April through June. Trailhead at Mile 8 of the Exit Glacier Road; turn west onto Exit Glacier Road from Milepost 3.7 of the Seward Highway. Related USGS Topographic maps: Seward A7, A8, B8.

Russian Lakes Trail. This 21.5-mile Chugach National Forest trail offers Dolly Varden, rainbow trout and salmon in the Russian River at one trailhead, rainbow trout at Lower Lake, Aspen Flats and Upper Lake and Dolly Varden at Cooper Lake. Black and brown bear may be encountered. Three public-use cabins are located along the trail. Trail closed to motorized vehicles May 1 to Nov. 30; closed to horses in April, May and June. Trailhead at Russian River Campground parking lot on the Sterling Highway at Milepost 52.8 from Seward; trailhead also at Mile 12 on the Snug Harbor Road, Cooper Landing. Related USGS Topographic maps: Seward B8, Kenai B1.

Saddle Trail. This 1-mile hike leads over the saddle between Halibut Cove and Grewingk Glacier in Kachemak Bay State Park. The trail, rated moderate, accesses the Alpine Ridge and Lagoon trails as well as the Grewingk Glacier Trail. It is steep on the Halibut Cove side. There is no transportation available from the trailhead to Glacier Spit or Halibut Cove unless you've made prior arrangements. Hiking the beach from the

trailhead to Right Beach isn't possible because of steep cliffs. The Saddle Trail trailhead is a popular spot to land boats during bad weather. Please respect private property near this trail. Hiking time is 25 minutes.

Seven Lakes Trail. Length 7 miles; relatively level; wet in some places; rated easy. Starts at Engineer Lake Campground parking lot; turn off on short side road at Mile 9.5 Skilak Lake Loop Road. This trail links Engineer Lake with Hidden, Kelly, Petersen and other smaller lakes in Kenai National Wildlife Refuge.

Silver Lake Trail. Trailhead at Mile 9.1 Swanson River Road in Kenai National Wildlife Refuge. Length 1 mile; rainbow trout and arctic char fishing.

Skilak Lookout Trail. Trailhead at Mile 5.5 Skilak Lake Loop Road off the Sterling Highway in Kenai National Wildllife Refuge. Length 2.6 miles; elevation range 700 to 1,450 feet; rated moderate. Trail offers glimpses of Skilak Lake and climbs to a knob that provides panoramic view of the lake and surrounding area. Round-trip is 4 to 5 hours.

Skyline Trail. Trailhead at Milepost S 61.4 Sterling Highway in Kenai National Wildlife Refuge. It is 3 miles round-trip; elevation gain 1,800 feet; rated very strenuous. Trail begins about 0.8 mile west of Lower Jean Lake Campground. The trail provides quick access to mountains, beginning in forest and emerging above tree line in about ³/₄ mile; it gradually disappears about 1¹/₄ mile from the trailhead in a beautiful alpine area. Spectacular views; berry picking. Winter travel not recommended because of avalanche hazard. Related USGS Topographic map: Kenai C-1.

Surprise Creek Trail. Trailhead on Skilak Lake Loop Road off the Sterling Highway in Kenai National Wildlife Refuge. Length 4.2 miles; elevation range 300 to 2,500 feet; steep, rated strenuous; minimum maintenance. A river crossing is necessary to reach the trailhead.

Turnagain Arm Trail. This trail, formerly called the Old Johnson Trail, parallels the coastline and the Seward Highway from Potter to Windy Corner. The 9.4-mile trail leads hikers through spruce forests, birch and alder groves, and flower-filled meadows. Scenic overlooks provide views of the Chugach Mountains to the north and the Kenai Mountains across Turnagain Arm.

Turnagain Arm earned its name in 1778 when two of Captain James Cook's ships — Discovery and Resolution — sailed into the arm in search of the Northwest Passage. The ships had to "turn again" when they reached the end of the arm.

The trail emerged in the 19th century as the vegetation was downtrodden by miners, trappers and prospectors. In 1915, the U.S. government improved the trail, as it intended to use it while continuing construction on a partially completed railroad that was to link Seward to Fairbanks and had been purchased from the bankrupt Alaska Central Railway. The trail was also used to deliver mail, and in 1917, telegraph lines were installed. Remnants of the railroad construction camps can still be seen along the trail.

Trailheads can be found at four places along the Seward Highway. At mile 115, the Potter Trailhead can be seen across from the Potter Section House. At mile 112, a trailhead can be found among the 30 picnic sites at McHugh Creek Picnic Area. Rainbow Creek Valley Trailhead is located at mile 108, and Windy Corner Trailhead is located at mile 106.

The trail begins at the Potter Section House, a state historic house that was once part of a railroad section camp that maintained 10 miles of railroad track. Chugach State Park Headquarters is in the basement of the house. From the Section House, the trail passes a billboard and heads uphill, where it levels off and follows a bluff east through birch, aspen and cottonwoods. At 1.9 miles, the trail slopes downward as it nears McHugh Valley. At 3 miles, two peaks can be seen inland — McHugh to the North and South Suicide to the northeast — and the trail splits. Stay to the right, where the trail will connect with the McHugh Creek Picnic Area.

To continue on to the Rainbow, pick up the McHugh Trailhead at the stairs in the lower parking lot of the picnic area. The trail crosses McHugh Creek and heads uphill to a fork in the trail. Take the eastern branch. The trail levels off and crosses a scree slope in an avalanche area.

At Mile 5, a side trail leads to Beluga Point, a good place to watch the bore tide come in if your timing's right. A bore tide is a wall of water coming in with the tide. It is created by a wide range between high and low tides (more than 35 feet in Cook Inlet) and by the narrow, shallow, gently sloping shape of the arm. Bore tides in Turnagain Arm range from 1/2 to 6 feet high and travel between 10 and 15 mph. Minus tides, new or full moons and high winds contribute to a large bore tide, which may sound like a

train. The bore tide generally occurs about 45 minutes after the predicted Anchorage low tide.

Beluga Point also has the earliest evidence of humans along Turnagain Arm. It was the lookout of choice for prehistoric hunters in search of beluga whales and Dall sheep. The best time to see belugas is at high tide from mid-July through August when salmon make their spawning runs.

At Mile 7.35, the trail crosses Rainbow Creek and winds toward the Rainbow trailhead and parking lot. From here, the trail continues through the spruce trees to its end at Windy Corner, mile 9.4. Windy Corner is popular with the local Dall sheep population. While it is not uncommon to see several ewes and lambs gathered there, the rams prefer higher ground.

Wosnesenski Trail. This 2-mile trail, rated easy to moderate, begins from the China Poot Peak Trail, about 10 minutes after crossing the inlet stream bridge at China Poot Lake in Kachemak Bay State Park. It winds along the shoreline of 3 lakes formed by a geologic fault. After about 25 minutes on the trail, you will find a good camping area in a stand of cottonwoods by the lake. After another 25 minutes of hiking, the trail climbs over a low saddle and drops down into the valley. Crossing the glacial rivers in the valley can be hazardous. Hiking time is 1 hour, 15 minutes.

River Running

Anchorage/Mat-Su Area

Chulitna and Tokositna rivers. The Chulitna, located along the George Parks Highway north of Talkeetna, runs partially through Denali State Park. The Middle Fork is clear water, generally shallow and rocky. The East Fork is clear, too, but fast (4 to 5 mph). Below the West Fork confluence, the Chulitna moves even faster (5 to 7 mph) and is braided in spots. Canoes, kayaks or rafts may be used on this river.

The upper section of the river drops 28 feet per mile and offers exciting white water (up to Class III). Fallen trees and sweepers are hazards. The water volume can change river conditions drastically. From the Parks Highway bridge (Milepost 132.8 from Anchorage), near the southern boundary of Denali State Park, to Talkeetna its gradient is 10 feet per mile and it is an easy river to float, although fast and very cold. Below Talkeetna, the river joins the Susitna. It is recommended that only skilled white-water paddlers with wilderness river experience test the section north of the Chulitna bridge.

Along this river boaters may see eagles, black bear and other wildlife. There also are views of the Alaska Range, including Mount McKinley. Fishing for grayling above Honolulu Creek is poor to moderate.

The Middle Fork is accessible at a bridge at Milepost 194.5 from Anchorage on the George Parks Highway just below Broad Pass. There is an undeveloped parking area southwest of the bridge below the highway. The East Fork can be reached from the same highway farther south at Milepost 185.1. From the Alaska Railroad the Chulitna can be reached at Broad Pass, Colorado, East Fork bridge, Honolulu, Hurricane and Talkeetna. The trip is 98 river miles from the bridge put in on the Middle Fork; other alternatives are shorter. Trip length is 1 to 5 days.

Another alternative is to start on the Tokositna River, described as one of the most scenic and easy to run rivers in the area. It has glaciers along its course and Mount McKinley towers above it. The Tokositna can be reached in a few minutes by air charter from Talkeetna to Home Lake. Its flow is moderately swift, but it presents no special obstacles down to its confluence with the Chulitna River just above the bridge on the Parks Highway. Distance is about 26 river miles from the usual put in point to the Chulitna River.

Related USGS Topographic maps: Healy A-5 and A-6; Talkeetna B-1, C-1; Talkeetna Mountains D-6.

Kahiltna River. This river heads at Kahiltna Glacier, 35 miles northeast of Talkeetna between Mount Foraker and Mount Hunter in the Alaska Range, and flows southeast to the Yentna River, 53 miles northwest of Anchorage.

This Class II braided river flows through an immense valley. The gradient in the first 28 miles is 8 feet per mile. Just above the Peters Creek confluence the pace quickens appreciably, the gradient increases to 15 feet per mile for the last 46 miles and huge boulders create numerous rapids. Silty and ice cold, this is considered a challenging river. Decked canoes, kayaks or rafts are suitable.

The Kahiltna is accessible by air charter from Talkeetna or Anchorage, landing a few miles from where it emerges from the glacier. Exit is by small plane from the Yentna River, or voyagers may continue down the Yentna to the Susitna River and Cook Inlet.

Related USGS Topographic maps: Talkeetna B-3, B-2, A2; Tyonek D-2, D-3.

Klutina River. This river heads at Stevenson Glacier in the Chugach Mountains and flows 63 miles northeast to the Copper River at Copper Center on the Richardson Highway, 66 miles northeast of Valdez.

This Class III river offers excellent whitewater paddling at low water volume. It is more dangerous at high water, which is usually in mid-July to August. The usual put in point is at 16-mile-long Klutina Lake. The first 10 miles of the river from the lake has a gradient of 17 feet per mile. The pace quickens for the last 16 miles, where the gradient increases to 23 feet per mile. Kayaks or rafts are suitable for this river; canoes and riverboats only for the very experienced. The trip takes 1 day.

The river offers excellent mountain scenery and fishing for king and red salmon in June and July. Dolly Varden and grayling are available in Klutina Lake.

Access to the Klutina River is possible by 4-wheel-drive vehicle over a bad road through private land from Copper Center bridge to the outlet of Klutina Lake. Access also is by floatplane to the lake. Exit at Copper Center, or continue on the Copper River to Chitina or the Gulf of Alaska.

Related USGS Topographic maps: Valdez C-5, C-6, D-4 and D-5.

Lake Creek. This clear-water stream heads in Chelatna Lake and flows southeast 56 river miles to the Yentna River, 58 miles northwest of Anchorage.

Lake Creek is rated Class I to IV for the first 48 miles. About halfway downriver is a severe Class IV canyon with huge boulders which should be scouted or portaged. It is possible to line the boat along the right bank. Portage is only 150 to 200 yards. It is possible to depart the river near this point via 2 portage trails. One well-marked trail leads to Shovel Lake where there is floatplane access. The other trail, marked with black ink on gray rock, leads to Martana Lake. From the canyon the river is a rocky and challenging Class III. The last 8 miles are rated Class I. Kayaks or rafts are suitable for this river. The trip takes 3 to 4 days, depending on conditions.

This river offers spectacular views of the Alaska Range and Mount McKinley to the northeast. Fair fishing for grayling and rainbow trout.

Access is by floatplane from Anchorage or Talkeetna to Chelatna Lake. Exit via floatplane or riverboat from the Yentna River.

Related USGS Topographic maps: Talkeetna A-2, A-3, B-3; Tyonek D-3.

Little Susitna River. The "Little Su" heads at Mint Glacier in the Talkeetna Mountains and flows southwest 110 miles to Cook Inlet, 13 miles west of Anchorage.

This is a fairly small river, ranging in width from 20 to 40 feet. Except for the upstream stretch, where the gradient is 20 feet per mile, it's also a slow river (2 to 4 mph) and meanders considerably as it makes its way through spruce, birch and willow forest. Be alert for sweepers, shallows, logjams, and air and jet boats.

There are 2 common put in points: at the Schrock Road bridge about 7 miles north of the Parks Highway and at the Parks Highway bridge at Milepost 57 from Anchorage. From the first put in, the river is rated Class III for 26 miles, after which it is flat water for about 106 river miles. Canoes, kayaks or rafts are suitable. The trip takes 1 to 3 days.

Fishing in the Little Susitna is excellent for king salmon from late May through June and for silver salmon in July and August. There also are red salmon to 10 pounds in mid-July. Other fish available include Dolly Varden and rainbow trout.

Exit from this river may be by prearranged charter flight or takeout at Burma Road, which starts 0.2 mile west of the Lake Marion turnoff on Big Lake Road.

Related USGS Topographic maps: Anchorage C-7 and C-8; Tyonek B-1, C-1.

Maclaren River. This river heads at Maclaren Glacier in the Clearwater Mountains and flows southwest 55 miles to the Susitna River.

The Maclaren flows from the high tundra country into the forests of the Lake Louise basin. From the usual access point on the Denali Highway, the river flows 52 miles with a gradient of 18 feet per mile. It is rated Class II and III and is rocky with many shallow rapids. Voyagers should take plenty of boat repair materials. Water volume can change rapidly. Canoes, kayaks and rafts are suitable.

Wildlife that may be seen along the way includes bear, moose and caribou.

Put in point is at the end of a state road which leaves the Denali Highway at Milepost 43.3 from Paxson. Once on the Susitna River it is possible to exit via the Tyone River to the road at Lake Louise. Or continue down the Susitna to the portage to Stephan

A tributary of the Chitina River, the Nizina River should be run only by experienced paddlers. (Karen Jettmar)

Lake. Related USGS Topographic maps: Mount Hayes A-5, A-6; Gulkana D-6, D-5; Talkeetna Mountains D-1.

Skwentna River. This river heads at South Twin Glacier below Mount Spurr and flows north and east 100 miles to the Yentna River near the settlement of Skwentna, 70 miles northwest of Anchorage.

The Skwentna is considered one of the most difficult and remote, but spectacular, wilderness rivers in Alaska. *CAUTION: This river is recommended only for expert paddlers who are experienced in wilderness travel.*

The Skwentna is extremely fast. It has many difficult rapids and steep-walled canyons. From its headwaters the gradient is 40 feet per mile. The first 24 miles are rated Class IV. The next 40 miles, also with a gradient of 40 feet per mile, are rated Class II and IV. Then the gradient changes to 17 feet per mile for 50 miles, rated Class II and III. The final 55-mile stretch is rated Class II; the gradient is 10 feet per mile. Decked 2-man canoes or kayaks are recommended for this river.

Moose, bear and an occasional wolf may be encountered along this river.

The Skwentna is not easy to get to. It is possible to reach the headwaters via a portage from Chakachamna Lake, but this route is difficult and takes at least a week. The primary means of access is by helicopter to the headwaters. Exit is at Skwentna, which has accommodations and scheduled air service. Related USGS Topographic maps: Tyonek B-8, C-8, D-8, D-7, D-6, D-5, D-4.

Susitna River. This large river heads at Susitna Glacier in the Alaska Range and flows southwest 260 miles to Cook Inlet, 24 miles west of Anchorage. The river's Tanaina Indian name, said to mean "sandy river," first appeared in 1847 on a Russian chart.

The Susitna offers 2 very different trips on its upper and lower sections.

A few miles from its origin the river emerges from the eastern Alaska Range. The mountains provide a magnificent backdrop to the swift, silty water. Wildlife that may be observed includes moose, bear, caribou, wolf and beaver. The best access is at the Susitna River bridge on the Denali Highway at Milepost 79.5 from Paxson. From this point the river has a gradient of 7 feet per mile and is rated Class III for 55 miles. Braided gravel flats alternate with a single river channel; some difficult rapids are in this section. Sparse forest growth clings to the shores along the river. Approximately 30 miles downriver from the bridge, the beautiful

Maclaren River joins from the east. Then after 10 miles of braided gravel flats, the Tyone River comes in from the east.

The Tyone River connects Lake Louise and the Susitna. The slow, meandering Tyone can be used as a connecting waterway to leave the Susitna Valley for the extensive Lake Louise plains. A small outboard motor on a canoe speeds an otherwise slow upriver paddle; it takes about a day to get to Tyone Lake with a motor.

Below the Tyone River confluence, the Susitna has several huge oxbow bends and approximately 20 miles of swift water and rapids rated Class II. Gradient increases to 20 feet per mile.

After this stretch, the river slows for the next 70 miles, rated Class I to II. Gradient is 10 feet per mile. This tame section ends at treacherous Devil Canyon, which should not be attempted. Look for Log Creek on the left, shortly after a sharp right bend. Pick-up may be made by floatplane at this point or it is possible to portage 5 miles to Stephan Lake, for a prearranged pickup by floatplane.

The Upper Susitna trip should be attempted only by experienced wilderness travelers. Decked canoes, kayaks, rafts or riverboats are suitable for this river.

The Lower Susitna is a Class I river that poses no technical difficulties, although its many channels do test water-judging abilities. There are no rapids, but there are boils and upwellings. Some branches and sloughs may be blocked by logjams and may be hazardous. Access points are the Alaska Railroad station at Gold Creek; Talkeetna; and the Susitna River bridge on the Parks Highway at Milepost 104.3 from Anchorage. Exit at Talkeetna, the Parks Highway bridge or via floatplane pickup at the river mouth. Distance from Gold Creek to Cook Inlet is about 120 river miles. Trip takes 1 to 3 days, depending on put in point. Canoes, kayaks, rafts or riverboats are suitable. Related USGS Topographic maps: Healy A-1, A-2; Talkeetna Mountains D-1, D-2, D-3, D-4, D-5, D-6, C-1, C-2, C-6; Talkeetna C-1, B-1, A-1; Tyonek D-1, C-1, C-2, B-2.

Talachulitna River. This river heads on Beluga Mountain and flows south and northwest to the Skwentna River, 14 miles upriver from the settlement of Skwentna, which is 70 miles northwest of Anchorage.

The upper reaches of Talachulitna Creek, which drains Judd Lake, may be shallow and have logjams. The upper river is slow and rated Class I to II. The river flows faster through a section of canyons in the lower 20 miles, rated Class II to III. Just below the Hiline Lake put in near the mid-point of the river there is a tricky drop rated Class III. Kayaks or rafts are suitable for this river. The trip takes 3 to 5 days depending on put in point.

The Talachulitna offers excellent views of Beluga Mountain and the Alaska Range. Moose and black bear may be seen. Fishing is good for 5 species of salmon, grayling and rainbow trout (catch and release only).

Access is by floatplane to Judd Lake or to the Talachulitna River at midpoint just south of Hiline Lake. Exit is by floatplane from the confluence with the Skwentna River, or continue down the Skwentna River and exit via scheduled air service at Skwentna or floatplane pickup from the Yentna River at its confluence with the Skwentna.

Related USGS Topographic maps: Tyonek C-4, C-5 and D-4.

Tazlina, Nelchina and Little Nelchina rivers. These rivers offer a variety of water conditions and trip alternatives. The Tazlina River drains Tazlina Lake and flows east 30 miles to the Copper River, 7 miles southeast of Glennallen and about 140 miles east of Anchorage. The Nelchina River heads at Nelchina Glacier and flows north and south-east 28 miles into Tazlina Lake. The Little Nelchina is a 48-mile-long tributary to the Nelchina.

Access is from the Glenn Highway via the Little Nelchina River at Milepost 137.5 from Anchorage. Access is also by floatplane to Tazlina Lake.

From the Glenn Highway put in, the Little Nelchina is a fast, narrow and rocky clear-water stream. It is shallow during low-water times. It flows 4 river miles rated Class IV and drops 50 feet per mile, before joining the Nelchina River. The glacial Nelchina flows 22 river miles rated Class I to II to Tazlina Lake. This section drops 20 feet per mile.

It's an 8-mile paddle on Tazlina Lake to the Tazlina River. Be alert for a whirlpool at the lake outlet. The Tazlina flows about 50 river miles to the Copper River. This stretch, with a gradient of 15 feet per mile, is rated Class II to III. Exit at the Tazlina River Bridge on the Richardson Highway at Milepost 110.7 from Valdez or continue down the Copper River.

Water volume on these rivers should be judged carefully. The rivers are generally least difficult before spring runoff in May and June, late in a dry summer or after cold weather slows glacial runoff. The Little Nelchina may have logjams. Kayaks or rafts are suitable, or canoes for the experienced. This trip takes 2 to 3 days to the Richardson Highway, depending on put in point.

Related USGS Topographic maps: Gulkana A-3, A-4, A-5 and A-6; Valdez D-7 and D-8.

Tyone River. This river heads at Tyone Lake and flows northwest 30 miles to the Susitna River, 68 miles northwest of Gulkana. This trip combines lake paddling with an easy river journey. About half the distance is across 3 adjoining lakes: Louise, Susitna and Tyone. The flat-water river flows slowly and meanders. This route is suitable for riverboats and canoes with small motors, as well as for kayaks and paddled canoes. The river can be run upstream from the Susitna by strong paddlers. This is considered a good trip for less experienced paddlers who are experienced in the wilderness.

Access is by floatplane to Lake Louise or via the 19.3-mile-long Lake Louise Road, which leaves the Glenn Highway at Milepost 159.8 from Anchorage. Exit is by floatplane from the Susitna River.

Lake Louise and Susitna Lake have excellent fishing for grayling, lake trout and ling-cod. Related USGS Topographic maps: Gulkana C-6; Talkeetna Mountains C-1.

Yentna River. This river is formed by its east and west forks, and flows southeast 75 miles to the Susitna River, 30 miles north-west of Anchorage.

This flat-water glacial river winds in graceful sweeps through the basin south of Mount McKinley. It has a large volume; white-water problems are minimal, but boaters should be alert for sweepers, logjams and floating trees. Canoes, kayaks, rafts and riverboats are all suitable.

Moose and bear may be seen; there is good fishing on clear-water tributary streams and creeks. There are several homesteads on the Yentna and riverboats may be encountered.

Access is by small plane to the headwaters. Exit is by prearranged floatplane pickup from the Susitna, or continue floating down the Susitna. Related Topographic maps: Talkeetna B-4, A-4, A-3; Tyonek D-4, D-3, D-2, C-2, B-2.

Copper River/Wrangell-St. Elias Area

Chitina River. This silty glacial river is located in the Chugach Mountains in Wrangell-St. Elias National Park and Preserve. The river heads at Chitina Glacier and flows west-northwest 112 miles to the Copper River, 1.2 miles east of Chitina and 66 miles northeast of Valdez.

This river is considered Class I to Class II from its headwaters and has a gradient of 10 feet per mile. It is a fast but not technically difficult river. At about its midpoint, the Chitina is joined by the Nizina River, which should be run only by experienced paddlers. It flows through a steep canyon and is considered Class II, fairly fast with difficult rapids.

Another alternative is to put in on the Kennicott River at McCarthy. The Kennicott to the Nizina is Class II, swift and braided. It is also shallow and may need to be lined or portaged. From where the Nizina joins it, the Chitina is braided with many gravel bars. Kayaks or rafts are recommended for these rivers.

The Chitina runs through wild mountain country with nearby peaks over 10,000 feet. Paddlers may see moose, brown bears and Dall sheep.

Access to the Chitina's glacial headwaters is by chartered wheel plane. The Kennicott River is accessed by the Chitina-McCarthy Road, which is usually passable by 2-wheel-drive vehicles. Check in Chitina for road conditions. Exit is at Chitina, below the highway bridge.

Related USGS Topographic maps: McCarthy A-6, B-6, B-7 and B-8; Valdez B-1, C-1 and C-2.

Copper River. This major glacial river heads on the north side of the Wrangell Mountains and flows south 250 miles through a gap in the Chugach Mountains to the Gulf of Alaska, just east of Cordova. Although the Richardson and Glenn highways parallel the river, they are rarely within sight or sound. This braided river passes through true wilderness country and features silty, but always swift water. The Copper forms the western boundary of Wrangell-St. Elias National Park and Preserve and flows by glacier-clad peaks ranging up to 16,000 feet, including Mount Sanford, Mount Drum, Mount Wrangell and Mount Blackburn. The lower portion passes through Chugach National Forest.

This is considered a Class II river. No difficult white water is encountered except at the end of Miles Lake, where the ice of Childs Glacier forms the western bank of the river. The river narrows here and the glacier calves directly into it. The powerful current frequently creates eddies and whirlpools of frightening dimensions. There also are some holes to avoid in Abercrombie Rapids above Miles Lake. This river's gradient is 7 feet per mile for about 150 river miles from Slana to Copper Center; 6 feet per mile for the next 60 miles to Chitina; and 5 feet per mile from Chitina to the gulf. The trip takes 7 to 9 days, depending on put in and takeout points. Canoes, rafts or kayaks are suitable.

Paddlers will be treated to outstanding scenery including mountains, glaciers, canyons and the river delta. Eagles, bears, seals and an abundance of waterfowl may be seen.

Access is from a bridge over the Gakona River, 1.8 miles from the Gakona junction on the Tok Cutoff (Glenn Highway), and a short distance from the confluence of the Gakona and Copper rivers. Access also at Copper Center on the Richardson Highway and Chitina on the Edgerton Highway. Once past Chitina, the next exit is more than 100 river miles away near the head of the Copper River Delta at a bridge on the Copper River Highway at Milepost 27 from Cordova. Or it is possible to paddle west into Cordova along the shoreline.

Related USGS Topographic maps: Gulkana A-3, B-3; Valdez A-3, B-2, B-3, C-2, C-3, D-3 and D-4; Cordova B-3, C-2, C-3, D-2 and D-3.

Delta River. The Delta River flows north out of Tangle Lakes, near Milepost 21.5 on the Denali Highway. It is open early June to mid-September. The trip takes 2 to 3 days, covers 29 miles of lakes and river, and is suitable for canoe, kayak or 12- to 14-foot craft. The upper portion of this national wild and scenic river is clear water; below Eureka Creek it is cold, silty glacial water with debris.

BLM classifies the Delta as Class I, II and III to Milepost 212.5 on the Richardson Highway. A falls must be portaged. A 1/2-mile maintained trail around the falls and across steep, rocky terrain is available. From Milepost 212.5 to Black Rapids, the Delta is Class III and IV with standing waves. From Tangle Lakes to Milepost 212.5 the trip is 35 miles or about 2 days. From that point it is 17 miles to Black Rapids, or less than a day's travel. Canoes, kayaks or rafts are suitable.

Start the trip at BLM's Tangle Lakes Campground on the Denali Highway, 22 miles west of Paxson. There are two commercial lodges on the Denali Highway near the Tangle Lakes and another at Paxson that provide gas, food and lodging. A public phone is available at Paxson Lodge. Paddle north through the lakes. There is a falls 2 miles below the last lake. A quarter-mile portage on the right bank crosses the Denali

Fault, one of the longest fault zones in Alaska. Two hundred yards after reentering the river, traverse to the left bank to run a difficult rapid or line on the right bank. Class II-III water for the next 2 miles requires quick maneuvering around the rocks. *NOTE: Boaters must have white-water experience. Each year 5 or 6 canoes are damaged beyond repair along this stretch. It is a long walk out.* The remainder of the river to the takeout at Milepost 212.5 is mostly Class I, with some Class II. There is a view of Rainbow Mountain to the right.

From Milepost 212.5, continue in raft or kayak only. There are long stretches of rapids with high, irregular waves and hidden boulders. End the float trip at Milepost 227.4 on the Richardson Highway.

Wildlife that may be seen along the Delta River includes moose, bear, Dall sheep, caribou, beaver, muskrat, golden eagles, bald eagles and many species of waterfowl. Fish available includes lake trout, arctic grayling, whitefish and burbot.

For more information about the Delta River contact: Bureau of Land Management, Box 147, Glennallen, AK 99588; phone 822-3217. Related USGS Topographic maps: Mount Hayes A-4, B-4, A-5, C-5; Gulkana D-4.

Gulkana River. A river trip of nearly 300 miles is possible by using this nationally designated wild and scenic river. Start at the Denali Highway, paddle and portage through the Tangle Lakes canoe trail, then float the Middle Fork Gulkana to the very popular Gulkana River, which joins the Copper River for the final leg to the Gulf of Alaska.

The Middle Fork Gulkana is generally Class I with some Class II, III and IV, according to the Bureau of Land Management, which manages this river.

Start this trip at the BLM's Upper Tangle Lakes Campground at Milepost 21.7 from Paxson on the Denali Highway. Paddle south through Tangle Lakes; 300-foot portage between first lake and Upper Tangle Lake. At the southwest end of Upper Tangle Lake, a 0.3-mile portage leads to Lake 2865. A shallow wadeable portage between Lake 2865 and the southernmost Tangle Lake is necessary, followed by a 1.3-mile portage to Dickey Lake. No trail markings, but most of the portage is low tundra brush.

The Middle Fork Gulkana flows out of Dickey Lake at the extreme southeast corner. The first 3 miles of the river are runnable, but less than 1 foot deep. The river is extremely swift, shallow and rocky for the

next 3 miles (Class III and IV); generally too swift and rocky to float. Toward the end of this stretch there is a small rock canyon with very steep gradient which requires careful lining. The next 19 miles to the main Gulkana is easy Class I and II; the river meanders a lot and has sweepers and logjams in some sections, especially between Swede Lake and Hungry Hollow Creek. The 9-mile trip from the Denali Highway to the river takes 1 to 2 days; the 25 miles to the Gulkana takes 2 to 3 days.

Paddlers floating the Gulkana also can start at Paxson Lake. Access is at Paxson Lake Campground, Milepost 175 from Valdez on the Richardson Highway. Paddle across lake to river outlet in southwest corner. (Old cabins may be seen on the lakeshore; do not trespass.)

The first 3 miles on the Gulkana River are Class II-III. From the confluence of the Middle Fork, the next 15 miles are Class I, followed by the Class III-IV Canyon Rapids, which should be run by experienced paddlers only. A sign marks a quarter-mile portage around the rapids on the left bank. The following 8 miles are Class II, requiring careful maneuvering around boulders and logs. Several canoes are wrecked here each year. At the first bend after the portage there is a 1-mile side trip to Canyon Lake, which has excellent grayling fishing; trail begins on the left bank. The remainder of the trip to Sourdough is Class I. There is road access at the Sourdough Campground, Milepost 147.6 from Valdez on the Richardson Highway. The remainder of the river to the takeout at Gulkana and the Gulkana River's confluence with the Copper River is Class I-II, with the last 8 miles ranging from Class I to Class II.

Use canoes or kayaks on Tangle Lakes; canoes, kayaks or rafts are suitable on the rivers.

Fish available includes rainbow trout, whitefish, arctic grayling, red and king salmon, lake trout and burbot, depending on location and season. Wildlife includes moose, bear, wolf, fox, caribou, muskrat, beaver, eagle, hawk and waterfowl.

For additional information contact: Bureau of Land Management, Box 147, Glennallen, AK 99588; phone 822-3217. Related USGS Topographic maps: Mount Hayes A-5; Gulkana B-3, B-4, C-4, D-4 and D-5.

Maclaren River. This river heads at Maclaren Glacier in the Clearwater Mountains and flows southwest 55 miles to the Susitna River.

The Maclaren flows from the high tundra country into the forests of the Lake Louise basin. From the usual access point on the Denali Highway, the river flows 52 miles with a gradient of 18 feet per mile. It is rated Class II and III, and is rocky with many shallow rapids. Voyagers should take plenty of boat repair materials. Water volume can change rapidly. Canoes, kayaks and rafts are suitable.

Wildlife that may be seen along the way includes bear, moose and caribou.

Put in point is at the end of a state road that leaves the Denali Highway at Milepost 43.3 from Paxson. Once on the Susitna River it is possible to exit via the Tyone River to the road at Lake Louise. Or continue down the Susitna to the portage to Stephan Lake. Related USGS Topographic maps: Mount Hayes A-5, A-6; Gulkana D-6, D-5; Talkeetna Mountains D-1.

Nabesna River. This river heads at Nabesna Glacier and flows northeast to join with the Chisana River to form the Tanana River near Northway Junction on the Alaska Highway. The river begins in Wrangell-St. Elias National Park and Preserve and flows through Tetlin National Wildlife Refuge.

This cold stream is in a wide graveled valley and is braided and quite fast at the start. Eventually it slows to meander through the foothills and taiga forest east of the Wrangell Mountains. The first 10 miles from the put in point are rated Class I to II, with a gradient of 20 feet per mile. The gradient for the next 15 miles of flat water is 13 feet per mile, and the gradient for the last 40 miles is 5 feet per mile. Canoes, kayaks or rafts are suitable.

The river can be reached from the 45-mile-long Nabesna Road, which leaves the Glenn Highway (Tok Cutoff) at Milepost 65.2 from Tok. This gravel road becomes very rough after Milepost 28.5; check on road conditions at Sportsman's Paradise Lodge at this point. There are several creeks that must be forded. A trail approximately 5 miles long leads to the Nabesna River from Milepost 41. Exit the river at Northway or at the Alaska Highway at the confluence of the Chisana River. Related USGS Topographic maps: Nabesna B-4, C-4, C-3, D-3, D-2; Tanacross A-2.

Tangle Lakes. The name Tangle is a descriptive term for the maze of lakes and feeder streams of the Delta and Gulkana river drainages. The system includes Long Tangle, Round Tangle, Upper Tangle and Lower Tangle Lakes. The Upper Tangle Lake canoe trail goes south through Tangle Lakes (portages required) to Dickey Lake, then follows the Middle Fork of the Gulkana River. Access is from Milepost 21.7 on the Denali Highway at BLM's Upper Tangle Lakes Campground.

The Lower Tangle Lakes, accessed from Tangle Lakes BLM campground at Milepost 21.5 Denali Highway, drain into the Delta River. Put in at Round Tangle and follow the Tangle Lakes for 9 miles to the Delta River. The 4 lakes are connected by shallow channels of moving water.

See the Gulkana River and Delta River this section. For more information contact: Bureau of Land Management, Box 147, Glennallen, AK 99588; phone 822-3217. Related USGS Topographic Maps: Mount Hayes A-4, B-4, C-4.

Kenai Peninsula Area

Kenai River. This river heads at Kenai Lake on the Kenai Peninsula and flows west 75 miles to Cook Inlet at Kenai. Much of this river is located in the Kenai National Wildlife Refuge. It ranges from Class II to III and features an exciting white-water canyon for the experienced paddler. This trip is suitable for kayak, raft or experienced canoeists.

Access this river at turnouts near the Kenai River bridge on the Sterling Highway at Milepost S 47.8, about 100 miles from Anchorage, for the 17-mile stretch to Skilak Lake. Or put in at the bridge at Milepost S 53. Be alert for the Class III rapids at Schooner Bend below the second put in point; stay close to the right bank. The most exciting rapids on this river are just downstream from Jean Creek; the 2-mile-long canyon is rated Class II to III. This stretch should be run by experienced paddlers only; vertical walls prevent lining. The river braids before it enters Skilak Lake and there may be sweepers or logjams.

Paddle 6 miles on the lake to the Upper Skilak Lake Campground. Strong winds on the lake may be hazardous, so stay close to shore. There are several miles of rock bluffs along this stretch, which means there is no place to take out if the winds suddenly whip up. From the upper campground, it's 7 miles of paddling to Lower Skilak Lake Campground and 2 miles farther to the Kenai River outlet. There are Class III rapids 12 miles downriver from the outlet.

Fish available on this trip include Dolly Varden, rainbow trout, and pink, silver and red salmon. (Also see Sportfishing, this section.)

Exit the river at Soldotna or Kenai or at numerous other points in between.

Related USGS Topographic maps: Seward B-8; Kenai B-1, B-2, B-3, C-2, C-3 and C-4.

THE DELTA RIVER: FROM FLAT TO FIERCE IN 80 SCENIC MILES

Fall comes quickly to the alpine country around the Tangle Lakes. In August, when most of the nation is gripped in the hottest days of summer, the days are already getting shorter along the Delta River, and the evening air starts nibbling at the inner corners of your lungs. At the headwaters of the river, crisp night air slaps the Tangle Lakes, their shallow waters warmed by 24-hour sunlight in June and July. Tremendous fog banks appear in the morning, dew dripping from any clothing or equipment left out overnight.

I found that August was a fine time to visit the Delta, but any time between mid-June and mid-September is certainly worth the effort.

Larry Kajdan, BLM's recreation planner in Glennallen, has been down the Delta River more than two dozen times. "I like hiking in the area around the Lower Tangle Lakes.

"You can scramble up on the glacial features and look around in all directions. There's no thick brush, so the hiking is easy and the views are fantastic. In August, the blueberries are plentiful and the afternoons can be warm and sunny. What more could you want?" asks Kajdan.

The Delta has outstanding grayling fishing. "There's been lots of them on every trip I've taken," says Kajdan, "and when the ice goes out on the lakes, usually in early June, the lake trout are real hungry. They'll head for the outlet and feed on snails in the shallows."

It's hard to take a trip on the Delta without seeing some wildlife, too. "I've seen moose above and below the portage. A few miles farther down, Garrett Creek comes in. Scope out the hillsides towards the east and look for grizzly bears. They are there more often than not," says Kajdan.

Wayne Boden has been visiting the Delta since 1962. "It's one of my favorite parts of Alaska. There is variety in the landscape, and you actually travel right through the Alaska Range," he notes.

His most memorable experience on the Delta was in its headwaters up in the Upper Tangle Lakes area, south of the Denali Highway. "We were up there on a moose hunt in mid-September. The weather was perfect. I climbed up on a small ridge to look around and was surprised to see a raft of 93 trumpeter swans staging for their fall migration. That same trip we counted about 50 tundra (whistling) swans, and maybe 500 ducks, mallards, teal, widgeons, pintails and shovelers, all staging too. We also saw 31 caribou and 11 moose. It was heavenly, just what you'd expect in Alaska."

Boden has noticed changes since his first visit. "For one thing, there are superior boat launch facilities and a nice portage trail. Back in '62 you had to pack your canoe through the brush, and there was little evidence of use. You really had a wilderness experience. You still can have a fantastic trip, but you will see that people have camped before in some of the choicer spots. But the fishing is every bit as good as I remember it 30 years ago."

The Delta River is one of the few rivers in Alaska with convenient road access at both the put in and takeout points. In August the average maximum temperature is 62.5°F, and the average minimum is 38.7°F. August 1, daylight is 5 A.M. to 10:33 P.M.; August 31, daylight is 6:27 A.M. to 8:55 P.M.

—Story by Ed Bovy, reprinted courtesy of the Bureau of Land Management, Public Affairs Office

Swan Lake. Established canoe trail within Kenai National Wildlife Refuge, managed by U.S. Fish & Wildlife Service. This 60-mile route connects 30 lakes with forks of the Moose River. Terminus of the trip is the confluence of the Moose and Kenai rivers at the Moose River bridge on the Sterling Highway at Milepost 82.1. This route can be traveled in less than a week. Longest portage is about 1 mile. Rainbow trout, Dolly Varden and silver salmon are found in most lakes, except for Birch, Teal, Mallard, Raven, Otter and Big Mink lakes. West entrance to the canoe route is at Canoe Lake on Swan Lake Road off the Swanson River Road, 21.2 miles from the Sterling Highway. East entrance is from Portage Lake, 5.8 miles beyond Canoe Lake on Swan Lake Road.

Consult the canoe pamphlet described under Swanson River. Related USGS Topographic map: Kenai C-2.

Swanson River. Established canoe trail within Kenai National Wildlife Refuge, managed by U.S. Fish & Wildlife Service. This 80-mile route links more than 40 lakes with 46 miles of the Swanson River. The entire route can be traveled in less than a week. Portages between lakes are generally short and cross level or slightly hilly terrain. Longest portage is about 1 mile. Rainbow trout, Dolly Varden and some red and silver salmon are found in most of the lakes, except Berry, Redpoll, Twig, Eider, Birchtree and Olsjold lakes. The first trailhead is on the Swanson River Road at Milepost 14.9 from the junction with the Sterling Highway. Enter the Swanson River at a campground here and float downstream 1 or 2 days to Swanson River canoe landing at Mile 38.6 on the Kenai Spur Highway within Captain Cook State Recreation Area. To make the entire 80-mile trip, take Swan Lake Road, which turns off to the right from Swanson River Road. Drive about 12 miles to near the end; take a branch to the left and drive a bit farther to a parking area. Carry your canoe or kayak down to Paddle Lake. Refer to the Fish and Wildlife Service pamphlet *Canoeing in the Kenai National Wildlife Refuge* for a map of all the routes and other details. Related USGS Topographic maps: Kenai C-2 and C-3, D-2 and D-3.

Sea Kayaking

Kachemak Bay. Attractions include abundant wildlife. Since one can drive to Homer and enter Kachemak Bay, this is one of the most easily accessed kayaking destinations. (Homer is 226 miles by highway from Anchorage.) There is a lot of private property within Kachemak Bay State Park so kayakers should take care to obtain permission before camping in these areas. Because of a prevailing southwesterly wind on sunny summer days one should plan to return to Homer before 11 A.M. or after 7 P.M. (See also Kachemak Bay State Park this section.)

Kenai Fjords National Park. Attractions include tidewater glaciers and abundant wildlife. Access is by air or boat charter from Seward. Kayaks can be rented in Seward or Anchorage. A number of guides and outfitters offer trips in this area. (See also Kenai Fjords National Park this section.)

Prince William Sound. Attractions in Prince William Sound include tidewater glaciers and abundant wildlife. Most kayakers enter the western Sound from Whittier. The Alaska Railroad provides a shuttle service from Portage, about 47 miles south of Anchorage on the Seward Highway, to Whittier. It is a 35-minute train ride. The shuttle train carries both passengers and vehicles. Kayakers with a lot of gear already loaded onto their vehicle might opt for paying extra and having their vehicle shipped to Whittier. While more expensive than traveling as passengers and paying a small fee for the kayak to travel as baggage, it saves loading and unloading at both stations and makes hauling everything to the dock in Whittier much easier.

Easy access from Anchorage has drawn many paddlers to western Prince William Sound, and in recent years the number of ocean kayakers in the area has exploded. Campsites along Passage Canal during peak holiday weekends are often full, and many kayakers are seeking charter boat service to more remote areas.

Charter boat service is available in Whittier, Valdez and Cordova. Charter prices depend on destination and number of persons in the party. One 4-hour charter boat trip for 6 persons and 4 kayaks from Whittier to Derickson Bay at the terminus of Nellie Juan Glacier, for example, costs $500 round-trip.

The paddle from Valdez to Whittier is growing in popularity. The Alaska Marine Highway ferry connects the communities; it is about a 7-hour ferry ride. The trip averages about 140 miles, depending on how closely one hugs the coast and explores the fjords and bays. (See Marine Parks this section for more information on state recreation areas in Prince William Sound.) Further information on boating conditions in Prince William Sound may be found in *Cruising Guide to Prince William Sound, Vol. 1, Western Part and Vol. 2, Eastern*

Part, by Jim and Nancy Lethcoe.

The eastern section of Prince William Sound is accessible by air or from Valdez and Cordova.

Changing wind direction and tidal currents can make paddling Prince William Sound a tricky business at best. Also keep in mind the weather can change abruptly. Be prepared for wind and rain.

Resurrection Bay. Attractions include abundant wildlife and challenging conditions. Seward is the access point which can be reached by highway or train. Kayaks can be rented in Seward. (See Seward under Communities this region for more information.)

Sportfishing

Anchorage/Mat-Su Area Fishing

Alexander Creek. Heads in Alexander Lake and flows southeast 35 miles to the Susitna River, 27 miles northwest of Anchorage. One of the best fishing streams in southcentral Alaska. Numerous lodges in the area. Primary access by floatplane from Anchorage. Fish available: king salmon excellent from late May through June, use egg clusters, spinners or spoons; silver salmon mid-July to September, use spinners or cluster eggs; pink salmon in even-numbered years, mid-July through mid-August, use small spoons; rainbow trout excellent late May through Sept. 1, use flies and spinning-type lures; grayling in late May and early June, use flies and small spinners.

Bull Lake. Fly-in lake located 20 minutes by small plane from Chulitna River Lodge, George Parks Highway, Milepost 156.2 from Anchorage. Fish available: lake trout to 5 pounds July and August, use spoons or spinners; grayling, use flies.

Chulitna Lake. Fly-in lake located 20 minutes by small plane from Chulitna River Lodge, Parks Highway, Milepost 156.2 from Anchorage. Fish available: rainbow trout to 4 pounds, July, August and September, use flies, lures and bait.

Deshka River. Located about 60 miles northwest of Anchorage. One of the best fishing streams in southcentral Alaska. Primary access by floatplane from Anchorage and riverboat from Susitna Landing. Numerous lodges in the area. Fish available: excellent fishing for king salmon, 20 to 25 pounds and up, late May to early July, use egg clusters, spinners or spoons; silver salmon, 4 to 6 pounds, mid-July through September, use spinners or cluster eggs; pink salmon in even-numbered years, mid-July to mid-August, use small spoons; rainbow trout excellent late May through September, use flies and spinning-type lures; grayling, 10 to 16 inches, best late May and early June, use flies and small spinners; northern pike June through September, use bait.

Donut Lake. Fly-in lake located 20 minutes by small plane from Chulitna River Lodge, Parks Highway, Milepost 156.2 from Anchorage. Dolly Varden to 2 pounds, available July and August, use spinners, spoons and flies.

High Lake. A 1-mile-wide lake at the 3,006-foot elevation in the Chugach Mountains southwest of Glennallen, 5.2 miles southeast of Tazlina Lake. Accessible by floatplane from Glennallen. Lake trout to 22 inches, June and early July with small spoons; some rainbow fly-fishing. Cabins, boats and motors available.

Jan Lakes. Fly-in lakes located 5 miles from Lake Louise or 12 miles from Tolsona Lake at Milepost 160 on the Glenn Highway. Accessible by floatplane from Lake Louise, Lee's Lake or Tolsona Lake. North Jan Lake has good rainbow trout fishery. South Jan Lake has landlocked silver salmon and king salmon.

Angler shows off a king salmon taken from the Deshka River. (Bill Sherwonit)

Judd Lake. Lake 0.9 mile across located on the Talachulitna River, about 65 miles northwest of Anchorage. Primary access by floatplane from Anchorage. Lodge on lake. Fish available: silver salmon average 6 to 8 pounds, best in August; red salmon average 7 to 8 pounds, best mid-July to early August; chum salmon average 10 to 12 pounds, best mid-July to early August; pink salmon in even-numbered years, average 3 to 4 pounds, best mid- to late July; grayling and Dolly Varden mid-June through September, best early and late.

Lake Creek. Flows from the foothills of Mount McKinley, about 70 miles northwest of Anchorage. One of the best fishing streams in southcentral Alaska. Primary access by floatplane from Anchorage. Numerous lodges in the area. Fish available: king salmon excellent late May through early July, use egg clusters, spinners and spoons; silver and chum salmon mid-July through August, use spinners or cluster eggs; pink salmon in even-numbered years, mid-July through mid-August, use small spoons; rainbow trout and grayling excellent just after breakup and just before freezeup, use flies and spinning-type lures for rainbows, flies for grayling.

Lewis River. Heads on Mount Susitna and flows 30 miles to Cook Inlet, 30 miles west of Anchorage. Accessible by small wheel plane from Anchorage. Fish available: king salmon late May through June, use egg clusters, spinners or spoons; silver salmon July to September, use egg clusters, spinners or spoons; pink salmon July and August, use small spoons; rainbow trout year-round, use flies or lures.

Little Susitna River. Heads at Mint Glacier in the Talkeetna Mountains and flows 110 miles southwest to Cook Inlet. Tremendous king salmon run and one of the largest silver salmon runs in Southcentral. Access from Milepost A 57.4 George Parks Highway by riverboat. Fish available: king salmon to 30 pounds, late May and June, use large red spinners or salmon eggs; silver salmon to 15 pounds, biggest run in late July, use small weighted spoons or fresh salmon roe; red salmon to 10 pounds, mid-July, use coho flies or salmon eggs.

Lucy Lake. Fly-in lake 1.6 miles long located within Denali State Park near Eldridge Glacier terminus, 40 miles north of Talkeetna. Access by small plane from Talkeetna or Chulitna River Lodge, Parks Highway, Milepost 156.2 from Anchorage. Fish available: lake trout to 20 pounds, June and July, use spinner and spoons; grayling use flies.

Portage Creek. A 1.5-mile-long tributary to the Susitna River, located 2.5 miles southwest of Curry and 18 miles northeast of Talkeetna. Access by small plane from Talkeetna or Chulitna River Lodge, Parks Highway, Milepost 156.2 from Anchorage. Fish available: rainbow trout, grayling, salmon July, August and September, use spoons, spinners or flies.

Shell Lake. A 5-mile-long lake located 85 miles northwest of Anchorage, 15 miles from Skwentna. Primary access by floatplane in summer, skiplane in winter. Shell Lake Lodge located on lake. Fish available: red and silver salmon late July through September; large lake and rainbow trout; some grayling. Winter ice fishing for burbot. Also wildlife-watching and photography, cross-country skiing and dog mushing.

Spink Lake. A 1.3-mile-long fly-in lake located in Denali State Park, 31 miles north of Talkeetna, 15 minutes by air west of Chulitna River Lodge, Parks Highway, Milepost 156.2 from Anchorage. Fish available: rainbow trout to 8 pounds; a few Dolly Varden July, August and September, use spinners and spoons.

Susitna River. This major Southcentral river heads at Susitna Glacier in the Alaska Range and flows southwest 260 miles to Cook Inlet. Access to fishing spots by boat or fly-in. Road access at Willow Creek Parkway, Milepost A 70.8 George Parks Highway. Fish available: king, sockeye, coho, pink and chum salmon; Dolly Varden; rainbow trout, lake trout, northern pike, burbot, grayling and whitefish.

Talachulitna River. Located about 65 miles northwest of Anchorage. Primary access by floatplane from Anchorage. One of the best fishing streams in southcentral Alaska. Lodges in the area. Fish available: king salmon, 25 to 50 pounds, best mid-June through early July, use big spoons and spinners; silver salmon average 6 to 8 pounds, best August through early September, use flies or lures; red salmon average 7 to 8 pounds, best mid-July to mid-August; chum salmon average 10 to 12 pounds, best mid-June through mid-July; pink salmon in even-numbered years averaging 3 to 4 pounds, best mid- to late July; rainbow trout average 1 to 3 pounds; grayling average 1 to 2 pounds; Dolly Varden average 2 to 4 pounds, mid-June through September, best early and late. *NOTE: Single hook, artificial lures only, release rainbow trout.*

Talkeetna River. Heads at Talkeetna Glacier in the Talkeetna Mountains and flows 85 miles southwest to the Susitna River near the community of Talkeetna. Access by riverboat from Talkeetna to fishing streams. Fish available: 5 species of Pacific salmon, rainbow trout and lake trout.

Theodore River. This river flows southeast 35 miles to Cook Inlet, 32 miles west of Anchorage. Accessible by small wheel plane from Anchorage. Fish available: king salmon late May through June, use egg clusters, spinners or spoons; silver salmon July to September, use egg clusters, spinners or spoons; pink salmon July and August, use small spoons; rainbow trout year-round, use flies or lures.

Yentna River. Located about 50 miles (35 minutes by small plane) northwest of Anchorage. Primary access by floatplane from Anchorage. Excellent fishery. Lodges on river. Fish available: king salmon late May to early July, use spoons; red salmon mid-June to late July, use spoons or flies; silver, chum and pink salmon mid-July through August, use spoons; rainbow trout and grayling year-round in season, best late August through September.

Copper River/Wrangell-St. Elias Area Fishing

Copper Lake. A 5.5-mile-long fly-in lake located within Wrangell-St. Elias National Park and Preserve, west of Tanada Lake. Accessible via Nabesna Road, which leaves the Glenn Highway (Tok Cutoff) at Milepost 65.2 from Tok. Turn off Nabesna Road at Milepost 23 for flying service at Long Lake or at Milepost 26.1 for 2-mile drive to Jack Lake and flying service. Cabins, boats and motors available. Fish available: lake trout 10 to 12 pounds, mid-June to September, use red-and-white spoons; kokanee 10 to 12 inches, mid-June to July, use small spinner; grayling 12 to 20 inches, July through September, use flies; burbot, use bait.

Crosswind Lake. An 8-mile-long fly-in lake located northwest of Lake Louise, 23 miles northwest of Glennallen. Accessible by floatplane from Glennallen. Deep, clear lake offers excellent fishing. Open water from early June through October. Best fishing early June to early July. Fish available: lake trout use spoons or plugs; whitefish use flies or eggs; grayling use flies.

Deep Lake. A 1.8-mile-long fly-in lake at the head of Dog Creek in the Copper River Basin, 30 miles north-northwest of Glennallen. Accessible by floatplane from Glennallen. Good fishing all summer for lake trout to 30 inches.

Gulkana River. Located near the community of Gulkana. Foot and vehicle access at various points between Milepost 123 and 148 from Valdez on the Richardson Highway. Excellent king salmon fishery. Fly-fishing only below highway bridge. Above bridge, use bright lures and/or salmon eggs. Also good fly-fishing for red salmon. River guides for float fishing available. (See The Rivers this section.)

Hanagita Lake. A 1-mile-long fly-in lake located in the Chugach Mountains, 32 miles southwest of McCarthy. Accessible by small plane from Glennallen. Excellent grayling fishing all summer; lake trout and steelhead in September.

Klutina Lake. A 16-mile-long lake, 27 miles from the Copper Center bridge via extremely bad road. Excellent grayling and Dolly Varden fishing.

Klutina River. Located at Milepost 100.7 from Valdez on the Richardson Highway. Foot and vehicle access; river guides available for float fishing. King salmon in June and July, with peak in August, use bright lures and/or salmon eggs; red salmon use streamer flies; Dolly Varden also available.

Lake Louise. An 8.5-mile-long lake located in the Copper River Basin, 32 miles northwest of Glennallen. Accessible by floatplane or skiplane from Anchorage, Glennallen and other communities. Access also via the 19.3-mile Lake Louise Road from the Glenn Highway at Milepost 159.8 from Anchorage. Lodges on lake. Excellent grayling and lake trout fishing. Lake trout average 10 pounds, up to 20 to 30 pounds, good year-round, best spring through July, late September, early season use herring or whitefish bait, cast from boat, later (warmer water) troll with #16 red-and-white spoon, silver Alaskan plug or large silver flatfish; grayling, 10 to 12 inches, cast flies or small spinners, June, July and August; burbot (freshwater lingcod) average 5 pounds, still fish from boat using hook with herring, dangle on bottom, in winter set lines with herring-baited hook through ice holes or jig for lake trout. Lake can be rough; small, underpowered boats not recommended.

Susitna Lake. A 10-mile-long lake located just northwest of Lake Louise in the Copper River Basin, 42 miles northwest of Glennallen. Accessible by boat across Lake Louise or by small floatplane or skiplane from Anchorage, Glennallen or other communities. Excellent fishing for lake trout, use spoons or plugs; grayling, use flies. Lake can be rough; underpowered boat is not recommended.

Tanada Lake. A 5.7-mile-long, 1-mile-wide fly-in lake located within Wrangell-St. Elias National Park and Preserve, 11 miles west of Nabesna. Accessible via Nabesna Road, which leaves the Glenn Highway (Tok Cutoff) at Milepost 65.2 from Tok. Turn off Nabesna Road at Milepost 23 for flying service at Long Lake or Milepost 26.1 for 2-mile drive to Jack Lake. Lodge on Tanada Lake. Considered one of the top lake trout fisheries in the state. Fish available: lake trout 3 to 10 pounds, occasionally up to 30 pounds, excellent last week of June and first 2 weeks of July, use large lures; grayling 14 to 16 inches, best last of June and first 2 weeks of July, use flies; whitefish and burbot available.

Tebay Lakes. Located in a line 7 miles long trending northeast in the Chugach Mountains, southwest of McCarthy and 68 miles east of Valdez. Accessible by small plane from Glennallen. Excellent fishing for rainbow trout 12 to 15 inches, all summer, use small spinners. Cabin, boat and motor rentals.

Kenai Peninsula Area Fishing

Anchor River. King salmon fishing permitted only on 5 consecutive weekends beginning Memorial Day weekend; trout and steelhead from July to October; closed to all fishing from Dec. 31 to June 30, except for king salmon weekends. Excellent fishing for 12- to 24-inch sea-run Dollies in July and late summer. Also saltwater trolling for king salmon to 80 pounds, halibut to 200 pounds. Access from Anchor River Beach Road; turn off Sterling Highway at Milepost 156.9 near Anchor Point. Fishing guides and charters available locally.

Bench Lake. A 1-mile-long lake located on the Kenai Peninsula in Chugach National Forest at the head of Bench Creek, 0.5 mile from Johnson Lake and 22 miles southeast of Sunrise. Lake is about halfway in on the 23-mile-long Johnson Pass trail. Arctic grayling available, best June to September, use flies or small spinners. No cabin on trail; lake above tree line.

Cook Inlet. From Kachemak Bay at Homer north to the waters between Deep Creek and Ninilchik, Cook Inlet is known for its fishing. Fish available include: king salmon to 76 pounds year-round, best May through July, use #5 and #6 spoons and herring; halibut, up to 350 pounds, from June through October. Other fish: bottom fish, use herring or clams; king salmon up to 70 pounds, troll with herring or large lures, June and July; pink salmon 4 to 5 pounds, July

and August, use small spoons; silver salmon to 15 pounds, August and September, use small weighted spoons, eggs and herring; red salmon to 4 pounds, July and August, use small weighted spoons, wet flies and coho streamers; Dolly Varden June through September, use small weighted spoons, eggs, or shrimp; rainbow trout taken from nearby streams from April to October, try candlefish (eulachon) for bait. Fishing guides and charters available locally. Several varieties of clams can be dug on nearby beaches from February to May and September to December. Shrimp also are available.

Crescent Lake. A 6-mile-long lake on the west side of Madson Mountain on the Kenai Peninsula in Chugach National Forest. Fish available: grayling best July to September, use flies or small spinners. Check ADF&G regulations for restrictive seasons and bag limits. Accessible by 15-minute floatplane flight from Moose Pass or via the 6.2-mile Crescent Lake trail. See Hiking Trails this section. Public-use cabin at lake outlet.

Crooked Creek. Fishing for coho salmon from Aug. 1, peaks in mid-August; steelhead from Aug. 1, bait prohibited after Sept. 15; closed to king salmon fishing and closed to all fishing near hatchery. Fishing access to confluence of Crooked Creek and Kasilof River is through the state recreation site on Coho Loop Road. Fishing access to Crooked Creek frontage above confluence is through a private RV park on Coho Loop Road; fee charged.

Deep Creek. Freshwater fishing for king salmon to 40 pounds, May 30 and 3 weekends in June, use spinners with bead lures; Dolly Varden in July and August; silver salmon to 15 pounds, August and September; steelhead to 15 pounds, late September through October, use large red spinners. No bait fishing permitted after Sept. 15. Access to mouth of Deep Creek is from Deep Creek State Recreation Area at Milepost S 137.3 Sterling Highway. Salt water south of the mouth of Deep Creek is known for producing top king salmon fishing in late May, June and July, with kings to 50 pounds.

Fuller Lakes. Located in Kenai National Wildlife Refuge. Accessible by the 4.8-mile-long Fuller Lakes trail from the Sterling Highway. Spring, summer and fall fishery for grayling in South Fuller Lake, use flies; Dolly Varden available year-round in North Fuller Lake, use bait, spinners, flies. This is bear country.

Grayling Lake. This 0.3-mile-long lake is located on the Kenai Peninsula 4.5 miles south of Kenai Lake and 10 miles north of Seward. Accessible by the Forest Service's 1.6-mile-long Grayling Lake trail, which leaves the Seward Highway at Milepost 13.2 from Seward. Fish available: 10- to 20-inch grayling, May to October, use flies. Watch for moose in the area.

Hidden Lake. Access from improved Hidden Lake Campground on the Skilak Lake Loop Road. Fish available: lake trout average 16 inches and kokanee 9 inches, year-round, best from mid-May to July 1, use spoons, red-and-white or weighted, by trolling, casting and jigging. This lake is a favorite with local ice fishermen from late December through March.

Johnson Lake. A 0.8-mile-long lake located within Chugach National Forest on the Kenai Peninsula, at the head of Johnson Creek, 0.5 mile from Bench Lake, 22 miles southeast of Sunrise. Lake is about halfway in on the 23-mile-long Johnson Pass trail. Fish available: rainbow trout, use flies, lures or bait. No cabin on trail; lake above tree line. (See Hiking Trails this section.)

Juneau Lake. A 1-mile-long lake located within Chugach National Forest on the Kenai Peninsula, 25 miles southwest of Hope. Accessible via the Resurrection Pass trail from the Sterling Highway at Milepost 53.1 from Seward. (See Hiking Trails this section.) Lake located 6 miles up trail. Fish available: summer fishery for rainbow trout, use flies, lures or bait; lake trout, use spoons or plugs; whitefish, use flies or eggs. Campground at lake.

Kasilof River. Fishing available: king salmon, late May through July, best in mid-June; coho salmon, mid-August to September, use salmon egg cluster, wet flies, assorted spoons and spinners; steelhead in May and September.

Kenai Lake. Fish available: lake trout, mid-May to Sept. 30; Dolly Varden and rainbow trout, May to September. Kenai Lake and tributaries are closed to salmon fishing.

Kenai River. From Kenai Lake to Skilak Lake: closed to king salmon fishing. Use artificial lures only. Silver salmon 5 to 15 pounds, August through October; pink salmon 3 to 7 pounds, July and August; red salmon 3 to 12 pounds, late May through mid-August (be familiar with regulations on closed areas); rainbow and Dolly Varden, April to November. Also whitefish.

Kenai River from Skilak Lake to Soldotna: consult regulations for legal tackle, limits and seasons. King salmon 20 to 80 pounds, use spinners, excellent fishing June to August;

red salmon 6 to 12 pounds, best July 15 to Aug. 10, use flies; pink salmon 4 to 8 pounds, Aug. 1 to Sept. 1 in even years, use spoons; silver salmon 6 to 15 pounds, mid-August to November, use spoons; rainbow, Dolly Varden 15 to 20 inches, June through September. There are a number of fishing guides in the Soldotna area.

Lost Lake. A 1.5-mile-long lake located at the head of Lost Creek on the Kenai Peninsula within Chugach National Forest, 10 miles north of Seward. Accessible via the 7-mile-long Lost Lake trail from the Seward Highway at Milepost 5.2 from Seward. Obtain permission from landowner to hike in from the south or hike from the north via Primrose Trail. (See Hiking Trails this section.) Rainbow trout available, use flies, lures or bait. Trail not free of snow until July. No cabins. Lake above tree line; no wood for fires, campers should carry stove and tent.

Moose River. From Moose River bridge at Milepost 82.1 on the Sterling Highway to confluence with Kenai River there is fishing for sockeyes in June. Big summer run of reds follows into August; silvers into October. Dolly Varden, rainbow and salmon (red, king, pink and silver) available at confluence of Kenai and Moose rivers, but check regulations for closures and restrictions.

Resurrection Bay. Seward has all facilities for fishermen, including marine supplies, fuel, guides, charter boats and a small-boat harbor. Inquire locally for best fishing locations. Fish available includes the following: silver salmon to 20 pounds, use herring, troll or cast, July to October (Silver Salmon Derby with more than $100,000 in prizes takes place in August); bottom fish includes flounder, halibut to 200 pounds, and cod, year-round, jig with large lures and bait.

Russian Lakes. Located on the Kenai Peninsula within Chugach National Forest about 25 miles northwest of Seward. Accessible via the 21-mile-long Russian Lakes trail from the Sterling Highway at Milepost 52.8 from Seward. Rainbow trout available at Lower Russian Lake (Mile 2.6) and at Upper Russian Lake (Mile 12), use flies, lures or bait. Dolly Varden available at Cooper Lake (Mile 21), use bait, spinners or flies. Black and brown bears may be encountered. Public-use cabins available. (See Hiking Trails this section.)

Russian River. Closed to all fishing April 15 through May 30. No bait area. Check regulations for limits and other restrictions. Red salmon run starts during first half of June, lasts 2 to 3 weeks. A second run of larger fish in July lasts about 3 weeks, must use flies only (streamer or coho). Silver salmon to 15 pounds, run begins mid-August, flies only; rainbow (hook and release only) averages 15 inches. Accessible from Russian River Campground at Milepost S 52.8 Sterling Highway.

Seldovia Area. The community of Seldovia is located 20 miles across Kachemak Bay from Homer. Accessible by boat, scheduled and charter air service from Homer and Alaska Marine Highway System from Homer or Kodiak. Area fishing includes the following: Seldovia Bay, king, silver and red salmon June 20 through September, use small spinners; halibut, average size, June 20 to September, use herring. Excellent bottom fishing. Fishing guides and skiffs available in Seldovia, which has food and lodging facilities. Outside Beach, 1.9 miles from Seldovia, has great fishing, casting from beach into surf for silver salmon, July 1 to 30, use any shiny lure. Silver and chum salmon and trout fishing available in Rocky River, 17 miles southeast of Seldovia, during August, use red spinning lures. *NOTE: Rocky River is on Native-owned lands, and a fee for fishing is required. Contact Port Graham Corporation, Port Graham, via Homer, AK 99603, for details.*

Skilak Lake. Fish available: salmon (sockeye, coho, pink), Dolly Varden, rainbow trout, lake trout and whitefish. Red (sockeye) salmon enter lake in mid-July. Access from Skilak Lake Campground on Skilak Lake Loop Road or boat-in. The lake is cold and winds are fierce and unpredictable.

Swan Lake. A 2-mile-long lake near the head of the Chickaloon River on the Kenai Peninsula within Chugach National Forest, 22 miles southwest of Hope. Accessible via the Resurrection Pass trail from the Sterling Highway at Milepost 53.1 from Seward. Lake located 9 miles up trail. Summer fishery for rainbow trout, use flies, lures or bait; lake trout, use spoons or plugs; Dolly Varden, use bait, spinners or flies; and red salmon, use spoons or flies. Campground at lake.

Swanson River. Access via Swanson River canoe route from Paddle Lake on Swan Lake Road. The river has a significant Dolly Varden and rainbow trout fishery, May through December.

Tustumena Lake. Located 6.4 miles from the Sterling Highway south of Soldotna, this huge lake is 6 miles wide and 25 miles long, subject to severe winds. Fish available: coho salmon, Dolly Varden, rainbow trout, brook trout and sheefish. Boat launch on the Kasilof River at campground.

Prince William Sound Fishing

Air charter operators in Prince William Sound know some of the best fishing locations, and several have cabins and tents near hot spots. Winter fishing for king salmon (up to 30 pounds) from Cordova can prove to be the fishing trip of a lifetime. Other species available are halibut, pollock, Dolly Varden, cutthroat trout, and pink, sockeye and chum salmon.

Cordova Area. Cordova has all facilities for fishermen, including marine supplies, fuel, guides, charter boats and a small-boat harbor. Inquire locally for best fishing locations. Fish available in nearby waters includes the following: silver salmon late July through mid-September, best in August and September, use herring or spoons (Silver Salmon Derby with top prize of $5,000 takes place mid-August to Sept. 1); pink and chum salmon good in July and August, use large red spinner or small spoons; halibut and other bottom fish, best fishing in small bays, jig with large lures and bait. Dungeness, king and tanner crab available in nearby bays or coves. Steamer clams common on gravel-mud beaches, razor clams in Orca Inlet and south of the Copper River Delta.

Valdez Area. Valdez has all facilities for fishermen, including marine supplies, fuel, guides, charter boats and a small-boat harbor. Inquire locally for good fishing locations. Fish available include the following: silver salmon late July through mid-September, excellent in August, use herring, spoons (Silver Salmon Derby with $10,000 top prize takes place the month of August); pink salmon during the summer, use large red spinner or small spoons; king salmon best late winter and early spring, use herring or large trolling lures; halibut, red snapper and shrimp available all summer, generally in small bays, jig with large lures and bait. Littleneck clams on most gravel-mud beaches in protected bays at half-tide level in Valdez Arm. Tanner, king and Dungeness crab also available in bays or coves.

Whittier Area. Whittier has all facilities for fishermen, including marine supplies, fuel, guides, charter boats and a small-boat harbor. Inquire locally for good fishing locations. Fish available in area waters includes the following: silver salmon in August, use large red spinner and spoons, herring and large trolling spoons; pink and chum salmon late summer, use large red spinner and spoons; king salmon June and early July, use herring, large trolling lures, spoons and spinners; red snapper in Passage Canal and Dungeness crab in Shotgun Cove.

SPECIAL FEATURES

Lighthouses

Cape Hinchinbrook Light Station. This light, which stands 235 feet above the water, marks Hinchinbrook Entrance, main entrance to Prince William Sound from the east. Cape Hinchinbrook, named on May 12, 1778, by the English explorer Capt. James Cook for Viscount Hinchinbroke, is located on the south tip of Hinchinbrook Island, 35 miles southwest of Cordova. Construction of the station was completed on Nov. 15, 1910, at a cost of about $100,000. It was rebuilt after earthquakes in 1927 and 1928 for $91,000. The U.S. Coast Guard automated the station in 1974. The original fresnel lens, approximately 5 feet high, is now on display at the museum in Valdez.

Cape St. Elias Light Station. This light, 85 feet above the water, is located on the southernmost tip of Kayak Island on Cape St. Elias. The cape was named by Captain Commander Vitus Bering on July 20, 1741, for the saint whose day it was according to the Russian Orthodox Church calendar. This 1,665-foot-high cape forms an unmistakable landmark for mariners. The waters south of the cape were regarded as "one of the most dangerous points along the entire coast." Congress appropriated money for the project in 1913, and construction of the lighthouse was completed on Sept. 16, 1916, at a cost of $115,000. It was equipped with the most modern equipment available. At one time

there were 3 lighthouse keepers in residence; the light was automated by the U.S. Coast Guard in 1974. It is listed on the National Register of Historic Places and is considered the best existing 1916 architectural example of a major Alaska lighthouse. The original fresnel lens, approximately 5 feet high, is now on display at the museum in Cordova.

Columbia Glacier

Star attraction of Prince William Sound, Columbia Glacier is one of the largest and most magnificent of the tidewater glaciers along the Alaska coast. Part of Chugach National Forest, the glacier, named by the Harriman Alaska expedition in 1899 for Columbia University in New York City, spreads over about 440 square miles. It is more than 40 miles long with a tidewater terminus more than 6 miles across. The glacier has receded almost a mile in recent years. Scientists are studying its retreat and increased iceberg production, which could pose a hazard to oil tankers from Valdez, about 25 miles to the east. Columbia is expected to recede about 22 miles in the next 20 to 50 years, leaving behind a deep fjord.

The face of the glacier, visible from Columbia Bay, varies in height above sea level from 164 to 262 feet. The glacier extends below sea level as much as 2,300 feet in some places. The bay teems with life at the face of the glacier. An abundance of plankton (microscopic water plants and animals) thrives here, attracting great numbers of fish, which in turn attract bald eagles, kittiwakes, gulls and harbor seals. Seals usually can be seen resting on ice floes or swimming in the frigid water.

The glacier heads in the perpetual snows of Mount Einstein (elev. 11,522 feet), in the Chugach Mountains. Near the glacier's source is Mount Witherspoon (elev. 12,012 feet). Both peaks are visible from the face of the glacier in clear weather.

Boaters can enjoy close-up views of the glacier face and watch giant icebergs calve (break off) from the ice wall. Don't get too close; calving bergs create high waves that can swamp a boat. There are daily and weekly charters by yacht and sailboat from Whittier, Valdez and Cordova as well as several tour boat operations departing from these ports too. Flightseeing tours over the glacier also are available from these communities or Anchorage. And, the glacier may be seen from the Alaska Marine Highway System ferries, which sometimes approach as close as half a mile from the face of the glacier. Forest Service interpreters staff the weekend runs of these ferries during the summer to point out features of the glacier and the national forest.

Copper River Delta

The 400-square-mile delta of this major glacier-fed river is noted for its spectacular waterfowl and shorebird migrations each spring and, to a lesser extent, each fall. Visitors will have the opportunity to view thousands to millions of birds.

The habitats of the region range from hemlock and spruce forest, to thickets of tall shrubs, lakes, rivers and coastal wetlands, to remote islands and marine waters.

The largest and most conspicuous of the waterfowl is the trumpeter swan, which has a wingspan of 6 to 8 feet. At one time this was an endangered species; now the greatest concentration of these swans in North America is along the Copper River and its tributaries. The Copper-Bering river deltas and adjacent areas also provide nesting grounds for dusky Canada geese.

The most abundant duck is the pintail.

Hundreds of thousands pass through in the spring and many remain to breed and nest. Other species of ducks and geese found in the delta are white-fronted geese, snow geese, teals, wigeons, shovellers, scaups and goldeneyes.

Many thousands of sandhill cranes stop to rest and feed on the flats on their way north to nest. Flocks of western and dunlin sandpipers occur in late April and early May. Densities of more than 250,000 shorebirds per square mile have been observed feeding on the delta. Other bird species seen on or near the delta include arctic tern, red-throated loons, mergansers, parasitic jaegers, Bonaparte's gulls, short-eared owls, northern harriers, bald eagles, great blue herons, black-legged kittiwakes, common murres, tufted puffins, American black oystercatchers, and double-crested, pelagic and red-faced cormorants.

Black and brown bears may be seen in the spring as they leave their dens to feed on grasses and in late summer and fall when they return to feed on spawning salmon. Other mammals that may be seen include black-tailed deer, moose, beaver, muskrat, mink and otter.

Icebergs calved from Columbia Glacier float in Prince William Sound. (Jerrianne Lowther)

The Delta moose herd, which thrives on the abundant supply of willow in the area, was first introduced in 1949.

Visitors are cautioned not to approach bears or moose and not to disturb nesting birds. Calving glaciers can produce waves 6 feet high, so don't get too close. When traveling on the mudflats, use great caution and pay attention to tide tables; tidewaters come in quickly and it's easy to become stranded by tidal sloughs and softening mud.

Access to the delta is by floatplane or boat from Cordova (see Communities this section) or by the Copper River Highway.

The 48-mile Copper River Highway from Cordova provides access to a number of national forest recreation and interpretive facilities in the Copper River Delta. Alaganik Slough at Milepost 16.9 has informal camping, fishing and an information sign on the Delta moose herd. At Milepost 25.4, a short trail leads to interpretive signs on spawning channels for salmon and on the salmon life cycle. The Cordova Ranger District of the Chugach National Forest has also developed hiking trails, canoe routes, picnic areas, and viewing platforms and displays along the Copper River Highway.

For additional information contact: Chugach National Forest, Cordova Ranger District, P.O. Box 280, Cordova, AK 99574; phone 424-7661. For a detailed mile-by-mile log of the Copper River Highway, see *The MILEPOST®*, a complete guide to Alaska's road and marine highway systems.

Katalla

Although a ghost town today, Katalla *(ka-TELL-a)* once was an oil and coal boom town. Katalla, located near the mouth of the Katalla River on Katalla Bay 50 miles southeast of Cordova, is near the site of one of the first oil discoveries in Alaska, made in 1896, and the state's first oil well, drilled in 1902. The town was established about 1903 as a supply point for the oil field, 3.5 miles to the east. The Bering River coalfields are about 15 miles to the northeast and once were connected to Katalla by a railroad. The

boom town's population may have been as high as 10,000 at one time, but had dwindled to 188 by 1910 and 23 by 1940. Today, a caretaker and his family are the only residents of Katalla. The town's post office, opened in 1904, was closed in 1943.

Around 1910, the government restricted coal mining and other mineral development in Alaska, and Katalla lost much of its population practically overnight. From 1902 to 1931 a total of 36 wells were drilled in the Katalla oil field, 18 were successful. A small refinery built in 1911 produced gasoline and heating oil for local markets until part of the plant burned in 1933, and the entire operation was abandoned.

Katalla also is noteworthy as the location where the coastal steamer *Portland,* which ran from Seattle to St. Michael at the mouth of the Yukon River, was wrecked in 1910. The *Portland* gained fame when it arrived in Seattle on July 17, 1897, with a ton and a half of gold from the Klondike on board and helped set off one of the biggest gold rushes in history.

Much of the land surrounding Katalla is part of Chugach National Forest and is pristine wilderness. However, 500 acres at the old refinery site are privately owned and new exploration is under way by the Alaska Crude Corp. About 11,000 acres are owned by the federal government, but subject to selection by Chugach Alaska Native regional corporation and likely will be developed. Another 30,000 acres at the coalfield is privately owned and development is planned by a Chugach Alaska joint venture. A road connecting Katalla with the Copper River Highway and Cordova is proposed and if built would mean the old boom town may see some new development.

The only way to get to Katalla is by charter plane or helicopter from Cordova, the nearest major community. (For information on service and facilities in Cordova, see Prince William Sound this section.) It is possible to get to Katalla by boat, but not usually feasible. Katalla is exposed to the full force of North Pacific storms, and waters in the area are often extremely rough.

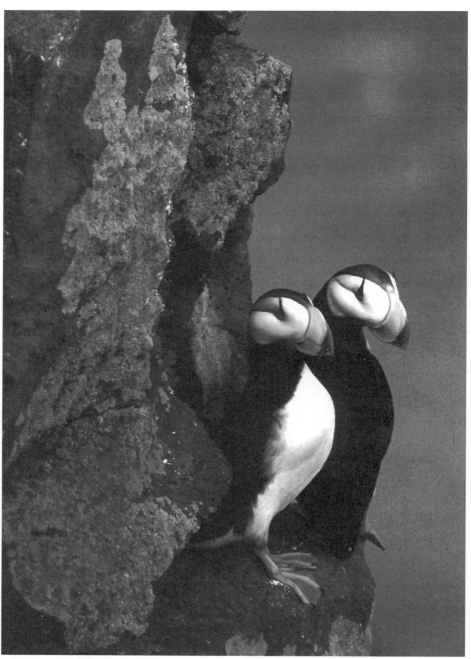

Common in Southwestern, horned puffins nest in rock crevices, among boulders, on sea cliffs or on grassy slopes. (Loren Taft)

SOUTHWESTERN

Active volcanoes, fish-rich rivers, huge brown bears and remote storm-washed islands characterize this beautiful region full of critical wildlife habitat that draws fishermen, hunters and bird-watchers from all over the world. Historically, it was the abundant marine mammal populations with their valuable furs that drew the first Russians to the Aleutians. Kodiak was Russian Alaska's first capital city. After 1867, when the United States took control of Alaska, the marine mammal populations were again hunted to near extinction. Later fox farming and fishing stirred the region's economy.

The Aleutians bore the brunt of WWII activities on Alaskan soil when the Japanese invaded Attu and Kiska islands and bombed Dutch Harbor. Kodiak bore the brunt of the 1964 Good Friday earthquake, which measured 9.2 on the Richter scale. The tidal wave that followed virtually destroyed downtown Kodiak.

Today most residents in the region live by fishing or seafood processing or are in the military. Kodiak is one of the largest commercial fishing ports in the United States, followed by Dutch Harbor-Unalaska. The federal government maintains bases in the Aleutians and on the Alaska Peninsula.

Access to the region is usually by air, although a state ferry regularly serves Kodiak and makes the run down the peninsula to the Aleutians about 4 times annually.

Location: This region takes in the Alaska Peninsula, which curves about 500 miles southwest from Naknek Lake to the first of the Aleutians, and the 200 islands of the Kodiak Archipelago in the Gulf of Alaska. The more than 124 islands of the Aleutian chain and the Pribilof group to the north in the Bering Sea make up the rest of the region. The Aleutians, extending more than 1,000 miles from Unimak to remote Attu, separate the Bering Sea from the North Pacific in a divide known as the "birthplace of winds."

Geography: The Aleutians and Pribilofs are treeless tops of submerged mountains. Few rivers etch their steep slopes. The Aleutians sit atop the "Ring of Fire," a necklace of volcanoes around much of the Pacific Rim. Shishaldin Volcano on Unimak Island, highest point in the Aleutians, rises 9,372 feet above sea level and 32,472 feet from the ocean floor. Off the Pacific side of the region lies the Aleutian Trench, 2,000 miles long, 50 to 100 miles wide, and up to 25,000 feet deep, where continental plates meet and the Pacific plate is carried down into the earth. To the north, the Bering Sea slopes downward in a shallow underwater valley, 249 miles long and up to 10,677 feet deep.

In summer the Aleutians and Pribilofs are covered with a carpet of lush grass and decorated with abundant wildflowers. The islands are treeless except for a few stands transplanted from other regions which have survived in sheltered nooks.

The Alaska Peninsula is a slender spine, steep-sloped and topped with volcanoes on the Pacific side. Pavlof Volcano and Mount Veniaminof on the peninsula are very active volcanoes, although neither has matched the huge and violent eruption of Novarupta Volcano in 1912, which created the Valley of Ten Thousand Smokes in Katmai National Park and Preserve. On the Bering Sea side, fish-clogged rivers drain from the peninsula's lakes down to the rich, coastal wetland along Bristol Bay.

Kodiak Island is known as the Emerald Island, and summers bring lush, tall green grass dotted with wildflowers. It is the largest island within the Kodiak Island group, followed in size by Afognak, Sitkalidak, Sitkinak, Raspberry, Tugidak, Shuyak, Uganik, Chirikof, Marmot and Spruce islands.

Climate: Rain is common in this region. Measurable precipitation occurs more than 200 days each year. Annual average is 33.44 inches at Cold Bay near the tip of the peninsula and 28.85 inches at Shemya in the western Aleutians. Kodiak averages 6 inches of rain a month during September, October and May, its wettest months, and planes can be grounded by fierce storms off the Gulf of Alaska.

Aleutian weather has been called the worst in the world. Storm fronts generally move from west to east here. But, climatic conditions on the Pacific side often differ vastly from those on the Bering side, placing the islands in the middle of a continual weather conflict.

Aleutian temperatures usually are milder than elsewhere in Alaska because of the chain's southern location and the moderating influence of surrounding waters. At Shemya summer temperatures range from 39°F to 53°F, with 28°F to 39°F in winter. Summer temperatures at Dutch Harbor in the eastern Aleutians range from 40°F to 60°F in summer and 27°F to 37°F in winter.

Wildlife: Brown/grizzly bears inhabit Unimak, easternmost of the Aleutians, but are absent from the rest of the chain and the Pribilofs. They are abundant on the peninsula, and Katmai rangers claim to have the largest unhunted brown/grizzly population in Alaska within their park's boundary. Hunters from all over the world come to Kodiak for its trophy-class brown bear.

The natural range of wolves, wolverine and most small mammals does not extend beyond Unimak Island. Only introduced mammal species inhabit the rest of the Aleutians with the possible exception of the arctic fox population in the western islands. Norway rats arrived aboard sailing ships in the mid-1800s and the Rat Islands were named for them.

Marine mammals from the great baleen whales to sea lions, northern fur seals, true seals and sea otters are found in numerous colonies. Seabirds, shorebirds and waterfowl by the millions throng to the peninsula, Aleutians and Pribilofs. More than 230 species have been recorded in the region.

Sockeye salmon clog the rivers of the peninsula in season; other species of salmon, grayling, arctic char, Dolly Varden and trout also fill the streams in this fishermen's paradise.

Offshore, commercial fishermen seek halibut, salmon, bottom fish, crab and shrimp.

A floatplane takes off from Naknek Lake in Katmai National Park. (Loren Taft)

▼ C O M M U N I T I E S ▼

Adak

[MAP 10] Located on Kuluk Bay on Adak Island in the Aleutians, 1,200 miles southwest of Anchorage. Adak is a restricted military installation not open to casual visitors or tourists.

Transportation: Military or scheduled airline from Anchorage. **Population:** More than 5,000, all military service members and their dependents, civil service employees and their dependents, and civilian contractors. **Zip code:** FPO Seattle, WA 98791. **Emergency Services:** Navy Security, phone 592-8051; Navy Branch Hospital.

Elevation: 20 feet. **Climate:** The average relative humidity is 83 percent. Precipitation occurs throughout the year, including an average of 102 inches of snow during the winter months (November through March). Rain in the summer and occasional blizzards during the winter are common. Drizzle, ice, snow and fog occur at various times of the year. Adak is occasionally buffeted by intense storms which migrate east-north-eastward. Average wind velocity throughout the Aleutian chain is 16 knots; however, winds in excess of 40 knots are not uncommon. The highest recorded gust is 109 knots in March 1954. Hence, Adak's well-known nickname, "birthplace of the winds."

Private Aircraft: Mitchell Field 1 mile from town; elev. 18 feet; length 7,880 and 7,600 feet; asphalt. No public transportation to town. Prior approval from the Navy required for all civilian aircraft.

Visitor Facilities: There is no tourist or unsponsored casual visitation to Adak. All requests to visit Adak are denied, except bona fide official visitors or temporary guests of island residents. There is no private civilian sector or community on the island of Adak. Except for one McDonald's and a Baskin-Robbins, all dining facilities are operated by the military. Banking,

laundromat/dry cleaning, barber/beauty shop and recreational services are available. Navy exchange and commissary are the only sources for supplies and commodities. Fishing/hunting licenses available; no guide services. Repair services available for autos. Rental cars available for island residents and authorized visitors. Available fuel limited to unleaded gasoline and JP5 (substitute for diesel). Moorage facilities available only for U.S. Navy or other military vessels, and vessels under government contract.

The U.S. Navy base on 28-mile-long Adak Island, in the Andreanof group, is the westernmost city in the United States. It is Alaska's largest naval base and is "home" for the Naval Air Station, Naval Security Group Activity, Naval Facility, Marine Barracks and several other associated tenant commands and activities.

There is archaeological evidence of earlier habitation, but Adak was unoccupied in 1942 when the military arrived after the outbreak of WWII. The installations on Adak are significant in the history of the Aleutian campaign because they allowed U.S. forces to mount a successful offensive against the Japanese-held islands of Kiska and Attu. Facilities from the old Adak Army base and Adak naval operating base have been nominated to the National Register of Historic Places. The Adak Community Museum houses WWII memorabilia, wildlife displays and Native artifacts.

The southern part of the island is part of Alaska Maritime National Wildlife Refuge. The U.S. Fish and Wildlife Service maintains a headquarters on the island.

Communications at Adak include phones, radio and TV. The base is served by 2 chapels and 2 schools with grades preschool through 12. College courses are offered through the University of Alaska Extension Service. All utilities and services are provided by the military.

Akhiok

[MAP 3] *(AH-ke-awk)* Located at Alitak Bay on the south side of Kodiak Island 80 miles southwest of the city of Kodiak, 340 miles south-southwest of Anchorage. **Transportation:** Boat; scheduled or charter air service from Kodiak. **Population:** 109. **Zip code:** 99615. **Emergency Services:** Village Public Safety Officer, phone 836-2205; Alaska State Troopers, Kodiak, phone 486-4121; Health Aide, phone 836-2230 (clinic) or 836-2218; Volunteer Fire Department.

Elevation: 50 feet at airport. **Climate:** Strong marine influence, characterized by moderately heavy precipitation, cool temperatures, high clouds and frequent fog. Humidity generally high, temperature variation small. Little or no freezing weather. Average temperatures from 25°F to 54°F. Annual precipitation 35 inches.

Private Aircraft: Airstrip 1 mile southwest, elev. 50 feet; length 3,100 feet; gravel; no fuel; unattended. Runway condition not monitored; visual inspection recommended prior to using. No public transportation to village.

Visitor Facilities: Arrange for accommodations at Community Building by contacting the City of Akhiok office, phone 836-2229. No other facilities or services available here. According to the city office there is a store at Alitak, 7 miles by skiff. Fuel available: marine gas, diesel, regular.

The name Akhiok was reported in the 1880 census. The village was renamed Alitak during WWI to avoid confusion with a village near Bethel called Akiak. The name later was changed back to Akhiok. Residents of Kaguyak relocated to Akhiok after the 1964 earthquake and tsunami washed out their village. The community was incorporated as a second-class city in 1972.

No roads connect Akhiok to any other town on Kodiak Island; a foot trail leads to the cannery.

The village is located adjacent to Kodiak National Wildlife Refuge. The community's Russian Orthodox church, Protection of the Theotokos Chapel, which was built around 1900 on the site of an earlier structure, is on the National Register of Historic Places.

The community originally was a sea otter hunting settlement. With the decline of the sea otter industry, however, the village became oriented toward fishing, which today forms the basis of its economy. Many of the residents are commercial fishermen.

A seiner works Kalsin Bay off Kodiak Island. (George Wuerthner)

Other employers include the cannery, school, health services, the city and occasional construction jobs. Almost all of Akhiok's residents depend on subsistence fishing and hunting for various food sources. Species harvested include salmon, crab, shrimp, scallop, clam, duck, seal, deer, rabbit and bear.

Communications in Akhiok include phones, shortwave radio, mail plane and TV. The community has a school with grades kindergarten through 12. There are community electricity, water and sewage systems. Freight arrives by barge or plane. Village government address: City of Akhiok, P.O. Box 5050, Akhiok, AK 99615; phone 836-2229, fax 836-2209. Village corporation address: Akhiok/Kaguyak Inc., Akhiok Rural Station, Akhiok, AK 99615.

Akutan

[MAP 9] Located on the north shore of Akutan Harbor on the east coast of Akutan Island, one of the Krenitzin Islands of the Fox Island group in the mid-Aleutian chain, 45 miles east of Unalaska, 750 miles southwest of Anchorage. **Transportation:** Boats; scheduled and charter amphibious aircraft from Cold Bay or Dutch Harbor. **Population:** 103 plus 500 temporary processor workers. **Zip code:** 99553. **Emergency Services:** Police, phone 698-2315; Clinic, phone 698-2208; Volunteer Fire Department, phone 698-2227.

Climate: Maritime, characterized by mild winters and cool summers. High winds with gusts up to 100 mph are common in winter. There is frequent cloudy weather and there is fog 64 percent of the days in July. The warmest month of the year is August; the coldest is February. Precipitation averages 28 inches per year.

Private Aircraft: Akutan has no airstrip; amphibious or floatplane only, seaplane landing ramp.

Visitor Facilities: Accommodations available at Akutan Bayview Plaza (698-2206); meals at Grab-A-Dab Cafe (698-2260). There is a laundromat. Groceries, clothing, first-aid supplies, hardware, camera film and sporting goods are available in the community at Native Dockside Store (phone 698-2226, fax 698-2207). No fishing/hunting licenses available; no guide service. Repair service for marine engines and boats may be available. Arrangements may be made to rent boats. Fuel available includes diesel and regular gasoline. Moorage facilities available.

The village was established in 1878 as a fur storage and trading port by the Western Fur and Trading Co. The company's first resident agent helped establish a commercial cod fishing and processing business. Residents of nearby villages moved to Akutan and a church and school were built in 1878. The community was incorporated as a second-class city in 1979.

After the Japanese attacked Dutch Harbor and seized Attu and Kiska in June 1942, the U.S. government evacuated Akutan residents to the Ketchikan area. They were allowed to return in 1944, but many chose not to. The exposure to the outside world brought about many changes in the traditional lifestyle of the community. Although the Aleut language is still spoken in many homes, it is dying out. However, the community is making an effort to relearn its Native heritage through such things as traditional arts and crafts.

Librarian Doug Welch describes Akutan as "a quiet community of neighbors bridged together by a maze of boardwalks replacing roads. A place where people truly care and share."

Commercial fishing and fish processing dominate Akutan's economy. Trident Seafoods has one of the largest onshore fish processing plants in Alaska. There is also employment at the school, post office, store, tavern and clinic. Subsistence hunting and fishing also are important. Game includes seals, wild cattle, ducks and geese. Fish include salmon, pogies, black bass, cod, herring, halibut, flounder and trout. Shellfish include clams, sea urchins and "bidarkies" (chitons).

Alexander Nevsky Chapel, a Russian Orthodox church built in 1918 to replace the 1878 structure, is listed on the National Register of Historic Places.

Akutan Island is mountainous and rugged, and 4,275-foot Akutan Volcano is considered active, belching fire and smoke throughout the fall of 1978. Lava flows occasionally run into the sea on a distant side of the peak. Akutan village also is within an area affected by tsunamis. In 1946 a tsunami run-up reached 115 feet and destroyed Scotch Cap Lighthouse on the west side of Unimak Island facing Unimak Pass, less than 30 miles east of Akutan.

Communications in Akutan include phones, radio, fax, mail plane and TV. The community has a school with grades kindergarten through 12. There are community electricity, water and sewer systems. Freight arrives by ship or by air. Government address: City of Akutan, P.O. Box 109, Akutan, AK 99553. Village corporation address: Akutan Corp., Box 8, Akutan, AK 99553; phone 698-2206, fax 698-2207. Aleutians East Borough, P.O. Box 349, Sand Point, AK 99661; phone 383-2699.

Atka

[MAP 9] Located on Atka Island in the Andreanof Island group, 90 miles east of Adak, 1,100 miles southwest of Anchorage. **Transportation:** Scheduled aircraft from Unalaska. **Population:** 107. **Zip code:** 99547. **Emergency Services:** Village Public Safety Officer, phone 839-2202 or 839-2224; Clinic, phone 839-2232; Volunteer Fire Department.

Elevation: 40 feet. **Climate:** Atka's maritime climate is characterized by mild winters and cool summers. The wind is calm only 2.5 percent of the time. The warmest month is August; the coldest is February. Mean annual precipitation is 60 inches, including 61 inches of snow.

Private Aircraft: Airstrip 1.5 miles north; elev. 33 feet; length 3,100 feet; asphalt; unattended. Runway condition not monitored; visual inspection recommended prior to using. A small supply of avgas and Jet 100 fuel is kept by Peninsula Airways.

Visitor Facilities: The city of Atka has 2 rooms with kitchen facilities for rent. No banking services or laundromat. Groceries, first-aid supplies, hardware and camera film are available for purchase at Atka Native Store and Island Store. Traditional grass baskets may be sold locally. Fishing/hunting licenses available. No guide or repair services. Fuel available includes marine gas, diesel and regular gasoline. No moorage facilities.

Atka is the most western and most isolated Native village on the Aleutian chain. The island has been occupied for at least 2,000 years and recent archaeological evidence suggests that the present village site may have had human use even earlier. The town was settled in the 1860s.

Atka residents were evacuated to the Ketchikan area after the Japanese attack on Dutch Harbor and seizure of Attu and Kiska in June 1942. The community was almost completely burned during the war by the Navy to keep the Japanese from using it. The Navy rebuilt it after the war. Many Attuans who had been held captive in Japan resettled in Atka after their release in 1945.

The community has persisted through the decades despite a lack of local jobs. After the end of the sea otter hunting era in the late 1800s, Atka had no cash economy, although it became relatively affluent during the fox farming boom in the 1920s. The economy today is based primarily on subsistence hunting and fishing and wages earned from seasonal employment in the crab and salmon fisheries elsewhere in the Aleutians.

The village is located within Alaska Maritime National Wildlife Refuge. Fish include halibut, salmon, black cod, Pacific Ocean perch and king crab. Reindeer introduced in 1914 have multiplied to 2,500 to 3,500 head and provide meat for the villagers. Foxes, seals and sea lions are also common.

Forming the northern end of the island is 4,852-foot Korovin Volcano, which has been active in recent years.

Communications in Atka, which incorporated in 1988 as a second-class city, include phones, fax, and mail plane. The community is served by St. Nicholas Russian Orthodox Church and a school with grades kindergarten through 12. Sale and importation of alcohol are prohibited. Freight arrives at the community by ship once a year. Government address: City of Atka, P.O. Box 47070, Atka, AK 99547; phone 839-2233. Village corporation address: Atxam Corp., P.O. Box 47001, Atka, AK 99547.

Attu

[MAP 10] Located on Attu Island in the Aleutian chain, 1,700 miles west of Anchorage, 500 miles east of the USSR mainland. **Transportation:** Air charter or U.S. Coast Guard aircraft. **Population:** 29. **Zip code:** 99502.

Elevation: 60 feet. **Climate:** Storms and dense fog are common. Mean annual precipitation is 54 inches, including 86 inches of snow.

Private Aircraft: Airport at southeast end of island; elev. 40 feet; length 6,300 feet; asphalt. Civilian authorization other than emergency must be obtained from U.S. Coast Guard District 17, Juneau. No transient service or maintenance available.

Visitor Facilities: No accommodations; camping only.

Attu Island is farthest west of the Aleutian chain and westernmost of the Near Islands. A Coast Guard loran station is located at Massacre Bay on the southeast coast of the island.

A granite memorial was dedicated at Attu in 1981 to honor American soldiers who fought and died in the Aleutians during WWII. Attu was the site of a brutal 19-day battle during May 1943 between American forces and Japanese entrenched on the island, second only to the Pacific theater's Iwo Jima in terms of troops involved. U.S. forces suffered 2,300 casualties, including 549 killed. While only 29 Japanese were captured on Attu, Americans counted 1,851 bodies and estimated 650 others had been buried in the hills. The Japanese have erected several monuments to their dead since the war. Much evidence of the battle still remains on the east end of the island. The Attu battlefield and old Army and Navy airfields have been named national historic landmarks; listed on the National Register of Historic Places is the wreckage of a P-38 fighter aircraft on the east bank of the Temnac River a mile from its mouth.

The entire island is part of Alaska Maritime National Wildlife Refuge, administered by the U.S. Fish and Wildlife Service. Arctic fox, sea otters, whales and a variety of North American and Asiatic birds can be seen on the island. Although remote, the island is popular for spring birding expeditions. For information about the refuge contact Refuge Manager, Aleutian Islands Unit, Alaska Maritime National Wildlife Refuge, PSC 486, Box 5251 (NAS), FPO, AP Adak, AK 96506-5251; phone 592-2406.

Belkofski

(See **King Cove**)

Chignik

[MAP 8] Located on the south shore of the Alaska Peninsula at the head of Anchorage Bay, 5 miles southeast of Chignik Lagoon, 450 miles southwest of Anchorage. **Transportation:** Boat; scheduled airline and air charter from King Salmon; limited state ferry service from Kodiak in summer. **Population:** 190. **Zip code:** 99564. **Emergency Services:** Alaska State Troopers, King Salmon, phone 246-3346; Subregional Clinic with 2 health aides and a physician's assistant on staff, services include x-ray and pharmacy, phone 749-2282; Village Public Safety Officer/Fire Chief, phone 749-2273.

Elevation: 30 feet. **Climate:** Chignik's maritime climate is characterized by cool summers, relatively warm winters and rainy weather. Precipitation averages 127 inches annually with 58 inches of snow. Average temperature in January is 20°F; average in July is 65°F.

Private Aircraft: Airstrip 2 miles from village; elev. 50 feet; length 2,800 feet; gravel; no fuel; unattended. Runway condition not monitored; visual inspection recommended prior to using. Birds on and in vicinity of airfield. No airport facilities or public transportation to village.

Visitor Facilities: Accommodations available at Aleutian Dragon Fisheries guest house. Groceries and supplies at Chignik Community Store and Chignik Pride Store. Restaurants are Grandma's Kitchen and The Bakery. There is a variety store, laundry and post office. Check with the City of Chignik about rental equipment. Fishing/hunting licenses available; no guide service. There is a 600-foot dock and boat haulout available. Marine vessel repair available. Fuel available includes marine gas, diesel, propane and regular gasoline; no avgas. Fuel is available through the fisheries.

Chignik, also called Chignik Bay, is an Aleut village established as a fishing village and cannery in the late 1800s on the site of an earlier Native village, Kaniagmuit, destroyed by the Russians in the 1700s. Chignik is a second-class city, incorporated in 1983.

Chignik's economy is based on commercial fishing for salmon, halibut, black cod and tanner crab. Aleutian Dragon Fisheries and Chignik Pride Fisheries operate year-round fishing processing plants here. During the summer, some 500 additional people come here to work in the commercial fishing and processing industry.

Most people in Chignik depend on subsistence hunting and fishing. Salmon are caught year-round. Other fish caught are rainbow trout and Dolly Varden. Dungeness, king and tanner crab, clams and octopus also are taken. Game includes moose, caribou, ptarmigan, ducks and geese.

The village is located within 3.5-million-acre Alaska Peninsula National Wildlife Refuge. During the winter, warm ocean currents keep much of the water relatively ice free and thousands of Steller's, common and king eiders, scoters, harlequins, oldsquaws and loons winter there. Brant and Canada geese fly over Chignik in the spring and fall. There are many seabird colonies along the coast and cormorants, puffins, murres, black-legged kittiwakes, gulls, terns and jaegers are occasional visitors at Chignik. Bald eagles, common along the coast, concentrate along streams during the salmon runs and along lagoons and bays in the winter. Peregrine falcons nest in the area, usually near seabird colonies.

A variety of marine mammals are present near Chignik, including harbor seals, sea otters, Steller sea lions, Dall porpoises and several species of whales.

Communications in Chignik include phones, mail plane and TV. The community is served by a church and a school with grades kindergarten through 12. There are public water, sewer and electricity systems. Freight arrives by barge. Government address: City of Chignik, P.O. Box 110, Chignik, AK 99564; phone 749-2280, fax 749-2300. Village corporation address: Far West Inc., General Delivery, Chignik, AK 99564; phone 749-2230.

Chignik Lagoon

[MAP 8] Located on the south shore of the Alaska Peninsula 5 miles west of Chignik, 450 miles southwest of Anchorage. **Transportation:** Boat; charter plane from King Salmon, Dillingham or Kodiak. **Population:** 46. **Zip code:** 99565. **Emergency Services:** Alaska State Troopers, King Salmon, phone 246-3346; Health Aide, phone 840-2214; Volunteer Fire Department.

Elevation: 50 feet. **Climate:** Maritime climate characterized by cool summers, relatively warm winters and rainy weather. Total precipitation averages 127 inches annually, with an average of 58 inches of snow. Summer temperatures range from 39°F to 60°F; winter temperatures range from 21°F to 36°F.

Private Aircraft: Airstrip adjacent southwest; elev. 50 feet; length 1,700 feet; gravel; unattended. Runway condition not monitored; visual inspection recommended prior to using. Seabirds on and near airfield. No airport facilities or transportation to village. Public domain seaplane base.

Visitor Facilities: Accommodations available at Chignik Lagoon School during school months. No laundromat, banking services or restaurant. Groceries, clothing, first-aid supplies, hardware, some camera film and ammunition may be purchased at Ward Cove Packing Co. Boots, rain gear, limited fishing gear available. No arts and crafts available for purchase. Fishing/hunting license available, as well as guide service. Marine engine and boat repair at cannery in

summer only, and at a local Johnson dealer which provides outboard maintenance and warranty work, plus other fishing essentials. Fuel available at the cannery includes marine gas, diesel, propane and regular gasoline. No public moorage facilities.

Chignik Lagoon took its name from its proximity to Chignik. The area was originally populated by Kaniagmiut Eskimos. After the Russian occupation, the intermarriage of the Kaniags and Aleuts produced the Koniags who now reside in Chignik Lagoon. The village was a fishing village and now serves, along with Chignik, as a regional fishing center. The community is not incorporated.

Subsistence hunting and fishing are the mainstay of the local economy, with commercial fishing providing seasonal employment. Fish include pink, chum and silver salmon, cod, black bass, halibut, rainbow trout and Dolly Varden. Also taken are Dungeness, king and tanner crab, clams and octopus. Game includes moose, caribou, ptarmigan, ducks and geese. In the fall, residents pick blueberries, cranberries, raspberries and salmonberries.

Veniaminof Volcano (erupted in 1983) dominates the horizon to the west, sending up occasional puffs of steam. Wildflowers abound along the beaches and there is fossil hunting along the north side of the lagoon. The nearby valley provides hiking opportunities, although care must be taken not to surprise brown bears. Eagles can be observed nesting and hunting in the area. There is beach recreation along Ocean Spit, which protects the lagoon from the open sea.

Communications in Chignik Lagoon include phones, mail plane, post office, radio and TV. There are church services in the summer. One school has grades kindergarten through 8. No community electricity, but there are water and sewer systems. Freight arrives by plane, barge and ship. Government address: Chignik Lagoon Village Council, General Delivery, Chignik Lagoon, AK 99565. Village corporation address: Chignik Lagoon Native Corp., General Delivery, Chignik Lagoon, AK 99565.

Chignik Lake

[MAP 8] Located on Chignik Lake on the Alaska Peninsula, 15 miles southwest of Chignik, 265 miles southwest of Kodiak. **Transportation:** Scheduled airline and air charter from Anchorage. **Population:** 153. **Zip code:** 99548. **Emergency Services:**

Clinic, phone 845-2236; Volunteer Fire Department.

Climate: Cool summers, warm winters. Summer temperatures range from 39°F to 60°F. Average winter temperatures range from 21°F to 50°F.

Private Aircraft: Airstrip adjacent southwest; elev. 50 feet; length 3,100 feet; gravel; unattended. Runway condition not monitored; visual inspection recommended prior to using. No airport facilities or transportation to village.

Visitor Facilities: Groceries can be purchased from J&K Co. (845-2228). Fuel available from local fuel company.

Established in the 1950s, the village has developed as a fishing village. During the summer, most residents move to a fish camp near the village of Chignik Lagoon.

Communications include phone, mail plane, radio and TV. There is a washeteria and community well. Electricity is purchased from the school. Sewage system is private septic tanks. There are 15 HUD homes and a sewage treatment lagoon. The community has an old and a new Russian Orthodox church. School offers preschool through grade 12. Freight arrives by air transport and barge. Village corporation address: Chignik River Limited, P.O. Box 4, Chignik Lake, AK 99548. Government address: Chignik Lake Village Council, General Delivery, Chignik Lake, AK 99548; phone 845-2212.

Cold Bay

[MAP 7] Located on the west shore of Cold Bay, 40 miles from the extreme westerly tip of the Alaska Peninsula, 630 miles southwest of Anchorage. **Transportation:** 40-mile gravel road system; boat; scheduled service from Anchorage via Reeve Aleutian Airways and MarkAir; scheduled and charter service from Anchorage and local area via Peninsula Airways; limited state ferry access in summer. **Population:** 137. **Zip code:** 99571. **Emergency Services:** Alaska State Troopers, Sand Point, phone 383-3535; Clinic, phone 532-2000; Volunteer Fire Department, phone 532-2416.

Elevation: 100 feet. **Climate:** The area has frequent but light rains, cool temperatures, high clouds and fog. Measurable precipitation occurs approximately 200 days per year. Mean annual precipitation is 35 inches, including 55 inches of snow.

Private Aircraft: Airport adjacent north; elev. 98 feet; length 10,400 feet; asphalt; fuel 100, Jet A; attended. The paved, crosswind runway is one of the largest in the state. All facilities at airport; no public transportation to town.

Visitor Facilities: Pavlof Services (532-2437) operates a restaurant, bar and hotel and sells groceries. There is a laundromat. No banking services. Fishing/hunting licenses available. Truck rental available from Cold Bay Truck Rental (532-2404). Fuel available includes white gas, kerosene, diesel and regular gasoline. No moorage facilities. New dock under construction (1993).

Cold Bay was near the southern edge of the Bering Land Bridge and probably played an important role in the migration of Asiatic peoples to North America. Although not yet excavated, the presence of numerous middens in the area suggests that it was inhabited by a relatively large population of Native people. Russian ships wintered nearby during the first coastal explorations by Europeans. The name Izembek was bestowed on the region in 1827 by Count Feodor Lutke when he named Izembek Lagoon after Karl Izembek, surgeon aboard the sloop *Moller*.

After the onset of WWII a large air base was built at Cold Bay. The airstrip is the third longest in Alaska and the airport now serves as the transportation and communications hub for the entire Aleutian-Pribilof islands region. An FAA office is located here. Cold Bay is used to visitors and welcomes tourists, fishermen and others coming through this isolated community.

Cold Bay is the gateway to Izembek National Wildlife Refuge and the southwestern portion of 3.5-million-acre Alaska Peninsula National Wildlife Refuge. Izembek refuge attracts 142 species of birds, but was established in 1960 primarily to benefit the brant. Izembek Lagoon has the world's largest eelgrass beds on which more than 100,000 brant, the North American continent's entire population, feed during spring and fall migrations. For more information, contact the Refuge Manager, Izembek National Wildlife Refuge, Pouch 2, Cold Bay, AK 99571. (See also Izembek National Wildlife Refuge in Attractions.)

Cold Bay has been called the Canada goose hunting capital of the world. Up to 70,000 Canada geese migrate through Cold Bay in the fall. Also plentiful in the area are red, blue and cross fox, brown bear and park squirrels.

The west side of the Izembek Lagoon also is the site of the wreck of the 3-masted schooner *Courtney Ford* in 1902. It is a good example of commercial ships used in the late 19th century and is the oldest intact hull in the state.

The land surrounding Cold Bay is rolling and treeless. Mount Frosty, a 5,785-foot-high volcano, is located 9 miles southwest of town. Two active volcanoes, Pavlof (35 miles east) and Shishaldin (60 miles west), are visible from Cold Bay when weather permits. The weather in this broad, exposed area is among the worst along the Alaska Peninsula and probably has contributed more to limiting development than any other factor.

There is good fishing in the area for Dolly Varden, salmon, steelhead, arctic char, Pacific cod, flounder and halibut. Contact the Alaska Dept. of Fish and Game, Box 127, Cold Bay, AK 99571, for more information. The City of Cold Bay and the Emergency Medical Squad sponsor a Silver Salmon Derby every Labor Day weekend. It is not unusual for 18 to 20 lb. silver salmon to be caught, according to city clerk Tara Nielsen.

Communications in Cold Bay, a second-class city incorporated in 1982, include phones, fax, mail plane and radio. The community is served by a church and a school with grades kindergarten through 12. Community water, sewer, electricity available. Freight arrives in the community by cargo plane and barge. Government address: City of Cold Bay, P.O. Box 10, Cold Bay, AK 99571; phone or fax 532-2401. Aleutians East Borough, P.O. Box 349, Sand Point, AK 99661; phone 383-2699.

Danger Bay

(See **Kazakof Bay**)

Dutch Harbor

(See **Unalaska**)

Egegik

[MAP 8] *(EEG-gah-gik)* Located on the northwest coast of the Alaska Peninsula near the mouth of the Egegik River, 50 miles south of King Salmon and 340 miles west of Anchorage. **Transportation:** Boat; scheduled and charter plane. **Population:** 120 in winter; 1,000 to 3,000 in summer. **Zip code:** 99579. **Emergency Services:** Public Safety Officer, phone 233-2202; Clinic, phone 233-2229; Village office, phone 233-2211.

Elevation: 50 feet. **Climate:** The predominantly maritime climate is characterized by cool, humid and windy weather. Average

summer temperatures range from 42°F to 63°F; average winter temperatures range from -29°F to 40°F. Total precipitation averages 20 inches annually; average annual snowfall is 45 inches.

Private Aircraft: Airstrip adjacent northeast; elev. 100 feet; length 2,100 feet; gravel; fuel limited 80, 100; unattended. Runway condition not monitored; visual inspection recommended prior to using. Tie-down chain available. Transportation to village with air carrier agent.

Visitor Facilities: Accommodations in private homes. A community-owned facility has a few rooms with showers available. Phone 233-2211 for more information. Meals at lodge or at restaurants in town during summer. Laundromat available; no banking services. Groceries, some clothing, hardware, camera film and sporting goods may be purchased in the community. Arts and crafts available for purchase include carved ivory and fur hats. Fishing/hunting licenses available, as well as guide service. Marine engine and boat repair available in summer. No rental transportation. Fuel available includes marine gas, diesel, propane and regular gasoline. No moorage facilities.

This village was first reported as a fish camp called Igagik during the early U.S. administration of 1867 to 1890. In 1895, the Alaska Packers Assoc. established a salmon saltery at the mouth of the river. The town developed around a cannery in the early 1900s, that also was established at the river's mouth. Egegik is unincorporated.

The economy in Egegik is based on commercial fishing, and residents there claim one of the largest red salmon runs in the world. Several canneries in the area provide seasonal employment from May to August. Residents supplement their income with subsistence hunting and fishing.

Becharof National Wildlife Refuge is accessible by plane or skiff up the Egegik River. There is sportfishing for salmon and trout and hunting for caribou and bear. (See also Wildlife Refuges in Attractions.)

Communications in Egegik include phones, mail plane, radio and TV. The community is served by the Egegik Bible Church and a school with grades kindergarten through 12. There is a community electricity system and public water and sewer. Freight arrives by cargo plane and barge. Government address: Egegik Improvement Corp., P.O. Box 189, Egegik, AK 99579. Village corporation address: Becharof Corp., P.O. Box 145, Egegik, AK 99579; phone 233-2235.

False Pass

[MAP 7] Located on the east end of Unimak Island on Isanotski Strait which separates Unimak Island from the Alaska Peninsula, 35 miles southwest of Cold Bay, 646 air miles southwest of Anchorage. **Transportation:** Boat; scheduled and charter airline from Cold Bay. **Population:** 84, plus 300 temporary processor workers. **Zip code:** 99583. **Emergency Services:** Village Public Safety Officer; Clinic; Village Health Aide; Fire Department.

Elevation: 20 feet. **Climate:** Mild winters and cool summers. The warmest month is August; the coldest is February. Average annual precipitation at Cold Bay is 33 inches, including 56 inches of snow.

Private Aircraft: Airstrip adjacent south; elev. 20 feet; length 2,700 feet; gravel; fuel 80, 100; unattended. Runway condition not monitored; visual inspection recommended prior to using. Surface may be soft during spring thaw and heavy rains.

Visitor Facilities: No accommodations available. No restaurants, laundromat or banking services. Food available at Peter Pan Seafoods cookhouse (May through August); groceries and supplies may be obtained at Peter Pan Seafoods store year-round. Fishing/hunting licenses available. No guide service. Rental transportation includes boats, charter aircraft. Fuel available includes marine gas, diesel, propane and regular gas. Moorage facilities available. New (1993) deep-water city dock.

Isanotski is the Russianized Aleut word "Issanak" or "Isanax" which means The Pass. Americans whose large ships could not navigate through the narrow Isanotski Strait into the Bering Sea from the Gulf of Alaska called it False Pass. The name stuck for the village. The strait is used extensively by vessels under 150 feet and the U.S. Coast Guard has buoyed the entrance to guide the vessels.

False Pass was settled in the early 1900s by homesteader William Gardner. A cannery, established by P.E. Harris, was relocated to False Pass from Mozhovoi Bay. As the cannery grew, additional people moved to the area. An airstrip and school were built in the early 1960s, and the city was incorporated in 1990. The cannery, now Peter Pan Seafoods, is owned by the Nichiro Corp. of Japan.

The local economy is based on the commercial salmon, halibut, herring and cod fisheries. False Pass is also an important stop for fishing fleets enroute to Bristol Bay and the Bering Sea fishing grounds.

Subsistence hunting and fishing also play an important role in the local economy. The area has abundant geese, ducks, caribou, bear, seals, octopus, cod, halibut, salmon and a variety of berries. The Ikatan River offers sportfishing.

The village is located within Alaska Maritime National Wildlife Refuge. Bears are often seen near the village. During migrations, spectacular concentrations of waterfowl rest and feed in the freshwater and saltwater wetlands, lagoons and shoals bordering the Bering Sea side of the pass. St. Catherine's Cove is a highly recommended bird-watching spot. Shorebirds frequent the beaches, tidal flats and shallow areas. Harbor seals are abundant; sea lions are present; an occasional walrus also is observed. The once-rare sea otter reestablished itself in the area and is now abundant.

Communications in False Pass include phones, fax, mail plane, radio and TV. There are no churches. The community has a school with grades kindergarten through 12. Freight arrives by cargo plane, barge and ship. Government address: False Pass Tribal Council, P.O. Box 29, False Pass, AK 99583; phone 548-2227, fax 548-2214. Village corporation address: Isanotski Corp., P.O. Box 9, False Pass, AK 99583; phone 548-2217, fax 548-2314. City of False Pass, P.O. Box 50, False Pass, AK 99583; phone 548-2319, fax 548-2214.

Ivanof Bay

[MAP 8] Located on the Alaska Peninsula at the north end of Ivanof Bay on the northeast end of the Kupreanof Peninsula, 200 miles from Sand Point, 510 miles southwest of Anchorage. **Transportation:** Scheduled air service available. **Population:** 35. **Zip code:** 99695. **Emergency Services:** Alaska State Troopers, Sand Point; Clinic; phone 669-2213.

Climate: Maritime climate characterized by cool summers, relatively warm winters and rainy weather. Total precipitation at Chignik, the nearest weather station 50 miles away, averages 127 inches annually. Average annual snowfall is 58 inches.

Private Aircraft: Airstrip 0.3 mile from village; length 1,500 feet; gravel; no airport facilities; no transportation to village. Approximately 10,000 feet of open water used for seaplane landing. High winds occasionally create violent turbulence.

Visitor Facilities: The local Community Hall accommodates 4 people in 2 rooms;

kitchen and dining area. Contact Elizabeth or Archie Kalmakoff at the Ivanof Village Council (669-2207). The Kalmakoffs also run the K-Family Market. No restaurant, laundromat or banking services. No arts and crafts available. Fishing/ hunting licenses not available. No guides, major repair service, rental transportation or moorage facilities. Fuel may be available.

The bay on which this predominantly Aleut village is located was named by Lieutenant Dall of the U.S. Coast and Geodetic Survey in 1880. The village occupies the site of a former salmon cannery which operated from the 1930s to the early 1950s.

Almost all residents of Ivanof Bay fish for a living. Most families move to cabins in Chignik for the summer salmon fishing season. A few residents work for the store, school and village, and most of the men run traplines in the winter for mink, otter, red fox, wolverine, ermine and lynx. Subsistence hunting and fishing also play a big role in the economy of Ivanof Bay.

Fish include salmon, cod, black bass and halibut. Also taken are king and Dungeness crab, cockles and clams. Game includes moose, caribou, bear, ptarmigan, ducks, geese, seals, porcupine and rabbits.

Communications include phones, mail plane, radio and TV. There is no church. A school has grades kindergarten through 12. There are community electricity and water systems. Freight arrives by air. Government address: Ivanof Bay Village Council, P.O. Box K1B, Ivanof Bay, AK 99695-0050; phone or fax 669-2207. Village corporation address: Bay View Inc., 11480 Doggie Ave., Anchorage, AK 99576.

Karluk

[MAP 3] Located on Karluk Lagoon on the west coast of Kodiak Island 75 air miles from Kodiak. **Transportation:** Boat; scheduled and charter air service from Kodiak. **Population:** 107. **Zip code:** 99608. **Emergency Services:** Village Public Safety Officer, phone 241-2230; Alaska State Troopers, Kodiak, phone 486-4761; Health Aide; Kodiak Hospital; Volunteer Fire Department.

Elevation: 137 feet at airport. **Climate:** Kodiak Island has a strong marine influence, characterized by moderately heavy precipitation, cool temperatures and frequent clouds and fog, with little or no freezing weather. Humidity is generally high and the temperature variation is small. Temperature at Karluk ranges from 31°F to 54°F.

Private Aircraft: Airstrip 1 mile east; elev. 137 feet; length 2,000 feet; gravel; no fuel; unattended. Runway condition not monitored; visual inspection recommended prior to using.

Visitor Facilities: No overnight accommodations or restaurant available at the village. Accommodations in summer at a private fishing lodge located across Karluk Lagoon from the village. No banking services or laundromat. Limited groceries, first-aid supplies and hardware available at small store operated by tribal council; most supplies obtained from Kodiak. No arts and crafts available for purchase. Fishing/hunting licenses and guide services available. No rental transportation, major repair services, moorage facilities or fuel available.

Prior to 1979, the village was located on both sides of the Karluk River at Karluk Lagoon. A spit and footbridge connected Old Karluk on the northeast side of the lagoon with Karluk on the southwest side. On January 7 and 8, 1978, waves driven by northeasterly winds reaching 100 mph breached the spit at the mouth of the river. Travel between the 2 settlements was disrupted and the residents decided to relocate to an entirely new site about 0.75 mile upstream on the south side of the lagoon.

Russian hunters established a trading post in Karluk in 1786; however, the mouth of the Karluk River is thought to have been populated several hundred years before the Russians arrival. In 1805, Capt. U.T. Lisianski of the Imperial Russian Navy reported the name of the settlement as "Carlook" or "Karloock." Between 1790 and 1850 many tanneries, salteries and canneries were established in the area. In 1890, Karluk was renowned for having the largest salmon cannery in the world and the river was known as the greatest red salmon stream in the world.

In the early 1900s, canneries were constructed by the Alaska Packers Assoc. Overfishing of the area forced the canneries to close in the 1930s, and today the buildings stand vacant and deteriorating.

Karluk is located adjacent to the Kodiak National Wildlife Refuge. The community's Ascension of Our Lord Russian Orthodox Chapel, built in 1888, is a national historic site.

Fishing is the primary source of livelihood for Karluk residents; there are a few year-round, part-time positions. Almost all residents depend on fishing and hunting as a food source. Species found in the area include salmon, trout, steelhead, flounder, duck, seal, deer, reindeer, rabbit and ptarmigan.

NOTE: Land along the Karluk River as well as the riverbed is owned by Koniag Inc. and the village corporations of Karluk and Larsen Bay. There is a $50 per person/per day fee for fishing or camping on the Karluk River. Permits may be obtained from Koniag Inc., 201 Kashevarof, Suite 6, Kodiak, AK 99615; phone 486-4147.

Communications in unincorporated Karluk include phones, daily mail plane, commercial radio from Kodiak and satellite TV. The community has a school with grades kindergarten through 10. There are community electricity, water and sewage systems. Freight arrives by mail plane and charter planes, fishing boats and occasional barges. Government address: Karluk Tribal Council, General Delivery, Karluk, AK 99608; phone 241-2224. Village corporation address: Koniag Inc., 201 Kashevarof, Suite 6, Kodiak, AK 99615; phone 486-4147.

Kazakof Bay

[MAP 3] Located at Kazakof (Danger) Bay on Afognak Island, approximately 20 miles north of Kodiak. **Transportation:** Boat or charter air service. **Population:** Private logging camp; size varies. **Zip code:** 99615. **Emergency Services:** EMT aide at logging camp; Alaska State Troopers, Kodiak; Kodiak Hospital, phone 486-3281; Coast Guard, call operator and ask for Zenith 5555.

Climate: Summers moist and cool, with highs occasionally up to 75°F. Winters windy, wet and gray, with low temperatures reaching 0°F. Average temperature from November to the first of March is 20°F.

Private Aircraft: No airstrip. Floatplane landings only.

Visitor Facilities: Fishing and hunting cabins are available for rent from Afognak Native Corp., phone 486-6014. No restaurant, laundromat or banking services. No stores; supplies are obtained from Kodiak. No rental transportation; public moorage facilities available.

Alaska's only elk herds live on Afognak and nearby Raspberry Island. Other wildlife includes Sitka black-tailed deer and Kodiak brown bear, as well as otter, fox and marten. Fishing is active from late May to mid-September for pink, red, chum and coho salmon, Dolly Varden and rainbow trout. Halibut also are available. Waters around Afognak are fished commercially for salmon, tanner and Dungeness crab, halibut, and

herring. Photography, hiking and kayaking are also favorite pastimes.

Air and boat charters are available in Kodiak for the 15-minute flight or 1½- to 3-hour boat trip to Kazakof Bay. Communications at the camp include daily mail planes and telephone service. The camp has its own electricity, water and sewer services. Freight arrives by plane, barge or charter boats.

Much of Afognak Island is owned by the Afognak Native Corp., Box 1277, Kodiak, AK 99615; phone 486-6014, fax 486-2514. Contact the corporation to reserve cabins or to use private lands.

King Cove

[MAP 7] Located on the Pacific Ocean side of the Alaska Peninsula, 18 miles southeast of Cold Bay, 630 miles southwest of Anchorage. **Transportation:** Boat; scheduled and charter aircraft from Cold Bay or Sand Point. **Population:** 832, plus almost double that number during fishing season. **Zip code:** 99612. **Emergency Services:** Police, phone 497-2211; Clinic, phone 497-2311; Volunteer Fire Department, phone 497-2211.

Climate: King Cove's maritime climate is characterized by mild winters and cool summers. The warmest month is August; the coldest is February. Precipitation averages 33 inches per year at Cold Bay.

Private Aircraft: Airstrip 4.8 miles northeast; elev. 148 feet; length 4,300 feet; gravel; no fuel; unattended. No airport facilities. Public transportation available to town. Runway condition not monitored; visual inspection recommended prior to using.

Visitor Facilities: Accommodations at Fleets Inn (497-2312). There are 2 restaurants: Fleets Inn (497-2312) and Dobsons Pizza (497-2292). A laundromat is available at the hotel for guests. No banking services. Groceries, clothing, first-aid supplies, hardware, camera film and sporting goods may be purchased at Peter Pan Seafoods (497-2234) or John Gould & Sons (497-2212). No arts and crafts are available. Fishing/hunting licenses available. There is no guide service. Auto repair service is available and arrangements may be made to rent autos. Fuel available includes marine gas, diesel, propane and regular gas. Moorage facilities are available.

King Cove, one of the larger communities in the Aleutian region, was founded in 1911 when Pacific American Fisheries built a salmon cannery. It is a first-class city, incorporated in 1947. Although the cannery burned down in 1976, it was immediately rebuilt and is now the largest cannery operation under one roof in Alaska.

The community has a fairly stable economy, dependent almost entirely on fishing and seafood processing. Other employment locally is with the store, school and city government. Subsistence activities add salmon, halibut, caribou, waterfowl, eggs of marine birds, ptarmigan and berries to local diets.

King Cove is located near the 4.3-million-acre Alaska Peninsula National Wildlife Refuge. The Alaska Peninsula has long been a major big game hunting area, especially for huge brown/grizzly bears. Other mammals found in the refuge are caribou, wolves and wolverine.

King Cove is 20 miles east of 5,784-foot Frosty Peak, a dormant volcano. The active Pavlof Volcano complex and Cathedral Ledge are 40 miles east of King Cove.

Twelve miles southeast of King Cove lies the ghost town of Belkofski, which was settled in 1823 by Russians. Reported as Selo Belkovskoe by the Russians, from the word "belka," meaning squirrel. They came to harvest sea otters in the Sandmand Reefs and other nearshore banks. During the height of this exploitation, Belkofski was one of the most affluent villages in the area. The near extinction of the sea otter forced residents to seek subsistence elsewhere.

An imposing Holy Resurrection Russian Orthodox Church was built in Belkofski in the 1880s, and the village became an administrative center for the church. The structure is on the National Register of Historic Places. When the last of the Belkofski residents moved to King Cove in the early 1980s, they took the church's bell and icons with them and built a new Orthodox church at King Cove. A seldom-used trail connects the former village to King Cove.

King Cove goes all out for the Fourth of July with a fishing derby, games, contests, a community barbecue and fireworks display.

Communications at King Cove include phones, mail plane and TV. Radio reception is occasional. The community has 2 churches and a school with grades kindergarten through 12. There are community electricity, water and sewer systems. Freight arrives by cargo plane, barge and ship. Government address: City of King Cove, P.O. Box 37, King Cove, AK 99612; phone 497-2340. Village corporation address: King Cove Corp., General Delivery, King Cove, AK 99612. Aleutians East Borough, P.O. Box 349, Sand Point, AK 99661; phone 383-2699.

King Salmon

[MAP 8] Located on the Alaska Peninsula on the Naknek River, 15 miles east of Naknek, 290 miles southwest of Anchorage. **Transportation:** Scheduled airline from Anchorage. **Population:** 434. **Zip code:** 99613. **Emergency Services:** Police, phone 246-4222; Alaska State Troopers, phone 246-3346; Camai Clinic, Naknek, phone 246-6155; Volunteer Fire Department.

Elevation: 50 feet. **Climate:** Cool, humid and windy weather. Average summer temperatures range from 42°F to 63°F; average winter temperatures range from 29°F to 44°F. Total precipitation averages 20 inches annually, including an average snowfall of 48 inches. Cloud cover is present an average of 76 percent of the time year-round. Naknek River is ice free between May and October.

Private Aircraft: Airport adjacent southeast; elev. 57 feet; length 8,500 feet; asphalt; fuel 100, Jet A; attended. *CAUTION: Air Defense aircraft may scramble at any time. Passenger and freight terminals, ticket counter, restrooms, traffic control tower at airport. Transportation available.*

Visitor Facilities: Accommodations at Quinnat Landing Hotel (246-3000) and King Ko Inn (246-3377); both offer restaurants and lounges. Area lodges include Wood-Z Lodge (246-3449) and Prestage's Sportfishing Lodge (246-3320). No laundromat available. Banking services available. Groceries, clothing, first-aid supplies, hardware, camera film and sporting goods may be purchased in the community. Arts and crafts available for purchase include carved ivory, baskets and masks. Fishing/hunting licenses available, as well as guide service. Major repair service for marine engines, boats and aircraft. Rental transportation includes autos in summer, boats and charter aircraft. Fuel available includes marine gas and regular gas. Moorage facilities available. *NOTE: Land on the south side of the Naknek River from King Salmon is owned by the Alaska Peninsula Corp. Contact the corporation for details on use and fees.*

In the 1930s, an air navigation silo was built at the present site of King Salmon. At the onset of WWII an Air Force base was constructed that continues today as the major military installation in western Alaska. In 1949, the U.S. Army Corps of Engineers built the road connecting King Salmon to Naknek. The community, located in the Bristol Bay Borough, has continued to develop as a government, transportation and service center.

King Salmon is the gateway to several large lakes on the Alaska Peninsula (Naknek, Iliamna, Becharof, Ugashik) and to Katmai National Park and Preserve. A 10-mile unimproved road leads from King Salmon to the park's western boundary and there are floatplane connections from King Salmon to the lodge at Brooks River, the National Park Service ranger station and public campground on Naknek Lake. There are 2 other lodges in the park. Independent travelers must make their own arrangements for visiting Katmai, including air service to King Salmon and Brooks River. Campers can purchase meals and scenic bus tour tickets at the lodge. The visitor center in the MarkAir building at the King Salmon airport offers trip planning assistance for USF&WS and National Park Service lands in the area. The center is open daily in summer (June to September) from 8 A.M. to 4:30 P.M. There is a staffed information desk; phone 246-4250.

Communications in King Salmon include phones, mail plane, radio and TV. The community is served by a church. Children are bused to school in Naknek. There is a community electricity system and sewage system; water is from individual wells. Freight arrives by air cargo or by barge to Naknek then is trucked to King Salmon. Government address: Bristol Bay Borough, Box 189, Naknek, AK 99633; phone 246-4224. King Salmon Visitors Center, P.O. Box 298, King Salmon, AK 99613; phone 246-4250. Village corporation address: Alaska Peninsula Corp., Box 104360, Anchorage, AK 99510; phone 274-2433, fax 274-8694.

Kodiak

[MAP 3] Located at the north end of Chiniak Bay near the eastern tip of Kodiak Island. **Transportation:** Commercial jet service from Anchorage; commuter air service from Anchorage; Alaska State Ferry System from Seward and Homer. **Population:** 7,229, city; 15,535, borough. **Zip code:** 99615. **Emergency Services:** Dial 911 for emergencies. Alaska State Troopers, phone 486-4121; City Police, phone 486-8000; Fire Department, phone 486-8040; Kodiak Island Hospital, phone 486-3281; Coast Guard emergency, dial operator and ask for Zenith 5555.

Elevation: Sea level. **Climate:** Average daily temperature in July 54°F; in January 32°F. Average annual precipitation 74 inches. September, October and May are the wettest months, each averaging more than 6 inches of rain.

Private Aircraft: Kodiak state airport, 7 miles southwest; elev. 73 feet; length 7,500 feet; asphalt; fuel 80, 100, Jet A-1. Kodiak Municipal Airport, 2 miles northeast; elev. 139 feet; length 2,800 feet; asphalt; attended daylight hours. Kodiak (Lilly Lake) seaplane base, 1 mile northeast; elev. 130 feet. Inner Harbor seaplane base, adjacent north; unattended; docks; watch for boat traffic; no fuel.

Visitor Facilities: Accommodations at several motels/hotels and about a dozen bed and breakfasts. There are several restaurants, sporting goods stores, gift shops, hardware stores and general merchandise stores. There are several air charter services in Kodiak for flightseeing trips, brown bear viewing, fly-in hunting and fishing or side trips to nearby points of interest. Boats can be chartered for fishing and hunting trips, sightseeing and photography. There are 5 car rental agencies, an airport bus service, taxi cabs, several year-round van touring services and seasonal sightseeing bus tours. (Kodiak has about 100 miles of roads which offer beautiful scenery and access to tidewater but not to the Kodiak National Wildlife Refuge. Kodiak's world famous brown bears are rarely seen from the roads.)

Kodiak Island, home of the oldest permanent European settlement in Alaska, is about 100 miles long. Kodiak is the largest island in Alaska, and second largest in the United States, with an area of 3,670 square miles. The Kodiak Borough includes some 200 islands, the largest being Kodiak.

Commercial fishing is the backbone of Kodiak's economy. Kodiak was the largest commercial fishing port in the United States in 1988 for product landed. Some 3,000 commercial fishing vessels use the harbor each year delivering salmon, shrimp, herring, halibut and whitefish, plus king, tanner and Dungeness crab to the 15 seafood processing companies in Kodiak.

Kodiak also is an important cargo port and transshipment center. Container ships stop here to transfer goods to smaller vessels bound for the Aleutians, the Alaska Peninsula and other destinations.

Kodiak, a home-rule city incorporated in 1940, has all the amenities of a medium-sized city, including radio stations, TV via cable and satellite and a daily newspaper, the *Kodiak Daily Mirror*. City government address: City of Kodiak, P.O. Box 1397, Kodiak, AK 99615; phone 486-8636, fax 486-

8600. Borough address: Kodiak Island Borough, 710 Mill Bay Road, Kodiak, AK 99615; phone 486-9310. Kodiak Island Convention and Visitors Bureau, 100 Marine Way, Kodiak, AK 99615; phone 486-4782, fax 486-6545. Native corporation address: Kodiak Area Native Assoc., 402 Center Ave., Kodiak, AK 99615; phone 486-5725.

For more information see *The MILE-POST®*, a complete guide to communities on Alaska's road and marine highway systems.

Larsen Bay

[MAP 3] Located near the mouth of Larsen Bay on the west shore of Uyak Bay on the northwest coast of Kodiak Island, 62 miles west-southwest of Kodiak. **Transportation:** Boat; scheduled and charter air service from Kodiak. **Population:** 169. **Zip code:** 99624. **Emergency Services:** Village Public Safety Officer, phone 847-2262; Alaska State Troopers, Kodiak, phone 486-4761; Clinic, phone 847-2208; Volunteer Fire Department.

Elevation: 20 feet. **Climate:** Kodiak Island's climate is dominated by a strong marine influence, characterized by moderately heavy precipitation, cool temperatures and frequent high clouds and fog. There is little freezing weather. Humidity is generally high and temperature variation is small. Mean maximum temperatures range from 32°F to 62°F. Larsen Bay gets approximately 23 inches of precipitation a year, with 23 inches of snow.

Private Aircraft: Airstrip adjacent southwest; elev. 77 feet; length 2,400 feet; gravel; no fuel; unattended. Runway condition not monitored; visual inspection recommended prior to using. No public transportation to town.

Visitor Facilities: No hotel or restaurant. Arrangements may be made for accommodations in private homes. Accommodations by advance reservation at area lodges, including Amook Lodge (847-2312) and Bayside Inn (847-2313). No laundromat or banking services. Groceries, clothing, first-aid supplies, hardware, film and sporting goods may be purchased at Larsen Bay community store (847-2226). No arts and crafts available for purchase. Fishing/hunting licenses available. No guide or major repair services. Private boats may be rented; charter aircraft available locally. No public moorage facilities. Fuel available: marine gas, diesel, propane, regular gasoline.

Larsen Bay was named for Peter Larsen, an Unga Island furrier, hunter and guide.

The Native name for the town is Uyak. The area is thought to have been inhabited for 2,000 years by the Aleut people. In the early 1800s there was a tannery in Uyak Bay. The Alaska Packers Assoc. built a cannery in the village of Larsen Bay in 1911. The cannery is now owned by Kodiak Island Seafoods Inc.

Larsen Bay is a second-class city, incorporated in 1974. It is located adjacent to Kodiak National Wildlife Refuge.

The economy is primarily based on fishing and cannery work. A large majority of the residents depend on subsistence activities for their livelihood. Species found in the area include seals, sea lions, salmon, halibut, codfish, ducks, clams, sea urchins, gumboots (chitons), crab, deer and various types of berries. There are a few local jobs with the city, the tribal council, school, post office and stores.

The main attraction in the area is the Karluk River, which is located 2 to 3 miles from the head of Larsen Bay. This river is known for its excellent king salmon, silver salmon and steelhead fishing. Raft trips from Karluk Lake to Karluk Lagoon also are popular.

NOTE: Land along the Karluk River as well as the riverbed is owned by Koniag Inc. and the village corporations of Karluk and Larsen Bay. There is a $50 per person/per day fee for fishing or camping on the Karluk River. Permits may be obtained from Koniag Inc., 203 Marine Way, Kodiak, AK 99615; phone 486-4147.

Hunting in the area is good for Sitka black-tailed deer. Other wildlife includes Kodiak brown bear, fox, rabbit, ermine, otter, seal, whale, sea lion and porpoise. Bird-watchers may see eagles, gulls, petrels, kittiwakes, mallards, green-winged teals, wigeons, pintails, lesser Canada geese, puffins, loons, cormorants and more. (Approximately 120 species of birds have been recorded in the Kodiak area, although most are migratory.)

Communications in Larsen Bay include phones, mail plane, commercial and single sideband radio and satellite TV. The community is served by 2 churches and a school with grades kindergarten through 12. There are community electricity, water and sewer systems. Freight arrives by cargo plane, barge, ship and charter plane. Government address: City of Larsen Bay, P.O. Box 8, Larsen Bay, AK 99624; phone 847-2221. Village corporation address: Larsen Bay Tribal Council, General Delivery, Larsen Bay, AK 99624; phone 847-2207.

Naknek

[MAP 8] Located on the Alaska Peninsula on the Naknek River near its mouth, 15 miles west of King Salmon, 300 miles southwest of Anchorage. **Transportation:** Daily passenger and freight service from Anchorage and Dillingham via MarkAir, Alaska Airlines, Peninsula Airways and Northern Air Cargo; local scheduled and charter flights via Peninsula Airways, MarkAir, Bristol Air, King Air Service, Windy's Mag Air and Katmai Air Service. A 15-mile paved road connects Naknek with King Salmon. **Population:** 565 (borough 1,451). **Zip code:** 99633. **Emergency Services:** Police, phone 246-4222; Alaska State Troopers, King Salmon, phone 246-3346; Camai Medical Center, phone 246-6155; Volunteer Fire Department.

Elevation: 50 feet. **Climate:** Cool, humid and windy weather predominates. Average summer temperatures at nearest weather station in King Salmon range from 42°F to 63°F. Average winter temperatures range from 29°F to 44°F. Total precipitation in King Salmon averages 20 inches annually, with an average snowfall of 48 inches. Kvichak Bay and the Naknek River freeze solid from late October to April.

Private Aircraft: Airstrip 1 mile north; elev. 70 feet; length 2,500 feet; gravel; fuel 80, 100; attended and a 1,500-foot gravel crosswind runway. Runway condition not monitored; visual inspection recommended prior to using. Airstrip is equipped with lights. Aircraft parking along entire length. Seaplane base adjacent north; elev. 30 feet; fuel 80, 100.

Visitor Facilities: Accommodations at 2 hotels. There are 3 restaurants. Laundry facilities and banking services available. Groceries, clothing, first-aid supplies, hardware, camera film and sporting goods may be purchased in the community. Arts and crafts available for purchase include ivory, baskets and masks. Fishing/hunting licenses available, as well as guide service. Major repair service for marine engines, boats, autos and aircraft. Rental transportation includes autos, boats and aircraft. Fuel available includes marine gas, diesel and regular gasoline. Moorage facilities available.

Naknek is the seat of the 531-square-mile Bristol Bay Borough, the state's oldest borough incorporated in 1962. The region was settled more than 6,000 years ago by Yup'ik Eskimo and Athabascan Indians. The Russians built a fort near the village and fur

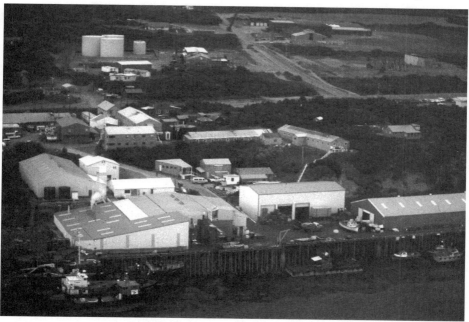

Naknek is a major center for commercial fishing and fish processing. (Karen Jettmar)

trappers inhabited the area for some time prior to the U.S. purchase of Alaska.

By 1883, the first salmon cannery opened in Bristol Bay; in 1890, the first cannery opened on the Naknek River. By 1900, there were approximately 12 canneries in Bristol Bay.

The community was developed as a major center for commercial fishing and processing, which today form the base of the area's economy. There are 9 salmon processors on the Naknek side of the river and Naknek bustles during the summer as a couple of thousand people arrive in June to fish and work in the canneries. Borough government also is a significant source of employment. Many residents also depend on subsistence hunting and fishing.

Hunting, fishing, camping and photography provide most of the outdoor recreation for borough residents. The Naknek River is famous for its excellent sportfishing; caribou and bear hunting are popular. There are scores of excellent fishing streams throughout the region.

The Russian Orthodox St. John the Baptist Chapel in Naknek, reportedly constructed in 1886, is on the National Register of Historic Places. Naknek also has the Bristol Bay Historical Museum, P.O. Box 43, Naknek, AK 99633. The collections of this "living history museum" feature archaeology, history and ethnology, and document Naknek's history as one of the largest commercial salmon fishing and canning headquarters in the world. Displays show the progression from the early subsistence-oriented lifestyle of the first Bristol Bay residents to the coming of the Russian fur traders on up to the oral histories and family trees of present residents. The museum building is the original Fisherman's Hall, an early meeting place for fishermen. Facilities include a gift shop, a library and parking. Open 4 hours every day except Sunday during the summer. Open in winter by appointment. No admission fee; donations accepted.

Communications in Naknek include phones, radio and TV. The community is served by 4 churches and a school with grades preschool through 12. There is an indoor community swimming pool. There is a community electricity and sewage system; water is from individual wells. Freight arrives in the community by cargo plane and barge. Government address: Bristol Bay Borough, Box 189, Naknek, AK 99633. Village corporation address: Paug-Vik Incorporated, Ltd., Box 61, Naknek, AK 99633; phone 246-4278.

Nelson Lagoon/Port Moller

[MAP 7] Located on a narrow spit that separates Nelson Lagoon and low-lying north coastal areas of the western Alaska Peninsula from the Bering Sea, 30 miles west of Port Moller, 550 miles southwest of Anchorage. **Transportation:** Air charter from Cold Bay. **Population:** 60. **Zip code:** 99571. **Emergency Services:** Clinic; Volunteer Fire Department; Village Public Safety Officer, phone 989-2292.

Climate: The area's maritime climate features mild winters and cool summers. The warmest month is August; the coldest is February. Precipitation averages 37 inches per year at Port Moller, including 99 inches of snow.

Private Aircraft: Airstrip 1 mile east; elev. 13 feet; length 3,300 feet; gravel; unattended. Runway condition not monitored, visual inspection recommended prior to using. Large seabirds feed along beach adjacent to runway.

The following description of Nelson Lagoon is provided by students of Nelson Lagoon School courtesy of principal Mark Massion. Our thanks to Priscilla Brandell, Valerie Johnson, Leona Nelson, Melinda Nelson and Craig Rysewyk.

Visitor Facilities: "Harold Johnson Sr. owns an apartment building called the Bering Inn. There are 5 rooms available with cable TV and phone. They all have bathrooms and some have small kitchenettes. Rates are $102 a night; $300 a week; and $800 a month. Harold's phone number is 989-2209.

"We do not have a restaurant. Newcomers that stop in should bring their own food, or stop at the Coho Commercial general store. It carries a little bit of everything you want. Summer hours are 1 P.M. to 4 P.M. Winter hours are from noon to 4 P.M. You can reach the store at 989-2230.

"Nelson Lagoon is located on a picturesque spit and is surrounded by the Bering Sea on one side. Nelson Lagoon is very small, but peaceful. In the summer, the lagoon is a professional fishing site. It attracts lots of fishermen and visitors. The winter brings high winds and lots of snow.

"Our community isn't very large, but it is growing slowly. About 75 to 80 residents live here year-round. In the summer, the population grows to about 95 to 110 people. That is because people come here to fish. Almost everyone in town is related and of

Aleut descent. We hunt for caribou, geese, ducks and other land mammals.

"Our town is well-kept. Some people might think our town is boring, but there are fun things to do here. You can go out and have picnics when it is sunny. You can go for a ride on 4-wheelers down the coast to Dick's camp if you like. In the winter you go on snowmobile rides. The people in Nelson Lagoon are very friendly, kind and helpful. They enjoy visitors. There are several great cooks in town. You may even get invited to dinner."

The community derived its name from the lagoon, which was named in 1882 for Edward William Nelson of the U.S. Signal Corps, an explorer in the Yukon delta region between 1877 and 1920. The area was settled in 1906 when a salmon saltery was built there. A cannery operated between 1915 and 1917. Peter Pan Seafoods currently operates in the area. For many years Nelson Lagoon was a seasonal camp, but families began to settle there and a school was established in 1965. Nelson Lagoon is part of the Aleutians East Borough.

According to its students, Nelson Lagoon School is the first place you see upon arriving in town. The school has a "great gym", used by students and community members alike. The school also has several computers and students learn several computer programs.

Nelson Lagoon has phones and mail service. Water is from individual wells or hauled from lakes; sewage system is flush toilets and seepage pits. There is a community electricity system. Freight arrives by ship or by barge via Port Moller. Government address: Nelson Lagoon Village Council, General Delivery, Nelson Lagoon, AK 99571. Village corporation address: Nelson Lagoon Corp., General Delivery, Nelson Lagoon, AK 99571. Aleutians East Borough, P.O. Box 349, Sand Point, AK 99661; phone 383-2699.

Nikolski

[MAP 9] Located on Nikolski Bay on Umnak Island, one of the Fox Island group in the mid-Aleutian chain, 116 miles from Dutch Harbor, 880 miles southwest of Anchorage. **Transportation:** Scheduled or charter flights from Dutch Harbor. **Population:** 54. **Zip code:** 99638. **Emergency Services:** Alaska State Troopers, Unalaska; Clinic.

Elevation: 73 feet. **Climate:** Mild winters and cool summers characterize the climate.

The warmest month is August; the coldest is February. Precipitation is 21 inches annually; snowfall averages 41 inches annually.

Visitor Facilities: Supplies available in the community. Availability of all other visitor facilities and services is unknown.

Nikolski was actively involved in sea otter hunting during the Russian period. A sheep ranch that is still operating today was established in Nikolski in 1926 as part of the Aleutian Livestock Co.

After the Japanese attacked Dutch Harbor and seized Attu and Kiska in June 1942, Nikolski residents were evacuated to the Ketchikan area until 1944. In the mid-1950s, the Air Force built a White Alice site which was later operated by RCA Alascom. It was abandoned in 1977.

Most residents work outside the village at crab canneries and processing ships during the fall season, fishing in the summer or at seasonal jobs in Cold Bay or St. Paul. Subsistence hunting and fishing provide a substantial part of the villagers' diets. Most families catch Dolly Varden and halibut in the bay. They also hunt ducks and seals. Octopus, fish and sea urchins can be gathered from the reef.

Ananiuliak (Anangula) Island on the north side of Nikolski Bay is the site of the earliest presently documented evidence of human habitation in the Aleutian Islands. Radiocarbon dating indicates occupation as far back as 8,000 years.

The Chaluka site in the village of Nikolski exhibits 4,000 years of virtually continuous occupation and is listed on the National Register of Historic Places. Also on the register is Nikolski's St. Nicholas Russian Orthodox Church, built in 1930.

Communications include phones and mail plane. The community has a school with grades kindergarten through 12. There are community electricity and water systems. The sewage system is septic tanks. Freight arrives by ship once or twice a year. Nikolski is unincorporated under state law, but is incorporated as an IRA village under the Indian Reorganization Act. Government address: Nikolski Village Council, General Delivery, Nikolski, AK 99638. Village corporation address: Chaluka Corp., General Delivery, Nikolski, AK 99638.

Old Harbor

[MAP 3] Located on the southeast shore of Kodiak Island on the west shore of Sitkalidak Strait across from Sitkalidak Island, 54 miles from Kodiak. **Transportation:** Scheduled and charter air service from Kodiak; private boat. **Population:** 284. **Zip code:** 99643. **Emergency Services:** Village Public Safety Officer, phone 286-2295; Alaska State Troopers, Kodiak, 486-4761; Clinic, phone 286-2205; Volunteer Fire Department.

Elevation: 20 feet. **Climate:** Kodiak Island's climate is dominated by a strong marine influence, characterized by moderately heavy precipitation, cool temperatures, frequent high clouds and fog. Humidity is generally high and temperature variation small. Average temperature at Old Harbor in January is 20°F; July temperatures average 50°F. Precipitation averages 60 inches per year, with 18.5 inches of snow.

Private Aircraft: Airstrip adjacent northeast; elev. 15 feet; length 2,200 feet; gravel; no fuel; unattended. Runway condition not monitored; visual inspection recommended prior to using. Vehicles may be on runway. Severe erosion adjacent to runway; usable runway width is 70 feet. No public transportation into town.

Visitor Facilities: Accommodations and meals at Sitkalidak Lodge (286-9246). No laundromat or banking services. Some groceries, clothing, first-aid supplies, hardware and film may be purchased at Old Harbor Food Store and Walt's Village Store. Most supplies are obtained from Kodiak. No arts and crafts available for purchase. Fishing/hunting licenses not available. Guide services and charter boats can be arranged locally. No major repair services. Moorage facilities and boat haul-out available. Diesel and regular gasoline available.

The area around Old Harbor is thought to have been inhabited for nearly 2,000 years. Grigori Shelikov, considered to be the founder of the Russian-American colonies, entered a harbor on the south coast of Kodiak Island in 1784. His flagship, the Three Saints, is the namesake for the harbor as well as the first Russian settlement in Alaska, Three Saints Bay. In 1788, a tsunami destroyed the settlement; it was hit by 2 more devastating earthquakes before 1792. In 1793, Alexander Baranov, who replaced Shelikov, relocated the town to Saint Paul Harbor, now known as Kodiak. A settlement at Three Saints Harbor was reestablished in 1884. The census of 1890 designated the settlement in that area as Staruigavan, meaning "old harbor" in Russian. The town was nearly destroyed by a tidal wave from the 1964 Good Friday earthquake; only 2 homes and the church remained standing. Old Harbor has since been rebuilt in the same location.

Visitor attractions in Old Harbor include the historic Russian Orthodox church and wildlife. Nearby Three Saints Bay, site of the first Russian settlement, has kittiwake rookeries and sea lion haul-outs. Old Harbor Native Corp. is the major landowner in Old Harbor; contact them for permission to use corporation lands. Old Harbor is adjacent Kodiak National Wildlife Refuge.

Many of Old Harbor's residents are commercial fishermen; however, most of the residents depend to some extent on subsistence activities for some food sources. Species harvested for subsistence use include salmon, halibut, cod, Dolly Varden, crab, herring, shrimp, clams, duck, seal, deer, rabbit and bear. Berries are also harvested. There are a few jobs locally with the stores, school, city and post office. Old Harbor is a second-class city, incorporated in 1966.

Communications in Old Harbor include phones, mail plane, commercial radio reception from Kodiak and satellite TV. The community is served by a Russian Orthodox church and a school with grades kindergarten through 12. There are community electricity, water and sewer systems. Freight arrives by barge, mail plane or charter boat. Government address: City of Old Harbor, P.O. Box 109, Old Harbor, AK 99643; phone 286-2204, fax 296-2278. Village corporation address: Old Harbor Native Corp., P.O. Box 71, Old Harbor, AK 99643; phone 286-2286, fax 286-2287. Old Harbor Tribal Council, P.O. Box 62, Old Harbor, AK 99643; phone 286-2215.

Ouzinkie

[MAP 3] *(you-ZENK-e)* Located on the west coast of Spruce Island on Narrow Strait across from Kodiak Island, 10 miles north of the city of Kodiak. **Transportation:** Boat; scheduled or charter air service from Kodiak. **Population:** 216. **Zip code:** 99644. **Emergency Services:** Village Public Safety Officer, phone 680-2259; Alaska State Troopers, Kodiak, phone 486-4761; Clinic, phone 680-2265; Volunteer Fire Department. Medical emergencies evacuated by air to Kodiak.

Elevation: 55 feet at airport. **Climate:** Maritime, with moderately heavy precipitation (approximately 60 inches per year), predominantly cool temperatures with little variation and frequent clouds and fog. Mean maximum temperatures 62°F in July and August, 32°F December to February. Snowfall occurs from December through March and averages 87 inches per year. Winds can become quite strong.

Private Aircraft: State airstrip adjacent north; elev. 55 feet; length 2,500 feet; gravel; no fuel. Visual inspection recommended prior to landing. *CAUTION: Large red-and-white board markers identify end of 2,500-by-100-foot safety area and are 195 feet before runway landing threshold.*

Visitor Facilities: Make arrangements for accommodations with Ouzinkie Native Corp. (680-2208 or 2211) and the City of Ouzinkie (680-2209 or 2257). No restaurant, laundromat or banking services. Groceries available at Ouzinkie Community Store. No arts or crafts available for purchase. Fishing/hunting licenses available. No guide or major repair services, rental transportation or public moorage facilities. Fuel available: diesel.

Ouzinkie is one of the oldest settlements of the Kodiak Island group. The village is nestled in a small cove among tall stands of spruce and hemlock. Spruce Island is separated from Kodiak Island by a strait named Uskiy, meaning "very narrow" in Russian. The village name is a transliteration of Uzenkiy which is derived from Uskiy.

The town was originally settled as a retirement community for the Russian-American Co. In 1889, the Royal Packing Co. constructed a cannery at Ouzinkie. Shortly afterward, the Russian-American Packing Co. built another. In the mid-1800s, a Russian Orthodox church was built. In the early 1900s, almost all Ouzinkie residents owned cattle. Through the years, however, ranching became less popular and finally disappeared altogether.

Ouzinkie is a second-class city, incorporated in 1967. The Russian Orthodox Nativity of Our Lord Chapel, built in 1906 next to the older church, is a national historic site. The community celebrates Russian Orthodox holidays. Check with the church about guided tours of the holy sites and old gravestones at Monks Lagoon.

Other visitor activities include salmon and halibut fishing, deer and bear hunting, birding, hiking, camping (by permission only) and taking in the view from the top of Mount St. Herman.

The fishing industry flourished through the years with new canneries replacing those that were destroyed by fire. In 1964, a tidal wave resulting from the Good Friday earthquake destroyed the Ouzinkie Packing Co. cannery. Following that disaster, Columbia

Ward bought the remains and rebuilt the store and dock, but not the cannery. In the late 1960s, the Ouzinkie Seafoods cannery was constructed. The operation, sold to Glacier Bay, burned down in 1976 shortly after the sale.

Ouzinkie's economic base is commercial fishing. Since 1976 there have been no local fish processing facilities and Ouzinkie fishermen use those in Kodiak or floating processors. There are a few other jobs locally with the store, city government, Native corp., clinic and schools. There are 74 single family homes and 3 apartment buildings in Ouzinkie. The community also supports a library, school gym and community center.

Residents depend on subsistence activities for various food sources. Species harvested locally include salmon, king crab, tanner crab, Dungeness crab, herring, halibut, shrimp, scallops, clams, ducks, deer and rabbits.

Zack Chichenoff, mayor of the City of Ouzinkie, says: "Ouzinkie on Spruce Island is paradise as far as I'm concerned, with an abundance of spruce trees, and access to fishing and hunting." Mr. Chichenoff says he wouldn't want to live anywhere else.

Communications in Ouzinkie include phones, mail plane, commercial radio from Kodiak, satellite and cable TV. The community is served by Russian Orthodox and Baptist churches and a school with grades kindergarten through 12. There are community electricity, water and sewer. Freight arrives by barge or mail plane. Government address: City of Ouzinkie, P.O. Box 109, Ouzinkie, AK 99644; phone 680-2209, fax 680-2223. Village corporation address: Ouzinkie Native Corp., P.O. Box 89, Ouzinkie, AK 99644; phone 680-2208, fax 680-2268. Ouzinkie Tribal Council, P.O. Box 13, Ouzinkie, AK 99644; phone 680-2259, fax 680-2214.

Perryville

[MAP 8] Located on the south coast of the Alaska Peninsula, 215 miles south-southwest of Dillingham and 285 miles southwest of Kodiak. **Transportation:** Scheduled airline, air charter from Dillingham or King Salmon. **Population:** 107. **Zip code:** 99648. **Emergency Services:** Alaska State Troopers, Sand Point or King Salmon; Clinic, phone 853-2236; Fire Department, phone 853-2206.

Elevation: 25 feet. **Climate:** Cool summers, with a fair amount of rain. Winters are relatively warm. The average snowfall is 58.5 inches. Total precipitation at Chignik, the nearest weather station (40 miles away), averages 127 inches annually.

Private Aircraft: Airstrip adjacent south; elev. 25 feet; length 2,500 feet; gravel; unattended. Runway condition not monitored; visual inspection recommended prior to use. No airport facilities or transportation to village, though private vehicles may be available.

Visitor Facilities: Limited accommodations. No restaurant, laundromat or banking services. Clothing (few), first-aid supplies, hardware, camera film and sporting goods may be purchased in the community. No arts and crafts available. Fishing/hunting licenses not available. No guide service, major repair service, rental transportation or public moorage facilities.

Perryville was founded in 1912 as a refuge for Native people driven away from their villages by the eruption of Mount Katmai. It was named after Captain Perry, who rescued the people with his boat and took them to Ivanof Bay, and later to the location of Perryville.

St. John the Theologian Church, a Russian Orthodox church built sometime after the 1912 founding of Perryville, is on the National Register of Historic Places.

Nearby rivers and the ocean in front of the village are used for sportfishing, and most of the residents fish commercially. There is berry picking in season and hunting for bear, moose and caribou. The village is unincorporated. *NOTE: Much of the land around Perryville is owned by the local village firm, Oceanside Corp. You will need to contact the corporation in advance for permission to enter.*

Communications include phones, mail plane, radio and TV. Public electricity and water are available. Sewage system is individual septic tanks. The community is served by the Russian Orthodox church, and a school with grades preschool through 12. Freight arrives by cargo and mail plane. Government address: Perryville IRA Council, General Delivery, Perryville, AK 99648. Village corporation address: Oceanside Corp., P.O. Box 84, Perryville, AK 99648.

Pilot Point

[MAP 8] Located on the east shore of Ugashik Bay on the Alaska Peninsula, 90 miles south of King Salmon, 380 miles southwest of Anchorage. **Transportation:** Scheduled and charter air service from King Salmon. **Population:** 67. **Zip code:** 99649. **Emergency Services:** Alaska State Troopers, King Salmon, phone 246-3346; Clinic, phone 797-2212; Volunteer Fire Department.

Elevation: 50 feet. **Climate:** Cool, humid and windy. Temperature and precipitation data were collected at Pilot Point from 1939 until 1945. The city installed a weather monitoring station in 1992. Low cloud cover and fog frequently limit travel into Pilot Point.

Private Aircraft: Airstrip adjacent east; elev. 75 feet; length 3,500 feet; gravel; fuel; some avgas available from the store; unattended. Runway condition not monitored; visual inspection recommended prior to using. Runway soft when wet. No airport facilities; summer taxi service to village.

Commercial fishing boats "dry docked" for the winter in Pilot Point. (Bill Sherwonit)

Visitor Facilities: Accommodations available at Caribou Look-out Lodge (797-2216). Cabins also available; contact Aleck Griechen (797-2205). No banking services. A gift shop is open in summer. A laundromat is available. Groceries, clothing, first-aid supplies, hardware, camera film and sporting goods may be purchased in the community. Limited arts and crafts available. Fishing/hunting licenses available; no guide service. No major repair service. Charter flights available. Fuel available includes diesel, propane and regular gasoline. Bulkhead dock at Dago Creek available for temporary tie-up, load and off-load only.

This predominantly Aleut village, which had a fish saltery in 1900, originally was known as Pilot Station, for the Ugashik River pilots who were stationed there and took boats up the river to a larger cannery at Ugashik. By 1918 the saltery had developed into a large cannery, and was forced to close in 1958 because of deterioration of the harbor. In 1933, the name of the village changed to Pilot Point. The community incorporated in 1992.

Residents depend on commercial salmon fishing for the majority of their cash income. Other jobs are found with the store, school and government. Subsistence hunting and fishing play a major role in the economy, based primarily on salmon and caribou.

Record-sized grayling have been taken from Ugashik Lakes. Other sportfishing is for salmon and trout. Hunting is for moose, caribou and brown bear. The Kvichak River is a major migration corridor for the sandhill crane and whistling swans that nest near the village. White-fronted and emperor geese, Canada geese and loons rest in the area in the spring and fall; some stay to nest and molt. Ugashik Bay and the Ugashik, Dog Salmon and King Salmon rivers are important bald eagle feeding areas.

NOTE: The majority of the land surrounding the village, as well as the Ugashik One Airfield, is owned by the Pilot Point Native Corp. Use of this land for hunting, fishing, or recreation is forbidden without the express permission of the Pilot Point Native Corp. Board of Directors.

Communications at Pilot Point include phones, mail plane, radio and TV. The community is served by St. Nicholas Russian Orthodox Church, which was built circa 1912 and is on the National Register of Historic Places. There also is a school with grades kindergarten through 12. Community electricity system is available; public water and sewage systems. Freight arrives by cargo plane and barge. Government address: City of Pilot Point, Box 430, Pilot Point, AK 99649. Pilot Point Village Council, P.O. Box 449, Pilot Point, AK 99649. Village corporation address: Pilot Point Native Corp., P.O. Box 487, Pilot Point, AK 99649.

Pleasant Harbor

[MAP 3] Located on Spruce Island, 3 miles east of Ouzinkie, 12 miles north of Kodiak. **Transportation:** Boat; charter air service. **Population:** 26. **Zip code:** 99644. **Emergency Services:** Village Public Safety Officer, Ouzinkie; Alaska State Troopers, Kodiak; Ouzinkie Clinic.

Climate: Winters are usually mild with very little snow, but it can snow 3 feet when you least expect it, says one resident. Winter temperatures range from 25°F to 40°F. Summers are usually sunny with occasional rain showers. Temperatures range between 60°F and 70°F.

Private Aircraft: Airstrip at Ouzinkie. Floatplane landings at Pleasant Harbor.

Visitor Facilities: Private residences only, no accommodations, meals or other visitor services available. Marine engine and boat repair services may be available. Public moorage facilities available.

Pleasant Harbor was founded in 1923 when Chris Opheim homesteaded a piece of land which included Sunny Cove and Pleasant Harbor. He and his family operated a cod saltery in Sunny Cove. Son Ed Opheim inherited the homestead and in 1947 moved his family to Pleasant Harbor where the family earned a living salting and smoking salmon. Ed Opheim later built and operated a sawmill.

The tidal wave generated by the 1964 Good Friday earthquake washed away both the old house at Sunny Cove and the Pleasant Harbor home. The Opheims have since rebuilt on higher ground. The family has been selling homesites and there are now a dozen or more homes in the community.

Most residents earn their living by fishing. Others take seasonal jobs in Kodiak and a few work for the lodge.

Attractions include Monks Lagoon, about an hour's walk from Pleasant Harbor, where St. Herman lived and worked during the early days of Russian America. It is now a Russian Orthodox sanctuary. The chapel built over St. Herman's grave is a national historic site.

New Valaam Monastery is located at Pleasant Harbor and the monks who live there are more than willing to share their knowledge of the history of the church in Alaska with visitors.

Salmon fishing is particularly good in July and August. Halibut and Dolly Varden can be caught in May and June. There are clams nearby and tide pools where a variety of marine creatures hide. Dolphins, harbor seals and sea lions are plentiful. Deer and rabbits venture near the homes; eagles soar overhead and nest on a point overlooking the ocean. On a tiny island nearby many sea and land birds, their nests and young can be seen. This island is covered with wildflowers in season. Elk and deer hunting can be done on Kodiak and Afognak islands, about 2 hours by boat from Pleasant Harbor.

Communications in unincorporated Pleasant Harbor include radio and TV. Freight arrives by plane or ship.

Port Heiden

[MAP 8] Located on the Alaska Peninsula on the north shore of Port Heiden, 150 miles from King Salmon; 435 miles southwest of Anchorage. **Transportation:** Boat; scheduled airline from King Salmon. **Population:** 119. **Zip code:** 99549. **Emergency Services:** Village Public Safety Officer, phone 837-2223; Clinic, phone 837-2208; Volunteer Fire Department, phone 837-2238.

Elevation: 90 feet. **Climate:** Mean annual precipitation is 15 inches, including 53 inches of snow.

Private Aircraft: Airstrip 6 miles northeast; elev. 86 feet; length 6,100 feet; gravel; fuel Jet A and 100. Airport has passenger and freight terminal, ticket counter, restrooms. Taxi service to village.

Visitor Facilities: Accommodations at a boarding house. Meals at lodging facility. No laundromat or banking services. Groceries, first-aid supplies, hardware and camera film may be purchased in the community. Arts and crafts which may be purchased include carved ivory. Fishing/hunting licenses and guide service available. Everyone does their own marine engine, boat and auto repairs. Make arrangements with private owners to rent autos or boats. Charter aircraft available. Fuel available includes marine gas, diesel and regular gasoline. No moorage facilities.

Port Heiden was founded by a Norwegian who came to the area in the 1920s and married a Native woman. Other families moved in later. Prior to that time many Native people lived in the area, but many died during an influenza epidemic in the 1900s. Port Heiden is a second-class city, incorporated in 1972.

NOTE: Hiking, berry picking, camping and fishing are permitted on lands owned by the Alaska Peninsula Corp. upon payment of a $100-per-person fee. Hunting and woodcutting on corporation lands are not permitted. Contact the corporation for more information.

The community is the gateway to 514,000-acre Aniakchak National Monument and Preserve. Access by floatplane from King Salmon or Port Heiden to Surprise Lake inside the caldera. By foot, it's 10 miles from Port Heiden to the park boundary on a very difficult trail.

Communications in Port Heiden include phones, mail plane, radio and TV. The community is served by 2 churches and a school with grades kindergarten through 12. There are community electricity, water and sewage systems. Freight arrives in the community by cargo plane, air taxi and barge. Government address: City of Port Heiden, P.O. Box 49050, Port Heiden, AK 99549. Village corporation address: Alaska Peninsula Corp., P.O. Box 104360, Anchorage, AK 99510.

Port Lions

[MAP 3] Located on Settler's Cove near the mouth of Kizhuyak Bay on the north coast of Kodiak Island, 21 miles from Kodiak. **Transportation:** Boat; scheduled and charter air service from Kodiak; Alaska Marine Highway System from Homer and Seward via Kodiak. **Population:** 222. **Zip code:** 99550. **Emergency Services:** Village Public Safety Officer, phone 454-2330; Alaska State Troopers, Kodiak, phone 486-4761; Clinic, phone 454-2275.

Elevation: 52 feet at airport. **Climate:** Relatively cool summers and warm winters, moderately heavy precipitation and frequent high clouds and fog. Temperatures from 20° to 60°F. Approximately 60 inches of precipitation per year.

Private Aircraft: Airport 2 miles northeast; elev. 52 feet; length 2,600 feet; crushed rock runway and apron; no fuel; unattended. Runway equipped with marker lights, beacon and wind direction indicator. Subject to downdrafts during northeast winds. Runway width 100 feet between edge markers.

Visitor Facilities: Accommodations and meals by advance reservation at Port Lions Lodge and Lion's Den Wilderness Lodge (454-2301). No public laundry facilities or banking services. Groceries, clothing, hardware and camera film available. Some arts and crafts available for purchase. Fishing/hunting licenses and guide and charter services available locally. Marine engine repair available. Boats and off-road vehicles may be rented. Fuel available: diesel, regular gasoline. Public moorage facilities available.

Port Lions was founded in 1964 by Lions International, the Bureau of Indian Affairs and the Public Health Service for the displaced residents of Afognak. The village of Afognak was partially destroyed by tidal waves in the aftermath of the March 27, 1964, earthquake. Afognak was 1 of 10 permanent settlements founded by Russian-American Co. employees between 1770 and 1799.

For many years, Port Lions was the site of the large Wakefield Cannery on Peregrebni Point. The cannery burned down in March 1975. Floating crab processors have operated there in recent years. Port Lions incorporated as a second-class city in 1966.

The economy of Port Lions is based primarily on commercial fishing. There are a few other jobs with the lodges, stores, boat harbor, oil company, school, city and health clinic. All residents depend to some extent on subsistence activities. Food harvested includes salmon, halibut, crab, shrimp, scallops, clams, ducks, seals, deer, rabbits, berries and plants.

Port Lions has excellent recreational opportunities. Boating and riding all-terrain vehicles are very popular. The surrounding area offers good hunting and fishing and an abundance of wildlife for the photographer.

Communications in Port Lions include phones, mail plane, radio and TV. The community is served by a Russian Orthodox church and Hillside Bible Chapel, a library, and a school with grades kindergarten through 12. Electricity is provided by Kodiak Electric Assoc. Utilities include a community water supply, sewer and refuse collection. Freight arrives by air, ship and state ferry. Government address: City of Port Lions, P.O. Box 110, Port Lions, AK 99550; phone 454-2332. Village corporation address: Afognak Native Corp., P.O. Box 1277, Kodiak, AK 99615; phone 486-6014, fax 486-2514.

Port Moller

(See **Nelson Lagoon**)

Port William

[MAP 3] Located on the south shore of Shuyak Island, 45 to 50 miles north of Kodiak. **Transportation:** Boat; scheduled and chartered floatplane from Kodiak; chartered floatplane from Homer. **Population:** 10. **Zip code:** 99697. **Emergency Services:** Alaska State Troopers, Kodiak; Kodiak Island Hospital, Kodiak.

Climate: Summer temperatures are usually in the 60s and low 70s. Winters are normally mild; the temperature ranges from the upper 20s to the 30s.

Private Aircraft: Floatplane landings only.

Visitor Facilities: Accommodations and meals provided at Port William Lodge (688-2253). Laundry facilities, showers and saunas available. Fishing/hunting licenses are available. Public moorage and water available.

Port William originally was a cannery. For years it was the largest ice and cold storage plant in the Kodiak area, according to a resident. Now privately owned, the cannery is no longer operating. Port William is the only docking facility for large vessels from Kachemak Bay to Kodiak. Residents earn their livings from lodge and docking services, and commercial fishing.

Most of Shuyak Island is a wilderness. The northern end of the island is the Shuyak Island State Park, while a section along the east side has been proposed for a state game sanctuary. The middle of the island is part of the Kodiak Island Borough.

There is fishing for world-class halibut, Dolly Varden in the spring, and for silver and pink salmon in the fall. There are many birds, including bald eagles and puffins. Poor grade jade and jasper can be found on some beaches. There is hunting for deer, bear and elk (on Afognak Island just to the south). Other wildlife includes sea lions (on the Latax Rocks to the north), sea otters, land otters, beavers and whales.

Communications at Port William include mail plane and radio. There is no church or school. Supplies are obtained from Kodiak. Freight arrives by mail plane.

Sand Point

[MAP 7] Located on the north coast of Popof Island in the Shumagin Islands off the south coast of the Alaska Peninsula. **Transportation:** Scheduled air service from Anchorage; state ferry service in summer. **Population:** 1,162. **Zip code:** 99661. **Emergency Services:** Police, fire, medical, phone 911.

Private Aircraft: Airport 2 miles southwest; elev. 22 feet; length 3,800 feet; gravel; Jet A 50 fuel available; unattended. *CAUTION: 80- to 120-foot cliff on east side of runway.*

Visitor Facilities: Accommodations at a motel, and bed and breakfast. There are 4 restaurants, a pizza parlor, 2 bars and a laundry facility. Cab service available. Supplies available in the community. Fishing/hunting licenses available at the city office. Guide service available, also major repairs. Charter air service available, as well as diesel fuel and gasoline. Moorage facilities available. Shower facilities, 2 gyms, a teen center and an indoor swimming pool.

One of the most prosperous and modern Aleut communities, Sand Point has a cannery and a locally owned fishing fleet for crab, bottom fish and salmon. The community was founded by the Russians in the 1870s. The town became a supply center for the surrounding area after a cod-fishing station was built by the McCollam Fishing and Trading Co. In 1946, the first cold storage plant in Alaska was built there. A mining operation is currently under way in the area. Sand Point is a first-class city, incorporated in 1966.

Sand Point's St. Nicholas Russian Orthodox Church, constructed in 1936, is on the National Register of Historic Places.

The community has 2 churches and a school with grades kindergarten through 12. There are community electricity, water and sewer systems. Freight arrives by air cargo, ship and barge. Government address: City of Sand Point, P.O. Box 249, Sand Point, AK 99661; phone 383-2696. Village corporation address: Shumagin Corp., P.O. Box 174, Sand Point, AK 99661; phone 383-3525. Other addresses: Aleutians East Borough, P.O. Box 349, Sand Point, AK 99661; phone 383-2699. Eastern Aleutian Tribes, Box 527, Sand Point, AK 99661. Unga Corp., Box 130, Sand Point, AK 99661. Aleutian East Borough School District, Box 429, Sand Point, AK 99661.

Shemya

[MAP 10] *(SHEM-ee-a)* Shemya Island is located near the west end of the Aleutian Chain, 1,500 miles southwest of Anchorage. **Access:** Shemya is a private military base with access strictly controlled by the U.S. Air Force. Visitors must be on official military business to go to Shemya. The contact point for visit requests is AAC/LGX, Elmendorf AFB, AK 99506; phone 552-5202. Private aircraft are not authorized access to Shemya. **Transportation:** U.S. Air Force plane or military charter plane only. **Population:** Approximately 576. **Zip code:** 98736. **Emergency Services:** Air Force Security; Air Force Medical Aid Station, phone 392-3552.

Elevation: 90 feet. **Climate:** Generally winters are cloudy, windy and cold. Snow showers are numerous, but short. Considerable fog is experienced during the summer.

Clear, calm days are rare. Temperatures range from an average high of 51°F in August to an average low of 28°F in February. Mean annual precipitation is 30 inches, including 65 inches of snow.

Private Aircraft: Airport adjacent south; elev. 90 feet; length 10,000 feet; asphalt. Official business only. Civilians must obtain prior permission to land; contact HQ USAF/PRPJ, Washington, D.C. 20330, phone (202) 697-5967.

Visitor Facilities: Military transient lodging and dining facilities only.

Shemya, largest in the Semichi Islands group, measures 4.5 miles long by 2.3 miles wide. The island is entirely controlled by the U.S. Air Force, which conducts operations at Shemya Air Force Base.

Black volcanic sand on the island inspired Shemya's nickname of "The Black Pearl of the Aleutians." The island also is referred to as "The Rock" because of its steep cliffs and rocky terrain. Summer brings a profusion of wildflowers, some unique to the Aleutians. Driftwood, various types of rocks and shells, and many WWII relics and ruins abound on Shemya, making for interesting beachcombing and hiking.

Shemya's involvement in the war began in May 1943, when 2,500 Army troops landed on the island to construct runways. The plan was to use Shemya as a secret air base for the bombardment of Japan. The first bombing mission flew from Shemya on March 16, 1944; the last on Aug. 13, 1945.

Communications at Shemya include phones, mail plane, radio and TV. All utilities are provided on base.

South Naknek

[MAP 8] Located on the Alaska Peninsula on the Naknek River, 2 miles south of Naknek, 15 miles west of King Salmon and 300 miles southwest of Anchorage. **Transportation:** Scheduled airline and air taxi. **Population:** 185. **Zip code:** 99670. **Emergency Services:** Police, phone 246-4222; Alaska State Troopers, King Salmon, phone 246-3346; Clinic, phone 246-6546; Volunteer Fire Department.

Climate: Cool, humid and windy weather. Average summer temperatures at the nearest weather station in King Salmon range from 42F° to 63°F; average winter temperatures from 4°F to 29°F. Average annual precipitation 20 inches; average snowfall 45 inches.

Private Aircraft: State airstrip 1 mile southwest; elev. 130 feet; length 3,000 feet; gravel; unattended. Runway condition not monitored; visual inspection recommended prior to using. The strip is equipped with low-intensity lighting.

Visitor Facilities: No hotel. There is a store and bar. Fishing/hunting licenses available. Guide service available. Availability of repair service, rental transportation and fuel unknown. Borough-maintained dock.

South Naknek, located just across the river from Naknek, is part of the Bristol Bay Borough. It is a more traditional rural community than its neighbor. South Naknek is not connected by road to any other community.

Commercial fishing and salmon processing are the mainstays of South Naknek's economy. Three of the 5 canneries that line the south bank of the Naknek River are in operation and recruit 400 to 500 people from outside the village for the brief summer salmon season. Most other employment is in community service. About 75 percent of South Naknek's residents depend on subsistence hunting and fishing as a vital source of food. Hunting camps along the Naknek River date back to 3,000 to 4,000 BC. South Naknek was settled after the turn of the century as a result of salmon cannery development.

NOTE: Hiking, berry picking, camping and fishing are permitted on lands owned by the Alaska Peninsula Corp. upon payment of a $100-per-person fee. Hunting and woodcutting on corporation lands are not permitted. Contact the corporation for more information.

South Naknek's Russian Orthodox Elevation of the Holy Cross Church, built in the early 1900s, is listed on the National Register of Historic Places.

Communications in South Naknek include phones, radio, mail plane and TV. The community is served by 2 churches and a school with grades preschool to 6; older students are flown to Naknek daily to attend school. There is a community electricity system; water is from individual wells or hauled from a central watering point. Sewage collection system but no treatment facilities. Freight arrives by air and barge. Government address: Bristol Bay Borough, P.O. Box 189, Naknek, AK 99663; phone 246-4224. Village corporation address: Alaska Peninsula Corp., Box 104360, Anchorage, AK 99510; phone 274-2433.

St. George

[MAP 7] Located on St. George Island, southernmost of the Pribilof Island group, 780 miles west-southwest of Anchorage. **Transportation:** Scheduled airline from Anchorage via St. Paul and twice weekly flights from Anchorage. **Population:** 216. **Zip code:** 99591-0929. **Emergency Services:** Village Public Safety Officer, phone 859-2429 or 859-2263; Alaska State Troopers in Dutch Harbor; Clinic; Volunteer Fire Department.

Elevation: 100 feet. **Climate:** The climate is controlled by the cold waters of the Bering Sea; there is cool weather year-round. Temperatures ranging from a high of 63°F in summer to a low of -7°F in winter have been recorded. The warmest month is July; the coldest is March. Heavy fog is frequent from May through August. Mean annual precipitation is 30 inches, including 47 inches of snow.

Private Aircraft: Airstrip adjacent west; elev. 90 feet; length 3,100 feet; gravel; fuel 100; unattended; contact City of St. George. Avoid flying over seal rookeries on northwest end of island May through October. Airport facilities in Tanaq building. Cab service available into town.

Visitor Facilities: Accommodations at the St. George Tanaq Hotel (designated a national historic landmark). Hotel may close during winter months. Meals available at hotel. There is a laundromat. No banking services. Groceries, clothing, first-aid supplies, hardware and camera film are available at Tanaq Store or St. George Canteen. Arts and crafts available for purchase include seal pelts, model bidarkas (skin boats), model seals and baskets. Fishing/hunting licenses not available. Tour guide service available in summer. Repair service for marine engines, boats and autos available. Arrangements can be made to rent private autos. Fuel available includes marine gas, diesel, propane, unleaded and regular gasoline. Moorage facilities available.

St. George Island has perhaps the largest seabird colony in the northern hemisphere: 2.5 million seabirds nest on the cliffs each summer. In addition, an estimated 250,000 seals congregate in 6 rookeries on the island. Because of scientific research on the island, camping is not permitted. The St. George Tanaq Corp. offers guided tour programs in the summer, which include transportation, lodging and meals. Travelers should leave itineraries loose in case weather delays flights; keep baggage to a minimum.

The treeless uplands around St. George are inhabited by a diverse population of songbirds, blue foxes, lemmings and a few reindeer that are descendants of 3 bucks and 12 does introduced in 1911.

Communications in St. George, a second-class city incorporated in 1983, include phones, mail plane, radio and TV. The community's St. George the Great Martyr Russian

Orthodox Church, built circa 1932-35, is on the National Register of Historic Places. There is a school with grades kindergarten through 8. There are community electricity, water and sewer systems. Freight arrives by cargo plane, barge, ship and mail. Government address: City of St. George, P.O. Box 929, St. George, AK 99591; phone 859-2263, fax 859-2212. Or City of St. George, 4000 Old Seward Hwy., Suite 301, Anchorage, AK 99503; phone 561-2124. Village corporation address: St. George Tanaq Corp., P.O. Box 939, St. George, AK 99591. Or St. George Tanaq Corp., 3000 C St., Suite 201, Anchorage, AK 99503; phone 562-3100, fax 562-3155.

St. Paul

[MAP 7] Located on St. Paul Island, northernmost of the Pribilof Island group. **Transportation:** Ship; scheduled and charter plane from Anchorage via Cold Bay or Dutch Harbor. **Population:** 763. **Zip code:** 99660. **Emergency Services:** Village Public Safety Officer, phone 546-2333 or 911; Chief of Police, Clinic, phone 546-2310; Volunteer Fire Department, EMTs, VHF Channel 16.

Elevation: 20 feet. **Climate:** Cool year-round. Heavy fog is frequent May through August. Mean annual precipitation is 23 inches, including 56 inches of snow.

Private Aircraft: Airstrip 3 miles northeast; elev. 44 feet; length 5,100 feet; gravel; fuel 100 and jet; unattended. For runway lights contact the National Weather Service on 123.6 or phone 546-2215. No airport facilities. Public transportation to town available.

Visitor Facilities: Accommodations and food at King Eider Hotel/Restaurant (546-2312). Laundry and shower facilities available. No banking services. Groceries, clothing, first-aid supplies, hardware, camera film and sporting goods available in the community. Arts and crafts including ivory jewelry, photographs of local flora and fauna, dried wildflowers and fur seal garments are available at 4 gift shops. Guide service available, as well as local tours. Repair service available for marine engines, boats and autos. Off-road vehicles available for rent. Fuel available includes diesel, propane, and unleaded gasoline.

Each summer more than a million northern fur seals gather in rookeries on the shores of the Pribilof Islands and can be observed from 2 blinds. Access is by permit or with a tour group.

More than 200 species of birds have been sighted on St. Paul Island during the summer months. Many of these birds breed and nest on the coastal cliffs west and south of the village. The U.S. Fish and Wildlife Service acquired 1,000 acres of nesting area on St. Paul and 2,000 acres on St. George as additions to Alaska Maritime National Wildlife Refuge.

The uplands around St. Paul have a diverse population of songbirds, white and blue foxes and about 500 reindeer, descendents of 4 bucks and 21 does introduced in 1911.

Tourists are encouraged to visit Black Diamond Hill, where they may find shiny crystals of augite. Crystals of olivine and rutile found on the island may reach semiprecious gem size and quality.

Communications in St. Paul, a second-class city incorporated in 1971, include phones, mail plane, radio and TV. There are community electricity, water and sewage systems. The community is served by Saints Peter and Paul Russian Orthodox Church, which is on the National Register of Historic Places, an Assembly of God church and a school with grades kindergarten through 10. Freight arrives by cargo plane, ship and barge. Government address: City of St. Paul, P.O. Box 901, St. Paul Island, AK 99660; phone 546-2331 or 546-2332. Village corporation address: Tanadgusix Corp., P.O. Box 88, St. Paul Island, AK 99660; phone 546-2312. IRA Council, P.O. Box 86, St. Paul Island, AK 99660; phone 546-2211.

Uganik Bay

[MAP 3] *(you-GAN-ik)* Located on Uganik Bay on the northwest side of Kodiak Island, 40 miles west of Kodiak, 270 miles south-southwest of Anchorage. **Transportation:** Boat; scheduled and charter air service from Kodiak. **Population:** 15. **Zip code:** 99615 (via Kodiak). **Emergency Services:** Alaska State Troopers, Kodiak; Kodiak Island Hospital.

Elevation: 50 feet. **Climate:** Mean daily maximum temperature in July 64°F; mean daily maximum in January 36°F. Mean annual precipitation 44 inches, with 51 inches of snow.

Private Aircraft: No airstrip; seaplane landings only.

Visitor Facilities: None.

Village Islands in Uganik Bay was the location of an Eskimo village in the 1800s. There are a few homes at West Point and another in Mush Bay in the east arm of Uganik Bay. Fishing is the only industry, according to one resident. There were 3 canneries operating in the bay in the 1920s. Today all canneries are closed.

Uganik Bay is located within the Kodiak Island National Wildlife Refuge. Most visitors to the area are deer or bear hunters who fly in with air charter operators from Kodiak.

Steelhead, rainbow trout and silver salmon are available at Lake Uganik.

Communications in unincorporated Uganik Bay include mail plane and shortwave radio. Electricity is from individual generators; water is from streams. Sewage systems vary from flush toilets to pit toilets. There is no school or church. Freight arrives by mail plane, barge or ship.

Ugashik

[MAP 8] *(Yoo-GA-shik)* Located on the Ugashik River on the Alaska Peninsula, 90 miles south of King Salmon, 370 miles southwest of Anchorage. **Transportation:** Boat; scheduled and charter air service from King Salmon. **Population:** 17. **Zip code:** 99683. **Emergency Services:** Alaska State Troopers, King Salmon, phone 246-3346; Health Aide, Pilot Point; Camai Clinic, Naknek; Kanakanak Hospital, Dillingham.

Elevation: 25 feet. **Climate:** Cool, humid and windy. Temperature and precipitation data were collected at Pilot Point from 1939 to 1945. Average summer temperatures ranged from 41°F to 60°F. Average winter temperatures ranged from 12°F to 37°F. Total precipitation averaged 19 inches annually, with an average snowfall of 38 inches.

Private Aircraft: Airstrip 1 mile north; elev. 25 feet; length 3,500 feet; gravel. No airport facilities or public transportation to village.

Visitor Facilities: No visitor facilities or services available. Supplies obtained from Pilot Point.

Ivan Petroff recorded the Eskimo village of Oogashik in 1880. It was one of the largest villages in the region until the influenza epidemic of 1919 decimated the population. The village has since remained small. A cannery in the village has operated under several owners, the most recent being the Briggs-Way Cannery. This predominantly Aleut village is unincorporated.

Fishing is the basis of Ugashik's economy. Usually about 10 residents fish commercially for salmon each season. Subsistence hunting and fishing supplement this income.

Recreational opportunities include sportfishing at Ugashik Lakes, accessible by air taxi or boat. Ugashik Narrows Lodge (272-9401) offers fly-in fishing.

NOTE: Hiking, berry picking, camping and fishing are permitted on lands owned by the Alaska Peninsula Corp. upon payment of a $100-per-person fee. Hunting and woodcutting on corporation lands are not permitted. Contact the corporation for more information.

Communications in Ugashik are mail plane, radio and TV. It is the only community in the region without phones. Electricity is from individual generators; water from private wells. Sewage system is pit privies. There is no church. Children are flown to Pilot Point to attend school. Freight arrives by cargo plane or barge. Government address: Ugashik Village Council, General Delivery, Ugashik, AK 99683. Village corporation address: Alaska Peninsula Corp., P.O. Box 104360, Anchorage, AK 99510; phone 274-2433.

Unalaska/Dutch Harbor

[MAP 9] Unalaska is located on the northern end of Unalaska Island, second island in the Aleutian Chain, 800 miles southwest of Anchorage; Dutch Harbor (the major port area) is located across a bridge from Unalaska on Amaknak Island. **Transportation:** Boat; scheduled and charter airline from Anchorage; state ferry April to October. **Population:** 3,815. **Zip code:** Unalaska 99685; Dutch Harbor 99692. **Emergency Services:** For all emergencies, phone 911; Iliuliuk Family Health Clinic, phone 581-1202; Volunteer Fire Department, phone 581-1233; Volunteer Ambulance Service, phone 581-1233.

Elevation: 20 feet. **Climate:** This is the "Cradle of the Storms," where the warm Japan Current from the south meets the colder air and water currents of the Bering Sea. This mingling creates storm centers which sweep westward, influencing weather systems over most of North America. While the temperature is moderate, there can be tremendous winds and days of almost constant rain. Mean annual precipitation is 64.5 inches.

Private Aircraft: Airport 1 mile north; elev. 22 feet; length 3,900 feet; paved; fuel 100, Jet A; attended. Passenger terminal, ticket counters, restrooms, taxis.

Visitor Facilities: Accommodations at Uni Sea Inn (581-1325), Grand Aleutian Hotel (581-3844), Eagle Inn (581-2800), and Capt's Bay Inn (581-1825); bunkhouses, operated by several seafood canneries; 8 restaurants; 2 laundromats; and banking services available. Groceries, clothing, first-aid supplies, hardware, camera film and sporting goods may be purchased at local stores, which include Carl's (581-1234), Alaska Commercial, Petro Mart, Aleutian Mercantile Co. (581-1796), and Alaska Ship Supply (581-1284). Arts and crafts for purchase include Aleut grass baskets, wood block prints, paintings, and wood and ivory carvings. Fishing/hunting licenses available; no guide service. Major repair service available for ships and marine engines and equipment; limited repairs for autos; check with air carriers for aircraft mechanic or go to Cold Bay. Vehicle and boat rental available. Air and fishing boat charters available. Moorage facilities available, contact the Port Director, phone 581-1254. Several other commercial enterprises are located in the community.

Ounalashka, or Unalaska, was the early headquarters of the Russian-American Co. and a key port for the sea otter fur trade in the 1700s. After the United States purchased Alaska, the North American Commercial Co. became manager of the seal harvest in the Pribilofs and built a station at Dutch Harbor. Unalaska became a major stop for ships heading to and from the Nome goldfields in the early part of this century. In 1939 the U.S. Army and Navy began building installations at Unalaska and Dutch Harbor. In June 1942, the area was bombed by the Japanese and almost all of the local Aleut people were evacuated to southeastern Alaska. Military relics still dot the hillsides, although there has been a major cleanup program in recent years. The Dutch Harbor Naval Base and Fort Mears on Amaknak Island have been designated national historic landmarks.

Unalaska is the major civilian port west of Kodiak and north of Hawaii and is the gateway to the Bering Sea region. It is becoming a major international transshipment port and staging area. Unalaska/Dutch Harbor is also one of the most productive seafood processing ports in the United States and remains ice free year-round. There are several large seafood processing companies that help form the basis for the local economy.

Two local attractions are on the National Register of Historic Places. They are the Russian Orthodox Church of the Holy Ascension in Unalaska (built in 1825), and the Sitka Spruce Plantation in Dutch Harbor — 6 trees which were planted by the Russians in 1805 and have survived in the harsh climate of the naturally treeless Aleutians.

At the entrance of the airport is a memorial to those killed in the Aleutians in WWII; a special tribute to the Aleuts who died during their relocation to southeastern Alaska also is planned.

Hiking in the area is easy and there is no need for trails. There are no bears on Unalaska Island; however, hikers should watch for cliffs. Dress appropriately. Be prepared for the weather to change for the worse.

Fish include halibut; red, pink and silver salmon; and Dolly Varden. Shrimp, crab, "bidarkies" (chitons) and clams are taken, but there is no guarantee that shellfish are free of paralytic shellfish poisoning. There is no big game on Unalaska; local hunting is for ptarmigan, ducks or red fox. Contact the Alaska Dept. of Fish and Game office, phone 581-1239, for more information.

Unalaska is a first-class city, incorporated in 1942, which encompasses Amaknak Island and Dutch Harbor, and a portion of Unalaska Island. Communications in Unalaska include phones, mail, radio and TV. There are community electricity, water and sewer systems. Government address: City of Unalaska, P.O. Box 89, Unalaska, AK 99685; phone 581-1260.

Woody Island

[MAP 3] Located 2.6 miles east of the city of Kodiak. **Transportation:** Private boat; charter air service. **Population:** 1 to 4 in winter; 1 to 6 in summer. **Zip code:** 99615 (via Kodiak). **Emergency Services:** Alaska State Troopers, Kodiak; Kodiak Island Hospital.

Climate: Similar to Kodiak.

Private Aircraft: No airstrip; floatplane or helicopter landings only.

Visitor Facilities: Available in nearby Kodiak.

The island was named by the Russian explorer U.T. Lisianski in 1804. Woody Island figured in the early history of Alaska as a boat-building center and a port from which the Russian American Ice Co. and Kodiak Ice Co. shipped ice to California in the early and middle 1800s. It is believed the first horses in Alaska were brought to Woody Island in 1867, and that the first road built in Alaska — 2.7 miles long — was built around the island. Boat building flourished at both Kodiak and Woody Island during the late 1880s. The settlement of Woody Island gradually diminished as the population settled more and more at Kodiak.

Woody Island has few residents. A Baptist youth camp operates here in the summer.

Communications at Woody Island include radio and satellite TV. A public electricity system is available; water is from wells and a lake; residents have flush toilets. Freight arrives by private boat. Village corporation address: Leisnoi Inc., 4300 B St., Suite 407, Anchorage, AK 99503.

▼ A T T R A C T I O N S ▼

National and State Parks, Etc.

Aniakchak National Monument and Preserve

This 580,000-acre monument and preserve is located on the Alaska Peninsula 10 miles east of Port Heiden and 150 miles southwest of King Salmon. Its centerpiece is 6-mile-wide, 2,000-foot-deep Aniakchak caldera, which was created by the collapse of a 7,000-foot volcano some 3,500 years ago. Later activity built a 2,200-foot cone, Vent Mountain, inside the caldera.

The caldera remained hidden from the outside world until 1922, when a government geologist noticed that the taller peaks in the area formed a circle on the map he was making. Even today, few people have seen the crater; fewer still have walked upon its floor.

It is believed that the caldera at one time contained a deep lake. Eventually the lake waters began to spill over the caldera wall, and through time the fast-flowing Aniakchak River has gouged a spectacular 1,500-foot-deep gap in the wall called The Gates. The wild and scenic Aniakchak River heads in Surprise Lake inside the caldera, which is fed by hot springs. The river then flows 32 miles southeastward to the Pacific Ocean.

Aniakchak last erupted in 1931, adding a "small, but impressive," explosion pit to the pocked caldera floor and scouring the caldera of vegetation. The caldera today chronicles a history of volcanic activity in its lava flows, cinder cones and explosion pits, as well as the beginnings of revegetation bringing life to the barren landscape.

Climate: Aniakchak is remote, difficult to reach and has "notoriously bad weather," says the National Park Service. Temperatures vary greatly. Winter's maximum may range from the low 30s to -30°F. Summer temperatures range from the mid- and upper 40s to a high of 70°F. Violent windstorms in the caldera even when the weather is calm outside can make camping there difficult. In June and July 1973, a man's camp was destroyed twice in 6 weeks and his boat blown away. Local pilots have reported strong turbulent winds in the caldera, particularly through the narrow Gates, which make flying conditions extremely hazardous.

Wildlife: Caribou, brown bears and eagles are found in the area. Red salmon spawn up the Aniakchak River all the way to Surprise Lake (fish from here are recognizable by the flavor of soda and iron from the mineral-laden water).

Activities: Recreation in Aniakchak includes hiking, camping, fishing, photography, natural history study, rafting the Aniakchak National Wild and Scenic River (whose upper reaches are termed "challenging") and beach walking. The Park Service recommends that anyone spending time in Aniakchak be equipped with clothing suitable for cold and wet weather. Bring tent and food if camping and be sure your tent can withstand strong winds. Bear-proof food canisters are recommended for campers and backpackers. The Park Service further cautions that a number of dangers may confront the inexperienced and for safety a copy of your itinerary should be left at park headquarters in King Salmon.

Accommodations: There are accommodations at Port Heiden through Reeve Aleutian Airways or in King Salmon, which has several lodges. In the monument and preserve, there is primitive camping only in most areas, although there is a rustic shelter cabin on the north side of the mouth of the Aniakchak River.

Access: Getting to Aniakchak isn't easy. Reeve Aleutian Airways has a flight between Anchorage and Port Heiden 2 or 3 days per week. From Port Heiden you can charter a small floatplane to Surprise Lake or walk the

10 miles to the monument and preserve, a difficult day- to day-and-a-half-long hike through tundra meadows interspersed with thickets of willow, alder and birch. There is no trail and few people have attempted this route. There are daily commercial flights from Anchorage to King Salmon, where you also can charter a small airplane to Aniakchak. Seasonal ferry service from Kodiak serves a few villages in the region, some of which have air charter services. Charter costs are high, ranging from $150 to $400 an hour depending on the size of the plane. Aniakchak is about 1¹/₂ hours flying time from King Salmon and a half hour from Port Heiden.

For more information: Contact Superintendent, Aniakchak National Monument and Preserve, P.O. Box 7, King Salmon, AK 99613; phone 246-3305, fax 246-4286. Related USGS Topographic maps: Sutwick Island, Chignik, Bristol Bay, Ugashik.

Katmai National Park and Preserve

The original Katmai National Monument at the top of the Alaska Peninsula was created in 1918 to preserve the volcanic wonders of the Valley of the Ten Thousand Smokes, formed by a cataclysmic eruption just 6 years earlier. The June 6, 1912, eruption of Novarupta Volcano, in which Mount Katmai also collapsed, was one of the most violent ever recorded and it darkened the sky over much of the northern hemisphere for several days. Novarupta spewed 7 cubic miles of incandescent ash and pumice which buried the 40-square-mile Ukak River valley as much as 700 feet deep.

During the 1940s, Ray Petersen of Northern Consolidated Airlines built Brooks Camp. The camp catered to fishermen, who came for the salmon and rainbow trout in the Brooks River. Bears also came for the fish, and in increasing numbers.

Today, some 35 to 40 bears may be found in the Brooks River drainage during the peak sockeye salmon run in July, and some 80 percent of the visitors to Brooks Camp are tourists who have come to view the bears or visit the Valley of Ten Thousand Smokes.

The bears congregate at Brooks Falls, about a mile below Brooks Lake. The Park Service built a viewing platform at the falls in 1983. In July, people can be found crowding the viewing platform from 5 A.M. until nearly midnight to watch up to a dozen bears fishing for salmon at the falls.

The valley remains one of the prime attractions of the park, where streams have cut dramatic gorges through the volcanic debris. In the years since the eruption, the thousands of fumaroles have dwindled to a few active vents. The park has been enlarged several times, and is currently 4 million acres.

Sportfishing is still a major draw at Katmai. There are fish camps at Grosvenor

Dramatic cliffs of eroded volcanic ash in the Valley of Ten Thousand Smokes. (Don Francis)

Lake, Kulik Lake and at several other locations. Special restrictions apply to fishing
the Brooks River because of the bears. "Bears
are quick learners," according to park superintendent Alan Eliason. "As soon as they
hear that reel zinging, they come running."

Besides the salmon, Katmai's waters boast
grayling, Dolly Varden, lake trout, northern
pike and trophy-sized rainbow trout—all
of which make the fishing here world
renowned. Catch-and-release fishing is
encouraged throughout the park and
required on some streams for rainbows.
Brooks River is fly-fishing only.

Climate: Visitors to Katmai should be
prepared for stormy weather as well as some
sunshine. Summer daytime temperatures
range from the mid-50s to the mid-60s; the
average low is 44°F. Strong winds and
sudden gusts frequently sweep the area.
Skies are clear about 20 percent of the
summer. Light rain can last for days. Bring a
warm sweater, windbreaker or lightweight
fiberfill jacket, footgear that provides good
support, wool socks and a wool hat. Rain
gear should include raincoat and pants,
parka and hat. You will need insect repellent
and/or a headnet.

Wildlife: Katmai is becoming best known
for its world-class bear viewing. Brown bears,
the coastal equivalents of grizzlies, gather at
Brooks Falls for the salmon run. But bears
may also be encountered on trails leading to
the falls and elsewhere in the park. Visitors
are urged to follow park guidelines regarding
bear safety.

In addition to bears, other wildlife that
may be seen are moose, wolf, wolverine,
river otter, marten, weasel, mink, lynx,
muskrat, beaver and an occasional caribou.
Harbor seals, sea lions, sea otters, and
beluga, killer and gray whales can be found
in the coastal waters of Shelikof Strait. A
variety of birds, including bald eagles,
osprey, ptarmigan, spruce grouse, swans and
abundant waterfowl can be readily observed.

Activities: Recreation includes canoeing
and rafting, sportfishing, wildlife viewing,
day hiking and backpacking. If you aren't a
backcountry hiker, Brooks Camp—where
Brooks Lodge, the park visitor center
and campground are located—offers the
most accessible attractions within Katmai
National Park. Brooks Falls, where there is a
platform for viewing bears fishing for
salmon, is a 1-mile walk from Brooks Camp.
The rangers conduct guided nature walks
and evening programs at Brooks Camp from
June to September. Also from Brooks Camp,

a 4-mile trail leads up Dumpling Mountain
for a view of Naknek Lake.

The same concessionaire-operated Brooks
Lodge also offers van or bus tours out to
Three Forks Overlook and the Valley of
10,000 Smokes. The trip takes visitors out a
rough, narrow, 24-mile road to the overlook.
For the hardy, a 1-mile trail leads down
1,000 vertical feet from the overlook to the
Ukak River and the valley floor. The hike is
strenuous, especially on the way back up,
but it offers a closeup look at the deeply
eroded ash cliffs. Cost for the round-trip
tour is $50. For overnight valley hikes you
can arrange a van drop-off and pickup with
the concessionaire.

The serene Grosvenor River, the swifter
Savonoski River and a series of large lakes
connected by a portage form a circular
waterway of about 70 miles for canoeists and
kayakers. The wild and scenic Alagnak and
Nonvianuk rivers offer a good float trip to
the Kvichak River, which empties into Bristol Bay. (See River Running this section.)

Katmai's rugged wilderness offers rewarding experiences providing reasonable precautions are taken. Anyone planning backcountry hiking in Katmai should stop in King
Salmon to check in with park headquarters
before flying in to be dropped off. Cold winds
and icy waters pose great hazards. Carry extra
dry clothing. Read up on hypothermia and its
treatment. Be prepared to wait out storms:
carry matches, first-aid kit, and emergency
food. Rains or melting glaciers can make
stream crossings impassable. You need sneakers *and* hiking boots. Be extremely cautious
when crossing muddy waters. The Park Service also warns that firewood is limited and
asks that campers use stoves. At Brooks Camp
you can arrange in advance for meals at the
lodge. Otherwise, bring all food with you.

Limited camping and food supplies,
including white gas, and some fishing tackle
are sold at Brooks Lodge. Several commercial
operators are authorized to provide air taxi,
flightseeing, backpacking, canoe, and fishing
guide service. Write the park for a list.

Accommodations: There are hotels and
restaurants in King Salmon. Within Katmai
National Park, the park concessionaire, Kat-
mailand Inc. (243-5448), operates Brooks
Lodge, Kulik Lodge and Grosvenor Lodge.
Kulik Lodge on Kulik Lake, which accommodates 15 people, specializes in fishing, as
does Grosvenor Lodge on Grosvenor Lake,
which can accommodate 6. Other fishing
lodges in the area include Enchanted Lake
Lodge, Battle Lake Cabins, Nonvianuk Camp

and Katmai Lodge (206-337-0326) on the Alagnak River.

Most visitors will be visiting Brooks Camp, where Brooks Lodge, the Park Service campground, and a visitor center are located. Brooks Lodge consists of 15 4-berth cabins with hot water and private baths, and a central lodge which houses the restaurant, registration, a small store and tour services. Within walking distance of the lodge is the park visitor center, where nature talks and slide shows are presented. Books and guides are for sale at the visitor center, and there is a wildlife exhibit. The Park Service campground is located nearby. The campground has a kitchen shelter. Campsites must be reserved in advance with the Park Service and there is a 5-night maximum stay limit.

Because of limited accommodations, day trips to the park have become more popular.

Access: King Salmon is the transportation gateway to the park and preserve. There is daily jet service from Anchorage to King Salmon and commercial amphibious planes fly several trips a day to Brooks Camp in the park from June to September. Air charter service is available in King Salmon, Iliamna,

Kodiak and other towns, for access to other areas in the park from May to October. The park and preserve also is accessible by a 10-mile road from King Salmon to Lake Camp, on the western side of Naknek Lake, where there is a boat dock and ramp.

For more information: For informational leaflets on bear safety and other subjects, write the Superintendent, Katmai National Park and Preserve, P.O. Box 7, King Salmon, AK 99615; phone 246-3305, fax 246-4286. Related USGS Topographic maps: Katmai, Naknek, Iliamna.

Shuyak Island State Park

This 11,000-acre wilderness park created in 1984 is one of the newest in the state system. The park is located on the northwestern end of Shuyak Island, northernmost sizable island of the Kodiak Archipelago, and includes a number of smaller islands, rocks, passages and beaches. A section along the east side of the island has been proposed for a state game sanctuary. The middle of the island is Kodiak Island Borough land.

Shuyak Island is low — highest point is 660 feet — and mostly covered with a virgin

One of 4 cabins for rent in Shuyak Island State Park. The cabins come equipped with propane lights and wood stoves. (Bill Sherwonit)

forest of Sitka spruce, although there are open tundra areas. On clear days the volcanic peaks of the Alaska Peninsula across 30-mile-wide Shelikof Strait can be seen from the park.

Climate: Shuyak's climate is similar to Kodiak, where the average daily temperature in July is 54°F; in January, 30°F. Average annual precipitation at Kodiak is 54.52 inches. September, October and May are the wettest months, with each month averaging more than 6 inches of rain.

Wildlife: Seals, sea lions, brown bears, Sitka black-tailed deer, land otters, beavers and large numbers of sea otters may be seen on Shuyak Island. Birds, too, are abundant. Species that may be seen include a large number of bald eagles, gulls, cormorants, oystercatchers, guillemots, red-breasted mergansers, harlequin ducks, common and red-throated loons, horned and tufted puffins, eider ducks, terns, kittiwakes and scoters.

Pink and silver salmon spawn in the island's many streams; fishing for silvers is particularly good in August. Other sport fish include Dolly Varden. Halibut, crabs and clams also are available.

Activities: Hiking is good on the open tundra on the north and west sides of the island, where the ground cover is grass, lichens and low heath plants, such as crowberry, bearberry and blueberry. Flowers are everywhere during spring and summer. Small ponds and a few isolated spruce dot the tundra. Jaegers fly overhead searching for voles; deer browse on the heath and ducks raise their young in the ponds.

The virgin forest on Shuyak may be the last stand of pure Sitka spruce in Alaska; other coastal forests are generally a mixture of spruce, hemlock and sometimes cedar. The forested area is thick with devil's club, sometimes growing head high; hikers may find it easier to follow the deer and bear trails that lace the island.

Shuyak Island's convoluted coastline of protected bays, channels and lagoons offers safe cruising by canoe or kayak. Many of the bays are separated by short portages. Skiff Passage, a long, narrow channel, completely cuts through Shuyak park from north to south.

Accommodations: Four cabins are located in the park and are available through the Division of Parks and Outdoor Recreation. (See Cabins this section for details.) Camping is permitted. Minimum-impact camping should be practiced; all trash should be packed out. Boil or treat all drinking water.

Access: The park is easily reached by charter plane from either Kodiak or Homer, both of which have daily air service. From Kodiak it's a 45-minute flight; Homer is a little farther away. A suggested landing spot is Big Bay.

For more information or to reserve cabins contact: Alaska Dept. of Natural Resources, Division of Parks and Outdoor Recreation, Southcentral Region, P.O. Box 107001, Anchorage, AK 99510; phone 561-2020. Or, Division of Parks and Outdoor Recreation, Kodiak District, SR Box 3800, Kodiak, AK 99615; phone 486-6339, fax 486-3320.

Wildlife Refuges

Alaska Maritime National Wildlife Refuge

This refuge consists of more than 2,400 parcels of land on islands, islets, rock spires, reefs and headlands of Alaska coastal water from Port Franklin on the Chukchi Sea to Forrester Island in southeastern Alaska. The refuge totals about 3.5 million acres, most of which is in the Aleutian Islands Unit.

Nearly all of the more than 124 named islands in the Aleutians are included in the refuge. The Bering Sea Unit includes the Pribilofs, Hagemeister Island and St. Matthew Island. The Alaska Peninsula Unit includes Simeonof and Semidi Islands, the Shumagin Islands, Sutwik Island, islands and headlands of Puale Bay, and other lands south of the peninsula from Katmai National Park and Preserve to False Pass.

Wildlife: Alaska Maritime is synonymous with seabirds — millions of them. About 75 percent of Alaska's marine birds (40 million to 60 million birds among 38 species) use the refuge. The refuge has the most diverse wildlife species of all the refuges in Alaska, including thousands of sea lions, seals, walruses and sea otters.

Steller sea lions are listed as a threatened species. According to the Alaska Maritime National Wildlife Refuge, all sea lion rookeries west of 141° longitude — which includes the Gulf of Alaska — have a 3-nautical-mile buffer zone in which no vessels may operate. On land the buffer zone is one-half mile or within sight of a listed Steller sea lion rookery on Pye Islands, Barren Islands, Marmot Island, Semidi Islands, Shumagin Islands, Aleutian Islands and Walrus Island in the Pribilof Islands group.

Activities: Visitor activities in the refuge include wildlife observation, backpacking

THE BEARS AT McNEIL RIVER

The bears have always come first at Alaska's McNeil River State Game Sanctuary.

Created in 1967 by the Alaska Legislature and managed by the state's Department of Fish and Game, McNeil sanctuary — about 200 miles southwest of Anchorage — is intended to protect the world's largest gathering of bears.

The focal point of the gathering is McNeil Falls, where bears come to feed on chum salmon returning to spawn. During the peak of that July-August chum run, dozens of brown bears congregate. In 1988, biologists identified a record 84 individuals at the falls; including cubs, as many as 106 bears have been observed along the river in a single day.

Brown bears — the coastal equivalent of grizzlies — are by nature solitary creatures. For them to gather in such large numbers and in such close quarters is exceptional. That they do so while viewed by people is even more remarkable.

Regulations restricting human visitation to McNeil sanctuary during the prime-time bear-viewing period were enacted in 1973. Since then, no more than 10 people per day — always accompanied by 1 or 2 state biologists — have been allowed to visit bear-viewing sites during the permit period (which now runs from June 7 through August 25). Because demand is so high, the department conducts an annual drawing to determine permit winners.

That permit system has been highly successful. Since the state enacted its visitor restrictions the number of bears visiting the falls has increased dramatically. Even more significantly, no bears have been killed in defense-of-life-and-property situations and no humans have been injured by bears. This despite thousands of bear-human encounters, often at close range.

"It's widely assumed that bears and people don't mix," says Larry Aumiller, the sanctuary's manager since 1976. "But here we've shown that they can mix, if you do the right things. To me, that's the most important message of McNeil: humans can coexist with bears."

Peaceful coexistence is possible because of a simple fact: McNeil's bears are habituated to humans but view them as neutral objects. People do not pose a threat, nor are they a source of food.

To prevent any such association, feeding of bears is forbidden at McNeil (as it is throughout Alaska). Furthermore, a designated wood frame building is provided for food storage, cooking and eating. And a strict no bears allowed in camp policy is strictly enforced within a well-defined campground area.

Many visitors come to the sanctuary with irrational fears born of ignorance or sensationalized accounts of bear attacks. They carry the simplistic and inaccurate image of bears as dangerous creatures, unpredictable killers waiting to attack. McNeil helps to change such misconceptions. Visitors discover firsthand that bears aren't man-eating monsters as so often portrayed in literature and news accounts.

Nearly all visitors begin their McNeil experience in Homer, where they hop a float plane for the 1-hour flight across Cook Inlet. On arriving at McNeil, they're directed to a camping area 2 miles from the falls.

The campground is human turf. Bears are not allowed. But all sanctuary land beyond the campground is "the bear zone."

"Out there," Aumiller says, "bears have the right-of-way."

While bear viewing within the sanctuary begins in June at Mikfik Creek (a neighboring stream of McNeil River), McNeil Falls remains the primary focus in July and August. Located about a mile above McNeil River's mouth, the falls is actually a step-like series of small waterfalls, pools and whitewater rapids, stretched over 300 yards of the stream. Individual bears take up fishing positions based on their place in the ursine pecking order.

Prime spots are located along the western bank, opposite the viewing pads. Immediately below the upper falls, the most dominant bears — adult males, some weighing 1,000 lbs. or more — jockey for position.

Because bears are not normally social animals, there's often considerable tension among the animals feeding at McNeil Falls, especially when few salmon are available. Stress is signaled by heavy salivation, laid-back ears, body posture and deliberate movements. Rarely do encounters result in fights, however. Less dominant bears usually back away — slowly. The worst thing a bear (or human) can do is turn tail and run, since that will trigger an aggressive instinct in the more dominant bear.

McNeil's bears use a variety of techniques to fish for salmon. Some stand motionless in midstream or along the bank, patiently monitoring the stream. When a chum swims by, they pin it to the stream bottom with their paws, then bite into it. Others use snorkeling techniques, or dive for fish.

Although McNeil is most famous for the large number of bears that fish at the falls, humans who've been there have perhaps an even greater appreciation for the close look they get at members of *Ursus arctos*. It's not uncommon for the most tolerant bears to eat salmon, take naps or even nurse cubs within 10 feet of the falls' viewing pads.

—Bill Sherwonit is a freelance writer living in Anchorage.

and photography. Bird watching is popular on Attu Island, far out in the Aleutians, where Asian birds stop on their migrations.

The refuge provides a naturalist on board most summer sailings of the state ferry MV *Tustumena* between Homer, Kodiak, Seward and Dutch Harbor. The naturalist presents daily programs, including slide shows, and is available to help identify seabirds and marine mammals.

The refuge operates a visitor center at 509 Sterling Highway in Homer. The center features wildlife exhibits and films. It is open 10 A.M. to 6 P.M. daily, between Memorial Day and Labor Day.

Access: Most of the refuge is wild and lonely, extremely rugged and virtually inaccessible. Some portions are classified as wilderness. Swift tides, rough seas, high winds, rocky shorelines and poor anchorages hamper efforts to view wildlife. Some islands within the refuge have restricted access to protect wildlife. There is scheduled air service to Dutch Harbor and Cold Bay, which have hotels, restaurants and air charter operations. Military clearance is required to visit Adak, Shemya and Attu islands. In the Pribilof Islands, St. Paul and St. George have scheduled air service from Anchorage and locally guided tours of seabird rookeries and fur seal haul-out sites.

For more information: Contact Refuge Manager, Alaska Maritime National Wildlife Refuge, 509 Sterling Hwy., Homer, AK 99603; phone 235-6961, fax 235-7469. Or Alaska Maritime National Wildlife Refuge, Aleutian Islands Unit, PSC 486, Box 5251 (NAS), FPO, AP Adak, AK 96506-5251.

Alaska Peninsula National Wildlife Refuge

This 4.3-million-acre refuge on the Pacific side of the Alaska Peninsula extends southwest from Becharof National Wildlife Refuge to False Pass. Aniakchak National Monument and Preserve splits the refuge into 2 parts.

The refuge is one of the most scenically diverse, featuring active volcanoes, lakes, rivers, tundra and a beautiful stretch of rugged, rocky Pacific Ocean coastline. The Alaska Peninsula is dominated by the rugged Aleutian Range, part of a chain of volcanoes known as the "Ring of Fire" that encircles the Pacific Rim. Mount Veniaminof (elev. 8,224 feet) in the refuge is one of Alaska's active volcanoes, last erupting in June 1983. Other special features of the refuge are the

Ugashik lakes, renowned for trophy grayling fishing; Castle Cape Fjords, a famous landmark to ships with its distinctive light and dark rock layers; and the needle-pointed Aghileen Pinnacles and vertical buttresses of Cathedral Valley near recently active Pavlof Volcano.

Climate: This area is characterized by high winds, mild temperatures, cloud cover and frequent precipitation. Fog and drizzle are common in summer. Severe storms can occur year-round, often with intense winds, known as williwaws. Fall usually is the wettest season. July is the warmest month, with temperatures averaging 54°F. December is the coldest month, with temperatures averaging 12°F.

Wildlife: Besides bears, large mammals found in the refuge include moose, caribou, wolves and wolverines. The bears are especially attracted to the productive salmon streams. Large populations of sea lions, seals, sea otters and migratory whales inhabit the coastline and offshore waters. The population of sea otters on the Pacific side of the peninsula numbers at least 30,000. The entire refuge provides habitat for millions of birds — especially waterfowl — that use the area as a staging ground on their way to and from nesting grounds in the Arctic.

Activities: This refuge is renowned for big game hunting, especially for moose, caribou and brown bear. Fishing is outstanding for king and silver salmon, arctic char, lake trout, northern pike and grayling. A list of commercial guides holding permits to operate in the refuge is available from the refuge manager.

Access: The refuge is accessible by air or by boat. There is scheduled air service from Anchorage to King Salmon, Kodiak, Sand Point and Cold Bay, where small planes may be chartered to the refuge. There are no commercial facilities, roads or trails in the refuge; wilderness camping only.

For more information: Contact Refuge Manager, Alaska Peninsula/Becharof National Wildlife Refuges, P.O. Box 277, King Salmon, AK 99613; phone 246-3339. Trip planning assistance for the refuge is available at the King Salmon Visitor Center at the MarkAir building at King Salmon airport. Jointly operated by the USF&WS, the National Park Service and area boroughs, the center is open daily in summer (June to September) from 8 A.M. to 4:30 P.M. There is a staffed information desk, along with an audio-visual room with videos; phone 246-4250.

Becharof National Wildlife Refuge

This 1.2-million-acre refuge is located on the Alaska Peninsula, sandwiched between Katmai National Park and Preserve and the Alaska Peninsula National Wildlife Refuge. It is dominated by Becharof Lake, second-largest lake in Alaska, which covers a quarter of the refuge and is surrounded by low rolling hills, tundra wetlands in the northwest and volcanic peaks to the southeast. The lake area also includes abandoned Kanatak village and the Kanatak Portage trail that allowed people to traverse the Alaska Peninsula.

Climate: Becharof skies are usually cloudy. Less than 20 inches of precipitation falls annually in the western lowlands, while as much as 160 inches falls on the eastern side of the Aleutian Range. October is the wettest month. Temperatures in December, the coldest month, average 12°F. In July, the warmest month, they average 54°F. Vegetation does not begin growing until late May or early June and the first frost usually occurs in late September.

Wildlife: The salmon spawning streams attract a large concentration of brown bears, many of which make their dens on islands in Becharof Lake. Moose inhabit the refuge in moderate numbers and about 10,000 caribou migrate through and winter in the refuge. Other mammals include wolves, wolverines, river otters, red fox and beaver. In addition, thousands of sea mammals such as sea otters, sea lions, harbor seals and migratory whales inhabit the Pacific coastline. Waterfowl are common in the wetlands and coastal estuaries, while nesting eagles, peregrine falcons and thousands of seabirds inhabit the sea cliffs and islands. About 20 species of seabirds nest in 13 colonies in the refuge; 2 colonies in Puale Bay are among the largest on the Alaska Peninsula.

Activities: Becharof offers outstanding bear and caribou hunting. Sportfishing in the refuge so far has been light, although trophy-sized rainbow trout, arctic char, grayling and salmon exist. Write the refuge manager for a list of commercial guides holding permits for the refuge.

Access: The refuge is accessible by air or by boat. There is scheduled air service from Anchorage to King Salmon, Kodiak, Sand Point and Cold Bay, where small planes may be chartered to the refuge. There are no commercial facilities or roads in the refuge; wilderness camping only.

For more information: Contact the Refuge Manager, Alaska Peninsula/Becharof National Wildlife Refuges, P.O. Box 277, King Salmon, AK 99613; phone 246-3339. Trip planning assistance for the refuge is available at the King Salmon Visitor Center at the MarkAir building at King Salmon airport. Jointly operated by the USF&WS, the National Park Service and area boroughs, the center is open daily in summer (June to September) from 8 A.M. to 4:30 P.M. There is a staffed information desk, along with an audio-visual room with videos; phone 246-4250.

Izembek National Wildlife Refuge

One of the older national refuges in the state, Izembek is located at the tip of the Alaska Peninsula just across False Pass from Unimak Island, first in the Aleutian chain. It faces the Bering Sea and abuts the Alaska Peninsula National Wildlife Refuge. The 315,000-acre Izembek Unit of the refuge encompasses the entire Izembek Lagoon watershed. (The Izembek refuge office also administers the 415,000-acre Pavlof Unit of the Alaska Peninsula National Wildlife Refuge, and the 932,000-acre Unimak Unit of the Alaska Maritime National Wildlife Refuge.)

Izembek's landscape consists primarily of low brush tundra, alder thickets, willow patches, and numerous lakes and marshes. Lowland vegetation gives way to barren scree, snowfields and glaciers. The main feature of the refuge is Izembek Lagoon, protected by barrier islands from the Bering Sea. The lagoon falls under state ownership and is itself a state game refuge.

Climate: Izembek summers are characterized by fog, drizzle and cloud cover, but they can vary from year to year. Severe storms may occur year-round, often accompanied by intense winds. The average annual precipitation is about 35 inches, with most occurring in fall. Temperatures range from an average of 28°F in February to 51°F in August. Vegetation usually starts growing in late May or early June; the first frost usually occurs in October or November.

Wildlife: This lagoon, along with several smaller lagoons, hosts up to 300,000 geese, 150,000 ducks and nearly all of the world's population of black brant (120,000 to 150,000 birds) during the fall migration. These birds feed on Izembek Lagoon's 84,000-acre eelgrass bed, one of the largest in the world. Most waterfowl arrive in the refuge in late August or early September. By early November a second wave of northern waterfowl (primarily sea ducks) arrives to winter at Izembek. The colorful Steller's eider, which nests on the Arctic coast of Alaska and Siberia, is the most common wintering duck. In addition, thousands of shorebirds feed on the bay shore at low tide. At high tide they gather in such large flocks that in flight they look like smoke clouds.

Other wildlife includes brown bear, caribou, ptarmigan and furbearers. Fish in the refuge include 4 species of salmon, Dolly Varden, arctic char and steelhead trout. Sea lions, sea otters, harbor seals and gray, killer and minke whales are seen in bays and lagoons.

The refuge office can provide lists of mammals and fish present on the refuge.

Activities: Goose and duck hunting is at its peak from late September to late October. Popular areas, according to the refuge office, include the Izembek Lagoon shoreline and islands (especially for brant) and the wetlands within a few miles of the lagoon (for Canada geese). There are no commercial guides offering waterfowl hunting trips.

A guide is required for nonresident brown bear hunters participating in the annual spring and fall Unimak Unit brown bear hunt (available through drawing permit system). Brown bear hunting is available on the Izembek and Pavlof units on an alternate spring-even-year and fall-odd-year schedule. Caribou hunting is available only to local residents for subsistence purposes.

Fishing for red and pink salmon is best in June and July. Silver salmon are present from August to early October.

Hunters and fishermen can access the shorelines of Izembek Lagoon and Cold Bay, Russell Creek and the lower flanks of Frosty Peak from the Cold Bay road system. There are no designated trails, but there are unimproved trails used by hunters and wildlife observers at various locations on the Izembek Unit.

Primitive camping is allowed on the refuge at no charge. Campers must provide all of their own equipment. Trip planning assistance is available through the refuge office.

Bird watching is also popular on the refuge, with October offering the best goose and duck viewing. Other species of birds are present at various times of the year. The refuge office can provide a bird list and bird finding guide.

Access: The refuge boundary is less than a mile from refuge headquarters in Cold Bay and is accessible by a road system. Vehicles may be rented in Cold Bay. Motorized travel off the roads in the refuge is prohibited. Cold Bay is reached by scheduled air service from Anchorage and has food and lodging facilities. Aircraft are not permitted to land in the refuge; however, they can land adjacent to the refuge below the mean high tide line. The area around Moffet Point, at the north end of the refuge, is popular for landing aircraft.

The Alaska Marine Highway vessel MV *Tustumena* serves Cold Bay from Kodiak monthly between May and September. The Cold Bay-Dutch Harbor trip is recommended for its excellent seabird viewing.

For more information: Contact Refuge Manager, Izembek National Wildlife Refuge, P.O. Box 127, Cold Bay, AK 99571; phone 532-2445, fax 532-2549.

Kodiak National Wildlife Refuge

This refuge encompasses 1.9 million acres on Kodiak, Uganik, Afognak and Ban islands — all part of the Kodiak Archipelago. The city of Kodiak is some 250 air miles from Anchorage and about 21 miles northeast of the refuge boundary. Kodiak is accessible by commercial jet and the Alaska Marine Highway System. The refuge is larger than the state of Delaware, but because of its convoluted coastline, no place on the island is more than 15 miles from the sea.

The refuge's varied landscapes include glacially carved valleys, tundra uplands, lakes, wetlands, sand and gravel beaches, salt flats, meadows and rugged mountains to 4,000 feet. Spruce forests dominate the northern part of Kodiak Island and all of the Afognak Island portion of the refuge. The interior of the refuge is covered with dense vegetation in summer. Sedges and fireweed to 6 feet are often mixed with salmonberry, blueberry and rose bushes. Dense thickets of willow, alder and elderberry abound. Devil's club, with thorns that can penetrate leather, grows up to 6 feet high in the woods and on the slopes. The heathland in the southwest portion of the refuge is covered with hummocks — small knolls of grass and soil that make walking difficult.

Climate: The climate is mild and wet. Winter temperatures average between 24°F and 36°F and rarely fall below zero. Summer days average between 48°F and 60°F. The island has an average annual precipitation of 54 inches, including 75 inches of snow. The sky is completely overcast about half the time. Despite mild temperatures, the weather

and winds are unpredictable and change abruptly. Climatic conditions change within short distances because of the varied terrain. The weather can make flying conditions hazardous and flights often are delayed for days.

Visitors should be equipped with plenty of warm clothes, rain gear and appropriate footwear. Bring extra food and other supplies in case weather prolongs your stay. Use only dead or downed wood, and carry a camp stove. Trash must be burned or packed out. Take precautions against unwanted encounters with bears, especially along salmon-spawning streams in midsummer. Do not leave food uncovered in camp; make noise while hiking to alert bears of your presence.

Wildlife: This refuge was originally established in 1941 to protect the habitat of the huge Kodiak brown bear and other wildlife. The brown bear remains the refuge's most well-known feature, attracting visitors from all over the world. The refuge supports the highest density of brown bears in the world. The 3 largest brown bears ever taken and 33 of the 50 largest in the Boone and Crockett North American records are from Kodiak Island. Females weigh about 650 pounds; larger males up to 1,500 pounds.

Besides the bears, there are only 5 other native land mammals in Kodiak refuge: red fox, river otter, short-tailed weasel, little brown bat and tundra vole. Several other species, including Sitka black-tailed deer, elk and beaver, have been introduced. Whales, porpoises, sea otters and sea lions are found in bays.

More than 210 species of birds have been seen on the archipelago. At least 200 pairs of bald eagles nest in the refuge. An estimated 2 million seabirds winter in the refuge's bays and inlets, and at least 200,000 waterfowl also winter along shorelines.

The refuge's 11 large lakes and many rivers are major spawning grounds for king, red, silver, pink and chum salmon. The various species spawn from June through August and begin to decrease in numbers in September, although a few silver salmon continue to spawn until December. Steelhead, rainbow trout and Dolly Varden also are found in refuge waters.

Activities: Predominant activities in the refuge are hunting, fishing, photography and trapping. Other activities are hiking, wildlife viewing, beachcombing, berry picking and clamming.

Accommodations: There are motels and campgrounds in Kodiak. Wilderness camping is allowed throughout the refuge without advance reservations, permits or fees. There are 9 public-use cabins in the refuge which may be reserved in advance (see Cabins this section). A visitor center located in Kodiak provides orientation for anyone traveling to the refuge. The visitor center is open year-round 8 A.M. to 4:30 P.M. Monday to Friday and noon to 4:30 P.M. Saturday and Sunday.

Access: Kodiak Refuge is roadless and reached most easily by chartered floatplane or boat from the city of Kodiak. Hovercraft and off-road vehicles are not permitted on refuge lands. Helicopter access is restricted to special use permit holders and is not permitted for recreational users. Recreational airboats are not permitted.

For more information: Contact Refuge Manager, Kodiak National Wildlife Refuge, 1390 Buskin River Road, Kodiak, AK 99615; phone 487-2600, fax 487-2144.

McNeil River State Game Sanctuary

McNeil River is located approximately 200 air miles southwest of Anchorage and 100 air miles west of Homer. The river drains into Kamishak Bay in the shadow of Augustine Island, an active volcano with a history of violent eruptions, the most recent in March of 1986. McNeil River is bordered to the south and west by Katmai National Park and Preserve.

The McNeil River State Game Sanctuary draws photographers from all over the world, attracted by the large numbers of brown bears that congregate in the summer to feast on spawning chum salmon. The greatest numbers may be seen at the McNeil River falls, about 1 mile up from the river mouth. As many as 60 bears at a time have been observed fishing for chum salmon during the peak of the season. (See *The Bears At McNeil River* this section.)

In order to reduce disturbance of the bears and minimize the risk of human-bear encounters, the Alaska Dept. of Fish and Game allows visitors to the sanctuary by permit only. A special bear-viewing permit is required during the peak season June 7 through Aug. 25. A Fish and Game employee is stationed at the camp to escort visitors to the falls each day. No more than 10 permit holders per day are allowed to visit the falls during peak season; permittees are selected

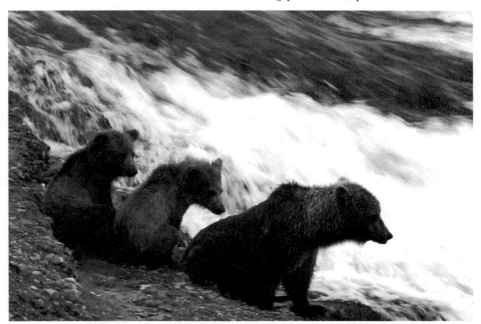

A sow and cubs at McNeil River falls. Large numbers of bears congregate here for the summer salmon run. (Bill Sherwonit)

KODIAK NATIONAL WILDLIFE REFUGE CABINS

	SLEEPS	AIR ACCESS	BOAT ACCESS	TRAIL ACCESS	HUNTING	FISHING	BEACHCOMB	SKIFF	STOVE
NORTHWEST KODIAK ISLAND									
Chief Cove	4	•	•		•	•	•		O
Little River *(Closed Dec. 1 to March 31)*	4	•			•	•			O
Uganik Lake *(Closed Dec. 1 to March 31)*	4	•			•	•	•		O
Viekoda Bay *(Clamming at minus tide)*	4	•	•		•	•	•		O
SOUTHWEST KODIAK ISLAND									
North Frazer Lake *(Closed Dec. 1 to March 31)*	4	•			•	•			O
O'Malley *(Closed Dec. 1 to March 31)*	4	•			•	•			O
Red Lake *(Closed Dec. 1 to March 31)*	4	•			•	•			O
South Frazer Lake *(Closed Dec. 1 to March 31)*	4	•			•	•			O
Uganik Island	4	•	•		•	•	•		O

The above chart gives a brief description of each cabin. Type of stove provided is oil (O) for heating only.

by a lottery drawing held March 15. The Dept. of Fish and Game receives about 2,000 applications for the roughly 280 permits available. Up to 3 people may be listed on one application. An application fee of $20 per name must accompany the application. The deadline for applications is March 1. Application forms are available at Alaska Dept. of Fish and Game offices in Anchorage, Fairbanks, Homer, Juneau, King Salmon and Soldotna.

Winners of the computer-generated lottery must pay a user fee: $100 for Alaska residents, $250 for nonresidents. The user fee helps defray the cost of operating the sanctuary visitor program.

Access to the sanctuary is usually by private or charter floatplane from Anchorage, Kenai or Homer, landing at high tide.

Visitors to McNeil River must be self-sufficient and prepared for a wilderness experience. There are no visitor facilities. Equipment and clothing must be adequate to withstand cold, wind and rain. Bring camping gear, rain gear, hip boots (you have to wade through water over knee-deep to reach the falls) and lots of film. Carry extra food in case bad weather prolongs your stay for several days. It also is recommended that photographers bring a packboard or packsack to carry camera equipment.

For more information and application forms, contact the Alaska Dept. of Fish and Game, Wildlife Conservation Division, 333 Raspberry Road, Anchorage, AK 99518; phone 267-2180.

Cabins

Kodiak National Wildlife Refuge Cabins

Kodiak National Wildlife Refuge maintains 9 recreational cabins available to the public by advance reservation (see chart). Cabins may be reserved for up to 7 days per year. Drawings for reservations take place Jan. 2 for April, May and June; April 1 for July, August and September; July 1 for October, November and December; and Oct. 1 for January, February and March. Cabins not reserved during the drawing are available on a first-come basis. Mail applications with choice of dates (including second choices if desired) to the refuge office. Fee for the cabins is $10 per night, due only after successful applicants have been notified.

All cabins have oil heating stoves. You must provide oil or kerosene for oil stoves; 5 gallons is usually sufficient for 1 week in mild weather. All cabins have pit toilets. No utensils or cook stoves are provided.

For a cabin pamphlet or reservation application contact: Refuge Manager, Kodiak National Wildlife Refuge, 1390 Buskin River Road, Kodiak, AK 99615; phone 487-2600, fax 487-2144.

Shuyak Island State Park Cabins

Alaska State Parks maintains 4 recreational public-use cabins on Shuyak Island, 2 on Big Bay, 1 on Carry Inlet and 1 on Neketa Bay. All are accessible by floatplane or boat, although floatplane is usually more practical.

The cabins can be rented for up to 7 days at a time with a maximum of 8 people per cabin. Rates are $25 per person per night to a maximum of $50 per night from June 1 to November 30; $15 per person per night to a maximum of $30 per night from December 1 to May 31. The fee is waived for children 15 years or younger if the child's name and date of birth are listed on the application.

The cabins are 12 feet by 20 feet and are equipped with wood stoves, propane lights and hot plate, 4 full-sized bunks with pads, manual shower and wash area, stainless steel sink, cooking utensils, and pit toilets.

Bring maps of the island, compass, first-aid kit, matches, rope, rain gear, garbage bags for packing out all garbage, sleeping bag, individual eating utensils and extra clothes and food in case bad weather prolongs your stay.

Anyone who is at least 18 years of age may apply for a cabin permit. Applications may be made in writing up to 180 days before the requested time. Reservations are accepted on a first-come basis and must be accompanied by a check.

Obtain additional information or make cabin reservations through Alaska State Parks, Kodiak District Office, SR Box 3800, Kodiak, AK 99615, phone 486-6339, fax 486-3320; or Dept. of Natural Resources, Public Information Center (PIC), 3601 C St., Suite 200, P.O. Box 107005, Anchorage, AK 99510-7005, phone 762-2261, fax 762-2236.

River Running

Alagnak and **Nonvianuk rivers.** (Part of the Kvichak watershed, Bristol Bay Wild Trout Area.) The 80-mile-long Alagnak River and its 11-mile tributary, the Nonvianuk, both originate within Katmai National Preserve. The Nonvianuk and the first 67 miles of the Alagnak were included in the National Wild and Scenic Rivers System in 1980. The Alagnak originates in Kukaklek Lake, then flows west-southwest to join the Kvichak River, which empties into Bristol Bay. Either the main branch or the Nonvianuk, which heads in Nonvianuk Lake, offers excellent boating.

The Alagnak leaves Kukaklek Lake at a moderate speed (3 to 4 mph), but quickly picks up speed (7 to 8 mph) as it drops through a canyon where there are 2 sets of Class III rapids, neither of which can be easily portaged because of extremely steep canyon walls. Below the canyon the river slows, braids and then becomes a broad channel (2 to 3 mph) as it empties into the Kvichak.

The Nonvianuk offers a leisurely float in its entirety, with some Class II rapids possible 4 to 5 miles from its origin during low water periods. High water season is during May, June and the first part of July. Inflatable rafts are recommended for the main branch; on the Nonvianuk rafts, kayaks and canoes are all suitable. The average trip takes approximately 4 to 5 days if just floating, 5 to 6 days if floating and fishing.

These rivers offer good fishing seasonally for all 5 species of salmon (especially sockeye), Dolly Varden, rainbow and lake trout, grayling and pike in side sloughs and lakes. Floaters also have a good chance of seeing brown bear, moose, wolf, red fox, wolverine, beaver, river otter and lynx. A variety of birds including bald eagles, osprey, ptarmigan, spruce grouse, swans and game ducks are readily observed. Hunting is allowed in the preserve in season.

Access to the river system is by scheduled air service from Anchorage to King Salmon, then by chartered floatplane to Kukaklek or Nonvianuk Lake, about 60 miles to the northeast. Exit is usually by floatplane from the lower 30 miles of the Kvichak, before the tidal influence in the last 10 miles. Trip planning assistance and information on the Alagnak is available from the Katmai National Park office in King Salmon (P.O. Box 7, King Salmon, AK 99615; phone 246-3305, fax 246-4286). Related USGS Topographic maps: Iliamna A-7, A-8; Dillingham A-1, A-2 and A-3.

Aniakchak River. The 32-mile-long Aniakchak River is unique in that it heads in a freshwater lake inside the caldera of an active volcano, which last erupted in 1931. The river, located entirely within Aniakchak National Monument, was included in the National Wild and Scenic Rivers System in 1980.

The river starts slowly from Surprise Lake and speeds up as it flows through a narrow

1,500-foot-high opening in the caldera wall called The Gates. The river is shallow and rocky, Class III to IV, and has low falls as it drops 70 feet per mile for the first 13 miles. Then the river meanders slowly, Class II to I, through flatlands to Aniakchak Bay on the Pacific Ocean side of the Alaska Peninsula. Inflatable rafts are recommended because of numerous, closely spaced boulders. The trip from Surprise Lake to Aniakchak Bay generally takes 3 days.

The number of groups on the river is increasing and 15 operators hold commercial use licenses for services in Aniakchak.

The caldera is scenic, featuring 2,000-foot walls, cinder cones and other volcanic wonders. There is good hiking in the monument. Fish available in the river include salmon, arctic char, Dolly Varden and rainbow trout. Wildlife that may be observed includes caribou, moose, brown bears, wolves, river otters, wolverines, sea otters, harbor seals, sea lions, bald eagles, waterfowl and shorebirds.

Weather in this area is generally miserable, with much rain, cold temperatures and high winds, especially through The Gates. (See cautionary notes in the section on Aniakchak National Monument.) Bad weather may delay put-in or takeout; floaters should be equipped with extra food and supplies. There is a shelter cabin on the north side of the mouth of the Aniakchak River where parties can wait for pickup.

Access to Aniakchak River is by chartered floatplane from King Salmon or Port Heiden to Surprise Lake. Exit is generally by floatplane from Aniakchak Bay; the bay often is too rough for floatplanes, but small, wheeled planes can land on the beach. Related USGS Topographic maps: Chignik D-1, Sutwik Island D-5, D-6.

Karluk River. This river heads in Karluk Lake on the west coast of Kodiak Island and flows north and west 24 miles through Karluk Lagoon to Shelikof Strait at the village of Karluk. This is a Class I river, but a portage is necessary around a fish weir about 1 mile up from Karluk Lagoon.

This is a very popular river for king, red and silver salmon, Dolly Varden and rainbow trout in season. *NOTE: Land along the Karluk River as well as the riverbed is owned by Koniag Inc., and the village corporations of Karluk and Larsen Bay. There is a $50 per-person/per day fee for fishing or camping on the Karluk River. Permits may be obtained from Koniag Inc., 201 Kashevarof, Suite 6, Kodiak, AK 99615; phone 486-4147. Canoes, kayaks,* *or rafts are suitable for this river. The trip takes 2 to 5 days.*

Access is by floatplane from Kodiak to Karluk Lake or to Larsen Bay, from where a 2-mile trail leads to the river. Access also by scheduled air service to Larsen Bay village. Exit is via the portage trail to Larsen Bay, or from Karluk village via charter or scheduled air service. Related USGS Topographic maps: Karluk B-1, C-1 and C-2.

Katmai Lakes. A series of large lakes and the Grosvenor and Savonoski rivers in Katmai National Park afford a circular trip of about 70 miles for kayakers and canoeists. This trip generally starts at Brooks Camp on Naknek Lake, then skirts the shore of Naknek Lake to the Bay of Islands, where there is a 1-mile portage to Grosvenor Lake. The portage begins at an old log cabin (available for public use on a first-come basis), then leads to a small lake which can either be paddled across or walked around on its eastern shore (do not take an obvious trail to the right as it will take you back to the Bay of Islands). After paddling the length of Lake Grosvenor, you'll enter the 3-mile, flat-water Grosvenor River which joins the Savonoski River, a braided, fairly slow glacial stream which will take you 12 miles to Iliuk Arm. Stay on the south shore of Iliuk Arm as the north shore is steep with few places to pull out in case of bad weather. Iliuk Arm joins Naknek Lake just a few miles from Brooks Camp.

These are very large lakes and easterly or westerly winds can quickly cause choppy water. Staying close to shore is highly recommended. Also, be aware that this is prime brown bear country; camping along the Savonoski River from mid-July to September is not recommended because large numbers of bears will be feeding on spawning salmon. A backcountry permit is required for this trip and can be obtained from the National Park Service in King Salmon or Brooks Camp. The trip, starting and finishing at Brooks Camp, generally takes 5 to 7 days.

This trip offers good fishing for sockeye salmon, rainbow and lake trout. Brush makes hiking difficult, except along the lake shores. Bear, moose, red fox, wolf, lynx, wolverine, river otter, mink, marten, weasel and beaver may be seen. Lake edges and marshes are nesting sites for whistling swans, ducks, loons, grebes and arctic terns.

Access to the lakes is by scheduled air service from Anchorage to King Salmon, then a scheduled flight or charter floatplane to Brooks Camp or Grosvenor Camp. Also, there is a road from King Salmon to Lake Camp at the west end of Naknek Lake. (See also Katmai National Park and Preserve this section.) Related USGS Topographic maps: Mount Katmai B-5, C-4 through C-6.

King Salmon River. This is a slow (1 to 2 mph), silty river flowing westward about 60 miles across a soggy, tundra-covered coastal plain to Egegik Bay. (Not to be confused with the King Salmon River farther south which flows into Ugashik Bay.) This river's headwaters are in Katmai National Park and it flows partially through Becharof National Wildlife Refuge. Raft, kayak and canoe are all suitable for this river. There can be strong upstream winds and tidal influences on the lower river. Stay in the far left channel of the King Salmon and Egegik rivers to reach the village of Egegik on Egegik Bay at low tide.

There is good scenery at the headwaters and observation of wildlife is good in season. King, sockeye and chum salmon are plentiful and rainbow trout, Dolly Varden and grayling also are present. Brown bears and Canada geese are abundant, caribou and moose also may be seen. The area is popular for big game sport hunting.

Access is by wheel or floatplane from King Salmon to a lake near the head of Gertrude Creek or to headwater gravel bars outside Katmai National Park. Exit is generally from the village of Egegik, which is served by commercial air service from King Salmon. Related USGS Topographic maps: Katmai A-6, Naknek A-1, A-2, A-4, A-5, B-2 to B-4.

Sea Kayaking

Kodiak Island. Kodiak's rocky, irregular coastline makes for miles and miles of fine sea kayaking opportunities. But precautions should be taken. The weather can change abruptly, and changing wind direction and tidal currents can make paddling a tricky business at best. Perhaps the prime area for ocean kayaking on Kodiak is Shuyak Island State Park, located on the northernmost sizable island of the Kodiak Archipelago. The inner coast, a maze of narrow, interconnected bays, inlets and passages, offers protected paddling for kayakers. Many of the bays are separated by short portages. Skiff Passage, a long, narrow channel, completely cuts through Shuyak park from north to south. Attractions include abundant wildlife and spectacular coastlines.

Access is by air charter from Homer or Kodiak. (See Shuyak Island State Park this section for more information.)

Sportfishing

This region offers some of the finest sportfishing in the world. Probably the most prized sport fish are the trophy-sized rainbow trout. Rainbows in this area regularly attain 10 pounds. All of Southwestern Alaska is part of the state's Wild Trout Area. Special regulations, designed to perpetuate the original wild rainbow trout stocks, apply here as do special management areas for catch-and-release and fly-fishing only.

Tackle-breaking king salmon are at their best from mid-June through July on the Alaska Peninsula. These fish are not uncommon at 30 pounds and up. Kodiak Island's Karluk River has one of the best king salmon runs in the world, with kings weighing more than 60 pounds. Chums and reds show up by July 1, pinks by mid-July (in even-numbered years) and silvers by mid-August. Salmon fishing is concentrated in the river systems.

Arctic char and Dolly Varden are found

A lake trout taken from Lake Grosvenor in the Naknek River System. (George Wuerthner)

throughout the region and are most abundant either in spring, when some migrate to the sea, or in midsummer, when large schools concentrate at river mouths to feed on outmigrating juvenile salmon.

Cloudy skies and light rain are common here. Bring warm clothing, rain gear and hip boots. Also be sure to bring lots of insect repellent. It's recommended that you purchase your fishing license in Anchorage. For more information about fishing on the Alaska Peninsula, contact: Area Management Biologist, Alaska Dept. of Fish and Game, P.O. Box 230, Dillingham, AK 99576; phone 842-2427. For the Kodiak area contact the Alaska Dept. of Fish and Game, Sport Fish Division, 333 Raspberry Road, Anchorage, AK 99518, phone 267-2218, or Alaska Dept. of Fish and Game, 211 Mission Road, Kodiak, AK 99615, phone 486-4791.

Afognak Island. Located approximately 30 air miles northeast of Kodiak, Afognak Island streams offer excellent remote fishing. Accommodations at Afognak Wilderness Lodge; phone 486-6442. This is brown bear country; try to avoid bears, make noise when traveling and carry a .30-06, or larger, rifle. Part of Afognak Island is within Kodiak National Wildlife Refuge and part is owned by Koniag Native Corp. **Afognak River** and **Afognak Lake** provide good fishing for Dolly Varden 10 to 20 inches, abundant most of the summer; red salmon peak runs in early June; silver salmon September best; pink salmon July and August; steelhead October and November; rainbow trout 10 to 16 inches, in the upper river June 15 to September. Steelhead and rainbow trout fishery is closed April 1 to June 14. This 6-mile-long lake is 32 air miles from Kodiak.

Other fishing waters on Afognak Island are: **Waterfall Lake**, 40 air miles from Kodiak, excellent fishing for Dolly Varden to 20 inches; **Pillar Lake**, small Dolly Varden; **Portage Lake**, 35 air miles north of Kodiak, **Malina Lake**, 36 air miles northwest of Kodiak, and **Laura and Pauls lakes**, 40 air miles northeast of Kodiak, all yield red salmon, silver salmon, Dolly Varden and rainbow trout. Portage, Malina and Laura lakes also yield pink salmon and steelhead.

Akalura Lake. Measures 2.5 miles across, located in the Kodiak Island National Wildlife Refuge approximately 80 air miles southwest of Kodiak, 3 miles north of Olga Bay. Access by floatplane from Kodiak. Fish available: rainbow trout best June 15 to

Fishermen at the mouth of Naknek Lake in Katmai National Park. (Loren Taft)

September, use flies, lures or bait, closed April 1 to June 14; small numbers of steelhead September to November, use spoons or eggs, closed April 1 to June 14; Dolly Varden May to October, best May and September, use bait, spinners or flies; silver salmon good mid-August through September, use herring or spoons; red salmon June to July, use spoons or flies; pink salmon July to August, use small spoons.

Alagnak River System. Located at the top of the Alaska Peninsula partially in Katmai National Preserve. Also within the state's Wild Trout Area; check the regulation book for special rules. The Alagnak River drains Battle and Kukaklek lakes and flows into Kvichak Bay. The Nonvianuk River, a tributary of the Alagnak, drains Kulik and Nonvianuk lakes. This drainage offers excellent fishing for 5 species of salmon. Excellent rainbow trout fishery; use unbaited, single-hook artificial flies June 8 through Oct. 31. Also available are grayling; arctic char, use spoons; northern pike, use spoons and spinners; and lake trout, use spoons and plugs. Air charter service available from Anchorage, Kenai, Homer, King Salmon, Dillingham and Iliamna.

Ayakulik (Red) River. Located in Kodiak National Wildlife Refuge approximately 85 air miles southwest of Kodiak. Fish available: rainbow trout season closed April 1 to June 14, best after June 15, use flies, lures or bait; steelhead good at lake outlet in late September and early October, use spoons or eggs; Dolly Varden May to October, best May and September, use bait, spinners or flies; king salmon, 15 to 40 pounds, best early June at mouth to mid-July in central river areas, use herring or spoons; silver salmon September through October, use herring or spoons; red salmon June to July, use spoons or flies; pink salmon July to August, use small spoons.

Barabara Lake. Located 21 air miles west of Kodiak within Kodiak Island National Wildlife Refuge. Access by floatplane from Kodiak. Fish available: small numbers of rainbow trout best after June 15, use flies, lures or bait, closed April 1 to June 14; Dolly Varden May to October, use bait, spinners or flies; red salmon June to July, use spoons or flies; silver salmon September through October, use herring or spoons.

Buskin River. Located a few miles south of Kodiak by road within Kodiak Island National Wildlife Refuge. The only roadside stream with a significant run of sockeye salmon, in June. King salmon June through

August, coho in August and September, pink salmon in August. Dolly Varden all year, best during May, September and October migrations; use spoons, spinners, eggs and flies. Rainbow, steelhead and chum salmon also available.

Egegik River System. Located approximately 40 miles south of King Salmon, partially within Becharof National Wildlife Refuge. Egegik River drains Becharof Lake and empties into Egegik Bay, as does one of the King Salmon rivers (the other one is in the Ugashik system farther south). Five species of salmon are found in this drainage; sockeyes spawn in Becharof Lake. Other fish present are grayling, use flies; arctic char, use spoons and eggs; northern pike, use spoons and spinners; and lake trout, use spoons and plugs. Air charter service available in King Salmon.

Karluk Lake, River and Lagoon. Located approximately 75 air miles southwest of Kodiak. Fish available: rainbow trout season closed April 1 to June 14, use flies, lures or bait; steelhead from 25 to 35 inches, best in October, use spoons or eggs, closed April 1 to June 14; Dolly Varden best in May and September, use bait, spinners or flies; excellent sockeye fishing with 2 runs of red salmon running strong in June and August and tapering off by mid-September, use spoons or flies; pink salmon best in July and early August, use small spoons; silver salmon plentiful late August through October, use herring or spoons; excellent for king salmon 10 to 40 pounds, early June (Karluk and Ayakulik Rivers), peak runs mid-June to the end of June, use herring or spoons. *NOTE: Land along the Karluk River as well as the riverbed is owned by Koniag Inc., and the village corporations of Karluk and Larsen Bay. Permits for fishing or camping on the Karluk River may be obtained from Koniag Inc., 201 Kashevarof, Suite 6, Kodiak, AK 99615; phone 486-4147.*

Kodiak Island saltwater. Halibut, rockfish, flounder and other marine fish are caught in Kodiak Archipelago waters throughout the year, although offshore fishing is best in summer. Pacific halibut commonly found in immediate offshore waters in late May or early June. Most halibut are taken off Long and Woody islands. Boat-caught halibut up to 50 to 100 pounds, averaging 15 pounds; use cut herring or large shiny lures near kelp beds. Other fish: Dolly Varden along rocky beaches from June through July, use herring strips and small- to medium-sized lures; pink salmon late June to mid-August, best from mid-July on, use small spoons; chum salmon 8 to 15 pounds arrive late July through early August, use spoons; silver salmon mid-August to November, use herring or spoons.

Lake Miam. A 1-mile-long lake on the east coast of Kodiak Island, a 15- to 20-minute flight by small plane from Kodiak. Fish available: small numbers of rainbow trout, season closed April 1 to June 14, use flies, lures or bait; small numbers of steelhead September to November, use spoons or eggs; Dolly Varden May to October, best May and September, use bait, spinners or flies; silver salmon September through October, use herring or spoons; red salmon June to July, use spoons or flies; pink salmon July to August, use small spoons.

Naknek River System. The Naknek system extends from the town of Naknek, adjacent to King Salmon, upstream approximately 75 miles to the east. Much of the system is in Katmai National Park and is subject to additional federal regulations. The Naknek River drains Naknek Lake, Brooks Lake, Lake Colville and Lake Grosvenor; its outlet is Kvichak Bay, a good fishing location for those operating on a restricted budget. King salmon fishing excellent on the Naknek River at King Salmon, where boats can be rented. Naknek Lake accessible by road from King Salmon. This drainage offers good fishing for 5 species of salmon. Excellent rainbow trout fishery. Also available are grayling, arctic char, northern pike, lake trout and whitefish. Smelt are available in winter. Outlying lakes served by air charter planes from King Salmon. Several commercial fishing lodges in the area.

Pasagshak River. Accessible by road from Kodiak, this stream supports the largest road accessible run of coho, beginning in August and continuing through September; coho average 10 to 12 pounds, use eggs, lures or flies. Sea-run Dolly Varden in mid-April, use flies or lures. King, sockeye and pink salmon also present.

Saltery Lake and River. Located 36 miles southwest of Kodiak via a 15- to 20-minute air charter from Kodiak. Fish available: rainbow trout 9 to 14 inches, present in small numbers most of the summer, use flies, lures or bait; small numbers of steelhead, closed April 1 to June 14, October through November, use spoons or eggs; Dolly Varden 10 to 18 inches abundant in May, August and September, use bait, spin-

ners or flies; silver salmon excellent late August through mid-October, use spoons; red salmon abundant in July, use spoons or flies; pink salmon abundant in mid-July to August, use small spoons.

Uganik Lake and River. Located 36 air miles southwest of Kodiak in Kodiak National Wildlife Refuge. Fish available: rainbow trout, season closed April 1 to June 14, best after June 15, use flies, lures or bait; steelhead September to November, use spoons or eggs; Dolly Varden May to October, best May and September, use bait, spinners or flies; silver salmon September through October, use herring or spoons; red salmon June to July, use spoons or flies; pink salmon July to August, use small spoons.

Ugashik System. Located approximately 80 miles south of King Salmon; Ugashik lakes are within Alaska Peninsula National Wildlife Refuge. The Ugashik River drains Upper and Lower Ugashik lakes and flows into Ugashik Bay, as does the King Salmon River, which drains Mother Goose Lake and the glacier-fed Dog Salmon River. Five species of salmon are found in this drainage; sockeyes spawn in the Ugashik lakes. The grayling fishery is closed in the Ugashik drainage due to conservation problems with that stock. Other fish present are arctic char, use spoons and eggs; northern pike, use spoons and spinners; and lake trout, use spoons and plugs. Air charter service available in King Salmon or Pilot Point.

Upper Station lakes. Located approximately 90 air miles southwest of Kodiak in Kodiak National Wildlife Refuge. Fish available: rainbow trout, season closed April 1 to June 14, best after June 15, use flies, lures or bait; small numbers of steelhead September to November, use spoons or eggs; Dolly Varden May to October, best May and September, use bait, spinners or flies; silver salmon September through October, use herring or spoons; red salmon June to July, use spoons or flies; pink salmon July to August, use small spoons.

Woody and Long Island lakes. Located 2 to 4 miles east of Kodiak. Accessible by small plane or boat. Good camping, hiking, picnicking and beachcombing. Fish available: rainbow trout year-round, best after June 15 and October, use flies, lures or bait; Dolly Varden May to October, best May and September, use bait, spinners or flies; silver salmon September through October, use spoons; grayling in Long Lake year-round, use flies.

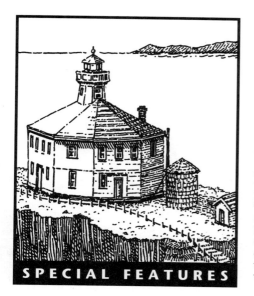

SPECIAL FEATURES

Anangula

Dating back at least 8,000 years, Anangula is the oldest known settlement in the Aleut world. This site is located on now-uninhabited Anangula (Ananiuliak) Island at the northern end of Samalga Pass off Nikolski village. Thousands of stone artifacts have been found at Anangula that link this culture to those of northern and central Asia, particularly the Kamchatka Peninsula. The fate of those who lived at Anangula is in question, however, as the site appears to have been occupied less than a century when a heavy cover of volcanic ash rained down from Okmok Volcano, probably killing local plants and animals on which the people depended. The 4,000-year gap between settlement here and evidence man again lived in the area appears to correspond to a period of volcanism.

Lighthouses

Cape Sarichef Light Station. This is the most westerly lighthouse in North America, located in the Aleutian Chain on the northwest side of Unimak Island overlooking Unimak Pass. Cape Sarichef began operating July 1, 1904. Construction crews reinforced the structures and the station was relighted in 1950. Now automated, the station serves as a National Weather Service forecasting center.

Scotch Cap Light Station. The first to be built on the outside coast of Alaska, Scotch Cap Light Station is the second most westerly lighthouse in North America and the most southerly in Alaska. The station is a monument also to many ship disasters, before and after its establishment. It was automated in 1971. The station began operation July 18, 1903. Partly because of the hazardous duty, each of Scotch Cap's 3 keepers received a year's vacation every 4 years. On April 1, 1946, an earthquake that registered 7.4 on the Richter Scale occurred southwest of Unimak Island, generating a 100-foot tsunami that swamped Scotch Cap and killed all 5 Coastguardsmen at the station. The wave crossed the Pacific Ocean and hit the north side of the Hawaiian Islands, killing 159 people. It then continued to Chile, rebounded and hit the southern side of Hawaii, causing what is rated as Hawaii's worst natural disaster ever because it hit with no warning.

Pribilof Islands

In 1786, when Russians searching for fur seals first encountered this isolated island group 200 miles out in the Bering Sea, they stumbled upon some of the continent's grandest wildlife spectacles. St. Paul and St. George islands claim North America's largest northern fur seal and seabird colonies, a wildlife extravaganza that still draws visitors to this remote corner of Alaska.

Archaeological records reveal no signs of habitation of the Pribilofs prior to their occupancy by Russian fur hunters who imported Aleuts from Unalaska and Atka and founded the island group's 2 communities, St. Paul and St. George.

From 1867, when the United States purchased Alaska, to 1909 the government contracted with private companies to harvest the fur seals. From 1910 federal officials managed the sealing operations, and the residents of the Pribilof Islands were treated as wards of the government.

During WWII, the entire population of the Pribilof Islands was evacuated and restricted to an abandoned cannery and mining camp at Funter Bay in southeastern Alaska. In 1983 the Pribilof people were given full control of their islands, and in 1987 they celebrated their bicentennial.

Although the fur seal industry has dominated the islands' economy in the past, it has been replaced by a growing fisheries industry and tourism. Subsistence centers around fur seal harvesting and fishing, especially for halibut.

(For more details on St. George and St. Paul, see Communities in this section.)

Unga Island Petrified Forest

Although the Aleutians are one of the most extensive treeless zones in the world, there is much evidence that trees thrived here before the ice ages. Some 150 acres of beach on the northwest coast of Unga Island, located west of Sand Point, contain black, yellow and gray petrified stumps measuring 2 to 4 feet in diameter. Petrified wood also is found on Amchitka and Atka islands. Unga's forest, experts claim, rivals those of national parks in the Lower 48. The rock stumps are the remains of metasequoia trees, thought to be an ancestor of the redwood trees of the western United States. Scientists estimate they lived 11 million to 25 million years ago, encouraged by the warm humidity of the Miocene period. These are angiosperms rather than gymnosperms (cone-bearing evergreens), which are the trees that do well today in the Aleutians, having been transplanted to sheltered areas at Unalaska, Atka,

Adak, Unga, Akutan and Squaw Harbor. Access to the Unga Island petrified forest is via charter plane or boat from Sand Point.

World War II Military Sites

Several sites in the Aleutians relating to WWII have been designated national historic landmarks including the following:

Adak Island, Adak Army Base and Adak Naval Operating Base. The bases have been nominated to the National Register of Historic Places. Adak, one of the Andreanof Islands in the Aleutian chain, is about 1,400 air miles southwest of Anchorage.

The island was unoccupied at the outbreak of WWII. Alaska's largest and most expensive wartime base of operations was established after the Japanese bombings of Unalaska and Dutch Harbor and the invasion of Attu and Kiska islands in June 1942. The need for an advance base farther west than Unalaska and Umnak islands became urgent and Adak was selected because of its all weather harbor. The first airstrip was built on Adak in 12 days and on Sept. 14, 1942, the first Liberators flew from Adak to bomb Japanese forces on Kiska. Permanent airfields later were built and Adak served as

Fur seal on St. Paul Island. The Pribilofs boast the largest northern fur seal and seabird colonies in North America. (Loren Taft)

the command post for the invasions of Attu and Kiska in 1943. Adak continued to serve as an active base throughout the war. In 1950, the Army Air Force turned it over to the Navy. Today, Adak Naval Air Station, located on the WWII site, occupies the northern half of the island; the southern half is part of the Alaska Maritime National Wildlife Refuge. As with many of the other islands that played a major role in WWII, Adak is littered with military Quonset huts and other buildings and relics. Adak is a restricted military installation not open to casual visitors or tourists.

Amaknak Island, Dutch Harbor Naval Operating Base and Fort Mears. At the time of the Dec. 7, 1941, Japanese attack on Pearl Harbor in Hawaii, these, along with top-secret Fort Glenn on nearby Umnak Island, were the only U.S. defense facilities in the Aleutians. Shortly after Pearl Harbor, a naval base was constructed at Unalaska. Some 60,000 men were stationed at Dutch Harbor/Unalaska, which was the target of Japanese bombing on June 3 and 4, 1942, in conjunction with the Battle of Midway. Much of the military installations remained at Dutch Harbor and Unalaska until June 1985, when a clean-up program began. Many of the old buildings are now gone, although old machine gun nests, barbed wire, trenches and bomb shelters will remain for years to come. The remains of the bombed-out ship *Northwestern*, which had been used for barracks, still lie partially submerged at the head of Captain's Bay, a short drive from town. Unalaska is accessible by commercial air service from Anchorage.

Attu Island, Attu Battlefield and the U.S. Army and Navy airfields. Site of the only WWII battle fought on the North American continent, Attu Island is at the western end of the Aleutian chain, 1,500 air miles southwest of Anchorage, 500 miles east of the USSR mainland.

The Japanese occupation of Attu and Kiska took place in June 1942, coordinated with the Battle of Midway. Attu was held for nearly a year before American troops invaded. During the bitterly fought, 19-day battle, most of the 2,500 Japanese troops were killed, many during a banzai attack out of the hills. Only 29 Japanese survived. U.S. casualties were heavy, too. Of 15,000 troops, 550 were killed, 1,500 wounded and another 1,200 disabled by Attu's harsh climate. During the remaining years of the war, the United States flew bombing raids on Japan from Attu. Today, there is much evidence of

the desperate battle on Attu's eastern end: thousands of shell and bomb craters in the tundra, Japanese trenches, foxholes and gun emplacements. American ammunition magazines and dumps and spent cartridges, shrapnel and shells are found at the scenes of heavy fighting. The steel-matted runways at Alexai Field and the asphalt runways at the U.S. Naval Air Station exist, the latter still operational. Portions of deteriorating piers stand at Massacre Bay. Roads may still be traced, but only 5 miles are maintained.

The only occupants today are a few U.S. Coast Guardsmen who operate a long-range navigation (loran) station. The Aleut village of Attu, whose residents had been captured and taken to Japan, was destroyed during the battle and no trace remains. The entire island is part of the Alaska Maritime National Wildlife Refuge, administered by the U.S. Fish and Wildlife Service. For information about Attu contact: Refuge Manager, Aleutian Islands Unit, Alaska Maritime National Wildlife Refuge, PSC 486, Box 5251, (NAS), FPO, AP Adak, AK 96506-5251.

Kiska Island, Japanese Occupation Site. Japanese withdrew from Kiska after the United States reclaimed Attu. Kiska, one of the Rat Islands group near the western end of the Aleutian chain, is 165 miles southeast of Attu.

On June 7, 1942, a Japanese task force invaded Attu and Kiska, overrunning a U.S. weather station on Kiska and constructing coastal and antiaircraft defenses, camps, roads, an airfield, submarine base, seaplane base and other installations. The occupation marked the peak of Japan's military expansion in the Pacific and caused great alarm in North America that a Japanese invasion would be mounted through Alaska. As Allied forces prepared to invade Kiska, 5,183 Japanese were secretly evacuated in less than an hour under cover of fog on July 28, 1943. On Aug. 15, 34,000 U.S. and Canadian troops invaded a deserted island. The Allies subsequently established their own camps. Kiska was abandoned after the war, but relics from Japanese and U.S. camps still litter the countryside.

Today Kiska is unoccupied and is part of Alaska Maritime National Wildlife Refuge. For information about access restrictions contact: Refuge Manager, Alaska Maritime National Wildlife Refuge, 202 Pioneer Ave., Homer, AK 99603; phone 235-6546. Or contact: Alaska Maritime National Wildlife Refuge, Aleutian Islands Unit, PSC 486, Box 5251, (NAS), FPO, AP Adak, AK 96506-5251.

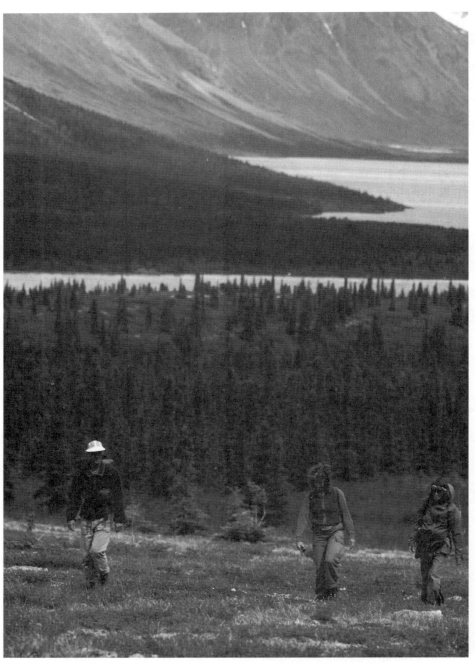

Hikers explore the foothills above Twin Lakes in Lake Clark National Park and Preserve.
(Bill Sherwonit)

WESTERN

Western Alaska encompasses fish-rich bays, an immense river delta, and the rugged Bering Sea coast and its offshore islands. Fishing and gold mining have lured outsiders to this Yup'ik Eskimo world, where many of the traditional ways are still followed.

Russians were the first visitors to enter the Eskimo world along the Bering Sea coast in the early 1800s. They explored along the coasts and established trading posts. Late in the century, after the United States purchased Alaska, missionaries, prospectors, traders and fishermen came to the region.

Today, mining and fishing stir the region's economy with commercial and transportation centers at Nome, Bethel, Naknek and Dillingham.

Residents of the region depend on salmon, including the great Bristol Bay sockeye run and a substantial fishery in the Yukon and Kuskokwim rivers, where species include grayling, trout, Dolly Varden, pike, arctic char, burbot and whitefish. In the Bering Sea, several species of shellfish and bottom fish feed a commercial and subsistence market.

Minerals have greatly influenced the region's economy. A gold rush led to the founding of Nome, and prospectors were some of the earliest settlers. The western region has led the state in gold production for several years. Near Goodnews Bay lies an important platinum deposit. The western Seward Peninsula has substantial tin deposits, while the Red Devil area near the delta contains mercury deposits.

Location: Western Alaska extends from the Arctic Circle south along the Bering Sea coast, across the top of the Alaska Peninsula to west Cook Inlet. It encompasses St. Lawrence Island, St. Matthew and Hall islands, Nunivak Island, the Yukon-Kuskokwim Delta and the Seward Peninsula.

This huge area is divided into 3 subregions: Bristol Bay, Yukon-Kuskokwim Delta and Seward Peninsula/Norton Sound. The text on Western Alaska's communities and attractions is divided according to these subregions.

Geography: South of the Arctic Circle, the Seward Peninsula reaches 200 miles west toward Asia. Cape Prince of Wales at the peninsula's tip points toward Little Diomede Island, about 25 miles offshore and 3 miles from the Soviet Union's Big Diomede Island. The international boundary and date line run between the islands. Norton Sound, a 125-mile finger of the Bering Sea, separates Seward Peninsula from the Yukon-Kuskokwim Delta, a wetland that stretches 250 miles south to Kuskokwim Bay and 200 miles inland.

Tundra carpets much of the region, where grasses, sedges, mosses, lichens and wildflowers grow beneath scrub willow and alder. Forests, which cover eastern Seward Peninsula and Norton Sound, give way to wetland tundra on the delta, then pick up again near Bristol Bay.

The Ahklun Mountains border the delta's flatlands on the south and separate them from Bristol Bay. The bay is renowned for its fishing, particularly the world's largest sockeye salmon run. The bay spans 200 miles from its base at Port Moller on the Alaska Peninsula to its northwest boundary at Cape Newenham, and stretches northeastward nearly the same distance to the mouths of the Nushagak and Kvichak rivers which drain its inland reaches.

The Nushagak and Kvichak are 2 of several major rivers in the region. The longest river in the region — and one of the most important — is the Yukon. These rivers, along with the Kuskokwim and Unalakleet, provide access for fish heading for spawning grounds and are the traditional route for inland travel.

Climate: The climate varies throughout the region, with temperatures ranging from the low 40s to low 60s in summer, and from -5°F to the low 20s in winter in the north. Farther south the weather moderates a bit. Highs in the 30s and lows around 0°F occur in winter; summers average from the mid-30s to mid-60s. Wind chill is an important factor in this region where few topographical features break its sweep across the land. Total annual precipitation is about 20 inches. The northern regions are drier than southern ones.

North of Bristol Bay rain and snow fall more frequently on the coast than farther inland. Near the bay the opposite is true.

Wildlife: Numerous big species make their home in mountainous areas of the region including bears, moose, caribou, wolves and Dall sheep. Musk-oxen, once hunted to near extinction in Alaska, were reintroduced to Nunivak Island in the 1930s and now thrive there and on the Seward Peninsula. Reindeer, introduced from Siberia just before the 20th century, roamed much of the Bering Sea Coast region but are now confined to the Seward Peninsula and Nunivak Island.

The Yukon-Kuskowkim Delta lacks suitable shelter for large mammals, but small furbearers such as foxes, muskrats, beaver, otters and weasels find the area a haven. Offshore pass bowhead, gray, killer and beluga whales, sea lions, fur seals, and several species of true seals.

The delta is also a breeding ground for millions of shorebirds and waterfowl. Seabirds crowd cliffs along the mainland coast and on offshore islands.

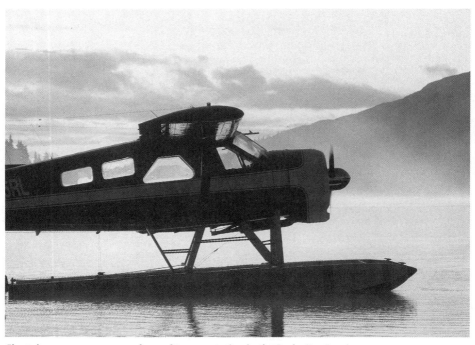

Floatplanes are a necessary form of transportation in the Bush. (Joe Prax)

BRISTOL BAY

World-class sportfishing and beautiful, remote rivers, perfect for floating, lure visitors from all over the world to Bristol Bay, known for its valuable commercial fishing and salmon processing industry. At the west end are the Kvichak River (which drains Lake Iliamna), the Nushagak, the Alagnak and the Naknek River, which drains Naknek Lake on the Alaska Peninsula (the Bristol Bay Borough encompasses Naknek, South Naknek and King Salmon). Farther east are the Yuyukuk, Tikchik, Wood and Togiak rivers. All offer fine floating and excellent fishing.

Just to stand on a riverbank and watch salmon swim by can be the experience of a lifetime. Each summer millions of salmon enter the drainages on the way to their spawning grounds. Anglers wanting to catch a particular species of salmon should time their trip carefully to coincide with the height of the run. In general, king salmon arrive first, in June, followed by red and chum, then pink and finally silvers, which can be fished in some areas through late September.

Freshwater fish include rainbow trout, grayling, char, Dolly Varden, lake trout and northern pike. These are available throughout the season, though timing and location are again important. (See Sportfishing in Attractions this region.)

The Kvichak-Alagnak watershed, except Lake Clark and its tributaries above Six-Mile Lake, has been designated a Wild Trout Area with fishing restrictions established to protect and perpetuate the high-quality wild rainbow trout fisheries and provide anglers a variety of fishing experiences. Anglers looking for arctic char might try the Wood River lakes chain in late May and June. The Nushagak is a favorite king salmon river, while the Togiak is known for its silvers. Information provided by fishing lodges and wilderness guides will help dedicated anglers plan their trip, and the Alaska Dept. of Fish and Game is also a helpful source of information.

Bristol Bay is bear country, and anglers should take special precautions. The very rivers, lakes and streams best for fishing are also the likeliest places to encounter bears, who also come to search for salmon. Make noise when traveling through tall brush: clap your hands, talk loudly, bang pots together, wear a bear bell on your day pack. Keep a clean camp; and Alaska Dept. of Fish and Game advises that you consider carrying a suitable firearm.

The Bristol Bay region is known for its sportfishing as well as its commercial salmon fishery. (Joe Prax)

Aleknagik

[MAP 12] *(a-LECK-nuh-gik)* Located where Wood River flows out of Lake Aleknagik, 25 miles north of Dillingham, 330 miles west of Anchorage. **Transportation:** Scheduled air service, car or taxi from Dillingham. **Population:** 182. **Zip code:** 99555. **Emergency Services:** Police, phone 842-5953; Clinic, phone 842-5512; Volunteer Fire Department.

Elevation: 70 feet. **Climate:** Cloudy skies, mild temperatures and moderately heavy precipitation. Annual precipitation ranges from 20 to 35 inches, with most occurring during the summer. Two-foot snowpack on ground in winter.

Private Aircraft: Airport 1 mile east; elev. 66 feet; length 2,100 feet; gravel; unattended. Fuel 80, 100 available. Condition not monitored, visual inspection recommended prior to use. Aleknagik Mission Lodge airstrip, private, adjacent northeast; elev. 150 feet; length 1,200 feet; silt and gravel; unattended. Unusable during winter months.

Visitor Facilities: No hotels or motels. Wilderness lodges in the area include Aleknagik Mission Lodge (842-2250). Groceries and hardware may be purchased locally. Arts and crafts for sale at Aleknagik Native Store. Hunting and fishing licenses not available. Guide service available. Marine engine, boat and car repair service available. Fuel available: marine gas, diesel and regular; Moody's Marina (842-5988).

The few early settlers in Aleknagik nearly all died in the influenza epidemic of 1918–19. Resettlement occurred around 1928, when a small Seventh-Day Adventist colony was established on the shores of Lake Aleknagik near the area now known as Mosquito Point. The settlement grew as former residents who survived the epidemic started drifting back and a school, churches and a small sawmill were established. There is an influx of people during summer when families return to summer homes for the fishing season.

Residents live by subsistence hunting for moose and caribou, and commercial fishing, mainly for salmon. Grayling and Dolly Varden are also harvested. Many varieties of berries are found in the area, although a local resident blames too many 3- and 4-wheelers for a diminishing berry crop. Many women in the community still practice traditional arts and crafts, such as basket weaving and skin sewing.

A scenic, 25-mile dirt road connects Aleknagik with Dillingham. The community is also the gateway to Wood-Tikchik State Park. Fishing in the park and surrounding watersheds is excellent with 5 species of salmon, char, grayling, northern pike, rainbow trout and Dolly Varden available.

Aleknagik is a second-class city, incorporated in 1973. Communications include phones, mail plane, radio and TV. The community is served by Seventh-Day Adventist, Russian Orthodox and Moravian churches, and a school with grades 1 through 8. Public electricity is available. Water is obtained from private wells or hauled from Aleknagik Lake. Freight arrives by air transport, barge or truck. Government address: City of Aleknagik, P.O. Box 33, Aleknagik, AK 99555; phone 842-5953, fax 842-2107. Village corporation address: Aleknagik Natives Ltd., P.O. Box 1630, Dillingham, AK 99576.

Clark's Point

[MAP 12] Located on a spit on the northeastern shore of Nushagak Bay, 15 miles south of Dillingham and 350 miles southwest of Anchorage. **Transportation:** Scheduled air service from Dillingham. **Population:** 83. **Zip code:** 99569. **Emergency Services:** Police, phone 842-5943; Clinic; Volunteer Fire Department.

Climate: Cloudy skies, mild temperatures and moderately heavy precipitation, with frequent strong surface winds. Average summer temperatures of 37°F to 66°F; winter temperatures from 4°F to 30°F. Annual precipitation from 20 to 26 inches, with most of the precipitation occurring in July and August.

Private Aircraft: Airstrip adjacent north; elev. 10 feet; length 2,700 feet; gravel; unattended. Runway condition not monitored; visual inspection recommended prior to landing. Watch for birds on runway and pedestrians and vehicles on west end. No fuel or airport facilities.

Visitor Facilities: None. Community store available with limited selection of items.

Settled in 1888, when Nushagak Packing Co. established a cannery there, the village was named for John W. Clark. He was manager of the Alaska Commercial Co. store at Nushagak, and was reputed to have operated a saltery on the spit prior to establishment of the cannery. The cannery closed and reopened several times during the years and shut down permanently in 1952. Since that time Alaska Packers Assoc. has operated the facility as a headquarters for its fishing fleet. A major flood occurred in 1929. Plagued by erosion and threat of floods, the village has since been relocated to higher ground.

The village, incorporated in 1971 as a second-class city, is a "designated anchorage" for scows, floaters and fishing boats working the bay during the summer fishing season. Commercial fishing is the primary base of the economy, and residents depend on subsistence activities for food sources.

Communications include phones, mail plane, radio and TV. The community has a Catholic church and a school with grades kindergarten through 12. Community water, sewer, electricity. Freight is transported by air transport and skiffs from Dillingham. Government address: Clark's Point, P.O. Box 7, Clark's Point, AK 99569; phone 842-5943. Village corporation address: Saguyak Inc., General Delivery, Clark's Point, AK 99569.

Dillingham

[MAP 12] Located on the south side of Snag Point at the confluence of the Wood and Nushagak rivers at the north end of Nushagak Bay, 175 miles southeast of Bethel, 320 miles west of Anchorage. **Transportation:** Scheduled airline from Anchorage. **Population:** 2,153. **Zip Code:** 99576. **Emergency Services:** Police and fire, emergency only, phone 911; Alaska State Troopers, phone 842-5641; Kanakanak Hospital, phone 842-5201; Fire Department, phone 842-2288.

Elevation: 80 feet. **Climate:** Transitional climate zone, affected primarily by the waters of Bristol Bay, but also by the arctic climate of the Interior. Cloudy skies, mild temperatures and fairly heavy precipitation. There are often strong winds. Heavy fog occurs often in July and August. Mean annual precipitation 25 inches, with 71 inches of snow.

Private Aircraft: Airport 2 miles west; elev. 85 feet; length 6,400 feet; asphalt, grooved; fuel 80, 100 and jet A; attended Monday to Friday. Airport has passenger and freight terminals, ticket counters, restrooms and traffic control tower. Public transportation to town available.

Visitor Facilities: Hotel accommodations at The Bristol Inn & Cannery Restaurant (842-2240 or 842-2222), Dillingham Hotel and Lake Road Cottage. Area wilderness lodges include Crystal Creek Lodge (842-2646) and Royal Coachman Lodge. Visitor center, open summers. Meals available at lodging facilities and at several restaurants. Laundromat, dry cleaners (alterations) and banking services available. Supplies available at several grocery and general mercantile stores, as well as specialty shops. Arts and crafts available for purchase include grass baskets, carved ivory, Eskimo dolls, masks, skin sewing and Eskimo yo-yos. Fishing/hunting licenses available, as well as guide services. Repair services available for marine engines, boats, autos and aircraft. Fuel available includes marine gas, white gas, diesel, propane, unleaded and regular gasoline. Moorage facilities available.

The area around Dillingham was long inhabited by various Eskimo and Indian groups. In 1818, Alexander Baranof, first governor of Russian America, ordered construction of a permanent post at the mouth of the Nushagak River. The post came to be known as Alexandrovski Redoubt and drew people from the Kuskokwim region, Cook Inlet and the Alaska Peninsula. The community was called Nushagak by 1837 when a Russian Orthodox mission was established there. In 1881 the U.S. Signal Corps established a meteorological station at Nushagak and in 1884 the first salmon cannery in the Bristol Bay region was constructed by the Arctic Packing Co. Two more canneries were established in the next 2 years, the second one at the present city of Dillingham, then known as Snag Point. In 1903, U.S. Sen. William Paul Dillingham of Vermont toured through Alaska with his subcommittee. The town was named after the senator in 1904.

Dillingham is a first-class city, incorporated in 1963.

Dillingham is the economic and transportation hub of the Bristol Bay region. Northbound cargo ships unload supplies for area villages at the Dillingham dock. The city-run dock handles 10,000 tons of freight and fish annually. The city also maintains a harbor serving more than 500 boats. The economy is augmented by commercial fishing, the cannery, trapping and tourism. An annual event, the Beaver Roundup, occurs each March. Bristol Bay is the world's largest producer of red salmon.

The Dillingham Heritage Museum (Pouch 202, Dillingham, AK 99576; phone 842-5610 or 842-5521) is an ethno-history museum featuring contemporary and traditional Alaskan arts, crafts and artifacts. The Yup'ik Eskimo culture of southwestern Alaska is represented in basketry, carving, skin sewing and dolls. The museum also hosts traveling exhibits from around the state. The museum shares a building with the public library. Hours are from noon to 6 P.M. Monday and Tuesday and Thursday through Saturday; 5-9 P.M. on Wednesday. No admission charge; donations accepted.

Numerous sportfishing lodges are located near Dillingham. There is a 25-mile road connecting the town with the Eskimo village of Aleknagik, located on Lake Aleknagik near Wood-Tikchik State Park, largest state park in the United States. The park also is accessible by floatplane from Dillingham.

In addition to salmon, trout, grayling and arctic char are the main species of fish caught in the area. There is hunting for brown bear, moose and caribou in the area and trapping for wolf, wolverine, fox, lynx, marten and beaver. Float trips down the Nushagak or Wood River systems are popular. (See River Running in the Attractions section.)

Much land in the Dillingham area is owned by the local Native corporation, Choggiung Ltd., which requires that a permit be obtained for any public use of its lands.

Communications in Dillingham include phones, radio, TV and 2 newspapers. The community is served by 8 churches, a public library, 3 public schools, a private school and a community college. There are community electricity, water and sewer. Freight arrives by cargo plane, barge and ship. Government address: City of Dillingham, P.O. Box 889, Dillingham, AK 99576; phone 842-5211. Village corporation address: Chog-giung Ltd., P.O. Box 889, Dillingham, AK 99576; Chamber of Commerce, City of Dillingham, P.O. Box 294, Dillingham, AK 99576.

Ekuk

[MAP 12] *(E-kek)* Located on the east shore of Nushagak Bay, 16 miles south of Dillingham and 340 miles west of Anchorage. **Transportation:** Small commercial and scheduled air service from Dillingham. **Population:** 2. **Zip code:** 99576. **Emergency Services:** Alaska State Troopers and health service at Dillingham.

Climate: Cloudy skies, mild temperatures and moderately heavy precipitation; subjected to strong surface winds, fog during winter months. Average summer temperatures from 37°F to 66°F; average winter temperatures from 4°F to 30°F. Annual precipitation from 20 to 26 inches, with most of the precipitation occurring in the summer months.

Private Aircraft: Private airstrip adjacent south; elev. 30 feet; lenth 1,200 feet; gravel and dirt; unattended. Runway not maintained during winter months; soft when wet. No fuel or airport facilities.

Visitor Facilities: None.

Ekuk, mentioned in Russian accounts of 1824 and 1828 (in the latter referred to as Village Ekouk and Seleniye Ikuk), was thought to be a major Eskimo village in prehistoric and early historic times. In Eskimo Ekuk means "the last village down," being the farthest village south of Nushagak Bay. St. Nicholas Chapel, a Russian Orthodox church in the village dating from 1917, is on the National Register of Historic Places. A cannery was opened in 1903 which drew many people to the area. Floods, erosion and lack of a school caused residents to leave.

Most local Ekuk residents maintain summer homes in the village for the commercial fishing season, which is the predominant activity in the village during the summer months, according to a spokesperson for Choggiung Ltd., the local Native corporation. The cannery employs and houses several hundred people during its peak activity time between May and August.

Fishing includes all species of salmon, as well as freshwater fish found nearby. The area supports a large and diverse population of small mammals and an abundance of birds.

Much of the land in the Ekuk area is owned by Choggiung Ltd., which requires that a permit be obtained for any use of its lands.

Communications in Ekuk, which is unincorporated, include phones, mail plane, radio and TV. Electricity and water supplied by individual generators and wells. Sewage system is honey buckets and outhouses. Freight arrives by air transport or barge. Village corporation address: Choggiung Ltd., P.O. Box 330, Dillingham, AK 99576; phone 842-5218, fax 842-5462.

Ekwok

[MAP 12] *(EK-wok)* Located on the Nushagak River, 48 miles east of Dillingham, 290 miles west of Anchorage. **Transportation:** Boat; snow machine; scheduled and charter air service from Dillingham. **Population:** 110. **Zip code:** 99580. **Emergency Services:** Village Public Safety Officer, phone 464-3326; Alaska State Troopers, phone 246-3346; Clinic, phone 464-3322; Volunteer Fire Department.

Elevation: 130 feet. **Climate:** Transition zone primarily maritime, also influenced by colder Interior weather. Cloudy skies, mild temperatures, fairly heavy precipitation and strong winds. Average summer temperatures from 30°F to 66°F; average winter temperatures from 4°F to 30°F. Annual precipitation from 20 to 35 inches, most of which occurs during summer. Fog and low clouds also in summer.

Private Aircraft: Airstrip adjacent south, elev. 130 feet; length 2,700 feet; gravel and dirt; no fuel; unattended. Runway condition not monitored; visual inspection recommended prior to using. Runway has 240-foot overrun at each end. No airport facilities or public transportation.

Visitor Facilities: Arrangements can be made to stay at private homes. No restaurant, banking services or laundromat. Groceries, clothing, first-aid supplies and sporting goods can be purchased in the community. Fishing/hunting licenses available. Arts and crafts available for sale include beaver hats, mukluks and ulus. Guide services available. No repair service. Rental transportation includes boats, charter aircraft and off-road vehicles. Fuel available includes diesel, regular and unleaded gasoline. No moorage facilities.

Ekwok is the oldest continuously occupied village on Nushagak River. Approximately 100 years ago the settlement was first used in spring and summer as a fish camp, and then in the fall as a base for berry picking. The village was reputed to be the largest settlement along the river by 1923. In 1930 the Bureau of Indian Affairs established a school there, and mail service began the same year. Ekwok is a second-class city, incorporated in 1974.

The main source of income for the village is commercial fishing, but most residents fish for subsistence purposes. A few residents trap beaver, mink, wolverine, otter, red fox and marten. Ekwok's entire population depends heavily on subsistence. Species commonly harvested include salmon, pike, Dolly Varden, char, duck, moose and caribou. Villagers pick blackberries, blueberries, salmonberries and highbush cranberries. Some of the women grow vegetable gardens. Ekwok residents exchange subsistence items with coastal communities.

A sportfishing lodge 2 miles downriver from Ekwok is owned by the village corporation and operates in summer only. It features modern accommodations and fishing for salmon, grayling, char, rainbow trout and pike. Near the lodge are the remains of several old sod houses used by previous Native residents of the area.

Communications in Ekwok include phones (village phone, 464-8001), mail plane, radio and TV. The community is served by 2 churches and a school with grades kindergarten through 8. Many residents celebrate Russian Orthodox holidays. Community electricity, water and sewer are available. Freight arrives by plane, barge and fishing boats. Government address: City of Ekwok, P.O. Box 49, Ekwok, AK 99580; phone 464-3311, fax 464-3328. Village corporation address: Ekwok Natives Ltd., P.O. Box 10064, Dillingham, AK 99576.

Igiugig

[MAP 12] *(ig-ee-AH-gig)* Located in the Western Cook Inlet area on the south shore of the Kvichak River at the southwest end of Lake Iliamna, 50 miles southwest of Iliamna and 50 miles northeast of King Salmon. **Transportation:** Scheduled air service from King Salmon. **Population:** 32. **Zip code:** 99613. **Emergency Services:** Health Aide.

Climate: Average summer temperatures from 42°F to 62°F; average winter temperatures from 6°F to 30°F. Total precipitation averages 26 inches annually, with an average snowfall of 64 inches.

Private Aircraft: Airstrip adjacent south; elev. 110 feet; length 2,700 feet; dirt and gravel; unattended. No airport facilities.

Visitor Facilities: Some supplies are available in the community. Accommodations available by advance reservation at several area fishing lodges, such as Igiugig Lodge (533-3216). Guide service for fishing; tackle is available for purchase. No other services available.

Igiugig began as a fishing village. Kiatagmuit Eskimos populated the village at the turn of the century. St. Nicholas Chapel, a Russian Orthodox church located in the village, is on the National Register of Historic Places. Igiugig is unincorporated.

Salmon fishing is the mainstay of Igiugig's economy. Some residents are employed in the community. During the red salmon season in late June and July, many leave the village to fish in Bristol Bay. In summer, sportfishing is popular in the Kvichak River-Lake Iliamna area. *NOTE: Contact Igiugig Native Corp. regarding land use fees before hunting, fishing or cutting wood.*

Communications include phones, mail plane, radio and TV. The community is served by old and new Russian Orthodox churches, and a school with grades 1 through 12. There are community electric and water systems. Residents use privies and honey buckets. Freight arrives in the village by air transport or barge. Native corporation address: Igiugig Natives Corp., P.O. Box 4009, Igiugig, AK 99613. Village council address: Igiugig Village Council, P.O. Box 4008, Igiugig, AK 99613.

Iliamna

[MAP 12] *(ill-ee-YAHM-nuh)* Located in the Western Cook Inlet area on the north side of Lake Iliamna, 17 miles from Nondalton, 187 miles east-northeast of Dillingham, 225 miles southwest of Anchorage. **Transportation:** Boat; scheduled or charter air service from King Salmon, Dillingham and Anchorage. **Population:** 119. **Zip code:** 99606. **Emergency Services:** Alaska State Troopers, phone 571-1236; Health Aide, phone 571-1386; Clinic, phone 571-1383; Volunteer Fire Department, phone 571-1246 or 571-1376.

Elevation: 190 feet. **Climate:** Transitional zone, with strong maritime influences. Average summer temperatures from 42°F to 62°F; average winter temperatures from 6°F to 30°F. Mean annual precipitation 26 inches; mean annual snowfall 61 inches.

Private Aircraft: Airport 3 miles west; elev. 207 feet; length 4,800 feet; gravel; fuel 100, jet A; attended on request. Runway

soft when wet. Airport facilities include ticket counter, restrooms and traffic control tower. Public transportation to town.

Visitor Facilities: Accommodations and meals available by advance reservation at several area wilderness lodges, such as Iliamna Lake Resort (571-1387). There is a laundromat. No banking services. Groceries, clothing, first-aid supplies, hardware, camera film and sporting goods available in the community. Arts and crafts available for purchase include grass baskets. Fishing/hunting licenses available, as well as guide service. Aircraft mechanic available. Rental transportation includes autos, boats, trucks and charter aircraft. Fuel available includes diesel, propane, marine gas, white gas, kerosene and regular and unleaded gasoline. No public moorage facilities.

"Old Iliamna" was located near the mouth of the Iliamna River. Around 1935, the Indian village moved to its present location, approximately 40 miles from the old site. The first of several hunting and fishing lodges opened in Iliamna in the 1930s. A few lodges stay open year-round for those interested in ice fishing and winter hiking. An 8-mile gravel road connects Iliamna to Newhalen, and there is an overland crossing from Old Iliamna to Iliamna Bay on Cook Inlet, still used for delivering freight and fishing boats.

Commercial fishing, sportfishing and hunting lodges are the major sources of income for the community. The majority of lodge employees, however, are hired from outside the village. There are several other jobs in the village with government agencies and local businesses.

Most Natives and an increasing number of non-Natives depend to varying degrees on subsistence hunting and fishing. Red and chum salmon are caught in summer. Freshwater fish, rabbit and porcupine are taken year-round. Moose, caribou, bear, ptarmigan, ducks and geese are hunted in season. Seals are taken occasionally from Lake Iliamna. In the fall, residents pick blackberries, blueberries, cranberries, salmonberries and raspberries. Wild celery, spinach and onions are gathered in spring.

Iliamna is a major gateway to the world-class fishing and hunting in the Kvichak River drainage. The system, with headwaters in Lake Iliamna and Lake Clark, is historically the most important spawning and rearing habitat for sockeye or red salmon in the world and the largest contributor to the Bristol Bay fishery. King, coho, chum and humpback salmon also are present, although in fewer numbers. State sportfishing regulations designate the Kvichak River system as a trophy fish area. Some of the largest rainbow trout in the world can be found in these waters.

Lake Iliamna, 75 miles long and 20 miles wide, is the largest lake in Alaska. It is reputedly the home of a "sea monster." Residents from villages around the lake claim to have seen the creature on several occasions.

Visitors planning to hike or canoe in the area should contact the National Park Service in Anchorage; much of the land is privately owned or owned by Native corporations. *NOTE: Iliamna Natives Ltd. charges fees for camping on corporation land: $25 per person per night for 1 or 2 people; $50 per night for a group of 3 or more people. Fees are payable in advance and are nonrefundable.* Hiking, berry picking and fishing also are permitted on corporation lands; hunting in general is not. Wood cutting is not permitted. These and other land-use regulations are available from the corporation office, P.O. Box 245, Iliamna, AK 99606.

Communications in Iliamna, which is incorporated, include phones, mail plane, radio and TV. The community is served by 2 churches and a school with grades preschool through 12. There are community electricity, water and sewer systems. Freight arrives by cargo plane. The sale of alcoholic beverages is prohibited. Government address: Iliamna Village Council, General Delivery, Iliamna, AK 99606; phone 571-1246. Village corporation address: Iliamna Natives Ltd., P.O. Box 245, Iliamna, AK 99606; phone 571-1256.

King Salmon

[MAP 8] Located on the Alaska Peninsula on the Naknek River, 15 miles east of Naknek, 290 miles southwest of Anchorage. **Transportation:** Scheduled airline from Anchorage. **Population:** 434. **Zip code:** 99613. **Emergency Services:** Police, phone 246-4222; Alaska State Troopers, phone 246-3346; Camai Clinic, Naknek, phone 246-6155; Volunteer Fire Department.

Elevation: 50 feet. **Climate:** Cool, humid and windy weather. Average summer temperatures range from 42°F to 63°F; average winter temperatures range from 29°F to 44°F. Total precipitation averages 20 inches annually, including an average snowfall of 48 inches. Cloud cover is present an average of 76 percent of the time year-round. Naknek River is ice free between May and October.

Private Aircraft: Airport adjacent southeast; elev. 57 feet; length 8,500 feet; asphalt; fuel 100, jet A; attended. *CAUTION: Air Defense aircraft may scramble at any time.* Passenger and freight terminals, ticket counter, restrooms and traffic control tower at airport. Transportation available.

Visitor Facilities: Accommodations at Quinnat Landing Hotel (1-800-770-3474) and King Ko Inn (246-3377); both offer restaurants and lounges. There are 3 additional restaurants. Area lodges include Wood-Z Lodge (246-3449) and Prestage's Sportfishing Lodge (246-3320). No laundromat available. Banking services available. Groceries, clothing, first-aid supplies, hardware, camera film and sporting goods may be purchased in the community. Arts and crafts available for purchase include carved ivory, baskets and masks. (Try the airport gift shop for carved ivory.) Fishing/hunting licenses available, as well as guide service. Major repair service for marine engines, boats and aircraft. Rental transportation includes autos in summer, boats and charter aircraft. Fuel available includes marine gas and regular gas. Moorage facilities available. *NOTE: Land on the south side of the Naknek River from King Salmon is owned by the Alaska Peninsula Corp. Contact the corporation for details on use and fees.*

In the 1930s, an air navigation silo was built at the present site of King Salmon. At the onset of WWII, an Air Force base was constructed that remains today as the major military installation in western Alaska. In 1949, the U.S. Army Corps of Engineers built the road connecting King Salmon to Naknek. The community, located in the Bristol Bay Borough, has continued to develop as a government, transportation and service center.

King Salmon is the gateway to several large lakes on the Alaska Peninsula (Naknek, Iliamna, Becharof, Ugashik) and to Katmai National Park and Preserve. A 10-mile unimproved road leads from King Salmon to the park's western boundary and there are floatplane connections from King Salmon to the lodge at Brooks River, the National Park Service ranger station and the public campground on Naknek Lake. There are 2 other lodges in the park. Independent travelers must make their own arrangements for visiting Katmai, including air service to King Salmon and Brooks River. Campers can purchase meals and scenic bus tour tickets at the lodge.

Communications in King Salmon include phones, mail plane, radio and TV. The community is served by a church. Children are bused to school in Naknek. There is a community electricity system; water is from individual wells. Sewage system is septic tanks. Freight arrives by air cargo or by barge to Naknek then is trucked to King Salmon. Government address: Bristol Bay Borough, Box 189, Naknek, AK 99633; phone 246-4224. Village corporation address: Alaska Peninsula Corp., Box 104360, Anchorage, AK 99510; phone 274-2433, fax 274-8694.

Kokhanok

[MAP 12] *(KOKE-a-nok)* Located in the Western Cook Inlet area on the south shore of Lake Iliamna, 25 miles south of Iliamna and 210 miles west of Anchorage. **Transportation:** Charter and air taxi service from Iliamna. **Population:** 154. **Zip code:** 99606. **Emergency Services:** Clinic, phone 282-2203; Volunteer Fire Department.

Elevation: 50 feet. **Climate:** Average summer temperatures from 40°F to 64°F; average winter temperatures from 3°F to 30°F. Total precipitation about 32 inches annually; average annual snowfall 89.4 inches. Fierce windstorms are characteristic of the area.

Private Aircraft: Airstrip 2 miles west; elev. 100 feet; length 3,400 feet; gravel; attended irregularly.

Visitor Facilities: No accommodations, except for cots in the Village Council Building (282-2202; bring own sleeping bag). Two stores are located in private homes. Groceries and supplies available at Nielson General Store (282-2239) or at Iliamna Trading Co. across Lake Iliamna (571-1225). The population of Kokhanok, also commonly called Kokhanok Bay, is primarily Aleut. Residents rely heavily on subsistence hunting and fishing for their survival. *NOTE: Hiking, berry picking, camping and fishing are permitted on lands owned by the Alaska Peninsula Corp. upon payment of a $100-per-person fee. Hunting and woodcutting on corporation lands is not permitted. Contact the corporation for more information.*

Community employment is available for some residents. The community is accessible only by air and water. In winter snow machines and trucks are used to cross the frozen lake to Iliamna and other villages. Village festivals take place in winter and sled dog racing is a popular pastime.

Communications include phones, mail plane, radio and TV. The community is served by the Saints Peter and Paul Russian

Orthodox Church, which is on the National Register of Historic Places, and by a school with grades preschool through 12. Electric power is provided from the school, September through May. Village power throughout the summer is provided by Kokhanok Electric. Water is hauled from Lake Iliamna, and residents have privies or honey buckets. Freight is brought in by air transport or by barge. The village bans the sale and importation of alcoholic beverages. Village corporation address: Alaska Peninsula Corp., P.O. Box 104360, Anchorage, AK 99510; phone 274-2433. Government address: Kokhanok Village Council, P.O. Box 1007, Kokhanok, AK 99606; phone 282-2202.

Koliganek

[MAP 12] *(ko-LIG-a-neck)* Located on the Nushagak River, 65 miles northeast of Dillingham, 280 miles west of Anchorage. **Transportation:** Scheduled air service from Dillingham. **Population:** 112. **Zip code:** 99576. **Emergency Services:** Alaska State Troopers, Dillingham, phone 842-5351; Volunteer Fire Department.

Private Aircraft: Airstrip adjacent south; elev. 240 feet; length 2,100 feet; gravel; fuel information unavailable; unattended. Runway condition not monitored; visual inspection recommended prior to landing. Runways unusable during breakup and after heavy rainfall.

Visitor Facilities: Information about most facilities and services unavailable; however, fishing/hunting licenses may be obtained in the community.

This Eskimo village is unincorporated. Many residents may be gone to fish camps during the summer.

The community has a school with grades kindergarten through 12. Electricity is obtained from private generators or from the school. There is a community water supply and a sewer system. Freight arrives by mail plane and barge. Village corporation address: Koliganek Natives Ltd., General Delivery, Koliganek, AK 99576.

Levelock

[MAP 12] *(Leev-lok)* Located on the west bank of the Kvichak River, 40 miles north of Naknek, 60 miles east of Dillingham, 280 miles southwest of Anchorage. **Transportation:** Scheduled and charter air service from King Salmon. **Population:** 127. **Zip code:** 99625. **Emergency Services:** Alaska State

Troopers, King Salmon; Clinic, phone 287-3011; Volunteer Fire Department.

Elevation: 60 feet. **Climate:** Transitional zone with primarily a maritime influence. However, because the village is located about 10 miles inland, the colder continental climate significantly affects local weather. Average summer temperatures from 30°F to 66°F; average winter temperatures from 4°F to 30°F. Annual precipitation from 20 to 35 inches. Most precipitation occurs during the summer.

Private Aircraft: Airstrip adjacent west; elev. 60 feet; length 1,900 feet; gravel; no fuel; unattended. Runway condition not monitored; visual inspection recommended prior to using. Runway surfaces soft and muddy during spring breakup or heavy rains. Sharp dropoff at west end of runway.

Visitor Facilities: Accommodations, meals and laundry facilities are available. No banking services. Groceries available at 2 stores. Arts and crafts available for purchase include carved ivory and pen-and-ink drawings. Fishing/hunting licenses available, as well as guide service. Boat and auto repair services available. Arrangements can be made to rent autos, off-road vehicles and boats. Fuel available includes marine gas, diesel, propane and regular gasoline. Moorage facilities available.

Early Russian explorers reported the existence of Levelock, which they called Kvichak. In 1908, a survey of Russian missions in the region referred to the village as Lovelock's Mission.

Levelock was likely devastated by a smallpox epidemic in the region in 1837, and again by a combination of measles and influenza in 1900 and flu in 1918-19.

Canneries operated at Levelock in 1925-26 and again in 1928-29. In 1929-30 the first school was built. A third cannery operated briefly in the 1950s.

Nearly all residents participate in the commercial salmon fishery, with about 75 percent of the residents going to Naknek during the fishing season. The entire community relies on subsistence hunting and fishing. Species commonly harvested include red, silver, chum, dog and king salmon, lake trout, rainbow trout and Dolly Varden; moose and caribou; and lowbush cranberries, blueberries, salmonberries and blackberries.

According to one resident the best reason to go to Levelock, besides its location in the designated sport trophy fishing area, is that Alaskan artist Ted Lambert used to live here and residents still have many of Lambert's paintings and block prints.

Communications in Levelock, which is unincorporated, include phones, mail plane, radio and TV. The community is served by Russian Orthodox and Baptist churches and a school with grades kindergarten through 12. There are public water, electricity and sewer systems. Freight arrives by cargo plane, barge and ship. Government address: Levelock Village Council, General Delivery, Levelock, AK 99625; phone 287-3030. Village corporation address: Levelock Natives Ltd., General Delivery, Levelock, AK 99625; phone 287-3040.

Manokotak

[MAP 12] *(Man-a-KOT-ak)* Located on the Igushik River, 25 miles southwest of Dillingham, 370 miles west of Anchorage. **Transportation:** Air charter service from Dillingham. **Population:** 370. **Zip code:** 99628. **Emergency Services:** Village Public Safety Officer; Alaska State Troopers, Dillingham; Clinic; Volunteer Fire Department.

Climate: Transitional zone with strong maritime influence; however it also is affected by the colder continental climate. Cloudy skies, mild temperatures and moderately heavy precipitation. Average summer temperatures from 40°F to 70°F; average winter temperatures from 4°F to 30°F. Annual precipitation from 20 to 26 inches, with most occurring from late June through August. Rain generally is accompanied by southwest winds.

Private Aircraft: Airstrip 1 mile north; elev. 107 feet; length 2,600 feet; gravel; no fuel; unattended. Runway condition not monitored; visual inspection recommended prior to using. Runway surface soft and muddy during spring breakup or heavy rains.

Visitor Facilities: No hotel, restaurant or banking services. Laundry facilities available. Groceries, limited clothing, first-aid supplies, hardware, camera film and sporting goods available in the community. Arts and crafts available for purchase include carved ivory, grass baskets, masks, fur hats and coats. Fishing/hunting licenses available. No guide service. No repair service or rental transportation. Fuel available includes marine gas, diesel and regular gasoline. Moorage facilities available.

Manokotak is one of the newer communities in the Bristol Bay region, although it is still strongly traditional, reflecting both its Eskimo heritage and Moravian Church influence. It became a permanent settlement in 1946-47 when several older villages consolidated. Beginning in 1949, school was conducted in a church which now serves as a workshop for students. A school was established in the community in 1958-59.

Almost everyone in Manokotak participates in the commercial salmon fishery. About 95 percent of the residents leave the village during the fishing season and most of them fish near the mouth of the Igushik River. About 40 percent of the residents also trap fox, beaver, mink, otter, lynx, wolverine and muskrat. Furs are sold at the Beaver Roundup held annually in Dillingham or to furriers in Anchorage.

The entire community depends heavily on subsistence hunting and fishing. Besides salmon, species taken include sea lion, beluga whale, caribou, herring, smelt, clams, grayling, trout, pike, sheefish, grouse and ptarmigan. Bird eggs, wild celery and various berries also are harvested. Trade with Togiak and Twin Hills brings Manokotak residents seal oil and whitefish.

Birds are abundant in the Manokotak area. The bald eagle is a summer resident and can be found nesting in the tops of trees or preying on seabirds, ground squirrels and fish. The Igushik River and its wetlands provide excellent habitat for migrating waterfowl and shorebirds in spring and fall. Peak migrations usually occur during the first week of May.

Communications in Manokotak, a second-class city incorporated in 1970, include a village phone (842-5978), mail plane, radio and TV. The community is served by a Moravian church and a school with grades kindergarten through 12. There are community electricity, water and sewer systems. Freight arrives by cargo plane and barge. Possession of alcoholic beverages is prohibited. Government address: City of Manokotak, P.O. Box 170, Manokotak, AK 99628; phone 289-1027. Village corporation address: Manokotak Natives Ltd., General Delivery, Manokotak, AK 99628.

Newhalen

[MAP 12] Located in the Western Cook Inlet area on the north shore of Iliamna Lake at the mouth of the Newhalen River, 4.5 miles southwest of Iliamna and 230 miles south-southwest of Anchorage. **Transportation:** Scheduled air service to Iliamna, then by road to Newhalen. **Population:** 172. **Zip code:** 99606. **Emergency Services:** Village Public Safety Officer, phone 571-1461; Clinic; Volunteer Fire Department, phone 571-1231.

Elevation: 190 feet. **Climate:** Transitional zone. Average summer temperatures from 42°F to 62°F; average winter temperatures from 6°F to 30°F. Annual precipitation averages 24 inches, with 50 inches of snow.

Private Aircraft: There is an old airstrip at Newhalen, but it has been out of use for years. Residents use the Iliamna airport.

Visitor Facilities: Accommodations and meals by advance reservation at several wilderness lodges in the Iliamna area. There is a washeteria with showers. Groceries and some camping and fishing supplies available at local stores. Fishing/hunting licenses available in Iliamna. No marine facilities or repair services. Fuel available: diesel and gasoline. *NOTE: Hiking, berry picking, camping and fishing are permitted on lands owned by the Alaska Peninsula Corp. upon payment of a $100-per-person fee. Hunting and woodcutting on corporation lands is not permitted. Contact the corporation for more information.*

The 1890 census listed the Eskimo name of Noghelingamiut, meaning "people of Noghelin," at this location. The present name is an anglicized version of the original. The village was established in the late 1800s to take advantage of the plentiful fish and game in the area. Today, it remains a fishing village. Newhalen was incorporated as a second-class city in 1971. It is connected by a 9-mile-long road to Iliamna and the airport.

During the red salmon season most residents leave Newhalen to fish in Bristol Bay; many return at the end of the red season, although a few stay to fish the smaller pink and silver salmon runs later in the summer and fall. Other employment is in the public sector, such as with the school district or seasonal firefighting for the Bureau of Land Management.

Income from these enterprises is supplemented by subsistence hunting and fishing. Freshwater fish, rabbit and porcupine are taken year-round. Moose, caribou, bear, ptarmigan, ducks and geese are hunted in season and seals are occasionally taken from Lake Iliamna. In the summer and fall, residents pick blackberries, blueberries, cranberries, salmonberries and raspberries. Wild celery and spinach are gathered in early spring.

Communications in Newhalen include phones, radio and TV. The community is served by a Russian Orthodox church and 2 schools with grades preschool through 12. There is a community electricity system. Most homes now have wells and bathrooms, and there are 15 new HUD homes. Freight arrives primarily by air cargo. Government address: City of Newhalen, P.O. Box 165, Iliamna, AK 99606; phone 571-1226. Village corporation address: Alaska Peninsula Corp., P.O. Box 104360, Anchorage, AK 99510.

New Stuyahok

[MAP 12] *(New STU-ya-hock)* Located on the Nushagak River, 51 miles northeast of Dillingham, 290 miles southwest of Anchorage. **Transportation:** Boat; snow machine; scheduled or charter air service from Dillingham. **Population:** 380. **Zip code:** 99636. **Emergency Services:** Village Public Safety Officer, phone 693-3170; Alaska State Troopers, Dillingham, phone 842-5641; Clinic, phone 693-3131; Kanakanak Hospital, Dillingham, phone 842-5101 or 842-5202; Health Aide, phone 693-3102 or 693-3133.

Elevation: 125 feet. **Climate:** Transitional zone; primary influence maritime. Because the village is inland the continental climate significantly affects local weather. Cloudy skies, mild temperatures and moderately heavy precipitation. There often are strong winds. Average summer temperatures from 37°F to 66°F; average winter temperatures from 4°F to 30°F. Annual precipitation 20 to 35 inches, with most of it occurring in August and September.

Private Aircraft: Airstrip 1 mile west; elev. 325 feet; length 1,800 feet; gravel; no fuel; unattended. Runway condition not monitored; visual inspection recommended prior to landing. Access road to parking apron not maintained; takeoffs and landings on road prohibited. No facilities at airport or public transportation into town.

Visitor Facilities: There is a roadhouse. Arrangements for accommodations in private homes also may be made. There is no restaurant, laundromat or banking facility. Groceries, clothing, first-aid supplies, hardware, camera film and sporting goods available in the community. Arts and crafts available for purchase include hand-sewn fur items. Fishing/hunting licenses not available. No guide or repair services, rental transportation, or moorage facilities. Fuel available: diesel and regular gasoline.

This Eskimo village was relocated several times because of flooding and has been at its present site since 1942. Stuyahok is an Eskimo word meaning "going downriver place." New Stuyahok got its first school, a log building, in 1961, and incorporated as a second-class city in 1972.

The community's economic base is the commercial salmon fishery, although about 30 people trap commercially and several are employed full time by the government or school district.

Beaver, lynx, fox and mink are the primary species trapped for fur; and muskrat, otter, wolverine, bobcat, marten and weasel also are taken. Furs are sold to buyers who pass through the village, at the Beaver Roundup in Dillingham, or at the annual New Stuyahok Beaver Festival.

The entire community depends heavily on subsistence activities for food. Many residents go to fish camps during the summer season. Moose, caribou and rabbit are the primary game animals. Beavers also are eaten. Fishing is for salmon, pike, grayling, smelt, whitefish, sucker, rainbow trout, lingcod and Dolly Varden. In the fall, blackberries, red berries, cranberries and some blueberries are gathered.

Communications include phones and radio. The community is served by a Russian Orthodox church and a school with grades kindergarten through 12. There are community electricity, water and sewer systems. Freight generally arrives by plane. Government address: City of New Stuyahok, P.O. Box 10, New Stuyahok, AK 99636; phone 693-3111. Village corporation address: Stuyahok Ltd., P.O. Box 50, Stuyahok, AK 99636; phone 693-3122.

New Stuyahok's distinctive Russian Orthodox church. (Bill Sherwonit)

Nondalton

[MAP 12] Located in the Western Cook Inlet area on the west shore of Six Mile Lake, 15 miles north of Iliamna and 200 miles southwest of Anchorage, within Lake Clark National Park. **Transportation:** Scheduled and charter air service from Anchorage and Iliamna. **Population:** 247. **Zip code:** 99640. **Emergency Services:** Police, phone 294-2262; Clinic, phone 294-2238; Volunteer Fire Department, phone 294-2262.

Elevation: 250 feet. **Climate:** Transitional zone. Weather information from Iliamna indicates average summer temperatures in Nondalton from 42°F to 62°F and average winter temperatures from 6°F to 30°F. Annual precipitation averages 26 inches, with 64 inches of snow.

Private Aircraft: Airstrip 1 mile northwest; elev. 250 feet; length 2,700 feet; gravel; fuel unavailable; unattended. Runway condition not monitored; visual inspection recommended prior to using. Transport to town available.

Visitor Facilities: Accommodations and meals by advance reservation at several area wilderness lodges. No bank or public showers, but laundromat available. Groceries, first-aid supplies, hardware, film, sporting goods and Nondalton hats and T-shirts available. Fuel includes marine gas, regular and unleaded gasoline, diesel, propane, white gas and kerosene. Arts and crafts available for purchase include birch-bark baskets and dolls from the local doll factory. Fishing/hunting licenses, guides and repairs to marine engines, boats and autos all available. Rental transportation includes automobiles, boats, aircraft and off-road vehicles.

Nondalton is a Tanaina Indian name, first recorded in 1909 by D.C. Witherspoon of the U.S. Geological Survey. The village originally was located on the north shore of Six Mile Lake. In 1940, firewood supplies were depleted and growing mudflats made it increasingly difficult to reach the lake, so the village relocated to the west shore. Nondalton was incorporated as a second-class city in 1971.

Nondalton's St. Nicholas Russian Orthodox Chapel, originally constructed in 1896 and moved with the rest of the village, is on the National Register of Historic Places.

Nondalton residents work seasonally in the commercial salmon fishery or fire-fighting for BLM. A few other jobs are with governmental agencies and the village Native corporation.

Residents depend heavily on subsistence hunting and fishing for food. Red salmon are caught in the summer and freshwater fish, rabbit and porcupine are taken year-round. Moose, caribou, bear, ptarmigan, ducks and geese are hunted in season. In late summer and fall, residents pick blueberries, blackberries and cranberries. Wild onions are gathered in the summer.

Communications include phones, TV via satellite and radio. The community is served by a school with grades preschool through 12. Nondalton has a new Russian Orthodox church. There are community electricity, water and sewer systems. Freight arrives by barge or small plane. The sale of alcoholic beverages is prohibited. Government address: City of Nondalton, General Delivery, Nondalton, AK 99640; phone 294-2235. Village corporation address: Kijik Corp., 4153 Tudor Centre Drive, Suite 104, Anchorage, AK 99508; phone 561-4487.

Nushagak

[MAP 12] *(NOOSH-a-gack)* Located on the east shore of Nushagak Bay, 5 air miles from Dillingham, 330 miles southwest of Anchorage. **Transportation:** Boat; charter plane from Dillingham. **Population:** Up to 100 during summer fishing season. **Zip code:** 99695. **Emergency Services:** Alaska State Troopers, Dillingham; Kanakanak Hospital, Dillingham.

Private Aircraft: No airstrip. Small planes land on the beach at low tide.

Visitor Facilities: None. Camp or sleep in one of several vacant huts (look for one with an intact roof). Supplies are airlifted from Dillingham.

Nushagak is a former Eskimo village established as a trading post about 1819. The Russians called it Aleksandrovsk. It was called Fort or Redoubt Alexander until 1899. The area is now used seasonally as a base for set-net fishermen.

The Russian Orthodox Transfiguration of Our Lord Chapel at Nushagak is on the National Register of Historic Places.

Pedro Bay

[MAP 12] Located in the Western Cook Inlet area at the head of Pedro Bay in Lake Iliamna, 180 miles southwest of Anchorage. **Transportation:** Scheduled or charter air service from Iliamna and Anchorage. **Population:** 67. **Zip code:** 99647. **Emergency Services:** Village Public Safety Officer, phone

850-2222; Health Aide, phone 850-2229; Volunteer Fire Department, phone 850-2225.

Climate: Transitional zone, with strong maritime influences. Weather data for Iliamna, 25 miles away, generally reflect conditions at Pedro Bay. Average summer temperatures from 42°F to 62°F; average winter temperatures from 6°F to 30°F.

Private Aircraft: Airstrip 1 mile west; elev. 45 feet; length 2,600 feet; crushed gravel topping; no fuel; unattended. Runway condition not monitored; visual inspection recommended prior to using. No transportation into village.

Visitor Facilities: Accommodations by advance reservation at Pedro Bay Lodge (850-2232) and bed and breakfast Triple K Services. No banking services. Laundry at Pedro Bay Public Health Building. Groceries and first-aid supplies available in the community. Some beadwork and skin sewing available for purchase. Fishing/hunting licenses available, as well as guide service. No repair services. Pedro Bay Lodge has skiffs for rent. No public moorage facilities.

The Denaina Indians have occupied this area for hundreds of years. A Denaina village was once located at the west entrance to Pedro Bay and the Denaina warred with Russian fur traders over trade practices in the early 20th century. Denaina Indians still live in the area. Much of the "old way of life" has changed, but some folklore still remains. According to Village Administrator Debi Wilson-Jacko, "You can walk from house to house and feel like you are in the middle of a beautiful, pristine wilderness." Pedro Bay is unincorporated.

Most Pedro Bay residents depend on subsistence hunting and fishing. Red salmon are caught in the summer and freshwater fish are taken year-round. Moose, rabbit, bear, ptarmigan and ducks are hunted in season. In early summer, residents gather wild celery and onions. In the fall, they pick blueberries, cranberries, blackberries and salmonberries.

Some residents obtain short-term or year-round government jobs. A few are fishermen, and several are slope workers. Others must leave the area to earn enough money to support themselves. Teachers leave during the winter and return in the summer.

St. Nicholas Russian Orthodox Chapel, built in 1890, is on the National Register of Historic Places.

During spring and summer, brown bears gather along the salmon streams near Pedro Bay. Black bears are numerous and can be a nuisance because they often wander into the village. Moose concentrate year-round in the area surrounding the village.

Pedro Bay is located within the Kvichak River system, with headwaters in Lake Clark and Lake Iliamna. This is historically the most important spawning and rearing habitat for sockeye salmon in the world. Sportfishing for rainbow trout, arctic char and Dolly Varden also is excellent. A winter carnival in March features shooting matches, team games and food.

Communications in Pedro Bay include phones, mail plane, radio and TV. The community is served by 1 church and a school with grades kindergarten through 12. There is a community electricity system. Water is from private wells. Sewage system is septic tanks. Freight arrives by barge and air taxi. Government address: Pedro Bay Village Council, P.O. Box 47020, Pedro Bay, AK 99647; phone 850-2225. Village corporation address: Pedro Bay Corp., P.O. Box 47015, Pedro Bay, AK 99647; phone 850-2232.

Pope & Vannoy Landing

[MAP 12] Located in the Western Cook Inlet area on Intricate Bay on Lake Iliamna, 25 miles from Iliamna. **Transportation:** Boat; air taxi from Iliamna. **Population:** 14. **Zip code:** Via Iliamna 99606. **Emergency Services:** Alaska State Troopers, Iliamna; Health Aide, Kokhanok.

Private Aircraft: No airstrip. Float or ski landings only.

Visitor Facilities: Accommodations and meals by advance reservation at Copper River Lodge (571-1248). Guide services available.

Pope & Vannoy Landing is a settlement primarily of Pope family members. Art Pope writes that his son bought a cabin and moved here in 1955. He was followed by Pope's brother-in-law in 1957, Pope and his wife in 1965, and a granddaughter, Marlene DeNeut, in 1980. Another couple from Iliamna moved over in 1983.

All residents of the area obtain their supplies from Anchorage. Art Pope and his wife, both in their 70s, set net for salmon in the summer and tend an 11,000-square-foot garden.

Electricity is from individual generators. Water is hauled from the lake or a spring. Sewage system is outhouses.

Portage Creek

[MAP 12] Located 30 miles southeast of Dillingham, 320 miles southwest of Anchorage. **Transportation:** Boat; charter air service from Dillingham. **Population:** 46. **Zip code:** 99695. **Emergency Services:** Alaska State Troopers, Dillingham; Kanakanak Hospital, Dillingham.

Climate: Transition zone, characterized by cloudy skies, mild temperatures and moderately heavy precipitation. Average summer temperatures from 30°F to 66°F; average winter temperatures from 4°F to 30°F. Annual precipitation from 20 to 35 inches. Most precipitation occurs during the summer months.

Private Aircraft: Airstrip east of village; elev. 137 feet; length 1,900 feet; gravel; no fuel; unattended. Runway condition not monitored; visual inspection recommended prior to landing. Runway surface soft and muddy during spring breakup or heavy rains; runway edges subject to erosion. Watch out for crosswind when landing.

Visitor Facilities: None.

This site was long used as an overnight camp. As the name implies, Portage Creek is part of a summer route from the head of Nushagak Bay to the mouth of the Kvichak River which avoided the open waters of Bristol Bay and a long trip around Etolin Point.

The first residence was built in 1961. At that time a few families had left Koliganek and other villages up to Nushagak River for settlement in Portage Creek. A school was established in 1963.

Portage Creek is an example of a phenomenon once common along the Nushagak River. Before the advent of expensive public institutions and development, villages were extremely mobile and the relocation of a few families could signal the beginning or ending of a village. Passage of the Alaska Native Claims Settlement Act and construction of schools have ended this practice except for summer fish camps.

The primary employment for Portage Creek residents is the fishing industry, but the entire population depends to some extent on subsistence hunting and fishing. Species commonly harvested include salmon, pike, whitefish, rainbow trout, moose, caribou, duck, geese, crane. There is also berry picking in season. Varieties available include salmonberries, blackberries, cranberries and blueberries.

There is superb king salmon fishing from the riverbank in front of the village in June and early July. Arrangements for guided fishing in the area are best made in Dillingham.

Land in the Portage Creek area is owned by the local Native corporation, Choggiung Ltd., which requires that a permit be obtained for any public use of its lands.

Communications in Portage Creek, which is unincorporated, include a phone in the council house (842-5966), mail plane, radio and TV. The community is served by a Russian Orthodox church and Ohgsenakale School with grades kindergarten through 12. Electricity is from individual generators in summer and the school in winter. Water is hauled from wells. Sewage system is outhouses. Freight arrives by barge or charter plane. Government address: Portage Creek Village Council, General Delivery, Portage Creek, AK 99695. Village corporation address: Choggiung Ltd., P.O. Box 196, Dillingham, AK 99576.

Port Alsworth

[MAP 12] Located in the Western Cook Inlet area on Lake Clark, 22 miles northeast of Nondalton, 180 miles from Anchorage. **Transportation:** Boat; scheduled and charter air service from Iliamna; Lake Clark Air charter service (781-2211). **Population:** 30. **Zip code:** 99653. **Emergency Services:** Alaska State Troopers, phone 571-1236; Health Aide, Iliamna, phone 781-2218.

Elevation: 230 feet. **Climate:** Summers are mild, according to one resident. Temperatures from 45°F to 80°F. Winters are usually mild, with temperatures from -30° to 40°F. Mean annual precipitation 17 inches; mean annual snowfall 68 inches.

Private Aircraft: There are 2 private airstrips in the center of the community. Aviation fuel 80, 100 available from The Farm Lodge for emergencies only. Airstrip use is by prior permission only from Glen or Wayne Alsworth, phone 781-2212 or 781-2204.

Visitor Facilities: Accommodations and meals at several area wilderness lodges: Alaska's Wilderness Lodge (781-2223), The Farm Lodge (781-2211), Koksetna Lodge (781-2227), Lakeside Lodge (781-2202) and Lake Country Lodge (283-5959). Meals available in the community. No banking services or laundry facilities. There are no stores; all supplies are obtained from Anchorage or Soldotna. Arts and crafts available for purchase include Indian and Eskimo hats, dolls, yo-yos, wood articles and local paintings. Fishing/hunting licenses available, as well as guide service. No major repairs available. Rental transportation includes boats and charter aircraft. No public moorage facilities.

Early Port Alsworth was a weather reporting station and stopover for airline flights to the Bristol Bay area, according to local residents. Pioneer bush pilot "Babe" Alsworth and his wife Mary, the settlement's first postmistress, were among the early settlers in the 1940s. They homesteaded on 160 acres and developed an airstrip and flying service. They also were involved in developing the Tanalian Bible Church and Camp. Port Alsworth now has several fishing lodges and is the local headquarters for Lake Clark National Park and Preserve. One resident describes it as "one of the finest places to live and visit in rural Alaska."

Most residents make their living either directly or indirectly from tourism. Employment is through the lodges, flying service, school, commercial fishing and a few local businesses.

Local attractions include 40-mile-long Lake Clark, one of the spawning grounds for the Bristol Bay red salmon run; the ruins of historic Kijik village, listed on the National Register of Historic Places; and picturesque Tanalian Falls. Activities include hiking, wildlife photography, bird watching, river rafting, fishing, cross-country skiing, sledding, snowmobiling and hunting for moose, caribou, bear and small game.

From Anchorage, air access to Port Alsworth is by way of 1,000-foot Lake Clark Pass through the Aleutian Range.

Lake Clark National Park and Preserve offers a prime wilderness experience. The area boasts steaming volcanoes, rugged mountains, craggy peaks, alpine valleys, blue-green glaciers, free-flowing rivers and sparkling lakes. Its wildlife includes eagles, hawks, waterfowl and seabirds; grayling, northern pike, trout and salmon; bear, moose, caribou and Dall sheep. For more information write: Superintendent, Lake Clark National Park and Preserve, 4230 University Dr., Suite 311, Anchorage, AK 99508.

Communications at Port Alsworth, which is unincorporated, include phones, mail plane, radio and TV. The community is served by Tanalian Bible Church and a school with grades 1 through 12. Electricity is from individual generators, water from private wells. Sewage system is septic tanks. Freight arrives by cargo plane and an occasional small barge.

South Naknek

[MAP 8] Located on the Alaska Peninsula on the Naknek River, 2 miles south of Naknek, 15 miles west of King Salmon and 300 miles southwest of Anchorage. **Transportation:**

Scheduled airline and air taxi. **Population:** 185. **Zip code: 99670. Emergency Services:** Police, phone 246-4222; Alaska State Troopers, King Salmon, phone 246-3346; Clinic, phone 246-6546; Volunteer Fire Department.

Climate: Cool, humid and windy weather. Average summer temperatures at the nearest weather station in King Salmon range from 42°F to 63°F; average winter temperatures from 4°F to 29°F. Average annual precipitation 20 inches; average snowfall 45 inches.

Private Aircraft: State airstrip 1 mile southwest; elev. 130 feet; length 3,000 feet; gravel; unattended. Runway condition not monitored; visual inspection recommended prior to using. The strip is equipped with low-intensity lighting.

Visitor Facilities: No hotel. There is a combined store, snack bar and bar. Fishing/hunting licenses and guide service available. Availability of repair service, rental transportation, fuel and moorage facilities unknown.

South Naknek, located just across the river from Naknek, is part of the Bristol Bay Borough. It is a more traditional rural community than its neighbor. South Naknek is not connected by road to any other community.

Commercial fishing and salmon processing are the mainstays of South Naknek's economy. Three of the 5 canneries that line the south bank of the Naknek River are in operation and recruit 400 to 500 people from outside the village for the brief summer salmon season. Most other employment is in community service. About 75 percent of South Naknek's residents depend on subsistence hunting and fishing as a vital source of food. Hunting camps along the Naknek River date back to 3,000 to 4,000 B.C. South Naknek was settled after the turn of the century as a result of salmon cannery development.

NOTE: Hiking, berry picking, camping and fishing are permitted on lands owned by the Alaska Peninsula Corp. upon payment of a $100-per-person fee. Hunting and woodcutting on corporation lands are not permitted. Contact the corporation for more information. (See address below.)

South Naknek's Russian Orthodox Elevation of the Holy Cross Church, built in the early 1900s, is listed on the National Register of Historic Places.

Communications in South Naknek include phones, radio, mail plane and TV. The community is served by 2 churches and a school with grades preschool to 6; older students are flown to Naknek daily to attend school. There is a community electricity system; water is from individual wells or hauled from a central watering point. Sewage collection system but no treatment facilities. Freight arrives by air and barge. Government address: Bristol Bay Borough, P.O. Box 189, Naknek, AK 99663; phone 246-4224. Village corporation address: Alaska Peninsula Corp., Box 104360, Anchorage, AK 99510; phone 274-2433.

Togiak

[MAP 11] Located at the head of Togiak Bay, 55 air miles west of Dillingham, 395 miles southwest of Anchorage. **Transportation:** Scheduled and charter air service from Dillingham. **Population:** 813. **Zip code:** 99678. **Emergency Services:** Police, phone 493-5212; Alaska State Troopers, Dillingham, phone 842-5351; Clinic, phone 493-5511; Volunteer Fire Department, phone 493-5212.

Elevation: 12 feet. **Climate:** Maritime; however, the arctic climate of interior Alaska also affects the Bristol Bay coastal region. Cloudy skies, mild temperatures, moderately heavy precipitation and strong winds. Average summer temperatures from 37°F to 66°F; average winter temperatures from 4°F to 30°F. Annual precipitation from 20 to 26 inches, with most of the precipitation occurring in the summer, when low clouds and rain can reduce visibility.

Private Aircraft: Airstrip adjacent southwest; elev. 21 feet; length 4,400 feet; gravel; no fuel; unattended; aircraft instructed to land. Runway condition not monitored; visual inspection recommended prior to using. No airport facilities. Public transportation into village: call city of Togiak.

Visitor Facilities: Accommodations are available at the Round House (493-5434 after 5 P.M.). Lodging may also be arranged with the City of Togiak (493-5820). Togiak Natives Limited (493-5520) operates a fishing lodge. No banking services. Food is available at Green House Restaurant and AC Store Deli. Groceries and supplies are available at Alaska Commercial (a.k.a., Our Store, 493-5334), Togiak Trading (493-5828), Kohok's Reliable Goods, Togiak Lumber and Togiak Village Co-op (493-5226). Arts and crafts available for purchase include grass baskets, some carved ivory, and fur hats and mittens. Fishing/hunting licenses available. *NOTE: Permission must be obtained from Togiak Natives Ltd. to hunt or fish on Native lands. Sportfishing guide service on Togiak River and charter boat trips to Walrus Islands State Game Sanctuary. No repair services. Moorage facilities available. Regular gasoline sometimes available.*

Many residents of the Yukon-Kuskokwim region migrated south to the Togiak area after a devastating influenza epidemic in 1918-19. "Old" Togiak, or Togiagamute, located across the bay from "New" Togiak where a cannery now is located, had a population of 276 in 1880 and only 94 in 1890. Heavy winter snowfalls made wood gathering difficult at "Old" Togiak, so gradually people settled at a new site on the opposite shore, where snow tended only to make deep drifts on the beach and a trail made wood gathering easier. In addition, a slough behind the new site provided good shelter for boats. The population of Togiak is 90 to 95 percent Eskimo with Yup'ik the primary language. Togiak was incorporated as a second-class city in 1969. A local resident classifies people in Togiak as "warm and friendly."

Togiak's economy is based primarily on commercial salmon fishing. Approximately 400 residents fish commercially. A fish processing facility is located near Togiak. The cannery across the bay from Togiak offers tours (493-5331 or 493-5531). The entire community also depends heavily on subsistence hunting and fishing. Species harvested include seal, sea lion, walrus, 5 species of salmon, herring, herring roe-on-kelp, smelt, clams, geese, ducks, ptarmigan and trout. Residents also gather gull and murre eggs.

Togiak is in the center of the Togiak National Wildlife Refuge and is the gateway to Walrus Island State Game Sanctuary. Round Island, one of the Walrus Islands group, is a popular place to view and photograph the 12,000 to 15,000 male walruses that summer on the island. Transportation to Round Island is by boat from Togiak or by charter plane from Dillingham or King Salmon. A trip to Round Island is a true wilderness experience; visitors must bring all their own food, shelter and equipment. Access to the game sanctuary is only by permit from the Alaska Dept. of Fish and Game offices in Anchorage, Dillingham or King Salmon. For information about permits and other information about the sanctuary, write the Alaska Dept. of Fish and Game, Division of Game, P.O. Box 199, Dillingham, AK 99576.

Some of the other islands in the Walrus Islands group also have large populations of seabirds such as puffins, murres, cormorants, kittiwakes, terns and gulls.

The Togiak River is known worldwide for its famous trout and salmon fishing. Fishing in the Togiak River is excellent during July, August and September for 5 species of salmon, rainbow trout and Dolly Varden.

Togiak is located within Togiak National Wildlife Refuge, a breeding and resting area for waterfowl and shorebirds. Peak migrations usually occur the first week in May.

Communications in Togiak include phones, mail plane, radio and TV. The community is served by a Moravian church and a school with grades kindergarten through 12. There are community electricity, water and sewer systems. Togiak prohibits the sale, importation and possession of alcoholic beverages. Freight arrives by cargo plane and barge. Government address: City of Togiak, P.O. Box 99, Togiak, AK 99678; phone 493-5820, fax 493-5932. Village corporation address: Togiak Natives Ltd., P.O. Box 169, Togiak, AK 99678; phone 493-5520.

Twin Hills

[MAP 11] Located near the mouth of a branch of the Togiak River known as Twin Hills River, 2 miles north of Togiak, 395 miles southwest of Anchorage. **Transportation:** Boat from Togiak; scheduled and charter air service from Dillingham. **Population:** 67. **Zip code:** 99576. **Emergency Services:** Alaska State Troopers, Dillingham, phone 842-5641; Clinic, phone 525-4326.

Elevation: 20 to 30 feet. **Climate:** Transitional zone; primary influence is maritime; however, the arctic climate of interior Alaska also affects the Bristol Bay coast. Cloudy skies, mild temperatures, moderately heavy precipitation and strong winds. Average summer temperatures 37°F to 66°F. Average winter temperatures 4°F to 30°F. Annual precipitation 20 to 26 inches, with most of the precipitation occurring in summer. Fog occurs often in winter.

Private Aircraft: Airstrip adjacent east; elev. 82 feet; length 2,000 feet; gravel; no fuel; unattended. Runway condition not monitored; visual inspection recommended prior to using. Bluff at north end may cause some turbulence when landing to the south. Loose rock on runway and apron up to 3 inches in diameter. Passenger terminal at airport; no public transportation into village.

Visitor Facilities: Arrangements may be made to stay in the school or in private homes. No restaurant, banking services or laundromat. Supplies available at The Cannery (5 miles away). Arts and crafts available for purchase include carved ivory, grass baskets and fur dolls. Fishing/hunting licenses not available. No guide or repair services. No rental transportation or moorage facilities. Fuel available: diesel, propane, unleaded and regular gasoline.

Located within Togiak National Wildlife Refuge, Twin Hills is a fairly new village located at the base of 2 hills which rise to 291 feet and 427 feet, prominent features in the generally flat coastal region. The village was established in 1965 following severe flooding in the upper Togiak Bay area. Some of the current residents migrated from Quinhagak, a small community on Kuskokwim Bay. The people of Twin Hills have strong cultural ties to the Yukon-Kuskokwim region not only because they have relatives there today, but also because many of their ancestors migrated south to the Togiak area following the devastating worldwide influenza epidemic of 1918–19.

Virtually all residents of Twin Hills participate in the commercial salmon fishery. A handful of jobs are available with the school, post office, clinic and the state. The entire community depends heavily on subsistence hunting and fishing, and people range great distances to obtain subsistence items. Species harvested include seals, sea lion, whale and walrus, 5 species of salmon, herring, herring roe-on-kelp, smelt, clams, geese, ducks, seagull and murre eggs, ptarmigan, trout and whitefish. In addition, Twin Hills residents trade food items with people from Manokotak.

There is a road leading from Twin Hills to the beach of Togiak Bay. From there it is possible to drive an auto or 3-wheeler to the Togiak Fisheries cannery on the bay across from Togiak.

NOTE: Twin Hills Native Corp. lands are closed to sportfishing, hunting and hiking by nonmembers. Before traveling in the Twin Hills area, check with the corporation about the location of restricted lands.

Communications in Twin Hills include phones, mail plane, radio and TV. There is a Moravian church and a school with grades preschool through 8; older students attend boarding school in other communities. There are community electricity, water and sewer systems. Freight arrives by cargo plane and barge. Government address: Twin Hills Traditional Council, General Delivery, Twin Hills, AK 99576. Village corporation address: Twin Hills Native Corp., General Delivery, Twin Hills, AK 99576.

▼ **A T T R A C T I O N S** ▼

National and State Parks, Etc.

Lake Clark National Park and Preserve

This 3.6-million-acre park and preserve is located north of Lake Iliamna, 150 miles southwest of Anchorage. The park and preserve boasts an array of features including a jumble of snow-capped, glacier-carved peaks, most unclimbed and unexplored, ranging up to 10,000 feet; 2 steaming volcanoes, including 10,197-foot Mount Redoubt, which last erupted in December 1989; countless glaciers; many lakes, ranging from 40-mile-long Lake Clark to shallow tundra ponds; deep U-shaped valleys with rushing streams; open, lichen-covered uplands where streams meander languidly; 3 wild and scenic rivers — the Mulchatna, Tlikakila and Chilikadrotna; and a coastline along Cook Inlet full of tidal bays and rocky inlets. Lake Clark is fed by hundreds of mountain waterfalls and is part of an important red salmon spawning ground. Some 56 archaeological sites have been located within the park and preserve, including the Kijik village site which is on the National Register of Historic Places. See "Lake Clark, The Undiscovered Park" on pages 284-285 for more on this destination.

Climate: The climate on the eastern Cook Inlet side of Lake Clark differs markedly from that on the northwestern slopes and plains. A maritime climate influences the former; drier, continental patterns dominate the latter. In summer the temperature ranges between 45°F and 65°F in the eastern portion and reaches into the 80s in the western part. Precipitation along the coast reaches 60 inches annually, while the interior gets only 20 inches. March and early April are best for cross-country skiing. From mid-April to late May thawing streams and lakes make all travel difficult. Strong winds,

severe in and near mountain passes, can occur at any time.

Wildlife: Along the coast is one of the northernmost stands of Sitka spruce rain forest, while inland are lowland boreal forests typical of Interior Alaska and several varieties of tundra, including arctic tundra usually found in northern Alaska. These varied ecosystems support more than 100 species of birds and nearly 40 species of mammals, including several of the state's most charismatic wildlife: black and brown bears, wolves, caribou and moose. Dall sheep reach the southern limit of their range in the Lake Clark mountains. Wolverine, marten, mink, land otter, weasel, beaver, lynx and red fox are found in the park and preserve. Whales and seals swim offshore along the coast, and the rocky coastal cliffs serve as rookeries for multitudes of puffins, cormarants, kittiwakes and other seabirds. Waterfowl are abundant along Tuxedni Bay and in the ponds and marshes of the tundra plains. Bald eagles, peregrine falcons and numerous other birds nest in the park and preserve.

The several major river and lake systems in the area offer world-class sport fishing opportunities for all five species of Pacific salmon and rainbow trout. Grayling and northern pike can be caught throughout most of the season of open water. Sport hunting is allowed in the preserve under Alaska Dept. of Fish and Game regulations.

Activities: Backpacking, river running and fishing are the primary activities in this predominantly wilderness area. Rangers recommend the hike to Turquoise Lake or Twin Lakes. Also highly recommended is the Chilikadrotna River float from the Twin Lakes put in. The Chilikadrotna also offers outstanding fishing.

Accommodations: Several private lodges on Lake Clark offer accommodations and services by advance reservation, and stores in Iliamna and Nondalton have limited supplies. Port Alsworth, on Lake Clark's southeast shore, is the park's field headquarters. There are no other public facilities in the park. Rangers are based at Twin, Telaquana and Crescent lakes in the summer.

The Park Service advises visitors to arrive self-sufficient and carry extra supplies in the event weather delays air or boat pickup. Warm clothing, good-quality camping and rain gear, and insect repellent or a head net are essential. The Park Service further cautions that this is a vast and sometimes hostile region; the animals are wild and must be respected. Also, local residents carry on subsistence hunting, fishing and other activities, and their camps and equipment are critical to their livelihood and should be left undisturbed.

Access: The region is accessible by air from Anchorage or the Kenai Peninsula. There is daily commercial air service to Iliamna, linked by road to Nondalton at the west end of Lake Clark. In addition, there are many air charter operators in Anchorage, the Kenai Peninsula, Iliamna and other communities who fly to the park or preserve. Pilots are allowed to land on any park lake,

gravel bar or glacier. There are no roads or trails in the park or preserve.

For more information: Contact the Superintendent for answers to questions regarding the park and preserve, guides, outfitters and lodges in the area. Superintendent, Lake Clark National Park and Preserve, 4230 University Dr., #311, Anchorage, AK 99508; phone 271-3751, fax 271-3707. Related USGS Topographic Series maps: Lime Hills, Lake Clark, Iliamna, Kenai, Seldovia, Tyonek.

Wood-Tikchik State Park

This 1.7-million-acre state park—largest in the system and in the country—is located about 30 miles north of Dillingham and 329 miles southwest of Anchorage. Wood-Tikchik is an undeveloped wilderness park containing 2 separate systems of large, interconnected pristine lakes that are spawning and rearing habitat for the Bristol Bay salmon fishery: 6 in the Tikchik River drainage and 6 in the Wood River drainage.

Rugged mountains 3,000 to 5,000 feet tall form a backdrop for some of the lakes on

The Twin Lakes area of Lake Clark National Park and Preserve offers hiking and river running. (Bill Sherwonit)

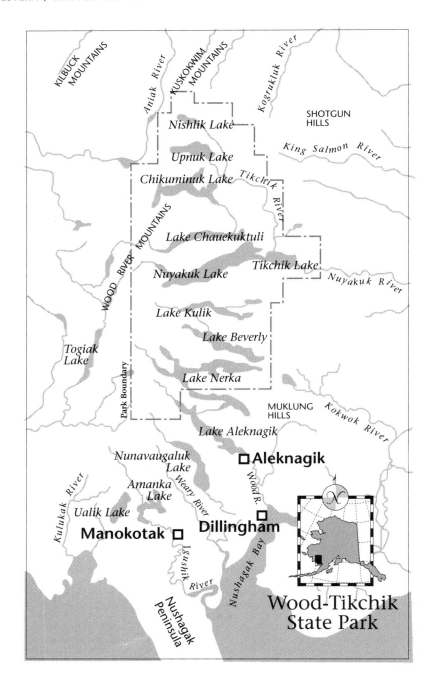

the western side of the park. Pinnacle peaks, high alpine valleys, hanging valleys and dramatic V-shaped incisions contribute to this area's fjordlike appearance. The eastern edge of the lakes overlooks numerous shoals and islands, gravel beaches and the broad tundra landscape of the Nushagak flats.

Climate: The area is characterized by cloudy skies, mild temperatures and fairly heavy precipitation. In August, some precipitation occurs 27 percent of the time along the coast. Average daily July temperatures range from 46°F to 65°F. Winds are usually moderate (0-30 mph), prevailing from the southeast/southwest in the summer, and the north and east in the winter. Although annual snowfall averages 60 to 70 inches at Dillingham, it may reach 160 inches at Lake Nerka. Snow and ice cover, especially on the upper lakes, is common until mid-June. Water levels in the connecting lakes drop during the summer months. By early October, the lakes start to freeze and snow begins to fall.

Wildlife: The area supports brown and black bears, moose, wolf, wolverine, fox, lynx, marten, beaver, porcupine, marmot, muskrat and squirrel. Fishing is excellent throughout the summer for arctic char, rainbow trout, northern pike, red salmon, Dolly Varden and grayling. Sportfishing and hunting are allowed in the park in season under Alaska Dept. of Fish and Game regulations. Catch-and-release fly-fishing for rainbow trout is encouraged.

Activities: The park offers excellent opportunities for boating, sightseeing, fishing and photography. Flying over the park, it might appear that there are opportunities for hiking ridgelines, but getting to the ridges is not easy. Since most access to the park is via the lakes, backpackers and hikers must bushwhack through the lower elevations to reach the beckoning ridges. There are no restrictions on camping in the park and boat motors are allowed on the lakes.

Floating and fishing are by far the most popular activities at Wood-Tikchik Lakes. The Alaska Division of Parks and Outdoor Recreation cautions that winds can quickly create rough water conditions on the lakes and white-water conditions may exist on streams, although most streams are navigable by canoe, kayak or inflatable raft. Water levels in the streams connecting the lakes drop as the summer progresses, revealing boulders which can challenge boaters. Some portages of upper streams are advised.

The trip from Lake Kulik to Aleknagik is about 140 miles of big lakes and short, fast rivers, suitable for canoeing and kayaking. From the drop off at Lake Kulik, this paddle leads down the Wind River to Mikchalk Lake; then down the Peace River to Lake Beverly; then down the Agulukpak River to Lake Nerka; and finally down the Agulowak River to Lake Aleknagik. (See River Running this section.)

The Alaska Division of Parks also warns those traveling by collapsible boat to be wary of porcupines. These creatures have demonstrated a taste for the coated canvas material used for many of these boats. One ranger advised anchoring boats offshore to keep porcupines from chewing on your boat and leaving you with an unseaworthy vessel. All travelers are also advised to leave a copy of their itinerary with a friend, the air charter operator or the park ranger.

Accommodations: There are hotel accommodations in Dillingham, as well as supplies and services. There are several commercial lodges in or near the park which cater only to fishing/sightseeing clients on an advance reservation basis — they are not equipped to accommodate drop-in visitors. In the park there are no developed facilities, trails, shelters, cabins, campsites, waste receptacles, sanitary facilities or emergency services. Visitors should arrive self-sufficient and the Division of Parks and Outdoor Recreation urges the pack-it-in, pack-it-out method of wilderness camping. Visitors should be prepared for cool nights, wind chill, rain and mosquitoes.

Lakeshores tend to be narrow and rocky, with willows and alders forming a barricade to whatever flat lands lie beyond the shore. The best sites for paddlers are found at stream washes that create gravel pads perfect for pitching a tent.

Access: Wood-Tikchik is accessible by scheduled air service to Dillingham, where charter air service to the park is available at about $325 an hour, depending on size of plane, party size and number of trips. Motorboats can access the Wood River Lakes system from Dillingham. The lakes are connected by shallow, swift rivers which generally require jet-equipped watercraft, according to the Alaska Divison of Parks. There is road access to Aleknagik village on Lake Aleknagik, which is adjacent to the southern end of the park. Much of the land around Aleknagik is private property and should be respected. Access to the Tikchik Lakes is primarily by aircraft. Pickup can be arranged from any of the lakes.

For more information contact: Wood-Tikchik State Park, P.O. Box 3022, Dillingham, AK 99576; phone 842-2375 (May 15 to October 1); or HC 52, Box 8999, Indian, AK 99540; phone 345-5014 (October 1 to May 15). Or contact Alaska Dept. of Natural Resources, Division of Parks and Outdoor Recreation, Chugach/Wood-Tikchik Area, P.O. Box 107001, Anchorage, AK 99510; phone 694-2108, fax 762-2535.

Wildlife Refuges

Togiak National Wildlife Refuge

This 4.3-million-acre refuge is located about 3 miles west of Dillingham at its closest point. More than half of the refuge is an established wilderness area. Adjacent to the refuge there are 0.7 million acres of private land: along lower river corridors this is village corporation land; property belonging to private individuals is scattered along the waterways. The refuge, 80 percent of which is in the Ahklun Mountains, offers outstanding scenery with a wide variety of terrain, including glacial valleys, tundra uplands, wetlands, sand and gravel beaches, rugged mountains and coastal cliffs. The myriad lakes range in size from tundra potholes to 13-mile-long Togiak Lake. Togiak Valley is the site of a rare geological feature: a 2-mile-long tuya, a flat-topped, steep-sided volcano formed when lava erupted under a glacier.

Climate: Summer months are usually moist and rainy, with temperatures ranging between 45°F and 75°F. Snow covers the mountains by early October. Ice forms on lakes and rivers in November and will remain until June. Winter temperatures range from -30°F to 45°F. The weather is unpredictable and it is not uncommon for a warm and sunny day to turn cold, windy and wet.

Wildlife: Togiak is a haven for migrating birds. As many as 200,000 waterfowl have been counted in the bays, lagoons and lakes along the coast of the refuge, where waterfowl await spring breakup in the Arctic. About 50 percent of the world's population of brant use the refuge—up to 50,000 birds can be seen at one time in Nanvak and Chagvan bays.

Thousands of emperor geese and common and Steller's eiders migrate through the refuge, along with significant numbers of king eiders, harlequin ducks and black scoters. Bald eagles nest inland and on coastal cliffs. The refuge is home to one of the largest populations of cliff-nesting seabirds in

the eastern Bering Sea. Cape Newenham, Cape Peirce, Bird Rock and Shaiak Island support an estimated population of 1 million common murres and black-legged kittiwakes.

Brown bear are the most numerous large mammal. Caribou occasionally migrate through the northeastern corner of the refuge. There is a thriving herd of caribou on the Nushagak Peninsula at the southeast corner of the refuge, which was transplanted there in 1988. Smaller mammals include the hoary marmot, beaver, wolverine, otter, mink, red fox and an occasional wolf. Walrus, Steller sea lions and harbor seals haul out on the shoreline. Gray whales feed close to shore; beluga and killer whales are sometimes seen along the coast.

The refuge attracts sportfishermen from around the world with major concentrations of 5 species of salmon, grayling, rainbow trout and Dolly Varden (arctic char) in the Togiak, Kanektok and Goodnews drainages. Other fish available are lake trout, burbot and northern pike.

Activities: Sportfishing and hunting are the major recreational activities on the refuge. Other activities are river floating (the Togiak, Goodnews and Kanektok rivers), hiking, sightseeing, camping and wildlife observation/photography.

One of the primary purposes of the refuge is to provide opportunities for subsistence activities: hunting, fishing and gathering. Commercial fishing occurs along the coast at nearly every river mouth. The Togiak has a major herring fishery.

Archaeological evidence indicates that humans have occupied the area for at least 2,000 and perhaps 5,000 years. Today, the residents of 6 nearby Eskimo villages use the refuge for subsistence activities. Their camps, fish nets and other equipment are critical to their livelihood and should be left undisturbed. Also, much of the land around the villages of Quinhagak, Platinum, Goodnews Bay, Togiak, Twin Hills and Manokotak is private property and should be respected. To avoid trespassing, consult the refuge office in Dillingham about the location of private lands.

The refuge office encourages anyone planning a trip to the refuge to discuss planned itineraries with the refuge staff as a safety precaution and also to allow the Fish and Wildlife Service to assess public use of the refuge. The refuge currently is in the planning stage and may in the future require visitors to obtain permits.

Accommodations: Hotel, food and medical services can be found in Dillingham and Bethel. There are limited facilities in Goodnews Bay, Togiak and Quinhagak. There are no campgrounds or established trail systems on the refuge. Camping on gravel bars below the high water mark is encouraged to reduce environmental impact and trespass on Native lands. The refuge office suggests that drinking water be boiled or chemically purified to avoid giardiasis, an intestinal disease. Several guides and outfitters operate within the refuge.

Access: The refuge can be reached by scheduled airline to Dillingham or Bethel, then a scheduled flight to one of the adjacent villages or a charter flight to the refuge.

For more information contact: Refuge Manager, Togiak National Wildlife Refuge, P.O. Box 270, Dillingham, AK 99576; phone 842-1063, fax 842-5402.

Walrus Islands State Game Sanctuary (Round Island)

This sanctuary in Bristol Bay offers an unsurpassed opportunity to view and photograph large numbers of bull walrus from May to September. There are 7 islands in the sanctuary, but Round Island 70 miles southwest of Dillingham is the one most used.

Wildlife: Between 6,000 and 8,000 male walruses return to the island each spring as the ice pack recedes northward. Females with young are seldom seen in Bristol Bay as they remain near the edge of the ice pack.

Hundreds of thousands of seabirds arrive on Round Island in the wake of the walruses. Murres, tufted and horned puffins, kittiwakes, auklets and others nest on the rocky cliffs until August. A colony of up to 200 Steller sea lions haul out on the southern shore of the island from May to September, and gray whales pass by during April and May as they migrate north. Year-round residents of the island are red foxes.

Accommodations: Round Island provides a true wilderness experience. There are no facilities or services available to visitors. Fresh water is available in the camping area, where there is also an outhouse. There is no firewood. Visitors must bring their own food, fuel, shelter and equipment. Tents should have waterproof flies and be able to withstand winds up to 60 mph. A full suit of rain gear and waterproof boots are essential. Fish and Game advises visitors to keep their schedules flexible and bring extra supplies since unpredictable weather can delay travel to or from the island.

Round Island is very rugged. The terrain is steep and the climate can be extremely inhospitable. Visitors should be experienced wilderness campers as well as in good physical condition. It is not recommended for the novice camper, the elderly, or families with children between the ages of 2 and 6, as the camping area is bordered by very steep rock cliffs. Medical facilities for emergencies are several hours to perhaps several days away, depending upon weather conditions.

Access: Travel to Round Island is difficult and regulated by permit from the Alaska Dept. of Fish and Game. Access is possible only by boat and is subject to weather conditions, which can quickly change for the worse at any time of year. A list of charter operators is available from the Fish and Game office in Dillingham. Don's Round Island Charter (493-5127) in Togiak provides regular service to the island.

Two wildlife technicians are stationed on the island to conduct walrus research and enforce Sanctuary regulations. They do not give tours. When you arrive at Round Island they will assist you in getting from your boat to the shore (a short trip on an inflatable raft). All beaches are off limits to visitors except in Boat Cove during loading and unloading. Boat Cove, on the north shore of Round Island, is the only access to the island.

Up to 12 visitors are permitted to camp on the island at one time. Permits are issued on a first-come, first-served basis and are

A walrus in the surf at Round Island. (Bill Sherwonit)

LAKE CLARK, THE UNDISCOVERED PARK

It's 11 P.M. on a July evening. The sun has disappeared behind a gentle hill, but the northwest horizon remains brightened by an afterglow of rich pastels. A band of yellow gradually yields to orange, then rose and finally purple.

Winds that swept in with an early evening rain shower have died, leaving the air utterly still yet surprisingly bug-free despite the midsummer warmth.

With the departure of the wind and rain, a shroud of silence has fallen. The quiet is broken only by the soft crunching of my boots on beach gravel, the occasional splash of grayling and the intermittent screeches of two young terns calling for their parents, out busily fishing for the evening meal. I share the beach with sandpipers and plovers that prowl the shoreline, skittering and dipping in their frenetic search for food. Just a few yards offshore, a family of old squaws swim past. And across the lake, an eagle circles over tundra brightened by multi-colored fields of wildflowers: blue monkshood and Jacob's ladder, yellow tundra rose, pink fireweed and prickly rose.

It is a magical, paradisiacal evening along Turquoise Lake in Lake Clark National Park and Preserve. Serene, yet bursting with life.

But less than 10 miles to the east, it's a different world, ominous and desolate. The tundra's greens, yellows and pinks give way to the blacks, grays and whites of rock, snow and ice. Rising darkly into the sky, 8,020-foot Telaquana Mountain is a natural fortress of solitude, its upper reaches guarded by jagged spires and pale-blue glaciers that overhang sheer rock cliffs. In fading light, it all makes for a magnificent spectacle.

Mountains, glaciers, wildlife, wildflowers, tundra, lake and sky. Wilderness that seems to stretch forever, in a park that epitomizes wild Alaska. Four-million-acre Lake Clark National Park may indeed be the quintessential Alaskan parkland. Within its boundaries are recreational opportunities for a wide spectrum of user groups, from hunters and anglers to river runners, sea kayakers, campers, backpackers, mountaineers and wildlife viewers.

Adding to the park's appeal is its close proximity to 2 of Alaska's most densely populated areas, Anchorage and the western Kenai Peninsula.

Lake Clark is therefore easily reached and has several access points. People can enter the park from Anchorage, Iliamna, Kenai or Homer.

Here, then, is a national park with fantastic scenery, easy access and diverse recreational opportunities. One would expect it to be among Alaska's most popular destinations. But it's not. In fact, Lake Clark is among the state's least known and least appreciated national parks.

"It's true," says Superintendent Ralph Tingey. "Lake Clark has a low profile. In a sense, it remains one of Alaska's 'undiscovered' parks. I'm not sure why, but I have some guesses. For one thing, it doesn't have any one focus. Denali, for example, has Mount McKinley and wildlife viewing. Katmai has its bears. Kenai Fjords has Exit Glacier and the coastal tour.

"The other big thing is that it's not

accessible by road. Sure it's easy to reach by plane and relatively inexpensive. But our society is so tied to the automobile. The bush plane is a very foreign experience for most people. And many don't like the feeling of being left in the middle of nowhere."

There's one other factor that likely acts as a crowd deterrent: the lack of visitor facilities.

The National Park Service's goal has been to keep development to a minimum within Lake Clark National Park. It contrasts sharply with Denali, which offers a hotel, visitor center, campgrounds and Park Road. Though park officials may eventually build some trails and campgrounds, such amenities aren't planned in the foreseeable future. To a large extent, the Park Service depends on the private sector to provide visitor-use facilities.

Several privately owned wilderness lodges are located within, or near, the park. But the simple fact is that their costs are beyond what most backcountry visitors are either willing or able to pay.

With no connection to Alaska's highway system, no singular attraction to catch the public's fancy and minimal visitor facilities, Lake Clark is likely to remain a low-profile park, at least for the near future. Which is fine with Tingey.

"If the people come, wonderful," he says. "We'd certainly like to heighten the public's awareness of the park. But I don't want to make Lake Clark a 'happening'; I wouldn't like to see it suddenly overrun by large numbers of people."

—Bill Sherwonit is a freelance writer living in Anchorage.

valid for a specified 5-day time period. The camping season extends from the first of May until the end of August. (During May, most of the island is still snow-covered and weather is usually cold and wet.) Permits are available after January 1; most prime viewing periods are booked up by April. (Walrus numbers, seabirds and wildflowers peak in July.) A maximum of 10 permits for any given time period may be issued more than 10 days in advance. Up to 3 additional camping permits may be issued for approved scientific or educational purposes.

To obtain a permit to camp on Round Island, you must fill out an application and return it to the Alaska Dept. of Fish and Game, Division of Wildlife Conservation Office, Dillingham, AK. A $50 application fee must accompany your completed application form. Detailed instructions are on the back of the application form.

Day-use permits are available for $10 for visitors who do not want to camp on the island. Up to 15 day-use visitors are allowed each day.

For more information: Contact Alaska Dept. of Fish and Game, Division of Wildlife Conservation, P.O. Box 1030, Dillingham, AK 99576; phone 842-1013.

River Running

Chilikadrotna River. This National Wild and Scenic River heads in Twin Lakes in Lake Clark National Park and Preserve and flows 60 miles to join the Mulchatna River 46 miles northwest of Nondalton on Lake Clark. The first 11 miles of the river are within the park and preserve. This swift (usually 5 mph) river flows through the forest west of the Alaska Range. It offers an excellent, but demanding, white-water experience with many stretches of fast water and rapids for the intermediate boater. The first 4 miles are Class II, followed by about 4 miles of flat water. Then it's 31 miles of Class II; there are many sweepers, which combined with the swift current and twisting course require constant alertness. About midway along this stretch (approximately 5 miles below the Little Mulchatna River) there is one Class III rapids. Rafts or kayaks are recommended; canoes should be used only by very experienced paddlers. The trip generally takes 4 days from Twin Lakes to the first Mulchatna River takeout.

This trip offers fishing for grayling, rainbow trout, Dolly Varden and pike. There also is lake trout fishing at Twin Lakes. Hiking is good throughout the course of the river and there is mountain scenery around Twin Lakes.

Access is by floatplane from Anchorage or the Lake Clark area to Twin Lakes. Exit is from the Mulchatna River 12 miles or more below the Chilikadrotna confluence, or from villages farther down on the Nushagak River. Related USGS Topographic Series maps: Lake Clark C-2 through C-7.

Copper (Iliamna) River. This fast, clear-water river heads in Meadow Lake and flows 40 river miles southwest into Intricate Bay on Lake Iliamna. The river connects Upper and Lower Copper lakes, and Upper and Lower Pike lakes. From Upper Pike Lake, the river offers a 1½-day-long trip with possible short portages suitable for relatively inexperienced boaters. This stretch features 6 miles of Class II consisting of 4 miles of Class I separating several larger rapids, some border on Class III. Boaters should be alert for right-angle turns. For white-water enthusiasts, the upper river offers a 2-mile stretch of Class III-IV between Upper and Lower Copper lakes, then 3 miles of Class III before 3 falls, which must be portaged on the left bank. From Upper or Lower Copper Lake the trip takes approximately 3 to 3½ days. Rafts are recommended.

The Copper River flows through a scenic forest and offers seasonally good fishing downstream from the falls for salmon and rainbow trout. Pike can be caught in side sloughs and lakes. Wildlife that may be seen includes bears, moose, eagles and beavers.

Access is by floatplane from Iliamna to Upper Pike Lake or to Upper or Lower Copper Lake. Exit is by floatplane from Intricate Bay or Lower Pike Lake. Related USGS Topographic Series maps: Iliamna C-3 through C-5.

Mulchatna River. This National Wild and Scenic River heads in Turquoise Lake in the foothills of the Chigmit Mountains in Lake Clark National Park and Preserve and flows 220 river miles to join the Nushagak River, 65 miles northeast of Dillingham. The first 24 miles of the Mulchatna are within the park and preserve. Above Bonanza Hills for the first 22 miles the Mulchatna is shallow Class II to Class III, rocky and fast. The alpine tundra around Turquoise Lake changes to spruce and hardwood forest downriver. Below the Bonanza Hills, the Mulchatna is an easy, leisurely float, wandering through a forest, although there is a 2- to 3-foot ledge drop about midway from the Bonanza Hills to the confluence of the Chilikadrotna River. Floaters also should be alert for numerous sweepers or logjams in the many channels of this section. Above Keefer Creek the river

passes through low hills; below Keefer Creek it meanders across the tundra of the Nushagak lowlands. Rafts are recommended above Bonanza Hills; rafts, canoes or kayaks are suitable for the rest of the river. This trip usually takes 2 days from Turquoise Lake to the end of the Bonanza Hills, then 4 days to the first takeout point. Thereafter, boaters average 12 to 18 miles per day.

Portions of the river valley are swampy, but many high places provide good campsites. Fishing varies from poor to good for grayling, rainbow trout, Dolly Varden and salmon, depending on water conditions and the time of year. There is beautiful scenery and good hiking around the Turquoise Lake area. Wildlife along the river includes a large beaver population.

Access is by floatplane from Anchorage or Lake Clark area communities to Turquoise Lake or to lakes along the Mulchatna below Bonanza Hills. Exit is by floatplane from the Mulchatna 12 miles or more below the Chilikadrotna River confluence, or from villages on the Nushagak served by scheduled air service. Related USGS Topographic Series maps: Lake Clark D-3 through D-6, C-6 through C-8, B-7 and B-8; Taylor Mountains B-1, A-1 and A-2; Dillingham D-1 through D-3, C-3.

Newhalen River. This large, clear white-water river heads in Sixmile Lake, then flows south 22 miles to Lake Iliamna. This beautiful turquoise-colored river has flat water for 8 miles from Sixmile Lake to an area called Upper Landing reached by road from Iliamna airport. Then there is 9 miles of Class I, with a few Class II riffles. Serious white water begins about 7 miles from the mouth of the river where there is a difficult Class V rapid, followed by 7 more Class IV rapids. The Class V rapid is signaled by a ledge extending nearly the width of the river at a right-hand bend. This ledge should be run on the left. Then there is a series of narrower ledges on a long, straight stretch, which should be run mid-stream. Boaters then reach a left-hand bend, below which an island divides the river into 2 chutes, with a rock pillar in the left chute. There are dangerous falls in the right chute, so run the left chute or portage on the left side. Portage can start from an eddy just above the island. This route requires a sure crossover from the midstream route around the series of ledges. A longer, safer portage begins at the wide ledge at the previous right-hand bend.

This river offers very good fishing in season for all salmon, grayling, arctic char, rainbow and lake trout.

Boaters should be aware that all of the land bordering the Newhalen has been selected by Native corporations. Contact BLM, 4700 E. 72nd Ave., Anchorage, AK 99507 for the location of public easements.

Access is by floatplane from Iliamna, by commercial air service, to Sixmile Lake. Or put in at Upper Landing via taxi. Exit is via a trail to Iliamna airport below a series of ledges called "The Falls" or float to the village of Newhalen. Related USGS Topographic Series maps: Newhalen dam site map or Iliamna C-6, D-5 and D-6.

Nushagak River. This river heads at 60°35'N, 156°06'W and flows southwest 275 river miles to the head of Nushagak Bay, 3 miles south of Dillingham. The Nushagak was the first river in this area ascended by the Russians in the early 1800s. Much of the river is edged by scattered forests, but the tundra is never very far away. The headwaters drain the Taylor Mountains, while the major tributaries — the Nuyakuk and Mulchatna rivers — carry drainage from the western lake country and glaciers to the east. The upper reaches of this river are very isolated. It is flat water all the way, but sweepers and logjams can be major obstacles. Canoes, kayaks and riverboats all are suitable for this river.

This river passes by the villages of Koliganek, New Stuyahok and Ekwok and boaters should be aware that there is much private property along the river corridor. Contact BLM, 4700 E. 72nd Ave., Anchorage, AK 99507 for the location of public easements.

Access is by charter plane from Dillingham to the upper reaches of the river or by scheduled air service to any of the villages. Exit can be from one of the villages or float to Dillingham. Dillingham has all facilities for visitors; there are limited accommodations in Ekwok and New Stuyahok.

Nuyakuk River. This river heads in Tikchik Lake in Wood-Tikchik State Park and flows about 50 miles to join the Nushagak. The upper 12 miles of the river are in the park. This river traverses a relatively flat valley and offers an easy float, with the exception of 2 short sets of rapids and a portage around a falls. The Class II rapids in the first 6 miles of the river can be easily portaged. The falls at the 6-mile point can be portaged by a well-used trail on the right that is clearly visible from the river. This trip generally takes 3 to 4 days from Tikchik Lake to Koliganek, the first village encountered going down the Nushagak. Rafts, canoes and kayaks are suitable for this river.

This trip offers very good fishing in season for all 5 species of salmon, arctic char, grayling, rainbow trout and pike. Moose, bear, beaver and waterfowl may be seen along the way. Campsites are adequate on the upper three-quarters of the river, but scarce on the lower quarter.

Access is by floatplane from Dillingham or King Salmon to Tikchik Lake. Exit is by scheduled air service from Koliganek, which has no visitor facilities, or one of the other villages farther down the Nushagak. Also, floatplanes can land on most of the Nuyakuk and Nushagak rivers. Related USGS Topographic maps: Dillingham D-4 through D-6.

Telaquana and Necons rivers. These rivers are semiclear-water tributaries to the silt-laden Stony River. The Necons heads in Two Lakes in Lake Clark National Park and Preserve and flows 16 miles to the Stony. It offers a relatively easy float on moderately swift water through an upland forest. There are 2 short (100 to 250 yards) stretches of Class II rapids on the Necons — a set near its outlet and another close to its confluence with the Stony River. Both may be lined or portaged. The Necons provides easier access to the Stony than does the Telaquana with the trip taking a day from Two Lakes to Stony River.

The Telaquana heads in Telaquana Lake, also located in Lake Clark National Park and Preserve, and flows 29 miles to the Stony. It offers more white water and better fishing for salmon than the Necons. There are 2 small falls on the Telaquana. The first is about 11 miles from its outlet and drops about 8 feet in 2 steps; the second drops 4 to 5 feet in several steps. Both may be portaged or the second drop may be lined or run. This trip generally takes 2 days from Telaquana Lake to Stony River.

Rafts, kayaks and canoes all are suitable for these rivers, although canoeists on the Telaquana should be experienced.

Telaquana and Two Lakes are scenic, offer good hiking and seasonally good hunting or viewing opportunities for moose, caribou, bear and waterfowl. Fishing is fair for Dolly Varden and grayling in both rivers and seasonally good for red salmon in the Telaquana River. Reportedly there are no good campsites at the outlet of Two Lakes.

Access is by floatplane to Telaquana or Two Lakes. Exit is by floatplane from the Stony River or lower Telaquana River, by mail plane from Lime Village or by scheduled air service from Stony River village, which has limited accommodations. Related USGS Topographic Series maps: For the Necons, Lime Hills A-3; for the Telaquana, Lake Clark D-3, D-4 and Lime Hills A-4.

Tikchik River. This river heads in Nishlik Lake in the Ahklun Mountains and flows 65 river miles south to Tikchik Lake in Wood-Tikchik State Park. This is a clear, gravelly stream. It is fast, and has sweepers but no rapids. Water conditions range from flat water to Class I, making this an excellent river for fishermen to float. For one of the most highly recommended trips in western Alaska, boaters can continue from Tikchik Lake down the Nuyakuk River to the Nushagak River and then to Bristol Bay. Canoes, kayaks and rubber rafts are suitable for the Tikchik.

This river has good fishing for rainbow trout, grayling and arctic char. Along its banks boaters may see ptarmigan, migratory birds, beavers and bears.

Access is to Nishlik Lake by chartered floatplane from Dillingham. Exit is by floatplane from Tikchik Lake for those not continuing down the Nuyakuk River.

Tlikakila River. *(ta-lick-a-KEEL-a)* This designated National Wild and Scenic River heads in Summit Lake and flows 51 miles to Lake Clark. This is an extremely fast but small glacial river that flows through a narrow, deep valley in the Alaska Range. A short portage may be necessary from Summit Lake to the river. Most of the river is Class I, but there are several hundred yards of Class III just below the North Fork confluence which can be portaged on the left side. This trip takes about 3 days from Summit Lake to

Lake Clark. Rafts or kayaks are recommended for this river, although canoes are suitable for experienced paddlers.

Access to the Tlikakila is by floatplane from Iliamna or Port Alsworth to Summit Lake. Exit is by floatplane from a small bay west of the river's mouth. Or boaters can paddle to Port Alsworth or farther down Lake Clark. Related USGS Topographic Series maps: Lake Clark B-2, B-3, C-1, C-2 and Kenai C-8 and D-8.

Togiak River. This river heads in 13-mile-long Togiak Lake in Togiak National Wildlife Refuge and flows 60 river miles to the village of Togiak on Togiak Bay. This river offers an easy, leisurely float ranging from flat water to Class I through tundra sparsely covered with willow, alder, cottonwood and some spruce. Low mountains flank the upper river. Boaters should use caution in crossing Togiak Bay from the mouth of the river to the village. Strong winds are possible and shallow sandbars may preclude staying close to the shoreline. It is possible to float the 12 miles between Upper Togiak Lake and Togiak Lake, but the river is small, multichanneled, meandering and obstructed in spots by logjams and many sweepers. There are riffles, but no rapids between the lakes.

The trip from Togiak Lake to the river mouth usually takes 4 days. Canoes, rafts and kayaks are suitable.

Refuge waters attract fishermen from all

A kayaker enjoys the flat water of Lake Beverly in Wood-Tikchik State Park. (Bill Sherwonit)

over the world. The Togiak River offers very good fishing for 5 species of salmon, grayling and arctic char. Moose, brown bear and eagles may be seen along the river.

There is private land along the river corridor. Check with the village of Togiak (493-5820) or contact Refuge Manager, Togiak National Wildlife Refuge, P.O. Box 270, Dillingham, AK 99576, regarding the location of private holdings.

Access is by floatplane from Dillingham to Togiak or Upper Togiak Lake. Exit is by scheduled airline from the village of Togiak where there are some visitor facilities, or by floatplane at numerous locations along the main river. Related USGS Topographic maps: Goodnews.

Wood-Tikchik Lakes. The 2 lake systems in Wood-Tikchik State Park north of Dillingham offer a combination of lake and river paddling, good fishing and beautiful mountain scenery. Many trip variations are possible. Favorite trips include floating the Tikchik River (Class I) from Nishlik Lake to Tikchik Lake; floating from Lake Kulik down the Wind River (Class II; white water, submerged boulders) and Peace River (flat water and Class I) to Lake Beverly, then the short Agulukpak River (Class I; short and swift, boulders) to Lake Nerka, and the 5-mile Agulowak River (Class I) to Lake Aleknagik, from which flows the Wood River (flat water) to Dillingham. *(NOTE: Nushagak Bay tides influence the lower half of the Wood River, making boating more difficult and creating tidal flats with few, if any, campsites.)* Other trip variations are exploring the fjords, enjoying the alpine setting of the Nishlik or Upnuk lakes area or floating the Nuyakuk. The Allen River connecting Chikuminuk Lake with Lake Chauekuktuli should be run only by experienced white-water boaters (per Alaska Division of Parks and Outdoor Recreation).

Kayaks, canoes or rafts with motors are recommended. No fuel for motors is available in the area. For lake travel, estimate 10 to 12 miles per day, paddling 5 hours per day. On the lakes the wind can quickly create white cap conditions; be sure to have survival gear and life jackets. Seasonally there is good fishing for 5 species of salmon, especially sockeye, and for rainbow and lake trout, grayling, arctic char and pike. Fishing is generally best in the rivers or at the river mouths. This area has beautiful mountain scenery. Hiking is generally hampered by dense brush separating lakes and alpine areas. Choose open, breezy spots to camp to avoid mosquitoes and other insects.

Access is by floatplane from Dillingham to any of the lakes. Exit is by floatplane from one of the lakes or by road from Lake Aleknagik to Dillingham. See Wood-Tikchik State Park this section.

Sportfishing

Except for a few roads around Dillingham, access to good fishing in the Bristol Bay area is primarily by airplane. If you have the time, however, you sometimes can walk or go by boat to a hot fishing spot. Boats occasionally can be rented or chartered at villages along the waterways. There are daily commercial flights to the transportation centers of the region where you can catch a commuter flight to a smaller village or charter a plane to a lake or river. In addition, commercial sportfish guides will handle logistics for you on guided fishing trips.

Bristol Bay is world famous for its sportfishing, particularly for trophy-sized rainbow trout which regularly attain 10 pounds. These fish are at their best in late summer and early fall. The Kvichak and Alagnak watersheds are within the state's Wild Trout Area. Special regulations designed to perpetuate the original wild rainbow trout stocks apply here, such as conservative bag limits and special management areas for catch-release and fly-fishing only.

Throughout the Bristol Bay area, the philosophy of catch-and-release is encouraged by everyone associated with the rainbow trout fishery, according to the Alaska Dept. of Fish and Game.

Tackle-breaking king salmon are at their peak from mid-June through July. These fish are not uncommon at 30 pounds and up. Chums and reds show up by July 1, pinks by mid-July (in even-numbered years) and silvers by mid-August. Salmon fishing is concentrated in the river systems.

Arctic char and Dolly Varden are found throughout this area and are most abundant in spring or in midsummer. Grayling can be caught most of the summer, but larger ones are more plentiful from August to October.

Farther west, rivers and their headwater lakes in Togiak National Wildlife Refuge provide excellent sportfishing for salmon, grayling, rainbow trout and arctic char. Lake trout are available in the lakes.

The Alaska Dept. of Fish and Game recommends that anyone traveling to remote areas should plan for the worst. Take a few days extra food, and fuel if necessary, and allow for a flexible schedule since weather can delay travel.

Although many villages have hunting and fishing license vendors, officials recommend that you purchase your license in Anchorage or another large community, since sometimes the local vendors themselves have "gone fishing." The Dept. of Fish and Game does not sell licenses.

More information about fishing in the Bristol Bay area may be obtained from: Alaska Dept. of Fish and Game, Sport Fish Division, 333 Raspberry Road, Anchorage, AK 99518, phone 267-2220; or Alaska Dept. of Fish and Game, P.O. Box 199, Dillingham, AK 99576-0199; phone 842-5925.

Chuitna River. Flows southeast 37 miles to Cook Inlet, 2 miles north of Tyonek. Fish available: king salmon June through early July, use cluster eggs, spinners or spoons; silver salmon July and August, use cluster eggs, spinners or spoons; pink salmon July and August, use small spoons or spinners; rainbow trout, use flies, lures or bait. Accessible by wheel plane (30 minutes flying time from Anchorage). NOTE: *Much of the land along the Chuitna River is owned by the Tyonek Native Corp. and fishermen must have a guide from Tyonek. Land on the north side of the Chuitna River mouth is public land.*

Goodnews River. Heads in Goodnews Lake in the Togiak National Wildlife Refuge and flows southwest 60 miles to Goodnews Bay at the village of Goodnews Bay. The river has 3 forks: the North Fork, 47 miles long; the Middle Fork, 42 miles; and the South Fork, 25 miles. The North and Middle forks are floatable with lake access; the South Fork has no headwater. The lower 22 miles of the North Fork and 15 miles of the Middle Fork are BLM and Goodnews Village Corp. lands. Excellent fishing. Fish available: 5 species of salmon, grayling, rainbow trout and Dolly Varden. Lake trout in Goodnews Lake. Access by air charter from Bethel or Dillingham. Land floatplanes below the confluence of the 3 forks (about 2.5 miles from the village). Wheel planes land at Goodnews Bay village. Sportfish guides offer fly-ins, a motorboat base camp and guided float packages.

Igushik River System. Located approximately 20 miles west of Dillingham. Heads in Amanka Lake in Togiak National Wildlife Refuge and flows south 50 miles to Nushagak Bay. (Nushagak Bay tides influence the lower half of the Igushik River, making boating more difficult and creating tidal flats.) Fish available include red salmon June to August; grayling best May to September; arctic char best June to September; rainbow trout best in late summer and early fall; and northern pike all year. Charter floatplanes available in Dillingham and King Salmon. No accommodations on lake or river.

Kanektok River. Heads at Kagati Lake in the Togiak National Wildlife Refuge and flows southwest 90 miles to Kuskokwim Bay, 1.5 miles west of Quinhagak. Excellent fishery. Fish available: salmon in season; rainbow trout best in late summer and early fall; arctic char best July to September; grayling year-round, best May to September; and lake trout. Access by charter floatplane from Bethel or Dillingham. No accommodations on lake or river, but several sportfish guides have motorboat base camps in the area. There are also several float guides. Not recommended for fly-in except at 1 or 2 floatplane landing locations on the river. No overnight accommodations at Quinhagak. The lower 17 miles of the river is Quinhagak Village Corp. land.

Kvichak River. This river heads in Lake Iliamna and flows southwest 50 miles to Kvichak Bay at the head of Bristol Bay. King and sockeye salmon, May through August, peaking in June and July; coho salmon to November; pinks in August, chums in July.

Lake Clark Area. Located approximately 30 miles north of Iliamna in Lake Clark National Park and Preserve. Excellent fishing. Fish available: lake trout, burbot, whitefish and northern pike year-round; red salmon June to August; arctic char, best June to September; grayling, best May to September. Accessible by small plane from Iliamna or Port Alsworth. Several private lodges in area require advance reservations. Other accommodations limited.

Lake Iliamna. Alaska's largest lake (1,000 square miles) helps support the largest sockeye (red) salmon run in the world. Iliamna, along with Lake Clark and tributary rivers, provides spawning grounds for the salmon, which grow to maturity in Bristol Bay then find their way back up the Kvichak River to lay their eggs, fertilize them and die. But sockeyes are only one of the salmon species that anglers go after in Iliamna Lake. There are also fine runs of kings, silvers, pinks and chums. Other fish include Dolly Varden, arctic char, lake trout and grayling.

The Alaska Board of Fisheries has designated the Kvichak-Alagnak watershed, which includes all of Lake Iliamna, as a Wild Trout Area. Regulations are conservative, designed to perpetuate the high quality wild rainbow trout fisheries while providing anglers a variety of fishing experiences. Large rainbow trout, probably the most sought-after sport fish in southwest Alaska, are available all season long, but most of the big ones (up to 18 pounds) are taken in late summer and early fall. During September the rainbows will leave the lake and enter clearwater streams to feast on salmon eggs and insects feeding on decaying salmon.

Besides the world-class fishing, anglers are treated to beautiful fall colors. Catch-and-release is practiced here, except for the occasional mortally hooked fish (kept for dinner) and the once-in-a-lifetime trophy saved for mounting.

Summers at Lake Iliamna tend to be cool and rainy, especially in August and September. When storms brew up, winds can whip the waters of the lake into high, dangerous waves. A wilderness lodge advises its visitors to bring down vests and jackets, wool shirts and good rain gear. Binoculars and, of course, a camera are also recommended.

Accommodations range from basic shelter to luxurious, first-class world renowned lodges. There are no established campgrounds around the lake. Some anglers prefer to stay in Iliamna itself (see Communities this section) and take day trips out via floatplane and hire a guide with a boat. Reservations at lodges should be made well in advance, but air taxi operators can usually accommodate the day fisherman.

The Alaska Dept. of Fish and Game reminds visitors that timing is critical, particularly for anglers targeting one or two species of fish. The department's Recreational Fishing Guide (available for $5 from Alaska Dept. of Fish and Game, Box 3-2000, Juneau, AK 99802-2000) provides preliminary information, and local guides and lodges can also help you plan your trip. Air taxi operators in Anchorage, Kenai and Homer can put you in contact with many of the sportfishing experts. The lake and its excellent fishing are accessible by scheduled and charter flights from Anchorage, Dillingham and King Salmon.

Lake Iliamna does not lie within any established park or refuge boundaries. Much of the land is owned by Native corporations. *NOTE: Iliamna Natives Ltd. charges fees for camping on corporation land; $25 per person per night for 1 or 2 people; $50 per night for a group of 3 or more. Fees are payable in advance and are nonrefundable.* Hiking, berry picking and fishing also are permitted on corporation lands; hunting in general is not. Wood cutting is not permitted. These and other land-use regulations are available from the corporation office, P.O. Box 245, Iliamna, AK 99606.

Nushagak-Mulchatna River System. This river system offers hundreds of miles of river fishing from Twin and Turquoise lakes in Lake Clark National Park and Preserve downstream to Dillingham. Float trips are popular. Fish available in the system: king salmon best in June and July; coho salmon best Aug. 15 to September; lake trout in headwater lakes year-round; grayling best May to September; arctic char best June to September; rainbow trout best in late summer and early fall; northern pike all year. Access by floatplane from Dillingham, King Salmon or Iliamna. Private lodges on the river.

Tikchik System. Located approximately 80 miles north of Dillingham in Wood-Tikchik State Park. Fish available: red salmon June to August; pink salmon July to August; grayling best May to September; arctic char best June to September; rainbow trout best in late summer and early fall; lake trout and northern pike year-round. Access by floatplane from Dillingham or King Salmon. Commercial lodges on lake require advance reservations; no other accommodations.

Togiak System. Located approximately 60 miles west of Dillingham. Togiak River heads in Togiak Lake in Togiak National Wildlife Refuge and flows southwest 58 miles to Togiak Bay, 2 miles east of Togiak village. A popular river to float. Easily accessible by floatplane (depending on water level), wheelplane and motorboat. Upper 38 miles of river is within Togiak Wilderness Area; lower 20 miles is Togiak Village Corp. land. Lakes in the system are Togiak Lake, Ongivinuk Lake, Gechiak Lake and Pungokepuk Lake. Fish available: all salmon in season; king salmon best June and July; coho salmon best Aug. 15 to September; grayling best May to September; arctic char best June to September; rainbow trout best in late summer and early fall; northern pike year-round. Access by charter floatplane from Dillingham, Bethel or King Salmon. Private accommodations on river.

Wood River System. Located 20 to 60 miles north of Dillingham. The lower lake, Lake Aleknagik, may be reached by road. Entire system navigable by riverboat or can be floated. Fishing best in rivers or at the river mouths. Fish available: all salmon in season; grayling best May to September; arctic char best June to September; rainbow trout best in late summer and early fall; northern pike year-round. Access by boat from Dillingham or Aleknagik village; or by charter floatplane from Dillingham or King Salmon. Commercial lodges located on the system require advance reservations.

YUKON-KUSKOKWIM DELTA

A vast, watery expanse of treeless lowland that supports millions of waterfowl and lies at the heart of the strong, traditional Yup'ik Eskimo culture—this is the Yukon-Kuskokwim Delta.

Villages, some 50 of them, are sprinkled generously up and down the Yukon and Kuskokwim rivers, around the shores of the Bering Sea and inland. Few of these villages have more than 500 residents. Bethel, the region's commercial and government hub, has fewer than 5,000.

In the delta outside Bethel, life goes on much as it has for generations. Subsistence hunting, fishing and trapping provide the livelihood, supplemented by seasonal fire fighting, construction and commercial fishing, and cottage industries such as basketry and skin sewing. Yup'ik is still spoken widely throughout the delta.

When Russian traders arrived in the early 19th century, their priests made converts to Russian Orthodoxy. The Moravians set off a second round of conversions in 1884 when they established a village which they renamed Bethel. But perhaps the strongest influence in the spiritual life of the Yup'iks is an older, intuitive connection to the land, the rivers, the sea, and the creatures that live there. Respect for animals taken in hunting runs deep in the Yup'ik culture and traditional festivals and dances honor animal spirits.

Most of the delta is encompassed in the Yukon Delta National Wildlife Refuge, which draws visitors for hiking, boating and bird watching. Those who venture into this remote, hauntingly beautiful country can count themselves lucky to catch glimpses of the Yup'ik culture manifested in racks of salmon drying in the open air or in women wearing *kuspuks* weaving baskets while listening to a radio newscast from Bethel delivered in both English and Yup'ik.

Tell-tale black wing tips identify adult snow geese in flight. These geese nest in grassy areas on the tundra. (Alissa Crandall)

Akiachak

[MAP 11] *(ACK-ee-a-chuck)* Located on the Kuskokwim River, 15 miles northeast of Bethel, 390 miles west of Anchorage. **Transportation:** Scheduled air service from Bethel. **Population:** 448. **Zip code:** 99551. **Emergency Services:** Village Public Officer, phone 825-4313; Alaska State Troopers, Bethel, phone 543-3494; Clinic, phone 825-4011; Volunteer Fire Department.

   Climate: Maritime; mean summer temperature 53°F; mean winter temperature 11°F. Mean annual precipitation 17 inches with 50 inches of snow.

   Private Aircraft: Airstrip adjacent southeast; elev. 25 feet; length 1,900 feet; gravel and dirt; no fuel; unattended. The runway is used year-round. Runway condition not monitored; visual inspection recommended prior to using. Runway has rough, rolling soft spots.

   Visitor Facilities: Lodging available at Yupiit School District or the IRA (Indian Reorganization Act) Council offices; make arrangements through the school, phone 825-4013. Food is available at Guy J's Restaurant. Groceries/supplies are available at Akiachak Enterprises, George Enterprises and General Merchandise Store. There is a washeteria. Fishing/hunting licenses available.

   Akiachak was founded in the early 1890s by former residents of another village; a population of 43 was recorded in the 1890 census. By 1895 the Moravian Church at Bethel had stationed a helper here.

   Akiachak's school was established in 1930 and an airstrip was built in 1967. Akiachak is located within Yukon Delta National Wildlife Refuge. Many village residents are likely to be gone to fish camps during the summer.

   This Eskimo community has a Moravian church. There is a school here which offers grades kindergarten through 12. There is a community electricity system and a community water supply at the washeteria; sewage system is privies and honey buckets. Freight arrives by barge or mail plane. Government

address: Akiachak IRA Council, P.O. Box 70, Akiachak, AK 99551; phone 825-4626, fax 825-4029. Village corporation address: Akiachak Ltd., P.O. Box 100, Akiachak, AK 99551; phone 825-4328.

Akiak

[MAP 11] *(ACK-ee-ack)* Located on the Kuskokwim River, 20 miles northeast of Bethel, 380 miles west of Anchorage. **Transportation:** Scheduled air service from Bethel. **Population:** 247. **Zip code:** 99552. **Emergency Services:** Village Public Safety Officer, phone 765-7527; Alaska State Troopers, Bethel, phone 543-3494; Clinic, phone 765-7527; Volunteer Fire Department.

   Climate: Maritime, summers cool, winters moderate.

   Private Aircraft: Airstrip adjacent southwest; elev. 22 feet; length 2,000 feet; gravel; no fuel; unattended. Runway condition not monitored; visual inspection recommended prior to using. Southwest 1,000 feet of runway subject to flooding during breakup.

   Visitor Facilities: Arrangements for accommodations may be made through the village office (765-7411); or at the school (P.O. Box 52227, Aniak, AK 99552; phone 765-7212). No restaurant or banking. Laundry facilities are available. Supplies available in the community at Ivan Gro and Kashatok Trading Post. Fishing/hunting licenses available.

   The name Akiak reportedly means "crossing over" and refers to a trail that connected the Kuskokwim River at Akiak with the Yukon River. The earliest census including Akiak was that of 1880 when 175 people were reported living here.

   An early convert to the Moravian Church, Helper Neck, who was noted for writing a syllabary of the Eskimo language, was born in Akiak and was stationed here in 1895.

   A school was established at Akiak in 1911 by John H. Kilbuck, co-founder in 1885 of the Moravian Mission at Bethel, the first Protestant mission on the Kuskokwim. Kilbuck was a Bureau of Education teacher at Akiak for several years; he died here of typhoid in 1922.

In 1907, gold was discovered along the upper Tuluksak River near present-day Nyac. Akiak was a supply point for the mining operations until an airstrip was built at Nyac.

An airport was completed in 1958 and a National Guard armory in 1960. Akiak, located within Yukon Delta National Wildlife Refuge, was incorporated as a second-class city in 1970.

Visitors may view commercial fishing on the Kuskokwim River. Jim Barker, school principal, describes the local Eskimo population as very warm and friendly.

The community is served by 2 schools with grades kindergarten through 12. There is a community electricity system. Water is from individual wells; the sewage system is septic tanks. Freight arrives by barge or mail plane. Government address: City of Akiak, P.O. Box 52167, Akiak, AK 99552; phone 765-7411. Village corporation address: Kokarmuit Corp., General Delivery, Akiak, AK 99552; phone 765-7228.

Alakanuk

[MAP 11] *(a-LACK-a-nuk)* Located at the east entrance to Alakanuk Pass (the major southern channel of the Yukon River delta) 160 miles northwest of Bethel and 110 miles south of Nome. **Transportation:** Jet service from Bethel or Nome. **Population:** 571. **Zip code:** 99554. **Emergency Services:** Police, phone 238-3421; Clinic, phone 238-3212; Bethel Hospital, phone 543-3711; Volunteer Fire Department.

Climate: Subarctic. Temperatures from -25°F in winter to 79°F in summer. Annual average snowfall 60 inches, precipitation 19 inches.

Private Aircraft: Airport adjacent southwest; elev. 10 feet; length 2,100 feet; gravel; no fuel; unattended; 60-foot gravel turnaround midway of runway. Condition not monitored; visual inspection recommended prior to using.

Visitor Facilities: Accommodations available for $35 per person per night at the city office (238-3313). The high school serves lunch daily from 11 A.M. to noon. Groceries, clothing, first-aid supplies, hardware, camera film and sporting goods can be purchased at 4 stores in the community: D.F. Jorgensen & Co., Alakanuk Native Store, Alstroms Store, and The Annex Store. Local arts and crafts available for purchase include carved ivory,

grass baskets, Eskimo boots and beading. Laundromat facilities available. No banking or major repair services. Rental transportation and taxi available. Diesel fuel available at the Native store. Moorage facilities available at city dock with depth of 7 feet. Water available from the city.

Alakanuk is a Yup'ik word meaning "wrong way," aptly applied to a village on a maze of watercourses. The Eskimo village was first reported by G.R. Putnam of the U.S. Coast and Geodetic Survey in 1899, although it was occupied before Russians arrived in the delta region in the 1830s. It is the longest village on the lower Yukon River, stretching for 3 miles along a slough. With the establishment of a school in 1959, population increased and the village became a second-class city with its incorporation in 1969. One local resident describes Alakanuk as "a wonderful place to live, with friendly people and fresh, clean air." There are 2 annual potlatches, one in mid-February, the other in mid-April.

Recreation is fishing and hunting. Fish include king, coho and chum salmon, whitefish, sheefish and lush. Traveling is done by snowmobile in winter and boat in summer. Larger boats should use caution at the entrance of the Yukon. The controlling depth is 10 feet and extreme caution is advised because of shifting sandbars. Pilot services available, phone 238-3629 or VHF16.

Communications include phones, mail plane, radio and TV. The community is served by Catholic and Assembly of God churches and a school with grades kindergarten through 12. Public water and electricity are available. Sewage system is honey buckets. Alakanuk prohibits the sale and importation of alcoholic beverages. Freight arrives by cargo plane and barge. Government address: City of Alakanuk, P.O. Box 167, Alakanuk, AK 99554; phone 238-3313. Village corporation address: Alakanuk Native Corp., P.O. Box 89, Alakanuk, AK 99554; phone 238-3117.

Andreafsky

(See **St. Marys**)

Aniak

[MAP 12] *(AN-ee-ack)* Located on the south bank of the Kuskokwim River at the head of Aniak Slough, 59 miles southwest of Russian Mission, 90 miles northeast of Bethel, 325 miles west of Anchorage. **Transportation:**

Scheduled or charter air service from Bethel. **Population: 518. Zip code: 99557. Emergency Services:** Village Public Safety Officer, phone 675-4326; Alaska State Trooper, phone 675-4398; Clinic, phone 675-4346; Fire Department, 911.

Elevation: 80 feet. **Climate:** Maritime in the summer and continental in the winter, thus summer temperatures are higher and winter temperatures colder than along the Bering Sea coast. Annual precipitation averages 17 inches, with 85 inches of snow. Expect snow between late September and early May. Strong winds common, especially in winter.

Private Aircraft: Airport adjacent south; elev. 88 feet; length 6,000 feet; gravel; fuel 80, 100; attended Monday to Saturday. Runway condition reports and snow and ice removal available only during duty hours. Passenger terminal, ticket counter and restrooms at airport. Transportation into village available. Seaplane landings in Aniak Slough and river in front of town.

Visitor Facilities: Accommodations available at Aniak Lodge (675-4317) and Benders Bed & Breakfast (675-4329). Food is available at Aniak Lodge and at Burt's Burgers. Laundry facilities available; no banking services. Groceries, clothing, first-aid supplies, hardware, camera film and sporting goods available in the community. Arts and crafts available for purchase include carved ivory. Fishing/hunting licenses available. Guide services available. Repair services available for marine engines, boats and airplanes. Rental transportation available. Fuel available includes marine gas, diesel, propane and regular gasoline. No moorage facilities.

Aniak is a Yup'ik Eskimo word meaning "place where it comes out," referring to the nearby mouth of the Aniak River. This river played a key role in the placer gold rush of 1900–01 when prospectors from Nome stampeded to the Kuskokwim Delta after hearing of discoveries along the "Yellow River" (later identified as the Aniak River), so-called because of its discoloration from silt. A Russian-era trader called Semen Lukin is credited with the discovery of gold near Aniak in 1832, but no 20th century settlement was started until Tom L. Johnson homesteaded the long-abandoned site of the old Eskimo village in 1914 and opened a general store. A territorial school opened in 1936. Construction of an airfield in 1939 was followed by the erection of a White Alice radar-relay station in 1956. The community started to grow as people from the surrounding area moved to Aniak to find jobs. Several businesses were started to serve the increased population and Aniak became the transportation hub for the mid-Kuskokwim region. Aniak today is the headquarters of the regional school district, as well as the regional offices of several state and federal agencies. Aniak is a second-class city, incorporated in 1972.

Aniak is the regional hub for the Kuskokwim Corp., the major landowner in the region. Land use permits are required to use lands owned by the Kuskokwim Corp. Uses include fishing, temporary camping, seasonal campsite, land crossing and research. There is a $100 administration fee. Big game hunting fee is $400. Seasonal campsite permits $50, annual use fee $250. Permits can be obtained at Aniak (675–4275) or in Anchorage, 645 G St., Suite 305, Anchorage, AK 99501; phone 276-2101.

Aniak has a mixed economy comprising income from private businesses and publicly funded programs. The community is closely knit and has several related families. The Yup'ik language is still commonly spoken among the elders. Subsistence lifestyles are still practiced.

Mail plane and charter service are provided to several area villages through a local air service and other independent carriers. Aniak also is a transfer point for the commercial fishing industry and a staging area for firefighting crews in the summer.

The Kuskokwim River is frozen 6 months of the year, with ice often 8 feet thick. Spring breakup is a spectacular and often disastrous event when ice moving downriver hangs up in horseshoe bends and on sandbars. These ice jams can cause flooding at Aniak.

Fish in the Aniak area include most species of salmon, trout, pike, whitefish, sheefish and lush. Game includes moose, black and brown bear, and caribou. Other wildlife common to the region are fox, rabbit, mink, eagles, ptarmigan, beaver, lynx, marten, songbirds and waterfowl.

Communications in Aniak include phones, mail plane and TV. The community is served by Catholic and Assembly of God churches and the Aniak school with grades preschool through 12. Public electricity is available. Water is from individual wells. Community sewage system to some homes; honey buckets also used. Freight arrives by cargo plane and barge. Government address: City of Aniak, P.O. Box 43, Aniak, AK 99557; phone 675-4481. Village corporation address: The Kuskokwim Corp., 645 G St., Suite 305, Anchorage, AK 99501; phone 276-2101.

Atmautluak

[MAP 11] *(at-MAUT-loo-ack)* Located on the Petmigtalek River in the Yukon-Kuskokwim Delta, 15 miles northwest of Bethel, 410 miles west of Anchorage. **Transportation:** Boat; snow machine; scheduled and charter air service from Bethel. **Population:** 234. **Zip code:** 99559. **Emergency Services:** Police, phone 553-5215; Health Aide, phone 553-5114; Fire Department.

Private Aircraft: Airstrip adjacent southwest; elev. 17 feet; length 2,000 feet; gravel; no fuel; unattended. Runway condition not monitored; visual inspection recommended prior to using. Passenger terminal, transportation into village available.

Visitor Facilities: Sleeping accommodations available at the school (553-5112). No restaurant, laundromat or banking services. Supplies available in the community. Carved ivory and beadwork available for purchase. Fishing/hunting licenses not available. No guide or major repair services. Arrangements can be made to rent boats. Marine gas, diesel and regular gasoline and moorage available.

Atmautluak, a second-class city incorporated in 1976, is located within the Yukon Delta National Wildlife Refuge.

Communications at Atmautluak include phones, mail plane and radio. The community has 2 churches and a school with grades preschool through 12. Community water and electricity systems available. Sewage system is honey buckets. Atmautluak prohibits the sale and importation of alcoholic beverages. Freight arrives by cargo plane and barge. Government address: City of Atmautluak, General Delivery, Atmautluak, AK 99559; phone 553-5511 or 553-5610. Village corporation address: Atmautluak Limited, General Delivery, Atmautluak, AK 99559; phone 553-5428.

Bethel

[MAP 11] Located on the north bank of the Kuskokwim River 90 miles from its mouth, 400 miles west of Anchorage. **Transportation:** Scheduled airline from Anchorage and all villages in the delta. **Population:** 4,868. **Zip code:** 99559. **Emergency Services:** Police, Fire Department, Ambulance, emergency only, phone 911; Alaska State Troopers, phone 543-2294; Yukon-Kuskokwim Delta Regional Hospital, phone 543-3711; Bethel Family Clinic, phone 543-3773.

Elevation: 10 feet. **Climate:** Maritime; mean summer temperature 53°F, mean winter temperature 11°F. Mean annual precipitation 17 inches, with 50 inches of snow. The last day of freezing usually is May 30 and the first freeze is usually about Sept. 9.

Private Aircraft: Airport adjacent southwest; elev. 131 feet; length 6,400 feet; asphalt; fuel 80, 100 and jet A; attended. Airport facilities include passenger and freight terminals, ticket counters, restrooms and traffic control tower. Taxi service to town available.

Visitor Facilities: There are many lodging facilities and about a dozen restaurants. Public laundry facilities and banking services. Several grocery stores, 3 shopping areas and several specialty shops. Arts and crafts available for purchase include carved ivory, grass baskets, masks, beadwork, mukluks, *kuspuks*, Eskimo yo-yos, and fur coats, clothing and slippers. Fishing/hunting licenses available, as well as guide service. Repair services for marine engines, boats, autos and airplanes. Rental transportation includes autos and charter aircraft; arrangements can be made to rent boats. Also 3 taxi services in town, and bus service on weekdays. All types of fuel available. Moorage facilities at small-boat harbor.

The popular Yugtarvik Regional Museum, first opened in 1967, closed in 1992. It is scheduled to reopen as part of the University of Alaska Fairbanks, Kuskokwim campus cultural center.

A visitor center for the Yukon Delta National Wildlife Refuge is located across from the Bethel Regional Hospital, on the main road to town from the airport. The center features exhibits, and refuge staff present periodic programs for schools and the public.

Bethel was settled in the 1800s and originally was known as Mumtrekhlagamute. The first trading post was established in 1867. When the Moravian Church established a mission here in 1885, its missionaries christened the place Bethel, in obedience to a scripture verse which commanded, "Arise, go up to Bethel, and dwell there." The community celebrated its centennial in 1985.

Bethel is one of the largest towns in western Alaska. It serves as the administrative hub for the area's villages, with a district court, superior court, and Alaska Dept. of Fish and Game, U.S. Fish and Wildlife Service, and Bureau of Indian Affairs offices.

The area's commercial fishing industry provides a major portion of Bethel's economy and employment. Bethel is the transportation center for 57 villages in the

Yukon-Kuskokwim Delta. Bethel's location at the head of Kuskokwim Bay provides access to the Bering Sea. The town has the only medium-draft port for ocean-going vessels in western Alaska. Bethel's airport is reported to be the third busiest in the state. Transportation and related industries contribute significantly to the town's economy.

While there are still many people living mainly by subsistence hunting and fishing in the surrounding villages, most of Bethel's residents work year-round in the growing private industries, Native corporations and government jobs.

The Kisaralik and Kwethluk rivers, 1 to 2 hours from Bethel by boat, offer good recreational fishing for grayling, Dolly Varden and rainbow trout, as well as silver and chum salmon. The Kisaralik also is used regularly in the summer for guided float trips sponsored by the City of Bethel Parks and Recreation Dept.

Ten nearby villages lie on lands owned by the Kuskokwim Corp. Land use permits are required to use lands owned by the Kuskokwim Corp. Uses include fishing, temporary camping, seasonal campsite, land crossing and research. There is a $100 administration fee. Big game hunting fee is $400. Seasonal campsite permits $50, annual use fee $250. For further information, contact Kuskokwim Corp., 645 G St., Suite 305, Anchorage, AK 99501; phone 276-2101, or in Aniak phone 675-4275.

Bethel is located within the 20-million-acre Yukon Delta National Wildlife Refuge, largest in the United States. Many species of waterfowl make the refuge their summer home.

There are several recreational events during the year in Bethel, including the Kuskokwim-300 Sled Dog Race, Yukon-Kuskokwim State Fair, Mink & Fox Festival, Fourth of July Fete and Eskimo dance festivals. The Kuskokwim Ice Classic in the spring is a fundraiser sponsored by Bethel Community Services. The winner is the person who predicts most closely the time the ice begins to break up.

Communications in Bethel include phones, radio, TV and weekly newspaper, the *Tundra Drums*. The community is served by 9 churches, 3 public schools, a private school, a community college, 3 day-care centers and a prematernal home. There are community electricity, water and sewage systems. Freight arrives by cargo plane, barge and ship. Bethel prohibits the sale of alcoholic beverages. Government address: City of Bethel, P.O. Box 388, Bethel, AK 99559; phone 543-2047, fax 543-4171. Village corporation address: Bethel Native Corp., P.O. Box 719, Bethel, AK 99559; phone 543-2124. Chamber of Commerce address: Bethel Chamber of Commerce, P.O. Box 329, Bethel, AK 99559.

Chefornak

[MAP 11] *(sha-FOR-nack)* Located at the junction of the Keguk and Kinia rivers in the Yukon-Kuskokwim Delta, 100 miles southwest of Bethel, 480 miles west-southwest of Anchorage. **Transportation:** Scheduled air service from Bethel; snow machines; outboards. **Population:** 299. **Zip code:** 99561. **Emergency Services:** Village Public Safety Officer, phone 867-8712; Alaska State Troopers, Bethel, phone 543-2294; Clinic, phone 867-8919; Volunteer Fire Department, phone 867-8712.

Private Aircraft: Airstrip adjacent east; elev. 40 feet; length 2,500 feet; gravel; no fuel; unattended. Runway condition not monitored; visual inspection recommended prior to using. Gulls and birds in airport area.

Visitor Facilities: Make arrangements for lodging at the high school, phone 867-8515 or 867-8700. Groceries, clothing, first-aid supplies, hardware, camera film, sporting goods, vehicles and boats available. Marine engine and boat repairs available; rental boats and off-road vehicles. No bank, laundromat or fishing/hunting licenses.

This Eskimo village, located within Yukon Delta National Wildlife Refuge, was incorporated as a second-class city in 1974. Many village residents are likely to be gone to fish camps during the summer.

Local recreation includes basketball games, dancing and Eskimo dancing, bingo, Sunday night gatherings for young adults and 2 arcades.

Communications include phones, CB radio, VHF radio, radio and TV. The community is served by a Catholic church and 2 schools with grades kindergarten through 12. There is a community electricity system. Water is hauled from a community watering point or rain water or ice is collected. Sewage system is honey buckets. Chefornak prohibits the sale and importation of alcoholic beverages. Freight arrives by plane and barge. Government address: City of Chefornak, P.O. Box 29, Chefornak, AK 99561; phone 867-8528. Village corporation address: Chefornamuit Inc., General Delivery, Chefornak, AK 99561; phone 867-8211.

Chevak

[MAP 11] *(CHEE-vak)* Located on the north bank of the Ninglikfak River, 17 miles east of Hooper Bay, 120 miles northwest of Bethel, 500 miles west of Anchorage. **Transportation:** Boats; snow machines; scheduled or charter air service from Bethel. **Population:** 601. **Zip code:** 99563. **Emergency Services:** Village Public Safety Officer, phone 858-7012; Alaska State Troopers, Bethel; Clinic, phone 858-7029; Volunteer Fire Department.

Climate: Maritime; temperatures range from -25°F to 79°F at nearby Cape Romanzof. Snow depth on the tundra averages between 2¹/₂ and 3 feet, with an average of 60 inches of snowfall per year. Freezeup occurs at the end of October; breakup in June.

Private Aircraft: Airstrip 1 mile north; elev. 75 feet; length 2,600 feet; gravel; no fuel; unattended. Runway condition not monitored; visual inspection recommended prior to using. Strong crosswinds. No transportation to village.

Visitor Facilities: Lodging sometimes available at the school, phone 858-7713. No restaurant or banking services. Laundry facilities available. Supplies available in the community at Chevak Company Corp., Lena's Store and Wayne Hill Co. Arts and crafts available include carved ivory, grass baskets, masks, beadwork and skin boots. Fishing/hunting licenses available. No guide service or rental transportation. Marine engine repair available. Fuel available: marine gas, regular gasoline. No moorage facilities.

Chevak is also known as New Chevak because residents inhabited another village called Chevak before 1950. "Old" Chevak, on the north bank of the Keoklevik River, 9 miles east of Hooper Bay, was abandoned because of flooding from high storm tides. The name Chevak refers to "a connecting slough" on which "old" Chevak was situated. Chevak was incorporated as a second-class city in 1967.

Employment in Chevak is at its peak in the summer months, with seasonal fire fighting for the Bureau of Land Management and summer construction projects. The city also usually hires several people for city improvement projects. Other jobs exist with the city, village corporation, local stores and the school.

Income is supplemented by public assistance programs and local subsistence activities. Residents hunt seal, walrus, geese, swans, ducks and ptarmigan. Additionally, clams, salmon, whitefish, blackfish, needlefish, sheefish, pike and tomcod are taken. In the fall, families gather greens and harvest berries.

Local recreation includes basketball games, dancing and Eskimo dancing.

Chevak is located within Yukon Delta National Wildlife Refuge, which is the summer home for many thousands of migratory birds.

Communications include phones, mail plane, radio and TV. The community has a Catholic church and a school with grades kindergarten through 12. There is community electricity; water is hauled from central watering points. Sewage system is primarily honey buckets. Freight arrives by barge or mail plane. Government address: City of Chevak, P.O. Box 136, Chevak, AK 99563; phone 858-7128. Village corporation address: Chevak Co. Corp., General Delivery, Chevak, AK 99563; phone 858-7920.

Chuathbaluk

[MAP 12] *(Chu-ATH-ba-luck)* Located on the north bank of the Kuskokwim River, 10 miles east of Aniak, 100 miles east of Bethel and 310 miles west of Anchorage. **Transportation:** Charter plane from Aniak. **Population:** 131. **Zip code:** 99557. **Emergency Services:** Alaska State Troopers, Aniak, phone 675-4398; Clinic, phone 467-4114; Volunteer Fire Department.

Climate: Continental; temperatures range between -55°F and 87°F. Annual snowfall 85 inches; precipitation 17 inches.

Private Aircraft: Airstrip 5 miles northeast; elev. 300 feet; length 1,800 feet; gravel; unattended. Runway condition not monitored; recommend visual inspection prior to using. No transportation to village; no airport facilities.

Visitor Facilities: Lodging at the school, phone 467-4129, or community center through the city office, phone 467-4115. Laundromat available. No banking services. Groceries and general merchandise available in the community. Fishing/hunting licenses and guide service not available. No major repair service or rental transportation. There are moorage facilities; the only fuel available is marine gas.

Land use permits are required to use lands owned by the Kuskokwim Corp. Uses include fishing, temporary camping, seasonal campsite, land crossing and research. There is a $100 administration fee. Big game hunting fee is $400. Seasonal campsite permits $50, annual use fee $250. For further information, contact Kuskokwim Corp., 645 G St., Suite 305, Anchorage, AK 99501; phone 276-2101, or in Aniak phone 675-4275.

The community existed as a Native settlement as early as 1833. It has been known by several names, most recently as "Little Russian Mission." However, this led to confusion between this community and a village on the lower Yukon River called Russian Mission. As a result, within the last 20 years the village was renamed Chuathbaluk, Yup'ik Eskimo for "big blueberries."

For many years the village had a small population. It grew considerably when permission to live on the property was given by the Russian Orthodox Church. It became a second-class city with its incorporation in 1975. The economy depends heavily on subsistence activities, supplemented by some construction work, and cottage industries such as skin sewing and basketry.

The community is served by a Russian Orthodox church established in 1891 and on the National Register of Historic Places, and a school with grades preschool through 12.

Communications available are phones, radio and TV. Community electricity available. Water hauled from a community well. Sewage system is honey buckets. Freight arrives by air cargo and barge. Government address: City of Chuathbaluk, General Delivery, Chuathbaluk, AK 99557; phone 467-4115. Village corporation address: Kuskokwim Corp., 645 G St., Suite 305, Anchorage, AK 99501; phone 276-2101.

Crooked Creek

[MAP 12] Located on the north bank of the Kuskokwim River, at its junction with Crooked Creek, in the Kilbuck-Kuskokwim Mountains, 50 miles northeast of Aniak, 145 miles northeast of Bethel, 280 miles west of Anchorage. **Transportation:** Scheduled air service from Bethel. **Population:** 119. **Zip code:** 99575. **Emergency Services:** Alaska State Troopers, Aniak, phone 675-4398; Health Aide; Volunteer Fire Department.

Elevation: 130 feet. **Climate:** Continental with low winter temperatures and high summer temperatures. Mean annual precipitation 15 inches, with 61 inches of snow.

Private Aircraft: Airstrip 2 miles south; elev. 128 feet; length 2,000 feet; gravel; fuel

100; unattended. Runway condition not monitored; visual inspection recommended prior to using. No line of sight from one end of runway to the other. Some erosion of south end of runway.

Visitor Facilities: Accommodations for 12 people at local roadhouse. No banking services. Supplies, laundry and shower facilities available. Fishing/hunting licenses not available. Information on guide and repair services, rental transportation, fuel and moorage unavailable.

Land use permits are required to use lands owned by the Kuskokwim Corp. Uses include fishing, temporary camping, seasonal campsite, land crossing and research. There is a $100 administration fee. Big game hunting fee is $400. Seasonal campsite permits $50, annual use fee $250. For further information, contact Kuskokwim Corp., 645 G St., Suite 305, Anchorage, AK 99501; phone 276-2101, or in Aniak phone 675-4275.

The village of Crooked Creek, or "Kipchapuk," was first reported in 1844 by Russian explorer L.A. Zagoskin, who noted that the site was used as a summer camp by residents of a nearby village. Crooked Creek also has been known as Portage Village. A more permanent settlement was established at the site in 1909 following a gold strike along the nearby upper Iditarod River. An influx of people to the area in 1909–10 led to the founding of the Flat and Iditarod mining camps. Crooked Creek was a supply point for those camps, which were within easy access of the Kuskokwim River.

Crooked Creek village, which is spread out on both sides of Crooked Creek, is unincorporated.

There are few year-round employment opportunities at Crooked Creek. Government programs, the regional school district and a few support services provide the only permanent jobs. Subsistence activities supplement this income.

Crooked Creek residents hunt beaver, muskrat, game birds, hare, moose, caribou and waterfowl. Income also is obtained from trapping and the sale of marten, wolverine, lynx, fox and mink. In summer, the Kuskokwim River and Crooked Creek yield king, silver, red and chum salmon, as well as whitefish, pike, grayling, Dolly Varden, sheefish and eel. In the fall, cranberries, blueberries, raspberries, blackberries, salmonberries and currants are harvested.

Communications in Crooked Creek include 4 private phones; a pay phone is located at the post office. Two air/ground radios are available for planes. TV signals are relayed to Crooked Creek via statewide satellite. The community is served by a Russian Orthodox church and a school with grades preschool through 12. Electricity is provided by the Middle Kuskokwim Electric Co-op, which serves 5 villages on the river. Water is hauled from the washeteria or laundromat. Sewage system is honey buckets. Freight arrives by mail plane or barge. Government address: Crooked Creek Traditional Council, General Delivery, Crooked Creek, AK 99575. Village corporation address: The Kuskokwim Corp., 645 G St., Suite 305, Anchorage, AK 99501.

Eek

[MAP 11] Located on the Eek River near the mouth of the Kuskokwim River on Kuskokwim Bay, 45 miles south of Bethel, 420 miles west of Anchorage. **Transportation:** Boat; snow machine; scheduled and charter air service from Bethel. **Population:** 273. **Zip code:** 99578. **Emergency Services:** Village Public Safety Officer, phone 536-5129; Alaska State Troopers, Bethel, phone 543-2595; Clinic, phone 536-5314.

Climate: Summers cool and rainy, winters cold, with a brisk north wind. Winter temperatures drop to -35°F to -40°F.

Private Aircraft: Airstrip 1 mile east; elev. 40 feet; length 1,300 feet; gravel; no fuel; unattended. Runway condition not monitored; visual inspection recommended prior to landing. No airport facilities or public transportation into village.

Visitor Facilities: Arrangements can be made to stay at the school during the school year, mid-August to mid-May. Cost $20 per person/per day, linens and bedding not supplied. Make prior arrangements with the principal, Eek School, P.O. Box 50, Eek, AK 99578; phone 536-5229. No restaurants or banking services. There is a laundromat with bathing facilities. Groceries, clothing, first-aid supplies, hardware, camera film and sporting goods available at Iqfijouaq Co. (536-5211), Billy's Trading Post (536-5212), Carter's Store (536-5327) and Wassilie Foster's Store (536-5213). Arts and crafts available for purchase include Eskimo dolls, grass baskets and fur hats. Fishing/hunting licenses available, but best to purchase before arriving in Eek. Arrangements may be made for guide service with local hunters and fishermen. No major repair service or rental transportation available. Fuel available includes marine gas,

diesel, propane and regular gasoline. No moorage facilities.

Eek was founded by residents who moved from an older village affected by erosion. Most Eek residents are commercial fishermen, but there also is subsistence hunting and fishing.

Eek is located within Yukon Delta National Wildlife Refuge. Traveling up the Eek River by boat is a treat, offering a real wilderness experience, according to one resident. There are birds, beavers and an occasional bear to be seen. Fish caught locally include salmon, pike, grayling, trout and smelt. Hunting is for moose, caribou, ptarmigan, rabbits and seal.

Some prospecting for gold has been reported in the area.

The village corporation, Iqfijouaq Co., has established no user fees or other restrictions on its lands. Check with the corporation regarding location of private lands.

Communications in Eek, a second-class city incorporated in 1970, include phones, mail plane, radio and TV. The community is served by Moravian and Russian Orthodox churches and a school with grades preschool through 12. There are community electricity and water systems. Sewage system is honey buckets. Eek prohibits the sale and importation of alcoholic beverages. Freight arrives by plane and barge. Government address: City of Eek, General Delivery, Eek, AK 99576; phone 536-5129. Village corporation address: Iqfijouaq Co., General Delivery, Eek, AK 99578; phone 536-5211.

Emmonak

[MAP 11] (e-MON-nuk) Located at the mouth of the Yukon River on the north bank of Kwiguk Pass in the Yukon-Kuskokwim Delta, 175 miles northwest of Bethel, 490 miles west-northwest of Anchorage. **Transportation:** Scheduled and charter air service from Bethel or Nome. **Population:** 660. **Zip code:** 99581. **Emergency Services:** Village Public Safety Officer, phone 949-1728; Clinic, phone 949-1511; Volunteer Fire Department.

Elevation: 10 feet. **Climate:** Maritime; mean precipitation 24.5 inches per year; mean snowfall 57 inches.

Private Aircraft: Airstrip adjacent east; elev. 10 feet; length 5,000 feet; gravel; fuel Jet A. Runway unattended and not monitored. Recommend visual inspection prior to using.

Visitor Facilities: Accommodations and meals available. There are 2 restaurants. Food is also available from the Emmonak

Tribal Government (949-1720). No banking services. Groceries, laundry, clothing, first-aid supplies, hardware, camera film and sporting goods available in the community. Arts and crafts available for purchase include carved ivory, grass baskets, fans, fur hats and spears. Fishing/hunting licenses available. No guide service. Marine engine repair available. Charter aircraft available. Fuel available includes marine gas, diesel, propane, unleaded and regular gasoline. No moorage facilities.

Emmonak was originally called Kwiguk, a Yup'ik Eskimo word meaning "big stream." Kwiguk Pass is one of the fingers of water leading from the Yukon River above its mouth to the sea. The village was first reported by G.R. Putnam of the U.S. Coast and Geodetic Survey in 1899. Later, commercial fishing became a major industry and Northern Commercial Co. built a cannery, which was washed away by floods in 1964. Heavy erosion affected the rest of the village and it was relocated in 1964–65 to a site 1.4 miles north. The new location was renamed Emmonak and is becoming a center for commercial fishing and processing on the lower Yukon River. Emmonak is a second-class city, incorporated in 1964.

Emmonak has a seasonal economy, with most activity in commercial fishing taking place in June, July and August. The Native-owned Yukon Delta Fish Marketing Cooperative operates a barge with a self-contained cannery at Emmonak. AMPAC also operates a fish-cleaning plant. Other jobs are provided by local businesses and government. Income from employment is supplemented by public assistance programs and subsistence activities. Residents hunt moose, beluga whale, seal, ptarmigan, hare and waterfowl, and fish for salmon, whitefish, blackfish, lush (burbot), sheefish and tomcod. In the fall, families travel upriver to harvest berries. Income also is derived from trapping mink, otter, red and arctic fox and lynx.

Recreational activities at Emmonak include winter potlatches for other nearby villages, and city league and high school basketball games. One local resident characterizes Emmonak as a progressive town, where everyone works together to build a better community.

Emmonak is located within Yukon Delta National Wildlife Refuge. Winter trails connect Emmonak with Kotlik, Alakanuk and Sheldon Point.

Communications include phones, mail plane, radio and TV. Emmonak is served by Catholic and Assembly of God churches and a school with grades kindergarten through 12. There are community electricity, water and sewer systems. Emmonak prohibits the sale and importation of alcoholic beverages. Freight arrives by cargo plane and barge. Government address: City of Emmonak, P.O. Box 9, Emmonak, AK 99581; phone 949-1227. Village corporation address: Emmonak Native Corp., General Delivery, Emmonak, AK 99581; phone 949-1129.

Georgetown

[MAP 12] Located on the north bank of the upper Kuskokwim River east of the mouth of the George River, 16 miles northwest of Red Devil, 22 miles northwest of Sleetmute. **Transportation:** Charter air service from Bethel or Red Devil; riverboat; snow machine. **Population:** 3 permanent. **Zip code:** 99656. **Emergency Services:** Alaska State Troopers, Aniak.

Climate: Continental; mean precipitation 15 inches per year, with 61 inches of snow. Greatest snowfall, according to Sleetmute data, is in January.

Private Aircraft: A private, 1,100-foot dirt airstrip adjacent to the north accommodates small planes. Heavy winds in the fall and winter often make air travel difficult or impossible for days.

Visitor Facilities: None. Land use permits are required to use lands owned by the Kuskokwim Corp. Uses include fishing, temporary camping, seasonal campsite, land crossing and research. There is a $100 administration fee. Big game hunting fee is $400. Seasonal campsite permits $50, annual use fee $250. For further information, contact The Kuskokwim Corp., 645 G St., Suite 305, Anchorage, AK 99501; phone 276-2101, or in Aniak phone 675-4275.

When Russian explorer L.A. Zagoskin passed by the George River in 1844, he called it by the Indian name Keledzhichagat and noted that there were summer houses nearby that belonged to people from Kwigiumpainukamiut.

Gold was found along the George River in 1909. An early mining settlement, located west of the mouth of the George River, and the George River itself, were named for the first 3 traders at the site: George Hoffman, George Fredericks and George Morgan. By summer 1910, about 300 prospectors were living in the vicinity. About 200 log cabins had been built when a fire swept through the settlement in July 1911, destroying all but 25 cabins along the riverbank and 2 general stores. By 1953 the only large structure that remained was the 2-story log house that belonged to George Fredericks.

In the 1950s, the present settlement of Georgetown began emerging east of the mouth of the George River opposite the earlier community. A school was established at the new site in 1965 and operated until 1970. The present community consists of 5 homes and an airplane hangar belonging to Vanderpool Flying Service of Red Devil.

Georgetown residents must travel to other communities for seasonal employment. Otherwise they depend on subsistence hunting and fishing. Moose, caribou, bear, waterfowl, game birds, rabbit and porcupine are hunted. Fishing yields salmon, whitefish, sheefish, burbot, grayling and trout. In the fall the tundra offers blueberries, blackberries and currants. Some income is obtained from trapping and selling beaver, marten, lynx, fox and mink pelts.

Communication is by radio; there are no phones. Fresh produce and other freight are shipped air freight from Anchorage to nearby Red Devil and then flown to Georgetown. There is no school or church. Electricity is from individual generators. Water from wells or the river. Sewage system is septic tanks or outhouses. Georgetown is not incorporated. Village corporation address: The Kuskokwim Corp., 645 G St., Suite 305, Anchorage, AK 99501; phone 276-2101.

Goodnews Bay

[MAP 11] Located on Goodnews Bay on the east shore of Kuskokwim Bay, 70 miles south of Bethel, 430 miles west of Anchorage. **Transportation:** Scheduled and charter air service from Bethel or Dillingham. **Population:** 230. **Zip code:** 99589. **Emergency Services:** Alaska State Troopers, Dillingham, phone 842-5641, or Bethel, phone 543-3781; Health Aide, phone 967-8128; Volunteer Fire Department.

Private Aircraft: Airstrip adjacent southeast; elev. 15 feet; length 2,500 feet; gravel; no fuel; unattended. Runway condition not monitored; visual inspection recommended prior to using. No airport facilities or public transportation into village.

Visitor Facilities: Accommodations available through the village or the school, phone 967-8213. No restaurant, banking services or laundry facilities. Clothing, first-aid supplies, hardware, camera film and sporting goods available in the community. Arts and crafts available for purchase include grass baskets, carved ivory, beadwork, hand-sewn skin garments and knitted goods. Fishing/hunting licenses available. Fishing guide service available. No major repair service or rental transportation. Fuel available includes marine gas, diesel and propane. Moorage facilities available.

Originally known as Mumtrak, the village's present name comes from the bay on which it is located. The name comes from the Russian Port Dobrykh Vestey, which probably was named by members of a Russian expedition in 1818–19.

The community grew because of nearby gold mining activities in the early 1900s. Goodnews Bay is a second-class city, incorporated in 1970.

Communications at Goodnews Bay include phones, mail plane, radio and TV. The community has a church and 2 schools with grades kindergarten through 12. There are community electricity and water systems. Sewage system is honey buckets. Goodnews Bay prohibits the sale and importation of alcoholic beverages. Freight arrives by cargo plane, barge and ship. Government address: City of Goodnews Bay, City Hall, P.O. Box 70, Goodnews Bay, AK 99589; phone 967-8614. Village corporation address: Kuitsarak Inc., General Delivery, Goodnews Bay, AK 99589; phone 967-8520. Also: Traditional Council, P.O. Box 56, Goodnews Bay, AK 99589.

Hooper Bay

[MAP 11] Located on Hooper Bay, 20 miles south of Cape Romanzof in the Yukon-Kuskokwim Delta, 120 miles northwest of Bethel, 540 miles west of Anchorage. **Transportation:** Scheduled and charter air service from Bethel. **Population:** 845. **Zip code:** 99604. **Emergency Services:** Police, phone 758-4615; Clinic, phone 758-4711; Volunteer Fire and Search and Rescue Department.

Elevation: 18 feet. **Climate:** Maritime. Mean annual snowfall and precipitation are 75 inches and 16 inches, respectively. Mean annual temperature is 29°F, with temperatures ranging between -25°F and 79°F. Winter ice pack and strong winds often cause severe winter conditions.

Private Aircraft: Airstrip 2 miles southwest; elev. 18 feet; length 3,600 feet; asphalt; lighted; unattended. Runway condition not monitored; visual inspection recommended prior to using.

Visitor Facilities: Accommodations available at Qavartarvik (Sea Lion Hotel; 758-4015). For groceries and general merchandise, contact Hooper Bay Native Store (758-4228), Sea Lion Retail Store (758-4015), Native Store Shop (758-4712), Hill's & Joe's Store (758-4431); also Bunyan's Trading and Naneng's Store. Crafts available at most stores. Laundromat with showers is available. Hooper Bay is famous for the grass baskets and tote bags produced by village women. Other crafts include sealskin boots, ivory and beaded earrings, and ulu knives. Fishing/hunting licenses available. Limited guiding services for bird watching, contact the Sea Lion Corp. Gasoline and diesel fuel are available at Hooper Bay Native Store. Limited motor repairs available.

The population of Hooper Bay is 98 percent Yup'ik Eskimo. The early Eskimo name for the community, Askinuk, refers to the mountainous area between Hooper Bay and Scammon Bay. The village was first reported in 1878 by E.W. Nelson of the U.S. Signal Service.

Hooper Bay incorporated as a second-class city in 1966. The local economy depends heavily upon subsistence activities. Clams, blackberries and tomcod are abundant in season. A small commercial herring fishery at Kokechik Bay takes place each spring. Full-time employment is principally with the village corporation stores, school and local government.

Communications include telephones, cable and state satellite TV. There are Catholic and Covenant churches and a school with grades kindergarten through 12. Community has electricity, and 2 public wells supply the community water. Sewage system for homes is honey buckets. Freight arrives by air and barge. The village prohibits the importation, sale and possession of alcoholic beverages. Government address: City of Hooper Bay, P.O. Box 37, Hooper Bay, AK 99604; phone, 758-4311. Village corporation: Sea Lion Corp., P.O. Box 44, Hooper Bay, AK 99604; phone 748-4015.

Kasigluk

[MAP 11] *(ka-SEEG-luk)* Located 20 miles northwest of Bethel, 425 miles west of Anchorage. **Transportation:** Boat; snow machine; scheduled and charter air service from Bethel. **Population:** 413. **Zip code:** 99609. **Emergency Services:** Alaska State Troopers, Bethel; Clinic, phone 477-6120; Volunteer Fire Department.

Climate: Average temperature in Kasigluk ranges from 65°F to 70°F during a dry, warm summer and 40°F to 55°F during a wet, cold summer, according to one resident.

Private Aircraft: Airstrip 2 miles south; elev. 40 feet; length 2,400 feet; gravel; fuel 80; unattended. Runway condition not monitored; visual inspection recommended prior to using. Runway badly rutted with dips and rolls. No summer or winter maintenance. Ice runway on river during winter. Watch for trucks and vehicles on runway.

Visitor Facilities: Arrangements can be made for accommodations at the school (477-6615), the clinic (477-6120) or private homes. No restaurant or banking services. Laundry facilities available. Groceries available in the community at Store #1 at Kasigluk (477-6126) and Store #2 at Akula Heights (477-6113 or 477-6114). Akula Heights is about 2 miles from Kasigluk. Arts and crafts available for purchase include Eskimo dolls, mukluks, beaver hats, Eskimo yo-yos and fur mittens. Fishing/hunting licenses available. No guide or major repair services, rental transportation or moorage facilities. Fuel available includes marine gas and propane.

The Eskimo village of Kasigluk, located on a small river, is one of a handful of tundra villages in the Yukon-Kuskokwim Delta. Most of the others are located on the seacoast or on a major river. Resident Anni Slim says, "If you visit Kasigluk in the summer, you will see a lot of green willow trees, and the tundra is filled with salmonberries, blueberries, red berries, cranberries and alive with other plants that the people gather up for the winter."

Kasigluk is situated within Yukon Delta National Wildlife Refuge.

Communications in Kasigluk, a second-class city incorporated in 1982, include phones, mail plane, radio and TV. There is a community electricity system. Water is hauled from a central watering point. Sewage system is honey buckets. The community is served by 2 churches and 2 schools with grades kindergarten through 12, Akula Elitnaurvik (477-6615) and Akiuk Memorial (477-6829). Kasigluk prohibits the sale and importation of alcoholic beverages. Freight arrives by cargo plane and barge. Government address: Kasigluk Traditional Council or Kasigluk Village Council, Box 19, Kasigluk, AK 99609; phone 477-6927, fax 477-6212. Village corporation address: Kasigluk Inc., General Delivery, Kasigluk, AK 99609; phone 477-6026.

Kipnuk

[MAP 11] Located on the Kugkaktlik River near the Bering Sea coast, 95 miles southwest of Bethel, 320 miles south of Nome, 500 miles west of Anchorage. **Transportation:** Scheduled air service from Bethel. **Population:** 600. **Zip code:** 99614. **Emergency Services:** Alaska State Troopers, Bethel, phone 543-3494; Clinic, phone 896-5927; Volunteer Fire Department.

Private Aircraft: Airstrip adjacent southeast; elev. 20 feet; length 2,100 feet; gravel; no fuel; unattended. Runway condition not monitored; visual inspection recommended prior to using. *CAUTION: Frequent crosswinds and heavy bird activity near runway. Erosion in safety area outside the gravel runway surface.*

Visitor Facilities: Lodging can be arranged with the Kipnuk Traditional Council, Box 57, Kipnuk, AK 99614; phone 896-5515. Groceries and supplies are available at Kipnuk Trading Co., Kugkaktlik Ltd. Corp. and Kashatok Bros. They offer a limited range of clothing, first-aid supplies, film and some hardware. Blazo available; no propane. No fishing/hunting licenses. Arts and crafts not available for purchase in stores, though they may be available from individual artisans. Local craftspeople usually sell their goods through the gift shop at the Alaska Native Service Center hospital in Anchorage or through the Alaska Native Arts and Crafts cooperative, with an outlet in Anchorage.

Kipnuk, which is not incorporated, is located within Yukon Delta National Wildlife Refuge.

The community is served by a Moravian church and 2 schools with grades kindergarten through 12. There is a community electricity system. Water is hauled from a central watering point. Sewage system is honey buckets. Kipnuk prohibits the sale and importation of alcoholic beverages. Freight arrives by mail plane and barge. Government address: Kipnuk Village Council, General Delivery, Kipnuk, AK 99614; phone 896-5515. Village corporation address: Kugkaktlik Limited Corp., General Delivery, Kipnuk, AK 99614; phone 896-5415.

Kongiganak

[MAP 11] *(kon-GIG-a-nuck)* Located on the west shore of Kuskokwim Bay, 70 miles west of Bethel, 460 miles west of Anchorage. **Transportation:** Scheduled air service from Bethel. **Population:** Approximately 305. **Zip code:** 99559. **Emergency Services:** Alaska

State Troopers, Bethel, phone 543-3494; Volunteer Fire Department.

Private Aircraft: Airstrip 8 miles northeast; elev. 25 feet; length 2,000 feet; gravel; no fuel; unattended. Runway condition not monitored; visual inspection recommended prior to using. Runway rough its full length.

Visitor Facilities: Lodging available at the school, phone 557-5126. There is a washeteria with bathing facilities. Supplies available in the community at Qemirtalik Store (557-5630). Arts and crafts available for purchase. Fishing/hunting licenses not available. Information on other visitor services and facilities unavailable.

This Eskimo village, located within Yukon Delta National Wildlife Refuge, is unincorporated. Many residents work seasonally in the summer commercial fishery or go to their own fish camps.

The community has a school with grades kindergarten through 12. There is a community electricity system. Water is hauled from the washeteria. Sewage system is honey buckets. Kongiganak prohibits the sale and importation of alcoholic beverages. Freight arrives by plane and barge. Village corporation address: Qemirtalik Coast Corp., General Delivery, Kongiganak, AK 99559; phone 557-5428.

Kotlik

[MAP 11] *(KOT-lick)* Located on the east bank of Kotlik Slough, 35 miles northeast of Emmonak in the Yukon-Kuskokwim Delta. **Transportation:** Scheduled and charter plane service from Nome or Bethel. **Population:** 503. **Zip code:** 99620. **Emergency Services:** Police, phone 899-4626; Alaska State Troopers, St. Marys, phone 438-2018; Clinic, phone 899-4511 or 899-4414; Volunteer Fire Department.

Climate: Subarctic. Temperatures range between -50°F and 87°F. Snowfall averages 60 inches annually; annual precipitation averages 16 inches.

Private Aircraft: Airstrip located adjacent southwest; elev. 5 feet; length 2,200 feet; gravel; no fuel; unattended. Runway condition not monitored; visual inspection recommended prior to using. No airport facilities or public transportation into village. *CAUTION: Cleared strip east of town unusable.*

Visitor Facilities: No hotel. Arrangements may be made to sleep at the Kotlik Lodge (899-4313) or the local school (899-4415). No restaurant. Groceries and supplies available at ACCO and Kotlik Laufkak. Arts and crafts available for purchase include grass baskets, parkas and mukluks, and carved ivory. Fishing/hunting licenses available. Information on guide and repair services, rental transportation, fuel and moorage facilities unavailable.

Prior to 1960, only 5 or 6 families lived at Kotlik. Early in the 1960s, people from surrounding villages moved there because a school had been built and accessibility was easier to the oil and freight barges serving the delta. By 1965, Kotlik emerged as one of the larger ports and commercial centers of the lower Yukon River, a status that it retains today.

Kotlik was incorporated in October 1970 as a second-class city. It has a seasonal economy which peaks in the June through August fishing season. Most families leave for their fish camps up the Yukon River, where they set their nets for king, silver and chum salmon. People also hunt for seals, ducks and geese. During the winter months, families ice fish, trap, hunt and hold potlatches. Traditional dances are celebrated on Christmas and Easter and other special days. February brings a village potlatch. Dog races are held each March.

Communications include phones, mail plane, radios and TV. Assembly of God and Catholic churches serve the community, as well as a school with grades kindergarten through 12. There is a community electricity system and a community water supply at the washeteria. Sewage system is outdoor pit privies and honey buckets. Freight is transported by air and barge. The village has banned the possession of alcoholic beverages. Government address: City of Kotlik, P.O. Box 20268, Kotlik, AK 99620; phone 899-4313, fax 899-4826. Village corporation address: Kotlik Yup'ik Corp., Kotlik, AK 99620; phone 899-4014.

Kwethluk

[MAP 11] Located on the Kwethluk River near its junction with the Kuskokwim River, 10 miles east of Bethel, 385 miles west of Anchorage. **Transportation:** Boat; snow machine; dog team; scheduled or charter air service from Bethel. **Population:** 541. **Zip code:** 99621. **Emergency Services:** Village Public Safety Officer, phone 757-6928; Alaska State Troopers, Bethel, phone 534-2294; Clinic, phone 757-6715; Volunteer Fire Department, phone 757-6928.

Private Aircraft: Airstrip adjacent south; elev. 28 feet; length 1,700 feet; gravel; no fuel; unattended. Runway condition not monitored; visual inspection recommended prior to using. Freight terminal at airport. There is no public transportation to the village.

Visitor Facilities: No hotel. Arrangements can be made to stay in private homes or the high school through the city office (757-6614) or the village corporation (757-6612). No restaurant or banking services. Laundry facility may be available. Groceries, clothing, first-aid supplies, hardware, camera film and sporting goods available in the community. Arts and crafts available for purchase include carved ivory, Eskimo dolls, ulus, baskets, model dogsleds, beadwork and fur garments. Fishing/hunting licenses not available. No guide services. No rental transportation or repairs. Fuel available includes marine gas, diesel and regular gasoline. Moorage facilities available.

The name Kwethluk means "bad river" in the Yup'ik Eskimo language. There is evidence that Kwethluk was occupied by Native people in prehistoric times.

Kwethluk apparently was the only place along the Kuskokwim River where a Moravian church worker was killed while doing missionary work. An Eskimo helper of missionary J.H. Kilbuck was assigned to Kwethluk in 1889. The following spring Kilbuck went to Kwethluk because he was told the helper might have gone insane. The men of Kwethluk became hostile and forced Kilbuck to leave. A few days later they took the lay missionary out of the village, killed him and left his body to be eaten by dogs. Another helper was later assigned to the village and in 1895 a Moravian chapel was built.

Gold prospectors worked the Kwethluk River after discoveries were made on the George River and Crooked Creek in 1909. Most efforts were unsuccessful, but at Canyon Creek on the upper Kwethluk River a small placer deposit was found and mined until WWII.

A Russian Orthodox church was built in Kwethluk in 1912 and a school was built in 1924. An airfield was constructed in 1956 and the community became a second-class city in 1975.

Communications in Kwethluk include phones, mail plane, radio and TV. There are 2 churches and 2 schools with grades kindergarten through 12. Community electricity and water; sewage system serves some homes, though many residents still use honey buckets. Kwethluk prohibits the sale and importation of alcoholic beverages. Freight arrives by cargo plane and barge. Government address:

City of Kwethluk, P.O. Box 63, Kwethluk, AK 99621; phone 757-6614 or 757-6711. Village corporation address: Kwethluk Inc., General Delivery, Kwethluk, AK 99621; phone 757-6613 or 757-6612.

Kwigillingok

[MAP 11] *(kwi-GILL-in-gock)* Located on the west side of Kuskokwim Bay, 85 miles south-southwest of Bethel, 465 miles west of Anchorage. **Transportation:** Scheduled air service from Bethel. **Population:** 246. **Zip code:** 99622. **Emergency Services:** Village Public Safety Officer; Alaska State Troopers, Bethel, phone 543-3494; Health Clinic, phone 588-8526; Volunteer Fire Department.

Private Aircraft: Airstrip 1 mile northwest; elev. 20 feet; length 2,600 feet; gravel; no fuel; unattended. Runway condition not monitored; visual inspection recommended prior to using. Erosion in safety area on fill outside the gravel runway surface.

Visitor Facilities: Arrangements may be made to stay in private homes through the IRA Council, phone 588-8114. Limited groceries and other supplies available at Kwik Inc. and Chaninik Co-op, Inc. Fuel includes marine gas, regular gasoline, diesel and kerosene. Fishing/hunting licenses available. Arts and crafts available for purchase include carved ivory and grass baskets.

This Eskimo village, located within Yukon Delta National Wildlife Refuge, is unincorporated. Many residents work seasonally in the summer commercial fishery or go to their own fish camps. Resident James Atti describes Kwigillingok as "a coastal village in a flat country with very little high ground. Residents spend most of the year gathering food like waterfowl, seals, wild berries, and fishing in season. There are activities for all ages at the church. Almost every evening the men meet with their friends to gather wood for the fires for the steam bathhouses."

Communications include phones, mail plane, radio and TV. The community has 2 schools with grades kindergarten through 12. Community electric system. Water is hauled from a central watering point. Sewage system is honey buckets. Kwigillingok prohibits the sale and importation of alcoholic beverages. Freight arrives by plane and barge. Government address: Kwigillingok IRA Council, P.O. Box 49, Kwigillingok, AK 99622; phone 588-8114. Village corporation address: Kwik Inc., General Delivery, Kwigillingok, AK 99622; phone 588-8112.

Lime Village

[MAP 12] Located on the Stony River, 90 miles south of McGrath, 85 miles northwest of Lake Clark and 190 miles west of Anchorage. **Transportation:** Scheduled or charter air service from McGrath or Aniak. **Population:** 40. **Zip code:** 99627. **Emergency Services:** Alaska State Troopers, McGrath, phone 524-3222, or Aniak, phone 675-4352; Clinic, phone 526-5113; Volunteer Fire Department. **Elevation:** 552 feet. **Climate:** Continental; temperatures range from -47°F to 82°F. Precipitation averages 22 inches per year, with 85 inches of snowfall.

Private Aircraft: Airstrip adjacent north; elev. 552 feet; length 1,500 feet; gravel; no fuel; unattended. Runway condition not monitored; visual inspection recommended prior to using. Heavy winds in the fall and winter can limit air travel to the village for days at a time.

Visitor Facilities: None.

Lime Village is named for the nearby Lime Hills, composed almost entirely of limestone. The earliest recorded settlement at the site was in 1907 when Paul, Evan and Zacar Constantinoff were year-round residents. The community was first cited in the 1939 census, when it was named Hungry Village after nearby Hungry Creek, where some prospectors are said to have starved.

A Russian Orthodox chapel, Saints Constantine and Helen, was constructed in 1923 and is on the National Register of Historic Places. A state school was established in 1974.

Income in Lime Village is primarily from government programs, supplemented by subsistence activities. Lime Village residents hunt black and brown bear, moose, caribou, waterfowl and ptarmigan. Seasonal fishing is for red, king, silver and chum salmon; whitefish, pike and grayling. Additional income comes from trapping and selling the pelts of beaver, muskrat, marten, mink, fox, lynx and wolverine. In the fall, blueberries, raspberries, highbush and lowbush cranberries and salmonberries are harvested.

Communication is by good AM/FM radio reception, and TV signals are received. The community has a school that offers grades preschool through 8. Electricity is from private generators. Sewage system is honey buckets. Freight arrives by mail plane once a week. Government address: Lime Village Traditional Council, General Delivery, Lime Village, AK 99627. Village corporation address: Lime Village Co., General Delivery, Lime Village, AK 99627.

Lower Kalskag

[MAP 11] Located on the Kuskokwim River, 65 miles north of Bethel and 350 miles west of Anchorage. **Transportation:** Scheduled air service from Bethel. **Population:** 273. **Zip code:** 99626. **Emergency Services:** Village Public Safety Officer; Clinic; Volunteer Fire Department.

Climate: Semiarctic with maritime influences from the Bering Sea. Annual precipitation 19 inches with 60 inches of snow.

Private Aircraft: Kalskag airport 2 miles upriver; elev. 49 feet; length 3,200 feet; gravel; no fuel; runway condition not monitored; visual inspection recommended prior to using. Runway is maintained by the state. Kalskag also has a grader to service the runway and main road between Upper and Lower Kalskag. Airport serves both Upper and Lower Kalskag. Transportation into village available.

Visitor Facilities: Arrangements may be made to stay at the school, phone 471-2318. Restaurant located in the community. No laundromat or banking services. Supplies available at a general store. Fishing/hunting licenses available. No guide or repair services. No rental transportation or moorage facilities. Fuel available: marine gas, diesel.

Land use permits are required to use lands owned by the Kuskokwim Corp. Uses include fishing, temporary camping, seasonal campsite, land crossing and research. There is a $100 administration fee. Big game hunting fee is $400. Seasonal campsite permits $50, annual use fee $250. For further information, contact The Kuskokwim Corp., 645 G St., Suite 305, Anchorage, AK 99501; phone 276-2101, or in Aniak phone 675-4275.

The site of this Eskimo village originally was used as a fish camp for families from Upper Kalskag. It wasn't until 1930 that people began living in Lower Kalskag year-round. The upper village was a Roman Catholic center, and because of religious differences, many of its residents moved to Lower Kalskag after the Russian Orthodox Chapel of St. Seraphim (now on the National Register of Historic Places) was built in 1940. Lower Kalskag was incorporated as a second-class city in 1969. It is located within Yukon Delta National Wildlife Refuge.

Lower Kalskag's economy is based primarily on subsistence activities. Employment is largely limited to public programs. Hunting is for moose, black bear, rabbit, game birds, porcupine and waterfowl; fishing for salmon, pike, whitefish, blackfish and eel; and trapping for muskrat, beaver, lynx, otter, wolverine and mink. In addition, the tundra yields raspberries, cranberries, blackberries, blueberries, strawberries and currants.

Communications include phones, mail plane, radio and TV. The community is served by 2 Russian Orthodox churches and 2 schools with grades 1 through 12. There are community electricity, water and sewer systems. Freight is transported by plane and barge. Government address: City of Lower Kalskag, P.O. Box 81, Lower Kalskag, AK 99626; phone 471-2228. Village corporation address: The Kuskokwim Corp., 645 G St., Suite 305, Anchorage, AK 99501; phone 276-2101.

Marshall

[MAP 11] (Also known as Fortuna Ledge.) Located on Poltes Slough, north of Arbor Island on the east bank of the Yukon River in the Yukon-Kuskokwim Delta, 75 miles north of Bethel, 400 miles west-northwest of Anchorage. **Transportation:** Boat; scheduled or charter air service from Bethel. **Population:** 295. **Zip code:** 99585. **Emergency Services:** Village Public Safety Officer; Alaska State Troopers, Bethel; Health Aide, phone 679-6226; Volunteer Fire Department.

Climate: Temperatures range between -54°F and 86°F. Rainfall measures 16 inches a year; the growing season lasts 100 days.

Private Aircraft: Airstrip 1 mile southeast; elev. 90 feet; length 1,700 feet; gravel; no fuel; unattended. Runway condition not monitored; visual inspection recommended prior to using. No airport facilities. Transportation to town for scheduled flights.

Visitor Facilities: Accommodations available at Hunter's Sales Room & Board (679-6111). No restaurant, banking services or laundromat. Groceries, clothing, first-aid supplies, hardware, camera film and sporting goods available at Hunter's Sales (679-6111) and Fortuna Ledge Co-op (679-6427). Arts and crafts available for purchase include fur and beadwork. Fishing/hunting licenses available. No guide service. Marine engine repair available. Arrangements can be made to rent boats or off-road vehicles. Fuel available includes marine gas, diesel, propane and regular gasoline. No moorage facilities.

This community has been known by several names since it was first recorded in

1880. After gold was discovered on a nearby creek in 1913, the settlement quickly became a placer mining camp and riverboat landing known as Fortuna Ledge, named after Fortuna Hunter, the first child born in the camp. Later the village was named Marshall's Landing for Thomas Riley Marshall, vice president of the United States under Woodrow Wilson from 1913–21. It was incorporated as a second-class city named Fortuna Ledge in 1970, but also was commonly referred to as Marshall. The community officially became Marshall in 1984.

Marshall residents work primarily during the summer salmon season, either in fishing or processing. Other seasonal employment includes fire fighting for the Bureau of Land Management. A few year-round jobs are available through the local government, school, village corporation and businesses. Income is supplemented by subsistence activities. Residents hunt black and brown bear, moose, rabbit, waterfowl and ptarmigan, and fish for salmon, whitefish, blackfish, sheefish, lush (burbot) and pike. In the fall, families harvest blueberries, blackberries, cranberries and salmonberries. Some residents also trap beaver, lynx, mink, otter and red fox.

Marshall is located at the northeastern boundary of Yukon Delta National Wildlife Refuge.

There are 2 gold mines in the area, which are reached by all-terrain vehicles.

The community is perhaps best described by resident Darcy Kameroff: "There is an uptown and downtown and it has 2 main roads. It is quite pretty when all the flowers and plants bloom. There are 2 big buildings, the school and Hunter's Sales. Marshall is special because of the history and the people. The people are special because they cooperate and care about each other. Marshall's attractions are the old gold mine, Soda Springs, and the trout in Wilson Creek."

Communications include phones, mail plane, radio and TV. The community is served by Russian Orthodox and Catholic churches. There are community electricity, water and sewer systems. Marshall prohibits the possession of alcoholic beverages. Freight arrives by cargo plane and barge. Government address: City of Marshall, General Delivery, Marshall, AK 99585; phone 679-6415. Village corporation address: Maserculiq Inc., P.O. Box 90, Marshall, AK 99585; phone 679-6512.

Mekoryuk

[MAP 11] *(ma-KOR-ee-yuk)* Located at the mouth of Shoal Bay on the north shore of Nunivak Island in the Bering Sea, 149 miles west of Bethel and 553 miles west of Anchorage. **Transportation:** Scheduled and charter air service from Bethel. **Population:** 197. **Zip code:** 99630. **Emergency Services:** Village Public Safety Officer, phone 827-8315; Alaska State Troopers, Bethel; Clinic, phone 827-8111; Volunteer Fire Department.

Elevation: 40 feet. **Climate:** Summer weather cool and rainy, with temperatures averaging 48°F to 54°F. Winter temperature averages 17°F to 20°F, but can get down to -30°F. Wind chill can force the temperature to -100°F. Mean annual precipitation 15 inches with majority falling as rain July to October; mean annual snowfall 57 inches.

Private Aircraft: Airstrip 3 miles west; elev. 48 feet; length 3,000 feet; gravel; no fuel; unattended. Runway condition not monitored; visual inspection recommended prior to using. Runway soft during heavy rains or spring breakup. Animals occasionally on runway. No airport facilities. Public transportation into village available.

Visitor Facilities: Lodging is available at Bering Sea Reindeer Products (827-8940). Food is available at the Mekoryuk Coffee Shop (827-8227) and at Olrun's Rec Room. Groceries, clothing, first-aid supplies, hardware, camera film and sporting goods available at NIMA Store (827-8313) and David's General Store. Laundromat available. Arts and crafts available for purchase include carved ivory, grass baskets, masks, beadwork, knitted items and fur garments. Fishing/hunting licenses available. Guide services, including lodging and meals, available. Private boats available for charter. Fuel available includes marine gas, propane, unleaded and regular gasoline. No moorage facilities. Residents rely on snow machines and 3- or 4-wheelers for local transportation.

Mekoryuk is the only community on Nunivak Island which is part of Yukon Delta National Wildlife Refuge. Approximately half the island is classified as wilderness. Nunivak, third largest island in Alaska, measures 60 miles long by 40 miles wide. The federal government built a school at Mekoryuk because its well-protected bay made it an easy place to unload goods.

The residents of Mekoryuk are socially and culturally distinct from the Yup'ik Eskimos of the Yukon-Kuskokwim Delta. They speak a separate dialect of Yup'ik, termed Cup'ik, and do not participate in many of the intervillage social activities of the mainland.

The people here live mostly off the land and sea, although there are a few federal government jobs. Many of the residents go to fish camps around the island during the summer. According to one resident, villagers hunt birds, walrus, seal, and red and arctic fox. The island has many rivers offering excellent fishing for salmon, trout, char and grayling, including the Mekoryuk River, which runs by the village. Halibut and cod are caught in the Bering Sea. Many of the people also are involved in reindeer herding and the roundups that take place usually in July. Approximately 3,000 head of reindeer roam the island, along with 400 head of musk-oxen, which were introduced in the 1930s. People come from all over the world to hunt musk-oxen during annual permit hunts.

Some of the finest ivory carving in the world is done here. Villagers also make unique wooden masks and knit qiviut wool from musk-oxen into lacy garments which are sold in Anchorage.

The island supports many species of birds, including ducks, geese, swans, murres, puffins, cormorants, several varieties of loon, ptarmigan and arctic tern.

Attractions for visitors include wilderness trips to see and photograph musk-oxen, reindeer, seal, walrus and birds. Advance arrangements should be made for lodging and meals.

Communications in Mekoryuk, a second-class city incorporated in 1969, include phones, mail plane, year-round plane service on Alaska/ERA airlines, 2 radio stations, TV and cable. The community is served by a Covenant church and a school with grades preschool through 12. There are community electricity and water. Sewage system is honey buckets. Mekoryuk has a 2 percent city sales tax and prohibits the possession of alcoholic beverages. Freight arrives in the community by cargo plane and barge. Government address: City of Mekoryuk, P.O. Box 29, Mekoryuk, AK 99630; phone 827-8314, fax 827-8626. Village corporation address: Nima Corp., General Delivery, Mekoryuk, AK 99630; phone 827-8313.

Mountain Village

[MAP 11] Located on the Yukon River, 20 miles west of St. Marys, 470 miles west-northwest of Anchorage. **Transportation:** Scheduled or charter air service from Nome or Bethel, and direct air service from Anchorage. **Population:** 665. **Zip code:** 99632. **Emergency Services:** Village Public Safety Officer; Alaska State Troopers, St. Marys, phone 438-2018; Area Clinic, phone 591-2926; Volunteer Fire Department.

Elevation: 40 feet. **Climate:** Both maritime and continental influences. Winters long and cold; summers short and cool, often cloudy but with little rainfall. Mean annual precipitation 17 inches; mean annual snowfall 45 inches.

Private Aircraft: Airstrip adjacent northeast; elev. 165 feet; length 2,200 feet; gravel; no fuel; unattended. Runway condition not monitored; visual inspection recommended prior to using. No airport facilities or public transportation into village.

Visitor Facilities: Food, groceries, clothing, first-aid supplies, hardware, camera film and sporting goods available in the community. No laundromat or banking services. Arts and crafts available for purchase include grass baskets and Eskimo clothing. Fishing/hunting licenses available. No guide service. Marine engine repair available. Autos and charter aircraft can be rented. Fuel available includes marine gas, propane and regular gasoline. There is a village marina.

Mountain Village was named because of its location at the foot of the first "mountain" encountered by those traveling up the Yukon River. Mountain Village was a summer fish camp site until the opening of a general store in the village in 1908 prompted immigration by the residents of 2 small upriver settlements. A salmon saltery was built in 1956 and a cannery in 1964. Mountain Village became a regional educational center after it was selected as headquarters for the Lower Yukon School District in 1976. It is a second-class city, incorporated in 1967.

The town's economy is expanding due to its relative accessibility, growing fishing industry and function as a regional education center. The school district, village corporation, government and local business provide year-round employment for about 70 people. This income is supplemented by subsistence hunting and fishing for moose, swan, geese, ducks, salmon, blackfish, sheefish, whitefish, burbot, grayling and pike. Income also is obtained from trapping beaver, muskrat, otter, mink and fox.

Mountain Village is located within Yukon Delta National Wildlife Refuge. A 17.7-mile road links Mountain Village with the communities of Pitka's Point, St. Marys and Andreafsky.

Communications at Mountain Village include phones, mail plane, radio and TV. The community is served by 3 churches and a school with grades kindergarten through 12. There are community electricity, water and sewer systems. Mountain Village prohibits the sale and importation of alcoholic beverages. Freight arrives by cargo plane and barge. Government address: City of Mountain Village, P.O. Box 32027, Mountain Village, AK 99632; phone 591-2920. Village corporation address: Azachorak Inc., P.O. Box 213, Mountain Village, AK 99632; phone 591-2026 or 591-2027.

Napaimute

[MAP 12] *(na-PAI-mute)* Located on the Kuskokwim River in the Kilbuck-Kuskokwim Mountains, 28 miles east of Aniak, 120 miles northeast of Bethel and 285 miles west of Anchorage. **Transportation:** Charter air service from Aniak or Bethel; riverboats; snow machines or dogsleds. **Population:** 2 permanent; 30 part time. **Zip code:** 99557. **Emergency Services:** Alaska State Troopers, Aniak.

Elevation: 200 feet. **Climate:** Napaimute's climate is continental. Annual precipitation averages 20 inches, with 85 inches of snow.

Private Aircraft: No airstrip; floatplanes land on river.

Visitor Facilities: None.

Land use permits are required to use lands owned by the Kuskokwim Corp. Uses include fishing, temporary camping, seasonal campsite, land crossing and research. There is a $100 administration fee. Big game hunting fee is $400. Seasonal campsite permits $50, annual use fee $250. For further information, contact The Kuskokwim Corp., 645 G St., Suite 305, Anchorage, AK 99501; phone 276-2101, or in Aniak phone 675-4275.

Napaimute, which reportedly means "forest people," was once called Hoffmans after George W. Hoffman, an Englishman who established a trading post at the site in 1906. The modern-day village grew around the trading post and was primarily occupied by non-Natives, although a significant number of Eskimo residents also lived here. Hoffman built a territorial school in the village in 1920. In 1942 the village had 47 residents. By the early 1950s, most residents had moved to nearby settlements, particularly Aniak. Reportedly there are only 2 permanent residents at Napaimute,

although there are a few other permanent residents a few miles upriver, and as many as 30 part-time residents arrive during the summer fishing season. Napaimute is unincorporated.

Communication is by a single-sideband radio; there are no phones. There is no school. Electricity is provided by private generators; rain water is collected or river water is hauled; sewage system is honey buckets or the community privy. Village corporation address: Kuskokwim Corp., 645 G St., Suite 305, Anchorage, AK 99501; phone 276-2101, or in Aniak phone 675-4275.

Napakiak

[MAP 11] *(na-PAK-ee-ack)* Located at the head of Kuskokwim Bay, 10 miles southwest of Bethel, 410 miles west of Anchorage. **Transportation:** Scheduled air service from Bethel. **Population:** 353. **Zip code:** 99634. **Emergency Services:** Police, phone 589-2920; Clinic, phone 589-2711; Volunteer Fire Department.

Private Aircraft: Airstrip adjacent west; elev. 20 feet; length 2,500 feet; gravel; fuel information unavailable; unattended. Runway condition not monitored; visual inspection recommended prior to using. Call Billy McCann (589-2026) for runway conditions. Unmarked poles located 200 feet west and 260 feet east of approach for runway 16.

Visitor Facilities: Arrangements may be made for accommodations at the school (589-2420) and Napakiak Washeteria; contact city offices (589-2611), 10 A.M. to 5 P.M. Groceries and supplies available at Jung's Trading Post and Naparyalruar (589-2227). Breakfast and lunch are available at the school on school days only. Fishing/hunting licenses available. Boats may be rented. Information on repair service and fuel at Mott's Marina (589-2811) and 2 other outlets.

This Eskimo community reportedly was established around 1890 by residents of an older village that had been located at the mouth of the Johnson River and also was known as Napakiak. A Moravian chapel was dedicated in 1930. An airport was completed in 1973. Napakiak was incorporated as a second-class city in 1970. It is located within Yukon Delta National Wildlife Refuge. Most of the people in Napakiak speak Yup'ik as their primary language. Many residents may be gone to fish camps during the summer.

There is year-round fishing, including salmon, pike, whitefish, sheefish and lush. In winter, Tri-Cab (589-2715) and McCann's (589-2026) offer winter drives on the ice road between Napakiak and Bethel, and tours of other villages. In summer, boat tours are available (589-2715).

Napakiak's school has grades kindergarten through 12. There are community electricity and water systems. Sewage system is honey buckets. Napakiak prohibits the possession of alcoholic beverages. Freight arrives by plane and barge. Government address: City of Napakiak, General Delivery, Napakiak, AK 99634; phone 589-2611. Village corporation address: Napakiak Corp., General Delivery, Napakiak, AK 99634; phone 589-2227, fax 589-2412.

Napaskiak

[MAP 11] (na-PASS-key-ack) Located on the Kuskokwim River 8 miles southwest of Bethel, 400 miles west of Anchorage. **Transportation:** Scheduled air service from Bethel and winter air and river taxi service. **Population:** 350. **Zip code:** 99559. **Emergency Services:** Police, phone 737-7639; Alaska State Troopers, Bethel, phone 543-3494; Clinic, phone 737-7329; Volunteer Fire Department.

Private Aircraft: Airstrip adjacent south; elev. 24 feet; length 2,400 feet; gravel; no fuel; unattended. Runway condition not monitored; visual inspection recommended prior to using. Center of runway is 20 feet of gravel. Runway rough due to dips and ruts, and it floods in spring.

Visitor Facilities: Accommodations at city building (737-7626). Supplies available at Napaskiak, Inc. (737-7413). Fishing/hunting licenses not available. Fuel available for snow machines, boat motors, and 3- and 4-wheelers. Information on other visitor services and facilities unavailable.

This Eskimo community may have been established around 1800 by residents of another village forced to move because of erosion. The population in 1880 was 196. Many people died in the influenza and measles epidemics of 1900 and the village was abandoned for a time.

In 1905 the first Russian Orthodox priest arrived and baptized the entire village. St. Jacob's Chapel, listed on the National Register of Historic Places, was built in 1931; a new church was constructed in 1978.

A Bureau of Indian Affairs school opened in 1939 and an airport was completed in

1974. Napaskiak, which is located within Yukon Delta National Wildlife Refuge, was incorporated as a second-class city in 1971. Many residents leave town during the summer season to go to fish camps.

The community is served by 2 schools with grades kindergarten through 12. There is a community electricity system and water supply. Sewage system is honey buckets. Napaskiak prohibits the sale and importation of alcoholic beverages. Freight arrives by plane and barge. Government address: City of Napaskiak, P.O. Box 6109, Napaskiak, AK 99559; phone 737-7626. Village corporation address: Napaskiak Inc., P.O. Box 6069, Napaskiak, AK 99559; phone 737-7413.

Newtok

[MAP 11] Located north of Nelson Island on the Kealavik River, 90 miles west-northwest of Bethel, 500 miles west of Anchorage. **Transportation:** Scheduled air service from Bethel. **Population:** 213. **Zip code:** 99559. **Emergency Services:** Alaska State Troopers, Bethel, phone 543-3494; Clinic, phone 237-2111; Volunteer Fire Department.

Private Aircraft: Airstrip 1 mile west; elev. 25 feet; length 2,100 feet; gravel; no fuel; unattended. Runway condition not monitored; visual inspection recommended prior to using.

Visitor Facilities: Lodging and meals are available at the high school (237-2126). Supplies are available at Newtok Corp. Store (237-2413) or Nick Tom Sr. Store (237-2114). Fishing/hunting licenses not available. Information on other visitor services and facilities unavailable.

Newtok, located within Yukon Delta National Wildlife Refuge, is a relatively new village established around 1949. It was incorporated as a second-class city in 1976. Many residents go to fish camps during the summer.

Newtok has a Catholic church and 2 schools with grades 1 through 12. There is a community electricity system. Water is hauled from a central watering point or ponds, and rain water is collected. Sewage system is honey buckets. Newtok prohibits the sale and importation of alcoholic beverages. Freight arrives by mail plane and barge. Government address: City of Newtok, General Delivery, Newtok, AK 99559; phone 237-2315. Village corporation address: Newtok Corp., General Delivery, Newtok, AK 99559; phone 237-2320.

Nightmute

[MAP 11] Located on the Toksook River on Nelson Island in the Bering Sea, 105 miles west of Bethel, 510 miles west of Anchorage. **Transportation:** Scheduled and charter air service from Bethel. **Population:** 153. **Zip code:** 99690. **Emergency Services:** Village Public Safety Officer, Toksook Bay; Alaska State Troopers, Bethel; Health Aide, phone 647-6312; Volunteer Fire Department.

Private Aircraft: Airstrip 2 miles north; elev. 14 feet; length 1,600 feet; gravel; no fuel; unattended. Runway condition not monitored; visual inspection recommended prior to using.

Visitor Facilities: Arrangements may be made for accommodations in private homes; contact the city of Nightmute (647-6426). Lodging also may be available at the school (647-6313). Meals available at the high school in winter. No banking services or laundromat. Groceries, clothing, first-aid supplies, hardware and camera film available in the community. Arts and crafts available for purchase include carved ivory, grass baskets and fur garments. Fishing/hunting licenses not available. Guide service available. No repair services or rental transportation. Fuel available includes marine gas, diesel and regular gasoline. Moorage facilities available.

According to local residents, the village grew as Native people gradually moved to Nelson Island. The Bureau of Indian Affairs established a school in the 1950s. Nightmute lost population in 1964 when many residents moved to Toksook Bay, 15 miles to the northwest, but the community was incorporated as a second-class city in 1974.

Nightmute is located within Yukon Delta National Wildlife Refuge. Residents work at seasonal jobs and engage in subsistence hunting for geese, ducks, rabbits, cranes, swans, ptarmigan, fox, beaver, muskrat, otter and mink. Fishing is for herring, king, silver, red and pink salmon, halibut, devil fish and pike. Most of the residents go to fish camp at Umkumute, 18 miles from Nightmute, during the summer.

Communications at Nightmute include phones, mail plane and TV. The community is served by a church and 2 schools with grades kindergarten through 12. There is a community electricity system. Water is hauled from a central watering point. Sewage system is honey buckets. Freight arrives by cargo plane and barge. Government address: City of Nightmute, Nelson Island, Nightmute, AK 99690; phone 647-6426. Village corporation address: NGTA Ltd., General Delivery, Nightmute, AK 99690; phone 647-6115.

Nunapitchuk

[MAP 11] *(nu-NA-pit-CHUCK)* Located on Johnson River 30 miles northwest of Bethel and 425 miles west of Anchorage. **Transportation:** Scheduled air service from Bethel. **Population:** 475. **Zip code:** 99641. **Emergency Services:** Police, phone 527-5718; Clinic, phone 527-5329; Volunteer Fire Department.

Climate: Transitional zone. Mean July maximum temperature 62°F; mean January minimum temperature 13°F. The village endures lots of wind and blowing snow in the winter, according to one resident.

Private Aircraft: Airstrip east of village; elev. 12 feet; length 2,000 feet; gravel; unattended. Runway condition not monitored; recommend visual inspection prior to using. There is a freight terminal and public transportation from airport. Seaplane base with small float on the river.

Visitor Facilities: Three rooms with kitchen area available at IRA Council building; contact the city office (527-5327) to make arrangements. No restaurant or banking services. Washeteria available. Groceries, clothing, first-aid supplies, hardware, camera film and sporting goods available in the community. Arts and crafts available for purchase include otter parkas, beaver hats, mukluks, knitted gloves and earrings. Fishing/hunting licenses available at the city office. Marine engine repair available. No guide service. Private off-road vehicles and boats may be rented. Fuel available: propane, regular gasoline. No moorage facilities.

In the 1930s, there were 5 or 6 families in the settlement. More families moved to the area after the federal government built a school in the 1940s. Nunapitchuk has an IRA (Indian Reorganization Act) Council that was established in the 1940s. It also had a second-class city status and was then incorporated with Kasigluk in 1969 as the city of Akolmiut. In October 1982 they split and went back to their individual status as second-class cities.

Residents depend on commercial fishing and subsistence activities. They hunt for moose, caribou and small game and fish for salmon and pike. They also trap for mink, muskrat, fox and land otters.

Communications include phones, mail plane, radio and TV. The community is served by Russian Orthodox, Moravian and Pentacostal churches, and a school with grades preschool through 12. There is an AVEC electricity system. Water is hauled from wells or the washeteria, or rain water is collected. Sewage system is honey buckets. Freight arrives by air transport and barge. The village bans the possession of alcoholic beverages. Government address: City of Nunapitchuk, c/o City Clerk, P.O. Box 190, Nunapitchuk, AK 99641; phone 527-5327. Village corporation address: Nunapitchuk Limited, P.O. Box 129, Nunapitchuk, AK 99641; phone 527-5717.

Oscarville

[MAP 11] Located on the north shore of the Kuskokwim River across from Napaskiak, 5 miles south of Bethel, 400 miles west of Anchorage. **Transportation:** Boat, snow machine and floatplane service from Bethel. **Population:** 39. **Zip code:** 99695. **Emergency Services:** Alaska State Troopers, Bethel, phone 543-3949; Clinic.

Visitor Facilities: Arrangements for accommodations may be made by contacting the school (737-7214). Supplies may be available at a general store. Fishing/hunting licenses are not available. Information on other facilities not available.

In about 1906, a man named Oscar Samuelson, born in Norway in 1876, and his Eskimo wife moved to Napaskiak and opened a small store. Samuelson became a mail carrier and in 1908 the Samuelsons moved across the river to what became known as Oscarville. Samuelson opened another small store that he ran until his death in 1953. His daughter and subsequent owners have operated the store. The first school opened in 1964. Oscarville is unincorporated.

Oscarville is served by a 2-teacher school with grades kindergarten through 12 depending on demand. Electricity is from individual generators. Water is hauled from the school well and ponds or rain water is collected. Sewage system is honey buckets. Freight arrives by plane or barge. Village corporation address: Oscarville Native Corp., General Delivery, Oscarville, AK 99695; phone 543-2066.

Pilot Station

[MAP 11] Located on the Yukon River, 11 miles east of St. Marys and 26 miles west of Marshall in the Yukon-Kuskokwim Delta,

430 miles west of Anchorage. **Transportation:** Scheduled and charter air service from Bethel. **Population:** 455. **Zip code:** 99650. **Emergency Services:** Village Public Safety Officer, phone 549-3213; Alaska State Troopers, St. Marys, phone 438-2019; Clinic, phone 549-3728; Volunteer Fire Department.

Climate: More maritime than continental, averaging 60 inches of snowfall and 16 inches of precipitation per year.

Private Aircraft: Airstrip 1 mile southwest; elev. 275 feet; length 3,000 feet; gravel; no fuel; unattended. Runway condition not monitored; visual inspection recommended prior to using. Heavy winds in fall and winter and crosswinds up to 50 mph year-round often limit access. No airport facilities. Transportation usually available for arriving passengers.

Visitor Facilities: Accommodations available. No restaurant, banking services or laundromat. Groceries, clothing, first-aid supplies and camera film available in the community. Arts and crafts available for purchase include carved ivory, wood carvings, grass and birch-bark baskets and masks. Fishing/hunting licenses available. No guide or major repair services. Rental transportation includes boats, off-road vehicles and charter aircraft. Fuel available includes propane, kerosene, marine gas and regular gasoline. No moorage facilities.

This Eskimo village was first called Ankachak, but later moved 0.3 mile upstream to another site called Potiliuk. R.H. Sargent of the U.S. Geological Survey noted that the village name was Pilot Station in 1916. Local riverboat pilots who used the village as a checkpoint were responsible for the name change.

Employment in Pilot Station is primarily related to the summer fishing season, supplemented with year-round enterprises and subsistence activities. There also is summer fire-fighting work with BLM.

Residents hunt black bear, moose, ptarmigan, waterfowl and porcupine, and fish for salmon, whitefish, blackfish, sheefish and pike. Berries are harvested in the fall. Income also is earned from trapping beaver, muskrat, marten, fox, lynx and wolverine.

Near Pilot Station is the old village site of Kurgpallermuit, designated by the Calista Regional Corp. as a historic place because it was occupied during bow and arrow wars between the Yukon and Coastal Eskimos.

Pilot Station is located within Yukon Delta National Wildlife Refuge. Favorite leisure activities include Eskimo dancing, square dancing, potlatches, and dog and snow machine racing.

Communications at Pilot Station, a second-class city incorporated in 1969, include phones, mail plane, radio and TV. The community is served by 2 churches and a school with grades kindergarten through 12. There are community electricity, water and sewer systems. Pilot Station prohibits the sale and importation of alcoholic beverages. Freight arrives by cargo plane and barge. Government address: City of Pilot Station, P.O. Box 5040, Pilot Station, AK 99650; phone 549-3211. Village corporation address: Pilot Station Native Corp., General Delivery, Pilot Station, AK 99650; phone 549-3512.

Pitkas Point

[MAP 11] Located near the junction of the Yukon and Andreafsky rivers, 5 miles northwest of St. Marys and Andreafsky, 445 miles west of Anchorage. **Transportation:** Scheduled airline from Bethel to St. Marys airport. **Population:** 67. **Zip code:** 99658. **Emergency Services:** Alaska State Troopers, St. Marys, phone 438-2019; Pitkas Point Clinic, phone 438-2546.

Climate: Both maritime and continental. Temperatures range from -44°F to 83°F at St. Marys. Annual precipitation 16 inches, with 60 inches of snow.

Private Aircraft: See St. Marys airport.

Visitor Facilities: Accommodations and supplies available in St. Marys. No accommodations, restaurant or banking services in Pitkas Point. There is a laundromat with showers. No arts and crafts available for purchase. Fishing/hunting licenses available at St. Marys. No guide service available. Repair service available for marine engines and boats in St. Marys. Autos may be rented for $70 a day. Fuel available includes marine gas, diesel, propane and regular gasoline. No moorage facilities.

Eskimos who first settled here called the village Nigiklik, a Yup'ik word meaning "to the north." The settlement was first reported by the U.S. Geological Survey in 1898. It was later renamed for a trader who opened a general store there, which was a branch of the Northern Commercial Co. station at nearby Andreafsky. Pitkas Point is unincorporated.

The village economy peaks during the summer fishing season, when most residents are involved in commercial salmon fishing. Summer also provides work in construction and fire fighting for BLM. There also are a few full-time jobs held by local people.

Public assistance payments and subsistence activities supplement this income. Residents of the area hunt moose, bear, hare, duck, geese, swan and ptarmigan. In the fall, berries are harvested from the surrounding tundra. Some income also is derived from trapping beaver, fox and otter.

Pitkas Point is surrounded by Yukon Delta National Wildlife Refuge.

The village is connected by a 17.7-mile road to St. Marys and Mountain Village. In winter, snow machines often are used for intervillage travel.

Communications in Pitkas Point include phones, mail plane and TV. The community is served by a Russian Orthodox church and a school with grades kindergarten through 12. There is a community electricity system. Water is hauled from the laundromat building. Sewage system is honey buckets. Freight arrives by cargo plane and barge. Government address: Pitkas Point Village Council, General Delivery, Pitkas Point, AK 99658; phone 438-2012. Village corporation address: Pitkas Point Native Corp., General Delivery, Pitkas Point, AK 99658; phone 438-2232.

Platinum

[MAP 11] Located on Goodnews Bay, 11 miles southwest of Goodnews Bay village, 135 miles south of Bethel, 445 miles southwest of Anchorage. **Transportation:** Scheduled air service from Bethel. **Population:** 62. **Zip code:** 99651. **Emergency Services:** Volunteer Fire Department.

Elevation: 20 feet. **Climate:** Summers are mild, with cool winds and some rain, according to one resident. Mean annual precipitation 22 inches; mean annual snowfall 43 inches.

Private Aircraft: Airstrip adjacent west; elev. 9 feet; length 3,800 feet; gravel; no fuel; unattended. Runway condition not monitored; visual inspection recommended prior to using. Runway soft when wet.

Visitor Facilities: Arrangements may be made for accommodations at the school (979-9111). No restaurant, banking services or laundromat. Supplies available in the community. Fishing/hunting licenses available. No guide services or rental transportation. Fuel available includes diesel, propane and regular gasoline. No moorage facilities.

Platinum got its name from an important lode of platinum that was discovered nearby in 1926 by an Eskimo named Walter Smith. The community was described as a boom town with 50 residents in 1937. The population reached a high of 72 in 1950. Platinum is a second-class city, incorporated in 1975.

People in Platinum work seasonally in commercial fishing, and also in the stores, post office, school and at odd jobs. Subsistence hunting and fishing are also important.

Residents fish in Goodnews Bay or up the Goodnews River for king, red and chum salmon and Dolly Varden. Hunting is for seals, sea lions, walrus, foxes, rabbits, squirrels, otters, beavers, mink, muskrat, ptarmigan, geese, ducks and sandpipers.

A long beach at Platinum offers good beachcombing, and the community is located within Togiak National Wildlife Refuge.

Communications at Platinum include phones and mail plane. The community is served by a church and a school with grades preschool through 12. There is a community electricity system. Water is hauled from a central watering point. Sewage system is honey buckets. Platinum prohibits the sale and importation of alcoholic beverages. Freight arrives by barge or mail plane. Government address: City of Platinum, P.O. Box 28, Platinum, AK 99651; phone 979-8114. Village corporation address: Arviq Inc., General Delivery, Platinum, AK 99651; phone 979-8113.

Quinhagak

[MAP 11] *(QUIN-a-hock)* Located on the southeast shore of Kuskokwim Bay, 70 miles south of Bethel, 425 miles west of Anchorage. **Transportation:** Boat; scheduled and charter air service from Bethel. **Population:** 520. **Zip code:** 99655. **Emergency Services:** Police, phone 556-8314; Clinic, phone 556-8320; Volunteer Fire Department.

Private Aircraft: Airstrip 1 mile northeast; elev. 10 feet; length 2,700 feet; gravel; no fuel; unattended. Runway condition not monitored; visual inspection recommended prior to using. Potholes entire length of runway. Equipment occasionally on runway. No airport facilities or public transportation into village.

Visitor Facilities: Lodging is sometimes available at the high school and washete-

ria. Laundry and shower facilities available. Groceries, clothing, first-aid supplies, hardware, camera film and sporting goods available in the community. No restaurants or banking facilities. Arts and crafts available include carved ivory, grass baskets and Eskimo yo-yos. Fishing/hunting licenses available, as well as guide service. Marine engine repair available, also air charter service. No rental transportation. Fuel available: marine gas, diesel, propane, regular gasoline. No moorage facilities.

Private sportfishing is prohibited on all property owned by the village corporation. All sportfishing must be from a boat, on state-owned land or with a guide.

This Eskimo village was reported by Lieutenant Sarichev in 1826. In 1975, Quinhagak was incorporated as a second-class city.

The village is located within Togiak National Wildlife Refuge.

Communications in Quinhagak include phones, mail plane, radio and TV. There is a community electricity system. Water is hauled from the washeteria. Sewage system is honey buckets. The village prohibits the possession of alcoholic beverages. Freight arrives by barge. Government address: City of Quinhagak, P.O. Box 90, Quinhagak, AK 99655; phone 556-8315. Village corporation address: Quanirtuuq Inc., P.O. Box 69, Quinhagak, AK 99655; phone 556-8211 or 556-8615, fax 556-8540.

Red Devil

[MAP 12] Located on the upper Kuskokwim River at the mouth of Red Devil Creek, 8 miles west of Sleetmute, 73 miles east of Aniak, 250 miles west of Anchorage. **Transportation:** Boat; scheduled and charter air service from Bethel or Aniak. **Population:** 27. **Zip code:** 99656. **Emergency Services:** Alaska State Troopers, Aniak; Health Aide; Volunteer Fire Department.

Climate: Continental. At nearby Sleetmute, temperatures range between -58°F and 90°F. Annual precipitation is 20 inches, with 85 inches of snow.

Private Aircraft: Airstrip 1 mile northwest; elev. 210 feet; length 5,200 feet; gravel; no fuel; unattended. Runway condition not monitored; visual inspection recommended prior to using. No airport facilities or public transportation.

Visitor Facilities: Accommodations and meals available. No banking services or laundromat available. Groceries available at combination roadhouse/bar/store. Hand-sewn fur items available for purchase. Fishing/hunting licenses available. No guide or repair services. Rental transportation includes boats and charter aircraft through local air service. Fuel available: marine gas, diesel and regular gasoline. No moorage facilities.

Land use permits are required to use lands owned by the Kuskokwim Corp. Uses include fishing, temporary camping, seasonal campsite, land crossing and research. There is a $100 administration fee. Big game hunting fee is $400. Seasonal campsite permits $50, annual use fee $250. For further information, contact The Kuskokwim Corp., 645 G St., Suite 305, Anchorage, AK 99501; phone 276-2101, or in Aniak phone 675-4275.

The village was named after the Red Devil Mine, which was established in 1933 by Hans Halverson after numerous quicksilver deposits were discovered earlier in the surrounding Kilbuck-Kuskokwim Mountains. The mine operated from 1939 to 1946 as the Kuskokwim Mining Co. and was reopened in 1952 as the DeCourcy Mountain Mining Co. Inc. The mine was last worked in 1971, when the mercury, cinnabar and antimony reserves were depleted. By that year the mine had produced some 2.7 million pounds of mercury—Alaska's total output. By 1971 a community had developed at the mining site. A school was established in 1958. The population was 152 in 1960, but declined when the mine closed.

In the summer of 1989 access to the inactive mine was closed because of a chemical hazard. An investigation revealed stored quantities of copper sulfate, potash and sodium hydroxide. In 1988, the federal Bureau of Land Management posted signs warning of potential health hazards and later removed 2 transformers containing polychlorinated byphenyls, or PCBs.

Employment opportunities in Red Devil today are limited. A few residents work for the school district, post office, clinic, store and flying service. There also is employment through the BLM's summer firefighting program. This income is supplemented by public assistance payments and subsistence activities. Local residents hunt bear, moose, caribou, rabbit, ptarmigan and waterfowl, and fish for king, chum, red and silver salmon, sheefish and whitefish. Trapping for marten, beaver, mink, wolverine, fox, otter and lynx also provides income.

Communications in Red Devil, which is unincorporated, include a phone (447-9901), mail plane, radio and TV. The community has a school with grades preschool through 12, but no church. Electricity is supplied by Middle Kuskokwim Electric Corp.; water is from private wells or the river. Sewage system is septic tanks or privies. Freight arrives by cargo plane and barge. Village corporation address: The Kuskokwim Corp., 645 G St., Suite 305, Anchorage, AK 99501; phone 276-2101, or in Aniak phone 675-4275.

Russian Mission

[MAP 11] Located on the Yukon River, 70 miles north of Bethel, 225 miles westnorthwest of Anchorage. **Transportation:** Scheduled and charter air service from Bethel. **Population:** 246. **Zip code:** 99657. **Emergency Services:** Village Public Safety Officer; Alaska State Troopers, St. Marys; Volunteer Fire Department.

Elevation: 50 feet. **Climate:** Both maritime and continental, with a greater maritime influence. Annual precipitation 16 inches; annual snowfall 60 inches.

Private Aircraft: Airstrip adjacent south; elev. 70 feet; length 2,700 feet; gravel; attended. Runway condition monitored, but visual inspection recommended prior to using. Airport has lighting system. No public transportation to village; 500 yards to village.

Visitor Facilities: Arrangements can be made for accommodations in private homes. There is 1 room available at the Russian Mission Pump House, run by the city of Russian Mission (584-5111). Lodging also may be available at the school (584-5615) and clinic (584-5529). Make arrangements with the mayor (584-5326) or health aides Anutka Nickoli or Olga Wigley. Food is available at various locations. Laundromat available. No banking services. Groceries, limited clothing, hardware and sporting goods available at P&K Trading Post and Native Store, Russian Mission Native Corporation, A&M's Outfit and Duffy's. Arts and crafts available for purchase include birch-bark baskets, masks and many other Native arts. Fishing/hunting licenses available. No guide services or rental transportation. Marine engine and boat repairs available. Fuel available: diesel, propane and regular gasoline. Moorage facilities available. Mary Belkoff, mayor, says, "Russian Mission is a wonderful place to visit, with friendly people and you are welcome anytime to stay."

The first Russian-American Co. fur-trading post was established at this village in 1837, but the Eskimos held the outsiders responsible for the smallpox epidemic that followed in 1838–39 and massacred the post's inhabitants. The first Russian Orthodox mission in the interior of Alaska was established here in 1851 by a Russian-Aleut priest, Jacob Netzuetov. Originally called Pokrovskaya Mission, the title Russian Mission replaced the previous name in 1900. The village was incorporated as a second-class city in 1970.

Employment opportunities in Russian Mission are concentrated in commercial fishing and public employment programs. Most residents of the community are directly or indirectly involved in commercial fishing from June through September. There are a few full-time jobs at the local stores, the post office, the school and the clinic. Summer work also includes fire fighting for BLM. This income is supplemented by subsistence activities. Residents hunt moose, black bear, ptarmigan, waterfowl, porcupine and rabbit. They fish for salmon, blackfish, whitefish, sheefish, pike and lush (burbot). Berries are harvested in the fall. Income also comes from trapping beaver, mink, lynx, marten and fox.

Communications include phones, mail plane, radio and TV. The community is served by Russian Orthodox and Catholic churches and a school with grades preschool through 12. There are community electricity, water and sewage systems. Freight arrives by cargo plane and barge. Sale and importation of alcoholic beverages are banned. Government address: City of Russian Mission, P.O. Box 49, Russian Mission, AK 99657; phone 584-5111. Village corporation address: Russian Mission Native Corp., General Delivery, Russian Mission, AK 99657; phone 584-5411.

St. Marys

[MAP 11] Located on the Andreafsky River near its confluence with the Yukon River, 37 miles northwest of Marshall, 450 miles west-northwest of Anchorage. **Transportation:** Boat up and down lower Yukon; scheduled and charter air service from Bethel and Anchorage; road from Mountain Village. **Population:** 525. **Zip code:** 99658.

Emergency Services: Police, phone 438-2911; Alaska State Troopers, phone 438-2019; Clinic, phone 438-2347; Volunteer Fire Department, phone 438-2911.

Elevation: 100 feet. **Climate:** St. Marys climate is both maritime and continental, with a greater maritime influence. Mean annual precipitation is 17 inches. Mean annual snowfall is 69 inches.

Private Aircraft: Airport 7 miles west; elev. 311 feet; length 6,000 feet; gravel; fuel available; attended variable hours. Runway conditions reported only during duty hours. Airport has passenger and freight terminals, ticket counter and restrooms; no traffic control tower. Hub airport of the Lower Yukon, served by 7 airlines. Taxi service to town.

Visitor Facilities: Food and lodging available at Bays Bed & Breakfast (438-2048) and the Road House. Meals also available at Papa's Pizza, St. Marys Marina and The Kids Center. Laundry facilities available. No banking services. Groceries, clothing, first-aid supplies, hardware, camera film and sporting goods available in the community. Arts and crafts available for purchase include carved ivory, grass baskets, beaded jewelry and hand-sewn skin garments. Fishing/hunting licenses available. Guide service available. Marine engine, boat and aircraft repair available. Charter aircraft available. Fuel available: marine gas, propane, regular gasoline. Public moorage facilities available.

St. Marys' history actually begins some 90 miles downriver at Akulurak. In 1903, Jesuit missionaries set up a mission at Akulurak to educate and care for children orphaned by a flu epidemic in 1900–01. Akulurak is an Eskimo word meaning "in-between place," aptly describing the settlement on an island in a slough connecting 2 arms of the Yukon River. The mission school flourished and by 1915 there were 70 full-time students. Over the years, though, the slough surrounding Akulurak silted in so severely that in 1948 the mission and village moved to higher ground.

Present-day St. Marys was chosen as the new mission site. Materials from an abandoned hotel built during the gold rush were used to construct the new mission and several village homes. The mission closed in 1987.

The names St. Marys and Andreafsky are sometimes confused. Andreafsky was established in 1899 as a supply depot and winter quarters for Northern Commercial

Co.'s riverboat fleet. The village took its name from the Andrea family, who settled on the river, originally called Clear River. The family built a Russian Orthodox church in the village. When St. Marys was incorporated as a first-class city in 1967, Andreafsky was not included within the new city's boundaries and remained a separate, unincorporated community until 1980.

Employment in St. Marys peaks during the summer fishing season, when 70 percent of the residents are involved in some form of commercial fishing activity. Other seasonal employment includes construction projects and fire fighting for BLM. Other jobs are with the school district, the city, airlines, state government and Native corporations. Cash income is supplemented by subsistence activities. Residents hunt for moose, bear, duck, geese, swan and ptarmigan; and fish for salmon, sheefish, blackfish, whitefish, grayling and trout. In the fall berries are harvested. Income also is earned from trapping beaver, fox, mink, otter and muskrat.

St. Marys has become a subregional center for air transportation. Its airport is capable of handling aircraft as large as a Boeing 727. St. Marys also is linked by a 17.7-mile road to Mountain Village.

St. Marys is surrounded by Yukon Delta National Wildlife Refuge. Locally, bird-watchers can see jaegers, falcons and numerous smaller passerines. There is good fishing on the Andreafsky River for Dolly Varden, grayling, pike and salmon. Favorite activities include annual potlatches, the Yukon 150 Dog Race in February and the Andreafsky 90 Sled Dog Race, held in mid-March.

In the slough opposite the dock is a burial ground for old river steamers. Rusting boilers can be seen above the water.

Communications in St. Marys include phones, mail plane, radios and TV. The community has 2 Catholic churches, public schools with grades kindergarten through 12 and a Catholic high school. There are community electricity, water and sewer systems. Freight arrives in the community by cargo plane and barge. Government address: City of St. Marys, P.O. Box 163, St. Marys, AK 99658; phone 438-2515, fax 438-2719. Village corporation address: St. Marys Native Corp., P.O. Box 162, St. Marys, AK 99658; phone 438-2315. Nerklikmute Native Corp., P.O. Box 87, St. Marys, AK 99658; phone 438-2332.

Scammon Bay

[MAP 11] Located on the Kun River 1 mile from the Bering Sea in the Yukon-Kuskokwim Delta, 145 miles northwest of Bethel, 525 miles west of Anchorage. **Transportation:** Scheduled and charter air service from Bethel. **Population:** 326. **Zip code:** 99662. **Emergency Services:** Police, phone 558-5529; Alaska State Troopers, Bethel, phone 543-2294; Clinic, phone 558-5511; Volunteer Fire Department.

Elevation: 22 feet. **Climate:** Maritime. Mean January temperature 9°F; mean July temperature 49°F. Temperatures range between -25°F and 79°F. Annual precipitation 14 inches; annual snowfall 65 inches. Easterly winds during the winter cause severe wind chill.

Private Aircraft: Airstrip adjacent north; elev. 22 feet; length 2,800 feet; gravel and dirt; no fuel; unattended. Runway condition not monitored; visual inspection recommended prior to using. Road to river crosses runway. Runway soft during breakup, after rains and during extreme high tides. No airport facilities or public transportation into village.

Visitor Facilities: Arrangements may be made for accommodations at the school (558-5312). No restaurant, laundromat or banking services. Groceries, clothing, first-aid supplies, hardware, camera film and sporting goods available at Askinuk Store (558-5211). Arts and crafts available for purchase include carved ivory, grass baskets and masks. No guide services. Marine engine repair available. Arrangements may be made to rent autos. Fuel available: marine gas, diesel, propane and regular gasoline. No moorage facilities.

The Eskimo name for this village is Mariak. The site is believed to have been settled in the 1700s because it had high ground and good water. The village was named after the nearby bay which honors Capt. Charles M. Scammon, who served as marine chief of the Western Union Telegraph expedition in Alaska in 1865–67. Scammon Bay was incorporated as a second-class city in 1967.

Peak economic activity in Scammon Bay occurs during the summer fishing season, when most residents are involved in commercial fishing. Other employment opportunities in the summer include fire fighting for BLM and various construction projects. There are a few year-round jobs with the city, stores, school and village corporation.

This income is supplemented by subsistence activities. Residents hunt beluga whale, seal, geese, swans, cranes, ducks, loons and ptarmigan. Fishing yields salmon, whitefish, blackfish, needlefish, herring, smelt and tomcod. Berries are harvested in the fall.

Scammon Bay is located within Yukon Delta National Wildlife Refuge. Winter trails connect Scammon Bay with nearby Hooper Bay and Chevak.

Communications in Scammon Bay include phones and mail plane. The community is served by Catholic and Covenant churches and a school with grades kindergarten through 12. There are community electricity, water and sewer systems. The village prohibits the possession of alcoholic beverages. Freight arrives by cargo plane and barge. Government address: City of Scammon Bay, P.O. Box 90, Scammon Bay, AK 99662; phone 558-5529 or 558-5626. Village corporation address: Askinuk Corp., General Delivery, Scammon Bay, AK 99662; phone 558-5311.

Sheldon Point

[MAP 11] Located on a south fork of the Yukon River, 18 miles southwest of Emmonak, 500 miles west-northwest of Anchorage. **Transportation:** Boat; scheduled or charter airline from Emmonak; snow machine. **Population:** 134. **Zip code:** 99666. **Emergency Services:** Village Public Safety Office; Alaska State Troopers, St. Marys; Clinic, phone 498-4228.

Climate: Climate is maritime, averaging 60 inches of snowfall and 18 inches of precipitation per year. Temperatures range from -40°F to 79°F.

Private Aircraft: Airstrip adjacent southeast of village; length 2,200 feet; gravel; unattended. No airport facilities or public transportation into village.

Visitor Facilities: Arrangements may be made for accommodations and meals in private homes; or at the school, phone 498-4112. No banking services. Groceries, clothing, first-aid supplies, hardware, camera film and sporting goods available at Swan Lake Store (498-4227). Arts and crafts available include Native jewelry, ivory, beadwork, wood carvings and Eskimo clothing. Fishing/hunting licenses not available. Arrangements may be made with local residents for guide services. No repair services. Fuel available: regular gasoline, fuel oil. No moorage facilities.

A relatively new Eskimo village, established in the 1940s, the community is named for a man called Sheldon, who owned and operated a fish saltery at the site. It is a second-class city, incorporated in 1974.

Commercial fishing supports the economy. Fish-buying companies from the lower Yukon, Bering Sea, Fort Yukon and the Yukon Delta Fish Marketing Co-op come here to buy fish. A few other employment opportunities exist with the store, post office, clinic, airlines, local government and schools. Income is supplemented by public assistance payments and subsistence activities. Residents hunt beluga whales, seals, moose, geese, ducks, ptarmigan and hares; and fish for salmon, whitefish, blackfish, sheefish, lush (burbot) and smelt. Additional income is gained from trapping fox, beaver, otter and mink.

Sheldon Point is surrounded by Yukon Delta National Wildlife Refuge.

Communications in Sheldon Point include phones, mail plane, radio and sometimes TV. The community is served by a Catholic church and a school with grades kindergarten through 12. There is a community electricity system and a water treatment plant. Sewage system is primarily honey buckets. Freight arrives by cargo plane, barge, small boat and snow machine. Sale and importation of alcoholic beverages are prohibited. Government address: City of Sheldon Point, General Delivery, Sheldon Point, AK 99666; phone, 498-4226. Village corporation address: Swan Lake Corp., General Delivery, Sheldon Point, AK 99666; phone 498-4227.

Sleetmute

[MAP 12] Located on the Kuskokwim River, 1.5 miles north of its junction with the Holitna River, 78 miles east of Aniak, 240 miles west of Anchorage. **Transportation:** Boat; scheduled and charter air service from Bethel or Aniak. **Population:** 74. **Zip code:** 99668. **Emergency Services:** Alaska State Troopers, Bethel, phone 675-4398; Clinic, phone 449-9901; Volunteer Fire Department.

Elevation: 290 feet. **Climate:** Continental with temperatures ranging between -58°F and 90°F. Mean annual precipitation 21.5 inches; mean annual snowfall 77 inches.

Private Aircraft: Airstrip adjacent east; elev. 178 feet; length 3,100 feet; gravel; no fuel; unattended. Runway condition not monitored; visual inspection recommended prior to using. No airport facilities or public transportation into village. High winds in the fall and winter can prevent planes from landing for days at a time.

Visitor Facilities: Accommodations may be arranged on floor of city offices (449-9901). A store carries groceries, first-aid supplies and sporting goods. Laundry facilities and public showers available. No banking services. Fishing/hunting licenses available. Guide services available. No repair services, rental transportation or moorage facilities. Fuel available: marine gas, diesel and propane.

Land use permits are required to use lands owned by the Kuskokwim Corp. Uses include fishing, temporary camping, seasonal campsite, land crossing and research. There is a $100 administration fee. Big game hunting fee is $400. Seasonal campsite permits $50, annual use fee $250. For further information, contact The Kuskokwim Corp., 645 G St., Suite 305, Anchorage, AK 99501; phone 276-2101, or in Aniak phone 675-4275.

The Native village of Sleetmute, which means "whetstone people," was named for nearby slate deposits. The village was founded by Ingalik Indians. In the early 1830s, the Russians developed a trading post near the present village site. By 1841, however, this post had been moved from Sleetmute to another site approximately 100 miles down the Kuskokwim River. Frederick Bishop established a trading post at Sleetmute's present location in 1906. A school was opened in 1921. Saints Peter and Paul Russian Orthodox Chapel was built in 1931. Sleetmute is unincorporated.

Most income in Sleetmute is from public employment programs, the school district and summer firefighting jobs with BLM. Some residents work in canneries in other villages during the fishing season. Residents rely on subsistence hunting for moose, bear, ptarmigan, waterfowl, porcupine and rabbit; fishing for salmon, whitefish, sheefish, trout, pike, grayling, lush (burbot), char and Dolly Varden.

Communications in Sleetmute include a phone (449-9901), radio, mail plane and TV. The community is served by a Russian Orthodox church and a school with grades preschool through 12. There are community electricity and water; sewage system is outhouses. The village prohibits the sale and importation of alcoholic beverages. Freight arrives by cargo plane and barge. Government address: Sleetmute Village, Box 9, New Road, Sleetmute, AK 99668; phone 449-

9901. Village corporation address: Kuskokwim Corp., 645 G St., Suite 305, Anchorage, AK 99501; phone 276-2101.

Stony River

[MAP 12] Located on Stony River Island in the Kuskokwim River near its junction with Stony River, 185 miles northeast of Bethel, 245 miles west-northwest of Anchorage. **Transportation:** Boat; snow machine; scheduled and charter air service from Aniak. **Population:** 73. **Zip code:** 99673. **Emergency Services:** Alaska State Troopers, Aniak, phone 675-4398; Clinic, phone 537-3228; Volunteer Fire Department.

Elevation: 220 feet. **Climate:** Continental. Record high was 85°F in July 1967; record low was -57°F in January 1951. Mean annual precipitation 23 inches; mean annual snowfall 93 inches.

Private Aircraft: Airstrip adjacent north; elev. 230 feet; length 2,900 feet; gravel; no fuel; unattended. Runway condition not monitored; visual inspection recommended prior to using. No airport facilities or public transportation into the village.

Visitor Facilities: Arrangements may be made for accommodations in private homes; or in the IRA Council building by contacting the Traditional Council. No restaurant, banking services or laundry facilities. Staple items, cigarettes and snacks available at local stores; most supplies are obtained from Sleetmute, Red Devil, Aniak or Anchorage. Arts and crafts available for purchase include birch-bark baskets, wooden bowls, moccasins, mukluks, beaver mittens and beaver-and-marten hats. Fishing/hunting licenses and guide service not available. Residents repair their own marine engines. No rental transportation or moorage facilities. Fuel available: marine gas, regular gasoline.

Land use permits are required to use lands owned by the Kuskokwim Corp. Uses include fishing, temporary camping, seasonal campsite, land crossing and research. There is a $100 administration fee. Big game hunting fee is $400. Seasonal campsite permits $50, annual use fee $250. For further information, contact The Kuskokwim Corp., 645 G St., Suite 305, Anchorage, AK 99501; phone 276-2101, or in Aniak phone 675-4275.

This unincorporated Eskimo and Indian village, which has been known as Moose Village and Moose Creek, began as a trading post and riverboat landing used to supply mining operations to the north. The first trading post was opened in 1930, followed by a post office in 1935. These facilities were used primarily by people who lived in one-family settlements nearby. In the early 1960s, villagers built cabins near the store. A state school opened in 1961 and work began on the airstrip the next year.

Most income in Stony River comes from public employment programs, including seasonal firefighting work with BLM. This income is supplemented by subsistence activities. Residents hunt for moose, caribou, bear, waterfowl, ptarmigan, rabbit and porcupine. They fish for salmon, whitefish, sheefish, burbot, grayling and trout. Income also is obtained from trapping beaver, marten, lynx, fox and mink.

Communications in Stony River include phones, mail plane, radio and TV. There is a community electricity system. Water is pumped from individual wells. Sewage system is honey buckets or outhouses. Freight arrives by barge or chartered plane. Government address: Stony River Traditional Council, General Delivery, Stony River, AK 99673. Village address: The Kuskokwim Corp., 645 G St., Suite 305, Anchorage, AK 99501; phone 276-2101.

Toksook Bay

[MAP 11] *(TOOK-sook)* Located on Nelson Island 5 miles southeast of Tununak, 100 miles west of Bethel and 505 miles west of Anchorage. **Transportation:** Scheduled and charter air service from Bethel. **Population:** 396. **Zip code:** 99637. **Emergency Services:** Alaska State Troopers, Bethel, phone 543-3494; Clinic, phone 427-7712; Volunteer Fire Department.

Private Aircraft: Airstrip adjacent west; elev. 95 feet; length 1,800 feet; gravel and dirt; no fuel; unattended. Runway condition not monitored; visual inspection recommended prior to using. Runway grade uneven. Deep dip at one end.

Visitor Facilities: Arrangements for accommodations may be made at the school (427-7815) or Nunakauiak Yupik Corp. Hotel (427-7928 or 427-7929) year-round. No restaurants, but a snack bar offers fast-food items. Groceries and supplies are available at NYC General Store and John's Store. Fishing/hunting licenses are also available.

Toksook Bay was established in 1964 when most of the population of Nightmute moved to what was considered a better village site. Toksook Bay, which is located within Yukon Delta National Wildlife Refuge, was incorporated as a second-class city in 1972.

Winter activities include occasional Eskimo dances, basketball tournaments, musk-oxen hunts sponsored by the Dept. of Fish and Wildlife, and tomcod jigging. Summers are spent at fish camps, subsistence fishing and drying fish.

Toksook Bay is served by a Catholic church and 2 schools with grades kindergarten through 12. There are community electricity, water and sewer systems. Toksook Bay prohibits the sale and importation of alcoholic beverages. Freight arrives by barge and plane. Government address: City of Toksook Bay, Nelson Island, Toksook Bay, AK 99637; phone 427-7613. Village corporation address: Nunakauiak Yup'ik Corp., General Delivery, Toksook Bay, AK 99637; phone 427-7929.

Tuluksak

[MAP 11] *(TOO-luck-sack)* Located on the south bank of the Kuskokwim River near the mouth of the Tuluksak River, 45 miles northeast of Bethel and 375 miles west of Anchorage. **Transportation:** Scheduled and charter air service from Bethel. **Population:** 302. **Zip code:** 99679. **Emergency Services:** Village Public Safety Officer; Alaska State Troopers, Bethel, phone 543-3494; Clinic, phone 695-6115; Volunteer Fire Department.

Private Aircraft: Airstrip adjacent southwest; elev. 30 feet; length 2,500 feet; gravel; no fuel; unattended. Runway condition not monitored; visual inspection recommended prior to using. Loose gravel to 2 inches in diameter on the northeast 1,000 feet of the runway. Potholes and ruts in runway.

Visitor Facilities: Arrangements for accommodations may be made through the city office (695-6212). There is a washeteria. Supplies available at 2 general stores. Fishing/hunting licenses not available.

This Eskimo village reportedly was named after a species of loon called "tulik" in the Eskimo language. It has been occupied continuously since early historic times and the Moravian missionaries had an Eskimo helper stationed there in 1895. Outside interest in the surrounding area was generated in 1907 when gold was found along Bear Creek on the upper Tuluksak River. The first Moravian chapel was built in 1912; a new chapel was completed in 1925. A Bureau of Education school opened in 1930.

Tuluksak, which is located within Yukon Delta National Wildlife Refuge, was incorporated as a second-class city in 1970. Many residents may be gone to fish camps during the summer season.

The community has 2 schools with grades kindergarten through 12. There is a community electricity system. Water is hauled from the washeteria. Sewage system is honey buckets. Tuluksak prohibits the sale and importation of alcoholic beverages. Freight arrives by mail plane and barge. Government address: City of Tuluksak, General Delivery, Tuluksak, AK 99679; phone 695-6212. Village corporation address: Tulkisarmute Inc., General Delivery, Tuluksak, AK 99679.

Tuntutuliak

[MAP 11] *(TOON-too-TOO-lee-ack)* Located on the north bank of the Kuskokwim River, 45 miles southwest of Bethel, 440 miles west of Anchorage. **Transportation:** Scheduled and charter air service from Bethel. **Population:** 203. **Zip code:** 99680. **Emergency Services:** Village Public Safety Officer, phone 256-2512; Alaska State Troopers, Bethel, phone 543-3494; Clinic, phone 256-2129; Volunteer Fire Department.

Private Aircraft: Airstrip 1 mile south; elev. 16 feet; length 1,900 feet; gravel; no fuel; unattended. Runway condition not monitored; visual inspection recommended prior to using. Runway has 40-foot gravel strip down the center; gravel edges may be soft.

Visitor Facilities: Arrangements for accommodations may be made with the school (phone 256-2415). There is a washeteria. Supplies available in the community. Fishing/hunting licenses available.

Unincorporated Tuntutuliak is located within Yukon Delta National Wildlife Refuge. Many residents may leave for fish camps in the summer.

The community has a church and 2 schools with grades kindergarten through 12. There is a community electricity system. Water is hauled from the washeteria. Sewage system is honey buckets. Tuntutuliak prohibits the possession of alcoholic beverages. Freight arrives by mail plane and barge. Government address: Tuntutuliak City Office, General Delivery, Tuntutuliak, AK 99680; phone 256-2112. Village corporation address: Tuntutuliak Land Ltd., General Delivery, Tuntutuliak, AK 99680; phone 256-2315.

Tununak

[MAP 11] *(tu-NOO-nak)* Located at Tununak Bay on the northwest coast of Nelson Island, 120 miles west of Bethel, 520 miles west of Anchorage. **Transportation:** Scheduled and charter air service from Bethel. **Population:** 337. **Zip code:** 99681. **Emergency Services:** Village Public Safety Officer, phone 652-6812; Alaska State Troopers, Bethel; Clinic, phone 652-6829; Volunteer Fire Department.

Private Aircraft: Airstrip adjacent southwest; elev. 17 feet; length 2,000 feet; gravel; no fuel; unattended. Runway condition not monitored; visual inspection recommended prior to using. Passenger terminal at airport; no public transportation into village.

Visitor Facilities: For sleeping accommodations in the school or clinic, contact the school (652-6827) or the city office (652-6312). Food is available at the Seaside Cafe. No banking services. Washeteria available. Groceries, clothing, first-aid supplies, hardware, camera film and sporting goods available at TRC General Store (652-6311), Tunanak Native Store (652-6813) and Charlie Sales (652-6027). Arts and crafts available for purchase include carved ivory, baskets and earrings. Fishing/hunting licenses available. No guide or repair services. Arrangements may be made to rent off-road vehicles. Fuel available: marine gas, propane and regular gasoline. No moorage facilities.

This Eskimo village was visited in December 1878 by E.W. Nelson of the U.S. Signal Service and reported as Tununuk, population 6. A Roman Catholic mission was established here in 1891. Tunanak was incorporated as a second-class city in 1975.

Tununak residents go to fish camps in the summer and also work on seasonal firefighting crews for BLM. Musk-oxen can be seen on the cliffs surrounding the village.

Communications in Tununak include phones and mail plane. The community is served by a Roman Catholic church and a school with grades kindergarten through 12. There is a community electricity system. Water is hauled from the washeteria. Sewage system is honey buckets. Tununak prohibits the sale and importation of alcoholic beverages. Freight is hauled by cargo plane and barge. Government address: IRA Council, P.O. Box 77, Tununak, AK 99681; phone 652-6527. Village corporation address: Tununrmuit Rinit Corp., General Delivery, Tununak, AK 99681; phone 562-6311.

Upper Kalskag

[MAP 11] (Also known as Kalskag) Located on the north bank of the Kuskokwim River, about 24 miles west of Aniak. **Transportation:** Scheduled and charter air service from Aniak or Bethel. **Population:** 165. **Zip code:** 99607. **Emergency Services:** Village Public Safety Officer; Clinic; Volunteer Fire Department.

Elevation: 49 feet. **Climate:** Semiarctic with maritime influences from the Bering Sea. Snowfall and precipitation are 60 inches and 19 inches, respectively. Weather records at nearby Aniak indicate that temperatures at Upper Kalskag range from a low of -55°F to a high of 87°F.

Private Aircraft: Kalskag airport adjacent west; elev. 49 feet; length 3,200 feet; gravel; no fuel. Runway is maintained by the state. Kalskag also has a grader to service the runway and main road between Upper and Lower Kalskag. Runway conditions not monitored; visual inspection recommended prior to using. Airport serves both Upper and Lower Kalskag. Transportation into village available.

Visitor Facilities: Arrangements for accommodations may be made at the school (471-2288) and Kalskag Store (471-2268). No laundromat or banking services. Groceries, clothing, first-aid supplies, hardware and sporting goods available at Ausdahl Mercantile, Betty's Gift Shop, Kalskag Store, Video Village Center and Morgan Fuel. Fishing/hunting licenses available in Lower Kalskag. No guide or repair services. No rental transportation or moorage facilities. Fuel available: marine gas, diesel, unleaded gas and propane.

Land use permits are required to use lands owned by the Kuskokwim Corp. Uses include fishing, temporary camping, seasonal campsite, land crossing and research. There is a $100 administration fee. Big game hunting fee is $400. Seasonal campsite permits $50, annual use fee $250. For further information, contact The Kuskokwim Corp., 645 G St., Suite 305, Anchor-

age, AK 99501; phone 276-2101, or in Aniak phone 675-4275.

Most of the inhabitants of Upper Kalskag were originally residents of the Eskimo village of Kaltkhagamute, located on a slough 4 miles southwest of Upper Kalskag. At the turn of the century, the people moved to the present site of Upper Kalskag. Paul Kameroff, Sr., is credited with founding the village of Upper Kalskag. He operated the only general store, which was established in the 1930s, and transported freight, groceries and fuel from Bethel on a barge he named for his daughter Pauline. A federal Bureau of Education school was built in 1931. At that time the community owned a herd of 2,100 reindeer. Through the years, residents of Ohagamiut, Crow Village and the Yukon River communities of Russian Mission and Paimute moved to Upper Kalskag. The community of Lower Kalskag, 2 miles to the southwest, was established during the same time period as Upper Kalskag. Upper Kalskag was incorporated as a second-class city in 1975.

Most income in Upper Kalskag comes from public employment programs. Subsistence activities account for about 70 percent of the total livelihood in the village. Some residents still go to fish camps, but most fish at or near the village. Seasonal fish catches include king, dog, silver and red salmon; grayling, whitefish, sheefish, blackfish, pike, burbot and eel. Moose are the most important meat source, supplemented by rabbit, waterfowl and game birds. Some income also is obtained from trapping and the sale of lynx, fox, wolf, otter, muskrat, mink, marten, beaver and wolverine pelts. Berries are harvested in the fall and some residents cultivate gardens.

Upper Kalskag is located within Yukon Delta National Wildlife Refuge. The setting is described by one resident as "beautiful, with the hills just behind Kalskag and the Kuskokwim River alongside."

Communications in Upper Kalskag include phones, mail plane, radio and TV. The community is served by 2 churches and 2 schools with grades 1 through 12. There are community electricity, water and sewer systems. Freight is transported by plane and barge. Government address: City of Upper Kalskag, Box 80, Upper Kalskag, AK 99607; phone 471-2220. Village corporation address: The Kuskokwim Corp., 645 G St., Suite 305, Anchorage, AK 99501; phone 276-2101.

Wildlife Refuges

Yukon Delta National Wildlife Refuge

At 19.6 million acres, this is the nation's largest wildlife refuge and encompasses the great deltas of the Yukon and Kuskokwim rivers, the 2 longest rivers in Alaska. This region is treeless and, apart from the Andreafsky and Kilbuck hills, is a seemingly limitless expanse of wetlands. The Andreafsky River, in the northern section of the refuge above St. Marys, is a designated wild river within an established wilderness area. The refuge also includes 1.1-million-acre Nunivak Island, 20 miles off the coast. On Nunivak the terrain includes volcanic craters, sand dunes, sea cliffs and rolling tundra. The southern half of the island is a designated wilderness area.

Climate: Weather in the refuge is unpredictable at best. January temperatures average near 0°F, although high winds often cause a wind chill factor exceeding -60°F. Winter in the delta region begins early in October. Annual snowfall may exceed 50 inches, but winter thaws prevent much accumulation. Ice breakup usually occurs in late May or early June. Summer temperatures in Bethel on the Kuskokwim River and St. Marys on the Yukon River average in the mid-50s, with occasional highs in the 70s and 80s.

Wildlife: This refuge is one of the most significant waterfowl breeding areas in North America. More than 220 species of birds have been observed and more than 140 species nest here, including more than 500,000 swans and geese, 1.6 million ducks and 10 to 20 million shore and water birds. More than half the continent's black brant population hatches in the refuge coast. All of the cackling Canada geese and 90 percent of the emperor geese are produced in the coastal lowlands. Large populations of Pacific white-fronted geese and tundra swans nest near the coast and on the inland tundra.

Nunivak Island shelters herds of reindeer and musk-oxen. Musk-oxen vanished from Alaska in 1865 because of overhunting. The Nunivak herd, introduced from Greenland in 1935, has provided breeding stock for establishing herds elsewhere in Alaska and the Soviet Union. The reindeer herd is a major source of food and income for residents of Mekoryuk, the only village on the island.

Other wildlife in the refuge includes moose, caribou, and grizzly and black bear. Wolves are found primarily in the northern hills and eastern mountains. Smaller mammals include beaver, muskrat, mink, land otter and fox. On Nunivak, native land animals include only red and arctic foxes, weasel, mink, shrews, voles and lemmings. Coastal waters support harbor, ribbon, ringed and bearded seals, walrus, and many species of whales during migrations.

Fish found in refuge waters include trout, arctic char and grayling in the mountain streams, and pike, sheefish, whitefish and burbot in lowland waters. Great numbers of king, silver, red, pink and chum salmon migrate through the delta rivers during the summer on their way to spawning grounds.

Activities: Major recreational activities in the refuge include wildlife observation, photography and boating. Other activities include hiking, camping, sled dog racing, snowmobiling and cross-country skiing. Hunting and fishing are allowed in accordance with state and federal regulations. Because of the refuge's remoteness and fickle weather, careful planning is necessary to ensure a safe trip. Top-quality equipment and a good insect repellent are essential, according to the Fish and Wildlife Service.

For many centuries, the abundance of wildlife has made the delta the heart of Yup'ik Eskimo culture. Residents of at least 56 villages depend on this region for subsistence purposes. Their equipment and camps are essential to their livelihood and should be left undisturbed. Also, ownership of large areas within the refuge has been conveyed to Native regional and village corporations, and this private property should be respected. Anyone planning a trip to the region should consult about the location of private lands with the Assoc. of Village Council Presidents, P.O. Box 219, Bethel, AK 99559, or with individual village corporations.

Accommodations: Lodging may be available in some villages, but should be arranged in advance. In general, travelers to the refuge should be self-sufficient. Wilderness camping is permitted in the refuge, but there are no established campgrounds or trails.

A visitor center for the Yukon Delta National Wildlife Refuge is located across from the Bethel Regional Hospital on the main road from the airport to downtown Bethel. The center features exhibits on the refuge, its wildlife and how the resources have been and are used by Eskimos in the region. Refuge staff present periodic wildlife programs for schools and the public.

Access: The refuge is accessible only by boat or airplane. There is scheduled airline service from Anchorage to Bethel, St. Marys and Aniak, where flights to other villages or remote areas can be arranged.

For more information: Contact Refuge Manager, Yukon Delta National Wildlife Refuge, P.O. Box 346, Bethel, AK 99559; phone 543-3151, fax 543-4413.

River Running

Andreafsky River. The Andreafsky is located within Andreafsky Wilderness, which is in the northern portion of Yukon Delta National Wildlife Refuge. The wild river consists of the Main Fork and the East Fork Andreafsky, which converge approximately 5 miles north of the village of St. Marys.

The river flows southwest 120 miles to the Yukon River at Pitkas Point. Both forks of the Andreafsky are scenic, and wildlife along the river includes black and brown bears, foxes, caribou, beavers, otters, bald and golden eagles, peregrine falcons, a variety of hawks, gulls and ducks, Canada geese

and tundra swans. Fish include chum, king and silver salmon, grayling and Dolly Varden.

Access to the Andreafsky River is difficult and expensive. The easiest method is to fly commercially to St. Marys. From there, arrange to have a raft towed upriver by jet-boat or charter a floatplane to take you up the river to a convenient dropoff point. A major problem is that there are no lakes along the rivers that a large floatplane can land on. A small floatplane is required to land along the river. A further problem is that charter and guide services either do not exist or are quite limited. A potential visitor will need to research extensively in order to set up a float trip on the river. Related USGS Topographic maps: Kwiglik A-2, A-3, B-1, B-2, C-1, C-2, D-1; St. Michael A-1; Unalakleet A-6; Holy Cross C-6, D-6.

Aniak River. The Aniak flows 140 river miles to the Kuskokwim River, 1 mile east of Aniak. This river has 3 distinct phases. It is clear, fast flat water over a gravel bed from its headwaters at Aniak Lake. It drops at 10 feet per mile for 40 miles through the forest and into the tundra. In its second phase, the course disintegrates into numerous channels filled with many sweepers, logjams and uprooted trees. It continues dropping at 10 feet per mile for 20 miles to where the Salmon River joins the Aniak. Below this very difficult stretch of Class II, the water becomes tame, flat water for the remaining 80 miles to Aniak. It is recommended that this isolated river be attempted only by the most experienced wilderness travelers. Decked canoes and kayaks are recommended.

Fishing on the Aniak is excellent for king, chum and coho salmon, pike, rainbow trout, sheefish and grayling. Aniak Lake has lake trout and grayling.

Access is by chartered floatplane from Bethel or Aniak. Exit is from Aniak, where there are overnight accommodations and other facilities. Related USGS Topographic maps: Bethel B-1, C-1, D-1; Russian Mission A-1, B-1, C-2.

Holitna River. This is a slow taiga river that was the Russians' first route into the Interior from Bristol Bay. Although it once saw much activity, today it is seldom visited. The Holitna flows northeast 200 river miles from its source at the confluence of Kogrukluk River and Shotgun Creek, to the Kuskokwim River across from Sleetmute village. The Holitna poses few technical problems for the boater; it is flat water all the way.

However, boaters must be alert for sweepers and logjams. The Holitna is isolated and recommended only for travelers with wilderness experience. Canoes, kayaks and riverboats all are suitable.

Five species of salmon are available in this river, but especially kings, chums and cohos, along with pike and sheefish. Also grayling and arctic char can be found upstream.

Access is by floatplane from Bethel. Exit is from Sleetmute, which has scheduled air service, but no overnight facilities. Related USGS Topographic maps: Taylor Mts. D-5; Sleetmute A-5, A-4, B-4, B-3, C-3.

Kanektok River. This river heads at scenic Kagati Lake in the Ahklun Mountains in Togiak National Wildlife Refuge and flows 90 miles to Kuskokwim Bay near the village of Quinhagak. The lower 17 miles of river are on Quinhagak Village Corp. land. The upper river flows through a mountain valley, while the lower portion wanders through flat tundra. There are numerous gravel bars and islands along the length of the river, particularly on the coastal plain. The first 25 miles are Class I, followed by 30 miles of Class I–II and then another 30 miles of flat water. There are no rapids in the middle 30 miles, but sweepers, combined with a moderately swift current and a winding course, require frequent maneuvering. Traveling the length of this river usually takes 5 to 7 days. Canoe, raft and kayak all are suitable.

Seasonally there is very good fishing for 5 species of salmon, arctic char, grayling and rainbow trout. The number of large fish in this river qualifies it as one of the premier sportfishing rivers on the North American continent, according to the Fish and Wildlife Service.

Access is by floatplane to Kagati Lake from Bethel or Dillingham. Exit is by scheduled commercial air service from Quinhagak, which has no overnight facilities. Several commercial float guides are available for the Kanektok. There is a float outfitter in Dillingham. Related USGS Topographic maps: Goodnews C-5, C-6, D-3, D-4, D-5, D-6, D-7, D-8.

Kisaralik River. This river heads in Kisaralik Lake in the Kilbuck Mountains and flows northwest 100 miles to the Kuskokwim River, 20 miles northeast of Bethel. This is considered an exciting whitewater float for boaters with intermediate skills. The river is swift, with long stretches of small rocky rapids. The upper half of the river flows through a tundra-covered valley bracketed by mountains rising 2,000 to 3,000 feet. Low bluffs parallel the river. Crossing the Kuskokwim lowlands, the river meanders slowly through paper birch, aspen and spruce forest. There are 4 short (50 yards or less) Class III rapids and then 20-yard-long Upper Falls (Class IV), which can be portaged easily on either side of the river. The left side is an easier portage but the right side has a better campsite. Quicksilver Creek, 3 miles downriver, and then the ridge through which the river cuts to form the falls, are recognizable landmarks. Upper Falls is followed by 12 miles of Class II, then the Class II Lower Falls, 4 miles of Class I–II and then Class III Golden Gate. The lower portion of the river consists of 35 miles of Class I and 25 miles of flat water. This trip generally takes 6 days. Rafts or kayaks are recommended; canoes for experienced paddlers.

There is superb mountain scenery and good hiking throughout the upper portion of the river. Downstream, boaters can take a break and explore tundra-covered ridges. Seasonally there is good fishing for all varieties of salmon, rainbow trout, grayling and arctic char. Lake trout are available in Kisaralik Lake.

Access is by floatplane from Bethel to Kisaralik Lake. Exit is by floatplane from the lower portion of the Kisaralik, or pickup by riverboat can be arranged at Bethel. There are accommodations and meals at Bethel. Related USGS Topographic maps: Bethel.

Kuskokwim River. This 540-mile-long river is Alaska's fourth longest. Its North Fork reaches far north to the Tanana basin and once served as a watercourse for Natives and, later, prospectors and trappers. Lake Minchumina is connected by a long, once well-trodden portage to the North Fork. There are few travelers today, so boaters must be prepared to rely on their own resources.

The first village reached is Medfra, located where the East Fork merges with the North Fork. From that point, the Kuskokwim is a wide river, flowing slowly through mountains southwest to the broad coastal plain and Kuskokwim Bay. The largest settlements are McGrath, Sleetmute, Chuathbaluk, Aniak and Bethel. This river is flat water all the way. Canoes, kayaks, rafts and riverboats all are suitable.

Access is by portage from Lake Minchumina or more easily by floatplane from Anchorage, Fairbanks or McGrath. Exit is by floatplane from any point on the river or by scheduled air service from most of the communities on the river. Related USGS Topographic maps: Kantishna River B-5, A-5, A-6; Mount McKinley D-6; Meafra D-1, C-1, C-2, B-2, B-3, A-3, A-4, A-5; McGrath D-5, D-6, C-6, B-6; Iditarod B-1, A-1; Sleetmute D-1, D-2, C-3, C-4, D-4, D-5, D-6, C-6, C-7, C-8; Russian Mission C-1, C-2, C-3, C-4, B-4, B-5, A-5, A-6; Bethel D-6, D-7, D-8, C-8; Baird Inlet C-1, B-1, B-2, A-2.

Stony River. This river heads at Stony Glacier in the Alaska Range and flows southwest and northwest 190 miles to the Kuskokwim, about 1 mile from Stony River village. This is a swift (averaging 5 mph), silty river flowing through a forest. Below its confluence with the Necons River, it flows through foothills, then passes into lowlands. Below its confluence with the Telaquana River, the Stony flows through a series of small, scenic canyons for 19 miles of Class II. Here there are short (100 yards or less) stretches of rapids, alternating with 1 to 4 miles of swift flat water. The remaining 90 miles of the river is flat water or Class I. The trip from the Telaquana confluence takes approximately 5 to 6 days. Rafts, kayaks and canoes all are suitable.

This river offers good grayling fishing in the clear-water tributaries; the river itself is too silty for sportfishing. There are numerous gravel bars for campsites. Mountain scenery upstream from the Necons River is good. This trip is popular with hunters; travelers who want only to sightsee should plan their trips before hunting season.

Access is by wheel plane or floatplane to the upper reaches of Stony River; or floatplane to Telaquana Lake, headwaters of the Telaquana River; or Two Lakes, headwaters of the Necons River. Exit is by mail plane from Lime Village on the Stony River; scheduled air service from Stony River village; or floatplane pickup from the lower river. Lime Village has no visitor facilities; Stony River has limited accommodations. Boaters also may continue down the Kuskokwim River to a larger village. Related USGS Topographic maps: Lime Hills A-4 through A-6, B-5 through B-8; Sleetmute B-1, C-1, C-2 and D-2.

Sportfishing

Access to good fishing in the Yukon-Kuskokwim area is primarily by air. If you have the time, however, you sometimes can walk or go by boat to a hot fishing spot. Boats occasionally can be rented or chartered at villages along the waterways. There are daily commercial flights to the transporta-tion centers of the region—Bethel, Aniak or St. Marys—where you can catch a commuter flight to a smaller village or charter a plane to a lake or river. In addition, commercial outfitters will handle logistics for you on guided fishing trips.

Tackle-breaking king salmon are at their peak from mid-June through July. These fish commonly weigh 30 pounds and up. Chums and reds show up by July 1, pinks by mid-July (in even-numbered years) and silvers by mid-August. Salmon fishing is concentrated in the clear-water or nonglacial river systems.

Dolly Varden are found throughout this area and are most abundant in late summer. These usually weigh 1 to 3 pounds, but an occasional 9- to 12-pounder has been reported. Grayling can be caught most of the summer, but larger ones are more plentiful from August to October. Grayling measuring 16 inches are not uncommon, and they can reach 23 inches. Arctic char are found in some of the area's alpine lakes.

Other species that may be encountered are whitefish, which can reach 5 pounds; burbot (also called lush or lingcod), which can weigh in at 10 to 12 pounds; and northern pike, which average 5 to 8 pounds but can attain 30 pounds. Pike have very sharp teeth, so beware.

The Alaska Dept. of Fish and Game recommends that anyone traveling to remote areas should plan for the worst. Take a few days extra food, and fuel if necessary, and allow for a flexible schedule since fickle weather can delay travel for days.

Although many villages have hunting and fishing license vendors, it is recommended that you purchase your license in Anchorage or another large community, since sometimes the local vendors themselves have gone fishing. The Dept. of Fish and Game does not sell licenses.

More information about fishing in the Yukon-Kuskokwim area may be obtained from the following: Alaska Dept. of Fish and Game, Sport Fish Division, 1300 College Road, Fairbanks, AK 99701-1599; phone 456-8819. Alaska Dept. of Fish and Game, P.O. Box 90, Bethel, AK 99559-0090; phone 543-2433, fax 543-2021. Alaska Dept. of Fish and Game, Sport Fish Division, P.O. Box 230, Dillingham, AK 99576-0230.

Andreafsky River. This is a National Wild and Scenic River located in the northeast corner of Yukon Delta National Wildlife Refuge. It joins the Yukon River just east of St. Marys. Excellent fishery. Fish available:

king, chum, coho and pink salmon, use spoons; grayling year-round, best in late summer, use flies; Dolly Varden best June to September, use spoons, eggs. Charter air service and accommodations available in St. Marys.

Aniak River. Joins the Kuskokwim River 1 mile east of Aniak village. Excellent fishery. Fish available: king, chum and coho salmon, use spoons; rainbow trout, use flies, lures or bait; Dolly Varden, best in fall, use spoons, eggs; grayling year-round, best in late summer, use flies; northern pike year-round, use spoons, spinners; sheefish, best May to September, use spoons; arctic char and lake trout in Aniak Lake, use spoons, plugs. Accommodations, guides and air charter service at Aniak.

Anvik River. This 140-mile-long river joins the Yukon 1.5 miles south of the village of Anvik. The Anvik has one of the largest chum runs in the world. The Anvik also has healthy populations of grayling and Dolly Varden. Chum salmon in season, use spoons; also good runs of kings, pink and coho; Dolly Varden, best in fall, use spoons, eggs; grayling year-round, best in late summer, use flies; northern pike excellent year-round, use spoons, spinners; sheefish good in June. Access by scheduled air service to Anvik or air charter to river from Grayling or St. Marys. Accommodations at Anvik River Lodge (663-6324).

Goodnews River. Heads in Goodnews Lake in the Togiak National Wildlife Refuge and flows southwest 60 miles to Goodnews Bay at the village of Goodnews Bay. The river has 3 forks: the North Fork, 47 miles long; the Middle Fork, 42 miles; and the South Fork, 25 miles. The North and Middle forks are floatable with lake access; the South Fork has no headwater lake. The lower 22 miles of the North Fork, and 15 miles of the Middle Fork, are BLM and Goodnews Village Corp. lands. Excellent fishing. Fish available: 5 species of salmon, grayling, rainbow trout and Dolly Varden. Arctic char and lake trout in Goodnews Lake. Access by air charter from Bethel or Dillingham. Land floatplanes below the confluence of the 3 forks (about 2.5 miles from the village). Wheel planes land at Goodnews Bay village. Sportfish guides offer fly-ins, a motorboat base camp and guided float packages.

Hoholitna River. Heads in Whitefish Lake and flows northwest 165 miles to the Holitna River, 13 miles southeast of its junction with the Kuskokwim River near Sleetmute. Fish available: northern pike year-round, use spoons, spinners; sheefish, best late June to August, use spoons; grayling, best in late summer, use flies; Dolly Varden, best June to September, use spoons, eggs. Access by air charter from Bethel or Aniak.

Holitna River. Joins the Kuskokwim River 1.5 miles south of Sleetmute. Fish available: 5 species of salmon in season, but especially kings, chums and coho. Other fish upstream are: northern pike year-round, use spoons, spinners; sheefish, best late June to August, use spoons; grayling year-round, best in late summer, use flies; Dolly Varden, best in fall, use spoons. Commercial lodge on river. Access by boat from Sleetmute, or air charter from Aniak or Bethel.

Kanektok River. Heads at Kagati Lake in the Togiak National Wildlife Refuge and flows southwest 90 miles to Kuskokwim Bay, 1.5 miles west of Quinhagak. Excellent fishery. Fish available: salmon in season; rainbow trout, best in late summer and early fall; Dolly Varden, best July to September; grayling year-round, best May to September; and lake trout and arctic char in headwater lakes. Access by charter floatplane from Bethel or Dillingham. No accommodations on lake or river, but several sportfish guides have motorboat base camps in the area. There are also several float guides. Not recommended for fly-in except at 1 or 2 floatplane landing locations on the river. No overnight accommodations at Quinhagak. The lower 17 miles of the river is Quinhagak Village Corp. land.

Kisaralik River. Flows into the Kuskokwim River 20 miles northeast of Bethel. Fish available: 5 species of salmon in season; rainbow trout, best in late summer and early fall, use flies, lures or bait; grayling year-round, best late summer, use flies; Dolly Varden, best in fall, use spoons, eggs. Rental boats and charter planes available in Bethel.

Kwethluk River. Flows into the Kuskokwim River 10 miles east of Bethel. Located in Yukon Delta National Wildlife Refuge. Fish available: 5 varieties of salmon in season; rainbow trout, best in late summer and early fall, use flies, lures or bait; grayling year-round, best in late summer, use flies; Dolly Varden, best in fall, use spoons, eggs. Rental boats available in Bethel.

Owhat River. Joins the Kuskokwim River 4.5 miles upriver from Aniak. Fishing best at its mouth. Fish available: sheefish, best late June to August, use spoons; grayling year-round, best in late summer, use flies; whitefish, use flies, eggs. Access by boat from Aniak.

SEWARD PENINSULA/NORTON SOUND

Successive waves of prehistoric migrations brought the first peoples to Alaska's Seward Peninsula. These nomads came across the ancient Bering Land Bridge from Asia, leaving evidence of their culture that archaeologists are still piecing together today.

Yup'ik and Inupiat Eskimos, descendants of these wanderers, continue the hunting, fishing and trapping which have supported them from time immemorial. In coastal and island villages marine mammals, whales, seals and walrus are the mainstays. More easterly villages rely on moose and caribou and salmon runs up the rivers.

Russian explorer Vitus Bering made the first documented sighting of the Diomede Islands in 1728, but it would be another century before the Russian-American Co. established a permanent settlement on the mainland, at St. Michael in 1833. European and American whaling crews had considerable contact with Eskimos along the coast. But not until the gold strike near Nome in 1898 did the Seward Peninsula receive another major wave of migration—this time of gold seekers.

In recent years, reindeer herding has been a needed source of cash for some Eskimo villages. (Pioneer missionary Sheldon Jackson originally introduced reindeer to the area as a new source of protein.) Both reindeer meat and horn are sold, much of it to South Korea for traditional Oriental medical uses. Recent changes in the official status of reindeer horn in the Oriental folk medicine market have threatened the economic health of this livelihood.

Another introduced mammal to the Seward Peninsula, the musk-ox, is thriving. A total of 61 musk-oxen were transplanted to the Seward Peninsula in 1970 and 1981, and their numbers have been increasing between 15 and 20 percent a year. A 1992 census by the BLM, Dept. of Fish and Game and Park Service found 700 musk-oxen in several small herds on the Seward Peninsula. The animals are off-limits to hunters.

Visitors to the Seward Peninsula and Norton Sound today enjoy seeing relics from the area's exciting gold rush past. Hiking, fishing, beachcombing, camping and watching birds are favorite activities. Serious birders can add checks to their life list with sightings of rare Asiatic species. Though much of the tundra is too boggy for hiking, the gentle mountains and alpine tundra make for excellent cross-country traveling, both winter and summer. Many visitors are especially drawn to the Norton Sound villages in March, when Iditarod Trail Sled Dog Race teams pass through Unalakleet, Shaktoolik, Koyuk, Elim, Golovin and Solomon on their way to the finish line at Nome. That city overflows with visitors during the exciting late winter event.

A visit to St. Lawrence Island, home of the Siberian Yup'iks, is a step back in time, where skin boats and drums made of walrus stomachs are taken for granted and family ties are much closer to the mainland of Siberia than to Alaska.

Musk-oxen were introduced to the Seward Peninsula in 1970. (Alissa Crandall)

Brevig Mission

[MAP 13] Located at the mouth of Shelman Creek on the north shore of Port Clarence on the Seward Peninsula, 6 miles northwest of Teller, 60 miles northwest of Nome, 481 miles west of Fairbanks. **Transportation:** Scheduled or charter air service from Nome. **Population:** 234. **Zip code:** 99785. **Emergency Services:** Village Public Safety Officer; Alaska State Troopers, Nome, phone 443-2835; Clinic, phone 642-4311; Volunteer Fire Department.

Elevation: 25 feet. **Climate:** Maritime climate, cool and damp, when the Bering Sea is ice free from early June to mid-November. Freezing of the sea causes a change to a more continental climate, with less precipitation and colder temperatures. Annual precipitation is 11.5 inches, with an average of 50 inches of snowfall. Average winter temperatures are between -9°F and 8°F; summer temperatures are between 44°F and 57°F.

Private Aircraft: Airstrip adjacent east; elev. 25 feet; length 2,400 feet; gravel; unattended. Runway condition not monitored; recommend visual inspection prior to using. Airport has lights and freight terminal. Transportation into village sometimes available.

Visitor Facilities: Arrangements can be made to stay in the high school during the school year by contacting the school principal (642-4021). The Washeteria building (642-4321) and the health clinic (642-4311) also offer lodging. No hotels, restaurants or banking services. Groceries, clothing, first-aid supplies, hardware, camera film and sporting goods available at Brevig Muit Store (642-4091). Arts and crafts available for purchase include carved ivory, fur slippers, mukluks, beadwork, crocheted and knitted items. Fishing/hunting licenses available. No guide service. Marine engine and boat repair available. Arrangements can be made to rent boats. Fuel available includes white gas, propane and regular gasoline. No moorage facilities.

The "Teller Reindeer Station" was established nearby in 1892 by Sheldon Jackson, who named it after Henry Moore Teller, U.S. senator and secretary of the Interior. The reindeer station was operated by the U.S. government from 1892 to 1900. The Norwegian Evangelical Lutheran Mission was established in 1900 at the present site of Brevig Mission and the settlement became known as Teller Mission. By 1906, the government role in reindeer herding had diminished and the mission became dominant. Brevig Mission is a second-class city, incorporated in 1969.

The Natives living around Port Clarence were Kauwerak Eskimos with no permanent settlement prior to 1892. They lived in migratory communities, pursuing fish and game. They traded furs with Siberia, Little Diomede and King Island, and alliances were formed with Wales, Little Diomede and others for protection.

Reindeer were the economic base of this community from 1892 to 1974, but their importance is now declining. Skin sewing for arts and crafts and jobs on seasonal construction projects bring in some income.

The people of Brevig Mission depend on both sea mammals and fishing for subsistence, going to seasonal hunting and fishing camps. Seal, oogruk and beluga whale are the most important subsistence mammals. Fish staples include salmon, whitefish, herring, tomcod, flounder, sculpin and smelt. Residents also rely on waterfowl, game birds, eggs, rabbits, squirrels, moose, berries and an occasional polar bear. According to one enthusiastic resident, "Fishing is great in the summer, spring hunting is even greater, and greatest of all: the community is friendly and we welcome visitors year round."

There is a winter trail to Teller used by snow machines and dogsleds.

Communications in Brevig Mission include phones, mail plane, radio and TV. The community is served by a Lutheran church and a school with grades preschool through 12. There are community electricity and water systems; sewage system is honey buckets. Brevig Mission prohibits the sale and importation of alcoholic beverages. Freight arrives by cargo plane and barge. Government address: City of Brevig Mission, P.O. Box 85021, Brevig Mission, AK 99785; phone 642-3851. Village corporation address: Brevig Mission Native Corp., General Delivery, Brevig Mission, AK 99785; phone 642-4091.

Buckland

[MAP 14] Located on the west bank of the Buckland River on the Seward Peninsula, 75 miles southeast of Kotzebue, 400 miles west of Fairbanks. **Transportation:** Boats; snow machine; scheduled air service from Kotzebue. **Population:** 365. **Zip code:** 99727. **Emergency Services:** Village Public Safety Officer, phone 494-2162; Alaska State Troopers, Kotzebue; Clinic, phone 494-2122; Volunteer Fire Department.

Climate: Transitional zone characterized by long, cold winters and cool summers. Temperatures in July and August average 60°F. Precipitation is light, less than 9 inches annually, with 35 to 40 inches of snow.

Private Aircraft: Airstrip 1 mile southwest from village; elev. 30 feet; length 2,200 feet; gravel. No airport facilities. Runway condition not monitored; recommend visual inspection prior to using. Subject to turbulent crosswinds during summer months. Public transportation into village available.

Visitor Facilities: No hotel, restaurant or banking service. Laundry facilities are available at the city washeteria, open daily. Groceries, clothing, first-aid supplies, hardware, camera film and sporting goods available at 4 stores. Fishing/hunting licenses available. No guide or major repair services. No rental transportation. Fuel available includes marine gas, propane and regular gasoline. No moorage facilities.

This village has existed at several other locations under various names in the past, including Elephant Point, so named because fossil mammoth or mastodon bones were found at the site in 1826. The presence of the fossil finds shows that this site was used by prehistoric man.

Buckland people moved repeatedly as conditions changed and the people depended at various times on reindeer or beluga whale or seal for survival. In the 1920s, they moved with their reindeer herd from Old Buckland, 1 mile downriver, to the present area. The townsite, however, was later relocated. Today, Buckland is a second-class city, incorporated in 1966.

Buckland has a primarily subsistence economy. In the fall and winter, residents hunt caribou; in spring they hunt beluga whale and seal off Elephant Point.

Some employment is provided with a locally owned reindeer herd, numbering 2,000 head. Herring, salmon, smelt, grayling, whitefish, rabbit, ptarmigan, berries and waterfowl and their eggs supplement the local diet.

Communications in Buckland include phones, mail plane and radio. The community is served by a church and 2 schools with grades preschool through 12. There is a community electricity system. Water is hauled from the washeteria. The city has its own honey-bucket haul system. Freight arrives by barge or by air. Government address: City of Buckland, P.O. Box 49, Buckland, AK 99727; phone 494-2121, fax 494-2138. Village corporation address: NANA Regional Corp., P.O. Box 49, Kotzebue, AK 99752. Buckland IRA Council, General Delivery, Buckland, AK 99727; phone 494-2171.

Candle

[MAP 14] Located on the Kewalik River, 90 miles southeast of Kotzebue. **Transportation:** Scheduled air service; charter plane; boat. **Population:** 4 year-round, 35 during summer mining season. **Zip code:** 99728. **Emergency Services:** Public Health Service Hospital in Kotzebue, phone 442-3321; Alaska State Troopers in Kotzebue, phone 442-3911.

Climate: June clear and cool, July hot and dry. In August, expect rain, then usually 2 or 3 weeks of Indian summer in September. Winters are cold, similar to Kotzebue.

Private Aircraft: Airstrip adjacent northeast; elev. 15 feet; length 5,200 feet; gravel; no fuel; unattended.

Visitor Facilities: None. Supplies are obtained from Kotzebue and Anchorage.

Candle is a mining community which started in 1904. Most of the town burned down approximately 20 years ago; just a few houses were left standing. There are 4 year-round residents, with the population increasing from May until freezeup or Oct. 1. Because the mining season is so short, July 4 is the only summer holiday, and residents hold a town picnic with horseshoes and a softball game.

There is an old deserted dredge about 6 miles from town. Fishing is good in the Kewalik River from July through September for salmon, grayling and trout. There are moose, caribou, reindeer and occasionally bear. Two mining operations in Candle are available for people to walk through and watch, as well as an old cemetery to view.

Council

[MAP 13] Located on the left bank of the Niukluk River on the Seward Peninsula, 33 miles northeast of Solomon, 74 miles northeast of Nome, 470 miles west of Fairbanks. **Transportation:** Boat, charter plane or auto from Nome. **Population:** 11 year-round, up to 50 in summer. **Zip code:** 99790. **Emergency Services:** Alaska State Troopers, Nome; Health Aide, phone 665-8001.

Elevation: 100 feet. Climate: Continental, with long, cold winters and short, mild summers. Average annual precipitation is 14 inches, with 46 inches of snowfall. Temperatures range between -9°F and 64°F.

Private Aircraft: Melsing Creek airstrip adjacent northeast; elev. 95 feet; length 2,000 feet; gravel; no fuel; unattended. Runway subject to crosswinds, not maintained in winter; unattended; recommend visual inspection prior to using. Runway connected to section of the road, which has been widened to serve as part of the airstrip. No airport facilities. Transportation into village sometimes available. Pederson airstrip adjacent east of mining camp; elev. 95 feet; length 2,100 feet; gravel; no fuel; unattended. Prior permission for use required in writing from owner. South end of runway rough. Runway doglegs; use east side runway by road. Grass on strip; use caution.

Visitor Facilities: Accommodations and meals available in summer at Camp Bendeleben fishing lodge (443-2880). No public laundry facilities or banking services. Limited groceries and sporting goods available at a small store in a local residence; most visitors bring their own supplies. No arts and crafts available for purchase. Fishing/hunting licenses not available. Guide services available. No repair service or rental transportation. Fuel available includes propane and regular gasoline. No moorage facilities.

Council, once one of the largest communities in Alaska, was founded in 1897 by Daniel B. Libby and his party. Libby had been 1 of 3 members of the Van Bendeleben expedition of 1896 who discovered gold in the area. Council became the site of the recording office and center of the Council Gold Mining District. By October 1897, it was a city of approximately 50 log houses and 300 people. The gold strikes at Council Creek predate major strikes at Nome, and a single claim on Ophir Creek was said to be almost the richest claim in the world, second only to a claim in Klondike. During the summers of 1897–99, Council's population was estimated to be as high as 15,000 people, and it was said to be bigger than Nome although the actual population was never documented. "Council City" was a genuine boom town with a hotel, wooden boardwalks, a post office, a 20-bed hospital and numerous bars. At one time 13 dredges worked streams and rivers between Solomon and Council, and the town was the southern terminus of a railroad that climbed a 600-foot ridge into Ophir Creek. Many of the boomers left Council in 1900 for the gold beaches of Nome, but a sizable community remained. Council, which still had a population of 686 in 1910, was for many years the second largest community in western Alaska. The influenza epidemic of 1918, the Great Depression and WWII contributed to its decline, and by 1950 only 9 people remained. The post office was closed in 1953.

Council is one of the few villages in the region connected to Nome by a road, which originated as a trail during the gold rush. The road was constructed in 1906–07. The road terminates across from Council at the river, which can be forded at low water periods. Three roads branch out from Council: one to Ophir Creek, the second to Melsing Creek and the airstrip, and a third over a hill northeast to Mystery. Except for the Ophir Road, 4-wheel-drive vehicles are necessary.

The movie *North to Alaska* starring John Wayne was filmed in this area. Remnants of gold mining activity are everywhere. The countryside is dotted with old cabins, roads, a railroad, mines and dredges, including an operating dredge at Ophir Creek. The old post office, school, hotel and numerous other buildings in various stages of deterioration still stand among newer buildings in the settlement.

All permanent residents of Council, and many of the seasonal residents, rely in part on local hunting and fishing for food. The Niukluk River provides some of the finest fishing on the Seward Peninsula. Arctic char, grayling, pike, whitefish, and chum, pink and king salmon abound. Rabbits, ptarmigan, moose, grizzly bears and wolves all inhabit the area. Some placer gold mining currently takes place in the area, primarily at Ophir Creek.

Communications in Council include a phone in the community building (665-8001) and radios. There is a community electricity system. Water is hauled from a central watering point. The sewage system is honey buckets. Freight is hauled over the Nome-Council Road for $500 per truckload. Council is unincorporated. Village corporation address: Council Native Corp., P.O. Box 727, Nome, AK 99762.

Deering

[MAP 14] Located at the mouth of the Inmachuck River on Kotzebue Sound, 57 miles southwest of Kotzebue, 150 miles north of Nome, 440 miles west-northwest of Fairbanks. **Transportation:** Scheduled and charter air service from Kotzebue; boat; snow machine. **Population:** 165. **Zip code:** 99736. **Emergency Services:** Village Public Safety Officer; Alaska State Troopers, Kotzebue, phone 442-3911; Health Aide, phone 363-2137; Volunteer Fire Department.

Climate: Transitional zone; long cold winters and cool summers. Precipitation is light and averages less than 9 inches per year, with 36 inches of snow.

Private Aircraft: Airstrip 1 mile southwest; elev. 15 feet; length 2,200 feet; gravel; crosswind; no fuel; unattended. Visual inspection recommended prior to landing. No airport facilities; private transportation to village.

Visitor Facilities: Accommodation with kitchen privileges at Deering Multipurpose facility (363-2136). Laundromat available. Groceries, clothing, first-aid supplies and camera film available at Deering Native Store (363-2159) and Beep's Store (363-2125). Some carved ivory available for purchase. Fishing/hunting licenses available. No guide service, major repair service or rental transportation. Fuel available includes diesel, propane and regular gasoline. No moorage facilities.

Deering, described as a beautiful oceanside community by one local resident, is built on a spit approximately 300 feet wide and 1.1 miles long. The village was established in 1901 as a supply station for Seward Peninsula gold mines and located near the historic Malemiut Eskimo village of Inmachukmiut. The village name probably was taken from the 90-ton schooner *Abbey Deering*, which was in the nearby waters in 1900. Deering is a second-class city, incorporated in 1970.

The economy is based on subsistence hunting and fishing and reindeer herding. Main sources of meat are moose, seal and beluga whale; residents go to hunting camps in the spring and fall.

A 26-mile road connects Deering with the mining area of Utica to the south. Also, many trails along major streams and across the tundra are used year-round for traveling to other villages, hunting and fishing.

Communications in Deering include phones, mail plane, radio and cable TV. The community has a church and a school with grades preschool through 12. There is community electricity. Water comes from a Public Health Service tank in summer; ice is hauled for water in winter. Sewage system is honey buckets. Deering prohibits the sale and importation of alcoholic beverages. Freight arrives by cargo plane and barge. Government address: City of Deering, P.O. Box 36049, Deering, AK 99736; phone 363-2136 or 363-2101. Village corporation address: NANA Regional Corp., P.O. Box 49, Kotzebue, AK 99752.

Diomede

[MAP 13] Located on the west coast of Little Diomede Island in Bering Strait, 80 miles northwest of Teller, 130 miles northwest of Nome, 650 miles west of Fairbanks. **Transportation:** Scheduled (in winter) and charter airplane service from Nome; helicopter. **Population:** 160. **Zip code:** 99762. **Emergency Services:** Alaska State Troopers, Nome, phone 443-2835; Health Clinic, phone 686-3311; Health Aide, phone 686-3071; Volunteer Fire Department, phone 686-3071.

Climate: Maritime climate when the strait is ice free June through November. When the strait and the Bering and Chukchi seas freeze, there is an abrupt change to a cold continental climate. Winters cold and windy, with average of 35 inches of snowfall. Annual precipitation, recorded at nearby Wales, 10 inches. Thick fog covers the island in May and June. Winter temperatures average between -10°F and 6°F. Summer temperatures average between 40°F and 50°F.

Private Aircraft: No airstrip. Helicopter landing pad. Floatplane access in summer; ski-equipped planes can land on the frozen strait in winter.

Visitor Facilities: A room with an efficiency kitchen is available through Inalik Native Corp. (686-3221). No restaurant or banking services. Laundromat with showers available. Limited groceries and supplies at Diomede Native Store (686-3611). Arts and crafts available for purchase include carved ivory and hand-sewn skin slippers and other garments. Fishing/hunting licenses not available. No guide or major repair services. Arrangements can be made to rent boats. Fuel available includes marine gas, diesel, propane and Blazo. No moorage facilities.

Residents of Diomede can look out their windows and see Russia's Big Diomede only 2.5 miles away. The international boundary between the United States and Russia lies between the islands. Early Eskimos on the island were great travelers to both Siberia and the Alaska mainland, conducting trade with both continents. The present village site, age unknown, was originally a spring hunting site. It gradually became a permanent settlement. The Native name for the village is Inalik, meaning "the other one" or "the one over there"; the village is commonly known as Diomede.

On Aug. 16, 1728, Captain Commander Vitus Bering named the islands in honor of St. Diomede. Explorers discovered that the Diomeders had an advanced culture with elaborate whale hunting ceremonies.

After WWII, the Soviet Union established the Iron Curtain and Big Diomede became a Soviet military base. All Native residents were moved to mainland Russia and the residents of Little Diomede never saw their relatives again. During the Cold War, Little Diomede residents who strayed into Soviet waters were taken captive and held as prisoners in Siberia for a whole summer. The villagers are very cautious about straying into Russian waters today.

Isolated and remote, Diomede has been perhaps less influenced by modern times than other Native villages in Alaska. Diomeders depend almost entirely on a subsistence economy. Blue cod, bullhead, flounder and tanner crab are harvested during the summer, and walrus, whales, seals and bears during spring and fall when these animals migrate through the area. Seal hides are used for mukluks, rope, harpoon lines and mittens, and walrus hides are used for boat hulls. Salmonberries, greens and some roots are found on the island. Diomede has abundant seabirds in summer, and these migratory birds and their eggs supplement the subsistence diet.

The Diomede people are excellent ivory carvers. Many villagers market their crafts in Anchorage, Teller, Kotzebue and Nome.

Communications in Diomede, a second-class city incorporated in 1970, include phones, mail plane, radio and TV. The community has a church and a school with grades preschool through 12. There are community electricity and water. Sewage system is honey buckets, except in the clinic and laundromat, which have flush toilets. Diomede prohibits the sale and importation of alcoholic beverages. Freight arrives by plane in winter, barge in summer. Delivery of freight can be hampered by ice or weather conditions. Government address: City of Diomede, Diomede, AK 99762; phone 686-3071. Village corporation address: Inalik Native Corp., General Delivery, Diomede, AK 99762; phone 686-3221, fax 686-3222.

Elim

[MAP 14] Located on the northwest shore of Norton Bay on the Seward Peninsula, 85 miles east of Solomon and 100 miles east of Nome. **Transportation:** Scheduled or charter air service from Nome. **Population:** 294. **Zip code:** 99739. **Emergency Services:** Police, phone 890-3081; Clinic, phone 890-3311; Volunteer Fire Department, phone 890-3441.

Climate: Subarctic, but changes to a more continental climate with the freezing of Norton Sound. Winter cold and relatively dry, average 40 inches of snowfall. Average annual precipitation 18.9 inches.

Private Aircraft: Airstrip adjacent southwest; elev. 130 feet; length 3,000 feet; gravel; no fuel; unattended; recommend visual inspection prior to using. Cliff south, runway rutted but usable. No line of sight between runway ends. Use caution.

Visitor Facilities: Accommodations may be arranged with the City of Elim (890-3441), which has 2 rooms available with 2 beds in each. Groceries, clothing and sundry items can be purchased at Elim Native Store and Eagles Cache Store. No restaurant. Fishing/hunting licenses available. Carved ivory available. No banking facilities or guide services. Boat, auto, aircraft repairs available; boats, autos and off-road vehicles available for rent. Fuel includes marine gas, diesel, propane, kerosene and regular gasoline.

Formerly the Malemiut Eskimo village of Nuviakchak, Elim is located on a former federal reindeer reserve, established in 1911, but dissolved with the Alaska Native Claims Settlement Act. A mission and school opened in the early 1900s increased the population. The village incorporated as a second-class city in 1970. Its economy is subsistence based, supplemented by seasonal employment in construction, fish processing and timber.

The Iditarod Trail passes through Elim, serving as a trail to Nome to the west and Unalakleet to the south.

Communications include phones, mail plane, radio and TV. The community has a church and a school for kindergarten through grade 12. Public electricity, water and sewage systems available. Freight arrives by air transport and barge. The village bans the sale and importation of alcoholic beverages. Government address: City of Elim, P.O. Box 39009, Elim, AK 99739; phone 890-3441, fax 890-3811. Village corporation address: Elim Native Corp., P.O. Box 39010, Elim, AK 99739-0010; phone 890-3741, fax 890-3091.

Gambell

[MAP 13] Located on Northwest Cape on St. Lawrence Island in the Bering Sea, 200 miles west of Nome, 675 miles west of Fairbanks. **Transportation:** Scheduled or charter air service from Nome. **Population:** 522. **Zip code:** 99742. **Emergency Services:** Police, phone 985-5333; Alaska State Troopers, Nome, phone 443-2835; Clinic, phone 985-5012; Volunteer Fire Department.

Elevation: 30 feet. **Climate:** Cool, moist maritime climate with some continental characteristics in the winter when much of the Bering Sea freezes. Winds and fog are common and precipitation occurs 300 days per year. Precipitation is usually very light rain, mist or snow, and total annual precipitation is only 15 inches. Average snowfall 80 inches, distributed evenly from November to May. Winter temperatures -2°F to 10°F. Summer temperatures 34°F to 48°F.

Private Aircraft: Airstrip adjacent south; elev. 27 feet; length 4,500 feet; asphalt; no fuel; unattended. No airport facilities or transportation into village.

Visitor Facilities: Accommodations and meals available at 1 lodge. Laundry facilities available; no banking services. Groceries, clothing, first-aid supplies, hardware, camera film and sporting goods available in the community. Arts and crafts available for purchase include carved ivory, baleen boats and Eskimo artifacts. Fishing/hunting licenses available. Contact the City of Gambell regarding guide service. No major repair service available. Arrangements can be made to rent off-road vehicles or boats. Fuel available includes diesel, propane and regular gasoline. No moorage facilities. Group tours available from Anchorage or Nome. *NOTE: Visitors to Gambell and Savoonga who wish to leave the city limits are required to pay a one-time fee of $25. The entire island is private property; the fee helps monitor use and serves as a registration system to make sure people don't get lost. The corporation also requires that any stories or photographs involving areas outside the townsite be submitted for prepublication approval.*

St. Lawrence Island has been inhabited for several thousand years. The island sits astride one of the great prehistoric migration routes—the Bering Land Bridge which linked Asia with the Americas. Evidence of Eskimo culture at Gambell dates back to 1700. Sivuqaq (Sivokak) is the Siberian Yup'ik name for the village and for St. Lawrence Island. The city was named in 1898 for Presbyterian missionaries and teachers Mr. and Mrs. Vene C. Gambell, who were lost in the schooner *Jane Grey* on their return from a leave of absence. The name was proposed by the new teacher, William F. Doty. The village was established under the Indian Reorganization Act of 1934 as the Native village of Gambell in 1939. It was incorporated as a second-class city under state law in 1963.

The economy in Gambell is largely based on subsistence hunting. Residents hunt walrus and bowhead and gray whales in spring and fall. During summer the people fish, crab, hunt birds, gather eggs and harvest seafoods, greens and berries. Seal, fish and crab are harvested throughout the winter. Arctic fox are trapped as a secondary source of cash income. Some reindeer roam the island, but most harvest activities take place out of Savoonga.

The Native people of Gambell still hunt from walrus-hide boats and follow many old customs. A whaling festival takes place in Gambell each spring when a whale is taken.

There are 5 prehistoric village sites at Gambell which had been on the National Register of Historic Places. That designation was recently stripped from the sites because of extensive looting by the villagers. For half a century artifacts have been dug up and sold to supplement meager village incomes on this harsh island where unemployment stays at about 25 percent.

Ivory carvings are a popular retail item, and the St. Lawrence Islanders are famous for their beautiful work.

Numerous species of birds, some of them rare Asiatic species, populate the island during summer.

Communications at Gambell include phones, mail plane, radio and TV. The community is served by Presbyterian and Seventh Day Adventist churches and a school with grades kindergarten through 12. There is a community electricity system. Water is hauled from the laundromat. Sewage system is honey buckets. Gambell prohibits the possession of alcoholic beverages. Freight arrives by cargo plane and barge. Government address: City of Gambell, P.O. Box 189, Gambell, AK 99742; phone 985-5112. Village corporation address: Gambell Native Corp., General Delivery, Gambell, AK 99742; phone 985-5826.

Golovin

[MAP 14] Located on a point between Golovnin Bay and Golovnin Inlet on the Seward Peninsula, 42 miles east of Solomon, 90 miles east of Nome and 450 miles west of Fairbanks. **Transportation:** Snow machine; scheduled and charter air service from Nome; boat. **Population:** 152. **Zip code:** 99762. **Emergency Services:** Village Public Safety Officer, phone 779-3911; Health Clinic, phone 779-3311; Volunteer Fire Department.

Elevation: 25 feet. **Climate:** Marine climate when the sea is ice free. Average annual precipitation 19 inches; average annual snowfall 40 inches. Average winter temperatures between -2°F and 19°F; average summer temperatures between 40°F and 60°F.

Private Aircraft: 0.5 mile east; length 2,600 feet; gravel.

Visitor Facilities: No hotel, restaurant or banking services. Laundromat available. Groceries/supplies available at Olson and Sons. Arts and crafts available for purchase include fur hats, some ivory and woven wool mittens. Fishing/hunting licenses available. No guide service. Fuel available includes diesel, propane and regular gasoline.

The Eskimo village of Chinik, located at the present site of Golovin, was originally settled by the Kauweramiut Eskimos who later mixed with Unaligmiut Eskimos. Lieutenant L.A. Zagoskin of the Imperial Russian Navy reported the village as Ikalikguigmyut in 1842. The name Golovin was derived from the name of Golovnin Lagoon, which was named after Captain Vasili Mikkailovich Golovnin of the Russian Navy.

Around 1890, John Dexter established a trading post at Golovin that became the center for prospecting information for the entire Seward Peninsula. Gold was discovered in 1898 and Golovin became the supply point for the Council goldfields to the northwest. Golovin incorporated as a second-class city in 1971.

Golovin's economy is based on subsistence food harvest and commercial fishing. Local businesses, government and construction work provide additional employment. Residents go to summer fish camps to catch salmon, whitefish, trout, grayling, pike and herring. Subsistence hunting includes seals, beluga whales, moose, ducks, geese and ptarmigans. Bird eggs and berries are gathered from the tundra.

The Iditarod Trail passes through Golovin and is used as a winter trail.

Communications in Golovin include phones, mail plane, radio and TV. The community has a Covenant church and a school with grades kindergarten through 12. Community electricity, water and sewage systems. Golovin prohibits the sale and importation of alcoholic beverages. Freight arrives in the community by cargo plane and barge. Government address: City of Golovin, P.O. Box 62059, Golovin, AK 99762; phone 779-3211. Village corporation address: Golovin Native Corp., General Delivery, Golovin, AK 99762; phone 779-3251.

Koyuk

[MAP 14] Located at the mouth of the Koyuk River, at the northeastern end of Norton Bay on the Seward Peninsula, 132 miles east of Nome and 75 miles north of Unalakleet. **Transportation:** Scheduled air service to Nome. **Population:** 216. **Zip code:** 99753. **Emergency Services:** Police, phone 963-3541; Clinic, phone 963-3311; Volunteer Fire Department.

Climate: Winters cold and relatively dry, with an average of 40 inches of snowfall. Summers cool, with most rainfall in July, August and September. Average annual precipitation 18.9 inches. Average winter temperatures -8°F to 8°F. Summer temperatures 46°F to 62°F.

Private Aircraft: Airstrip adjacent northeast; elev. 130 feet; length 3,500 feet; gravel; unattended. Runway condition not monitored in summer; recommend visual inspection prior to using. Turbulence on approach when wind from northwest. Caution advised.

Visitor Facilities: No hotel or restaurant. Lodging is available at the pool hall (963-3661). Washeteria available. Groceries, clothing, first-aid supplies, hardware, camera film and sporting goods available at the Beluga Store (963-3551) and at Koyuk Native Store (963-3451). Pay phone (963-9991) available. No arts and crafts available. Fishing/hunting licenses available, as well as guide service. No banking or major repair service; no moorage facilities or rental transportation. Fuel available includes marine gas, propane and unleaded gasoline.

The village known as Kuynkhakmuit was first recorded by Lt. L.A. Zagoskin of the Imperial Russian Navy in the 1840s. Prior to 1900, the village was nomadic, gradually settling around the present site where supplies could easily be lightered to shore. Located 40 miles downriver from the Norton Bay Station trading center and near a coal mine which supplied steamships and the city of Nome, Koyuk became a natural transfer point for goods and services.

The archaeological site of Iyatayak, with traces of early man 6,000 to 8,000 years old, is located south of Koyuk on Cape Denbigh.

The village was incorporated in 1970 as a second-class city. The economy is based on subsistence supplemented by part-time wage earnings. Some income is derived from reindeer herding, with hides and antlers being sold on the commercial market. Salmon, herring, grayling, beluga, seal, caribou, wildfowl, moose and berries are harvested.

Communications include phones, mail plane, radio and TV. The community has a Covenant church and a school with grades preschool to 12. Community electricity system is available. Sewage system is honey buckets. Water from a community well is hauled from the washeteria. Freight arrives by air transport and barge. The village bans the sale and importation of alcoholic beverages. Government address: City of Koyuk, P.O. Box 29, Koyuk, AK 99753; phone 963-3441. Village corporation address: Koyuk Native Corp., Koyuk, AK 99753; phone 963-3551.

Nome

[MAP 13] Located on the south coast of the Seward Peninsula, 550 air miles northwest of Anchorage. **Transportation:** Daily jet service from Anchorage available year-round. Charter air service to and from village; in winter, snow machines, dogsleds. **Population:** 4,503. **Zip code:** 99762. **Emergency Services:** Norton Sound Regional Hospital; Police, Fire and Ambulance, phone 911.

Elevation: 13 to 44 feet. **Climate:** Average temperature in January from -3°F to 12°F; average temperature in July from 45°F to 60°F. Mean annual precipitation 15.5 inches; mean annual snowfall 55 inches. Snow usually starts falling in early October; last snowfall in late April.

Private Aircraft: Nome airport 2 miles west; elev. 36 feet; length 6,000 feet; asphalt; fuel 80, 100, Jet A, A1. Three cab companies available for transportation to town. Nome city aerodrome 0.9 mile north; elev. 59 feet; length 3,200 feet; gravel.

Visitor Facilities: Accommodations available at 7 hotels and 1 bed and breakfast. For additional information, contact the Nome Convention and Visitors Bureau (443-5535). There are a number of restaurants, 1 bank, laundry and shower facilities. Groceries, clothing, first-aid supplies, hardware, camera film and sporting goods available at local stores. Native arts and crafts available at several excellent gift shops. Fishing/hunting licenses available, as well as guide service. Public moorage facilities available. Truck and van rentals available.

Nome owes its name to a misinterpretation of "? name" annotated on a manuscript chart prepared aboard the HMS *Herald* about 1850. The question mark was taken as a C (for cape) and the A in "name" was read as O.

Gold was found in the Nome area in September 1898, and the town got its start that winter when 6 miners met at the mouth of Snake River and formed the Cape Nome Mining District. Originally the settlement was called Anvil City, after Anvil Creek where the first major gold strike was found. During the following summer gold was found on the beaches of Nome. News of the gold strike set off a major rush in the summer of 1900 when the news reached Seattle. By August 1900, there were some 20,000 people in Nome. The Seward Peninsula is believed to hold 100 gold dredges from bygone days; 44 dredges lie in the immediate Nome area. Gold mining continues today as an important economic activity. Reactivated gold dredges operate near the main Nome airport and north of town.

Incorporated in 1901, Nome is the oldest first-class city in Alaska and has the state's oldest first-class school district.

Nome is the transportation and commerce center for northwestern Alaska. Alaska's reindeer industry is centered in the Nome vicinity. Almost half of all wage and salary jobs are with federal, state and local governments. Nome also is a major stopover on arctic tours and a jumping-off point for tours to surrounding Eskimo villages. It is also a jumping-off point for visits to Russia.

Provideniya is a 60-minute flight from Nome.

Nome is the location of Northwest College. The city has 1 parking meter in front of the newspaper office.

The Bering Sea is only a stone's throw from Front Street. The granite sea wall protecting Nome from the sea was built between 1949 and 1951 by the U.S. Army Corps of Engineers. The 3,350-foot-long seawall is 65 feet wide at its base, 16 feet wide at its top, and stands 18 feet above mean low water.

Carrie McLain Memorial Museum, P.O. Box 53, Nome, AK 99762, phone 443-2566, is located in the basement of the building containing the Kegoayah Kozga Library on Front Street. This history museum has a fascinating collection of some 6,000 photographs of the gold rush and early Eskimo life. Copies of the photographs can be purchased on request. Permanent exhibits include the Bering Land Bridge; natural history; Eskimo lifestyles and art; contemporary art; the Nome gold rush; and dog mushing history. Special exhibitions and demonstrations take place throughout the year. Hours vary according to season. No admission charge; donations accepted.

Nome's city hall, with turn-of-the-century decor, is on Front Street. A massive wood-burl arch sits in the lot next to city hall until March each year, when it is raised over Front Street for the Month of Iditarod festival celebrating the 1,049-mile Iditarod Trail Sled Dog Race from Anchorage to Nome. Hundreds of visitors come to Nome to take part in the various activities that include a statewide basketball tournament, the 200-mile Nome to Golovin snowmobile race and a snowshoe softball tournament. Another event that attracts national attention and participants is the Bering Sea Ice Golf Classic, a golf tournament played on the frozen Bering Sea in March. The highlight of the month comes with completion of the Iditarod Trail Sled Dog Race. All the townspeople turn out to welcome each tired musher and team at the finish line.

In June Nome celebrations include the annual Midnight Sun Festival, sponsored by the chamber of commerce. The highlight of the festival is a raft race on the Nome River, in which many unusual homemade craft take part. Winner of the raft race is traditionally awarded a fur-lined honey bucket.

The Anvil Mountain Run is scheduled for the Fourth of July. This 12.5-mile race follows a very rugged course from city hall to the top of 1,977-foot Anvil Mountain, so named because of the anvil-shaped rock on its peak, and down again via the face of the mountain.

Other events in the community are the Memorial Day Polar Bear Swim and the Labor Day Bathtub Race.

Three roads, maintained only in summer (mid-June through early October), extend east, north and west from the city: the 72-mile Nome-Teller Road, the 72-mile Nome-Council Road, and the 86-mile Nome-Taylor Road. Travelers can spot many varieties of wildflowers and birds along these roads. More than 184 species of birds have been identified in the Nome area. Moose, bear and musk-oxen can be viewed. Blueberries, salmonberries and cranberries ripen all over the Seward Peninsula around August.

For more information about attractions in Nome, contact the Nome Convention and Visitors Bureau, Box 251, Nome, AK 99762; phone 443-5535.

According to one resident, "The fall is beautiful, with the tundra in full foliage and long cool days with beautiful sunsets over the ocean and tundra. No trees to get in your way! You can see for miles."

Communications in Nome include phones, 2 radio stations, TV and the weekly *Nome Nugget* newspaper. There are community electricity, water and sewer systems. The community is served by 15 churches, elementary and high schools, a 19-bed hospital and port facilities for vessels up to 22 feet of draft in 30-foot depth. Government address: City of Nome, P.O. Box 281, Nome, AK 99762; phone 443-5242, fax 443-5349.

Port Clarence

[MAP 13] Located on Point Spencer on the Bering Sea coast, 80 miles northwest of Nome, 560 miles west of Fairbanks. **Transportation:** U.S. Coast Guard aircraft or charter air service from Nome. **Population:** 30. **Zip code:** 99762. **Emergency Services:** Alaska State Troopers, Nome; U.S. Coast Guard corpsman.

Elevation: 10 feet. **Climate:** Mean annual precipitation 10 inches; mean annual snowfall 47 inches. Snow starts falling in late October; last snowfall usually in late May.

Private Aircraft: Airstrip 1 mile northeast; elev. 10 feet; length 4,500 feet; asphalt; no fuel. Closed to the public. Available to private aircraft only in emergencies (contact 122.8 MMZ), unless prior permission obtained from Coast Guard District 17 headquarters in Juneau, phone 463-2000.

Visitor Facilities: None.

Port Clarence is a U.S. Coast Guard loran station with no public facilities. The airfield originally was constructed for bombers in WWII. In 1961 the Coast Guard station was built to aid in navigation for ships in the Bering Sea.

Residents of nearby communities use the Point Spencer spit during the summer fishing season.

St. Michael

[MAP 14] Located on St. Michael Island, 48 miles southwest of Unalakleet, 125 miles southwest of Nome and 420 miles northwest of Anchorage. **Transportation:** Boat; snow machine; scheduled and charter air service from Unalakleet and Nome. **Population:** 305. **Zip code:** 99659. **Emergency Services:** Village Public Safety Officer; Alaska State Troopers, Unalakleet, phone 624-3646; Clinic, phone 923-3311; Volunteer Fire Department.

Elevation: 30 feet. **Climate:** Subarctic with maritime influence in summer, when Norton Sound is ice free (usually June to November), and a cold continental influence during the winter. Summers are moist, with clouds and fog common, but annual precipitation is only 12 inches, much of which occurs in July, August and September. Annual snowfall averages 38 inches, with most of it during October and February. Winter temperatures average -4°F to 16°F; summer temperatures average 40°F to 60°F.

Private Aircraft: Airstrip adjacent north; elev. 30 feet; length 2,300 feet; gravel; no fuel; unattended; runway condition not monitored; visual inspection recommended prior to using.

Visitor Facilities: No hotel or restaurant. Arrangements for accommodations at the school or private homes can sometimes be made by contacting the school principal (923-3041) or the city office (923-3211). There is a washeteria. Supplies available in the community. Fishing/hunting licenses available. Information on other visitor services and facilities unavailable.

The Russians established a stockade post there in 1833, named after a governor of the Russian-American colony. Its name soon became Michaelovski or Redoubt St. Michael, and the post was the northernmost Russian settlement in Alaska. The Eskimo village of Tachik was located to the northeast.

During the gold rush era at the end of the century, St. Michael became the major gateway to the Interior via the Yukon River. A U.S. military post, Fort St. Michael, was established in 1897, but was closed in 1922. As many as 10,000 people were said to live in St. Michael during the Nome gold rush. The village remained an important transshipment point until the Alaska Railroad was built. St. Michael also was a popular trading post for Eskimos trading for Western goods.

Remnants of St. Michael's historic past can still be seen. Three Russian-built houses, the hulks of steamboats and several old cemeteries remain. The old Russian church and most military buildings have been torn down, and an old cannon and other Russian artifacts were moved to Sitka. The sites of the old U.S. fort and the Russian redoubt are on the National Register of Historic Places.

St. Michael is the closest deep-water port to the Yukon and Kuskokwim rivers. It remains a transfer point for freight hauled from Seattle on large oceangoing barges to be placed on smaller river barges or shipped to other Norton Sound villages. St. Michael incorporated in 1969 as a second-class city.

St. Michael's economy is based on subsistence food harvest supplemented by part-time jobs. Residents harvest sea mammals, including seals and beluga whales. Moose and caribou are important winter staples. Summer fishing provides salmon, whitefish, tomcod and herring. Waterfowl, particularly ducks and geese, are hunted in nearby marshes. The tundra yields salmonberries, blackberries, blueberries, raspberries and cranberries.

St. Michael is served by Catholic and Assembly of God churches, as well as a school with grades preschool through 12. There is a community electricity system. Water is hauled from a central watering point. Sewage system is honey buckets. St. Michael prohibits the sale and importation of alcoholic beverages. Freight arrives by barge and plane. Government address: City of St. Michael, P.O. Box 70, St. Michael, AK 99659; phone 923-3211. Village corporation address: St. Michael Native Corp., P.O. Box 70, St. Michael, AK 99659; phone 923-3231.

Savoonga

[MAP 13] *(suh-VOON-guh)* Located on St. Lawrence Island in the Bering Sea, 39 miles southeast of Gambell, 164 miles west of Nome and 700 miles west of Fairbanks. **Transportation:** Scheduled and charter air service from Nome. **Population:** 509. **Zip code:** 99769. **Emergency Services:** Police, phone 984-6011; Clinic, phone 984-6513; Volunteer Fire Department, phone 984-6234.

Climate: Cool, moist, subarctic maritime with some continental influences during winter, when the Bering Sea freezes. Mean annual precipitation 11 inches; mean annual snowfall 58 inches. Winter temperatures average -7°F to 11°F; summer temperatures average 40°F to 51°F.

Private Aircraft: Airstrip 2 miles south; elev. 53 feet; length 4,600 feet; gravel; no fuel; unattended. Passenger terminal at airport. There is usually transportation into the village with local people.

Visitor Facilities: Accommodations at Alunga Lodge, contact Ora Gologerger (984-6520), and at a city facility with kitchen, contact the City of Savoonga (984-6614). Washeteria with showers available. No banking services. Groceries, clothing, first-aid supplies, hardware, camera film and sporting goods available at Savoonga Native Store and Wayne Penaya's Grocery Store. Arts and crafts available for purchase include carved ivory, baleen baskets, hand-sewn skin garments and Eskimo artifacts. No repair services. Arrangements may be made to rent off-road vehicles. Fuel available: marine gas, diesel, kerosene, propane, unleaded and regular gasoline. Moorage on beach. *NOTE: Visitors to Gambell and Savoonga who wish to leave the city limits are required to pay a one-time fee of $25. The entire island is private property; the fee helps monitor use and serves as a registration system to make sure people don't get lost. The corporation also requires that any stories or photographs involving areas outside the townsite be submitted for prepublication approval.*

St. Lawrence Island has been inhabited for several thousand years. The Siberian Yup'ik Eskimos lived by subsistence for many years and had little contact with the rest of the world until European traders began to frequent the area. In the 18th and 19th centuries, St. Lawrence Island supported a population of about 4,000 people. A tragic famine from 1878 to 1880 decimated the population, and in 1903 only 261 people were reported on the entire island.

A herd of 70 reindeer was introduced to the island in 1900. The herd grew during the next 40 years, increasing to a peak of

Walrus are harvested in Savoonga, which is known for its walrus hunts. (Bill Sherwonit)

10,000 animals. The reindeer tended to remain on the eastern side of the island, and managing them from Gambell became impossible. A reindeer camp was established at Savoonga, 4 miles west of the abandoned village of Kookoolik, in 1916. Good hunting and trapping in the area attracted more residents. The population of Savoonga steadily increased, and in the 1980 census it surpassed that of Gambell. The community is built on wet, soft tundra and boardwalks crisscross the village, providing dry routes to all buildings. In 1969 Savoonga was incorporated as a second-class city.

The economy of Savoonga is based largely on subsistence hunting, with some cash income. Best known for its walrus hunts, Savoonga is called the "Walrus Capital of the World." The community holds a Walrus Festival every spring. Residents also hunt bowhead and gray whales in the spring and fall. During summer, the people fish, crab, hunt birds, gather eggs and harvest various seafoods, greens and berries. Seals, fish and crabs are harvested through the winter. Arctic foxes are trapped as a source of income, but there is no other commercial hunting or fishing. Reindeer roam free on the island, but the herd is not really managed. There are a few jobs in the village with the city, Native corporation, school and store.

St. Lawrence Islanders are famous for their ivory carvings, which are a popular retail item. Artifacts found at some of the older village sites on the island also are sold for income.

The area is rich in wildlife: polar bears, whales, walruses, seals and seabirds. Bird watching is popular with visitors, who come to view and photograph the 2.7 million seabirds that nest on the island.

Communications in Savoonga include phones, mail plane, radio and TV. There is a community electricity system. Water is hauled from 3 watering points. Sewage system is honey buckets. The community is served by Presbyterian and Seventh Day Adventist churches and 2 schools with grades kindergarten through 12. The village prohibits the sale and importation of alcoholic beverages. Freight arrives by plane, barge and ship. Government address: City of Savoonga, P.O. Box 87, Savoonga, AK 99769; phone 984-6614. Village corporation address: Savoonga Native Corp., P.O. Box 142, Savoonga, AK 99769; phone 984-6613.

Shaktoolik

[MAP 14] *(shack-TOO-lick)* Located on the east shore of Norton Sound, 33 miles north of Unalakleet, 180 miles east of Nome, 410 miles northwest of Fairbanks. **Transportation:** Boat; scheduled and charter air service from Nome or Unalakleet. **Population:** 197. **Zip code:** 99771. **Emergency Services:** Village Public Safety Officer; Alaska State Troopers, Unalakleet, phone 624-3646; Clinic, Health Aide, phone 955-3511; Volunteer Fire Department, phone 955-3661.

Climate: Subarctic with considerable maritime influence when Norton Sound is ice free, usually from May to October. Winters cold and relatively dry, with an average of 43 inches of snowfall. Winds from the east and northeast predominate. Summers cool, with most precipitation occurring in July, August and September. Average annual precipitation is 14 inches. Winter temperatures average between -4°F and 11°F. Summer temperatures average between 47°F and 62°F.

Private Aircraft: Airstrip 3 miles northwest; elev. 15 feet; length 2,200 feet; gravel; no fuel; unattended. Runway condition not monitored; visual inspection recommended prior to using. No airport facilities. Public transportation available to village.

Visitor Facilities: No hotel, restaurant or banking services. Arrangements may be made to stay at 1 bed and breakfast, in private homes, or on the school floor. Laundromat with showers available. Groceries, clothing, first-aid supplies, hardware, camera film and sporting goods available in the community. Arts and crafts available for purchase include carved ivory, wooden berry picking buckets, wooden masks, Eskimo dolls, parkas, mukluks and beadwork. Fishing/hunting licenses available. No guide services. Residents do their own marine engine, boat and auto repairs. Arrangements may be made to rent private off-road vehicles and boats. Fuel available: diesel, white gas, propane and regular gasoline. No moorage facilities.

Shaktoolik was first mapped in 1842–44 by Lt. L.A. Zagoskin of the Imperial Russian Navy, who called it Tshaktogmyut. The village moved from a site 6 miles up the Shaktoolik River to the river mouth in 1933, but was subject to erosion and wind damage at that location. In 1967 the village moved again to a more sheltered location 2.5 miles to the north. Shaktoolik is a second-class city, incorporated in 1969.

The economy is subsistence, supplemented by part-time earnings from jobs with the city, school, construction, store, airlines and Native corporation. About 1,500 privately owned reindeer provide meat, hides and additional income. Residents harvest moose, caribou, whales, seals, squirrels, rabbits, waterfowl and ptarmigans. They fish for salmon, arctic char, tomcod, flounder, sculpin, herring and smelt. In fall they pick berries.

The Iditarod Trail passes through Shaktoolik and links the village to Unalakleet and coastal villages to the west along Norton Sound.

Cape Denbigh, 12 miles to the northeast, is the site of Iyatayat, a national historic landmark 6,000 to 8,000 years old. Another attraction is Besboro Island off the coast, site of a major seabird colony.

Communications in Shaktoolik include phones, mail plane, radio and TV. The community is served by Covenant and Assembly of God churches and a school with grades preschool through 12. There are community electricity and water systems. Sewage system is flush toilets and seepage pits. The village prohibits the sale and importation of alcoholic beverages. Freight arrives by cargo plane. Government address: City of Shaktoolik, P.O. Box 10, Shaktoolik, AK 99771; phone 955-3441. Village corporation address: Shaktoolik Native Corp., General Delivery, Shaktoolik, AK 99771; phone 955-3451.

Shishmaref

[MAP 13] Located on Sarichef Island between the Chukchi Sea and Shishmaref Inlet, 5 miles from the mainland, 100 miles southwest of Kotzebue, 120 miles north of Nome, 550 miles west of Fairbanks. **Transportation:** Scheduled and charter air service daily from Nome. **Population:** 444. **Zip code:** 99772. **Emergency Services:** Police, phone 649-3411; Alaska State Troopers, Nome, phone 443-2835; Clinic, phone 649-3311; Volunteer Fire Department.

Elevation: 20 feet. **Climate:** Transitional zone; winters windy, cold and dry, and snowfall averaging only 33 inches. Winter temperatures average -12°F to 2°F. Spring can be foggy, with west winds prevailing and temperatures averaging 47°F to 54°F. Average annual precipitation is 8 inches.

Private Aircraft: Airstrip ½ mile southwest; elev. 8-10 feet; length 5,000 feet; asphalt; no fuel; unattended. Runway condition not monitored; visual inspection recommended prior to using. All air travel is "weather permitting," says one resident.

Visitor Facilities: Accommodations available in trailer owned by Nayokpuk General Store, in private homes, on school floor and at the Shishmaref city hall. Food is available at Che-Che's Snack Bar. No banking services. Washeteria available. Groceries, clothing, first-aid supplies, hardware, camera film and sporting goods available at Shishmaref Native Store and Nayokpuk General Store. Arts and crafts available for purchase include carved and etched ivory, fur slippers and mukluks, horn dolls and bone carvings. Fishing/hunting licenses available. No guide or repair services; no rental transportation. Fuel available: diesel, propane, white gas, kerosene and regular gasoline. No moorage facilities.

Shishmaref is just 20 miles south of the Arctic Circle and only 100 miles east of Siberia. The original Eskimo name for the island is Kigiktaq. Lieutenant Otto Von Kotzebue named the inlet Shishmarev in 1816 after Capt. Lt. Glieb Semenovich Shishmarev, who accompanied him on his exploration. Archaeologists excavated some of the sites at Kigiktaq around 1821 and found evidence of Eskimo habitation going back several centuries. After 1900, when a supply center was established to serve gold mines in the interior of the Seward Peninsula, the village was renamed after the inlet. The site offered a fairly good harbor and proximity to mining operations. Shishmaref was incorporated as a second-class city in 1969.

The Shishmaref economy is based on subsistence and part-time employment at local stores, the school district, city and Native corporations. In spring residents harvest *oogruk*, walrus, seals, rabbits, squirrels, ptarmigans, waterfowl, eggs, various greens and plants. Summer brings the harvest of herring, smelt, salmon, whitefish, trout, grayling, greens and plants. In fall berries, waterfowl, squirrels, moose, *oogruk*, seals, herring, grayling and lingcod are taken. In winter residents hunt for seals, polar bears, rabbits and ptarmigans; and fish for tomcod, flounder, sculpin and smelt. Two reindeer herds totaling 7,000 head are managed from Shishmaref, and reindeer meat and skins are sometimes available at a local store.

Shishmaref is the home of Eskimo artist Melvin Olanna and Iditarod Trail dog musher Herbie Nayokpuk.

Each year, the Shishmaref Spring Carnival, highlighted by the Seward Peninsula Open-Class Championship Sled Dog Races, takes place on the third weekend in April.

Shishmaref is surrounded by 2.6-million-acre Bering Land Bridge National Preserve, considered to be part of the land bridge over which prehistoric hunters traveled from Asia to North America. It offers a variety of arctic wildlife and plants, hot springs, lava beds and other volcanic phenomena, and archaeological sites. For more information write: Superintendent, Bering Land Bridge National Preserve, P.O. Box 220, Nome, AK 99762.

Winter travel in Shishmaref consists mainly of snow machines, dogsleds and snowshoes. There are winter trails to the mainland and along the coastline.

Communications in Shishmaref include phones, mail plane and radio. There is a community electricity system. The community is served by a Lutheran church and a school with grades preschool through 12. Water is hauled from the washeteria, collected from rain water or melted from ice hauled from the mainland. Sewage system is primarily honey buckets. The village prohibits the sale and importation of alcoholic beverages. Freight arrives by cargo plane and barge. Government address: City of Shishmaref, General Delivery, Shishmaref, AK 99772; phone 649-3781 or 649-4811. Village corporation address: Shishmaref Native Corp., General Delivery, Shishmaref, AK 99772; phone 649-3751.

Solomon

[MAP 13] Located on the west bank of the Solomon River, 1 mile north of Norton Sound, 32 miles east of Nome, 500 miles west of Fairbanks. **Transportation:** By auto on the Nome-Council Road; charter air service from Nome. **Population:** 8. **Zip code:** 99762. **Emergency Services:** Alaska State Troopers and Norton Sound Regional Hospital in Nome.

Climate: Solomon's climate is both maritime and continental. Summers are short, wet and mild. Winters are cold and windy. Weather data from Nome shows annual precipitation is 16.4 inches, with 54 inches of snowfall. Temperatures range from -30°F to 56°F.

Private Aircraft: Lee's (mining) Camp is a private strip, 5 miles north of Solomon. Permission necessary from owner to use this 1,000-foot unpaved runway.

Visitor Facilities: None.

This location was called Erok on a 1900 map of Nome Peninsula by Davidson and Blakeslee. Originally established as a mining camp in 1900 on a spit between the Solomon and Bonanza rivers, the townsite was destroyed by a 1913 storm. Townspeople decided to move Solomon east across the Solomon River to the site of the abandoned southern terminus of the Council City and Solomon River railroad, which had been known as Dickson. Flooding continued to threaten the low-lying town, and in the 1930s the townsite was moved once again to the base of Jerusalem Hill on the west side of the river.

During summer 1900, a thousand or more people lived in Solomon. The community had 7 saloons, a post office, and a ferry dock, and by 1904 was the terminus of a standard gauge railroad that ran north.

The town's boom was short-lived. Few held productive mining claims and several disasters befell the community. Besides the 1913 storm, the 1918 worldwide influenza epidemic devastated the population. Mining picked up a bit between the wars, but people moved out again during WWII to find work. In 1956 the Bureau of Indian Affairs school closed.

Rusting railroad equipment, the old school and the river ferry today offer reminders of Solomon's historic past. The Solomon Roadhouse, built in 1904 in Dickson, was nominated to the National Register of Historic Places in 1979.

The unpaved Nome-Council Road, which originated as a trail during the gold rush, runs through town. The road, maintained only in summer, brings many visitors to the area, including bird-watchers, fishermen, hunters and tourists. A section of the road is part of the Iditarod Trail from Seward to Nome, and a spur extends up the Solomon River into the Casadepaga River valley.

Communication is by radio. There is no public electricity system. Water is hauled from the Solomon River or Jerusalem Creek. The sewage system is honey buckets or outhouses.

Four families live in Solomon year-round. Many Nome residents have seasonal homes or camps there. Village corporation address: Solomon Native Corp., P.O. Box 243, Nome, AK 99762; phone 443-2844.

Stebbins

[MAP 14] Located on the northwest coast of St. Michael Island on Norton Sound, 53 miles southwest of Unalakleet, 120 miles southeast of Nome, 300 miles northwest of Anchorage. **Transportation:** Scheduled and charter air service from Unalakleet. **Population:** 384. **Zip code:** 99671. **Emergency Services:** Village Public Safety Officer, phone 934-3451; Clinic, phone 934-3311; Volunteer Fire Department.

Elevation: 26 feet. **Climate:** Subarctic with a maritime influence June to November when Norton Sound is ice free, and a cold continental influence in winter. Clouds and fog common in summer. Weather data for St. Michael indicates annual precipitation at Stebbins is 12 inches, with 38 inches of snow. Winter temperatures between -1°F and 16°F, summer temperatures between 40°F and 60°F, with a record high of 77°F.

Private Aircraft: Airstrip adjacent northwest; elev. 26 feet; length 3,200 feet; gravel; no fuel; unattended. Runway condition not monitored; visual inspection recommended prior to using. No airport facilities; public transportation to village available.

Visitor Facilities: Arrangements for lodging at small inn or in private homes may be made. No restaurant or banking services. Laundry facilities and showers available. Groceries, clothing, first-aid supplies, hardware, camera film and sporting goods available in the community. Arts and crafts available for purchase include carved ivory, masks and grass baskets. Fishing/hunting licenses available. For guide services, contact city office. No repair services. Arrangements may be made to rent off-road vehicles and boats. Fuel available includes marine gas, propane, diesel and regular gasoline. Moorage facilities available.

The Eskimo village of Atroik or Atowak was first recorded in 1898 by the U.S. Coast and Geodetic Survey at a site on the hillside north of Stebbins. The Native name for the village is Tapraq; the name Stebbins was first published on a USCGS map in 1900. In 1950, Stebbins was described as a village of Eskimos who made their livelihood by hunting, fishing and herding reindeer. Stebbins was incorporated as a second-class city in 1969.

The Stebbins economy is still based on subsistence hunting and fishing, supplemented by part-time wage earnings. There is presently an unmaintained herd of reindeer on Stuart Island just off the coast. Subsistence harvest includes bearded, ring and spotted seals, walrus, beluga whales, ptarmigans, rabbits, wildfowl, salmon, tomcod, flounder, sculpin, herring, smelt and berries. Commercial fishing in the area is on the increase.

Stebbins is located at the northern tip of Yukon Delta National Wildlife Refuge. Birdwatching is for peregrine falcons and a myriad of migratory wildfowl.

Recreational activities in Stebbins include basketball, bingo, Eskimo dances and an annual potlatch.

Overland travel is by snow machine in the winter. A number of trails link Stebbins with St. Michael.

Communications in Stebbins include phones, mail plane, radio and TV. The community is served by a church and a school with grades kindergarten through 12. There are community electricity and water. Sewage system is honey buckets. Stebbins prohibits the sale and importation of alcoholic beverages. Freight is hauled by cargo plane, barge and ship. Government address: City of Stebbins, P.O. Box 22, Stebbins, AK 99671; phone 934-3451 or 934-4561. Village corporation address: Stebbins Native Corp., General Delivery, Stebbins, AK 99671.

Teller

[MAP 13] Located on a spit between Port Clarence and Grantley Harbor on the Seward Peninsula, 72 miles north of Nome, 540 miles west of Fairbanks. **Transportation:** By auto on the Nome-Teller Road; scheduled and charter air service from Nome. **Population:** 275. **Zip code:** 99778. **Emergency Services:** Village Public Safety Officer, phone 642-3401; Alaska State Troopers, Nome, phone 443-2441; Clinic, phone 642-3311.

Elevation: 10 feet. **Climate:** Maritime when the Bering Sea is ice free, usually early June to mid-November. Freezing of the sea causes a change to a more continental climate with less precipitation and colder temperatures. Mean annual precipitation 11 inches; mean annual snowfall 50 inches. Winter temperatures average -9°F to 8°F; summer temperatures average 44°F to 57°F.

Private Aircraft: Airstrip 2 miles south; elev. 293 feet; length 2,300 feet; gravel; no fuel; unattended; lighted. Runway condition not monitored; visual inspection recommended prior to using. No airport facilities. Public transportation into town available. Public phone.

Visitor Facilities: No hotel, restaurant or banking services. Accommodations may be arranged at the school (642-3041). Washeteria available. Groceries, clothing, first-aid supplies, hardware, camera film and sporting goods available at Teller Commercial (642-3333), Teller Native Store (642-4521), Nanook Management Store and Sherman's Transportation. Arts and crafts available include carved walrus and mastodon ivory, hand-sewn seal skin items, and Eskimo dolls. Fishing/hunting licenses available. No guide or repair services. No rental transportation or moorage facilities. Fuel available: diesel and regular gasoline.

Captain Daniel B. Libby and his party from the Western Union Telegraph expedition wintered here in 1866 and 1867; the site was then called Libbyville or Libby Station. The first permanent settlement, named for U.S. Sen. H.M. Teller, was established around 1900 after the Bluestone Placer discovery 15 miles to the south. During those boom years at the turn of the century, Teller had a population estimated at 5,000 and was a major regional trading center. Although Teller's population had dropped to 125 by 1910 and continued to decrease through 1930, the number of residents has increased gradually since then. The community was incorporated as a second-class city in 1963.

The economy of Teller is based on subsistence food harvest supplemented by part-time wage earnings. Some foxes are trapped in the area and reindeer herding has been practiced since Teller's founding. Residents hunt for seals, beluga whales, moose, squirrels, rabbits, ptarmigans, wildfowl and their eggs. They fish for salmon, herring, smelt, whitefish, sculpin, tomcod and flounder.

Teller was the landing site of the *Norge,* the first dirigible to be flown over the North Pole. The craft, piloted by Roald Amundson, flew 71 hours from Spitzbergen, Norway. Its intended landing site was Nome, but bad weather forced it to land May 13, 1926, on the beach at Teller instead. Near the landing site, a plaque commemorating the event has been placed on an old 2-story false-front building in which some of the disassembled segments and gear from the *Norge* were stored. The storage site is on the National Register of Historic Places.

From May through October a 72-mile gravel road is open from Teller to Nome. Taxis will make the trip for $45 each way. Air taxis also operate between the 2 communities, charging $55 per person one way. Local resident Allan Okpealuk recommends the drive for its beautiful scenery, fishing spots, berry picking and bird watching.

Winter trails, traveled primarily by snow machines and a few dogsled teams, radiate from Teller to Brevig Mission, Marys Igloo and Nome. Area rivers lead to summer fish camps.

Communications in Teller include phones, mail plane, radio and TV. The community has Lutheran and Catholic churches served by itinerant pastors. It also has a school with grades preschool through 12. There are community electricity and water systems; sewage system is primarily honey buckets. Teller prohibits the sale and importation of alcoholic beverages. Freight arrives by cargo plane and barge. Government address: City of Teller, P.O. Box 548, Teller, AK 99778; phone 642-3401, fax 642-2051. Village corporation address: Teller Native Corp., P.O. Box 509, Teller, AK 99778; phone 642-4011.

Tin City

[MAP 13] Located at the mouth of Cape Creek, 7 miles southeast of Wales, 100 miles northwest of Nome, 600 miles westnorthwest of Fairbanks. **Transportation:** Boat; scheduled and charter air service from Wales. **Population:** 10 to 20. **Zip code:** 99762. **Emergency Services:** Village Public Safety Officer, Wales; Alaska State Troopers, Nome; Tin City Air Force Station Medic.

Elevation: 270 feet. **Climate:** Mean annual precipitation 12 inches; mean annual snowfall 45.5 inches. Snowfall usually starts in late September or early October; last snow in late May or early June. Temperatures in winter -10°F to 7°F. A record high of 84°F was reached in early July 1987.

Private Aircraft: Tin City Air Force Station airport 1 mile east; elev. 269 feet; length 4,700 feet; gravel. Closed to the public. Aircraft on official business may land only with 24-hour advance permission from airstrip supervisor, phone 552-3793. *CAUTION: Turbulence on approach due to high winds. Field on high bluff.*

Visitor Facilities: For accommodations contact Richard Lee, owner of the trading post and Tin City's sole resident not connected with the military. (General Delivery, Tin City, AK 99762; phone 664-3141.) Reservations should be made in advance. There is no food or lodging available to the public at the military site. No restaurant, banking services or laundry facilities available. Groceries, clothing, first-aid supplies, hardware, camera film and sporting goods available. Arts and crafts available for purchase include carved ivory, moccasins and other hand-sewn skin items from Diomede, Wales, Shishmaref, Brevig Mission and other villages. Fishing/hunting licenses not available. No guide or repair services. No rental transportation or moorage facilities. Fuel available includes marine gas and propane.

Tin City was established as a mining camp at the base of Cape Mountain in 1903 after tin ore was discovered on the mountain in 1902. Tin City Air Force Station was constructed in the early 1950s; military personnel have now been replaced by GE Government Services employees. The military site is closed to the public. An abandoned White Alice communications site is located on a nearby hill.

Tin is still mined in the area. Lee Mining Camp operated in the 1960s, but was sold to Lost River Mining Co. in the 1970s. Tin is mined from breakup to fall.

There are several privately owned cabins facing the beach. Tin ore, along with jade and other minerals, can be found on the beach, according to a Wales resident. Trout and salmon can be caught with rod and reel from the beach.

Communications in Tin City include mail plane, radio and TV. There is no church or school. There are community electricity and water systems and flush toilets on the Air Force site. Freight arrives by cargo plane and barge.

Unalakleet

[MAP 14] *(YOU-na-la-kleet)* Located on the east shore of Norton Sound at the mouth of the Unalakleet River, 145 miles southeast of Nome, 395 miles west-northwest of Anchorage. **Transportation:** Scheduled and charter air service from Anchorage and Nome. **Population:** 802. **Zip code:** 99684. **Emergency Services:** Police, phone 624-3008; Clinic, phone 624-3535; Medical Emergencies, phone 911; Volunteer Fire Department.

Elevation: 8 to 12 feet. **Climate:** Subarctic with considerable maritime influence

when Norton Sound is ice free, usually from May to October. Freezing of the sound causes a change to a colder, more continental climate. Winters cold and relatively dry, with an average of 41 inches of snowfall. Summers cool with most rainfall occurring in July, August and September. Average annual precipitation is 14 inches. Winter temperatures average -4°F to 11°F; summer temperatures average 47°F to 62°F.

Private Aircraft: Airport 1 mile north; elev. 21 feet; length 6,000 feet; gravel; fuel 80, 100; attended. Airport facilities include passenger and freight terminals, ticket counter and restrooms. Public transportation to town available.

Visitor Facilities: Accommodations and meals at Unalakleet Lodge (624-3333); food service at The Igloo (624-3640). No banking services. Laundromat. Groceries, clothing, first-aid supplies, hardware, camera film and sporting goods available at Alaska Commercial Co. (624-3272), UNC General Store (624-3322), Northwest Alaska Trading Co. (624-3711), Lowell's Hardware (624-3169) and Bill's Video (624-3084). Arts and crafts available for purchase include carved ivory, birch-bark baskets, grass baskets, masks, ulus, beadwork, mukluks and slippers, fur hats and other clothing. Fishing/hunting licenses available, as well as guide service. Marine engine, boat, auto and aircraft repair services available. Arrangements can be made to rent autos and boats, and charter aircraft. Fuel available includes marine gas, propane, diesel and regular gasoline. Moorage facilities available.

NOTE: Land surrounding Unalakleet is owned by the Unalakleet Native Corp. Trespassing laws are strictly enforced, but permits can be obtained from the corporation office in Unalakleet for camping, hunting, fishing, bird watching, boating, sledding and photography.

The Unalakleet area has been occupied for centuries. Archaeologists have dated house pits along the old beach ridge at 200 B.C. to 300 A.D. More than 100 of these pits extend for a quarter mile near the Unalakleet airport. The name Unalakleet means "place where the east wind blows." The Eskimo name Ounakalik was recorded by Lt. L.A. Zagoskin of the Imperial Russian Navy on an 1850 map. A village site inhabited before the smallpox epidemic of 1838–39 exists along the south side of the Unalakleet River. Reindeer herders brought to Alaska from Lapland in 1898 settled at Unalakleet and quickly established sound herding practices. Descendants of a few of them still live in Unalakleet. The community was incorporated as a second-class city in 1974.

Commercial fishing and subsistence hunting and fishing form the basis of Unalakleet's economy. A fish processing plant employs up to 50 persons from May through August. Other jobs are with the Bering Strait School District, airlines, local stores, Native corporation, city and schools. For subsistence, several species of salmon, char, grayling and herring are fished and seals, caribou, moose, bears, birds and waterfowl are hunted.

Unalakleet is the takeoff point for sportfishing in Norton Sound and the Unalakleet and North rivers.

The Unalakleet River, above its junction with the Chiroskey River, has been designated a wild and scenic river and is popular for float trips. The area is administered by BLM and additional information can be obtained from BLM, Anchorage District Office, 4700 E. 72nd Ave., Anchorage, AK 99507.

Unalakleet is the terminus of a long-used winter trail from Anvik, on the Yukon River, that forms a leg of the Iditarod Trail. Unalakleet is a checkpoint each March for the Iditarod Trail Sled Dog Race from Anchorage to Nome.

Communications in Unalakleet include phones, mail plane, radio and cable TV. The community is served by Covenant, Mormon, Assembly of God and Catholic churches. Elementary and high schools. There are community electricity, water and sewer systems. Freight arrives by cargo plane, barge and ship. Government address: City of Unalakleet, P.O. Box 28, Unalakleet, AK 99684; phone 624-3531 or 624-3474, fax 624-3130. Village corporation address: Unalakleet Native Corp., P.O. Box 100, Unalakleet, AK 99684; phone 624-3020 or 624-3411.

Wales

[MAP 13] Located on the western tip of the Seward Peninsula, on the coast of Cape Prince of Wales, 7 miles west of Tin City, 111 miles northwest of Nome, 595 miles west of Fairbanks. **Transportation:** Scheduled and charter air service from Nome. **Population:** 159. **Zip code:** 99783. **Emergency Services:** Village Public Safety Officer, phone 664-3671; Alaska State Troopers, Nome; Clinic, phone 664-3691; Volunteer Fire Department.

Elevation: 25 feet. **Climate:** Maritime when Bering Sea is ice free, usually June through November. Freezing of the sea causes abrupt change to a cold continental climate. Winters cold and windy; temperatures average -10°F to 6°F. One resident says the wind chill factor pushes the temperature as low as -100°F. Summer temperatures average 40°F to 50°F. Mean annual precipitation 11 inches; mean annual snowfall 41 inches.

Private Aircraft: Airstrip 1 mile northwest; elev. 25 feet; length 4,000 feet; gravel; unattended. Easterly winds may cause severe turbulence in the vicinity of the runway. Frequent fog, wind and occasional blizzards limit access to Wales. No airport facilities; transportation available to village.

Visitor Facilities: Accommodations may be arranged in a trailer of the Wales Native Corp. (664-3641) or in a room in the City of Wales (644-3501) dome building. No restaurant or banking services. Laundromat and showers available. Groceries, first-aid supplies, hardware and camera film available at Wales Native Store (664-3351). Arts and crafts available for purchase include carved walrus ivory, moccasins, Eskimo dolls, fur mukluks and knitted caps, gloves and socks. Fishing/hunting licenses available. Informal guide service may be available. No repair service. Arrangements may be made to rent private off-road vehicles and boats. Fuel available: marine gas, diesel and propane. Moorage on beach.

Cape Prince of Wales is the farthest west point of mainland Alaska; 2,289-foot Cape Mountain which rises above Wales is the terminus of the Continental Divide separating the Arctic and Pacific watersheds. The Wales area has been inhabited for centuries; archaeological evidence dates back to 500 A.D. A burial mound of the Birnirk culture (500 A.D. to 900 A.D.) was discovered behind the present village and is now a national historic landmark.

In historical times, the villages of Eidamoo near the coast and King-a-ghe farther inland were noted in 1827 by Captain Beechy of the Imperial Russian Navy. In 1880, Capt. E.E. Smith of the U.S. Revenue Cutter Service reported Kingigamute, meaning "the high place," with a population of 400. In 1890, the American Missionary Assoc. established a mission here and in 1894 a reindeer station was organized. Wales was incorporated as a second-class city in 1964.

Wales was a major center for whale hunting due to its strategic location on the animals' migratory route until the 1918–19 worldwide influenza epidemic claimed the lives of many of Wales' finest whalers. The village retains a strong Eskimo culture; ancient songs and dances are still performed and customs practiced.

The economy of Wales is based on subsistence hunting and fishing, trapping, some mining and Native arts and crafts. Wales artisans make excellent ivory carvings, especially birds, which are sold locally or marketed in Nome, Anchorage or Fairbanks. Other crafts such as skin sewing bring additional income to the community. There is some trapping of fox and wolverine. A private reindeer herd of about 1,500 head is managed out of Wales and local residents are employed during roundup. A few jobs are provided by the city, store, clinic, airlines, school and Native corporation.

The mining potential is great in the area. Tin placers located nearby have estimated reserves of 2,000 tons of tin. Gold also is plentiful in the region.

Vast herds of walrus and whales migrate through Bering Strait and villagers hunt them from early April to the end of June. Ice cellars are used to store and preserve the meat. Polar bear, moose, waterfowl, salmon, ptarmigan, tomcod and flounder supplement local diets, along with berries and various greens.

In Wales, the visitor will get a glimpse of Eskimo life relatively unaffected by Outside contact. During the summer, Wales is a base for residents of Little Diomede Island, and these Eskimos often can be seen traveling to and from their island in large traditional skin boats. Air service and tours to Wales are available out of Nome.

The city has established the George Otenna Museum in the community center, City of Wales, Wales, AK 99783, phone 664-3671. This local history museum features contemporary arts and crafts, as well as Eskimo artifacts and the history of Wales and the surrounding area.

Activities in Wales include the annual Fourth of July celebration with games for all ages, community feasts on Thanksgiving and Christmas, and competitive indoor games for men's and women's teams from Dec. 26 to Dec. 31 each year.

Winter trails connect Wales to Tin City and the interior of the Seward Peninsula. A tractor trail also runs to Tin City.

Many Bush residents rely on moose hunting to fill their larders. (Bill Sherwonit)

Communications in Wales include phones, mail plane, radio and TV. The community is served by a Lutheran church and the Wales-Kingikme School with grades kindergarten through 9; older students go to boarding schools in other communities. There is a community electricity system. Water is hauled from Village and Gilbert creeks in summer and ice blocks are cut in winter. Sewage system is honey buckets. Wales prohibits the sale and importation of alcoholic beverages. Freight arrives by ship, barge and plane. Government address: City of Wales, P.O. Box 489, Wales, AK 99783; phone 664-3671. Village corporation address: Wales Native Corp., P.O. Box 529, Wales, AK 99783; phone 664-3641.

White Mountain

[MAP 13] Located on the west bank of the Fish River near the head of Golovin Lagoon on the Seward Peninsula, 15 miles northwest of Golovin, 65 miles east of Nome, 490 miles west of Fairbanks. **Transportation:** Boat; snow machine; scheduled and charter air service from Nome; Nome-Council Road open late June, early July. **Population:** 189. **Zip code:** 99784. **Emergency Services:** Village Public Safety Officer, phone 638-3411 or 3351; Alaska State Troopers, Nome; Clinic, phone 638-3311; Volunteer Fire Department, phone 638-3411.

Elevation: 50 feet. **Climate:** Transitional, with less extreme temperature variations than interior Alaska. Colder continental weather during the icebound winter. Mean annual precipitation 16 inches, with 57 inches of snow. Winter temperatures average -7°F to 15°F; summer temperatures average 43°F to 80°F.

Private Aircraft: Airport 1 mile north; elev. 262 feet; length 2,100 feet; gravel; no fuel; unattended. Runway condition not monitored; visual inspection recommended prior to using. Runway slopes at both ends. Passenger terminal at airport; no public transportation into village.

Visitor Facilities: Accommodations available at 1 local lodge (open summers and for Iditarod Trail Sled Dog Race in March), or arrangements may be made for lodging in private homes. No restaurant or banking services. Washeteria with laundromat and showers available. Groceries, clothing and sporting goods available in the community. Arts and crafts available for purchase include knitted gloves and caps, moccasins, porcupine quill, beaded

and ivory earrings, beaver caps, and carved walrus ivory. Fishing/hunting licenses available, as well as sportfishing guide service. Boat repair available. Fuel available: diesel, marine gas, propane, white gas, kerosene and regular and unleaded gasoline. Moorage on beach.

The Eskimo village of Nutchirviq was located here prior to the influx of white settlers during the turn-of-the-century gold rush. Bountiful fish populations in both the Fish and Niukluk rivers supported the Native populations. In 1899, C.D. Lane erected a log warehouse as supply headquarters for his numerous gold claims in the Council district. The name White Mountain was derived from the color of the mountain located next to the village. White Mountain was incorporated as a second-class city in 1969.

"The community is located near a hill which breaks the northeast wind," writes city clerk Dorothy Barr. "It is special because it has a friendly environment, with the residents always smiling and welcoming people who come into White Mountain."

White Mountain residents rely both on subsistence hunting and fishing and on wages from seasonal work in commercial fishing, construction, fire fighting, wood cutting, trapping, some cannery work and reindeer herding. There are a few jobs locally with the school, city, store and airlines. Residents spend much of the summer at fish camps. The year-round diet includes lingcod, pike, whitefish, grayling, trout and skipjack. Assorted greens and roots, berries, wildfowl and squirrels are harvested in the fall; seals, moose, brown bears, reindeer, rabbit, ptarmigan, flounder and sculpin in the winter; rabbits, ptarmigans, *oogruk*, seals, wildfowl and eggs, and assorted roots and greens in the spring; and herring, smelt, salmon and beluga whales in the summer.

White Mountain serves as a checkpoint on the Iditarod Trail.

Communications include phones, mail plane, radio and TV. The community is served by a Covenant church and a school with grades kindergarten through 12 and a village library. Community electricity and water. Sewage system is honey buckets. Freight arrives by barge and cargo plane. Government address: City of White Mountain, P.O. Box 66, White Mountain, AK 99784; phone 638-3411. Village corporation address: White Mountain Native Corp., General Delivery, White Mountain, AK 99784; phone 638-3511.

National and State Parks, Etc.

Bering Land Bridge National Preserve

This 2.8-million-acre preserve is located just below the Arctic Circle on the Seward Peninsula, 50 miles south of Kotzebue and 90 miles north of Nome. It is a remnant of the land bridge that once connected Asia and North America 14,000 to 25,000 years ago. More than just a narrow strip across the Bering Strait, the land bridge at times was up to 1,000 miles wide. It rose as the formation of massive glaciers during the ice ages caused the water levels of the Bering and Chukchi seas to fall. Across this bridge people, animals and plants migrated to the New World and the preserve is considered one of the most likely regions where these prehistoric hunters crossed over. An archaeological site at Trail Creek caves has yielded evidence of human occupation 10,000 years old.

Other interesting features of the preserve are several lava flows around Imuruk Lake, some as recent as 1,000 years ago; low-rimmed volcanoes called maar craters, which have become lakes, in the northern lowlands around Devil Mountain; and Serpentine Hot Springs, long recognized by Natives for its spiritual and medicinal values. The Inupiat Eskimo name for these springs is Iyat, which means "cooking pot." Hillsides in the preserve are dotted with the remains of ancient stone cairns, their original purpose lost in the misty past. Also of interest are the more recent historical sites from early explorations and mining activities.

Today, Eskimos from neighboring villages pursue their subsistence lifestyles and manage reindeer herds in and around the preserve. Their camps, fish nets and other equipment are critical to their livelihood and should be left undisturbed.

Climate: Temperatures in the preserve vary. On the coast, January temperatures are -10°F to -20°F, while inland they may reach -60°F. Maximum July temperatures on the coast are in the lower 50s, while inland they are in the mid-60s. Summer is the wettest time, receiving 3 to 4 inches of the annual 10 inches of precipitation. Snowfall averages 50 to 60 inches per year. Insects are most bothersome from mid-June to early August.

During the short summer the preserve bursts into life and many of the 245 species of plants bloom with bright colors.

Wildlife: The preserve includes 112 species of migratory birds; marine mammals such as bearded, hair and ribbon seals, walrus, and humpback, fin and bowhead whales; grizzly bears, some wolves, caribou to the north and east, some muskoxen from transplanted herds, moose, red and arctic foxes, weasels and wolverines. Fish in preserve waters include salmon, grayling and arctic char.

Activities: Recreational opportunities in the preserve include hiking, camping, fishing, sightseeing, wildlife observation and photography.

Accommodations: Aside from the cabin at the hot springs, there are no accommodations or campgrounds in the preserve. There are hotel and restaurant facilities in Nome and Kotzebue (although during the summer most of the rooms are booked by tour groups), and limited accommodations in Shishmaref. Visitors to the preserve must arrive self-sufficient, with food, clothing, shelter, and in some cases fuel. There is driftwood on beaches, but wood is scarce inland. The Park Service further advises that visitors to the preserve should have good outdoor skills including hiking, backpacking and camping experience and the stamina to survive difficult conditions.

Access: Commercial jets to Nome or Kotzebue, which have connecting flights to Deering and Shishmaref, provide access to the preserve. Visitors to the preserve usually arrive by charter plane from Nome or Kotzebue, landing on lakes, gravel bars, beaches or private mining camp airstrips just outside the preserve. There also is an airstrip at Serpentine Hot Springs, location of a public-use cabin. That strip is 1,100 feet long and 50 feet wide; the runway slopes, crosswinds are common and the surface is muddy when wet. Access also is possible by driving from Nome on the 86-mile-long Taylor Highway to the Kougarok River, about 20 miles from the preserve, and then hiking in. You also can travel a road from Deering 25 miles along the Inmachuk River to within 5 or 10 miles of the preserve. Or it's possible to go by boat from Shishmaref to the preserve.

For more information contact: Superintendent, Bering Land Bridge National Preserve, P.O. Box 220, Nome, AK 99762; phone 443-2522. Related USGS Topographic Series maps: Kotzebue, Shishmaref, Bendeleben, Teller.

River Running

Unalakleet River. This designated National Wild and Scenic River flows southwest through the low, rugged Nulato Hills to the village of Unalakleet where it drains into Norton Sound. The river is approximately 105 miles long, but only the lower 76 miles is deep enough to float; often the river is floatable only from the confluence of Old Woman River. Sweepers line much of the river's banks. Canoes, kayaks or rafts all are suitable for this river.

The usual put in point is at the Unalakleet's confluence with Tenmile Creek about 29 miles from the river's source. Stream flow is relatively fast and there are many obstructions across the river. Fishing is excellent from this point to Old Woman River. The Old Woman Mountain can be seen as boaters approach Old Woman River. Many sand and gravel bars provide camping sites. The flow slows, depth increases and the river braids. About 4 miles beyond the Old Woman River confluence, the Unalakleet flows through a flat valley where marshes and oxbows can be seen. Around Mile 51, the North Fork joins

the Unalakleet. A series of braided channels flow through heavy cover, making identification of the main channel difficult. In this area there are several private cabins that are used seasonally for fishing, trapping and hunting. Do not trespass. The river widens as it stretches toward the confluence with the Chiroskey River, the end of the wild river corridor. For the remaining 24 miles, the river crosses Native corporation land. There also is one commercial fishing lodge on this lower portion. The trip from Tenmile Creek to the river mouth generally takes 6 days.

Fish in the Unalakleet include king, silver, chum and pink salmon, Dolly Varden and grayling. Wildlife that may be seen include moose, black and brown bears, wolves, waterfowl, beavers and foxes.

Access is by scheduled air service to Unalakleet, then a local guide or boat operator may be hired to take parties to Tenmile Creek by riverboat. Exit is from Unalakleet, where there are visitor facilities. Related USGS Topographic Series maps: Norton Sound A-1 and A-2, Unalakleet D-2 through D-4.

Sportfishing

Except for a few roads around Nome, access to good fishing in the Seward Peninsula/Norton Sound area is primarily by airplane. If you have the time, however, you sometimes can walk or go by boat to a hot fishing spot. Boats occasionally can be rented or chartered at villages along the waterways. There are daily commercial flights to the transportation centers of the region — Nome and Unalakleet — where you can catch a commuter flight to a smaller village or charter a plane to a lake or river. In addition, commercial outfitters will handle logistics for you on guided fishing trips.

King salmon are at their peak from mid-June through mid-July. These fish are commonly to 30 pounds. Chums show up by July 1, pinks by mid-July (in even-numbered years) and silvers by mid-August. Salmon fishing is concentrated in the river systems.

Dolly Varden are found throughout this area and are most abundant in the fall. Grayling can be caught all summer. Other species that may be encountered are whitefish, burbot (also called lush or lingcod) and northern pike.

In general the best fishing throughout the northern half of the Bering Sea Coast region is in July and August.

The Alaska Dept. of Fish and Game recommends that anyone traveling to remote areas should plan for the worst. Take a few days extra food, and fuel if necessary, and allow for a flexible schedule since fickle weather can delay travel.

Although many villages have hunting and fishing license vendors, officials recommend that you purchase your license in Anchorage or another large community, since sometimes the local vendors themselves have gone fishing. The Dept. of Fish and Game in Nome sells licenses.

For current information on closures, bag limits and up-to-date fishing data, contact: Alaska Dept. of Fish and Game, Sport Fish Division, 1300 College Road, Fairbanks, AK 99701-1599; phone 456-8819. Or, Alaska Dept. of Fish and Game, P.O. Box 1148, Nome, AK 99762-1148; phone 443-5796, fax 443-5893.

Agiapuk River. Heads 8 miles northeast of Black Mountain and flows southeast 60 miles to the Imuruk Basin, 21 miles southeast of Teller. Excellent fishery. Fish available: pink, chum and coho salmon, use spoons; grayling year-round, best in late summer, use flies; Dolly Varden best in fall, use spoons, eggs. Access by plane from Nome or Teller.

Bluestone River. Located at Mile 58.1 on the Nome-Teller Road. Named for the color of the stones in the river. Fish available: chum, pink and coho salmon, use spoons; Dolly Varden best in fall, use spoons, eggs; grayling year-round, best in late summer, use flies. Access by car from Nome or Teller.

Cripple River. Located at Mile 20.3 on the Nome-Teller Road, 9 miles beyond the Penny River. Narrow bridge crossing. Fish present include Dolly Varden best in fall, use spoons, eggs. Also available in season are chum, coho and pink salmon, use spoons. Access by car from Nome.

Feather River. Located at Mile 37.4 on the Nome-Teller Road. Fish available: chum, pink and coho salmon, use spoons; Dolly Varden best in fall, use spoons, eggs; grayling year-round, best in late summer, use flies. Access by car from Nome or Teller.

Fish River. Located about 35 miles east of Solomon on the Nome-Council Road. Fish available: king, chum, pink and coho salmon, use spoons; grayling year-round,

best in late summer, use flies; Dolly Varden best in fall, use spoons, eggs; northern pike year-round, use spoons, spinners. Access by car from Nome.

Grand Central River. Located 35 miles north of Nome on the Nome-Taylor (Kougarok) Road. Very small turnoff present. Excellent canoe/small boating river. Fish available: grayling year-round, best in late summer, use flies; Dolly Varden best in fall, use spoons, eggs; whitefish available year-round, use flies, eggs. Access by car from Nome.

Inglutalik River. Heads at Traverse Peak and flows 80 miles to Norton Bay north of Shaktoolik and south of Koyuk. Fish available: king, chum, pink and coho salmon; Dolly Varden best in fall, use spoons, eggs; grayling year-round, best in late summer, use flies. Access is by aircraft.

Koyuk River. Flows into Koyuk Inlet at the village of Koyuk at the head of Norton Bay off Norton Sound. Only river in immediate area with sheefish, best June to September, use spoons. Other fish available: northern pike year-round, use spoons, spinners; chum salmon July to August, use spoons; grayling year-round, best in late summer, use flies. Boats may be available for rental or charter in Koyuk.

Kuzitrin River. Located at Mile 68 on the Nome-Taylor (Kougarok) Road. Fine, clear-water fishery. Fish available: chum salmon July to August, use spoons; Dolly Varden best in fall, use spoons, eggs; grayling year-round, best in late summer, use flies; northern pike year-round, use spoons, spinners; few whitefish, use flies, eggs. Access by car from Nome.

Kwiniuk River. Flows into Norton Sound near Moses Point, northeast of Elim. Fish available: king, chum, pink and coho salmon; Dolly Varden best in fall, use spoons, eggs; grayling year-round, best in late summer, use flies. Access by charter air service from Nome or Unalakleet. No accommodations in Elim. The Moses Point airport is privately owned and permission is needed to land.

Niukluk River. Nome-Council Road ends at this river (Mile 72). There is good fishing in July and August for king, chum, pink and coho salmon, use spoons; Dolly Varden fishing good August and September, use spoons, eggs; other fish available: grayling year-round, best in late summer, use flies; whitefish, use flies, eggs; burbot in the fall, use bait. Access by car, or small plane from Nome to Council airstrip.

Nome River. Fishing locations 4 miles east of Nome on Main Street extension at the junction of the river and the ocean. Also, 10 miles north of Nome on Nome-Taylor (Kougarok) Road where river parallels road. There are numerous turnoffs. Spring and fall fishery best here. Fish available at both locations: chum and pink salmon July to August (check for closures), use spoons; coho salmon August to September, use spoons; Dolly Varden best in fall, use spoons, eggs. Closed to grayling fishing.

Penny River. Located at Mile 13.2 on the Nome-Teller Road. Old gold mining area. Turnout present. Fish available: Dolly Varden best in fall, use spoons, eggs; coho salmon, August to September. Access by car from Nome.

Pilgrim (Kruzgamepa) River. Located north of Nome at Mile 65 on the Nome-Taylor (Kougarok) Road, 19 miles beyond Salmon Lake. Old gold mining area. Turnoffs present. No accommodations, but there are undeveloped areas suitable for camping. Fish available below bridge near Pilgrim Hot Springs: pink and chum salmon and grayling July to August, use spoons; coho salmon August to September, use spoons; Dolly Varden best in fall, use spoons, eggs; northern pike year-round, use spoons, spinners. Above bridge, mostly grayling and Dolly Varden best in late summer or early fall. Access by car from Nome.

Safety Sound. Located east of Nome at Mile 17.6 on the Nome-Council Road. Bridge crosses lagoon outlet. Boat fishing recommended. Eskimo summer fishing camps throughout the area. Fish available: pink and chum salmon July to August, use spoons; Dolly Varden and coho salmon best in fall, use spoons, eggs; flounder use cut bait; burbot in the fall, use cut bait. Access by car from Nome.

Salmon Lake. Located at Miles 36 to 44 north of Nome on the Nome-Taylor (Kougarok) Road. The lake is parallel to the road; numerous side roads lead to the lakeshore. Camping area with picnic sites and outhouses available. No accommodations, but there is an airstrip. Fish available: Dolly Varden best in fall, use spoons, eggs; grayling year-round, best in late summer, use flies; northern pike year-round, use spoons, spinners; whitefish, use flies, eggs. The lake is closed to all salmon sportfishing.

Shaktoolik River. Flows into Shaktoolik Bay on Norton Sound just north of Shaktoolik village. Fish available: king, chum, pink and coho salmon, use spoons; Dolly Varden best in fall, use spoons, eggs; grayling year-round, best in late summer, use flies. Access by boat from Shaktoolik or by aircraft.

Sinuk River. Located at Mile 26.7 on the Nome-Teller Road. Fish available: chum and pink salmon in season, use spoons; coho salmon August to September; Dolly Varden best in fall, use spoons, eggs; large grayling year-round, best in late summer, use flies. Access by car from Nome.

Snake River. Bridge crossing at Mile 7.9 on the Nome-Teller Road. Turnoff present. Good fishery in spring and fall. Other fish available: chum and pink salmon July to August, use spoons; coho salmon August to September, use spoons; grayling year-round, best in late summer, use flies; Dolly Varden best in fall, use spoons, eggs; Access by car from Nome.

Solomon River. Located from Miles 40 to 50 on the Nome Council Road. River parallels road. Good fishing about 1 mile beyond Solomon. Fish available: pink and chum salmon July to August, use spoons; coho salmon August to September; Dolly Varden best in fall, use spoons, eggs. Closed to grayling fishing. Access by car from Nome.

Unalakleet River. Mouth is just south of Unalakleet village on Norton Sound. Commercial fishing lodge on lower river. Accommodations in Unalakleet. Boats may be available. Good fishing for king salmon in late June; use lures. Other fish available: coho July to September; chum and pink salmon July to August, use spoons; Dolly Varden best in fall, use spoons, eggs; grayling year-round, best in late summer, use flies. Access by boat from Unalakleet.

Ungalik River. Heads on Traverse Peak and flows southwest 90 miles to Norton Bay north of Shaktoolik and south of Koyuk. Fish available: king, chum, pink and coho salmon, use spoons; Dolly Varden best in fall, use spoons, eggs; grayling year-round, best in late summer, use flies. Access is by aircraft.

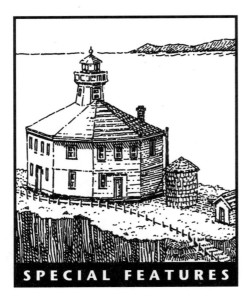

SPECIAL FEATURES

Cape Denbigh

The Iyatayat archaeological site at Cape Denbigh, 12 miles west-northwest of the village of Shaktoolik on Norton Sound, is a national historic landmark. Cape Denbigh was named by English explorer Capt. James Cook on Sept. 11, 1778; its Eskimo name is Nuklit. This site, excavated by archaeologist J.L. Giddings from 1948-52, is the type site for the Norton culture and the Denbigh Flint complex, and was a momentous discovery because it was older than previously known sites. The site is located on an old beach ridge and represents 3 cultural periods dating back as far as 5,000 B.C. Access is by boat from Shaktoolik, which is reached by scheduled air service from Unalakleet. Check with the city government or the village corporation about the location of private lands in the area.

Cape Nome Roadhouse

Located just east of Cape Nome at Mile 14 on the Nome-Council Road, this historic roadhouse is listed on the National Register of Historic Places. The original section was built in 1900 of logs hauled 70 miles from Council by horse. In 1913, after a flood destroyed the log building, an abandoned government building from Safety reportedly was moved to the site and became the present roadhouse. From about 1910 it was a major stopover for dog teams traveling the Iditarod Trail. It was the only roadhouse still standing that was used in the famous 1925 "race to Nome" to deliver serum during the diphtheria epidemic. The building also was used as a temporary orphanage. It has been converted to a private residence.

Hot Springs

Pilgrim Hot Springs. Located on the left bank of the Pilgrim River 13 miles northeast of Salmon Lake. This site of a gold rush resort and later a Catholic mission is listed on the National Register of Historic Places. In the days of gold mining on the Seward Peninsula about 1900, the property was known as Kruzgamepa Hot Springs and was a recreation center for miners attracted by its spa baths, saloon, dance hall and roadhouse. The roadhouse and saloon burned in 1908. The property was given to Father Bellarmine Lafortune, who turned the ranch into a mission and orphanage in 1917–18 and operated it until 1941, housing up to 120 children. Ruins of the mission school and other church properties remain at the site, which is still owned by the Catholic Church. Access is by charter air service from Nome to a small airfield at Pilgrim Hot Springs, or by car on an 8-mile gravel road that joins the Nome-Taylor Road at Cottonwood.

Serpentine Hot Springs. Located within Bering Land Bridge National Preserve. The waters of Serpentine Hot Springs have long been sought for their healthful properties. Eskimo shamans gathered here in earlier times. When the influence of the shamans had passed, native healers still relied on these waters to help their followers. Likely the most visited area of Bering Land Bridge National Preserve, Serpentine still offers a soothing break from the harsh surrounding climate, and the nearby granite tors create a dramatic landscape that lures hikers to explore. A public-use cabin is located at the springs. Winter trails from Shishmaref and other traditional villages lead to Hot Springs Creek near the tractor trail. Traversed by snow machine and dogsled in winter it reaches the springs from the end of the Nome-Taylor (Kougarok) Road. A 1,100-foot airstrip at the hot springs allows wheeled plane access.

Kigluaik Mountains

These mountains are located about 50 miles north of Nome on the Seward Peninsula, 100 miles south of the Arctic Circle. The range is oriented east to west and is approximately 75 miles long and 25 miles wide. It is bordered by the Kougarok Road (Nome-Taylor Road) on the east, the Nome-Teller Road on the west, and the Imuruk Basin and Kuzitrin River on the north.

Visitors will find a wide variety of recreational opportunities: hiking, dog mushing, cross-country skiing or snow machining. There is evidence of early-day gold seekers to explore as well as plenty of fish in the clear mountain streams. Access is easy, by western Alaska standards: You can rent a car in Nome and drive to either the east or west end of the range; you can arrange for an air charter to any number of potential landing sites within the range; and in the winter snow machines can get into areas that are not accessible during the rest of the year.

One area of particular interest starts at glacially formed Crater Lake, a deep, still pool that discharges into the Grand Central River. The Wild Goose Pipeline starts at Crater Lake and runs down the southern side of the Grand Central Valley. Built about 1920, the pipeline carried water to early mining operations near the Nome River, 10 to 20 miles away. The 21-inch pipeline is made of redwood slats held together with iron hoops. The wood has not deteriorated and the pipe is still intact in some places. (Please respect this historical artifact and help preserve the region's heritage by taking nothing but pictures!) The pipeline's name comes from the Wild Goose Railroad which carried supplies north from Nome to the early mining camps near Shelton, located on the Kuzitrin River. Remnants of old cabins, possibly built for maintenance personnel, still remain along the pipeline.

Another point of interest is the Mosquito Pass area. A hike from Windy Creek to the Cobblestone River through Mosquito Pass provides access to some spectacular side canyons, with abrupt peaks reaching nearly 3,000 feet above sea level. Cirque lakes in some of the side canyons offer outstanding photo opportunities. During the summer you can hike into the Mosquito Pass area by leaving the Nome-Taylor Road in the vicinity of the confluence of Hudson Creek and the Nome River.

In the Kigluaik Mountains (pronounced KIG-lee-uk or KIG-loo-ak) you may see wolves, grizzly bear, moose, red fox, ground squirrels and hoary marmots. Reindeer that are part of domesticated herds are also present throughout the year. The varied landscape provides nesting habitat for a variety of birds during the summer. Many Asiatic species frequent this region, making it particularly interesting for ornithologists. Among the species that have long migration routes and nest here are the wheatear, the arctic warbler, bluethroat, yellow wagtail and the white wagtail. Birds of prey such as the rough-legged hawk, golden eagle and gyrfalcon may also be observed soaring overhead, taking advantage of the updrafts in this mountainous region.

Facilities in the Kigluaiks are limited. There is a campground at Salmon Lake on the eastern end of the range near Mile 40 on the Kougarok Road. There is also a public shelter cabin in the Mosquito Pass area. There are no public trails in the mountains, and the Bureau of Land Management advises that visitors should be aware of the demands of the backcountry where help may be far away. Related USGS Topographic maps: Nome D-1, D-22, D-3; Teller A-1, A-2, A-3; Bendeleben A-6; Solomon A-6.

For additional information, contact the Bureau of Land Management, Kobuk District Office, 1150 University Ave., Fairbanks, AK 99709; phone 474-2330; or the Bureau of Land Management, Nome Field Office, P.O. Box 925, Nome, AK 99762; phone 443-2177.

King Island

This rocky, 1,196-foot-high island located in the Bering Sea, 40 miles west of Cape Douglas on the Seward Peninsula, is the ancestral home of the King Island Eskimos, who now live at Nome. The island was named by Capt. James Cook of the Royal Navy on Aug. 6, 1778, for Lt. James King, a member of his party. The Eskimo name for the island, and the tiny village on stilts that clings to the hillside, is Ukivok. The island today is inhabited only by thousands of seabirds: puffins, auklets, murres, sea gulls and kittiwakes. Villagers began moving away in the 1950s, attracted by job opportunities and health facilities in Nome. The BIA closed the school in 1959. The village was last inhabited in 1966. A group of former residents organized to keep their cultural traditions alive, and today the King Island Inupiat Singers and Dancers perform widely before appreciative audiences. The 2-mile-wide island is isolated 8 months of the year and reached only by a 6-hour boat ride. King Islanders still return in late May or June each year to pick greens, gather bird eggs and hunt walrus.

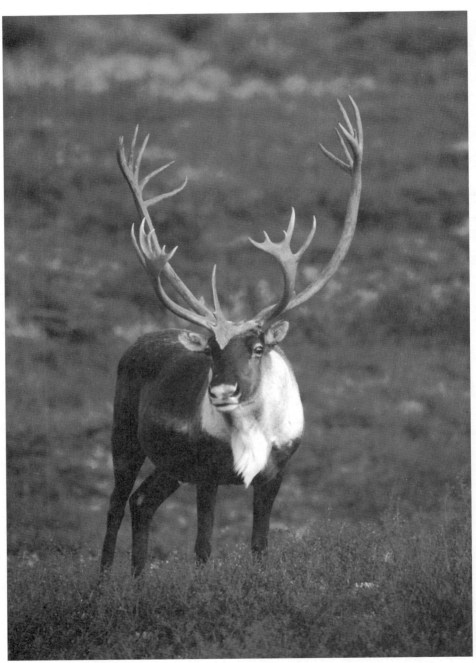

Large herds of caribou migrate through this region. Caribou are important to the subsistence economy of many villages. (Karen Jettmar)

BROOKS RANGE/ARCTIC

This last great wilderness of mountain range and arctic coastal plain stretches for miles across the top of Alaska, beckoning visitors with the promise of beauty and solitude and grandeur. The Brooks Range and the Arctic are true wilderness, immense and almost roadless, remote and sparsely populated.

In the Brooks Range the mountains stand like sentinels protecting the fragile ecosystem of the Arctic from casual intrusion. These mountains are themselves protected in a series of national parks and preserves that stretch from the Dalton Highway (North Slope Haul Road) west almost to the Chukchi Sea. And to the east of the highway the Arctic National Wildlife Refuge preserves the north and south slopes of the Brooks Range all the way to the Canadian border.

Oil, mining and subsistence hunting and fishing provide the majority of economic support for the Arctic. The 800-mile-long oil pipeline from Prudhoe Bay to Valdez on Prince William Sound began operation in 1977. The huge industrial complex on the North Slope created jobs for many arctic residents and provided the economic stimulus for new houses, schools, hospitals and civic buildings. Further oil field development in the region has been proposed in the Arctic National Wildlife Refuge (ANWR). In the western Arctic, the Red Dog mine promises to be the largest operating zinc mine in the western world.

Residents of smaller villages rely on subsistence and temporary work, usually in construction or government. Caribou are important to inland Eskimos, while coastal villagers depend on fish and marine mammals.

Location: The Arctic Circle and the southern foothills of the remote Brooks Range delineate the southern boundary of this region. The Chukchi Sea borders to the west. The Arctic Ocean with the Beaufort Sea in the northeast are the region's northern boundaries.

Geography: The Brooks Range, though not as high as Alaska's coastal mountains or the Alaska Range, rises majestically between Interior's flat expanses and the Arctic's coastal plains. Lying east to west across the width of the state, it consists of endless gentler mountains interrupted by the spectacular granite spires of Arrigetch Peaks.

The Brooks Range spawns a host of rivers running north and south, east and west. Many of these rivers have been designated wild and scenic, and are among the most beautiful and remote in the world.

A taiga forest on the south side of the Brooks Range gives way to tundra that stretches north to the Arctic Ocean. While the Arctic is covered by snow and ice for much of the year and veiled in darkness for up to 3 months, there is enough sunshine in the remaining months to transform the bleak winter tundra into a summer carpet of flowering plants.

Several varieties of tundra can be found in the Arctic. Higher elevations support alpine tundra, which is characterized by lichens, grasses, sedges and some herbs. Moss campion grows on drier slopes. Cotton grass, mosses, lichens, dwarf birch and willows cover the foothills. Sedges, mosses, cotton grass and lousewort predominate on the boggy plain, and high brush vegetation, featuring willow and alder, grows along major rivers.

The treeless Arctic is interlaced with meandering rivers and dotted with thousands of shallow thaw lakes. Permafrost, beginning a few inches under the surface and extending down as far as 2,000 feet, underlies most of the Arctic. Most areas receive less than 10 inches of precipitation a year, but soggy tundra and bogs are common in summer because there is little evaporation and poor drainage.

The Kobuk River, an important highway for prehistoric and contemporary people, and the Noatak, with its pristine watershed, drain much of northwestern Alaska. On the arctic plain, the Colville and north-flowing streams in the eastern Arctic provide access to the region's interior.

Climate: Winters are long and cold in the Brooks Range, with temperatures as low as -60°F. Summers on the south slopes are considerably warmer than on the north, and precipitation is low.

Strong winds, cold temperatures and low precipitation characterize the arctic climate. The Beaufort and Chukchi seas moderate temperatures in summer, but readings drop when ice covers the sea for 9 months each year. At Barrow, July and August temperatures average between 30°F and 40°F; in January and February between 15°F and -18°F.

Wildlife: Brown bears and grizzly bears, Dall sheep, wolves, and moose roam areas of the Brooks Range and the Arctic where there is suitable habitat. Two major caribou herds, the west-ern Arctic and Porcupine, migrate through the Brooks Range to summer calving grounds on the arctic plain.

After being hunted out of Alaska in the mid-1800s, musk-oxen were successfully reintroduced to Nunivak Island in western Alaska in the 1930s. Today several herds range the Arctic.

Wolverines, weasels, a few river otters, snow-shoe hares, lynx, arctic and red foxes, shrews, lemmings and voles also inhabit the Brooks Range and the Arctic.

The frigid waters of the Beaufort and Chukchi seas support polar bears, walrus, bow-head and beluga whales, and bearded and ringed seals. In summer when ice retreats from the coast, harbor seals, harbor porpoises, and killer and gray whales feed here. Rarer species of great whales—fin, sei and little piked—have been reported in Chukchi waters. Even more unusual are the occasional spottings of narwhals.

Many bird species migrate to summer breeding grounds in the Arctic although few winter here. Summer visitors can look for the conspicuous white snowy owl guarding its nest. Endangered arctic peregrine falcons nest along rocky ridges. Thousands of snow geese raise their young near the arctic coast. In the mountains look for hawks, owls, ptarmigan and migrating waterfowl.

All-terrain vehicles are a common mode of transportation in the Bush. (Lee Foster)

Ambler

[MAP 20] Located on the north bank of the Kobuk River near the confluence of the Ambler and Kobuk rivers, 125 miles east of Kotzebue, 320 miles northwest of Fairbanks. **Transportation:** Scheduled airline, air taxi from Kotzebue. **Population:** 271. **Zip code:** 99786. **Emergency Services:** Police, phone 445-2180; Clinic, phone 445-2129; Volunteer Fire Department.

Elevation: 135 feet. **Climate:** Continental climate, characterized by long, cold winters and warm summers. Average annual precipitation 16 inches, including 80 inches of snow.

Private Aircraft: Airstrip 1 mile north; elev. 289 feet; length 2,600 feet; gravel; fuel 80, 100; unattended. Runway condition not monitored; visual inspection recommended prior to using. No facilities at airport.

Visitor Facilities: Accommodations and meals available at 1 lodge. No laundromat or banking services. Groceries, clothing, first-aid supplies, hardware, camera film and sporting goods available. Local arts and crafts available for purchase include birch-bark baskets, masks, mukluks, beaver hats and yo-yos. Fishing/hunting licenses available, as well as guide service. Aircraft mechanic for major repair service only. Rental transportation available includes autos, off-road vehicles, boats and charter aircraft. Fuel available includes marine gas, diesel, propane and regular gasoline. Boat moorage on riverbank.

This Eskimo village was settled in 1958 when people from Shungnak and Kobuk moved here because of its spruce forest and the availability of game. The second-class city was incorporated in 1971. Ambler's economy is based on arts, crafts, and subsistence hunting and fishing. In the summer, many residents go to Kotzebue for commercial fishing. Some local employment is provided by government, school and local businesses.

Ambler is some 20 miles from the archaeological dig at Onion Portage, where artifacts dating back 10,000 years have been found. Kobuk Valley National Park lies about 15 miles downriver and the Great Kobuk Sand Dunes are approximately 35 miles away. Visitors often charter aircraft out of Ambler to Walker Lake in the Brooks Range, then float back down the Kobuk River.

Fishing near Ambler includes salmon, sheefish, grayling, whitefish and trout. The western Arctic caribou herd migrates near Ambler; other game includes moose, grizzly and black bear. Jade can be found in some local streams. A ski track is maintained in winter. Bird watching, especially good around breakup time, includes swans, cranes and other waterfowl.

Communications include phones, mail plane, radio and TV. The community is served by 2 churches and a school with grades preschool through 12. Public water, electricity and sewage systems available. Ambler prohibits the sale and importation of alcoholic beverages. Freight arrives in the community by cargo plane and barge. Government address: City of Ambler, P.O. Box 9, Ambler, AK 99786; phone 445-2122. Village corporation address: NANA Regional Corp., P.O. Box 49, Kotzebue, AK 99752.

Anaktuvuk Pass

[MAP 20] *(an-ak-TU-vuk)* Located on a divide between the Anaktuvuk and John rivers in the central Brooks Range, 260 miles northwest of Fairbanks. **Transportation:** Scheduled airline, air taxi from Fairbanks. **Population:** 364. **Zip code:** 99721. **Emergency Services:** Public Safety Officer, phone 661-3911; Clinic, phone 661-3914; Fire Department, phone 661-3529.

Elevation: 2,200 feet. **Climate:** Due to high elevation, temperatures remain below freezing most of the year, with daily maximum temperature higher than freezing only 142 days of the year. January is the coldest month; July is the warmest month. Mean annual precipitation is 10.3 inches. Average annual snowfall is 63 inches.

Private Aircraft: Airstrip adjacent to southeast; elev. 2,100 feet; length 5,000 feet; gravel; attended. Fuel includes avgas, and Jet A and B. A city bus provides transportation Monday through Saturday from 7:40 A.M. to 10 P.M.

Visitor Facilities: Public campground (check with National Park Service ranger station or village store). No banking services. Groceries available. Local arts and crafts available for purchase include caribou skin masks and carvings. Fishing/hunting licenses available. No guide service. No major repair service or rental transportation. Fuel available includes propane and regular gasoline.

This Nunamiut Eskimo village in Anaktuvuk Pass, a historic caribou migration route, is the last remaining settlement of the inland northern Inupiat Eskimo, whose ancestors date back to 500 B.C. The original nomadic Nunamiut bands left the Brooks Range and scattered in the early 1900s, primarily due to the collapse of the caribou population in 1926 and 1927, but also because of cultural changes brought about by the influx of western civilization. By 1938, however, several Nunamiut families returned to the mountains at Killik River

Caribou skin masks are sold in Anaktuvuk Pass. (Lee Foster)

and Chandler Lake. In the late 1940s, both groups joined at broad, treeless Anaktuvuk Pass, "the place of caribou droppings," to settle permanently. The community incorporated as a second-class city in 1957.

Subsistence hunting, primarily of caribou, and some construction work, in addition to arts and crafts, form the economic base. This is perhaps the most scenic village on the North Slope as it is surrounded by tall mountains, and is near rivers and lakes. Anaktuvuk Pass is located in Gates of the Arctic National Park and Preserve. There is public access to parklands across regional and village Native corporation lands; check with a park ranger about planned routes.

Simon Paneak Memorial Museum, P.O. Box 21085, Anaktuvuk Pass, AK 99721, is open all year. The museum focuses on recording and preserving the history of the Nunamiut. Exhibits are on the early natural, geological and cultural history of the Anaktuvuk Pass area, including the migrations of people across the Bering Land Bridge. Exhibits also feature clothing, household goods and hunting implements used by the Nunamiut Eskimos around the time of the first contact with Westerners. No admission fee.

Communications include phones, mail plane, radio and TV. The community is served by a Presbyterian church and the Nunamiut School with grades preschool through 12. Public electricity is available. Water is delivered by truck from the village well. Sewage is managed through the use of pit privies and honey buckets. Anaktuvuk Pass prohibits the possession of alcoholic beverages. Freight arrives by air transport. Government address: City of Anaktuvuk Pass, P.O. Box 21030, Anaktukvuk Pass, AK 99721; phone 661-3612. Village corporation address: Nunamiut Corp., General Delivery, Anaktuvuk Pass, AK 99721.

Arctic Village

[MAP 18] Located in the Brooks Range on the east bank of the East Fork Chandalar River, 100 miles north of Fort Yukon, 290 miles north of Fairbanks. **Transportation:** Scheduled air service from Fairbanks; winter trail to Venetie. **Population:** 109. **Zip code:** 99722. **Emergency Services:** Village Public Safety Officer; Clinic (with a Health Aide); Volunteer Fire Department.

Elevation: 2,250 feet. **Climate:** Mean temperature in July is 56°F; in January, -29°F.

Private Aircraft: Airstrip 1 mile southwest of village; elev. 2,086 feet; length 5,200 feet; gravel; unattended. Check for runway construction; watch for loose gravel on approach and vehicles on runway.

Visitor Facilities: The village council operates Arctic Village Lodge for visitors; phone 587-9320. A coffee shop is available. No banking services. Supplies and groceries are available at Midnight Sun Native Store (587-5127), Gilbert Store (587-5329) and the local coffee shop. There is a community-owned laundromat with showers. Arctic Village is a traditional Athabascan Indian village and crafts may be available for purchase locally. Gasoline and fuel oil are available at Arctic Village Gas & Oil.

The Neets'ik Gwich'in Indians, a once seminomadic people known for trading *babiche* "sinew lacings" and wolverine skins for seal oil and skins from the Barter Island Eskimos, settled Arctic Village.

Arctic Village elected to retain title to the 1.8-million-acre Venetie Indian Reservation under the Alaska Native Claims Settlement Act. The reserve and Arctic Village are bounded to the north by Arctic National Wildlife Refuge, although recreational access to the refuge is primarily from Kaktovik on Barter Island. Arctic Village is the northwesternmost Indian community in Alaska. It is also the migration route of the Porcupine caribou herd, which winters here.

Employment in Arctic Village is limited to the National Guard Armory, post office, clinic, school, village services, trapping and crafts.

There is an Episcopal chapel in the village, which replaced the old Mission Church now on the National Register of Historic Places. Under restoration, the old church (built entirely of logs with handcrafted finish and furnishings) reflects the skill of the Native artisans under Albert Tritt, who later became its minister.

Communications include phones, mail plane, radio and TV. There is a school with grades preschool through 12. Village services include the laundromat and showers, and electric generator. Honey buckets and outhouses are used. Freight delivery by plane. The sale and importation of alcoholic beverages is prohibited. Government address: Arctic Village Council, P.O. Box 22059, Arctic Village, AK 99722; phone 587-5428.

Atqasuk

[MAP 20] *(AT-ka-sook)* Located on the west bank of Meade River near Imakrak Lake, 58 miles southwest of Barrow. **Transportation:** Scheduled cargo airline, air taxi from Barrow; snow machines in winter. **Population:** 219. **Zip code:** 99791. **Emergency Services:** Public Safety Officer, phone 633-6911; Clinic, phone 633-6711; Fire Department, phone 633-6611; Search and Rescue, phone 633-6815; EMTs on standby 24 hours a day; ambulance, emergency aircraft (helicopter and twin beech) from Barrow.

Elevation: 65 feet. **Climate:** Temperatures remain below freezing for most of the year. July and August are the warmest months, with temperatures ranging from 40°F to 60°F. Many mosquitos. January and February are the coldest, with temperatures ranging from -30°F to -35°F. Windchill factor is significant. Annual precipitation averages 5 inches, with snowfall averaging 30 inches annually.

Private Aircraft: The Meade River airstrip south of the city runs east/west; elev. 95 feet; length 4,400 feet; gravel; rotating beacon light; runway lights can be turned on by aircraft remote or upon request; radio beacon; lighted windsock; no fuel available; unattended; runway condition monitored daily; visual inspection recommended prior to using. No facilities. No fuel available. Public and private transportation available.

Visitor Facilities: No hotel, restaurant, banking services or public restrooms. However, lodging is being developed and Meade River Store (633-6120) will sometimes cash checks. Groceries, clothing, first-aid supplies, camera film, laundromat and hardware are available from Meade River Store. Arts and crafts available for purchase include masks, mittens, dolls, yo-yos, ulus and parkas. Fishing/hunting licenses available. No guide service. No major repair service or rental transportation. Fuel available includes propane, regular gasoline, diesel and motor oil. No moorage facilities.

Laundromat, shower facilities and lavatory available at the Borough Washeteria (633-6320), which is open 7 days a week.

The area around this Inupiat Eskimo village has traditionally been hunted and fished by the Inupiat (northern Eskimo). During WWII, coal was mined here and freighted to Barrow. The mine was operated by residents for personal use from 1978-79 and opened again in 1987 for a trial period. The coal is now used by some residents as an alternative to diesel fuel year round.

The village had a post office from 1951 to 1957 under the name Meade River. The village was reestablished in 1977 by former Barrow, Meade River and Tikigluk residents and incorporated into a second-class city in

1982. Abandoned sod houses, an old cellar and gravesite near the village provide evidence of earlier settlements in the area.

Atqasuk's economy is based on subsistence caribou hunting, fishing and berry picking. Some of the hunters migrate to Barrow for whale, seal and walrus hunting. The area has many caribou, foxes (red, white and silver), wolverines, moose, wolves and lemmings. Fish in the Meade River include grayling, burbot, 3 types of whitefish and 3 species of salmon. Local hunters bag ptarmigan, ducks and geese.

Atqasuk now has a community center, which houses city offices, the recreation department and video game room; a gymnasium; a water-treatment plant; and waste disposal services.

Communications include phones, mail plane, CB radio, radio, a newspaper and TV. The community has a Presbyterian chapel and a school with grades kindergarten through 12. Public electricity is available. Lake water is hauled by truck. Most residences have honey buckets. Freight arrives in the community by air transport or sometimes by cat train from Barrow in winter. (After the cat-train has delivered freight and diesel a few times, residents use the tracks to drive to Barrow.) Atqasuk allows the possession of alcoholic beverages. Government address: City of Atqasuk, P.O. Box 91119, Atqasuk, AK 99791; phone 633-6811. Village corporation address: Atkasook Corp., P.O. Box 91021, Atqasuk, AK 99791.

Barrow

[MAP 20] Located on the Chukchi Sea coast, 10 miles southwest of Point Barrow, 500 miles northwest of Fairbanks. **Transportation:** Scheduled airline from Anchorage via Fairbanks. **Population:** 3,075. **Zip code:** 99723. **Emergency Services:** Public Safety Officer, phone 852-6111; Alaska State Troopers, phone 852-3783; Hospital, phone 852-4611; Volunteer Fire Department.

Elevation: 20 feet. **Climate:** Normal daily maximum temperature in July (warmest month) is 44°F. Normal daily minimum in January (coldest month) is -24°F. The sun rises May 10 and does not set until Aug. 2. When the sun disappears at noon Nov. 18 it does not appear again until noon, Jan. 24.

Private Aircraft: Wiley Post-Will Rogers Memorial Airport adjacent southeast; elev. 44 feet; length 6,500 feet; asphalt; fuel 80, 100, Jet A1; attended 4 to 10:30 P.M. or upon request; phone 852-7400.

Visitor Facilities: Accommodations are available at Top of the World Hotel (852-3900), Airport Inn (852-2525), Arctic Hotel (852-7786) and Lik-Narl Hotel (852-7800). Food is available at Pepe's North of the Border, Sam & Lee, Ken's Restaurant, Arctic Pizza, Browers Cafe (852-3435) and QFC. There are a dry cleaners and a bank. Groceries and supplies at AC/StuaqPak (852-6711), Arctic Coast Trading Post (852-7717) and Cape Smythe Trading (852-6178). Arts and crafts available for purchase include baleen boats, etched baleen, carved ivory, masks, parkas and fur mittens. Fishing/hunting licenses available. No guide service.

Major repair services include marine engine, boat, auto and aircraft mechanics. Air taxi service available. Fuel available includes marine gas, diesel, propane, aviation fuel, unleaded, regular and supreme. No moorage. Trucks are available for $75 a day at S&M Auto Rental (852-6593).

During the summer months tour operators offer package tours of the area. Contact Tundra Tours, Inc. (852-3900) or Arctic Safari Tours (852-4444) to set up a tour that can include polar-bear watching, photographing snowy owls or watching Inupiat Eskimos pull bowhead whales up the beach.

Barrow is one of the largest Eskimo settlements and the seat of the 88,000-square-mile North Slope Borough, the world's largest municipal government. It is also the furthest north frontier settlement in the United States. Traditionally, Barrow is known as Ukpeagvik, "place where owls are hunted." Barrow takes its name from Point Barrow, named for Sir John Barrow of the British Admiralty by Captain Beechey of the Royal Navy in 1825. Beechey had been assigned the task of plotting the Arctic coastline of North America in the HMS *Blossom*. Barrow was incorporated as a first-class city in 1959.

Across from the airport sits the Will Rogers and Wiley Post Monument, dedicated in 1982 to commemorate the 1935 airplane crash of the American humorist and the famous pilot. The accident happened 15 miles south of Barrow where the men had landed seeking directions to Barrow, a planned stop on their trip from Fairbanks to Siberia. Upon takeoff their plane rose to 50 feet, stalled and then plunged into a river below, killing both men. Two monuments, both on the National Register of Historic Places, are located where the men died. Other sites on the national register are the Cape Smythe Whaling and Trading Station in nearby Browerville and the Birnirk archaeological site approximately 2 miles north of the Barrow airfield. Cape Smythe was built as a whaling station in 1893 and is the oldest frame building in the Arctic. The Birnirk culture, which existed about 500–900 A.D., is represented by a group of 16 dwelling mounts and is considered a key link between the prehistoric cultures of Alaska and Canada.

Visitors also may view the Eskimos heading for whale camps in April and May. Despite the fact that the village is very much into the 20th century, hunting of whales, seals, walrus, caribou and ducks is still important for both traditional and economic reasons. It also provides a great portion of the food for the residents. If the whalers are successful, there is a festival called "Nalukataq" when whaling season ends in May.

Barrow residents work for the oil companies at Prudhoe Bay, for the borough, the Native corporation and various other local businesses.

Barrow has all communication services, including cable TV, a public radio station, as well as community electricity, water and sewer systems. Many homes are heated by natural gas from the nearby gas fields. The community is served by 7 churches, a high school, an elementary school and a post secondary Higher Education Center affiliated with the University of Alaska in Fairbanks. There is also a recreation center that includes a new gymnasium, 2 racquetball courts, a weight room and saunas, as well as adult dances and sport tournaments, exercise classes and cross-country skiing. The high school has a swimming pool, weight room and gymnasium that is open to the community evenings and weekends.

Freight arrives by cargo plane and barge. Barrow bans the sale of alcoholic beverages. Government address: City of Barrow, Box 629, Barrow, AK 99723; phone 852-5211. Regional corporation address: Arctic Slope Regional Corp., Box 129, Barrow, AK 99723; phone 852-8633. Village corporation address: Ukpeagvik Inupiat Corp., Box 427, Barrow, AK 99723. Borough government address: North Slope Borough, Box 69, Barrow, AK 99723; phone 852-2611.

Bettles

[MAP 20] (Includes the city of Bettles, Old Bettles, the native village of Evansville and Bettles Field post office.) Located on the south bank of the Upper Koyukuk River in the foothills of the Brooks Range, 180 miles northwest of Fairbanks. **Transportation:** Scheduled air service from Fairbanks (Frontier Flying Service and Wright's Air Service) and charter air service in Bettles (Brooks Range Aviation, 692-5444; Bettles Lodge, 692-5111; and Sourdough Outfitters, 692-5252). Also accessible by boat in summer, snow machine in winter. Winter ice-road to Dalton Highway at Prospect Creek usually open in March (call the city for conditions). Connected by trail to Allakaket and Anaktuvuk Pass. **Population:** 56. **Zip code:** 99726. **Emergency Services:** Clinic, phone 692-5035; Health Aide, phone 692-5141 or 692-5738; Fire Department, phone 692-5244.

Elevation: 624 feet. **Climate:** Semiarid and subarctic. January temperatures average -9°F, with winter winds making it colder. Winter temperatures range from 10°F to -60°F. Summer temperatures average 75°F, with rain and sun, and frost possible. Greatest mean monthly precipitation is in August with 2.63 inches.

Private Aircraft: Bettles airstrip adjacent north; elev. 643 feet; length 5,200 feet; gravel; fuel 100AV, A1+, B. FAA installation, runway maintained year-round. Evansville seaplane base 1 mile north of Bettles runway; river sometimes very low; visual inspection recommended prior to using. Alternate landing sites available; fuel available at river and airport from Koyukuk Inc. (692-5088) or Bettles Lodge (692-5111).

Visitor Facilities: Meals and overnight accommodations available at Bettles Lodge; bunkhouse at Sourdough Outfitters. Campground. Groceries, clothing, hardware, camera film, sporting goods, topographic maps and first-aid supplies may be purchased in the lodge or from outfitters. Arts and crafts available locally include furs, gloves, hats, parkas, ivory, baskets, masks and locally crafted gold jewelry. Fishing/hunting licenses available from Bettles Lodge and Bettles Trading Post. Visitor center at Gates of the Arctic National Park and Kanuti National Wildlife Refuge office. Outfitting and guiding services available, including trips by dog team, canoe, raft, snowmachine or foot. Northern lights viewing tours available. Ecological tours. Fly-out wilderness hunting and fishing trips available. Major repair available for aircraft; check locally for mechanics to work on other types of engines. Residents may lease transportation such as boats and autos. Moor boats on riverbank. Fuel available: diesel, propane, aviation and unleaded gas; Coleman fuel. Lubricating and hydraulic oils available.

Evansville, 5 miles east of Old Bettles and 1 mile north of Bettles Field, was founded by Wilfred Evans, who built the Bettles Lodge for Wien Air in 1952. Bettles began as a trading post in 1899 and was named for the proprietor, Gordon C. Bettles. It developed into a mining town and supply point for the upper Koyukuk Valley mines, and was eventually abandoned. Bettles Field, the airstrip, was built by the U.S. Navy upriver from Old Bettles in 1945. Employment here consists mainly of state and federal jobs. Bettles was incorporated in 1985.

Bettles is the gateway to Gates of the Arctic National Park and Preserve and Kanuti National Wildlife Refuge, and is generally receptive to the growing number of visitors. The community sees a number of hikers and river rafters in summer. Visitors are advised, however, not to pick up souvenirs. Camps, cabins and claims that appear to be abandoned may be privately owned and still in use. Also, Bettles is trying to preserve some of its local mining history. A museum is being planned. There is hunting and fishing in the area, but visitors should be aware of subsistence claims and rules governing park and preserve lands.

Communications include phones, mail plane, radio and TV. There is a nondenominational church in the community and a 2-classroom school with grades 1 through 12. There is community electricity service, but water is either hauled from the river or obtained from private wells, and the sewage system is flush toilets and septic tanks. Freight comes in by cargo plane or via winter ice road. Village government address: City of Bettles, Box 26023, Bettles, AK 99726; phone 692-5191.

Coldfoot

[MAP 18] Located at Mile 175 on the Dalton Highway in the southern slopes of the Brooks Range, 248 miles north of Fairbanks. **Transportation:** Dalton Highway from Fairbanks (no permit needed); charter air service from Fairbanks. **Population:** est. 35 summers; est. 12 winters. **Zip code:** 99701. **Emergency Services:** Alaska State Troopers, phone 678-5201 and leave message.

Climate: Subarctic winters average from 10°F to -20°F or -30°F; summer temperatures average 75°F.

Private Aircraft: State-maintained airstrip adjacent west; elev. 1,050 feet; length 3,500 feet; gravel; no fuel; unattended. No airport facilities.

Visitor Facilities: Coldfoot Services/ Arctic Acres Inn (678-5201) offers motel accommodations, restaurant, lounge, general store, post office, RV park with full hookups, laundromat, shower, dump station; automotive fuels; propane. No banking services. General store has groceries, some clothing, hardware, film, sporting goods, etc. Carved ivory, Eskimo dolls, silver jewelry available for purchase at gift shops. Fishing/hunting licenses available from Fish and Wildlife officer; no guide service.

Coldfoot is the site of a historic mining camp at the mouth of Slate Creek on the east bank of the Middle Fork Koyukuk River. Originally named Slate Creek, Coldfoot reportedly got its name in 1900 when gold stampeders got as far up the Koyukuk as this point, then got cold feet, turned and departed. The old cemetery still exists. Emma Dome (elev. 5,680 feet) lies to the west.

Coldfoot's one commercial facility is open year round. Coldfoot Services offers CB-equipped escort up and down the Dalton Highway. In summer, pipeline and wildlife presentations, flightseeing and recreational gold panning are available

The post office at Coldfoot opened in 1986, and postal service resumed for the first time since the early 1900s. With the increase in gold mining activities in the area, it is not unusual to find a miner bartering his gold for some cool refreshment at the local lounge.

The National Park Service, Bureau of Land Management, and U.S. Fish and Wildlife Service operate a visitor center here, offering travel information and nightly presentations on the natural and cultural history of the Arctic. The visitor center sells USGS topographical maps of the area and books of interest. It is open from June 1 through September. A Fish and Wildlife officer is stationed at Coldfoot.

Locals report good fishing for grayling at nearby creeks and a couple of hike-in lakes. Because the trans-Alaska pipeline is adjacent, there is no hunting nearby. (North of the Yukon River, hunting is prohibited within 5 miles on either side of the pipeline.) Motorcycles and all-terrain vehicles provide summertime leisure activity, and winters are taken up with dog mushing and snow machining.

The unincorporated community has no public utilities. The 4 private phones, all located at the motel, are for collect and credit card calls only. Mail arrives by truck; TV via satellite.

Deadhorse

[MAP 20] Located 487 miles by road north of Fairbanks near the Arctic Ocean. **Transportation:** Scheduled jet service from Fairbanks, or via the Dalton Highway. **Population:** between 3,500 and 8,600 including Prudhoe Bay oil-field workers. **Zip code:** 99734. **Emergency Services:** Public Safety Dept., 659-2515; emergency medical and fire handled by oil-field operators ARCO Alaska and BP Exploration Alaska.

Climate: Winter temperatures hover between -55°F and -60°F, but with wind chill factor can fall as low as -115°F. For 56 days in midwinter, the sun never rises. But from mid-April to mid-August, daylight is continuous, and temperatures can reach as high as 70°F.

Private Aircraft: State-maintained airport 2 miles north; elev. 57 feet; length 6,500 feet; paved, attended most days; fuel available.

Visitor Facilities: Accommodations are available at NANA Deadhorse Hotel (659-2840) and at several camps, but reservations should be made well in advance as increased oil drilling activity can result in a shortage of available rooms. Motel rooms are expensive ($90 and up a night); meals are included in some prices. A general store sells hunting and fishing licenses and some local handicraft items.

The Prudhoe Bay industrial complex on the Arctic Ocean is located a short distance from Deadhorse. Access to Prudhoe Bay is on roads owned by the oil companies and permission must be obtained. Prudhoe Bay is not a place for drop-in, independent visitors. Oil-field workers, tour groups and visitors on official business are accommodated. For security and safety reasons, however, unescorted visitors are not allowed on the docks or on area roads.

Communications include phones, mail plane, radio and TV. Church services are held at several camps. Freight arrives by cargo plane, by truck up the Dalton Highway, or is shipped in from the West Coast on barges to Prudhoe during the brief 6 weeks each summer when the arctic icepack moves offshore. For more information, contact ARCO Alaska, Inc., P.O. Box 100360, Anchorage, AK 99510; or BP Exploration Alaska, P.O. Box 196612, Anchorage, AK 99519-6612.

Kaktovik

[MAP 18] *(Kack-TOE-vik)* Located on the north coast of Barter Island on the Beaufort Sea, 390 miles north of Fairbanks. **Transportation:** Scheduled airline, air taxi via Fairbanks or Barrow. **Population:** 227. **Zip code:** 99747. **Emergency Services:** Public Safety Officer, phone 640-6911; Clinic, phone 640-6413; Fire Department, phone 640-6611.

Elevation: 40 feet. **Climate:** February is the coldest month; July the warmest. Mean annual precipitation is 6.5 inches, with 39 inches of snow.

Kaktovik, on Barter Island in the Beaufort Sea, is on the northern edge of the Arctic National Wildlife Refuge. (Karen Jettmar)

Private Aircraft: Airstrip 1 mile from village; fuel 80, 100; control tower. Transportation to village.

Visitor Facilities: Accommodations and meals are available at Waldo Arms (640-6513) and Sim's Camp (640-6615). Laundromat available. No banking services. Groceries and supplies are available at Kikitak Store (640-6620) and Sim's Store (640-6615).

Local arts and crafts that can be purchased include etched baleen, carved ivory and masks. Fishing/hunting licenses available, as well as guide service. Major repair services include auto and aircraft mechanic. Charter aircraft is the only rental transportation. Fuel available includes marine gas, diesel, propane, unleaded and regular. No moorage.

This Inupiat Eskimo village is on the northern edge of the 20.3-million-acre Arctic National Wildlife Refuge, the most northerly unit of the national wildlife refuge system. As the unofficial jumping-off point for the refuge, Kaktovik has experienced an influx of visitors the community is not prepared for. Hikers and campers in particular should note that camping is restricted. There are no public campgrounds, but arrangements may be made with private land holders. Contact Kaktovik Inupiat Corp. (640-6120) or Marx Sims (640-6615 or 640-6820).

The ruins of old Kaktovik can be seen from the road into the village from the airport. Hunting in the nearby area is for Dall sheep, moose, caribou and fox.

"Kaktovik is an Arctic desert," says one resident. "It is truly amazing to see such beauty evolve from the frozen tundra. Nowhere have I experienced such beauty and tranquility."

Communications in Kaktovik, which incorporated as a second-class city in 1971, include phones, mail plane, radio and TV. The community is served by a Presbyterian church and Harold Kaveolook School with grades preschool through 12. Public water and electricity are available; sewage system is honey buckets. Freight arrives by cargo plane and barge. Government address: City of Kaktovik, P.O. Box 27, Kaktovik, AK 99747; phone 640-6313. Village corporation address: Kaktovik Inupiat Corp., Box 73, Kaktovik, AK 99747.

Kiana

[MAP 19] *(ky-AN-a)* Located on the north bank of the Kobuk River, 57 miles east of Kotzebue, 390 miles west of Fairbanks.

Transportation: Boat; snow machine; scheduled airline and air taxi from Kotzebue. **Population:** 434. **Zip code:** 99749. **Emergency Services:** Police, phone 475-2129; Clinic, phone 475-2199; Volunteer Fire Department.

Elevation: 150 feet. **Climate:** Kiana is in the transitional climate zone and has long, cold winters and warm summers. Summer temperatures average 60°F. Precipitation averages more than 16 inches annually, including 60 inches of snow.

Private Aircraft: Bob Baker Memorial Airport 1 mile from village; elev. 150 feet; length 3,400 feet; gravel; no fuel available. Runway conditions monitored by airport manager. No facilities at airport. Public transportation usually available from airfield.

Visitor Facilities: No lodging facilities or banking services. A small restaurant and laundromat are available. Groceries, clothing, first-aid supplies, hardware, camera film and sporting goods can be purchased in the community. No arts and crafts available for purchase. Fishing/hunting licenses and guide service available. Outboard engine repair only. Rental transportation includes boats and charter aircraft. Fuel available includes marine gas, diesel, propane and regular gasoline. Moorage facilities available.

This Eskimo village was probably established as a seasonal camp or central village of the Kowagmiut Eskimos. Its name means "place where 3 rivers meet." It is the most modern of the villages in the Kobuk River area. It became a supply center for Squirrel River placer mines in 1909. It is a second-class city, incorporated in 1964.

Kiana has a subsistence economy based on moose, caribou, rabbits and various waterfowl. Fishing includes chum salmon, sheefish, whitefish, lingcod and grayling. In summer, many men go to Kotzebue, Red Dog mine or Prudhoe Bay to work in construction or commercial fishing.

The community is downstream from Kobuk Valley National Park, where winter's dry, cold climate still approximates that of late Pleistocene times, supporting remnant flora once common on the vast arctic steppe. From Kiana, a network of old trading trails is still used for intervillage travel, hunting and fishing. All-terrain vehicles, snow machines and, less frequently, dogsleds are used in the winter.

Communications include phones, mail plane 6 times daily, radio and TV. The community is served by 2 churches and 2 schools with grades preschool through 12. There are public electricity, water and sewer systems. Freight arrives by barge and air transport. Kiana bans the sale and importation of alcoholic beverages. Government address: City of Kiana, P.O. Box 150, Kiana, AK 99749; phone 475-2136. Village corporation address: NANA Regional Corp., P.O. Box 49, Kotzebue, AK 99752.

Kivalina

[MAP 19] *(Kiv-a-LEEN-a)* Located on an 8-mile-long barrier beach between the Chukchi Sea and Kivalina Lagoon, 90 miles north of Kotzebue, 465 miles west of Fairbanks. **Transportation:** Boat; snow machine; scheduled airline, air taxi from Kotzebue. **Population:** 290. **Zip code:** 99750. **Emergency Services:** Alaska State Troopers, Kotzebue, phone 442-3222; Clinic, phone 645-2141; Volunteer Fire Department.

Elevation: 11 feet. **Climate:** Located in the transitional climate zone, Kivalina has long, cold winters and cool summers. The Chukchi Sea is ice-covered from November to June. Precipitation is light, with an annual mean of 8.6 inches, including 57 inches of snow.

Private Aircraft: Airstrip adjacent; elev. 10 feet; length 5,000 feet; no fuel. Runway condition not monitored; visual inspection recommended prior to using. Support facilities and transportation to village.

Visitor Facilities: Accommodations sometimes available in private homes. No restaurant, laundromat or banking services. Groceries, clothing, first-aid supplies, hardware, camera film and sporting goods can be purchased in the community. Arts and crafts available for purchase include model skin kayaks, model dogsleds, whale bone masks, ivory carvings and baskets. Fishing/hunting licenses not available. No guide or major repair services. Boats can sometimes be rented. Fuel available: marine gas, diesel, propane, regular and unleaded. No moorage.

This Eskimo village, built on a flat sand and gravel spit, has long been a stopping-off place for seasonal travelers between the Arctic coast and Kotzebue Sound. Lieutenant L.A. Zagoskin of the Imperial Russian Navy recorded the name "Kivualinagmut" in 1847. It is a second-class city, incorporated in 1969.

Kivalina has a subsistence economy based on bowhead and beluga whales, walruses, seals, moose and caribou. There is fishing for salmon, grayling and arctic char in 2

rivers near the village. The Chukchi Sea usually is open to boat traffic from about mid-June to the first of November. Winter travel is by snow machine and dogsled from late October through May.

Communications include phones, mail plane, radio and TV. The community is served by 2 churches and 2 schools with grades preschool through 12. There are public electricity and water-supply systems. Sewage system is honey buckets. Kivalina prohibits the sale and importation of alcoholic beverages. Freight arrives in the community by plane, barge and ship. Government address: City of Kivalina, P.O. Box 50079, Kivalina, AK 99750; phone 645-2137. Village corporation address: NANA Regional Corp., P.O. Box 49, Kotzebue, AK 99752.

Kobuk

[MAP 20] Located on the right bank of the Kobuk River, 150 miles east of Kotzebue, 300 miles west of Fairbanks. **Transportation:** Scheduled airline, charter from Kotzebue. **Population:** 86. **Zip code:** 99751. **Emergency Services:** Village Public Safety Officer; Clinic and Health Aide; Volunteer Fire Department.

Elevation: 140 feet. **Climate:** Kobuk is located in the continental climate zone; winters are long and cold, summers relatively warm. Mean annual precipitation 16.7 inches, including 56 inches of snow.

Private Aircraft: Airstrip adjacent; elev. 145 feet; length 2,500 feet; gravel; no fuel; visual inspection recommended prior to using. Restroom facilities. No public transportation. Floatplane operation on lake. Also, 3,800-foot gravel airstrip at Dahl Creek, 3 miles from Kobuk.

Visitor Facilities: Accommodations at 1 hotel or arrangements can be made with private homes or clinic. Laundromat with showers available. No restaurant or banking services. Groceries, first-aid supplies, hardware, camera film and sporting goods can be purchased in the community.

Local arts and crafts available for purchase include birch-bark baskets and picture frames, mukluks, beaver hats and fur mittens. Fishing/hunting licenses available, as well as a fishing guide. No major repair services. Rental transportation includes boats and charter aircraft. Fuel available includes marine gas, diesel, propane, unleaded and regular gasoline. Moorage available.

This Eskimo community of log homes was founded in 1899 as a supply point for mining activities in the Cosmos Hills to the north and was then called Shungnak. Area residents gravitated to the trading post, school and mission. Riverbank erosion forced relocation of the village in the 1920s to present-day Shungnak, 10 miles downriver. The few people who stayed and those who returned named the old village Kobuk. The village is a second-class city, incorporated in 1973.

Kobuk has a subsistence economy largely based on fishing and hunting. Fish include sheefish (up to 60 pounds), salmon, grayling, whitefish, pike and trout. Game includes caribou, moose, black and grizzly bear, and Dall sheep. Residents also work for the local government, school district and village corporation. Firefighting provides summer work.

Kobuk is located near the headwaters of the Kobuk River. Visitors to Kobuk Valley National Park can fly into Kobuk from Nome or Kotzebue and float down the Kobuk to the national park and the Great Kobuk Sand Dunes, or fly to Walker Lake in Gates of the Arctic National Park in the Brooks Range and float the river from there. Also of interest is the jade mine, 3 miles from Kobuk by jeep, owned by Oro Stewart of Stewart's photo in Anchorage. Visitors are welcome in June and July to watch jade mining and cutting. No charge for cabins; bring sleeping bags and food. NANA Regional Corp. also operates a jade mine at nearby Jade Mountain. Historic trails along the river are still used for intervillage travel, hunting and fishing.

Communications include phones, mail plane, radio and TV. The community is served by a church and a school with grades preschool through 8. There are public water supply and electricity systems. The sewage system is honey buckets. Freight arrives by plane or barge. Kobuk bans the sale and importation of alcoholic beverages. Government address: City of Kobuk, P.O. Box 20, Kobuk, AK 99751; phone 948-2217. Village corporation address: NANA Regional Corp., P.O. Box 49, Kotzebue, AK 99752.

Kotzebue

[MAP 19] *(KOT-sa-byou)* Located on the northwest shore of Baldwin Peninsula in Kotzebue Sound, 26 miles above the Arctic Circle, 550 miles north of Anchorage. **Transportation:** Daily jet service from Anchorage via Nome. **Population:** 3,800. **Zip code:** 99752. **Emergency Services:** For police, fire, ambulance, phone 911; Women's Crisis Project, phone 442-3969; Maniilaq Medical Center, phone 442-3321.

Elevation: 10 feet. **Climate:** In summer the temperature averages between 40°F and 50°F. During winter, the average temperature is between -5°F and -8°F. Mean annual precipitation is 9.5 inches, including 25 inches of snow. During summer the sun does not set for approximately 36 days.

Private Aircraft: Ralph Wien Memorial Airport, 1 mile south; elev. 11 feet; length 5,900 feet; asphalt; fuel 80, 100, Jet A. Transportation to town available. Kotzebue seaplane base within city.

Visitor Facilities: Accommodations at Nullagvik Hotel (442-3331), Drake's Camp (442-2736) and Budget Inn Bed & Breakfast (442-2865). There are restaurants, banking services, several stores carrying all supplies, beauty salons, a library and taxis. Among the many Eskimo arts and crafts items that can be purchased are jade items made at a local factory as well as parkas and mukluks made locally. Fishing/hunting licenses and guide service available, as well as several air charter companies. All fuel is available.

Kotzebue is the commercial center for a 48,000-square-mile area of northwestern Alaska which includes 10 villages and a population of about 7,047. It is a second-class city, incorporated in 1958, and is the largest Eskimo village in Alaska.

The town is on a spit that is about 3 miles long and 1,100 to 3,600 feet wide. The site has been occupied for some 600 years and centuries before Europeans arrived "Kikiktagruk" was a busy trading center. It acquired its present name from the adjacent sound named for Polish explorer Otto von Kotzebue.

The population is more than 80 percent Eskimo. The economy is based on government services, commercial fishing and subsistence hunting and fishing. The wage economy of the entire region is concentrated in Kotzebue, which contains the regional offices of several state and federal agencies.

Local attractions include the NANA Museum of the Arctic, P.O. Box 49, Kotzebue, AK 99752; phone 442-3304, which features a 2-hour program that includes a diorama show unequaled anywhere in Alaska. Shows are scheduled at 9:15 A.M. and 3 P.M. daily; tickets for the show are $20. Collections in the museum reflect the ethnology and natural history of northwestern Alaska, along with wildlife exhibits. Also included in a trip to the museum are a visit to the jade manufacturing factory, a panoramic slide show, cultural heritage demonstrations featuring skin sewing, ivory carving, Eskimo dancing and other traditional arts, and an Eskimo blanket toss. The museum is open from June to September and hours are 8:30 A.M. to 5:30 P.M. daily. Winter hours are by appointment. General admission is free. The west end of the museum building houses administrative offices of the National Park Service, phone 442-3890; or write Superintendent, Northwest Alaska Areas, National Park Service, Box 287, Kotzebue, AK 99752 for information about national parks in the area. The Park Service public information center is down the street from the museum. The excellent city museum, Ootukahkuktuvik or "Place Having Old Things," City of Kotzebue, P.O. Box 46, Kotzebue, AK 99752 requires special arrangements to view; contact the city hall. Among the items to see are a raincoat made from walrus intestine and a coat fashioned from bird feathers.

Points of interest include the large cemetery, with graves lavishly decorated with artificial flowers, and spirit houses over some of the graves.

NANA Regional Corp. offers tours and viewings of native dances. Tundra tours are also available, including special trips to reindeer herds.

During the summer, tour groups are entertained with Eskimo blanket tosses and often dances and skin-sewing demonstrations. The July 4 celebration, followed closely by the Northwest Native Trade Fair, is the biggest event of the year in Kotzebue. The fair features traditional Native games. A muktuk eating contest, seal-hook throwing contest and an Eskimo buggy race are among the special events. People from all over the region come to trade handicrafts and participate in traditional dances and feasts. In September, the northern lights are visible. In winter, there are various dog mushing races.

Preliminaries to the Eskimo Olympics take place between Christmas and New Year's Day. Events include the knuckle hop, high-kicks, blanket toss, finger-pulling contest and greased pole walk.

In April, residents gather to watch snowmachine riders begin the Willie Goodwin Sr./Archie Ferguson Memorial Snowmachine race. The race, sponsored by the Kotzebue Lions Club, takes riders across some of the most demanding terrain at speeds of more than 100 mph. The course runs from Kotzebue to Noorvik, through the Kiana Pass and on to Selawik before turning back to Noorvik. The last stretch leads across Hotham Inlet and Melvin Channel back to Kotzebue.

As spring approaches, the ice in Kotzebue sound begins to melt and break apart, as does the ice in nearby rivers. As the ice passes the city, it begins jamming up, and pushes itself up towards shoreline streets. One resident says, "there have been times when there was a wall of ice all along Front Street." As spring becomes summer, ice floes take on the appearance of crystals and make the sound of tinkling glass. "At times, a moose or some other animal will get stranded on the moving ice," says a resident. "There isn't much that can be done except hope the ice floats or is pushed toward land so the animal can jump off."

Kotzebue has all communications systems, as well as community water, sewer and electricity. The community is served by 8 churches, 2 schools, a community college and a technical center. Freight arrives by ship, barge and air cargo planes. The community bans the sale of alcoholic beverages. Government address: City of Kotzebue, P.O. Box 46, Kotzebue, AK 99752; phone 442-3401. Native corporation: NANA Regional Corp., P.O. Box 49, Kotzebue, AK 99752.

Kuparuk

[MAP 18] *(Koo-PAH-ruk)* Located on the arctic coastal plain, 40 miles west of Prudhoe Bay, 400 miles north of Fairbanks. **Transportation:** Charter plane or gravel road from Prudhoe Bay. **Population:** Approximately 300 oil-field workers. **Emergency Services:** North Slope Borough Police, Prudhoe Bay; ARCO security officers; ARCO medical clinic.

Climate: Summer weather usually cool, windy and foggy, but temperatures can reach 70°F. Winter weather is cold, dark and very windy. Bugs can be ferocious during calm periods in June and July.

Private Aircraft: Airstrip 0.5 mile from camp is not open to private aircraft; state-operated airport at Deadhorse is available.

Visitor Facilities: The land is privately leased and there are no visitor facilities.

Kuparuk is the ARCO Alaska base camp for the second largest oil field in the United States. Communications include phones, mail plane, radio and TV. Freight arrives by cargo plane and barge, or by truck up the Dalton Highway to Prudhoe Bay.

Noatak

[MAP 19] *(NO-a-tack)* Located on the west bank of the Noatak River, 55 miles north of Kotzebue, 470 miles northwest of Fairbanks. **Transportation:** Boat; scheduled air service and air taxi from Kotzebue. **Population:** 305. **Zip code:** 99761. **Emergency Services:** Police, phone 485-2168; Alaska State Troopers, Kotzebue, phone 442-3911; Clinic, phone 485-2162; Volunteer Fire Department.

Elevation: 60 feet. **Climate:** Noatak is on the border between the transitional and continental climate zones; winters are long and cold; summers warm. Precipitation averages 10 to 13 inches annually, including 48 inches of snow.

Private Aircraft: Noatak airstrip adjacent southwest; elev. 99 feet; length 2,200 feet; gravel; fuel 80, 100. No airport facilities or transportation to village. Floatplanes can land on river usually from second week of June to first week of October.

Visitor Facilities: Arrangements can be made for sleeping at the school and in private homes. No restaurant, laundromat or banking services. Groceries, some clothing, hardware and some sporting goods available. Arts and crafts available for purchase include hand-knitted gloves, mukluks and beaver caps. Fishing/hunting licenses available. No guide or major repair services. Boats can be rented. Fuel available includes marine gas, propane and regular gasoline. No moorage facilities.

Noatak, a community of log and wood-frame homes 70 miles above the Arctic Circle, is situated on a bluff overlooking the river. It was established as a fishing and hunting camp in the 19th century and developed into a permanent settlement listed in Ivan Petroff's 1880 census as "Noatagamute," which meant "Noatak [River] people." The community is unincorporated. Its economy is based primarily on subsistence hunting and fishing. Fish include chum salmon, whitefish, grayling, pike, lingcod and Dolly Varden. Game includes caribou, moose, waterfowl, rabbits and Dall sheep. There is summer employment in Kotzebue or at the nearby Red Dog zinc mine.

Noatak is the only settlement along the 396-mile-long Noatak River, eighth longest river in Alaska. The 6.6-million-acre Noatak National Preserve encompasses the major portion of the river, except the headwaters located in Gates of the Arctic National Park and Preserve. Access to the lower river is by air charter from Kotzebue; access to the upper river for float trips is generally by air charter from Bettles to a lake along the river. Many historic trails along the Noatak are still used for intervillage travel, hunting and fishing.

Communications in Noatak include phones, TV, radio and mail plane. The community is served by a church and a school with grades preschool through 12. There are public water, electricity and sewer systems. Noatak prohibits the sale and importation of alcoholic beverages. Freight arrives by cargo plane and barge. Government address: Noatak Village Council, General Delivery, Noatak, AK 99761. Village corporation address: NANA Regional Corp., P.O. Box 49, Kotzebue, AK 99752.

Noorvik

[MAP 19] Located on right bank of the Nazuruk Channel of the Kobuk River, 45 miles east of Kotzebue, 400 miles west of Fairbanks. **Transportation:** Boat; scheduled and charter plane from Kotzebue. **Population:** 560. **Zip code:** 99763. **Emergency Services:** Police, phone 636-2173; Clinic, phone 636-2103; Volunteer Fire Department.

Elevation: 70 feet. **Climate:** Transitional, with long, cold winters and cool summers. Mean annual precipitation 16 inches, with 60 inches of snow.

Private Aircraft: Robert Curtis Memorial Airport 1 mile from village; elev. 63 feet; length 2,800 feet; gravel; no fuel; unattended; visual inspection recommended prior to using. Airport manager and freight terminal at airport. No transportation to village.

Visitor Facilities: Accommodations at 1 hotel. There is a restaurant. No banking services. Groceries, clothing, first-aid supplies, hardware, camera film and sporting goods may be purchased in the community. Fishing/hunting licenses available, as well as guide service. Repair services available for marine engines and boats. Arrangements can be made to rent autos, off-road vehicles and boats. Available fuel includes marine gas, diesel, propane and regular gasoline.

This village was established by Kowagmiut Eskimo fishermen and hunters from the village of Deering in the early 1900s. The village was first called Oksik, but became known as Noorvik around 1914. Noorvik is a second-class city, incorporated in 1964.

The economy is based primarily on subsistence hunting and fishing. There is some full-time employment in the village with local government and businesses and seasonal employment in Kotzebue, Fairbanks, the Red Dog zinc mine or Prudhoe Bay. Noorvik is downstream from Kobuk Valley National Park. Many historic trails in the area are still used for intervillage travel, hunting and fishing.

Communications include phones, mail plane, radio and TV. The community has a church and 2 schools with grades preschool through 12. There are public water, sewer and electricity systems. Noorvik bans the sale and importation of alcoholic beverages. Freight arrives by cargo plane and barge. Government address: City of Noorvik, P.O. Box 146, Noorvik, AK 99763; phone 636-2100. Village corporation address: NANA Regional Corp., P.O. Box 49, Kotzebue, AK 99752.

Nuiqsut

[MAP 20] *(noo-IK-sut)* Located on the west bank of the Nechelik Channel of the Colville River Delta, about 35 miles from the Beaufort Sea coast, 60 miles west of Prudhoe Bay, 380 miles north of Fairbanks. **Transportation:** Scheduled or charter plane from Prudhoe Bay or Barrow. **Population:** 314. **Zip code:** 99789. **Emergency Services:** Public Safety Officer, phone 480-6111; Clinic, phone 480-6729; Fire Department, phone 480-6611.

Elevation: 50 feet. **Climate:** Temperatures remain below freezing most of the year, rising above freezing only 122 days per year. July is the warmest month; February the coldest month. Precipitation is light, measuring 5 to 6 inches per year. Total snowfall averages 20 inches.

Private Aircraft: Airstrip adjacent; elev. 50 feet; length 4,600 feet; gravel; no fuel; unattended; visual inspection recommended prior to use. Runway soft or flooded during late spring breakup. No facilities at airport. Transportation to village.

Visitor Facilities: No hotel or restaurant. Laundromat available. No banking services. Groceries, clothing, first-aid supplies, hardware, camera film and sporting goods may be purchased in the community. Arts and crafts available for purchase include skin masks and boats, fur mittens and parkas and carved ivory. Fishing/hunting licenses available. No guide service. No major repair services or rental transportation. Fuel available includes marine gas, diesel, propane, white

gas, kerosene and regular gasoline. No moorage facilities.

The Colville River Delta has traditionally been a gathering and trading place for the Inupiat Eskimo people, and has always offered good hunting and fishing. The village was constructed in 1974 under sponsorship of Arctic Slope Regional Corp. after a winter overland move of 27 Barrow families with ties to the Colville River delta area. The new residents lived in a tent city for 18 months before permanent housing could be built. Nuiqsut, which encompasses 9 square miles, was incorporated as a second-class city in 1975.

The economy is based primarily on subsistence hunting and fishing, but many residents are employed in seasonal construction work. Fish include whitefish, burbot, arctic char and grayling. Game animals include bowhead and beluga whales, caribou, seals, moose and many species of waterfowl such as swans, geese, ducks and loons. Local recreational activities include riding snowmobiles and 3-wheelers, playing bingo, and activities at the Kisik Community Center. On the Fourth of July various outdoor games take place. Traditional dances are performed at these and other celebrations.

Communications include phones, mail plane, radio and TV. The community is served by a Presbyterian church and a school with grades preschool through 12. There is a public electricity system. Water is delivered from a freshwater lagoon. The sewage system is honey buckets. Nuiqsut prohibits the possession of alcoholic beverages. Freight arrives by barge or plane. Government address: City of Nuiqsut, P.O. Box 148, Nuiqsut, AK 99789; phone 480-6727. Village corporation address: Kuukpik Corp., P.O. Box 187, Nuiqsut, AK 99789.

Point Hope

[MAP 19] Located on a triangular foreland which juts into the Chukchi Sea 275 miles north of Nome, 570 miles northwest of Fairbanks, 325 miles southwest of Barrow. **Transportation:** Scheduled airline, air charter from Kotzebue. **Population:** 591. **Zip code:** 99766. **Emergency Services:** Public Safety Officer, phone 368-2911; Clinic, phone 368-2234; Fire Department, phone 368-2774.

Elevation: 13 feet. **Climate:** Temperatures cool year-round but much less severe than elsewhere in the North Slope Borough. Temperatures are above freezing 162 days of the year. February is the coldest month with temperatures averaging -15°F; August is the warmest month when the mercury soars to 44°F average. Mean annual precipitation is 10 inches, including 36 inches of snow.

Private Aircraft: Airstrip 2 miles southwest; elev. 14 feet; length 4,000 feet; asphalt; emergency fuel only; unattended. Tickets and reservations through Point Hope Native Store or other agents in town. City bus available to village.

Visitor Facilities: Accommodations, restaurant and laundry facilities available. Native store will cash checks. Groceries, clothing, first-aid supplies, hardware, camera film and sporting goods available in the community. Arts and crafts available for purchase include carved ivory, baleen baskets, carved whale bone masks and animals, caribou skin masks, etched baleen, Eskimo parkas, ivory-tipped harpoons and bird spears, and oosiks. Fishing/hunting licenses available, as well as guide service. Repair services available for marine engines, boats and autos. Arrangements may be made to rent private autos, off-road vehicles or boats, including skin boats. Fuel available: marine gas, diesel, propane, unleaded, regular and supreme. Public moorage available.

The village was named in 1826 by Capt. F.W. Beechey after Englishman Sir William Johnstone Hope.

The point's favorable location for harvesting bowhead whales attracted an earlier people to settle here some 2,000 years ago after they crossed a land bridge connecting Siberia and Alaska. The Point Hope peninsula is one of the longest continually occupied areas in North America. At Point Hope are the remains of the sod houses of Old Tigara Village, a prehistoric site, and an even earlier site with about 800 house pits known as Ipiutak, occupied from about 500 B.C. to 100 A.D. Ipiutak and the surrounding archaeological district are on the National Register of Historic Places.

The Point Hope people traditionally dominated an extensive area from the Utukok River to the Kivalina River and far inland. By 1848 commercial whaling activities brought an influx of Westerners, many of whom employed Point Hope villagers. By the late 1880s, the whalers established shore-based whaling stations on the peninsula, notably at nearby Jabbertown (so-named because of the many languages spoken there). These disappeared with the demise of the whaling industry in the early 1900s.

Point Hope village was incorporated in 1966 and 6 years later became a second-class city. Erosion and a threat of storm flooding from the Chukchi Sea led to its relocation to higher ground in the mid-1970s.

Construction work is the main source of income in Point Hope, while capital improvement programs create new jobs in operations and maintenance. Other jobs are available with the city, school, Native corporation and local businesses.

Nearly all men in the village participate in the spring whale hunt, in which traditional skin boats still are used. A festival, to which visitors are welcome, takes place after the whaling season, around June 1. There also are village-wide celebrations on the Fourth of July, Thanksgiving and Christmas.

In addition to the prehistoric village sites, there are old burial grounds in the area, including a cemetery marked by large whale bones standing on end. Beachcombing and rockhounding are available in the area and the point also is home to an abundance of tiny arctic wildflowers. Other activities include boating and bird, wildlife and whale watching, cold dip swimming in the lagoon, egg gathering at Cape Thompson and Cape Lisburne, and bingo 6 nights a week.

Fish available include salmon, trout, grayling and whitefish. Hunting is for caribou, moose, bear, ptarmigan, ducks and geese.

Communications in Point Hope include phones, mail plane, radio and TV. There are community electricity and water systems. Sewage system is honey buckets. The community is served by an Episcopal church (the oldest in the region, established in 1890) and Assembly of God and Church of Christ churches. The Tikigaq school has grades preschool through 12. Point Hope prohibits the sale and importation of alcoholic beverages. Freight arrives by cargo plane and barge. Government address: City of Point Hope, P.O. Box 169, Point Hope, AK 99766; phone 368-2537. Village corporation address: Tigara Corp., P.O. Box 9, Point Hope, AK 99766.

Point Lay

[MAP 19] Located on the Chukchi Sea, 550 miles northwest of Fairbanks, 300 miles southwest of Barrow. **Transportation:** Scheduled airline, air charter from Barrow. **Population:** 158. **Zip code:** 99723. **Emergency Services:** Public Safety Officer, phone 833-2911; Clinic, phone 833-2527; Fire Department, phone 833-2611.

Elevation: 10 feet. **Climate:** The temperature averages around 40°F in summer and -35°F in winter. July is the warmest month; January is the coldest month. Mean annual precipitation is 6.73 inches, including 18.5 inches of snow.

Private Aircraft: Seldom-used sand airstrip at old village site; length 700 feet. Airstrip at DEW line station; elev. 20 feet; length 3,500 feet; gravel; civilian aircraft need 5 days prior landing clearance from the U.S. Air Force.

Visitor Facilities: No hotel, restaurant, laundromat or banking services. There is a store. Arts and crafts available for purchase include baleen baskets, masks, carved ivory and fur parkas. Fishing/hunting licenses available. No guide service, major repair service, rental transportation or public moorage facilities. Fuel available includes propane and regular gasoline.

Kali, the Eskimo name for the village, means "mound" and refers to the elevated area on which it stands. It is probably the last remaining village of the so-called Kukpowruk people.

The deeply indented shoreline prevented effective bowhead whaling, and the village never fully participated in the whaling culture. People of the village engage in subsistence hunting including the harvesting of beluga whales and some construction work.

Recreational activities include snowmobiling, 3-wheeling, hunting, fishing and trapping. Point Lay is an unincorporated village within the North Slope Borough.

Communications include phones, mail plane, radio and TV. Water is delivered by truck from freshwater lakes. Sewage system is honey buckets. There are no churches. School has grades preschool through 12. Point Lay bans the sale and importation of alcoholic beverages. Freight arrives by air transport and barge. Village corporation address: Cully Corp., General Delivery, Point Lay, AK 99723.

Prudhoe Bay

(See **Deadhorse**)

Selawik

[MAP 19] *(SELL-a-wik)* Located at the mouth of the Selawik River, 90 miles southeast of Kotzebue, 375 miles west of Fairbanks. **Population:** 682. **Zip code:** 99770. **Emergency**

Services: Police, phone 484-2229; Alaska State Troopers, phone 911; Clinic, phone 484-2199; Volunteer Fire Department.

Elevation: 50 feet. **Climate:** Long, cold winters and cool summers. Precipitation is 8.7 inches annually, including 35 to 40 inches of snow.

Private Aircraft: Airstrip adjacent; elev. 25 feet; length 1,900 feet; gravel; no fuel; unattended. No facilities at airport. No transportation to village. Roland Norton Memorial Airstrip 12 miles north; elev. 360 feet; length 3,000 feet; gravel; attended upon request.

Visitor Facilities: Contact city office (484-2132) to arrange for accommodations in private homes or at the school. No restaurant or banking services available. Groceries, clothing, first-aid supplies, hardware, camera film and sporting goods may be purchased in the community. Arts and crafts available for purchase include masks, baskets and caribou jawbone model dogsleds. Fishing/hunting licenses available. No guide service. Repair services available for marine engines, boats and autos. Fuel available: diesel, propane and regular gasoline. No moorage facilities.

Lieutenant L.A. Zagoskin of the Imperial Russian Navy first reported Selawik's existence in the 1840s as the settlement of "Chilivik." Some traditional sod houses are still found in this Eskimo village. Selawik is a second-class city, incorporated in 1977.

The economic base is arts and crafts, and subsistence hunting and fishing. Some residents are employed as firefighters during the summer. Fish include whitefish, sheefish, grayling, northern pike and arctic char. Caribou and moose are the most important game animals.

Selawik is located near Selawik National Wildlife Refuge. The refuge includes the delta area formed by the Kobuk and Selawik rivers, an important breeding and resting spot for migratory waterfowl. The Selawik River is classified as a wild and scenic river.

Communications in Selawik include phones, mail plane, radio and cable TV. The community is served by Seventh-Day Adventist and Baptist churches and a Friends Mission. It also has 2 schools with grades preschool through 12. There is a cooperative electricity system, and parts of town have public water. The sewage system is honey buckets. Selawik prohibits the sale and importation of alcoholic beverages. Freight arrives by cargo plane and barge. Government address: City of Selawik, P.O. Box 49,

Selawik, AK 99770; phone 484-2132. Village corporation address: NANA Regional Corp., P.O. Box 49, Kotzebue, AK 99752.

Shungnak

[MAP 20] *(SHUNG-nak)* Located on the Kobuk River, 150 miles east of Kotzebue and 300 miles west of Fairbanks. **Transportation:** Boat; scheduled or charter airline from Kotzebue; snowmachine or dogsled in winter. **Population:** 245. **Zip code:** 99773. **Emergency Services:** Police, phone 437-2147; Alaska State Troopers, Kotzebue, phone 442-3222; Clinic, phone 437-2138; Volunteer Fire Department.

Elevation: 140 feet. **Climate:** Shungnak is in the continental climate zone and has long, cold winters and relatively warm summers. Mean precipitation is 16 inches, including 71 inches of snow.

Private Aircraft: Airstrip 0.5 mile from village; elev. 200 feet; length 3,300 feet; gravel; fuel 80, 100; unattended. No facilities at airport. Transportation available to village.

Visitor Facilities: Accommodations and other services available at Commack Lodge & Store (437-2157). Laundromat available. No banking services. Groceries and supplies available at Shungnak Native Store (437-2148) and Commack Lodge & Store. Arts and crafts available for purchase include birch-bark baskets, jade, beadwork, masks, mukluks, beaver hats, mittens, parkas and bone carvings. Fishing/hunting licenses available, as well as guide service for river floating, dog mushing and other activities. Some repair service available for marine engines, boats and autos. Fuel available includes marine gas, diesel, kerosene, propane and regular and unleaded gasoline. Moorage available for boats.

The original settlement of Shungnak was 10 miles upriver at the present location of Kobuk. Residents relocated in the 1920s because of riverbank erosion at the old site. Shungnak was incorporated as a second-class city in 1967.

Shungnak has a subsistence economy based on fishing and hunting. Fish include sheefish, whitefish, salmon and grayling. Game animals are caribou, moose and bear, as well as ducks and geese. There also is trapping for marten, beaver, fox, lynx, otter, wolverine and wolf.

There also is seasonal employment in construction, fire-fighting, mining and recreation, and some year-round employ-

ment with the local government and schools.

The 347-mile-long Kobuk, a wild and scenic river and the ninth largest in Alaska, begins in Gates of the Arctic National Park and Preserve. It has become popular for float trips to Shungnak and beyond to Kobuk Valley National Park. The upper river is excellent for bird watching in spring and summer. The river is generally safe for boats from the last week of May to the first week in October. (See also River Running this section).

Onion Portage Archaeological District, listed on the National Register of Historic Places, is 35 miles downriver from Shungnak. First discovered by Dr. J. Louis Giddings in 1941, this site containing 30 layers of middens and old dwellings is described as the most important ever found in the Arctic.

Other recreational activities in the area include camping, hiking, canoeing, gold panning and photography, as well as observing jade mines at Dahl Creek near Kobuk and at Jade Mountain.

Communications include phones, mail plane, radio and TV. The community is served by Friends, Baptist and Seventh-Day Adventist churches, as well as a school with grades preschool to 12. Shungnak has a strong and active elders council. There are community water, sewage disposal and electricity systems. Shungnak prohibits the sale and importation of alcoholic beverages. Freight arrives by cargo plane and barge. Government address: City of Shungnak, P.O. Box 59, Shungnak, AK 99773; phone 437-2161, fax 437-2176. Village corporation address: NANA Regional Corp., P.O. Box 49, Kotzebue, AK 99752.

Umiat

[MAP 20] Located on the Colville River, 75 miles south of Harrison Bay and 340 miles north-northwest of Fairbanks. **Transportation:** Charter aircraft from Prudhoe Bay. **Population:** 5. **Zip code:** 99790. **Emergency Services:** North Slope Borough Public Safety Officer, Prudhoe Bay; Small local dispensary or Prudhoe Bay Clinic.

Elevation: 340 feet. **Climate:** Cool, fairly dry summers, but it can be windy. Extremely cold winters; Umiat frequently is the coldest reporting station in Alaska. Mean annual precipitation is 6.5 inches including 34 inches of snow.

Private Aircraft: Airstrip adjacent; elev. 266 feet; length 5,400 feet; gravel; fuel 80, 100 and jet; attended regularly; visual inspection recommended prior to using. Mountain ridges north and south. Restrooms at airport.

Visitor Facilities: Rustic accommodations available at a lodge. Rates in excess of $100 per night, including meals. Single, family-style meals can be purchased. Facilities are managed by O.J. and Eleanor Smith, who staff the weather station. Their Umiat Enterprises can be contacted for fuel, sandwiches, rooms or guiding services. Address: Box 60569, Fairbanks, AK 99706; phone 488-2366 (North Pole) or 452-9158 (Umiat via Fairbanks). No laundromat, banking services or stores. No arts and crafts available. Fishing/hunting licenses not available. Fly-in hunting can be arranged. Limited aircraft repair available. Charter service is the only rental transportation. Float trips starting at the Killik River floating to Umiat on the Colville River are best in the fall when moose, caribou and grizzlies can be seen. Fuel available for aircraft only. No moorage facilities.

An emergency airfield was established here and in 1945 it became a supply and operations base for oil exploration. It still is a major airfield and refueling stop between Fairbanks and Barrow.

There is excellent moose and caribou hunting along the Colville River west of the village. Caribou hunting is usually best the week before moose season opens in early September. There are good landing areas for light planes on river bars, and coal from the riverbank can be used for fires.

Communications at Umiat include phones, mail plane, radio and TV. There is no church or school. Also, no public water, sewage or electricity systems. Freight arrives by cargo plane.

Wainwright

[MAP 19] Located on Chukchi Sea coast, 85 miles southwest of Point Barrow, 520 miles north-northwest of Fairbanks. **Transportation:** Scheduled airline or charter plane from Barrow. **Population:** 502. **Zip code:** 99782. **Emergency Services:** Public Safety Officer, phone 763-2911; Clinic, phone 763-2714; North Slope Borough Fire Department.

Elevation: 30 feet. **Climate:** Maximum daily temperature above freezing point only 123 days of the year. Mean annual precipitation is 5.85 inches.

Private Aircraft: Wainwright airstrip 0.3 mile south; elev. 30 feet; length 4,700 feet; gravel; no fuel; unattended; visual inspection recommended prior to using. No facilities at airport. Public transportation available to village.

Visitor Facilities: Accommodations and food available at Olgonik Corp. Hotel and Restaurant (763-2514). No banking services. Laundromat available. Groceries and other supplies at Wainwright Co-op (763-2715). Local arts and crafts available for purchase are carved ivory figurines and jewelry, baleen boats, whale bone carvings, clocks, knitted caps and gloves. Fishing/hunting licenses available, as well as guide service. No major repair service. Arrangements can be made to rent private autos, off-road vehicles and boats. Fuel available includes marine gas, diesel, propane, unleaded, regular and supreme. No moorage facilities.

For centuries villages have stood on the land between Wainwright Inlet and the sea, the most recent one being the Inupiat Eskimo village of Wainwright. Wainwright Inlet was named in 1826 by Capt. F.W. Beechey for his officer, Lt. John Wainwright. The present village was established in 1904 when the Alaska Native Service built a school. The community was incorporated as a second-class city in 1962.

Wainwright's subsistence hunting economy is based primarily on whales and caribou, but some residents work at local businesses, the borough government and seasonal construction. Villagers' lives revolve around whaling during the spring and summer months, and the taking of a bowhead or beluga whale is cause for celebration — a Nalukatak festival, which takes place usually in June. Eskimo dances also are performed occasionally by the villagers. Other recreational activities in the village include boating; riding snowmobiles and 3-wheelers; and smelt fishing on the lagoon in the spring. Bird watching can be done anywhere on the tundra away from the village and seashells can be found on the beach.

Communications in Wainwright include phones, mail plane, radio and TV. The community is served by 3 churches and a school with grades preschool through 12. Public water and electricity is available; sewage system is primarily chemical toilets. Wainwright prohibits the sale and importation of alcoholic beverages. Freight arrives in the community by cargo plane and barge. Government address: City of Wainwright, P.O. Box 9, Wainwright, AK 99782; phone 763-2815 or 763-2726. Village corporation address: Olgoonik Corp., General Delivery, Wainwright, AK 99782.

▼ A T T R A C T I O N S ▼

National and State Parks, Etc.

Cape Krusenstern National Monument

This 660,000-acre monument, 10 miles northwest of Kotzebue, contains some of the most important prehistoric sites in the Arctic. The 114 beach ridges of Cape Krusenstern and nearby bluffs contain a chronological record of some 4,000 years of prehistoric and historic use, primarily by Native groups. The ridges were formed by shifting sea ice, ocean currents and waves, each new one being used in succession by Eskimos for their hunting camps. Eskimos still hunt seals along the cape's outermost beach. At shoreline campsites, the women trim and render the catch for the hides, and the meat and seal oil that are still vital to their diet.

Climate: Cloudy skies, frequent fog, westerly winds and minor fluctuations in daily temperatures are normal in the monument. Average daily summer temperatures range from 43°F to 53°F, with the highest temperatures occurring in July. Coldest months are January until early March, when average daily temperatures range between -20°F and 0°F. August is the wettest month, with a mean monthly precipitation of 2.26 inches.

Wildlife: The monument includes grizzly bears, Dall sheep, caribou, moose, wolves, lynx and an occasional musk-ox. Walrus, polar bears and several species of seals and whales can be seen offshore at various times of the year. Many species of waterfowl nest around the lagoons in summer. Fish in monument waters include whitefish, arctic char, 2 species of salmon (including chums), northern pike, burbot, Dolly Varden and herring.

Activities: Recreational activities in the monument include primitive camping, hiking, bird watching and fishing. Visitors to the monument should be self-sufficient and prepared for a variety of weather conditions. Contact the Park Service for specific information before traveling to the area; leave a copy of your planned itinerary with the regional office.

The National Park Service office maintains a list of businesses licensed to provide services within the monument. Nonlicensed businesses may provide services outside the monument boundaries only. Contact the business for information on services and prices.

Accommodations: There are no accommodations or campgrounds within the monument. A hotel is located at Kotzebue. Camping is permitted throughout most of the monument, except in archaeological zones, where it would interrupt subsistence activities, or on private land holdings located primarily along river and beachfronts. There is a dilapidated shelter cabin in the monument, but no National Park Service facilities, trails or services.

Access: There are daily commercial jet flights from Anchorage to Kotzebue. From Kotzebue, access to the monument is by chartered light aircraft (1-hour roundtrip) or boat. When there is adequate sea ice in winter, access by snow machine and dogsled is possible. Weather is extremely variable and can curtail travel to the monument at any time of year. Airplanes may not be used in pursuit of subsistence hunting and fishing. Helicopter landings are not permitted unless authorized by written permit from the monument superintendent.

For more information: Contact or visit the Park Service visitor information center in Kotzebue or contact: Superintendent, Cape Krusenstern National Monument, P.O. Box 1029, Kotzebue, AK 99752; phone 442-3890. Related USGS Topographic maps: Noatak, Kotzebue, Point Hope and DeLong Mountains.

Gates of the Arctic National Park and Preserve

The major feature of this 8-million-acre park and preserve is the Brooks Range, an extension of the Rocky Mountains that stretches across Alaska from the Canadian border almost to the Chukchi Sea. Gates of the Arctic was the name that Robert Marshall, a forester who explored the then-unmapped areas north and west of Wiseman in the 1920s and 1930s, gave Boreal Mountain and Frigid Crags. Marshall named both, and they rise like sentinels on either side of the North Fork Koyukuk River.

Climate: Long, cold winters and short, mild summers are the rule. On the Brooks Range's south slopes midsummer temperatures range from 32°F to 85°F; winter temperatures range from 32°F to -60°F. North of the Brooks Range, summer temperatures are much cooler; winter temperatures are somewhat milder but there is more wind. Annual precipitation of 8 to 10 inches classifies the area as semiarid, but this can be hard to believe while slogging through frequent showers and boggy tundra during the summer, particularly August. Mid-May through mid-August, the area has 18 to 24 hours of daylight. North of the Continental Divide snow may fall every month of the year and freezing temperatures occur by early September, sometimes in mid-August.

Wildlife: Thirty-six species of mammals live in the park and preserve, ranging in size from lemmings to grizzly bears. There are moose, caribou, Dall sheep, black bears, wolves, beavers, hoary marmots, wolverines, otters, martens, mink, weasels, lynx, red foxes, porcupines and an assortment of small rodents. Eagles and many migratory birds inhabit the area. Fish include grayling in clear streams and lakes; lake trout in larger, deep lakes; char in streams on the North Slope; and sheefish and chum salmon in the Kobuk and lower Alatna rivers. The productivity of fisheries is low due to the short seasons and cold waters of the Arctic.

Activities: Six designated wild rivers flow within and out of Gates of the Arctic: Noatak, Alatna, John, Kobuk, Tinayguk and North Fork Koyukuk. These, plus the Killik, are considered floatable by the National Park Service. (See River Running this section.) The Mount Igikpak and Arrigetch areas offer superb rock and mountain climbing, as well as impressive photographic opportunities. Hiking in the Arctic is made more difficult by tussocks and abundant wet areas. Hikers should plan on no more than 5 miles per day. Boaters and backpackers generally are dropped off and picked up by chartered aircraft. Winter activities include cross-country skiing, snowshoeing and dogsledding. Sport hunting is allowed in the 2 preserve areas in the northeast and southwest.

Gates of the Arctic is a remote wilderness. Animals are wild and unpredictable. Keep a clean camp and use common sense. Cook away from your camp. Local residents carry on subsistence activities within the park and preserve, and their camps, fishnets and other equipment should not be disturbed.

Accommodations: Bettles has a lodge, general store and canoe rentals. There are no campgrounds in the park, but wilderness camping is allowed. To minimize impact, visitors are asked to camp on gravel bars or areas with hardy heath or moss. There are no established Park Service facilities, roads or trails in the area. Some cases of giardiasis, a parasitic infection of the intestines, have been reported and visitors may wish to boil or purify drinking water.

Access: Most people get to the central Brooks Range via scheduled flights from Fairbanks to Bettles, where they charter small aircraft for flights into the park and preserve. Charter flights also can begin in Fairbanks, Kotzebue and Ambler, and additional scheduled flights are available from Fairbanks to Allakaket and Anaktuvuk Pass. There is overland access from the Dalton Highway at Coldfoot and Wiseman at the southeast corner of Gates of the Arctic. Ultralights or helicopters are not permitted to land in the park or preserve.

For more information: Contact Superintendent, Gates of the Arctic National Park and Preserve, P.O. Box 74680, Fairbanks, AK 99707; phone 456-0281. Related USGS Topographic maps: Chandler Lake, Wiseman, Survey Pass, Killik River, Hughes, Ambler River, Philip Smith Mountains, Chandalar.

Kobuk Valley National Park

This 1.7-million-acre park encompasses a nearly enclosed mountain basin on the middle section of the Kobuk River in northwestern Alaska, 350 miles west-northwest of Fairbanks and 75 miles east of Kotzebue. Today's cold, dry climate approximates that of the ice age and supports similar plants. During the Pleistocene epoch, the Kobuk Valley provided an ice-free corridor joined to the land bridge that periodically formed between Alaska and Siberia. The valley contains artifacts dating 12,500 years of human occupation. At Onion Portage, near the eastern boundary of the park, Dr. J. Louis Giddings, the same archaeologist who made the discoveries at Cape Krusenstern, found what has been described as the most important archaeological site unearthed in the Arctic. The diggings are now within a designated National Register Archaeological District. Great herds of caribou still cross the Kobuk River at Onion Portage, attracting hunters today just as they did long ago.

Covering 25 square miles south of the Kobuk River are the wind-sculpted Great Kobuk Sand Dunes, some up to 100 feet high and overrunning the nearby forest. These, along with the Little Kobuk Sand Dunes near Onion Portage, and the Hunt River Dunes, are among the few dune fields found in the Arctic.

Within the park, the Salmon River has been classified a wild and scenic river. The Kobuk River is designated a wild and scenic river from where it flows out of Walker Lake to the western boundary of Gates of the Arctic National Preserve, located east of Kobuk Valley National Park.

Climate: Long, cold winters and warm, brief summers characterize the park. Summer highs in the mid-80s to 92°F have been recorded, but the mean July temperature is in the mid-50s. Winter temperatures can drop to -60°F, and -20°F is common. Freezeup usually occurs from early to mid-

October and breakup in mid- to late May. Mosquitoes appear in late May, are worst in June and disappear in August, when the whitesox and gnats come on the scene until the September frosts.

Wildlife: Animals found in the park include grizzly and black bears, caribou, moose, wolves, lynx, martens, wolverines and some Dall sheep. Numerous ponds and oxbows provide excellent waterfowl habitat; more than 100 species of birds have been spotted in the area. Arctic peregrine falcons may pass through the park during migrations. Fish found in park waters include 3 species of salmon, grayling, pike and sheefish.

Activities: Most visitors float through the park on the Kobuk River. (See River Running this section.) Some start at the headwaters in Gates of the Arctic National Preserve, while others begin their trips in Ambler, Shungnak or Kobuk. The Great Kobuk Sand Dunes can be reached by an easy hike from the river. The lower Salmon River offers good canoeing and kayaking. Other activities include backpacking in the Baird and Waring mountains, fishing and photography. Sport hunting is prohibited.

In Kobuk Valley National Park, human settlement and use of the land is part of the area's heritage. People have hunted and fished in this region for centuries and continue to do so. Please do not interfere with local subsistence activities. Private land

Hikers explore the Great Kobuk Sand Dunes in Kobuk Valley National Park. (Karen Jettmar)

within the park boundaries, mostly along the Kobuk River corridor, should not be used without permission.

Accommodations: No accommodations are available in the park and none are planned. There are no established campgrounds; primitive camping is permitted throughout the park, except in archaeological zones and on private lands along the Kobuk River. There is a hotel at Kotzebue and a lodge at Ambler. Limited amounts of groceries, gasoline and other supplies can be purchased in the villages. There are no Park Service facilities, roads or trails. The only public-use facility in the park is an emergency shelter near the mouth of the Salmon River.

Access: Aircraft provide the primary access to the park, although boats can be taken from Kotzebue during the ice-free season to the 5 villages on the Kobuk River. The Upper Kobuk River can be reached from Kotzebue, Ambler, Bettles or Fairbanks. There are regularly scheduled flights from Kotzebue to the villages on the Kobuk. Flights may be chartered from Kotzebue, Kiana, Ambler or Bettles to land on sand bars or beaches. Other means of travel in the region are snow machines and dogsleds during the winter.

For more information: The national park office maintains a list of businesses licensed to provide services within the park. Nonlicensed businesses may provide service outside the park boundaries only. Contact the specific business to find out information about their services and prices. For the list and other information, write Supervisor, National Park Service, Northwest Alaska Areas, P.O. Box 1029, Kotzebue, AK 99752; phone 442-3760.

Noatak National Preserve

This 6.6-million-acre preserve, located 350 miles northwest of Fairbanks and 16 miles northeast of Kotzebue, protects the largest untouched mountain-ringed river basin in America. Of its area, 5.8 million acres have been designated wilderness. The 396-mile-long Noatak River is contained within a broad and gently sloping valley which stretches more than 150 miles east-west. The river, from its source in Gates of the Arctic National Park to its confluence with the Kelly River in Noatak National Preserve, is part of the National Wild and Scenic Rivers System. This is one of the finest wilderness areas in the world and

UNESCO has designated it an International Biosphere Reserve.

The Noatak River passes through 6 regions on its way to the sea: headwaters at the base of Igikpak Mountain; the great Noatak Basin with its rounded mountains and plentiful wildlife; the 65-mile-long Grand Canyon of the Noatak and the much steeper, 7-mile Noatak Canyon; plains dotted with spruce, balsam and poplar; the rolling Igichuk Hills; and finally the flat coastal delta.

Climate: Long, cold winters and short, mild summers are the rule in this area. Temperatures during June, July and August range from 40°F to 85°F, with average midsummer daytime temperatures in the 60s and 70s. However, subfreezing temperatures can occur on summer nights. June is generally the clearest summer month; clouds increase in July and August. Fog around Kotzebue during the summer can create transportation problems. Winter temperatures sometimes drop to -50°F, and -20°F occurs often. Strong winds produce a severe windchill. Mosquitoes appear in late May, are worst in June and disappear in August. Whitesox are present from August until September frosts. Good insect repellent and a head net are essential.

Wildlife: The western Arctic caribou herd, numbering about 200,000 animals, crosses the preserve in April and August on migrations. Other wildlife seen in the preserve are moose, Dall sheep, grizzly bears, wolves, foxes, lynx, martens, beavers and muskrats. Approximately 125 species of birds have been identified in the preserve and another 31 are thought to occur, including the arctic peregrine falcon. Fish present in preserve waters include grayling, char, salmon, lake trout, burbot, pike and whitefish.

Activities: Recreational activities in the preserve include floating down the Noatak by raft, canoe or kayak; backpacking along the river and in the foothills; wildlife observing; and photography. (For more information on floating the Noatak see River Running this section.) Sportfishing and hunting are allowed in season. The National Park Service cautions that the Noatak basin is one of the least-traveled areas in Alaska. A passing aircraft may not even be seen for days. You are truly "on your own" here. For safety, leave a copy of your itinerary with the Park Service in Kotzebue and carry a few days extra supply of food. Local residents carry on subsistence activities within the preserve. Their camps, fishnets and other equipment should not be disturbed.

Accommodations: There are no accommodations or campgrounds within the preserve. Camping is permitted throughout the preserve; however, there are numerous private holdings along the lower Noatak River in the preserve and these properties should be respected.

Access: The preserve can be reached by charter aircraft from Kotzebue, Ambler, Bettles or Kiana. Chartered flights usually land on gravel bars in the river. Numerous gravel bars suitable for landing most of the season are located throughout the preserve. Float-planes may also be landed throughout the preserve and are available from some of the charter services. Other means of travel are by boat from Kotzebue in summer, and by snow machine and dogsled in winter. All travel is dependent on the weather. There are no trails or roads in the preserve.

For more information: The National Park Service maintains a list of businesses licensed to provide services within the preserve. Nonlicensed businesses may not provide services inside the preserve boundaries. Contact the specific businesses for informa-

tion about their services and prices. For a copy of the list and other information, write the Supervisor, National Park Service, Northwest Alaska Areas, P.O. Box 1029, Kotzebue, AK 99752; phone 442-2760. Related USGS Topographic maps: Survey Pass, Ambler River, Howard Pass, Baird Mountains, Misheguk Mountain.

Wildlife Refuges

Arctic National Wildlife Refuge

The 19.3-million-acre Arctic National Wildlife Refuge (ANWR) in the northeastern corner of Alaska encompasses some of the most spectacular arctic plants, wildlife and land forms in the world. Designed to preserve a large portion of the migration routes of the great Porcupine caribou herd, numbering about 160,000 animals, ANWR is also home to musk-oxen, Dall sheep, moose, packs of wolves and such solitary species as wolverine, polar bear and grizzly bear. Some 160 species of birds can be seen in the refuge. Thousands of ducks, geese, swans and loons breed on coastal tundra, and birds throng coastal migration routes all summer. Snowy owls, peregrine falcons, gyrfalcons, rough-legged hawks and golden eagles nest inland.

The refuge extends from the Porcupine River basin near the Canadian border north through the Sheenjek River valley and across the eastern Brooks Range down to the Arctic Ocean. Much of this land is above tree line and offers rugged, snowcapped, glaciated peaks, and countless streams and rivers that drain north into the Beaufort Sea and south into the Porcupine and Yukon drainages.

Climate: Winter in the refuge is long and severe; summer is brief and intense. Snow showers can occur at any time, but days can be warm in June and July. Mountain lakes usually are ice free by mid-July; south slope lakes usually open by mid-June. Daylight is nearly continuous in summer. Frost is not uncommon in August; by early August autumn has turned the tundra scarlet. Snow usually covers the ground at least 9 months of the year. Arctic plants survive even though permafrost is within 2 feet of the surface. Annual growth of trees and shrubs is slight. It may take 300 years for a white spruce at tree line to reach a diameter of 5 inches; small willow shrubs may be 50 to 100 years old.

Activities: Visitors to the refuge have rapidly increased in the last few years. Development interests, especially oil, have

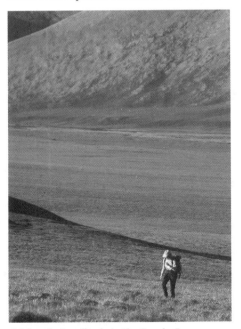

A hiker finds solitude in the Brooks Range. (Karen Jettmar)

focused on the refuge, helping to create an unprecedented interest in recreational visits. Rivers, especially the Kongakut, Hulahula, Canning and Sheenjek, are getting high numbers of visitors. Recreational activities include kayaking and rafting on rivers both north and south of the Brooks Range. Plane charters out of Fort Yukon, Deadhorse and Fairbanks land parties at access sites throughout the refuge for excellent hiking and backpacking. Though not common, mountain climbing on 9,020-foot Mount Chamberlin and 8,855-foot Mount Michelson is possible. Coastal lagoons and other areas of the refuge offer excellent wildlife observation opportunities. The refuge includes 3 wild and scenic rivers: the Ivishak, Sheenjek and Wind. (See River Running this section for more information.)

This area, possibly more than anywhere else in America, can provide a true wilderness experience in which the wild has not been taken out of the wilderness. There is little information about specific hiking areas and rivers in the refuge, and there are no established trails or campsites. Visitors planning a trip to ANWR should be prepared mentally and physically, be well-equipped and understand the risks involved.

Accommodations: There are no lodges or other commercial facilities in the refuge. Food and equipment should be purchased in Fairbanks. Some supplies may be available in Kaktovik, but travelers should come prepared and not count on being able to buy essential items there. Camping is permitted throughout the refuge; use of stoves is recommended because wood supplies are scarce. To avoid giardiasis, boil or purify drinking water. Mosquitoes are most numerous in June and July; a good insect repellent and a head net are recommended.

Access: The only access to the refuge is by air. Commercial air service is available from Fairbanks to Fort Yukon, Arctic Village, Deadhorse and Kaktovik on Barter Island, the usual jumping-off sites for refuge visitors. Charter air service is available at Deadhorse and Fort Yukon, and should be prearranged whenever possible. Private aircraft are permitted in the refuge; helicopter use requires a special permit from the refuge manager. Off-road vehicles are not permitted.

For more information: Contact Refuge Manager, Fish and Wildlife Service, Arctic National Wildlife Refuge, Room 266, Federal Bldg. and Courthouse, 101 12th Ave., Box 20, Fairbanks, AK 99701; phone 456-0250.

Selawik National Wildlife Refuge

This 2.15-million-acre refuge straddles the Arctic Circle in northwestern Alaska, 360 miles northwest of Fairbanks. The northeastern part of the refuge (240,000 acres) is wilderness. The refuge's northern boundary abuts Kobuk Valley National Park, and its southeastern corner joins Koyukuk National Wildlife Refuge. Its northwestern edge lies along Hotham Inlet across from Baldwin Peninsula and Kotzebue, the region's largest town. Selawik is a showcase of estuaries, lakes, river deltas and tundra slopes. Its most prominent feature is an extensive system of tundra wetlands nestled between the Waring Mountains and Selawik Hills.

The refuge is located near the Bering Land Bridge that once connected Asia and North America. Many years ago animals and humans migrated across here. In later years prospectors searched for gold. The refuge contains relics of these ancient and recent migrations.

Climate: Temperatures in June and July reach 70°F and 80°F, and there is 24-hour daylight. Insects become bothersome by mid-July. Winter comes quickly and temperatures reach the -20°F mark in October. Temperatures are coldest in January and February, when it can drop to -60°F. By the winter solstice there is only 1 hour and 43 minutes of daylight each day.

Wildlife: Selawik is a vital breeding and resting area for a multitude of migratory waterbirds. Nesting ducks number nearly 100,000. Tundra swans, sandhill cranes, Canada and white-fronted geese, and several species of loons are also common in the area. Thousands of caribou winter in the refuge, feeding on lichen-covered foothills. Other common mammals include moose, grizzly bears and other furbearers. Sheefish (some weighing 40 pounds), whitefish, grayling and northern pike inhabit lakes, ponds, streams and rivers.

Activities: Recreation in the refuge includes hiking, boating, camping, wildlife viewing and photography. Portions of the Selawik River are designated as a wild river, and it provides good river rafting and sportfishing. Limited commercial guide service is available. Hunting, trapping and fishing are permitted in accordance with state and federal regulations. Main activities in the refuge are subsistence hunting, fishing and edible plant gathering by local residents. There are more than 500 Native allotments in the refuge, which are private land and should not be trespassed. These allotments are mainly along the rivers, including the wild river portion of the Selawik River.

The Fish and Wildlife Service cautions that the Selawik Refuge, like most of Alaska, has changeable weather. Visitors must be self-sufficient and prepared for emergencies as well as inclement weather.

Access: The refuge is accessible by boat, aircraft, snowmobile, dog team, foot and cross-country skis depending on the season and weather. There are no roads. Scheduled air service is available to Kotzebue from Anchorage, and to Selawik, Kiana and Noorvik from Kotzebue. Charter air service to the refuge is available at Kiana, Ambler, Galena and Kotzebue. In the summer, floatplane and boats are the only practical way of visiting refuge islands and waters.

For more information: Contact Refuge Manager, Selawik National Wildlife Refuge, P.O. Box 270, Kotzebue, AK 99752; phone 442-3799.

River Running

Rafts, canoes, kayaks and klepper boats can all be used on the rivers; however, rafts are the most popular because of their portability in aircraft. Unless they are collapsible, canoes and kayaks are expensive to transport and are more hazardous in the whitewater sections found on many rivers, especially those found on the north slope of mountains in the Arctic National Wildlife Refuge.

Rivers must always be evaluated and run according to current conditions. River ratings are somewhat subjective and can change slightly depending on the stage of the river at any one time. Although rivers are generally open June through September, the safest water levels and best weather occur during July and early August. Visitors should be cautious of the higher-than-average flows that can occur any time of the year, especially after localized heavy rains upstream. It is usually possible to line through or portage the most difficult sections of the rivers.

Spring breakup generally occurs on north-slope rivers during late May and early June. Water levels are often at flood stage during this time, and navigation is haz-

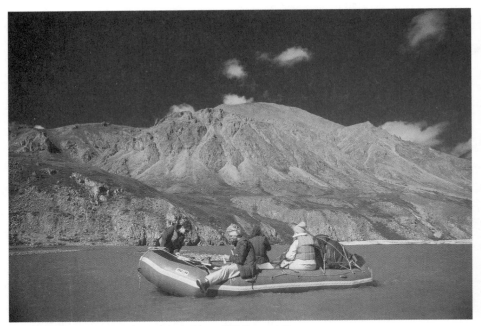

Rafters stop for a rest on the Hulahula River. (Bill Sherwonit)

ardous because of ice floes and aufeis (thick layers of ice formed by successive freezing of stream overflows during winter). During breakup, rivers carve vertical-walled canyons through aufeis fields that can be a mile or more in length. During early summer or high water later in the season, it can be dangerous to attempt travel through such areas. By mid- to late June, the channels are generally carved and melted wide enough to allow passage. However, aufeis fields can be dangerous any time during the summer if river levels rise as a result of rains upstream. Visitors should scout all ice areas prior to floating through to ensure that the river is not flowing under or through tunnels in the ice.

Aichilik River. The Aichilik begins among the high glaciated peaks of the Romanzof Mountains and flows north to the Arctic Ocean. Steep-sided valleys of the river's upper reaches provide scenic hiking but poor access; rapids, braiding and low flows combine to discourage floating. On the coastal plain, the river is the eastern boundary between the 1002 area and designated wilderness.

Alatna River. The upper portion of this designated wild and scenic river flows in Gates of the Arctic National Park on the south slope of the Brooks Range. River trips on the Alatna start in an area famous for the dramatic granite spires of Arrigetch Peaks to the west. The Alatna then meanders through the Endicott Mountains and the Helpmejack Hills, before winding through the lowlands of the Koyukuk River.

Highly advanced paddling skills are not required on this trip, but the country is a remote wilderness. Float trips start either at the headwater alpine lakes or from Arrigetch Creek, 47 miles downstream. For the first 5 miles out of the headwater lakes lining is necessary; then there is a short stretch of Class III rapids just above Ram Creek that is easily portaged. The next 22 miles to Arrigetch Creek is fast-flowing, with sweepers present. From Arrigetch Creek the Alatna flows slowly, offering a good float for those with moderate river experience.

There are numerous hiking and backpacking opportunities, as well as fishing for grayling, whitefish, arctic char and pike.

Access is by floatplane from Bettles or Fairbanks to the headwater lakes or to lakes near Arrigetch Creek. Exit is possible from the Indian village of Allakaket on the Koyukuk, where there are no accommodations, but there is scheduled air service to Fairbanks. The floater can also continue

down the Koyukuk. For more information contact Gates of the Arctic National Park, P.O. Box 74680, Fairbanks, AK 99707; phone 456-0281. Related USGS Topographic maps: Survey Pass, Hughes, Bettles.

Canning River. This is a fast whitewater river in the Arctic National Wildlife Refuge, beginning in the Franklin Mountains and flowing 125 miles northward, emerging west of Camden Bay on the Beaufort Sea. It flows through a scenic mountain valley and then through the arctic coastal lowlands. The clear Marsh Fork, the Canning's main tributary, passes through a narrow valley between mountains that rise sharply on both sides of the river. The main stem of the Canning River leaves the mountains about halfway from its origin. Portions of the main stem below the confluence of Marsh Fork are heavily braided and the channel must be carefully selected. Strong headwinds may impede progress on the lower river. The Marsh Fork has a couple of rocky stretches up to 4 miles long that have rapids in the upper limit of Class II.

Rafts or small whitewater kayaks may be used on the Marsh Fork or the main stem, while a folding boat is suitable only on the main stem.

This river corridor offers good hiking, arctic scenery, wildlife viewing opportunities, and fishing for arctic char, grayling and whitefish.

Access to the Canning is from Fairbanks, Deadhorse or Fort Yukon, or by charter wheel plane with short landing and takeoff capability to gravel bars on the Marsh Fork or the main stem. Pickup can be arranged from gravel bars in the Canning delta.

The Arctic National Wildlife Refuge is remote, weather is unpredictable and trips should be carefully planned. Information and assistance are available by writing Refuge Manager, Arctic National Wildlife Refuge, Room 266, Federal Bldg. and Courthouse, 101 12th Ave., Box 20, Fairbanks, AK 99701; phone 456-0250. Related USGS Topographic maps: Arctic and Mount Michelson.

Coleen River. The clear, shallow Coleen, which flows south on the east side of the Arctic National Wildlife Refuge, was a traditional route for Eskimos seeking trade with the Athabascan Indians. The river's upper tributaries are braided, have poor aircraft access and flow through scenic, but undramatic mountains. Although its forested middle and lower sections have good access, the Coleen is one of the refuge's less-floated rivers.

PORTAGING AND LINING ON THE KOBUK

From its headwaters on the southern slopes of Arrigetch Peaks, the Kobuk River flows 347 miles to the Chukchi Sea. For most of its course, it is a gentle Class I and II float. But the upper river and the small unnamed tributary feeding the Kobuk from Walker Lake have some dangerous white water. Most paddlers choose to portage and line their boats on these sections of the river, rather than risk wrecking a boat far from civilization. Karen Jettmar describes navigating this upper portion of the Kobuk in an August trip with a client and two friends. To reach the Kobuk, Karen, Kaci, Yolanda and Jo flew from Bettles into Walker Lake with two 2-person folding kayaks (airfare for all: about $700). The entire float, from Walker Lake to their pull-out at Kiana, took 15 days.

Less than a mile below the outlet of Walker Lake is a mile of Class IV-V rapids, with four major drops of several feet, boulders, haystacks, serious hydraulics and no clear path through which to steer a boat. Portaging this section is essential. For us that meant pulling out the kayaks, completely unloading them (after we had just packed them up a half hour before), and making 3 trips per person to carry the boats and gear over rough trail (or no trail), climbing over fallen trees, and squeezing the 17-foot-long boats between standing trees. All to avoid the impassable rapids.

Hours later, with sweat dripping from our brows, twigs clinging to our shirts, and a hole punched in one boat from a sharp tree branch, we had all our gear a half-mile downriver. The white water above had intimidated us; we decided to

hike downriver a distance to scout out more of the river.

Finding no more white water in the next mile, we returned to our mound of gear, patched one boat and reloaded both of them. After a snack, we gingerly pushed off into the current and made our way through Class II riffles and a few rocks. We had smooth traveling for the rest of the day.

The following day we reached Upper Kobuk Canyon, marked by a tall canyon wall on the left and a huge boulder mid-river. We pulled out on the right side of the river to scout it. There were rocks and riffles for more than a quarter of a mile. We probably could have run it, but we decided to play it safe. With one of us holding a 30-foot-long line attached to the bow of the kayak, and the other holding a line on the stern of the kayak, we walked the boats down the right shore of the river, pulling them in close and occasionally allowing them to run through the riffles.

Later that day we reached the Lower Kobuk Canyon (Class III-IV). We again pulled out on the right to scout. The water was high, with three sections of rapids. The first section had several large rock outcrops and standing waves. We opted to line the boats. Following a set of fresh bear tracks to a shale ledge, we walked along above the river, carefully pulling the boats in to shore as close as we could to prevent them from drifting into the rocks. Below our feet, the riverbank dropped off sharply.

The white water grew worse as we made our way downriver. There were more rocks and a couple of chutes with 5-

to 6-foot ledge drops, and a nasty hydraulic at the bottom, followed by a nearly unbroken line of boulders with narrow chutes and several more drops. I imagined my kayak cracking in half as it dropped down one of the chutes, and decided to continue lining the boat, despite the difficulty in maintaining my balance on the rock ledge, which was at that moment about to disappear into a rock wall.

Suddenly, over the roar of water reverberating through the canyon, I heard Kaci yell, "Bear!" Sure enough, there was a black bear swimming across the river toward us. The bear pulled out on the ledge where we had stood just moments before, apparently unaware of our presence.

Yolanda and I scaled the cliff to see how much farther the white water continued. Below this last ledge drop were a few rocks, and below that the way was clear. Ripe raspberries clung to a steep hillside, and we paused to eat a few sweet morsels. Then we pulled the kayaks down to the base of a sheer cliff where we could all hop into them again and make the last run through a few rocks. Bouncing through the last riffles, we pulled in to an island just below the canyon to take a breather. We were home free on the Kobuk River. Below us lay over 300 miles of pristine wild river, which we would come to know intimately over the next two weeks.

—*Karen Jettmar, who lives in Anchorage, is a writer/photographer and a guide for Equinox wilderness trips. She is also author of* The Alaska River Guide: Canoeing, Kayaking and Rafting in the Last Frontier *(Alaska Northwest Books, 1993).*

Colville River. This is Alaska's largest river north of the Continental Divide and is the seventh-longest in the state at 428 miles. The Colville heads in the De Long Mountains, part of the Brooks Range, and bisects the arctic lowlands as it flows east-northeast into Harrison Bay on the Arctic Ocean.

From its headwaters to the Kiligwa River, the Colville's water levels are shallow in some sections and must be lined. From the Kiligwa confluence to Umiat, 225 miles downriver, the Colville consists of several 1- to 4-mile pools connected by shallow riffles. The Colville is not considered a difficult river to run, but this is extremely remote country and travelers should be experienced with wilderness camping.

The North Slope of the Brooks Range has much wildlife, including lots of grizzly bears. Thousands of migratory birds breed and nest here. Most notable are nesting peregrine falcons (avoid disturbing these birds!), gyrfalcons and rough-legged hawks. Dall sheep, caribou, moose and fox also may be spotted. Other activities along the river include hiking and photography. Fishing is so-so for whitefish, arctic char, grayling, chum salmon, pike and trout.

Access is generally by scheduled commercial air service to Bettles, Kotzebue, Barrow or Prudhoe Bay, then charter plane to the Kiligwa River confluence. Exit is at Umiat or Nuiqsut, where there is air service to Barrow, Prudhoe Bay or Fairbanks. Related USGS Topographic maps: Misheguk Mountain, Utukok River, Howard Pass, Ikpikpuk River, Killik River, Umiat, Harrison Bay.

East Fork Chandalar River. The Chandalar is a major Yukon River tributary. The East Fork of the river flows swiftly south from its high mountainous headwaters nearly 60 miles through a wide, mountain-rimmed valley. From there it meanders slowly through a forested, lake-dotted valley. The river passes Arctic Village and serves as a highway to subsistence hunting, fishing and trapping areas.

Hulahula River. This river in the Arctic National Wildlife Refuge flows west and north 100 miles to Camden Bay on the Beaufort Sea about 20 miles from Barter Island. The trip generally takes 8 days from the headwaters (although this is highly variable) and gets a fair amount of use.

This river offers magnificent views of some of the highest mountains in the Brooks Range, then continues through canyons and gorges to the lowlands of the Arctic Slope.

Rapids between Class II and Class IV can be portaged or lined. Rafts and kayaks are suitable for this trip. It is recommended that anyone taking this trip be in top physical condition and an expert river runner, as this is a fast-flowing river with many boulders, drops and rapids. This river tends to carry a substantial glacial silt load in summer, and low water can be a problem in August, but generally is not a serious concern.

There are excellent hiking and photography opportunities. Wildlife viewing includes Dall sheep in the hills and vast herds of caribou on the coastal plain.

Access to the Hulahula is generally by scheduled air service from Fairbanks to Kaktovik. Charter flights are available from Kaktovik to and from the river. The river is generally accessed at a place called Grassers Strip. A narrow twisting pass across the continental divide between the headwaters of the Hulahula and Chandler rivers provides a natural hiking route and a frequently used corridor for airplanes. The river is heavily hunted and fished by Kaktovik villagers.

Arctic National Wildlife Refuge is remote, weather is unpredictable and trips should be carefully planned. Outfitters offer float trips on the Hulahula. Also, information and assistance with planning trips to the refuge are available by writing Refuge Manager, Arctic National Wildlife Refuge, Room 266, Federal Bldg. and Courthouse, 101 12th Ave., Box 20, Fairbanks, AK 99701; phone 456-0250. Related USGS Topographic maps: Barter Island A-5; Flaxman Island A-1; Mount Michelson B-1, C-1, D-1.

Ivishak River. A National Wild and Scenic River in Arctic National Wildlife Refuge, the Ivishak heads in the Philip Smith Mountains and flows northwest 95 miles through treeless arctic tundra to the Sagavanirktok River. Fed by flows from relic hanging glaciers, it is a highly braided, swift river, rated Class I white water, Class C flat water. The upper half of the Ivishak flows through tundra covered mountains with excellent hiking terrain. Floaters can continue down the Sagavanirktok River, traversing the North Slope. The lower Ivishak and the Sagavanirktok cross a broad open floodplain with scrub willow. Overflow ice on the floodplain can remain much of the summer, and scouting may be needed to be sure the river doesn't disappear under an ice shelf. Best time of year to float the river is July. Popular trip length is 95 to 150 miles. Although scenic, the river's shallow water, poorly defined channels and marginal access result in low use by floaters.

For more information: Contact Refuge Manager, Arctic National Wildlife Refuge, Room 266, Federal Bldg. and Courthouse, 101 12th Ave., Box 20, Fairbanks, AK 99701; phone 456-0250.

John River. This designated wild and scenic river in Gates of the Arctic National Park offers a rewarding voyage for the adventuresome traveler. It is possible to paddle the length of the river by starting at the Eskimo village of Anaktuvuk Pass. A short portage and lining on the small creek near the village is necessary. Experience is essential for safe negotiation of some fast water and easy rapids above Hunt Fork.

Most float trips, however, start at Hunt Fork and continue 100 miles to the confluence with the Koyukuk. The John, a clearwater tributary to the Koyukuk, then offers an exciting but safe trip through an extremely scenic area of the Brooks Range, which has not yet been exploited by large numbers of people. Rugged mountains along the way offer excellent hiking and are home to Dall sheep. Other wildlife that may be seen are grizzly bears, moose and wolves. Fishing is fair for grayling, whitefish, burbot, pike in the lakes, and chum salmon.

Access to the river is by floatplane from Bettles or Fairbanks to Hunt Fork Lake or Anaktuvuk Pass. It generally takes 5 days to float from Hunt Fork to the mouth of the John, then another half a day to line 5 miles up the Koyukuk to Bettles, where there are overnight accommodations and regularly scheduled air service to Fairbanks. Related USGS Topographic maps: Wiseman A-4, A-5, B-4, B-5, C-5, D-5; Bettles D-4.

Killik River. This scenic river heads in Gates of the Arctic National Park at the Continental Divide and flows northward 105 miles to the Colville River. The river passes through mountainous terrain and then into the lowlands of the Arctic Slope. The trip generally takes 10 days from the usual put-in point at Easter Creek to Umiat, on the Colville River about 70 miles downstream from the Killik River confluence.

The Killik offers Class I and Class II conditions throughout its course. About halfway to the Colville, Sunday Rapids might be Class I or Class II, depending on water levels and should be inspected before passage is attempted. A whitewater kayak is recommended for this river.

There is good hiking in the mountainous region, where Dall sheep can be seen. Wildlife viewing also can be excellent in the river valley, where grizzly bear, moose, caribou, wolf, fox, lynx and wolverine may be spotted. Fossils can be seen in rock outcroppings below Sunday Rapids. Fishing is for grayling, arctic char and pike.

Access is generally by scheduled airline from Fairbanks to Bettles, then charter floatplane from Bettles to the Easter Creek area. Pickup from gravel bars on the Colville just upstream from the Killik River confluence can be arranged. Or there is air service out of Umiat to Prudhoe Bay and Fairbanks. Related USGS Topographic maps: Survey Pass, Killik River, Ikpikpuk River.

Kobuk River. This 347-mile-long river is the ninth longest in Alaska and one of the most popular for float trips. (See "Portaging and Lining on the Kobuk" this section.) The Kobuk is designated a wild and scenic river from its headwaters at Walker Lake in Gates of the Arctic National Park to the park's western boundary. Lower stretches of the Kobuk pass through Kobuk Valley National Park.

The Kobuk flows between the Baird Mountains to the north and low-lying Waring Mountains to the south, and the wide, forested valley offers sweeping views. After 2 sets of rapids, which are usually portaged, the Kobuk winds through 2 canyons, then meanders serenely to the sea. The 125-mile journey to Kobuk, where most floaters stop, can be made in about 6 days by raft, kayak or canoe. Some floaters continue on to Kiana.

River floaters can fish for sheefish, northern pike, grayling, whitefish, chum salmon and, in Walker Lake, lake trout. Wildlife that may be seen along the river includes bears, moose, caribou and wolves.

The Kobuk has for centuries been a major river highway for both coastal and inland Eskimos and still is used as such today. Recreational river travelers are cautioned not to interfere with any subsistence activities taking place along the Kobuk. Also check with the National Park Service about the location of private lands.

Access to the Kobuk River is by floatplane from Bettles or Ambler to Walker Lake. All 5 villages along the river have scheduled air service to Kotzebue or Fairbanks. There are overnight accommodations in most of the villages. It's a good idea to contact the village ahead of time if you plan to spend time there. Several outfitters offer a variety of float trips down the Kobuk. Related USGS Topographic maps: Survey Pass, Hughes, Shungnak, Ambler River, Baird Mountains, Selawik.

Kongakut River. This is a high-use river in Arctic National Wildlife Refuge that flows through country of primeval beauty and wildness on the north slope of the Brooks Range. The Kongakut flows northeast from the Davidson Mountains, ending 100 miles away at Siku Lagoon, 8 miles northwest of Demarcation Point in the far northeast corner of Alaska. The trip generally takes 11 days from the headwaters.

Rafts or folding boats are suitable for this trip, which is suggested for the intrepid explorer in good condition. Recommended for experienced paddlers only, the river does have some Class III waters, although rapids are generally Class I and II.

The Fish and Wildlife Service says North Slope rivers tend to be swift and rocky. They also are icy cold, and life jackets should have pockets to carry waterproof matches, candles, insect repellent and other survival gear. Rivers on the North Slope usually are free-flowing by mid-June, and remain high and silty for several weeks, depending on the weather. Low water can be a concern in August, but is generally not a problem.

Wildlife viewing can be excellent in the refuge, particularly during migrations of the Porcupine caribou herd.

A kayaker lines a section of the Canning River (George Wuerthner)

Access to the Kongakut is generally by scheduled air service from Fairbanks to Kaktovik on Barter Island. Charter flights are available from Kaktovik to and from the river. The river is generally accessed fairly high in the headwaters at a place called Drain Creek. Most floaters take out at Caribou Pass, although some float all the way to Beaufort Sea.

Arctic National Wildlife Refuge is remote, weather is unpredictable and trips should be carefully planned. Information and assistance with planning trips to the refuge are available by writing Refuge Manager, Arctic National Wildlife Refuge, Room 266, Federal Bldg. and Courthouse, 101 12th Ave., Box 20, Fairbanks, AK 99701; phone 456-0520. Related USGS Topographic maps: Table Mountain, Demarcation Point.

Nigu-Etivluk. Both the Nigu and Etivluk rivers are small, swift and clear tributaries to the Colville River. The Nigu's headwaters are in Gates of the Arctic National Park, and it tumbles for 70 miles before joining the Etivluk. Then it's another 70 miles to the Colville.

The Nigu generally has shallow Class I water, with frequent Class II rapids. The Nigu is floatable by raft only until about the third week of June or by canoe or kayak until the last week of June. The Etivluk has fast Class I water, with scattered Class II rapids. Canoes or small rafts are recommended, although kayaks also are used. This trip passes through majestic mountains, rolling hills and level coastal plain. Animals that may be seen are grizzly bears, Dall sheep, caribou, wolves and foxes.

There is good hiking in the treeless valleys, and on the tundra ridges and lower mountains. Fishing is good for grayling, whitefish and arctic char.

Access is by floatplane from Bettles or Fairbanks to lakes at the Nigu headwaters (be prepared to portage a mile over soggy tundra from the headwaters) or to Nigtun Lake at the Etivluk headwaters. Arrange for pickup from lakes or gravel bars along the lower Etivluk or the Colville River. Or travel down the Colville to Umiat, which has air service to Prudhoe Bay and Fairbanks. Related USGS Topographic maps: Killik River, Howard Pass.

Noatak River. This 396-mile-long designated wild and scenic river winds through Gates of the Arctic National Park and Noatak National Preserve before flowing into Kotzebue Sound. Considered by many to be the finest wilderness river in the Arctic, the Noatak flows through forest and tundra

country entirely above the Arctic Circle. Highlights of this river are the mountains along the upper river, Noatak Canyon and the run to the sea below the village of Noatak. There are several stretches of Class II rapids, but the river is generally smooth flowing. The trip from the headwaters to the village of Noatak generally takes 16 days.

The Noatak features changing scenery along with a variety of animals and birds. The Noatak basin is particularly rich in migratory birds during spring and summer and the river traveler also may glimpse moose, caribou, wolves or grizzly bears. Fishing is good for grayling, whitefish, arctic char, pike and chum salmon. Wild berries are abundant in July and August.

Access to the Noatak generally begins with a commercial flight from Fairbanks to Bettles and a charter floatplane flight to any of several lakes along the upper river. There is scheduled air service from Noatak village to Kotzebue, or pickup can be arranged from scattered lakes, the river itself or gravel bars. For more information contact the Supervisor, National Park Service, Northwest Alaska Areas, P.O. Box 1029, Kotzebue, AK 99752; phone 442-3760. Related USGS Topographic maps: Survey Pass, Ambler River, Howard Pass, Misheguk Mountains, Baird Mountains, Noatak.

North Fork Koyukuk. This is a designated wild and scenic river in Gates of the Arctic National Park that provides a good family-type wilderness boating experience.

Canoe, raft or kayak can be used. The river is not difficult, but there are some sharp turns and obstacles to watch for. The river offers good hiking and scenery—waterfalls, jagged peaks and hanging valleys. Old cabins dot the banks—silent reminders of a historic mining past. Fishing is good for grayling, pike and whitefish.

Access to the river is generally by floatplane from Bettles to Summit Lake, or to lakes near the mouth of Redstar Creek. From Redstar Creek it takes approximately 4 to 5 days to float to Bettles. Bettles is served by scheduled commercial air service from Fairbanks and has meals and lodging.

For more information and a list of guide services licensed to operate in Gates of the Arctic contact the National Park Service, Box 74680, Fairbanks, AK 99707; phone 456-0281. Related USGS Topographic maps: Wiseman D-1, D-2, C-2, C-3, B-2, A-2, A-3; Bettles D-3, D-4; Chandler Lake A-1.

Redstone and Cutler rivers. These rivers in northwestern Alaska offer access from the

Kobuk River to the Noatak River. The traverse crosses some extremely remote country, but connects the 2 major river systems with an 8-mile portage.

Heading north from the village of Ambler to the Redstone River is recommended. The slow-flowing Redstone permits upstream paddling and easy lining.

A low valley opening shows one obvious route for the portage. A second, somewhat shorter portage is through the next valley, about 6 miles upriver. The clear and shallow Cutler River, which has a string of easy rapids, is just over the divide from the Redstone.

The traverse in the opposite direction (from the Cutler to the Redstone) is possible, but involves a longer upstream paddle and more lining.

Access to Ambler, which has overnight accommodations, is by plane from Kotzebue. Before making the traverse, it's advisable to contact the village of Ambler regarding your plans. Related USGS Topographic map: Ambler River.

Salmon River. A National Wild and Scenic River in Kobuk Valley National Park, the Salmon heads in the Baird Mountains and flows south 60 miles to the Kobuk River near its confluence with the Tutksuk River northeast of Kiana. The Salmon descends through a poplar-spruce forest in the western Brooks Range then meanders finally into the Kobuk. In its upper navigable reaches, below Anaktok and Sheep creeks, this clear small river alternates short shallow pools and riffles. Downriver, the pools lengthen and the river deepens. The river is also noted for its many beautiful rock outdroppings. It is rated Class I white water, Class A flat water. Best time of year to float is July to September. Popular trip length is 140 miles. For more information contact the Supervisor, National Park Service, Northwest Alaska Areas, P.O. Box 1029, Kotzebue, AK 99752; phone 442-3760.

Selawik River. This National Wild and Scenic River is located in Selawik National Wildlife Refuge. The Selawik heads in the Zane Hills and flows west 140 miles to Selawik Lake, an expansive body of water only 5 to 15 feet deep. A long, low-lying river, the Selawik rises at about 600 feet in spruce forests and follows a looped, meandering pattern west through treeless, pingo-dotted wetlands. The upper third of the river has numerous boulders and sweepers; on the lower 25 miles, the current is slow but strong west winds can build waves up to 3

feet high. It is rated Class I white water. Best time of year to float is July to September. Popular trip length is 230 miles. For more information contact the Refuge Manager, Selawik National Wildlife Refuge, P.O. Box 270, Kotzebue, AK 99752; phone 442-3799.

Sheenjek River. This National Wild and Scenic River flows 200 miles south to the Porcupine River. It is located in the Arctic National Wildlife Refuge. A gentle, clear-water river flowing through a broad valley, the Sheenjek drains the south slopes of the Romanzof Mountains and skirts some of the highest peaks in the Brooks Range. Providing a long, relatively easy float, it flows south from open tundra through subarctic boreal forest to the Yukon River wetlands. Since overflow ice can remain most of the summer, scout ahead to be sure the channel is open all the way through. Rated Class II white water and Class B flat water. Can be floated July to mid-September. Popular trip length is 270 miles. For more information contact the Refuge Manager, Arctic National Wildlife Refuge, Room 266, Federal Bldg. and Courthouse, 101 12th Ave., Box 20, Fairbanks, AK 99701; phone 456-0250.

Squirrel River. This is a clear water, free-flowing stream that originates in the Baird Mountains of northwestern Alaska. It flows for about 95 miles through a broad, mountain-flanked valley before entering the Kobuk River near the village of Kiana. The valley supports a variety of vegetative systems ranging from alpine tundra to upland spruce/hardwood and bottomland spruce/poplar forest. The Squirrel River is readily accessible by light aircraft from Kotzebue (approximately 30 minutes flying time, one way). It provides a relatively safe, easy float, although there is some white water in the upper few miles of the river. Sportfishing for arctic char, chum salmon and grayling is available. There is good hiking terrain in the headwaters area. Good overnight campsites are plentiful along most of the river. Additional information is available from the BLM office located in Kotzebue, Box 1049, Kotzebue, AK 99752; phone 442-3430. Related USGS Topographic maps: Baird Mountains A-3, A-4, A-5, B-5, B-6; Selawik D-3.

Tinayguk River. This National Wild and Scenic River rises in the Endicott Mountains and flows 44 miles south through alpine valley in the Brooks Range to the North Fork Koyukuk River. It is located in the Gates of the Arctic National Park. Rated Class II whitewater, the Tinayguk has extensive rocky rapids, especially at low water. Can be floated July to September. Popular trip length is 120 miles. For more information contact the Superintendent, Gates of the Arctic National Park and Preserve, P.O. Box 74680, Fairbanks, AK 99707; phone 456-0281.

Wild River. This clear, fast tributary of the Koyukuk flows from Wild Lake, where fishing is good for grayling, pike and lake trout, to the Koyukuk.

Trips on this river generally take place only in June, before water levels drop.

Floaters pass through beautiful mountain scenery, then into typical arctic taiga where the river occasionally slows on its meandering course to the Koyukuk River. Brief shallow areas may be encountered.

Access is possible by chartering a plane from Bettles to Wild Lake. The trip down the Wild River generally takes 4 to 6 days. After reaching the Koyukuk River, it's only a few miles downriver to Bettles where there are overnight accommodations and regularly scheduled flights to Fairbanks. Related USGS Topographic maps: Bettles D-3, D-4; Wiseman A-3, B-3, B-4, C-4.

Wind River. This river heads at 68°34'N, 147°18'W in the Brooks Range and flows southeast 80 miles within Arctic National Wildlife Refuge to the East Fork Chandalar River.

The Wind River at moderate to high-water stages is swift and is considered an exciting white water river for intermediate boaters. At these water levels, the river is Class II from the vicinity of Center Mountain for 22 miles, then there's a 10-mile stretch of Class I, followed by 7 miles of Class III and 25 miles of Class II. The last 6 miles are Class III. This trip generally takes 4 days. Rafts or kayaks are recommended; canoes are suitable for advanced paddlers. Below its confluence with the Wind River, the East Fork Chandalar is Class I, with some Class II rapids at low water levels. Lining through some boulder rapids may be necessary at low water.

On the Wind there is good mountain scenery and hiking, particularly along the upper river. There is fishing for arctic grayling, pike and whitefish. Travelers also can hike into several lakes close to the river for good pike fishing.

Access is by charter air service from Fairbanks or Fort Yukon to a lake behind Center Mountain or lakes farther downriver. Gravel bars in this area, or farther upriver, may be suitable for wheel planes; consult local pilots. Exit is from a lake located 5 miles below the confluence with the East Fork Chandalar River, possibly from East Fork itself, or continue on to Venetie, which has scheduled air service but no visitor facilities.

Related USGS Topographic maps: Christian, Arctic A-5, Philip Smith Mountains A-1, B-1.

Sportfishing

Rivers and lakes in the Arctic are accessible for sportfishing primarily by air, although riverboats occasionally can be rented or chartered at villages along the waterways. In the Far North there is virtually no sportfishing around communities such as Barrow, Kaktovik, Wainwright or Point Lay. However, there are lakes and rivers on the Arctic Slope that contain arctic char or Dolly Varden trout, which average 4 to 6 pounds, but can reach 12 to 15 pounds.

Lakes in the Brooks Range are popular for lake trout, which can reach 30 pounds. Anyone planning a trip to one of these mountain lakes should be aware that they may not be totally ice free until July. Listed in this section are some of the largest and most scenic of these lakes.

At other locations anglers can encounter sheefish, which can reach in excess of 50 pounds (53 pounds is the state record) in the Selawik-Kobuk area. Other species present in arctic waters are whitefish, which can reach 5 pounds; burbot (also called lush or lingcod) which can weigh in at 20 pounds; northern pike, which average 4-8 pounds, but can attain 30 pounds; and arctic grayling, which can reach 4 pounds and which fisheries biologists say can be found "everywhere it's clear and wet."

Most sportfishing in the Arctic takes place in August and September, with anglers flying their own planes or chartering aircraft in Fairbanks, Bettles, Kaktovik or Kotzebue. A general rule from the Alaska Dept. of Fish and Game is to "plan for the worst" when traveling in the Arctic. Take a few days extra food and allow for a flexible schedule since fickle weather can play havoc with the best laid plans.

For more information contact the Alaska Dept. of Fish and Game, Sport Fish Division, 1300 College Road, Fairbanks, AK 99701.

Anaktuvuk River. Located in the Brooks Range in Gates of the Arctic National Park near Anaktuvuk Pass. Good arctic char fishery at its best in September, use spoons and eggs. Air charter available at Bettles.

Canning River. Located at the western boundary of Arctic National Wildlife Refuge. Good arctic char fishery at its best in September, use spoons and eggs. Air charter service available in Fairbanks or Kaktovik.

Chandler Lake. Fly-in lake located on the north slope of the Brooks Range 26 miles west of Anaktuvuk Pass, about 1 hour by floatplane or small wheel plane from Bettles. Short, rough airstrip at lake. Ice may be present until July. Excellent lake trout and grayling fishing. Lake trout fishing best as ice is leaving, good through the season, use spoons or plugs; grayling year-round, use flies; arctic char through the season, best in fall, use spoons, eggs; whitefish also present, use flies, eggs. Air charter available in Bettles.

Elusive Lake. Located on the north slope of the Brooks Range 80 miles northeast of Anaktuvuk Pass. A popular lake trout fishery best just after the ice leaves, use spoons, plugs; grayling also present. Air charter available in Fairbanks or Bettles.

Fish Lake. Fly-in lake located south of the Brooks Range about 1 hour by floatplane from Bettles. Excellent lake trout, grayling and arctic char fishing. Lake trout fishing best in spring and good through the season, use spoons or plugs; arctic char through the season, best in fall, use spoons, eggs; grayling year-round, use flies; whitefish use flies, eggs. Air charter available in Bettles.

Helpmejack Lake. Fly-in lake located south of the Brooks Range west of Bettles about 35 minutes by floatplane. Lake trout fishing best in spring and good through the season, use spoons or plugs; northern pike year-round, best June 1 through Sept. 15, use spoons, spinners; whitefish use flies, eggs. Air charter available in Bettles.

Iniakuk Lake. Fly-in lake located south of the Brooks Range 50 miles west of Bettles. Lake trout fishing best in spring and good through the season, use spoons or plugs; northern pike year-round, best June 1 through Sept. 15, use spoons, spinners; whitefish use flies, eggs. Iniakuk Lake Lodge on lake. Air charter available in Bettles.

Itkillik Lake. Located on the north slope of the Brooks Range 60 miles northeast of Anaktuvuk Pass. A popular lake trout fishery best in spring just after the ice leaves, use spoons, plugs; grayling also present. Air charter available in Fairbanks or Bettles.

Kobuk River (Upper and Lower). Flows from Walker Lake in Gates of the Arctic National Park to Kotzebue Sound. Boats may be chartered from residents of villages along the Kobuk: Kiana, Noorvik, Ambler, Shungnak and Kobuk. The Kobuk is famous for sheefish, use spoons. It also has the northernmost commercial salmon (chum) fishery in the state. Northern pike year-round, best June 1 through Sept. 15, use spoons, spinners; grayling year-round, use flies; whitefish present in upper river, use flies, eggs. Air charter available in Kotzebue.

Kongakut River. Located within Arctic National Wildlife Refuge. Good arctic char fishery at its best in September, use spoons and eggs. Air charter service available in Fairbanks or Kaktovik.

Kurupa Lake. Located on the north slope of the Brooks Range 75 miles west of Anaktuvuk Pass. A popular lake trout fishery best in spring just after the ice leaves, use spoons, plugs; arctic char and grayling also present. Air charter available in Fairbanks or Bettles.

Nanushuk Lake. Fly-in lake located on the north slope of the Brooks Range northeast of Anaktuvuk Pass, about 1 hour by floatplane from Bettles. Lake trout fishing best as ice is leaving, good through the season, use spoons or plugs; grayling year-round, use flies; whitefish use flies, eggs. Air charter available in Bettles.

Noatak River. Fly-in river located in northwestern Alaska flows through Gates of the Arctic National Park and Noatak National Preserve to Kotzebue Sound. Arctic char fishing excellent in the fall, use spoons and eggs; grayling use flies; chum salmon July 15 through Sept. 30, peaking in August, use spoons; some pike also present. Arrangements may be made for accommodations at Noatak village. Commercial and charter air service available from Kotzebue.

Nutuvukti Lake. Fly-in lake located south of the Brooks Range in Gates of the Arctic National Preserve. No camps or boats available. Good summer fishery. Lake trout through the season, use spoons or plugs; grayling year-round, use flies; northern pike year-round, best June 1 through Sept. 15, use spoons, spinners; burbot throughout the season, best in fall and winter, use bait such as head or tail of lake trout. Charter floatplane available in Bettles or Kotzebue.

Round Lake. Fly-in lake located on the North Slope of the Brooks Range about 1 hour by floatplane from Bettles. Lake trout fishing best as ice is leaving, good through the season, use spoons or plugs; grayling good year-round, use flies; arctic char use spoons, eggs; whitefish use flies, eggs. Air charter available in Bettles.

Sagavanirktok River. Also known as "The Sag." Located on the Arctic Slope with its outlet near Prudhoe Bay. Good arctic char fishery at its best in September, use spoons and eggs. Char fishery outstanding on Ivishak River, a tributary to the Sagavanirktok. Air charter service available in Fairbanks, Prudhoe Bay or Kaktovik.

Schrader Lake. Located on the Arctic Slope 65 miles south of Barter Island. A popular lake trout fishery best in spring just after the ice leaves, use spoons, plugs; arctic char and grayling also present. Air charter available in Kaktovik or Fairbanks.

Selawik River. Fly-in river about 70 miles southeast of Kotzebue. Fishing excellent for small- to medium-sized sheefish in summer and fall, use spoons; northern pike year-round, best June 1 through Sept. 15, use spoons, spinners. Air charter available in Kotzebue.

Selby Lake. Fly-in lake located south of the Brooks Range in Gates of the Arctic National Preserve. Summer fishery is excellent. Lake trout through the season, use spoons or plugs; grayling year-round, use flies; northern pike year-round, best June 1 through Sept. 15, use spoons, spinners; burbot throughout the season, best in fall and winter, use bait such as head or tail of lake trout. Charter floatplane available in Bettles or Kotzebue.

Shainin Lake. Fly-in lake located on the north slope of the Brooks Range, 22 miles northeast of Anaktuvuk Pass, about 1 hour by floatplane from Bettles. Excellent lake trout and grayling fishing. Lake trout fishing best as ice is leaving, good through the season, use spoons or plugs; grayling year-round, use flies; whitefish use flies, eggs. Air charter available in Bettles.

Walker Lake. Fly-in lake located in the Brooks Range within Gates of the Arctic National Park, about 45 minutes northwest of Bettles by floatplane. Lake trout fishing excellent through the season, use spoons or plugs; northern pike year-round, best June 1 through Sept. 15, use spoons, spinners; arctic char use spoons, eggs; whitefish use flies, eggs. Walker Lake Wilderness Lodge on lake. Air charter available in Bettles.

Wulik River. Located in northwestern Alaska near Kivalina 90 miles northwest of Kotzebue. Excellent arctic char fishery in spring and fall, use spoons and eggs; grayling use flies. Midnight Sun Lodge located 30 miles upriver from Kivalina. Commercial and charter air service available in Kotzebue.

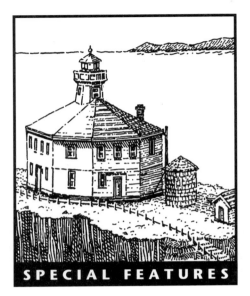

SPECIAL FEATURES

Kasegaluk Lagoon

Stretching southwest along the Chukchi Sea coast from just south of Wainwright to beyond Point Lay, this shallow 120-mile-long body of water (pronounced *ka-SEE-ga-luk*) is the largest barrier island-lagoon system in North America. It offers excellent wildlife viewing, as well as kayaking in shallow (3- to 6-foot) waters protected from ocean waves by the low barrier islands. During July, August and September half a million migrating eiders and thousands of terns, gulls, jaegers, loons, brants and old-squaws can be seen. Many beluga whales move into the lagoon in late June. At other times of the year it is possible to see arctic foxes, lemmings, caribou, brown bears, various types of seals and gray whales. Kasegaluk Lagoon is considered an important and productive habitat by the Alaska Dept. of Fish and Game. South of Icy Cape, near the mouth of the Utukok River, is the abandoned village of Tolageak, marked by the remains of Eskimo sod huts.

The only access to the lagoon area is by chartered plane from Barrow or Kotzebue. There is a landing strip at an abandoned DEW line site at Icy Cape which is not maintained and may be in poor or unusable condition. Lodging is available at Barrow or Kotzebue, but it's wilderness camping only at the lagoon. Campers and kayakers should be prepared for high winds and cold weather year-round. Take a few extra days supply of food in the event you get weathered in. Do not in any way harass nesting birds or other wildlife. And, be aware that there is considerable subsistence hunting, fishing and other activity in the area at various times of the year. The village of Wainwright owns some of the land at the north end of the lagoon. For additional information contact: Arctic District Manager, Bureau of Land Management, 1541 Gaffney St., Fairbanks, AK 99703; phone 356-5130.

Leffingwell Camp

On southcentral Flaxman Island stand the remains of what is believed to be the camp established by explorer and geologist Ernest de Koven Leffingwell in 1907 to carry out important permafrost studies, mapping and other studies of arctic conditions. The camp is on the National Register of Historic Places.

Leffingwell spent 6 years between 1901 and 1914 in the Canning River region and compiled the first accurate maps of that part of the northern coast. A cabin at the campsite was built from the timbers of the expedition's ship, the Duchess of Bedford, which had been damaged by the ice pack. The camp, about 4.5 miles west of Brownlow Point located west of Kaktovik on Barter Island, also contains the remains of 3 traditional Eskimo houses, a storage shed, ice cellar and 2 large iron ship tanks.

Teshekpuk Lake

This large lake lies just a few miles from the Arctic Ocean in the wet, low tundra region southeast of Barrow. Teshekpuk Lake, which is 22 miles across, and smaller surrounding lakes, are considered a crucial waterfowl and caribou habitat area. Wildlife viewing and photography are excellent. The region is home to migratory brants, greater white-fronted and Canada geese, which arrive in July and August from the Alaska Peninsula, Canadian Arctic and Siberia. The lake system protects these large birds from predators while they molt and regrow their wing feathers. Other birds that nest in the region include plovers, sandpipers, phalaropes, dunlins, loons, oldsquaws, jaegers, gulls and snowy owls. Caribou, arctic foxes and lemmings also can be seen.

The only access to the area is by charter plane from Barrow or Prudhoe Bay. There is lodging in Barrow, but wilderness camping

only in the lake area. Special use regulations are in effect in the summer to minimize aircraft and other disturbance of wildlife. For additional information, contact: Arctic District Manager, Bureau of Land Management, 1541 Gaffney St., Fairbanks, AK 99703; phone 356-5130.

Tunalik

This 5,000-foot airstrip is located south of Icy Cape in the vicinity of Kasegaluk Lagoon. The Tunalik River mouth, 10 miles south of Icy Cape at 70°11 N, 161°44 W, is 5 to 10 miles downstream from the airstrip, which was built to supply oil exploration expeditions. The strip is reported to be still usable, although it is not maintained and should be inspected before a landing is attempted. There is a gravel pad on one side of the runway for camping. This open tundra region offers a real arctic tundra wilderness experience, with good opportunities for wildlife viewing and photography in the summer. There are no facilities here. You are on your own and should be prepared with adequate clothing and extra food and supplies in the event the weather changes for the worst.

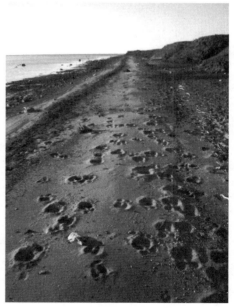

Caribou tracks on a sandy stretch of beach along the Arctic Ocean. (George Wuerthner)

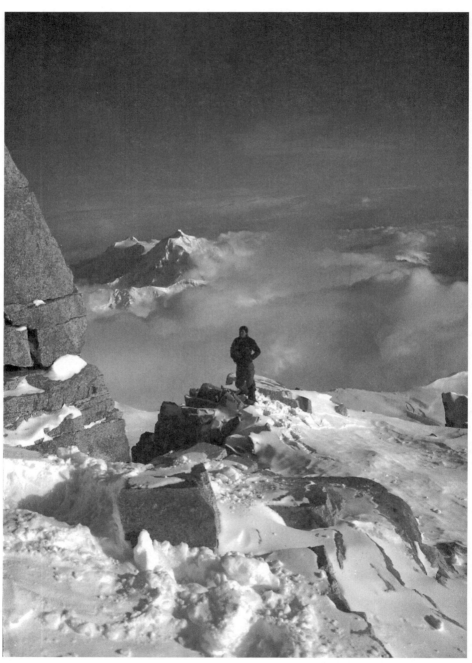

Karen Jettmar gets a good view of the Alaska range from 16,500 feet on Denali. Mount McKinley (Denali), at 20,320 feet, is the highest peak in North America. (Karen Jettmar)

INTERIOR

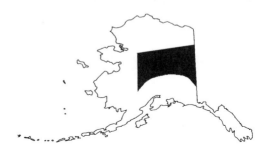

Alaska's Interior is a land of superlatives. Majestic Mount McKinley crowns the region's southern border. The Yukon, Alaska's longest river, carves a swath across the entire region. The Interior encompasses almost one third of the state, most of it wilderness. Rivers were, and are, the Interior's natural highways.

Gold discoveries of the 1880s and 1890s brought the major influx of non-Natives to the Interior. Abandoned dredges and active mining claims may still be seen in the Fairbanks mining district. Gold Dredge Number 8, now a tourist attraction, is 10 miles from Fairbanks. Other dredges rest near Chicken and Jack Wade camp not far from the Fortymile River, where active gold mining continues. At Healy, southwest of Fairbanks, the state's only operating coal mine produces coal used to generate electricity in the Interior.

Fairbanks is Alaska's second largest city and administrative capital of the Interior. It began in 1903–04 as a gold-mining community, then grew as a service and supply point for the Interior. Fairbanks played a key role during construction of the trans-Alaska pipeline in the 1970s, and continues to be important to Arctic industrial activities.

The 800-mile-long trans-Alaska pipeline cuts through the Interior and is visible from several highways. The 48-inch-diameter pipeline crosses the Yukon River north of Fairbanks, passes through rolling hills 10 miles east of the city, then goes south past Delta Junction to the Alaska Range before descending to the Copper River basin and the marine terminal at Valdez.

Location: Encompassing the Alaska Range on the south, stretching to the southern foothills of the Brooks Range and the Arctic Circle on the north. The Canadian border is to the east. Alaska's Interior blends with the Bering Sea Coast region on the west. The state's geographic center is located near Lake Minchumina, about 60 miles northwest of Mount McKinley.

Geography: Great rivers have forged Alaska's Interior. The Yukon, Tanana, Porcupine, Koyukuk and many others provided avenues of exploration for the Athabascan Indians and later white explorers, trappers and miners. South of the Yukon, the Kuskokwim River rises in the hills of the western Interior before beginning its meandering course across the Bering Sea Coast region.

Two distinct environments, forests and tundra, characterize the Interior. Below 2,000 feet and in river valleys, forests of white spruce, birch and aspen are broken by stands of balsam poplar and tamarack. Cottonwood thrive near river lowlands, and hardy black spruce grow in bogs. Willows, alders, berries, wildflowers, grasses and sedges abound, as does reindeer moss, a type of lichen which makes up a substantial portion of the diet of caribou.

In northern and western reaches of the Interior, the forests give way to slow-growing tundra. Above 2,500 feet, most mountains are bare, except for flowering plants and rock lichens.

Climate: The climate here is largely governed by latitude. The Arctic Circle sweeps through the region. Shining almost 24 hours a day in summer, the sun is nearly absent in winter. The aurora borealis illuminates long winter nights.

Temperatures in the Interior range widely, from winter lows of -50°F to -60°F to summer highs of 80°F to 90°F. Stagnant air masses typify the semiarid continental climate, which averages about 12 inches of precipitation annually.

Wildlife: Caribou from several different herds spend all or part of the year in the Interior. Moose are common in second-growth forests, on timberline plateaus and along the rivers. Grizzly bears, black bears and wolves range throughout the region. Dall sheep are found in the high mountains. All these species may be seen at Denali National Park and Preserve. Wolverines are classed as big game but are seldom seen. An introduced bison herd ranges near Delta

Junction, and a smaller, private herd grazes near Healy.

Coyotes, red fox, lynx and snowshoe hare may be hunted or trapped. Porcupine may be hunted. Beaver, marten, mink, weasel, muskrats, land otter, flying squirrel, arctic ground squirrel, red squirrel, hoary marmot and pika are protected from hunting, though all but the pika may be trapped.

Millions of birds make their homes in this region including wigeon; pintail; green-winged teal; northern shoveler; canvasback; Canada geese; several species of scoter, scaup and swans; and many other species. Endangered peregrine falcons nest in Yukon-Charley Rivers National Preserve. Minto Flats State Game Refuge is an important staging area for waterfowl from the Yukon Flats and North Slope during fall migration.

Common year-round in the Interior, ptarmigan often roost at the top of spruce trees. Ptarmigan have distinct color phases in summer and winter. (Bill Sherwonit)

Alatna

[MAP 16] Located on north bank of the Koyukuk River, 2 miles downriver from Allakaket, 182 miles northwest of Fairbanks. **Transportation:** Boat or snow machine from Allakaket. **Population:** 35. **Zip code:** 99790. **Emergency Services, Elevation, Climate** and **Private Aircraft:** See Allakaket.

The village is situated on a high open plateau where Kobuk Eskimos and the Koyukukhotana Athabascans met to trade goods. The Indians settled across the river in what is now Allakaket.

The Eskimo village of Alatna has no visitor facilities. Water is hauled from the Koyukuk River. Electric service is provided by a generator. Sewage system is outhouses. Most services and facilities are available at Allakaket.

Allakaket

[MAP 16] *(alla-KAK-it)* Located on south bank of the Koyukuk River at the mouth of the Alatna River, 2 miles upriver from Alatna, 180 miles northwest of Fairbanks. **Transportation:** Scheduled air service from Fairbanks; boat or snow machine to Alatna and Hughes. **Population:** 202. **Zip code:** 99720. **Emergency Services:** Village Public Safety Officer; Clinic, phone 968-2210; Volunteer Fire Department.

Elevation: 600 feet. **Climate:** Warmest month is July with a mean temperature of 58°F and 2.06 inches of precipitation. Coldest month is January, averaging -18°F. Snow from about September through May.

Private Aircraft: Airstrip adjacent village beside river (river floods south end of runway in spring); elev. 350 feet; length 2,800 feet; gravel; unattended. Runway condition not monitored; visual inspection recommended prior to using (watch for children and dogs on runway). No facilities.

Visitor Facilities: No accommodations or meals available, though arrangements can be made to sleep on the school floor. Two stores in the community carry groceries, clothing, hardware, camera film and sporting goods. No banking services but there is a community-owned laundromat (washeteria) which is also the village watering point. Beaded arts and crafts and fur hats available for purchase. Fishing/hunting licenses available. Diesel, white gas and gasoline are available and boats may be rented.

This area was originally a place where the Kobuk Eskimos and the Koyukukhotana Athabascans met to trade goods. The Eskimos settled on the north bank of the river (now Alatna) and the Athabascans on the south bank. The population declined with the influx of Russians in 1838. In 1906, Archdeacon Hudson Stuck established a mission here.

"A hard subsistence life" is how one Allakaket resident describes it here. Fishing in local rivers includes sheefish, grayling and whitefish. Gates of the Arctic National Park and Preserve are located to the north of the village, and Kanuti Wildlife Refuge is adjacent. The village has first priority for subsistence hunting, but caribou and moose are scarce.

Communications include phones, mail plane, CB radios, radio and TV. There is an Episcopal church (St. John's-in-the-Wilderness) and a school with grades preschool through 10. There are a municipal electric service and small private generators. Water is obtained from the river and the laundromat. Sewage system is outhouses. Freight comes in by plane. Allakaket bans the possession of alcoholic beverages. Government address: City of Allakaket, P.O. Box 30, Allakaket, AK 99720; phone 968-2241.

Anvik

[MAP 15] Located on the Anvik River at its mouth just west of the Yukon River and east of the Nulato Hills; 34 miles north of Holy

Cross, 160 miles northwest of Bethel and 350 miles west-northwest of Anchorage. **Population:** 83. **Zip code:** 99558. **Emergency Services:** Police, phone 663-3644; Clinic; Volunteer Fire Department.

Elevation: 325 feet. **Climate:** In the continental climate zone. Annual average snowfall is 110 inches; total precipitation per year is 21 inches.

Private Aircraft: Airstrip 1 mile southeast; elev. 325 feet; length 2,800 feet; gravel and dirt; unattended. Runway condition not monitored; visual inspection recommended prior to using. Runway dish-shaped; severe erosion adjacent to runway shoulder 800 feet from south end.

Visitor Facilities: Reserved accommodations with meals at R & L's Anvik River Lodge (262-6324). Groceries, general merchandise, gifts and novelties, local arts and crafts available. There is a laundromat. Fishing/hunting licenses may be obtained locally. Major repair services, charter aircraft available. All fuels available except premium gasoline. No banking services.

Anvik, 1 of 5 villages inhabited by the Ingalik Athabascan Indians, was incorporated as a second-class city in 1969. In 1834, Russian Andrei Glazanov reported several hundred people living here. Anvik was originally located across the Yukon River at an area called the point. Spring flooding forced people to move from the point to a higher location where, in 1887, the Episcopalians established a mission. Anvik has been known by many names throughout the years.

Anvik has a seasonal economy which shows an upswing in summer when local construction programs get under way. Most families have fish camps and rely heavily on subsistence activities such as hunting, fishing and home gardening.

The site of the Christ Church Mission with its remaining structures, founded in 1888, is on the National Register of Historic Places.

Every other year, Anvik is a checkpoint in the 1,049-mile Iditarod Trail Sled Dog Race held in March.

Communications include phones, mail plane, radio and TV. The community is served by an Episcopal church and a school with grades preschool through 12. Public electricity is available. Water is provided by a city well. Sewage system is privies and honey buckets. Freight arrives by air transport and barge. Government address: City of Anvik, General Delivery, Anvik, AK 99558; phone 663-6328. Village corporation address: Ingalik Inc., General Delivery, Anvik, AK 99558; phone 663-6330.

Arctic Village

[MAP 18] Located in the Brooks Range on the east bank of the East Fork Chandalar River, 100 miles north of Fort Yukon, 290 miles north of Fairbanks. **Transportation:** Scheduled air service from Fairbanks; winter trail to Venetie. **Population:** 109. **Zip code:** 99722. **Emergency Services:** Village Public Safety Officer; Clinic (with a Health Aide); Volunteer Fire Department.

Elevation: 2,250 feet. **Climate:** Mean temperature in July is 56°F, in January, -29°F.

Private Aircraft: Airstrip 1 mile southwest of village; elev. 2,086 feet; length 5,200 feet; gravel; unattended. Check for runway construction; watch for loose gravel on approach and vehicles on runway.

Visitor Facilities: The village council operates Arctic Village Lodge for visitors; phone 587-9320. A coffee shop is available. No banking services. Supplies are available at Midnight Sun Native Store (587-5127), Gilbert Store and Tritt's Store (587-5426). There is a community-owned laundromat with showers. Arctic Village is a traditional Athabascan Indian village and crafts may be available for purchase locally. Gasoline and fuel oil are available.

The Neets'ik Gwich'in Indians, a once seminomadic people known for trading *babiche* "sinew lacings" and wolverine skins for seal oil and skins from the Barter Island Eskimos, settled Arctic Village.

Arctic Village elected to retain title to the 1.8-million-acre Venetie Indian Reservation under the Alaska Native Claims Settlement Act. The reserve and Arctic Village are bounded to the north by Arctic National Wildlife Refuge, although recreational access to the refuge is primarily from Kaktovik on Barter Island. Arctic Village is the northwesternmost Indian community in Alaska. It is also the migration route of the Porcupine caribou herd, which winters here.

Employment in Arctic Village is limited to the National Guard, post office, clinic, school, village services, trapping and crafts.

There is an Episcopal chapel in the village, which replaced the old Mission Church now on the National Register of Historic Places. Under restoration, the old church—built entirely of logs with handcrafted finish and furnishings—reflects the skill of the Native artisans under Albert Tritt, who later became its minister.

Communications include phones, mail plane, radio and TV. There is a school with grades preschool through 12. Village services include the laundromat and showers, and electric generator. Honey buckets and outhouses are used. Freight delivery by plane. Arctic Village is a dry village; the sale and importation of alcoholic beverages is prohibited. Government address: Arctic Village Council, P.O. Box 22050, Arctic Village, AK 99722; phone 587-9320.

Beaver

[MAP 16] Located on the north bank of the Yukon River, 60 miles southwest of Fort Yukon, 110 miles northwest of Fairbanks. **Transportation:** Scheduled air service from Fairbanks. **Population:** 65. **Zip code:** 99724. **Emergency Services:** Clinic, phone 628-6228; Volunteer Fire Department. **Elevation:** 365 feet.

Private Aircraft: Airstrip adjacent north; elev. 365 feet; length 3,600 feet; gravel; unattended; recommend visual inspection prior to using.

Visitor Facilities: There are no hotels, restaurants, banks or other services. Lodging may be arranged through the Beaver Tribal Office; contact Arlene or Cindy, phone 628-6126. Food, groceries and supplies are available at the Innuit Co-op (628-6127) or at Florida Gierke's. There is a post office, a community laundromat with bathing facilities. Some supplies and fishing/hunting licenses are available in the community. Diesel and gasoline are available.

Beaver is an unincorporated Eskimo and Indian village. The village was founded by Frank Yasuda, whose interest in the location was two-fold. Married to an Eskimo woman, Yasuda saw Beaver as a place to relocate his Eskimo family and friends, who were facing hard times with the decline of whaling in arctic waters. Yasuda was also a partner of J.T. Marsh and Tom Carter, who had prospected for gold throughout the Arctic before settling in the Chandalar region to the north. Yasuda founded Beaver as a river landing for the Chandalar quartz mines started by Marsh and Carter in about 1909. In 1910, the Alaska Road Commission pushed through a trail from the mines south some 100 miles to Beaver, and Marsh and Carter spent the next several years trying to turn a profit from the modest amount of gold in the mines. A stamp mill was shipped in to crush the quartz for gold, although only parts of the 28-ton mill survived the

rugged trail to the mines. With the Great Depression and the subsequent withdrawal of financial backing, mining ceased.

Communications include phones, mail plane, radio and TV. The 2 churches in the community are St. Matthew Episcopal and Assembly of God. The school has grades preschool through 12 and also houses both the health clinic and generator for the community. Water is available at the laundromat. The sewage system is privies. Freight service is by plane or via Yutana Barge service 4 times a year. Government address: Beaver Tribal Council, General Delivery, Beaver, AK 99724; phone 628-6126, fax 628-6812.

Birch Creek

[MAP 16] Located on Lower Birch Creek, 26 miles southwest of Fort Yukon, 152 miles northeast of Fairbanks. **Transportation:** Mail and charter plane. **Population:** 53. **Zip code:** 99790. **Emergency Services:** Volunteer Fire Department; police and medical aid available from Fort Yukon or Fairbanks.

Elevation: 450 feet. **Climate:** According to a Birch Creek resident, "summers dry and warm, winters cold and lots of snow."

Private Aircraft: Airstrip 1 mile north; elev. 450 feet; length 2,500 feet; gravel; runway condition not monitored; visual inspection recommended; radio operated landing lights.

Visitor Facilities: Plans are under way at this community to establish a store, meal service and other visitor facilities. Currently, accommodations and meals must be arranged for ahead of time by contacting the council office (221-9113 or 221-2212). Supplies, including fuel, are obtained from Fort Yukon and Fairbanks. Birch Creek has no restaurant, laundromat or banking services.

Birch Creek was an Athabascan Indian village in the 1800s and became a mining community with the discovery of gold. According to a local resident, the community got its start after a break with Fort Yukon. The people here hunt moose and bear, fish northern pike and trap furs for a living.

Communications include phones, radio, TV and a mail plane. There is a 2-classroom school with grades kindergarten through 12. There is a waterplant and a community power system, but honey buckets still comprise the sewage system. Freight comes in by cargo plane. Birch Creek bans the possession of alcoholic beverages. Village corporation address: Birch Creek Corp. Office, General Delivery, Birch Creek, AK 99790.

Chalkyitsik

[MAP 17] *(chal-KEET-sik)* Located 45 miles north of Fort Yukon, 170 miles northeast of Fairbanks, on the Black River. **Transportation:** Boat; charter or scheduled air service from Fort Yukon or Fairbanks. There is a winter trail to Fort Yukon. **Population:** 85. **Zip code:** 99788. **Emergency Services:** Village Public Safety Officer, phone 848-8212; Alaska State Troopers in Fort Yukon; Clinic, phone 848-8215; Volunteer Fire Department.

Elevation: 560 feet. **Climate:** Summers are generally hot with some cool and rainy weather; mean temperature in July is 80°F. Winters are cold, with the mean monthly temperature in January -60°F.

Private Aircraft: Airstrip adjacent southwest; elev. 560 feet; length 2,600 feet; gravel. Airport facilities include fuel, navigational aids and lighting.

Visitor Facilities: Lodging is available at the local school (848-8113; 662-2515 in summer). Meals available from Minnie Salmon (848-8411). Chalkyitsik Native Corp. Store (848-8112) carries groceries, camera film, hardware and sporting goods. Propane and gasoline are available, but there are no other services or facilities.

Originally an Athabascan seasonal fish camp, Chalkyitsik means "fish with a hook at the mouth of the creek." James Nathaniel of the village council says Chalkyitsik is so beautiful and serene in the summer that three visitors said they'd like to move there. "Chalkyitsik is a small town with a lot of nice people. Although employment is limited, there are seasonal jobs. Subsistence plays a major role in the village." The people work for the school, clinic, post office, Native store and village council. There is fishing for jackfish, whitefish and dog salmon; trapping; and hunting for ducks, grouse and ptarmigan.

Communications include phones, mail plane, radio and TV. Public buildings in town include the log community hall, the health clinic, the village council office and the Native Corp. store and office. There is a school with grades preschool through 12 and there are 2 churches. A community utility service provides power, but water is hauled from the river (the pipes at the pump house freeze in winter) and the sewage system is honey buckets. The sale and importation of alcoholic beverages has been banned here. Freight arrives by cargo plane. No moorage facilities. Government address: Chalkyitsik Village Council, P.O. Box 57, Chalkyitsik, AK 99788; phone 848-8893. Village corporation address: Chalkyitsik Native Corp., General Delivery, Chalkyitsik, AK 99788; phone 848-8212 or 848-8211.

Chicken

[MAP 17] Located on the Taylor Highway, 78 miles from Tok, 95 miles from Eagle. **Transportation:** Auto in summer (Taylor Highway closed in winter). **Population:** 37. **Zip code:** 99732. **Emergency Services:** Alaska State Troopers (Tok), phone 883-5111; Tok Community Clinic, phone 883-5855 during business hours; Tok Public Health Clinic, phone 883-4101; Tok Fire Department, phone 883-2333.

Private Aircraft: Tok airstrip; elev. 1,670 feet; length 2,700 feet; paved; unattended; fuel 80, 100.

Visitor Facilities: The Goldpanner and the Chicken Mercantile Emporium offer meals, groceries, gas and repairs, along with local gifts, gold and souvenirs. There is no phone.

A mining camp and post office established in 1903, Chicken probably got its name from the plentiful ptarmigan in the area. In the North "chicken" is a common name for that bird. One story has it that the early-day miners wanted to name their camp "Ptarmigan" but were unable to spell it and settled for Chicken instead. Chicken was the home of the late Ann Purdy, whose autobiographical novel *Tisha* recounted her adventures as a young schoolteacher in the Alaska Bush.

Below the airstrip at Chicken is an access point for the South Fork Fortymile River, a route which avoids the more challenging waters of the North Fork. (See River Running in the Attractions section for more information on floating the Fortymile.)

NOTE: All gold-bearing ground in the Fortymile area is claimed. Do not pan in streams.

For more information about Chicken, see *The MILEPOST®*, a complete guide to communities on Alaska's road and marine highway systems.

Circle

[MAP 17] Located on the banks of the Yukon River, at Mile 162 Steese Highway, 125 miles northeast of Fairbanks. **Transportation:** Via the Steese Highway. **Population:** 94. **Zip Code:** 99733.

Elevation: 700 feet. **Climate:** Mean

monthly temperature in July is 61°F; in January, -10°F. Snow from October through April.

Private Aircraft: Airstrip adjacent north, elev. 610 feet; length 3,500 feet; gravel; unattended.

Visitor facilities: Accommodations and meals are available. Other facilities include a grocery store, gas station, post office, trading post and general store. Hunting/fishing licenses are available. A campground on the banks of the Yukon at the end of the road offers tables, toilets and a grassy parking area.

Before the Klondike gold rush of 1898, Circle was the largest gold mining town on the Yukon River. Today, Circle is a popular put in and takeout spot for Yukon River boaters. For more information see *The MILEPOST®*, a complete guide to communities on Alaska's road and marine highway systems.

Eagle

[MAP 17] Located on the banks of the Yukon River, at mile 161 Taylor Highway, near the Alaska-Yukon Territory border, about 200 miles east of Fairbanks. **Transportation:** Scheduled and charter air service year-round; auto in summer via Taylor Highway (closed in winter); tour boat downriver (100 miles) from Dawson City, YT. **Population:** 168. **Zip code:** 99738. **Emergency Services:** Health Aide, phone 547-2218; Village Public Safety Officer, phone 547-2246; Fire Department, phone 547-2282.

Elevation: 820 feet. **Climate:** Mean monthly temperature in July 59.4°F, in January -13.3°F. Record high, 95°F (July 1925), record low -71°F (January 1952). Mean precipitation in July, 1.94 inches; in December, 10.1 inches.

Private Aircraft: Airstrip 2 miles east; elev. 880 feet; length 3,500 feet; gravel; no fuel; unattended. Runway condition not monitored; visual inspection recommended prior to landing.

Visitor facilities: Accommodations, meals, gas and groceries available at Eagle Trading Co. (547-2220) and the Village Store (547-2270). Accommodations only at Jackie Helmer's cabins (547-2222). Meals only at Riverside Cafe (547-2250). Public and private campgrounds available. There is also a hardware store and automotive service center. Laundromat, showers, fishing/hunting licenses and gifts available.

The old courthouse in Eagle houses the museum. Eagle is a popular jump-off point for float trips through Yukon-Charley Rivers National Preserve. (Jerrianne Lowther)

Local historian Elva Scott describes Eagle as a "remote rural community on the bank of the Yukon River, surrounded by mountains. Eagle retains an atmosphere of an isolated gold mining town, steeped in history." The Eagle Historical Society conducts daily tours in summer of the community's historic buildings. Eagle began in the early 1880s as a fur-trading post, then boomed with the 1898 gold rush. It became Alaska's first incorporated city in 1901.

Eagle is a popular jumping-off point for Yukon River travelers. Headquarters for Yukon-Charley Rivers National Preserve is located on the bank of the Yukon River at the base of Fort Egbert; phone 547-2233.

For more information on Eagle, see *The MILEPOST®*, a complete guide to communities on Alaska's road and marine highway systems.

Fairbanks

[MAP 16] Located 263 air miles north of Anchorage and 1,519 air miles north of Seattle. **Transportation:** Several international, interstate and intrastate airlines provide scheduled service; auto and bus access via the Alaska Highway or the George Parks Highway; railroad access via the Alaska Railroad from Anchorage. **Population:** 30,843, borough 77,720. **Zip code:** 99701. **Emergency Services:** Alaska State Troopers, 1979 Peger Road, phone 452-1313 or, for non-emergencies, phone 452-2114; Fairbanks Police, 656 7th Ave., phone 911 or, for nonemergencies, the Dept. of Public Safety, phone 459-6500; Fire Department and Ambulance Service (within city limits), phone 911. Hospitals: Fairbanks Memorial, 1650 Cowles St., phone 452-8181; Bassett Army Hospital, Fort Wainwright, phone 353-5281; Eielson Clinic, Eielson AFB, phone 377-2296. Crisis Line, phone 452-4357. Civil Defense, phone 452-4761. Borough Information, phone 452-4761.

Elevation: 434 feet at Fairbanks International Airport. **Climate:** The weather changes dramatically here. A record high 100°F in June 1915; the record low -66°F in January 1989. The average temperature is 2°F in winter, 59°F in summer. In June and July, daylight lasts 21 hours. Annual precipitation is 10.4 inches, with an annual average snowfall of 68.4 inches. Ice fog forms over the city when the temperature is -25°F or lower.

Private Aircraft: Facilities for all types of aircraft. Consult the *Alaska Supplement* for information on the following airports: Eiel-son AFB, Fairbanks International, Fairbanks International Seaplane, Phillips Field and Wainwright AAF.

Visitor Facilities: Fairbanks has about 30 major hotels and motels; reservations are a must during the busy summer season. There also are many bed-and-breakfast operations and a youth hostel. The town has more than 100 restaurants with a range of prices. Banks, laundromats and a wide variety of stores are available. All major repair services are available. Many air taxi operators, guides and outfitters are based in Fairbanks. Boats also may be rented. For a free copy of the Fairbanks Visitors' Guide, contact the Fairbanks Convention and Visitors Bureau, 550 1st Ave., Fairbanks, AK 99701; phone 456-5774 or 1-800-327-5774, fax 452-2867. For information on Alaska's recreational lands, contact the Alaska Public Lands Information Center, 250 Cushman St., Suite 1A, phone 451-7352. The center offers free exhibits, films and brochures on forests, parks and refuges in Alaska.

In 1901, Capt. E.T. Barnette set out from St. Michael by steamer up the Yukon River with supplies for a trading post he planned to establish at Tanana Crossing (Tanacross), the halfway point on the Valdez to Eagle trail. But the steamer could not navigate the fast-moving, shallow Tanana River beyond the mouth of the Chena River. The captain of the steamer finally dropped off the protesting Barnette on the bank of the Chena River, near what is now 1st Avenue and Cushman Street. A year later, Felix Pedro, an Italian prospector, discovered gold about 15 miles north of Barnette's temporary trading post. The site is now marked at Mile 16 Steese Highway. The opportunistic Barnette quickly abandoned his plan to continue on to Tanana Crossing.

The ensuing gold rush in 1903–04 established the new gold mining community, which was named at the suggestion of Barnette's friend, Judge James Wickersham, for Sen. Charles Fairbanks of Indiana, who later became vice president of the United States under Theodore Roosevelt. The town became an administrative center in 1903 when Wickersham moved the headquarters of his Third Judicial District Court from Eagle to Fairbanks.

The city's economy is linked to its role as a service and supply point for interior and arctic industrial activities, with emphasis in recent years on the operation of the trans-Alaska oil pipeline. Active mining is taking place in the Fairbanks Mining District.

Tourism also plays an important role in the Fairbanks economy. During the winter, several sled dog races are staged in Fairbanks, including the Yukon Quest International Sled Dog Race, which starts in February from Fairbanks in even-numbered years. The 2-week-long Winter Carnival takes place in early March. The Festival of Native Arts takes place on the University of Alaska campus at the end of February. During the summer, Fairbanks hosts a number of events, including the largest summertime event in Alaska, Golden Days held in July to commemorate the discovery of gold near Fairbanks in 1902. The World Eskimo-Indian Olympics attracts international attention and is held in July. Each August, Fairbanks hosts the Tanana Valley Fair and the Fairbanks Summer Arts Festival.

Creamer's Field Migratory Waterfowl Refuge, which lies about a mile north of downtown between College and Farmer's Loop roads, provides opportunities for viewing, photography and study of plants, wildlife and geological features. The refuge is best known for its spring and fall concentrations of ducks, geese and cranes that stop over on the refuge fields during migration. Visitors also enjoy a 2-mile, self-guided nature path complete with moose-viewing tower. The path passes through a variety of habitats common to Interior.

Wilderness exploration is easy from Fairbanks, either on your own or with one of the many tour operators. Mount McKinley, the Gates of the Arctic National Park and the mighty Brooks Range are accessible from Fairbanks. Flightseeing over the forests and mountains, rafting, camping in remote areas, sportfishing, and photographic safaris are all available.

Fairbanks has all the amenities of a large city, including 12 radio stations, 4 TV channels (plus cable) and a newspaper, the *Fairbanks Daily News-Miner*. City government address: City of Fairbanks, 410 Cushman St., Fairbanks, AK 99701; phone 452-6770. Borough government address: Fairbanks North Star Borough, P.O. Box 1267, Fairbanks, AK 99707; phone 452-4761.

For more information, see *The MILE-POST®*, a complete guide to communities on Alaska's road and marine highway systems.

Flat

[MAP 15] Located on Otter Creek, 8 miles southeast of Iditarod, 59 miles northeast of Holy Cross, 85 miles southwest of McGrath, 375 miles west of Anchorage. **Transportation:** Charter plane from Anchorage or Fairbanks. **Population:** 5 in winter, 30 in summer. **Zip code:** 99584. **Emergency Services:** Alaska State Troopers, Aniak; McGrath Health Center.

Elevation: 309 feet. **Climate:** According to residents, Flat is dry during June and July. August and September are wet. Winter is cold and windy and the temperature can drop to -50°F.

Private Aircraft: Airstrip adjacent east; elev. 309 feet; length 2,500 feet; turf and gravel; state-maintained; no fuel; unattended. Runway condition not monitored; visual inspection recommended prior to using. Runway slick when wet. Both sides of runway used as road. Trees and tailings along runway edge.

Visitor Facilities: None.

This gold mining town was reported in 1910 by A.G. Maddren of the U.S. Geological Survey. At that time, Flat was the leading settlement on Otter Creek with a population of about 400. Its population was 158 in 1920 and 124 in 1930. Flat is unincorporated.

The area around Flat is mostly private mining claims and owners carefully watch for trespassers, according to one resident.

Some of the buildings in Flat were moved from the ghost town of Iditarod. A padlocked store and bank gather dust. A tramway once connected the 2 communities; a gravel trail now parallels the old tramway route.

Today only 1 family lives in Flat year-round, Mark and Sherri Kepler and their 3 children. Sherri teaches the children by correspondence, talking to a teacher twice a week by radio. Mark, a pilot and a wizard at making things run, is the postmaster, complete with Zip code and flag: "I fly the flag by the rules," he told a reporter for the Associated Press in 1989. "I raise it at dawn, which here in Alaska happens in April, and I take it down at sunset, in September."

The summer population swells when miners, who scatter to warm climates in winter, return to work their claims. The sluice boxes still show color, and if nobody is getting rich, Flat's isolation and simple lifestyle still prove a draw.

Flat has no phones ("Alascom hasn't found us yet," explains Mayor Zeke Grundoon.) There is no community electricity system. Most homes have indoor running water and sewer systems. Supplies are obtained by plane from McGrath or Anchorage.

Fort Yukon

[MAP 16] Located at the confluence of the Porcupine and Yukon rivers, 140 miles northeast of Fairbanks and about 8 miles north of the Arctic Circle. **Transportation:** 6 airlines provide scheduled service from Fairbanks; charter air service available; accessible by boat. **Population:** 708. **Zip code:** 99740. **Emergency Services:** Police, phone 662-2311; Alaska State Troopers, phone 662-2509; Clinic, phone 662-2460; Volunteer Fire Department, phone 662-2311.

Elevation: 420 feet. **Climate:** Dry and warm in summer, with a mean temperature of 61°F and mean precipitation of 0.94 inch in July. Winters are very dry and cold, with a mean temperature of -20°F and mean precipitation of 0.41 inch in January.

Private Aircraft: Airstrip 0.3 mile north of town; elev. 433 feet; length 5,800 feet; gravel; fuel 80, 100, A1+. Transportation to town via municipal transit, phone 662-2379 or 662-2479, or by taxi.

Visitor Facilities: Accommodations and meals are available at the Sourdough Hotel (662-2402) and at the Northern Lights Lodge (622-2800). There is no bank, but there is a laundromat. Supplies are available in the community. Groceries and supplies are available at M&A Enterprises (662-2582), Alaska Commercial Co. (662-2330) and CNC Store (662-2703). Beaded moose skin accessories and clothing, furs and carved ivory jewelry are available for purchase in local trading posts. Fishing/hunting licenses are available and local fishing trips may be arranged. Major marine engine, boat and auto repair is available. Charter aircraft and boats may be rented. Fuel is available. Boat moorage on riverbank.

In 1847, Alexander Hunter Murray founded a Hudson's Bay Co. trading post near the present site of Fort Yukon. After the purchase of Alaska in 1867, it was determined that Fort Yukon was within U.S. territory. By 1873, the Alaska Commercial Co. was operating a steamer on the Yukon and had established a post here run by trader Moses Mercier. The gold rush of 1897 dramatically increased both river traffic and the white population of Fort Yukon, while disease reduced the population of Kutchin Athabascans. Fort Yukon remained the largest settlement on the Yukon below Dawson for many years, and was headquarters for a hospital and pioneer missionary Hudson Stuck, who is buried here. Fort Yukon was incorporated as a second-class city in 1959.

Hub of the Yukon Flats area, Fort Yukon has just about everything a big city has except it is in the Bush. Employment is in sales and service, local, state and federal government, and also the traditional subsistence fishing (salmon, pike, etc.), hunting (moose, bear, small game) and trapping (lynx, beaver, fox). Recreation includes boating and canoeing the Yukon River, camping, softball, swimming and driving 3-wheelers in summer; cross-country skiing, dog mushing, snow machining, ice skating, ice fishing and bingo in winter. The community itself is the attraction for visitors, as one resident points out. Subsistence fish wheels, traps and garden plots exist alongside utility poles and cable TV. The Old Mission House here is on the National Register of Historic Places.

Communications include phones, mail plane, radio and TV. The community is served by Assembly of God, Baptist and Episcopal churches. The sizable school here has grades preschool through 12. The city has public water, power and sewage systems. Freight is delivered by cargo plane and by Yutana Barge Service. Government address: Fort Yukon, P.O. Box 269, Fort Yukon, AK 99740; phone 662-2379 or 662-2479, fax 662-2717. Village corporation address: Gwitchyaa Zhee Corp., P.O. Box 57, Fort Yukon, AK 99740; phone 662-2325.

Galena

[MAP 15] Located on the north bank of the Yukon River, 270 miles west of Fairbanks, 350 miles northwest of Anchorage. **Transportation:** Scheduled air service from Fairbanks and Anchorage; accessible by boat or barge service from Nenana, and over marked snow machine trails. **Population:** 833. **Zip code:** 99741. **Emergency Services:** Police, phone 656-1303; Alaska State Troopers, phone 656-1233; Clinic, phone 656-1266; Fire Department, phone 911.

Elevation: 120 feet. **Climate:** Mean monthly temperature in January is -12°F. Warm and sunny in summer with a mean monthly temperature in July of 60°F. August is the wettest month with 2.31 inches mean precipitation. Mean snow and sleet in January is 7.2 inches.

Private Aircraft: Galena airport adjacent northwest; elev. 152 feet; length 6,200 feet; asphalt/concrete; caution—work may be in progress. Galena airport is the commercial air center for 6 surrounding villages and is also the forward U.S./A/F Air Force base for F-15 jet fighters. An FAA station is located here. All facilities, including passenger terminal. Taxi service available.

Visitor Facilities: For accommodations contact Gana-a'Yoo, Ltd. (656-1606). No banking services. Public laundromat and showers are available. Groceries and supplies are available at Galena Commercial, Galena Store and Huhndorf's. Local arts and crafts available for purchase include Indian beadwork, birch-bark baskets, skin moccasins, fur hats and ivory work. Fishing/hunting licenses available from the local Alaska Dept. of Fish and Game officer and guide service. All types of fuel and repair service are available. Autos and boats may be rented in Galena. Moorage facilities are also available.

Galena was founded as a supply point for nearby galena (lead ore) prospects in 1919. The airstrip was built in 1940 by the U.S. Army. Galena was incorporated in 1971. Koyukon Athabascans comprise most of the town's population. The population increases in summer with firefighters. There is some construction and commercial fishing in summer, and year-round employment in government jobs, but traditional subsistence hunting and fishing support many residents. There is sportfishing for salmon, grayling, whitefish, sheefish, burbot and pike in nearby clear-water lakes and streams. Koyukuk National Wildlife Refuge lies to the north of Galena, and the northern portion of the Innoko refuge lies across the Yukon River to the south.

As transportation hub for several outlying villages, Galena sees many visitors in summer. In winter, when the Yukon is frozen solid, neighbors come in by dogsled or snow machine. Galena is the turnaround point for the Yukon 800 boat race from Fairbanks, held in June. The town has its own Fourth of July softball tournament, a Native arts and crafts bazaar on Thanksgiving weekend, and a Winter Carnival the last weekend in March.

Communications include phone, mail plane, radio and TV. There are 2 churches: St. John Berchman's Catholic Church and the Galena Bible Church. The community is proud of its city schools, which include an elementary school (grades kindergarten through 6), a high school (grades 7 through 12) and a branch of the University of Alaska. There are community electric, water and sewage systems, although honey buckets and a water haul system are also used. Freight arrives by air cargo plane and Yutana Barge Service. Government address: City of Galena, P.O. Box 149, Galena, AK 99741; phone 656-

1301. Village corporation address: Gana-a'Yoo, Ltd., P.O. Box 38, Galena, AK 99741; phone 656-1301.

Grayling

[MAP 15] Located on the west bank of the Yukon River east of the Nulato Hills, 21 miles north of Anvik, 350 miles west-north-west of Anchorage. **Transportation:** Scheduled and charter air service from McGrath or Bethel. **Population:** 211. **Zip code:** 99590. **Emergency Services:** Alaska State Troopers, Aniak, phone 675-4398; Health Aide; Volunteer Fire Department.

Elevation: 90 feet. **Climate:** Continental; mean annual precipitation 21 inches; mean annual snowfall 110 inches.

Private Aircraft: Airstrip 1 mile south; elev. 99 feet; length 2,400 feet; gravel; unattended. Runway condition not monitored; visual inspection recommended prior to using. North end of runway and taxiway floods in spring.

Visitor Facilities: Lodging is available through Yukon Enterprises (453-5145) or arrange for rooms with the City of Grayling (453-5148). There are no restaurants. Groceries and supplies from Grayling Native Store (453-5153), Ten Little Indians Store (453-5118) and Walker's Store (453-5170). No banking services. Arts and crafts available for purchase include birch-bark baskets, grass baskets, skin boots, fur hats and beadwork. Fishing/hunting licenses available. No guide service. Aircraft mechanic available, as well as charter aircraft. Fuel available includes diesel, propane and regular gasoline. Moorage facilities available.

When the U.S. Revenue Service steamer *Nunivak* stopped here in 1900, Lt. J.C. Cantwell reported an Indian village of approximately 75 residents. They had a large stockpile of wood to supply fuel for steamers. When gold mining in the area diminished, the village was abandoned until 1962, when residents of Holikachuk on the Innoko River moved to the site. Grayling today is a second-class city, incorporated in 1948 under the name of Holikachuk, Territory of Alaska. The name was changed to Grayling in 1964.

Grayling's economy depends on subsistence, and employment is primarily seasonal summer work in construction, road work and commercial fishing. Most families fish for salmon, whitefish, sheefish, pike and eels, and hunt for moose, black bear, small game and waterfowl. Residents also trap marten, mink, otter, beaver, wolf, lynx and wolverine, and sell the pelts.

Grayling is located across the Yukon River from Innoko National Wildlife Refuge.

Every other year Grayling is a checkpoint on the 1,049-mile Iditarod Trail Sled Dog Race.

Communications in Grayling include phones, mail plane, radio and TV. The community is served by St. Paul's Episcopal Church and the Arctic Mission, as well as a school with grades kindergarten through 12. There are community electricity, water and sewer systems. Grayling prohibits the sale and importation of alcoholic beverages. Freight arrives by barge or mail plane. Government address: City of Grayling, P.O. Box 89, Grayling, AK 99590; phone or fax 453-5148. Village corporation address: Hee-Yea-Lingde Corp., General Delivery, Grayling, AK 99590; phone 453-5133 or 453-5126.

Holy Cross

[MAP 15] Located on the west bank of Ghost Creek Slough (on Walker Slough), off the Yukon River, 34 miles southeast of Anvik and 420 miles southwest of Fairbanks. **Population:** 296. **Zip code:** 99602. **Emergency Services:** VPSO, phone 476-7180; Clinic, phone 476-7174; Volunteer Fire Department.

Elevation: 150 feet. **Climate:** Summer temperatures average 70°F to 80°F; winter temperatures -50°F to 50°F. Annual precipitation averages 18.97 inches, with snowfall averaging 79.4 inches a year.

Private Aircraft: Runway 1 mile south; elev. 61 feet; length 4,000 feet; gravel; fuel 80, 100; unattended. Runway condition not monitored; visual inspection recommended prior to use.

Visitor Facilities: Accommodation and meals available at Holy Cross Lodge. Food, groceries and supplies available at Holy Cross Mercantile and Holy Cross Stop & Shop. Arts and crafts include beaded jewelry and skin-sewn items such as mukluks, mittens and hats. Fishing/hunting licenses available. No guide service, banking services, moorage facilities or rental transportation. Fuel available is propane and regular gasoline.

Holy Cross first had contact with Europeans in the early 1840s when Russian explorer Lt. L.A. Zagoskin sighted the village which was called Anilukhtakpak. Population increased with establishment of a Jesuit mission and school in 1886. The founder of the mission was Father Aloysius Robaut who came to Alaska across the Chilkoot Trail.

The village was incorporated in 1968 as a second-class city. The economy is seasonal with its peak in the summer fishing season. Community and construction employment is supplemented by subsistence hunting, fishing and gardening.

Communications include phones, mail plane and TV. The community has a Catholic church and a school with grades kindergarten through 12. Public electricity, water and sewage systems available. Most residents have flush toilets; some use honey buckets. Freight arrives by air transport and barge. Village bans the sale and importation of alcoholic beverages. Government address: City of Holy Cross, P.O. Box 203, Holy Cross, AK 99602; phone 476-7139, fax 476-7141. Village corporation address: Deloycheet Inc., P.O. Box 53, Holy Cross, AK 99602; phone 476-7177.

Hughes

[MAP 15] Located on the Koyukuk River, 120 miles northeast of Galena, 215 miles northwest of Fairbanks. **Transportation:** Scheduled air service from Galena; accessible by boat; trails to Allakaket, Alatna, Huslia and Indian Mountain. **Population:** 80. **Zip code:** 99745. **Emergency Services:** Alaska State Troopers in Galena, phone 656-1233; Clinic, phone 889-2206; Volunteer Fire Department.

Elevation: 550 feet. **Climate:** Fair weather in the summer, with both hot, sunny days and rainy, cool days. It can get windy here since the community is in a valley surrounded by rolling hills and mountains. Mean temperature in July is 60°F; in January -10°F. August is the wettest month with 2.48 inches of precipitation. Mean snow and sleet in January is 6.6 inches.

Private Aircraft: Airstrip 0.9 mile southwest; elev. 289 feet; length 4,000 feet; gravel; runway condition not monitored.

Visitor Facilities: Lodging at the school ($20 per night) or visitors may arrange with local residents to stay in private homes for a fee. Meals, laundry and banking services are not available. Supplies may be purchased in the community. Native beadwork and sometimes snowshoes, baskets and baby sleds may be available for purchase. If you can catch Alfred S. Attla, Sr., in town, you can purchase a fishing/hunting license from him; if he's not around, the nearest outlet is the Alaska Dept. of Fish and Game office in Galena. No major repair services are available, but visitors can rent the town pickup or local 3-wheelers, autos or boats. Regular gasoline, diesel and propane are available. Public moorage on the riverbank.

Some of the older citizens here remember when Hughes was a riverboat landing and supply point for gold mining camps in the nearby mountains about 1910. It was named for Charles Evans Hughes (1862–1948), then governor of New York. The store remained here and Hughes became a Koyukon Indian village. The post office was reestablished in 1942 and the city was incorporated in 1973. There are about 27 military personnel stationed at Indian Mountain Air Force Station, 15 miles east of Hughes. Employment in Hughes is in local services with seasonal firefighting and trapping. There is fishing for grayling, chum, sheefish and salmon.

Communications include phones, mail plane, radio and TV. An Episcopal church is here and a school with grades kindergarten through 8. There are municipal water and electric services; sewage is individual septic tanks or honey buckets. Freight arrives by cargo plane or barge. Government address: City of Hughes, P.O. Box 45010, Hughes, AK 99745; phone 889-2206.

Huslia

[MAP 15] *(HOOS-lee-a)* Located on the Koyukuk River, 70 miles north of Galena, 250 miles northwest of Fairbanks. **Transportation:** Scheduled air service from Galena; accessible by boat. **Population:** 258. **Zip code:** 99746. **Emergency Services:** Alaska State Troopers, phone 656-1233; Health Clinic, phone 829-2204; Volunteer Fire Department.

Elevation: 180 feet. **Climate:** Conditions at Huslia are similar to those of Galena with cold winters, hot summers and generally low precipitation. In June and July, the average maximum temperature is in the lower 70s. During the winter months below zero temperatures are common. Local residents report a record low of -65°F and a record high of above 90°F. Most precipitation occurs between July and September with a total annual precipitation of only 13 inches. Annual snowfall is about 70 inches and generally persists from October through April.

Private Aircraft: Airstrip 1 mile northeast; elev. 180 feet; length 3,000 feet; gravel. Runway condition not monitored; no facilities.

Visitor Facilities: No accommodations

or meals, though arrangements can be made to stay in private homes or in the school or clinic. Most supplies available in the community at R&M Mercantile (829-2209) and other local stores. There is a laundromat but no bank. Beadwork, knitted gloves and other arts and crafts may be purchased. No local guides; fishing/hunting licenses available. There is no major repair service. Rental transportation is available. Diesel, propane and regular gasoline are available.

Huslia was originally settled in the late 1940s by Koyukon Indians from Cutoff trading post. The community takes its name from a nearby stream. Huslia was incorporated in 1969. Employment here includes seasonal firefighting, construction and trapping, along with positions at the school, church and in local government. Many local residents spend the summer at fish camps. Other summer activities include softball, berry picking, camping and gardening.

Communications include phones, mail plane, air service from Fairbanks and Galena, and TV. There are Catholic and Episcopal churches and a school with grades kindergarten through 12. The community has water, sewage and electrical systems as well as privies. Huslia bans the sale of alcoholic beverages. Freight arrives by barge and cargo plane. Government address: City of Huslia, P.O. Box 10, Huslia, AK 99746; phone 829-2266, fax 829-2224.

Kaltag

[MAP 15] Located on the Yukon River, 90 miles southwest of Galena, 330 miles west of Fairbanks. **Transportation:** Scheduled air service from Galena; trails to Nulato and Galena; accessible by boat. **Population:** 295. **Zip code:** 99748. **Emergency Services:** Alaska State Troopers in Galena, phone 656-1233; Village Public Safety Officer; Clinic, phone 534-2209; Volunteer Fire Department, phone 534-9221; Search and Rescue Team, phone 534-9221.

Elevation: 200 feet. **Climate:** Warm summers with high temperatures in the 70s. Rainiest months are August and September. Winters are cold with average temperatures of -20°F and lows of -60°F. A resident reports up to 6 feet of snow accumulates in winter.

Private Aircraft: Airstrip 0.25 mile from village; elev. 200 feet; length 3,200 feet; gravel; unattended. Runway condition not monitored; recommend visual inspection prior to use.

Visitor Facilities: No formal accommodations or restaurants. However, the local fire hall offers beds (b.y.o. sleeping bag), and kitchen and bathroom facilities. Some supplies are available at Victor's Store (534-2231) and Kaltag Co-op (534-2235). Marine gas, diesel, propane, kerosene and regular gasoline are available. No other services available.

This is an Indian village called Kaltag by the Russians. An 1880 census listed a Lower Kaltag and Upper Kaltag here. The present village is believed to be the former Upper Kaltag, while Lower Kaltag is now referred to as the Old Kaltag site. Kaltag was incorporated in 1969. Marion Nickoli says, "Folks are always welcome, and friendliness awaits all."

One resident describes Kaltag's way of life like this: "The people still rely on subsistence for their living. They fish during the summer (for salmon and grayling) and stay out at fish camps; they sell the fish or put some away for the winter; they also go hunting for moose, bear and other animals for food. They set traps in the winter for animals such as marten, rabbits or beaver. They sell the fur or make clothing out of it for themselves. The people mostly make a living for themselves and raise their families."

There is a Catholic church and a school with grades kindergarten through 12. There is also a community water and sewer system, although some homes still haul water and have privies. A generator provides the community's power. Freight is shipped in by plane or barge. Government address: City of Kaltag, P.O. Box 9, Kaltag, AK 99748; phone 534-2230, fax 534-2236.

Koyukuk

[MAP 15] Located at the confluence of the Koyukuk and Yukon rivers, 30 miles northwest of Galena, 300 miles west of Fairbanks. **Transportation:** Scheduled air service from Galena; accessible by boat. **Population:** 131. **Zip code:** 99754. **Emergency Services:** Public Safety Officer, phone 927-2214; State Troopers in Galena; Clinic; Volunteer Fire Department.

Salmon are cut in strips and hung to dry at a fish camp near Kaltag. (Alissa Crandall)

Elevation: 115 feet. **Climate:** Described as typical of interior Alaska, with warm summers, and cold, dry winters, with a temperature range of -60°F to 90°F.

Private Aircraft: Airstrip adjacent west of village; elev. 115 feet; length 2,600 feet; gravel; unattended; no facilities.

Visitor Facilities: No formal accommodations or restaurants. Visitors may arrange to stay in private homes or at the school, phone 656-1201. There are showers and a laundromat at the community watering facility. Some supplies available in the community. Arts and crafts include beadwork, marten hats, moose skin gloves and sleds. Fishing/hunting licenses may be purchased in the village. Propane and gasoline are available.

Originally a Koyukukhotana Indian village, a trading post was established here in the late 1800s. The village served the growing number of miners in the area and the increasing river traffic. Today, people here make their living as trappers and fishermen; in seasonal construction or in local clerical and maintenance jobs; or they commute to larger communities for work. Fishing for salmon in the Yukon and Koyukuk rivers is done both commercially and for subsistence purposes, and local summer fish camps are active. Local people do occasional guiding, but visitors should be well prepared with equipment and supplies since none are available locally. Moose hunting is good in the fall and black bear are prevalent.

Communications include mail plane, phones, radio and TV. Freight arrives by plane or by barge. Koyukuk has a school (grades kindergarten through 10), a public library, recreation center, a community generator and a safe-water plant. Sewage system is private privies. Government address: City of Koyukuk, Box 49, Koyukuk, AK 99754; phone 927-2215.

Lake Minchumina

[MAP 16] *(min-CHEW-min-a)* Located on the northwest shore of Lake Minchumina, 205 miles northwest of Anchorage, 150 miles southwest of Fairbanks. **Transportation:** Scheduled air service from Fairbanks. **Population:** about 30. **Zip code:** 99757. **Emergency Services:** Alaska State Troopers in Fairbanks; trained rescue group, no phone.

Elevation: 640 feet. **Climate:** Summers are cool and wet with a monthly mean temperature in July of 59°F. June is the driest summer month with 1.7 inches of precipitation. Winters are cold with moderate snowfall; monthly mean temperature in January is -6°F, mean snow/sleet for January is 9.5 inches.

Private Aircraft: Airstrip adjacent southeast; elev. 684 feet; length 4,100 feet; gravel; unattended; no facilities.

Visitor Facilities: Accommodations at Denali West Lodge (733-2630). Groceries and supplies available from Minchumina Mercantile that opens 1 day a week and upon request. Originally a Tanana Indian village until a flu epidemic wiped it out early this century, Lake Minchumina saw further settlement with construction of the airstrip in 1941. The lake yields some pike. There is no central utility or sewage system here. Water is hauled from the lake or obtained from wells. Communication is through a radiophone at the lodge and a single public phone booth near the runway (939-4000) which has an answering machine. Freight is delivered by small plane.

Manley Hot Springs

[MAP 16] Located at Mile 152 Elliott Highway, 90 miles west of Fairbanks. **Transportation:** Scheduled and charter air service from Fairbanks; road via the Elliott Highway. **Population:** 88. **Zip Code:** 99756.

Elevation: 330 feet. **Climate:** Mean monthly temperature in July is 59°F; in January, -10°F. Snow from October through April, with traces in September and May.

Private Aircraft: Airstrip adjacent southwest; elev. 270 feet; length 2,500 feet; gravel; fuel 80, 100; unattended. Runway condition not monitored; visual inspection recommended prior to using.

Visitor facilities: Meals and accommodations are available at Manley Hot Springs Resort (672-3611) and the Manley Roadhouse (672-3161). Groceries, gas, gifts, liquor and post office at Manley Trading Post (672-3221). There is a public campground; fee is $3 per night. The hot springs are a short walk from the campground. Manley Hot Springs Slough offers good pike fishing, May through September.

Once a busy trading center for nearby Eureka and Tofty mining districts, today Manley Hot Springs is a quiet settlement. For more information see *The MILEPOST®,* a complete guide to communities on Alaska's road and marine highway systems.

McGrath

[MAP 15] Located on the Upper Kuskokwim River opposite the junction with the Takotna River, 220 miles northwest of Anchorage, 250 miles northeast of Bethel, and 280 miles southwest of Fairbanks. **Transportation:** Scheduled air service from Anchorage and Yukon River communities; on-demand air charter service to outlying communities; river travel May to October; 21.8 miles of local roads. **Population:** 535. **Zip code:** 99627. **Emergency Services:** Public Safety Officer, phone 524-3075; Fish and Wildlife Protection, phone 524-3222; Clinics, phone 524-3299 or 524-3104; Emergency Fire and Medical, phone 911.

Elevation: 337 feet. **Climate:** Average daily maximum temperatures in summer in the upper 60s, with highs in the 80s; minimum winter temperatures below zero, with lows to -60°F. More than 40 percent of the normal annual precipitation occurs between July and September. Comparatively low precipitation in winter, with accumulated snowfall averaging 86 inches.

Private Aircraft: Airport adjacent west; elev. 337 feet; length 5,400 feet; asphalt; fuel 80, 100, A1+. All facilities including flight service station and passenger and freight terminals. McGrath seaplane base on the Kuskokwim River east of east/west taxiway; fuel 80, 100.

Visitor Facilities: Accommodations and meals are available at Rosa's Riverside Cafe and Rooms (524-3666), Takusko House (524-3198), Caoline's Kitchen and Rooms (524-3466), and Fly On In Bed and Breakfast (524-3947). Food also available at Miner's Cafe (524-3026). Groceries and other supplies available at B.J.'s Pik N Pak (524-3545), Alaska Commercial Co. (524-3588), The Shoppe (video and variety), and General Service hardware and sporting goods (524-3485). Limited arts and crafts available for purchase include birch-bark baskets, carvings and fur items. There are no banking services here. The laundromat has shower facilities. Fishing/hunting licenses are available, as well as local guides/outfitters. All types of fuel (marine, aircraft, diesel, propane, etc.) and major repair of vehicles and heavy equipment available. Repair and annual inspections of aircraft also available. Charter aircraft flights are available. Boats and off-road vehicles may be rented from private individuals.

Prospecting in the upper Kuskokwim and Innoko River valleys in the late 1800s brought increasing numbers of non-Native people into the area. In the spring of 1907, Peter McGrath, U.S. Commissioner sent from Nome, established a trading post and recording office at Old McGrath (across the Kuskokwim River from current site). Strikes on Ganes Creek and other Innoko Valley streams in 1906, and on Otter Creek and adjacent streams in 1908, made McGrath's location strategic as a supply point. Today it continues to serve as a supply point for a number of active gold mines in the area. The town relocated to its current location on the left bank of the Kuskokwim River in 1938. In February 1924, McGrath became the first Alaska town to receive mail by air, delivered by pioneer aviator Carl Ben Eielson. An Army base was located in McGrath from 1942 to 1943, and the new runway was an alternate stop for fueling lend-lease aircraft during WWII. Since early days, McGrath has been a transportation and supply center for the region. It was incorporated as a second-class city in 1975. The majority of employment is in government jobs, the school district and local services. Many residents also rely on subsistence activities, including fishing, hunting, vegetable gardening, and harvesting berries and timber for food and fuel.

One resident describes McGrath as "only a 35-minute jet ride from Anchorage, yet it has the attitude of the bush community. The people are independent and self-reliant, yet come together in times of celebration or crisis."

The oldest celebration in McGrath is held on the Fourth of July with floats, a parade, a huge potluck picnic and games for all ages. The annual KSKO Music Festival is held in mid-July and the McGrath State Fair is in late August. The Iditarod Trail Sled Dog Race takes mushers through McGrath each year, and dog mushing is a major winter activity in the area. The Upper Kuskokwim Mushers Assoc. sponsors many local races for all age groups.

Communications include phone, daily mail, public radio station KSKO and cable TV. Public services and organizations include the McGrath Community Library, 4 Rivers Counseling Service, the Upper Kuskokwim Mushers Assoc., McGrath Native Village Council, Tanana Chiefs Conference subregional office, Tochak Historical Society, University of Alaska Cooperative Extension Service and the Kuskokwim Valley Rescue Squad, VFW, Civil Air Patrol and Girl Scouts. There are 4 churches: McGrath

Christian Fellowship, St. Michael Catholic Church, McGrath Community Church and Spiritual Assembly of Baha'is. School includes grades preschool through 12 and postsecondary classes are available through the University of Alaska Rural Education Center. Homes are heated with wood or oil stoves. Most homes have individual cesspools (FAA and the Dept. of Natural Resources have their own sewage treatment plants) and a city-owned/maintained piped water system is utilized by most homes. Electrical power is generated by McGrath Light and Power. Barge service from Bethel delivers fuel products, heavy equipment and building materials. Other freight arrives by air. Government address: City of McGrath, P.O. Box 30, McGrath, AK 99627; phone 524-3825. McGrath Native Village Council address: P.O. Box 134, McGrath, AK 99627; phone 524-3024.

Medfra

[MAP 15] Located on the Kuskokwim River 30 miles east northeast of McGrath, 210 miles northwest of Anchorage. **Transportation:** Charter air service only. **Population:** 1 year-round resident. Population doubles in summer. **Zip code:** 99627. No emergency services.

Elevation: 435 feet. Climate: Weather conditions are similar to those found in McGrath with warm summers and cold winters with relatively low precipitation.

Private Aircraft: Airstrip adjacent west; elev. 435 feet; length 2,200 feet; turf; unattended. No winter maintenance or snow removal. Runway is soft during spring thaw and the north end is potholed.

Visitor facilities: None.

Perhaps a native campsite originally, modern-day Medfra began when F.C.H. Spencer operated a trading post here in the early 1900s. Travelers to the 1917 gold strike on Nixon Fork of the Takotna River found that the easier route was along the Kuskokwim River to a landing near the site of Medfra, then traveled overland to the gold fields.

Arthur Berry bought out Spencer and for a time the site was known as Berrys Landing. By 1920 Berrys Landing had become an important transfer point for upper Kuskokwim area gold fields. In 1922 a post office was established and the settlement renamed, perhaps after an early settler to the area. Arthur Berry operated a fur farm in the area and ran the store until 1937 when he sold it

to Clint W. Winans, who kept the store going until he died in 1958. Winan's widow, Bertha, operated the store until 1963 when she turned it over to Jack Smith, who continued operations until sometime in the late 1970s or early 1980s when a store opened in Nikolai.

Minto

[MAP 16] Located on the Tolovana River, 11 miles from the Elliott Highway on the Minto Road, adjacent to the Minto Flats State Game Refuge, 50 miles west of Fairbanks. **Transportation:** Via the Elliott Highway; charter air from Fairbanks. **Population:** 233. **Zip Code:** 99758.

Elevation: 460 feet. Climate: Temperatures range from 55°F to 90°F in summer and from 32°F to -50°F in winter. Snow from October through April with traces in September and May.

Private aircraft: Airstrip 1 mile east of village; elev. 460 feet; length 3,500 feet; gravel; unattended. Runway condition not monitored; recommend visual inspection prior to using.

Visitor facilities: Reserved accommodations and meals available at Lakeview Lodge (798-7448), where crafts are available. Groceries and supplies are available at North Fork Store (798-7512).

The Athabascan Indian village was moved to its present location from the east bank of the Tanana River in 1971 because of flooding. The original site, Old Minto, was established in 1915. Minto is a major access point for the Minto Flats State Game Refuge, a popular duck hunting area. Most residents make their living by hunting and fishing. Some local people also work making birch-bark baskets and beaded skin and fur items. Minto bans the sale and importation of alcoholic beverages. Government address: Minto Village Council, P.O. Box 26, Minto, AK 99758; phone 798-7112.

For more information see *The MILEPOST®*, a complete guide to communities on Alaska's road and marine highway systems.

Nikolai

[MAP 15] Located 40 miles northeast of McGrath, 195 miles northwest of Anchorage. **Transportation:** Scheduled air service from McGrath and Anchorage; charter air service based in McGrath; winter trails to McGrath, Medfra and Telida; accessible by river (May to October). **Population:** 119.

Zip code: 99691. **Emergency Services:** Clinic, phone 293-2328; other services in McGrath.

Elevation: 450 feet. **Climate:** Mean monthly temperature in July is 54°F; in January, -15°F. More than half of the normal annual precipitation occurs between July and September. Relatively low snowfall in winter.

Private Aircraft: Airstrip adjacent northwest; elev. 450 feet; length 2,500 feet; dirt and gravel; unattended.

Visitor Facilities: A city-owned hotel/apartment building provides limited accommodations for visitors. A coffee shop in the community center serves breakfast and lunch. A laundromat is also located in the community center. There are no banking facilities. All supplies available at the general store. Arts and crafts, such as snowshoes, moccasins, slippers and beaded items, may be available for purchase locally. Fishing/hunting licenses may be purchased in the village and there is a local guide. Villagers use 3-wheelers, snow machines and dog teams for transportation. Gasoline is available; no major repair service.

Like other communities in this region, Nikolai was an Athabascan Indian village in the late 1800s and has been relocated since its original settlement. A trading post and roadhouse here served miners during the Innoko gold rush. Nikolai was incorporated as a second-class city in 1970.

Heavily dependent on subsistence, Nikolai residents rely on hunting (moose, caribou, rabbits, ptarmigan and waterfowl) and fishing (king, chum and coho salmon, whitefish, sheefish and grayling). Some residents spend the summer at Medfra at fish camps. There is also trapping and vegetable gardening. Seasonal construction and fire fighting offers some employment.

Communications include phones, mail plane, TV and radio, with most residents tuned to McGrath's KSKO radio station. There is a school with grades preschool through 12, housed in a building completed in 1983. The Russian Orthodox church here was built in 1927. A large community building houses the post office, clinic, a laundromat and showers, library, poolroom, coffee shop and city offices. The city provides electricity and cable TV to Nikolai residences and home heating is with wood stoves. While some homes, the school, hotel and store have indoor plumbing and running water, most residents haul water from private wells or the community center. Sewage

system is primarily outdoor privies. Fuel and heavy equipment are delivered by barge; other freight is delivered by plane. Government address: City of Nikolai, P.O. Box 25, Nikolai, AK 99691; phone 293-2113.

Northway

[MAP 17] Located 7 miles south of the Alaska Highway within the Tetlin National Wildlife Refuge, about 100 miles west of the Canadian border. **Transportation:** Auto via side road from Alaska Highway 256 miles southeast of Fairbanks; charter air service from Fairbanks, Gulkana. **Population:** est. 360 in area. **Zip code:** 99764. **Emergency Services:** Alaska State Troopers, phone 778-2245; Emergency Medical Service, phone 778-2211; Fire Department.

Climate: Mean monthly temperature in July, 55°F; in January, -21°F.

Private Aircraft: Northway airport, adjacent south; elev. 1,716 feet; length 5,147 feet; asphalt; fuel 80, 100, jet; customs available; FAA station.

Visitor Facilities: Northway Airport Lodge & Motel (778-2266), groceries, liquor store, bar, propane, gas stations, air taxi service. Hardware, camera film, fishing/hunting licenses available. Wide range of Athabascan Indian crafts including beadwork, birch-bark baskets, moose hide and fur items such as moccasins, mukluks, mittens and hats.

Historically occupied by Athabascan Indians, Northway was named to honor the village chief who adopted the name of a riverboat captain in the early 1900s. The rich Athabascan tradition of dancing, crafts, and hunting and trapping continue in Northway today. The community has a community hall, post office and modern school.

Northway's airport was built in the 1940s as part of the Northwest Staging Route. This cooperative project of the United States and Canada was a chain of air bases from Edmonton, AB, through Whitehorse, YT, to Fairbanks. This chain of air bases helped build up and supply Alaska defense during WWII and also was used during construction of the Alcan and the Canol projects. Lend-lease aircraft bound for Russia were flown up this route. Northway is still an important port of entry for air traffic to Alaska, and a busy one.

For more about Northway, see *The MILE-POST®*, a complete guide to communities on Alaska's road and marine highway systems.

Nulato

[MAP 15] Located on the Yukon River, 25 miles west of Galena, 310 miles west of Fairbanks. **Transportation:** Scheduled air service via Frontier Flying Service and Larry's Flying Service; local air charter; accessible by boat. **Population:** 378. **Zip code:** 99765. **Emergency Services:** Public Safety Officer, phone 898-2290; Clinic, phone 898-2209; Volunteer Fire Department.

Elevation: 510 feet. **Climate:** Mean monthly temperature in July, 57°F; in January, -6°F. The greatest mean precipitation occurs in August, with 2.81 inches.

Private Aircraft: Airstrip 1 mile northeast; elev. 310 feet; length 2,500 feet; gravel; unattended; no facilities.

Visitor Facilities: No formal overnight accommodations or restaurants, but there is a small lodge with 3 beds, kitchenette and privy; water must be hauled. Arrangements can be made by calling 898-2205. Some supplies available in the community. There is a laundromat with showers at the safe-water facility. Fishing/hunting licenses are available, but there are no registered guides (ask local people about fishing). Diesel, propane and gasoline are available, and visitors may be able to rent boats and autos from area residents. Charter aircraft is available. There are no major repair services.

Nulato is the site of one of the most chronicled events in Alaskan history, the murder of Lt. John J. Barnard by Koyukuk Indians in 1851. Barnard came to Alaska as part of the British search party sent after Sir John Franklin. While Barnard was staying with the agent in charge of the Russian-American Co.'s post at Nulato, the Koyukuk Indians attacked the Russian fort, killing both Barnard and the Russian (Darabin), and the Indian village below the fort, killing 53 inhabitants. Various reasons have been given for the Nulato massacre, among them the traditional rivalry of the Lower Koyukon and Upper Koyukon, a possible insult by the British lieutenant of the Koyukon shaman, or the assumed challenge by the British to the Koyukuk trade monopoly. Barnard's gravesite is about 0.5 mile downriver from present-day Nulato.

The village was incorporated as a second-class city in 1963. Communications include phones, mail plane and TV. The 12-classroom school has grades kindergarten through 12. There is electric service. Water is hauled from the river or available through the village safe-water facility. Sewage system

is honey buckets. Freight arrives by barge or plane. Government address: Nulato City Council, P.O. Box 65009, Nulato, AK 99765; phone 898-2205.

Rampart

[MAP 16] Located on the Yukon River, 61 miles northeast of Tanana, 85 miles northwest of Fairbanks. **Transportation:** Scheduled air service from Fairbanks; charter air service; river travel except during breakup and freezeup. **Population:** 49. **Zip code:** 99767. **Emergency Services:** Clinic, phone 358-3219; Volunteer Fire Department.

Elevation: 380 feet. **Climate:** Cold in winter and warm in summer. Mean monthly temperature in January, -11°F; in July 57°F.

Private Aircraft: Airstrip 2 miles east; elev. 275 feet; length, 3,000 feet; gravel; no fuel; unattended. Inspection recommended prior to using. Frequent crosswinds at both ends; no line of sight between runway ends.

Visitor Facilities: No accommodations or meals available. Groceries and supplies available from Rampart Trading Post (358-3113). Local arts and crafts include marten hats and slippers. The village does have a laundromat. There are no banking services, rental transportation or any repair facilities. Regular gasoline, marine gas, diesel and propane are available. Fishing/hunting licenses may be purchased here, but there are no guides.

Originally an Indian village, the community grew with the influx of miners following the 1896 gold discovery on Minook Creek. Today, Rampart is an unincorporated Athabascan village where some residents trap and fish for a living. The community is friendly and accommodating to visitors. There are still gold mines in the area. Employment also includes commercial fishing and fish processing. Residents fish for salmon in the summer. Rampart's location also makes it a good stop for anyone traveling the Yukon River, although one resident warns that there are many bears in the area.

Communications include some private phones, mail plane, radio and TV. Rampart has a school with grades preschool through 12. Generators provide electrical service, but water is hauled from the Yukon River or the school well. The sewage system is outhouses. Freight arrives via cargo plane and barge. Tribal government address: Rampart Traditional Council, General Delivery, Rampart, AK 99767. Village corporation address:

Baan o yeel Kon Corp., P.O. Box 74558, Fairbanks, AK 99707; phone 456-6259.

Ruby

[MAP 15] Located on the Yukon River, 50 miles east of Galena, 220 miles west of Fairbanks. **Transportation:** Scheduled air service; river travel except during breakup and freezeup; dogsled, snow machine or skis in winter. **Population:** 287. **Zip code:** 99768. **Emergency Services:** Public Safety Officer, phone 468-4460; Fire station, phone 468-4412; Clinic, phone 468-4433.

Elevation: 710 feet. **Climate:** Fair in summer with temperatures to 80°F, lows in winter to -50°F. The mean monthly temperature in January is -2°F; in July it is 58°F.

Private Aircraft: Airstrip 1 mile southeast of community; elev. 635 feet; length, 3,000 feet; gravel. No facilities. Transportation to town available.

Visitor Facilities: The school student council rents an apartment to raise money for school events (468-4465). There are no restaurants. Groceries and supplies are available at Ruby Trading Co. and McCarthy's Services. No banking services available. There is a laundromat and most types of fuel are available. Automobiles may be rented and there are charter aircraft, but no major repair services available. Fishing/hunting licenses are available as well as guide service. Public moorage available on the river.

Gold was discovered on Ruby Creek near the present-day townsite in 1907, but the gold rush did not take place until 1911 with a second gold discovery on Long Creek. Today Ruby is a peaceful, friendly village. Its residents make a living by commercial fishing, subsistence fishing, hunting, trapping (marten, beaver, mink, fox, wolf), logging, or working for the school, city or private businesses. There are some summer jobs in construction and at the sawmill.

Recreation for residents in summer includes swimming, waterskiing or fishing in clear pools on the Melozi River. In winter there are races by dogsled, snowshoe, snow machine or skis. Ruby is also a checkpoint for the annual Iditarod Trail Sled Dog Race in alternate years.

Communications include phones, mail plane and TV. Ruby has a Bible church and a Catholic church (St. Peter In Chains), a school with grades kindergarten through 12 and a library. There is a public electric power system and a community well. Indi-vidual residences have private wells and septic tanks or privies. Freight arrives by cargo plane and barge. Government address: City of Ruby, P.O. Box 90, Ruby, AK 99768; phone 468-4401, fax 468-4443. Village corporation address: Dineega Corp., P.O. Box 28, Ruby, AK 99768; phone 468-4405.

Shageluk

[MAP 15] *(SHAG-a-luck)* Located on the Innoko River, 20 miles east of Anvik, 34 miles northeast of Holy Cross, 330 miles west of Anchorage. **Transportation:** Scheduled and charter air service from Bethel, Aniak, Grayling, Anvik and McGrath. **Population:** 167. **Zip code:** 99665. **Emergency Services:** Village Public Safety Officer, phone 473-0221; Clinic; Volunteer Fire Department.

Elevation: 70 feet. **Climate:** Continental. Temperatures range from -60°F to 87°F. Average annual precipitation 21 inches, with 110 inches of snow. Snowfall usually starts in October and ends in April.

Private Aircraft: Airstrip 1 mile north; elev. 70 feet; length 2,300 feet; gravel; no fuel; unattended. Runway condition not monitored; visual inspection recommended prior to using. Floods during breakup, may be soft after heavy rain. Transportation to village available for $5 per person/per ride.

Visitor Facilities: Accommodations available at Innoko River School (473-8233) for $25 per person/per night. There is a washeteria with showers. Groceries and supplies are available at Shageluk Native Store, The Outpost and G&P's video. Fuel available: gasoline, propane. Information on other visitor services and facilities unavailable.

Shageluk is an old Ingalik Indian village first reported in 1850 as Tiegoshshitno, by Lt. L.A. Zagoskin. In 1861, P. Tikhmenien, considered to be the chief historian of the Russian-American Co., noted 6 villages. These were collectively called the Chageluk settlements in the 1880 census. Shageluk became one of the permanent communities in the area; however, the village was relocated to its present location in the mid-1960s because of flooding. Shageluk, which is located about 10 miles south of Innoko National Wildlife Refuge, was incorporated as a second-class city in 1970.

About half of the buildings in Shageluk are built of logs, including a 6-sided *kashim*, a structure used for traditional social gatherings.

Although many residents own snow machines, dog teams are popular in Shageluk. Every other year the village is a checkpoint on the 1,049-mile Iditarod Trail Sled Dog Race from Anchorage to Nome. There also are trails connecting Shageluk with Anvik and Grayling.

There are a few full-time jobs with the school, city, clinic, post office, store or village corporation and some seasonal construction work on public projects or fire fighting. This income is supplemented by subsistence activities. Residents hunt moose, black bear, small game and waterfowl, and fish for salmon, whitefish, sheefish and pike. They also trap and sell the pelts of beaver, marten, mink, fox, otter, wolverine, lynx and muskrat. Some families also grow potatoes, cabbage, onions, carrots, turnips and lettuce.

Communications in Shageluk include phones, commercial radio and TV via satellite. The community is served by St. Luke's Episcopal Church and a school with grades kindergarten through 12. There is a community electricity system. Water is hauled from the washeteria, rain water is collected in summer and fall, and ice blocks are cut in winter. Sewage system is outhouses or honey buckets. Shageluk prohibits the sale and importation of alcoholic beverages. Freight arrives by barge several times each summer or by mail plane. Government address: City of Shageluk, P.O. Box 107, Shageluk, AK 99665; phone 473-8221. Village corporation address: Zho-Tse Inc., General Delivery, Shageluk, AK 99665.

Stevens Village

[MAP 16] Located on the Yukon River, 90 miles north of Fairbanks. **Transportation:** Scheduled air service from Fairbanks via Frontier Flying Service and Larry's Flying Service; river travel except during breakup and freezeup. **Population:** 94. **Zip code:** 99774. **Emergency Services:** Alaska State Troopers in Fairbanks; Clinic with Health Aides; Volunteer Fire Department. **Elevation:** 310 feet.

Private Aircraft: Airstrip adjacent north; elev. 310 feet; length, 2,000 feet; gravel; unattended. Runway condition not monitored; visual inspection recommended prior to using. Prevailing winds from west and southwest.

Visitor Facilities: No accommodations or restaurants. Visitors may arrange with the Village Council office (478-7114) to stay in the old school. Groceries and supplies are available at Pitka's Store and George's Store. Local women may have arts and crafts (mostly beadwork) for sale. Marine gas and regular gasoline are available. Visitors may arrange to rent boats and boat repair is available. There are no banking services.

According to local tradition, this Indian village was founded by 3 brothers: Old Jacob, Gochonayeeya and Old Steven. When Old Steven was elected chief in 1902, the village was named for him.

Stevens Village is unincorporated. People here today make their living working in the post office or store, the Native corporation clinic, in maintenance, or at the school. Villagers also do some trapping and spend summers at fish camp.

There are 2 churches: Assembly of God and Episcopal. Stevens Village School has grades preschool through 12. There is a community power supply and safe-water supply. Sewage system is privies. Most residents have phones and there is a public pay phone in the village office. Freight comes in by plane or barge. Stevens Village bans the sale and importation of alcoholic beverages. Government address: Stevens Village Council, General Delivery, Stevens Village, AK 99774; phone 478-7114. Village corporation address: Dinyea Corp., 544 9th Ave., Suite 107, Fairbanks, AK 99701; phone 456-2871.

Takotna

[MAP 15] Located on the Takotna River, 17 miles west of McGrath, 230 miles northwest of Anchorage. **Transportation:** Scheduled passenger and mail plane from McGrath; charter plane; river travel June through September; snow machine and dogs. Takotna has more roads than most Interior communities. About 90 miles of road connect the community with Tatalina Air Force Station; Sterling Landing, on the Kuskokwim River, where the barge docks; Ophir, an old mining community with a few occupants in summer; and other mining areas. **Population:** 67. **Zip code:** 99675. **Emergency Services:** Alaska State Troopers in Bethel; Public Safety Officer in McGrath; Clinic with Health Aide, phone 298-2214; Volunteer Fire Department.

Elevation: 825 feet. **Climate:** With more than 40 percent of the normal precipitation occurring between July and September, summers are "more wet than dry" as one resident puts it. Average daily maximum temperatures during summer are in the upper 60s. Winters are drier and cold, with minimum temperatures to -60°F.

Private Aircraft: Village airstrip adjacent north; elev. 825 feet; length 2,000 feet; gravel; unattended.

Visitor Facilities: There are no formal lodges, but the community hall has beds for rent. Limited groceries are available. There is a laundromat with showers. Marine gas and diesel are available. Meals, banking services, rental transportation and major repair service are not available.

Takotna started as a supply town for gold mines in the upper Innoko region. The town prospered through the 1930s, when gold mining in the region declined and McGrath replaced Takotna as the supply center. Nearby Tatalina Air Force Station was established in 1949. Community capital improvement projects have employed many village residents in construction during the summer, although as these projects slow down, some residents may have to go to Anchorage for summer work. Takotna is a checkpoint for the Iditarod Trail Sled Dog Race.

Most residents are involved in subsistence activities. Hunting for moose, the staple red meat, is fair. There is some duck hunting and local fishing for grayling, pike and trout. Local residents also grow vegetable gardens and harvest wild berries.

Communications include phones, mail plane, radio and TV. There are no churches. The new 2-classroom schoolhouse has grades preschool through 12. There is a community electricity system. Most residents heat their homes with wood stoves. Water is hauled from the PHS building or from a nearby stream (referred to locally as Takotna Waterworks). Some residents use indoor honey buckets, but most houses have indoor plumbing with wells; the community hall and PHS building are on septic tanks and have running water. Freight arrives by plane or by barge to Sterling Landing. Takotna is unincorporated and within the unorganized borough and therefore is without a regional government. Native residents of Takotna are shareholders in MTNT Ltd., P.O. Box 104, McGrath, AK 99627; phone 524-3391.

Tanana

[MAP 16] *(TAN-a-nah)* Located near the confluence of the Yukon and Tanana rivers, 135 miles northwest of Fairbanks. **Transportation:** Scheduled air service from Fairbanks and local charter; river travel in summer;

snow machine and dogs. **Population:** 414. **Zip code:** 99777. **Emergency Services:** City police, phone 366-7158; Clinic, phone 366-7223; Fire Department, phone 366-7158.

Elevation: 227 feet. **Climate:** Hot and dry in June and July, cooler in August, cold October through February. One resident says September (sunny and cool) and March and April (cold and sunny) are the best months.

Private Aircraft: Ralph M. Calhoun Memorial Airport, 1 mile west; elev. 227 feet; length 4,400 feet; gravel. Runway condition not monitored; visual inspection recommended before use. Restrooms at airstrip; transportation to town available.

Visitor Facilities: Meals and accommodations available at Tanana Lodge (366-7165). Groceries and supplies are available at Terry's I (366-7233) and Tanana Commercial (366-7188). All supplies available in the community. There is a laundromat. Beadwork, parkas, mukluks, birch-bark baskets and other crafts may be purchased. Fishing/hunting licenses available. There are no banking services. Charter aircraft are the only rental transportation available. Diesel, propane, unleaded and regular gasoline are available. Major marine engine repair available; minor repairs also available. Charter aircraft available to rent, and other vehicles may be rented from private individuals.

Tanana is located at a historic Indian trading locality known as Nuchalawoya, meaning "place where the 2 rivers meet." A Nuchalawoya Indian festival, with potlatch and contests, is held in Tanana every June. Arthur Harper established an Alaska Commercial Co. trading post here in 1880, and in 1891 the U.S. Army built Fort Gibbon (the fort was abandoned in 1923). Tanana was incorporated as a first-class city in 1983. Under restoration today is the wood plank Mission of Our Savior Church, which overlooks the Yukon and Tanana rivers. The church was part of an Episcopal mission established here in 1891 by Rev. J.L. Prevost.

Residents cite the mission, Indian festival and Tanana's sled dog races as some of its attractions. The Yukon River sled dog championships are held in early April, and several outfitters offer sled dog trips or freighting on ski trips in winter. In summer, the Yukon River is swimmable ("65°F and silty in July"), and fish wheels can be seen operating, especially in August and September. Boating is good throughout the area, and boat races are held over Labor Day weekend. There is canoeing on tributary streams. Tanana's residents make their living trapping, fishing and in government jobs.

Communications include phones, mail plane, radio and TV. There are 3 churches: St. Aloysius Catholic Church, St. James Episcopal Mission and Arctic Mission Bible Church. The school has grades kindergarten through 12. Tanana Power provides electricity to the city. Water is from community wells and the sewage system is both outhouses and flush toilets. Freight comes in by cargo plane and by barge. Government address: City of Tanana, P.O. Box 249, Tanana, AK 99777; phone 366-7159 or 366-7202. Village corporation address: Tozitna Native Corp., P.O. Box 202, Tanana, AK 99777; phone 366-7255.

Telida

[MAP 16] *(Ta-LIE-da)* Located 80 miles northeast of McGrath, 185 miles northwest of Anchorage. **Transportation:** Scheduled mail plane; charter plane; small riverboat; winter trail to Nikolai. **Population:** 32. **Zip code:** 99627. **Emergency Services:** Alaska State Troopers in McGrath, phone 524-3222; Clinic, phone 843-8126; Volunteer Fire Department.

Elevation: 650 feet. **Climate:** Average daily maximum temperatures in summer in the 60s, with occasional highs in the 80s. Minimum temperatures in winter below zero, with lows to -60°F. More than half the normal precipitation occurs between July and September.

Private Aircraft: Airstrip adjacent south; elev. 650 feet; length 1,100 feet; turf; unattended; no facilities. Some rough spots on runway.

Visitor Facilities: Rental cabin available from Steve and Olga Eluska (843-8115). No meals, restaurants or stores. Supplies are obtained from McGrath and Anchorage. Some beadwork is done in the village. Gasoline is available and boats may be rented, but there are no other visitor services.

This old Indian village has had 3 locations since white explorers first camped in the village in 1899. The village's second location, 4 or 5 miles upstream from present-day Telida, was abandoned and is now referred to as Old Telida. New Telida was settled by the Carl Sesvi family. The lifestyle here is heavily subsistence. The Athabascan residents hunt moose, bear, waterfowl and small game; fish for whitefish, sheefish, chum salmon, grayling, pike and Dolly Varden; and trap fox, lynx, wolverine, beaver, muskrat, marten and mink. There is some vegetable gardening and families harvest wild berries in late summer and fall.

Communications in Telida, which is unincorporated, include phones, mail plane, radio and a TV set at the school. There is a Russian Orthodox church in the village and a 1-classroom schoolhouse with grades 1 through 4. The school also supplies the community's water. The village has electricity. The school has a self-contained sewer system; each Telida home has an outhouse. Freight comes in by plane. Tribal government address: Telida Traditional Council, General Delivery, Telida, AK 99627. Village corporation address: MTNT Ltd., P.O. Box 104, McGrath, AK 99627; phone 524-3391.

Venetie

[MAP 16] *(VEEN-e-tie)* Located on the Chandalar River, 140 miles north of Fairbanks. **Transportation:** Scheduled air service from Fairbanks and Fort Yukon; winter trail from Arctic Village and Fort Yukon. **Population:** 208. **Zip code:** 99781. **Emergency Services:** Alaska State Troopers in Fort Yukon, phone 662-2509; Health Aides.

Elevation: 620 feet. **Climate:** Mean monthly temperature in January, -18°F. Mean monthly temperature in July, 57°F. Greatest mean monthly precipitation is in August, with 1.5 inches.

Private Aircraft: Airstrip adjacent northeast; elev. 550 feet; length 4,100 feet; dirt and gravel; unattended. Runway soft and muddy after rain. Some dips in runway. *NOTE: Airstrip is privately owned and landing fees may be assessed.*

Visitor Facilities: No meals or overnight accommodations available. Some supplies available in the community.

An Indian village settled in 1900, Venetie is unincorporated and is part of the 1.8-million-acre Venetie Indian Reservation. Residents are employed in seasonal trapping and fire fighting. Some year-round employment in the school and store. Venetie school, established in 1938, has grades preschool through 12. There is also an Episcopal church here. Electrical power is provided by a village generator. Homes are on septic tanks. Freight comes in by plane. Venetie is a dry village; the sale and importation of alcoholic beverages is prohibited. Tribal government address: Arctic Village-Venetie IRA Council, General Delivery, Arctic Village, AK 99722; phone 587-5129.

▼ A T T R A C T I O N S ▼

National and State Parks, Etc.

Chena River State Recreation Area

This 254,080-acre recreation area straddles the Chena River, taking in the river valley and adjoining ridges, 30 miles east of Fairbanks between Mileposts 26.1 and 50.7 of Chena Hot Springs Road.

Wildlife: The recreation area offers opportunities to view many species, including beaver, snowshoe hare, red squirrel, weasel, mink, muskrat, porcupine and marten. Wolves, wolverines and lynx are present but rarely seen. Waterfowl and shorebirds can be seen along the river. Black bears are occasionally observed along the river during salmon migrations and in berry patches on hillsides in August and September. Grizzly bears periodically wander through the area as part of their territory. Hunting in the recreation area is allowed in season, except within 0.25 mile of a developed facility.

According to Park Ranger Wayne Biessel, "The area boasts one of the highest road-accessible moose concentrations in the state. From late June until September, watch for moose along the highway, feeding in old river channels and ponds. Drive carefully — moose are often crossing the roadway."

The Chena River arctic grayling fishery is one of the most popular in the state. However, recent decline in grayling numbers has forced the grayling fishery to become catch-and-release only. (See Alaska Dept. of Fish and Game regulations for additional information.) Grayling can be caught from May to October on a variety of small flies and lures. The Chena also has a small run of king and chum salmon that migrate up from the Yukon and Tanana rivers in July and August. However, fishing for salmon upstream from the Chena flood control dam (which is well below the recreation area) is prohibited.

Activities: The recreation area offers a full range of outdoor activities associated with the river, adjacent spruce and birch forests, alpine ridges and historic trails. Summer activities include fishing, camping, hiking, canoeing, bicycling, berry picking, target shooting, hunting, ATV use, sightseeing and horseback riding.

Winter activities include dog mushing, snowmobiling, snowshoeing, trapping, hunting and cross-country skiing. Several sled dog races cross the recreation area, including the Yukon Quest.

The road paralleling the clear-water Chena River offers several access points for float trips. Popular launch sites are at Mileposts 48.9, 44.1, 39.5 and 37.9. Easy takeout points are Mileposts 44.1, 39.5, 37.9 and 27. Float times vary according to stream flow, type of craft and ability of the paddlers.

There are many backcountry routes for summer hiking along the river and on hillsides, and 3 established hiking trails: the Angel Rocks Trail, Chena Dome Trail and the Granite Tors Trail (see Hiking Trails this section).

Weather in this area is unpredictable; take suitable clothing for a range of conditions. Mosquitoes can be a nuisance, so bring repellent. Water sources on the trails are unreliable in dry weather; carry enough drinking water for the trip. Bears inhabit this area, so act accordingly: keep food containers sealed and away from your tent, and carry out all trash.

Accommodations: There are 2 developed campgrounds in the state recreation area. Rosehip Campground at Milepost 27 has 38 sites; Tors Trail Campground at Milepost 39.5 has 20 sites. Both campgrounds charge $6 per night (annual pass available) for overnight camping; campsites will accommodate large RVs and have tables, fireplaces and tent pads. Potable water, latrines and visitor information displays are provided.

For more information: Contact Alaska State Parks, 3700 Airport Way, Fairbanks, AK 99709; phone 451-2695.

Denali National Park and Preserve

This national park is located 120 miles south of Fairbanks and 240 miles north of Anchorage. The main attraction is the wildlife. Grizzly bear, caribou, moose and Dall sheep are seen frequently along the park road. A looming backdrop for this wildlife preserve is Mount McKinley, the tallest peak on the North American continent. The north summit reaches a height of 19,470 feet; the south, 20,320 feet.

The Athabascan Indians called McKinley *Denali*, meaning "the high one," and in 1980 the name of the park was changed to Denali. That year, too, the park was enlarged from 3.2 million acres to its present 6 million acres to protect Mount McKinley on all sides and also to preserve the habitat of the many species of animals found in the area.

Other interesting features of the park are Wonder Lake, the Savage River Canyon, the Outer Range, Sanctuary River, Muldrow Glacier and the Kantishna Hills—all of which can be seen from a 90-mile road that traverses the park.

The Outer Range is located just north of the central Alaska Range and is composed of some of Alaska's oldest rocks, called Birch Creek Schist, which can be seen clearly in the Savage River canyon. The 22.5-mile-long Sanctuary River passes through the Outer Range between Mount Wright and Primrose Ridge. Caribou calving grounds are located near its headwaters. Muldrow Glacier, largest on the north side of the Alaska Range, flows for 32 miles and descends 16,000 feet from near Mount McKinley's summit.

Wonder Lake, 4 miles long and 280 feet deep, is a summer home for loons and grebes, as well as many migrating species, and also provides a wonderful reflection of Mount McKinley. The Kantishna Hills were first mined in 1906, when the town of Eureka boomed with gold seekers. The area was included in the park in 1980.

Climate: Typical summer weather in the park is cool, wet and windy. Visitors should bring clothing for temperatures that range from 40°F to 80°F. Rain gear, a light coat, sturdy walking shoes or boots, and insect repellent are essential. Mount McKinley is clouded more often than not. (From June through August the chances of seeing the summit on any given day run about 35 percent to 40 percent.) Winter weather is cold and clear, with temperatures sometimes dropping to -50°F at park headquarters. In the lowlands, snow seldom accumulates to more than 3 feet.

There are more than 450 species of trees, shrubs, herbs and flowering plants growing in the taiga and tundra of Denali National Park and Preserve. The major species of the taiga are white spruce in dry areas and black spruce where it's wet, intermingled with aspen, paper birch and balsam poplar. Wet tundra features willow and dwarf birch, often with horsetails, sedges and grasses along pothole ponds. Dry tundra covers the upper ridges and rocky slopes above the tree line from about 3,500 feet to 7,500 feet.

Wildlife: Denali Park is most famous for the high visibility of its wildlife. In the shadow of Mount McKinley live 37 species of mammals including caribou, grizzly bear, wolf, wolverine, moose, Dall sheep, red fox, lynx, ground squirrel, snowshoe hare and voles.

About 155 species of birds occur in the park. Year-round residents include the great horned owl, raven and the white-tailed, rock and willow ptarmigan. The majority, however, visit the park only during summer. Some of these are sandhill cranes, oldsquaws, sandpipers, plovers, gulls, buffleheads and goldeneyes. Sport fish in park waters includes lake trout and grayling.

Activities: Recreational activities include ice and rock climbing, photography and wildlife viewing, nature walks, slide programs, sled dog demonstrations, cross-country skiing, and bus and flightseeing tours.

There are few established trails in the park, and these are near the park entrance. Check at the Visitor Access Center (located 1 mile west of the George Parks Highway) for information about backcountry hiking. A permit is not required for day-use hiking. All hikers should obtain a free map indicating special wildlife closure areas. Backpackers must obtain a free backcountry permit and bear-resistant food container at the Visitor Access Center. Camping gear should include a gasoline or propane stove; a tent or waterproof shelter because of frequent rains; and rain gear. Water should be boiled or treated. Pets are not allowed in the backcountry.

Accommodations: Denali Park Hotel is open mid-May to mid-Sept., reservations advised. Several hotels and campgrounds are located just outside the park. Food is available at a restaurant and snack shop at the hotel and also from a grocery store. Gasoline, oil, propane and air are available at a gas station near the hotel; 228 campsites are available at 6 Park Service campgrounds within the park, on a first-come basis. Campgrounds typically fill by midmorning for the following day during peak season. It is advised that you stop at an Alaska Public Lands Information Center in either Anchorage or Fairbanks when you arrive in the state to check on campground status.

Access: Denali National Park and Preserve can be reached by the Alaska Railroad, or by auto or bus from Anchorage or Fairbanks on the George Parks Highway. The best time to visit the park is from late May to early September; the park is open year-round, but the road into the park is not plowed in winter.

Private vehicles are restricted on the Park Road past Savage River, 15 miles from the park entrance. Several campgrounds are accessible only by camper shuttle buses. There is a wildlife tour bus operated by the park concession. A free shuttle bus service between the park entrance and Wonder Lake will pick up and drop off visitors anywhere along the way. Boarding coupons for the free shuttle bus service are available at the Visitor Access Center in person for the same day (when space is available) or up to 2 days in advance. During peak season, bus coupons are all handed out by midmorning for the following day.

Admission fees are charged for anyone who travels beyond the Savage River Check Station. Fees are collected at the Visitor Access Center where tickets for shuttle buses are obtained.

During the peak summer season, visitors should allow a minimum of 2 full days in order to obtain bus seats and campground accommodations within the park. This time can be well spent enjoying park programs and activities at the park entrance area. There are also a variety of activities immediately outside the park entrance. The Denali experience is considered well worth the wait, especially for those who schedule their visit accordingly and avoid the frustration of too little time to enjoy the park. Parking space is limited within the park. It is advised that you carpool with fellow travelers and bring the smallest vehicle available when coming to the Visitor Access Center. You should also come prepared to park in the overflow parking lot in Riley Creek Campground and walk or take the mini-shuttle to the Visitor Access Center.

Cross-country skiers at Ruth Glacier in the Great Gorge. (Karen Jettmar)

For more information: Contact Superintendent, Denali National Park and Preserve, P.O. Box 9, Denali Park, AK 99755; phone 683-1266 (summer), 683-2294 (winter). Related USGS Topographic maps: McKinley, Talkeetna, Healy.

Tanana Valley State Forest

Created in 1983, this 1.81-million-acre state forest is located almost entirely within the Tanana River basin and includes 200 miles of the Tanana River. It extends from near the Canadian border approximately 265 miles northwest to Manley Hot Springs and encompasses areas as far south as Tok, and is interspersed with private and other state lands throughout the basin. The elevation varies from 275 feet along the Tanana River below its confluence with the Kantishna River to more than 5,000 feet in the Alaska Range, south of Tok. The Bonanza Creek Experimental Forest west of Fairbanks is located within the State Forest.

Almost 90 percent of the land base is forested by spruce and hardwoods. Seven percent is shrubland. The major tree species are paper birch, quaking aspen, balsam poplar, black spruce, white spruce and tamarack. Over 60 percent of the forest, about 1.1 million acres, is suitable for timber production. Forty-four rivers, streams and lakes within the forest have significant fish, wildlife, recreation and water values and will receive additional protection. Nearly all of the land will remain open for mineral development.

Climate: The Tanana basin includes some of the warmest and coldest areas of the state. The continental climate is characterized by cold, dry winters and warm but relatively moist summers. The mean July daytime high temperature in Fairbanks is 72°F, while the mean January daytime low in Tok is -30°F. Precipitation averages about 12 inches each year for the entire region; however, variations in altitude influence the amount of precipitation.

Wildlife: The Tanana River valley provides habitat for moose, caribou, bears and bison. A large population of beaver is found in the region, especially in the Chena River drainage. Other furbearers include muskrat, mink, red fox, lynx, marten, land otter, weasel and wolverine. Three species of salmon — king, chum and coho — are found in the Tanana River drainage. Arctic grayling and northern pike are found throughout the clear-water streams and lakes of the area. Waterfowl nest on the lakes,

sloughs and ponds scattered throughout the lowlands. Spruce grouse are found in the forested regions; peregrine falcons have been reported in the bluffs along the Tanana River; and bald eagles are known to overwinter in the southeastern section near the Delta-Clearwater rivers.

Activities: Fishing, hunting, hiking, boating, cross-country skiing, dog-mushing, snowmachining and some all-terrain vehicle use are pursued throughout the forest. Some 250 miles of trails have been identified in the forest, some of which are maintained. The Tanana Basin Trails Management Plan, which is not complete, inventories trails in the borough, several of which are located within the State Forest, and will provide more detailed information on existing trails and plans for their management. Many rivers, lakes and streams within the forest offer sportfishing and boating opportunities.

Accommodations: The Eagle Trail State Recreation Site is the only developed facility within the State Forest and has 40 campsites. Additional campgrounds, public use cabins, boat launches and waysides are planned. Eighteen communities are located near the forest, including Fairbanks, the second largest city in Alaska. Supplies, lodging, charter transportation, rentals and guides are available in Fairbanks or may be found in some of the smaller communities.

Access: Approximately 85 percent of the forest is located within 20 miles of a highway, making it one of the more accessible public lands in the Interior. Rivers and trails throughout the river basin provide additional access to areas within the forest.

For more information: Contact the Department of Natural Resources, Northern Region, Division of Forestry, 3700 Airport Way, Fairbanks, AK 99709; phone 451-2660. Other sources of information include: Alaska Dept. of Fish and Game, 1300 College Road, Fairbanks, AK 99709, phone 452-1531; Department of Natural Resources, Division of Parks and Outdoor Recreation, 3700 Airport Way, Fairbanks, AK 99709, phone 451-2695; or the Fairbanks North Star Borough, P.O. Box 1267, Fairbanks, AK 99707, phone 452-4761.

White Mountains National Recreation Area

The 1-million-acre White Mountains National Recreation Area, managed by the Steese/White Mountain District of the Bureau of Land Management, is located

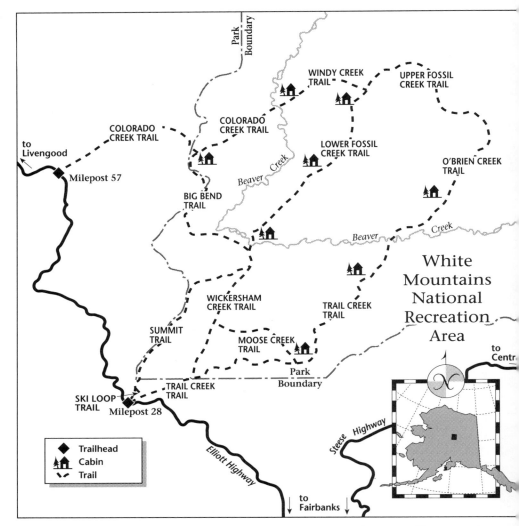

between the Elliott and Steese highways, approximately 30 miles north of Fairbanks. Access is via trail from Milepost 27.8 and 57 on the Elliott Highway or by road from Milepost 57.3 on the Steese Highway.

Climate: From May to September temperatures may range from 20°F to 80°F, with snow possible at any time at higher elevations. Wind can become a problem in areas with little shelter, such as treeless ridges on the summer trail. Winter temperatures may dip as low as -70°F. Any wind will drop the chill factor to a critical level, so adequate protection from the cold and wind is necessary at all times.

Activities and Access: The recreation area has more than 200 miles of winter trails and 20 miles of summer hiking trails. (The Summit Trail is the only summer hiking trail.) The trails connect with 10 recreation cabins managed by the BLM (see Cabins this section for details). The trails are used throughout the winter by dog mushers, snowmobilers, cross-country skiers and snowshoers. The BLM uses snow machines to maintain the winter trails, although they are not always packed early in the season. (Check with the BLM for current trail conditions.) The trails are: Big Bend, Colorado Creek, Fossil Gap, Lower Fossil Creek, Moose

Creek, O'Brien Creek, Ski Loop, Summit, Trail Creek, Upper Fossil Creek, Wickersham Creek and Windy Creek. Only Colorado Creek, Ski Loop, Summit and Wickersham Creek have trailheads on the Elliott Highway; all other trails branch off these. (See Hiking Trails this section for details.)

The White Mountains recreation area also includes major portions of Beaver Creek, a national wild and scenic river, and encompasses the Nome Creek Valley, site of both historic and active placer gold mining.

There is a 4-mile stretch of Nome Creek in the recreation area that is designated for recreational gold panning. Access is from Milepost 57.3 on the Steese Highway, where U.S. Creek Road leads north 6 miles to the Nome Creek gold panning area (marked by white signs). The road in fords Nome Creek. At most water levels, passenger cars with high ground clearance should have no problem fording the stream; watch for large rocks in stream channel. Recreational gold panning is limited to hand tools and light equipment, such as gold pans, rocker boxes, sluice boxes, picks and shovels. Pan only in the designated area to avoid encroaching on surrounding established mining claims.

For more information: Contact Steese/White Mountains District Office, Bureau of Land Management, 1150 University Ave., Fairbanks, AK 99709; phone 474-2350.

Yukon-Charley Rivers National Preserve

This 2.5-million-acre preserve is located in east-central Alaska north and west of Eagle. The preserve includes a 128-mile stretch of the Yukon River, as well as the entire 106 miles of the wild and scenic Charley River.

The broad, swift Yukon flows by old cabins and the remains of old mining camps. The Park Service is preserving a dredge, camp buildings and equipment as a clue to the region's mining history. Gold was discovered on Coal Creek in the early 1900s by miner Frank Slaven. His claims were later sold and the company that bought them had a dredge shipped up from San Francisco. It was the first gold dredge to operate in Yukon-Charley and continued operation until the early 1960s. A roadhouse named for Slaven is on the National Register of Historic Places. It opened about 1930, taking advantage of the traffic along the Yukon River, as well as up Coal Creek. The main mining camp on Coal Creek is also part of the donation. The camp

includes 10 cabins that served a variety of uses. They were built on skids so they could be moved along with the floating gold dredge. Some gold discoveries at Circle and other eastern Yukon localities preceded the Klondike gold rush.

By contrast, the Charley River watershed is virtually untouched by modern man. It flows crystal clear and is considered to be one of Alaska's finest recreational streams. The 2 rivers merge between the early-day boom towns of Eagle and Circle.

Humans have lived in the Yukon-Charley country since long before recorded time. Archaeological surveys are only beginning, but evidence found so far indicates people have been present for at least 10,000 years. Much of the preserve was unglaciated during the last ice age and there is a good chance that sites older than 10,000 years will be found. Because it was in the ice-free corridor, the area also contains a diverse cross section of vegetation.

Climate: The preserve is located in a sub-arctic climate zone, characterized by exceptionally cold winters, relatively warm summers, low annual precipitation and generally light winds. Summer highs average in the low 70s and lows in the mid-40s, although freezing at night can occur any month of the year at higher elevations. Winter lows can reach -40°F and lower for extended periods. Normal winter temperatures range from -5°F to -25°F. Precipitation is light, about 8 to 10 inches annually, mostly falling as rain in summer. Thunderstorms are common in summer. Snow cover is light but continues for about 7 months of the year. Breakup of the Yukon River ice usually occurs in early May. In mid-May 24-hour daylight begins. The transition from summer to winter is rapid; peak fall colors occur in the high country in late August and by mid-September most aspens and birches at lower elevations have turned golden. Ice begins flowing in the Yukon in October, with freezeup usually by mid-November.

Wildlife: The preserve includes caribou from the Fortymile herd which migrate to Canada and back. A moderate number of moose browse along streams and lowland areas, while Dall sheep occupy heights above the Charley River. Other wildlife includes grizzly and black bears, wolves and many small mammals.

More than 200 species of birds have been reported to occur in the preserve, including bald and golden eagles, rough-legged hawks and gyrfalcons. In its cliffs and rocky peaks the preserve contains some of North America's finest habitat for the peregrine falcon, an endangered species. Yukon-Charley lies along a major flyway for waterfowl that breed on the Yukon Flats and winter in the continental United States.

Fish in preserve waters include king salmon in July and chum salmon in September or October. A few coho also are taken. Other species include sheefish, whitefish, northern pike and burbot. Sportfishing centers primarily on arctic grayling, found at the mouths of tributary streams early in the season and farther upstream as the summer progresses. Northern pike are found in the lower reaches of most tributary streams and in the back-water sloughs of the Yukon. Dolly Varden are found in one nameless tributary of the upper Charley River.

Activities: The float on the Yukon River from Eagle to Circle is a great trip for a 1- or 2-week family vacation. Both Eagle and Circle are accessible by road. Besides river floating and camping, recreational opportunities in the preserve include hiking, fishing, wildlife observation and photography, cross-country skiing, dogsledding, snowmobiling and snowshoeing. Sport hunting is permitted in season.

The Park Service cautions that the preserve is a vast and sometimes hostile environment. The preserve's small staff can provide only minimal patrol or rescue services. Self-sufficiency is the rule; visitors are completely on their own once they leave the well-traveled Yukon River corridor. Weather conditions or equipment failure often can cause schedules to go awry; visitors should bring extra supplies to be prepared. As a safety precaution, visitors may leave a copy of their planned itinerary with the rangers at the Park Service office in Eagle. Also, local residents carry on subsistence activities within the preserve. Their camps and equipment are crucial to their livelihood and should be left undisturbed.

Accommodations: There are no accommodations in the preserve. In the summer, food service, basic supplies, gas and limited lodging facilities are available in Eagle and Circle. Both communities also have campgrounds and public boat landings. There are no formal campgrounds in the preserve, but camping is permitted on any federally owned land. Campsites on river bars are recommended because there is usually a breeze to keep the insects at bay. Minimum-impact camping, leaving no garbage, is encouraged.

NOTE: Private land owned by the Hungwitchin Native Corp. of Eagle is located on both sides of the Yukon River from Calico Bluff near Eagle to just below the Tatonduk River mouth. They request that visitors not camp on their land.

Access: The preserve is accessible primarily by small plane or boat from Eagle, 12 river miles south of the preserve on the Taylor Highway, or Circle, 14 river miles to the north on the Steese Highway. Both Eagle (pop. 198) and Circle (pop. 101) are easily accessible by auto or plane from Fairbanks. Floating the 154 miles of the Yukon River from Eagle to Circle is the most popular means of visiting the preserve. Most travelers spend about 4 days on this section. July and August are the most popular months for floaters. (See also River Running this section.)

Charter Super Cub access can be arranged to an unimproved gravel strip above Copper Creek. Most people prefer to float the Charley River in late June to mid-July. There are no roads or maintained trails within the preserve. No fees or permits are required to use any of the rivers. Inflatable raft rentals, charter boat service and fixed-wing and helicopter charters are available in nearby communities.

For more information: Contact headquarters for the Yukon-Charley Rivers National Preserve at the foot of Fort Egbert on the bank of the Yukon River in Eagle. Books and USGS maps are sold and a library of reference material is available there, or write, Superintendent, Yukon-Charley Rivers National Preserve, P.O. Box 167, Eagle, AK 99738; phone 547-2233. Related USGS Topographic maps: Eagle, Charley River, Big Delta, Circle.

Wildlife Refuges

Innoko National Wildlife Refuge

This refuge is located about 300 miles northwest of Anchorage in the central Yukon River valley. Its 2 units encompass approximately 3.85 million acres. The northern unit is administered by the Koyukuk National Wildlife Refuge office in Galena. The southern or main unit of approximately 3.5 million acres includes the middle portion of the Innoko River and its drainage. The Yukon River borders on the west, the Kaiyuh Mountains on the north, the Kuskokwim Mountains on the east, and the Beaver Mountains on the south.

About half of the refuge consists of black spruce muskeg, wet meadow, and sedge or horsetail marsh. The other half is mostly white spruce and birch-covered hills, most of which do not exceed 1,000 feet in elevation. The rivers are lined with a combination of cottonwood, alder, aspen and white spruce, as well as extensive willow bars. Thousands of lakes and ponds dot the wetlands area. Approximately 1.24 million acres (all of the refuge land south of the Innoko River) is designated Wilderness Area, with restrictions on the use of certain motorized equipment and vehicles other than boats and floatplanes.

Climate: Summer temperatures may exceed 80°F although 60s and 70s are more common. Visitors should anticipate rain at any time during the spring, summer or fall and carry rain gear. Also, a surprise freeze can happen even in the summer, particularly in June or August, so visitors should prepare accordingly. During the fall, it is wise to expect cold, wet weather. Winters are cold; the temperature may drop to -60°F.

Wildlife: This refuge was established to protect waterfowl nesting and breeding habitat. More than 100,000 waterfowl and shorebirds use the wetlands, which encompass nearly 80 percent of the refuge lands. This is an important nesting area for white-fronted and lesser Canada geese, pintail, wigeon, shoveler, scaup, scoter, red-necked grebe, lesser yellowleg and hudsonian godwit.

The refuge is home to moose, black and grizzly bears, and wolves. Caribou use the refuge in winter when deep snow drives them down from the mountains. This area also is renowned for its beaver population. Other furbearers include muskrat, marten, wolverine, lynx, river otter and red fox.

Fish found in refuge waters include salmon, sheefish, grayling, blackfish, whitefish and northern pike.

Activities: Recreational opportunities include moose hunting, trapping, floating the Innoko and Iditarod rivers, hunting black bear, fishing, wildlife observation and photography. The refuge staff will assist in planning trips.

Access and Accommodations: Chartered aircraft from McGrath or Galena provide access to the refuge. Supplies and commercial lodging are available in McGrath and Galena; some supplies and limited lodging in Grayling; and limited supplies in Shageluk.

There are no facilities in the refuge; wilderness camping only. No roads or trails exist. Campers should be prepared for a wet environment and be sure to bring waterproof boots, a tent and warm sleeping bag. Drinking water should be boiled or purified to protect against giardiasis. A first-aid kit and plenty of mosquito repellent are recommended. The Fish and Wildlife Service also recommends that anyone planning to enter the refuge check in with the refuge manager in McGrath for safety purposes.

For more information: Contact Refuge Manager, Innoko National Wildlife Refuge, P.O. Box 69, McGrath, AK 99627; phone 524-3251. Related USGS Topographic maps: Ophir, Holy Cross, Iditarod and Unalakleet for the lower unit and Nulato for the upper unit.

Kanuti National Wildlife Refuge

This 1.6-million-acre refuge straddles the Arctic Circle approximately 150 miles northwest of Fairbanks and south of Bettles. It extends westward to the villages of Allakaket and Alatna. The refuge encompasses a portion of the Koyukuk River basin and the Kanuti flats near the southern foothills of the Brooks Range. It is characterized by lakes and marshes dotting the broad, rolling plain of the Kanuti and Koyukuk river valleys.

Climate: Kanuti's climate is typically continental. The long summer days are mild, with maximum temperatures mostly in the high 60s and low 70s. The sun does not set from June 2 through July 9. From November through March, minimum temperatures average below zero and readings of -45°F to -55°F are common. Annual precipitation averages approximately 14 inches. Snow has occurred during all months but July. Winds prevail from the north 10 months of the year, but are seldom strong.

Wildlife: Some 105 species of birds have been observed on the Kanuti, which provides important nesting habitat for waterfowl, particularly white-fronted geese, Canada geese, pintail, wigeon, scaup and scoters.

Portions of the large western Arctic caribou herd winter within the refuge. Black bears, grizzly bears, wolves, wolverines and moose are found there, along with numerous smaller mammals. Fish in refuge waters include 4 species of salmon, arctic char, grayling, whitefish, sheefish, lake trout, burbot and northern pike.

Activities: Fishing, hunting, trapping, wildlife observation, photography, camping and boating are the main activities in Kanuti. Backpacking is good in only a few areas due to the terrain.

Access and Accommodations: The refuge is accessible by charter air service from Bettle and by boat down the Koyukuk River from Bettles to Allakaket. Commercial and charter air service is available in Fairbanks to Bettles and in Allakaket. Overnight accommodations are available in Bettles, but not Allakaket. On the refuge there are no facilities; wilderness camping only. Visitors should arrive self-sufficient. As a safety precaution, visitors should leave a copy of their itinerary with a friend.

For more information: Contact Refuge Manager, Kanuti National Wildlife Refuge, Federal Bldg. and Courthouse, 101 12th Ave., Box 11, Fairbanks, AK 99701; phone 456-0329.

Koyukuk National Wildlife Refuge

This 3.5-million-acre refuge is located 270 miles west of Fairbanks. Lying in the circular floodplain formed by the lower Koyukuk River, the refuge is heavily forested and contains much wetlands. Fourteen rivers and hundreds of creeks meander throughout the refuge providing habitat for salmon, beaver and waterfowl. More than 15,000 lakes also are found in the refuge. The topography is relatively gentle. Lowland forests gradually merge with tundra vegetation at the 3,000-foot elevation.

The refuge has a 400,000-acre wilderness area surrounding the 10,000-acre Nogahabara Sand Dunes. These, along with the Great Kobuk Sand Dunes, are the only large, active dune fields in interior Alaska. Both were formed some 10,000 years ago by windblown deposits during the mid- to late Pleistocene period.

Wildlife: Moose are abundant and are important to the subsistence economy of villages in the area. The entire region is part of the winter range of the western Arctic caribou and Galena Mountain herds. With the presence of both moose and caribou, wolves also are common. Black bears are abundant in forests and grizzly bears inhabit the open tundra at higher elevations. The refuge is productive beaver country and excellent habitat for other furbearers.

Fish available in the refuge include king and chum salmon. Whitefish and northern pike are abundant in lowlands and arctic grayling are found in colder headwater streams.

Access and Accommodations: Access to the refuge is by boat, snowmobile or charter plane from Fairbanks. There are no accommodations in the refuge; wilderness camping is permitted.

For more information: Contact Complex Manager, Koyukuk/Nowitna Refuge Complex, P.O. Box 287, Galena, AK 99741-0287; phone 656-1231.

Minto Flats State Game Refuge

Created in 1988, this state refuge encompasses more than 500,000 acres 35 miles west of Fairbanks and is bordered to the south by the Tanana River. An enormous low-lying wetlands, Minto Flats is dotted with numerous lakes, oxbows and potholes. One of the highest quality waterfowl habitats in Alaska and probably in all of North America, Minto Flats is the third most popular duck hunting area in the state. The wetland is also an important year-round hunting, fishing and trapping area for local villagers and others, and archaeological evidence suggests use of the area by Athabascan Indians predates historic contact.

Wildlife: The flats produce as many as 150,000 ducks annually and support a breeding population averaging 213 ducks per square mile. Trumpeter swans nest on numerous lakes dotting the area and white-fronted geese, sandhill cranes, common and arctic loons nest on the flats. The flats are also an important staging area for waterfowl from the Yukon Flats and the North Slope during the fall migration. Predominant species are tundra swan, mallard, pintail, scaup, green-winged teal, redhead, bufflehead and gadwall.

Also found in the refuge are moose, black bear, a large beaver population, river otter, lynx, wolverine, wolf, red fox, mink, muskrat and marten.

Activities: The Alaska Dept. of Fish and Game reports more than 5,000 hunter days are logged each year and more than 11,000 ducks and 700 geese are taken. Fishing for northern pike, burbot, sheefish, humpback whitefish, grayling, and king, silver and chum salmon is also popular. Tolovana Lodge offers float trips throughout Minto Flats.

Accommodations: There are no developed public-use facilities in the refuge. A general store is located in Minto, a village adjacent to the flats. Accommodations by advance reservation at Tolovana Lodge, located at the confluence of the Tanana and Tolovana rivers, 55 miles west of Nenana. (The lodge is accessed from Nenana; phone 832-5569.) Generally, those using the flats camp on one of the islands in the flats. Fresh water should be carried, and anyone headed for the area during the fall hunting season should be prepared for any type of weather, from 70°F to rain to snow. Hip boots are a must, and a boat or inflatable raft is also recommended.

Access: The flats can be reached by float-plane from Fairbanks; by boat from Minto, which can be reached from Fairbanks via the Elliott Highway; by boat from Nenana down the Tanana River, then up Swanneck Slough into the flats; or by the Murphy Dome Road. In winter, snow machines and skiplanes can be used.

For more information: Contact Alaska Dept. of Fish and Game, 1300 College Road, Fairbanks, AK 99701; phone 452-1531.

Nowitna National Wildlife Refuge

This 2.1-million-acre refuge is located approximately 200 miles west of Fairbanks in the central Yukon River valley. It protects a lowland basin bordering the Nowitna and Yukon rivers and encompasses forested lowlands, hills, lakes, marshes, ponds and streams. The dominant feature is the Nowitna River, part of which is a nationally designated wild river. This river is considered outstanding for float trips and also provides spawning grounds for northern pike and sheefish. However, the primary reason the refuge was established was to protect furbearers, waterfowl and their habitat.

Nowitna is 1 of 4 refuges (the others are Innoko, Kanuti and Koyukuk) encompassed by solar basins, which are characterized by encircling hills, light winds, low rainfall, severe winters and short, warm summers.

Wildlife: The forested lowlands of Nowitna Refuge provide excellent wetland habitats that support good populations of fish and waterfowl. More than 250,000 birds, including the trumpeter swan, breed on the refuge. Other wildlife found here include black and grizzly bear and moose.

Activities: Moose and bear hunting are major activities on the refuge. Marten, mink, wolverine, beaver and muskrat are important furbearers that provide income, food and recreation for local residents. Fishing for northern pike and sheefish is excellent. Other fish found in refuge waters include salmon, whitefish and arctic grayling.

Access and Accommodations: Access to Nowitna is by boat or charter air service from Fairbanks.

For more information: Contact Complex Manager, Koyukuk/Nowitna Refuge Complex, P.O. Box 287, Galena, AK 99741-0287; phone 656-1231.

Tetlin National Wildlife Refuge

This 730,000-acre refuge is located in east central Alaska. It is bordered on the north by the Alaska Highway, on the east by the Canadian border, on the south by Wrangell-St. Elias National Park and Preserve and on the west by the Tetlin Reserve (formerly the Tetlin Indian Reservation).

Tetlin Refuge is a showcase of natural features created by wildfires, permafrost and fluctuating river channels. The refuge features an undulating plain broken by hills, forests, ponds, lakes and extensive marshes. The glacial Chisana and Nabesna rivers dominate the valley where they meander before joining to form the Tanana River. Parabolic sand dunes, formed by windblown glacial flour, are found southeast of Northway and at Big John Hill.

Tetlin's vegetation is a good example of the benefits of wildfires. These natural phenomena help create diverse plant habitats such as grasslands or birch forests. Spruce forests are usually the dominant vegetation in

Eighty percent of the world's population of trumpeter swans nest in Alaska.
(Jerrianne Lowther)

a subarctic environment. When fire destroys such a forest, a series of habitats follow until once again spruce trees dominate.

Climate: Temperatures in June and July often exceed 80°F, with lows to 40°F. During these months it is light around the clock. By mid-September daytime temperatures of 45°F and nighttime temperatures of 25°F are common. Winter temperatures can drop to -70°F, and often stay below -40°F for a week or below 0°F for several months. Weather can change rapidly. Snow can occur as early as August.

Wildlife: These varied habitats are home to a diverse group of animals: moose, black and brown bears, ptarmigan, wolf, lynx and red fox. Caribou winter in the refuge and Dall sheep can be seen on mountain slopes. The refuge is a stopover for migrating birds and its wetlands provide important summer breeding habitat. Refuge wetlands are critical when drought in Canada sends birds farther north. The refuge supports a growing population of trumpeter swans, as well as the largest population of nesting osprey in Alaska. As many as 100,000 sandhill cranes pass through the refuge each fall. Other large birds found in the refuge include arctic and common loons, bald eagles and golden eagles. Birds that are rarely, if ever, seen in other parts of Alaska (because their usual range is farther south) may be seen here, including blue-winged teals, ruddy ducks, ring-necked ducks, red-winged blackbirds and mountain bluebirds. The refuge also is the western or northern limit of distribution of the American coot, rail and brown-headed cowbird.

Arctic grayling, whitefish, lake trout, burbot and northern pike inhabit lakes and streams. There are no significant salmon runs, although a few chum salmon run up the Tanana and its tributaries.

Activities: Recreational activities popular on Tetlin refuge include fishing and hunting, wildlife observation and photography. Fishing and hunting guide service is available in Tok; a big game guide operates within the refuge. The refuge office is located on the Alaska Highway in Tok directly across from the Alaska Public Lands Information Center at Milepost 1314.1. The refuge sponsors wildlife movies at the center. Tetlin National Wildlife Refuge Visitor Center is located at Milepost 1229 Alaska Highway; open 7 A.M. to 7 P.M. from Memorial Day to Labor Day. The center has an excellent scenic vista, interpretive displays, animal mounts and general information on natural resources.

Seven interpretive turnouts on the Alaska Highway also offer scenic vistas and the opportunity to view wildlife.

Visitors to the refuge should leave an itinerary with a friend or the refuge office in Tok and contact that person or office upon returning.

Accommodations: Camping at 2 refuge campgrounds on the Alaska Highway. Wilderness camping is allowed throughout the refuge. The best summer campsites are river bars and ridges where breezes reduce the insect problem. Choose sites carefully to avoid possible flooding from rainstorms or rising rivers. Dead or downed wood is usually available on river bars or in spruce stands. Pack out all unburnable trash and bury firepits. Human waste should be buried at least 100 yards from the water source. Camping supplies, as well as gas, food and lodging, are available in Tok and Northway.

Access: The Alaska Highway provides access along 65 miles of the refuge's northern border. Foot access is possible along the highway from the Canadian border to Gardiner Creek and at other points. The refuge is accessible by small boat from the Alaska Highway at Desper Creek and from the Northway Road at the Chisana River bridge. Charter planes are available in Tok. Riverboats are available at Tok and Northway. There are no designated roads or trails for motorized vehicles in the refuge. The refuge has no foot trails; some appear on maps but are not identifiable on the ground. Topographic maps and a compass are necessary for cross-country trips.

For more information: Contact Refuge Manager, Tetlin National Wildlife Refuge, P.O. Box 779, Tok, AK 99780; phone 883-5312.

Yukon Flats National Wildlife Refuge

This refuge, about 100 miles north of Fairbanks, encompasses 8.6 million acres in east-central Alaska. This area is primarily a complex of wetlands of more than 30,000 lakes, ponds and sloughs.

The refuge is bisected by the Yukon River, America's fifth largest river, which meanders for 225 miles. Here the river breaks free from canyon walls and spreads out through the vast floodplain. In the spring, millions of migrating birds converge on the flats before the ice moves from the river. The refuge has one of the highest nesting densities of waterfowl in North America and contributes more than 2 million ducks and geese to the continent's flyways.

The Porcupine River is the major tributary of the Yukon River within the refuge, joining the Yukon just downstream from Fort Yukon. Others include the Chandalar, Christian, Hadwenzic, Hodzana, Sheenjek and Dall rivers and Birch and Beaver creeks. All are important for salmon spawning except the Christian River.

Climate: Yukon Flats has a continental subarctic climate characterized by great seasonal extremes of temperature and daylight. Summer temperatures regularly top 90°F and have hit 100°F, the highest ever recorded above the Arctic Circle. Winter minimums to -50°F and lows in excess of -70°F have been recorded. Precipitation is low, averaging about 6.5 inches annually at Fort Yukon. July and August are the wettest months. Freezeup usually occurs in October. Breakup occurs at Fort Yukon around May 15; larger lakes are not free of ice until later.

Wildlife: Mammals on the refuge include a substantial population of moose, as well as Dall sheep in the White Mountains, caribou, wolves, grizzly and black bear, marten, lynx, snowshoe hare, beaver, muskrat and some red fox and wolverine.

King, coho and chum salmon from the Bering Sea pass through and spawn in the flats each summer — the longest salmon run in the United States. Other fish found in refuge waters include Dolly Varden, arctic grayling, whitefish, sheefish, cisco, burbot and northern pike.

Activities: Residents of 7 communities — Beaver, Birch Creek, Chalkyitsik, Circle, Fort Yukon, Stevens Village and Venetie — use the refuge for subsistence activities. Their camps and equipment are crucial for their survival and should be left undisturbed. Subsistence accounts for 90 percent of the public use of the refuge. The remaining uses center on sport hunting and river floating (see River Running this section). There are considerable private holdings within the refuge, particularly along river corridors; contact the refuge office for the location of these lands to avoid trespassing.

Accommodations: There are no accommodations within the refuge. There are commercial visitor facilities at Fort Yukon and Circle, but not at the other villages in the area.

Access: Yukon Flats Refuge can be reached by air and water. Scheduled commercial air service is available to all communities on the refuge. Charter air service to remote areas of the refuge is available in Fairbanks, Fort Yukon and Circle. A few bush airstrips, numerous lakes, and sand or gravel bars make most areas of the refuge accessible by light aircraft. Local residents use riverboats, canoes, kayaks and rafts for river floating and other recreational activities. There is no road access to the refuge, although the Dalton Highway runs adjacent to the refuge's southwestern boundary.

For more information and assistance in planning a trip to the refuge contact: Refuge Manager, Yukon Flats National Wildlife Refuge, Federal Bldg. and Courthouse, P.O. Box 14, Fairbanks, AK 99701; phone 456-0440.

Cabins

BLM Cabins

The Bureau of Land Management (BLM) has 10 recreational cabins (see chart) and 1 shelter cabin available to the public in the Interior. Many of the cabins are most easily accessed during the winter, although several cabins may be reached by trail in summer. Each of the cabins has a wood stove, Coleman lantern and cook stove (bring white gas), ax, bowsaw and outhouse. Carry out garbage. Cut firewood available, but please replenish pile for next visitor. Use only dead or downed wood.

Cabin reservations are accepted up to 30 days in advance with payment. Reservations are required. The fee for all recreational cabins is $20 per night on Friday and Saturday, $15 Sunday to Thursday; use is restricted to 3 consecutive nights. Payment must be received at the time the reservation is made. A receipt will be issued which should be taken along as proof of cabin reservation. No reservations are required and no fee is charged for the Wickersham Creek Trail Shelter (Mile 11.2 Wickersham Creek Trail; sleeps 2).

For more information: Contact the BLM Steese/White Mountain District Office, phone 474-2350. Make reservations and payments in person or by mail to the BLM Land Information Office, 1150 University Ave., Fairbanks, AK 99709; phone 474-2350.

Chena River State Recreation Area Cabins

The Division of Parks and Outdoor Recreation maintains 5 public-use recreation cabins in Chena River SRA that can be rented for up to 3 consecutive nights for $25 per night. Reservations can be made up to 180 days in advance; fees must be paid when reservations are submitted.

Access to each of the cabins varies. Some are located up to 6 miles from the road and are reached by snow machine, dogsled, cross-country skiing, hiking or boat. A detailed map of the cabin's location is provided when reservations are made.

All cabins will accommodate at least 4 people. Each cabin is furnished with plywood sleeping platforms, a woodstove, table, benches, fire extinguisher, bow saw and ax. An outhouse is located nearby.

For more information or to reserve a cabin, contact Alaska State Parks, 3700 Airport Way, Fairbanks, AK 99709; phone 451-2695.

Hiking Trails

Angel Rocks Trail. Trailhead at Milepost 48.9 Chena Hot Springs Road in Chena River State Recreation Area. This is a short (3.5-mile), relatively easy hike. It is less than 2 miles to the spectacular rock outcropping. At the top, there are 3 alternatives: return on the same improved trail, continue up to the end of the tor formations for beautiful views of the Alaska Range, Chena Dome and Far Mountain, or continue on the loop trail that

is currently under construction. Approximate hiking time is 3 to 4 hours. Related USGS Topographic maps: Big Delta D-5 and Circle A-5.

Big Bend Trail. A White Mountains National Recreation Area trail, this 15-mile trail begins at Mile 14.5 on the Colorado Creek Trail and ends at Mile 19.5 on the Wickersham Creek Trail. It is rated moderate with an elevation change of 1,325 feet. Because of wet, muddy sections of trail in the summer, it is easiest to use this trail in winter. From the Colorado Creek Trail junction, the trail passes Colorado Creek Cabin and continues through a large open meadow for 3 miles, then climbs steeply for 1 mile to the top of the ridge. The trail follows the ridgeline south for 3 miles over its highest elevation of 2,675 feet. The trail then descends for 3 miles before crossing a bridge near the "Big Bend" on Beaver Creek and continuing 5 miles through open meadows and black spruce forests to junction with the Wickersham Creek Trail. For more information contact the BLM, Steese/White Mountains District, 1150 University Avenue, Fairbanks, AK 99709; phone 474-2350. Related USGS Topographic map: Livengood B-2.

Chena Dome Trail. Trailhead at Milepost 50.5 Chena Hot Springs Road in Chena River State Recreation Area. (Also trailhead

BLM CABINS

	SLEEPS	AIR ACCESS	BOAT ACCESS	TRAIL ACCESS	HUNTING	FISHING	BEACHCOMB	SKIFF	STOVE
FAIRBANKS AREA									
Borealis–LeFevre *(Mile 20 Wickersham Creek Trail)*	5	•	•		•				W
Cache Mountain *(Mile 6 O'Brien Creek Trail)*	6			•					W
Caribou Bluff *(Mile 1 Fossil Gap Trail)*	4		•						W
Colorado Creek *(Mile 14 Colorado Creek Trail)*	5		•						W
Cripple Creek *(Summer cabin; road access from Mile 60 Steese Highway)*	3		•		•				W
Crowberry *(Mile 21 Trail Creek Trail)*	4		•						W
Lee's *(Mile 1 Trail Creek Trail)*	6		•						W
Moose Creek *(Mile 9 Trail Creek Trail)*	3		•						W
Windy Gap *(Mile 22 Lower Fossil Creek Trail)*	4		•		•				W
Wolf Run *(Mile 1.5 Windy Creek Trail)*	6		•						W

The above chart gives a brief description of each cabin. Type of stove provided is indicated as follows: O=oil stove, W=wood stove, G=outdoor grill, OH=oil heater.

for Angel Creek Cabin ATB Trail.) This 30-mile loop trail circles Angel Creek Valley and rejoins Chena Hot Springs Road at Milepost 49.1. The trail crosses Chena Dome at its highest point (4,421 feet), and offers high alpine scenic views not seen elsewhere in the recreation area. At each end of the loop a 3-mile section of trail has been cut through the forest to tree line. The rest of the trail traverses tundra ridges marked by rock cairns and blanketed with wildflowers in late May, June and July. The loop provides a good 3- to 4-day trip for backpackers. Some portions of the trail are steep; wear suitable footgear. Water may be a problem in late summer. Additional information about this hike is available on bulletin boards at the trailheads. Related USGS Topographic maps: Big Delta D-5, Circle A-5 and A-6.

Colorado Creek Trail. A White Mountains National Recreation Area trail, this 23-mile trail begins at Milepost 57 Elliott Highway and ends at Beaver Creek. It is rated as moderate with an elevation change of 1,015 feet. Because of wet, muddy sections of trail in summer, it is easiest to use this trail in winter. From the Elliott Highway trailhead, the trail climbs gently for about 11 miles, increasing in steepness for the next 3 miles to the top of the ridgeline at 1,625 feet. About 0.5 mile beyond the ridge there is a trail junction: the left trail continues 9 miles to Beaver Creek, the right trail goes 0.5 mile to Colorado Creek Cabin. From this trail junction, the 9-mile stretch to Beaver Creek goes through an old burn area then through forested sections of spruce, occasionally breaking into open meadows which provide good views of the White Mountains. In the forested areas, the cut trail is visible and marked, but high winds may drift snow across open sections of trail, making it difficult to follow. This also may happen on the last 2 miles before Beaver Creek when the trail passes through open meadow. Once across the meadow, the trail crosses Beaver Creek and connects with the Windy Creek Trail. For more information contact the BLM, Steese/White Mountains District, 1150 University Avenue, Fairbanks, AK 99709; phone 474-2350. Related USGS Topographic maps: Livengood B-2, B-3, C-2, C-3.

Granite Tors Trail. Trailhead at Tors Trail Campground, Milepost 39.5 Chena Hot Springs Road in Chena River State Recreation Area. Tors are high, isolated pinnacles of jointed granite jutting up from the tundra. Follow the dike (levee) on west side upstream 0.3 mile from campground to trail sign. It is

6 miles to the nearest tors, 8 miles to the main grouping. The upper portion of the trail is rocky and suitable footgear should be worn. A trail guide is available at the bulletin board in the campground. Related USGS Topographic map: Big Delta D-5.

Lower Fossil Creek Trail. This White Mountains National Recreation Area trail is 23 miles long, rated moderate to difficult, with a 550-foot elevation change. It begins at Beaver Creek at Mile 20 Wickersham Creek Trail and ends at the Windy Creek Trail junction. It is recommended for winter use. The trail crosses 2 frozen lakes in the first 7 miles. Watch for overflow and open water. At Mile 13 the trail drops onto Fossil Creek and pretty much parallels the creek to trail end at the Windy Gap Cabin at the Windy Creek Trail junction. For more information contact the BLM, Steese/White Mountains District, 1150 University Avenue, Fairbanks, AK 99709; phone 474-2350. Related USGS Topographic maps: Livengood B-1, B-2, C-1.

Moose Creek Trail. This White Mountains National Recreation Area trail is 10 miles long, rated moderate, with a 275-foot elevation change. One end of the trail connects at Mile 11.2 Wickersham Creek Trail and the other end of the trail connects at Mile 10 Trail Creek Trail. Because of wet, muddy sections of trail in summer, it is recommended for winter use. The trail passes through spruce forests and open burn and meadow areas and follows several creek drainages. The Moose Creek Cabin is just beyond the junction with the Trail Creek Trail at the eastern end of the meadow. For more information contact the BLM, Steese/White Mountains District, 1150 University Avenue, Fairbanks, AK 99709; phone 474-2350. Related USGS Topographic maps: Livengood A-2, B-2.

O'Brien Creek Trail. This White Mountains National Recreation Area trail is 19 miles in length, rated moderate to difficult, with a 1,725-foot elevation change. The trail begins at Beaver Creek, Mile 27 Trail Creek Trail, and ends at the Cache Mountain Divide, Upper Fossil Creek Trail. Because of wet, muddy sections of trail in summer, it is recommended for winter use. From Beaver Creek the trail heads northeast for 3 miles through a burn area and open spruce forests, then turns north and parallels O'Brien Creek for 9 miles. Cache Mountain Cabin is at Mile 6 on the trail. At Mile 12 there is a small trapper cabin that can be used in an emergency. Two miles past the trapper cabin the trail turns left and follows a side drainage 3.5 miles into high alpine meadows. The last 1.5 miles of the trail climbs steeply up to the saddle that separates the O'Brien Creek and Fossil Creek drainages. At the top of the Cache Mountain Divide, the trail junctions with Upper Fossil Creek Trail. For more information contact the BLM, Steese/White Mountains District, 1150 University Avenue, Fairbanks, AK 99709; phone 474-2350. Related USGS Topographic maps: Livengood B-1, C-1.

Pinnell Mountain National Recreation Trail. This rugged, 27.3-mile trail is accessible from the Steese Highway at Twelvemile Summit (Milepost 85.6) or Eagle Summit (Milepost 107.1). Day hikes or overnight stays can be enjoyed from either trailhead. Allow at least 3 days to travel the entire trail. The trail is clearly marked by rock cairns and mile markers. The trail traverses talus slopes and alpine tundra above tree line. It is quite steep and rugged, so hikers must be physically prepared.

Pinnell Mountain Trail is the first national recreation trail to be established in Alaska. It is also the only recreational development in the Steese National Conservation Area, a 1.2-million-acre area administered by the Bureau of Land Management.

This is one of the most accessible northern alpine tundra areas in the Interior. The trail winds along mountain ridges and through high passes mostly above 3,500 feet; the highest point reached is 4,721 feet. Along the trail are vantage points with views of the White Mountains, Tanana Hills, Brooks Range and Alaska Range. Between June 18 and 25 hikers can see the midnight sun from many high points along the trail, including the Eagle Summit trailhead parking area.

Some of Alaska's large carnivores — wolves, grizzly bears and wolverines—are occasionally spotted from the trail by an attentive eye. More frequently seen is the hoary marmot, perched atop a lookout rock issuing its shrill call. Also living in the rocky slopes is the small pika or "rock rabbit" with its brief, high-pitched squeak. Small groups of caribou can sometimes be seen from the trail.

Birdlife includes rock ptarmigan, gyrfalcons, ravens, northern harriers, golden eagles, northern wheatears, lapland longspurs and various surf birds. Wildflowers bloom in profusion along some sections. Look for moss campion, alpine azalea, oxy-

Ptarmigan Creek trail shelter, 1 of 2 shelters on the Pinnell Mountain National Recreation Trail. (George Wuerthner)

trope, frigid shooting star, arctic forget-me-not, lousewort and mountain avens.

Some of the oldest rocks in Alaska are found along this trail. These rocks are made up from sediments first deposited over a billion years ago.

No horses or motorized vehicles are allowed on the trail. Water is scarce; carry your own supply and boil or treat any water from streams. Backcountry camping is allowed along the trail; 8-by-12-foot shelter cabins are located near Mile 10 (Ptarmigan Creek Trail Shelter) and Mile 18 (North Fork Trail Shelter) from the Eagle Summit trailhead. Be prepared for mosquitoes and cool, windy weather. Bring a camp stove and a windscreen. Lodging is available at Fairbanks, Chatanika, Central and Circle Hot Springs; a few campgrounds are located along the Steese Highway. The state maintains the Steese Highway during the winter, but for current road conditions call the Alaska State Dept. of Transportation and Public Facilities in Fairbanks, phone 452-1911.

For more information contact the Bureau of Land Management Information Office, 1150 University Ave., Fairbanks, AK 99708-3844; phone 474-2350. Related USGS Topographic maps: Circle B-3, B-4, C-3, C-4.

Ski Loop Trail. The trailhead for this White Mountains National Recreation Area trail is at Milepost 27.8 Elliott Highway. It is an easy 5-mile loop from the highway trailhead following 1.5 miles of the Wickersham Creek Trail and 2 miles of the Summit Trail. The Summit Trail portion climbs for 1 mile to an overlook at 2,660 feet, with views of the Alaska Range on a clear day. Trail can be used year-round, although there are wet and muddy sections. For more information contact the BLM, Steese/White Mountains District, 1150 University Avenue, Fairbanks, AK 99709; phone 474-2200. Related USGS Topographic map: Livengood A-3.

Summit Trail. The trailhead for this White Mountains National Recreation Area trail is at Milepost 27.8 Elliott Highway. The 20-mile trail has been designed for summer use, with boardwalk installed over most wet areas. It is rated as moderate, with an elevation change of 1,775 feet. From the highway trailhead, the trail gently climbs and descends Wickersham Dome for the first 7 miles. After 2 miles of spruce forest, it climbs to 3,100 feet near Mile 10, then descends for 2 miles to 2,150 feet before climbing back to 2,505 feet at Mile 13. The final 7 miles of trail descends to 1,325 feet at Beaver Creek. The last 2 miles to Beaver

Creek are along the Wickersham Creek Trail. The Borealis-LeFevre Cabin is located on the north side of Beaver Creek. Use caution crossing Beaver Creek at high water. For more information contact the BLM, Steese/White Mountains District, 1150 University Avenue, Fairbanks, AK 99709; phone 474-2200. Related USGS Topographic maps: Livengood A-3, B-2, B-3.

Trail Creek Trail. A White Mountains National Recreation Area trail, rated moderate, with an elevation change of 825 feet. Because of wet, muddy sections of trail in summer, this trail is recommended for winter use. The 27-mile-long trail begins at Mile 6 on the Wickersham Creek Trail and ends at Beaver Creek. From the Wickersham Creek Trail junction, the trail follows a forested ridgeline for 4 miles, then climbs 2 miles to 2,245 feet. It junctions with the Moose Creek Trail at Mile 10; access to Moose Creek Cabin. The trail reaches its highest point of 2,387 feet at Mile 12, then gently descends for the next 12 miles to the Beaver Creek drainage. The last 3 miles drop steeply to Beaver Creek and connects with the O'Brien Creek Trail. Use caution while traveling on Beaver Creek as the overflow ice may be thin. For more information contact the BLM, Steese/White Mountains District, 1150 University Avenue, Fairbanks, AK 99709; phone 474-2200. Related USGS Topograhic maps: Livengood A-2, B-1, B-2.

Upper Fossil Creek Trail. This White Mountains National Recreation Area trail is 14 miles in length, rated moderate to difficult, with a 1,400-foot elevation change. Because of wet, muddy sections of trail in summer, this trail is recommended for winter use. The trail begins at Mile 23 on the Windy Creek Trail and ends at the O'Brien Creek Trail junction. The trail follows Fossil Creek most of the 14 miles to the Cache Mountain Divide. Watch for overflow; it is very easy to break through into water. There is a steep climb up to the saddle that separates the Fossil Creek and O'Brien Creek drainages. At the top of Cache Mountain Divide, the Upper Fossil Creek Trail connects with the O'Brien Creek Trail. Access to Windy Gap Cabin near Windy Creek Trail junction. For more information contact the BLM, Steese/White Mountains District, 1150 University Avenue, Fairbanks, AK 99709; phone 474-2200. Related USGS Topographic map: Livengood C-1.

Wickersham Creek Trail. This White Mountains National Recreation Area trail is 20 miles in length, rated easy to moderate, with a 1,150-foot elevation change. The trail begins at Milepost 27.8 on the Elliott Highway and ends at Beaver Creek. Because of wet, muddy sections of trail in summer, this trail is recommended for winter use. From the Elliott Highway trailhead, the trail follows a forested ridgeline 5 miles east to a 2,545-foot peak; good view from top of Alaska Range and White Mountains. The Wickersham Creek Trail junctions with Trail Creek Trail at Mile 6 and with Moose Creek Trail at Mile 11. At Mile 11.2 is the Wickersham Creek Trail Shelter. This small cabin sleeps 2 people and has a wood stove. This shelter need not be reserved in advance. From the shelter, the trail descends through spruce forests for 4 miles, then climbs the next 3 miles, breaking into open forest. The trail drops steeply the last 2 miles to Beaver Creek. The Borealis-LeFevre Cabin is visible through the trees on the north side of Beaver Creek. For more information contact the BLM, Steese/White Mountains District, 1150 University Avenue, Fairbanks, AK 99709; phone 474-2200. Related USGS Topographic maps: Livengood A-2, A-3, B-2.

Windy Creek Trail. This White Mountains National Recreation Area trail is 10 miles in length, rated moderate to difficult, with a 1,000-foot elevation change. It begins on Beaver Creek at Mile 23 on the Colorado Creek Trail and ends at Fossil Creek. Because of wet, muddy sections of trail in summer, it is recommended for winter use. The Wolf Run Cabin is at Mile 1.5 on the trail. Beyond the cabin, the trail parallels Windy Creek and follows the creek drainage 5 miles up the valley, winding through black spruce forests and open meadows. The trail climbs steeply for 2 miles through Windy Gap and emerges on top of a plateau overlooking the Fossil Creek drainage with views of the White Mountains, Limestone Gulch and Windy Arch. The trail then descends into forest and drops steeply 1 mile to Fossil Creek and the Windy Gap Cabin. For more information contact the BLM, Steese/White Mountains District, 1150 University Avenue, Fairbanks, AK 99709; phone 474-2200. Related USGS maps: Livengood C-1, C-2.

River Running

Beaver Creek. Beaver Creek, a National Wild and Scenic River, originates within White Mountains National Recreation Area north of Fairbanks and then flows in a northerly direction through Yukon Flats National Wildlife Refuge into the Yukon River.

This clear-water stream is classified as Class I overall by BLM. Canoes, kayaks and rafts are suitable. From its headwaters the river drops 9 feet per mile to the end of the wild river corridor below Victoria Creek 127 miles away. The trip to this point usually takes 7 to 10 days. Exit from this point is by floatplane or gravel bar landing in the Victoria Creek area. It is possible to continue on through Yukon Flats Refuge to the Yukon River and exit at the Yukon River bridge on the Dalton Highway. This segment is another 268 miles, which takes approximately 8 to 14 days.

Fish available in Beaver Creek include grayling, burbot, whitefish and northern pike.

Access is by auto from Milepost F 57.3 on the Steese Highway via U.S. Creek Road to Nome Creek.

For additional information about Beaver Creek contact: Steese/White Mountains District office, phone 356-5367; or Bureau of Land Management, Fairbanks Support Center, 1541 Gaffney Road, Fairbanks, AK 99703; phone 356-2025. Related USGS Topographic maps: Circle B-6, C-6, D-5 and 6; Livengood B-1 and 2, C-1 and 2, D-1.

Birch Creek. Birch Creek, a wild and scenic river, originates about 70 miles northeast of Fairbanks and flows generally east then north into the Yukon River. Most of Birch Creek is within the Steese National Conservation Area.

BLM classifies this river as Class I and II, with some Class III rapids above the confluence of Wolf Creek. From the put in point it is generally Class I water; the upper 8 miles may be shallow and require lining through riffles. There is a stretch of Class II rapids just below the confluence of Clums Fork. Canoes, kayaks or rafts all are suitable. From the usual put in point to the usual exit point is 126 miles; the river drops 10 feet per mile. The trip generally takes 7 to 10 days. Fishing for grayling, northern pike and whitefish. There is extensive mining above the put in point and outside the river corridor which has muddied the water of this stream; it may be difficult to identify submerged rocks. *NOTE: Respect the rights of others; avoid actively mined areas.*

This stream is accessible at both ends by auto from the Steese Highway. The usual put in point is near Milepost F 94, where a short road leads down to a parking area and canoe launch. The usual takeout point is the Steese Highway bridge at Milepost F 147.1.

For additional information about Birch Creek contact: Steese/White Mountains District Office, phone 356-5367 or Bureau of Land Management, Fairbanks Support Center, 1541 Gaffney Road, Fairbanks, AK 99703; phone 356-2025. Related USGS Topographic maps: Circle A-3 and 4, B-1 through 4, C-1.

Black River. This slow, meandering stream flows some 200 miles to join the Porcupine River, about 17 miles northeast of Fort Yukon. Much of the river is within Yukon Flats National Wildlife Refuge. The section above the confluence of the Salmon Fork flows moderately fast (3 to 4 mph) through forested lowlands of white spruce and willow. Below the Salmon Fork confluence, the river slows to 2 to 3 mph as it widens and passes along numerous bluffs. Below Chalkyitsik the river slows further to 1 to 2 mph as the meanders increase in size.

This trip takes approximately 13 to 16 days from the vicinity of Birch Lake to Fort Yukon or 9 to 10 days from Birch Lake to Chalkyitsik. Canoes or kayaks are suitable for this trip.

Above the Salmon Fork, and again upstream from Chalkyitsik, sand or gravel bars are infrequent or not suitable for campsites. Upstream winds on the lower river can create whitecaps in a short time. There is low water after July 1 and the river usually is not floatable above Chalkyitsik. Views generally are limited to the river corridor because of high banks, although bluffs below Salmon Fork add variety.

Fishing varies from poor to fair depending on water conditions and season for grayling, Dolly Varden, northern pike, whitefish and sheefish. Moose, bear and other wildlife inhabit the area, but high vegetation limits viewing. Waterfowl are numerous.

Access is by floatplane from Fort Yukon to the river or to adjacent lakes between Salmon and Grayling forks. Exit is by floatplane from the Black or Porcupine rivers, by scheduled air service from Chalkyitsik, or float to Fort Yukon. To reach Fort Yukon, paddle 3 miles up the Sucker River from its confluence with the Porcupine River to a road-accessible landing.

Related USGS Topographic maps: Black River A-3, B-3 and 4, C-4 through 6; Fort Yukon C-1 through 3.

Chandalar River. Both main forks head in the Brooks Range and flow south to become the Chandalar River, which empties into the Yukon River south of Venetie. Below the confluence of the North and East Fork Chandalar rivers, it is quite fast and never dull. The Junjik River, which joins the east fork above Arctic Village, offers whitewater challenges. The upper East Fork Chandalar is very fast, but not spiked with rapids. The more difficult North Fork flows through Chandalar Lake.

From the usual put in on the East Fork Chandalar, there are 72 miles of fast, flat water to Arctic Village. For those trying the Junjik, it's Class II, descending at 6 feet per mile, to the East Fork Chandalar, then on to Arctic Village for a total of 40 river miles. From Arctic Village, the East Fork Chandalar is Class II, dropping at 7 feet per mile for 160 river miles, to its confluence with the North Fork. From the usual put in at Chandalar Lake, the North Fork offers 120 miles of Class II and III, dropping at 15 feet per mile. Below the confluence of the North and East forks, the Chandalar is 90 river miles of flat water, dropping at 5 feet per mile, to the Yukon.

The East Fork Chandalar is bounded on the east by the Venetie Indian Reservation, owned by the people of Venetie and Arctic Village, and by Arctic National Wildlife Refuge to the north and west. The Chandalar River is bounded to the northeast by the reservation and to the southwest by Yukon Flats National Wildlife Refuge. Camping is permitted on wildlife refuge lands; do not use reservation lands without permission.

Access is by charter air service from Fairbanks or Fort Yukon to the rivers. Exit is by scheduled air service from Arctic Village, which has limited overnight accommodations, or Venetie, which has no visitor facilities.

Charley River. All 106 miles of this wild and scenic river flow within Yukon-Charley Rivers National Preserve. The Charley originates at the 4,000-foot level and flows northeast to join the Yukon River.

The Charley is rated Class II, or intermediate, with a few areas rated Class III, or more difficult. Paddlers should be experienced; canoes, kayaks or rafts are suitable because they are very portable, and inflatable rafts are most commonly used.

Maximum stream flow is in late May and early June. The boating season generally begins in June and there is usually sufficient flow for small boats through August, although exposed rocks and bars necessitate portaging during August. The Charley flows from its headwaters with an average gradient of 31 feet per mile and an average current of 6 to 8 mph. During high water the upper two-thirds of the river provide a good whitewater experience. As the water level lowers, maneuvering becomes a constant necessity and some rapids must be scouted to determine the best channel. Rapid runoff from rainstorms during June and July, and occasionally in August, can cause the river to rise as much as several feet within hours, posing a hazard for floaters. From the usual put in point at Copper Creek, it is usually a 4-day float to the Yukon, then another 2 days to Circle.

The Charley is considered good to excellent for grayling fishing. Northern pike are found as far as 16 miles upstream. Sheefish and king, chum and coho salmon are occasionally found in the river.

Access is generally by helicopter from Tanacross to the Copper Creek area. A primitive landing strip located just above Copper Creek provides limited fixed-wing aircraft access to the Charley River. Exit is by riverboat up the Yukon River to Eagle, floating down the Yukon to Circle, or by floatplane from the Yukon. Circle is accessible by auto from Fairbanks via the Steese Highway.

Ranger patrols are infrequent and visitors should exercise caution and be prepared for any hazard.

For additional information about the Charley River contact: Yukon-Charley Rivers National Preserve, P.O. Box 167, Eagle, AK 99738; phone 547-2233. Related USGS Topographic maps: Charley River A-4 and 5, B-4 through 6; Circle D-1; Eagle C-6, D-5 and 6.

Chena River. A tributary of the Tanana River, the Chena is the focal point for the Chena River State Recreation Area. There are several launch points along Chena Hot Springs Road. Local paddlers suggest a float from Milepost 39.5 to 37.9 for easy paddling; Milepost 44.1 to 37.9 for a longer float; and Milepost 52.3 to 47.3 for paddlers with more skill. Allow about 1 hour on the river for each road mile traveled. The Chena should not be underestimated. The river is cold and the current very strong. Watch for river-wide logjams and sweepers. Access to the Chena is from Fairbanks via the Steese Highway to Chena Hot Springs Road. Related USGS Topographic maps: Fairbanks D-1 and D-2.

Fortymile River. This clear-water wild and scenic river is located in east-central Alaska. It is fed by numerous creeks and streams and flows eastward into the Yukon River at Fortymile in Canada.

There are 2 major options for trips on the Fortymile: via the Middle or South forks.

The Middle Fork is classified by BLM as Class I overall. However, there are several

Class II rapids, a Class III and a Class V rapid known as "The Kink." In general the rapids become progressively more difficult downstream, but all can be checked out on foot first and easily portaged. In late July and August the river may be low, making for a safer if slower voyage. Mining claims cover several stretches of the Fortymile and virtually all of the bed of the South Fork is claimed. (Although the Fortymile River is a national wild and scenic river, the riverbed belongs to the state, which allows underwater mining claims.) Travelers may see some suction dredging. *NOTE: Mining claims are posted. Please avoid these areas!* There is fishing in these rivers for arctic grayling and burbot.

If floating the Fortymile to the Yukon River, travelers will cross into Canada and then back into the United States. Upon arriving in Clinton, YT, travelers must report to Canadian customs in Whitehorse, phone (403) 667-6471. After reentering the United States on the Yukon River, check in again with U.S. customs at Eagle.

There are numerous access points, both road and fly-in, and a number of float trips can be made on the various forks. For the Middle Fork trip, charter flights can be taken from Tok on the Alaska Highway, to the abandoned mining settlement of Joseph at the confluence of Joseph Creek and the Middle Fork Fortymile. The Joseph airstrip is unmaintained. Access to the river is by a 50-yard trail from the east end of the runway. There are takeouts at the O'Brien Creek bridge, Milepost 113.2 on the Taylor Highway, and at the Clinton Creek bridge at Clinton, YT, Canada. The 90-mile trip from Joseph to the O'Brien Creek bridge usually takes 4 to 5 days; the 182 miles from Joseph to Eagle via the Yukon River takes about 7 to 9 days.

The Class III rapids, called "The Chute," is on the North Fork Fortymile just below its confluence with the Middle Fork. Exercise extreme care at the first right turn after the confluence. Canoes can be lined on the right bank. Rafts should stay close to the right bank. A few miles farther is "The Kink." Now on the National Register of Historic Places, The Kink was a major engineering feat in 1904 when a narrow channel was blasted 100 feet through a ridge of land forming the neck in what was a sharp bend in the river. The channel rerouted the river and left the riverbed open for mining. The Kink today is a Class V rapids and should be portaged. (For more information on The Kink, see Special Features this section.)

If leaving the river at the O'Brien Creek bridge, land 100 yards upstream from the bridge on the right bank. There is a trail to the parking lot.

A few miles downriver from O'Brien Creek is the Class III rapids known as "Deadman Riffle," which is hazardous for canoes. This area is not far from the Canadian border. Shortly before reaching Clinton there is a Class IV rapids called "The Canyon." Line from either bank depending on water level. This rapid is in 2 sections separated by a quarter mile of calm water; it is very dangerous during high water. There is road access once again at the Clinton Creek bridge, or floaters can continue on to the Yukon River and float the 57 miles to Eagle. At Eagle, there are 2 boat landings. The upstream landing is generally preferred because vehicles can be driven very close to the water. The downstream landing requires a 2-story climb up a steep stairway to reach downtown Eagle.

Floating the clear-water South Fork Fortymile will avoid The Chute and The Kink. This fork is Class I overall, with some Class II and III rapids.

There are numerous accesses from the Taylor Highway: at the BLM recreation site at Milepost 48.8; via an unmaintained 2-track trail that heads south from the airstrip at Chicken (Milepost 66.4); and at the South Fork bridge, Milepost 75.3.

The trip is 72 miles from Milepost 48.8 to O'Brien Creek bridge and takes 3 to 4 days; from O'Brien Creek to Eagle via the Yukon River it's 92 miles and takes 4 to 5 days. A few miles above the confluence of the South and North forks, floaters will pass by the site of Franklin, a small mining community established about 1887. It was the hub of mining activity for the southern portion of the Fortymile mining district.

For additional information about the Fortymile River system contact: Bureau of Land Management, Steese/White Mountain District Office, 1150 University Ave, Fairbanks, AK 99709; phone 474-2250; or Bureau of Land Management, Field Office in Tok (behind the Alaska Public Lands Information Center), P.O. Box 307, Tok, AK 99780; phone 883-5121. Related USGS Topographic maps: Eagle B-3 through 5, C-3. Canadian Maps: 40-Mile 116-C7, Cassiar Cis. 116-C8, Shell Creek 116-C9, Mount Gladman 116-C10. Purchase Canadian maps from dealers or Canada Map Office, 615 Booth St., Ottawa, ON, Canada K1A 0E9.

Innoko River. The Innoko River heads south of Cloudy Mountain in the Kuskokwim Mountains, northwest of McGrath, and flows northeast and southwest 500 miles to junction with the Yukon River. The middle portion of the river flows through Innoko National Wildlife Refuge and is accessible for an easy Class I to Class II float for experienced wilderness paddlers.

The river, from put in at Ophir to Cripple Landing, is very scenic with wildflowers along the hillsides and abundant wildlife, including grizzly and black bear, moose, wolf, otter, marten, beaver, porcupine and a variety of waterfowl. Fishing for grayling and pike. Numerous small waterfalls tumble into the Innoko along the way.

Historic sites along the upper river include the site of Folger, near the mouth of Folger Creek, and Cripple Landing, just above the North Fork. Little evidence of a town remains at Folger, once a thriving community that supplied mines to the northeast. At Cripple Landing there is an old trading post/post office building (privately owned) and 3 abandoned cabins. Like Folger, Cripple Landing was a supply point for area mines during the early 1900s.

Closer to the junction of the Innoko and Dishna rivers is Rennie's Landing, where 2 buildings and a warehouse remain. Privately owned, this site serves as a fall and winter trapping headquarters. The site of Simel's trading post, also known as Fairview, is 2.6 miles above the confluence and is marked only be a few foundation outlines on the rapidly eroding river bank. Across the river at Simel's, hidden by willow and cottonwood trees, are the boiler and paddlewheel from one of the old steamers that plied the river during the gold rush days.

Eighteen miles below the mouth of the Dishna River is the site of Diskaket, an Athabascan Indian winter village that became a crossroads on the gold rush trails. Remains of three buildings and a cemetery are all that's left of the old village, which has been nominated as a National Historic Site. From Diskaket to the abandoned village of Holigachuk (privately owned), just upriver from Shageluk, only occasional cabin sites show evidence of man's presence.

Watch for sweepers. Wind and rain can slow progress, and paddling will be necessary as the river slows. Best time for a river trip is usually in July. Normally clear, the Innoko may be muddy during mining season.

Recommended float is from Ophir to

Shageluk, near the mouth of the Innoko. Takeout point during low water is by wheel aircraft at Cripple Landing or by float-equipped aircraft from the Dishna River down (upriver below North Fork only during high water). Arrange with air taxi operators in Galena, McGrath, Bethel or Aniak. Ophir is accessed by road from Takotna.

For more information contact: Refuge Manager, Innoko National Wildlife Refuge, P.O. Box 69, McGrath, AK 99627; phone 524-3251. Related USGS Topographic maps: Ophir A-2, B-2, C-1, C-2, C-3, D-1, and D-2.

Kantishna River. The Kantishna is an ancient route between the Tanana and the Kuskokwim (via the Lake Minchumina portage). In later years, many prospectors and trappers traveled up the river, summer and winter, to work their claims or traplines along the foothills of Mount McKinley.

This river is not difficult. It meanders and flows slowly. More skillful paddlers may wish to try an alternate route on the tributary stream, Moose Creek, which has some rapids and shallow stretches in dry seasons. Canoes, kayaks and riverboats are suitable.

Access is by air charter service from Anchorage to Lake Minchumina or by scheduled air service to the community of Lake Minchumina. Float the Muddy River, which drains Lake Minchumina, east 25 miles to Birch Creek, which joins shortly thereafter with the McKinley River to become the Kantishna. From the outlet of Lake Minchumina to the confluence of the Kantishna and the Tanana River is 220 miles of flat water. Related USGS Topographic maps: Mount McKinley D-3, D-4, C-4, B-4, B-3, A-3; Kantishna River B-2, B-1, C-1.

Nabesna River. This river heads at Nabesna Glacier and flows northeast to join with the Chisana River to form the Tanana River near Northway Junction on the Alaska Highway. The river begins in Wrangell-St. Elias National Park and Preserve and flows through Tetlin National Wildlife Refuge.

This cold stream is in a wide graveled valley and is braided and quite fast at the start. Eventually it slows to meander through the foothills and taiga forest east of the Wrangell Mountains. The first 10 miles from the put in point are rated Class I to II, with a gradient of 20 feet per mile. The gradient for the next 15 miles of flat water is 13 feet per mile, and the gradient for the last 40 miles is 5 feet per mile. Canoes, kayaks or

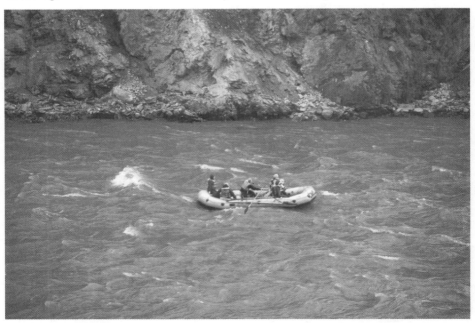

Commercial raft outfitters run the difficult portion of the Nenana River near the Denali Park entrance. (Jerrianne Lowther)

rafts are suitable.

The river can be reached from the 45-mile-long Nabesna Road, which leaves the Glenn Highway (Tok Cutoff) at Milepost 65.2 from Tok. This gravel road becomes very rough after Milepost 28.5; check on road conditions at Sportsman's Paradise Lodge at this point. There are several creeks that must be forded. A trail approximately 5 miles long leads to the Nabesna River from Milepost 41. Exit the river at Northway or at the Alaska Highway at the confluence of the Chisana River. Related USGS Topographic maps: Nabesna B-4, C-4, C-3, D-3, D-2; Tanacross A-2.

Nenana River. The Nenana River heads at Nenana Glacier in the Alaska Range and flows north 140 miles to the Tanana River at the town of Nenana. This river is easily accessible at several locations on the Denali and George Parks highways and the Alaska Railroad.

A popular put in is 18 miles from Cantwell where the Denali Highway closely parallels the Nenana River. The trip from this point to the Tanana usually takes 5 days. Put ins on the Parks Highway: McKinley Village, Milepost 231; the Riley Creek bridge, Milepost 237; Nenana River bridge, Milepost 238; Healy, Milepost 248.8; Rex Bridge over Nenana, Milepost 275.8. Put ins along the Alaska Railroad: Windy Station; Denali Park Station; Riley Creek bridge; Healy; and Nenana.

From the Denali Highway put in, the Nenana River is Class I to Class II for the 38 miles to McKinley Village. From this point for the next 32 miles to below Healy, heavy water and very difficult rapids rated at Class IV to Class V through a narrow canyon make the river suitable only for expert paddlers. Others should skirt this section via the Parks Highway. (Organized raft tours are offered down this part of the river by outfitters based near the entrance to Denali National Park and Preserve.) Below this canyon area, the Nenana's course to the Tanana has braided channels, but no difficult rapids. Canoes, kayaks and rafts are suitable for the upper and lower river. Kayaks or rafts only on the middle river.

Related USGS Topographic maps: Fairbanks A-5, B-5, C-5; Healy B-3 and 4, C-4, D-4 and 5.

Nowitna River. This National Wild and Scenic River heads in the forested uplands of the Kuskokwim Mountains and flows northeast 250 miles to the Yukon River. It is located in Nowitna National Wildlife Refuge.

Broad, clear and deep, it is rated Class 1 white water and Class C flat water. High water and ice dams can back up the river in spring. Popular trip length is 310 miles. For more information contact the Refuge Manager, Nowitna National Wildlife Refuge, P.O. Box 287, Galena, AK 99741; phone 656-1231.

Porcupine River. This river heads in Canada at 65°28 N, 139°32 W and flows 460 miles to the Yukon River, 2 miles north of Fort Yukon. Difficulties along the river are minor, so the trip is considered suitable for families with older children. Canoes or kayaks are recommended for the trip; rafts also are suitable, but progress may be slower due to upstream midafternoon winds.

The Porcupine is generally slow moving (2 to 4 mph) flat water to Class I with somewhat swifter current (4 to 6 mph) through multi-hued, steep-walled canyons beginning a few miles upstream from New Rampart House, in Yukon Territory. From the border to Fort Yukon the river flows within the Yukon Flats National Wildlife Refuge. Downstream from Canyon Village, AK, the canyons give way to low rolling hills on either side of the river. Farther downstream, the river meanders across the wetlands of the Yukon Flats. To reach Fort Yukon, paddle 3 miles up the Sucker River from its confluence with the Porcupine River to a road-accessible landing.

The most common put in is at Old Crow, YT. From there it generally takes 6 to 10 days to float the 250 miles to Fort Yukon. It also is possible to charter a plane to the upper Porcupine or to Summit Lake on the Bell River, a tributary to the Porcupine, and extend the trip some 250 additional miles. For a description of the trip from Summit Lake, send for a Parks Canada booklet titled *Wild Rivers: Yukon Territory* available for a nominal fee from Printing and Publishing, Supply and Services Canada, Ottawa, ON, Canada K1A 0E9.

Grayling, whitefish, northern pike, sheefish and burbot are present in the Porcupine. Coho, king and chum salmon from the Bering Sea migrate up this system, one of the longest fish migrations in North America.

Old Crow is served by scheduled commercial air service from Whitehorse or Dawson, YT. Fort Yukon, where travelers can clear customs upon reentering the United States, is served by scheduled commercial air service from Fairbanks.

Related USGS Topographic maps: Coleen A-1 through 4, B-1 through 2; Black River D-4 through 6; Fort Yukon C-1 through 3, D-1. Canadian maps may be purchased from

Canada Map Office, 615 Booth St., Ottawa, ON, Canada K1A 0E9.

Yukon River. The Yukon River originates in the coastal mountains of Canada and flows 2,300 miles in a great, wide arc to the Bering Sea.

Historically, travelers on the Yukon have used all manner of watercraft from log rafts to stern-wheelers. Today, most visitors use canoes, kayaks, inflatable rafts or outboard-powered riverboats. Freight-loaded barges are also seen on this major transportation corridor.

If starting your float trip in Canada, be sure to check in with U.S. customs upon arrival at Eagle. Between Eagle and Circle, the Yukon flows for 128 miles through Yukon-Charley Rivers National Preserve and then, shortly after Circle, into Yukon Flats National Wildlife Refuge for 300 miles.

According to the National Park Service, "The segment of the Yukon beginning at Dawson and continuing downstream through [Yukon-Charley] preserve comprises one of the most scenic yet safely traversable stretches of any large river in North America."

Floaters generally take 4 to 10 days to travel from Eagle to Circle, depending on whether they take any side trips up tributaries or day hikes. Most camp on open beaches or river bars where winds keep down the insects.

Downriver from Eagle, the vivid black-and-white limestones of Calico Bluff form one of the most striking attractions on the river. NOTE: Land on both sides of the Yukon River from Calico Bluff to just below the Tatonduk River mouth is owned by the Hungwitchin Native Corp. of Eagle, which requests that visitors not camp on its land.

As the river enters Yukon-Charley Preserve 12 miles north of Eagle, it flows across a narrow floodplain flanked by high bluffs and heavily forested hills. The bluffs become less prominent as the river leaves the preserve near Circle, 14 miles north of the preserve, and enters Yukon Flats.

Through the preserve the river drops 230 feet for an average gradient of 1.5 feet per mile, producing a 6- to 8-mph current. Flows of 10 to 11 mph occur during and just after breakup, which usually takes place in early May. Width of the river along this stretch varies from less than a half mile to several miles near Circle, where the stream becomes braided, making it difficult to pick out the main channel. There are no rapids on this section, but reef-formed riffles may be encountered in the low water of late

summer, and debris may be encountered in early summer. Beware of the occasional whirlpool. In any season strong winds may develop, building waves of 2 or 3 feet over exposed stretches; small boats should head for shore at such times.

There are numerous cabins in this area to explore that date back to the last century. NOTE: Respect private property. Take only photographs!

The Yukon River enters Yukon Flats National Wildlife Refuge along its southern boundary approximately 10 miles downstream from Circle. Then it flows northwesterly in a braided channel for some 60 miles to Fort Yukon, where it bends and flows southwest for another 240 miles in a meandering course with many sloughs before leaving the refuge in a narrow valley between the Ray and White mountains.

Fort Yukon is the primary community along this stretch of the river. Floaters generally take 4 to 7 days to pass through the refuge.

Downstream from the wildlife refuge is the Ramparts section, from the Dalton Highway to Tanana. This 128-mile section of the river classified as Class I has broad vistas, mile-wide river channels, high rock bluffs and hills covered with spruce and paper birch.

From the Dalton Highway, it generally takes 5 days to float to Tanana.

After the village of Rampart, the river passes between the high walls of Rampart Canyon.

Popular put ins for the Yukon River are at Dawson, YT, Canada; Eagle, located at the end of the Taylor Highway; Circle at the end of the Steese Highway; and about a half mile upstream from the Yukon River bridge on the Dalton Highway (Milepost 56). Exit can be at Eagle, Circle, Fort Yukon, the Dalton Highway or Tanana, all of which have scheduled air service. Or pickup by charter air service can be arranged from the river. Floaters also can continue from Tanana down the broad, flat-water Yukon to the Bering Sea. Some communities along the way have overnight accommodations, and most of the larger ones have scheduled air service.

Related USGS Topographic maps: From Eagle to Circle—Charley River A-1 and 2, B-2 through 6, C-6, D-6; Circle C-1, D-1; Eagle C-1, D-1.

From Circle to Dalton Highway—Fort Yukon, Beaver.

From Dalton Highway to Tanana—Livengood C-6, D-6; Tanana A-3 through 5, B-1 through 3, C-1, D-1.

Sportfishing

Access to sportfishing in Alaska's Interior can be as simple as climbing in your car and heading down one of several highways in the region. But the majority of the lakes and rivers of the Interior are reached only by plane or boat. (For good fishing locations along Interior highways consult *The MILE-POST®*.)

Northern pike live throughout the Interior. These fish average 2 to 5 pounds and occasionally attain trophy status of 15 pounds. Some lucky anglers have even caught 25- to 30-pound pike. Watch out for their sharp teeth! Use a wire leader and carry pliers for unhooking your catch.

Another enthusiastic fighter commonly found in Interior waters (particularly Yukon River tributaries, the Minto Flats and the lower Chena River) is the sheefish. Sheefish average 7 to 12 pounds in these waters, but occasionally attain 30 pounds.

Other fish found in the Interior are whitefish, which average 1 to 2 pounds; burbot (also called lush or lingcod) which average 2 to 5 pounds, but can attain 20 pounds; and arctic grayling. Grayling like clear, cold water and are found throughout much of the state; any grayling over 3 pounds is considered trophy size.

Access to most off-the-road sportfishing in the Interior is via small planes, usually chartered in Fairbanks, which can land on lakes or rivers, or on bush airstrips or gravel bars. However, boats occasionally can be rented in villages along the waterways. Fishing and hunting licenses can often be purchased from village vendors, but it is recommended that licenses be purchased in Fairbanks or another large community since rural vendors may be out hunting or fishing themselves.

For those traveling in the wilderness, a general rule from the Alaska Dept. of Fish and Game is to "plan for the worst." Travelers should take a few days extra food and other necessary supplies and allow for a flexible schedule in the event the weather turns bad and prevents pickup from remote sites.

For more information about fishing in the Interior, contact the Alaska Dept. of Fish and Game, Sport Fish Division, 1300 College Road, Fairbanks, AK 99701.

Birch Creek. Located 70 miles northeast of Fairbanks, Birch Creek is accessible from the Steese Highway. Grayling up to 12 inches may be caught in this stream from June to October. Northern pike and whitefish also available.

Black River. Located about 17 miles northeast of Fort Yukon; accessible by floatplane from Fort Yukon. Fair fishing (depending upon water conditions) for grayling, Dolly Varden, northern pike, whitefish and sheefish.

Charley River. The Charley River is considered good to excellent for grayling fishing. Northern pike are found as far as 16 miles upstream. Sheefish and king, chum and coho salmon are occasionally found in the river. Access is by aircraft.

Chena River. The Chena River flows southwest 100 miles to the Tanana River near Fairbanks. It has the most popular arctic grayling fishery in the state. However, recent decline in grayling numbers has forced the grayling fishery to become catch-and-release only. Access to the river within Chena River State Recreation Area is via Chena Hot Springs Road, 30 miles east of Fairbanks. Grayling from May to October on a variety of small flies and lures. The Chena also has a small run of king and chum salmon. Check current regulations concerning the Chena River grayling fishery.

Delta–Clearwater River. A spring-fed stream near Delta Junction shown as Clearwater Creek on USGS topographic maps; tributary of the Tanana River. Access from Milepost 1414.8 Alaska Highway. Boat needed for best fishing. Tops for grayling May 1 to Sept. 30, use flies or lures; whitefish in spring and summer, use flies; burbot also available; silver salmon spawn here in October.

East Twin Lake. Fly-in lake located in the Tanana Lowlands approximately 85 air miles southwest of Fairbanks, 40 miles east of the Bitzshtini Mountains. Trophy-sized pike use spoons, spinners. Air charter service available in Fairbanks.

Goodpaster River. Located northeast of Delta Junction. Accessible by boat via the Delta Clearwater and Tanana rivers. Excellent grayling fishing April 1 to Sept. 30, use flies, lures or bait.

Koyukuk River. Joins the Yukon River 22 miles northeast of Nulato. Boats may be available for rental at communities on the river. Pike and sheefish available at Huslia. Sheefish in late September and pike year-round at Hughes. Sheefish in September; grayling and pike year-round at Allakaket.

Lake Minchumina. Fly-in lake located 66 miles northwest of Mount McKinley, 150 miles southwest of Fairbanks, 205 miles northwest of Anchorage. Pike averaging 5 to

15 pounds, use spoons or spinners. Lodge on lake. Scheduled air service from Fairbanks to Lake Minchumina village. Charter air service available in Fairbanks or Anchorage.

Mansfield Lake. Fly-in lake located 7 miles north of Tanacross on the Alaska Highway. Fish available: northern pike year-round, use spoons or spinners; burbot year-round, use bait. Air charter service available in Tanacross or Tok.

Melozitna River. Tributary of the Yukon River; mouth located 2 miles upstream from Ruby. Good sheefish fishery upriver in July, use spoons. Boat accessible from Ruby.

Minto Lakes. Located in Minto Flats about 40 miles northwest of Fairbanks and southeast of the village of Minto. Good spring, summer and fall fisheries. The Fish and Game Dept. says this area has some of the best pike fishing in Alaska; pike up to 20 to 25 pounds can be caught here. Pike fishing expected to be fair as they rebound from a year of low water and low numbers caught. Other fish available: sheefish in midsummer, use spoons; whitefish year-round, use flies or eggs; burbot year-round, use bait. Accessible by small plane from Fairbanks; boat from Minto village, which is reached via the Elliott Highway; or via the Murphy Dome Extension Road from the top of Murphy Dome down to the Chatanika River.

Mystic Lake. Located in the foothills of the Alaska Range near the upper Tonzona River, 48 miles west of Mount McKinley, 158 miles northwest of Anchorage. Fish available: lake trout to 4 to 5 pounds, use spoons or plugs; northern pike to 4 feet, use spoons or spinners. Access by floatplane from Anchorage.

Nowitna River. Flows into the Yukon River 38 miles northeast of Ruby. Fish available: northern pike year-round, use spoons or spinners; sheefish in late summer, use spoons; grayling in abundance, use flies.

Salmon also spawn in this river.

Nulato River. Flows into the Yukon River 1 mile southwest of Nulato. Fish available: arctic char in late summer, use spoons and eggs; grayling May to October, use flies, lures or bait; king and chum salmon arrive in July, use spoons. Access by boat from Nulato.

Porcupine River. Heads in Canada at 65°28 N, 139°32 W and flows 460 miles west to join the Yukon River 2 miles northwest of Fort Yukon. Fish available: arctic grayling May to October, use flies; sheefish July to October, use spoons; northern pike year-round, use spoons. Access by boat or air charter service from Fort Yukon.

Quartz Lake. Excellent fishing for rainbow and silver salmon near Delta Junction. Developed campsites on a loop road, with firepits, water, tables, toilet and boat launch. A trail connects Lost Lake and Quartz Lake camping areas. Black Spruce Lodge located on lake; phone 895-4668.

Rainbow Lake. Located approximately 8 air miles across the Tanana River from Big Delta. Excellent rainbow trout fishing, use flies or lures. Access by floatplane during summer or by winter trail.

Tetlin Lake. Located 16 miles southeast of Tok. Excellent northern pike fishery, use spoons or spinners. Access by riverboat up the Tetlin River from the Tanana River, or by floatplane from Tok, Tanacross, Northway or Fortymile on the Alaska Highway.

Tozitna River. Flows into the Yukon River 6 miles downstream from Tanana. Fish available: northern pike year-round, use spoons, spinners; sheefish July to October, use spoons. Access by boat or small plane from Tanana.

Wien Lake. Fly-in lake located 60 miles south of the Yukon River between the Nowitna and Kantishna rivers. Good fishing for northern pike up to 18 pounds. Lodge on lake. Access by floatplane from Fairbanks.

SPECIAL FEATURES

Ghost Towns

Gold seekers came to the Interior before the turn of the century and built their towns and camps along its rivers. Some, like Fairbanks, flourished. Others died when the miners' luck ran out. Their picturesque remains still can be seen today, although sometimes they are overgrown with brush and difficult to find. We've listed a few of the old camps here. *NOTE: Respect private property. State and federal laws prohibit removing or destroying relics. Take only photographs.*

Caro. Located on the north bank of the Chandalar River at the mouth of Flat Creek, 26 miles south-southeast of Chandalar, 45 miles north of the Arctic Circle. The cluster of log cabins on a slight, brush-covered rise is not visible from the river. This settlement was named for Caro Kingsland Clum, the daughter of Fairbanks postmaster John P. Clum, in 1907 when the Caro post office opened. The post office was discontinued in 1912. A wagon trail known as the Government Road, now overgrown with brush, once led to Caro from Beaver on the Yukon River.

Chandalar. Located on the east shore of Chandalar Lake at Rosalie Creek about 75 miles north of the Arctic Circle. This mining camp was established in 1906-07 and named after John Chandalar, who operated a Hudson's Bay Co. trading post there. Chandalar had a post office from 1908 to 1944.

Diamond (or Diamond City). Located at the junction of Moose Creek and Bearpaw River, which flows out of Denali National Park and Preserve into the Kantishna River. This mining camp was the head of small-boat navigation on the Bearpaw and probably was a supply point for miners working farther upriver. Several buildings are still standing; a trapper may be using one during the winter. Check with the Park Service about any restrictions.

Fortymile. Located at the junction of Bullion Creek and North Fork Fortymile River, 37 miles southwest of Eagle. The U.S. Army Signal Corps established a telegraph station called North Fork here in 1903. Prospectors later called the place Fortymile. A few cabins remain standing.

Franklin (or Franklin Gulch). Located at the junction of Franklin Creek and the South Fork Fortymile River, 48 miles southwest of Eagle. A post office was established at this mining camp in 1902; it was discontinued in 1945. A few buildings remain.

Glacier (or Glacier City). Located at the junction of Glacier Creek and Bearpaw River within Denali National Park and Preserve. Dozens of old homes, warehouses and the like remain from this mining community that thrived from about 1908 until the 1920s, when it was abandoned. This ghost town is virtually invisible from the air when leaves are on the trees; it's easiest to visit in winter when overland access is possible. Check with the Park Service about any restrictions.

Kemperville (also known as Buckholtz Roadhouse). Located on the right bank of the Tanana River at the mouth of Hot Springs Slough, approximately 6 miles downstream from Manley Hot Springs. A trading post was established here in 1909 in one of the log cabins still standing. The camp, reportedly named for prospector George Kemper, was active until 1911.

Mastodon. Located on Mastodon Creek, south of the Yukon River, 40 miles southwest of Circle. The first gold strike was made in this area in 1894. The creek, and subsequently the camp, were named by miners after they found mastodon bones and tusks at their diggings. This camp was active from 1902 to 1906.

Nation (or Nation City). Located on the south bank of the Yukon River, 2.2 miles below the mouth of the Nation River. This was a mining camp and supply point for the Fourth of July placer mining area from 1908 to 1924. Only 2 cabins remain standing; 13 more are in ruins.

Rooseveldt (or Roosevelt). Located on the Kantishna River near the confluence of the Bearpaw River. This town was a regular stop for stern-wheelers in the early days. Cargo was unloaded here and placed in smaller craft for shipment to Diamond, Glacier and points farther upriver. The river has washed most of the buildings away, but a few still stand. There are many old sod doghouses behind the existing buildings; at least one cache has been used in recent years.

Woodchopper Creek. Located on Woodchopper Creek at the mouth of Iron Creek, 19 miles west of the junction of the Charley and Yukon rivers. This mining camp was established about 1907 and was active between 1919 and 1936.

Hot Springs

Chena Hot Springs: Located about 50 air miles northeast of Fairbanks, this popular private resort can be reached via the Steese Highway and Chena Hot Springs Road. The road cuts through Chena River State Recreation Area, an exceptional area offering picnic sites, campgrounds and easy access to the Chena River's grayling fishery (catch-and-release only).

Chena Hot Springs were first reported in 1907 by U.S. Geological Survey field teams. The resort offers food, lodging and swimming in the mineral springs; phone 452-7867. There is also an airstrip at the lodge. Overnight camping is available for a fee in the parking area at the end of the road.

Circle Hot Springs: About 100 miles northeast of Fairbanks, the springs are 8 miles off Mile 127.8 Steese Highway. Ketchum Creek BLM Campground is located at Mile 5.7 of the Circle Hot Springs Road, offering 12 campsites with toilets, tables and firepits. At the hot springs, year-round swimming, lodging, food, groceries, bakery, gas and camper parking are available; phone 520-5113.

Circle Hot Springs was discovered in 1893 by prospector William Greats. In 1905, Franklin Leach homesteaded around the springs. Tents were used as the first bath-houses. Many miners wintered over at the springs when they could not work on the creeks.

The springs provide warm water for irrigating the resort's garden, which produces vegetables of great variety and size. Many buildings have been extensively renovated.

Manley Hot Springs: Located 151 miles from Fairbanks via the Elliott Highway, the springs are on a hillside just outside the community of the same name. One spring runs 35 gallons a minute with a temperature of 136°F, another runs 110 gallons per minute at 135°F, for a total of some 208,800 gallons every 24 hours. Manley Hot Springs Resort (672-3611) offers food, lodging, camping and swimming in a hot mineral spring-fed pool. The resort is open year-round.

Melozi Hot Springs: Located on Hot Springs Creek, 30 miles northeast of Ruby. There is a group of 20 or so springs along the creek. A 1911 U.S. Geological Survey team reported finding a 2-room cabin and 2 small bathhouses on the springs. Today Melozi Hot Springs is the site of a private fly-in wilderness lodge; phone 892-6987.

The Kink

Originally the name of a sharp bend in the North Fork Fortymile River, it came to mean the 15-foot-wide channel (eroded to 50 feet by the 1970s) that was blasted 100 feet through a ridge that formed the neck in the bend.

The channel was blasted through in 1904 by miners to divert the flow of the river and leave an approximately 2.8-mile area of riverbed open for mining. It was abandoned in 1905 when prospects turned out to be unprofitable. Now on the National Register of Historic Places, The Kink was a major engineering feat at its time and place and is considered a permanent monument to man's undertakings in the pursuit of gold at the turn of the century.

The Kink is located 40 miles southwest of Eagle on the east side of the North Fork Fortymile River, about 1 mile south of the confluence of Hutchinson Creek.

ADVENTURE TRAVEL DIRECTORY

This Adventure Travel Directory is a listing of businesses offering services to travelers to Alaska's wilderness. The list was compiled from information provided by businesses that responded to a questionnaire sent out by *The Alaska Wilderness Guide* and does not purport to be comprehensive. The listings are based on information provided by these businesses and their appearance here should not be considered a recommendation by the publisher. Readers are urged to request brochures and names and addresses of former customers when investigating these services.

Categories included in this section are:

Fishing/Hunting Guides & Outfitters
Boat Charters
Wilderness & Fishing Lodges
Air Taxi and Air Charter Operators
Adventure Guides & Outfitters
River Running/Sea Kayaking/Boating
Other

Listings appear alphabetically by name except for Wilderness & Fishing Lodges, which is arranged alphabetically by location. The region, area or community served appears at the end of each listing in most categories.

Readers should be aware that rarely does a wilderness operator fall clearly into one category of service. A hunting guide and outfitter may also have a wilderness lodge; a wilderness lodge may offer guided fishing, flightseeing and river running. We have tried to list each business under its primary service, but read through all related categories for the most complete look at what is available.

Fishing/Hunting Guides & Outfitters

Alaska Backcountry Angling, P.O Box 81483, Fairbanks, AK 99708; phone 479-7882. Multi-day, guided float trips on fishing rivers. Specializing in the Gulkana River. *Statewide.*

Alaska Fair Chase, P.O. Box 19443, Thorne Bay, AK 99919; phone 828-3989, fax 828-3374 (city hall). Brown bear, black bear and goat hunts in southeast Alaska. Hunting from 54-foot modern cruiser; fishing too. Seasonal service April 1-Oct. 30. *Southeast.*

Alaska Luxury Charters, P.O. Box 1324, Homer, AK 99603; phone 235-2283. All-day guided halibut fishing aboard 37-$\frac{1}{2}$-foot tollycraft, departing from Homer Harbor. Also bear hunting, sightseeing, bay cruises. *Southcentral.*

Alaska Safaris and Brooks Range Arctic Hunts, HC33 Box 32810, Nenana, AK 99760-9303; phone 452-8751. Guided and outfitted big game trophy hunting by gun, bow or camera for Dall sheep, grizzly, caribou, moose, wolf, wolverine in Brooks Range; or Interior Alaska for black and grizzly bear, moose, caribou, wolf and wolverine. Outfitted, non-guided Interior Alaska hunts are available. *Interior, Brooks Range/Arctic.*

Alaska Trophy Safaris, Inc., P.O. Box 670441, Chugiak, AK 99567; phone or fax 696-2484. Hunting for Kodiak bear and Sitka black-tailed deer on Kodiak Island; for brown bear in Southeast; and for Dall sheep, moose, caribou, black and grizzly bear in Alaska Range. Guided fishing trips for 5 species of salmon, rainbow trout, steelhead, grayling and char. *Southwestern.*

Alaska Wilderness Expeditions, P.O. Box 375, Mercedes Dr., Talkeetna, AK 99676; phone 733-2704. Guided daily fishing charters for salmon, trout. Fly-out wilderness lodge. Guided hunting; specializing in bow hunts for dangerous game. *Southcentral.*

Arctic Grayling Guide Service, P.O. Box 83707, Fairbanks, AK 99708; phone 479-0479. One- to 7-day trips for arctic grayling, king and silver salmon. Streamside cabin, canoe float trips. Guided and unguided trips available from the Fairbanks area. *Interior, Brooks Range/Arctic.*

B&C Charters, P.O. Box 4024, Homer, AK 99603; phone 235-7916. Guided fishing for halibut and salmon; equipment and bait furnished. Six passenger capacity. *Southcentral.*

Bob Elliott, 5920 Airport Way, Fairbanks, AK 99709; phone 479-6323. Fly-in to remote lakes for grayling, silver salmon, northern pike and rainbow trout. *Interior.*

Fishing/Hunting (continued)

Aurora Sportfishing, P.O. Box 2824, Homer, AK 99603; phone 235-7765. Halibut and salmon charters May to September. Custom-designed trips also available for groups. *Southcentral.*

Big Sky Charter and Fish Camp, 13120 Saunders Rd., Anchorage, AK 99516; phone 345-5760; 262-9496 (summer). Fishing lodge on the Kenai river. Cabin rentals and guided charter boatfishing (power and drift) to all locations of the Kenai. Additional drift boat service to Kasilof River. *Southcentral.*

Bob's Trophy Charters, P.O. Box 1775, Homer, AK 99603; phone 1-800-770-6400 or 235-6544. Full-day charters for "barndoor" halibut, mid-May through mid-September; also king and silver salmon. Unguided hunting trips for black bear in spring, deer and elk in fall. Bunkroom accommodations. Overnight trips also available. *Southcentral.*

Brightwater Alaska Inc., P.O. Box 110796, Anchorage, AK 99511; phone 344-1340, fax 344-4614. Completely outfitted fishing float trips for rainbow trout, Dolly Varden/arctic char, grayling and all 5 species of Pacific salmon. Specialize in fly fishing. Since 1975. *Southcentral/Western.*

Clearwater Adventures, P.O. Box 2369, Homer, AK 99603-2369; phone 235-8030. Fishing charters in Lower Cook Inlet for halibut and salmon. Bed and breakfast apartment available. Season April 15-Sept. 15; also winter fishing for king salmon. Brochures. *Southcentral.*

F.I.S.H.E.S., P.O. Box 245-MP, Hoonah, AK 99829; phone 945-3327. Guided saltwater fishing for halibut, salmon and trout aboard 43-foot yacht. Overnight or day trips. Meals, gear, fish processing, land transportation included. Year-round. Brochure. *Southeast.*

Glacier Guides, Inc., P.O. Box 66, Gustavus, AK 99826; phone or fax (907) 697-2252 (summer). P.O. Box 460, Santa Clara, UT 84765; phone (801) 628-0973 (winter). Hunting and fishing with master guide; 72-foot yacht. *Southeast.*

Homer Ocean Charters, Inc., P.O. Box 2543, Homer, AK 99603; phone 1-800-478-6212 (in AK); 1-800-426-6212 (nationwide). Full-day and long-range halibut fishing trips. Hunting for black bear and Sitka black-tailed deer. Brochure. *Southcentral.*

Hook-M-Up Tours, P.O. Box 116, Aniak, AK 99557; phone 675-4376, fax 675-4419. Base camp on Kuskokwim River features sportfishing for 4 species of salmon, plus char, grayling, northern pike, rainbow and sheefish. Walled tent cabins, running water and sauna. *Western.*

Kichatna Guide Service, P.O. Box 670790, Chugiak, AK 99567; phone 696-3256. Guided hunting trips in the Alaska Range for moose, brown/grizzly bear, caribou, black bear and Dall sheep, in the Brooks Range for Dall sheep; caribou and wolf; on Kodiak Island for Kodiak brown bear and Sitka black-tailed deer. *Southcentral, Southwestern, Brooks Range/Arctic.*

Kniktuk Outfitters, Inc., P.O. Box 882, Delta Jct., AK 99737; phone 895-5285, fax 895-1003. Guided fishing for rainbows, Dolly Varden, grayling and 5 salmon species. Camp with tents, oil stoves, hot showers and electric lights. Access via Iliamna. Season mid-June to mid-September. Hunting also available for trophy caribou, black bear, moose and fall brown/grizzly bear. Dall sheep and spring bear hunt; mid-August to mid-October. *Western/Bristol Bay.*

Lake Country Lodge, HC2 P.O. Box 852, Soldotna, AK 99669; phone 283-5959, fax 283-9177. Hunting and fishing lodge on Lake Clark. Fly-out fishing trips for all species within 2 hours of Lake Clark; boat trips (guided or unguided) big game guide and outfitter for moose, caribou, brown bear, black bear and Dall sheep. *Southcentral, Western.*

Martana Enterprises, P.O. Box 141345, Anchorage, AK 99514; phone 333-7692. Remote cabins and boats for fishing Lake Clark area; guides available; fully equipped for up to 6 persons. *Western/Bristol Bay.*

Meekin's South Fork Outfit, HC03 Box 8485, Mile 110 Glenn Hwy., Palmer, AK 99645; phone 746-4290. Guided horsepack expeditions and hunts, 3-21 day tours. Explore alpine glaciers of the Chugach Mountains. Brochure. *Southcentral.*

Morning Peace River Guides, P.O. Box 124, Aniak, AK 99557; phone 675-4343, fax 675-4301. Guided fishing and eco-tourism trips by river boats on western Alaska wilderness rivers. Day fishing from Aniak, June to September, salmon, trout, sheefish, pike, drop-off camping. Family groups welcome. Since 1975. *Western.*

Ouzel Expeditions Inc., P.O. Box 935, Girdwood, AK 99587; phone (907) 783-2216 or 1-800-825-8196, fax (907) 783-3220. Guided fly-in float fishing trips. Five species of salmon, rainbow, char, grayling. 25 years of experience. *Southcentral, Brooks Range/Arctic, Western.*

Radar's Alaskan Bush Adventures Inc.,

P.O. Box 1908, Bethel, AK 99559; phone 1-800-841-0688, fax (907) 543-2277. Two-day to 1-week fly-out fishing excursions. One-week trips include stay at wilderness base lake with daily fly-out trips. Six-person maximum. *Western.*

Saltwater Safari Company, P.O. Box 241225, Anchorage, AK 99664; phone 277-3223, fax 274-5977. Halibut and salmon fishing. Sightseeing, hunting, and kayak dropoffs. Exclusive day and night charters. *Statewide.*

Sportfishing Alaska, 1401 Shore Dr., Anchorage, AK 99515-3206; phone 344-8674, fax 349-4330. Professional fishery biologist assists anglers in developing personalized Alaska fishing vacations, providing when, where, and how-to for great sportfishing. Guides, lodges, rental equipment. Year-round service. Brochure. *Statewide.*

Tom Hundley, P.O. box 2772, Palmer, AK 99645; phone 745-2084. Fair chase big game hunts in the Chugach Mountains; dall sheep, brown bear, black bear, mountain goat. *Southcentral.*

Ugashik Narrows Lodge, P.O. Box 101068, Anchorage, AK 99510; phone 272-9401, fax 272-0251. Private cabin on Alaska Peninsula; fishing for salmon, trout, char, northern pike. Guided fly-out service available. *Southwestern.*

Willard's Moose Lodge, 40520 Waterman Rd., Homer, AK 99603; phone 235-8830. Big game guiding for moose, black bear, brown bear. Lake and stream fishing. Fly-in lodge on Caribou Lake (20 minutes from Homer). Est. in 1946. All trips on horseback. *Southcentral.*

Wrangell R Ranch, P.O. Box CZN, Tok, AK 99780; radio phone 345-1160 (summer). P.O. Box 222475, Anchorage, AK 99522; phone or fax 349-8159 (winter). August and September hunts by horseback in Wrangell Mountains for sheep, caribou, moose, grizzly bear, wolf and wolverine. Tent camps with shower. *Southcentral.*

Boat Charters

Alaskan Star Charters, P.O. Box 2027, Wrangell, AK 99929; phone 874-3084, fax 874-3068. Multiday, live-aboard charters in southeast Alaska on the 60-foot Star Queen. Whale watching, wildlife photography, black bear hunts, fishing, steelheading. Specializing in family trips. *Southeast.*

Anderson Charters, P.O. Box 7118, Ketchikan, AK 99901; phone 225-2456. Sportfishing, hunting, sightseeing and some diving. 50-foot motor yacht. *Statewide.*

Auke Bay Sportfishing/Charters, P.O. Box 32744, Juneau, AK 99803; phone 789-2562 or 789-9783, fax 789-1444. Half-, full- and multiday boat charters for fishing or sightseeing. Plane tours also available. *Southeast.*

Brownie's Charters and Bed & Breakfast, 2038 Halibut Point Hwy., Sitka, AK 99835; phone 747-5402. Half- and full-day fishing charters for halibut and salmon. Free vehicle and freezer space. *Southeast.*

Captain Mike's Charters, P.O. Box 269, Homer, AK 99603; phone 235-8348. Fleet of 4 6-person boats, plus 2 larger boats for up to 16 passengers. Specializing in halibut fishing; salmon fishing and sightseeing also. *Southcentral.*

Central Charters Booking Agency, Inc., 4241 Homer Spit Rd., Homer, AK 99603; phone 235-7847. Halibut fishing, Cook Inlet. *Southcentral.*

Chan IV Charters, P.O. Box 624, Petersburg, AK 99833; phone 772-4859. Trawl and pull pots on a commercial gill-net boat, then enjoy an on-board meal of shrimp, crab or sole, and wine. *Southeast.*

Choice Marine Charters, 6530 Lakeway Dr., Anchorage, AK 99502; phone 243-0069, fax 243-0069 (on call only). Marine charter serving Prince William and Blying sounds. Overnight and extended charters for sightseeing, fishing, hunting or research. Modern 50-foot motor yacht, 4 to 6 passengers. April through December. *Southcentral.*

Don's Round Island Boat Charters, P.O. Box 68, Togiak, AK 99678; phone 493-5127. Boat service from Togiak Cannery to Round Island for walrus viewing. *Western.*

Ellis Inc., P.O. Box 1068, Petersburg, AK 99833; phone 772-3039 or 772-3240. Custom and commercial charters on 50-foot twin screw steel vessel. Also extended Stikine River trips as far as navigation allows. In business 33 years. *Southeast.*

Grafin Marine Services, P.O. Box 6081, Ketchikan, AK 99901; phone 225-3747. Charter vessel service, casual fishing trips and sightseeing. *Southeast.*

Grand Pacific Charters, P.O. Box 5, Gustavus, AK 99826; phone (907) 697-2288, fax (907) 697-2289 (summer). P.O. Box 2557, St. George, UT 84771; phone (801) 673-8480, fax (801) 673-8481 (winter). Whale watching, halibut and salmon fish-

Boat Charters (continued)

ing. Rates include gear, bait and preparation of catch. Personalized overnight excursions in Glacier Bay. *Southeast.*

Gustavus Marine Charters, P.O. Box 81, Gustavus, AK 99826; phone 697-2233, fax 697-2414. Salmon and halibut day fishing in Icy Strait. Multiday adventure tours in Glacier Bay National Park aboard 42-foot yachts. *Southeast.*

Homer Charter Assoc., P.O. Box 148, Homer, AK 99603. Free list of members offering fishing charters out of Homer. *Southcentral.*

Hoonah Charters, P.O. Box 384, Hoonah, AK 99829; phone 945-3334. Personalized adventure, whale watching, fishing or relaxing cruises. Four to 6 guests on 44-foot vessel for overnight, week-long or day trips in northern southeast Alaska waters. *Southeast.*

Inside Passage Charter Boat Assoc., 369 S. Franklin St., Suite 200, Juneau, AK 99801; phone 463-3466, fax 463-4453. Service for people seeking a boat to charter for a wilderness multiday cruise. *Southeast.*

Islander Charters, P.O. Box 20927, Juneau, AK 99802; phone 780-4419. Salmon fishing charters. *Southeast.*

Ken's Charters, P.O. Box 9609, Ketchikan, AK 99901; phone 225-7290. Multiday, live-aboard charters and day trips for groups of up to 4 (6 on day trips), for salmon, halibut, bottomfish, sightseeing, photography, beach combing and marine animal viewing. Trips in Inside Passage, Misty Fiords and Ketchikan area. *Southeast.*

Ketchikan Sportfishing, P.O. Box 3212, 435 Water St., Ketchikan, AK 99901; phone 225-7526, fax 225-7525. Half-day, full-day and overnight fishing and sightseeing excursions. *Southeast.*

Klawock Bay Charters, P.O. Box 145, Klawock, AK 99925; phone 755-2329. Salmon and halibut charters, sightseeing and lodging. *Southeast.*

Knudson Cove Marina, 407 Knudson Cove Rd., Ketchikan, AK 99901; phone 247-8500. Charter boats, moorage, boat rentals, full-service tackle shop. *Southeast.*

Kodiak Island Charters, P.O. Box 3750, Kodiak, AK 99615; phone 486-5380. Fishing, hunting, sightseeing and whale watching. Specializing in salmon trolling. 43-foot USCG-inspected boat, 16 passengers, 6 overnight. *Southwestern.*

Last Frontier Charters, P.O. Box 19443,

Thorne Bay, AK 99919; phone 828-3989, fax 828-3374 (city hall). Comfortable accommo-dations and fine food aboard a 54-foot modern cruiser. Fish for salmon and halibut; see bears, eagles and whales. *Southeast.*

58°22' North Sailing Charters, P.O. Box 32391, Juneau, AK 99803; phone 789-7301. Bareboat and skippered sailing charters in northern southeast Alaska. Fully equipped Catalina 30 and 36 yachts. *Southeast.*

Puffin Charters, Inc., 4418 Mint Way, Juneau, AK 99801; phone 789-0001. Cruising, fishing, sightseeing waters of southeast Alaska. Specializing in salmon and halibut fishing. Day trips, 6 people; overnight trips, 4 people. *Southeast.*

Reel Em' Inn/Cook Inlet Charters, 13641 Venus Way, Anchorage, AK 99515; phone 345-3887. Charters out of Deep Creek offer world-class fishing for king salmon and barndoor halibut. Also lodging, fish freezing. *Southcentral.*

Rock 'n' Rollin' Charters, 11380 Alderwood St. N. Suite C, Ketchikan, AK 99901; phone 225-6919. Day trips for salmon, halibut or sightseeing. 28-foot silverton with twin turbo diesels. *Southeast.*

Sablefish Charters, P.O. Box 1588; Seward, AK 99664; phone 224-3283. Fishing charters and sightseeing. Catch halibut, ling cod, red snapper, black bass, silver, pink and king salmon. Fish Resurrection Bay, Chiswell Islands, Kenai Fjords and the Gulf of Alaska. All gear and bait provided. *Southcentral.*

Seawind Charters, P.O. Box 240126, Douglas, AK 99824; phone 364-3341. Day, evening or extended trips to Glacier Bay, Tracy Arm, Admiralty Island, Petersburg, Wrangell and Ketchikan. 42-foot boat has 2 private cabins, modern electronics. Service April through October. *Southeast.*

Sportsman Charters, 821 Charles St., Sitka, AK 99835; phone 747-8756. Day fishing trips. Pickup and drop-off service for hikers, campers, kayakers. Wildlife viewing and photography trips. *Southeast.*

Yukon Explorer, 3330 Riverside Dr., Fairbanks, AK 99709; phone 452-8251 (ext. 3245) or 479-8817, fax 459-3851. Boat charters on the Yukon River, from Holy Cross to Dawson City. Fishing, sightseeing, photography, hiking, camping, touring Native villages and other historical sites. All equipment provided. All trips custom arranged. Seasonal service. *Brooks Range/Arctic.*

Winter King Charters, P.O. Box 14, Cordova, AK 99574; phone 424-7170. Year-round fishing for salmon, halibut and bottom fish. Transportation for binding, photography, hunting or camping. Custom trips. *Southcentral.*

Wilderness Lodges & Fishing Lodges

Afognak Wilderness Lodge, P.O. Box 5, Seal Bay, AK 99697; phone 486-6442. Lodge and cabins for 12 guests; local cuisine; salmon and halibut fishing; wildlife photography; floatplane access. Color brochure, international references. *Afognak.*

Mission Lodge, 200 W. 34th #1160, Anchorage, AK 99503; phone 349-2753, fax 344-4594. Full-service, fly-out fishing lodge; single occupancy; sauna, hot tub. *Aleknagik.*

Wilderness Place Lodge, P.O. Box 190711, Anchorage, AK 99519; phone 733-2051 or 248-4337, fax 733-2051. Full-service fishing lodge, 75 air miles northwest of Anchorage. Guided fly fishing and spin fishing for all 5 Pacific salmon, grayling and rainbow trout. Maximum 15 guests. *Anchorage.*

R & L's Anvik River Lodge, General Delivery, Anvik, AK 99558; phone 663-6324. Fishing and hunting lodge. Fishing for king, chum and silver salmon, grayling, char, northern pike. Guided big game hunts: brown/grizzly and black bear, caribou, moose. Maximum 8 guests. *Anvik.*

Bettles Lodge, P.O. Box 27, Bettles, AK 99726; phone 1-800-770-5111, fax (907) 488-7909. Fly-in lodge with rooms, cabins and restaurant; outfitting. *Bettles.*

Minakokosa Lake Camp, P.O. Box 27, Bettles, AK 99726; phone 1-800-770-5111, fax (907) 488-7909. Fly-in fish camp; lake and stream fishing for lake trout, pike, grayling; Kobuk River float for sheefish. *Bettles.*

Alaska Rainbow Lodge, P.O. Box 39, King Salmon, AK 99613; phone or fax 287-3059. Full-service lodge on the Kvichak River. Fly-out and riverboat fishing for 5 species of salmon, arctic char, grayling, northern pike, Dolly Varden, sheefish, and lake and trophy rainbow trout. Float trips also available. *Bristol Bay area.*

Big Mountain Lodge Inc., 14940 Longbow Dr., Anchorage, AK 99516; phone 345-2459, fax 345-7934. Full-service lodge; guided local and fly-out fishing in Kvichak River, Iliamna/Bristol Bay region; meals;

sauna; tackle and fish packaging. June to October. *Bristol Bay area.*

Crystal Creek Lodge, P.O. Box 3049, Dillingham, AK 99576; phone 1-800-525-3153, fax (602) 437-8780. Full-service lodge. Guided, daily fly-out fishing by helicopter or floatplane to area streams for 11 species of freshwater fish. *Bristol Bay area.*

Iniakuk Lake Lodge, P.O. Box 80424, Fairbanks, AK 99708; phone 479-6354. Operating since 1974, the lodge offers painting and photography workshops, bird watching, canoeing, fishing and wildlife viewing. *Brooks Range/Arctic.*

Peace of Selby, P.O. Box 86, Manley Hot Springs, AK 99756; phone or fax 672-3206. Full-service lodge, cabins, tent camps; fishing, hiking and rafting in Gates of the Arctic National Park. *Brooks Range/Arctic.*

Camp Bendeleben, P.O. Box 1045, Nome, AK 99762; phone 443-2880. Fishing lodge 75 miles northeast of Nome. Full-service base camp, remote permanent tent camp with canoes for do-it-yourselfers. Fishing for 4 species of salmon, arctic char, large grayling. *Council.*

Black Spruce Lodge, HC 60 Box 4840, Delta Junction, AK 99737; phone 895-4668. Fishing lodge on Quartz Lake; cabins, boat rentals; rainbow and silver salmon fishing; cross-country skiing in winter. *Delta Junction.*

Camp Denali, P.O. Box 67, Denali Park, AK 99755; phone or fax (907) 683-2290 (summer). P.O. Box 369, Cornish, NH 03746; phone (603) 675-2248, fax (603) 675-9125 (winter). Nature center/wilderness lodge; cabins; guided hiking, photography, canoeing, biking, flightseeing and other activities. June to September. *Denali National Park.*

Denali Backcountry Lodge, P.O. Box 810, Girdwood, AK 99587; phone 1-800-841-0692, fax (907) 783-2928. Full-service lodge; 1- to 4-night all-inclusive packages; guided hikes, natural history programs and other activities. *Denali National Park.*

Denali Wilderness Lodge, P.O. Box 50, Denali Park, AK 99755 (summer). P.O. Box 71784, Fairbanks, AK 99707 (winter). Phone 1-800-541-9779 or (907) 683-1287, fax (907) 683-1286 (year-round). Full-service fly-in lodge; horseback riding, naturalist programs and other activities. *Denali National Park.*

Tokosha Mountain Lodge, P.O. Box 13-188, Trapper Creek, AK 99683; phone 733-2821. Lodging, fishing, rafting and river-boat trips. *Denali National Park.*

Lodges (continued)

Deshka Silver-King Lodge, P.O. Box 1037, Willow, AK 99688; phone 733-2055. On Deshka River; lodge, private cabins, all meals; outfitted fishing boat, tackle, guides; private airstrip; 2-day, 4-day and custom packages. King salmon May 25 to July 13; silvers July 22 to Aug. 15. Winter sled dog tours, Jan. 1 to April 1. *Deshka River.*

Royal Coachman Lodge, P.O. Box 1887, Anchorage, AK 99519; phone 346-2595, fax 346-3733. Fly-in fishing lodge; 5 species of freshwater fish including all 5 Pacific salmon; maximum 12 guests. *Dillingham.*

Cross Sound Lodge, P.O. Box 85, Elfin Cove, AK 99825; phone 1-800-323-5346, fax (907) 239-2210. Full-service fishing lodge; salmon and halibut; May to September. *Elfin Cove.*

Elfin Cove Lodge, P.O. Box 44, Elfin Cove, AK 99825; phone (907) 239-2212 (summer). P.O. Box 4007, Renton, WA 99057; phone 1-800-422-2824, fax (206) 939-0902 (winter). Waterfront lodge; 4- and 5-day fishing trips for salmon and halibut; light tackle specialists; 26-foot boats with licensed skippers. May to September. *Elfin Cove.*

Tanaku Lodge, P.O. Box 49, Elfin Cove, AK 99825 (summer). 1060 Old Salem Rd. NE, Albany, OR 97321 (winter). Phone 1-800-285-7211. Sportfishing lodge with 5-night packages; maximum 12 guests. *Elfin Cove.*

Iliamna Lake Resort, P.O. Box 208, Iliamna, AK 99606; phone 571-1387, fax 571-1430. Lodging and dining; fly-out fishing, float trips, flightseeing; bear viewing at Katmai National Park; whitewater jet boat trips; boat and raft rental, tackle shop, fishing and camping equipment rental. *Iliamna.*

Iliaska Lodge Inc., P.O. Box 228, Iliamna, AK 99606; phone 571-1221. Lodging and meals; fly fishing only, 7-day package on 7 different rivers; floatplanes, guiding in boats or rafts. *Iliamna.*

Newhalen Lodge, 3851 Chiniak Bay Dr., Anchorage, AK 99515; phone 522-3355, fax 522-3555. Fly-out fishing, sightseeing and wildlife photography. *Iliamna.*

Ole Creek Lodge, 506 Ketchikan St., Fairbanks, AK 99701; phone 533-3474 (summer), 452-2421 (winter). Full-service fishing lodge on Kvichak River and Lake Iliamna; guides. *Iliamna.*

Melozi Hot Springs Lodge, P.O. Box 52081, Big Lake, AK 99652; phone 892-6987. Lodge with family-style dining, log cabin accommodations; fishing, hiking, hunting; hot springs. *Interior.*

Battle River Wilderness Retreat, 8076 Caribbean Way, Sacramento, CA 95826; phone (916) 381-0250, fax (916) 362-8785. Lodging, meals and guided fishing for trophy rainbow trout, salmon, arctic char and grayling; hiking; unguided moose and caribou hunting. July 1 to Oct. 1. *Katmai National Park.*

Brooks Lodge, 4700 Aircraft Dr., Anchorage, AK 99502; phone (907) 243-5448 or toll-free for reservations in Alaska 1-800-478-5448, in the rest of the U.S. 1-800-544-0551, fax (907) 243-0649. Lodging, restaurant, bar, trading post; volcano tours; bear viewing, fishing. *Katmai National Park.*

Grosvenor Lodge, 4700 Aircraft Dr., Anchorage, AK 99502; phone (907) 243-5448 or toll-free for reservations in Alaska 1-800-478-5448, in the rest of the U.S. 1-800-544-0551, fax (907) 243-0649. Full-service fishing lodge; 3-, 4- or 7-night packages; boat and guide service; license and equipment. *Katmai National Park.*

Kulik Lodge, 4700 Aircraft Dr., Anchorage, AK 99502; phone (907) 243-5448 or toll-free for reservations in Alaska 1-800-478-5448, in the rest of the U.S. 1-800-544-0551, fax (907) 243-0649. Full-service fishing lodge; 3-, 4- or 7-night packages; boat and guide service; daily floatplane fly-outs; license and equipment. *Katmai National Park.*

Mink Bay Lodge, 1515 Tongass Ave., Ketchikan, AK 99901; phone 225-7906, fax 247-3875. Fishing lodge in Misty Fiords National Monument; fishing for halibut, salmon, trout and steelhead. *Ketchikan.*

Salmon Falls Resort, P.O. Box 5700, Ketchikan, AK 99901; phone 225-2752, fax 225-2701. Fishing lodge with 52 rooms and main lodge with restaurant. Guided fishing on 26-foot cabin cruisers for halibut and salmon. Self-guided and fly-out packages available. *Ketchikan.*

Unuk River Post, P.O. Box 5065, Ketchikan, AK 99901; phone (206) 293-5972. Log cabins, meals; guided fresh and saltwater fishing (trout, salmon, bottom fish); Misty Fiords sightseeing boat trips; Unuk River jet boat trips. *Ketchikan.*

Yes Bay Lodge, 1515 Tongass Ave., Ketchikan, AK 99901; phone 225-7906, fax 247-3875. Full-service fishing lodge; halibut, salmon and freshwater fishing for trout and steelhead. Wildlife viewing. Located 50 miles north of Ketchikan. *Ketchikan.*

Katmai Lodge, 2825 90th St. SE, Everett, WA 98208; phone (206) 337-0326, fax (206) 337-0335. On the Alagnak River. Main lodge and out buildings with private rooms and cabins; all amenities. Buffet-style dining; sauna. Fishing for salmon, trophy rainbow trout and grayling, arctic char, Dolly Varden, northern pike; guides, fishing boats (including 12 jet boats); tackle. Floatplanes available for fly-out fishing; private airstrip. *King Salmon.*

Munsey's Bear Camp, Amook Pass, Kodiak, AK 99615; phone 847-2203. Lodge offers photo safaris for brown bear and other wildlife; fishing for halibut and salmon. *Kodiak Island.*

Olga Bay Lodge, Inc., 321 Maple St., Kodiak, AK 99615; phone or fax 486-5373. Full-service fishing lodge; guides, fly-out and jet boat fishing; freshwater fishing for salmon, trout and steelhead. *Kodiak Island.*

Port Lions Lodge & Charters, Inc., P.O. Box 51, Port Lions, AK 99550; phone 454-2264 (summer), 486-6079 (winter), fax 486-6079. Full-service lodge; guided fishing, duck hunting. *Kodiak Island.*

Saltery Lake Lodge, 1516 Larch St., #1, Kodiak, AK 99615; phone 1-800-770-5037, fax (907) 486-3188. Fishing for 5 species of salmon, trout, Dolly Varden, steelhead and halibut; hunting for deer, ducks and bear; float trips on the Karluk River. Packages available, send for brochure. *Kodiak Island.*

Zachar Bay Lodge, P.O. Box 2609, Kodiak, AK 99615; phone 486-4120. 50 miles southwest of Kodiak by floatplane. Former cannery with 8 rooms, shared or private bath, dining hall. Fishing for king salmon, silvers, reds, pinks, Dolly Varden and halibut. Bear viewing trips. Includes shared twin accommodations, all meals, guides, halibut tackle and bait, fish cleaning. *Kodiak Island.*

Lakeside Lodge, #1 Lakeside Dr., Port Alsworth, AK 99653; phone 781-2202. Full-service lodge on Lake Clark; kitchenette cabins and boat rentals also available. *Lake Clark.*

Denali West Lodge, P.O. Box 40, Lake Minchumina, AK 99757; phone or fax 674-3112. Lodge with cabins, full-guided natural history tours, hiking, canoeing, fishing. Dog sledding in winter. *Lake Minchumina.*

Lisianski Inlet Lodge, Box 776, Pelican, AK 99832; phone 735-2266. Beachfront homestead with cabin; fishing, hiking and wildlife viewing. Floatplane or boat access. May 1 to Sept. 20. *Pelican.*

Gold Coast Lodge, P.O. Box 9629, Ketchikan, AK 99901; phone (907) 225-8375 or 1-800-333-5992. Custom-built floating fishing lodge; fishing for salmon, halibut and other bottom fish with guide David Ausman; maximum 8 guests. *Prince of Wales Island.*

Sportsman's Cove Lodge, P.O. Box 2486, Olympia, WA 98507; phone (206) 956-3442, reservations 1-800-962-7889, fax (206) 956-0345. Lodge with meals, private baths at Saltery Cove (20 minutes from Ketchikan by floatplane); fully guided salmon and halibut fishing on 36-foot yachts; sightseeing cruises; tackle and fish packaging. Mid-May to September. All inclusive. Full-service travel agency. *Prince of Wales Island.*

Port William Lodge, P.O. Box 670556, Chugiak, AK 99567; phone or fax 688-2253. Full-service fishing lodge, originally a cannery, located 30 minutes from Kodiak by air; also accessible by boat. Sauna, game room, library. Fishing for halibut, salmon, trout and bottomfish; filleting and packaging; licensed captains operate cruisers and skiffs. Sightseeing brown bear and other wildlife. Maximum 24 guests. *Shuyak Island.*

Northwoods Lodge, P.O. Box 66, Skwentna, AK 99667; phone (907) 733-3742 or 1-800-999-6539. Fly-in fishing lodge; fully guided and outfitted fishing for 5 species of salmon, trout and pike. Tent camps and float fishing available. *Skwentna/Lake Creek area.*

Mother Goose Lodge, Donkey Lake, Skwentna, AK 99667; phone 733-2166. Full-service lodge or cabins for do-it-yourselfers; fishing for salmon, grayling, trout and northern pike; registered hunting guide. *Skwentna.*

Skwentna Lodge, 8051 Rabbit Creek Rd., Anchorage, AK 99516; phone 345-1702, fax 345-5216. Full-service, year-round lodge catering to anglers; Skwentna and Yentna rivers, Lake Creek and other streams. Packages include air from Anchorage, guide, bait and motor, lodging and meals. *Skwentna.*

Stephan Lake Lodge, P.O. Box 770695, Eagle River, AK 99577; phone 696-2163, fax 694-4129. Fishing for king salmon, silvers and reds, rainbow trout, lake trout and grayling; hiking and hunting. *Stephan Lake.*

Air Taxi & Air Charter Operators

Alaskan Airventures, Inc., HCO 3 Box 8758, Palmer, AK 99645; phone 822-3905, fax 822-3905. Air taxi; floats; skis. *Statewide.*

Bear Lake Air & Guide Service, HCR 64, Box 386, Seward, AK 99664; phone 224-5725. Floatplane service; flightseeing; fly-in hunting and fishing; Kenai Peninsula. *Southcentral.*

Bering Air, Inc., P.O. Box 1650, Nome, AK 99762; phone 443-5620 (Russian desk) or 443-5464 (gen. reservations), fax 443-5919. Scheduled service to over 30 villages from bases in Kotzebue and Nome. Two- and 4-night charter - tour packages to Russian far east. *Western.*

Bettles Air Service, P.O. Box 27, Bettles, AK 99726; phone 1-800-770-5111, fax (907) 692-5655 (summer) or (907) 488-7909 (winter). Flightseeing/fly-in Brooks Range, Gates of the Arctic National Park. Wilderness trips. Fairbanks - Bettles flightsee with brunch daily. *Brooks Range/Arctic.*

Branch River Air Service, 4540 Edinburgh Dr., Anchorage, AK 99515 (winter); P.O. Box 545, King Salmon, AK 99613 (summer); phone 248-3539 or 246-3437, fax 248-3539. Regional floatplane air taxi service based in King Salmon. Offering floatplane service for fishermen, rafters, hunters, flightseeing, photography and air charter service. *Western.*

Bush Pilots Air Service, P.O. Box 190389, Anchorage, AK 99519; phone 243-1434, fax 349-6724. General air taxi for charter. Fly-out fishing and hunting packages. *Southcentral.*

Cordova Air Service Inc., P.O. Box 528, Cordova, AK 99574; phone 424-7611. Charter service on Prince William Sound. Flightseeing, drop-offs for hunting and fishing. *Southcentral.*

Doug Geeting Aviation, P.O. Box 42, Talkeetna, AK 99676; phone 733-2366, fax 733-1000. Flight tours with glacier landing in the Alaska Range. Aerial photography, overnight guided wildlife safaris. Tours of Mount McKinley, 6 passengers. *Southcentral.*

Era Aviation, 6160 South Airpark Dr., Anchorage, AK 99502; phone 243-6633, fax 266-8383. Regional carrier. Scheduled service between Anchorage and Kenai, Homer, Kodiak, Iliamna and Valdez. Additional flights from Bethel to 17 villages in Western Alaska. Charter service available throughout the state. *Statewide.*

Frontier Flying Service, Inc., 3820 University Ave., Fairbanks, AK 99709; phone 474-0014, fax 474-0774. Daily departures available for trips through the Gates of the Arctic. Daily service to over 20 Interior and Arctic destinations. *Brooks Range/Arctic.*

Haines Airways, Inc., P.O. Box 470, Haines, AK 99827; phone 766-2646, fax 766-2780. Southeast Alaska package tours. Scheduled service between Haines, Juneau, Gustavus and Hoonah. Rafting fly-in specialists. *Southeast.*

Harbor Air Service, P.O. Box 269, Seward, AK 99664; phone 224-3133, fax 224-3679. Daily commuter service to Anchorage; air tours to Kenai Fjords National Park, Harding Ice Cap; air taxi service to Forest Service cabins; fly-in hunting and fishing. *Southcentral.*

Homer Air, 2190 Kachemak Dr., Homer, AK 99603; phone (907) 235-8591 or 1-800-478-8591. Daily flights between Homer and Seldovia and other Kenai Peninsula destinations; flightseeing, charter. *Southcentral.*

Hudson Air Service, Inc., P.O. Box 648, Talkeetna, AK 99676; phone 733-2321. Scenic trips, prospecting, charters, kayakers, rafters and hunters. *Statewide.*

K2 Aviation, P.O. Box 545, Talkeetna, AK 99676; phone 733-2291, fax 733-1221. Glacier landings, fly-in fishing and hunting, Mount McKinley circle flights and summit overflights. *Southcentral.*

Kachemak Air Service, Inc., P.O. Box 1769, Homer, AK 99603; phone 235-8924. Flightseeing glaciers, floatplane service. *Southcentral.*

Katmai Air, 4700 Aircraft Dr., Anchorage, AK; (907) 243-5448, reservations 1-800-478-5448 (AK), 1-800-944-0551 (U.S.), fax (907) 243-0649. Air taxi service to and in Katmai National Park, Alaska Peninsula and Bristol Bay area. Flightseeing, charters, floattrips (guided and unguided), hunter drop-offs. *Western.*

Kenai Lake Adventures, P.O. Box 830, Cooper Landing, AK 99572; phone 595-1363. Fly-in hunting and fishing; air taxi to Forest Service cabins; charter; flightseeing. *Southcentral.*

Ketchum Air Service, Inc., P.O. Box 190588, Anchorage, AK 99519-0588; phone 243-5525. Flightseeing Columbia Glacier; drop-off hunting; day fishing tours. *Southcentral.*

Lake Clark Air, Inc., The Farm, Box 1, Port Alsworth, AK 99653; phone 781-2211, fax 781-2215. Statewide charter service. Package guided and unguided fly-out fishing and hunting trips. Also boating, rafting, hiking, flightseeing. Each package is custom-made. *Statewide.*

Larry's Flying Service, Inc., P.O. Box 2348, Fairbanks, AK 99707; phone 474-9169, fax 474-8815. Scheduled air service; air tours to Fort Yukon, Bettles, Anaktuvuk Pass. *Brooks Range/Arctic, Interior.*

Loken Aviation, 8995 Yandukin Dr., Juneau, AK 99801; phone 789-3331, fax 789-7076. Scheduled and charter trips. Flightseeing, bear watching at Pack Creek in Admiralty Island National Monument Wilderness Area. *Southeast.*

McCarthy Air, Box MXY, McCarthy, AK 99588; phone 1-800-478-6909. Charters based in the heart of the Wrangell-St. Elias National Park. Flightseeing, backcountry air support, photography. 22 years experience. VS, MC, AX accepted. *Southcentral.*

Merrill Field Municipal Airport, 800 Merrill Field Dr., Anchorage, AK 99501-4129, phone 276-4044, fax 276-8421. 1,422 tiedowns for general aviation aircraft, both transient and permanent. Six public aviation fueling facilities and a mobile fuel truck. Public aircraft washing area and public Compass Rose. Near downtown Anchorage, shopping mall next to airport. *Southcentral.*

Olson Air Service, Inc., P.O. Box 142, Nome, AK 99762; phone 443-2229, fax 443-5017. Daily schedules, air taxi, charters, flightseeing tours. *Western.*

Talkeetna Air Taxi, P.O. Box 73, Talkeetna, AK 99676; phone 733-2218. Glacier landings on Mount McKinley; climbing expedition support. Sportfishing and hunting flights. *Southcentral.*

TEMSCO Helicopters, Inc., 1650 Maplesden Way, Juneau, AK 99801; phone 789-9501, fax 789-7989. Helicopter glacier tours from Juneau and Skagway; all tours feature glacier landings. *Southeast.*

Tundra Air, P.O. Box 87, Manley Hot Springs, AK 99756; phone 672-3692, fax 457-2475. Charter flights. Pike and sheefish trips; cabins and boats available. Brooks Range trips for rafting, kayaking, hiking, fishing, hunting. Bush flying on wheels and skis also. *Statewide.*

Uyak air Service, P.O. Box 4188, Kodiak, AK 99615; phone 486-3407, fax 486-3267. Air taxi service. *Southwestern, Brooks Range/Arctic.*

Warbelow's Air Ventures, Inc., 3758 University Ave. S., Fairbanks, AK 99709;

phone 474-0518. Scheduled and charter service; mail flights, fly-in packages. *Brooks Range/Arctic, Interior.*

Wrangell Mountain Air, Inc., McCarthy, P.O. Box MXY, Glennallen, AK 99588; phone (907) 345-1160 or 1-800-478-1160, fax (907) 345-0614. Based in the heart of the Wrangell-St. Elias National Park at McCarthy near Kennicott. Specializing in fly-in backcountry wilderness trips. Flightseeing tours and charters. Service from Chitina, Glennallen, Anchorage. Year-round service. *Statewide, Southcentral.*

Wright Air Service, P.O. Box 60142, Fairbanks, AK 99706; phone 474-0502, fax 474-0375. Scheduled service to various villages, charters, flightseeing. *Brooks Range/Arctic, Interior.*

Adventure Guides & Outfitters

Air Adventures, P.O. Box 22, Kenai, AK 99611-0022; phone 776-5444, fax 776-5445. Guided and unguided fishing trips; flightseeing tours; unguided hunting; bear watching tours. Wilderness camp, cabin or lodge accommodations. *Southcentral, Southwestern, Western.*

Alaska Bush Adventures, 610 W. 91st Ave., Anchorage, AK 99515; phone 522-1712, fax 563-6789. Guided and unguided hunting and fishing trips; wilderness hiking; photography trips. Motor home rental. *Statewide.*

Alaska Cross Country Guiding and Rafting, P.O. Box 124, Haines, AK 99827; phone 767-5522. Guided hunts for brown and black bear and mountain goat. Fly-in, raft-out wilderness tours supported by remote cabins, including optional glacier and alpine hiking. All activities located in and around the Chilkat Bald Eagle Preserve. October eagle photo blinds. *Southeast.*

Alaska Cruises/Outdoor Alaska, P.O.Box 7814, Ketchikan AK 99901; phone 225-6044, fax 225-8036. Cruise/fly to Misty Fjords National Monument; kayaker transportation; fly-in fishing and camping. *Southeast.*

Alaska-Denali Guiding, Inc., P.O. Box 566, Talkeetna, AK 99676; phone 733-2649, fax 733-1362. Mount McKinley expeditions, mountaineering and seminars; rugged hiking trips and custom-designed trips. *Statewide.*

Alaska Fish and Trails Unlimited, 1177 Shypoke Dr., Fairbanks, AK 99709; phone 479-7630. Specializing in guided or unguided expeditions into the Gates of the Arctic. Backpacking, rafting, fishing tours, skiing. *Brooks Range/Arctic.*

Alaska Rainforest Tours, 369 S. Franklin St., Suite 200, Juneau, AK 99801; phone 463-3466, fax 463-4453. Central booking agency for adventure tours, mainly in northern southeast Alaska but also throughout the state. Also a central booking service for bed and breakfasts. Specializing in individual and small group trip planning. *Southeast.*

Alaska Tolovana Adventures, P.O. Box 281, Nenana, AK 99760; phone or fax 832-5569. Fully guided custom river trips, wildlife observation, fishing trips and winter dog sled trips. Accommodations and meals available at Tolovana Lodge, a restored 1923 roadhouse on the Tanana River. Fly-in or riverboat from Nenana. *Interior, Brooks Range/Arctic.*

Alaska Wildland Adventures, P.O. Box 389, Girdwood, AK 99587; phone 1-800-334-8720 outside AK, (907) 783-2928 in AK, fax (907) 783-2130. Nationally recognized natural history/ecotourism operator. Seven-, 10- or 12-day wildland safaris plus 8-day "Senior" safari. Experience-oriented trips to Denali, Kenai Fjords, wildlife refuges and seacoast glaciers. Free color brochure. *Statewide.*

Alaska Women of the Wilderness, P.O. Box 773556, Eagle River, AK 99577; phone 688-2226. A year-round non-profit wilderness program for women, designed to develop competence and confidence in and through the outdoors. Activities include: climbing, backpacking, canoeing, kayaking, skiing, bicycling, rafting, llama and horse packing, fishing, women's retreats and an annual film festival. *Southcentral.*

Alaskan Sojourns, P.O. Box 871410, Wasilla, AK 99687; phone 376-2913, fax 376-7100. River running; sportfishing; backpacking; watercolor painting; photography. *Southcentral, Western.*

Alaskan Wilderness Outfitting Company, Inc., P.O. Box 1516, Cordova, AK 99574; phone 424-5552, fax 424-5564. Fly-in salt and fresh water fishing packages. Tour Alaska by seaplane, outpost cabins, floating cabins, rafting. Also lodge facilities. *Statewide, Southcentral, Brooks Range/Arctic.*

Alatna Headwaters Wilderness Cabin, P.O. Box 80424, Fairbanks, AK 99708; phone 479-6354. Witness major caribou migrations, wolves and grizzlies 100 miles above the Arctic Circle. Arctic valleys to explore and numerous mountains to climb. Since 1967. *Brooks Range/Arctic.*

Arctic 7 Tours, P.O. Box 80890, Fairbanks, AK 99708; phone 479-0751, fax 479-2229. Wildlife and nature excursions; fishing adventures year-round; shuttle service to Denali Park; local sightseeing tours; charter trips available; winter northern lights viewing. Summer and winter schedules. *Brooks Range/Arctic.*

Baranof Sportsman's Vacations, 325 Seward St., Sitka, AK 99835; phone or fax 747-4937. Large modern cabin on private 4-acre island in Sitka Sound. Boat rentals to 24-foot equipped for offshore salmon and halibut fishing. Guided saltwater fishing and sightseeing. Wilderness camping transport. *Southeast.*

Chandalar River Outfitters, P.O. Box 74877, Fairbanks, AK 99707; phone 488-8402 or 451-6587, fax 488-7899. Guided and outfitted hunting, fishing, canoeing, camping, horseback trips, horse-drawn sleigh and hay rides. Remote cabins for rent, bed and breakfast, guide and trapping schools. *Interior, Brooks Range/Arctic, Western.*

Chazman Charters, P.O. Box 2826, Kodiak, AK 99615; phone 486-6780, fax 486-5666. Fishing and sightseeing charters, whale watching. *Southwestern.*

Chilkat Guides Ltd., P.O. Box 170, Haines, AK 99827; phone 766-2491, fax 766-2409. One- to 14-day raft trips. Tatshenshini-Alsek helicopter hiking tours. Mountain guiding and hiking trips. *Southeast.*

Earth Tours, 705 W. 6th Ave., #205, Anchorage, AK 99501; phone 279-9907, fax 279-9862. Custom-designed wilderness adventures to suit any budget. Multilingual staff. *Statewide.*

Gates of the Arctic Wilderness Cabin, P.O. Box 80424, Fairbanks, AK 99708; phone 479-6354. Situated along wild and scenic Alatna River, 15 miles from Arrigetch Peaks. Exclusive bookings, comfort and privacy. Since 1967. *Brooks Range/Arctic.*

Golden Plover Guiding and Air, Colville Village via Pouch 340109, Prudhoe Bay, AK 99734; phone 659-3991. Lodging and guides in remote Arctic Alaska. Bird tours, photography, museum, boating, sightseeing. Air taxi charter service, flightseeing. *Brooks Range/Arctic.*

Great Land Birding Tours, SRA Box 1415, Slana, AK 99586; phone 822-3003. Bird watching, hiking, rafting, flying trips to Copper River Delta. *Southcentral.*

High Adventure Air Charter Guides and Outfitters, P.O. Box 486, Soldotna, AK 99669; phone 262-5237. Fly-in hunting, fishing, flightseeing, backpacking, brown bear viewing. *Southcentral, Western.*

Hugh Glass Backpacking Co., Inc., P.O. Box 110796, Anchorage, AK 99511; phone 344-1340, fax 344-4614. Guided backpacking, sea kayaking, raft trips, canoe trips into ANWR, Kenai Fjords, Katmai, Wrangell-St. Elias and Shuyak Island parks. *Southcentral, Brooks Range/ Arctic, Western.*

Kachemak Bay Adventures, P.O. Box 1196, Homer, AK 99603; phone 235-8490. Sightseeing tours featuring bird watching and wildlife viewing. Natural history tour to historic Seldovia. *Southcentral.*

Katmai Adventures, P.O. Box 418, King Salmon, AK 99613; phone 1-800-770-FISH, fax (907) 246-6200. Guided fishing, rental boats, boat tours of Katmai National Park, raft trips, flightseeing. Non-guided drop-off caribou hunts. Fly-out fishing to remote destinations. Lodging. *Western.*

Kayak Ventures, P.O. Box 8630, Kodiak, AK 99615; phone 1-800-462-5634, fax (907) 486-5666. Guided kayak day trips to multi-day expeditions. Novices welcome. *Southwestern.*

Kodiak Island Charters, P.O. Box 3750, Kodiak, AK 99615; phone 486-5380, fax 486-5666. King salmon and halibut fishing, sightseeing and group tours, whale watching. *Southwestern.*

Lost Creek Ranch, P.O. Box 84334, Fairbanks, AK 99708; phone 672-3999. Rustic lodging and cabins off the Elliott Highway northwest of Fairbanks. Horseback riding, camping, fishing, gold panning, mountain climbing, fall-spring northern lights. Homemade meals and baked goods. *Interior.*

Max Schwab, Registered Guide, P.O. Box 295, Talkeetna, AK 99676; phone 733-2681. River rafting; air charter for backpacking and camping, fishing, hunting. *Statewide.*

Mountain Trip, P.O. Box 91161, Anchorage, AK 99509; phone 345-6499. Guided climbs and instruction in the Alaska Range. Expeditions to Denali, Mount Hunter, Mount Sanford; climbing classes in the Anchorage area. *Southcentral.*

Muskomee Bay Lodge, P.O. Box 1234, Kodiak, AK 99615; phone 1-800-462-5634, fax (907) 486-5666. Full-service remote lodging, fishing, wildlife photography, hiking. *Southwestern.*

North Star, P.O. Box 1724, Flagstaff, AZ 86002; phone (602) 773-9917 or 1-800-258-8434. Guided sea kayaking in Prince William Sound and Kenai Fjords National Park. Rafting, canoeing, backpacking in the Brooks Range/Arctic . Natural history tours to different national parks of Alaska: Denali, Katmai, Kenai Fjords, Wrangell-St. Elias. Focus on natural history. *Southcentral, Brooks Range/Arctic.*

Outland Expeditions, P.O. Box 92401, Anchorage, AK 99509-2401; phone 522-1670, fax 522-4633. Custom trips. Dog-mushing, back country skiing,. mountaineering, rafting, sea kayaking, photography safaris, hunting and fishing, cultural experiences. *Statewide.*

Personal Alaskan Adventures, 12,900 Norak Place, Anchorage, AK 99516; phone 345-4493. Bush plane flights, rafting and canoeing, riverboating, ferry tours. Specializing in private group sightseeing tours; fishing safaris; wilderness treks. Accommodations and meals. *Southcentral.*

St. Elias Alpine Guides, P.O. Box 111241, Anchorage, AK 99511; phone 277-6867. Statewide expeditions with a focus on the Wrangell-St. Elias National Park. Backpacking expeditions such as the Chitistone Canyon, rafting trips, and mountaineering adventures specializing in first ascents in very remote ranges. Also glacier seminars, raft/hike combinations, and day trips out of McCarthy. *Statewide.*

Sea Hawk Air, Inc., P.O. Box 3561, Kodiak, AK 99615; phone 1-800-770-HAWK, fax (907) 486-5666. Bear viewing, flightseeing, helicopter tours, fly-in fishing, camping, kayaking. Kodiak, Katmai National Park area. *Southwestern.*

Seaside Farms, 58335 East End Rd., Homer, AK 99603; phone 235-7850. Horseback trips on Kachemak Bay. Accommodations in cottages and private rooms; common shower, bath and kitchen; bunkhouse; tent sites available (farm work in exchange for camping). *Southcentral.*

Simpson's Alaska Flocations, Rt. 1 Box 73, Decatur, NE 68020; phone (402) 374-1430, fax (402) 374-1430. Sightseeing; fishing on upper Anvik River; rafting. Fly-out pike fishing. Bird watching and wildlife viewing. Food and lodging. *Western.*

457

Adventure (continued)

Sourdough Outfitters Inc., P.O. Box 90, Bettles, AK 99726; phone or fax 692-5252. Wilderness guide and outfitting service. Backpack/trek Arrigetch, Gates of the Arctic, Noatak and ANWR. Canoe and raft trips on arctic rivers. Exploratory trips, caribou migration, dog sledding, snowmobile, base camps, wilderness cabins, world-class fishing and equipment rentals. Year-round service from our headquarters on the south slope of the Brooks Range. Brochure and video. VS, MC, AX accepted. *Brooks Range/Arctic.*

TAK Outfitters, P.O. Box 66, Moose Pass, AK 99631; phone 288-3640. Guided horse packing trips, Kenai Peninsula. *Southcentral.*

Teklanika Tours, P.O. Box 83298, Fairbanks, AK 99708; phone 457-7194. Wilderness guiding, fishing, river trips, back-packing and outfitting. *Brooks Range/Arctic.*

Ultima Thule Outfitters, P.O. Box 109, Chitina, AK 99566; phone 344-1892, fax 258-0636. Fly-in wilderness lodge. Rafting, fishing, hunting, glacier exploration, wildlife, Flightseeing horses, climbing, dog mushing, yearround. Wrangell-St. Elias National Park. *Southcentral.*

Wilderness Alaska, P.O. Box 113063, Anchorage, AK 99511; phone 345-3567. Custom and scheduled river and hiking trips. Base camping and consulting. Natural history excursions. *Brooks Range/Arctic.*

Wilderness: Alaska/Mexico, 1231 Sundance Loop, Fairbanks, AK 99709; phone 479-8203. Backpack, raft and kayak trips in Gates of the Arctic National Park, Arctic National Wildlife Refuge, Noatak National Preserve, Kobuk Valley National Preserve; and sea kayaking trips in Prince William Sound. *Southcentral, Brooks Range/Arctic.*

River Running/Sea Kayaking/Boating

ABEC's Alaska Adventures, 1550 Alpine Vista Ct., Dept. W., Fairbanks, AK 99712; phone 457-8907, fax 457-6689. Guided backpack and river trips in the Brooks Range and other wildlands. Backcountry expeditions, ranging from 7 to 21 days, explore the Gates of the Arctic, Noatak, Arrigetch and the Arctic National Wildlife Refuge. *Brooks Range/Arctic.*

Alaska Discovery, 234 Gold St., Juneau, AK 99801; phone 463-5500. One-day guided sea kayaking trips in Glacier Bay and Juneau area; kayak rentals; canoe trips to Pack Creek bear sanctuary; other wilderness trips available. *Southeast.*

Alaska River Adventures, 1831 Kuskokwim St., Suite 20, Anchorage, AK 99508; phone 276-3418, fax 272-9839. Photo safaris, float and fishing trips, ocean kayak tours and custom adventures from the Arctic to the Kenai. *Southcentral.*

Alaska Rivers Co., P.O. Box 827, Cooper Landing, AK 99572; phone 595-1226. Scenic floats or guided fishing using drift boats or rafts on the Upper Kenai River. April 1 through Nov. 1. Brochure. *Southcentral.*

Alaska River Charters, P.O. Box 81516, Fairbanks, AK 99708; phone 455-6827, fax 455-4041. Powerboat trips on tributaries of Tanana and Yukon rivers. Fly out to wilderness areas and hot springs. Cabins or tent camping. Float trips, backpacking, fishing, wildlife observation, spring snow machine and dog mushing trips. *Interior, Brooks Range/Arctic.*

Alaska Wilderness Sailing Safaris, P.O. Box 1313, Valdez, AK 99686; phone 835-5175, fax 835-5679. Guided sailing and sea kayaking trips in Prince William Sound. Whale and bird watching, glacier viewing. Bareboat, skippered. 3-14 days. *Southcentral.*

Anadyr Adventures, P.O. Box 1821, Valdez, AK 99686; phone 835-2814, fax 835-4845. Guided sea kayaking tours. Overnight and extended trips throughout Prince William Sound. Kayak rentals. *Southcentral.*

Arctic Treks, P.O. Box 73452M, Fairbanks, AK 99707; phone 455-6502. Backpacking and rafting in Gates of the Arctic National Park and Arctic National Wildlife Refuge. *Brooks Range/Arctic.*

Denali Floats, P.O. Box 330, Talkeetna, AK 99676; phone 733-2384. Custom-guided rafting expeditions throughout Alaska and Siberia. *Statewide.*

Denali Raft Adventures Inc., Drawer 190 Mile 238 George Parks Hwy., Denali Park, AK 99755; phone 683-2234, fax 683-1281. Guided 2-hour, 4-hour and full-day scenic, whitewater, or combination raft trips on the Nenana River. Paddle rafts available. *Southcentral.*

Eruk's Wilderness Float Tours, 12720 Lupine Rd., Anchorage, AK 99516; phone 345-7678. Float trips for fishing and wildlife viewing; guided hunts. Five- to 14-day fly-in expeditions. *Brooks Range/Arctic, Western.*

Glacier Bay Sea Kayaks Inc., P.O. Box 26, Gustavus, AK 99826; phone 697-2257.

Kayak rentals in Glacier Bay National Park. Camper/kayaker transportation to remote areas. *Southeast.*

Keystone Raft and Kayak Adventures Inc., P.O. Box 1486, Valdez, AK 99686; phone (907) 835-2606 or 1-800-328-8460. Rafting and kayak adventures statewide. Fishing, whitewater, wildlife and sightseeing trips. *Statewide.*

Marine Adventure Sailing Tours, 945 Fritz Cove, Juneau, AK 99801; phone 789-0919. Custom-designed charters. Sailing, fishing, hiking, kayaking and beach-combing. *Southeast.*

Nichols Expeditions Inc., 497 N. Main St., Moab, UT 84532; phone 1-800-635-1792 or (801) 259-7882, fax (801) 259-2312. Guided tours rafting the Copper River, sea kayaking Kenai Fjords and combination rafting/backpacking trips. 6-10 days. *Statewide.*

Quest Expeditions, P.O. Box 671895, Chugiak, AK 99567; phone 688-4848. River trips in the Arctic National Wildlife Refuge and Gates of the Arctic National Park. Also float-fishing trips on the Kobuk, Kisaralik and other rivers for salmon, rainbow and sheefish. *Brooks Range/Arctic, Western.*

Raven Charters, P.O. Box 2581, Valdez, AK 99686; phone 835-5863 or 835-4960 (message). Customized sailboat charters into Prince William Sound. Day, overnight and extended trips available. *Southcentral.*

Southeast Exposure, P.O. Box 9143, Ketchikan, AK 99901; phone 225-8829. Guided sea kayaking trips; 4-, 6- and 8-day trips. Custom trips, kayak rentals and instruction. *Southeast.*

Spirit Walker Expeditions, P.O. Box 240, Gustavus, AK 99826; phone (907) 697-2266 or 1-800-478-9255 (AK only), fax (907) 697-2266. Guided wilderness sea kayaking expeditions in Inside Passage. All equipment provided. Custom trips and beginners are our specialties. *Southeast.*

Stan Stephens Cruises, P.O. Box 1297, Valdez, AK 99686; phone (907) 835-4731 or 1-800-992-1297, fax (907) 835-3765. Depart Whittier or Valdez, cruise Prince William Sound to Growler Island camp. Meals; private heated tent. Mid-May to late September. Brochure. *Southcentral.*

Yukon River Tours, 214 2nd Ave., Fairbanks, AK 99701; phone 452-7162, fax 452-5063. Cruise the Yukon River to a traditional working Athabascan Indian summer fish camp. Meet the Athabascan people and learn how they harvest and preserve salmon. *Interior.*

Other

EQUIPMENT RENTALS & SERVICE

Alaska Grocery Shippers, P.O. Box 200246, Anchorage, AK 99520; phone 276-1656. Groceries shipped to the Bush. In business since 1976. *Statewide.*

Aldersheim Lodge, P.O. Box 210447, Auke Bay, AK 99821; phone or fax 780-4778. Kayak rentals. *Southeast.*

Backcountry Logistical Services, P.O. Box 82265, Fairbanks, AK 99708; phone 457-7606. Raft and canoe rentals. *Interior, Western.*

Clem's Backpacking Sports, 315 Wendell St., Box 222, Fairbanks, AK 99707; phone 456-6314. Specialized lightweight camping gear for mountain climbing, hiking, trekking, hunting, river running; tents, backpacks, sleeping bags, boots, stoves and cook gear, dry food. *Statewide.*

Independent Rental Inc., 2020 S. Cushman St., Fairbanks, AK 99701; phone 456-6595, fax 456-2927. Rental rafts, canoes, tents, camping equipment, small fishing skiffs with motors, video cameras. *Statewide.*

Ken's Alaskan Tackle, P.O. Box 1168, Soldotna, AK 99669; phone 262-6870. Boats and canoes for rent; also rods and reels, hip waders, fishing tackle and lures. *Southcentral.*

Recreational Services, P.O. Box 1112, Palmer, AK 99645; phone 745-2447. Inflatable boat and related equipment rental. One, 7- and 10-day rates, delivery available. *Statewide.*

7 Bridges Boats & Bikes, P.O. Box 80890, Fairbanks, AK 99708; phone 479-0751, fax 479-2229. Rental boats, hourly or day rate; rental bikes, day rate. Van transport upriver and pickup downriver. *Interior.*

Tippecanoe, P.O. Box 1175, Willow, AK 99688; phone 495-6688. Canoe and raft rentals; serving the Nancy Lake recreation area and surrounding lakes and streams in the Susitna River Valley. *Southcentral.*

Wildlife Canoe Adventures, P.O. Box 80488, Fairbanks, AK 99708; phone 479-0751, fax 479-2229. Canoe rentals for self-guided float trips; transport by van upriver and pickup downriver available. *Interior.*

PERMITS

Choggiung Ltd., Box 330, Dillingham, AK 99576; phone 842-5218, fax 842-5462. Land use permits for campsites. *Western.*

Other (continued)

PUBLICATIONS & CLASSES

Alaska Alpine School, P.O. Box 111241, Anchorage, AK 99511; phone 277-6867. Statewide expeditions, glacier trekking, high altitude mountaineering, first ascents courses, river rafting, backpacking, ski mountaineering and touring, leadership courses, mountain photography and naturalist hikes. *Statewide.*

Alaska Wilderness Recreation & Tourism Assoc., P.O. Box 1353, Valdez, AK 99686; phone 835-4300. Publishes a directory of business members offering a variety of wilderness experiences. *Statewide.*

Alaska Wilderness Studies, College of Community and Continuing Education, University of Alaska Anchorage, 3211 Providence Dr., Anchorage, AK 99508; phone 786-1468. Credit classes in climbing and mountaineering, canoeing, rafting, kayaking, wilderness emergency medicine, natural history, camping and backpacking. Summer credit class expeditions to various remote locations. *Statewide.*

National Outdoor Leadership School, P.O. Box 981, Palmer, AK 99645; phone 745-4047, fax 745-6069. Wilderness education expeditions. Two weeks to semester length courses in sea kayaking, backpacking, mountaineering and river paddling. *Southeast, Southcentral, Brooks Range/Arctic.*

Northern Writing Services, P.O. Box 670790, Chugiak, AK 99567; phone 696-3256. Publishers of the *Alaska Hunting Journal,* a quarterly hunting newsletter featuring profiles of Alaska hunting guides and game units, along with information on guide areas and hunting resorts. *Statewide.*

San-Alaska Statewide Yellow Pages, 4504 Spenard Rd., Anchorage, AK 99517; phone 248-2014, fax 243-0250. Yellow page directory with listings of hotels by region and city. *Statewide.*

TOURS, TRAVEL & BOOKING AGENCIES

Alaska Booking & Reservation Center, 329 F St. #206, Anchorage, AK 99501; phone 277-6228, fax 272-7766. All Alaska tours and excursions. *Statewide.*

Alaska Rainforest Treks, 369 S. Franklin St. #200, Juneau, AK 99801; phone 463-3466, fax 463-4453. Hiking and backpacking with naturalist guide. Day hikes for everyone, Chilkoot Trail tours, women's backpacking tours. *Southeast.*

All Ways Travel Inc., 302 G St., Anchorage, AK 99501; phone 276-3644, fax 258-2211. Complete booking and ticketing for adventure travel. *Statewide.*

Denali National Park Central Reservations, 2815 2nd Ave. #400, Seattle, WA 98121; phone (206) 728-4202, fax (206) 443-1979. Central booking agency for lodging, tours, transportation and wilderness resorts in the Denali National Park area. *Interior.*

Dockside Services, P.O. Box 1503, Homer, AK 99603; phone 1-800-478-8338 in Alaska, 1-800-532-8338 rest of U.S. Provides information and reservations for Homer area wilderness activities and lodging. *Southcentral.*

Puffin Travel, Box 3, Gustavus, AK 99826; phone 697-2260, fax 697-2258. Custom packages for Glacier Bay and Juneau icefield. *Southeast.*

Sanctuary Travel Services, Inc., 3701 E. Tudor Rd., Anchorage, AK 99507; phone (907) 561-1212 or 1-800-247-3149, fax (907) 563-6747. Full-service travel agency specializing in customized wilderness trips. *Statewide.*

World Express Tours, Inc., 200 W. 34th Ave. #412, Anchorage, AK 99503; phone 1-800-544-2235, fax (907) 786-3298. Custom travel planning for fishing, rafting and lodges. *Statewide.*

TRANSPORTATION

Alaska Marine Highway System, P.O. Box 25535, Juneau, AK 99802-5535; phone 1-800-642-0066.

Alaska Railroad Corp., Passenger Service Dept., P.O. Box 107500, Anchorage, AK 99510-7500; phone (907) 265-2494 or 1-800-544-0552.

VISITOR INFORMATION CENTERS

Anchorage Visitor Information Center, 4th Ave. & F St., Anchorage, AK 99501; phone 274-3531.

Bethel Visitors Center, P.O. Box 388, Bethel, AK 99559; phone (907) 543-2098.

Cordova Visitors Center, P.O. Box 391, Cordova, AK 99574; phone 424-7443.

Delta Junction Visitor Information Center, P.O. Box 987, Delta Junction, AK 99737; phone 895-9941 (summer), 895-5068 (winter).

Denali Visitor Information Center, P.O.

Box 7, Cantwell, AK 99729; phone 768-2420, fax 768-2942.

Gustavus Visitors Assoc., P.O. Box 167, Gustavus, AK 99826; phone 697-2358.

Hyder Community Assoc., P.O. Box 149, Hyder, AK 99923; fax (604)636-9148.

Juneau Visitor Information, Davis Log Cabin, 134 Third St., Juneau, AK 99801; phone 586-2201.

Kenai Peninsula Tourism Marketing Council, 110 S. Willow St. #106, Kenai, AK 99611; phone 283-3850, fax 283-3913.

Kenai Peninsula Visitor Information Center, P.O. Box 236, Soldotna, AK 99669; phone 262-1337, fax 262-3566.

Kenai Visitor Information Center, P.O. Box 497, Kenai, AK 99611; phone 283-7989.

King Salmon Visitors Center, P.O. Box 298, King Salmon, AK 99613; phone 246-4250.

Kodiak Island Visitor Information Center, 100 Marine Way, Kodiak, AK 99615; phone 486-4070, fax 486-6545.

Mat-Su Visitors Center, HC01 Box 6166J-21, Palmer, AK 99645; phone 746-5002.

Prince William Sound Tourism Coalition, P.O. Box 243044, Anchorage, AK 99524-3044; phone 338-1213, fax 333-9642.

Southeast Alaska Tourism Council, 369 S. Franklin St. #205, Juneau, AK 99801; phone 586-4777, fax 463-4961.

Alaska's Southwest, 3300 Arctic Blvd. #203, Anchorage, AK 99503; phone 562-7380, fax 562-0438.

Unalaska Visitors Center, The Henry Swanson House, P.O. Box 89, Unalaska, AK 99685; phone 581-1483.

Valdez Visitor Information Center, P.O. Box 1603, Valdez, AK 99686; phone 835-4636.

White Mountain Visitor Information Center, c/o City Hall, White Mountain, AK 99784; phone 638-3411.

CULTURAL CENTERS AND MUSEUMS

Anchorage Museum of History & Art, 121 W. Seventh Ave., Anchorage, AK 99501; phone 343-6173 (recorded message).

Alaska State Museum, 395 Whittier St., Juneau, AK 99801-1718; phone 465-2901.

Alaska Natural History Assoc., 250 Cushman St., #1A, Fairbanks, AK 99701; phone 451-7352.

Carrie McLain Memorial Museum, P.O. Box 53, Nome, AK 99762; phone 443-2566, fax 443-5349.

Cordova Historical Museum, P.O. Box 391, Cordova, AK 99574; phone 424-6665, fax 424-6000.

Juneau Douglas City Museum, 155 South Seward, Juneau, AK 99801; phone 586-3572.

Oscar Anderson House Museum, 420 M St., Anchorage, AK 99501; phone 274-2336, fax 235-2764.

Samuel K. Fox Museum, P.O. Box 273, Dillingham, AK 99576; phone 842-2322.

Sheldon Jackson Museum, 104 College Dr., Sitka, AK 99835-7657; phone 747-8981.

State of Alaska Railroad Museum, P.O. Box 419, Nenana, AK 99760; phone 832-5566.

Tongass Historical Museum, 629 Dock St., Ketchikan, AK 99901; phone 225-5600, fax 225-5075.

Totem Heritage Center, 629 Dock St., Ketchikan, AK 99901; phone 225-5900, fax 225-5075.

Trail of '98 City Museum, P.O. Box 415, Skagway, AK 99840; phone 983-2420.

Valdez Museum, P.O. Box 307, Valdez, AK 99686; phone 835-2764.

Wales Museum, City of Wales, Wales, AK 99783; phone 664-3501, fax 664-3671.

Wrangell Museum, P.O. Box 1050, Wrangell, AK 99929; phone 874-3770.

INDEX

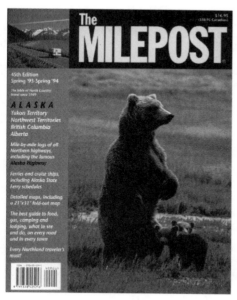

"The Bible of North Country Travel"

The MILEPOST®

provides the best, most current information available on the highways of Alaska and northwestern Canada. Updated every year by a team of experienced field editors, The MILEPOST® contains mile-by-mile logs of all roads in Alaska and Yukon Territory, plus major routes in British Columbia, Alberta and Northwest Territories.

* More than 600 pages.
* Over 200 color photos.
* 42 highway maps and 42 city and area maps.
* Free pull-out Plan-A-Trip map.

Called the "quintessential reference" by The Associated Press, The MILEPOST® has been guiding travelers up the Alaska Highway since 1949.

The MILEPOST® offers detailed information for every traveler on everything — from food, gas, lodging and camping to ferry travel, sightseeing attractions and activities. $18.95 / $20.95 Canadian. Softbound.

The MILEPOST® SOUVENIR LOG BOOK is the perfect companion to The MILEPOST®. This 64-page travel diary makes it easy to keep track of all the highlights of your trip. There's

room to record gas, mileage, food, lodging and wildlife sightings. Historical photos and captions in the book commemorate the construction of the Alaska Highway in 1942. $4.95 / $5.95 Canadian. Softbound.

NORTHWEST MILEPOSTS

is the most complete guide available to the highways of the greater Pacific Northwest. From the Editors of The MILEPOST®, NORTHWEST MILEPOSTS offers mile-by-mile logs of the major highways of Washington, Oregon, Idaho, western Montana and southwestern Canada. $14.95 / $18.95 Canadian. 328 pages softbound.

see next page for ordering information

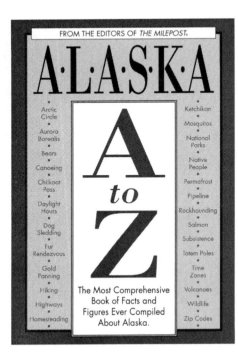

Inclusion of Disabled Children in Primary School Playgrounds

Helen Woolley
with Marc Armitage, Julia Bishop,
Mavis Curtis and Jane Ginsborg

Joseph Rowntree Foundation

The Joseph Rowntree Foundation has supported this project as part of its programme of research and innovative development projects, which it hopes will be of value to policy-makers, practitioners and service users.

National Children's Bureau

NCB promotes the voices, interests and well-being of all children and young people across every aspect of their lives. As an umbrella body for the children's sector in England and Northern Ireland, NCB provides essential information on policy, research and best practice for its members and other partners.

NCB aims to:
- challenge disadvantage in childhood
- work with children and young people to ensure they are involved in all matters that affect their lives
- promote multidisciplinary, cross-agency partnership and good practice
- influence government through policy development and advocacy
- undertake high-quality research and work from an evidence-based perspective
- disseminate information to all those working with children and young people, and to children and young people themselves.

The views expressed in this book are those of the authors and not necessarily those of the National Children's Bureau, the Joseph Rowntree Foundation or the University of Sheffield.

Published by the National Children's Bureau for the Joseph Rowntree Foundation

National Children's Bureau, 8 Wakley Street, London EC1V 7QE
Tel: 020 7843 6000.
Website: www.ncb.org.uk
Registered Charity number 258825

NCB works in partnership with Children in Scotland (www.childreninscotland.org.uk) and Children in Wales (www.childreninwales.org.uk).

© The University of Sheffield 2005

Published 2005

ISBN 1 904787 66 5

British Library Cataloguing in Publication Data
A catalogue record for this book is available from the British Library

Contents

Acknowledgements

First and foremost we are very grateful to the children who shared their experiences of the playground with us in such a meaningful and informative way, providing a wealth of information. We also thank the parents of the children for agreeing to their involvement.

Many people have contributed to the research upon which this publication draws. Our major thanks go to the pilot school and the six schools that were involved in the main study; the headteachers who agreed that their schools could be involved; the class teachers who allowed the disruption of taking small groups of children out of class for discussions; special educational needs coordinators for sharing their experiences and insights; personal support assistants for being helpful; lunchtime supervisors for sharing their experiences; and school caretakers.

Bradley Crompton, Anika Syeda Fahreen, Jordan Mathers and Louise Myers were involved in a special way as members of the young people's advisory group and we would like to thank them for their reflections on the methods, process and study as a whole. The adult advisory group was extremely supportive, patient and constructive and we would like to thank the members for their individual and group cooperation throughout the project. The members of this group were Virginia Morrow (School of Early Childhood and Primary Education, Institute of Education, University of London), Jane Stoneham (The Sensory Trust), Judy Denziloe (Action for Leisure), Claire Tregaskis (Independent Consultant and Research Fellow at Plymouth University), Michelle Moore (University of Sheffield), Fraser Brown (Leeds Metropolitan University), Diana McNeish (Barnardos) and Judith Gwynn (Talbot Special School, Sheffield).

Neither this research nor this publication would have been possible without the generous support of the Joseph Rowntree Foundation, whose willingness to invest in this project has allowed the importance of play in primary school playgrounds and issues relating to inclusion for disabled children to be documented. Special thanks go to Susan Taylor, the coordinator of the 'Understanding Children's Lives' research programme at the Joseph Rowntree Foundation, for her ongoing support and patience throughout the project.

The research was undertaken by a multi-disciplinary team based in, and associated with, the Department of Landscape at the University of Sheffield. The project was coordinated by Helen Woolley, a chartered landscape architect, senior lecturer and a director of the Centre for the Study of Childhood and Youth at the University of Sheffield. The three research associates who undertook the fieldwork were Julia Bishop, an academic folklorist, Mavis Curtis, a specialist in children's folklore and Marc Armitage, an independent play specialist who works under the name Playpeople. Jane Ginsborg, Research Fellow at the Royal Northern College of Music, made a significant contribution to the project during the analysis and writing-up stages. Joan Beal, director of the National Centre for English Cultural Tradition at the University of Sheffield, was also associated with the project.

Summary

The increasing integration of many disabled children into mainstream education since the Special Educational Needs and Disability Act (2001) has led to an examination of the physical and educational needs of disabled children in and around the school buildings. However, little attention has been paid to disabled children's experiences in the playground. Thus this research sought to develop an understanding of the experience of play in the playground for disabled children in a series of primary schools, with particular regard for issues of inclusion and exclusion.

The aims of this research were:

- to develop an understanding of disabled and non-disabled children's experiences in mainstream primary school playgrounds
- to document their knowledge, activities and use of the play space together with their explanations and commentary
- to compile perspectives on the dynamics of contemporary playground culture in the children's own terms and in the light of their participation in that culture.

This research was undertaken in six schools in Yorkshire, England and included a study of relevant publications and policy documents provided by each school. In order to listen to the voices of the children, multiple methods were used consisting of interviews with small groups of children, observations in the playground – taking field notes, photographs and videos – and a mapping exercise. To understand the issues from the staff perspective, a series of interviews were undertaken with the headteachers, class teachers, the special educational needs coordinators (SENCO), personal support assistants (PSAs) and lunchtime supervisors.

The research has confirmed that a variety of play is undertaken in primary school playgrounds, and that many of the children take an inclusive approach to play participation. However, some barriers to inclusion were identified. It is anticipated that the suggestions made will be adopted as tools to improve the experiences for all in the playground.

Disabled children's inclusion in play

A wide range of play was observed in all six schools involved in the study. This play was classified as play with high verbal content, play with high imaginative content, play with high physical content and less structured play such as walking, talking, sitting and watching. Many of the disabled children – identified as focus children – were included across all four categories of play identified. In some situations, focus children were included in play without any adaptations, while in other situations the focus children adapted play or used their technical aids as a tool of inclusion. Sometimes inclusion of the focus children was facilitated by the adaptation of play by other children. In other situations inclusion of the focus children was enabled by the PSA or lunchtime supervisor. Some of the focus children created their own play opportunities, either by themselves or with other children.

How the social world of playgrounds can influence inclusion

Children who were good to play with were friends who were well behaved and had positive attributes, such as being kind. Children who were not good to play with were poorly behaved and exhibited negative attributes, exemplified by swearing and fighting. Play was reinforced by friendship bonds and friendship groups were an important part of this. It was observed that the focus children might have large or small friendship groups. Moving school could create issues about developing friends and getting to know people to play with. This was particularly an issue for some of the focus children. Initiation of play took place in several ways: gathering people to play something particular; finding a group and then deciding what to play; and finding friends and then deciding what to play. Sometimes a child was perceived as the 'boss' of play, because they were very skilful or owned the equipment for play. Solitary play sometimes took place by choice and sometimes because of exclusion. Various ways were found to overcome being left out of play. These included finding alternative people to play with, playing alone, spending time with a member of staff or persuading them – or a friend or relative – to intercede on their behalf, or finding a younger child to play with.

Barriers to inclusion in playgrounds

Barriers to inclusion in play for the focus children were identified as *organisational, social* and *physical.* Organisational barriers were identified as relating to the time available for play, staff training, and the balance between risk and health and safety. Only one school in the study had an afternoon playtime for all its children, while half of the schools did not have an afternoon playtime for any children. The playtime and outside play opportunities at lunchtime were reduced in time for some of the focus children because of routines. Some of these were individual routines but some related to how the disabled children were treated as a group within a school. Many of these routines appeared to be historic in origin, without recent review or involvement of the children concerned. Training of staff with responsibilities for disabled children in the school, was, in the main, related to issues such as health and safety. Finding the balance between safety and taking risks was not easy for all school staff dealing with the focus children. Social barriers sometimes related to negative aspects of a child–staff relationship. Sometimes this might be due to a focus child spending more time with adults than their peers, or because being with an adult attracted other children and influenced other social interactions in the playground. Sometimes the organisational barrier of concern about health and safety was compounded by a member of staff's attitude, resulting in limitations to the exploration of play. Some physical barriers existed to the inclusion of disabled children in play in the primary school playgrounds investigated. These mainly related to access to playgrounds and the fixed equipment within them, the design of the playground and the fixed equipment, and details in the playing surfaces and access between them.

Some examples of good practice

Good practice was identified in some organisational and social aspects of the schools visited. However, little good practice, except for the provision of ramps, was found with respect to physical issues in the playgrounds. The retention of morning and afternoon playtimes in one school, together with mixed age groups sharing playtimes in another school, was considered to be good practice. In some schools, routines for individual focus children were identified that did not impinge on play or lunchtimes. In one school, staff had been on relevant courses; their contribution and value was acknowledged and they were retained in the school. Some of the PSAs benefited from experience over a period of years, and learned more about the child they were responsible for by talking with parents and professionals such as physiotherapists. In order to help the transition from one school to another for disabled children, some teachers discussed the situation with their class before the new child arrived. Some teachers used PE lessons as an opportunity for focus children to be included in activities, develop skills and transfer these skills to playtime. Two of the PSAs would take the focus child they were responsible for to the playground during class time if they felt that the child would particularly benefit from such extra time. Perhaps one of the most pertinent aspects of good practice, which took place over a period of time, was when school staff were able to help a focus child develop confidence to such an extent that they were enabled to go into the playground by themselves.

Suggestions for the future

Acknowledging the limitations of this qualitative study, the following suggestions are made which it is anticipated will improve the inclusion of disabled children in play opportunities in primary school playgrounds:

- **School routine**: the retention – or reintroduction – of afternoon playtimes; the possible introduction of playtimes allowing mixed age groups to play together.
- **Individual routine**: the inclusion of free time – playtimes and lunchtimes – in disabled children's reviews.
- **Staff experience**: the acknowledgement and reward of good quality work by staff responsible for disabled children.
- **Training**: staff should be offered and receive a variety of training relevant to their situation and responsibilities. Once staff have been trained, they should be encouraged to stay with a school. It might be appropriate for trained and experienced staff to remain responsible for a particular disabled child over a period of time in order to help develop their confidence.
- **The role of staff in the playground**: staff should be helped to understand the constructive and supporting, but not dominating, role that they can take in the playground with respect to disabled children's play. This could be by awareness training and a mentoring system.
- **Power relations**: decisions about disabled children, their routines, desires and aspirations relating to outdoor play in the playground should be based upon a dialogue between child, parents or guardians, school staff and, if appropriate, external support staff.
- **Audit of play and playground and action on the audit**: an audit should be undertaken in all primary school playgrounds. Any such audit should be

accompanied by a fully resourced action plan detailing priorities, responsibilities and costs. Such audits should include access to playgrounds and the fixed equipment within them, the design of the playground and the fixed equipment, and details in the playing surfaces and access between them.

1. Introduction and methods

Background to the research

While some disabled children have for many years been included in mainstream education, this situation was formalised in 2001 with the *Special Educational Needs and Disability Act*. This has resulted in increasing numbers of disabled children being integrated into schools with consideration being given to their educational entitlements in the classroom. However, little consideration has been given to the entitlements and experience of disabled children with respect to play and activities in school playgrounds. This research focused on the experience of disabled children in a selection of primary school playgrounds in Yorkshire, England, and the extent to which these children were included in play.

The importance of play for all children

There have been many discussions as to what the word 'play' means. For the purposes of this report the following definition will be adopted: 'play is freely chosen, personally directed and intrinsically motivated behaviour that actively encourages the child' (NPFA and others 2000).

Children's right to play has been detailed in the United Nations (UN) *Convention on the Rights of the Child* (Unicef 1989), with a number of the articles specifically relating to children's access to and experiences of their local environment and their access to play (Cole-Hamilton and others 2002). The UN convention was ratified by the United Kingdom government in 1991 and since then policy for children has been expressed in the *Children Act* and *Every Child Matters*, both published in 2004. These documents assert that disabled children have the same rights as non-disabled children.

There is increasing evidence that play and outdoor activities provide opportunities for the development of children's different skills. This includes the development of negotiating and collaborative skills, confrontation and resolution of emotional crises, the management of conflicts and the development of moral understanding (Taylor 1998; Cole-Hamilton and others 2002). Play is also important for the development of cognitive skills such as language and language comprehension, experimentation and problem-solving skills. Play also engages the mind, body and spirit, facilitates the practice of new skills and consolidates previous learning. It can also assist flexibility in problem solving, help develop creative and aesthetic appreciation, and facilitate the expression of emotions. Thus play is considered to be an important element of children's motivation and participation in society (Rogers and Sawyers 1988).

The benefits of play are believed to be of significance not only for individuals but also for families and society as a whole. To this end, play can provide a focus for informal networks and contribute to children's development into adults who are creative and effective, both socially and economically. Play also provides opportunities for exploring cultural identity, similarities and differences and can be a tool for tackling social exclusion through community development (NPFA and others 2000).

One issue concerning play in contemporary western society is that of risk and the balance between risk and health and safety. Many children want stimulating and challenging play opportunities with some degree of risk. However, many providers and managers of play opportunities are often more concerned about liability and any legal consequences that might result from an accident (Moorcock 1998). Parents, too, are concerned about risk, and some of them are perceived to be over-protective of their children (Bateson and Martin 1999). Yet, it has been acknowledged that 'an appropriate level of risk' is fundamental to play, allowing children to develop confidence and abilities and it is the responsibility of play providers to respond with 'exciting and stimulating environments that balance risks appropriately' (NPFA and others 2000).

Play in primary schools

In the primary school context, it has been shown that playtime breaks during the school day not only provide all the above-mentioned benefits but also mean that children learn more quickly and in a more meaningful way than when there is no playtime break (Pellegrini and Blatchford 1993; Coalter and Taylor 2001).

The first national survey of school breaktimes, covering 1990/91 and 1995/96, (Blatchford and Sumpner 1998) revealed interesting trends. This research identified that in this five-year period 56 per cent of the primary schools in the study had made changes to their breaktimes, with 26 per cent of the junior schools changing, usually shortening, the length of the lunchtime. The other major change was the abolition of the afternoon breaktime, with 12 per cent of infant and 26 per cent of junior schools stating that they had abolished the afternoon breaktime. The main reasons given for the changes to breaktimes were to increase teaching time and to reduce behavioural problems, even though these related to only a small number of pupils. Other research has revealed that the reduction in lunchtime has made pupils angry because it reduced the time they had to play and because the change appeared to have been made because of problems with a few children.

Disabled children and play

A small amount of research has been undertaken about disabled children and their play environments. Problems with the existence of and access to play provision were identified by Petrie and others (2000) while provision for disabled children in kids' clubs had also been identified as inadequate (Kids' Club Network 2001). A good-practice guide about providing accessible play space (ODPM, 2003), which is the result of government-funded research, is available.

The social context of play has been emphasised as an important issue in inclusive education. It should be geared to responding to and developing the self-determination, control and identity of young disabled children becoming disabled adults in a disabling society (Bishop and others 1999).

In a school setting, it is important that disabled children have opportunities to play with non-disabled children. This is partly because in both mainstream and special schools there is a tendency for disabled children to spend most of their time in the company of school staff rather than other children (Watson and others 2000) and it is known that children are not only socialised by adults but work on their own socialisation (Delalande 2001). It has been suggested that the likelihood of contact between disabled children and their peers in a mainstream school can be affected by a range of factors (Hegarty and Pocklington 1981). These were identified as the disabled pupils themselves (personality, age, nature of impairment), their peers (their familiarity with and understanding of an impairment, and peer pressures) and the school (the nature of the site and opportunities for contact). Research into social inclusion of children with physical impairments revealed four themes affecting the social interactions of these children: reciprocity, characteristics of social play and play interactions, effects of adult involvement and the quality of occupational engagement (Richardson 2002). Others have argued that schools will be not become fully inclusive until the adults who control them take account of children's views and are allowed to challenge structural, cultural and individual conditions which create disability (Davis and Watson 2000).

Other research has revealed parental concerns about their disabled children joining mainstream schools, with one mother saying that she feared her son might be bullied and experience bullying and name-calling. Her son settled in well, however, and had a small close-knit group of friends, whom he had chosen. Other parental concerns related to a desire for disabled children not to be segregated in the playground and the length of time an assistant spent with a child in the loo (Alderson and Goodey 1998).

Research design

Aims of the research

This research sought to develop an understanding of the experience of play in the playground for disabled children in a series of primary school playgrounds, with a particular focus on issues of inclusion and exclusion. (The research design is briefly summarised here; for more details see the Appendix.)

The aims of the research were:

- to develop an understanding of disabled and non-disabled children's experiences in mainstream primary school playgrounds
- to document their knowledge, activities and use of the play space together with their explanations and commentary
- to compile perspectives on the dynamics of contemporary playground culture in the children's own terms and in the light of their participation in that culture.

Selection of schools

A set of seven, individually diverse schools, in North, West and South Yorkshire, was identified using the selection criteria. One of these schools was involved in the pilot study and the remaining six schools, two in each of the three locations, were the focus of the main study.

Pilot study

Three research associates worked together in the pilot school in order to foster consistency in methods and learn from each other's experiences. A review of the pilot study led to the refining of methods, which included modifications to specific questions and a reduction in the number of focus children and classes to be involved in the main study.

Methods within each school

In order to listen to and elicit children's views, data were obtained through discussions which were taped and transcribed, and through 'mapping' exercises with the children in the selected classes. Researcher observations of play at playtimes and lunchtimes were recorded by the taking of field notes and the use of still and video cameras. This was supplemented by a review of relevant documentation from each school and interviews with school staff who were responsible for playtime and behaviour policies, who were responsible for the outdoor playing spaces at the school, and who had particular contact with the focus children.

Selection of focus children and their classes

In each school, two classes that included several disabled children were identified in consultation with the headteacher. Table 1 lists the focus children by their age, gender and impairment, and provides the pseudonym given to each child for the purposes of this study. These are the only children mentioned by name in the report. Once the focus children had been identified, their classes were selected to be involved in the research.

Development of tools for interviews

A set of questions was developed for use with all the children and another with school staff. These were employed as a general guide for semi-structured discussions. The aim of the questions was to elicit the views of the children about what happened in the playground, where it happened and with whom, and to explore the associated social dynamics. There were also questions designed to enquire about inclusion and

Table 1 Focus children with details of their age, gender and impairment

School	Pseudonym	Age	Gender	Impairment
1	Elizabeth	8	Girl	Severe autism
	Danny	10	Boy	Autism
2	Jessica	9	Girl	Down's syndrome
	David	10	Boy	Muscular dystrophy
3	Wajid	8	Boy	Muscular dystrophy
	Akram	8	Boy	Visual impairment
	Stacey	7	Girl	Epilepsy
	Usman	9	Boy	Registered blind, impaired growth and difficulties with balance
4	Euan	6	Boy	Hearing impairment
	Laura	6	Girl	Developmental delay and language impairment
	Jodie	8	Girl	Cerebral palsy resulting in severe language impairment and limited physical control
5	Andrew	6	Boy	Global developmental delay and visual impairment
	Sally	11	Girl	Cerebral palsy
6	Joe	6	Boy	Cerebral palsy, congenital heart disease, spastic quadriplegia and visual impairment
	Rowan	6	Boy	Communication difficulties
	Helen	8	Girl	Spina bifida and hydrocephalus

exclusion in play. The aim of the questions for the school staff was to explore their perspective on what happened in the playground, especially from the angle of social inclusion, and their perceptions of their own role and the role of the school as an institution in the management of inclusion in the playground.

Ethical considerations

The Social Research Association *Ethical Guidelines* (2002) were the framework for the project. In addition the research team welcomed the deliberations that took place with the adult advisory group on various ethical issues.

Advisory groups

An adult advisory group was established which included people with academic, practice and policy experience. This was supplemented by a young people's advisory group, and included one focus child from the pilot school.

Permission from the individual schools

From the beginning, the research team and the adult advisory group were most concerned about the issue of permission to be involved in the research. Schools with a number of disabled children were identified and those that were willing to be included in the study were sent a letter explaining the research and asking for the headteacher's consent for the school to be involved in the project.

Permission from individual parents or carers

The schools informed parents in their regular school newsletter or in a letter sent to them, that the research was about play and activity in the playground. Parents and guardians were asked to let the school know if either the parents or the children did not want to be involved in the research.

Presentation of the research to the children

The researchers and the research were introduced to the children at several stages of the project and at each stage children were given the opportunity to opt out of the research. Initially this took place during a school assembly immediately prior to the beginning of the fieldwork period. The purpose of the research was explained as being 'what the children did in the playground at playtimes and lunchtimes'. It was also explained that the researcher would work with two classes. Each research associate introduced themselves to the members of their two classes and, at this point, children were given the possibility of opting out. When the researchers met with each small group an additional opportunity for individual pupils to withdraw from the interview was given. In one school, one girl and one boy chose to opt out of the research at this stage.

Feedback to schools

Headteachers in half of the schools were keen to have feedback directly from the research associate who had been in their school and this was facilitated while the research was being written up. In addition, each school has been sent a letter of thanks and a copy of the report.

Summary

- Play is a right of all children, whether disabled or non-disabled, and this right is detailed in the UN *Convention on the Rights of the Child*. The national policy context also includes *Every Child Matters*.
- Play promotes many different aspects of a child's development. This is not only of benefit to the individual child but also to families and society as a whole.
- Breaktimes in school are an important opportunity for outdoor play, providing additional academic benefits. Yet in recent years there has been a reduction in the length of break and lunchtimes, and even the omission of afternoon breaktimes in many schools.
- Previous research has revealed that disabled children in a primary school setting may have both positive and negative experiences associated with playtimes and lunchtimes and the opportunities for play in the primary school playground.
- Using a set of criteria, seven schools were selected to be involved in the research: one as a pilot and six for the main study.
- Two classes that included disabled children in each school were selected to be involved in the study.
- In order that children's views could be heard, small-group discussions, mapping exercises and observations of the playground were undertaken.
- Relevant staff in each school were interviewed.
- Schools, families and individual children were given several opportunities to be involved or to opt out of the research.

2.   Disabled children's inclusion in play

This chapter draws on the children's accounts, researcher observations and playground maps to exemplify the range of play undertaken by the children in the six schools. This is discussed in relation to a classification system developed as part of the research. In particular, the knowledge and experience of the focus children are highlighted.

Playtime activities

The many things that children do at playtimes can appear chaotic and haphazard to adults (Opie 1993; Armitage 2001; Delalande 2001). However, this apparent chaos can be understood using a classification based on one developed by Bishop and Curtis (2001) and further developed during this research. This classification has four major categories:

- play with high verbal content
- play with high imaginative content
- play with high physical content
- less structured play, including walking, talking, sitting and watching.

In practice, activities sometimes straddle several categories but the relative prominence of the verbal, physical and imaginative content of each determines its classification. In general, children's play preferences vary according to their age, with imaginative play being more commonly found in Key Stage 1 (KS1) and play involving more rule-based games in Key Stage 2 (KS2) (Blatchford and Sharp 1994). Play preferences can also be affected by gender; football, for example, tends to be dominated by boys, while clapping and skipping tend to be undertaken by girls (Thorne 1993; Blatchford 1998).

Children's knowledge of play and games can be thought of as a repertoire that evolves with age, ability, confidence, and new experiences and social encounters.

Knowledge is acquired from a wide range of sources through a continuous process of listening, watching, interpreting, copying and mastering play. Invention and adaptation are also part of this process, resulting in new and varied activities. This gives all children the potential to respond flexibly to different play circumstances, and to include children with abilities and talents different from their own.

Play with high verbal content

Language

Purely verbal forms encompassed narratives, such as urban myths and ghost stories, and jokes, including topical ones referring to the contemporary conflict in Iraq. Other forms of verbal play, such as nicknames which is often associated with bullying (Crozier and Dimmock 1999), played on children's surnames ('Mozza' for 'Morris') and taunts ('Liar, liar, pants on fire') were documented, although not extensively. No examples of this kind were recorded from any of the focus children, although Joe was noted for his sense of humour, for example, commenting, when surrounded by girls, that it was 'just like being at the hairdresser's'.

Language, music and movement

Songs and chants, and play combining language with music and movement, such as clapping and dance routines with singing, were popular at all six schools, principally among girls. Games reported or observed ranged from so-called traditional games, like 'The farmer's in his den' and 'In and out of the winding bluebells', to song-and-dance routines based on imitation of current pop music. The Asian English girls at one school also emulated music and dances from Bollywood films which they had seen on video.

Stacey, the only white girl in her class, had only been at the school for three months at the time of the study. She was, nevertheless, highly active in dancing and singing both western pop and Indian music, and had learnt rhymes in Punjabi. Jodie and her friend made up dances that involved Jodie turning round in her wheelchair while her friend pirouetted alongside her. Helen had enjoyed music and movement play when she was in KS1 and, with her friends, had performed S Club 7 and S Club Junior dance routines for her designated lunchtime supervisor. In KS2, Helen occasionally played clapping games, which were very popular at her school at the time.

Play strategies

A range of strategies was used in other forms of play, such as methods of choosing football teams or 'counting out', using a chant to determine the person to be 'It' or 'On' at the start of a chase game. Counting out was commonplace in all schools. Rowan was familiar with a counting out chant used among his peers, 'Car, bus, lorry', but his description of the procedure – 'You have to do "Car, bus, lorry" three times, then you're on' – was hotly contested by another child in the interview group.

Play with high imaginative content

Role enactment

Role-enactment games were an important part of the play repertoire in every school. The roles were either generic ones, such as in 'Mums and dads', or specific characters. The latter were particularly popular with boys and often employed characters and storylines, such as *Lord of the Rings*, *Power Rangers* and Formula One motor racing, drawn from computer games, video and other mass media products.

Role-enactment games were prominent among the play preferences of focus children. Andrew played 'Puppies' with a group of classmates and also made initial contact with children on the playground by pretending to be a monster and making roaring noises, and many classmates accepted him despite this unconventional approach. Joe had an extensive repertoire of role-enactment games, cultivated largely in association with his PSA and lunchtime supervisor, who pushed his manual wheelchair in the playground before he acquired a motorised one. Joe's games included 'Police car' or 'Fire engine', in which the lunchtime supervisor was the siren and the children lay down and pretended to need rescuing. Laura joined in imaginative play with her classmates but was usually given the more passive role, such as the little girl who was petted and had her hair plaited in 'Families'.

Space-related imaginative play

Imaginative play may be associated with a particular feature or space. At one school, the climbing apparatus was the basis for an exceptional number of pretend games, such as 'Archaeologists', 'Jungle' and 'Pirate ship', although Helen noted that much of the equipment was inaccessible to her, excluding her from many such games.

However, she and her playmates made use of the playground markings in 'Witches', and a particular tree in 'Mission girls', where she described the play thus: 'I'm a computer and when I go beep-beep-beep, it means that there's a mission for them to solve. And on this tree they've got to press what the problem is and then they go and solve the problem.'

Imaginative play with playthings

Toys such as Barbie dolls or cars also stimulated imaginative play among children both in KS1 and KS2. An expansion of this involved the use of focus children's technical aids as playthings in imaginative play. In Joe's 'Space game', for example, his wheelchair became a rocket, which his PSA made tremble prior to 'blast off', Joe pressing buttons on the chair and 'steering' it. Similarly, Wajid used his wheelchair as a motorbike in 'Power Rangers'.

Play with high physical content

There was a large variety of physical play at all the schools. Previous play research shows that this kind of play can be a cause of tension, both among children, and between children and school staff (Armitage 2001). This is because it often requires space and some games may dominate the available play space while involving only a limited number of players (Swain 2000). A number of schools in the study had grass areas, resulting in a greater amount of play space for the children at the time of year that the field research took place and probably reducing the amount of conflict relating to physical play. On the other hand, the grass areas were not accessible to some focus children, or could only be reached by them with difficulty.

High physical content without playthings

Games such as 'Handstands', 'Roly-poly' and balancing on walls and fixed play equipment were common, and were played by children individually and in groups. There were also many games involving an It-role, in which one or more group members acted in opposition to the group. A classic example is the game of 'Touch-chase', which in northern England, and hence at the schools in the study, is called 'Tig', 'Tigs' or 'Tiggy' (Opie and Opie 1969). Numerous variants were played, depending on the location of the game and the ways of gaining respite from the chaser.

Sally was particularly inclined to physical play, including 'Tiggy' and 'Bouncing up on the bridge'. The 'bridge' consisted of a series of logs suspended close to the ground like a hammock, between two fixed, vertical supports. Children of all ages played 'Bouncing up on the bridge', where a player on the end support jumped onto the logs (the 'bridge') and 'bounced up' one or several children who were standing on them. Helped by her friends, Sally would sit on the bridge and her friends took it in turns to bounce her up, to Sally's obvious enjoyment. On other occasions Sally had climbed up a grass bank and, leaving her walking frame at the top done a roly-poly down, despite the reservations of various staff members. Her response was: 'I just want to be like the other children. I just want to be tret like everybody else.'

Some games involved a 'high-power' It-role, in which the It-player can make strategic choices and control the other players' actions (Gump and Sutton-Smith 1955). Helen played one such game, 'Farmer, farmer, can I cross your golden field?':

> There's a person that's on and these other people at the other side. The people have to say, 'Farmer, farmer, may I cross your golden field?' And the person that's on has to say 'Only if' and they can say anything they like, 'Only if you've got blonde or red hair.'

Those who did not manage to cross the field were chased by the It-player and the one caught then became It. Helen liked to be the It-player but was thwarted by the fact that her playmates, apparently in an effort to favour her, often chose things which only she had, enabling her to cross rather than be among those chased. Ultimately, Helen simply said, 'I want to be on' and the children let her. Joe, on the other hand, played 'What time is it, Mr Wolf?' and often took the high-power It-role in the game.

Many of the focus children played 'Tig'. Variants of the game had evolved that enabled Sally and Joe to participate. Sally's friends, for example, preferred not to play 'Tiggy steps' because they were aware that the steps were inaccessible to her, but played 'Tiggy colour', 'Tiggy scarecrow' and 'Tiggy offground' with her. In 'Tiggy offground', Sally could avoid being caught by sitting on the bench or the back of her walker, and in 'Tiggy colour' could again use her frame when the colour was blue because the frame was blue. In 'Tiggy scarecrow', the children slowed down or ran near her at times so that she could catch them, and also commented with genuine feeling that 'she's fast' and was clearly not to be underestimated. Joe's friends did likewise, dancing round him while he wheeled his chair, and after a while holding out their arms to be tigged by him. David took part in a game of 'Bob down tig' and indicated that if he held his head slightly to one side this meant he was 'bobbing down' and could not be caught.

Andrew played chase games too, and 'Hide and seek'. He also became involved in rough and tumble play with other boys who, according to his PSA, did not make any concessions for him in the play: 'They don't treat him different to anybody else. They'll rough and tumble with him and he'll rough and tumble with them back. They don't wrap him in cotton wool.' Rowan participated in 'Spiderman tigs' on a regular basis.

High physical content with plaything

Individual and group skipping was played in most of the schools but was not immediately accessible to Joe and Helen. Turning the rope was the main manner of their participation, a role less favoured and less active than that of being the skipper. Helen commented: 'I twined the rope because I can't skip properly. I can't skip at all, not even if I tried.' Jodie also turned the rope for skipping, initiated by her PSA. Joe had also been encouraged to do this in PE lessons. Sometimes he participated in other play using a skipping rope, 'Limbo', in which he was able to go under the rope like the rest of the players.

Team games with plaything

Team games were also very popular at all schools, particularly football. Both boys and girls generally saw it as the province of the boys, although certain girls played occasionally. Ability was a key criterion in the organisation of the game, and admiration for relevant skills was common and often conferred on children who took part in out-of-school football training clubs. Andrew took part in playground football, although less regularly than many other boys in his class. Joe was a keen fan of professional football and, prior to a chest operation and the transition to the motorised wheelchair, had thoroughly enjoyed participating in the playground game. According to his PSA:

> I can remember this little group, they were playing [football] there at the time. I did ask them, 'Is it okay if Joe plays?' And they were brilliant. They said, 'Of course he can, of course he can!' I was just running round and we

were catching the ball in the wheelchair. And he thought that were wonderful. Because he joined in. And I sort of kicked it and passed it to one of our team and our team scored.

Walking, talking, sitting, watching

Walking, talking, sitting down and watching whatever was going on are easily overlooked as playtime activities, but were widespread and provided an alternative to the more structured play. Elizabeth, for example, appeared to spend most of her playtimes and lunchtimes on her own, and it was thought by staff that she did not pay any attention to other children. Closer observation, however, revealed that she often copied the actions of individuals or groups of children, usually after they had stopped what they were doing. Helen was clear about the value of talking with her peers: 'We don't play that much but we talk and tell secrets to each other.' Jodie's PSA stated that she 'normally finds they [i.e. a group of girls] want to take her [Jodie] away into a corner where the benches are. They sit around and have a girlie chat.'

Walking round with a staff member on playground duty was sometimes chosen by children who felt isolated, usually on a temporary basis, perhaps because of a conflict or because their particular friend was away from school. Joe often spent playtimes talking with his PSA or lunchtime supervisor who, in turn, attracted other children to them whom they would encourage to interact with Joe.

Summary

- A wide range of play was observed in all six schools involved in the study. This play was classified as play with high verbal content, play with high imaginative content, play with high physical content and less structured play, such as walking, talking, sitting and watching.
- Many of the focus children were included across all four categories of play identified.
- Inclusion of the focus children, in some situations, was made possible by the focus child themselves or the use of their equipment.
- Inclusion of the focus children, in some situations, was facilitated by the adaptation of play by other children.

- Inclusion of the focus children, in some situations, was enabled by the PSA or lunchtime supervisor.
- Some of the focus children created their own play opportunities, either by themselves or with others.

Beyond knowledge of play activities themselves, children also need skills and experience in the social conventions that surround play. These include interacting appropriately with their peers and knowing how to approach potential playmates and form and maintain friendships. Chapter 3 therefore turns to the social world of the playground, and the experiences of the focus children within it.

3. How the social world of playgrounds can influence inclusion

For the majority of children, playtimes are occasions when they want to associate with and play with others. This depends on a child being able to find suitable playmates, make friends, develop notions of generally accepted ways of initiating and orchestrating play activities, and take steps if they are rejected or excluded. The children taking part in this study were asked questions about their social experience of the playground, such as, who do you play with (in relation to particular games), what makes people good, or not good, to play with, how do you decide what to play, is anyone ever left out of play, and what needs to happen when people are left out? This chapter reports on the children's responses to these questions and draws upon the playground observations to highlight the children's views on, and experiences of, inclusion and exclusion. This is done with respect to the focus children in particular.

Previous research has identified that belonging to a group is important, and that the words 'group' and 'boss' have a central place in younger children's vocabulary (Delalande 2001). This research adds that friendship does not seem to be formed following a first approach in class, but seems to happen as a result of a shared educational or recreational activity.

Friends

The qualities of friends

The responses given to the above questions support many of Blatchford's (1998) findings in relation to friendship and play in the school playground. Play is a key way in which children make, break and re-negotiate friendships. Children played with their friends, and friends, in turn, were people who were good to play with or be with, across all six schools of the study. Positive personal qualities were often cited as the reason for friendships and emphasised as 'being nice to you', 'kindness', 'making you laugh' and 'good manners' (saying 'please' and 'thank you', sharing). The qualities of friends were sometimes related specifically to play: 'They always want to play with me', 'They play by the rules', 'We agree with stuff that we want to play'.

Views on the qualities that made people not good to play with were even more readily expressed by many, and often emphasised the inverse of the positive qualities, such as being aggressive (shouting, hitting), naughty (swearing, challenging the teacher), impolite (not listening, not sharing), or overbearing ('bossy'). Again, some of these qualities were seen in terms of play etiquette, such as being disruptive of a game (abandoning it part-way through) or dismissive ('I don't want to play your stupid game'). One group of boys and one group of girls also highlighted crying too readily as an undesirable quality.

Sally had many friends within the class and the year groups above and below it. This popularity could be attributed, in part, to her determination to participate in play. She and her friends had identified and created a number of games in which they could all participate, and she continued to take physical risks and challenge the limits in her play. Within this larger circle, Sally had a set of special friends with whom she played regularly. Like many of the children, Sally felt that what made people good to play with was 'because we have a good time'.

The role of play in reinforcing friendship bonds was observed for Euan in a game that he regularly played with three girls. In this, they ran up and down the banking where they imagined a river was running down, and they rescued people from the flood. Euan was also fully engaged with this group of friends when they played on the climbing frame, when the grass in the middle was turned into a pool full of crocodiles.

Types of friends and friendship groups

Although the children in this study mostly chose friends of the same age as themselves, they sometimes played with siblings and cousins of different ages who attended the same school. However, this could create tensions: 'I want to play with my sister at football but all the year 5 and 6s wouldn't let me play ... Because I were younger than them ... I were just walking away and my sister came up to me and I felt more better.' For some, on the other hand, playing with siblings and cousins was prevented because of the school's different timing of breaks for children of different ages, or playground rules forbidding children at KS1 to go into the physical space of those in KS2 and vice versa.

Some children talked about varying degrees of friendship, often expressed in relation to play. A group of eight-year-old boys distinguished between 'ordinary friends and real friends': ordinary friends being those you might play football with and real friends being those you have known for a long time and can talk with. Another group of girls expressed their changing notions of what friendship was, saying that in year 2 they were friends, in year 3 they used to fall out with each other and then get back together, 'and now that we're in year 4 and we're older we really know what it is to have friends'.

Danny was part of a regular friendship group of about five or six children, exclusively boys, who were observed to be together at all breaktimes, despite not being in the same class. Danny was often mentioned when his friends described the play of their group, although Danny was on holiday when the interview took place. At no point was Danny's impairment mentioned; he was simply a member of their group.

Friendship was related to loyalty, especially in terms of commitment to games once they had started. According to one nine-year-old girl, 'You know when you pick a friend and start playing with them? Sometimes, some friends, if they're not true friends, they just run away. True friends stay with you and play with you.'

Some of the focus children were observed to only have one friend. One girl, who was excluded from play because other children perceived her as smelly, played exclusively with Jodie. Staff revealed that, as a result of this friendship, Jodie's play repertoire and participation in the playground had increased, the two girls having made up dances together, and the other girl having made up various ball games for them to play. However, on an occasion when the other girl was away from school, Jodie found people to play with and participated in their games, suggesting that she could expand her circle of friends and play possibilities if, and when, she wanted to.

Wajid played with Akram all the time but, unlike Jodie and her friend, their special relationship was embedded in a bigger friendship group. Their friendship had developed after Wajid had acquired a motorised wheelchair and became more independent.

Rowan tended to be more peripatetic in the playground and appeared to be more superficially involved in play, although he was included in play by his classmates to some extent. He played with children in his class but did not have any close friends. He was seen by some of the boys as not having any friends at all and they mimicked his way of talking. He attracted the attention of some for the ways in which his behaviour sometimes broke accepted norms but, while they saw this as amusing in the classroom, it did not win him friends in the playground.

Duration and extent of contact in and out of school

Knowing someone for a long time, knowing someone from a context out of school, and sitting on the same table in class were also reasons children gave for specific friendships. Being in school together since nursery or reception, attending breakfast club or the same out-of-school activity, and being invited to play at someone's house all provided continuity and reinforcement and could endow the relationship with a special quality.

One of the reasons that the other children so readily accepted Jodie was because she had been in the school since reception class. Her PSA said 'people guess what she wants. If she points they'll get her things. They are very good like that. She's been in school since reception so they're used to her being around.'

Joe was well liked and had been invited to the birthday parties of most of the children in his class. He knew the names of many of the children in KS1 and enjoyed talking to them. He also had several best friends, of both genders, among his classmates. These children would run up to him in the playground to engage him in conversation and help him by moving obstacles.

The impact of moving school on play and friendships

Many children interviewed who had come new to a school, without previous contacts, had found a way to make friends and become accepted into play. Initial contacts in the classroom seemed to be particularly significant in this process. One boy had started by playing with the boy he sat next to in class, and he explained: 'We were always talking to each other. Then we started playing together.' Through this initial contact the new boy was accepted into existing friendship groups and the games they played.

Sally had joined the school at the beginning of the school year and was a year older than her classmates. Her teacher had had general discussions with her class prior to Sally's arrival about everyone being different and having strengths and weaknesses, and also the fact that Sally had a mobility impairment. When Sally started at the school, the children were curious about her physical condition and asked Sally and the teacher about it. The teacher emphasised that 'her legs are not as strong as yours, they need a bit of support' and 'basically, she's the same as you lot. She just needs a bit of help getting round, a bit of consideration, a few doors opening.' On reflection, the teacher felt she may have overdone the preparation for Sally since the children 'smothered her', all rushing at once to open the door in an effort to show that they were considerate and aware.

Stacey, however, was potentially doubly isolated in that she had recently moved to the school because she had been bullied at her previous school, and there were other markers of difference for her because she was the only white child in the class. She had not yet had time to develop a particular group of friends, although she did join in singing and dancing pop music, both western and Indian.

The social etiquette of play

Initiating play

The initiation of play depended on the nature of friendships and who was available at any given breaktime. The children identified a number of possible scenarios. These involved wanting to play something particular and collecting together a suitable group of children to play it with ('Who wants to play —?'), seeking out a group first and then reaching agreement on what to play ('Do you want to come and play with me?'), or locating friends directly and deciding what to play ('I find my friends and then we think of a game to play and start playing it'). One example of this was given by a group of boys, aged nine:

> If it's sort of a wet day and (playtime) is not on the grass and it's not our day to play football and it's not our day to play basketball, then what we'll do is, we'll say, 'Well, what you want to do?' And so we'll have a discussion and we'll say, 'Right, shall we play Tigs?' And if someone says 'No' then we'll not play it because it would not be fair. So we have everyone's ideas. And we once made us own game up and it were an idea from Josh, Anthony and me. And then we put all our ideas together.

Children also drew attention to certain people's ownership of a game and their role in leading it (cf. Blatchford 1989). A particular game of football was known as one boy's game, for example, because the particular boy was sometimes 'boss of the game'. The role of 'boss' resulted from having an acknowledged high level of skill or owning the means of play. This role sometimes endowed the person with responsibility for choosing team members and making refereeing decisions.

The 'boss' role was not confined to football, nor was it exclusive to boys. A seven-year-old girl explained that a certain girl went first in 'Hopscotch' because it was her game. A group of five-year-old girls described how their friend made games up and how 'she's the boss of us', 'because we let her say what we have to do, don't we?'

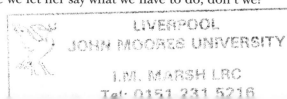

Helen usually could find people to play with, but her relationships could be strained because she was perceived as 'bossy'. The line between being 'boss' of a game and being 'bossy' was evidently the fact that she often reserved the best or most high-status parts for herself, such as being the lead singer when playing 'Pop bands'. This resulted in friends losing interest and going off. Helen seemed to resort to playing with a group of girls who appeared to have a more marginalised status within the class, because of learning and behavioural difficulties, and with whom she shared her PSA in the classroom.

Joining play in progress

Joining in play once it was under way could be difficult because this was disruptive and might necessitate returning to the discussions that initiated play. The children's examples indicated that a newcomer was expected to ask whether they could join in. Sometimes they were accepted, perhaps after some investigation of their reasons for wanting to participate. One eight-year-old boy described how he asked his regular friendship group of girls if they would play with him. They said 'no' because they wanted to play with their other mates. They then came up to him when he was in the middle of a game and asked if they could play. He said no at first, because they had said 'no' in the classroom. They said, 'Well, we didn't mean it,' and he then let them play.

Refusal to allow participation in play could be due to a range of factors. These included negative personal qualities described above but such refusal was also sometimes because games had the generally agreed number of players already, or because the task of reorganising the game to accommodate a newcomer was felt to be too disruptive or time-consuming:

> If they want to play a game and you've only just started, they could wait until you've finished the game. But if they say, 'Can I join in?' and they say, 'Yes,' the game will get complicated and they'll have to start, they'll have to wait ... If it's a game of 'Bulldog's charge' or 'My grandfather's chest' even, you'd do a round and they could join in.

Solitary play

Participation in play with others was not seen as a universal, constant or necessarily desirable goal by all. There was a distinction between those who opted to play on their own and those who were solitary because of being left out of play. A small number chose to play on their own, either occasionally or regularly. They might be engaged in structured play, such as the eight-year-old boy who played 'Ninjas' and 'Army' on his own, or see themselves as opting out because 'sometimes if you don't want to play, you don't have to'. An example of this was Helen, who explained, 'Sometimes I want to be on my own when I'm sad because something's happened at home.'

Elizabeth was a solitary figure in the playground. Both her PSA and lunchtime supervisor saw her as not having any friends or participating in play, observing that 'she likes to be on her own' and that she was 'just in her own little world, skipping around'. Her PSA played with her a lot outside during class time and taught her social skills, such as taking turns. The PSA cited the intensity of their relationship in the classroom as the reason that she stood back and let Elizabeth play on her own at breaktimes. Some children were observed deliberately moving away from Elizabeth on the playground. Some children included her, occasionally, such as when a group accommodated her into their imaginative game in the playhouse or when she jumped over the rope in skipping. Although solitary for much of the time, however, Elizabeth was not disengaged from play, often watching what the others were doing and copying them from a distance.

Joe became more solitary for a while when he acquired his motorised wheelchair. This was partly because he was engrossed in learning how to operate it and because his PSA was no longer so near to him. At the same time, Joe felt more self-conscious because he was the only child in the school with a motorised wheelchair and he was aware that all the children were looking at him.

Leaving out and being left out

The negative qualities referred to above, which made people not good to play with, were the most commonly cited reasons for leaving people out of play. Such qualities could also threaten the well-being of one's friends and prompt a desire to protect them: 'Me and my friends leave you out of our games because you keep hurting my best friend' (boy, aged five).

Exclusion also occurred when someone was not being allowed to join in play part-way through, or because one's friends were unavailable because they were still eating their dinner, had a differently timed break or were away from school.

Disagreements over games and how to play them, and the resulting breaking-off of friendships, were commonly cited as reasons for being left out. At such times, it was advantageous to be popular and have a wide circle of friends:

> I've been left out before. Sometimes I've got friends. And then they don't want to be friends any more. Because I want to play something that they don't want to play. And then somebody comes to me and asks me if I want to play with them. And I just play with them. And then next day they might be my friend again. [Interviewer: Is this okay?] It's fine. Because I've got a lot of friends. (*girl, aged eight*)

In such cases, the experience of exclusion was reported to last from two minutes to one day.

Many children could identify at least one experience of being left out of play or seeing someone else left out of play. They said that this made them cry, or feel sad; as one child put it, 'I felt like my heart was hurting.' There was a recognition that most people 'want to be part of something'. At least one child said he had learnt to be more inclusive from his experience of being excluded:

> What happened were, one day, I never used to let anybody play with me if they were left out. But then when I got left out I realised how sad it were. It weren't right good for you to be left out. So that's why I started letting people try to play with other people or play with me. (*boy, aged eight*)

Most said that, if they saw someone who was unhappy and left out, they would ask them to play.

Usman was a solitary figure and lacked confidence in the playground setting. Some of the other children asked him to play games such as Tig, but he often opted not to join in. His PSA considered that he needed more game-playing skills such as taking turns. When he did play with other children, it tended to be with girls because this was less physically demanding. At the time of the study, he had just learnt to jump, could do four hops and found it difficult to throw a ball straight. He played on his own, one of his favourite games being walking along the coloured lines painted on the playground.

Dealing with being left out

Being excluded for one reason or another, left a child in the situation of having to find alternative people to play with or alternative play which they could pursue on their own. Some looked for groups of people and were successful in joining in their game, while others looked for children who were on their own and initiated play with them. This appeared to be successful, at least on a temporary basis.

Another strategy was to approach a member of staff, either to walk round with them for a time or to persuade them to intercede on their behalf. Sometimes a friend or relative performed a similar function to the member of staff. Other excluded children found younger children to play with. This was the approach of one girl, who was regarded as bossy by others in her class.

Some children who had been left out opted to use equipment which developed individual skills, such as a skipping rope or assault course: 'I'm left out all the time because [a boy] and [a girl] play with each other and I ask if I'm allowed to play with him and he says, 'No,' and then I go up to the climbing frame and play on that' (girl, aged eight). Playing on one's own might also be an option for a while, before going back to the group or telling a member of staff in order to get the children told off, and finding someone else to play with.

Wajid knew what it was to be left out of play. In KS1, before he had the motorised wheelchair, he spent most of his outdoor playtimes being pushed around by a member of staff, unable to join in any games. The motorised wheelchair freed him from this restraint and he could take an equal part in the play he was actually able to participate in. On the other hand, the chair was seen by staff as having a deleterious impact on his physical condition because it reduced the amount of exercise he was getting. The social confidence he had gained was evident when, on one occasion, he was left out of 'Power Rangers' and decided to start up his own breakaway game with Akram.

Summary

- Children who are good to play with were friends, and these were people who were well-behaved and had positive attributes.
- Similarly, people who were not good to play with were people who were badly behaved and had negative attributes.
- One way that friendship was expressed was through play and this in turn reinforced friendship bonds.
- Friendship groups were important for play for many children – focus children had large or small friendship groups.
- Contact outside school, such as at birthday parties, can enhance friendships.

- Moving school creates issues about developing friendships and getting to know people to play with.
- Initiation of play can take place in several ways: gathering people to play something particular; finding a group and then deciding what to play; and finding friends and then deciding what to play
- Sometimes a child is perceived as the 'boss' of play, because they are very skilful or own the equipment for play.
- Solitary play sometimes takes place by choice and sometimes due to exclusion.
- Various ways were found to overcome being left out of play. These included finding alternative people to play with, playing alone, spending time with a member of staff or persuading them – or friend or relative – to intercede on their behalf or finding a younger child to play with.

4. Barriers to inclusion in playgrounds

Barriers to inclusion in play for the focus children in this study fell into three broad categories: *organisational, social* and *physical.* These related to issues such as how long they had at playtimes and lunchtimes, who they played with, what they played, how they played, equipment they played with and where they could play.

Organisational barriers

Three organisational issues were identified as having a major impact on inclusion in play for some of the focus children. These were constraints of time, lack of staff training, and health and safety considerations.

Time constraints – length and number of playtimes

All schools had a morning playtime of 15 or 20 minutes. In two of the schools, this playtime was staggered for KS1 and KS2 children. At another school playtimes were staggered. Children from reception and years 5 and 6, with some from year 2, had one playtime, while children from years 1 through 4, including the other year 2 children, had a separate playtime. Lunchtimes varied in length between 50 minutes and 1 hour 15 minutes. In some schools, the times were staggered for KS1 and KS2 children, while in one there was a rolling programme with the children in each year group having 50 minutes. Three of the schools had no afternoon playtime. Two of the schools had afternoon playtime for KS1 children only and one school had an afternoon playtime for both KS1 and KS2 children. This lack of afternoon playtimes is in line with the findings of the national survey mentioned in chapter 1 (Blatchford and Sumpner 1998). The benefit of playtime was acknowledged by a teacher in one school who commented that, 'they're generally fidgety and hard to settle when they've not had the chance to be outside'.

Discussions with children and interviews with staff revealed a difference in understanding as to when a playtime started. Most of the teaching staff considered that playtime started at the end of a teaching session, but for children their actual playing time only started when they arrived in the playground. Before they could play, the children had to undertake several activities that reduced playing time. Thus they had to leave the classroom, change their shoes, put on coats, go to the toilet, have a drink, line up and then line up again at the end of playtime.

Lunchtime breaks were longer in order 'to feed as many children as possible in as short a time as possible', as one member of staff commented. The amount of playing time depended on the speed with which children ate their dinner, and the logistics of going in and coming out of the dining room and playground. In some schools, the younger children were fed first and given a longer lunchtime break because they tended to be slower eaters than the older children.

Boys at one school had fitted their play to accommodate the different lengths of the playtimes; they used the morning playtime to practise ball skills and the longer lunchtime playtime for a 'proper game of football'.

Time constraints – individual routines affecting length of playtimes

Some focus children had certain routines and support sessions that curtailed the length of time that they had for outdoor play during the school day. The routines, usually adult determined, revolved around such matters as going to and from lunch and going to the toilet, while support sessions included things like physiotherapy.

In one school, for example, all the disabled children were treated as a group at lunchtime, when they were collected together and taken to the dining room. Their peers went to the dining room using a different route, which took them outside the building. However, because the disabled children were in different classes, some time was spent waiting for the members of the group to assemble before going to the dining room. Similarly, when the disabled children had all eaten, they were taken to the toilet together and they had to wait until they were all ready before they could go out to play. On one occasion it was observed that this resulted in these children having only five minutes in the playground before afternoon school started.

Some focus children had no morning playtime at all. One example of this was David, who had his regular physiotherapy sessions at this time. His PSA stated that 'this is the most convenient time of day'. David, however, acknowledged that he liked to go outside: 'My favourite bit is lunchtime, is playing outside ... My less favourite bit is playtimes because I have to stay in. So I only go out at lunchtimes.'

Another example was Elizabeth, who had a drink before going out at playtime. She left the class with her PSA at the same time as the other children but, in order to encourage her speech and language development, the PSA would wait until she 'requested' her coat. She was then helped to put on her coat. All this resulted in her getting to the playground later than her peers. The PSA stated that the delay was 'only a couple of minutes', but it was observed to be five minutes on some occasions, a significant proportion of a 15-minute playtime. Not only did Elizabeth lose the amount of time she had to play, but she was denied being present at the beginning of playtime, when friends are located and play gets under way, as described in chapter 3. At lunchtime, Elizabeth spent longer in the dining room than her peers, again with a resultant loss of time in the playground.

Joe's situation was similar in that he had to change from one wheelchair to another to go outside, which inevitably made him late into the playground. He also took some time to eat his food and was regularly observed to have only five to ten minutes for play at lunchtime, sometimes not getting outside at all. His lunchtime supervisor was aware of this and had raised the matter, but had been told that he needed to eat his food as he needed to put on weight following an operation.

Staff training

Only a small number of supervisory staff and PSAs who were interviewed had received training of any kind with respect to play, or guidance as to what roles they might take on as an adult with a child, in a child-led play situation. Many had relied upon their own ideas, parenting skills and experiences with other disabled children and children with emotional and behavioural difficulties in order to construct their own role in the playground context. Lunchtime supervisors in one school had received training about how to teach children games, and some schools had a 'playground activity pack'. It appears that there had been no consultation with the focus children as to their wishes regarding the role of these staff in relationship to them.

Some staff members saw children's role-playing based on media sources as impoverished play, one headteacher commenting, for example, that 'the lunchtime supervisors are keen not to intrude on play but to introduce different games, encouraging children to do more than act out television programmes'. Yet, there are often creative and imaginative aspects in this common activity (Marsh 2001). This dismissal of certain kinds of play is a barrier to all children, in that it devalues play and represents children as lacking in imagination.

Health and safety versus risk

There is an ongoing debate in all areas of play about the issue of safety and risk with respect to children's play (Council for Disabled Children 2004), some fearing that any risk is unacceptable while research clearly shows that some level of risk is important for learning to cope with risk and other situations in adult life.

Health and safety issues were a major concern in all the schools in respect of all the children. This was demonstrated, for example, in regard to fixed play equipment such as climbing frames and their use, doing handstands and cartwheels on the field (which was discouraged at one school 'in case you have an accident', or 'you might [get] bits in your hands' or 'you might break your neck'), or playing 'Peetoo', which involved piling up stones to make a kind of wicket.

The tension between risk and independence versus safety in play was particularly acute for many of the focus children. School staff or parents' desire to reduce risk and promote safety constituted a barrier to inclusion for some focus children, because it reduced their play opportunities and ability to participate alongside their peers. In some instances, school staff supported a focus child's right to play. For example, Usman's spectacles broke while he was playing in the playground. His father was annoyed about this but the school was keen to encourage Usman's independence and the SENCO discussed the matter with him at a meeting. The father agreed that, on balance, it was better for his son to risk having his glasses broken if it meant that he could participate more in play.

Social barriers

Relationships were an important part of determining whether children were included in play. Aspects of both child–child relationships and child–staff relationships could influence this.

Child–child relationships

There were many examples of focus children being included in play by their peers in the playground, as described in chapters 2 and 3. This reflects the findings of earlier research, mentioned in chapter 1, where the children led the way towards inclusion in personal friendships, mutual support and matter-of-fact acceptance of difference in schools (Alderson and Goodey 1998). There were also some who were solitary, and some whose participation in play and friendship networks was less than that of many of their peers.

Some focus children attracted helpers or befrienders who, motivated by a desire to be considerate and aware, were responding to the child's impairment. This was sometimes influenced by the way staff had prepared for the arrival of the focus child into a new class or school. Nevertheless, friendships based on a more balanced appreciation of the focus child's personality and identity seem to have developed from some of these situations.

As seen in chapter 3, behaviour that was regarded as unconventional or unacceptable militated against the full participation of children who behaved in these ways because such qualities were clearly regarded as making a person not good to play with. This was particularly observed to reduce the level of Rowan's participation in the playground and affect the quality of his peer relationships.

Child–staff relationships

Relationships that focus children had with staff could be a positive aid to play and are discussed in chapter 5. However, negative aspects of child–staff relationships were also observed. The focus children spent a great deal more time than many of the non-disabled children with staff, both medical staff and PSAs, in one-to-one situations. Therefore, they sometimes displayed more confidence in their dealings with staff than with other children. The second aspect observed was that staff who spent time associated with one or two particular children became a magnet for other children, thus influencing other social interactions within the playground.

In addition to this, the issue of safety and risk was closely tied in with the attitude of the staff member who might be with a focus child at any one time. Sometimes children wanted to do things but were prevented, or thought not capable of the activity, by a member of staff. Elizabeth, for example, was observed waiting to use the tyre playground. When no staff member arrived, she and some other children started playing on it anyway. Elizabeth was obviously keen and showed herself able to take part in this play. Elizabeth's PSA, however, considered her 'not capable of using it without hurting herself' and actively prevented her from using it.

Sally demonstrated how empowering and self-affirming risk-taking could be. She recounted her dissatisfaction that she could not do all the things that her peers could do. However, she was keen to show that she could do a roly-poly down a grass slope. A PSA tried to dissuade her on the grounds that she might bang her head. The PSA encouraged her to climb the slope with her walking frame by the 'safe' route, where the incline was gentler, because recently Sally had fallen backwards on the steeper slope. Nevertheless, Sally chose the steep route and persuaded her PSA to let her roll down, which she did. She stopped, when she felt dizzy, and began to crawl to finish the route, to the cheers of her peers. The whole thing was accomplished without incident and with a great sense of achievement.

Physical barriers

Constraints due to physical details in the playground

The design of the playground or access to it created physical constraints to the inclusion of some focus children. Access issues had been dealt with in the building, in most schools. There were, for instance, lifts and ramps for children with mobility impairments, and staff were aware of the need to provide manoeuvring room for wheelchairs within classrooms. Access to power points for computers was also provided and, in some situations, significant amounts of money had been spent on upgrading toilet facilities. One school was about to undertake an audit of the interior of the school to assess its suitability for children with a variety of impairments.

Access to the playground, design of the playing space as a whole, and access to facilities such as fixed equipment had not been so comprehensively addressed. There were ramps to the playing area, in some schools, but little attention had been given to paving or ground materials, edges between different surfaces, changes of level, gradients and gates. This particularly applied to children with mobility impairments or who were wheelchair users. David, for example, was not able to get onto the field. There was a big dip along the boundary between the field and the playground and, as he recognised, 'my wheelchair nearly tips up'. Joe had a similar problem with his newly acquired motorised wheelchair which, once identified, the school had noted and promised to address. Helen sometimes left her walker and crawled onto the grass in order to sit with a playmate and chat or make daisy chains. Jodie was unable to get to both the field and the climbing frame because her wheelchair could not cope with the steep path to these facilities.

Constraints due to fixed playground equipment

Five of the schools in the study had climbing or other types of large, fixed play equipment. However, most of this equipment was not designed to be accessible to children with mobility impairments and did not specifically facilitate use by disabled children. Helen could only use a small part of the fixed play equipment and found difficulty traversing the bark chippings under it. Sally felt keenly aware of what she could not do when she saw her friends on the fixed play equipment, although, as described in chapter 2, she participated in 'Bouncing up on the bridge' with her friends.

Constraints due to technical aids

Technical aids such as a motorised wheelchair or walking frame could enable children with mobility impairments to participate in some forms of play, and sometimes became an important element within the game, as noted in the foregoing chapters. This gave some focus children independence and increasing confidence. Wajid, for example, liked his motorised wheelchair because it allowed him to go where the other children went. He still felt at a disadvantage, however, in that 'when I go at full speed, this is only walking place, so I cannot join in running games'. He clearly wished he could go faster in his wheelchair but also expressed the concern that 'then I might crash into things'.

Summary

- Barriers to inclusion in the playground for the focus children were identified as *organisational, social* and *physical.*
- Only one school in the study had an afternoon playtime for all its children, while half of the schools did not have an afternoon playtime for any children.
- The amount of morning and lunchtime play was reduced for some of the focus children because of routines. Some of these were individual routines but some related to how disabled children were treated as a group within a school.
- Staff members responsible for focus children at playtimes received little or no guidance on the nature of this role or how to perform it from a social and from a health and safety point of view.
- Balancing risk-taking and health and safety issues was an ongoing issue, regarding which children and adults sometimes had different points of view.

- Some of the focus children spent more time with staff than their peers did, which meant that these children sometimes appeared less confident with their peers and also that staff might become a magnet for other children, thus influencing other social interactions within a playground.
- The approach of some staff, sometimes related to risk and health and safety issues, resulted in focus children not being allowed to participate in play when they wanted to and were able to.
- Physical barriers included access to playgrounds and the fixed equipment within them.
- The design of the playground and the equipment was also a barrier.
- Details in the playing surfaces and access between them were also identified as physical barriers.

5. Some examples of good practice

All the schools sought to take social inclusion seriously, although there were a variety of approaches to the understanding of how this might be implemented. Most schools had an equal opportunities policy statement, an inclusion statement and behaviour management policies. Some of the schools had rules that pertained to movement around the buildings, to and from the playground and the use of play equipment in the playground. Notably, one headteacher discussed his role as relating, not just to the national curriculum, but also the 'hidden curriculum', which he defined as 'that vital part of the curriculum in which we ensure the physical and social, and the mental well-being and development of the children', which he felt was very undervalued, 'especially in the present climate when everything has to be tested'.

This chapter looks beyond the policies and provides some examples of good practice that were identified. This is discussed within the *organisational and social* themes identified in chapter 4. Physical issues are not discussed separately because most of the good practice in this area related to the buildings and not the play and playgrounds. The limited examples of physical good practice related to the provision of ramps, which had been put in before the commencement of this research.

Organisational good practice

Playtimes and lunchtimes

The many benefits that can be provided by outdoor play opportunities during a primary school day were acknowledged by the continued existence of an afternoon playtime for both KS1 and KS2 children in one of the schools. Two of the other schools had an afternoon playtime for the KS1 children only. One school had two morning playtimes for mixed age groups in an attempt to facilitate play between some siblings and cousins.

Individual routines

Chapter 4 discussed how some of the focus children have physiotherapy in playtimes. However, this was not the case for all of the focus children. An example of good practice was arranging physiotherapy for Susie, a focus child, during some assembly times or quiet reading times, allowing her to participate in playtime.

In one of the schools where the children were supervised whenever they moved around the school, the disabled children were escorted to and from the play area by an adult, when using the steps to the playground. However, as part of encouragement towards their own development, if a child was considered capable, they were allowed to use the ramp, accompanied by another child. This was taken further for Usman, who was encouraged by his PSA to go up the steps alone so that he got experience of using steps.

Staff training

Training for work with particular children and understanding of their impairments was patchy across the schools. Any such training received usually related to health and safety issues, such as lifting or manual handling. Good practice was identified at one school, where support assistants were encouraged to go on training courses and remained at the school, passing on their expertise to their colleagues. This training allowed the support assistants to take on additional responsibilities that they would not have done otherwise. However, this good practice was not repeated in other schools in the study. Indeed, in one school some of the staff who had received some training had moved on to better-paid posts, and there was a constant – and expensive – need to train others.

Lunchtime supervisors in one school had received some training on a course called 'Happy Heart'. The supervisors had learnt from the training and were shown some equipment for use with children with special needs, which they felt would really help one of their children 'bridge the gap with others in the playground'. However, the supervisors were unhappy because, as far as they were aware, money allocated for special needs play had not been spent.

In another school, support staff experienced a training session where they began to understand something of what it was like to have a visual impairment, and this had resulted in an increased respect for the way a particular focus child was coping. It also led to a greater awareness of how to help visually impaired children join in ball

games. The staff particularly found this to be helpful when playing cricket with
Akram, because they learned to bowl more slowly than they would have done, thus
allowing Akram to respond to the movement of the ball.

The benefit of staff experience

Some PSAs felt a great deal of job satisfaction from their financially unrewarding job.
This appeared to be because the PSAs were appreciated by the teaching staff and
specialists, such as physiotherapists and speech therapists, and by the children's
parents. This resulted, in some instances, in long-term service within a particular
school, allowing the PSA to build up a high level of skill. It was the custom, in some
schools, to move the PSAs round from one child to another, thus increasing their
breadth of experience and giving them new challenges. These PSAs appreciated this,
although one of them expressed the opinion that while she enjoyed this, she was not
sure the child she was supporting did.

Moving to a new school

Some of the focus children had moved to a school out of their immediate local area
because another school had better facilities, as was particularly the case with at least
one of the schools in the study. Children who changed schools, especially if this was
part way through a school year, were particularly disadvantaged since friendship
groups within a class had already had some time to become established.

The class teachers in some schools discussed the situation with the class before the
new child arrived. This was done to explain aspects of the new child's impairments,
while encouraging the children to befriend the new child. This had resulted, in one
situation, in the new child being almost overwhelmed with potential friends when
she first arrived, but the situation settled down and she developed specific friends.

Physical education lessons translated into the playground

Examples were identified where teachers used the opportunity of PE lessons to help
focus children develop aspects of skills and play, and some of these were translated to
the playground. In her previous school, Sally had not taken part in physical
education. The class teacher at the school in the study had fully expected Sally to get

changed for PE, get in the hall and participate in the lesson, when she first arrived. At first, Sally was reticent but became involved as she gained confidence. The teacher recalled that, 'Sally gets involved as much as possible. She was the first person to score a rounder when we were doing indoor rounders, and I'm sure that in the playground she could do equally as well ... with that sort of activity.' Sally was also encouraged to go out into the playground because the teacher felt that, '[at the previous school] I don't think that she was let out to play very often and bond and make relationships with the other children'.

Another teacher tried to adapt activities within the PE lesson to enable Joe to participate. This meant the opportunity to become involved in skipping by turning the rope and, although this was not full involvement, it was play in which he participated.

The teacher in another school encouraged Wajid to use his PE lesson to practise reversing his wheelchair round the hoops that the other children were jumping round. The teacher saw this as a way of developing his skills with his wheelchair, enabling him to be more active in the playground.

The benefits of extra time outside for some focus children

There were two situations where a focus child spent more time outside playing than the other children in their class. One PSA revealed that she took the focus child she was responsible for outside to play on the equipment when the child lost concentration or became noisy in the classroom. They played together in the playground and sometimes on the fixed play equipment. The PSA stated that, 'We go out more than the other kids really.' This approach could be seen as excluding the individual child from the classroom, thus missing some formal teaching time, but it could also be seen as responding to the individual child's needs by taking her outside to her benefit.

Social good practice

School staff encouraging confidence in children

The balance between taking risks and developing confidence emerged as an issue for some of the focus children and the school staff working with them. A group of support assistants in one school stated that they felt that, if they supervised the children too closely in the playground, this interfered with the children's ability to form relationships.

There were some situations where a PSA would encourage a focus child to try things that at first the child thought they might not be able to undertake. The school staff were encouraging confidence and ability in these situations. One example of this was Joe, who felt very secure in his wheelchair and when his PSA suggested anything different he tended to say 'no' straight away. However, the PSA encouraged him to go onto the grass and he found that he could go over the edge between the path and the grass: 'Now he's found he can play like everyone else on the grass': at the end of playtime or lunchtime he went into the building with his class. The PSA encouraged him to be 'the same as everybody else apart from the equipment for his physical needs'. Joe's PSA also recalled how she tried to get the children to talk directly to Joe and not to talk to him through her, thus building up his confidence and that of the other children. Joe had recently started to use a motorised wheelchair at the time of the fieldwork, so during playtimes he was often absorbed in mastering this on his own. However, for Wajid, another of the focus children, a motorised wheelchair meant that he could go out into the playground without an accompanying adult.

The PSA in another school had, over a period of time, encouraged Jessica in the playground. Jessica's PSA and class teacher took a joint decision that, as her confidence grew, Jessica need not be accompanied in the playground. The decision was made upon observing Jessica's maturity and feeling that she was able to cope 'without disappearing' and after they had 'made sure she was happy'. The school staff realised that Jessica needed the PSA less and was actually coming to the PSA less: 'We felt it was time she was doing things on her own.'

Summary

Good practice was identified in some organisational and social aspects of the schools visited. However, little good practice relative to physical issues was identified, except for the provision of ramps. The following areas of good practice have been highlighted:

- Retention of morning and afternoon playtimes in one school in order to maximise play opportunities for all children.
- The possibility of mixed age groups sharing playtimes in order to enable siblings and cousins to spend time with each other.

- The adoption of routines for individual focus children that maximised playtimes: such as having physiotherapy at other times, for example, during assembly time or in a quiet reading time.
- Training of school staff on relevant courses accompanied by acknowledgement of their value and resulting in their retention in the school.
- The experience of some PSAs, over a period of years, accompanied by talking with parents and professionals such as physiotherapists, resulted in an increased understanding of a focus child's potential.
- Helping the transition into a school for a focus child who had moved from another school.
- PE lessons being adapted so that focus children could be included in activities, and could develop and use skills in the playground.
- Some of the PSAs realising that an individual focus child would benefit from extra time playing in the playground and acting on this.
- Some of the school staff being able to help a focus children develop confidence to such an extent that, over a period of time, they were enabled to go into the playground by themselves.

6.   Suggestions for the future

The importance of play for all children

This study investigated the inclusion of a selection of disabled children within play in a series of six primary school playgrounds in Yorkshire, England. This was a qualitative study and the results and conclusions should be understood in that context and not generalised. However, the findings can give pointers for thought, policy and action in order that disabled children might be more included in primary school playgrounds. This research is further limited because every child is different from each other, with individual desires and needs for play. The organisation within each school and the design of each playground might also be variables that impact on inclusive play.

Under the UN Convention on the Rights of the Child (1989) play is enshrined as a right for all children. There is also evidence, some of which is reported in chapter 1, that reveals the importance of play for children in the development of a range of skills and academic achievement. National, local and school policy should properly reflect this importance, and value and resource play in the school playground. Issues relating to the inclusion of disabled children should not only be reflected in policy and action within the context of buildings, but also with respect to playgrounds and the play that takes place there.

Organisational issues

A range of organisational barriers has been identified that contribute to the lack of full involvement of disabled children in the play of the playground. Some of these relate to general school routines or the routines of individual children, often imposed by adults.

The following suggestions are made with respect to organisational issues.

School routines

Schools that have reduced the length of playtimes, or have stopped having an afternoon playtime should reconsider this in light of the importance of the opportunities playtimes offer for the social, physical and academic development of all children.

Individual routines

Disabled children have regular reviews of their educational progress, to which parents, staff and the children themselves have access. It is suggested that the routines of disabled children for playtimes and lunchtimes should be included in this review, so that the child has the opportunity to influence their playtime and lunchtime routines and maximise their opportunities for play.

Staff experience

Support staff and lunchtime supervisors should all receive encouragement for good quality work they undertake with disabled children. Such good quality work should be acknowledged and rewarded in some way. This might include being invited to pass on good practice to other members of staff.

Training

PSAs, lunchtime supervisors and class teachers should be offered and receive a variety of training relevant to their situation and responsibilities. This training might include how to be sensitive to the dynamics of play and inclusion, and how to identify when children might benefit from adult intervention to increase their participation and confidence in play. This could include aspects of play, language development and how to build confidence while balancing the issue of risk.

Experienced PSAs, disabled adults, play workers and other workers experienced in this field would be best placed to provide such training, and links could be made with local agencies for disabled people. There might also be disabled parents among the school's own community who would welcome the opportunity to be involved in this way.

Social issues

Much of the play observed was inclusive and participatory, and children had strong and clear ideas about inclusion and exclusion in playgrounds. However, the approach and actions of staff could also have an impact on the inclusion of disabled children in play in the playground. Sometimes staff behaviour and interaction, both with each other and with disabled children, could affect the extent to which disabled children were included in play.

The following suggestions are made with respect to social issues.

The role of staff in the playground

Staff should be helped to understand the constructive and supporting, but not dominating, role that they can take in the playground with disabled children's play. Staff would also benefit from knowing how to help a disabled child to develop independence in the best way for the individual. Some of this may be achieved by awareness training but it is also suggested that a mentoring system be established where experienced staff, acknowledged to be suitably trained, could provide such mentoring.

Power relations

It is suggested that decisions about disabled children, their routines, desires and aspirations relating to outdoor play in the playground, should be based upon a dialogue between child, parents or guardians, staff at the school and, if appropriate, external support staff. The lunchtime supervisors and support staff, in particular, are staff who should be considered in this process, because of the contact time that they have with the children. Issues can be discussed and explained, the child's point of view can be considered and there is a better chance of the result being beneficial to the child, in this way, rather than just fitting into the constraints under which the school may find itself operating.

Physical issues

Physical barriers included access to playgrounds and the fixed equipment within them, together with the design of the playground and the equipment. Details in the playing surfaces and access between them were also identified as physical barriers. Most of the playgrounds studied, and the equipment within them, had not been assessed for their suitability in terms of providing opportunities for inclusive play and opportunities for all children, and this is considered to be a significant omission.

The following suggestions are made with respect to physical issues.

Audit of play and playground and action on the audit

It is recommended that an audit should be undertaken in all primary schools, in order to comply with the *Disability Discrimination Act 1995*, and because it is good practice.

Such an audit should include access to playgrounds and the fixed equipment within them, the design of the playground and the equipment, and details in the playing surfaces and access between them. It is suggested such audits would be enhanced if they also addressed issues relating to organisation and social factors as identified in this study.

The choice of auditor is critical. It is suggested that children themselves, as the users of the playground spaces, are well positioned to undertake such audits, with suitable adults facilitating. The use of multiple methods, as undertaken in *The Mosaic Approach* (Clark and Moss 2001) is suggested as a suitable way forward for gathering children's views.

Any such audit should be accompanied by an action plan outlining the priorities and costs associated with undertaking the plan. Individuals or teams responsible for undertaking the actions should also be identified, and, if a member of staff leaves, then someone else should be identified to follow on with the particular responsibility. Funding sources might need to be identified and funding made available to follow up some of the actions identified in the audit. The audit itself should be reviewed on a regular basis.

Future research

Options for future research following from this work are many. The recent comment by Baroness Warnock – who raised the issue of including disabled children in mainstream school some 30 years ago – that mainstream education might not be suitable for all disabled children adds other dimensions which could be explored with respect to disabled children and play in the context of primary schools. Here a few suggestions are made, based upon the themes of organisation, social and physical issues, some of which could be applied to not only primary schools but also nurseries and secondary schools.

Organisation

- An exploration of the value and importance placed on play, particularly for disabled children, by school staff to identify the culture of play.
- An investigation into what training is available for PSAs and how much of this is taken up and what impact it has. This would lead to an improved understanding of training opportunities that might be worthwhile.
- Identify what PSAs know about their responsibilities for disabled children and what they would like to know to help them in their job. Similarly for lunchtime supervisors.
- Explore the integration or isolation of PSAs and lunchtime supervisors in the school network, and find what support and information networks exist for them. Then identify how this impacts on their work and relationships with children and each other, and suggest ways of improving this.

Social

- An exploration of friendship groups of disabled children in the primary school playground context. This could investigate whether they play in smaller friendship groups than non-disabled children and what affects long-term friendships with their peers. It could also investigate whether disabled children are more comfortable with adults than non-disabled children.
- An investigation of the issues surrounding play for disabled children in schools with special units or in schools where a number of disabled children have one particular impairment.

Physical

- Investigate the role that different staff have in choosing fixed and loose play equipment, and whether its use is monitored.

- An investigation into the design of playgrounds and any options for fixed equipment in them to make them inclusive.
- Explore or review existing information about the types of experiences that would be of most benefit to children with particular impairments, so that these could become part of an inclusive design process.

Appendix: Research design

Selection of schools

The research was undertaken in primary schools in South, North and West Yorkshire, England. This region was chosen because it offered a wide variety of schools in terms of the selected research criteria (set out below) and because the research team had previously worked in other schools in the region. Six schools were selected for the study, two in each of the three counties. The criteria for the selection of the schools were:

- The attendance of disabled children – identified by numbers of children, not individuals, through the special needs register – to ensure that there were children who could be the focus of the study.
- The socio-economic status of the community served by the school – identified by the percentage of children receiving free school meals – to provide a variety of socio-economic backgrounds.
- The geographic location – ensuring both urban and rural schools were represented in the study.
- The cultural background of the children in the school – in order to incorporate a range of cultural backgrounds, from schools with a predominantly white British population, through populations of mixed ethnicity, to a school in which almost all of the children were from minority ethnic backgrounds.

Following an initial approach to several local educational authorities in the region, 21 schools were approached and invited to participate in the research. In each case the approach was made to the headteacher. From these schools, a set of seven, individually diverse schools was identified, which together covered the above criteria. One of these schools was involved in the pilot study and the remaining six schools were the focus of the main study.

The six schools in the main study had geographic locations varying from an inner-city situation, through urban to a village and former mining community. The smallest school had 130 children in KS1 and KS2, while the largest had over 400. The percentage of children in receipt of free school meals ranged from 5 per cent to 46 per cent. Most of the schools comprised mainly white British children but one had 97 per cent of its pupils from a British Pakistani background, 3 per cent from a British Indian background and less than 1 per cent from a white British background. The percentage of children with special educational needs varied from 1.2 per cent to 33 per cent.

The schools were sent a confirmatory letter and the headteacher was asked to sign and return a form consenting to the school's involvement in the project. The fieldwork was undertaken in spring and summer 2003, the schools for the main study being visited between March and July. Each of the three research associates worked in two schools: one working with schools in South Yorkshire, one in West Yorkshire and one in North Yorkshire. During the fieldwork the weather was generally fine, with some rain, thus providing many opportunities for observing the outdoor play of children in school playgrounds.

Pilot study

One of the schools that responded positively to the initial invitation to be involved in the research was chosen as the school for the pilot study, because children came from a range of socio-economic and cultural backgrounds. The pilot study took place in February and early March 2003. The three research associates worked together in the pilot school in order to foster consistency in methods and learn from each other's experiences. A review of the pilot study by the research associates and project coordinator led to the refining of the methods. This included modifications to specific questions and a reduction in the number of focus children and classes to be involved in the main study due to the length of time needed to undertake the qualitative methods. The pilot study also revealed that the school caretaker who had been interviewed knew little about activities in the playground, but a decision was taken to interview caretakers in the six main study schools because it was felt that the situation might vary from school to school.

Methods within each school

Within each school the aim was to develop an in-depth understanding of the play and activities of disabled children, and the issues that might affect their experience, within the context of the play and experiences of all the children in KS1 and KS2. There was a particular desire to listen to the voices of the children themselves and understand issues from their perspective. Thus data was obtained through discussions and 'mapping' with the children in the selected classes, and researcher observations of play at playtimes and lunchtimes. This was supplemented by interviews with selected adult members of the school and a review of relevant documentation from each school.

Review of school documentation

As part of their orientation to the school, the research associates familiarised themselves with relevant policies and documents developed by the school. Although they varied slightly from school to school, these usually included

- the school prospectus
- the inclusion policy
- special educational needs policy
- the health and safety policy
- the anti-bullying/positive behaviour policy
- the manual handling policy
- the play policy (where one was available).

Selection of focus children and their classes

In each school two classes that included several disabled children were identified in consultation with the headteacher. In this context, disabled children were children who had physical and/or sensory impairments and/or severe learning difficulties. There was also liaison within the project team in order to ensure that children with a range of impairments and learning difficulties were included in the study. The team members were aware that this meant seeing the focus children initially in terms of their impairment, but the aim of the research was to go beyond the labels and discover the experiences of the children themselves. The focus children are listed in Table 1, chapter 1, and are identified only by their age, gender and impairment. The pseudonym given to each child for the purposes of this study is also noted in Table 1. Once the focus children had been identified, the classes that they were part of became the classes to be involved in the research.

Involvement of children

Methods were selected to enable the voices of the children to be expressed with respect to their past experiences and knowledge of playtimes, their current activities, their conceptualisations of the playing space and inclusion. Three methods were therefore used: *researcher observations* of the children in the playground, *small-group discussions* and *'mapping' of playtime activities* with all of the children in the two classes selected in each school. The observations were undertaken during a selection of playtimes, including lunchtimes. The research associates took notes, still photographs and video-recordings of the play of the playground. Special attention was given to the focus children and their classes, but children from other classes were also included, to gain a holistic view of playtimes. The observations were done overtly and the researchers interacted with the children, who often brought games and observations to the researcher's attention. In two of the schools, the researcher video recorded specific play activities during playtime at the request of the children.

Small-group discussions were generally undertaken with groups of four children, allowing each child to contribute without the discussion becoming dominated by one or two children (Woolley and others 1999).

The 'mapping' exercise was intended to identify where different types of play were undertaken within the available playing space. The children were asked what they did in each part of the play area, and the results were plotted on a map of the school grounds. In five of the six schools, this process took the form of one or more groups of children from the focus classes, including the focus children, taking the research associate on a 'guided tour' of the playground, pointing out salient features and describing the forms of play undertaken. In one school, the children themselves drew on plans of the playground where they played which games.

Interviews with school staff

The school staff interviewed were those responsible for playtime and behaviour policies, those who had particular responsibilities in relation to the outdoor playing spaces at the school and those who had particular contact with the focus children, and included:

- headteacher
- special educational needs coordinator (SENCO)
- class teachers of the classes involved in the research

- classroom assistants of the classes involved in the research
- support assistants of the disabled children
- lunchtime supervisors on duty in the playground at lunchtimes
- caretakers.

Development of tools for interviews

A set of questions was developed for use with the children, and another with school staff. These were employed as a general guide but not a rigid questionnaire. They were tested in the pilot study and somewhat revised for the main study. The aim of the questions for the children was to understand, from their points of view, what happened in the playground, where it happened and with whom, and to explore the social and aesthetic dynamics related to these matters. There were also questions designed to enquire about inclusion and exclusion in play. The aim of the questions for the staff was to explore their perspective on what happened in the playground, especially from the angle of social inclusion, and their perceptions of their own role and the role of the school as an institution in the management of playtimes.

Analysis of the data

Analysis of the data was undertaken by identifying the themes that were revealed from the different sources. This process involved the research team having whole-day discussions about the findings and a study of the transcripts, field notes, mapping, and still and video photographic data.

Ethical considerations

The Social Research Association *Ethical Guidelines* (2002) were the framework for ethical considerations for the project. In addition, the research team welcomed the deliberations that took place with the adult advisory group on various ethical issues.

Advisory groups

An adult advisory group was established, which included people with academic, practice and policy experience. This was supplemented by a young people's advisory group from the pilot school, and included one focus child.

Permission from the individual schools

From the beginning, the research team and the adult advisory group were most concerned about the issue of permission to be involved in the research. Schools with a number of disabled children were identified, and those that were willing to be included in the study were sent a letter explaining the research and seeking informed, written consent from the headteacher.

Permission from individual parents or guardians

The schools informed parents of the research being about play and activity in the playground in their regular school newsletter or in a letter sent to parents. Parents/guardians were asked to let the school know if they were not happy for their children to be involved in the research. It was made clear that the videos would be used as a research tool only, and thus would only be viewed by the research team.

Presentation of the research to the children

The research associates were introduced to the children at several stages of the project and at each stage children were given the opportunity to opt out of the research. Initially this took place during a school assembly immediately prior to the beginning of the fieldwork period. The purpose of the research was explained as being 'what the children did in the playground at playtimes and lunchtimes'. It was also explained that the researcher would work with two classes. In addition, each research associate introduced themselves to the members of each of their two classes, and the possibility of opting out was given to the children. When each researcher met with the small interview groups, an opportunity for each pupil to withdraw from the interview was given again. In one school one girl and one boy chose to opt out of the research at this stage.

Focus of the research

After discussion between the adult advisory group and the research team it was decided not to tell the children that the specific focus of the research was disabled children. This was not an easy decision to make because of the desire to be honest about the research and its aims and to listen to the views of the children. On balance it was decided that we did not want to draw attention to the fact that the research was interested in the focus children and their play because we did not want to give children labels, nor reinforce any that might already exist, based upon the children's impairments. The headteachers were told that the focus of the research was upon disabled children.

Feedback to schools

Half of the schools were keen to have feedback directly from the research associate who had been in their school and this was facilitated while the research was being written up. In addition, each school has been sent a letter of thanks and a copy of this publication.

References

Alderson, P and Goodey, C (1998) *Enabling Education*. London: Tufnell Press.

Armitage, M (2001) 'The ins and outs of school playground play', in Bishop, J and Curtis, M (eds) *Play Today in the Primary School Playground: Life, Learning and Creativity*. Buckingham: Open University Press.

Bateson and Martin (1999) writing in the Guardian, 31/08/99.

Bishop, J and Curtis, M (eds) (2001) *Play Today in the Primary School Playground: Life, Learning and Creativity*. Buckingham: Open University Press.

Bishop, A, Swain, J and Bines, H (1999) 'Seizing the moment: reflections on play opportunities for disabled children in the early years', *British Journal of Educational Studies*, 47, 2, 170–83.

Blatchford, P (1989) *Playtime in the Primary School: Problems and Improvements*. Windsor: NFER-Nelson.

Blatchford, P (1998) *Social Life in School: Pupils' Experiences of Break-time and Recess from 7 to 16 Years*. London: Falmer.

Blatchford, P and Sharp, S (eds) (1994) *Break-time and the School*. London: Routledge.

Blatchford, P and Sumpner, C (1998) 'What do we know about break-time? Results from a national survey of break-time and lunch-time in primary and secondary schools', *British Educational Research Journal*, 24, 79–94.

Children Act (2004). London: The Stationery Office.

Clark, A and Moss, P (2001) *Listening to Young Children: The Mosaic Approach*. London: National Children's Bureau on behalf of the Joseph Rowntree Foundation.

Coalter, F and Taylor, J (2001) *Realising the Potential: The Case for Cultural Services – Play*. Edinburgh: Centre for Leisure Research, University of Edinburgh.

Cole-Hamilton, I, Harrop, A and Street, C (2002) *Making the Case for Play – Gathering the Evidence*. London: National Children's Bureau.

Council for Disabled Children (2004) *The Dignity of Risk*. London: Council for Disabled Children.

Crozier, WR and Dimmock, PS (1999) 'Name-calling and nicknames in a sample of primary school children', *British Journal of Educational Psychology*, 69, 505–16.

Davis, JM and Watson, N (2000) 'Disabled children's rights in everyday life: problematising notions of competency and promoting self-empowerment', *International Journal of Children's Rights*, 8, 211–28.

Delalande, J (2001) *La Cour de recreation: pour une anthropologie de l'enfance (The Playground: Towards an Anthropology of Childhood)*. Rennes: Presses Universitaires de Rennes.

Every Child Matters: Change for Children (2004) London: HM Government. Available online (consulted October 2005): www.everychildmatters.gov.uk

Gump, PV and Sutton-Smith, B (1955) 'The "It" role in children's games', *American Association of Group Workers*, 17, 3 (Feb.), 3–8; reprinted in Avedon, EM and Sutton-Smith, B (eds) (1971) *The Study of Games*. New York: John Wiley.

Hegarty, S and Pocklington, K (1981) *Educating Pupils with Special Needs in the Ordinary School*. Windsor: NFER-Wilson.

Kids' Club Network (2001) *Providing for Disabled Children in your Kids' Club*. London: Kids' Club Network.

Marsh, K 'The influence of the media, the classroom and immigrant groups on children's playground singing games', in Bishop, J and Curtis, M (eds) (2001) *Play Today in the Primary School Playground: Life, Learning and Creativity*. Buckingham: Open University Press.

Moorcock, K (1998) *Swings and Roundabouts: The Danger of Safety in the Outdoor Play Environment*. Sheffield: Sheffield Hallam University Press.

NPFA (National Playing Fields Association), Children's Play Council and Playlink (2000) *Best Play: What Play Provision Should Do for Children*. London: National Playing Fields Association.

ODPM (Office of the Deputy Prime Minister) (2003) *Developing Accessible Play Space – A Good Practice Guide*. London: ODPM.

Opie, I (1993) *The People in the Playground*. Oxford: Oxford University Press.

Opie, I and Opie, P (1969) *Children's Games in Street and Playground*. Oxford: Clarendon Press.

Pellegrini, AD and Blatchford, P (1993) 'Time for a break', *The Psychologist*, 63, 51–67.

Petrie, P and others (2000) *Out of School Lives, Out of School Services*. London: The Stationery Office.

Richardson, PK (2002) 'The school as social context: social interaction of children with physical disabilities', *American Journal of Occupational Therapy*, 56, 3, 296–304.

Rogers, C and Sawyers, J (1988) *Play in the Lives of Children*. Washington DC: National Association for the Education of Young Children.

Social Research Association (2002) *Ethical Guidelines*. Available online (consulted October 2005): www.the-sra.org.uk

Special Educational Needs Disability Act 2001. London: The Stationery Office.

Swain, J (2000) 'The money's good, the fame's good, the girls are good: the role of playground football in the construction of young boys' masculinity at junior school', *British Journal of Sociology*, 21, 1, 95–109.

Taylor, J (ed) (1998) *Early Childhood Studies: An Holistic Introduction*. London: Arnold.

Thorne, B (1993) *Gender Play: Girls and Boys in School*. Buckingham: Open University Press.

Unicef (1989) *UN Convention on the Rights of the Child*. New York: Unicef.

Watson, N and others (2000) *Life as a Disabled Child: A Qualitative Study of Young People's Experiences and Perspectives*. Edinburgh: Department of Nursing Studies, University of Edinburgh.

Woolley, H and others (1999) 'Children describe their experiences of the city centre: a qualitative study of the fears and concerns which may limit their full participation', *Landscape Research*, 24, 3, 287–310.

Also available in the Understanding Children's Lives series

Children and Decision Making
Ian Butler, Margaret Robinson and Lesley Scanlan
2005. ISBN 1 904787 54 1

Children's Perspectives on Believing and Belonging
Greg Smith
2005. ISBN 1 904787 53 3

Children's Understanding of their Sibling Relationships
Rosalind Edwards, Lucy Hadfield and Melanie Mauthner
2005. ISBN 1 904787 48 7

Other titles published for the Joseph Rowntree Foundation by NCB

'Involved' Fathering and Child Well-being
Father's involvement with secondary school age children
Elaine Welsh, Ann Buchanan, Eirini Flouri and Jane Lewis
2004. ISBN 1 904787 24 X

It's Someone Taking a Part of You
A study of young women and sexual exploitation
Jenny J Pearce with Mary Williams and Cristina Galvin
2003. ISBN 1 900990 83 0

Listening to Young Children
The Mosaic approach
Alison Clark and Peter Moss
2001. ISBN 1 900990 62 8

Monitoring and Supervision in 'Ordinary' Families
The views and experiences of young people aged 11 to 16 and their parents
Stephanie Stace and Debi Roker
2005. ISBN 1 904787 42 8

Parenting Programmes and Minority Ethnic Families
Experiences and outcomes
Jane Barlow, Richard Shaw and Sarah Stewart-Brown, in conjunction with REU
2004. ISBN 1 904787 13 4

Understanding What Children Say
Children's experiences of domestic violence, parental substance misuse and parental health problems
Sarah Gorin
2004. ISBN 1 904787 12 6

Young People, Bereavement and Loss
Disruptive Transitions?
Jane Ribbens McCarthy with Julie Jessop
2005. ISBN 1 904787 45 2

To order these titles, or any other title published by NCB, call +44 (0)20 7843 6087,
email booksales@ncb.org.uk or visit www.ncb-books.org.uk

Children in difficulty

Written by two practising clinicians, this book is designed as a guide to those who work with children. In clear, simple language it focuses upon some of the most common, yet often incapacitating, difficulties which are frequently encountered by young children and adolescents.

After introducing and discussing different forms of therapy and treatment used in clinical work with children, the book provides a series of chapters, each dealing with a specific difficulty. Drawing upon recent research findings, and employing detailed case illustrations, it seeks to help the reader to understand the nature of each problem and offers a guide as to how the child in difficulty can best be helped.

The book is designed to be of particular value to those working in education, social work, health and childcare settings, and anyone who needs to be able to recognise and help children in difficulty.

Julian Elliott is Professor of Educational Psychology at the University of Sunderland. Formerly, he was a teacher in special and mainstream schools and an LEA educational psychologist. **Maurice Place** is a consultant child and adolescent psychiatrist, and Visiting Professor at the University of Northumbria. In addition to working directly with children and their families, he acts as a consultant to a variety of special educational establishments which deal with difficult and troubled children.

Children in difficulty

A guide to understanding and helping

Julian Elliott and Maurice Place

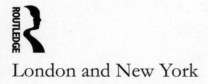

London and New York

First published 1998
by Routledge
11 New Fetter Lane, London EC4P 4EE

Simultaneously published in the USA and Canada
by Routledge
29 West 35th Street, New York, NY 10001

Typeset in Garamond by RefineCatch Limited, Bungay, Suffolk
Printed and bound in Great Britain by
TJ International Ltd, Padstow, Cornwall

British Library Cataloguing in Publication Data
A catalogue record for this book is available from the British Library

Library of Congress Cataloging in Publication Data
Elliott, Julian, 1955–
    Children in difficulty: a guide to understanding and helping /
    Julian Elliott and Maurice Place.
        p.   cm.
    Includes bibliographical references and index.
    1. Child psychotherapy. 2. Child psychopathology. 3. Adolescent
    psychotherapy. 4. Adolescent psychopathology. I. Place, Maurice.
    II. Title.
    RJ504.E43   1998   97–42582
    618.92′8914—dc21   CIP

ISBN 0–415–14458–2 (hbk)
ISBN 0–415–14459–0 (pbk)

Contents

Figures

1   Introduction

There are few issues which can raise stronger feelings in the average person than those which relate to children. Be it outrage at their challenging behaviour, or distress at injury or neglect, adults quickly become moved by issues which involve children. Even more fascinating is the way that each person knows how the situation or behaviour should be handled – and usually this means that the delinquent needs more punishment, or the hurt child needs more care. While such emotional responses are very understandable, they are not always the correct way to intervene in a situation to ensure that matters will be improved. But how should you intervene in delicate situations and be confident that you are helping?

Helping takes a number of forms from being a sympathetic listener to the employment of highly specialised and complex approaches. What is presented in this book is not only what an individual might do, but what is undertaken by others working in the caring professions. Readers, therefore, need to judge whether they have the expertise to undertake some of the techniques described and must carefully consider the point at which it is necessary to refer to others.

The general rules of child management can be easily stated with the three 'C's – care, consistency and control. The emphasis upon a particular element of this triad depends upon the circumstances – a sick child tends to need more care, a wayward child more control. However, all three must be present in reasonable degree if problems are to be managed or prevented.

Louise was fifteen years of age and was having difficulties in school. When challenged by the teachers over trivial matters she would become angry and storm from the classroom. Her parents said that she had behaved like this at home ever since being a toddler. The parents said that when these episodes occurred at home they either gave in to her wishes or tried to calm her down by offering treats or rewards. The parents adopted this placating style when Louise was eighteen months of age, because it was then that she was diagnosed as having a major hormonal problem, and the doctors said it would be dangerous for her if she became upset. Over the years the parents had continued to believe that Louise's life would be in danger if she became too upset and so made every effort to avoid such situations ever arising.

Situations such as this are not common, but seeing children whose behaviour is troublesome because they have not been managed with a balanced regime is. Too much control, which is not tempered by a caring warmth, creates angry, and at times violent, children. Too little control, and the young person will live to the limit of that control, quickly exceeding it and usually only being pulled up by the limits which society imposes in the form of laws.

When confronted with a challenging situation, how is the best course of action determined, and perhaps even more crucially, how is that action carried out? In the following chapters there are descriptions of how to deal with the more common challenges that arise within everyday life. To be able to intervene effectively it is important to have a structured way of understanding the information that is gathered by locating it in the context of the child's development, current functioning and the wider issues of family and environment.

DETERMINING THE ORIGIN OF THE DIFFICULTIES

There are many influences which work upon a child and help to determine how he or she will behave. First, there is the genetic make-up which the child has inherited from the parents. The belief that problems within the parents can be passed on to their children has been persuasive since biblical times. The advent of scientific study, and the work of George Mendel, the Augustinian monk, gave a clear understanding of the principles of heredity, and prompted research in many areas to try to determine the part genetics plays in the origin of many disorders and syndromes. For example, Heston (1966) looked at the children of schizophrenic patients and found that they were more likely to develop the disease than the general population. Such studies, together with studies of twins, have gradually supported a view that genetic influences often make a contribution to the emotional and behavioural difficulties which children may show.

A related theme to genetic influences is that of physical make-up, and particularly the complex chemical structures which control all of our bodily systems, and alter emotions and behaviour. The detail and complexity of such elements make them beyond the scope of this text, but by way of illustration we can look at one particular body chemical: serotonin (or 5-HT). Work over the years has highlighted that certain disorders (particularly depression, anxiety and eating disorders) are more frequently seen in females, whereas others (such as alcoholism, aggressiveness and suicide) are seen more frequently in males. In animals as well as humans the female shows a tendency to an increased synthesis and turnover of serotonin, and evidence is now accumulating that this may be the chemical which moderates the emotional responses to adverse experiences throughout the animal kingdom (Steiner *et al.* 1997). Any dysfunction in serotonin's action and emotional problems are therefore likely to arise. This leads to the speculation that this brain chemical may have a significant role in the origin or maintenance of these disorders, so opening a new avenue of potential treatment for them.

The second key area of influence is a child's temperament. Whether this can be totally divorced from genetic influences is difficult to say, but there can be no doubt that some children appear placid in the face of adversity, while others are challenging at every turn. These characteristics are particularly startling when neither parent has such traits, and often prompt great exasperation from the parents as it seems out of context from their family.

The third great influence is history. The history of the child's life often contains important clues and themes which have clearly had a strong influence in shaping the child's present pattern of behaviour. The death of a parent, serious illness in brothers or sisters, being the victim of abuse or neglectful parenting – such themes are very powerful in prompting behavioural and emotional reactions which can quickly become part of a child's routine responses. Sometimes the history is more a family myth than actual events – but if powerful enough it may establish patterns of behaviour.

John was seven years of age and lived with his mother in a quiet part of town. He was seen in the neighbourhood as a helpful and pleasant boy, and school had only praise for his work there. John's mother presented to the adult mental health services because she was miserable. She explained that since her husband had left she had found it hard to manage John's behaviour. John's father had been the main disciplinarian because she had never been able to control John's outbursts. She explained that as a teenager she had been expected to look after her older brother, who had also been called John. He had often been violent towards her and seemed to take particular delight in tormenting her. On the night of her son's birth her brother John had been killed while committing a robbery, and she was convinced that her son had taken on this malevolent spirit. The family's wish to have her child named after her dead brother compounded this belief.

The important theme here is not the veracity of John's mother's belief but merely the strength with which she believed it. Growing up with a parent who expects you to be difficult and violent towards her is very likely to encourage such behaviour to surface.

As we shall see later, a child's development occurs in stages and the established elements of development that result from each stage are incorporated into the next one. In this way, early life experiences are used to develop competencies, and a child who has successfully met all the challenges of a particular developmental stage is well equipped to take on the next stage (Sroufe and Rutter 1984). If there have been difficulties or upheavals, however, these can create vulnerabilities which are also carried forward, with the result that the child arrives at the later stages of development with less than the optimal resources to respond to new challenges. This is known as

Werner's Orthogenetic Principle (Werner 1948) and illustrates how problems at a particular age can still be exerting influence many years later.

The next strand to be considered when addressing why a problem is happening is the present family atmosphere. We are social animals and feel most comfortable when part of a group which wants us to be there. We respond to subtle changes in atmosphere, and will often do things we would not have chosen to do because the group we are with makes it seem right. This is even more true for children who have still to acquire the sense of personal determination which allows adults to resist these influences and expectations. It is not surprising, therefore, that a young person's behaviour can be powerfully influenced by the relationships within the family and the way that these relationships are expressed. For example, if a child feels a close alliance with a particular member of the family, or becomes caught in conflict between parents, then he or she may try to deal with the confusion of feelings by reacting in a challenging or distressed way. In practice many problems that present are in fact signposts to troubles within the family, and if these troubles are not recognised and addressed then resolution of the problems is far less likely.

Finally, there is the influence of the peer group and the subculture in which the young person is living. The need to conform to the wishes and plans of significant people is a feature of all humans' make-up, but at different phases of life the significant people tend to change. For example, in infancy the parents are central, but in adolescence the peer group becomes more influential. If conformity to the peer group demands involvement in dangerous or troublesome activity then the teenager is clearly at risk if the need to participate is felt strongly. Much of the delinquent behaviour seen in society is committed by teenagers who are part of a group pursuing excitement or physical gain. Similarly, if a peer group is criticising or teasing a young person, these negative statements can be powerful in making the adolescent feel badly about himself or herself.

Peer group influence is but one specific example of the impact which subculture can have upon the behaviour or emotional state of a child. A further example is given by the work of Rutter, who in his detailed study of the influence of schools (Rutter *et al.* 1979) highlighted the relationship between a school's ethos and children's behaviour, as well as the levels of vandalism and graffiti, irrespective of the type of area from which the pupils of the school were drawn.

Understanding the areas which can influence functioning allows the information that is gathered to be used to clarify the influences which underlie the difficulties. It also points to certain areas of enquiry which it is wise to pursue if a full understanding of the problem is to be achieved.

DEVELOPMENTAL THEMES

As well as these elements of influence it is important to remember that children are also developing organisms. This means that each child has to proceed through various stages of development in a variety of ways. Each of these helps to equip them for their future life as an adult. There have been many suggestions as to how to conceptualise these processes, focusing on many different aspects of development, but in the context of this text the psychological/social sequence described by Erikson (1959) is perhaps the most helpful (Figure 1.1). This developmental process illustrates the elements that are most influential in a child's life at each stage of development, and although others will still exert some influence, this process highlights the features which are exerting most influence at each age level. For example, in the Industry phase it is teachers and peers who exert the most influence. All parents will have experienced this when trying to help a child

Trust v Mistrust Birth to 1 year	Infants must learn to trust others. There must be minimal uncertainty, and with each demand satisfied the infant grows in trust. Maternal care fosters identification. Insufficient warmth and care and the infant views the world as a dangerous place. The mother figure is the primary agent.
Autonomy v Shame and Doubt 1 to 3 years	The child's self-will emerges and self-esteem begins to emerge. This striving needs to be matched by the adults maintaining a clear sense of care and security.
Initiative v Guilt 3 to 6 years	Children at this age attempt to act grown up and, possessing some sense of self-control, they seek to broaden their horizons and strive to achieve a physical independence from their parents. They begin to notice sex and role differences. The members of the family are key agents.
Industry v Inferiority 6 to 12 years	Relates to parents and other adults on an equal basis. The child compares self to peers. Teachers and peers have the greatest influence.
Identity v Confusion Adolescence	Seeking a path through a maze of life options to establish their own unique identity and achieve emotional independence from their parents. Key influences are peers, significant adults (usually not parents) and society.

Figure 1.1 Erikson's developmental process

with homework, and the child becomes distressed because 'it is not the way my teacher said to do it'. The possibility that there may be other methods is not something the child can recognise easily at this age, but, more importantly, the way teachers demonstrated the task must be right because of their importance in the young person's world.

These stages should not be seen as gateways. The completion of the tasks in each stage is not a prerequisite to moving on to the next stage, but they do equip the child to cope with the next stage better and in a more robust fashion. This means that problems during any stage do not prevent the child developing, but make it more difficult for them since crucial knowledge and skills may be lacking. For example, a child who has not fully developed social skills during the Industry phase will find negotiating the process of dating in adolescence especially difficult. Of course the earlier that the difficulties occur the more profound the disruption might be, and many developmental theorists have linked major illness processes, such as psychopathic personality disorder, to difficulties in the first months of life. The young person may traverse the remaining stages well, and this may correct much of the initial disturbance, but the disruption of those early stages presents the young person with a far steeper hill to climb.

A key factor, therefore, in trying to predict how a traumatic event might be dealt with is to consider the child's age. After eighteen months of age infants begin to understand that they are independent entities separate from their parents. Self-regulation becomes increasingly important, but to achieve this the child has also to learn frustration tolerance. Marked tantrums are common as this is developed, but if the relationship with parents has been solid and secure up to this point then these 'explosions' are facilitated by an internal picture that the child has of the parents being available and sensitive to emotional needs. This helps the infant to feel free to express negative feelings directly, confident that the parents will be supportive through times of distress. It is interesting to note that the quality of this attachment between an infant and parents can be in great measure predicted from the mother's description of her baby while she is pregnant (Benoit *et al.* 1997). This suggests that in the early stages of this evolving attachment it is the contribution of the parents which is the most influential.

In young children the usual medium for coming to understand such emotions and the events occurring around them is through the world of play. By about two years of age toddlers' sense of self provides sufficient differentiation for them to begin to recreate experiences in play. It is interesting to note that children who have been abused at this young age find it difficult to develop all the skills of this stage, and so they engage in less symbolic play, find it difficult to play with peers, and are generally more aggressive (Alessandri 1991).

Although children can recognise that events have occurred through the mechanical processes of repetition that play offers, their sense of the world is not sufficiently developed for them to set the events in any context. This means that at this age a child can't anticipate events or consequences very easily, because the context that would act as a warning is missing.

By four years of age the child can repress one view in preference to another and so there is the beginning of a recognition that there can be alternative origins for problems other than the child's action. Now the recognition of other sources of influence begins to become apparent, and the play takes on a richer content as the roles of others in making things happen are gradually explored. By six years of age this ability is fully developed and the child is able to relate the cause of events to origins which the child recognises they can't influence. They also begin to evaluate their competence by comparing themselves to others (Dweck and Elliott 1983), and with this comes the start of seeing peer approval as important, an influence which reaches its peak in adolescence. The areas of this influence tend, however, to be different in boys and girls, for while boys seek approval for their actions, it is a girl's view of herself that is most strongly influenced by the views of others (Cole *et al.* 1997).

The significance of this developing awareness is that if traumatic events should occur early in a child's life it is likely that they will believe themselves responsible. The help offered to children has therefore not only to take account of what the child may have experienced but at what age it has occurred so that the correct emphasis can be given to the therapeutic help.

A STRUCTURED ASSESSMENT

When confronted with any type of problem, the first impulse may be one of bewilderment: where to start? It is nearly always best in such situations to recognise that there is no danger in silence. A quiet and reflective style will probably start the information flowing, and if all that is happening is weeping and distress then silent support is equally comforting. Although there is a need to know in order to be able to understand, the first response should be one of availability and support. From this basis the immediate issues can usually be clarified, and together these two themes give an excellent platform from which to begin to obtain the detail upon which decisions can be based.

THE WAY FORWARD

Armed with the detail of the situation it is then possible to formulate the next steps. There may be a clear recognition that more specialised help is needed, and the task then becomes to help the child, and the family, to see how important this may be.

In most cases, however, the information is used to inform the process of assistance being offered by the concerned adult. For most situations, being clear and decisive can prove very beneficial. The young person feels less confused because an adult is bringing clarity, and if they are agreeable to help then they feel less frightened and alone. Not all young people want to be

Initial themes

1 Clarify the issues, who is concerned, and why? If there are discrepancies, this may be significant.
2 Details of the current problem – duration, intensity, circumstances and consequences.
3 The attitudes of the key people – the youngsters themselves, parents, teachers, etc.

Developmental history

Is there anything in the child's history which might be influencing the behaviour?

School functioning

The key areas here are academic performance – is the youngster struggling in lessons?

• relationships with teachers;
• relationships with other children – don't forget the powerful impact of being bullied.

Peer relationships

Are there any friends, what are they like, how much of an influence do they wield?

Hobbies and interests

Are there elements of variation in the child's life or is he or she overly focused on a single issue or area, or perhaps even on no areas at all?

Traumatic events

Have significant things happened in the life of the family or directly to the youngster which seem linked to the present issues?

Family relationships

Although these can be asked about, the most effective way of evaluating family relationships is to observe them in action – who speaks most?

• the tone of exchanges
• who holds the authority (it might be a child!)

The child's behaviour

How does the child behave, restless/settled, calm/sad, etc. All such observations help to clarify the type of difficulties that may exist.

Figure 1.2 The structured assessment

helped, and sadly there are a few who are set on a self-destructive path from which they will not be deviated. Knowing one's personal and professional limitations, while not underestimating innate skills, is the starting point for deciding what a particular individual's role should be. If the problem is one detailed in the following pages then the themes described will help to clarify how best to proceed.

REFERENCES

Alessandri, S.M. (1991). Play and social behaviours in maltreated pre-schoolers. *Developmental Psychopathology* 3, 191–206.

Benoit, D., Parker, K.C.H. and Zeanah, C.H. (1997). Mothers' representations of their infants assessed pre-natally. Stability and association with infant attachment classifications. *Journal of Child Psychology and Psychiatry* 38, 307–13.

Cole, D.A., Martin, J.M. and Powers, B. (1997). A competency-based model of child depression: a longitudinal study of peer, parent, teacher, and self-evaluations. *Journal of Child Psychology and Psychiatry* 38(5), 505–14.

Dweck, C. and Elliott, E. (1983). Achievement motivation. In P. Mussen (ed.) *Handbook of Child Psychology, Volume IV: Socialization, Personality and Social Development.* New York: Wiley.

Erikson, E. (1959). *Identity and the Life Cycle.* New York: International University Press.

Heston, L.L. (1966). Psychiatric disorders in foster home reared children of schizophrenic mothers. *British Journal of Psychiatry* 112, 819–25.

Rutter, M., Maughan, B., Mortimore, P., Ouston, J. and Smith, A. (1979). *Fifteen Thousand Hours: Secondary Schools and their Effects on Children.* London: Open Books.

Sroufe, L.A. and Rutter, M. (1984). The domain of developmental psychopathology. *Child Development* 55, 17–29.

Steiner, M., LePage, P. and Dunn, E.J. (1997). Serotonin and gender specific psychiatric disorders. *International Journal of Psychiatric Clinical Practice* 1, 3–13.

Werner, H. (1948). *Comparative Psychology of Mental Development.* New York: International University Press.

2 The basics of being helpful

INTRODUCTION

Perhaps the most important distinction between the child and the adult clients is that children with difficulties rarely seek help themselves. Rather, they are typically referred for help by concerned others, usually the child's family or teachers. It should not be assumed that because the child is deeply unhappy about his or her circumstances and strongly desires change to take place that professional intervention will be welcomed or accepted. Many forms of therapy, particularly the psychotherapies, are based upon an assumption that the client is a willing participant who actively wishes to change. The reality is that many children who are brought to therapists come unwillingly and respond only because of the power imbalances which they perceive. Furthermore, successful work with children is likely to involve direct support and intervention from others, such as parents, teachers, social workers and peers.

This chapter cannot provide an exhaustive account of the many differing forms of therapy. Where this is required the reader is advised to examine the specialised texts referred to in each section.

THE TALKING THERAPIES

Talking with others, outlining the difficulties we are experiencing and receiving advice on how to remedy a difficult situation, is a natural, effective and everyday way of tackling problems. The old adage, 'a problem shared is a problem halved' reflects the fact that merely by unburdening ourselves to others our difficulties may often appear less arduous, our sense of confusion and powerlessness less overwhelming. In a world where communication is often brief or misunderstood, where there often appears to be insufficient time for one another, the availability of another who, in a non-judgemental fashion, will try to understand your problems, concerns and frustrations, who will provide a sounding board for your own, often confused understandings and who may suggest ways forward is often rare.

Despite the efficacy of problem-solving discussion between a child and a concerned adult in everyday situations, the types of problem outlined in this book are unlikely to be resolved solely by such means. Unlike the common scene in television sitcoms where the question 'Can we talk about this?' can usually be relied upon to result in greater understanding and awareness of the complexity of interpersonal relationships, the problems of the highly anxious, phobic, aggressive or defiant child are unlikely to be resolved in such a fashion.

A term increasingly used to describe supportive forms of talking is counselling. The use of this as a description of the process of discussing problems has now become so widespread as to render the term virtually meaningless; parents counsel their children, teachers their students, police counsel potential lawbreakers, finance brokers their clients. With regard to children, counselling is frequently used to describe the process of listening to problems, advising on action and explaining the constraints within which the child should operate. Indeed, counselling is misguidedly used as a euphemism for controlling behaviour – the headteacher who asked one of the present authors to 'severely counsel' a wayward five-year-old was by no means exceptional. As is shown in Chapter 8, counselling is often misunderstood and misused.

Such a criticism, however, does not imply that counselling, undertaken appropriately and skilfully, is of little therapeutic value. Indeed, the basic elements of counselling and psychotherapy have shown a tendency to converge over the years, with much cross-fertilisation of approach and technique resulting. Counselling uses a variety of techniques to help people, but often involves assistance to help them express emotion over painful events (Lindemann 1944), communicate their feelings more accurately and develop problem-solving behaviour, and employs empathy and displays of concern to increase self-esteem (Rogers 1951, 1961). In contrast to the psychotherapies, there is, perhaps, less reliance on a theory of development to which themes are referenced, and this makes it very suitable, for instance, as a way of helping people come to terms with traumatic events that are still troubling them (see Chapter 7). In recent years there has also been a rapid growth of pre-emptive counselling: offering assistance to people in the immediate aftermath of an incident. This approach assumes that early intervention, and the rapid ventilation of feelings in a controlled way will prevent problems later. Although this has some theoretical attraction, the results of such processes suggest that this is not totally successful (Bisson *et al.* 1997).

Counselling has perhaps also seen a great expansion because, unlike the psychotherapies, training is easily available. Many academic settings offer basic counselling certificates and diplomas, and there is a well-structured development path up to post-degree level. A danger, however, is that it is often easy for individuals to claim counselling expertise on the basis of very limited training.

While there may be much overlap between the everyday process of listening to and supporting another, and the operation of the many forms of talking therapy (Garfield and Bergin (1994) identified 400 in their review), the latter is marked by the presence of a theoretical base which underpins practice. While theoretical perspectives vary greatly, talking therapies have several elements in common; these were first pointed out by Frank (1974). At the heart of this commonality is the establishment of a therapeutic relationship. The sense of regard and concern shown by the therapist for the client is a foundation point from which other elements can emerge. A second key theme common to all psychotherapies is facilitating the emergence of emotional arousal. The linking of emotions with recalled events or memories provides the basic material from which therapy proceeds because being able to tolerate such emotions and then recognising their associations is a key element of working through the areas of difficulty.

At the heart of each psychotherapy, however, is the aim of giving the person insight into their problems, and their origins, on the assumption that from such self-knowledge they will begin to change and the difficulties will be eased. This is perhaps seen at its clearest when dealing with someone who has experienced a traumatic early life and now has difficulties that the therapist believes are occurring as a consequence of those experiences. By helping the person see these links their growing understanding modifies their sense of inevitability and helps them to find new ways of behaving.

The therapist works from a specific theoretical base and the responses reflect the theory of development being used. For example, Freud (1976) used psychosexual development, and the way that basic drives (id) and the higher morality of conscience (superego) interacted with each other to influence behaviour. Such theories offer the child a context in which to view the traumas, and so build a framework from which to analyse beliefs, feelings and reactions. This gives a sense of structure to the emerging understanding. These theoretical frameworks also have common elements: for example, the offering of a predictable space and time dedicated to exploring the themes. Within each session information is gathered which helps the therapist to refine the understanding of the specific difficulties, and these hypotheses are tested by subsequent information. Therapists will then use their specific understanding and the theoretical base to reflect upon the origins of specific behaviours, feelings or beliefs. Most of these therapies also depend upon using the emotion generated within sessions to inform the process. So, for instance, a passage in which the client becomes upset may be specifically noted – because people sometimes experience emotions but have no name for them or, more commonly, may display emotions without realising they are doing so. 'I notice you become angry whenever you mention your father' could be the starting point for a young person to realise such a link. In some hands these interpretations can be quite confrontational (Ashurst 1991).

Another theme which is common to many of the psychotherapies is the way that a therapist uses emotions that arise within themselves to highlight the unspoken emotions and feelings of the client. This is described as transference and can arise in many situations. For example, when a mother is spoken of by a child, it is possible that the therapist also feels a personal sense of sadness. The commenting on such feelings is seen in some therapeutic styles (particularly psychoanalysis) as a key element of the process.

The best-known therapy is psychoanalysis (Freud 1976), which was the first psychotherapy and whose basic tenets are still at the core of many therapeutic approaches. Its requirement of three to four sessions a week for two years or more means it is not the routine approach in many centres. At the heart of psychoanalytical theory are the assumptions that:

- no item of mental life or pattern of behaviour is accidental, rather it is the outcome of previous experiences
- thoughts, feelings and other aspects of mental activity and behaviour are trying to achieve something; that is, they are goal directed
- unconscious determinants mould and affect the way we perceive and react. These are thoughts of a primitive nature and are shaped by impulses and feelings within the individual of which he or she is unaware
- early childhood experiences are overwhelmingly important and pre-eminent over more recent experiences

Other theorists have also seen therapeutic approaches developed from their theories, the most important of which for work with children is that of Melanie Klein (Segal 1964).

Most psychotherapy offered today is less frequent and far less lengthy than that offered by Freud and his followers. Known as short-term dynamic (Davanloo 1980) or brief psychotherapy (Malan 1963) this work uses similar principles to the longer-term analyses, but there is a greater emphasis upon specific issues, and indeed most brief dynamic therapies depend upon finding a focus from which themes can be explored. Although in such approaches it is still seen as important to make the client aware of unconscious fantasies, the most fundamental therapeutic lever is seen as helping the client to rework relationship patterns that have been damaging. This is achieved through the relationship they develop with the therapist, a process that has been described as the 'corrective emotional experience' (Alexander and French 1946). Because of this emphasis, transference is perhaps of even greater importance in these types of approach, as is the need to establish a good therapeutic relationship quickly.

The appropriateness of the brief psychotherapy approach is illustrated by the finding that the success of psychotherapy in general often depends upon the quality of the relationship that is established between client and therapist (Orlinsky and Howard 1986). This type of brief psychotherapy is indicated if there is also a motivation to change, and the person has a circumscribed problem, with an absence of severe mental disorder (Malan 1976).

The effectiveness of psychotherapy has been examined in over 250 studies. On average, the results from these indicate that about 79 per cent of children will show some benefit from psychotherapy (Weisz *et al.* 1987), although on average children show only a 20 per cent improvement in their functioning (Weiss and Weisz 1990). Work with adults is beginning to suggest that no one type of psychotherapy is more effective than another (Andrews 1993), although techniques which focus upon observable behaviour may be particularly valuable for work with children (Kazdin 1990).

PLAY THERAPY

Play is the medium by which a child gains an understanding of the world. When confronted by difficult or poorly understood situations the child's natural reaction is to incorporate this into play, and by regular repetition there emerges an explanation and understanding which the child can adopt. The accuracy of this explanation is, however, dependent on many factors, not least of which is the child's limited understanding of the world and its complexities. It is not surprising then that play should be seen as the obvious medium by which to work therapeutically with a young child. The therapeutic approaches are broadly similar to the talking therapies, but the emphasis is shifted to using play as the medium of communication. It can operate on several levels. The play can be used as a method of communicating inner world feelings and so becomes the exact equivalent of the psychotherapy used in adults. Such work is again rooted in a theoretical model of child development, the most well known being those described by Anna Freud (1966) and Melanie Klein (Segal 1964).

The client-centred non-directive approach described by Rogers (1951, 1961) also has its equivalent in play therapy. The leading exponent of this type of approach is Axeline (1947), whose description of play therapy is the foundation for the many play therapists who are not practising within a formal psychoanalytical structure. She described eight rules for such practice:

1 quickly develop a warm, and friendly relationship;
2 accept the children as they present themselves, not as they should be;
3 the relationships should be permissive, allowing the children to express their feelings freely;
4 recognise and reflect feelings so that the child gains insight;
5 the responsibility for making changes is the child's;
6 the child's wishes give direction;
7 sessions are at the child's pace;
8 the only limitations are those of safety and responsibility within the therapeutic relationship.

Allan was referred at ten years of age because of the aggressive and hostile behaviour he was showing both at home and school. Allan had been adopted by his present family when he was five years of age, his life with his birth family having been one characterised by violence and neglect from being a baby. Allan had no explanation for his behaviour other than to say that he became angry when people 'bugged' him.

A regular sequence of play sessions was established which quickly became dominated by themes of tragedy (people being killed or seriously injured; rescue attempts being sabotaged). Gradually the therapist became a participant in the play and verbalised that it seemed that there was no way to help the characters of the games. Some three months into the sessions an additional theme began to emerge from the play. When the models and toys had been injured or hurt they would seek revenge, and would let nothing stand in the way of it being achieved.

Later, these elements faded somewhat and there were several sessions which focused upon being small and helpless in large, complex and confusing worlds. The therapist reflecting on how small and vulnerable that must feel increased the tempo of the play and its chaotic quality. Almost immediately after commencing the sessions Allan's aggressive behaviour at school faded, but became more evident at home. Seven months after commencing therapy Allan's behaviour at home began to moderate, but when therapy stopped after a year he was still seen by the family as more difficult than his siblings.

This description illustrates how play can be used by a child to portray his or her inner world. It also shows how recognising the link between apparently distinct play activities is often the key to understanding this portrayal. This example also illustrates a key factor that must be considered when deciding if therapy is appropriate. Effective therapy reduces the defences which the child is using to cope with the world, and this can be a very frightening experience. As a result, in the early stages of therapy there is often a deterioration rather than an improvement. Similarly, if the child is not in an environment in which he or she feels safe and secure the ability to take risks in therapy evaporates and little meaningful work is achieved. With the potential for so much emotional impact to occur within the sessions, and the possibility that the child does not feel secure enough to share, it is crucial that the pace of any work done within the sessions is set by the child.

As well as being a medium through which psychotherapy is pursued, play therapy can also be used more directly. As the child works through a difficulty or a painful experience, the play is usually transparent enough for an acute observer to see the underlying themes. This can be used as a basis for exploring such issues in more detail, and can also be used to offer alternative views and explanations. As with all psychotherapies, the sharing of emotions becomes an important element of healing, although within a play context it is easy to transfer such feelings on to other elements of the activity – for example, 'the doll is naughty and must be smacked'.

BRIEF (SOLUTION FOCUSED) THERAPY

As is discussed below, it is a fundamental tenet in the management of all animal behaviour that more is achieved by reward than by punishment. It is, however, only very recently that this fundamental has seen its expression in a dynamic (i.e. interpersonal) therapy. Brief solution focused therapy is an approach which can be seen as using this position as a starting point underpinned by the assumption that successful work depends upon knowing where the client wants to get to. From this flow the principles that understanding the problem is not necessary, and indeed focusing on the problem more than is needed for the client to feel heard is probably counterproductive. The philosophy here is that successful work depends upon taking the positive path, which means determining what the client is trying to achieve, working out the quickest way of achieving this goal, and detailing what they are already doing that might start them on this path (de Shazer 1991). This philosophy has become summarised in three rules:

1 If it ain't broke, don't fix it.
2 Once you know what works, do more of it.
3 If it don't work, then do something else.

Work usually, therefore, begins by identifying 'exceptions to the rule' of the problem, in other words identifying what is already working, even if this is only in very small pockets. The drive towards emphasising the positive means that even small acknowledgements that things are moving in a positive direction can be the start of a cascade of change which gathers momentum, carrying the client towards their desired goals.

There are several aspects to this type of approach which harness these basic themes. For example, a question like 'If a miracle has occurred and the problem is solved what will be the first thing you notice?' (usually described as 'the miracle question') may begin the process of clarifying the desired goals, and identifying the first steps that need to be taken to achieve them. These are then built upon by asking what the first small step they need to take might be to progress towards their goal. As with any therapy, the client will frequently doubt the progress, and usually does so by highlighting times when things have not gone as expected. However, these exceptions can also feed the therapeutic process, because subsequent questions can continue to emphasise the positive – 'Tell me about times it doesn't happen' or, if the statement is that it never stops, then the question might be, 'When does it happen least?' It is also important to realise that any pattern of improvement will consist of both forward and backward steps. When such situations occur the therapist can help the client to identify what resources, skills and techniques have been used to prevent slipping too far backwards, and through this recognition, additional strengths are acknowledged.

The content of a therapeutic session is flexible, the goal for each often being established by simple questions such as, 'How will you know at the end of the session that it was useful to come today?' The general aim of every session, however, is always to follow the basic behavioural principle of emphasising the positive, and to identify with the client those exceptions when the problem was stopped or did not occur. Techniques such as rating the occurrence and intensity of good spells can be used to demonstrate progress, but can also be valuable in identifying the next step towards the full solution. The framing of the questions around such elements adds to the overall emphasis upon the positive. For example, examining the most recent scores on the rating scale could prompt the question, 'What will be happening when you are just one point higher on the scale?', a question which contains an implicit assumption that the next point will be achieved.

This therapy approach is still relatively new, and detailed outcome studies of its effectiveness are not yet available. However, preliminary indications suggest that perhaps 60 per cent of cases report improvement (Macdonald 1997), and on average this is achieved by a three-session intervention (Berg and de Jong 1996).

GROUP THERAPY

Dynamic group therapy is useful to broadly the same type of person as the individual approach. It adds the extra dimensions of sharing difficulties with others and tends to reduce the sense of isolation, and thoughts that 'I'm the only one'. However, it does require the group members to be able to tolerate the frustrations which arise in sharing relationships, although for some this can have a therapeutic benefit in its own right.

These themes tend to result in groups being run for children, or parents, who have a shared experience or difficulty. In child abuse, for instance, this type of intervention is commonly used because the sense of personal isolation is reduced. In addition, if the group is working well there can be a tremendous sense of support which allows participants to share far more than they might have done in other circumstances.

FAMILY THERAPY

Children grow up not in isolation but with myriad influences playing upon them. These influences shape, alter and colour the child's evolving feelings and beliefs so that each adult becomes a unique individual, made up of the way that these developmental experiences interact with the person's genetic make-up and current life events. Recognising the importance of these influences opens a major branch of potential intervention, for if these influences can be changed in a helpful way, a lasting impact upon the adult that is to come may be achieved. In the 1960s many centres began to explore the potential for bringing about such change, and the main focus of this work was the family, for as Erikson has pointed out (see Chapter 1) it is the family which exerts the most powerful influence in the formative years.

Some therapy styles seek to detail the family's belief system, and acknowledging with them its content can help the family to explore new ways of relating (Byng-Hall 1995). This may involve working with the family in the construction of their family tree (known as a genogram), not only to record linkage, but more especially to recognise family traits and similarities (Lieberman 1979).

Today the most common style of family therapy is that based upon systems theory (Burnham 1986). The approach is less rooted in family history, concentrating instead upon day-to-day interactions and the impact one person's behaviour has on the other members of the family. By way of illustration, consider the child who is fearful of attending school. By considering the child in isolation the conclusion might be that an illness is present, a phobia of school. However, if a wider perspective is taken, it may be discovered that the child has a particularly close relationship with his mother, that he is not fearful of attending school but that his real difficulty is leaving his mother at home alone. His fear, perhaps, might stem from concerns about her health, particularly as she has been prescribed medication similar to that taken by his uncle, who died suddenly some six months ago.

Clearly this story may be greatly expanded, but hopefully it shows how links can arise between apparently disparate elements to cause a problem. The significance of this is that if these links are not identified and dealt with, the problem will not be resolved. Here, for instance, a programme aimed at helping the child overcome a fear of school would fail even though it is the apparent problem. Family therapy tries to clarify what influences are operating to maintain a problem, and then attempts to change them. This can sometimes be achieved merely by making the influences explicit, but usually also involves the setting of tasks.

Within this main thrust there emerge two broad schools. Structural therapy recognises that certain family patterns and make-ups are more helpful than others and seeks to set tasks and goals that move families towards these patterns. For instance, a child may be acting as a parent, with the new stepparent marginalised and prevented from taking any role within the family. The stepfather's complaint that the child will not go to sleep except in the parental bed has to be seen in this context. Helping the parents develop an equal relationship, to which the children are subordinate, and recognising that there is a boundary around the adults which children have to respect become key in resolving such problems (Mann *et al.* 1990). It is, of course, not always possible to help families achieve such change, but any movement along the path may be deemed to be helpful.

Alternatively, the family pattern of functioning can be used to identify the issues which are specifically maintaining the problem. In this type of approach it is assumed that the symptoms that are presented are in fact an unsatisfactory solution to the family's difficulties, and that by making the present symptoms even less successful at reducing the underlying difficulties a new pattern of family functioning will emerge. The therapeutic strategies used may be the same as a structural approach would identify but in general they tend to be more circumscribed and hence the tasks also tend to be more focused. For instance, asking the stepfather to take charge of bedtime routines in the above example may bring about a structural change, but its primary purpose is to evict the child from the parental bed. A variation on such strategic work can be the use of paradox (Cade 1984), where families who seem to fail to act on professional advice are approached with that very expectation in mind. The underlying principles for the interventions remain the same, but the tasks take on a more challenging quality.

One of the approaches which can be used in a paradoxical approach is that of reframing. Here the symptom is accepted and a different, positive explanation for its occurrence is offered. By offering this positive explanation its value in suppressing the more deep-rooted family problems is reduced, and so it becomes redundant. An example of such an approach might be to identify a child's soiling as a helpful thermometer of the parents' relationship.

In recent years the ethics around paradoxical work have been questioned, but the core elements probably still have a place in the strategic therapist's armoury (Shoham-Solomon and Jancourt 1985).

The effectiveness of family therapy

Research into family therapy has shown that such work, no matter what its style, can bring about major changes in a child's environment and presenting problems (Weisz *et al.* 1992). Summarising the results from nineteen outcome studies, 76 per cent of families improved through therapy, and improvement reached a peak some ten months after therapy had ceased (Markus *et al.* 1990). Five years after discharge these improvements had largely dissipated.

Work is also proceeding to try to identify what parts of the family work are the most powerful influences of change. These process studies show how reducing coalitions between a parent and child, and so establishing appropriate parental authority, helps to reduce problem behaviour (Mann *et al.* 1990), as does moving the parent's focus from organisational issues (such as bedtimes) to wider, more emotional themes (Heatherington and Friedlander 1990).

Brief solution focused family therapy

As was described above, recently there has been a rapid increase in interest in using this type of therapy, and this enthusiasm has also been evident within family therapy work. This is not surprising since the therapy was largely developed from a systemic perspective (de Shazer *et al.* 1986), the techniques are easily transferred into the family context, and the approach is proving to be equally effective when used with families (Berg 1994). As its name implies, the task of the therapist within sessions is continually to guide the conversation in the session towards solution talk. To do this the therapist fits in with the family process while highlighting exceptions to the rule that 'the problem is always there', the potential solutions they have already found, and the individual, or family, strengths which they themselves identify.

Sarah was twelve years of age when she was brought by her mother and grandmother because of their concern about the difficult behaviour she was displaying. Problems had begun after her grandfather's death a year ago. Since that time she had been stealing, lying and avoiding school at every opportunity. Both mother and grandmother clearly found Sarah's behaviour very annoying, and although they had identified the onset as coinciding with Sarah's grandfather's death, they found it difficult to understand why she was behaving like this.

The 'miracle question' was used to clarify that Sarah wanted to feel as she had before her grandfather's death, and that the adults wished she would behave as she did then. With this goal in mind, questions were asked which focused upon what they would notice about themselves after they had reached this goal, and by using scaling questions they clarified for themselves how close they were to achieving it. The first session showed they had already moved three points from the low ebb they had been at immediately after Sarah's grandfather died, recognising how this had been achieved and identifying strengths and resources which the family possessed and which they could use to move further forward.

Over the next three sessions each small positive change was highlighted and emphasised. When talk about problems began, exceptions were sought and so the focus was persistently kept upon encouraging solution talk. The homework at the end of each session was to record when each family member saw signs that her goal was being achieved. As this task highlighted the genuine affection which they had for each other, the irritation of the adults towards Sarah dissipated and the problem behaviour stopped. The last session was dominated by descriptions of how much they were now enjoying their time together, and how helpful Sarah had become once more.

BEHAVIOURAL APPROACHES AND THERAPIES

In contrast with the talking therapies, behavioural therapies place less emphasis upon helping the client to achieve insight into why he or she is exhibiting problem behaviour. Rather than dwelling upon the past or considering hypothetical underlying causes of problems, behaviourists are primarily concerned with observable, measurable behaviour in the here and now. In most cases the goal of therapy is to assist the client to change specific problem behaviour in ways which are predetermined.

Behavioural techniques have their origins in experimental studies of animal learning where it was found that behaviour could be systematically changed (conditioned) by modifying its consequences (reinforcement). Behavioural therapies are based upon the principle that all behaviour (adaptive and maladaptive) is learned and can thus be unlearned or replaced by alternative behaviours. Therapy consists of altering the client's environment in such a way that desirable behaviour replaces that which was giving rise to problems.

Behaviour therapies draw upon two major types of learning: classical and operant conditioning. Classical conditioning refers to the process by which a naturally occurring, largely involuntary, behaviour becomes linked with a neutral object or event (a stimulus) in such a way that the two become associated. As a result, the presence of the stimulus results in the behaviour's occurrence. This principle resulted from the famous studies of Ivan Pavlov at the beginning of the twentieth century, which showed how sounding a tuning fork when presenting food to dogs led to an association between the sound and the feeding process. As a result, the dogs would salivate (their typical response when anticipating food) when hearing the tuning fork, even if no meat were presented. Thus the dogs had, through classical conditioning, been taught to salivate at the sound of the tuning fork – a naturally occurring response had been linked to a new stimulus.

The findings from animal studies were subsequently applied to human situations. In a highly influential study, Watson and Rayner (1920) demonstrated the effectiveness of classical conditioning with an eleven-month-old child, Albert. When initially presented with a white rat, Albert showed no fear; when, subsequently, the rat's presentation was accompanied by a sudden, very loud noise, Albert became highly anxious and fearful. After several presentations of the rat and the noise together, the child became intensely fearful of the rat alone. In essence a previously neutral object, the rat, had become the source of a conditioned fear response.

A further study at about this time (Jones 1924) concerned another child, Peter, who was inordinately fearful of rabbits, and furry objects. Treatment involved gradual and systematic exposure to a rabbit while he was engaged in pleasurable eating activity. Positive, rather than negative, associations with furry animals were made and Peter's phobia disappeared.

Drawing upon these early studies of classical conditioning, many sophisticated techniques for treating problem behaviours have been developed. Perhaps the simplest example is the bell and pad treatment for nocturnal enuresis (bedwetting). When the sleeping child begins to urinate, a bell awakens the child and further urination is inhibited. This process is repeated nightly and, over time, the child associates the sensations from the bladder as it fills with the exercise of sphincter control. Eventually, the bladder's contents are contained all night without waking.

As Albert's case might suggest, classical conditioning underpins many treatments for phobias and other forms of emotional disorder. Techniques such as systematic desensitisation and emotive imagery (see Chapter 3), for example, through the process of association, involve the gradual substitution of a pleasant, relaxed state for the unpleasant anxiety or fearfulness previously experienced.

Operant conditioning, based upon the pioneering work of B.F. Skinner, is a rather different behavioural technique which emphasises the importance of consequences in maintaining and shaping an individual's behaviour. Where a behaviour is followed by a positive consequence, it is more likely to recur (i.e.

it can be said to have been reinforced). Where behaviour is not reinforced, it is less likely to be repeated.

Reinforcement is a key conceptual tool for analysing why people behave as they do and is of particular value for understanding and treating problem behaviour. Frequently, one finds that undesirable behaviour is reinforced in ways that are not always obvious.

Samantha, aged four, was a member of a class of children who were listening to the teacher read from a giant-sized book full of colourful illustrations. She was bored, restless and kept fidgeting. This was beginning to disturb the other children. As a means of deflecting her behaviour, Samantha's teacher asked her to come to the front of the class and help her hold up the book for the other children to see.

While the reactions of the teacher are likely to have resolved the immediate problem caused by Samantha's disruptiveness, a behavioural analysis would suggest that, in the long term, her reaction may have made things worse. The child's undesirable behaviour was rewarded by attention and the allocation of a 'high-status job'. If such situations were repeated, Samantha is likely to associate 'being a nuisance' with desirable outcomes and, as a consequence, the undesirable behaviour would be 'reinforced', that is, it would become stronger and be exhibited more frequently (see Chapter 7 for further case studies).

In contrast, there are many situations where desirable behaviours are not reinforced as frequently or as strongly as they should be. For some adults, because children are expected to behave appropriately, they are rarely rewarded by thanks, praise or more tangible rewards when exhibiting desired behaviour. Over time, the child finds that 'good' behaviour goes unrewarded while 'bad' behaviour often gains adult attention and can alleviate boredom.

It is exceedingly rare for any human behaviour to be reinforced each time it is exhibited and the term 'intermittent reinforcement' describes situations where behaviour is reinforced in an unpredictable fashion. In such situations one can never be certain when rewards will follow behaviour. When reinforcement is stopped completely, the individual will tend to persist in the undesired behaviour for a much greater period of time than in other situations where behaviour had consistently been reinforced. The principle of intermittent reinforcement helps to explain the immense hold which fruit machines exert over people, for the customer always hopes that reinforcement will take place next time!

Alan, aged nine, was allowed one chocolate biscuit a day by his mother, although continually pestered for more. His mother would usually refuse his requests for a second biscuit and, invariably, this would result in scenes where the boy would become highly demanding, either by pleading and coaxing or by becoming verbally aggressive.

On some occasions, his mother's resolve was strong and, however poor Alan's behaviour, her determination to 'stick to her guns' meant that he could not get his own way. On other days, however, her son's temper tantrums and pleading often became too much for her and on such occasions she would give in 'for a quiet life'.

The above case study represents a classic illustration of intermittent reinforcement. Because Alan can never be certain whether prolonging his undesirable behaviour will eventually result in the achievement of his desires, he is likely to persevere with demanding behaviour even when it is not being reinforced. The expectation that his goal will eventually be met is often so strong that parental resolve to resist is unlikely to modify the child's behaviour in the short term. Given such a scenario, it is hardly surprising that parents who decide to 'stand up to their child' often come to believe that their new stance is not working and are tempted to give up. Where this happens, the pattern of intermittent reinforcement is continued and future attempts to take charge are likely to be met by even greater resistance.

In work with challenging children, the selection and effective use of reinforcement to shape behaviour is often more difficult than it might first appear. Children vary greatly in what is reinforcing for them; for example, some may respond to stars and stickers, others may see these as childish and prefer more tangible rewards. While many parents perceive yelling and scolding to be a form of punishment, for some children, receiving parental attention, in whatever form, is highly reinforcing.

It is also often difficult to control reinforcement. The range of possible reinforcers is limited and these may be insufficient to counter the perceived rewards which are associated with the problem behaviour. The child may find peer admiration when disrupting a class, the excitement and emotional rush from stealing a car, the satisfaction obtained from baiting a family member to be far more attractive outcomes than any rewards which parents or teachers might be able to offer.

There are many behavioural techniques which are employed as parts of treatment programmes. Some of the most common forms of therapy are listed in Figure 2.1.

Behaviour therapies have been shown to be among the most effective types of child therapy (Kazdin 1990). They are the cornerstones of treatment for phobias and anxieties and are highly valuable in work with conduct disordered, challenging children and adolescents. They are accessible to clinicians operating in a wide range of disciplines and under appropriate supervision programmes can be operated by parents, teachers and many other relevant parties.

Unlike the use of medicines, behaviour therapy has no side-effects; unlike the talking therapies, it does not demand high-level verbal ability; and

positive reinforcement (e.g. praise, pocket money) follows the occurrence of a desired response (e.g. making one's bed). Such behaviour should occur more frequently in future. A process where positive reinforcement is used to change behaviour over a number of gradual stages is known as shaping (Chapters 3, 7, 8);

negative reinforcement an undesirable situation (e.g. being kept in at playtime) is removed upon the occurrence of a desired response (e.g. classwork is completed). Such behaviour should occur more frequently in future (Chapters 7, 8);

punishment an unpleasant situation (e.g. detention) follows the occurrence of an undesired response (e.g. failure to complete classwork). Such behaviour should occur less frequently in future (Chapters 7, 8);

extinction undesirable behaviour is not reinforced and, as a result, gradually disappears (e.g. the child exhibiting a tantrum is completely ignored until he or she exhibits acceptable behaviour) (Chapter 7);

token economy symbolic rewards (e.g. points, stars, tokens) are given in response to desirable behaviour. These can subsequently be exchanged for material items, such as money and sweets, or privileges, such as staying up to watch TV. In some programmes undesirable behaviour may result in a 'fine' where rewards are removed (sometimes known as 'response cost') (Chapters 7, 8);

contingency contracting an explicit agreement is drawn up between two or more parties which sets out desired and undesired behaviours and the rewards and sanctions which will be made contingent upon these (Chapters 3, 7, 8);

time out when specific, undesirable behaviours occur, the child is removed from all sources of positive reinforcement (e.g. the child is required to sit alone in the hall for a fixed period of time) (Chapter 7)

systematic desensitisation through relaxation training and a gradual exposure to a feared situation (via the imagination or in reality), a fearful or anxious state is gradually substituted by one of relaxation and calmness (Chapter 3);

emotive imagery closely allied to systematic desensitisation, this involves developing an association between the feared object and a heroic figure with whom the child identifies. This association permits the child to confront and reduce the feared situation (Chapter 3);

flooding/implosive therapy rather than introducing, through gradual exposure, that which is most feared (as in systematic desensitisation), the child is asked to imagine, or actually experience, this from the outset. Sometimes the feared object or situation is deliberately exaggerated to maximise its initial impact. The situation does not permit escape from the feared object or event and gradually the high level of anxiety lessens. The child comes to realise that the fear is unrealistic and that it can be controlled (Chapter 3);

modelling the child is asked to observe and imitate behaviour modelled by another (e.g. family member, therapist). Successful performance is subsequently reinforced. Modelling may be used in respect of phobias (e.g. holding a spider in one's hand) or conduct disorders (e.g. tidying up one's toys at bedtime) (Chapter 3).

Figure 2.1 Major forms of behavioural therapy (chapters where these are outlined, or form part of case illustrations, are listed in brackets)

unlike the group and environmental therapies it does not require the involvement of a range of other people or the regulation of wider environmental factors. Its non-diagnostic and non-stigmatising language helps prevent the formation of negative and excusatory self-concepts, particularly among adolescents with deep disorders and who search for ploys which neutralise therapeutic intervention.

(Hoghughi 1988: 98)

It has become increasingly recognised that narrow behavioural conceptions are often insufficient for understanding and treating complex behaviour disorders. For this reason, behaviour therapists now more readily take into consideration broader issues relating to the functioning and belief systems of the child and the family together with the impact of the wider social context (Messer *et al.* 1993).

COGNITIVE THERAPY

Cognitive therapy uses techniques from several sources to pursue its aim of helping people change the way they think about their problems, and their general functioning. As described in the context of treating depression (see Chapter 10), the basic principle on which cognitive therapy is based is that moods and feelings are directly influenced by thoughts and ways of thinking – known as cognitions. These cognitions include the inner dialogue we use to understand events, and the template by which we always judge certain events. So, for example, a summons to the boss's office may always prompt the spontaneous thought 'What have I done wrong?' even though there is nothing to suggest that this is the reason for the request. Using such 'spontaneous' explanations is not usually a cause of problems, but if they become routinely negative and make the person permanently anxious, angry or depressed, they become a source of major difficulty. Cognitive therapy seeks to change such explanations, and so produce a more accurate, and hopefully healthier, view of the world for the individual to live by.

The first major description of this type of therapy was given by Beck (1963, 1964) who studied its use with people who had severe depression. Since that time the therapy has undergone major development, and is now seen as a cornerstone of treatment for several conditions, for example, depression (Williams 1992), eating disorders (Hartmann *et al.* 1992) and stress-related conditions (Solomon *et al.* 1992). This value is especially true in children for whom, for instance, drug treatment in depression is not very useful and so cognitive therapy tends to be the first line of response (Vostanis and Harrington 1994).

DRUG TREATMENTS

Drug treatments can only be prescribed by doctors, and so for many situations where problems are being considered by other professionals, the role of drugs is not considered. In adults drug treatments have been a significant part of the way that doctors try to help people with major psychiatric problems. It is not surprising, therefore, that similar endeavours have been seen when trying to assist with emotional and behavioural difficulties that arise in childhood. The efforts have, however, been more muted because of concern about the long-term effects of giving any drug to a child. In addition there is the ethical dilemma that since problems in childhood can be strongly influenced by many factors, is it right to subdue the symptom and not tackle the cause? This dilemma can be illustrated by the child who demonstrates aggressive behaviour primarily as a result of his or her parents' own marital violence. Should such a child be treated with potent drugs to minimise what is, in effect, a natural response to such behaviour in his or her care-givers? Interestingly, the response to this question has tended to differ depending on which side of the Atlantic you live. In the UK the giving of drugs to children who do not have physical or demonstrable major psychiatric illness is rare. By contrast, American clinicians are much more likely to explore drug regimes (Campbell and Cueva 1995). These American studies have tended to confirm that for certain major psychiatric illnesses, such as schizophrenia (Spencer and Campbell 1994) and obsessional compulsive disorder (De Veaugh-Geiss *et al.* 1992), drugs are as useful in young people as they are in adults. For some major diseases however, most notably depression (Puig-Antich *et al.* 1987), drugs prove to be of little value.

The difference of approach is perhaps most clearly seen when thinking about aggressive behaviour. In the UK using drugs in an effort to modify conduct disorder or aggressive behaviour is very rare. By contrast, American physicians have explored several possible regimes, the most popular of which is lithium. Lithium is a drug used primarily in manic depressive illness to reduce the intense mood changes that are a feature of that disorder. The drug is very successful in achieving this, although there can be significant side-effects, and the dangers if the person becomes dehydrated are severe. The work which has been undertaken to look at its usefulness in reducing aggressive behaviour in children does not show that this drug is particularly helpful (Alessi *et al.* 1994), which perhaps tends to support adopting a general attitude of caution towards drug prescription in children. In most situations in the UK, therefore, it would be unusual for drugs to be seen as the first response to be offered.

MILIEU THERAPY AND INTENSIVE APPROACHES

Residential units

It has been a traditional response when confronted with someone who has severe emotional or behavioural problems to look to place them in a residential setting which can not only offer continuous assistance and treatment to the individual, but removes them from the community where their problems may be prompting concern or distress. In psychiatry this residential setting has been a hospital, in education a residential school, and in the social services arena may range from a residential family group home to a secure accommodation provision.

Such settings can offer an intensive intervention, and may permit specific treatment approaches (such as token economy schemes) to be implemented which would be impractical in more limited provisions. Over recent years, however, the role of residential settings has been severely questioned, and their use has tended to dwindle. Removal of children from their families and the community is always a detrimental step and must be weighed against the potential advantages. Hospital admission now tends to be of briefer duration, and is often used to provide a more detailed picture of the difficulties before deciding upon the best treatment regime.

The programmes offered in residential settings have to take account of the developmental stage which the child has reached. Regimes that would be suitable for young children would clearly be inappropriate for adolescents, and offering a suitable range of responses in what are usually quite small units is one of the major challenges which residential settings face. As with any effective intervention its content must be tailored to the needs of the individual but usually there are elements of work with the child individually as well as group activities. One of the most powerful elements that is at work in any treatment setting is the milieu. Because so much time is spent in residential settings, the power which this exerts in such environments is particularly important.

Milieu is difficult to define, and yet we all experience it several times a day. As human beings we are sensitive to the mood in a room, or the 'atmosphere' that exists in some meetings. Children are especially sensitive to ambience, and can be strongly influenced by it. Any therapeutic environment, therefore, is not only influencing the child by the stated treatment programme but by way the unit 'feels'. 'First impressions' and 'prevailing atmosphere' are indicators of the milieu which the unit is offering. This is partly to do with the physical environment, but is mostly made up of a blend of warmth and personal regard combined with clear expectations about behaviour and general conduct. A staff view that 'we care about you too much to let you do this' is an excellent foundation for a positive milieu, and once accepted as genuine can be far more powerful at bringing about change than a formal treatment strategy.

Day units

As mentioned above, one of the difficulties with residential treatment is the way that it separates the child from family and community. In recent years there has been a great upsurge in the provision of day treatment programmes (called partial hospitalisation in the United States) as a way of providing an intensity of care with the minimum of disruption to the day-to-day functioning of the child. As well as offering a greater intensity of involvement than can be achieved by outpatient appointments, such programmes allow the child to remain within the family, and this in turn produces issues and information that can be used to inform and progress family change. By remaining within their community children may also develop support networks through friends, school, and so on. These become particularly important when the day programme comes to an end.

While residential admission can be seen to be of assistance by immediately removing the child from the dysfunctional or damaging situation, day programmes expect improvement by gradually reducing the dysfunction, and building supports for the remainder to minimise its impact. In addition, with careful planning it is possible to provide very focused treatment packages which are age specific, and use the continued attendance at school and so on as a positive lever for change (Place *et al.* 1990).

Confronting and challenging inappropriate behaviour is a key element of the programmes offered by a variety of residential settings and day units. Many use the interpretative style described by Redl (1959) and which he called 'the life-space interview'. This seeks to use such situations not only to help the child recognise patterns and repetitions in their behaviour, but to assist them in developing new responses which are more appropriate.

The diversity of day unit programmes and the differing goals which they aspire to make it difficult to offer a general view on the effectiveness of such programmes. In units which deal with psychological difficulties about three-quarters of the children continue to have improved functioning two years after discharge (Place *et al.* 1990). These improvements are often not only in the presenting problem but also in the child's self-esteem and hopefulness about the future (Grizenko *et al.* 1993). Long-term follow-up studies show that for both residential and day treatment programmes two-thirds of the children have sustained their improvement after ten years (Erker *et al.* 1993).

Treatment foster care

With the issues of cost and separation from family making residential programmes less attractive, there has been a growing interest in whether children could be helped to overcome their difficulties by placing them in a substitute family whose purpose is to offer a therapeutic regime. For some children whose family of origin is limited in its parenting resources, moving to a family which offers good-quality care may be sufficient to bring about positive change. However, for more damaged children these substitute families have to offer a deliberately therapeutic regime, similar to those that might be offered in an inpatient unit. Interest in using treatment foster care has been increasing (Clark *et al.* 1994), and the initial results are quite encouraging. However, whether children who have received such treatment will maintain the improvement in their functioning in the longer term is still to be determined (Reddy and Pfeiffer 1997).

Voluntary agencies

In any locality there is a variety of voluntary and charitable agencies that may be helpful in dealing with difficulties. For instance:

- Relate is a voluntary agency that will help couples to explore, and hopefully resolve, relationship difficulties. Although the agency's workers are volunteers, as with other voluntary agencies, they are trained to ensure they can offer the appropriate skills necessary to help couples address their problems.
- Cruise is a voluntary service which helps both adults and children cope with bereavement.
- Victim Support gives practical advice and support to anyone who has been the victim of crime.
- Rape Crisis offers help and support to people who have been the victims of rape, though they usually only offer services to teenagers and adults.

In addition to such focused agencies the children's charities, for example, NSPCC, Barnardos, National Children's Homes (NCH), are increasingly developing specialised sources of help for specific situations – such as the victims of sexual abuse, or supporting children from very damaging homes who have been adopted. Such services tend to be patchy, but your local social services department will know what is available in your locality.

REFERENCES

Alessi, N., Naylor, M.W., Ghaziuddin, M. and Zubieta, J.K. (1994). Update on lithium carbonate therapy in children and adolescents. *Journal of the American Academy of Child and Adolescent Psychiatry* 33, 291–304.

Alexander, F. and French, T. (1946). *Psychoanalytic Therapy. Principles and Application*. New York: Ronald Press.

Andrews, G. (1993). The essential psychotherapies. *British Journal of Psychiatry* 162, 447–51.

Ashurst, P. (1991). Brief psychotherapy. In J. Holmes (ed.) *Textbook of Psychotherapy in Psychiatric Practice*. Edinburgh: Churchill Livingstone.

Axeline, V. (1947). *Play Therapy*. Boston: Houghton-Mifflin.

Beck, A.T. (1963). Thinking and depression. I. Idiosyncratic content and cognitive distortions. *Archives of General Psychiatry* 9, 324–33.

Beck, A.T. (1964). Thinking and depression. II. Theory and therapy. *Archives of General Psychiatry* 10, 561–71.

Berg, I.K. (1994). *Family Based Services: A Solution Focused Approach*. New York: W.W. Norton.

Berg, I.K. and de Jong, P. (1996). Solution-building conversations: co-constructing a sense of competence with clients. *Families in Society* 2, 376–91.

Bisson, J.I., Jenkins, P.L., Alexander, J. and Bannister, C. (1997). Randomised controlled trial of psychological debriefing for victims of acute burn trauma. *British Journal of Psychiatry* 171, 78–81.

Burnham, J.B. (1986). *Family Therapy*. London: Routledge.

Byng-Hall, J. (1995). *Re-writing Family Scripts*. New York: Guilford Press.

Cade, B. (1984). Paradoxical techniques in therapy. *Journal of Child Psychology and Psychiatry* 25, 509–16.

Campbell, M. and Cueva, J.E. (1995). Psychopharmacology in child and adolescent psychiatry: a review of the past seven years. II. *Journal of the American Academy of Child and Adolescent Psychiatry* 34, 1262–72.

Clark, H.B., Prange, M.E., Lee, B.L. and Adlai, L.B. (1994). Improving adjustment outcomes for foster children with emotional and behavioral disorders: early findings from a controlled study on individualized services. *Journal of Emotional and Behavioral Disorders* 2, 207–18.

Davanloo, H. (1980). *Short-term Dynamic Psychotherapy*. New York: Aronson.

de Shazer, S. (1991). *Putting Difference to Work*. New York: W.W. Norton.

de Shazer, S., Berg, I.K., Lipchik, E. and Nunnally, E. (1986). Brief therapy: focused solution development. *Family Process* 25, 207–22.

De Veaugh-Geiss, J., Moroz, G. and Biederman, J. (1992). Clomipramine hydro-chloride in childhood and adolescent obsessional-compulsive disorder: a multicenter trial. *Journal of the American Academy of Child and Adolescent Psychiatry* 31, 45–9.

Erker, G.J., Searight, H.R., Amanat, E. and White, P.D. (1993). Residential versus day treatment for children: a long term follow-up study. *Child Psychiatry and Human Development* 24, 31–9.

Frank, J.D. (1974). Therapeutic components of psychotherapy. A 25 year progress report of research. *Journal of Nervous and Mental Disease* 159, 325–42.

Freud, A. (1966). *The Writings of Anna Freud. Vol. 2. The Ego and Mechanisms of Defense*. New York: International University Press.

Freud, S. (1976). *Introductory Lectures on Psychoanalysis*. Harmondsworth: Penguin.

Garfield, S. and Bergin, A. (1994). Introduction and historical overview. In A. Bergin and S. Garfield (eds) *Handbook of Psychotherapy and Behaviour Change*. Chichester: Wiley.

Grizenko, N., Papineau, D. and Sayegh, L. (1993). Effectiveness of a multimodal day treatment program for children with disruptive behavior problems. *Journal of the American Academy of Child and Adolescent Psychiatry* 32, 127–34.

Hartmann, A., Herzog, T. and Drinkman, A. (1992). Psychotherapy of bulimia nervosa: what is effective? A meta-analysis. *Journal of Psychosomatic Research* 36, 159–67.

Heatherington, L. and Friedlander, M.L. (1990). Complementarity and symmetry in family therapy communication. *Journal of Counselling Psychology* 37, 261–8.

Hoghughi, M. (1988). *Treating Problem Children*. London: Sage.

Jones, M.C. (1924). The elimination of children's fears. *Journal of Experimental Psychology* 7, 382–90.

Kazdin, A.E. (1990). Psychotherapy for children. *Annual Review of Psychology* 41, 21–54.

Lieberman, S. (1979). *Transgenerational Family Therapy*. Guildford: Biddles Ltd.

Lindemann, E. (1944). Symptomatology and management of acute grief. *American Journal of Psychiatry* 101, 101–48.

Macdonald, A.J. (1997). Brief therapy in adult psychiatry–further outcomes. *Journal of Family Therapy* 19, 213–22.

Malan, D.H. (1963). *A Study of Brief Psychotherapy*. London: Social Science Paperbacks.

Malan, D.H. (1976). *The Frontiers of Brief Psychotherapy*. London: Hutchinson.

Mann, B.J., Borduin, C.M., Henggeler, S.W. and Blaske, D.M. (1990). An investigation of systematic conceptualizations of parent–child coalitions and symptom change. *Journal of Consulting and Clinical Psychology* 58, 336–44.

Markus, E., Lange, A. and Pettigrew, T. (1990). Effectiveness of family therapy: A meta-analysis. *Journal of Family Therapy* 2, 205–21.

Messer, S.C., Morris, T.L. and Gross, A.M. (1993). Clinical behavior therapy with children. In A.S. Bellack and M. Hersen (eds) *Behavior Therapy in the Psychiatric Setting*. New York: Plenum Press.

Orlinsky, D. and Howard, K. (1986). Process and outcome in psychotherapy. In S. Garfield and A. Bergin (eds) *Handbook of Psychotherapy and Behavioural Change*. Chichester: Wiley.

Place, M., Rajah, S. and Crake, T. (1990). Combining day patient treatment with family work in a child psychiatry clinic. *European Archives of Psychiatry and Neurological Sciences* 239, 373–8.

Puig-Antich, J., Perel, J.M. and Lupatkin, W. (1987). Imipramine in prepubertal major depressive disorders. *Archives of General Psychiatry* 44, 81–9.

Reddy, L.A. and Pfeiffer, S.I. (1997). Effectiveness of treatment foster care with children and adolescents: a review of outcome studies. *Journal of the American Academy of Child and Adolescent Psychiatry* 36, 581–8.

Redl, F. (1959). A strategy and technique of the life-space interview. *American Journal of Orthopsychiatry* 29, 1–15.

Rogers, C.R. (1951). *Client-centred Therapy*. London: Constable.

Rogers, C.R. (1961). *On Becoming a Person*. London: Constable.

Segal, H. (1964). *Introduction to the Work of Melanie Klein*. London: Heinemann.

Shoham-Solomon, V. and Jancourt, A. (1985). Differential effectiveness of paradoxical interventions for more versus less stress-prone individuals. *Journal of Counselling Psychology* 32, 499–513.

Solomon, S., Gerrity, E. and Muff, A. (1992). Efficacy of treatments for post traumatic stress disorder: an empirical review. *Journal of the American Medical Association* 268, 633–8.

Spencer, E.K. and Campbell, M. (1994). Children with schizophrenia: diagnosis, phenomenology, and pharmacotherapy. *Schizophrenic Bulletin* 20, 713–25.

Vostanis, P. and Harrington, R. (1994). Cognitive-behavioural treatment of depressive disorder in child psychiatric patients–rationale and description of a treatment package. *European Child and Adolescent Psychiatry* 3, 111–23.

Watson, J.B. and Rayner, R. (1920). Conditioned emotional reactions. *Journal of Experimental Psychology* 3, 1–14.

Weiss, B. and Weisz, J.R. (1990). The impact of methodological factors on child psychotherapy outcome research: a meta-analysis for researchers. *Journal of Abnormal Child Psychology* 18, 639–70.

Weisz, J.R., Weiss, B., Alicke, M.D. and Klotz, M.L. (1987). Effectiveness of psychotherapy with children and adolescents: a meta-analysis for clinicians. *Journal of Consulting and Clinical Psychology* 55, 542–9.

Weisz, J.R., Weiss, B. and Donenberg, G.R. (1992). The lab versus the clinic: effects of child and adolescent psychotherapy. *American Psychology* 47, 1578–85.

Williams, J.M.G. (1992). *The Psychological Treatment of Depression*. (2nd edn). London: Routledge.

3　School refusal

INTRODUCTION

Children may not wish to attend school for many reasons, ranging from boredom in class, fear of classmates, to a reluctance to leave their parents. The list of reasons is long and applies to most children at some time during the 15,000 hours that they typically spend in school.

Most children are likely to miss occasional days from school at some stage during their childhood because of what may often appear to an onlooker to be trivial fears or anxieties. Perhaps a lesson has been misunderstood and a teacher's anger is feared, or a best friend has teamed up with someone else. Usually such difficulties are resolved or quickly forgotten and school attendance soon resumes. Some children maintain a strong dislike of school throughout their childhood but accept the requirement to attend regularly. A much smaller proportion cease to attend school for a prolonged period of time; these are the individuals who usually come into contact with helping agencies.

TRUANTS OR SCHOOL REFUSERS?

A major distinction is often drawn between truants and school phobics (the latter are now more commonly termed school-refusers). Although truants also choose not to attend school they are usually perceived as experiencing no major psychological difficulty in attending; rather they prefer not to. In contrast, school refusers may wish to attend but often find that they cannot. To some extent, then, one distinction between truancy and school refusal centres upon volition. Truancy is widely perceived as one variant of acting-out behaviour, often associated with delinquency and disruptiveness, whereas school refusal is typically perceived as a form of neurosis characterised by anxiety and fearfulness. This widely held distinction is complicated because some writers (e.g. Kearney 1995) include all those who refuse to attend school, both truants and school phobics, under the broader, all encompassing heading of school refusal. This chapter, however, will maintain the generally accepted distinction between truants and school refusers.

In distinguishing school refusal from truancy, Berg *et al.* (1969) noted that unlike truants, refusers tend to share the following features:

- severe difficulty in attending school, often amounting to prolonged absence
- severe emotional upset. This may involve such symptoms as excessive fearfulness, temper tantrums, misery or complaints of feeling ill without obvious organic cause when faced with the prospect of going to school
- during school hours, the child remains at home with the knowledge of the parents
- absence of significant antisocial disorders such as juvenile delinquency, disruptiveness and sexual activity

In contrast, truants are more likely to attend school on a sporadic basis. They are typically not excessively anxious or fearful about attending school, nor do they usually complain about physical discomfort. Truants are more likely to conceal the absence from their parents, often by wandering the streets during the day, and are more likely to engage in antisocial acts. In a comparative study of truants and school refusers (Galloway 1983) parental reports indicated that truants were more influenced by peers and had a greater history of lying, stealing and wandering from the home out of school hours. In contrast, school refusers were reported as having more concerns about academic matters, were more anxious about parental well-being and were reluctant to leave the home. There were, however, no significant differences in peer relationships, the frequency of eating and sleeping difficulties or the proportion of cases of enuresis.

It should be recognised, however, that truants and school refusers do not always fall into clear-cut groups and a relatively small proportion of absentees show features of both truancy and school refusal. In one study of one hundred chronic absentees, for example, Bools *et al.* (1990) found that approximately 10 per cent of the sample demonstrated both emotional and antisocial conduct disorders.

PREVALENCE

Estimates of the prevalence of school refusal vary considerably, primarily because of the differing criteria that have been used to define the term. Where estimates of school refusal, not including truancy, are employed (consistent with the use of the term in this chapter) figures in the USA and UK generally range from 0.4 per cent to 2 per cent of the population.

TYPES OF SCHOOL REFUSER

Hersov (1977: 458–9) outlines a common picture of school refusal immediately recognisable to those with experience of such difficulties:

The problem often starts with vague complaints about school or reluctance to attend progressing to total refusal to go to school or to remain in school in the face of persuasion, entreaty, recrimination and punishment by parents and pressures from teachers, family doctors and education welfare officers. The behaviour may be accompanied by overt signs of anxiety or even panic when the time comes to go to school and most children cannot even leave home to set out for school. Many who do return home halfway there and some children, once at school, rush home in a state of anxiety. Many children insist that they want to go to school and are prepared to do so but cannot manage it when the time comes.

In addition to the psychological distress noted above, such children often complain of physical illness such as headaches, stomach aches, dizziness or vomiting for which there are no organic causes. In many cases these physical symptoms disappear once the child is allowed to remain at home. The high levels of anxiety may also be compounded by depression leading to tearfulness, sleeping difficulties, irritability and low self-esteem.

Although such a picture is common, it is important to recognise that there is no single form of school refusal. Major areas of controversy centre on, first, the extent to which school refusal should be seen as a consequence of fear of being in school rather than of separating from parents and home, and, second, whether there is a difference between those children whose non-attendance is sudden, as opposed to developing over a long period. In both issues the influences of age and gender are seen as important mediating factors.

Although Broadwin (1932) is credited as being the first writer to describe a form of persistent school absence marked by fearfulness and prolonged refusal to attend, Johnson *et al.* (1941) coined the term 'school phobia' to describe this phenomenon. According to these early theorists, the school refusing child had an excessively strong love attachment to the parent and fantasised about returning to the nourishing and protective maternal situation enjoyed in infancy. The mothers of such children were perceived as having similarly unfulfilled emotional needs and, as a result, became overprotective of their child and overdemanding of attention. It was thought that anger, resentment and hostility experienced by both mother and child in the resolution of the quest for independence/dependence resulted in anxiety about separation directly resulting in school refusal. This view became highly popular in the 1950s and 1960s to the extent that some writers (e.g. Johnson 1957) saw school phobia being replaced by separation anxiety as the key diagnostic criterion.

Separation anxiety is now seen by many practitioners as an inadequate explanation for all cases of school refusal. The theory does not explain why the peak age for school refusal is between the ages of eleven and thirteen (Last *et al.* 1987) rather than in the early years of schooling as the theory would suggest. Furthermore, many school phobic children appear to have little difficulty in separating from their parents for other social/recreational activities. Given these weaknesses in the theory, many contemporary writers tend to place equal emphasis upon the school itself as the source of anxiety (Pilkington and Piersel 1991).

In identifying differing types of school phobia, a distinction is often drawn between acute and chronic school refusal, a factor that may be important in the devising of appropriate interventions. Berg *et al.* (1969) suggested that where absence had been preceded by at least three years' trouble-free attendance, irrespective of current duration, the school refusal should be considered as acute. Other cases should be considered as chronic. Studies comparing children falling into these two categories have repeatedly demonstrated that chronic refusal is associated with a greater dependency, neurosis, a higher incidence of parental mental illness, less sociability and lower self-esteem. In contrast, acute refusal is associated with higher levels of depression.

Given the greater incidence of problems experienced by chronic cases and findings indicating that such children are often unlikely to be provided assistance by support services for several months, it is hardly surprising that the prognosis for chronic refusal is poorer than for acute cases (Berg 1970). Indeed, it is arguable that chronic cases are merely acute cases that have been allowed to persist over time.

Studies have been inconsistent and variable in determining both age and sex differences (Trueman 1984), although there is some evidence to suggest that separation anxiety is more a feature of younger female children while fear of school tends to be more prevalent in older male children (Last *et al.* 1987). There is some evidence, however (e.g. Smith 1970), that cases are high at the time of school entry and peak between the ages of eleven and thirteen (at a time when most children transfer from primary to secondary schooling). In general, studies suggest that older school refusers suffer from more severe disorders and have a poorer prognosis (Atkinson *et al.* 1985). Intellectual functioning in school refusers, contrary to earlier thinking, tends to mirror that of non-school refusers of comparable ages (Trueman 1984).

It is now widely accepted that school refusal is not a unitary syndrome but, rather, multi-causal and heterogeneous. As such, rather than focusing upon simple school phobia/separation anxiety or acute/chronic onset distinctions, it may be more helpful for practitioners to examine the needs of the child that are met by non-school attendance (Kearney and Silverman 1990). Understanding what the child gains by not attending school should help the practitioner derive the most effective forms of intervention. Kearney and Silverman's clinical and research work has led them to the conclusion that, for each individual, school refusal is maintained by one or more of four major categories (see Figure 3.1). Preferred modes of intervention for each of these categories can be outlined (see Chapter 2) and their effectiveness measured over time.

Category 1 Avoidance of specific fearfulness or general overanxiousness related to the school setting. This includes cases where one or more particular features of school (a corridor, toilets, test situations, a particular teacher) are feared. **Category 2** Escape from aversive social situations. This focuses on situations where problems centre upon unsatisfying relationships with others (peers and/or teachers). Often this incorporates an evaluative element. **Category 3** Attention-getting or separation-anxious behaviour. This may be manifested by tantrums and/or somatic complaints where the child's intention is primarily to stay at home with a parent or important other. **Category 4** Rewarding experiences provided out of school. Children who fall into this category may wish to remain at home because this provides opportunities for engaging in preferred activities such as watching the television or associating with friends.

Figure 3.1 Kearney and Silverman's functional categories for school refusal

ASSESSMENT

The heterogeneous nature of school refusal is such that a detailed assessment of the child is necessary in order to derive the most appropriate intervention. It is important that consideration is given to the child's affective, cognitive and behavioural functioning both generally and in relation to the specific context of the refusal. Most practitioners favour the employment of a range of procedures, including child interviews (in both one-to-one and whole family settings), the employment of self-report questionnaires, ratings of the child by significant others (e.g. parents and teachers), self-monitoring by the child (e.g. the use of a diary to record feelings and behaviours), direct behavioural observation of the child in the home and school setting and an assessment of family dynamics.

At the initial stages information about the child's general functioning at home and at school is sought. The precise nature of the refusal is explored in greater detail in order to ascertain the extent of the child's difficulty. Subsequently, consideration of specific aspects of the child's environment that induce fearfulness, together with examination of the responses of others to this, are examined. At this early stage, the practitioner may discover that school refusal is a secondary symptom of another, more pervasive difficulty. This may be a genuine physical illness, severe depression, agoraphobia, a complex learning difficulty, or more generally defiant or challenging behaviour.

Many practitioners advocate the use of self-report instruments that gauge children's perceptions of their feelings and emotions. Widely used measures include the Children's Manifest Anxiety Scale – Revised (Reynolds and Paget 1983), the Fear Survey Schedule for Children – Revised (Ollendick 1983), the

Children's Depression Inventory (Kovacs and Beck 1977; see Chapter 10) and the Social Anxiety Scale for Children – Revised (La Greca and Stone 1993).

Such scales typically ask children to respond to a variety of situations printed on a questionnaire. The Fear Survey Schedule for Children – Revised, for example, lists eighty situations that are potentially fearful (e.g. spiders, being in a fight, failing a test, having to go to hospital). For each, the child is asked to indicate whether he or she experiences no fear, some fear or a lot of fear. As a number of the situations relate to school contexts, this measure provides a useful means of differentiating between those whose difficulties relate specifically to one or more aspects of school life and those who experience a wider form of separation anxiety (Ollendick and Mayer 1984).

The only self-report measure that specifically addresses school refusal behaviour is the School Refusal Assessment Scale (Kearney and Silverman 1993) which attempts to ascertain what needs are served by the child's school refusal behaviour. This scale, which is available in child, teacher and parent versions, contains sixteen items, of which four questions each measure the relative influence of one of the four maintaining conditions (see Figure 3.1).

An important issue to assess in understanding what maintains any phobic behaviour is whether it is negatively or positively reinforced, that is whether the 'reward' is escaping from something unpleasant (negative reinforcement) or achieving a pleasing experience (positive reinforcement). In relation to school refusal, such an analysis involves considering whether avoidance of school is maintained because:

1 it results in the reduction or elimination of unpleasant experiences, such as no longer being teased by schoolmates (negative reinforcement); or
2 avoidance of school results in an increase in the experience of desirable outcomes, such as playing at home on one's computer (positive reinforcement).

Clearly, the intervention programme will differ greatly according to the nature of the factors that maintain the behaviour. An illustrative example is provided below.

Richard, a fourteen-year-old, was an only child living at home with his mother and her partner. Two years earlier his natural parents separated, and shortly after her new boyfriend moved in on a permanent basis. Richard spoke wide-ly of his liking for his mother's new partner although readily admitted that he would like to see his parents reunited.

Richard was referred to an educational psychologist on the grounds of his prolonged absence from school. His parents informed the psychologist that in order to persuade the boy to return to school they had bought him a motorcycle for use in the woods near his home. Richard, however, sub-sequently reneged on his promise to return to school and was now stating that he would only return to school if he were bought a more powerful machine. His mother informed the psychologist that she was prepared to accede to this request if it led to a return to school but she wasn't optimistic that this would be the case.

Detailed examination of Richard's situation resulted in the following observations:

1 There was little evidence of fearfulness and/or anxiety when Richard was in school (prior to the onset of the refusal and during a brief, ultimately unsuccessful, staged return trial programme).

2 Richard's day at home was undemanding and generally pleasurable. He got up late, watched the television or played with his computer. His mother and her partner were at work all day so he spent his time at home alone. Most evenings he met his schoolmates in the woods and rode his motorcycle. Occasional attempts to restrict his use of the motorcycle had been introduced but these appeared to make no impact upon his unwillingness to attend school. His mother had therefore ceased to use this threat as a means of persuasion.

3 Richard enjoyed good relations with most people with whom he came into contact. Apart from friction concerning his non-attendance at school, there was little conflict or hostility in the home. Richard appeared to have accepted his mother's partner and enjoyed going out with him to fish or to play sports. There was no indication of any specific difficulties at school (e.g. academic problems, bullying or harassment). His behaviour in class was good and his teachers were mystified by his unwillingness to attend.

4 From the outset, Richard was eager to establish a positive relationship with those professionals who were attempting to help him. His presentation of himself as relaxed and sociable was backed up by a rather jocular manner that appeared somewhat inappropriate.

5 Richard could not articulate any reasons for not attending school other than to state that he 'couldn't face it'. When pressed, he would clam up and become silent. If another topic was raised he would immediately become communicative once more. When asked about his bargaining over the replacement motorcycle he replied that he wanted it so badly that he would force himself to attend school.

6 Richard's mother was meeting regularly with her husband in order to persuade him to exert influence over their son. Father was coming to the house on a regular basis but family discussions usually ended with Dad losing his temper with Richard.

The investigation of Richard's case indicated that his school refusal was maintained primarily by the fourth of Kearney and Silverman's (1993) categories, that is, his school refusal behaviour was being positively reinforced by his out of school experiences. His enjoyable daytimes, together with the power he was exerting over the adults in his life, appeared to combine in the maintenance of his school refusal. This power not only resulted in his bargaining for material things but gave him control over his parents, frequently bringing them together, possibly in the hope that they might ultimately be reunited. School refusal may be a powerful weapon for a child who feels generally powerless to control a break-up of the family.

There was no indication that the other three functional categories had any bearing on this case. The implications for intervention were clear: change the reinforcement schedules operating at home (by relating access to enjoyable activities at home and in the evenings to school attendance and establishing a more appropriate daily routine (e.g. bedtimes, getting up in the morning); and engage the family in therapeutic work geared to the resolution of the family-based problems and tensions that were leading to the school refusal.

INTERVENTION APPROACHES

The many different conceptions and manifestations of school refusal, each with differing underlying causes and symptoms, have led to fierce debate about the most appropriate interventions and it has proven impossible to derive any one strategy that has proven effective or appropriate for all school refusers. What is clear is that if either support agencies or the school fail to work collaboratively, and fail to understand the contribution that other professionals will be making, the chances of a successful return are greatly reduced. The following sections deal initially with types of clinical intervention and then go on to consider the central role which the school plays.

In treating school refusal, a distinction is often made between psychodynamic approaches, which are concerned with disturbances of thought, feeling and behaviour, and which are typically addressed by means of some form of individual, group or family therapy, and behaviour therapy approaches based upon the premise that disordered behaviour is learned and can thus be unlearned through the use of a variety of 'behavioural' techniques. With regard to school refusal, behavioural approaches usually involve a graduated weakening of the relationship of school attendance with associated negative emotions, and ensuring that rewards and sanctions in the child's life become contingent upon desired behaviour (i.e. school attendance).

A number of techniques are used to address school refusal. These are based upon applications of talking therapy, behavioural techniques and medication (see Chapter 2). The most widely advocated techniques are:

- systematic desensitisation through relaxation
- emotive imagery
- shaping and contingency management
- modelling
- social skills training
- cognitive therapy
- family therapy
- medication

Each of these will be briefly described below:

Systematic desensitisation

Systematic desensitisation usually consists of a three-stage procedure (the reader is referred to Kratochwill and Morris (1991) for a more detailed account):

1 Teaching the client to become progressively relaxed. King *et al.* (1995) outline a helpful format of relaxation training that involves progressive muscle relaxation. The programme involves systematically tensing and relaxing muscle groups (e.g. arms and shoulders, legs and feet) with, for younger children, the assistance of associated mental imagery. It is suggested that no more than three muscle groups should be introduced in each 15–20-minute session.
2 Constructing a hierarchy of anxiety-evoking situations. The child and practitioner agree upon a target fear (such as attending school). The child is presented with a number of blank cards and is asked to write down briefly about each situation (e.g. undressing for PE) where that fear is evoked. The child is asked to outline situations where there are differing degrees of fearfulness or other forms of emotional discomfort. Cards are then ranked in order of fearfulness. Additional cards are completed as necessary in follow-up sessions until there is a hierarchy ranging from zero-level fearfulness to that which evokes the most extreme emotions.
3 Replacing anxiety by relaxation for each of these situations. Once the child has become skilled at practising relaxation techniques he or she is asked to imagine each of the situations on the cards, commencing in ascending order. Usually, three or four situations are considered in any one session. The intention is that the fearful situation becomes associated with being in a relaxed state and, as a result, anxiety is diminished.

Emotive imagery

Emotive imagery is another fear reduction method that closely resembles systematic desensitisation. First employed by Lazarus and Abramovitz, it involves the association between each situation on the fear hierarchy with imagined scenes which 'arouse feelings of self-assertion, pride, affection, mirth and similar anxiety-inhibiting responses' (1962: 191). Typically, the child's usual hero images (e.g. a famous footballer) or activities that are greatly desired (e.g. driving a speedboat) are elicited, imagined and then related to items in the fear hierarchy by means of a narrative. As with systematic desensitisation, as anxiety is gradually inhibited in each of the lower-level items, the procedure is repeated until the highest item can be considered without undue anxiety. Despite the caveat expressed by Kratochwill and Morris (1991) that this method has yet to be supported by controlled research studies, the approach is recommended widely by clinicians and is considered to be particularly effective with primary-aged children (King *et al.* 1995).

Shaping and contingency management

Contingency management procedures are based upon behavioural principles whereby the influence of events taking place before and after specific behaviours is highlighted and subsequently modified to effect desired behavioural change. For school refusal, this approach involves maximising rewarding experiences for being in school and minimising the rewards for remaining at home during the school day. Common elements include the reduction of parental or sibling attention when the child is at home, the removal of pleasures such as the use of television and computer during school time and during evenings and weekends.

Shaping refers to a procedure where the child's behaviour is gradually modified by means of contingent reinforcement, until a desired result is achieved. This may involve a number of steps: for example, rewards for undertaking homework at home, progressing to undertaking homework in a friend's house, undertaking homework in a classroom with a parent after school hours, attending school for one lesson each day, attending for half a day, and so on. At each step, the child's successful behaviour is reinforced by praise and attention and by those more tangible rewards that are deemed appropriate.

Modelling

This approach is based upon the premise that an individual may acquire behavioural dispositions as a result of the process of observing another individual. A popular approach for many child phobias, it involves the child observing a model (e.g. the therapist, peer or significant other) engaging in the behaviour that is feared. This may take place either by means of live modelling or through film and imagination. The child observes the model successfully handling the situation with no adverse consequences. Subsequently, the child is asked to imitate the performance of the model. As a result, the child's anxiety is reduced and appropriate skills acquired.

It is important to note, however, that many of the studies reported in the literature deal with less complex social situations than those relating to school attendance. Typically, these studies concern a fear of animals (often dogs) dental or medical procedures. Although modelling techniques have also proven valuable in work with children who lack social skills/confidence (King *et al.* 1995), many fearful situations (e.g. showering in public, going to the toilet, performing in PE) are not easily modelled. Furthermore, controlled studies of the effectiveness of this technique for cases of school refusal are very few (Kratochwill and Morris 1991).

Social skills training

Closely allied to modelling approaches, social skills training involves assisting the child to perceive and understand the behaviour of others and to respond in a more appropriate and skilled fashion. In relation to school refusal, such training is geared to help the child manage interpersonal situations more effectively, so reducing anxiety about evaluation by peers and/or teachers. Social skills training typically includes such skills as listening, non-verbal and verbal expression, recognising the position of others and self-assertion.

Cognitive therapy

Underlying many cognitive therapy approaches is the assumption that patterns of thinking and self-statements about one's ability to cope with potentially challenging situations result in the maintenance of adverse emotions and unpleasant physical sensations and inappropriate, maladaptive patterns of behaviour. A range of approaches has been designed to tackle such faulty thinking, among the most popular being rational-emotive therapy (Ellis 1984), cognitive therapy (Beck 1976) and self-instruction-training (Meichenbaum and Goodman 1971).

With regard to school refusal, such approaches operate on the basis that the child perceives an aspect of school attendance as dangerous (usually because it is considered that harm may result to the child at school or to the caregiver at home). The child does not consider himself or herself to be capable of managing the situation and as a result anxiety/fearfulness increases. By remaining at home, the problem is avoided, anxiety is reduced and school refusal is reinforced.

Cognitive approaches involve the clinician and child in an investigation of unhelpful, inappropriate and unrealistic beliefs that are subsequently challenged and, hopefully, replaced by new understandings. During this process the child is helped to identify and monitor self-statements that lead to anxiety or fearfulness. Maladaptive thoughts (e.g. 'My classmates will laugh at me if I answer a question incorrectly') are contrasted with competing, more positive conceptions (e.g. 'Everyone makes mistakes from time to time; other children are unlikely to take much notice of me') and the child is shown how these may alternatively result in anxiety production or reduction. (See Chapter 10 for a description of how cognitive therapy is used in practice.)

Family therapy

This technique is outlined in greater detail in Chapter 2 so will be only briefly discussed here. In the case of school refusal, the problem is often not seen as merely residing in the child, or even in the mother–child relationship, but rather as a product of faulty family functioning. Kearney and Silverman (1995) describe five differing types of family of school refusers: enmeshed and overdependent; coercive and marked by conflict; detached with little interaction among family members; isolated, with little interaction with people outside of the family; healthy families with a child with an individualised psychopathology. According to these writers, each of these types of family will require different forms of therapeutic intervention. Such interventions will also be heavily influenced by the theoretical form of family therapy to which the therapist subscribes.

It should be noted that while assessment of family functioning and some form of family work are universally advocated, it is rare that family therapy, in isolation, is seen as the preferred mode of treatment. In a recent survey of treatment approaches operated by a large sample of American psychologists, Kearney and Beasley (1994) found that work with families tended to focus upon parent training and contingency management (see Chapter 8); family therapy did not register as a specific treatment. It is possible, however, that a rather different picture would have emerged if psychiatrists and social workers, rather than psychologists, had been canvassed.

Medication

Drug treatment, usually in the form of antidepressants or tranquillisers, is frequently employed in the United States as one element of intervention programmes. Perhaps the most widely employed form of medication in the United States is imipramine hydrochloride, an antidepressant that can reduce panic attacks (Last and Francis 1988). Although these writers state that the advantages of using this drug as an adjunct to behaviour therapies are 'extraordinarily clear', a note of caution is introduced by King *et al.* (1995), who point to the existence of a number of side-effects including rare incidents of damage to the heart and more common symptoms of nausea, weight loss and allergic reactions (see also Waters 1990). In Britain, the use of medication for school refusal is far more controversial. In a recent review Murphy and Wolkind (1996: 148) looked at the evidence for the use of antidepressants for school refusal and concluded that: 'given the availability of safer psychological therapies, antidepressant treatment is not generally recommended'.

Combining methods to create individual programmes

Kearney *et al.* (1995) argue that practitioners should assess the particular needs that are served by school refusal and suggest that these are usually typified by one of four categories (see Figure 3.1). Such an assessment can provide clear guidance as to appropriate intervention. Kearney *et al.*'s suggestions are outlined below.

Where school refusal is predominantly the result of a *strongly phobic reaction to being in school*, intervention would normally involve the gradual reduction of anxiety or fear by means of some form of desensitisation. In essence, the goal is to assist the child to be able to think of, and subsequently attend, school with progressive reduction in emotional reaction.

Where school refusal is primarily a *means of avoiding social and/or evaluative situations*, modelling, role play and social skills training techniques are widely advocated. In addition, counselling which aims to change the nature of the child's perceptions, thoughts and beliefs (cognitive therapy) is advocated.

Where the problem results primarily from a *desire to obtain caregiver attention*, parent training focusing upon the use of contingent use of attention and the use of reward systems is advocated (see Chapter 8 for further details).

Where school is refused because *home has more attractions* (for example, television, staying in bed, playing computer games), family therapy and the systematic use of rewards and sanctions (contingency contracting) are suggested. In such situations, there may often be conflict between family members on the appropriate way of dealing with the problem (typically, one family member advocating a 'get tough' line, another arguing for a need to be sympathetic and indulgent). Such conflict often provides the child with attention and an inconsistent parenting regime. The systematic and contingent use of rewards may include the use of computer/TV, pocket money, outings, toys. Sanctions for non-attendance may involve the removal of such incentives and limitations placed upon evening and weekend activities.

It is important to recognise, however, that these approaches should not be limited to particular categories and that in many cases school refusal may result from a combination of factors. As with all problems, interventions should be closely tailored to the needs and dispositions of the individual child in a flexible and sensitive fashion.

The role of the school in intervention

The majority of published studies and reviews have been produced by American researchers (often with a medical background) who have little expertise or professional involvement in educational matters. The focus for these writers is usually the child and family system and school is often taken as a given to which the child should accommodate. It is perhaps for this reason that the literature makes little reference to examining the ways by which the school can help a child to overcome a reluctance to attend. It is clear, however, that school settings where bullying, truancy or disruption proliferate, where there is rigid streaming that can result in the child being placed in a class containing a significant proportion of disaffected, alienated peers, where teacher–pupil relationships are impersonal or generally hostile, where toilets and other public areas are not closely monitored by staff, are all likely to be important factors in contributing to school refusal. In such cases operating at the level of the child and the immediate family may prove insufficient for resolving non-attendance.

The role of teachers is crucial both in identifying difficulties at an early stage and in providing as supportive and as facilitative a school environment as possible. Early signs of persistent school refusal may include occasional absences, excessive anxiety and frequent complaints about feeling unwell. Some children may seem preoccupied with concerns about home and the well-being of family members, others may seem hypersensitive to seemingly trivial incidents in school. Given widespread agreement that a swift return to school increases the likelihood of successful reintegration, it is essential that teachers are alert to possible present or future cases of school refusal and, where the child's needs cannot be catered for by school-based personnel, readily seek the assistance of support agencies at an early stage. Where teachers, particularly those in senior management, and education social workers have a sound understanding of school refusal and appropriate intervention techniques, however, much of the early diagnostic and treatment work can be undertaken before other services become involved. Thus, training teachers in skilled and effective management of school refusal can lead to a reduction in the referral rate of school refusers to psychologists and psychiatrists (Blagg and Yule 1984).

Unlike truancy, the child's absence may be explained by parents on the grounds of minor medical ailments such as head or stomach aches. In such cases school registers will indicate absence on medical grounds and scrutiny of attendance patterns by education welfare services may not identify the existence of a problem until a later, and potentially more intransigent, stage. Here, the vigilance of the school nurse may also prove particularly valuable.

In cases of school refusal teachers also have an important role to play in managing the school environment. This may involve making short-term modifications to the child's timetable, ensuring that opportunities for the child to be unsupported in threatening situations (e.g. break and lunch times) are reduced, that inquisition of the child about recent absences is minimised and that the child has ready access to teachers should additional guidance, support or counselling be required.

Blagg (1987) outlines a number of school-based considerations that are important for an effective return to school:

1 Academic-related concerns. Does the child need help to catch up with work that has been missed? Will individual tutorials by specialist teachers be necessary? Does the child have learning difficulties that will need to be addressed? Will it be possible to set up a graduated reintegration package where, initially, only some lessons will be attended? Will the child remain in school at other times?
2 Peer-related concerns. Are measures necessary to ensure that victimisation, in the form of bullying or taunting, does not take place? Does the child require a means of avoiding potentially threatening break- and lunch-time settings? Are teachers aware that the child may need to have a low profile in the classroom (e.g. by avoiding situations where they are required to read aloud or answer questions in front of their classmates)?
3 Teacher-related concerns. Does the child have a particular anxiety about one or more teachers? Is it appropriate to change the child's class in order to accommodate specific teacher- (or peer-)related anxieties or can the problem be resolved through other means?

It is essential that the school can provide a suitably quiet area where the child can begin the school day and be based when not in class. At the early stages of reintegration it is possible that the child may show signs of panic or anger and it is advisable that an area free from onlookers is reserved for dealing with such difficulties. A trusted teacher who greets the child at the beginning of the school day and prepares them for entry to the classroom can help to minimise potential difficulties, as can the involvement of close friends who are sympathetic to their classmate's difficulty.

It is important that teachers recognise that the child's seemingly irrational fears are meaningful rather than dismissed as attention-seeking or fanciful. It should be recognised that even where a child's physical discomfort does result from psychological rather than organic causes, the adversity of the experience is no less real or unpleasant. Nevertheless, while demonstrating a sensitivity to the child's feelings, it is unwise to engage in lengthy and repeated discussion with the child about these symptoms as this may have a reinforcing effect.

Where school refusal is seen as genuine by teachers, school-based factors that contribute to the problem are often de-emphasised in favour of a focus upon the excessive child–parent dependency of separation anxiety theories (King *et al.* 1995). Some teachers may fail to recognise the effect their interpersonal style has upon the highly sensitive child and find references to this, however sensitively handled, by senior colleagues or support professionals to be demeaning or inaccurate.

It is also important to be sensitive to wider, whole-school influences. A number of practitioners (Hersov 1985; Blagg 1987; King *et al.* 1995) have noted that school refusal is associated with high staff and student absenteeism rates, low levels of achievement, large class sizes, high levels of indiscipline, low staff morale, a management style characterised by authoritarianism and rigidity, and teachers who are themselves authoritarian, anxious or eager to obtain student approval. Despite such considerations, it is rare that a change of school is recommended in the literature. In cases where children do change school difficulties often recur but are now compounded by the child's unfamiliarity with teachers and peers. A change of school is usually only advisable where the child's school refusal is wholly related to a specific educational context that is unlikely to be successfully modified. Even then, anxiety may be displaced to the new setting (see case study, Stacey, below).

Stacey, a thirteen-year-old girl, had displayed anxiety about attending her local secondary school after a child in another class had been murdered in front of her schoolmates by an intruder. Concurrently, she had also been subject to bullying by other girls who had teased and tormented her. After periods of sporadic attendance, marked by frequent arguments, crying fits and somatic complaints, absence became almost total. Stacey's mother (a single parent with no other children), believing that school was not recognising the nature of her daughter's difficulties, arranged for her daughter to transfer to another secondary school several miles away. As there had been no difficulties in primary school, it was anticipated that Stacey's problems would be left behind her.

At first, Stacey settled happily into her new school and enjoyed good relations with her new schoolmates. There was no recurrence of the bullying and she liked her new teachers. After four months, however, she began to become increasingly anxious before school each morning and her sleep pattern became disturbed. After six months she stopped attending school totally. Investigation by the school's educational psychologist suggested that Stacey's difficulties did not relate to a specific feature of her new school; rather, the earlier trauma had continued to haunt her. A graduated return programme, involving attendance at some lessons and, at other times, the provision of work in a quiet room, was established and appeared initially to be succeeding. After a few weeks, however, this programme failed as Stacey's mother unexpectedly withdrew her daughter from school with the stated intention of educating her daughter at home. Mother stated that she did not have the emotional strength to continue to insist that Stacey attend school each day and could no longer cope with the stress that was being experienced at home. She then declined to have any further involvement with clinical support services.

In the light of the discussion above, this case study illustrates two important points:

1 The unwillingness of the staff at the first secondary school to demonstrate a recognition of, and sympathy towards, Stacey's difficulties alienated the family, reduced mother's commitment to seeking a school-based solution and delayed the involvement of appropriate support agencies.
2 A change of school may not resolve a problem even if its origins are clearly located in the original setting.

Immediate or gradual return to school?

A major issue in school refusal is whether the child should be forced to return immediately or through a more graduated procedure, perhaps after a period at a specialised off-site education unit. Clearly, prolonged absence from school increases the difficulty of reintegration:

> With each day out of school more lessons are missed, difficulties in keeping up with other children mount, work accumulates, the embarrassment in finding suitable excuses for teacher and children increases, and the advantages of 'staying away from it all' become greater every day. Return to school becomes progressively more difficult. These secondary factors . . . very often overshadow the (original) cause and make it difficult to isolate the precipitating events. They may form a barrier to effective treatment.
>
> (Glaser 1959: 219)

Kennedy (1965) argues that forced procedures (technically known as *in vivo* flooding) are appropriate for school refusal, particularly for acute cases where onset is rapid and there has been no prior history of similar problems. The advantage of such an approach is that return to school can be immediately reinforced, opportunities for the child's non-attendance to be reinforced by being at home are minimised, and the problem is not compounded by the factors noted by Glaser above. Such an approach, however, can prove highly stressful for both child and parents and may be perceived as unethical by some parties. In addition, the programme may require a high level of ongoing supervision from support agencies that proves to be unavailable.

One of the strongest advocates of forced return approaches is Blagg (1987) who outlines a detailed programme focusing upon each of the steps necessary for establishing a return to school. This outline provides helpful and practical guidance, particularly for those practitioners with limited experience of school refusal. Topics covered include: preparing the child, parents and teachers for return; establishing what changes are necessary at school and at home; establishing an effective system for ensuring the child arrives at school each day (initially, with one or more escorts); and establishing monitoring and follow-up procedures. Although forced return approaches require that the child remain in school all day, it is accepted that the child's placement on the normal school timetable may be introduced in a step-by-step fashion.

In contrast, gradual exposure approaches involve returning the child to school initially for those situations that cause minimal anxiety. Gradually the period in school is increased until full attendance is achieved. Often an emphasis is put upon attending for the last part of the day in order that the natural reinforcer of going home at the end of the school day is operative. This approach is generally less stressful than full forced return for the child and family, although the risks of the child's non-attendance being reinforced by spending more time at home are greater.

Blagg and Yule (1984) compared the relative efficacy of differing intervention techniques for a sample of sixty-six children who were refusing school. Thirty children received behaviour therapy consisting of contingency contracting and enforced return to school (*in vivo* flooding), twenty received home tuition for two hours a day and psychotherapy on a fortnightly basis at a child guidance clinic. The remaining sixteen were hospitalised, received regular therapy inputs and tranquillisers as appropriate. At a one-year follow-up, the return to school group demonstrated significantly improved attendance with 93.3 per cent of the sample having been judged as successfully returning to school, while the hospitalised and home tuition groups had made very little progress (37.5 per cent and 10 per cent success rates respectively). In examining attendance rates at follow-up, it was discovered that 83 per cent of the forced return group were attending school more than 80 per cent of the time, while only 31 per cent of the hospitalised group and none of the home tuition group reached this level.

What form of intervention is the most effective?

Despite the relatively detailed literature on intervention with school refusers, it is widely noted that the vast majority of publications refer to individual or multiple case studies that have not been subject to experimental control. Often, the nature of the children's difficulties is inadequately discussed so that it is unclear to what extent problems are related to separation anxiety rather than to school-based factors. There is also no indication of the extent to which there is evidence of severe emotional difficulties, such as clinical depression. Where the outcomes of interventions have been examined (e.g. Blagg and Yule 1984), it has been assumed that school refusers are essentially alike, a proposition that does not appear to be justifiable. A further difficulty in judging the efficacy of treatment results from the use of a number of techniques in combination (e.g. systematic desensitisation, contingency management and drug therapy). As a result, it is difficult to ascertain the unique contribution of each.

PROVISION FOR SCHOOL REFUSERS

Legal considerations

Under the 1969 Children and Young Persons Act those of statutory school age who failed to receive an appropriate education could be placed in the care of the local authority. This resulted in many chronic non-attenders (both truants and school refusers) being placed in foster or children's homes. Many children's homes provided education on the premises and, thus, the legal requirement that the child received education was met. Such establishments often catered for delinquent, conduct-disordered children and in the minds of many professionals these homes were often more appropriate for truants than school refusers. It is perhaps for this reason that legal proceedings were more likely to be pursued where the child was perceived as an unwilling truant rather than as psychologically unable to attend school.

The introduction of the Children Act in 1989 removed the use of care orders solely on the grounds of non-school attendance. In their place Section 36 created a new education supervision order that provides a framework for education welfare services to work with the child and the family. Where the child's parents can demonstrate that they are doing everything they can to encourage the child to return to school, the supervision order does little more than ensure a continued forum for the continuance of professional support (see Robertson (1996) for further details).

It is possible for parents to provide education in the home setting, either by the employment of a home tutor or by educating their child themselves. The relevant local education authority must be satisfied as to the suitability of the education and will inspect the nature of the arrangements. Although this may be a highly attractive proposition to parents struggling with a highly anxious child (see case study, Stacey, above), and the quality of the child's learning could be high given the availability of appropriate tutors, it is questionable whether such an option would maximise such a child's future adult functioning.

The role of support services

In most cases of prolonged absence from local authority schools, the first point of contact for school staff will be the education welfare officer (EWO), sometimes known as an education social worker (ESW), who is often attached to a patch of schools in a defined geographical area. The EWO has particular responsibility for screening school registers and intervening in cases of poor school attendance at an early stage. Depending upon local circumstances, those whose absence appears to stem from fearfulness, anxiety or depression may be considered to require more specialised help and would then be likely to be referred to one or more support agencies, usually the LEA educational psychology service, the district health child and family psychiatry or child guidance services or the local authority social services department. In some cases, parents will seek specialist referral to these services themselves, usually via the school or the family doctor.

Many of these services incorporate a variety of professionals, psychologists, psychiatrists, social workers, occupational therapists, nurses and child therapists. Most of the techniques outlined in this chapter may be undertaken by any of these professionals, although emphases will differ. It is likely, for example, that the educational psychologist would have a greater role in addressing important school-based factors (e.g. exploring how the child may be assisted with academic difficulties) whereas the child psychiatrist would be more likely to be closely involved in working with medical colleagues and in prescribing medication. Given the differing perspectives that can be held by professionals involved in tackling school refusal, it is essential that close liaison exists and opportunities for the provision of conflicting advice are minimised. As Blagg (1987) notes, a failure to achieve such liaison can result in the anxious parent becoming even more confused and unsure how to proceed. Furthermore, it may help the resistant parent to ignore any recommendations for action. Blagg recommends that educational psychologists, by virtue of their educational and clinical expertise, are best placed to co-ordinate multi-professional involvement, although recent changes in psychologists' work patterns have made this more problematic. Particular stresses result from the pressure upon educational psychology services to undertake increasing numbers of statutory assessments of children with special educational needs and the widespread use of time-contracting, by which educational psychologist time is allocated to each school on a pro rata basis. These factors often reduce the educational psychologist's availability and flexibility in responding to individual cases. There may be little time for intensive, ongoing casework and this may preclude the psychologist from monitoring the child's progress and intervening where necessary on a sufficiently intensive basis.

Provision alternative to school

Home tuition

In the United Kingdom many local education authorities provide home tuition for school refusers. This may involve a visit to the home by a peripatetic support teacher for one or two sessions per week with periodic review by an education social worker or educational psychologist. Given that Blagg and Yule's (1984) study found home tuition with psychotherapy to be a highly unsuccessful technique (to such an extent that the authors queried whether this might have even inhibited spontaneous remission), there must be serious doubts as to the efficacy of such an approach. Where such provision is complemented by local authority support services working actively to ensure a return to school, the prognosis may be more favourable (see, for example, Tansey 1995).

Pupil referral units

A number of local education authorities have established off-site provision, pupil referral units, which cater for children with various difficulties that preclude them from attending mainstream school on a temporary or permanent basis. Although the majority of units cater primarily for children whose disruptive behaviour has resulted in exclusion from school, they may include children with other needs: for example, school refusers or pregnant schoolgirls. Usually, these units each address specific difficulties as it would generally be inappropriate to group together highly aggressive, disruptive children with those whose difficulties are very different (Department for Education 1994). There has been little systematic research to examine the effectiveness of such units with school refusers.

Hospitalisation

Inpatient treatment for school refusal is rare in the United Kingdom although part-time placement in child psychiatry department day units is more widely employed. Usually, inpatient treatment is associated with more severe symptoms, particularly depression, and greater incidence of family disruption and dysfunction (Borchardt *et al.* 1994).

Berg (1991) states that while it may be difficult to get the child to accept admission to hospital, once achieved, emotional upset usually improves and a graduated return to school can be planned. The relatively generous availability of psychiatric staff permits support in escorting the child to school and in the provision of a range of appropriate therapies. Murphy and

Wolkind (1996) support the use of hospitalisation where other approaches have failed, the child is becoming increasingly anxious or depressed and/or parents have effectively lost control of their child. They add, however, that potential dangers of this procedure are that hospitalisation can increase the likelihood that the child becomes scapegoated for all the family's problems and is emotionally or physically excluded. In return, the hospitalised child may feel rejected by the family and hostile to its members.

OUTCOMES

As noted above, the likelihood of a positive outcome appears to be related to the severity of the disorder, the age of onset, and the immediacy of treatment intervention. Studies of adults suffering from neurotic disorders (particularly agoraphobia) indicate that a significant number were school refusers as adolescents (e.g. Berg *et al.* 1974). A number of studies have followed up school refusers in adulthood (e.g. Berg and Jackson 1985; Flakierska *et al.* 1988, 1997). In general, these suggest that approximately one-third of cases continues to experience severe emotional disorders and/or problematic social relationships into adulthood, although it should be noted that samples often contain children who were hospitalised – usually the most severe cases.

REFERENCES

Atkinson, L., Quarrington, B. and Cyr, J.J. (1985). School refusal: the heterogeneity of a concept. *American Journal of Orthopsychiatry* 55, 83–101.

Beck, A.T. (1976). *Cognitive Therapy and the Emotional Disorders.* New York: International Universities Press.

Berg, I. (1970). A follow-up study of school phobic adolescents admitted to an inpatient unit. *Journal of Child Psychology and Psychiatry* 11, 37–47.

Berg, I. (1991). School avoidance, school phobia and truancy. In M. Lewis (ed.) *Child and Adolescent Psychiatry: A Comprehensive Textbook.* London: Willliams and Wilkins.

Berg, I. and Jackson, A. (1985). Teenage school refusers grow up: a follow-up study of 168 subjects, ten years on average after inpatient treatment. *British Journal of Psychiatry* 119, 167–8.

Berg, I., Nichols, K. and Pritchard, C. (1969). School phobia – its classification and relationship to dependency. *Journal of Child Psychology and Psychiatry,* 10, 123–41.

Berg, I., Marks, I., McGuire, R. and Lipsedge, M. (1974). School phobia and agoraphobia. *Psychological Medicine* 4, 428–34.

Blagg, N. (1987). *School Phobia and its Treatment.* London: Croom Helm.

Blagg, N. and Yule, W. (1984). The behavioural treatment of school refusal – a comparative study. *Behaviour Research and Therapy* 22, 119–27.

Bools, C., Foster, J., Brown, I. and Berg, I. (1990). The identification of psychiatric disorders in children who fail to attend school: a cluster analysis of a non-clinical population. *Psychological Medicine* 20, 171–81.

Borchardt, C.M., Giesler, J., Bernstein, G.A. and Crosby, R.D. (1994). A comparison of inpatient and outpatient school refusers. *Child Psychiatry and Human Development,* 24(4), 255–64.

Broadwin, I.T. (1932). A contribution to the study of truancy. *American Journal of Orthopsychiatry* 2, 253–9.

Department for Education (1994). *Circular 11/94: The Education by LEAs of Children Otherwise than at School*. London: DFE Publications.

Ellis, A. (1984). *Rational-emotive Therapy and Cognitive Behaviour Therapy*. New York: Springer.

Flakierska, N., Linstrom, M. and Gillberg, C. (1988). School refusal: a 15–20-year follow-up study of 35 Swedish urban children. *British Journal of Psychiatry* 152, 834–7.

Flakierska, N., Linstrom, M. and Gillberg, C. (1997). School phobia with separation anxiety disorder: a comparative 20–29 year follow-up study of 35 school refusers. *Comprehensive Psychiatry* 38, 17–22.

Galloway, D. (1983). Truants and other absentees. *Journal of Child Psychology and Psychiatry* 24(4), 607–11.

Glaser, K. (1959). Problems in school attendance: school phobia and related conditions. *Pediatrics* 23, 371–83.

Hersov, L. (1977). School refusal. In M. Rutter and L. Hersov (eds) *Child Psychiatry. Modern Approaches*. Oxford: Blackwell.

Hersov, L. (1985). School refusal. In M. Rutter and L. Hersov (eds) *Child and Adolescent Psychiatry. Modern Approaches* (2nd edn). Oxford: Blackwell.

Johnson, A.M. (1957). School phobia. *American Journal of Orthopsychiatry* 27, 307–9.

Johnson, A.M., Falstein, E.I., Szurek, S.A. and Svendsen, M. (1941). School phobia. *American Journal of Orthopsychiatry* 11, 702–11.

Kearney, C.A. (1995). School refusal behaviour. In A.R. Eisen, C.A. Kearney and C.E. Schaefer (eds) *Clinical Handbook of Anxiety Disorders in Children and Adolescents*. Northvale, NJ: Aronson.

Kearney, C.A. and Beasley, J.F. (1994). The clinical treatment of school refusal behavior: a survey of referral and practice characteristics. *Psychology in the Schools* 31, 128–32.

Kearney, C.A. and Silverman, W.K. (1990). A preliminary analysis of a functional model of assessment and treatment of school refusal behavior. *Behavior Modification* 14, 340–66.

Kearney, C.A. and Silverman, W.K. (1993). Measuring the function of school refusal behaviour: the School Refusal Assessment Scale. *Journal of Clinical Child Psychology* 22, 85–96.

Kearney, C.A. and Silverman, W.K. (1995). Family environment of youngsters with school refusal behavior. *American Journal of Family Therapy* 23(1), 59–72.

Kennedy, W.A. (1965). School phobia: rapid treatment of fifty cases. *Journal of Abnormal Psychology* 70, 285–9.

King, N., Ollendick, T.H. and Tonge, B.J. (1995). *School Refusal: Assessment and Treatment*. Massachusetts: Allyn and Bacon.

Kovacs, M. and Beck, A.T. (1977). An empirical-clinical approach toward a definition of childhood depression. In J.G. Schulterbrandt and A. Raskin (eds) *Depression in Childhood: Diagnosis, Treatment, and Conceptual Models*. New York: Raven Press.

Kratochwill, T.R. and Morris, R.J. (eds) (1991). *The Practice of Child Therapy*. New York: Pergamon Press.

La Greca, A.M. and Stone, W.L. (1993). Social Anxiety Scale for Children Revised: factor structure and concurrent validity. *Journal of Clinical Child Psychology* 22, 17–27.

Last, C.G. and Francis, G. (1988). School phobia. In B.B. Lahey and A.E. Kazdin (eds) *Advances in Clinical Child Psychology*, Vol. II. New York: Plenum.

Last, C.G., Francis, G., Hersen, M., Kazdin, A.E. and Strauss, C. (1987). Separation anxiety and school phobia: a comparison using DSM-III criteria. *American Journal of Psychiatry* 144, 653–7.

Lazarus, A.A. and Abramovitz, A. (1962). The use of 'emotive imagery' in the treatment of children's phobias. *Journal of Mental Science*, 108, 191–5.

Meichenbaum, D.H. and Goodman, J. (1971). Training impulsive children to talk to themselves: a means of developing self-control. *Journal of Abnormal Psychology* 77, 115–26.

Murphy, M. and Wolkind, S. (1996). The role of the child and adolescent psychiatrist. In I. Berg and J. Nursten (eds) *Unwillingly to School* (4th edn). London: Gaskell.

Ollendick, T.H. (1983). Reliability and validity of the Revised Fear Survey Schedule for Children (FSSC-R). *Behaviour Research and Therapy* 21, 685–92.

Ollendick, T.H. and Mayer, J.A. (1984). School phobia. In S.M. Turner (ed.) *Behavioral Theories and Treatment of Anxiety*. New York: Plenum.

Pilkington, C. and Piersel, W.C. (1991). School phobia: a critical analysis of the separation anxiety theory and an alternative conceptualization. *Psychology in the Schools* 28, 290–303.

Reynolds, C.R. and Paget, K.D. (1983). National normative and reliability data for the Revised Children's Manifest Anxiety Scale. *School Psychology Review* 12, 324–36.

Robertson, I. (1996). Legal aspects. In I. Berg and J. Nursten (eds) *Unwillingly to School*. (4th edn). London: Gaskell.

Smith, S.L. (1970). School refusal with anxiety: a review of sixty-three cases. *Canadian Psychiatry Association Journal* 15, 257–64.

Tansey, K. (1995). This can't be my responsibility: it must be yours! An analysis of a reintegration programme for a school refuser. *British Journal of Special Education* 22(1), 12–15.

Trueman, D. (1984). What are the characteristics of school phobic children? *Psychological Reports* 54, 191–202.

Waters, B. (1990). Pharmacological and other treatments. In B.J. Tonge, G.D. Burrows and J.S. Werry (eds) *Handbook of Studies on Child Psychiatry*. Amsterdam: Elsevier.

4 Attention deficit disorder and hyperactivity

Children who present with difficult and disruptive behaviour are a major concern both to parents and schools. Children with these difficulties who are also restless, find it difficult to settle to tasks, and have poor impulse control, have for some years been distinguished as perhaps presenting a different problem from that of merely poor behaviour.

Labelling of this group of children has undergone many changes with terms such as hyperactivity, hyperkinesis and attention deficit becoming almost interchangeable as different views and emphases have held sway. Unfortunately, the usefulness of such concepts has become devalued, not only because of this confusion of labelling, but because the terms have come into common parlance where they have been applied to any child whose behaviour is difficult, and who in certain settings demonstrates a resistance to comply with tasks. This obviously intensifies the confusion about what people mean when they refer to someone as 'hyperactive' and it becomes even harder to make sense of the bewildering amount of information which exists on this topic.

TERMS IN USE

Over the years, various features and difficulties have been associated with this condition but there are three elements of key importance.

- Attention deficit is a pattern of behaviour in which the child shows only a brief concentration to tasks imposed by adults, and over any period of play the young person will often change activities quite rapidly. This is increasingly seen as the core feature of this problem.
- Overactivity (often called hyperactivity, and sometimes called hyper-kinesis) is an increased tempo of physical activity. The commonest element is fidgeting, but it may take the form of not being able to sit still for more than a few moments, or of restlessly pacing up and down the room. It is important to realise that this is a true increase of physical activity, as has been demonstrated when the physical movements of these young people are compared to resting levels (Porrino *et al.* 1983).

- Impulsiveness is where a child will act upon a wish or desire without thought to its consequence. In some situations this can take the form of quite dangerous behaviour (such as running into roads), but most often it is a pattern of breaking rules without thought to what might happen as a result.

DIAGNOSTIC CONSIDERATIONS

The confusion over labelling has, over recent years, become especially marked. As already pointed out the core feature is increasingly being seen as a difficulty with attention, and now the term attention deficit disorder (ADD) has become widely accepted, and is the term used in the American diagnostic standard manual (DSM-IV) (American Psychiatric Association 1994). Such children show persistent difficulties with attention span, and distractibility. If there is also a picture of restlessness then it is said to be attention deficit hyperactivity disorder (ADHD). The details of the diagnostic criteria for this condition are set out in Figure 4.1.

In defining the international classification, however, the World Health Organisation has retained the term hyperkinetic disorder (World Health Organisation 1992). This definition is far more stringent than the ADD one and requires features of restlessness to be present as well as difficulties with attention.

The proposal that problems with maintaining attention are at the heart of the difficulties is an attractive one, and much research effort has been concentrated on trying to delineate the mechanism. The attraction comes in the way that the observed symptoms would be logically explained by a difficulty in regulating the wealth of sights, sounds and information which press in upon all of us. If our filtering mechanisms should falter it must have a profound effect upon our functioning.

However, it has been pointed out (Taylor 1995) that attention problems could take several forms – problems with controlling attention, selecting what to attend to, sustaining attention, or not attending intently enough. Determining the exact nature of the deficit is clearly important, and there is increasing evidence that these children have a difficulty in processing information (Leung and Connolly 1994), and so a key mechanism may be the child's difficulty in inhibiting responses to the inappropriate elements of this information deluge (Schachar and Logan 1990). Taylor (1995) has described this as cognitive impulsiveness, and there is a great deal of work now going on to try to understand its exact role in causation.

A POTENTIAL CLASSIFICATION STRUCTURE

How can we bring some structure to this confused situation? In fact the way forward begins by recognising that attention deficit disorder is an encompassing term, and that within it there are different subgroups of

A *EITHER* Six (or more) of the following symptoms of *inattention* have persisted for at least six months to a degree that is maladaptive and inconsistent with developmental level:

- often fails to give close attention to details or makes careless mistakes in schoolwork, work or other activities
- often has difficulty sustaining attention in tasks or play activities
- often does not seem to listen when spoken to directly
- often does not follow through on instructions and fails to finish schoolwork, or chores (not due to oppositional behaviour or failure to understand instructions)
- often has difficulty organising tasks and activities
- often avoids, dislikes or is reluctant to engage in tasks that require sustained mental effort (such as schoolwork or homework)
- often loses things necessary for tasks or activities (e.g. toys, schoolwork, pencils, books)
- is often easily distracted by extraneous stimuli
- is often forgetful in daily activities

OR Six (or more) of the following symptoms of *hyperactivity/impulsivity* have persisted for at least six months to a degree that is maladaptive and inconsistent with developmental level:

- often fidgets with hands or feet or squirms in seat
- often leaves seat in classroom or in other situations in which remaining seated is expected
- often runs about or climbs excessively in situations in which it is inappropriate (in adolescents this may be subjective feelings of restlessness)
- often has difficulty playing or engaging in leisure activities quietly
- is often 'on the go' or often acts as if 'driven by a motor'
- often talks excessively
- often blurts out answers before questions have been completed
- often has difficulty waiting turn
- often interrupts or intrudes on others (e.g. butts into conversations or games)

B Some hyperactive–impulsive or inattentive symptoms that caused impairment were present before seven years of age.

C Some impairment from the symptoms is present in two or more settings.

D There must be clear evidence of clinically significant impairment in social or academic functioning.

E The symptoms do not occur exclusively during the course of another condition.

Figure 4.1 Attention deficit disorder (DSM-IV)

people with distinctive characteristics, each of which will probably require a different emphasis when it comes to intervention.

If, for example, we consider the British research, then the children that meet the diagnostic criteria tend to fall into two groups. The first is a group whose problems appeared early in life, often with a history of difficulties around the birth. They are clumsy, and have delays in motor, cognitive and language skills, such as speech acquisition. These young people are in contrast to the members of the other group who present later in life with difficulties which are most evident in school. This group often has associated learning difficulties.

To these two distinct groups can be added those children whose difficulties appear to be mostly within the home, and, indeed, are often only apparent when the child is in the care of one particular parent. If we finally add in the studies which have identified that for some children the problems seem to be related to specific foods (Egger *et al.* 1985), then we have the basis for a logical structure to describe this problem.

Within this structure, attention deficit disorder, as determined by the DSM-IV, would have four subtypes:

- *Subtype I – Predominantly a school-based problem* – the difficulties emerge after the school career has started and there is usually a pattern of not settling to task, frequently leaving the seat, and disturbing other children. The child's parents or carers generally have few concerns about behaviour, and would not seek help without the urging of teachers. Careful analysis and assessment usually reveals educational difficulties – either through specific difficulties such as dyslexia, or a more generalised inability to cope with the schoolwork.
- *Subtype II – Family focus* – here the problems are primarily seen within the home, and consist of persistent defiance and disobedience. There may be problems with destructiveness, or even fire setting, and friction with siblings is very common. There is usually family adversity either in the form of marital conflict, or social deprivation and poverty. Teachers generally report fewer problems with the child's behaviour, and there are no real difficulties when they are with relatives or family friends.
- *Subtype III – Conduct/oppositional* – as will be seen later, there is frequently a conduct component to the profile of a child with attention deficit. If conduct problems dominate the picture then these should be the principle focus for any intervention.
- *Subtype IV – Pervasive hyperactivity* – this pervasive subtype is typified by a young person who has difficulties evident both at home and at school. They often began very early in life, and show the features of poor attention, and overactivity. This subtype can probably be further divided into three sub-classifications:

  1 Organic – children who had a difficult birth, are delayed in some of their milestones and subsequently are clumsy and unco-ordinated.

Sometimes there are symptoms to suggest that the child may be experiencing some seizure activity.

2 Dietary – the child's problems often developed upon weaning, and in many cases a cow's-milk allergy may have been identified. The child has other signs of an allergic tendency, such as asthma or eczema, and often the family has already identified that certain foods seem to make the behaviour much worse.

3 Undifferentiated – this group has the features in all parts of their life but none of the above aspects pertain.

In the present state of knowledge this classification gives a sound basis from which to consider not only other aspects of this disorder but, more importantly, how to intervene in a helpful manner. The origins and causes of the pervasive subtype have attracted the most interest, and there is now strong evidence from twin and genetic studies to suggest a genetic origin (Faraone *et al.* 1992), and in approximately one-quarter of the siblings of this group of children similar problems will be seen (Faraone *et al.* 1996).

PREVALENCE

Differences in diagnosis between Europe and North America explain why there is as much as a twentyfold difference in the rate of children identified with attention deficit between the two continents (Taylor 1994). It also means that conclusions drawn from clinical studies need to be considered in the light of the type of diagnosis that was being used.

This difference in approach can be illustrated by the finding that among British children perhaps as many as a quarter show features that are similar to those used to diagnose attention deficit disorder in America (Goodman and Stevenson 1989). The US rates, therefore, which range from 9 per cent to 14 per cent of all children (Weiss 1991), are an estimate of the encompassing disorder which includes all of the subtypes described. Using the tightest definition, which is the basis for the pervasive disorder described above, the rate in Britain is between 1 and 3 per cent of the population (McArdle *et al.* 1993), and is four times more likely in boys (Ross and Ross 1982).

ASSOCIATION WITH CONDUCT DISORDER

One of the features which has been inextricably linked with this disorder since its first description is conduct disorder, which is a pattern of antisocial behaviour where there may be episodes of stealing, lying and truanting. Of course, there are many reasons which can account for the onset of conduct disorder, the major one being persisting family difficulties (Loeber and Stouthamer-Loeber 1986). However, the frequency with which attention problems and conduct disorder occur together has prompted much research into whether there is a link between the two.

One of the most interesting studies in this area shows that if at three years of age a child has the hyperactivity component as part of their attention difficulties, then this is a strong predictor of conduct disorder in later childhood (Stevenson *et al.* 1985). If the hyperactivity does not emerge until eight or nine years of age, however, the likelihood of conduct disorder is no greater than in the general population (Fergusson *et al.* 1993). All of these children are, however, at risk of educational failure which tends to reaffirm that the early onset, pervasive subtype of attention deficit is distinct from those who show most of their difficulties in educational settings.

The conclusions from the research into this area are that the two problems of attention deficit and conduct disorder tend to coexist, rather than one being the direct consequence of the other. However, if attention deficit is present, this does increase the likelihood of conduct disorder occurring especially if there is also psychosocial adversity, such as poverty or marital violence (Schachar and Tannock 1995). It is also worth noting that conduct and attention deficit disorders seem to have an intensifying effect on each other, so the problems which occur when both are present are greater than the problems which either attention deficit or conduct disorder exerts on its own (McArdle *et al.* 1995).

Martin was a seven-year-old boy presenting with violent outbursts towards his younger sister and a continuous refusal to comply with his mother's wishes. In the evenings she found it hard to prevent him destroying toys which he did when he became frustrated in any way. Martin was always difficult to settle to bed, constantly demanding his mother's attendance and the routine had therefore become that Martin would sleep in his mother's bed. The day was always punctuated with battles – over dressing, washing, what to have for breakfast, and so on. This picture contrasted starkly with that seen in school where Martin was settled, performing well and presented no behavioural difficulties to the staff. Such a stark contrast between two environments points to a problem within relationships, and it became evident over time that Martin's mother was struggling with a significant depressive illness which had prevented her from establishing a clear and consistent pattern of management with him.

Treatment of this depressive illness, and a series of sessions focusing upon management, allowed Martin's mother to establish a clear and decisive parenting approach. With its introduction Martin said he now felt happier, and that he could cope with no longer being allowed to sleep in his mother's bed.

This illustrates the importance of assessing a child's behaviour in several settings. A pattern of behaviour problems specific to one area is a strong indication not of attention deficit but that there are issues within that setting that the child is reacting to.

INTERVENTION

The evaluation of what is the most helpful way to deal with such children has been made more difficult by the different types of definition that have been used. Because of this, studies have often not been looking at the same types of child and this has made it difficult to compare one study with another. However, using the classification set out here we can follow a logical path of assessment to determine how to intervene most successfully.

If there is a suspicion that there is a problem with attention deficit the first need is to confirm that the types of symptom described in Figure 4.1 are present, and to what degree. Within school it is common to compare children with their peers to make such judgements, and a qualitative difference with the rest of the children on the areas mentioned is a good starting point. The picture can be obtained not only by asking detailed questions about the child's history and performance in other settings, but by using one of the many questionnaires which specifically identify attention deficit symptoms – such as the Revised Ontario Child Health Study Scales (Boyle *et al.* 1993), the Child Behaviour Checklist (Achenbach and Edelbrock 1991) or the modified Rutter Parent Questionnaire (Goodman 1994).

In such cases it is also worthwhile carrying out an assessment of how long the child can stay on everyday tasks, such as reading, drawing, watching television, playing computer games. This type of information gives a good insight into whether staying with a task is a persistent problem.

With confirmation that this is a case of attention deficit disorder the next stage is to determine into which subtype it falls. Information about the child's present difficulties, when they started, and the child's educational functioning help to determine whether the problems are present in just one setting, such as school, which gives a strong clue that issues within that setting are likely to be at the heart of the difficulties that are being seen.

At this stage professional help can then be sought. The family doctor can arrange for a referral to the local child psychiatry service, or the school's doctor can be approached to advise about the best way of further assessing the child. If the issues have a strong school theme, then the educational psychologist for the school is going to be a valuable source of help. If the problems are particularly family focused, then social services or the health visitor can also be approached for help and advice.

If the major focus of concern, and indeed the reported history, is one of conduct/oppositional-type problems then these behaviours need to be examined and their origins understood. For some, sometimes referred to as 'adrenaline junkies', it is the thrill and excitement of the misdeeds, while for others the problems may be driven by a need to challenge parental authority as part of the adolescent process. In many there are clearly longstanding problems with control by the family. Having gained such an understanding, intervention should be focused upon bringing about change, and this often has a significant component of behavioural management.

Social services may already be involved if these problems are of a significant degree, and often these services have a range of strategies that they can offer to help with such problems.

As the name implies, the family focus subtype will need a careful family assessment to detail the themes and issues which are contributing to the problem behaviour. This may indicate that a course of family therapy is appropriate, or there may be evidence that the principal carer is suffering from a depressive illness which demands treatment in its own right.

An early onset, developmental delays and a problem in various settings point to a pervasive hyperactive subtype, and often the first step in responding to such children is to consider the possibility of a dietary component.

DIETARY APPROACH

The interest in how diet influences behaviour had a significant boost from the work of the team at Great Ormond Street Hospital in the mid-eighties (Egger *et al.* 1985). This work showed that hyperactive behaviour could, in some young people, be significantly influenced by diet. The work also highlighted the difficulties there are in finding an effective approach to assessing and treating such children. In particular the work showed that each child had a unique pattern of allergies, so no universal diet could be offered, and that each young person was allergic to more than one item, with the result that simply stopping one or two things was unlikely to be helpful.

The only way to carry out a successful assessment is therefore to minimise food item intake over a test period and monitor the response. This is called an oligoantigenic diet because, by having so few food items, the number of problem items (antigens) that the young person might face is minimised. Figure 4.2 shows the type of advice sheet that could be given to parents to carry out such a dietary trial.

As with all such trials of treatment, the progress needs to be monitored as accurately as possible. This can be done either by means of a specific scoring sheet or by using one of the questionnaires described above.

ORGANIC CAUSES

As was pointed out in discussing the features of this pervasive subtype, children who find it hard to maintain attention often have features in their history suggesting developmental delay or birth difficulties. This should raise the question of whether the child's problems are arising because of physical anomalies in the brain. Most commonly this may show as epilepsy. If any such elements are suspected, then a medical opinion should be sought through the family's or the school's doctor. The assessment will involve various neurological tests, and probably an electroencephalogram (EEG), which records the electrical activity of the brain. If anything is found, then it may be necessary to offer medication or other treatments which are specific for the problem detected.

THE PROBLEM

For a small number of children and young people, eating specific foods and/or additives can lead to unmanageable behaviour.

The research

A large research study at Great Ormond Street Hospital showed that it was common for two or three substances to be affecting any one child, so that it was useless to look for the guilty food by stopping one thing at a time. They also found that each child was unique in the combination of food that affected them. Their research identified that there are very few foods where there is no reaction by any child. To find the culprit, virtually everything has to be given up then restarted.

THE SOLUTION

The solution is in three stages.

Stage One – The Comparison

It is necessary to compare the child's behaviour before and during the specific diet to see if it has changed significantly. A chart is used to help assess the child's behaviour for the week before the specific diet starts. Using the scale of 0 – 10, where 0 is normal behaviour for a child of that age and 10 is unacceptable, the child's behaviour is recorded for each of three time periods in the day. It is very important to record this at the end of *each* period, rather than trying to remember later on.

Stage Two – The Diet

The child must eat only the food on the list. *Nothing* else may be eaten or drunk. Cooking should be by boiling, grilling, baking or microwaving, but without adding anything: oil, butter and so on. This is kept up for three weeks (twenty-one days). During the twenty-one days, the behaviour for each time period of each day should be scored.

At the end of the twenty-one days, the behaviour scores for the diet days are compared with the before-diet days. If there is a big difference, then clearly some combination of foods has been having an effect and we move on to Stage 3. If there is not a big difference, then food is not the problem and the programme stops.

Stage Three – Finding the Guilty Foods

While keeping to the special diet, one new food is added to the child's diet, starting with their favourite. A new food is started every two days until your child's behaviour changes rapidly for the worse. Stop the food most recently started and do not add any more new items to the diet until your child's behaviour settles down again. Continue in this way, until all normal food is being eaten *except* those foods which caused a deterioration in behaviour. Remember that some cooking needs oil, butter, and so on, and they count as new items.

WHAT CAN BE EATEN?

Lamb, chicken, potato, rice, cabbage, lettuce, celery, cauliflower, banana, apple, can be eaten. It is very difficult to make different meals from this very limited list but it is the best way to decide if there is a food allergy and which combination is causing the problems. The child should be encouraged to drink plenty of water.

It is important to remember that the most restricted diet lasts for only three weeks, then gradually returns to nearly normal.

Figure 4.2 Finding the guilty foods

Shane was a six-year-old boy who had a three-year history of being unable to settle to any game or task. He frequently destroyed his toys, and would lash out at other children if they thwarted him in any way, and was particularly vindictive towards his younger brother. He was a very poor sleeper, and his mother described a sense of total exhaustion in trying to control him.

Soon after Shane's birth his mother had become pregnant with his younger brother, and as a single parent this had placed great pressure on her coping resources. Shane's early development was not problematic but his acquisition of speech had been very slow and he had had a significant amount of speech therapy when he was four years old.

An EEG revealed abnormal spikes throughout the record, indicating seizure activity. Shane's mother was relieved that a physical cause had been found because she believed that many of the professionals she had met blamed her for Shane's difficult behaviour. He was prescribed anti-convulsants and over the next six weeks Shane's behaviour dramatically improved. At three-month follow-up his mother reported that his behaviour had greatly improved, though he could still be cruel towards his younger brother at times.

The recognition of such an underlying problem is clearly important. As in this particular case, the family often feels great relief that the problem has turned out to be a physical one, and not a reflection of their parenting. In all such cases, however, it is important not to lose sight of the influence that family issues can still be exerting. If a family has struggled with a difficult young person for some time they will have developed mechanisms of responding which, if they continue, may, in themselves, keep prompting problems. All types of treatment, therefore, need to include a close examination of family dynamics if the full benefit of a treatment regime is to be realised.

MEDICATION

Stimulants

Medication, and, in particular, the use of central nervous system stimulants, has been the area to receive most research attention. The drug most commonly used is methylphenidate (usually known as Ritalin), but sometimes dexamphetamine (known as Dexedrine) is prescribed. These drugs, which are part of the amphetamine family, change the level of brain chemicals and appear to help some children to concentrate. However, they are sometimes drugs of abuse, and are potentially addictive (see Chapter 9). In addition, these drugs can cause many side-effects for the child because they can prevent sleeping and may make the child more irritable and restless. Other side-effects may be a dry mouth, sweating, palpitations, headaches and pains in the stomach. It has been suggested that if the drug is taken for a long period it may interfere with a child's growth (Gittelman and Mannuzza 1988), but it is becoming clear that any shortness of stature is probably due to the ADHD and not its treatment (Spencer *et al.* 1996a). As was mentioned in Chapter 2, drug prescribing for children is relatively rare in the United Kingdom, and this has been as true for ADHD as for any other emotional or behavioural problem.

Studies in America have shown that methylphenidate can give moderate improvements in symptoms in pre-school children, with somewhat more powerful responses in older children (Spencer *et al.* 1996a). The most obvious improvements tend to be a reduction in the overactivity and impulsivity which the child shows, as well as an improvement in overall attention levels (Wilens and Biederman 1992), and increases in academic productivity, improved cognitive functioning and recall (O'Toole *et al.* 1997).

It is still not clear whether these changes in attention are exerting influence in other aspects of the young person's life or whether the drug directly affects other aspects of the child's functioning. For instance, these drugs do improve the young person's social interaction and increase the sensitivity in perceiving communications (Whalen *et al.* 1990). A more obvious link to the improved attention is the fact that such medication also improves classroom performance (Du Paul *et al.* 1994). An especially interesting phenomenon is the way that methylphenidate suppresses aggressive outbursts (Murphy *et al.* 1992), and this perhaps illustrates how difficulties with attention and concentration help to fuel behaviour problems, because without addressing the conduct problems directly they fade when the young person's attention improves.

There had been concern in earlier studies that the genuine benefits offered by medication were at the expense of sedating the child, or risking the development of addiction, but more recent work suggests that neither of these is the case (Spencer *et al.* 1996b). It is because of concerns such as these, however, that in the United Kingdom the use of stimulants has tended to be reserved for severe cases.

If medication may be of assistance, the speed of action of methylphenidate allows a very rapid trial of its value to be made. It is, of course, important for families to understand the nature of the drug being used, and Figure 4.3 shows a typical information sheet which should be given to the family of any young person who is receiving the medication.

Antidepressants

In some cases the poor concentration and restlessness which are typical of a pervasive disorder are associated with a picture of sadness and misery. This combination of hyperactivity and signs of depression prompted some practitioners to examine the effects of prescribing antidepressants for young people with hyperactivity. The results indicate that it has a positive effect on all age groups, but especially in adolescents (Wilens *et al.* 1993). This makes this type of treatment a reasonable alternative to the stimulants, especially if there is any suspicion that a stimulant drug would be abused.

Antidepressants do not have the same instant response which is seen with

FORM: Short-acting tablets of 5mg, 10mg or 20mg.

DOSAGE: Very individual but average is 5–20mg morning and lunchtime.

DURATION OF ACTION: Rapid acting, the effects become apparent in 15 – 20 minutes. Its effects last for about 4 hours.

EFFECTS: It specifically improves concentration and memory. If these are major sources of difficulty then there may also be improvement in the control of frustration and anger.

POSSIBLE SIDE-EFFECTS:
- Nervousness and insomnia.
- Reduced appetite and associated weight loss.
- A few children initially have abdominal pain, nausea and vomiting but these generally fade over time.
- Occasionally headaches, drowsiness, dizziness.
- If the young person has tics, these can get worse.
- A few children become irritable or tearful.
- Occasionally growth can be slowed, and the drug must at least be stopped on weekends, and if possible stopped completely.
- On very rare occasions a young person can develop anaemia.

PRECAUTIONS: As with any powerful drug it should only be used if the benefits are marked. Because of the potential for addiction, periods without the medication are worth considering at least two or three times a year.

Figure 4.3 Medication for attention deficit disorder – methylphenidate (Ritalin)

the stimulants, and so there is a need to persevere for a few weeks before the full benefit of such medication can be determined. It needs to be carefully explained to everyone involved that there will be no instant improvement, and so the drug must not be stopped prematurely.

Much of this work has been done with one particular family of anti-depressants – the tricyclics. There is another group of antidepressants which can have a positive effect on this disorder: the monoamine oxidase inhibitors (MAOIs), a title which refers to their action upon certain chemical transmitters which are found in nerve endings. These drugs have also produced improvements in most cases (Barrickman *et al.* 1995), and especially in aggressive symptoms (Simeon *et al.* 1986). Unfortunately, these drugs have significant problems because they react with many other types of drug, such as cough mixtures, and certain foods, such as cheese and yeast extracts. These reactions can still occur even a few weeks after the drug has been stopped, and so great care must be taken if they are to be used.

BEHAVIOURAL TECHNIQUES

Behavioural techniques have a part to play in helping a young person attend to tasks, and gradually increase the period that attention can be sustained.

They are also helpful in curbing some of the conduct elements which may be part of the picture. The principles outlined in Chapter 7 would apply equally to this type of problem. However, the emphasis where the child has attention problems is upon trying to improve attention and to increase the child's general sense of self-esteem and self-worth. It is also worth remembering that such young people often don't fully register instructions, or information generally. It is therefore important that instructions and information are regularly repeated, with information being given in various ways, such as saying it, writing it down, and perhaps using diagrams or pictures.

As a starting point it is important with any task to recognise what the child's limit of sustained attention is, and to tailor activities to fit within that time span. To achieve this, it may be necessary to take the task and divide it into small segments which the young person can definitely manage. Having set this to a realistic level, expecting them to complete the task becomes important not only to ensure that there is a sense of achievement, but to avoid the excuse of poor attention being used simply to avoid work.

Children with attention deficit need structure and routine. They should be helped to make schedules and break assignments down into small tasks to be performed one at a time. It may be necessary to ask them repeatedly what they have just done, how they might have acted differently, and why others react as they do. Especially when young, these children often respond well to the strict application of clear and consistent rules.

Family conflict is one of the most troublesome consequences of attention deficit. Especially when the symptoms have not yet been recognised and the diagnosis made, parents blame themselves, one another, and the child. As they become angrier and impose more punishment, the child becomes more defiant and alienated, and the parents become still less willing to accept the child's excuses or promises. A father or mother with adult attention deficit sometimes compounds the problem. Constantly compared unfavourably with his brothers and sisters, the child with attention deficit may become the family scapegoat, blamed for everything that goes wrong. When attention deficit is diagnosed, parents may feel guilty about not understanding the situation sooner, while other children in the family may reject the diagnosis as an excuse for attention-getting misbehaviour.

To avoid constant family warfare, parents need to learn to distinguish behaviour with a biological origin from reactions to the primary symptoms or responses to the reactions of others. They should become familiar with signs indicating imminent loss of self-control by a child with attention deficit. A routine with consistent rules must be established; these rules can be imposed on young children but must be negotiated with older ones and with adolescents. The family should have a clear division of responsibility, and the parents should present a united front. It helps to write down the rules, and it is important to praise good behaviour immediately. Role-playing may help a child with attention deficit to see how others see him. Family therapy or counselling, parent groups, and child management training are sometimes useful.

Most children with attention deficit are taught in the regular classroom, but their pattern of difficulties presents a challenge to the teachers who work with them because they often need some special approaches to help them learn. For example, the teacher may seat the child in an area with few distractions, provide an area where the child can move around and release excess energy, or establish a clear set of rules and rewards for appropriate behaviour. Sometimes just keeping a card or a picture on the desk can serve as a visual reminder to use the right school behaviour, like raising a hand instead of shouting out, or staying in a seat instead of wandering around the room. The regular repetition of instructions or writing instructions on the board can be helpful, as can closely monitoring the child's own recording, and offering quiet study areas. It is also very helpful to offer short study periods broken by activity (including permission to leave the classroom occasionally), and to use brief directions which are often repeated. Teaching the child how to use flashcards, outlines and underlining can all keep the attention focused on the task. Even simple structures such as giving lists of the books and materials needed for the task may make it possible for disorganised, inattentive children to complete the work. Many of the strategies of special education are simply good teaching methods. Telling students in advance what they will learn, providing visual aids, and giving written as well as oral instructions are all ways to help students focus and remember the key parts of the lesson. Timed tests should be avoided as much as possible because the child will tend to underperform under such pressure. Other children in the classroom may show more tolerance if the problem is explained to them in terms they can understand.

Children with attention deficit often need to learn techniques for monitoring and controlling their own attention and behaviour. For example, children may be taught several alternatives to use when they lose track of what they are supposed to do. These strategies may involve looking for instructions on the chalkboard, raising a hand, waiting to see if they remember, or quietly asking another child. The process of finding alternatives to interrupting the teacher can make the child feel more self-sufficient and create an atmosphere of co-operation. With fewer interruptions there is also an increase in praise and a reduction in reprimands. It helps if the teacher can frequently stop to ask children to notice whether they are paying attention to the lesson or if they are thinking about something else, and to record their answer on a chart. As students become more consciously aware of their attention, they begin to see progress and feel good about staying focused. These young people are quite capable of learning, but their hyperactivity and inattention make learning difficult.

Rewards for success are key, and they may be something as simple as the opportunity to run around for five minutes – which is not only a reward but also a release that will help the child settle to the next segment. Gradually extending the time of each segment shapes the young person's behaviour, and begins to create a more durable concentration span. Encouraging the young person to do regularly things they are good at, such as sport, helps to give a strong sense of success. This prevents the child from feeling a total failure because tasks requiring concentration are difficult.

OUTCOME

Although the overactivity tends to fade in adolescence, the attention problems often persist (Cantwell 1985). Indeed, up to half of affected children still show difficulties related to hyperactivity in adulthood (Mannuzza *et al*. 1993). Using these figures, about 1 per cent of the adult population will have problems with hyperactivity (Spencer *et al*. 1996b). In fact it seems probable that only a small proportion of children with attention deficit are at risk of major problems in adulthood. The present state of knowledge indicates that those children that appear most at risk are those with family adversity and those who have poor peer relationships. However, it does not seem that the severity of the attention problems in anyway predicts the likelihood of long-term difficulties (Taylor 1995).

It might be expected that having social and family difficulties as well as attention problems would cause addition difficulties to arise, and the research evidence does tend to suggest that these young people have wider difficulties than hyperactivity as adults (Weiss and Hechtman 1986).

CONCLUSION

Despite the vast amount of effort that is being put into answering the fundamental questions around attention deficit and hyperactivity it is only now that some sort of structured understanding of these problems is emerging. As well as the concentration difficulties, these young people are very prone to have conduct problems and educational failure. Indeed, it is becoming clear that despite average cognitive abilities, these young people fare academically less well than their peers (Wilson and Marcotte 1996). For example, work in New Zealand (Fergusson and Horwood 1992) has shown that at twelve years of age the child's level of attention deficit directly influences his or her level of reading achievement. There can therefore be no doubt that this is a very important condition to understand, not only because it is common, but because of the profound effect it has upon young people's lives.

SOURCES OF FURTHER HELP

The ADD/ADHD Family Support Group, 1a The High Street, Dilton Marsh, nr Westbury, Wiltshire BA13 4DL. Telephone (01373) 826045.

ADD Information Services, PO Box 340, Edgware, Middlesex, HA8 9HL. Telephone (0181) 9052013.

REFERENCES

Achenbach, T.M. and Edelbrock, C.S. (1991). *Integrative Guide to the 1991 CBCL 4–18, YSR and TRF Profiles.* Burlington: University of Vermont.

Barrickman, L., Perry, P. and Allen, A. (1995). Bupropion versus methylphenidate in the treatment of ADHD. *Journal of the American Academy of Child and Adolescent Psychiatry* 34, 649–57.

Boyle, M.H., Offord, D.R., Racine, Y., Fleming, J.E., Szatmari, P. and Sanford, M. (1993). Evaluation of the Revised Ontario Child Health Study Scales. *Journal of Child Psychology and Psychiatry* 34, 189–213.

Cantwell, D.P. (1985). Hyperactive children grown up. *Archives of General Psychiatry* 42, 1026–8.

Du Paul, G., Barkley, R. and McMurray, M. (1994). Response of children with ADHD to methylphenidate: interaction with internalizing symptoms. *Journal of the American Academy of Child and Adolescent Psychiatry* 33, 894–903.

Egger, J., Carter, C., Graham, P. and Gumley, D. (1985). A controlled trial of oligoantigenic treatment in the hyperkinetic syndrome. *Lancet* I, 540–5.

Faraone, S.V., Biederman, J. and Chen, W.J. (1992). Segregation analysis of attention deficit hyperactivity disorder: evidence for a single gene transmission. *Psychiatric Genetics* 2, 257–2.

Faraone, S.V., Biederman, J., Mennin, D. and Gershon, J. (1996). A prospective 4-year follow-up study of children at risk of ADHD. *Journal of the American Academy of Child and Adolescent Psychiatry* 35, 1449–59.

Fergusson, D.M. and Horwood, L.J. (1992). Attention deficit and reading achievement. *Journal of Child Psychology and Psychiatry* 33, 375–85.

Fergusson, D.M., Horwood, L.J. and Lloyd, M. (1993). Confirmatory factor models of attention deficit and conduct disorder. *Journal of Child Psychology and Psychiatry* 32, 257–74.

Gittelman, R. and Mannuzza, S. (1988). Hyperactive boys almost grown up: III. Methylphenidate effects on ultimate height. *Archives of General Psychiatry* 45, 1131–4.

Goodman, R. (1994). A modified version of the Rutter Parent Questionnaire including extra items on children's strengths. *Journal of Child Psychology and Psychiatry* 35, 1483–94.

Goodman, R. and Stevenson, J. (1989). A twin study of hyperactivity–I. An examination of hyperactivity score and categories derived from Rutter Teacher and Parent questionnaire scores. *Journal of Child Psychology and Psychiatry* 30, 671–90.

Hallowell, E. M. (1996). *Responding to ADD.* Private communication.

Leung, P.W.L. and Connolly, K.J. (1994). Attention difficulties in hyperactive and conduct disordered children: a processing deficit. *Journal of Child Psychology and Psychiatry* 35, 1229–45.

Loeber, R. and Stouthamer-Loeber, M. (1986). Family factors as correlates and predictors of juvenile conduct problems and delinquency. In M. Tonry and N. Morris (eds) *Crime and Justice: An Annual Review of Research.* Vol. VII. Chicago: University of Chicago Press.

Mannuzza, S., Klein, R.G., Bessler, A. and Malloy, P. (1993). Adult outcome of hyperactive boys: educational achievement, occupational rank and psychiatric status. *Archives of General Psychiatry* 50, 565–76.

McArdle, P., O'Brien, G. and Kolvin, I. (1995). Hyperactivity: prevalence and relationship with conduct disorder. *Journal of Child Psychology and Psychiatry* 36, 279–303.

Murphy, D., Pelham, W. and Lang, A. (1992). Aggression in boys with ADHD: methylphenidate effects on naturalistically observed aggression, response to provocation and social information processing. *Journal of Abnormal Child Psychology* 20, 451–66.

O'Toole, K., Abramowitz, A., Morris, R. and Dulcan, M. (1997). Effects of methylphenidate on attention and nonverbal learning in children with ADHD. *Journal of the American Academy of Child and Adolescent Psychiatry* 36, 531–8.

Porrino, L.J., Rapoport, J.L., Behar, D., Sceery, W., Ismond, D. and Bunney, W.E. (1983). A naturalistic assessment of the motor activity of hyperactive boys: I. Comparison with normal controls. *Archives of General Psychiatry* 40, 681–7.

Rapport, M.D., Carlson, G.A., Kelly, K.L. and Pataki, C. (1993). Methlyphenidate and desipramine in hospitalized children: I. Separate and combined effects on cognitive function. *Journal of the American Academy of Child and Adolescent Psychiatry* 32, 333–42.

Ross, D.M. and Ross, S.A. (1982). *Hyperactivity: Current Issues, Research and Theory*. New York: Wiley.

Schachar, R. and Logan, G.D. (1990). Impulsivity and inhibitory control in development and psychopathology. *Developmental Psychology* 26, 1–11.

Schachar, R. and Tannock, R. (1995). Test of four hypotheses for the comorbidity of attention deficit hyperactivity disorder and conduct disorder. *Journal of the American Academy of Child and Adolescent Psychiatry* 34, 639–48.

Simeon, J.G., Ferguson, H.B. and Fleet, J. (1986). Bupropion effects in attention deficit and conduct disorders. *Canadian Journal of Psychiatry* 31, 581–5.

Spencer, T., Biederman, J., Harding, M. and O'Donnell, D. (1996a). Growth deficits in ADHD children revisited: evidence for disorder-associated growth delays? *Journal of the American Academy of Child and Adolescent Psychiatry* 35, 1460–9.

Spencer, T., Biederman, J., Wilens, T. and Harding, M. (1996b). Pharmacology of ADHD across the life cycle. *Journal of the American Academy of Child and Adolescent Psychiatry* 35, 409–32.

Stevenson, J., Richman, N. and Graham, P. (1985). Behaviour problems and language abilities at three years and beavioural deviance at eight years. *Journal of Child Psychology and Psychiatry* 26, 215–30.

Taylor, E. (1994). Syndromes of attention deficit and overactivity. In M. Rutter, E. Taylor and L. Hersov (eds) *Child and Adolescent Psychiatry: Modern Approaches*. Oxford: Blackwell.

Taylor, E. (1995). Dysfunctions of attention. In D. Cicchetti and D.J. Cohen (eds) *Developmental Psychopathology*. New York: Wiley & Sons.

Taylor, E., Scharchar, R., Thorley, G. and Weiselberg, M. (1987). Which boys respond to stimulant medication? A controlled trial of methylphenidate in boys with disruptive behaviour. *Psychological Medicine* 17, 121–43.

Taylor, E., Sandberg, S., Thorley, G. and Giles, S. (1991). *The Epidemiology of Childhood Hyperactivity*. Maudsley Monographs No. 33. Oxford: Oxford University Press.

Weiss, G. (1991) Attention deficit hyperactivity disorder. In M. Lewis (ed.) *Child and Adolescent Psychiatry: A Comprehensive Textbook*. Baltimore: Williams & Wilkins.

Weiss, G. and Hechtman, L.T. (1986). *Hyperactive Children Grown Up*. New York: Guilford.

Whalen, C., Henker, B. and Granger, D. (1990). Social adjustment processes in hyperactive boys: effects of methylphenidate and comparison with normal peers. *Journal of Abnormal Child Psychology* 18, 297–316.

Wilens, T.E. and Biederman, J. (1992). The stimulants. *Psychiatric Clinics of North America* 15, 191–222.

Wilens, T.E., Biederman, J., Geist, D.E. and Steingard, R. (1993). Nortriptyline in the treatment of ADHD: a chart review of 58 cases. *Journal of the American Academy of Child and Adolescent Psychiatry* 32, 343–9.

Wilson, J.M. and Marcotte, A.C. (1996). Psychosocial adjustment and educational outcome in adolescents with a childhood diagnosis of ADHD. *Journal of the American Academy of Child and Adolescent Psychiatry* 35, 579–87.

World Health Organisation (1992). *The ICD-10 Classification of Mental Health and Behavioural Disorders: Clinical Descriptions and Diagnostic Guidelines*. Geneva: World Health Organisation.

5   Eating disorders

INTRODUCTION

Eating is one of the fundamental requirements, along with breathing, necessary to sustain life. If a person does not breathe for some minutes death occurs very quickly; for someone not eating, although it may take several weeks, the fact of death is no less inevitable. Perhaps this is why, throughout the animal kingdom, feeding is such a major part of the daily routine and has become in some species a part of ritual. In primates in particular, feeding routines have assumed particular importance, and are regularly used to placate aggressors. In humans mutual feeding has also evolved as a major mechanism for showing affection or sexual interest (Morris 1967).

This may go some way to explain why children's problems with eating can so quickly become emotionally charged, and can so often become an area of persisting conflict and difficulty. The high level of concern which feeding problems can provoke provides an excellent mechanism for children to manipulate adult views and achieve their own desires over the expressed wishes of their parents.

INFANT FEEDING

The newborn infant has no capacity to feed itself, and can only respond to danger or discomfort by crying. The main caregiver, usually the mother, has to respond to these signals if the baby is to be reassured. Feeding is an integral part of this process, and so if it becomes disrupted in any way, the impact for both mother and child can be quite profound.

Chatoor and Egan (1987) considered the way that such problems arose and their system of classification is very useful not only for offering some structure, but for giving a direction in how to improve the situation. In the first two months of life the baby is learning the mechanics of feeding, and so it is most likely that feeding problems at this very young age are physical ones. They may be mechanical in that the baby cannot co-ordinate the movements necessary for effective feeding, or they may be medical – for instance, colic or respiratory problems that make sucking a problem. The main focus then for a young infant with difficulties in feeding is the mechanics of the process, and the nature of the difficulties can usually be determined by means of a careful medical review.

Between two and six months the infant begins the crucial process of developing a specific emotional attachment to the primary caregiver. Therefore, problems arising in this age group usually reflect problems in this developing relationship. The commonest cause is for the mother to be depressed, or simply worn out with the childcare routine. The responses to the young person are then poorer, or in the worst case non-existent, and the child becomes fretful and upset. If matters continue, the baby may start to reduce its demands and become remote and self-stimulating, but usually the response is to demand attention by escalating resistance, and so force the mother to interact, albeit in an irritated and perhaps punitive way. These sorts of interaction are very commonly seen in children who present as being very small, and apparently undernourished – the non-organic failure to thrive syndrome. When in a different environment they usually have insatiable appetites, and characteristically put on significant weight and growth spurts during periods when not in their parent's care. Recent work has indicated that problems with feeding at this young age can, if persistent, lead to the young person having significantly poorer intellectual functioning than his or her peers (Puckering *et al.* 1995). The solution in such potentially damaging situations is to try to identify the origin of the interaction problem, and correct it. It must be borne in mind however, that if it persists, it does so as an interactional difficulty, and so both the parent's and child's contributions need to be carefully evaluated. Any solution must address both parent and child, and usually joint play sessions which develop periods of positive interaction are the starting point for a successful intervention.

ANOREXIA NERVOSA

Anorexia nervosa is a condition which has been known for some time, but was first formally identified by Gull in 1873. It has, however, become far better known in recent years as the image of being thin has become the one to which youth has increasingly been urged to aspire. This idealised image is experienced by the young at a time when they are searching for a personal identity, and trying to navigate the difficult route from childhood to becoming an adult. As has been mentioned in Chapter 1, one way that adolescents cope with these pressures is to seek conformity with stereotypes, and peer-group expectations. It is perhaps not surprising, then, that becoming totally focused on body image is a mechanism that some young people use to cope with these difficult pressures. In one survey 40 per cent of teenage girls and 10 per cent of teenage boys were dieting significantly, and for 7 per cent of the girls (and 1 per cent of the boys) this was extreme (Patton *et al.* 1997).

Anorexia nervosa rarely emerges before puberty, and if a younger child is showing problems with weight loss and a reluctance to eat, it is very important that all physical illnesses are carefully excluded before any attempt to diagnose anorexia nervosa is made. In these younger children it is easy for bowel problems to masquerade as anorexia, and caution is therefore very important. The key factor for diagnosis in this age group, as in all others, is the presence of distortion in how the young person sees his or her body.

Anorexia nervosa affects 0.1 – 0.2 per cent of the adolescent population (Whitaker *et al.* 1990), and occurs in girls ten times more commonly than in boys (Lucas *et al.* 1991). In younger children the problem is quite rare, but here the proportion of boys is as great as 30 per cent (Jacobs and Isaacs 1986). One of the interesting questions to ask is whether the pressures of modern life are resulting in anorexia occurring ever more frequently. From his detailed analysis of the literature, Fombonne has concluded that the rate of occurrence of anorexia nervosa is not increasing over time, which offers some reassurance about the future (Fombonne 1995a).

Anna, at fifteen years of age, was a girl who greatly enjoyed tennis. In the winter her relative inactivity caused her to put on weight and several people within school began calling her 'Pug'. This made her quite distressed, and she determined to lose the extra weight.

Over the next few weeks she embarked upon a severe diet which involved eating low-fat yoghurt for breakfast and lunch and a salad for tea. On occasions Anna would 'cheat' by eating biscuits or chocolate, and afterwards she felt so guilty that she would sometimes not eat for two days to remove this 'weight'.

After three months her periods had stopped and she was 15 per cent below the weight that was typical for her height and age. When seen in individual sessions Anna could not accept that she was thin and was worried that if she began eating again she would rapidly become overweight. Family reassurance did not seem to help ease this anxiety for her. Using a cognitive therapy approach (see Chapter 2), Anna was gradually able to develop new ways of thinking about her weight. Having achieved this it was then possible slowly to change her dietary regime so that it maintained her at a weight appropriate to her height. As part of this programme, she began keeping a diary which listed her positive qualities as well as the nice things which people had said about her on that day. Three times a week she would read recent entries and over the next few months she confirmed that she was now seeing herself in a different light. Two years on, Anna continues to maintain her weight appropriately, and plays tennis for her university.

The problems presented by Anna are relatively clear, although for many young people with anorexia there are underlying problems of which the unwillingness to eat is merely an external manifestation.

This case illustrates the importance of recognising the key elements which lead to a diagnosis of anorexia nervosa. A desire to be slim, a wish to diet, a feeling of being overweight do not in themselves confirm that the young person has anorexia. The diagnosis requires that the young person has a dread of being overweight which is accompanied by an unshakeable belief that she is too large, even if to the objective observer the young person is in fact very thin. This distortion of body image is the key element in determining that anorexia nervosa is present, and if it is absent, then other possible causes of the problem should be considered.

In addition to this key element the young person is usually very thin, and in girls the periods have stopped. In about a third of cases there is also a soft, downy hair on the arms, legs and face, but this is a symptom arising because of the starvation; it is not part of the anorexia nervosa itself.

In the midst of the illness the young person diets very severely, and is very knowledgeable about food; this will tend to be a constant theme of the young person's conversation. Such young people are often good cooks, and will take delight in cooking for others, though they themselves maintain a strict dietary regime. Indeed, once established, being able to maintain the strict regime is often a major source of pleasure for the young person, and in more reflective moments he or she may well recount how good it felt to be able to resist a particular food or treat. For some, the diet is not sufficient, and there may also be a punishing exercise regime, which is often justified as part of a health drive. In a few the weight loss is assisted by taking large quantities of laxatives on a daily basis, or regularly vomiting after meals.

In the midst of the illness such dieting may be the only source of self-praise and when considering other aspects of their life they may view themselves with scorn or even disgust. They often stop meeting friends or taking part in social occasions and generally seem more solitary and preoccupied. In day-to-day things they often are more irritable and bad tempered, with an air of gloominess which can lead people to think that they are becoming depressed (Strober 1991).

The cessation of menstruation is the first sign of the significant impact which the starvation is having, but if the severe dieting is prolonged, damage can occur to important body organs (see Table 5.1) such as the liver and kidneys (Sharp and Freeman 1993). If the dieting is at all prolonged, there is also a thinning of the bones (Bachrach *et al.* 1990). This osteoporosis is also

Table 5.1 Physical problems which can occur in anorexia nervosa

Symptom	%
Heart abnormalities, especially slowing of heart rate	87
Hypotension (low blood pressure)	85
Kidney abnormalities (giving changes in kidney function)	70
Thinning of spinal bone	50
Anaemia	30
Nutritional hepatitis	30
Stomach ulcers	16
Pancreatitis	occasional

Source: Sharp and Freeman (1993)

seen in older women whose periods have stopped and so is probably due to the drop in oestrogen levels rather than a direct consequence of starvation (Biller *et al.* 1989).

Rachel's parents had been concerned about her for many months. They knew that she ate very little, and her mother believed that her periods had stopped at least six months ago. Rachel had refused professional help, but had finally agreed when her favourite aunt, with whom Rachel felt an affinity, insisted that she must see someone.

The dietary history Rachel gave indicated that she was eating only 450 calories a day, and when she was weighed it was found that her weight was 40 per cent below the weight that was typical for her height and age. After much discussion she agreed to be admitted to hospital on a voluntary basis, and over the next few days more details of her routines emerged. She had been eating almost nothing but low-fat yoghurt and salad for some months, and over the same period she had been pursuing a very intensive fitness regime which involved jogging daily and swimming four times per week.

Rachel could recite the calorific value of almost every food item, and described her greatest pleasure as cooking Sunday lunch for the family. The ward staff commented that in her first few days in hospital she kept very active, and never seemed to stay still for a moment.

Although finishing meals was expected as part of the programme, increasingly Rachel did not finish her meals when junior nurses supervised them. These nurses said that Rachel had told them how frightened and upset she felt whenever she was expected to eat. They felt sorry for Rachel and felt that they were being cruel in insisting that she ate.

After three weeks Rachel's weight gain was minimal, and a search revealed the remains of meals outside of the room window, and within the room the staff found plastic bags filled with food behind furniture, and even in the springs of a chair.

Boys tend to develop similar symptoms (Oyebode *et al.* 1988), but they usually prove to have much greater underlying psychological problems.

The causes of anorexia nervosa

As the concerns about anorexia nervosa have grown, so have the attempts to explain why some adolescents develop such a potentially profound problem. Family and twin studies suggest there is an important genetic influence in developing anorexia nervosa (Fombonne 1995b). However, for many, the origins of anorexia nervosa are to be found in the young person's own struggle with the pressures of maturity (Crisp 1980). The cessation of periods, the maintaining of the angularity of youth, and the delay in other secondary sexual characteristics are all certainly consequences of starvation. This type of theory is given added credence because many girls with anorexia nervosa tend to dress in a childish manner, perhaps emphasising their desire to avoid becoming an adult. In clinical samples a fear of growing up is certainly a common feature if the anorexia began before fourteen years of age, whereas in older girls it is a desire to be thin which dominates their thinking (Heebink *et al.* 1995).

This difference in emphasis between the two age groups is also reflected in the response to therapy. For those in whom the problem started at a young age, family therapy which focuses upon relationships and maturation tends to be most successful, whereas for those in whom the problem started late in adolescence, the best response tends to be achieved by an individual psychotherapy approach (Russell *et al.* 1987).

Whatever the usual cause, it is clear that certain groups are particularly prone to developing the problem. Ballet dancers in particular show rates far in excess of the general population, as do models (Garfinkel and Garner 1982; Strober 1991). This is perhaps not surprising when one considers the tremendous pressure on such people to stay 'in shape' and avoid getting fat. It is interesting to speculate, though, whether these groups are merely experiencing an intense version of what everyone with anorexia experiences or whether the problem is of a different sort – a necessary routine which has become so habitual that it becomes a goal in its own right. With the interest which this problem prompts being so high, it will not be too long before answers to these conundrums are found.

Intervention

The first stage of any intervention process is to recognise that a problem is developing. With the modern emphasis upon slimness it can be difficult for families, or other concerned adults, to realise that there is a cause for concern. The first worry is usually the marked thinness of the young person, but it can also be concern that the diet seems too severe. Asking about eating is usually dismissed, and it is often only when considerable weight has been lost, and there can be no doubt about the matter, that professional help is sought. The first requirement is then to seek a referral to the local psychiatry service.

After gaining an understanding of the history of the problem, and the issues which are sustaining it, the first aim of intervention is to limit further weight loss. The programme which has traditionally been used for this is based on behavioural principles. The exact make-up of the programme varies depending upon the philosophy of the institution, but most would expect that if the young person is 35 per cent below the ideal body weight for height and age, then a hospital admission is indicated. Recent legal concerns about consent by teenagers to medical procedures has helped in understanding how to respond to young people with anorexia nervosa who do not wish to be admitted to hospital. In the case of Re W (Consent) [1991] a girl of fifteen years with severe anorexia nervosa refused to be moved to a special treatment setting. The court said that it was appropriate in such cases to use the powers available under the Mental Health Act (1981) because the illness did adversely affect the young person's ability to make rational decisions. It must be remembered, however, that each case is judged on its merits, and diagnosing that someone has anorexia nervosa does not automatically mean that they can be admitted to hospital against their will.

Whether in hospital or not, the first aim is to bring the body weight back to a more normal level. It is important to have a clear idea of the usual food intake because the new regime must very slowly increase from that level to one which is gradually producing a weight gain. The increase in weight is usually quite frightening to the young person and so the process demands great tact, care and lots of reassurance that they will not be made fat. It is sometimes helpful in these early stages to give a sedative medication, which can help reduce the intense feelings of panic that many feel as the weight chart slowly climbs. This gradual gaining of weight is accompanied by agreed rewards and, supplementing this, there needs to be a continuous educational and support programme to reduce the concern about the steady weight gain.

In the early stages the young person will usually talk of nothing but food and weight targets, and it is important to establish a sequence of meetings where this is not the focus, but rather the focus is upon their life and their aspirations for the future. These become the kernel of the individual psychological programme which gathers momentum as the weight concerns reduce. This psychological support may take many forms from formal psychotherapy to approaches based upon problem solving. All, however, use the young person's own feelings and ideas, and in the process specific events which may have initiated the problem may be uncovered.

As already mentioned, the family's role both in the origin of the difficulties and in their solution may prove pivotal. Most families find exploration of their intimate workings very difficult, but without major shifts in attitude and approach relapse is very likely. One of the first major works in this area was by Minuchin and his team who explored family structures and functioning in what he described as 'psychosomatic families' (Minuchin *et al.* 1978). He described a pattern in which families were quite overinvolved, with a feeling that the family members were very enmeshed with each other. He also found that, typically, conflict between members of the family was avoided, and that if there was marital conflict it was very common for the young person to become caught in the middle of it.

A somewhat similar pattern of findings was noted by Selvini-Palazzoli in her work with anorexic girls in Italy (Selvini-Palazzoli 1974). She also noted that secret alliances between family members were often present, as was a strong expectation that family members would preserve the outward appearance of a settled family life. Although some of the conclusions from such work have been eroded over time, the basic approach to family issues still remains (Humphrey 1994). Understanding the family's functioning remains a fundamental requirement of any intervention programme, especially in the younger patient. The type of family work that is undertaken is largely dictated by the philosophy of the unit treating the young person, but often it has a systems theory basis (see Chapter 2).

Alongside the dynamic exploration of family issues, it is important that a consistent approach is agreed with the parents towards eating. In milder weight loss situations this may be the only direct management of the eating, and its success is necessary for any lasting progress. The home regime is based upon agreed menus, and a constant expectation that plates will be cleared. The steady increase in amounts offered is still necessary, and using large dinner plates can help with the illusion that the quantity is small. A single exchange item on each menu is permitted, otherwise the meals are as agreed, and the adults of the family stay with them until all is eaten. Resisting excuses and ploys, and maintaining a solid insistence, is not only necessary to maintain the weight, but is often the first indication of a major shift in how the family functions.

Any concerned adult can offer the opportunity to listen to worries or concerns, but if they become food or weight orientated, these discussions should be diverted by saying 'those are issues to discuss with your specialist'. Within school, projects on anorexia may be sought out, and may offer the opportunity to ventilate certain feelings or ideas. It is important that the illness does not become too dominant, however, because maintaining a wide range of interests and having success in different arenas are crucial to the recovery process. Gently steering into new tasks, highlighting success and praising positive progress can all help in reducing the drive to be thinner.

There is no medication which specifically helps young people overcome this problem, and so the role of medication in anorexia nervosa is limited to two situations. The first is to help with the initial difficulties over establishing a weight-gain programme; the second is where the anorexia nervosa is occurring alongside a depressive illness. In the latter cases the use of antidepressants can help speed recovery (Pryor *et al.* 1990), but the psychological efforts to understand the problem's origins, and establish solutions, are still required.

Outcome

Although the general approach to anorexia nervosa has been established for several years, the outcome is still very variable. This is because recovery is determined far more by how successful the psychological efforts have been than whether an appropriate weight was achieved. In general over half of the girls will achieve a reasonable weight and see their periods restored, but boys have a much poorer course (Steinhausen *et al.* 1991).

The earlier that the illness starts, the poorer tends to be the outcome (Walford and McCune 1991). This could be because the illness has a somewhat different psychological make-up in the younger girl, for as we have already seen, younger girls tend to be troubled by fears of growing up, rather than preoccupied with being thin – which is the more common driving force in older teenagers. Alternatively, of course, this poorer outcome may arise because the illness delays the onset of full puberty, and as a result alters the ultimate course of physical development (Russell 1985).

Although most recover their weight, and often restart their periods, in the longer term only about 44 per cent will maintain normal eating habits. As many as 20 per cent go on to develop a chronic illness that can be directly attributed to their anorexia. Perhaps most worrying of all is the fact that despite the best efforts of clinicians and families about 5 per cent of young people who have had anorexia nervosa die of a condition which can be directly attributed to their eating disorder (Patton 1988). This level of mortality, which is six times that of the general population, makes it a condition that, when recognised, must be treated with the greatest of respect.

BULIMIA NERVOSA

Bulimia nervosa is a variation of anorexia nervosa which was initially distinguished as a separate problem by Russell in 1979. He described a group of girls who had an intense fear of becoming fat, but, unlike typical anorexic girls, most of this group were not extremely thin. This group was also distinctive because their dietary routine was not extremely restrictive, but rather had episodes when they would eat a very large quantity of food, and afterwards they would vomit, use large amounts of laxatives, or exercise to an extreme degree to prevent the binge meal causing them to put on weight.

Bulimia tends to begin well after puberty, and occurs in about 1 per cent of adolescent and young adult women (Fairburn and Beglin 1990). It can occasionally occur in girls before they start their periods, but this is unusual (Schmidt *et al.* 1992). There is no evidence that it is inherited and, indeed, life events seem to be the main precipitants (Fombonne 1995b); a substantial minority of the girls suffering from bulimia have been victims of sexual abuse (Pope and Hudson 1992).

Amanda was seventeen years of age and during a school field trip a teacher became worried because Amanda seemed to spend long periods in the toilet after each meal. The teacher wanted to send Amanda home, but Amanda said that this had been happening for some time and that she had a stomach problem. As the week progressed Amanda began to confide in the teacher and in response to the teacher's obvious concern Amanda confessed that she in fact made herself sick after meals. Amanda considered herself to be ugly, and felt fat. She had tried many types of diet and had had slimming pills from her doctor, but couldn't seem to lose weight.

In the last year she had started to be sick after meals, and felt much happier after she had been sick, because she knew this food would not add to her weight problem. After much discussion Amanda agreed to be referred to a specialist clinic.

Initially, Amanda found it hard to talk about her eating problems, but eventually described how upset she was about her appearance, and how desperately she wanted to be thinner. She explained how sometimes the desire to eat became overwhelming, and on these occasions she would literally eat everything in the kitchen. She described how on these occasions she would even eat packets of butter as though they were some sort of ice-cream bar. Afterwards she had to be sick, and then could rest. At other times she felt the need to be sick only after large meals, and said that she was taking thirty laxative tablets a day to help keep her weight down.

In many regular bulimics the vomiting has created a characteristic pattern of enamel erosion on the teeth and enlarged salivary glands in the cheeks. The frequent vomiting also exposes the oesphagus to stomach acid and so is likely to provoke ulcers, and in rare cases it may cause the oesphagus to rupture (Overby and Litt 1988).

Intervention

Identifying a problem of bulimia nervosa can be very difficult. Hearing someone being sick may be the only clue, because otherwise there are few outward signs to notice. Therefore, it is the young person's declaration that there is a problem which tends to be the first indication. A referral to the local psychiatric services is the usual route of response, but experienced counsellors or community psychiatric nurses may be other avenues of help. The first task is to distinguish bulimia from anorexia nervosa, since the treatment emphasis is quite different. In trying to assist young people with bulimia various approaches have been used, but most clinical effort has been focused upon two avenues, the first of which is trying to understand the problems which are prompting the difficulties. The second has been trials of various behavioural techniques which aim to extinguish the symptoms. This work has pointed to two interventions which seem to hold the most promise for assisting in this condition. The first is the use of cognitive therapy (discussed in Chapter 2) which engages the patient in a careful examination of how the problem is viewed and thought about. When used in bulimia nervosa, the focus of cognitive therapy is upon seeking thoughts that are closely associated with the episodes of vomiting, and then seeking alternatives to reduce the urge to be sick.

The second avenue is the use of medication. Work in various centres has produced evidence that certain antidepressants can reduce episodes of bulimia and the preoccupation with body size (Goldstein *et al.* 1995). This work is still being evaluated, and so the long-term benefits have still to be defined. However, the evidence suggests this could be a helpful approach.

The family's role in helping to resolve the problems depends upon whether direct family themes, such as conflict or abuse, are seen to be underlying the behavioural pattern. The use of family therapy can sometimes deal with such issues in a way that allows the young person to escape what feels like an oppressive atmosphere. If such themes are not dominant, then the family role tends to be one of support – both in terms of offering time for quiet reflection, and in terms of routine and structure. If it is clear that the hour after mealtimes is a particularly difficult time, then restructure routines so that there is no opportunity to vomit. This can be achieved by chores, playing board games or even taking a walk together. Such plans work best when agreed with sufferers, and this also allows them to be challenged if they try to excuse themselves.

Within other settings, such as school, assistance in breaking patterns is harder to organise. Keeping occupied is the most important requirement: empty time is dangerous time. A routine of going to clubs or assisting with the library can be quite powerful, but direct help means that the problem has to be shared, and that specific things are asked of the adult. It is unusual for school staff even to know that one of their students has bulimia, and so positive help tends to be very uncommon.

Friends can be a great source of help. They can be asked to be vigilant and close friends can be empowered to be quite forceful in stopping trips to the toilet unaccompanied. These types of intrusion are, however, only of value if the young person wants them, and they are part of a structured plan. As isolated measures they offer little, and if not sought by the sufferer, they can ruin relationships, and make matters worse by deepening the sense of isolation.

Outcome

Bulimia has been identified as a separate condition for less than twenty years, and so there has not been the opportunity to study the long-term effects in any detail. In the studies which have been carried out, over half of the women are reported to have fully recovered ten years after they have been diagnosed. In contrast to anorexia nervosa, it appears that women with bulimia nervosa tend to recover better the earlier the onset. It also seems that the seriousness of the initial psychological problems does not help to predict how good the recovery will be (Johnson-Sabine *et al.* 1992).

Although many do seem to be able to put this problem behind them, in those who do not make a full recovery there continue to be symptoms typical of a wide variety of different psychological problems, but to date there is no specific association to other specific psychiatric illnesses (Collins and King 1994).

CONCLUSION

Eating is a crucial part of every person's life, and any disruption to it is potentially life threatening. It is therefore not surprising that disruption to eating, by whatever mechanism, provokes extreme concern from family and professionals alike. The research in the areas described here shows a steady move towards understanding what is the most effective way to intervene in such situations, hopefully giving the young person the best chance of minimising the impact of the eating disorder upon future life.

SOURCES OF FURTHER HELP

Anorexics Anonymous. 24 Westmoorland Road, London. Telephone (0181) 748 3994.

Eating Disorder Association. 44–48 Magdalen Street, Norwich, Norfolk NR3 1JE. Telephone (01603) 621414.

REFERENCES

Bachrach, L.K., Guido, D. and Katzman, D. (1990). Decreased bone density in adolescent girls with anorexia nervosa. *Pediatrics* 86, 440–7.

Biller, B.M.K., Saxe, V. and Herzog, D.B. (1989). Mechanisms of osteoporosis in adult and adolescent women with anorexia nervosa. *Journal of Clinical Endocrinology and Metabolism* 68, 548–54.

Chatoor, I. and Egan, J. (1987). Etiology and diagnosis of failure to thrive and growth disorders in infants and children. In J. Noshpitz (ed.) *Basic Handbook in Child Psychiatry*. New York: Basic Books.

Collins, S. and King, M. (1994). Ten year follow up of 50 patients with bulimia nervosa. *British Journal of Psychiatry* 164, 80–7.

Crisp, A.H. (1980). *Anorexia Nervosa: Let Me Be*. London: Academic Press.

Dare, C. and Eisler, I. (1992). The family therapy of anorexia nervosa. In P. Cooper and A. Stein (eds) *The Nature and Management of Feeding Problems in Young People*. New York: Harwood Academics.

Fairburn, G. and Beglin, S.J. (1990). Studies of the epidemiology of bulimia nervosa. *American Journal of Psychiatry* 147, 401–8.

Fombonne, E. (1995a). Anorexia nervosa: no evidence of an increase. *British Journal of Psychiatry* 166, 462–71.

Fombonne, E. (1995b). Eating disorders: time trends and possible explanatory mechanisms. In M. Rutter and D.J. Smith (eds) *Psychosocial Disorders in Young People: Time Trends and Their Causes*. Chichester: John Wiley.

Garfinkel, P. and Garner, D. (1982). *Anorexia Nervosa–A Multidimensional Perspective*. New York: Brunner.

Goldstein, D.J., Wilson, M.G. and Thompson, V.L. (1995). Long term Fluoxetine treatment in bulimia nervosa. *British Journal of Psychiatry* 166, 660–6.

Gull, W.W. (1873). Anorexia hysterica (apepsia hysterica). *British Medical Journal* 2, 527–9.

Heebink, D.M., Sunday, S.R. and Halmi, K.A. (1995). Anorexia nervosa and bulimia nervosa in adolescence: effects of age and menstrual status on psychological variables. *Journal of the American Academy of Child and Adolescent Psychiatry* 34, 378–82.

Humphrey, L.L. (1994). Family relationship. In K.A. Halmi (ed.) *Psychobiology and Treatment of Anorexia Nervosa and Bulimia Nervosa*. Washington, D.C.: American Psychiatric Press.

Jacobs, B. and Isaacs, S. (1986). Pre-pubertal anorexia nervosa: a retrospective controlled trial. *Journal of Child Psychology and Psychiatry* 27, 237–50.

Johnson-Sabine, E., Reiss, D. and Dayson, D. (1992). Bulimia nervosa: a follow up study. *Psychological Medicine* 22, 951–9.

Lucas, A.R., Beard, C.M. and O'Fallon, W.M. (1991). Fifty year trends in the incidence of anorexia nervosa in Rochester, Minnesota: a population-based study. *American Journal of Psychiatry* 148, 917–22.

Minuchin, S., Rosman, B. and Baker, L. (1978). *Psychosomatic Families. Anorexia Nervosa in Context.* Cambridge, MA; Harvard University Press.

Morris, D. (1967). *The Naked Ape: A Zoologist's Study of the Human Animal.* London: Jonathan Cape.

Overby, K.J. and Litt, I.F. (1988). Mediastinal emphysema in an adolescent with anorexia nervosa and self-induced emesis. *Pediatrics* 81, 134–6.

Oyebode, F., Boodhoo, J.A. and Schapira, K. (1988). Anorexia nervosa in males: clinical features and outcome. *International Journal of Eating Disorders* 7, 121–4.

Patton, G.C. (1988). Mortality in eating disorders. *Psychological Medicine* 18, 947–51.

Patton, G.C., Carlin, J.B., Shao, Q. and Hibbert, M.E. (1997). Adolescent dieting: Healthy weight control or borderline eating disorder. *Journal of Child Psychology and Psychiatry* 38, 299–306.

Pope, H. and Hudson, J. (1992). Is childhood sexual abuse a risk factor for bulimia nervosa? *American Journal of Psychiatry* 149, 455–63.

Pryor, T., McGilley, B. and Roach, N.E. (1990). Psychopharmacology and eating disorders – the dawning of a new age. *Psychiatric Annals* 20, 711–22.

Puckering, C., Pickles, A., Skuse, D. and Heptinstall, L. (1995). Mother–child interaction and the cognitive and behavioural development of four-year-old children with poor growth. *Journal of Child Psychology and Psychiatry* 36, 573–95.

Russell, G.F.M. (1985). Premenstrual anorexia nervosa and its sequelae. *Journal of Psychiatric Research* 19, 363–9.

Russell, G.F.M., Szmukler, G.I., Dare, C. and Eiser, M.A. (1987). An evaluation of family therapy in anorexia nervosa and bulimia nervosa. *Archives of General Psychiatry* 44, 1047–56.

Schmidt, U., Hodes, M. and Treasure, J. (1992). Early onset bulimia nervosa—who is at risk? *Psychological Medicine* 22, 623–8.

Selvini-Palazzoli, M. (1974). *Self Starvation: From Individual to Family Therapy in the Treatment of Anorexia Nervosa.* New York: Aronson.

Sharp, C.W. and Freeman, C.P.L. (1993). The medical complications of anorexia nervosa. *British Journal of Psychiatry* 162, 452–62.

Steinhausen, H.Ch., Rauss-Mason, C. and Seidel, R. (1991). Follow up studies of anorexia nervosa: a review of four decades of outcome research. *Psychological Medicine* 21, 447–54.

Strober, M. (1991). Family-genetic studies in eating disorders. *Journal of Clinical Psychiatry* 52 (suppl. 10), 9–12.

Walford, G. and McCune, N. (1991). Long term outcome of early onset anorexia nervosa. *British Journal of Psychiatry* 159, 383–9.

Whitaker, A., Johnson, J., Shaffer, D. and Rapoport, J. (1990). Uncommon troubles in young people; prevalence estimates of selected psychiatric disorders in a non-referred psychiatric population. *Archives of General Psychiatry* 47, 487–96.

6   Traumatic and stressful situations

GENERAL CONSIDERATIONS

It is an interesting observation that while some people can cope with adversity without experiencing great distress others become stuck in remembrance, misery and fear. It is not fully understood why there should be such a variation in reaction, but it does seem that in general adverse life events are linked to the development of psychiatric illness in adolescence. These effects are relatively non-specific in that such adverse events do not predict what type of psychiatric illness the teenager may develop or how severe that illness may prove. The work in this area is, however, beginning to show that some children are protected from the harmful effects of negative life events by their own inner strengths (Goodyer 1993).

A key factor in trying to predict how a traumatic event might be dealt with is the child's age. At about two years of age the toddler can distinguish individuals and begin to recreate experiences in play. Through this the child can recognise that events have occurred but cannot set them in any context. This means that at this age a child can't anticipate events or consequences very easily because the context that would act as a warning is missing. By the age of three years the child's play is becoming more sophisticated and is starting to become the medium through which the child seeks to gain an understanding of the world. With this development also comes a fundamental change of thinking as the child begins to shed the belief that the world is governed solely by their actions.

Around the age of four years the child develops the ability to recognise alternative ways of proceeding and can favour one over another, which is the beginning of the child recognising that there can be alternative origins for problems other than the child's own action. By six years of age this ability is so fully developed that the child is then able to relate the causes of events to origins which the child recognises he or she can't influence. The importance of this developmental sequence is that a child younger than five years of age is likely to view any traumatic event as something that they caused to occur. The death of a parent, for instance, will be linked to some fleeting thought about wishing them dead, or a sequence of abuse will be seen by the child as something that they are responsible for. Such an attribution can be a major source of guilt for a child, and act as the stimulus for the development of a variety of psychological difficulties at the time, and into the future.

SPECIFICALLY STRESSFUL SITUATIONS

Bereavement

As with all other aspects of coping with stressful events, the age at which children are asked to cope can have a crucial impact on how they deal with stressful events. Following bereavement, children younger than five years of age see death as reversible and so the person has simply gone somewhere else, and may perhaps return one day. This belief is simultaneously reassuring to the child and disconcerting for adults, who may feel that the child's lack of marked distress is because 'they don't care' or because 'it hasn't sunk in yet'. In fact neither of these is the case – the child simply believes the person is elsewhere, a fact which is not a cause for distress.

By the age of seven years the child can recognise that death is an ending and is permanent. As a result, in children of this age the loss of a loved one can have quite an impact, for the child can recognise the loss but does not have the emotional experience or maturity with which to deal with it. In children over seven years of age, therefore, the sense of loss can provoke reactions which approximate those seen in adults. Immediately upon learning of the loss there is a sense of shock and disbelief. The young person often appears dazed, but in the following days there is the emergence of misery, and possibly an attempt to withdraw from company. There is usually a deterioration in sleep patterns and concentration, and eating habits change. There are broadly two patterns that young people may display in the weeks following the death of significant figures in their lives. The first is where the child may find it so difficult to come to terms with the loss, that he or she tries to retain a 'relationship' in some way. This often takes the form of retaining a keep-sake, or having feelings that the person is still with them (Silverman *et al.* 1992). Sometimes the child may report seeing or hearing the person, but these events are not of the same quality as the hallucinations seen in major psychotic illnesses. In such young people reunion fantasies are quite common, and this pattern can cause adults to become quite concerned about the child.

The second type of reaction is typically seen after a traumatic death. Children feel overwhelmed by the distress and so seek to avoid any remembrance of it. They will avoid items, or situations, that could act as reminders, and begin to fear that other significant people may also suddenly be taken from them. This can be compounded if they associate the death with some threat or wish that they uttered in anger, for the magical thinking that is so prevalent in the early school years can easily link two such events. This leads children to believe that others may be in danger from their anger, and prompts further withdrawal from social groupings. This pattern of avoidance and withdrawal can significantly distort the grieving process, and if prolonged may need professional intervention.

Commonly, in the aftermath of a significant bereavement, children will lose motivation to do schoolwork, and will often report intrusive thoughts or images associated with the dead person crowding into their minds when they try to work or study. There may be a sequence of minor illnesses, which can be an effective way of obtaining adult concern and care for a child who does not fully understand that being bereaved can obtain such support in its own right.

Over the subsequent weeks these intense emotions give way to a more blunted pattern of sadness and irritability, and sometimes there is the emergence of aggression. If the children are able to share their feelings they often report feeling particularly distressed by remembrances, items that remind them of the person, or dates that have particular significance. Over the subsequent months these features fade and become less frequent, so that by eighteen months most have effectively dealt with their feelings and stop grieving. Very few young people go on to have adult problems as a result of a bereavement (Fristed *et al.* 1993), and the strongest determinant of whether this will occur is the quality of childcare offered in the aftermath of the bereavement (Breier *et al.* 1988). Indeed, some young people take on a more mature perspective as the result of suffering a bereavement and emerge better equipped to cope with future adversity (Balk 1990). This in itself can sometimes be problematic, for if a child with this sense of responsibility feels obliged to assume a parenting role within the family (to allow the parents the space to grieve themselves), then this can, if prolonged, begin to distort the developmental path of the young person.

The other crucial factor which influences a child's reaction to a death is the relationship that existed before the bereavement. The death of a distant relative will prompt little in the way of direct grief, and most of the child's behaviour will be in response to the parents' reactions to the news. If, however, the death is of a parent with whom the child had a close relationship, then the child can feel a keen sense of abandonment and quite a profound bereavement reaction will ensue.

Responses and intervention following bereavement

When children are faced with coping with the loss of a significant adult it is important to consider the child's age. In younger children it is necessary to be prepared for indifference, and perhaps a surprising lack of distress. Indeed, in younger children it is often the adults who need reassurance that the child's reaction is quite age appropriate, and not a sign that there are deeply repressed feelings that will later cause the young person major problems.

In older children the first need is to establish a supportive and caring environment. It is important to recognise that the child will have questions and strong emotions that must be dealt with. The child may not feel able, or feel they have permission, to grieve, or may not know how to respond to the emotions that they are experiencing. The supportive response is to let the child feel that it's acceptable to be upset, and perhaps even confirm that being tearful at such times is a natural reaction. It is also usually helpful if the child attends the funeral. Most children express a desire to attend the ceremony, and research indicates that attendance is generally beneficial to their ultimate adjustment (Weller *et al.* 1988).

Following an intensely distressing bereavement it is important to keep a special watch for a young person who, in the aftermath of a bereavement which has severely touched a parent, becomes a parent to the rest of the family. Initially, this can be seen as helpful – getting other children in the family ready for school or accepting more household tasks so that the parent can rest. To a certain degree such a shift in role can also make a positive contribution to the child's maturation process, but if too intense, or if the child is too young to assume such responsibility, then their longer-term development may be adversely affected. In the shorter term such a shift in family roles may also limit the amount of grieving which the child can actually do, and so leave unresolved problems which may manifest in other ways – for instance, as physical symptoms such as headaches.

Another way that children may miss out on their own grieving process is if their sense of duty prompts them to making efforts to distract their parents from their grief. This often takes the form of misbehaviour, since this is the most potent way of obtaining parental attention, and certainly is capable of demanding a high priority in their parents' concerns.

Alex presented at eight years of age with a six-month history of being difficult and truculent at home. His mother said he had become defiant and everything had become a battle. Alex's parents saw the behaviour as particularly problematic because their younger child had developed leukaemia some months ago and they felt they had enough worries without having to respond to Alex's tantrums and defiance.

When seen alone, Alex quickly became weepy and distressed, saying that he was very concerned about his brother, but since he had developed his illness his parents spent all their spare time with him, and Alex felt he had no time with them. He said of the last few weeks that 'they aren't crying all the time now, they're too busy shouting at me'.

A further mechanism by which poor behaviour can emerge is if the parents have been so deeply affected by the loss that their parenting abilities have become blunted, or they have lost the motivation to keep insisting upon good behaviour. Looser boundaries and less certain responses to challenge can allow poor behaviour to surface and it often reaches quite a marked level before the parent realises how much things have deteriorated.

Work with adolescents suggests that young people of this age feel better if they can talk about their feelings of loss with their peers (Gray 1989), but many worry that their emotional distress will be too much for their friends to cope with, or may not know how to express how they are feeling. This awkwardness and uncertainty about how to behave tends to drive the young person to withdraw into solitude. This is probably why many teenagers report that their friendships deteriorate in the aftermath of a bereavement (Balk 1990).

If the young person retains good social links and is keeping up with schoolwork, then they are coping well with the situation and do not require outside assistance. As Dyregrov (1991) has outlined, however, there are several elements that are worth pursuing after a bereavement in order to make sure that the grief is dealt with appropriately.

- Ensure that the child gets information on the illness or circumstances of the death. It is important that they understand the situation properly, and to this end the explanations must be concrete and explicit.
- Correct any misunderstandings or wrong information.
- Give the child explicit permission to grieve, and offer opportunities to do so in a safe environment. In younger children features of the death may dominate pictures and play for some weeks after, and this should be accepted as the norm.
- Give information on how people grieve, in particular confirming that it's appropriate to have a range of feelings, not only sadness at the loss, but anger that they have been deserted.
- Re-establish routines as soon as practicable – returning to the familiar and the predictable helps to minimise the fears that the young person's own future is threatened by the loss.
- Help retain peer links, but this should be by offering opportunities not by creating any sense of pressure.
- Re-enforce parental strength and control, and ensure that rules are still enforced. This gives the necessary sense of support to the young person, as well as offering the same predictability as existed before the loss.
- Parents should also be encouraged to plan how they will respond to their children so that they can reaffirm that they are solid and dependable.
- Most children benefit from being given the opportunity to say 'goodbye' properly. The younger the child the more concrete this expression tends to be – for example, a young child may wish to place a favourite toy upon the grave.

As well as these typical bereavement processes there are two special situations that are worthy of mention. The first is when the child is witness to a particularly horrific death. In these situations professional help from the local social services department, or through the family doctor, is nearly always necessary if the child is to resolve fully the feelings such an experience provokes. A variation on this theme, which brings with it myriad emotional problems, is the thankfully rare situation when one parent kills another. Although the processes are not very different, specialised assistance, through the agencies mentioned, is necessary (Hendriks *et al.* 1993).

The second situation is when a classmate has a terminal illness, and so it can be seen that a whole class will have to cope with a bereavement. In such a situation it is helpful to prepare the class by giving the information in a structured way, and prompting class members to plan how they will react and respond (Yule and Gold 1993).

Growing up in a violent household

There is increasing concern that growing up in a household where there is violence has a damaging effect upon a child's development. This arises not only because of the direct impact that witnessing or being a victim of violence causes, but indirectly because of the way that the violence prevents effective parenting from being given.

Research in this field has indicated that physically abused toddlers tend to show far more angry non-compliance than their peers, and are easily frustrated in tasks or games (Erickson *et al.* 1989). Older children tend to show disruptive and aggressive reactions (Shields *et al.* 1994). A particularly interesting observation is that boys who have grown up in violent households appear to become more aroused by angry exchanges than peers, and perhaps as a consequence are far more likely to involve themselves in the angry exchanges (Cummings *et al.* 1994). This pattern tends to recur throughout their lives, and so when teenagers and young adults they are particularly prone to having romantic relationships which are punctuated by violent and abusive episodes (Riggs *et al.* 1990).

Cicchetti and Toth (1995) have described how growing up in a violent household, or being the victim of any type of abuse, has the potential to distort four areas of a child's functioning:

- emotional regulation
- attachment
- sense of self
- peer relationships

Emotional regulation comprises the way the young person copes with feelings and, as already pointed out, this can mean exaggerated reactions, or responses which are too quick and ill thought out, to situations of potential aggression. In other situations the emotion may be more the expected ones of misery or distress, but prompted by trivial, and unrelated situations, which can give the impression that the young person is moody or suffering from a depressive illness when in fact the problem is a distorted regulatory mechanism.

Attachment to the parent is the first, and perhaps most fundamental, relationship which a child achieves. It helps to establish a pattern of emotions, thoughts and expectations which become the yardstick for all future relationships to be judged by. Abused children have more insecure attachments (Crittenden 1988) and this often means that the toddler finds it difficult to cope with separation, giving a 'disorganised', disorientated quality to the pattern of dealing with the daily separations which are part of any child's life (Carlson *et al.* 1989). However, if toddlerhood is without major incident, and the negative experiences begin later in life, then the risk of disturbing attachment markedly decreases (Lynch and Cicchetti 1991). As parents, young people who have experienced disturbed attachment have poorer parenting practices, and are more likely to maltreat their own children (Main and Goldwyn 1984). This is largely because, since they have not developed solid attachments in childhood, they find it particularly difficult to develop such attachments with their own children.

The child's sense of self becomes established by the age of two years, and, as already mentioned, with this begins the process of developing a capacity to use play to represent situations, which in turn helps the child understand what he or she is responsible for, and what part others play in bringing events about. If young people have abusive experiences before this age, then this sense of self is distorted. Such children find it harder to engage in the symbolic play so typical of toddlerhood (Alessandri 1991) and they tend to be more aggressive and less competent with their peers. Such young people show a low self-esteem and have less sense of being able to cope (Cicchetti and Toth 1995).

As has already been pointed out in Chapter 1, establishing effective peer relationships is a key developmental issue for all children. Violent experiences can distort this process because such young people have heightened levels of physical and verbal aggression and may respond in this way to friendly overtures and even signs of distress in others (Mueller and Silverman 1989). The other reaction which is commonly seen, and which can significantly disturb peer-relationship development, is a withdrawal from peer interactions and an avoidance of activities where the young person is expected to mix with peers (Rogosch and Cicchetti 1994).

Interestingly, parents who maltreat their children often have high expectations of their performance, and yet they do not provide the support necessary to achieve the goals they set. For instance, they provide less verbal stimulation to their children and do not encourage autonomy, both of which are important in fostering achievement (Trickett *et al.* 1991). In addition, these parents see child rearing as less enjoyable and use more controlling disciplinary techniques than average. Because these children tend to be quite challenging, schools can easily replicate this pattern of management, and with it become identified with the parents. The antipathy which is felt for the parents can, in these circumstances, then be acted out against the school.

In the longer term young people who have grown up in violent households, or experienced significant abuse as children can develop depression

(Toth *et al.* 1992), but most commonly they go on to have problems with delinquency (Lewis *et al.* 1989), and to show a violent tendency in their relationships (Malinosky-Rummell and Hansen 1993).

Responding to children who are growing up in a violent household

Helping young people who have experienced a violent upbringing has many similarities to the response offered to children who have been the victims of abuse. The intervention focuses on three areas, the first of which is the family element. It is essential that the functioning of the parental figures is well understood, in particular their own childhood history, and their perceptions, feelings and reactions to the child. If any of these elements show distortion, intervention may need to be offered using either cognitive approaches or family therapy techniques (see Chapter 2). If there are problems within the parent–child interaction then parental depression must be excluded as a cause. If it is truly interactional then play sessions with parent and child can help to establish the necessary rapport and so help correct potential problems with the attachment process (Lieberman *et al.* 1991).

The second element is work with the child. This can only begin once it is clear that the child is now safe from violent or abusive experiences. A child cannot begin to deal with painful issues of this kind unless it is clear that such events are now in the past. To ask a child to explore such issues when they may recur invites them to expose themselves to even greater harm. This is because within any therapeutic process young people must question and challenge their beliefs, ventilate the anger which they have harboured, and perhaps ask difficult questions of their parents. To attempt this when further violence or abuse is possible is dangerous indeed.

If the young person can feel trust and security within the treatment relationship, then these emotions and themes can be explored in a gradual manner. As the process progresses the expressions of emotion become more marked before a gradual subsidence of the difficulties occurs. It is important to be alert to these changes: good therapy makes things worse before it makes them better.

The last element of an intervention programme focuses on the environment in which the child is living. One aspect of this is clearly to remove the potential for further violence or abuse, but there are also the important themes of maintaining routines and allowing the child experiences of success. In addition, positive relationships of all kinds are important in offering alternative experiences to those that are being worked with in the therapeutic alliance.

The importance of intervention is not only due to its effect on immediate disturbances and difficulties, but because it decreases the probability of the young person developing major problems in later life. In particular, effective intervention reduces the likelihood of there being relationship problems in adulthood, as well as reducing the risk of the pattern being repeated when the former victims become parents themselves (National Research Council 1993).

Being the victim of sexual abuse

Many of the themes relevant to children growing up in a violent household are commonly found in other forms of abusive situation, but being the victim of sexual abuse does carry with it specific issues and reactions which are worthy of separate consideration.

Sexual abuse is a term which can encompass a wide range of inappropriate sexual activity from fondling to full intercourse, with about 5 per cent of reported incidents involving penetrative intercourse (Baker and Duncan, 1985). Girls are 2.5 times more likely to be the victim than boys (Finkelhor 1986), and although the child can be any age, it is most common for it to begin between the ages of eight and twelve years (Monck *et al.* 1993). Such abuse occurs irrespective of social status or religious persuasion and in many of the cases the abuse is a repeated act over several years. Most cases are never reported, and it has been estimated that as few as 2 per cent of cases are brought to the attention of the authorities (Russell 1983), with incest with a sibling probably being the most common (Finkelhor 1979), and yet least reported. The type of difficulty experienced by the young person depends on five factors:

- the age and stage of development at the time of the abuse
- the type of abuse that occurred
- the sophistication of the young person's own coping mechanisms for dealing with the emotions it provokes
- the caregiver's reactions and innate mechanisms for coping with the feelings which the abuse raises
- the environmental factors: for example, does the abuser still see the child?

Generally, sexual abuse results in significant psychiatric impairment in the victims, most typically oppositional-defiance, anxiety or depression (Merry and Andrews 1994). Evidence is also emerging that sexual abuse of boys may in the long term have greater effects and be more complex in nature than we have yet realised (Garnefski and Diekstra 1997).

In the immediate aftermath anxiety symptoms tend to be the most evident – evidenced by insomnia, nightmares and somatic complaints, with half of the cases having the severe symptoms associated with post-traumatic stress disorder (PTSD) – re-experiencing the trauma, flashbacks and avoiding situations which might act as reminders (McLeer *et al.* 1988). Indeed, for some children the trauma of the experience can be so great that they try to distance themselves from the events by 'forgetting' that they occurred. This defence against pain is known as denial and can be sustained for quite long periods of time, but for some the memories do return in later life; indeed, it is now becoming increasingly common for adults with psychiatric illnesses to disclose that they have been the victims of sexual abuse as children, raising questions as to the part that such traumas play in the causation of psychiatric illness (Sheldrick 1991).

The other defence mechanism that some children use is dissociation. Here the child escapes into 'another life' where such painful experiences do not occur. There are periods of amnesia, intense daydreaming and going into a trance-like state which can occasionally lead to the child developing multiple 'personalities', each with its own characteristics, a disorder which is very disruptive to functioning when an adult.

Although such defence mechanisms can clearly have a profound effect upon long-term functioning, lesser effects can cause havoc to the self-image of a child. Most victims of abuse see themselves as 'damaged goods' because of their experiences (Sgroi 1982), and this compounds the feelings of depression and misery that are so common for the children to have. This is why so many victims in adult life have marked psychiatric problems such as major depressive illnesses (Livingstone 1987), eating disorders (Pope and Hudson 1992) and drug abuse (Goodwin *et al.* 1990). In addition to such defined problems there are often difficulties in relating to peers (Sgroi 1982) and a trend towards excessive aggression when thwarted or angry (Friedrich *et al.* 1986).

About 16 per cent of children report feelings of arousal within the abusive relationship (Monck *et al.* 1993). The sense of conflict between these feelings and the knowledge of being abused can be a powerful force in creating psychiatric problems.

One of the most consistent observations is the way that sexually abusive experiences distort the child's own sexual functioning, and this seems especially true if the abuse occurred before the age of seven years (McClellan *et al.* 1996). Public masturbation and the tendency to repeat sexually abusive experiences are very common patterns (Monck *et al.* 1993). Infants who have been abused find it difficult to distinguish appropriate displays of affection from the episodes of sexual activity (Yates 1982), leading to abused toddlers showing quite explicitly sexual behaviour. It is important to remember that children learn about sexuality, they are not born with an innate knowledge; so if they are sexually explicit, this is because of what they have seen or experienced.

Sara was four years of age when her nursery became concerned at her sexualised play. She would openly masturbate while playing, and would sit on adults' knees, rocking slowly while making a moaning sound and becoming quite excited. Investigations revealed that Sara had been subjected to repeated sexual abuse from the age of two years of age, as had her elder sister.

It is within the nature of any painful or traumatic event that extreme reactions can take the form of seeking out more, similar experiences, or trying to avoid them. So it is with sexual abuse, for as well as sexual acting out the child can react by avoiding sexual situations, and attempting to repress sexual feelings (Finkelhor 1979). While this may not be too problematic in childhood, such a way of coping with the painful experiences can have a profound effect upon adult relationships, especially when they are also influenced by disturbance of gender identity. This disturbance can show itself in girls as a drive to be more masculine in demeanour, and to express a strong preference to become a boy (Cosentino 1993). Similar gender confusion has been noted in abused boys and it is postulated that such confusion may prompt experimentation with homosexuality (Singer 1989).

The age of children can quite markedly influence the pattern seen, because if children are very young, then, as was described earlier, the ability to distinguish whether they caused the abuse is poorly developed and they will tend to accept it as part of routine adult–child interaction. In addition, the belief in the authority of adults means that if the abuse is perceived as wrong, the child is likely to see it as occurring because of the bad things they have done. Such beliefs can form a powerful foundation for children to believe they are bad, unlovable, or worthy of punishment – all strong causes for having major adjustment problems in adult life.

In considering the list on p. 93, it is clear that only the last three factors can be influenced, and so it is important that all three of these aspects are addressed if any meaningful help is to be offered (Cicchetti and Toth 1995). Sexually abused children are often seen within school to be anxious, inattentive and unable to understand classroom expectations. They tend to be unpopular with peers, and show an increased frequency of withdrawal and aggressive outbursts in any interactions they have with them. Typically, they tend to get by because they are highly dependent upon teachers (Erickson *et al.* 1989).

Intervention with children who have been sexually abused

The first requirement of any intervention is to recognise that abuse is occurring. The majority of cases comes to light because of a disclosure by the child, and so an essential first principle is to accept the child's statements when first told. Being the victim of abuse can provoke quite significant behavioural difficulties and so it is dangerous to dismiss a child's report of abuse simply because they have been troublesome in the past.

If you are the recipient of a disclosure of any type of abuse, then offer a calm and accepting demeanour. Responses should be in a supportive tone, and either a repetition of their last phrase, or simple requests for them to continue. The information must be passed on to the relevant professionals and so any promise to 'keep the secret' must be avoided. Record as accurately and as soon as possible what was said, and then follow the advice about making a referral that is contained in the Child Protection Procedures manual.

The professional network of social workers and police acts on the disclosure by carrying out a careful investigation. The first priority is always to ensure that the child is safe from further abuse, and in half of the families the concern about how supportive the family will be is sufficient for the child to be accommodated away from home (Monck *et al.* 1993).

Upon completion of the assessment there may be legal action in the form of civil proceedings (care order applications and so on) or criminal proceedings against the abusing adult. The timing of therapy has to be considered in the light of such proceedings because any formal intervention needs to occur in the context of a supportive and consistent parenting regime. The sense of control and parental containment enhances the sense of safety that is crucial if children are to surrender their defences and allow themselves fully to explore the emotions and beliefs that are associated with their abuse experiences. The choice of timing is also important in ensuring that the courts, in the case of criminal proceedings, do not feel that therapeutic work has contaminated the child's evidence.

Initial intervention is focused upon ventilating feelings, and this is achieved by repeatedly exploring the events and exposing the associated emotional elements. With such processes the distress should gradually subside and children develop a better understanding of the events and their part within them (Berliner 1991). If the child remains cool and detached despite evidence of traumatic abuse experiences, then it is likely that he or she is trying to cope with the events by dissociation or denial (see above). This is especially likely if the abuse experiences are multiple or occur over a long period. In such situations formal psychiatric help is indicated, and the situation is likely to demand a lengthy intervention.

In most cases a variety of approaches is necessary in order to address the various types of difficulty that abuse can cause. The sexualised components are addressed initially by age-appropriate sex education and establishing with the child what are the age-appropriate ways of dealing with sexual needs and urges (Berliner 1991). Group therapy can help significantly in dealing with children's belief that they are the only ones to whom this has happened, as well as helping to reduce the intensity of behavioural problems (Nekli and Watters 1989). Cognitive therapy has also been shown to offer specific assistance in reducing the difficulties associated with abuse (Cohen and Mannarino 1996). In addition, work with the abuser, and the wider family, is usually occurring at the same time and is primarily looking to understand why it occurred and exploring how such abusive behaviour can be prevented in future.

It is important within this process not to lose sight of parental distress, since the success of such programmes can be strongly influenced by how well the parents are coping (Cohen and Mannarino 1996).

There are three potential solutions to the problem of ensuring that in future the child has a safe and supportive environment:

- re-integration back into a complete family; however, this is possible in only about 15 per cent of cases (Bentovim *et al.*, 1988)
- remaining with the non-abusing parent: this is the commonest solution
- being accommodated with an alternative family: this is the solution when the family's support and protection is deemed inadequate

Outcome for sexually abused children

The studies carried out among adults reveal the potential that exists for sexually abusive experiences in childhood to prompt major psychiatric difficulties in adult life. In particular there is concern that abused children may become abusing adults, and a great deal of therapeutic effort is focused upon trying to break this cycle. It is clear that the present intervention programmes are effective at reducing the symptoms which show themselves after disclosure of abuse (Monck *et al.* 1993), but whether they will reduce the longer-term problems only time will tell.

Coping with parental separation and divorce

Parental separation is one of the most common traumatic events that a child can face. In fact children who have experienced a separation or divorce are up to three times more likely to have emotional and behavioural difficulties than the average. However, it is very rarely a single event, for, in the vast majority of cases, there has been ongoing relationship difficulty between the parents before the specific act of separation occurs. Wallerstein and Blakeslee (1989) describe three phases of separation:

1 Acute – a highly emotional phase with tense conflict between the parents and one (or even both) may develop depression or even become suicidal. This phase is usually relatively brief, but can last for several years if the couple becomes trapped in a sequence of legal battles, personal recriminations or ploys to try to re-establish the relationship.
2 Transitional – the parents begin to distance themselves from each other and establish new relationships. This is a period of excitement but also of uncertainties.
3 Settlement – new patterns of living are established and there is no longer direct emotional linkage to the ex-partner.

With the separation of parents come changes in income and perhaps of home and school. As the phases described above indicate, there is also a change in the emotional tenor of the parents, which may lead to psychiatric illness. With the fracture of the previous parenting system and these marked emotional changes in the immediate aftermath of the separation, the parenting offered to the child may diminish. This can become an ongoing problem if the custodial parent does not establish a new equilibrium quickly, or if the search to replace the lost partner detracts too much from the reassertion of appropriate parenting patterns. Equally problematic is if the child becomes a parent's prop through this difficult period, for a dependency on the child can then develop which makes normal development tasks far harder for the child to achieve.

A sadly common consequence of separation is the pattern of ongoing friction between the parents which superficially can be focused upon contact or financial settlements, but in fact is a continuation of their relationship conflict. Within this type of conflict there can be competition for the affection and allegiance of the child which can take many forms, few of which are helpful to the child's development.

Michael was six years old when his parents separated. Michael's mother was very bitter at her husband's departure and the way that he had 'deserted the family'. She resisted any idea of ongoing contact between Michael and his father because she feared he would 'pick up his habits and his ways'. The court imposed regular contact at a neutral venue and before each meeting Michael's mother would remind him that his father was 'a bad man'. After the visits she would closely question Michael about his father's present lifestyle, whether he had a new partner and so on.

A situation such as this imposes major stress upon the child. Not only is there a need not to upset the parent who looks after you, but any suggestion of liking the other parent is seen as disloyalty. Equally, the contact sessions cannot be enjoyed for their own sake because of the danger of fuelling the battle by some inadvertent comment.

Coping with the separation and divorce is actually the final stage of the process which has entangled the family in ongoing friction and emotional upheaval, usually for a lengthy period. Indeed, such marital friction is more damaging to a child than the separation itself, especially for boys where such problems usually prompt acting-out behaviour (Cherlin *et al.*, 1991). The elements described in the section on violent households (see above) are equally relevant here, as are the concerns about how the friction might affect the future functioning of the child.

Faced with the distress of parental separation, children react as they would to any very painful situation. Initially, the dominant feeling is one of their present world collapsing, and a sense of anxiety, perhaps even dread of the future. Their grief at the loss of their family is usually compounded by concern at the distress shown by their parents, and bewilderment as their loyalty to both parents is challenged. Pre-school children resist separation, become more demanding, cry frequently, and may 'lose' acquired routines such as table manners or developmental skills such as toileting. Sleep disturbances are common, as is behaving more aggressively towards parents, siblings and peers.

When the separation occurs at a time when the children are just established in school, they have vivid concerns as to whether the departed parent will continue to care for them and they show open grief at the separation. Children of this age find it difficult to understand the complexities of the situation and often seek to resolve the hurt by trying to reunite the parents.

Jeanette was seven years old at the time her parents separated. To that point there had been no concern about her development or functioning, but in the weeks following the separation her behaviour in school deteriorated and she became more challenging towards her mother within the home. These episodes of refusal to comply were only stopped by Jeanette's father coming to the home and 'taking charge'. Jeanette told her father that she liked it when he came back to the house and she would stop being naughty if he moved back permanently.

When the separation occurs just before puberty, the child's ability to understand the issues is greater and the child's own reactions are more complex. However, overall, the reaction still is rather black and white and is often typified by anger at the 'bad' parent for causing the separation, and an intense commitment to care for the 'hurt' one. Such commitment can interfere with peer relationships and school performance, as these elements are given second place to being with the parent that 'needs them'.

Parental separation during children's adolescence complicates a time when they are endeavouring to cope with their own emotional storms brought on by this developmental stage. The additional stress of the separation tends to intensify the existing emotional features and can precipitate the emergence of acting-out behaviour, depression or even suicidal feelings. At this age, the concrete thinking of the child is giving way to a more abstract and complex understanding of situations which can often lead to the adolescent reaching a strongly held view as to how the events leading up to the separation should be interpreted.

Although in general boys appear to fair somewhat worse than girls in the aftermath of parental separation (Block *et al.* 1981), when adolescence is reached girls of separated parents do experience greater difficulty than the average in separating from their mothers (Kalter *et al.* 1985). A good relationship with one or both parents predicts a better outcome (Emery 1982), and a helpful supportive adult outside the family can offer additional benefit in helping the child cope with the stresses within the family. However, overall, it is how parents cope with the trauma of separation and divorce that is the major determinant of how children will cope (Guidubaldi and Perry 1985), and to what extent they will carry a fear of failed relationships into their adult lives.

Assisting the process of coming to terms with parental separation

The first strand of intervention is to endeavour to establish an amicable and flexible atmosphere between the separating parents to minimise the child's sense of being 'in the middle'. Successful resolution of the family law issues of custody, contact and maintenance is crucial to setting the tone in which the child's future functioning will be determined. There are six tasks that children must achieve if they are to minimise the impact of parental separation (after Wallerstein 1983):

- acknowledge the reality of the separation
- distance themselves from parental conflicts and distress, and re-establish normal routines
- come to terms with the losses that separation has prompted
- resolve their sense of anger and self-blame
- accept the permanence of the separation
- set realistic goals for future relationships with parents and new parental figures

Adults in contact with the child can facilitate this process by being available, understanding and supportive, and being so without being drawn into the value judgements about parental behaviour which often dominate the child's thinking in the early stages.

Children trapped in acrimonious separations, or who are reacting badly to the family changes, may require more focused help. This commonly takes the form of group work where the child can share feelings and recognise he or she is not the only one to whom this has happened. In addition, an active group process can help to reduce the intensity of emotional and behavioural problems, as well as improving peer skills. Individual work needs to address the child's beliefs, attitude and feelings about the separation, and examine closely the child's position within the new domestic arrangements. Seeing the family as a whole can also be helpful in dealing with situations where the child is caught between warring parents, but such intervention needs to be finely judged, because a child may be punished by one of the parents if their contribution within the session was not seen as supportive enough of the parent's point of view.

Coming to terms with physical illness

In the western world about 5 per cent of children have a significant, handicapping physical disorder (Pless and Nolan 1991). How such children react to their difficulties is very varied, but the trend is that the more severe the handicap, the greater the risk of the young person developing a psychiatric disorder (Daud *et al.* 1993). However, most young people do cope, and those who seek to cope actively by thinking of other things or using calming self-statements tend to fare much better than those who simply hope things will be all right (Gil *et al.* 1991). When problems do occur, they tend to show themselves either as emotional symptoms or as eating anomalies (Pearson *et al.* 1991).

Paradoxically, although the development of a significant disability obviously has a major impact upon the young person, it is the impact that it has upon the parent which is often the most significant for predicting future psychological difficulties. As a result of coming to terms with their child's disability or illness, the parents may become depressed or overprotective, or lose interest in the child, all of which can have a marked effect upon the child's development. However, if support can be mobilised for the parents through counselling or formal psychiatric help, then the attentiveness to the child can become more average, and hence more healthy for the child (Reynolds *et al.* 1988).

Illnesses or injuries which involve the brain are particularly problematic and evidence suggests that children with epilepsy, for instance, may be up to four times more likely to develop psychiatric problems than the general population, particularly if there are other neurological abnormalities evident (Rutter *et al.* 1970). It is not only the direct impact of the illness which causes the problems, however, for children with epilepsy are also more prone to show an inappropriate level of dependency than their peers (Hoare 1984). In some people it is clear that seizures can be provoked by becoming emotional or feeling stressed. This observation has prompted the development of programmes which look to control seizures using psychological methods, and there is evidence that teaching appropriate psychological and behavioural techniques can offer some people a degree of control (Motofsky and Balaschak 1977).

Head injuries may result in a child developing a seizure problem, but such an injury may prompt psychological difficulties even without the emergence of post-traumatic epilepsy. It is possible that even mild head injuries may result in psychological difficulties (Middleton 1989), but the vast majority of such injuries cause problems that are transient and quickly resolved. In severe head injuries, however, up to 50 per cent of victims will show long-term psychiatric problems (Rutter *et al.* 1983), and this is most likely in those who had some emotional or behavioural difficulties before the injury occurred. The likelihood of future difficulties can also be predicted by how much of the immediate post-accident events the child can't remember. If the period of this post-traumatic amnesia is for the events which have occurred more than a week after the accident then psychiatric difficulties are increasingly likely (Chadwick *et al.* 1981).

Dealing with the emotional aspects of physical illness

In any situation where there is physical illness this must be treated by the appropriate methods. As the above shows, however, it is also important to be aware of the psychological elements that may be occurring, and perhaps contributing, to the picture. The first element of concern should be to help the child cope with the illness and the limitations it imposes. If the illness is a life-threatening one, then a variation of bereavement counselling may be necessary to help the child find some resolution to the questions that such a devastating diagnosis prompts. Such efforts may be concentrated into a brief time span in the case of acute illnesses, or may have a far more protracted make-up if the illness is one that shortens life expectancy to some degree.

In some illnesses the more pressing issue is coming to terms with limitations. For example, diabetes requires a degree of dietary vigilance that other children do not require, or children with cerebral palsy have physical and mobility restrictions that prevent them participating fully in all the activities of their friends. If the illness gives the child an unusual appearance or oddity of action, then feeling self-conscious is to be expected. There may need to be intensive work, however, to ensure such children do not avoid such feelings by isolating themselves, but rather look at their feelings and develop mechanisms, using behavioural and cognitive techniques, that ensure they push through the feelings and maintain an active and full life.

The child's reaction to illness or disability is strongly influenced by the reaction of the family. It is very natural for parents to see a child's distress at being teased by peers as a reason to allow the child to avoid and withdraw. It is far harder to help them find ways of coping so that they can continue and face the situation. As part of any intervention, families must be given appropriate information and education about the illness, its problems and clinical management. It is also necessary that they are advised how to respond to the problems and difficulties which day-to-day living throws up. A pattern of caring and concern has to be balanced with a recognition that some pushing to try to overcome is necessary if the full potential is to be reached.

Part of that process begins by ensuring that parental expectations are realistic. There is great danger in not recognising that certain skills and abilities have been lost, for the child will not achieve and the resulting sense of disappointment erodes everyone's self-esteem. Equally as important is to avoid underestimating capabilities, and indeed this is often the more damaging extreme. Most children are far more capable than might appear at first sight, and it is vital that each child lives to the limit of his or her capabilities. A child with epilepsy, for instance, need not have a parent in attendance constantly – trips out with friends are a necessary milestone that even children with epilepsy have to experience at some point. Precautions are important, foolhardiness is to be avoided, but having taken sensible steps, it is necessary sometimes for the parents to adopt that classical parental role of sitting at home and worrying.

A key element for any child, no matter what the underlying problem or difficulty, is to encourage maximum involvement with peers. So much of a child's learning and experience of life comes from peer interaction that to limit this in any way is to begin to deprive the young person of a significant element of life. With such contact comes the risk of teasing or cruel comments, but it is better for children to learn how to cope with such things than to withdraw and never risk themselves in the world. Adults can help in this process, not only by minimising the opportunity for teasing to occur, but by giving the child mechanisms for dealing with such situations when they arise. Many schools now have anti-bullying programmes and the techniques they teach are just as applicable to children with illness or disfigurement.

With regard to the particular case of problems associated with illnesses affecting the brain, there is a variety of drugs available to control seizure activity. The use of such drugs can sometimes prompt psychiatric problems in their own right (Taylor 1991), and this has led to certain drugs, such as phenobarbitone, falling out of favour. The choice of drug regime is governed by a variety of factors, and needs to be carefully tailored to suit the needs of each individual case. The elements described above for psychological management are especially applicable to families where there is a child with epilepsy, for appropriate usage may help to reduce the rate of seizure activity in its own right.

In children who, after a head injury, are disinhibited, aggressive or emotionally quite volatile the anti-epilepsy drug carbamazepine has proven to be quite helpful (Lewin and Sumners 1992). Such treatment, however, must be considered in the context of a strong behavioural management programme which focuses upon rewarding the sought behaviour and minimising the response to difficult or challenging behaviours. These programmes are very difficult for families to carry through and there needs to be a high degree of support from health agencies and social services if they are to be effectively implemented.

In addition to such specific programmes it is important for the adults involved with the child to:

- determine the present level of skills and abilities
- use this evaluation to establish clear rules and expectations which are very slowly increased over time
- offer appropriate experiences so that the child can reacquire skills such as pencil control and so on
- slow the pace of presenting information
- minimise background distraction
- recognise that the child may need additional time to complete tasks

Such a package gives the best chance for children who have suffered setbacks through head injury, or illness, to achieve their maximum potential.

Recovering after a traumatic event

Work with victims of disasters, such as the sinking of a cross-channel ferry (Duggan and Gunn 1995), highlights the sequence of events that people experience when they have been involved in extreme trauma. One of the first studies to look at the effects of intense trauma on children was the Chowchilla study (Terr 1979) which examined twenty-six children who were kidnapped and held in a darkened trailer for twenty-six hours. This very traumatic event affected the children deeply, and it was clear that all children, regardless of their previous adjustment, can demonstrate features of an intense stress reaction if the events are significant enough. However, the child's previous development, relationship with parents, and other stresses within the family all tend to influence how the youngster copes with such events in the longer term (Terr 1983).

In the general population less than 1 per cent can be expected to show the features of a full-blown post-traumatic stress disorder, but up to 15 per cent may show symptoms of distress at any one time (Helzer *et al.* 1987). When faced with a major traumatic episode, children tend to remain quiet, but then show acute distress in the immediate aftermath (Terr 1979). Almost immediately they begin to try to think of some reason why this should have happened to them, a process called 'causal attribution' (Joseph *et al.* 1991). This 'search for a reason' can go on for months and is one of the aspects which tends to become a persistent feature of the child's thinking in later years.

In general, any child over three years of age will have good recall of the events unless they were unconscious or concussed. This will not be the case, however, if there were several traumatic events (see the section on being the victim of abuse earlier in this chapter), or if the single event has a long-lasting effect – such as the death of a parent (Terr 1991).

In the days and weeks following the event(s) images associated with the trauma keep recurring either in quiet moments or when any reminder occurs. Fearfulness quickly becomes a feature of the child's functioning – not only a fear that events may be repeated, but of more mundane elements such as being separated from parents, the dark or the presence of strangers. Sleep is often disturbed by vivid dreams, which are often life-like re-enactments of the events. Children's play becomes dominated by the events, as do their drawings, and they may demonstrate a need to keep recounting the story. The play elements tend to have an obvious link to the trauma, and become quite monotonous in content. This is especially so for children under the age of three years who cannot fully verbalise their experiences and so play out their feelings and experiences over and over again. In older children intrusive 'flashbacks' occur, which bring with them not only elements of the events but the emotions which are associated with them. Such emotional intensity is very draining, as well as distressing, and so the person usually tries to avoid being reminded of the event and generally may appear emotionally flat. There is some variation in these specific features depending upon the age of the child.

Within months some of the features, especially the emotional elements such as sleeplessness, irritability and the anxious striving to be close to parents, fade, but the re-enacting of events in play tends to persist. This monotonous preoccupation may cause the child either to become in-creasingly withdrawn or perhaps to victimise others as they have been victimised.

Intervention following traumatic events

Although early intervention to prevent problems is tempting, it is not clear that it has a positive effect (Bisson *et al.* 1997), and indeed it appears to be the presence, or absence, of other factors (such as previous psychological problems and adequate social support) that are more likely to affect the outcome than whether early protective intervention occurred (Bisson and Deahl 1994).

The early days after such traumatic events can be very distressing for all and the impact upon the child may be lessened by the use of drugs – particularly anxiety-reducing medications such as beta-blockers and cloni-dine. In the longer term the use of groups to help children share their experiences and feelings has proved helpful, especially if they were all exposed to the same event. Such groups need to focus upon the sharing of feelings and reactions, with encouragement offered for each member to speak out, but the leaders also need to remain acutely aware that the degree of trauma experienced by each child is likely to be different.

Although cognitive techniques can be used in the older child to intrude upon the difficult remembrances which can become so much part of the child's routine, it is play therapy which has long been the mainstay of helping traumatised children (Webb 1991). Such an approach can help obtain a great-er detail of events, but it is its function of helping children to express their feelings and to understand the emotional context which is the key. In older, more verbal children the move is towards more formal psychotherapy – with a particular emphasis upon ventilating their feelings, discussing symptoms and their meaning, and looking at what the children are doing 'to cope'. Such processes also allow the 'why me' question to be addressed. As was indicated earlier, this is a persistently negative theme and its eradication can have a major impact upon reducing symptoms and emotional distress.

Experience with adult victims indicates that by two years after the event little remains, but avoiding things that are reminders of the trauma is still often present (Duggan and Gunn 1995). For a significant minority (12 per cent), however, their problems have increased and they have developed clear psychiatric problems. In the five-year follow-up of the children from Chowchilla (Terr 1983) nearly all found it hard to imagine having a full and happy life, career, and so on, which may indicate how much more such events may blight a child.

REFERENCES

Alessandri, S.M. (1991). Play and social behaviours in maltreated pre-schoolers. *Developmental Psychopathology* 3, 191–206.

Baker, A.W. and Duncan, S.P. (1985). Child sexual abuse: a study of prevalence in Great Britain. *Child Abuse and Neglect* 9, 457–67.

Balk, D.E (1990). The self-concept of bereaved adolescents: sibling death and its aftermath. *Journal of Adolescent Research* 5, 112–32.

Bentouim, A., Van Elburg, A. and Boston, P. (1988). The results of treatment. In A. Bentouim, J. Hildebrand, M. Tranter and E. Vizard (eds) *Child Abuse within the Family: Assessment and Treatment.* London: John Wright.

Berliner, L. (1990). Clinical work with sexually abused children. In C.R. Hollin and K. Howells (eds) *Clinical Approaches to Sex Offenders and their Victims.* Chichester: John Wiley.

Bisson, J.I. and Deahl, M.P. (1994). Psychological debriefing and prevention of post traumatic stress. *British Journal of Psychiatry* 165, 717–20.

Bisson, J.I., Jenkins, P.L., Alexander, J. and Bannister, C. (1997). Randomised controlled trial of psychological debriefing for victims of acute burn trauma. *British Journal of Psychiatry* 171, 78–81.

Block, J.H., Block, J. and Morrison, A. (1981). Parental agreement–disagreement on child rearing orientations and gender-related personality correlates in children. *Child Development* 52, 965–74.

Breier, A., Kelsoe, J.R., Kirwin, P.D. and Beller, S.A. (1988). Early parental loss and development of adult psychopathology. *Archives of General Psychiatry* 45, 987–93.

Carlson, V., Cicchetti, D., Barnett, D., Braunwald, K. (1989). Disorganised/disorientated attachment relationships in maltreated infants. *Developmental Psychology* 25, 525–31.

Chadwick, O., Rutter, M. and Brown, G. (1981). A prospective study of children with head injuries. II. Cognitive sequelae. *Psychological Medicine* 11, 49–61.

Cherlin, A.J., Furstenberg, F.F., Chase-Lansdale, P.L., Kiernan, K.E., Robins, P.K. and Morrison, D.R. (1991). Longitudinal studies of effects of divorce on children in Great Britain and the United States. *Science* 252, 1386–9.

Cicchetti, D. and Toth, S.L. (1995). A developmental psychopathological perspective on child abuse and neglect. *Journal of the American Academy of Child and Adolescent Psychiatry* 34, 541–65.

Cohen, J.A. and Mannarino, A.P. (1996). Factors that mediate treatment outcome of sexually abused preschool children. *Journal of the American Academy of Child and Adolescent Psychiatry* 35, 1402–10.

Cosentino, C.E. (1993). Cross-gender behavior and gender conflict in sexually abused girls. *Journal of the American Academy of Child and Adolescent Psychiatry* 32, 940–7.

Crittenden, P.M. (1988). Relationships at risk. In J. Belsky and T. Negworski (eds) *Clinical Implications of Attachment Theory.* New Jersey: Erlbaum.

Cummings, E.M., Henness, K., Rabideau, G. and Cicchetti, D. (1994). Responses of physically abused boys to inter-adult anger involving their mothers. *Developmental Psychopathology* 6, 31–42.

Daud, L.R., Garralda, M.E. and David, T.J. (1993). Psychosocial adjustment in pre-school children with atopic eczema. *Archives of Diseases in Childhood* 69, 670–76.

De Young, M. (1984). *Sexual Victimization of Children.* Jefferson, NC: McFarland.

Duggan, C. and Gunn, J. (1995). Medium term course of disaster victims: A naturalistic follow-up. *British Journal of Psychiatry* 167, 228–32.

Dyregrov, P. (1991). *Children in Grief. A Handbook for Adults.* London: Jessica Kingsley.

Emery, R.E. (1982). Interparental conflict and the children of discord and divorce. *Psychological Bulletin* 92, 310–30.

Erickson, M., Egeland, B. and Pianta, R. (1989). The effects of maltreatment on the development of young children. In D. Cicchetti and V. Carlson (eds) *Child Maltreatment: Theory And Research on the Causes and Consequences of Child Abuse and Neglect.* New York: Cambridge University Press.

Finkelhor, D. (1979). *Sexually Victimized Children.* New York: Free Press.

Finkelhor, D. (1986). *Sourcebook on Child Sexual Abuse.* New York: Sage.

Friedrich, W.N., Urquiza, A.J. and Beilke, R. (1986). Behavioral problems in sexually abused young children. *Journal of Pediatric Psychology* 11, 47–57.

Fristed, M.A., Jedel, R., Weller, R.A. and Weller, E.B. (1993). Psychosocial functioning in children after the death of a parent. *American Journal of Psychiatry* 150, 511–13.

Garnefski, N. and Diekstra, R.F.W. (1997). Child sexual abuse and emotional and behavioral problems in adolescence: gender differences. *Journal of the American Academy of Child and Adolescent Psychiatry* 36, 323–9.

Gil, K.M., Williams, D.A., Thompson, R.J. and Kinney, T.R. (1991). Sickle cell disease in children and adolescents: the relation of child and parent pain coping strategies to adjustment. *Journal of Pediatric Psychology* 16, 643–63.

Goodwin, J.M., Cheeves, K. and Connell, V. (1990). Borderline and other severe symptoms in adult survivors of incestuous abuse. *Psychiatric Annals* 20, 22–32.

Goodyer, I.M. (1993). Recent stressful life events: their long term effects. *European Journal of Child and Adolescent Psychiatry* 2, 1–9.

Gray, R.E. (1989). Adolescent perceptions of social support after the death of a parent. *Journal of Psychosocial Oncology* 7, 127–44.

Guidubaldi, J. and Perry, J.D. (1985). Divorce and mental health sequelae for children: a two year follow-up of a nationwide sample. *Journal od the American Academy of Child Psychiatry* 24, 531–7.

Helzer, J.E., Robins, L.N. and McEvoy, L. (1987). Post traumatic stress disorder in the general population: findings of the Epidemiologic Catchment Area Survey. *New England Journal of Medicine* 317, 1630–4.

Hendriks, J.H., Black, D. and Kaplan, T. (1993). *When Father Kills Mother. Guiding Children through Grief.* London: Routledge.

Hoare, P. (1984). Does illness foster dependency? A study of epileptic and diabetic children. *Developmental Medicine and Child Neurology* 26, 20–6.

Joseph, S.A., Brewin, C.R. and Yule, W. (1991). Causal attribution and psychiatric symptoms in survivors of the *Herald of Free Enterprise* disaster. *British Journal of Psychiatry* 159, 542–6.

Kalter, N., Reimer, B., Brickman, A. and Chen, J.W. (1985). Implications of divorce for female development. *Journal of the American Academy of Child Psychiatry* 24, 538–44.

Lewin, J. and Sumners, D. (1992). Successful treatment of episodic dyscontrol with carbamazepine. *British Journal of Psychiatry* 161, 261–2.

Lewis, D.O., Mallouh, C. and Webb, V. (1989). Child abuse, delinquency and violent criminality. In D. Cicchetti and V. Carlson (eds) *Child Maltreatment: Theory And Research on the Causes and Consequences of Child Abuse and Neglect.* New York: Cambridge University Press.

Lieberman, A.F., Weston, D. and Pawl, J.H. (1991). Preventive intervention and outcome with anxiously attached dyads. *Child Development* 62, 199–209.

Livingstone, R. (1987). Sexually and physically abused children. *Journal of the American Academy of Child and Adolescent Psychiatry* 26, 413–15.

Lynch, M. and Cicchetti, D. (1991). Patterns of relatedness in maltreated and non-maltreated children: connections among multiple representational models. *Developmental Psychopathology* 3, 207–26.

Main, M. and Goldwyn, R. (1984). Predicting rejecting of her infant from mother's representation of her own experience: implications for the abused–abusing intergenerational cycle. *Child Abuse and Neglect* 8, 203–17.

Malinosky-Rummell, R. and Hansen, D. (1993). Long term consequences of childhood physical abuse. *Psychological Bulletin* 114, 68–79.

McClellan, J., McCurry, C., Ronnei, M. and Adams, J. (1996). Age of onset of sexual abuse: relationships to sexually inappropriate behaviors. *Journal of the American Academy of Child and Adolescent Psychiatry* 35, 1375–83.

McLeer, S.V., Deblinger, E. and Atkins, M.S. (1988). Post traumatic stress disorder in sexually abused children. *Journal of the American Academy of Child and Adolescent Psychiatry* 27, 342–53.

Merry, S.N. and Andrews, L.K. (1994). Psychiatric status of sexually abused children 12 months after disclosure of abuse. *Journal of the American Academy of Child and Adolescent Psychiatry* 33, 939–44.

Middleton, J. (1989). Thinking about head injuries in children. *Journal of Child Psychology and Psychiatry* 30, 663–70.

Monck, E., Bentovim, A. and Goodall, G. (1993). *Child Sexual Abuse: A Descriptive and Treatment Study.* London: HMSO.

Motofsky, D. and Balaschak, B. (1977). Psychological control of seizures. *Psychological Bulletin* 843, 723–7.

Mueller, E. and Silverman, N. (1989). Peer relations in maltreated children. In D. Cicchetti and V. Carlson (eds) *Child Maltreatment: Theory And Research on the Causes and Consequences of Child Abuse and Neglect.* New York: Cambridge University Press.

National Research Council (1993). *Understanding Child Abuse and Neglect.* Washington D.C.: National Academic Press.

Nekli, J. and Waters, J. (1989) A group for sexually abused young children. *Child Abuse and Neglect* 13, 369–77.

Pearson, D.A., Pumariega, A.J. and Seilheimer, D.K. (1991). The development of psychosomatic symptomatology in parents with cystic fibrosis. *Journal of the American Academy of Child and Adolescent Psychiatry* 30, 290–7.

Pless, I.B. and Nolan, T. (1991). Revision, replication and neglect – research on maladjustment in chronic illness. *Journal of Child Psychology and Psychiatry* 22, 347–65.

Pope, H. and Hudson, J. (1992). Is childhood sexual abuse a risk factor for bulimia nervosa? *American Journal of Psychiatry* 149, 455–63.

Reynolds, J.M., Garralda, M.E. and Jameson, R.A. (1988). How parents and families cope with chronic renal failure. *Archives of Diseases in Childhood* 63, 821–6.

Riggs, D., O'Leary, K. and Breslin, F. (1990). Multiple correlates of physical aggression in dating couples. *Journal of Interpersonal Violence* 5, 61–73.

Rogers, C.N. and Terry, T. (1984). Clinical intervention with boy victims of sexual abuse. In I.R. Stuart and J.R. Greer (eds) *Victims of Sexual Aggression: Treatment of Children, Women, and Men.* New York: Van Nostrand Reinhold.

Rogosch, F.A. and Cicchetti, D. (1994). Illustrating the interface of family and peer relations through the study of child maltreatment. *Social Development* 3, 291–308.

Russell, D.E. (1983). The incidence and prevalence of intrafamilial and extrafamilial sexual abuse of female children. *Child Abuse and Neglect* 7, 133–46.

Rutter, M., Chadwick, O. and Shaffer, D. (1983). Head injury. In M. Rutter (ed.) *Developmental Neuropsychiatry.* London: Churchill Livingston.

Rutter, M., Graham, P. and Yule, W. (1970). A neuropsychiatric study in childhood. *Clinics in Developmental Medicine.* No. 35/36. London: Heinemann.

Sgroi, S. (1982). *Handbook of Clinical Intervention in Child Sexual Abuse.* Lexington, MA: Lexington Books.

Sheldrick, C. (1991). Adult sequelae of child sexual abuse. *British Journal of Psychiatry* 158 (Suppl. 10) 55–62.

Shields, A.M., Ryan, R.M. and Cicchetti, D. (1994). The development of emotional and behavioral self regulation and social competence among maltreated school children. *Developmental Psychopathology* 6, 57–75.

Silverman, P.R., Nickman, S. and Worden, J.W. (1992). Detachment revisited. The child's reconstruction of a dead parent. *American Journal of Orthopsychiatry* 62, 494–503.

Singer, K.I. (1989). Group work with men who experienced incest in childhood. *American Journal of Orthopsychiatry* 59, 468–72.

Sroufe, L.A. and Fleeson, J. (1986). Attachment and the construction of relationships. In W. Hartup and Z. Rubin (eds) *Relationships and Development*. New Jersey: Erlbaum.

Taylor, E. (1991). Developmental neuropsychiatry. *Journal of Child Psychology and Psychiatry* 32, 3–47.

Terr, L.C. (1979). Children of Chowchilla. *Psychoanalytical Study of the Child* 34, 547–623.

Terr, L.C. (1983). Chowchilla revisited. *American Journal of Psychiatry* 40, 1543–50.

Terr, L.C. (1991). Childhood traumas: an outline and overview. *American Journal of Psychiatry* 148, 10–20.

Toth, S.L., Manly, J.T. and Cicchetti, D. (1992). Child maltreatment and vulnerability to depression. *Developmental Psychopathology* 4, 97–112.

Trickett, P.K., Aber, J.L. and Carlson, V. (1991). The relationship of socioeconomic status to the etiology and development sequelae of physical child abuse. *Developmental Psychology* 27, 148–58.

Wallerstein, J.S. (1983). Children of divorce: the psychological tasks of the child. *American Journal of Orthopsychiatry* 53, 230–43.

Wallerstein, J.S. and Blakeslee, S. (1989). *Second Chances: Men, Women and Children a Decade after Divorce*. New York: Ticknor & Fields.

Webb, N.B. (1991). *Play Therapy with Children in Crisis: A Casebook for Practitioners*. New York: Guilford Press.

Weller, E.B., Weller, R.A. and Fristad, M.A. (1988). Should children attend their parent's funeral? *Journal of the American Academy of Child and Adolescent Psychiatry* 22, 559–62.

Yates, A. (1982). Children eroticized by incest. *American Journal of Psychiatry* 139, 482–5.

Yule, W. and Gold, A. (1993). *Wise before the Event: Coping with Crisis in Schools*. London: Calouste Gulbenkian Foundation.

7 Noncompliance and oppositional behaviour in young children

INTRODUCTION

On one occasion, one of the present authors was visiting the home of an eight-year-old child, Simon, who, although highly intelligent and often friendly with visitors, frequently found himself in conflict with parents and teachers. Seated in the family living room, the child had repeatedly engaged in a variety of attention-seeking behaviours such as waving household materials in front of an open fire, switching television channels with the remote control and jumping on the furniture. When admonished by his mother, he immediately sought to engage her in an argument and clearly delighted in her subsequent inability to manage him.

Simon then pushed his face up to his mother's and said that it was time for his medication for nocturnal enuresis (bedwetting). His mother told him that he was mistaken and asked him to be quiet. Simon then pawed at his mother, grabbed her arm and attempted to lead her to the tablets that were carefully situated on top of a clock hanging on the wall – well out of reach. Simon's mother, who had tried to maintain an air of dignified resignation during the early stages of the interview, became increasingly anxious and, as Simon tried to knock the clock off the wall, it was apparent that she was beginning to be overcome by panic. Eventually, her resolve snapped and she told the boy that he could have the tablets.

Having taken two tablets from the container, Simon's mother asked her son to come and take them from her. Simon pretended not to hear and started to take a renewed interest in the television. During the next few minutes the author witnessed an increasingly agitated mother struggling to get the tablets into the mouth of her son who was furiously clamping his mouth shut to deny her. For Simon, the act of opposing others, and winning, was a major element of his interactions.

This chapter addresses the origins, development and management of oppositional behaviour in young children aged from two to ten years. Oppositional or noncompliant behaviour is common to everyone but is perceived as particularly evident (and problematic) in childhood. The child watching the television who does not 'hear' the call for bed, the child who reacts to the word 'no' by storming upstairs, slamming the doors, the child who won't turn down the volume on the radio are all failing to comply with adult instructions or requests. When does such behaviour become a major problem worthy of professional intervention and become a form of child 'tyranny' (Barcai and Rosenthal, 1974) or an example of the 'brat syndrome', as described by Bernal *et al.*: 'a child who often engages in tantrums, assaultiveness, threats etc., which are highly aversive and serve to render others helpless in controlling him' (Bernal *et al.* 1968: 447).

The current edition of the American Psychiatric Association's *Diagnostic and Statistical Manual* (APA 1994: 94) states that oppositional defiant disorder (ODD) is 'a recurrent pattern of negativistic, defiant, disobedient and hostile behaviour toward authority figures that persists for at least six months'.

The manual adds that ODD is characterised by the frequent occurrence of at least *four* of the following behaviours:

- losing one's temper
- arguing with adults
- actively defying or refusing to comply with the requests or rules of adults
- deliberately doing things that will annoy others
- blaming others for his or her own mistakes or misbehaviour
- being touchy or easily annoyed by others
- being angry and resentful
- being spiteful or vindictive

The manual states that to qualify as ODD, the above behaviours must occur more frequently than is typically observed in individuals of comparable age and at a similar developmental level. Furthermore, they must lead to significant impairment in social, academic or occupational functioning.

The prevalence of severe noncompliance in children varies greatly from one study to another. The APA study states that rates of ODD vary from 2 per cent to 16 per cent depending upon the sample and method of assessment. In 1989 the US Institute of Medicine estimated that 4–10 per cent of children in the United States met the criteria for ODD and/or conduct disorder.

The infant years are marked by a growing sense of individuation and autonomy and, as such, the emergence of oppositional behaviour in the toddler is age-appropriate and largely desirable. Indeed, many parents might become concerned for the well-being of their child if he or she never displayed stubbornness, resistance or negativism. Starting at the age of eighteen to twenty months, oppositional behaviour often peaks between three and four before declining as children approach their sixth birthday. As noted by Haswell *et al.*

> The child's intellectual conquest of the meaning of the word 'no' and the concept of negation, along with the realisation of the self as a separate

being with a separate will, makes possible the refusal of others' wills. The struggle for autonomy is thus at the heart of oppositional behaviour as the preschool child grows in mastery and explores her/his growing need for independence. Thus, whereas oppositional . . . behaviour is frustrating for parents . . . it is a normal and crucial aspect of early childhood development.

(Haswell *et al.* 1981: 440)

It is those children whose oppositional behaviour appears particularly intense or long lasting who become the subject of parental and professional concern. Johnson *et al.* (1973), found that noncompliance in a normal sample of children occurred in 26 per cent of the total opportunities for compliance. In contrast, in studies of children described as 'deviant' non-compliance ratios were in the 57–80 per cent range (e.g. Forehand and King 1977). It is important to note, however, that some of these differences may reflect parental desires to heighten their child's deviant status, in order to justify professional intervention.

Gard and Berry (1986), in a review of the literature, argue that oppositional children differ from normal children in that they engage in a range of problem behaviours to a greater degree and intensity. In particular they:

- are exceedingly non-compliant to those in authority
- refuse to conform to ordinary rules and conventions
- are perceived as wilful and contrary
- appear to derive satisfaction in provoking adults
- may display tantrum behaviours, which may be aggressive and destructive
- tend to demonstrate poor school performance
- exhibit an inability to delay gratification and accept frustrations
- appear to develop serious problems in social relationships
- tend to have a negative outlook towards themselves and others
- often lack basic social skills
- tend not to be as responsive to normal social reinforcement or punishment

The psychiatric literature distinguishes between oppositional defiant disorder and conduct disorder, the former being seen as a somewhat less severe difficulty lacking the aggression towards others, the destruction of property and the theft and deceit which are frequently features of conduct disordered children. It is recognised, however, that conduct disordered adolescents who demonstrated symptoms of ODD, and subsequently conduct disorder, in their pre-school years are likely to be more chronically antisocial in later life than those children who experience difficulties in adolescence after a normal history of social and behavioural development (White *et al.* 1990). Given this scenario, the importance of intervening at an early stage is clear.

WITHIN-CHILD FACTORS

All parents know that some children seem temperamentally more difficult to socialise than others, and differences between children within the same family cannot be sufficiently explained solely by environmental factors. Similarly, it is widely accepted that biological characteristics by themselves are unlikely to account for antisocial behaviour; rather, these interact with environmental experiences in establishing deviant behaviour (Plomin and Hershberger 1991). Although there is some evidence suggesting that there is a genetic link to antisocial behaviour which is exhibited from an early age and persists throughout the lifespan, this appears to have a weaker effect than environmental factors (Dishion *et al.* 1995).

Temperamental (or dispositional) factors are likely to play an important mediating role between the child's genetic make-up, environmental experiences and behaviour. Research suggests that negative temperamental characteristics of infants (e.g. difficultness, unadaptability and negative emotions and feelings) are related to later behavioural difficulties, although this relationship is substantially weaker than key parental and family factors (Bates *et al.* 1991). A promising line of enquiry with respect to conduct disordered children (e.g. Dodge 1993) concerns the extent to which particularly aggressive and challenging children are less able to recognise and understand social cues and thus respond appropriately.

Oppositional behaviour tends to be more common in males before puberty, although gender differences tend to disappear subsequently.

PARENTAL AND FAMILY FACTORS

General behavioural difficulties in young children have been found to be associated with parental conflict leading to divorce (Kazdin 1987), although it is the degree and nature of the parental conflict, rather than divorce per se, which appear to be the most important factors (O'Leary and Emery 1982). It is also widely noted in the literature (Webster-Stratton 1993) that parents of young children with behavioural difficulties tend to encounter a greater incidence of major stressors (unemployment, divorce, poverty) and more minor everyday troubles which can result in depression, impatience, irritability and the adoption of a coercive approach to family relations.

A key issue is whether highly oppositional children are the product of poor parenting or whether the deficiencies in parenting skills often observed in such cases are by-products of the anxiety and tensions which result from having to contend with a difficult child. Similarly, findings that oppositional children tend to have overcontrolling, aggressive, depressed mothers and distant, passive, non-communicative fathers are open to similar questions regarding causality. Research studies have indicated that parents of challenging children tend to exhibit fewer positive behaviours towards their children, are more likely to threaten, criticise, nag and humiliate their children, are less likely to monitor their children's behaviours and don't give them enough time to comply with commands (Delfini *et al.* 1976; Forehand *et al.* 1975; Webster-Stratton and Spitzer 1991).

Most practitioners will recognise a series of behaviours frequently exhibited by parents with oppositional children. Commands are given in an anxious or irritable voice, spoken rapidly. The parent may maintain a tense posture and observant manner and be quick to intervene if the child fails to comply. Alternatively, the parent may deliberately avoid following up a request as noncompliance is expected and, as such, an effort is made to avoid conflict. Some parents signal resignation by distancing themselves from the child, speaking in a flat, toneless fashion and giving directions in the form of questions, 'Don't you think it's time that you went upstairs to bed?' Such questions are often accompanied by defensive postures (e.g. arms and or legs crossed) and an accompanying lack of voice projection.

Patterson (1982) coined the term 'coercive process' to describe a pattern of behaviour in which children come to realise that they can have their desires met, or avoid censure, by increasingly escalating their negative behaviours until their parents capitulate. Although such patterns of interaction occur in all families from time to time, it is considered that a high rate of such exchanges acts as a form of training to interact in a coercive fashion.

In line with this thinking, Gard and Berry's (1986) review of the research literature described the following common pattern of interaction (Figure 7.1):

Parent issues instruction/command.

Child perceives command as aversive/undesirable and responds with noncompliance.

Parent EITHER: withdraws command – this reinforces the child's noncompliance.

OR attempts to reason/persuade the child to comply – again, this reinforces the unwanted behaviour.

Parent fails to persuade child to comply, becomes increasingly frustrated and begins to shout, threaten or physically chastise.

EITHER
child eventually complies – parent's aggressive/aversive behaviour is reinforced and increases the perception that such behaviours are 'the only way to get through to the child'. Child is resentful, and less likely to push parent to the limit subsequently;
OR
increased anger and punishment continue to be ineffective. Child recognises own power to defy parent even when threat is great. Perception of power is reinforcing for the child.

Figure 7.1 Common pattern of interaction

INTERVENTION ISSUES

It has been generally found that behavioural approaches to noncompliance are the most effective means of effecting change. These can take the form of:

- group parent training
- individual parent training
- child's individual behaviour programme
- behavioural training incorporating some form of family therapy

Parent management programmes for oppositional and other conduct disordered children have been subject to more detailed evaluation than any other form of therapy. These studies suggest that such programmes are among the most promising types of intervention (Kazdin 1997). With a strong psychological focus, they are typically co-ordinated by social work, psychology or psychiatry services. Often teachers, nursery nurses and other childcare professionals have an important role, either by sharing in the delivery of programmes or by offering encouragement and support to parents who are struggling to change their child management behaviours.

Group parent training

Although practices vary, the most common model of parent training involves a short presentation by the therapist for approximately thirty minutes for each of the six to ten weeks of the programme. The presentation is then followed by either large or small group discussion depending upon the number of trainers available. Each presentation introduces a particular issue or theme (e.g. how to operate a time-out procedure) which can subsequently be incorporated into a plan of action. In the early stages the presentations serve to provide an understanding of behavioural principles and methods and how parents may react in counterproductive ways. The focus subsequently shifts to the recording and assessment of behaviour and, finally, to issues of intervention.

After each presentation and group discussion, each parent is asked to feed back on the results of the previous week(s) and to consider the implementation of the technique under consideration in the week ahead.

An example parent programme is outlined, below.

Week 1 What is normal behaviour? What is problem behaviour?

This first session provides a gentle introduction to the programme. It introduces parents to the notion that defiance, aggression and other challenging behaviours are common in young children and seeks to help them become less threatened and intimidated by their situation. An important element of this first session is the reduction of feelings of isolation and separateness often encountered by such parents.

Opportunities are provided for parents to talk about the difficulties they encounter with their children and the distress and anxiety that can result. The group leader should be careful not to allow this activity to degenerate into a negative spiral of complaint but, rather, to draw upon the accounts provided to help parents to recognise that their problems are common to others and their frequent feelings of heightened anxiety are a common yet undesirable consequence of child defiance.

The homework task may be to focus upon one aspect of their child's behaviour and to consider how they (and, perhaps, other members of the family) typically respond. Parents are asked to jot this information down in a notebook shortly after an event has taken place. This serves to introduce the idea of systematic recording, an important aspect of behavioural approaches.

Week 2 Measuring and recording behaviour

This session is designed to assist parents to focus more closely upon problematic behaviours and, in particular, to gain a more detailed grasp of when and how frequently these occur. During this session it is hoped that those who believe that their child's problematic behaviours 'take place all the time' may be assisted to gain an accurate picture of the circumstances. Parents are asked to focus upon a particular problem behaviour exhibited by their child and are shown how a simple recording system can be established. An example is provided below (Figure 7.2).

Each parent is asked to devise a simple recording chart, similar to that in Figure 7.2, that records the incidence of one or more problem behaviours exhibited by their child. The homework task may be the maintenance of the chart during the forthcoming weeks.

The frequency chart helps parent and therapist to gain a realistic picture of the true frequency of the problem behaviour and the times when this is most prevalent. This serves both to indicate when the potential for difficulty is greatest and as a baseline upon which to gauge the effectiveness of the subsequent intervention.

Week 3 The relationship between behaviour and consequences

Participants are provided with a number of scenarios involving a child's problem behaviour and examples of parental responses. One example would be a child crying for sweets in a supermarket, an escalating temper tantrum and, as a result of the public humiliation, immense parental anxiety and eventual capitulation. Parents would be asked to record whether these scenarios reflected their own experience and the extent to which the parental compliance outlined in the scripts reflected their own circumstances.

A key skill is the ability to ignore a child's problematic behaviour while not responding emotionally. Often the parent's continued watchfulness, anxiety

	Sun	Mon	Tues	Wed	Thur	Fri	Sat
7.00–8.00							
8.00–9.00							
9.00–10.00							
10.00–11.00							
11.00–12.00							
12.00–1.00							
1.00–2.00							
2.00–3.00							
3.00–4.00							
4.00–5.00							
5.00–6.00							
6.00–7.00							
7.00–8.00							
8.00–bedtime							

Week beginning . . . .

Figure 7.2 Chart demonstrating the number of times each day that a child disobeys parents

or interruption is highly reinforcing to the child and thus maintains the unwanted behaviour. Participants are instructed to ignore the irritation. One of the writers has found the common childhood game of 'Knock Down Ginger' or 'Knocky Nine Doors', where the child rings a doorbell and runs and hides, to be a productive metaphor. Most parents grasp the message that the occupant who rages and yells is more likely to become a frequent victim of the game. (For further details of the use of such strategies with parents, see Beaver (1996: 193–201).)

A major difficulty concerns when to ignore and when to intervene, as unfamiliar 'ignoring' behaviour can result in the child seeking to restore the usual pattern of interaction by accentuating the problem behaviour to a point where the child, or significant other, is at physical risk. Parents often need guidance as to when they should intervene, how to avoid being too emotionally charged at such times, and how to minimise the rewarding nature of such attention.

The scenarios would provide a contextualised introduction to key behavioural principles, in particular to the concept of reinforcement. From this would be developed the antecedents–behaviour–consequences (ABC) model of behaviour analysis that is common to most behavioural programmes.

John (aged four) is sitting in his front room and is bored. He has repeatedly tried to gain his mother's attention but she keeps shooing him away in order to complete her domestic tasks. John has nothing to do and is uninterested in the television programme he has been instructed to watch. He decides to play with some of his parents' ornaments but clumsily knocks one over and it is destroyed. Mother runs into the room horrified, shouts at her son and gives him a smack. She then takes him into the kitchen with her and gives him the task of helping her to stir the cake mix which she has prepared.

Mary (aged six) is with her father in the supermarket. He is not happy about having to do the shopping and has little patience with his daughter's repeated whining. She usually helps her mother collect items from the shelves but her father wants her to stay by his side and be quiet. At the checkout, Mary demands a chocolate bar from the prominent display. Father, irritated by the store's cynical promotion, refuses, saying that she will be having dinner shortly. Mary exhibits a major temper tantrum, shouts that she hates her father and then grasps the counter, refusing to budge. Father becomes increasingly embarrassed and has a sense of guilt that he has mishandled the situation. Reluctantly, he purchases the chocolate bar while telling his daughter that she is a very naughty child who doesn't deserve the treat she is to receive.

In both of the scenarios above, it is tempting for parents to focus upon the problem behaviour (carelessness with treasured possessions, the display of a temper tantrum) without considering the events which took place before and afterwards. As the incidents demonstrate, parental handling prior to each event was a contributory factor. More sensitive awareness of each child's frustration and a little imagination may have prevented the incidents from occurring.

One should also consider the extent to which each parent's reaction was likely to increase the likelihood of similar behaviour in the future. Although John's mother may consider a smack and a telling off to be a punishment, she may fail to recognise that, for most children, any attention is better than no attention: 'Attention to a child is like sunshine to a flower'. Subsequently, John is further 'rewarded' by being allowed to help her in the kitchen. Mary's father also rewards his daughter for undesirable behaviour, although in this case with the purchase of the chocolate bar. His public labelling of her as 'naughty' only serves to compound matters, as the internalisation of the label by Mary may result in her becoming more obstructive on future occasions.

Consideration of the events leading up to such incidents (antecedents) and those which follow (consequences) is a cornerstone of all behavioural programmes. Most involve assisting parents to analyse a series of difficult situations in the form of an ABC chart (see Figure 7.3).

Antecedents	Behaviour	Consequences
Monday teatime: John and Mary were watching the television. They started to argue about which channel to watch. I told them that I would turn it off if they didn't stop shouting.	John punched Mary and threw his toys around the room.	I sent Mary upstairs to play. John was told to settle down to the television or he'd be sent to bed.
Tuesday breakfast: John fussed over which cereal to eat. He wanted the toy from the bottom of one of the packets.	John refused to eat anything until the toy was retrieved. He 'accidentally' spilt milk over the table.	The toy was retrieved but only after a lot of fuss!
Tuesday evening: John was irritating Mary by running into her bedroom and taking her dolls. Mary scratched his face.	John kicked Mary, hard, and ran screaming into the kitchen where I was washing up.	Both children were told off. I said that I would play with them both later if they stopped arguing.
Wednesday teatime: A fun time! John and Mary told us about some amusing events at school. I couldn't see trouble ahead although both kids were getting rather excited. John began to get silly and made stupid noises at the meal table. Mary was encouraging him. I told him that if he didn't settle down he would have to go to his room.	He got worse! Eventually his dad had to carry him forcibly to his room to calm down. John was kicking and biting in temper.	When he eventually calmed down, he was allowed to watch television.

Figure 7.3 Extract from a weekly ABC chart

Although the above brief extract provides an incomplete picture, it is clear that much useful data are beginning to emerge. There are occasions, for example, when parental responses reinforce John's poor behaviour. At other times his behaviour is not tolerated – possibly when his father is present. In a real-life situation, parents might be asked to consider each situation and consider alternative options. Many of the difficulties appear to arise from sibling conflict. It may be valuable for parents in such situations to consider how such situations can be prevented or minimised.

A homework task for those undertaking a parent training programme might be to complete a simple ABC chart, similar to that above during the forthcoming week. This would form the basis for a group exploration of the above issues.

Week 4 Increasing desirable behaviour – how to apply reinforcement

This session would develop from Week 3 by focusing upon how reinforcement can be used to increase desirable behaviour in children. The importance of ensuring that reinforcement follows desired behaviour relatively swiftly, particularly in the initial stages, would be stressed. Differing forms of reinforcement from smiling and approving to more tangible forms such as sweets and pocket money and their impact are discussed and evaluated. The powerful effect of intermittent reinforcement (see Chapter 2) would be described with reference to everyday experiences (e.g. the attraction of fruit machines). Case examples of the use of contingent reinforcement would be presented with the aim of helping participants to grasp the fact that they can be proactive and influential in shaping children's behaviour.

The homework task may be to consider the reinforcers that are, or are potentially, available in the home. Parents would be asked to consider how these may become contingently related to desired behaviours.

Week 5 Decreasing inappropriate behaviour – the role of punishment

The literature indicates that many parents place too great a reliance upon harsh and frequent punishments. The difference between negative reinforcement (where desired behaviour is increased by the removal of an aversive stimulus) and punishment (where an aversive response is designed to reduce a given behaviour) is a distinction that, in the opinion of the present writers, may prove unnecessarily sophisticated and unnecessarily complex for many participants. Thus, punishment here is taken as any response that the child may perceive as unwelcome.

The limited role of many punishments in reducing inappropriate behaviour is outlined. Participants are asked to discuss the current operation of punishment in their homes and its effectiveness. The reinforcing effect of parental attention (even if this takes an aversive form) is outlined and parents are helped to greater understanding of the seemingly paradoxical effect of their actions.

The most important means of reducing undesirable behaviour (removing reinforcement, employing a time-out procedure, as illustrated in Figure 7.4) are outlined and the relevance to participants' own situations is highlighted.

Time-out is short for 'time-out from positive reinforcement' and usually involves the removal of the child to a location where positive reinforcers (e.g. attention, peer approval, interesting toys and objects) are unavailable. In the home setting this is often a bedroom, a corridor, a corner of a room or a chair. It is important, however, that the particular location is not disturbing to the child (e.g. a dark area in a confined space) and that parents have some opportunity to maintain a degree of vigilance.

Although a highly effective strategy, it is important that it is carried out systematically and in keeping with a predetermined schedule. Most comment-ators consider a period of from three to fifteen minutes to be sufficient (the longer period being more appropriate for older children) and it is important that parents do not become over-punitive by increasing the period in order to gain a greater sense of control.

McAuley and McAuley (1977: 103) outline a three-stage time-out procedure:

Stage 1 – the child is commanded to do something or to stop doing some-thing; stage 2 – the child is rewarded if he complies; if he has not complied within a reasonable length of time (which is judged according to the con-tent of the command) then a second command is given with a punishment warning; stage 3 – the child is rewarded if he complies; if he has not complied within a further reasonable time he is sent to time-out.

McAuley and McAuley note that instituting time-out procedures often involves three problems, refusal to go to time-out, refusal to stay in time-out and refusal to leave time-out. With young children, it may be necessary for the parent to use physical means of ensuring that the procedure is followed. The child's frustration may often result in screams, assault and tantrums and it is essential that the parent appears unmoved emotionally throughout this time. In general, timing should not commence until the child is quiet. On the first few occasions this may last for an hour or more and require considerable doggedness and determination on the part of the rapidly tiring parent. Sub-sequently, however, the child will usually cease such behaviours relatively quickly. If the child refuses to leave time-out, the parent should avoid re-entering a power struggle by attending to such statements which are usually ploys by the child to appear unconcerned by the technique. Close monitoring of the child's behaviour over time should provide a clear indication of the true effectiveness of the intervention.

It is important that the use of time-out is complemented by an attempt to teach the child prosocial behaviours such as how to share with others, or how to tidy away one's toys.

Figure 7.4 Time-out

Homework for this parent training session involves consideration of how reinforcement and punishment may operate with one's child – the implication being that this will be operationalised in an actual intervention.

Week 6 Communicating with others

This session (which may take place earlier in the programme) provides an opportunity for consideration of the verbal and non-verbal behaviours which signal authority to the child and help to ensure compliance. A focus of the session will be upon the use of eye contact, posture, voice, position, the articulation of simple, straightforward, concrete instructions (rather than taking the form of questions or rationales) and the conveyance of 'I mean it!' messages. Other important issues include the importance of providing verbal alerts (e.g. 'In five minutes you will need to put your toys away and come upstairs for your bath'), supporting the child's desire for autonomy by offering choices where possible, giving the child time to comply with instruction (four–five seconds) and the need to exercise some flexibility in interacting with the child.

The inputs from the group leader(s) may be supported by the use of role-played videotaped interactions. While permitting the parents the opportunity to distance themselves to some extent, the use of critical incidents can help parents to recognise and reflect upon examples of ineffectual communication that may mirror that in which they engage themselves.

An advantage of introducing this topic in a later session is that the development of group identity and trust may permit opportunities for participants to engage in practical development through role-play.

Homework may require participants to reflect upon one or more incidents during the forthcoming week where they have attempted to communicate authority and ensure compliance.

Week 7 Family factors

Many behavioural programmes fail because of inconsistency within the family and the wider social network. This session is geared to help participants recognise how family members may consciously or unconsciously undermine an attempt to introduce a behavioural programme. This may be for many reasons, for example, a sibling's desire to scapegoat, the other parent's assertion that there is no problem to address or grandparental indulgence. This session must be handled skilfully as highlighting such difficulties can result in increasing tension and heightened disharmony within the family that are likely to exacerbate the difficulties encountered. Rather, the aim must be to help participants to gain greater understanding of family dynamics and, in the light of this, to find creative ways of ensuring that the family has ownership of, and commitment to, the programme.

Weeks 8–12 Establishing and operating the programme

By Week 8, participants will have identified those behaviours that are to be addressed, will have data as to their incidence and frequency, have considered the availability of the means of reinforcement and punishment, and have greater understanding of their own and their family's impact upon the child under consideration. The programme's design permits change in parental handling (and, hopefully, the child's behaviour) from its outset, an important element in ensuring continued parental engagement. Week 8, however, is geared to pulling these threads together to produce a more comprehensive and systematic intervention intended to operate over the next few weeks.

Following a 'weight watchers' motivational model, the goals and operation of the programmes are made explicit and each week participants report upon progress. Where difficulties arise, the group works with the parent to modify the programme or redouble his or her efforts. The active support of the group is highly reinforcing and empowering for many parents, particularly those who feel isolated and helpless to effect change.

There has been much consideration in the parent training literature as to the most effective means of providing information. Reviews of evaluation studies (e.g. Moreland *et al.* 1982) would appear to suggest that the modelling of appropriate parental behaviour and the supervision of behaviour rehearsal are key features in ensuring that parents acquire and continue to maintain important skills of using commands, providing attention at appropriate times and operating time-out. The provision of written materials, telephone contact and audio and videotaped sequences is likely to provide further valuable assistance. It is widely agreed that some programmes have placed too great an emphasis upon a translation of behavioural principles rather than upon the articulation, modelling and practice of skills.

Many writers have expressed concern at the relatively high drop-out rates of those engaged in parent training: on average 25–30 per cent of those who commence the programme (Forehand *et al.* 1983). It is clear that there are certain categories of parent who are particularly at risk of failing to complete. McMahon *et al.* (1981) found that drop outs from parent training programmes were more likely to be from low socio-economic-status groupings, show greater incidence of maternal depression, and tended to offer more commands to their children. Maintenance of initial gains was less likely to occur in families where the mother was isolated or had poor relationships with members of the local community (Wahler 1980). While these mothers had shown an ability to utilise the behavioural techniques during the programme, these were not maintained and they continued to understand their children's behaviour in general, blame-oriented terms. Wahler *et al.* (1981) noted that these mothers' widespread experience of interpersonal dealings marked by conflict and attrition had generalised to their children. In such cases approaches might need to incorporate family therapy approaches which permit consideration of broader intra-familial and extra-familial relationships (Griest and Wells 1983).

In comparison with an individual programme, group training has a number of advantages and disadvantages:

Advantages

1 Because several parents are seen together the approach is relatively cost-effective.
2 Parents value and are encouraged by the knowledge that others are encountering similar difficulties.
3 Group discussion about ideas and practices covered during the training helps to ensure understanding of the material.
4 Parents serve as models for one another.
5 The recording and discussion of individual family outcomes can prove highly motivating and helps to maintain adherence to agreed programmes.

Disadvantages

1 It is rare that the therapist is able to observe or gain accurate measures of actual parent behaviours in the home setting.
2 It is difficult to set up simulation exercises involving guided feedback to parents.
3 It may prove easier for parents to drop out of a group programme.

In general, however, research studies suggest that group training programmes are as effective as individual programmes and, of course, can prove far more cost-effective.

Individual parent training

This employs many of the same principles as group parent training but, operating in clinic and home contexts, permits more tailored intervention to meet the needs of the particular parents. A number of programmes, based upon the work of Forehand and his colleagues (1977; 1981) have incorporated sophisticated simulation techniques in which parents (usually mothers) practise issuing instructions and responding to noncompliance in their young children. In one study (Powers and Roberts 1995), for example, parents were trained in a simulation room equipped with a 'bedroom', 'dining table' and 'play area'. A doll, held by a co-therapist played the child's role. The simulation involved the parent responding to a predetermined script with the lead therapist, situated behind a one-way window, speaking to the co-therapist by means of an ear 'bug'. Findings indicated that parent training undertaken in these clinic-based simulation sessions resulted in significantly improved performance in the home.

Individual behavioural programme

Many interventions involve both an individual behavioural programme and an element of parent training (although the training element may often be rather less structured and overt than that described above). In such cases, the focus may be upon examining the pay-offs for the child's negative behaviour and in ascertaining how inappropriate antecedent conditions and typical reinforcements may be amended. In this approach, parental handling and management of the child is shaped primarily through the operation of the programme. Key elements include reducing the child's capacity for negotiation, ensuring that instructions are complied with and taking care that rewards and sanctions are clearly signalled and operate contingently.

Adam, aged eight, was referred to the educational psychologist by his school at parental request. He was perceived by his teachers as being rather idiosyncratic – he would occasionally make funny noises in class, demonstrated some rather unappealing personal habits, was something of a loner and, in his interests and sense of humour, appeared to function as a somewhat younger child. Although he had some learning difficulties, for example, he was only a beginning reader and required additional help from a support teacher, he was generally well behaved in class and responsive to his teachers. On occasions he had been brought to the headteacher for his involvement in minor misdemeanours (e.g. writing on the walls, teasing younger children).

At home, his behaviour was radically different. Here, he was often argumentative, irritating, destructive and refused to respond to his parents' direction. Many of the arguments centred upon requests for sweets, toys and television or refusal to undertake self-help tasks such as washing himself, getting dressed or preparing for bedtime.

Adam's father worked long hours and was often away from home. Although supportive, the demands upon him were such that he was often unable to impact greatly upon the family's functioning. When Father was at home, Adam's behaviour was markedly better and this resulted in Father becoming frustrated at his wife's inability to cope at other times. His mother, a caring, concerned parent, was frequently overwhelmed by the demands of her son, particularly in public settings where his noisy and overbearing manner frequently brought anxious glances from members of the public. Adam's maternal grandparents, while indulging the boy, were exasperated by his behaviour and often fuelled the tension within the family. For them, Adam was a lost cause who was regularly compared unflatteringly with his younger sister (Sasha, aged five) who could 'do no wrong'.

Adam was essentially a good-natured boy with a loving disposition. He would often cuddle his parents and grandparents affectionately and his behaviour appeared to stem primarily from poor social learning rather than from any latent hostility or antagonism towards his family.

The educational psychologist came to the conclusion that a number of therapeutic outcomes were desirable:

1 Adam's behaviour needed to be shaped by a more explicit and contingent use of reinforcement with the aim of encouraging greater compliance.
2 Adam's family (particularly his mother) needed to appear more confident and strong in their interactions with him. In particular, his power in public settings should be eroded.
3 The family needed to work together in a more supportive and collaborative fashion.
4 The family scapegoating of Adam should be reduced. Continued comparison with his younger sibling should cease.
5 The significant influence of the school (in particular, the headteacher) should be drawn upon to add greater weight to the intervention.

Baseline measures of Adam's noncompliant behaviour, completed by Mother, indicated that bickering and non-compliance were almost continuous occurrences. As a result, it was agreed to set up a behavioural programme which would monitor sequences of thirty minutes – a highly intrusive and demanding schedule.

Capitalising upon Adam's love of the *Power Rangers* television characters, Adam and his mother designed a Monopoly-style Power Rangers game board on a large piece of card. Each segment of the pathway represented a thirty minute time period. There were sufficient segments to cover morning and evening sessions during weekdays and all day on Saturday and Sunday. The number of boxes totalled approximately one hundred.

At the end of each thirty-minute period an entry was made. If the target behaviours were achieved (no arguing with parents, compliance with instructions), Adam drew or coloured in the square. If these were not achieved, a large cross was drawn in the square with a felt pen.

Rewards, in the form of pocket money, sweets, television programmes and other treats, were tied in tightly and explicitly to daily and weekly targets. It was made clear to Adam that there would be no negotiation or debate about parental judgements or the operation of reinforcement. Adam was required to take the chart to school at the end of each week to show his classteacher and headteacher. In addition, the educational psychologist indicated that he would review progress at three-week intervals.

Although somewhat daunted by the schedule, Adam's parents agreed to establish the programme and to adhere to the measures agreed. His grandparents, however, thought that the scheme was 'daft' and was unlikely to be any more effective than earlier attempts to tackle Adam's misbehaviour. This perception provided an opportunity for the psychologist to tackle issues 2 and 3 (see above) and to highlight the importance for the family of maintaining a united and determined position. Reluctantly, the grandparents agreed to 'give it a try'. Discussion focused upon the ways to give instructions, to pause afterwards to permit time for compliance, and to ensure that all verbal and non-verbal messages signalled an air of authority.

The effects of the programme surpassed all expectations. During the next few weeks, Adam's behaviour continually improved to a level which astounded all participants, including the psychologist. The displays of public non-compliance gradually disappeared as Adam's goals shifted to the gaining of public recognition for positive behaviour and the rewards which were contingent upon this.

A crucial factor, somewhat obscured by the demands of the intensive behavioural programme, was the very real change in the family functioning, particularly that of Adam's mother. In interview she stated, 'Whereas before I was often hesitant and anxious in talking to Adam, he now knows that I am determined to see matters through. The new programme and the support of school and the psychologist have made me feel a lot less isolated and, as a result, my confidence has increased.'

This air of self-assurance and confidence that instruction will be complied with are important elements in all interpersonal dealings (see Chapter 8) and are elements that can be overshadowed by behavioural technologies. The change in the way in which Adam was handled may well have been the most important element in the intervention. The complex and detailed behavioural programme may have been the means by which this change could be best effected.

Three months after the programme was completed, a follow-up interview was conducted. As is often the case with such programmes, Adam's behaviour had deteriorated somewhat but by no means to a level commensurate with the original position. Regression to earlier patterns of behaviour is common in many behavioural programmes, although the goal that new patterns of reinforcement and concomitant changes in management will have lasting and positive effects remains. As Adam's mother stated during the follow-up interview, 'Yes, he can still be difficult at times but things are different now. I know that I can handle whatever happens. I'm no longer overwhelmed by feelings of panic. Adam knows that I won't be intimidated as I used to be and that I'll stand my ground. Nevertheless, I think that I'll always find him to be a handful!'

This case study demonstrates the complex interaction between a simple behavioural model, the nature and quality of child–adult communication and the wider family and school contexts within which these operate. In the opinion of the writers, the failure of many behavioural interventions results from a simplistic focus upon a mechanistic technology and a corresponding neglect of key interpersonal/parenting skills and wider family dynamics.

Behavioural training involving family therapy

As noted in the case study above, it is often necessary to complement the operation of a behavioural programme (whether through a child-focused programme or parent training) with some form of wider family work. This is particularly important where difficulties relating to intrafamilial roles, communication and/or tensions serve to exacerbate the child's problems. In many cases it becomes clear that one or more members of the family have their needs satisfied as a result of the child's challenging behaviour (e.g. acting as a convenient scapegoat, drawing attention from marital tensions, permitting displacement of hostility) and thus such individuals may consciously or subconsciously seek to subvert any externally directed initiative. In such circumstances it may prove necessary for the therapist to help the family members gain greater understanding of their roles and relationships with one another.

OUTCOMES

Although oppositional behaviour in children can be highly distressing and disempowering for parents, the voluminous number of existing studies clearly indicates that where parents (and other key family members) take a full and active part in a structured intervention programme, improvements in the child's behaviour usually occur relatively speedily. Given such programmes, the prognosis for oppositional children appears to be markedly superior than for those whose behaviour is marked by hyperactivity or significant learning difficulty.

REFERENCES

American Psychiatric Association (APA) (1994). *Diagnostic and Statistical Manual of Mental Disorders* (4th edn). Washington, D.C.: Author.

Bates, J.E., Bayles, K., Bennett, D.S., Ridge, B. and Brown, M.M. (1991). Origins of externalising behaviour problems at eight years of age. In D.J. Pepler and H.H. Rubin (eds) *The Development and Treatment of Childhood Aggression*. Hillsdale, NJ: Erlbaum.

Barcai, A. and Rosenthal, N. (1974). Fears and tyranny: observations of the tyrannical child. *Archives of General Psychiatry* 30, 302–96.

Beaver, R. (1996). *Educational Psychology Casework: A Practical Guide*. London: Jessica Kingsley.

Bernal, M., Durgee, J., Pruett, H. and Burns, B. (1968). Behaviour modification and the brat syndrome. *Journal of Consulting and Clinical Psychology* 32, 447–55.

Delfini, L., Bernal, M. and Rosen, P. (1976). Comparison of deviant and normal boys in home settings. In E. Marsh, L. Hammerlynek and L. Handy (eds) *Behaviour Modification and Families*. New York: Brunner/Mazel.

Dishion, T.J., French, D.C. and Patterson, G.R. (1995). The development and ecology of antisocial behavior. In D. Cicchetti and D.J. Cohen (eds) *Developmental Psychopathology* Vol. 2. Chichester: John Wiley and Sons.

Dodge, K.A. (1993). Social-cognitive mechanisms in the development of conduct disorder and depression. *Annual Review of Psychology*, 44, 559–84.

Forehand, R. and King, H. E. (1977). Noncompliant children: effects of parent training on behavior and attitude change. *Behavior Modification* 1, 93–108.

Forehand, R. and McMahon, R. J. (1981). *Helping the Noncompliant Child*. New York: Guilford.

Forehand, R., King, H.E., Peed, S. and Yoder, P. (1975). Mother–child interactions: comparisons of a noncompliant clinic group and a nonclinic group. *Behaviour Research and Therapy* 13, 79–84.

Forehand, R., Middlebrook, J., Rogers, T. and Steffe, M. (1983). Dropping out of parent training. *Behavior Research and Therapy* 21, 663–8.

Gard, G.C. and Berry, K.K. (1986). Oppositional children: taming tyrants. *Journal of Clinical Child Psychology* 15(2), 148–58.

Griest, D. and Wells, K. (1983). Behavioral family therapy with conduct disorders in children. *Behavior Therapy* 14, 37–53.

Haswell, K., Hock, E. and Wenar, C. (1981). Oppositional behaviour of preschool children: theory and intervention. *Family Relations* 30, 440–6.

Johnson, S.M., Wahl, G., Martin, S. and Johansson, S. (1973). How deviant is the normal child? A behavioural analysis of the preschool child and his family. In R.D. Rubin, J.P. Brady and J.D. Henderson (eds) *Advances in Behavior Therapy*. Vol. 4. New York: Academic Press.

Kazdin, A.E. (1987). Treatment of antisocial behaviour in children: current status and future directions. *Psychological Bulletin* 102, 187–203.

Kazdin, A.E. (1997). Psychosocial treatments for conduct disorder in children. *Journal of Child Psychology and Psychiatry* 38(2), 161–78.

McAuley, R. and McAuley, P. (1977). *Child Behaviour Problems*. London: Macmillan.

McMahon, R.J., Forehand, R. Griest, D.L. and Wells, K. (1981). Who drops out of treatment during parent behavioral training? *Behavioral Counselling Quarterly* 1, 79–85.

Moreland, J.R., Schwebel, A.I., Beck, S. and Wells, R. (1982). Parents as therapists: a review of the behavior therapy parent training literature – 1975 to 1981. *Behavior Modification* 6, 250–76.

O'Leary, K.D. and Emery, R.E. (1982). Marital discord and child behavior problems. In M.D. Levine and P. Satz (eds) *Middle Childhood: Developmental Variation and Dysfunction*. New York: Academic Press.

Patterson, G.R. (1982). Coercive Family Process. Eugene, OR: Castalia.

Plomin, R. and Hershberger, S. (1991). Genotype–environment interaction. In T.D. Wachs and R. Plomin (eds) *Conceptualization and Measurement of Organism–environment Interaction*. Washington, D.C.: American Psychological Association.

Powers, S.W. and Roberts, M.W. (1995). Simulation training with parents of oppositional children: preliminary findings. *Journal of Clinical Child Psychology* 24(1), 89–97.

Wahler, R.G. (1980). The insular mother: her problems in parent–child treatment. *Journal of Applied Behaviour Analysis* 13, 207–19.

Wahler, R.G., Hughey, J. and Gordon, J. (1981). Chronic patterns of mother–child coercion: some differences between insular and non-insular families. *Analysis and Intervention in Developmental Disabilities* 1, 145–56.

Webster-Stratton, C. (1993). Strategies for helping early school-aged children with oppositional defiant and conduct disorders: the importance of home–school partnerships. *School Psychology Review*, 22(3), 437–57.

Webster-Stratton, C. and Spitzer, A. (1991). Reliability and validity of a parent Daily Discipline Inventory: DDI. *Behavior Assessment* 13, 221–39.

White, J., Moffit, T., Earls, F. and Robins, L. (1990). Preschool predictors of persistent conduct disorder and delinquency. *Criminology*, 28, 443–54.

8 Disruptiveness in schools and classrooms

INTRODUCTION

Most pupils believe that they and their teachers have different interests. In their view, it is his business to exact of them hard service, theirs to escape from it; it is his privilege to make laws; theirs to evade them. He is benefited by their industry, they by their indolence; he is honoured by their obedience, they by their independence. From the infant school to the professional seminary this moral warfare exists.

(*English Journal of Education* 1858: 373; cited in Furlong 1985: 1)

Historical accounts of childhood misbehaviour in school (Pearson 1983) remind us that problem behaviour is no recent phenomenon. Nevertheless, concern about rising misbehaviour in school is currently a worldwide concern. In Britain the perception of rising indiscipline is resulting in increasing use of formal exclusion from school and in calls for an expansion of special provision such as schools for children with emotional and behavioural difficulties and/or units for disruptive children.

Although labels such as 'emotional and behavioural difficulties' and 'disruptive' may be helpful to educationalists in accessing specialist provision for children whose behaviour disrupts classes (Galloway and Goodwin 1987), it is important to note that such terms are largely subjective and often do not clearly relate to specific behaviours. In many cases such labels are reflections of a teacher's mounting concern or anxiety about the impact of a child's behaviour upon others. In his review of the genesis of the 'disruptive pupil', Turkington (1986: 103) notes:

The definitions adopted for surveys and in published reports were invariably so broad as to allow the inclusion of any incident of misbehaviour. The guiding criterion was the interpretation of the incident rather than the incident itself. This problem was frequently commented on and inevitably implied that pupils defined as 'disruptive' by one teacher or one school would not be defined in this way by other teachers in the same school or other schools.

Although labelling may be directly related to the freeing of additional resources, in seeking to reduce classroom misbehaviour it is rarely helpful to concern oneself overly with psychological classifications or diagnoses. Rather, it is more important to consider what approaches can be introduced to alleviate or resolve the situation. Such considerations involve a close examination of many factors at three different levels. These, and the approaches associated with them, form the basis of this chapter.

LEVELS OF ANALYSIS

The 1980s witnessed a proliferation of interest in ways by which disruptive and challenging behaviour might be tackled in schools. Essentially, approaches were adopted which addressed problems at one or more of three levels: that of the child, the classroom and the school (Elliott and Morris 1991).

When asked to consider the reasons for a child's misbehaviour, many teachers will understandably point to aspects of the child's environment, history or psychological make-up. Environmental factors that are often employed to account for misbehaviour include disruption to family life, poor parenting, socio-economic hardship and physical or sexual abuse. Psychological accounts may focus upon such factors as the child's personality, attitudes, temperament and interpersonal style.

In such accounts, the prime focus usually involves 'within-child' analyses where the source of the problem is located within the child. The child enters the school each day, along with his or her problems, and clashes with teachers and other children are an inevitable consequence. As, in such analyses, the origin of the child's problems is perceived to be located outside of the school gates, it is not surprising that schools feel unsure how best to respond. Often the 'answer' is seen as remedying the child's home circumstances, transferring the child to alternative educational provision, or providing some form of psychological therapy.

It is universally accepted, however, that for the majority of children classroom behaviour may vary considerably, depending upon who is teaching at any given time. Although 'within-child' analyses can provide an indication as to why an individual child has a *propensity* to exhibit problem behaviour in school, these are insufficient as a comprehensive explanation for disruptiveness. A focus on the background and interpersonal dynamics of an individual child neglects the importance of the impact of the teacher in determining what *actually transpires*. The highly skilled teacher may often be able to secure a settled, industrious classroom despite the fact that many of the children have the potential to be extremely challenging. In contrast, a less skilled teacher may be confronted with major disruption even by groups of children who can usually be relied upon to conduct themselves admirably.

During the 1980s attention shifted somewhat from the impact of *individual teachers* upon children's behaviour to that of *schools* as social organisations. Unlike studies conducted during the 1960s that appeared to suggest that differences between schools made little or no impact upon student behaviour and attainment, research during the 1970s (Reynolds *et al.* 1976, Rutter *et al.* 1979) began to suggest that the impact of individual schools as social organisations upon children's general level of performance was significant. Teachers also recognised that the difficulties presented by individual children were often exacerbated or ameliorated by a transfer to an alternative school. It is not simply that the classroom skills of the child's teachers may differ from one school to another but, rather, that the overall general ethos or social climate of each school communicates different messages to the child. For many teachers during the late 1980s and 1990s, it was this 'whole school effect' upon children's behaviour that was targeted as the focus for professional development sessions (Elliott and Morris 1991).

Intervention at the within-child level

The major ways of tackling problems at the within-child level involve a variety of forms of counselling or behavioural techniques. These approaches, of course, have long been misguidedly perceived by some teachers as 'a good talking to' and 'school detention'. Misunderstanding of the precise nature of counselling and behavioural approaches and their potential for teachers has arguably reduced their impact and, in extreme cases, resulted in their being dismissed as of little value for school contexts.

At the most simplistic level, counselling attempts to enable the individual to gain a clearer understanding of his or her attitudes, beliefs, attributions, expectations and values, the impact of others upon his/her behaviour, the nature and impact of his/her behaviour upon others and the relationship of these to the child's psychological and social functioning. In the specific context of challenging behaviour in school, it is generally hoped by school staff that the outcome of counselling will be that the child gains greater self-understanding and that this will lead to a change of behaviour.

Behavioural approaches, in contrast, make rather less demands upon the child's ability to reason and ultimately consider what is the preferred pattern of behaviour (see Chapter 2). With regard to disruptiveness in school, the most widely used technique is contingency contracting. This involves establishing a programme that systematically provides rewards and sanctions demonstrably contingent upon behaviour. The desired behaviours are negotiated, specified and explained to the child. Outcomes directly related to these specified behaviours are made explicit and a system of close monitoring and evaluation is established.

Although it is common for both approaches to be employed in combination, it is important to recognise that, within the context of school, it is the latter approach that often sits more easily within the prevailing power structures.

Counselling, and other forms of talking therapy, are generally based upon the premise that the client recognises that he/she has a problem and wishes

to work with another in order to find a solution. Where children have problems that do not directly intrude upon the smooth running of school (e.g.
anxiety about peer relationships, grief concerning the loss of a loved family
member) the practice of counselling is unlikely to lead to role conflict for the
teacher concerned. Many young people who engage in disruptive behaviour
in school, however, do not actively seek, or wish to enter into, a counselling
relationship, nor do they necessarily wish to reflect upon or change their
present circumstances, for often their disruptiveness is proving reinforcing
to them.

Although a vast array of differing models of counselling exist, they have
in common a general principle that it is the client who has ultimate control,
freedom and responsibility to choose what he or she feels is the most effective way forward. The counsellor's task is to help the child gain greater understanding of relevant issues and to empower him/her to decide on a course
of action. The decision taken should be accepted and valued by the counsellor. This begs the important question, who in the school can and should
engage in the counselling process?

During the 1960s, the notion of the school counsellor, already a fully
qualified teacher, who could be non-judgemental and non-authoritarian,
gained a degree of popularity. Following the model of the school-based
guidance counsellor in the USA, it was anticipated by many that each secondary school would employ a counsellor who would help the child with
social, educational and vocational issues. Although the child might be
referred by school staff, there would be no doubt that the client was the child
rather than the school. In such cases, counsellors would not necessarily see a
resolution of those difficulties identified by schools as the central goal of
their work.

As educational resources declined and conceptions of the role of the
teacher changed to incorporate views of teaching the 'whole child', the
notion of the teacher as counsellor gained in popularity. Heads of year or
house were increasingly expected to engage in counselling children with a
variety of personal and social, as well as educational, problems. Gradually
this role was taken up by increasing numbers of classteachers, and skills of
counselling (e.g. active listening, reflecting, clarifying and summarising) were
widely taught by means of inservice training and published materials (e.g.
Langham and Parker 1989).

The value of teachers having basic counselling skills in working with
colleagues, young people and their parents has now become widely accepted
(Elton Report 1989), although an important distinction should be drawn
between the operation of such skills in day-to-day school life and the
employment by teachers of counselling as the primary strategy in work with
a highly challenging individual.

In contrast with the school counsellor, the teacher's perceived task in
'counselling' challenging children is often to ensure that they are persuaded
to change their behaviour in a desired fashion. In such circumstances all of

the adult's skills of persuasion may be brought to this task, and existing power differentials are likely to be exploited. In such circumstances is counselling appropriate? Consider, for example, the child who is refusing to wear school uniform and is summoned to the head of year to be 'counselled'. Does the description of the ensuing exchange as counselling mean that the child has a real freedom to make a decision? If the child chooses not to act in accordance with the requirements of the school, is the head of year in a position to accept and value the child's decision? To suggest, as is often the case, that a disinterested head of year is merely helping the child to understand the consequences of continued non-acquiescence, that the child is free to make up his or her own mind in the full knowledge of the likely outcomes, is to debase the notion of what true counselling sets out to achieve. In such situations, and however justifiable it may be, the process is not counselling but exhortation, persuasion and/or threat.

> Counselling is about change – personal change – and as such we cannot, and should not, talk in terms of enforcing counselling on others. It is almost impossible to make people change the more fundamental aspects of themselves *unless they want to*. It is also unethical to try to impose such changes on another person. This is allied at worst to brainwashing or intimidation, and at best to social control.
>
> (Cowie and Pecherek 1994: 55; emphasis in original)

Such a difficulty, albeit to a lesser extent, may also be encountered by other professionals whose responsibility is to provide support to children with behavioural difficulties. The educational psychologist or LEA behaviour support teacher, although freed from the day-to-day pressure that a child may exert on the classteacher or school management, is still likely to feel a degree of pressure to effect the desired change in the client, to encourage the child to respond in ways which the school, local authority and they themselves might find desirable. This is not, of course, to suggest that the interests of the child are overlooked but, rather, that it may become apparent that the child's interests are best served by ensuring that problem behaviour is reduced. In many circumstances, therefore, it is not clear whether a professional is actually engaging in counselling as understood by the counselling literature or is actually guiding the child to behave in a desired fashion. To illustrate this dilemma, consider the example of Colin.

Colin, aged fourteen, was becoming an increasing problem for his teachers. Although not aggressive or directly challenging to teachers, his continual use of argument, name-calling and general banter towards peers was becoming increasingly disruptive and undermining the quality of many lessons. Colin was somewhat overweight and had a marked physical resemblance to a famous comedian. This attracted risible comment from peers to which he would reply in kind.

At his first interview with the educational psychologist, Colin professed unhappiness at his circumstances and a strong desire that those who were provoking him should be silenced. He agreed to meet with the psychologist over a period of weeks in the hope that ways forward might be deduced.

At an early stage in their sessions, the educational psychologist considered Colin to be locked in a spiral of peer antagonism. As a result, the boy appeared to be unthinkingly engaged in a series of self-defeating behaviours that met neither his needs nor those of others. For this reason, it was considered that counselling should focus upon events in school and Colin would be asked to explore what happened and determine whether he wished change to take place. It was anticipated that Colin's generally good-natured disposition and his obvious desire for a comfortable existence, together with a greater understanding of his own role in provoking conflict, would result in a desire and an ability to modify his behaviour.

Over a number of counselling sessions, Colin's behaviour in school was examined and analysed. Events antecedent to conflict were identified and, using flow-charts on large sheets of paper, Colin was shown how his reactions would often maintain difficulties for himself. Over time, Colin appeared to have much greater insight into the dynamics of his classroom setting and the ways by which he interacted with others.

Once a degree of insight was gained, Colin was reminded that he had earlier expressed a desire to change his circumstances. He was asked what would have to change in order that the verbal aggression and ensuing classroom disruption might be reduced. Colin persisted in his argument that it was his peers, not he, who would have to change, even though he clearly understood his impact upon them. (This is a common feature of work with children where highly contradictory perceptions can be held simultaneously, the less desirable of which may often be maintained by a powerful need to attribute blame to a third party.) During the course of further sessions, Colin came to accept that meaningful change would be likely to take place only if he were to change his normal pattern of classroom behaviour. At this point he announced that he enjoyed the classroom banter – it alleviated the tedium of lessons – and that he had made a decision that he did not want his present circumstances to change. This position was maintained during further follow-up sessions.

The educational psychologist was now in a difficult situation. Within the counselling relationship it had been suggested that Colin should come to his own decisions about future action, based upon the insights and understandings obtained during the sessions. The boy had, however, chosen an unwelcome path that placed him in direct conflict with the school. If he did not change it was clear that a likely outcome would be exclusion followed by an enforced transfer to a disruptive unit. In the opinion of the psychologist this was a most undesirable placement given Colin's circumstances. To what extent, therefore, could the psychologist seek to place greater pressure upon Colin to change his behaviour? The use of behavioural techniques, family controls and school sanctions could be integrated into a programme that may be able to enforce compliance yet would this indicate that the pose adopted in the counselling interview was little more than a sham, that freedom of choice for the child existed only in so far as this represented the desired outcomes of others? On the other hand, was it sufficient for the psychologist to inform the school and local authority that he had done his best but, unfortunately, Colin did not wish to change and thus the case would be closed? The pressure upon local authorities to provide services perceived by schools to be 'effective' might further reduce the appeal of the latter alternative.

In the final analysis it was considered that the risks to Colin of permanent exclusion were so great that the employment of a behaviour modification programme geared to reducing his disruptive behaviour was the most appropriate course of action. Such a programme was subsequently established. This involved itemising and agreeing desired behaviours with Colin, his teachers and his parents. After each lesson his teachers provided him with a score which was recorded on a form. His total daily score was then used to establish the extent to which he would receive a variety of rewards such as pocket money and television.

This programme proved highly effective and, despite his initial reluctance, Colin soon became an enthusiastic participant.

One is left to consider, however, whether this satisfactory end justified the action taken – was it right to take control from the child once he had refused to change in the desired fashion? Despite the fact that Colin appeared not to recognise the contradictions above, it is likely that, with hindsight, the psychologist would have specified the limitations upon the boy's freedom to choose.

It is important to note that fairly intrusive behavioural techniques were required to help Colin to change. While it is widely accepted that the *skills* of counselling are of value to teachers in working with child, parents and colleagues, counselling as a *therapeutic process* is only rarely an effective and sufficient technique for teachers confronted by acts of major indiscipline. Indeed, the series of DfE circulars addressing 'Pupils with Problems' (DfE 1994) virtually ignore talking therapies as strategies for helping children with behaviour difficulties.

Behavioural approaches, in contrast to counselling approaches, have as their primary focus observable behaviours and how these may be modified or shaped (see Chapter 2). Such approaches place particular stress upon the relationship between behaviours and their consequences. Put simply, it is considered that behaviour followed by a positive experience is more likely to recur. Behaviour that has no 'pay-off' or, alternatively, an adverse consequence should become less likely to recur. This very simple maxim, stemming originally from work with animals, becomes somewhat problematic, however, when applied to complex social situations such as classrooms or playgrounds.

Unlike animals in experimental situations, humans engage in complex social behaviours, and experience positive and negative results in ways that are not easily reducible to simple cause and effect. The sources of perceived outcomes are similarly many and the ability of those in authority to control these is comparatively limited. For example, for many adolescents, peer approval is a significantly more powerful factor than any reinforcer (tangible or intangible) which may be at the teacher's disposal.

Behavioural techniques tend to be most effective in settings where the ability to control rewards and sanctions in a consistent and uniform fashion is at its greatest. For this reason, such approaches have become particularly popular in secure settings for children with highly complex and challenging behaviour, as these have relatively high and sustained control over the child's environment and, thus, to the sources of reinforcement. An example of such a setting is Boston Secure Treatment (BST), a maximum-security setting in Massachusetts for children who have been convicted of serious offences such as rape and murder (Elliott 1987). BST operates a highly complex points system for every phase of the child's day from getting up in the morning, having breakfast, attending classes, engaging in group work and therapy, engaging in evening recreation, to going to bed at night. Aggregated scores for the week lead to the children being placed at one of four levels. A child's level is the key factor in determining the privileges that can be enjoyed for the rest of the week. These include such rewards as pocket money, use of radio/TV/computers, use of phones, bedtimes, and the delivery of pizza. Because the children are incarcerated for twenty-four hours a day and privileges are so tightly controlled, the behavioural programme is immensely powerful and provides strong controls on the behaviour of a highly volatile and disordered population.

Although similar programmes can be found in residential special schools for children with behavioural difficulties, it is very difficult to apply these in mainstream school settings. Clearly, such a high degree of control over reinforcement is impossible (and, for many people undesirable) in mainstream schools. These settings can usually offer only a very restricted range of rewards and sanctions, and, given the length of the school day, can exert a direct influence for only six hours on five days a week.

To illustrate, consider the case of Mary, aged fourteen, who is proving to be highly disruptive in her classes. You, as one of her teachers, wish to encourage her to become more responsive to you by relating such desired behaviour to positive outcomes. What rewards (reinforcements) are open to you? The list is likely to be limited and involve few items that will be perceived as particularly attractive by Mary. Now consider likely rewards that result directly from her disruptiveness. These may include peer approval, amusement at the teacher's discomfort, an escape from perceived boredom, an opportunity to take out her anger towards someone else (a parent? sibling? boyfriend?) on a 'safe' target, an opportunity to mask her insecurities about academic work, the opportunity to exert power/control over another. Where Mary is struggling with major unresolved issues (parental separation, an abusive family, social isolation, low self-esteem) the power of such reinforcers is often likely to be greater than those which adults can substitute.

Furthermore, you are in contact with Mary for only a fraction of her time in school. Although she appears to be presenting difficulties in other lessons, her behaviour does seem inconsistent and clearly differs from one teacher to another. To what extent could you rely upon your colleagues to support you by following the behavioural programme even if you could persuade senior management to establish one? How could you be certain that whatever is set up will not be undermined by Mary's parents, relatives or friends?

The establishment of a behavioural programme for a highly challenging child in a school setting will usually involve close collaboration between teachers, senior management, parents and, in many cases, an external consultant such as an educational psychologist or behaviour support teacher. In drawing up a behavioural programme the following issues will need to be clearly specified (see also Chapter 7):

- a clear definition of the behaviours which are giving cause for concern. Information will be required concerning their nature, frequency, intensity, the settings in which they occur; in particular, the extent to which they are situation or person specific. This usually requires the establishment of a detailed system of measuring and recording which can provide a pre-intervention baseline and demonstrate what gains, if any, are made subsequently
- precipitating factors which appear to trigger the behaviour and the usual consequences for the child of the behaviour
- the present and potential range of rewards and sanctions that can be applied at home and at school
- factors which may undermine the operation of the programme and the means by which these may be overcome
- complementary ways by which the behaviour difficulties can be addressed (e.g. use of counselling, peer support, amendments to timetabling/ curriculum content and delivery)
- the clear commitment to the programme of all those involved in its operation
- roles and responsibilities for all those involved in operating and monitoring the programme

Many attempts to operate individual behavioural programmes founder because there is insufficient attention to detail, progress is not monitored closely and those involved do not adhere closely to agreed action in response to the child's behaviour. Where such failings are not in evidence, behavioural programmes can be very successful. One example, that of Carl, is illustrated below.

Carl, aged nine, attended Hilltown primary school. Located in a highly socially disadvantaged urban area, the school was very experienced in dealing with disaffected, volatile and aggressive children and its teachers were generally highly competent and confident in tackling misbehaviour. Carl, however, was proving too taxing and was at severe risk of being permanently excluded.

Carl could be a pleasant and amiable boy yet he was prone to become defiant and aggressive to adults in authority. When asked to engage in classroom tasks he would often refuse outright and seek to amuse himself by taunting other children or playing with equipment/toys. When confronted by his teacher, he would rapidly become verbally aggressive and begin to shout that no one was going to tell him what to do. If his teacher persisted in demanding that he should acquiesce, Carl would hurl materials around the room prior to running out of school. Although Carl had experienced some difficulties during his infant education, the intensity and frequency of his recent classroom outbursts were not in keeping with his earlier behaviour.

Within the peer group, Carl was perceived as a leader who, through his physical prowess and personal qualities, could control the behaviour of the other members of class. He was skilled in his interactions with peers and appeared to enjoy his influential position. When he wished, he appeared able to relate well to adults. Carl's academic ability was not perceived as problematic, although his behaviour was resulting in underachievement.

Carl was the oldest of three children living at home with their divorced mother. Although Carl's mother was highly concerned about her son's behaviour in school, her attempts to reason with him had proven to be ineffective and she was at a loss to know how to proceed. On occasions, she had stopped him playing out with his friends in the evening or had stopped his pocket money but this 'had not taught him a lesson' and his behaviour had continued unabated.

In his interviews with all concerned, the educational psychologist built up a picture of a boy who had a clear grasp of the nature of his behaviour and its effect upon others. Unlike some children with emotional and behavioural difficulties, Carl appeared not to be overwhelmed by inner tensions, not to have confused attributions as to the intentions of others, did not demonstrate an inability to tolerate perceived provocation or experience an incapacity to maintain acceptable control of his emotions. Rather, it seemed that he enjoyed the exercise of power, found his behaviour in class to be rewarding both in offering him prestige and influence and in providing him with opportunities to avoid undesirable tasks. As Carl's influence with peers grew, and as he passed through to the junior section of the school, he appeared to have gained in confidence to a level that he was now more prepared to challenge school in an outright, defiant fashion. A series of short-term exclusions had made no impact upon his behaviour and it appeared that an inevitable outcome of continued misbehaviour would be permanent exclusion. In such circumstances it appeared essential that Carl should come to recognise the authority of his parents and teachers and be encouraged to participate fully in his education.

In discussions with Carl's mother and teachers, it was agreed that a behavioural programme would be established. This would make highly explicit to Carl exactly what was desired behaviour in school and how this would be related to the exercise of privileges at home. Carl's mother proved highly willing to ensure that agreed outcomes were effected and demonstrated her conviction that she was able to ensure that Carl could not subvert these. (Note: this is an essential element in the operation of such pro-grammes and a lack of parental resolve in carrying out agreed action is often a reason for failure.)

It was decided that the key behaviour to tackle was Carl's propensity to temper tantrums in class and his tendency to storm out of the room. It was explained to him that he would receive a coloured sticker each day if he were able to avoid such responses. If he received a sticker he would be awarded points based upon his behaviour; these would be directly related to pocket money. Stickers and points were entered each day on a chart held by his teachers which would be taken home to be scrutinised by his mother each evening.

In the operation of such programmes, it is important that the child is made aware that privileges such as pocket money, sweets, treats are not always an automatic right. Rewards for desired behaviour, therefore, would normally tend to total little more than that which is already being made available; the key issue is that they are now contingent upon the child's actions. Such a stance helps to reduce the possibility that the child is seen as being rewarded for poor behaviour, or that rewards are perceived as bribes.

Carl's mother wished to add a sanction for severe misbehaviour (i.e. when the sticker was not awarded) and after discussion it was decided that in such cases he would be put into his pyjamas and kept in the house after tea. As Carl enjoyed playing out most evenings, it was clear that he would find this undesirable.

Extensive discussion took place between the educational psychologist, Carl, his mother and teachers in order to ensure that the procedures were fully understood. These were also set out in a letter (see Figure 8.1).

Dear Mrs X,

Following our discussion at Hilltown School on 26 March 1997, I thought it would be helpful to make a note of what we agreed about Carl's home–school programme.

1 Carl will be responsible for bringing the form home each evening and returning it to school the following day.
2 The sticker will be necessary each day for Carl to receive any treats that same evening. Should he fail to receive the sticker, he will be sent to his room after tea.
3 When he is successful in obtaining the sticker, Carl may be rewarded with the agreed treats. To receive these, however, he must also obtain a total of nine points for that day.
4 When Carl receives at least nine points he will:
   • be allowed to watch television
   • be permitted to play outside with his friends (if such circum-stances as the weather, etc., are favourable)
   • receive 40 pence pocket money
   • receive 20 pence for his savings account

continued

We agreed that we should stress to Carl that this sum reflects the amount he currently receives and by no means should it be perceived as an *additional* incentive or a bribe to be well behaved. I understand that if Carl succeeds in saving enough money, you are prepared to take him on a shopping trip in order that he might buy some football boots.

5 Any further allowances and treats which you provide will depend upon Carl scoring highly on his weekly total. Attempts will be made, wherever possible, however, to limit the availability of money, sweets, treats and the like from other sources (e.g. relatives, friends), as these will reduce the effectiveness of the programme.

7 Carl will not attempt to influence his teachers by entering into negotiation with them. If this does transpire, his teachers have been asked to place a zero on the record form.

8 Carl's teacher, Mrs Wright, will total the points scored each day and return it to him. You have kindly indicated your willingness to sign the form each evening so that she will be aware that you have seen it.

9 If Carl fails to bring the form home, it should be assumed that he has not behaved appropriately that day and, therefore, the agreed rewards will not follow.

10 I have explained the system to Carl and he appears to understand how it will work.

11 Finally, may I stress again the importance of focusing upon good behaviour and using praise as an important added reward.

I hope that you will feel that this letter represents an accurate account of our agreement. Please contact me as soon as possible if you feel that any changes are needed. If not, we shall aim to start the programme from the beginning of the new term.

We are grateful for your support and obvious commitment to helping Carl make the most of his education.

Figure 8.1 Letter from the educational psychologist to Carl's mother

Figure 8.2 provides an example of the daily record form.

In these cases a common pattern involves the child obtaining scores which are initially high (a honeymoon period) often followed by a sudden deterioration in behaviour. At such a time, it is easy for the adults concerned to become disheartened and to give up. It is important, therefore, to ensure that everyone concerned adheres closely to the agreed procedures and the child recognises that, unlike many other past attempts to tackle his or her behaviour, the present intervention will be maintained in a consistent and sustained fashion. Such a procedure took place with Carl.

Unlike many children, Carl very quickly reneged on his agreement to maintain a more desirable pattern of behaviour in class. Although Day One had witnessed major improvement in his usual behaviour, on the second day he returned to his former behaviour of shouting out, picking arguments with others and refusing to undertake any work. As his teacher attempted to

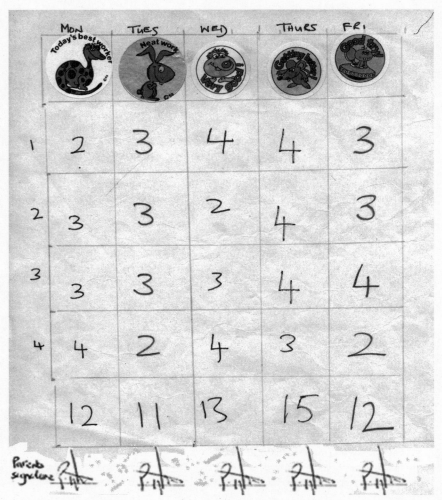

Figure 8.2 A completed record form employed for Carl

address the situation, Carl threw his books across the room and ran out swearing. Carl did not receive his sticker.

Consequently, that evening the educational psychologist visited Carl's home. Carl was asked to discuss the events of the day and consider the outcomes of his behaviour. He seemed surprised that his mother had stuck to the agreement as in the past she had often been inconsistent in seeing through her threats. As the educational psychologist spoke with Carl and his mother and arranged a home visit later that week from an educational social worker, it would have become clear to Carl that this intervention was not going to go away. Carl's behaviour was subsequently transformed and, during the time that the programme operated (ten weeks), there was no recurrence of such extreme behaviour.

Often behaviour scores are placed on a graph. This helps the practitioner to track changes in behaviour over time. Visual representation of progress can also be highly motivating for all those involved as the child's progress can be made visible and thus provides frequent opportunities for praise and congratulations. In Carl's case, the graph proved highly reinforcing.

It should be recognised that such programmes generally set out to reduce extreme behaviours, to make what are perceived to be intolerable situations manageable. In many cases one would expect children's behaviour to regress after completion of the programme. In successful interventions, however, they do not regress to the former level of severity, intensity or frequency. Although, after the programme was terminated, Carl continued to have difficulties in school from time to time, he was no longer perceived to be particularly difficult, nor did his behaviour warrant further referral to external support agencies.

Factors which reduce the likelihood of effective intervention

It is important to recognise that the successful outcome of the above intervention is not a feature of all behavioural programmes. In the experience of the writers the following factors, if present, greatly reduce the likelihood of a successful home–school behavioural programme:

- The child's behaviour is the result of major emotional confusion and/or a manifestation of severe psychological trauma.
- The child does not have a clear understanding of exactly which behaviours are being addressed and how these will relate to subsequent outcomes.
- The child does not consider that he/she is working with all parties to effect a change in behaviour which is perceived to be helpful for him/her. A strong desire to subvert the programme is clear from the outset.
- Parents are unable or unwilling to suggest rewards which can be made available for desirable behaviour.
- Parents are ambivalent about following through the agreed procedures because they lack the authority or mechanisms of control or because they are concerned that the child will think 'that I don't love him/her' any more.
- Parents do not consider that the behaviour is sufficiently problematic to warrant such concerted intervention.
- Parents are preoccupied with other concerns to an extent that they have insufficient energy/motivation to address the needs of their children.
- Teachers do not have a clear understanding about exactly which behaviours are being addressed. Other issues (e.g. homework completion, where this is not part of the programme) are allowed to affect scores.
- Teachers do not ensure that the monitoring of the scheme is tightly managed. The child's performance is not checked and, where appropriate, praised each day. In secondary schools one member of staff does not

assume responsibility for keeping an overview of the programme and addressing weaknesses.

- Teachers fail to appreciate that the programme must be underpinned by skilled and sensitive classroom management.
- External agencies, where these have established the programme, do not maintain an active involvement. As a result, child, parents and teachers may consider that interest in the programme has decreased.
- Regular case discussions are not held and attended by all parties concerned with the operation of the programme.

Intervention at the level of teacher–pupil interaction

It is a truism that however difficult the child in class, manifest behaviour is determined, to a significant extent, by the effectiveness of the teacher. During the 1980s, approaches that aimed to tackle school-based disruption concentrated largely upon teacher management skills. These concerned, first, the skills involved in delivering an appropriate curriculum in an educationally sound fashion and, second, those aspects of interpersonal effectiveness by which the authority of the teacher was respected and accepted. It is the ineffective exercise of these latter skills that is often related to classroom misbehaviour.

The seminal work of Kounin (1970) in the United States suggested that those teachers who were considered to be superior in their management of classroom situations differed from their less effective colleagues not in their response to major acts of indiscipline but, rather, in their ability to prevent difficulties from occurring in the first instance. Kounin's work pointed to the importance of teacher vigilance (or 'withitness'), the need to manage effectively the many demands upon the teacher's attention in the classroom, and the skills involved in keeping children alert and free from distraction.

In Britain, the work of Robertson (1990) built upon American studies. This work emphasised the nature of teacher authority and how this was signalled through a range of highly subtle verbal and non-verbal cues. From the first meeting of teacher and child, such communication serves to increase or decrease the likelihood of a challenge to the teacher's authority. Many teachers, particularly the less experienced, are unaware of the subtle ways by which children may test them out and only become aware of the potential threat to their authority at a later time. Key non-verbal and verbal behaviours, which add to or diminish the teacher's air of authority, are summarised below:

- eye contact (scanning groups of children)
- one-to-one eye contact
- rate of speech
- volume and pitch of speech
- rhythm, fluency and intonation in delivery

- pitch of voice
- body posture and kinaesthetics
- use of territory/space

Eye contact

Eye contact is an important element in maintaining alertness, holding the listener's concentration and signalling vigilance. Some speakers have a tendency to focus on objects immediately in front of them or to stare blankly out into space. Others address one part of the audience (usually those in the central region) and appear to ignore the others. It is widely accepted that in addressing any group it is important to suggest to each individual that it is he or she to whom the presentation is being addressed. For teachers, the ability to sweep the classroom visually and give the impression to each child that it is to him or her that the message is being addressed denotes a capacity for vigilance, alertness and a grasp of a professional skill that will be perceived even by very young children.

The individual who controls eye contact in an interaction is generally perceived to be the dominant partner. In direct dealings with children eye contact is likely to be used to convey differing forms of challenge to the teacher. Eyes downcast are usually understood to represent submission or deference to authority; a gaze away, often in a slightly upward direction, suggests sufficient compliance to remain in the speaker's presence but an unwillingness to listen to, or heed, what is being said; a fixed and intense stare, often allied to a rigid posture and a reduction of physical distance, may signal an overt and direct challenge to one's authority and be associated with a degree of physical threat.

It is important to note that these behaviours are conditioned significantly by age, gender and cultural factors. Although enraged infants may stare in a hostile, albeit brief, fashion at the objects of their anger, young children seeking challenge are more likely to employ indirect methods such as averting their eyes and refusing to take notice of the adult. Adolescent girls who wish to signal defiance may similarly avert their gaze while feigning an air of indifference or boredom. The more confrontational 'locked-gaze' behaviours, in a school context, are usually the product of male teacher–male adolescent interactions. This latter situation is particularly problematic and may quickly escalate into physical confrontation.

It is important to note, however, that for children from minority cultures, for example, those of Afro-Caribbean heritage, avoiding eye contact when being chastised is a sign of respect. A failure to recognise cultural differences may increase the likelihood of subsequent conflict.

The skilled teacher reads such signals and draws upon a range of other contextual and interpersonal cues to determine how best to respond, whether to attempt to establish authority in an overt fashion, for example, by saying, 'Look at me when I'm talking to you!', or by using other methods of signalling authority, such as skilfully controlling the dialogue, similarly withholding eye gaze, or appearing not to notice the challenge.

Voice

The voice is another key element in preventing and managing behaviour difficulties. Many individuals project the impression of a lack of confidence in themselves as authority figures by speaking too rapidly or breathlessly, allowing the pitch of their voice to rise when anxious, speaking in a flat, monotone way with little rhythm or cadence and by stammering or struggling to find appropriate words to explain themselves. A common failing resides in the false belief that raising one's voice (by shouting, rather than voice projection) necessarily suggests authority. Although cultural differences vary to the extent that shouting at children is deemed acceptable (e.g. American teachers are often horrified by the raised voices they hear in British classrooms), the effective use of this measure by skilled teachers often serves as an unhelpful model for those who are struggling to demonstrate their authority. What many fail to recognise is that a lowered voice carries a greater suggestion of intent, self-control and authority.

Body language

The third key area concerns the awareness and use of body language (O'Neill 1991). Anxious teachers tend to adopt rigid, tense postures. They may cross their arms or legs across their body defensively and may feel challenged by a young person's overly relaxed, non-responsive posture (e.g. leaning back in a chair with arms behind head). Relaxed postures reflect status differentials and are a means by which teacher authority may be tested. Similarly, teachers who lack confidence may not circle the classroom environment in a sufficiently casual or extensive manner to suggest that the classroom is their 'territory'. Standing rigidly at the front of the classroom for prolonged periods, staring at the class as a unit in an unfocused manner and adopting defensive mannerisms such as crossing one's arms or rubbing one's face are all behaviours which dramatically increase the likelihood of indiscipline.

Control over communication

At the verbal level it is essential to recognise that authority is usually vested in the individual who is in control of the content and flow of the dialogue. Children may test out adults in authority by posing questions (the answers to which they may have little interest), making requests, ignoring statements or questions, pausing before replying, and generally seeking control over the communication. Less experienced members of staff may be overly responsive to the child – answering all questions, seeking to maintain a relationship by acquiescing to the child's wishes to as great an extent as possible and

proceeding to speak without first gaining the child's full attention. To persevere in such behaviours is to signal to the child that one lacks experience
and/or sufficient strength to manage the complexities of classroom life.

Brian, a newly qualified teacher with a class of eight-year-olds, was experiencing considerable difficulties in managing classroom behaviour, despite
the fact that he was popular with the class and no one child was displaying
severely challenging behaviour. The difficulties he was encountering were
largely the result of his own behaviour, as the following event exemplifies.

It was the beginning of the afternoon session and Brian was finishing off
his introduction to the class who, seated on the carpet, were breaking off into
groups to begin their allotted tasks. The final group, who were going to work
in the craft area, were eager to get started, spurred by the knowledge that the
area contained a small amount of furry material which was greatly prized by
all the children.

Brian's first mistake was to omit to impart some important information
about the groups' tasks during the briefing. As the children hurried to the craft
table he realised his mistake. His second error was to call further instructions
across the room while the children rooted through the materials. As he tried
to gain the children's attention (most of whom had their backs to him) he
spoke louder with his voice carrying a rather higher pitch. Finally, he was
distracted by another child's desire for attention and he left the group to work
unassisted for several minutes. Brian's behaviour signalled to the whole
class that he did not have control over communication and was unsure as to
how this could be gained.

Brian immediately and independently recognised the mistake he had
made with respect to the imparting of directions and, as such, was unlikely to
repeat this error. He had not, however, appreciated that the tone and pitch of
his speech was helping to undermine his authority and was surprised when
this was pointed out to him by an observer. Fortunately, he was willing to
accept help and agreed to the use of audio recordings of him speaking in the
classroom. By modelling voice projection and intonation and analysing
the tapes, Brian's adviser helped him to become more skilled in the use of
his voice, particularly when he found himself in stressful situations.

Advising and supporting teachers with classroom management problems is
problematic for many reasons: often a conceptual framework for understanding behaviour is lacking, opportunities for colleagues to observe and
advise are limited, and resistance to being observed or accepting proffered
advice is strong.

Skilled professional behaviour often operates at a tacit level and many
highly able teachers find it difficult to articulate what it is exactly that they do
which maintains classroom discipline. The common response of many
experienced teachers when asked about their practice, 'It's just experience,
actually!', is of little help to the novice teacher beset by difficulties.

Although general advice about good practice can be helpful, it is often only detailed observation of practice which can highlight professional short-comings; unfortunately, constraints upon staffing rarely render such support possible.

An ability to control one's classroom is a key skill which lies at the heart of the teacher's professional identity. Thus, for many teachers, in particular those who are relatively experienced, the suggestion that the misbehaviour in their classroom stems in part from poor management is highly threatening and a source of shame. In such cases, there may be strong pressure to attribute responsibility to the child or children rather than to oneself. For this reason, struggling teachers may be loath to be observed, and any advice concerning classroom management may be perceived as a threat to their professional dignity and thus met by defensiveness, resistance and an inability to accept personal responsibility.

Despite these difficulties, helping the struggling teacher to develop inter-personal and management skills is generally the single most important means of reducing the prevalence and intensity of disruptive incidents. Such a view was endorsed by the Elton Report (1989) which stated that:

1 Teachers' group management skills are probably the single most import-ant factor in achieving good standards of classroom behaviour.
2 These skills can be taught and learned.
3 Practical training in this area is inadequate.

A number of training packages have been produced to aid teachers in devel-oping skills for preventing challenging behaviour (e.g. Rogers 1994; Chisholm *et al.* 1986). While the delineation of these skills can offer the new or trainee teacher a valuable conceptual framework to consider his or her developing knowledge, as has been noted above, for the more experienced teacher, the ability to manage behaviour is a core professional skill which it is often considered shameful to lack. For this reason, some teachers may approach professional development sessions in a defensive manner and feel constrained in their ability to discuss their difficulties, strengths and weak-nesses. If such a dialogue does not take place, professional development in this area becomes little more than a series of mechanistic prescriptions that are unlikely to become accommodated within the teacher's existing behavioural repertoire.

Intervention at the whole school level

Research in the 1960s and 1970s had appeared to suggest that schools, as individual units, made little impact upon student behaviour or attainment. Large-scale surveys in the United States (Coleman *et al.* 1966; Jencks *et al.* 1972) and in Britain (Plowden Report 1967) placed far more emphasis upon family influences. Subsequently, however, the seminal work of Power *et al.* (1967) led to a succession of studies (e.g. Reynolds *et al.* 1976; Rutter *et al.* 1979; Mortimore *et al.* 1988) which provided strong support for the suggestion that schools as social institutions had a significant and differing effect upon the behaviour and attainment of children.

These findings, together with a general emphasis upon whole-school planning and development, have resulted in most schools attempting to develop whole-school behaviour policies. Such policies emphasise the importance of shared visions, values and understandings, consistency of expectations, response and management, the structured use of rewards and, to a lesser extent, sanctions for children's behaviour.

Other whole-school initiatives draw upon rather more narrow behavioural principles in the belief that these will result in a climate in which teachers act consistently to reinforce desirable behaviour and eliminate disruptive and unco-operative behaviour. An early programme of this kind for primary schools, BATPACK (Wheldall and Merrett 1985) was commended by the Elton Report, although this has been overtaken in popularity by a highly structured, yet relatively straightforward, American programme, Assertive Discipline (Canter and Canter 1992). Although perceived by some as failing to respect children's and parents' rights (Robinson and Maines 1994), the approach is popular with many teachers who welcome a structured programme in which classroom rules are made clear and relate in contingent fashion to specified rewards and sanctions.

The Assertive Discipline programme is the result of Lee Canter's perception that many teachers with classroom management difficulties are either lacking in assertiveness or are hostile in their dealings with children. It emphasises the importance of making classroom rules and procedures clear and explicit and communicating a strong resolve to back up their instructions with actions where necessary. Where children do not observe the rules, the programme offers a series of punishments, the severity of which usually depends upon the number of times the rules are broken. Sanctions usually range from a warning from the classteacher at the first instance to referral to the headteacher for multiple occurrences.

To date, there has been little structured evaluation of the impact of Assertive Discipline upon schools and much of the current controversy has centred upon philosophical issues concerning the ethics of the techniques advocated (Maines and Robinson 1995; Robinson and Maines 1994; Swinson and Melling 1995). One detailed study of fifteen British primary school classrooms (Nicholls and Houghton 1995), however, indicated that, for some classes, the introduction of Assertive Discipline resulted in an increase in on-task behaviour and a concomitant decrease in the frequency of disruptive behaviour.

A difficulty with programmes such as Assertive Discipline is that while teacher management skills are emphasised in the training manuals, these may be subsequently overlooked in the desire to implement punitive structures for those who misbehave. Thus, the programme may become little more than a highly structured system of providing in-class sanctions and referrals to senior management. Rather than using interpersonal skills to prevent or deflect problem situations, the teacher may feel tempted to highlight the 'problem' and seek to invoke punitive consequences in order to demonstrate his or her authority. Thus, any attempt to introduce whole-school behaviour programmes should ensure that the day-to-day, preventive skills of the classroom teacher, rather than the school's formal disciplinary procedures, are emphasised.

Furthermore, while the adoption of a whole-school approach is invaluable for increasing the positive climate of school, and should, over time, inevitably reduce the frequency and intensity of disruption (see, for example, Elliott and Morris 1991), it is unlikely that establishing and operating a whole-school policy on behaviour is sufficient as a solution to problems currently posed by a particularly difficult child. In such circumstances, an examination of interpersonal dealings at school and in the home, exploration of the potential of behavioural approaches, and a detailed analysis of the suitability of the educational tasks that are being presented are likely to be more promising in the short term.

SUMMARY – WHAT SORT OF INTERVENTION STRATEGY IS APPROPRIATE?

In attempting to prevent or manage a disruptive situation in the classroom it is necessary to consider the impact of individual child factors, the interactional pattern and skills of teachers' classroom management and the impact of the school as a social institution. The intervention strategy that is adopted will depend upon individual circumstances, particularly the extent to which the difficulty is specific or general (see Figure 8.3).

It is important to note that Figure 8.3 refers to an underlying *emphasis* rather than to the employment of discrete strategies. A coherent and structured whole-school approach should reduce the likelihood and frequency of severe behavioural difficulties. Where these do exist, however, improving teachers' classroom management skills and ensuring a high quality of curriculum

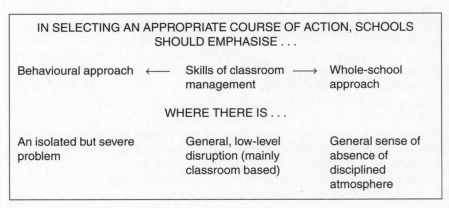

Figure 8.3 Intervention strategies

delivery are more likely to produce a solution in the short term. Where a school is experiencing difficulty with a particular child, especially where this is not specific to one teacher, a behavioural intervention may be the most productive solution. Ideally, however, intervention should operate at all three levels and, indeed, classroom management and behavioural approaches are often considered as part of a broader whole-school approach (e.g. Galvin *et al.* 1990).

REFERENCES

Canter, L. and Canter, M. (1992). *Assertive Discipline.* Santa Monica: Lee Canter Associates.

Chisholm, B., Kearney, D., Knight, G. Little, H. Morris, S. and Tweddle, D. (1986). *Preventive Approaches to Disruption.* London: Macmillan.

Coleman, J.S., Campbell, E., Hobson, C., McParland, J., Mood, A., Weinfeld, F. and York, R. (1966). *Equality of Educational Opportunity.* Washington, D.C.: US Government Printing Office.

Cowie, H. and Pecherek, A. (1994). *Counselling: Approaches and Issues in Education.* London: David Fulton Publishers.

Department for Education (DfE) (1994). *Pupils with Problems.* London: DfE.

Elliott, J. (1987). The treatment of serious juvenile delinquents in Massachusetts. *Educational Psychology in Practice* 3(2), 49–52.

Elliott, J. and Morris, J. (1991). Teacher in-service and the promotion of positive behaviour in school. *British Journal of In-service Education* 17(2), 111–19.

Elton Report (1989). *Discipline in School.* London: HMSO.

Galloway, D. and Goodwin, C. (1987). *The Education of Disturbing Children.* New York: Longman.

Furlong, J. (1985). The Deviant Pupil: Sociological Perspectives. Milton Keynes: Open University Press.

Galvin, P., Mercer, S. and Costa, P. (1990). *Building a Better Behaved School.* Harlow: Longman.

Jencks, C., Smith, M., Acland, H., Bane, M.J., Cohen, D., Gintis, H., Heyns, B. and Michelson, S. (1972). *Inequality: A Reassessment of the Effect of Family and Schooling in America.* New York: Basic Books.

Kounin, J.S. (1970). *Discipline and Group Management in Classrooms.* New York: Holt, Rinehart and Winston.

Langham, M. and Parker, V. (1989). *Counselling Skills for Teachers.* Lancaster: Framework Press.

Maines, B. and Robinson, G. (1995). Assertive Discipline: no wheels on your wagon – a reply to Swinson and Melling. *Educational Psychology in Practice* 11(3), 9–11.

Mortimore, P., Sammons, P., Stoll, L., Lewis, D. and Ecob, R. (1988). *School Matters: The Junior Years.* Wells: Open Books.

Nicholls, D. and Houghton, S. (1995). The effect of Canter's Assertive Discipline Program on teacher and student behaviour. *British Journal of Educational Psychology* 65(2), 197–210.

O'Neill, S. (1991). *Classroom Nonverbal Interaction.* London: Routledge.

Pearson, G. (1983). *Hooligan: A History of Respectable Fears.* Macmillan.

Plowden Report (1967). *Children and their Primary Schools.* London: HMSO.

Power, M.J., Alderson, M.R., Phillipson, C.M., Schoenberg, E. and Morris, J.N. (1967). Delinquent schools. *New Society* 10, 542–3.

Reynolds, D., Jones, D. and St Leger, S. (1976). Schools do make a difference. *New Society* 37, 321.

Robertson, J. (1990). *Effective Classroom Control*. London: Hodder and Stoughton.

Robinson, G. and Maines, B. (1994). Jumping on a dated wagon. *Educational Psychology in Practice* 9(4), 195–200.

Rogers, W. (1994). *Behaviour Recovery*. London: Longman.

Rutter, M., Maughan, B., Mortimore, P. and Ouston, J. (1979). *Fifteen Thousand Hours*. London: Open Books.

Swinson, J. and Melling, R. (1995). Assertive Discipline: four wheels on this wagon – a reply to Robinson and Maines. *Educational Psychology in Practice* 11(3), 3–8.

Turkington, R. (1986). In Search of the Disruptive Pupil: Problem Behaviour in Secondary Schools. Unpublished PhD thesis, University of Leeds.

Wheldall, K. and Merrett, F. (1985). *The Behavioural Approach to Teaching Package (BAT-PACK)*. Birmingham: Positive Products.

9 Drug and solvent abuse

The use of drugs to create a sense of well-being has been a feature of many cultures throughout the centuries. Within our own culture the use of alcohol and tobacco has been quite acceptable for many years, although health concerns around the use of tobacco are now greatly reducing its acceptability. For almost as long, the use of illicit drugs has also been an accepted part of life for the literary elite, as Thomas De Quincy's *Confessions of an English Opium-eater* testifies. However, in the past forty years the use of illicit drugs such as heroin, cocaine and cannabis has shown a dramatic increase and has become so endemic that in certain parts of western culture such drug use must be considered the norm. Images of drug use constantly press upon us, and part of that image is of drug abuse being routine among the young; but is this really the case?

Of course, under-age drinking is a routine way for many teenagers to demonstrate rebellion and individuality, and drug experimentation is becoming more common – a recent study in the north-west of England found that half of the children had tried drugs before they were sixteen years of age (Parker *et al.* 1995). Despite such worrying findings, the regular use of harder drugs is still relatively rare in the United Kingdom. In the United States, however, there has been a dramatic increase in the use of the harder drugs, in particular cocaine (Kosten and Kleber 1992).

REASONS FOR DRUG USAGE

Adolescence is a time of transition when young people are seeking to establish their own identities. This is partly achieved by experimentation and by challenging adult concepts and expectations. There are, of course, many ways to do this, two of which are under-age drinking and experimenting with drugs. No matter how adolescents try to establish a sense of separate identity, they are very adept at justifying their behaviour, and this can be extremely exasperating for the adults around them. They tend to win in any debate, in part because with adolescence comes the ability to think hypothetically, which is in contrast to the very concrete pattern of thinking which is typical of childhood (Piaget 1952). Because of this, it is important to avoid trying to offer discipline only through debate – such an approach is liable to see the adult losing.

Perhaps even more critically from a drug usage point of view is the fact that this phase of development is one where the young person feels a need to place great reliance upon friends. Copying the group in dress or behaviour and behaving in ways that win their approval are felt as key elements of being successful as a teenager. If the group of friends views drug experimentation as part of their pastimes, then this can exert a powerful influence upon steering a young person to drug usage.

A great deal of work has been carried out in an effort to try to predict who might become a significant drug user. Consistently, such work shows that although drug users often have personality problems, such as being considered immature, there is no specific personality type that predicts future drug addiction (Ghodse 1995). It is therefore important to look at the functioning of the individual in order to understand the origins of the problem, and the factors that are helping to maintain it. Although there can be many reasons for someone to begin taking drugs, a key distinction which needs to be made is between drugs that are being used to cope with the stress of a severe psychiatric illness and their use to be part of a particular youth culture. The former type of user is usually a solitary individual, and often demonstrates many other problems and difficulties. Indeed, recent studies have suggested that perhaps up to one-third of young people who have an addiction problem may have other psychiatric disorders (Hovens *et al.* 1994) and these often started before the drug abuse began (Christie *et al.* 1988).

As already mentioned, the origins of abuse are very individual but it has been recognised for some time that such problems can run in families, which has prompted considerable interest in whether addiction problems may actually be inherited. There is evidence that becoming dependent on alcohol may have an inheritable component counting for up to 60 per cent of the influence (Pickens *et al.* 1991), but it has not been shown that a similar inheritance pattern exists with other forms of addiction. Genetics is not the only way that families influence their children, and indeed a child's desire to copy parents is one of the stronger determinants of future patterns of behaviour. This mechanism is a powerful factor in drug use, for if there is a pattern of parental drug abuse there is a greatly increased likelihood that the child will also develop such a habit (Bewley *et al.* 1974). For many teenagers, however, one of the strongest influences on their immediate behaviour remains the peer group with which they spend their time.

WHEN IS DRUG USE A PROBLEM?

For some drugs, such as alcohol and tobacco, usage is so common that it cannot be considered an abnormal activity. In addition, discovering that a teenager has been trying cigarettes or drinking alcohol should not provoke an overreaction. Offering long lectures, or too intense a display of disappointment, runs the risk of seeing the behaviour repeated. Isolated episodes should be treated as such. Recognising that usage is now becoming regular obviously increases adult concern, and encouraging the young person to seek counselling from local youth projects or drug treatment teams is helpful. The ways that parents, teachers and other concerned adults can help are described towards the end of this chapter.

The pattern of usage can be described as addiction when it is causing problems to the young person's health, or alters social or psychological functioning. At this stage advice from the nearest community addiction team can be invaluable, but it is very rare that real help can be given to drug users until they are willing to receive it. It is helpful to realise that among persistent addicts the average age of starting significant drug taking is nineteen years and there is no difference in frequency between men and women (Gossop *et al.* 1994b).

When a young person is addicted to drugs the addiction is not only maintained because of the sense of physical craving, but often, more powerfully, by a sense of psychological dependence. In this the addict believes that he or she cannot cope without the drug, and anticipates significant problems if the drug is stopped. It is this anticipation which powerfully contributes to feeling the need to continue. In addition to these elements of dependence, and the problems experienced as a result of the withdrawal of the specific drug, the sense of needing to keep using drugs can also be reinforced if there are significant environmental and social factors. Difficulties within the family, such as seeing marital violence or feeling that parents no longer care about you, can be very potent sources of distress which the young person can only relieve by becoming intoxicated (Braucht *et al.* 1973). Indeed, sometimes the driving force may be to try to blot out some passage within the adolescent's own past which is just too painful to come to terms with.

Donna was nine years old when her father died in a car crash. In the year before his death there had been concern within the police and social services that he was sexually abusing Donna, but sufficient proof was not found. From the age of twelve years Donna began missing school, and she was frequently in trouble with the police for stealing. No matter what the time of day, or night, she was usually to be found sitting in the local park with a group of older boys, in an intoxicated state. On several occasions she needed to be taken to the local hospital because she had taken a cocktail of pills and alcohol which had rendered her incoherent.

Donna's mother acknowledged that she was not able to control her daughter's behaviour, and four weeks after her fourteenth birthday she was received into the care of the local authority. Initially, she went to live with a local foster family, but she continued to stay out until very late at night, and was usually returned in an intoxicated state either by her friends or the police.

After three months Donna was moved to a children's home which offered closer supervision than the foster family could manage. The first few days were quiet, but Donna gradually became more moody, and would fly into violent rages when thwarted or challenged in any way. She began absconding from the home, and would often be missing for days at a time. When found, she was unkempt and would openly recount stories of criminal activity, drug usage and sexual activity which sometimes included prostitution.

Donna was referred to the local adolescent psychiatry service, and in the sessions there Donna would describe the vivid dreams she had when she tried to sleep. These were always scenes from her early abuse – her bedroom, a sense of being trapped, and feelings of pain and self-disgust. She described how during the day she would sometimes see a flash image of herself in which the front of her nightdress was covered in blood. Donna would avoid looking in a mirror because she said her body disgusted her and explained that the only way she could escape these feelings and images was to 'numb herself' with pills. Donna was, however, adamant that she did not want any psychiatric treatment because she was not a 'nutter'.

After four months in the children's home Donna was arrested for breaking into a chemist's shop. She was remanded to secure accommodation and within two days of arriving began to show the symptoms of withdrawal from sedatives. She successfully completed a withdrawal programme within the secure setting, and after several weeks she began to talk to staff on the unit about her recollections of her abuse.

Donna's story illustrates several of the problems that professionals face when confronted with someone who is routinely abusing drugs. The pattern of self-destruction in this case was being fuelled by recollections of early abuse which were too painful for Donna to deal with. Her method of 'escape' was to be almost permanently intoxicated. Although professional intervention could assist her to deal with these issues, she did not want to co-operate with it, leaving the adults around her feeling powerless to help. Similarly, her drug usage could not be dealt with without her co-operation, and it was only when her general behaviour became totally unruly that formal legal action could be taken. It is sadly true that for most cases of persistent drug usage the situation has to sink to a considerable depth before those concerned for the addict are permitted to offer real help.

DRUGS OF ABUSE

Alcohol

The vast majority of senior secondary schoolchildren admit to under-age drinking. Indeed, in a recent survey it was found that over half of fifteen-year-olds in Scotland and Wales had been drunk twice in the previous year (King *et al.* 1996). In some this can be a pattern of quite heavy alcohol consumption, but the problems of dependence tend not to occur until adulthood. As with drug use generally, it is said that the drinking has become problematic when there is a deterioration in day-to-day functioning or in general health. It is important to realise that young people who use many different drugs will frequently also use alcohol, and so a young person who is clearly intoxicated may not only have been drinking.

Effects

Research in recent years has suggested that small amounts of alcohol may be helpful to health by reducing the potential for heart disease (Doll *et al.* 1994). However, chronic abuse of alcohol is clearly not healthy. As with most drugs of abuse, one of the first signs of addiction is that of tolerance. This is where the young person finds that there is a need to drink increasing amounts in order to achieve the same effect of well-being and intoxication. Tolerance occurs because the body, and in particular the liver, becomes more adept at dealing with the alcohol and so minimises its effect more rapidly as time goes on. It is also worth noting that women appear to metabolise alcohol less well than men, and so smaller amounts, at least in the initial stages of chronic abuse, are capable of producing equivalent levels of intoxication (Frezza *et al.* 1990).

Features of withdrawal

The body's increased capacity to cope with alcohol gradually leads to a steady state in which the normal functioning of the body's systems requires a persistent level of alcohol. When this state has been achieved the young person is said to be showing physiological dependence. At this point, if there is a sudden withdrawal of the alcohol, the young person gradually becomes restless, agitated and tremulous. In severe cases the adolescent may become confused, disorientated and have vivid hallucinations. This severe withdrawal picture (known as the delirium tremens) is uncommon in adolescents, but if it should occur, it needs immediate medical treatment.

Initial intervention and responses to acute intoxication

Most adolescents will have episodes when they become significantly intoxicated. The first priority in such situations is to ensure their safety. Because they are liable to vomit, they should not be allowed to lie on their backs, but kept on their sides. With intoxication comes confusion, so a warm soothing tone should be used to keep reassuring them where they are, and that they are safe. Dehydration always follows excess, and is the main cause of the hangover. The drinking of small quantities of water should be encouraged on a frequent basis, and vigilance maintained so that any vomiting does not obstruct the breathing.

If the adolescent is too young to drink, then action needs to be taken. Long lectures or too intense a display of disappointment should be avoided, for this may be counterproductive. It is also important to avoid letting anger colour the intervention. Rather, it should be assumed that such events will happen and the sanction for such behaviour planned in advance. The next day the planned sanction should then be imposed with the minimum of comment. It is the imposition of a sanction that has an impact, not its severity. The cool, brisk intervention is far more effective than long speeches and lengthy punishments. If the episodes begin to form a regular pattern, then a formal behavioural programme (such as described in Chapter 7) may help, recognising, of course, that regular drinking of alcohol is a quite acceptable element of many people's lives.

If the drinking is clearly to excess, and is beginning to cause ill-health or problems with maintaining a daily routine, then the situation has reached the abuse stage. The management of alcohol abuse demonstrates many of the approaches that are used to deal with any drug addiction. First, it is important to recognise that the young person must be willing to co-operate with any treatment regime if it is to stand any chance of success. Admitting adolescents to hospital against their will is possible, but can only be achieved by using the powers of the Mental Health Act (1983). This requires that two doctors agree that the young person:

• is suffering from mental disorder of a nature or degree which warrants the admission, and
• ought to be detained in the interests of his or her own safety or with a view to the protection of another person.

Practitioners are very reluctant to detain people in hospital against their will, and so such a course of action for someone with a drug problem would be very rare, and probably reserved for someone who was acutely intoxicated and out of touch with reality. They would also need to be at risk of harm, or harming others, and even in such circumstances they would be kept in hospital only for as long as they were confused and disorientated.

Detoxification

If the young person is willing to co-operate with the treatment, then referral to the community addiction team is the first step. Usually the team can be approached directly, or the adolescent's general practitioner can make a referral. The first stage of the process is to look for any physical illness that may be increasing the difficulties. Most regimes routinely give courses of vitamins because young people who have been drinking excessively for any period of time usually have had a very poor diet. The second stage is gradually to reduce the amount of alcohol within the young person's system. This detoxification can cause the adolescent to become very ill, and so it is usual to give regular tranquillisers which help to reduce the worst of the effects that withdrawing the alcohol can cause. Once the effects of stopping the alcohol have been overcome the tranquillisers can be gradually withdrawn and the detoxification programme is complete.

Psychological support

If stopping the drinking is to have any chance of success, it is important that at an early stage the issues which started the drinking, and are maintaining it, are carefully explored and addressed. This forms a routine part of all addiction programmes, but for most young people detoxification is not necessary, and it is the psychological management which is the central requirement. Community addiction teams obviously have great expertise in this area, but skilled counsellors within doctors' surgeries and schools, as well as psychiatry teams, can offer appropriate support providing they have experience of dealing with such difficulties.

In some young people there are clearly social and psychological problems behind the drinking, and dealing with them can be quite a lengthy process. Many drinkers have developed a belief that they cannot get through a day successfully without drinking, and the use of cognitive techniques can help to address these issues. Many programmes involve the use of groups which allow the members to feel they are not alone in trying to deal with their difficulties, and some organisations such as Alcoholics Anonymous offer a very intensive programme of self-analysis and mutual encouragement.

Over the years there have been various attempts to use behavioural techniques to control drinking habits. The most well established of these is the use of a drug called disulfram, which is better known as Antabuse. With this drug in the bloodstream any alcohol creates strong feelings of nausea and physical discomfort, including throbbing headache and palpitations, and the intention is to create a sense of aversion to the thought of any further drinking. The decision to use Antabuse needs to be taken with some care, because if the young person is determined to drink despite the treatment, potentially life-threatening complications can occur, such as irregular heartbeat or a dramatic drop in blood pressure.

Sedatives

Effects

As the name implies, this group of drugs tends to reduce brain activity and clinically they are often used to reduce anxiety or induce sleep. They are also capable of reducing muscle activity and so are sometimes used to help with muscle strains and other such injuries. Although barbiturates were the initial drugs of abuse in this group, the benzodiazepines are now mainly used, with temazepam being the drug which has prompted the most recent concern (Ruben and Morrison 1992).

Young people who abuse sedatives often use other types of drugs as well, especially alcohol. Episodes of violent behaviour are sometimes seen in regular abusers, but generally the picture is one of intoxication similar to alcohol.

ALCOHOL

Method of use Drinks.

Effects on user Relaxation and reduced inhibition. Effects begin within ten minutes and can stay in the bloodstream for several hours. Although the user is not aware of it, judgement and manual dexterity are impaired, and so driving while intoxicated is especially dangerous.

In excess Slurred speech and unco-ordinated movements. Moods may be exaggerated. Alcohol will increase the effects of any other drugs that are taken.

What to look for Slurred speech and unsteady gait. Very distinctive smell.

Upon withdrawal After acute intoxication – headache and clouded thinking, often with nausea and abdominal pains.
   When dependent upon alcohol – tremors and visual hallucinations. Can become confused and disorientated (delirium tremens).

SEDATIVES

Other names Barbs, and benzodiazepines such as temazepam ('wobbly eggs').

Method of use Ingested, though occasionally injected.

Effects on user Intoxication, with drowsiness, lack of co-ordination and sleepiness.

In excess Sedation and coma.

What they look like Commercial products – usually as tablets or capsules.

What to look for Intoxication, with marked sedation.

Upon withdrawal Depressed or paranoid.

Typical cost A tablet costs £1.

Figure 9.1 Comparison of alcohol and sedatives
Source: Adapted from National Drugs Helpline information

Features of withdrawal

The drugs within this group cause physical dependence and so if a regular user is deprived of the drug, there can be a withdrawal syndrome which is similar to the one seen with chronic alcoholism. In mild cases the addict becomes restless and anxious, and has great difficulty sleeping. In more severe cases the young person may go on to have seizures, become delirious, develop a high body temperature (hyperthermia) and a very rapid heartbeat (tachycardia). Such a reaction can be life threatening and so when present immediate medical attention is necessary. While waiting for medical attention, the person should be kept calm, and someone who understands first aid and resuscitation must remain with them.

Withdrawal from barbiturates usually resolves in about eight to ten days but the longer-acting benzodiazepines cause problems for much longer. Some people still show the effects of withdrawal many months after stopping the drug. The most potent drugs within the group, such as alprazolam (Xanax) and triazolam (Halcion) can produce some of the most severe withdrawal symptoms if they have been the drug of regular abuse.

Detoxification

When it is suspected that someone has a sedative addiction it is important to form a clear picture of how much of the drug they have been taking. A regular heavy user will need the assistance of the community addiction team to detoxify. The first stage in such a process is to transfer from the sedative to a long-acting drug such as diazepam. This is given to minimise the withdrawal effects of the abuse drugs, and ideally a mild intoxication should be created. After stabilisation the dose of diazepam can gradually be reduced, and such a process often needs a lengthy stay within hospital.

Psychological Support

Even after a successful detoxification programme young people often continue to experience difficulties with sleep, anxiety, depression, headaches and muscle-aches which is known as the abstinence syndrome. The chronic presence of such symptoms is a very common reason for the person to revert to being a drug user, and so the psychological support described above is an important element in any attempt to stop sedative addiction. Again, if the usage is not severe, then skilled counsellors can help the young person to explore the issues which may have caused the problem, and may develop strategies to reduce the risk of reuse.

Stimulants

Effects

As the name implies, this group of drugs increases certain aspects of thinking and sensation which has led to the use of names such as 'uppers' and 'speed' being used to describe them. Methylamphetamine (crystal, meth, ice) creates a rapid feeling of well-being, vigour and physical power. This is described as the 'rush'. Four to six hours later these feelings of increased well-being give way to a sense of unhappiness, anxiety and depression which is known as 'the crash'. This can sometimes be quite profound and suicidal gestures are not uncommon. The tremendous sense of health decreases each time the drug is used. This increasing tolerance to the drug means that larger and larger doses need to be taken in order to create a similar effect.

Some of the most potent stimulants, for example, smoking methyl-amphetamine, can produce so intense a change of thinking that the sense of well-being is replaced by a complete disorganisation of thoughts and psychotic symptoms emerge. These psychotic symptoms can usually be distinguished from a severe psychiatric illness because the hallucinations are vivid visual ones and occur at a time when the young person is confused and disorientated (Poole and Brabbins 1996).

One of the best-known drugs within this group is cocaine. This comes from the leaves of the coca plant which originally grew in the Andes of South America. It was used by the Incas for some time before becoming a regular treatment in western medicine for such diverse problems as hysteria and asthma. Although Coca-Cola derived its name from the fact that it contained cocaine, this was actually replaced in 1903 by caffeine and, indeed, in the early part of the century cocaine was a little-used drug, only being popular with artists and people of a bohemian lifestyle.

In the 1960s the drug experienced a renewed popularity and rapidly gained the reputation of being 'glamorous', with the commonest methods of use being by injection or inhaling the powdered form. In the 1970s it was found that the potency of taking cocaine could be increased if it was inhaled while being heated with a solvent. This became known as 'freebasing'. A further refinement to the process was developed in the 1980s, when drug suppliers began to heat cocaine and solvents at higher temperatures, which removes

---

STIMULANTS

Other names Speed, uppers, whiz, amph.

Method of use Sniffed or taken by mouth. Occasionally it is injected.

Effects on user Quickly creates a feeling of energy and confidence, which lasts for about four hours. The typical side-effects are a dry mouth, constipation and an inability to sleep.

In excess Increased pulse rate and blood pressure. There can be marked mood swings, episodes of aggressive behaviour, a sense of panic and even paranoia.

What they look like White, pink or yellow powder, or tablet.

What to look for Energetic, and more intense than usual. Significant mood swings and complaints about side-effects.

Upon withdrawal Depressed, or paranoid.

Typical cost A gram costs £10.

Figure 9.2 Features of stimulants
Source: Adapted from National Drugs Helpline information

the hydrochloride part of the chemical structure. This process also allows impurities to settle to the bottom, leaving brown crystals. It is these crystals which are heated and inhaled, and because of the distinctive crackling sound that they make when they are heated, this form of cocaine has become known as 'crack'. Both refined forms of cocaine give a very intense sense of well-being which lasts only for a brief time and is inevitably followed by a very profound 'crash'. The intensity of both the positive rush and the after-effects make this a highly addictive drug, though there is evidence that smoking the drug is less addictive than injecting it (Gossop *et al.* 1994a)

Cocaine creates a sense of well-being, with the young person often talking excessively and perhaps becoming quite agitated. The crash produces sleeplessness, depression and an increasing craving for more cocaine (Gawin and Ellinwood 1988). The effects can remain evident for several weeks afterwards, with the user showing marked lethargy, apathy and depression.

In the UK about 2 per cent of eleven to sixteen-year-olds have experimented with cocaine (Wright and Pearl 1990). Regular cocaine usage carries with it significant physical problems. If the drug is taken by means of injection, obviously there are concerns to do with HIV and hepatitis as well as the potential for infections within the blood. The drug itself can cause irregular heartbeats, heart attacks and seizures. Crack, in particular, can damage lungs and cause marked breathing difficulties (Cregler and Mark 1986), and if it is used regularly in pregnancy the baby is always of a low birth weight, and there is an increased likelihood of foetal abnormalities.

Large doses of cocaine can cause people to start having paranoid ideas and sometimes they will have psychotic episodes, with visual and tactile hallucinations, which could last for several days. These are often associated with episodes of violent and antisocial behaviour. These symptoms subside as the drug leaves the system, and if they persist, it may be that the young person has a true psychiatric illness and taking the drug was perhaps their way of trying to cope with it.

Features of withdrawal

The features of withdrawal may begin quite insidiously, with the young person having no idea why he/she is feeling tired, irritable and lethargic, but usually it is characterised by a more dramatic sense of agitation and depression which begins some hours after the last dose. This is followed by an inability to sleep, despite an increasing sense of fatigue, and a gradual reduction in the sense of craving for more cocaine. This initial withdrawal phase ends with the young person feeling totally exhausted, but with an increasing appetite, and sleep patterns which are returning to normal.

After this initial phase there may be several more sequences in which the young person slips into a period of feeling miserable and lethargic, and then returns to feeling more settled and comfortable.

COCAINE AND CRACK

Other names Charlie, coke, snow, freebase, rock.

Method of use Sniffed, smoked or injected. When smoked crack has an immediate effect which lasts for ten to fifteen minutes.

Effects on user Increases alertness and gives sense of energy. There is a sense of enhanced confidence.

In excess Increased pulse rate and blood pressure. Eyes become light sensitive and pupils dilate. Crack, in particular, also produces agitation, aggressive outbursts and sometimes psychosis or convulsions.

What it looks like White powder, or crystal 'rocks' of crack.

What to look for Energetic, and more intense than usual. To be sniffed the powder needs to be 'cut' so look for razor blade, and tube such as straw. Pipe or syringe if being taken in those ways.

Upon withdrawal Intense craving to repeat experience, and then marked lethargy, with young person becoming depressed, or paranoid.

Typical cost A crack 'rock' for one hit can cost £20. Cocaine powder costs up to £100 an ounce.

Figure 9.3 Features of cocaine and crack
Source: Adapted from National Drugs Helpline information

Psychological support

The immediate support of someone in an intoxicated state has been described above. It is always worthwhile to try to determine what the intoxicating agent may be, but always within the context of maintaining a tranquil atmosphere. Treating cocaine addicts rarely requires an alternative drug to be prescribed, and most treatments depend upon using psychological methods of counselling and support. As with all drug problems, the source of expert help and advice is the community addiction team. Unfortunately, relapse rates are very common with this drug which is why its use is such a cause for concern.

Opiate drugs

Opiate drugs such as heroin have been prescribed by the medical profession over many years, and at the turn of the century opium dens were features of most large cities. Heroin in the UK is not used as commonly as other drugs of abuse such as alcohol or solvents, but because it can quickly become the dominant focus of the young person's life, addiction is easily established. Many users become criminals to finance the habit. It is reported that in the UK approximately 2 per cent of senior secondary school pupils have tried the drug (Wright and Pearl 1990).

HEROIN

Other names H, horse, scag, smack, snuff.

Method of use Sniffed, smoked ('chasing the dragon') or injected ('main lining').

Effects on user Calming, with a sense of warmth and well-being while intoxicated. Dependence quickly develops.

In excess Increased agitation, aggressive outbursts and sometimes psychosis or convulsions.

What it looks like White powder or tablets.

What to look for Rather an apathetic mood, and pinpoint pupils. If injecting, then the paraphernalia may be in evidence – needles, syringes, blackened spoons. Needle marks on arms, legs and feet indicate injecting something.

Upon withdrawal Increasing feelings of craving. Sweating and diarrhoea becoming more severe with time, bone pains and pupils dilate.

Typical cost A fingernail-sized bag of heroin costs £10.

Figure 9.4 Features of heroin
Source: Adapted from National Drugs Helpline information

Features of withdrawal

The opiates can be smoked, injected under the skin ('skin popping') or injected into a vein ('main lining'). Tolerance to the drug develops quite quickly, and since the young person feels quite unwell as the effect of the drug wears off, addiction to it is rapidly established. If addicts attempt to withdraw they experience severe abstinence symptoms, which begin to appear about eight to twelve hours after the last dose. There is an intense craving to reuse the drug and this is associated with nausea, diarrhoea, a running nose, goosebumps and severe pain within the bones and joints. The young person also begins to sweat profusely, the pupils are very dilated and extreme lethargy is apparent, with repetitive yawning. As well as these physical symptoms, the addict will appear to be markedly anxious, restless and depressed.

Even when these profound problems have been overcome, the young person can, for several months, feel depressed and anxious and have marked difficulty in sleeping.

An habitual user of opiates can experience physical problems from their use. There are problems associated with injecting a drug, but in addition the drug itself can prompt fluid to develop on the lungs or depress the breathing. If the young person takes too large a dose, then a profound reduction in vital signs is seen, with a slowing of respiration and the tell-tale pinpoint pupils.

Psychological support

In an acutely intoxicated situation the general advice of protection and tranquil atmosphere apply. The health risks associated with overdose require extra vigilance for breathing problems, which in extreme cases may need resuscitation measures to be started.

If an addict is seeking help to overcome a drug habit, the addiction team first look to substitute the drug with a synthetic opiate, methadone. If the young person is also abusing other drugs, then these have to be reduced before any effort is made to reduce the dose of methadone. For some abusers, establishing them on a regular programme of methadone is the most that can be achieved. The remainder of the programme is focused on offering psychological insight and support, and the slow and at times faltering process of helping the user rebuild a life.

Hallucinogens

Perhaps the best-known drug within this group is lysergic acid diethylamide (LSD). This drug became very popular in the 1960s and its popularity has continued to rise steadily since then, with 4 per cent of the population reporting having tried it in 1985 compared to 10 per cent in 1992 (Institute for the Study of Drug Dependence 1993). More recently 5–4–4–methylamphetamine (MDMA) has become popular among the young. This drug is better known as 'ecstasy'. Also within the group is phencyclidine (PSP), which is also known as 'angel dust', but this has not really become established as a drug of abuse in the UK.

Effects

Hallucinogenic drugs tend not to be drugs of habitual use, but are rather used intermittently to enhance social activities, such as rave dancing. Tolerance rapidly develops and so the young person has to take increasing doses to produce the same effect. These drugs alter perception – visual images will flow together and objects will appear to melt. Thoughts assume an unusual clarity and there is often an apparent distortion of time which can make things appear to move very quickly, or very slowly. When intoxicated with the drug there is usually a feeling of euphoria, but users can feel very panicky, or become paranoid. Switching between such moods can occur abruptly and the distortion of time can make it appear that the bad feelings are lasting for ever. In fact the effects of MDMA and PSP will last for up to eight hours in most cases, although the effects of LSD can last up to twenty-four hours.

When the mood changes are those of panic and fearfulness it is said that the young person is having 'a bad trip'. Such feelings are often associated with breathlessness, and many young people report fearing that they are losing their sanity during such episodes. Although these feelings tend to fade after some hours, they can recur some weeks or months after the drug was last taken. Such re-experiences are known as 'flashbacks' and although usually mild and brief, they can, on occasion, cause a great deal of fear and concern for a loss of sanity in the user.

MDMA – ECSTASY

Other names E, adam, XTC, fantasy, white doves, disco burgers, new yorkers

Method of use Taken orally, effects start after twenty minutes, and can last for several hours.

Effects on user Gives sense of energy, acute thirst.

In excess inability to sleep, depression and paranoia.

What it looks like White, brown, pink or yellow tablets or capsules. Often they may also contain caffeine or household substances.

What to look for Energetic, restless and drinking large amounts of soft drinks.

Upon withdrawal Not considered to be addictive, but can make young person depressed, or paranoid.

Typical cost A tablet may sell for £12 to £25.

Figure 9.5 Features of ecstasy
Source: Adapted from National Drugs Helpline information

LSD

Other name Acid.

Method of use By mouth.

Effects on user Hallucinations, especially associated with sounds and colours. Dilated pupils.

In excess Increased pulse rate and blood pressure. Hallucinations can be frightening and can prompt acute anxiety or paranoia.

What it looks like Small tablet or absorbed on to a piece of coloured paper.

What to look for Change in behaviour, with disorientation and recounting of hallucinations.

Upon withdrawal Not known as a problem.

Typical cost A dose costs £2.

Figure 9.6 Features of LSD
Source: Adapted from National Drugs Helpline information

Psychological support

If PCP is taken in high doses, it is likely to provoke quite marked violent behaviour, often with psychotic symptoms. In such situations the young person is often unco-ordinated, blood pressure is quite high and the heart is often erratic in its beat. In such severe toxicity cases the young person needs to be admitted to hospital to minimise the physical effects. For most young people, however, it is a matter of being supportive and offering a calming influence until the effect of the drug subsides. This also involves reassuring them of their safety, and that the effects of the drug will pass.

If the young person is experiencing flashbacks then a similar supportive stance is appropriate. The effects are not a sign that they are going crazy, but in the midst of the experience this might be difficult for them to accept. Referral to a drug counselling service or to their own doctor can put them in touch with people who can re-emphasise this reassurance and this is especially necessary if the flashbacks are becoming a regular occurrence.

Inhalants

Solvents, glues, lighter fuel and the propellants within aerosols have all had a vogue with young people as drugs of abuse. Young people normally experiment with such drugs within groups and continued use is often part of a social routine. The dangers of this type of abuse partially arise from their inflammable nature, and also from the associated risks of choking and suffocation. In the UK the number of deaths appears to be rising, with the 82 deaths in 1983 increasing to 149 in 1990 (Institute for the Study of Drug Dependence 1993).

Effects

Drugs of this group create an immediate sense of light-headedness and this is usually associated with a floating sensation. There is a clouding of thinking and the young person may appear quite drowsy, usually with an associated lightening of mood. Commonly, the organic solvents are put in a plastic bag and inhaled to intensify the effect, and, of course, such a mechanism increases the risk that accidental suffocation will occur. The use of aerosol propellants can also be quite dangerous if the spray is a noxious chemical such as fly spray, and some young people will spray through a cloth to try to strain out these other chemicals.

One of the most dangerous of the group is lighter fuel. This is used by spraying the fuel on to the back of the throat, and because of its irritant nature it tends to prompt swelling of the throat lining, which can cause severe breathing problems.

A young person intoxicated with solvents appears rather drunken, with slurring of speech and a slowing of thought processes. The eyes may be red from the irritant nature of the fumes being inhaled, and some users develop inflamed skin round the nose and mouth, also as a result of this irritation.

Sometimes the young person can have a toxic reaction to a particular inhalant and this causes breathing problems, an increased pulse rate and rapid unconsciousness. This is a potentially fatal situation and requires close medical supervision until the crisis has passed.

Psychological support

Although usually cheerful and biddable, intoxication can prompt a sense of panic, and during this acute phase the aim should be to offer a calm and non-threatening environment in which the effects can wear off. It is important to monitor breathing and pulse to detect any complications that are arising, but usually the effects will simply pass. The decision as to whether medical assistance is needed is determined by whether physical complications, such as breathing problems, are starting to appear. It is unusual for hospital admission to be needed.

There is little evidence to suggest that young people who regularly use solvents experience withdrawal, and so the major thrust of assistance is trying to understand the origins of the use while looking for signs of underlying psychiatric illness. The approach for families needs to strike a balance between offering support and maintaining a clear rule system which consistently emphasises disapproval of inhalant use. The process of intervention tends to be a slow one. Inhalant use is usually a social activity, and so many young people have no motivation to stop until they outgrow their peer group.

INHALANTS

Types Glue, gas, aerosols, lighter fuel.

Method of use Sniffed or inhaled.

Effects on user Dizziness and intoxication with loss of inhibition. The effects are immediate and last for about thirty minutes.

In excess May experience hallucinations and can kill.

What they look like Commercial produce.

What to look for Signs of intoxication. Possibly smell of solvents, soiled plastic bags or discarded empties.

Upon withdrawal Some tolerance, but withdrawal is psychological.

Typical cost Cost of commercial product.

Figure 9.7 Features of inhalants
Source: Adapted from National Drugs Helpline information

Robert was a fifteen-year-old boy who had begun sniffing glue when he was thirteen. His friends within the neighbourhood had introduced him to its use, and most evenings they would gather in a remote corner of a small wood which was next to the estate where they all lived. Glue had become popular because it was easier to steal than alcohol, and there had been a gradual progression from glue to solvents of various kinds.

Robert and his friends began to miss those lessons at school that they didn't enjoy, preferring to spend the time in the local shopping centre. Robert's group became very adept at stealing from shops, and would plan what they could do to liven up their evenings – on occasion they would bring offroad motorcycles to ride in the wood, or steal a car and drive it at great speed through the estate.

The search for greater excitement led Robert and his friends into more daring thefts, after which the group would gather in their corner of the wood and inhale solvents to enhance their feelings of elation. At fifteen Robert and four of his friends appeared in court on several charges of breaking and entering, and two further court appearances eventually resulted in Robert being given a custodial sentence.

Robert's history illustrates the commonest theme to be found among solvent users. A mixture of peer-group pressure, the search for excitement and accepting delinquent activity as the norm are the elements which tend to maintain solvent use. The lack of motivation to stop means that concerned adults have no real opportunity to intervene. Occasionally the solvent use is a solitary activity to block out psychological or emotional problems, and such users do sometimes recognise that help with these underlying problems is a better solution than solvent usage.

Cannabis

Cannabis is a common drug of experimentation among adolescents and is derived from the cannabis sativa plant. This drug is grown throughout the world and has been used by many cultures over the centuries. In the UK 3–5 per cent of senior schoolchildren report having tried the drug (Health Education Authority 1992). It occurs in two forms – a mixture of the dried stems, seeds and leaves which is known as marijuana, and the far more potent resin which is derived from the flowering tops of the plants and is known as hashish. Both forms can be taken orally or smoked.

There is a movement which argues that because cannabis in itself is no more dangerous than tobacco and is in such common use it should be legalised. Opponents of this stance point to the fact that most hard drug users have a history of cannabis use. However, most cannabis users do not go on to become users of hard drugs.

The effects of cannabis begin within a few minutes and last for an hour or two. Perception of visual and tactile stimuli are often enhanced, and there is

---

CANNABIS

Other names Pot, dope, grass, puff, ganja, weed, herb, spliff, marijuana, hashish, blow, hemp, draw, smoke, joint, skunk.

Method of use Smoked or occasionally by ingestion with food.

Effects on user Relaxation, sometimes with a heightened awareness of colour and music. Reduced co-ordination, dilated pupils.

In excess Increased pulse rate and blood pressure. Rarely may be a sense of anxiety which can prompt temporary paranoia.

What it looks like Either a mixture of leaves, stalks and seeds (marijuana), or a solid brown cake (hashish).

What to look for Relaxed, dilated pupils and perhaps rather disinterested demeanour. A strong herbal smell, and sometimes the eyes are reddened.

Upon withdrawal Very rarely a problem.

Typical cost A quarter-ounce of hash is about £15, and is sufficient for twenty cigarettes.

Figure 9.8 Features of cannabis
Source: Adapted from National Drugs Helpline information

some distortion in the perception of time. At the same time the heart rate may often increase, and fine tremors are not uncommon. The user may feel hungry, and usually the drug increases relaxation, though on occasions it can prompt the young person to become agitated and feel anxious.

In someone who uses the drug quite regularly there can be a pattern of mild withdrawal with irritability and restlessness. Anyone wishing to withdraw from the drug should be encouraged to pursue the type of approach which is advocated for stopping smoking.

Anabolic steroids

There has in recent years been an increasing concern that anabolic steroids are being used by athletes and body builders to increase their performances. In such cases it is quite common for two or even three different steroids to be used (Perry *et al.* 1990). While this is not strictly a drug of addiction, some young people can come to believe that they must regularly take the drug to maintain a high performance.

In young people regular use of the drug can cause depression, irritability, hostility, aggression and even psychosis. If these drugs are used by children, growth problems can develop. There is no recognised withdrawal programme, but many of the psychological principles used in helping other types of drug abuser will apply to these young people too.

GENERAL RECOGNITION AND MANAGEMENT OF AN ADDICT

Certain aspects of teenage rebellion occur so frequently that they should be considered normal. Under-age drinking is an example of this type of behaviour, but although this might be quite typical for this age group, a young person who has developed a dependence on alcohol clearly is not. The regular use of drugs has the potential to have a profound effect upon a young person's future life and functioning and quite naturally parents, and others who come into contact with the young person, become very concerned by such behaviour. However, it is important to realise that many young people move away from drug use without any formal treatment (Biernacki 1986).

Sudden changes of behaviour may be the first indication that a young person is starting to establish a drug habit. The sudden onset of stealing, a marked drop in school performance, changing friendships and alliances, and becoming more irritable and bad tempered can all be features of a young person trying to cope with adolescence, but should also prompt consideration that they may also be abusing drugs.

At this stage it is important to voice suspicions in the correct way. Direct confrontation will only provoke denial and prompt the young person to be more secretive. Suspicion should be followed by a period of looking for supporting signs, especially periods of intoxication. If a drug habit is developing it will be increasingly difficult for a young person to hide the drug's effects.

If the young person presents in an intoxicated state, then protection from harm, and monitoring of breathing and so on, in a calm, reassuring style, is the first priority. Identifying the drug is helpful, because, as indicated above, certain drugs may cause specific health concerns. If the source of the intoxication cannot be identified, then referral to the local casualty department is prudent.

The pattern of response described for alcohol is generally applicable to all drug usage situations. If the young person agrees to professional help then the local addiction service will decide whether detoxification will be necessary. Although such detoxification is an important step in a successful programme, engaging the young person in appropriate psychological support is the fundamental factor in determining whether drug usage can be stopped. As part of this process it is important to determine whether the young person has any concurrent psychological problems, and, with regard to this, the responses offered by family or classroom may be a significant arena for change. For example, marital conflict may be prompting misery that can only be escaped through drug use. If this family issue is not addressed, then no real progress with the drug use is likely. Similarly, teenagers who are being bullied at school, or are finding the work expectations beyond them, will need to have changes in these areas if motivation for change is to be secured.

Some young people may lack the motivation to stop drug usage, and in such cases the approach needs to be a careful mix of education and gentle encouragement. For some, the most that can be achieved in the short term is harm minimisation – and developments such as needle exchange programmes and education about which inhalants carry the greatest risk are examples of this approach (Anderson 1990). These young people are often the most frustrating for adults to deal with. They seem deliberately to refuse to accept the advice being offered, and this prompts concerned parents, and teachers, to demand that 'something be done'. Unfortunately, the lack of things that can be done tends to frustrate the adults even more, which can result in the young person losing the adults' support. Recognising that they have to decide about their own life is one of the hardest lessons for any concerned adult to learn. The most assistance that can be offered is to establish clear expectations for behaviour and to stick to them totally. If the drug use is too disruptive for a household or school to tolerate, then intoxication may mean being barred. This is not a punishment for misbehaviour, it is protection for the home or school from further disruption. This 'tough love' approach places a great strain on caring adults but helps to impress upon a user the terms on which they can rejoin their family or community.

Formal treatment programmes

Professional agencies, such as drug addiction teams, tend to offer treatment which falls into two categories. The first are treatments which focus upon the young person, and may take the form of counselling, behavioural techniques or group meetings. Self-help groups can be beneficial in helping users to recognise that the problems they face are commonly shared, but young people tend to be reluctant to participate in such meetings. The second approach is to focus upon the family, and the network in which the adolescent lives. Whichever type of approach is adopted the aims are broadly similar – to encourage abstinence and enhance those areas of life that are not linked to drug usage.

If there is active therapy going on then at crucial times within that process the young person's mood and behaviour may deteriorate. These episodes need to be anticipated and understood, but if rules are broken, the necessary sanction needs to be applied. Understanding that this is a difficult time does not mean changing the rules, for although on the surface the young person may complain about the rules, it is the very predictability of those rules which offers the strongest reassurance and support.

SOURCES OF FURTHER HELP

The Standing Conference on Drug Abuse (SCODA). 1 Hatton Place, Hatton Garden, London EC1N 8ND. Telephone (0171) 4302341.

The Institute for the Study of Drug Dependence (ISDD). 1 Hatton Place, Hatton Garden, London EC1N 8ND. Telephone (0171) 4301993.

ADFAM National is a charity which helps families of drug users. Telephone (0171) 4053923.

REFERENCES

Anderson, H.R. (1990). Increase in deaths from deliberate inhalation of fuel gases, and pressurised aerosols. *British Medical Journal* 301, 41.

Bewley, B., Bland, J. and Harris, R. (1974). Factors associated with the starting of cigarette smoking by primary school children. *British Journal of Preventative and Social Medicine* 28, 37–44.

Biernacki, P. (1986). *Pathways from Heroin Addiction: Recovery without Treatment.* Philadelphia PA; Temple University Press.

Braucht, G.N., Brakarsh, D. and Follingstad, D. (1973). Deviant drug use in adolescence: a review of psychosocial correlates. *Psychological Bulletin* 79, 92–106.

Christie, K.A., Burke, J.E. and Regier, D.A. (1988). Epidemiologic evidence for early onset of mental disorders and higher rates of drug abuse in young adults. *American Journal of Psychiatry* 145, 971–5.

Cregler, L.L. and Mark, H. (1986). Medical complications of cocaine abuse. *New England Journal of Medicine* 315, 1495–500.

Doll, R., Peto, R. and Hall, E. (1994). Mortality in relation to consumption of alcohol: 13 years' observations on male British doctors. *British Medical Journal* 309, 911–18.

Frezza, M., di Padova, C. and Pozzato, G. (1990). High blood alcohol levels in women: the role of decreased gastric alcohol dehydrogenase activity and first pass metabolism. *New England Journal of Medicine* 322, 95–9.

Gawin, F. and Ellinwood, E.H. (1988). Cocaine and other stimulants: actions, abuse and treatment. *New England Journal of Medicine* 318, 1173–82.

Ghodse, H. (1995). *Drugs and Addictive Behaviour: A Guide to Treatment.* 2nd edn. London: Blackwell Scientific Publications.

Gossop, M., Griffiths, P. and Powis, B. (1994a). Cocaine: patterns of use, route of administration and severity of dependence. *British Journal of Psychiatry* 164, 660–4.

Gossop, M., Griffiths, P. and Strang, J. (1994b). Sex differences in patterns of drug taking behaviour. *British Journal of Psychiatry* 164, 101–4.

Health Education Authority (1992). *Tomorrow's Young People. 9–15 Year Olds Look at Alcohol, Drugs, Exercise and Smoking.* London: Health Education Authority.

Hovens, J.G.F.M., Cantwell, D.P. and Kiriakos, R. (1994). Psychiatric co-morbidity in hospitalised adolescent substance abusers. *Journal of the American Academy of Child and Adolescent Psychiatry* 33, 476–83.

Institute for the Study of Drug Dependence (1993). *National Audit of Drug Misuse in Britain 1992* London: Institute for the Study of Drug Dependence.

King, A., Wold, B., Tudor-Smith, C. and Harel, Y. (1996). *The Health of Youth: A Cross-National Survey.* European Series No. 69. Geneva: WHO Regional Publications.

Kosten, T. and Kleber, H. (1992). *A Clinician's Guide to Cocaine Addiction.* New York: Guilford Press.

Parker, H., Measham, F. and Aldridge, J. (1995). *Drug Futures. Changing Patterns of Drug Use amongst English Youth.* London: Institute for the Study of Drug Dependence.

Perry, P.J., Andersen, K.H. and Yates, W.R. (1990). Illicit anabolic steroid use in athletes. A case series analysis. *American Journal of Sports Medicine* 18, 422–8.

Piaget, J. (1952). *The Origins of Intelligence in Children.* New York: International University Press.

Pickens, R.W., Svikis, D.S. and McGue, M. (1991). Heterogeneity in the inheritance of alcoholism: a study of male and female twins. *Archives of General Psychiatry* 48, 19–28.

Poole, R. and Brabbins, C. (1996). Drug induced psychosis. *British Journal of Psychiatry* 168, 135–8.

Ruben, S.M. and Morrison, C.L. (1992) Temazepam misuse in a group of injecting drug users. *British Journal of Addiction.* 87, 1387–92.

Wright, J.D. and Pearl, L. (1990). Knowledge and experience of young people regarding drug abuse, 1969–1989. *British Medical Journal* 300, 99–103.

10 Depression in children

Over recent years, there has been an intense interest in the concept of depression in childhood. The issue is particularly complex because sadness and tears are common parts of all children's lives and so cannot form any true basis for a diagnosis of a depressive illness. In addition, the term itself has become so much part of common usage that it has begun to lose value as a description of a particular illness process. Even within professional circles the word 'depression' is used synonymously to describe three discrete levels (Kadzin 1990):

Depressed mood

A state of profound unhappiness and sense of dejection (dysphoria) that is more than normal sadness. The person cannot see any real bright spots to his or her life, and there is a loss of emotional involvement with either other people or activities. Often it is associated with negative styles of thinking about the young people themselves (giving rise to feelings of failure and guilt) or about the future (giving a sense of hopelessness). Figure 10.1 shows how such thoughts create a wider shift in mood, which then becomes attributed to all aspects of life. The presence of some such feelings is a normal reaction to a distressing event, but they are in proportion to the importance of the event, and the overall intensity is not great.

When reflecting upon:	Personal achievements	Ability to influence events
The past	Feelings of guilt and shame	Fearful of acting in case repeats 'mistakes'
The present	Believes self to be a failure	Feels helpless
The future	Expects the worst to happen	Feels hopeless

Figure 10.1 The way that negative thoughts can become attributed to all aspects of life

Depressive syndrome

A cluster of symptoms including depressed mood, tearfulness, irritability, loss of appetite, sleep disturbance, poor concentration and loss of energy.

Depressive disorder

A psychiatric diagnosis of depression, such as the one given in the *Diagnostic and Statistical Manual* (DSM-IV) of the American Psychiatric Association (1994), is based on typical symptoms but they must be present for a specific time, and clearly impair the person's functioning. Persistence and impairment are what distinguishes the disorder from the syndrome.

However, this is not the end to the confusion of terms. For example, some people prefer to use the term 'affective disorder' to describe the family of emotional illnesses, and recently diagnostic labelling has moved from terms such as depression to 'unipolar disorder'. Not surprisingly, with a subject so littered with terms and titles it is sometimes difficult to understand what is being referred to. (See the glossary for definitions of some of the other terms used when referring to depression and other emotional illnesses.)

It is important to realise that the classification of depressive illness has remained contentious for many years, and over that time there have been many variations in the classification. The discussion so far has looked at what are usually referred to now as major depressive episodes, and are described in the World Health Organisation's classification (1992) as endogenous depression. But what about the person who is easily, or chronically, distressed and unhappy. These types of problem have been called neurotic depressions, and they can be distinguished from the other group because the causes, and to some degree the reactions, are merely exaggerations of what we all might feel in similar circumstances. The DSM-IV classification uses a different term for this group, describing it as dysthymic. This aspect of classification is also not settled, but most of the work in children has been concerned with major (endogenous) type illness, and the following is focused upon this disorder. However, it is important not to lose sight of other emotional reactions in children and adolescents that can at first sight appear similar. An excellent example of this is the mood lability which is common in the early teenage years, and presents as rapid changes of mood which are sometimes marked. It is occasionally difficult to distinguish this type of marked mood swing from the illness process where profound depression alternates with a very elated and over-cheerful period (known as bipolar illness), but the distinction is important since the ways to respond to these two types of mood variation are substantially different.

REACHING A DIAGNOSIS

To confirm that a depressive syndrome is present, the young person must not only appear miserable and unhappy, but demonstrate a negative style of thinking and present a daily routine which illustrates a loss of interest and concentration. For some clinicians, there must be clear anhedonia – which means that the young person has lost all enjoyment of life and now portrays a picture dominated by gloom and despondency.

Julie, a fourteen-year-old girl, presented with a six-week history of not attending school. When asked about this, she explained that for some months she found it difficult to concentrate at school and was concerned that all of her friends had turned against her, and that the teachers no longer liked her. Her mother said that Julie was previously a happy and cheerful girl, but over recent months she had become quiet and withdrawn, and would quickly become tearful and distressed at any difficulty or problem. She no longer went out with her friends, preferring to spend most of her time in her bedroom watching television. She had stopped eating and, although she constantly felt tired, was finding it difficult to settle to sleep and was waking consistently at 4.00a.m. Throughout the interview, Julie emitted a sense of sadness and misery, and when asked directly confirmed that she saw no future for herself, and had thought about suicide, although she insisted she would not kill herself since she did not want to cause additional distress to her family.

It is only in recent years that it has been established that the definitions of the depressive syndrome and disorder which are used in adults are also the ones to use when trying to assess children. Previously, there had been a view that depression did not occur until adult life, or that if it did present in children, it was in a 'masked' form. This theory suggested that a variety of difficulties within childhood, for example, soiling and wetting, were the manifestations of depression in a childhood (Frommer 1968). This theory drew its support, in part, from the fact that conditions such as bedwetting improved when treated with antidepressants, an interesting reversal of the present view on the relevance of antidepressants in depression, as we shall see later.

With the acceptance that adult-type depression is present in children, there has been an increasing interest in whether the mixture of depression and mania, which is seen in adults, can occur in childhood. There has been a gathering agreement that this type of disorder does occur in young people, and that children with the bipolar illness should be differentiated from those with depression only (Weller *et al.* 1995), although the symptoms of depression that both groups show are remarkably similar (Depue and Monroe 1978).

PREVALENCE

Having confirmed that the adult diagnosis can be used in children, the next problem is to determine how often such illnesses occur in young people. The summary of results from such studies has pointed to about 2 per cent of children developing a depressive illness before they reach puberty (Kashani *et al.* 1983), with perhaps as many as 30 per cent of those who present with depression before puberty going on to show the bipolar illness in later life (Geller *et al.* 1994).

Most of the studies with adults have predicted that the number of people who will have at least one episode of depression before they die (lifetime prevalence of depression) to be 15–18 per cent of the population (Wittchen *et al.* 1994), with about 9 per cent of the adult population having a significant depressive illness in any one year. Of course, when considering prevalence, it is important to bear in mind the distinction between the presence of depressive symptoms and the more profound depressive disorder. For example, a community-based study in Cambridge found 21 per cent of the girls reported having symptoms of depression in the previous year, but when a syndrome definition was used the rate was 6 per cent (Cooper and Goodyer 1993). Overall 5–10 per cent of adolescents will have a major depressive illness during their teenage years (Fleming and Offord 1990), with the majority of these starting at around fifteen years of age (Lewinsohn *et al.* 1994).

As has already been pointed out, having symptoms of depression does not mean that the disorder of depression is actually present. Indeed, up to 25 per cent of the general adolescent population show some symptoms of depression at some point (Roberts *et al.* 1990), and although only a small proportion of these will go on to develop the full disorder, this group is more likely to show the full disorder in the following two years than the general population (Weissman *et al.* 1992).

IMPACT OF THE DISORDER

As already described, depressed young people are persistently miserable, gloomy, and unhappy. They may feel so bad that the effort to express such negative emotions is too much, and they then become inert and withdrawn. There is often an associated slowing of speech and movement which can sometimes be mistaken by the uninformed as disinterest. Not surprisingly, such behaviours cause these young people to have impaired peer and family relationships, and there is usually a deterioration in school performance (Puig-Antich *et al.* 1993). In some cases these features rather than the depressive symptoms themselves may be more evident to the casual observer (Kent *et al.* 1995).

A particular problem can occur in adolescence because this period of development does tend to exaggerate existing psychological traits such as needing to tidy or compulsively checking that lights are switched off. If the young person was already prone to be gloomy, then adolescence itself may make this more marked, but such symptoms still fall short of the features that would allow it to be called a depressive illness.

The nature of the disorder can have a significant impact on trying to find out details of history from the young person. The withdrawal and general slowing up of thought processes mean that they are unlikely to volunteer information and any answers they do give are likely to be slowly given. Many questions will be met with 'don't know', but since this is almost a universal adolescent reply, it is not very helpful diagnostically.

CAUSES OF DEPRESSION

There has been a great deal of scientific endeavour focused on trying to understand what causes depression. But this has largely been focused on the illness in adults, and it is only comparatively recently that the same interest has been shown in understanding the disorder in children. The lines of enquiry have been those followed for adults – genetic, brain chemistry, the role of historical themes and significant life events. None of these has so far been proven to be the total explanation for the onset of depression, and all seem unlikely to be so, for environmental pressures and life events also clearly play parts (Kendler *et al.* 1992). Children, perhaps even more than adults, are sensitive to atmospheres and the expectations of a particular situation. Living in an environment that is limited financially, and has few opportunities for play or stimulation, is therefore quite capable of sapping a child's sense of the positive and rendering the start of each day a gloomy prospect.

When considering genetics it is important to distinguish those patients who have bipolar or severe major depressive illness, because this group has inheritability estimates of around 80 per cent. This contrasts with milder forms of the disorder (which make up the vast majority of cases) where the inheritability estimate is between 10 and 50 per cent (McGuffin and Katz 1989). In fact the evidence for any significant genetic effects in these only moderate depression disorders is weak, and it is probably the influence which the family environment exerts which is the most significant factor in these cases (Radke-Yarrow *et al.* 1992). As a general rule the evidence for children and adolescents is that if the illness starts before puberty or is severe, then it is very likely that there is a genetic influence at work (Strober 1992).

One of the most enduring theories in the causation of depression is the amine hypothesis (Deakin and Crow 1986). This suggests that depression arises because there is a problem with a particular family of chemical transmitters, the monoamines. If these are depleted, then depression is said to result. The evidence for this comes from the fact that if drugs are given which are known to reduce monoamines, then depression occurs, and, conversely, many of the drugs used to ease depression are known to increase these brain chemicals. However, depressed young people do not show the same positive response to these drugs that adults do, although it is not clear what implication this has for this particular hypothesis.

Alongside the interest in chemical causes, there has been a vast amount of work done with adults looking at how environmental issues, stress, life events and other such changes in a particular person's circumstances might effect the onset of depressive illness. The facts that for each successive generation the prevalence of depression is increasing and the age of onset is decreasing (Klerman and Weissman 1989) have tended to reinforce the belief that life issues play a significant part in the causation of depression.

One observation which has fuelled much speculation is the way that the prevalence of the illness changes in men and women over time. The rate of depression in adult women has consistently been found to be about twice that of men, although the difference is gradually reducing over time. In children under the age of twelve years, however, it is boys who tend to present more frequently with depression problems (Angold and Rutter 1992). For this difference to be explicable there must be a phase of life when the sex pattern shifts over; that is, a time when the frequency in girls increases and overtakes that of boys. It does, indeed, seem the case that with the onset of adolescence girls begin to show a greater likelihood of developing a depressive illness (McGonagle *et al.* 1994), with the shift of prevalence having fully occurred by mid-adolescence (Whitaker *et al.* 1990). How could such a shift be explained? A pointer may be the ways in which the sexes deal with the stress that adolescence imposes. For boys there tends to be an externalising of emotion – they gather in groups and become very action based. This is often as innocuous as kicking a football around, but can involve more risk-taking behaviour such as driving stolen cars. For girls the mechanism of coping is more typically one of internalising the emotion – long, intimate and heart-felt discussions with close friends are common pastimes, and perhaps this analysing of emotion establishes this as a mechanism to be used when more marked difficulties arise.

One of the factors which is consistently shown to be influential is the family, where it has consistently been shown that severe parental psychiatric illness increases the risk of a poor outcome in their child's illness (Rutter and Quinton 1984). In addition, other strands of work in this area have clearly demonstrated a link between being exposed to marital discord and divorce and developing depressive symptoms (Hetherington *et al.* 1985). It is less easy to know how to interpret the fact that children of clinically depressed parents are more likely to suffer from a major depressive illness than their peers (Weissman *et al.* 1987). This could arise from a genetic inheritance, but equally could be the influence of living with a depressed parent and the family environment that such an illness creates.

ASSOCIATIONS WITH OTHER DISORDERS

The type of situation where more than one disorder appears to be present at the same time is called co-morbidity, and with regards to depression there is a strong co-morbidity with oppositional and conduct disorder (Angold and Costello 1993). Why there should be a link with conduct problems is not understood, but it is probably significant that the overall outcome for young people with conduct problems does not seem to be influenced by whether they have depression or not (Harrington *et al.* 1991). Since there is also no strong family history of depression in such cases, it seems likely that this depression may be a product of young people reflecting upon their adverse life events, rather than a depressive illness acting in a way that causes conduct problems to arise.

Although links with conduct problems have been found, the commonest association with depression has been with anxiety disorder, because as many as 75 per cent of depressed young people will show anxiety features (Merikangas and Angst 1994). In the more marked forms, the anxiety tends to precede the onset of the depressive illness (Brady and Kendall 1992) and may herald a more severe form (Bernstein 1991). However, there is no evidence to suggest that this is a particular type of illness, rather that having two such difficulties occurring together multiplies the impact upon the sufferer's life.

INTERVENTION

As one might imagine, a young person presenting with a depressive illness often has other difficulties and problems associated with it, and it is important that these are assessed and dealt with appropriately (Goodyer *et al.* 1991). In many cases the correct resolution of wider family difficulties, and addressing issues such as poor peer relationships, can have a major beneficial effect upon the young person's mood. It is therefore important to recognise all the elements which may be contributing to the low mood, and to ensure that each element is given due weight in the intervention plan.

The treatment of depressive illness in adults has been exhaustively researched, and several approaches have been delineated. Although somewhat dependent upon the philosophy of the service offering treatment, and the views of the individual, the use of medication has been the first approach to such problems for a long time.

Medication

The evidence that medication is helpful in the treatment of depression in adults has become increasingly robust in recent years, with most authorities stating that it has a clear part to play in any treatment approach (Paykel and Priest 1992). As was mentioned earlier, the view that children used to demonstrate depression in a 'masked' way had in part arisen because certain symptoms in children seemed to improve with antidepressants. It is not surprising, therefore, that when the criteria used in adults to diagnose depression began to be applied to children and teenagers, the treatments which had emerged as valuable in adults began to be tried with young people.

The drugs most commonly used with adult patients are the tricyclic antidepressants. These drugs have proved effective in treating the disorder in about 80 per cent of cases. There is usually little response in the first two weeks, but then the features which are associated with depression, such as appetite, sleep and being slow in movements, begin to improve. The patients usually do not actually feel any better themselves at this stage, but observers see the improvements. It is usually six to eight weeks before the full impact of the drug is felt upon mood. There are many drugs in this group but the commonest, and the only two approved for use with children, are imipramine and amitriptyline. Although these have proved very useful in adults, patients are often troubled by the side-effects they cause, particularly the heart problems, such as irregular heartbeats. Most patients experience drowsiness, a constant dry mouth, and constipation, and, for some, problems with blurred vision and urine retention can cause discomfort.

These drugs can be dangerous if they are taken in overdose, and this limits their use in very depressed, suicidal patients. In adults who show such features the use of electroconvulsive therapy (ECT) needs to be considered. However, although the use of electroconvulsive therapy has been found to be valuable in the stringent reviews carried out in adults, it is rarely, if ever, used in the younger age group.

The fact that a lack of monoamines appears to play a part in causing depression has prompted much research into methods that can change the concentration of these chemicals in the brain. Drugs which interfere with the chemical's destruction, the monoamine oxidase inhibitors (MAOIs), have also been found to help some patients with depression. These drugs do have to be used with great care because they react with many other drugs, such as cough mixtures, and certain foods, such as cheese and yeast-extract products. These effects can last for a few weeks after the drug has been stopped, and so there needs to be great care taken if they are to be used.

The discovery of another brain chemical transmitter that influences depression (serotonin) has produced a new family of drugs which can be used to treat the condition. These are usually known as selective serotonin reuptake inhibitors (SSRIs) and they have become almost the first choice treatment because they are as effective as the tricyclic drugs but have fewer side-effects. The most commonly used drug in this family is fluoxetine (Prozac) which has become very popular with middle-class patients, and is the first antidepressant that it is almost fashionable to admit to be taking. Others in the family include fluvoxamine (Faverin) and paroxetine (Seroxat). Although these drugs are far less toxic than the older tricyclics, they do have side-effects of their own, most notably gastrointestinal problems such as nausea and vomiting, which are dose related. Although none of these drugs has been formally approved to be given to children, researchers in America have used various drugs from this family in clinical trials.

The proven value of such drugs in treating adults with depression has not been found in children. Indeed, there is no evidence that antidepressants are superior to a placebo in treating childhood or adolescent depression (Ambrosini *et al.* 1993). This raises the interesting conundrum of whether childhood depression is actually the same as that seen in adults, or whether the drugs are simply ineffective in the younger age group. Certainly, it is not that the antidepressants are inert when given to children, for there is a great deal of evidence that they exert effects in children with regard to other disorders, such as bedwetting and attention deficit disorder (see Chapter 4). There will need to be much more information gathered before this question can be answered, but if drugs are not going to be beneficial, what can be done to help a depressed young person?

Psychological approaches

Almost since the beginning of modern psychiatry there have been efforts to help people overcome psychological difficulties by using techniques which work with mental processes directly. These have taken many forms, and work which proves that they are as effective as other types of intervention has only recently been forthcoming (Tillett 1996). These approaches may focus upon:

- changing behaviour directly through behavioural programmes
- changing the thinking processes which are influencing the mood and behaviour; this is known as cognitive therapy
- exploring the young person's inner world by looking at history, belief systems and issues such as loss; this is the basis of most psychotherapies

Behavioural approaches are discussed in detail elsewhere (Chapter 2), and although the focus will be different for a depressed child, the principles are very similar. The fundamental aim is to focus on behaviours which are maintaining the problem, and reduce them, or introduce new behaviours which are incompatible with being depressed. So, for example, each task completed can be followed by a small reward, and planning the future rewards is an important first step in establishing such programmes. In addition, it is very helpful to establish routine sessions of physical activity, or regularly play favourite games to intrude upon the gloomy mood and, if well chosen, to give islands of positive feeling which can be gradually expanded and intensified. In practice behavioural programmes are not used in isolation, but as part of a wider psychological approach using cognitive therapy.

In recent years the use of cognitive therapy for people with depression has become recognised as a helpful approach, and some work has also been done with children using this technique (Vostanis and Harrington 1994). As described in Chapter 2, this type of therapy is based on the assumption that behaviour and moods are produced as a result of what the person is thinking, and so changing the thinking can change the behaviour. Since its original focus was dealing with depressive illness, it is perhaps not surprising that its value in treating young people has been explored.

In practice this type of intervention depends upon understanding the processes which are governing a particular person's thinking. Although there are several elements to the thinking process, two of the key ones from a therapeutic point of view are cognitive processes and cognitive products. Cognitive processes are the procedures which the brain uses to perceive and interpret experiences. The cognitive products are the thoughts which result from the interpretation and its interaction with experience, opinions and so on. If the young person has distortions in the cognitive processes then it becomes very easy to develop a distorted view of the world, and the depressing thoughts that stem from this act as strong reinforcement that the original view was a correct one. For example, if a young person believes he or she is useless at schoolwork, every low mark or comment by a teacher helps to confirm for the young person that this is a true summary of the situation. This view has been supported by the finding that such negative cognitions (such as self-criticism) are stable and often precede the emergence of depressive symptoms (Nolen-Hoeksema *et al.* 1992).

These cognitive processes can give rise to problems such as depression in two different ways. The first is that there is a necessary skill or area of understanding which the young person still has to grasp fully. An example of this might be needing to develop a way of controlling temper outbursts, or learning to cope with a cutting remark without taking it to heart. The second type of problem is that the thinking becomes distorted in some way, for instance, seeing a group of people talking always makes the young person believe that they are being discussed in a derogatory way.

This type of therapy has been used to treat depression in adults very successfully, and work with depressed young people shows that they have the sort of difficulties that should respond to this type of approach. In particular, these young people do not have the skills to solve interpersonal problems easily (Sacco and Graves 1984), and often show a pattern in which they set themselves too high a standard, only then to criticise and punish themselves when these standards are not achieved (Kaslow *et al.* 1984). Perhaps most significant of all, depressed young people always tend to attribute the good things that happen to them to external, specific factors, and the bad things as due to themselves and characteristics that they can't change (Bodiford *et al.* 1988).

The basic approach in cognitive therapy is always one of collaboration, with therapist and patient working as a team. For depressed young people this is often hard to establish, since they feel worthless and without a future. Engaging them in the therapy process usually means that initially they have to be led, and that enthusiasm for help needs to be nurtured and encouraged rather than being the prerequisite to commencing which it is in other types of therapy.

To be of any help it is necessary to gain an understanding of the thoughts that are fuelling the depressive feelings. Typically, this process has three stages. First, it is important to confirm that the young person understands the concepts of emotion – happiness, sadness and so on. Much of the work requires an accurate reporting of feelings and emotions, and so it is vital that these are fully recognised and labelled correctly. Using the knowledge, the young person begins to self-monitor, recording feelings and moods – when they occur and what they are associated with. This allows the young person and therapist together to identify the behavioural sequences which are associated with the problem. In this way the elements that require changing are clarified. This is the starting point for looking at the thought processes. If thought triggers mood which triggers behaviour, then examining the sequences most associated with gloomy moods should help to bring out the originating thoughts.

Having found the thought, then the cognitive restructuring can begin. The overall aim is to help the young person change the underlying cognitive processes which determine the interpretation that is being placed upon events. This is done in as concrete a way as possible, trying all the time to challenge the child's 'beliefs' with evidence that cannot be misinterpreted. Using such techniques helps the young person gradually to replace belief with knowledge, and with that knowledge comes a lessening of symptoms.

Marie was a fifteen-year-old girl who for the last year had felt increasingly miserable and unhappy. One morning her mother had not been able to rouse her for school, and hospital investigations revealed that she had taken about twenty of the tablets her grandmother was prescribed for her anxiety illness. Although her mother said Marie had been a little more subdued in recent weeks, she was shocked by this event, for the family saw Marie as sensible and very level headed. The parents could not identify any particular stresses in Marie's life which might have prompted the overdose, but accepted that since becoming a teenager she had tended to stay in her room and no longer confided in her mother about her problems or worries.

Marie described a pattern of increasing sadness in which she had lost interest in schoolwork and hobbies. She felt her friends no longer liked her, and the overdose had been prompted because she had finally become convinced that all of the girls in her class despised her. She had reached this conclusion because she had come to realise that whenever the girls were whispering together they were making derogatory remarks about her.

The thought identification approach drew out this negative attribution and Marie was asked to think of an alternative explanation for the huddle. She decided upon 'so the boys can't hear', and every time she saw the huddle she used a particular sequence which commenced with visualising a road stop sign and repeating 'stop' under her breath. She then took a deep breath and repeated the new explanation to herself. Self-scoring showed that over the subsequent week her concern about these huddles of girls reduced. Similar measures were used to tackle the other specific issues which arose through the course of therapy, and Marie showed a full return to school-work and hobbies, and a new interest in boyfriends, over the next three months. Marie still did not share with her parents, but when therapy ended she was talking intently with her two best friends and was telling them 'everything'!

It is important to realise that there are many variations of the approach that can be adopted, although most use elements of the process described. A more detailed programme for a cognitive therapy package to be used with children is given by Vostanis and Harrington (1994).

Whatever the specific content of the sessions, it does appear that this type of approach is not only helpful with the immediate symptoms of depression, but may be more successful than drugs in preventing relapse (Evans *et al.* 1992).

The last intervention which is regularly used to reduce the symptoms of depression is psychotherapy. This is another term that has gradually assumed a wider definition, and so has become rather devalued. In this text psychotherapy is a therapy which uses a relationship between patient and therapist as a basis for change, and the focus is very much upon the individual's inner world. The primary aim of such therapy is to give insight into the events and situations that prompted the difficulties, and more importantly into the unresolved issues which are maintaining them. A more detailed discussion of psychotherapy can be found in Chapter 2, but in this context the therapy is often focused on exploring painful historical events or losses. The theoretical assumption is that the emotional effort of avoiding dealing with these painful elements is prompting the depression, and so recalling them fully and gaining an understanding of them will allow the person to progress. In such a treatment sequence there is nearly always an initial phase in which symptoms become more marked, and new problems may actually arise. This needs to be prepared for, and concerned adults should be primed to expect such a period. The advice for handling such a phase is to recognise the origin of the behaviour, but to maintain the usual rules and expectations. The continuing predictability of all other aspects of the young person's world is a key element in allowing unimpeded concentration on the painful areas which the therapy is addressing.

OUTCOME

In trying to form a view of how young people with depression might fair in adult life it is important to distinguish those who only have a moderate form of depression from those with severe depression or bipolar illness. As was described earlier, there may be a genetic loading in this last group which makes the development of longer-term problems more likely.

The research evidence suggests that having an episode of depression in childhood does make it more likely that there will be episodes of depression in adult life, but if the young person has only a single episode of depression throughout the teens and twenties, then the outlook is good (Rao *et al.* 1995). There are factors that can offer reassurance that this may be the only episode. High self-esteem, good coping skills, school achievement, outside interests and positive relationships with family and friends all seem to exert a positive influence and mitigate against further recurrence (Compas 1994; Merikangas and Angst 1994).

The outlook for the severely ill group may be less positive, for it has been estimated that the risk of a repeat episode of depression is about 60 per cent (Harrington *et al.* 1990), and that as many as 80 per cent of adults with bipolar illness report that their illness started pre-pubertally (Geller *et al.* 1994). This issue of repeat occurrence is of importance because of the major impact that recurring depressive illness has upon a person's life. It has been established that an adult with a confirmed major depressive illness experiences, on average, between five and six recurrences during his or her lifetime (Zis and Goodwin 1979). These usually take about nine months to be resolved, although about 20 per cent of patients experience depressions that last almost two years (Post and Ballenger 1984). Such predictions have prompted Keller (1994) to conclude that as a general principle depression should be seen as a long-term disorder where patients are vulnerable to relapse.

No matter which type of illness it is, there can be more subtle long-term problems, for although treatment may reduce the immediate depressive symptoms, this is not always followed by improvement in other areas, such as social functioning (Kovacs and Goldston 1991). If the young person has a second episode of depression in adolescence, then there is a far greater likelihood of disruption to interpersonal relationships and a persistent sense of dissatisfaction with life (Rao *et al.* 1995). Also, as adults, they are more likely to present with overdoses and other suicidal gestures than is the general population (Kovacs *et al.* 1993).

As well as the factors within the child, there are wider influences which can affect the likelihood of further depressive episodes. For example, if the mother suffers from mood disorders, then this increases the risk of recurrence (Hammen *et al.* 1990).

PREVENTATIVE STRATEGIES

With the knowledge that exists about predicting the frequency of future problems in at-risk groups, it is natural to ask what is being done to try to prevent this heavy psychological toll on these young people. Some work in adults has looked at whether the continued prescription of antidepressants is able to prevent relapse, and the results suggest long-term treatment does reduce the likelihood of relapse but does not abolish the likelihood of some symptoms returning (Paykel 1993). There is no proven value in treating depression in the young with medication, and no evidence that continued usage reduces the likelihood of relapse.

In young people the evidence suggests that cognitive therapy is both a positive treatment and that it may reduce the likelihood of recurrence. This therapeutic approach can be combined with the factors which seem to be protective against further relapse: encouragement in developing outside interests; assistance offered to help foster positive relationships with family and friends; teaching good coping skills; correcting any educational deficits so that the young person can experience school achievement. Such a range of measures will also strengthen self-esteem and so reduce the likelihood of further problems.

As might be expected, it has also been shown that a positive emotional atmosphere at home and a perceived sense of family support for the child are far more important in protecting against mental illness than merely having the appearance of an average family make-up (Garrison *et al.* 1997). Family work in such cases therefore needs to focus on trying to strengthen the genuine emotional climate and produce a tangible sense of support if maximum assistance is to be offered.

This is a challenging list, but there are signs that group cognitive therapy focusing on some of these themes with young people who have depressive symptoms can reduce the risk of them having a full depressive episode (Clarke *et al.*, 1995). It is clearly very early days for this type of preventive work, but such protective programmes must be the way forward if they can demonstrate their effectiveness.

CONCLUSION

Depressive illness is a debilitating and often recurrent problem, which exerts influences far beyond the immediate way that it effects the patient. It often seems to begin in adolescence, and although our understanding of it in this age group is increasing there is still much to learn about how it influences the young person's adult life. The treatment in adults has been principally by medication, but increasingly cognitive therapy approaches are being introduced. Although work still continues to try to find drug treatments that will work in the young, it is cognitive therapy that is attracting most interest in this age group. The early results are promising, and this may prompt the use of drugs in adults to be moderated in favour of these psychological treatments, which may prove more persistently effective in the long term.

SOURCES OF FURTHER HELP

Depression Alliance. 35 Westminster Bridge Road, London SE1 7JB. Telephone (0171) 6339929.

Young Minds. 102–108 Clerkenwell Road, London EC1 55A. Telephone (0345) 626376 (during office hours).

REFERENCES

Ambrosini, P.J., Bianchi, M.D., Rabinovich, H. and Elia, J. (1993). Antidepressant treatments in children and adolescents. I. Affective disorders. *Journal of the American Academy of Child and Adolescent Psychiatry* 32, 1–6.

American Psychiatric Association (1994). *Diagnostic and Statistical Manual of Mental Disorders.* 4th edn. Washington D.C.: American Psychiatric Association Press.

Angold, A. and Costello, E. (1993). Depressive co-morbidity in children and adolescents: empirical, theoretical and methodological issues. *American Journal of Psychiatry* 150, 1779–91.

Angold, A. and Rutter, M. (1992). Effects of age and pubertal status on depression in a large clinical sample. *Developmental Psychopathology* 4, 5–28.

Bernstein, G.A. (1991). Comorbidity and severity of anxiety and depressive disorders in a clinic population. *Journal of the American Academy of Child and Adolescent Psychiatry* 30, 43–50.

Bodiford, C.A., Eisenstadt, R.H., Johnson, J.H. and Bradlyn, A.S. (1988). Comparison of learned helpless cognitions and behaviour in children with high and low scores on the Children's Depression Inventory. *Journal of Clinical Child Psychology* 17, 152–8.

Brady, E.U. and Kendall, P.C. (1992). Comorbidity of anxiety and depression in children and adolescents. *Psychological Bulletin* 111, 244–55.

Clarke, G.N., Hawkins, W., Murphy, M., Sheeber, L.B. and Lewinsohn, P.M. (1995). Targeted prevention of unipolar depressive disorder in an at-risk sample of high school adolescents. *Journal of the American Academy of Child and Adolescent Psychiatry* 34, 312–21.

Compas, B.E. (1994). Promoting successful coping during adolescence. In M. Rutter (ed.) *Psychosocial Disturbance in Young People: Challenges for Prevention.* Cambridge: Cambridge University Press.

Cooper, P. and Goodyer, I. (1993). A community study of depression in adolescent girls. I. Estimates of symptom and syndrome prevalence. *British Journal of Psychiatry* 163, 369–74.

Deakin, J.F.W. and Crow, T.J. (1986). Monoamines, rewards and punishments—the anatomy and physiology of the affective disorders. In J.F.W. Deakin (ed.) *The Biology of Depression.* London: Royal College of Psychiatrists.

Depue, R. and Monroe, S. (1978). The unipolar–bipolar distinction in the depressive disorders. *Psychological Bulletin* 85, 1001–29.

Evans, M., Hollon, S. and De Rubeis, R. (1992). Differential relapse following cognitive therapy and pharmacology for depression. *Archives of General Psychiatry* 49, 802–8.

Fleming, J. and Offord, D. (1990). Epidemiology of childhood depressive disorders: a critical review. *Journal of the American Academy of Child and Adolescent Psychiatry* 29, 571–80.

Frommer, E. (1968). Depressive illness in children. *British Journal of Psychiatry* Spec. Pub. 2, 117–36.

Garrison, C.Z., Waller, J.L., Cuffe, S.P. and McKeown, R.E. (1997). Incidence of major depressive disorder and dysthymia in young adolescents. *Journal of the American Academy of Child and Adolescent Psychiatry* 36, 458–65.

Geller, B., Fox, B.S. and Clark, K.A. (1994). Rate and predictors of prepubertal bipolarity during follow-up of 6 to 12 year-old depressed children. *Journal of the American Academy of Child and Adolescent Psychiatry* 33, 461–8.

Goodyer, I.M., Germany, E., Gowrusankur, J. and Altham, P. (1991). Social influences on the course of anxious and depressive disorders in school age children. *British Journal of Psychiatry* 158, 676–84.

Hammen, C., Burge, D., Burney, E. and Adrian, C. (1990). Longitudinal study of diagnoses in children of women with unipolar and bipolar affective illness. *Archives of General Psychiatry* 47, 1112–17.

Harrington, R.C., Fudge, H., Rutter, M., Pickles, A. and Hill, J. (1990). Adult outcomes of childhood and adolescent depression. I. Psychiatric status. *Archives of General Psychiatry* 47, 465–73.

Harrington, R.C., Fudge, H., Rutter, M., Pickles, A. and Hill, J. (1991). Adult outcomes of childhood and adolescent depression. III. Risk for antisocial. *Journal of the American Academy of Child and Adolescent Psychiatry* 30, 434–9.

Hetherington, E.M., Cox, M. and Cox, R. (1985). Long term effects of divorce and remarriage on the adjustment of children. *Journal of the American Academy of Child and Adolescent Psychiatry* 24, 518–30.

Kashani, J., McGee, R.O., Clarkson, S.E. and Anderson, J.C. (1983). The nature and prevalence of major and minor depression in a sample of nine-year-old children. *Archives of General Psychiatry* 40, 1217–27.

Kaslow, N.J., Rehm, L. and Siegel, A.W. (1984). Social-cognitive and cognitive correlates of depression in children. *Journal of Abnormal Child Psychology* 12, 605–20.

Kazdin, A. (1990). Childhood depression. *Journal of Child Psychology and Psychiatry* 31, 121–60.

Keller, M.B. (1994). Depression: a long term illness. *British Journal of Psychiatry* 165 (suppl. 26), 9–15.

Kendler, K., Neale, M., Kessler, R., Heath, A. and Eaves, L. (1992). A population-based twin study of major depression in women: the impact of varying definitions of illness. *Archives of General Psychiatry* 49, 257–66.

Kent, L., Vostanis, P. and Feehan, C. (1995). Teacher reported characteristics of children with depression. *Educational and Child Psychology* 12, 62–70.

Klerman, G.L. and Weissman, M.M. (1989). Increasing rates of depression. *Journal of the American Medical Association* 261, 2229–35.

Kovacs, M. and Goldston, D. (1991). Cognitive and social cognitive development of depressed children and adolescents. *Journal of the American Academy of Child and Adolescent Psychiatry* 30, 388–92.

Kovacs, M., Goldston, D. and Gatonis, C. (1993). Suicidal behaviors and childhood onset depressive disorders: a longitudinal investigation. *Journal of the American Academy of Child and Adolescent Psychiatry* 32, 8–20.

Lewinsohn, P., Clark, G., Seeley, J. and Rohde, P. (1994). Major depression in community adolescents: age of onset, episode duration, and time to recurrence. *Journal of the American Academy of Child and Adolescent Psychiatry* 33, 809–18.

McGonagle, K., Zhao, S. and Nelson, C. (1994). Lifetime and 12 month prevalence of DSM-III-R psychiatric disorders in the United States: results from the national comorbidity survey. *Archives of General Psychiatry* 51, 8–19.

McGuffin, P. and Katz, R. (1989). The genetics of depression and manic depressive disorder. *British Journal of Psychiatry* 155, 294–304.

Merikangas, K.R. and Angst, J. (1994). The challenge of depressive disorders in adolescence. In M. Rutter (ed.) *Psychosocial Disturbances in Young People: Challenges for Prevention*. Cambridge: Cambridge University Press.

Nolen-Hoeksema, S., Girgus, J. and Seligman, M. (1992). Predictors and consequences of childhood depressive symptoms. *Journal of Abnormal Psychology* 101, 405–22.

Paykel, E.S. (1993). The place of antidepressants in long-term treatment. In S.A. Montgomery and J.H. Corn (eds) *Psychopharmacology of Depression*. Oxford: Oxford University Press.

Paykel, E.S. and Priest, R.G. (1992). Recognition and management of depression in general practice: consensus statement. *British Medical Journal*, 305, 1198–202.

Post, R. and Ballenger, J. (1984). *Neurobiology of Mood Disorders*. Baltimore: Williams and Wilkins.

Puig-Antich, J., Kaufman, J., Ryan, N. and Williamson, D. (1993). The psychosocial functioning and family environment of depressed patients. *Journal of the American Academy of Child and Adolescent Psychiatry* 32, 244–53.

Radke-Yarrow, M., Nottelman, E., Martinez, P., Fox, M.B. (1992). Young children of affectively ill parents: A longitudinal study of psychosocial development. *Journal of the American Academy of Child and Adolescent Psychiatry* 31, 68–77.

Rao, U., Ryan, N.D., Birmaher, B. and Dahl, R.E. (1995). Unipolar depression in adolescents: clinical outcome in adulthood. *Journal of the American Academy of Child and Adolescent Psychiatry* 34, 566–78.

Roberts, R.E., Andrews, J.A., Lewinsohn, P.M. and Hops, H. (1990). Assessment of depression in adolescents using the Center for Epidemiological Studies Depression Scale. *Journal of Consulting and Clinical Psychology* 2, 122–8.

Rutter, M. and Quinton, D. (1984). Parental psychiatric disorder: effects on children. *Psychological Medicine* 14, 853–80.

Sacco, W.P. and Graves, D.J. (1984). Childhood depression, interpersonal problem-solving and self ratings of performance. *Journal of Clinical Child Psychology* 13, 10–15.

Strober, M. (1992). Relevance of early age-of-onset in genetic studies of bipolar affective disorder. *Journal of the American Academy of Child and Adolescent Psychiatry* 31, 606–10.

Tillett, R. (1996). Psychotherapy assessment and treatment selection. *British Journal of Psychiatry* 168, 10–15.

Vostanis, P. and Harrington, R. (1994). Cognitive-behavioural treatment of depressive disorder in child psychiatric patients: Rationale and description of treatment package. *European Journal of Child and Adolescent Psychiatry* 3, 111–23.

Weissman, M.M., Fendrich, M., Warner, V. and Wickramaratne, P. (1992). Incidence of psychiatric disorder in offspring at high and low risk for depression. *Journal of the American Academy of Child and Adolescent Psychiatry* 31, 640–8.

Weissman, M., Gammon, G., John, K. and Merikangas, K. (1987). Children of depressed parents. *Archives of General Psychiatry* 44, 847–53.

Weller, E.B., Weller, R.A. and Fristad, M.A. (1995). Bipolar disorder in children: misdiagnosis, underdiagnosis, and future directions. *Journal of the American Academy of Child and Adolescent Psychiatry* 34, 709–14.

Whitaker, A., Johnson, J., Shaffer, D. and Rapoport, J. (1990). Uncommon troubles in young people: Prevalence estimates of selected psychiatric disorders in a non-referred adolescent population. *Archives of General Psychiatry* 47, 487–96.

Wittchen, H.-U., Knauper, B. and Kessler, R.C. (1994). Lifetime risk of depression. *British Journal of Psychiatry* 165, (suppl. 26), 16–22.

World Health Organisation (1992). *The ICD-10 Classification of Mental and Behavioural Disorders. Clinical Descriptions and Diagnostic Guidelines*. Geneva: World Health Organisation.

Zis, A.P. and Goodwin, F.K. (1979). Major affective disorder as a recurrent illness: a critical review. *Archives of General Psychiatry* 36, 835–9.

11 Dyslexia

INTRODUCTION

In every country one can find a significant number of children whose performance in reading, writing and spelling falls considerably below the average range. Although the origins of such difficulties can be easily explained for some children, for example, because of hearing/visual impairment, autism, brain damage, there are many others, often in mainstream schools, for whom the cause is less evident. Many of this latter group are considered to have a specific disorder, dyslexia, which although far from understood, is believed to have an underlying neurological cause and be particularly related to language.

The focus of this chapter concerns not only what is meant by the term dyslexia but, perhaps more importantly, whether this term adds to our ability to understand and remedy the problems of children who have difficulty in learning to read.

In 1994 the Orton Dyslexia Society defined dyslexia as:

> one of several distinct learning disabilities. It is a specific language-based disorder of constitutional origin characterized by difficulties in single word decoding, usually reflecting insufficient phonological processing abilities. These difficulties in single word decoding are often unexpected in relation to age and other cognitive and academic abilities; they are not the result of generalized developmental disability or sensory impairment. Dyslexia is manifested by variable difficulty with different forms of language, often including, in addition to problems reading, a conspicuous problem with acquiring proficiency in writing and spelling.
>
> (Lyon 1995: 9)

Such a definition of dyslexia, far more focused than those which had appeared a decade earlier, reflects the influence of a growing, and increasingly sophisticated, research base which appears to point strongly towards language processing as the basis for the problems observed. Despite this, dyslexia remains a highly controversial condition, with some denying its very existence and others arguing that the diagnosis, however valid, is of little value to practitioners.

An increasing number of educationalists, objecting to dyslexia's quasi-medical tone, prefer to speak of 'specific learning difficulties'. This term is somewhat broader and refers to any area of learning where the child's level of functioning is significantly less than one would expect on the basis of his or her general performance in other areas. Rather than being wholly synonymous terms, then, dyslexia may be considered to be one common type of specific learning difficulty.

There have been many accounts in the popular press of children who have struggled through their education under great stress, who, it was subsequently discovered, were shown to be dyslexic. This finding, it is sometimes alleged, proved to be a turning point in their lives as they could now benefit from remedial teaching geared for dyslexics and begin to make the gains which one would anticipate given their intellectual abilities. For other individuals, however, a failure to diagnose the condition, it is frequently alleged, resulted in a ruined education and limited options in adult life. For some, litigation is now a justifiable consequence. The following quotation, taken from a newspaper article, is representative of many:

> A 22 year old woman was condemned to 'temporary menial tasks' because her former schools did not realise she was dyslexic, the High Court heard yesterday. Pamela Phelps claims that she is of average intelligence but because her learning difficulty was not discovered until two months before she left school, she never learned to read and write properly . . . It was not the disorder that prevented her from being able to read. She had originally been 'lumped in' with children of low intelligence when she needed special tuition.
>
> Tests were carried out on her at infant, junior and comprehensive schools. At the age of 10 she was found to be four years behind in reading and writing skills but the reason was never identified.
>
> (*Guardian*, 27 July 1997: 5)

The above account suggests that if a diagnosis of dyslexia had been arrived at earlier, appropriate treatment would have resolved her difficulties. As will be shown later, this may not necessarily have been the case.

In order to ascertain the educational value of a diagnosis of dyslexia three important issues relating to conceptualisation, intervention and the provision of resources need to be considered:

1 Is dyslexia a meaningful condition? Can one locate children with literacy difficulties into clear dyslexic/non-dyslexic groupings?
2 To what extent does the dyslexic label guide the educator in devising appropriate forms of intervention?
3 To what extent should the dyslexic label result in the child receiving additional school/LEA resources and/or special examination arrangements which would not otherwise be made available?

IS DYSLEXIA A MEANINGFUL CONDITION? CAN ONE LOCATE CHILDREN WITH LITERACY DIFFICULTIES INTO CLEAR DYSLEXIC/NON-DYSLEXIC GROUPINGS?

While there is no such thing as a typical dyslexic, there are a number of underlying signs and symptoms which are often associated with the condition. These may include:

- speech and language difficulties (particularly as a young child)
- poor short-term verbal memory
- difficulties in ordering and sequencing
- clumsiness
- lack of consistent hand preference
- frequent use of letter reversals (b for d, p for q)
- poor verbal fluency

Such difficulties, however, are also frequently found in people without reading difficulties and in poor readers who are not considered to be dyslexic. Furthermore, it is a point of some debate whether such symptoms are causes or consequences of reading failure. Thus, as is so often the case with the types of problem discussed in this book, the existence of certain signs and symptoms does not necessarily assist the practitioner in making a diagnosis.

There are many reasons why a child may experience difficulties in learning to read. Heaton and Winterton (1996) suggest that key factors are:

- low intelligence
- inadequate schooling in the form of poor teaching or inappropriate content
- socio-economic disadvantage
- physical disability (e.g. hearing or visual difficulties)
- 'visible' neurological impairment which goes beyond reading and writing
- emotional and behavioural factors which might affect attention, concentration and responsiveness to teacher direction, thus jeopardising the child's ability to learn
- dyslexia

One of the major difficulties of such analyses is that dyslexia may simply be defined and identified by the absence of the first six factors (Lyon 1995). Difficulties abound here particularly with respect to the relationship of intelligence to dyslexia (see below) and the significance of socio-economic factors. Dyslexia has been criticised as a 'middle-class syndrome', for, as Rutter (1978) points out, consideration of social factors may rule out the possibility of a diagnosis of dyslexia in those from disadvantaged backgrounds. A further difficulty concerns the role of visual factors. It is often alleged that dyslexics have difficulties in visual processing, for example, exaggerated sensitivity to light (this is discussed below).

For dyslexia to be meaningfully differentiated from other forms of reading difficulty, one would require differences in underlying cause, presenting symptoms, prognosis and/or responsivity to differing forms of intervention (Pumfrey 1996). For each of these, however, evidence is currently inconclusive. This is largely because of theoretical disagreement about the more general development of language and the particular patterns of difficulty which are encompassed by the terms dyslexia and specific learning difficulties (Pumfrey and Reason 1991).

It is highly likely, however, that dyslexia will eventually become more tightly defined and have a clearer relevance to educational practice than at present.

Given the lack of current consensus about what constitutes dyslexia, it is hardly surprising that estimates of its prevalence vary substantially. One estimate (Crisfield 1996) suggests that as much as 10 per cent of the population may have 'mild' developmental dyslexia and 4 per cent 'severe' dyslexia. In contrast, the Dyslexia Institute estimates that approximately 15 per cent of boys and 5 per cent of girls, totalling 350,000 pupils in UK schools, are currently affected by dyslexia.

What causes dyslexia?

Biological factors

No single cause of dyslexia has been discovered and it is highly likely that the various difficulties with which this term is associated have differing causes. Much work has focused on biomedical accounts which emphasise brain structure and genetic influences. Although, in most individuals, the left hemisphere of the brain is usually larger than the right, this is less evident in dyslexics. This, together with other neurological findings, has led to the suggestion that dyslexia results from ineffective operation of the two sides of the brain. The widely promulgated, although somewhat inconclusive, work in this area has, however, often resulted in rather oversimplistic and sweeping analyses being presented to practitioners (see e.g. Attwood 1994).

The common finding that dyslexia runs in families has resulted in a familiar genes versus environment debate. While it is quite possible that the quality of a child's literacy experiences will be significantly affected by living with one or more parents who have encountered difficulties in learning to read, it is highly likely that there is also a biological explanation to reading difficulty (Pennington 1995). In the Colorado Family Reading Study, for example, it was found that boys born to a dyslexic parent ran a 35–40 per cent risk of developing dyslexia themselves (tending to the higher figure if the dyslexic parent was male), whereas girls ran a 17–18 per cent risk irrespective of the parent's gender. Where neither parent was dyslexic, the risks for boys and girls was 5–10 per cent and 1–2 per cent respectively (De Fries 1991).

Pumfrey's (1996) review of current research concludes that while it is unlikely that a specific gene defect will be identified, there may prove to be a genetic susceptibility for some individuals which can be minimised or maximised by subsequent life experiences.

Visual processing factors

The role of visual processing deficiencies has often been seen as a key element of dyslexia, although its perceived relative importance to language processing deficits has tended to fluctuate during the past two decades (Rayner 1993). The development of our understanding of the role of visual factors has not been assisted by journalists' overenthusiasm for much heralded 'miracle cures' which have often promised more than could be delivered and have not been subsequently validated by well-designed research evaluations.

Key areas of debate in this field concern the effectiveness of eye movements, the difficulties that may result from an inability to co-ordinate binocular vision and the inhibiting effect of oversensitivity to light.

The importance of eye movements

It has been noted by clinicians that many dyslexics scan from right to left rather than in the direction of normal western print order. Pavlidis (1981) argued that, in reading, dyslexics tend to be less skilled in scanning texts, experience difficulties in fixating upon text and are less likely to make jumps (saccades) from one chunk of print to the next in the most efficient fashion. Such ideas, however, are now less influential and it is increasingly considered that, rather than a cause of dyslexia, the role of eye movements may be a reflection of an underlying language processing difficulty (Miles and Miles 1990).

Difficulties in co-ordinating binocular vision

It has been argued (Stein and Fowler 1982; Stein 1993) that many dyslexic children fail to establish dominance in one eye when reading print, thus giving the reader the perception that the words are moving around the page. For such individuals, Stein recommends monocular occlusion, a process which involves children wearing glasses with one lens frosted over or covered by tape. These are then worn for reading and close work for a period of approximately six months. Although Stein reports that reading performance improves greatly when binocular difficulties are stabilised, it is important to note that others are critical of the data interpretation (Bishop 1989) or have not found replication studies to be supportive of the theory (Wilsher 1990). It is no longer thought that addressing ocular dominance difficulties represents a significant method of treatment.

Sensitivity to light (scotopic sensitivity syndrome)

During the 1980s there was much newspaper speculation about a wonder cure for dyslexics which involved the use of tinted lenses to reduce glare from bright lighting or white page backgrounds and limit the strain upon eyes resulting from sustained focusing (e.g. Brace 1993). Irlen (1983), who is largely credited with developing this technique, claimed that between 50 and 75 per cent of children with dyslexic profiles may suffer from such sensitivity.

In response to the widespread publicity which resulted from Irlen's work the Intuitive Colorimeter, a piece of apparatus which can throw light of various shades and strength on to texts, is now employed by some optometrists. Assessment, with the aid of this machine, it is argued, permits the prescription of coloured lenses individually tailored to the client's specific requirements.

The validity of such procedures continues to be a topic of debate. While practitioners may be able to identify individual children whose reading appeared to have improved following the prescription of coloured lenses, research evidence is largely unsupportive of the notion of 'scotopic sensitivity' (Shute 1991) and the designs of those studies which have shown treatment gains have been criticised as being unsatisfactory (Reeves 1988). It is possible that reported gains often reflect the child's belief that something important or valuable is happening (the Hawthorne effect) and this, in turn, results in greater motivation, attention and concentration resulting in superior performance on reading tests.

Research into the field of visual processing suggests that it is highly unlikely that these factors can be considered to be significant causes of dyslexia. While it is possible that physical discomfort resulting from visual difficulties may result in a disinclination, or unwillingness, to read, most researchers now tend to believe that the origins of dyslexia lie with linguistic, rather than visual, processing difficulties.

Phonological processing

The most influential theories about dyslexia now focus upon deficits in phonological awareness (i.e. the ability to recognise different sounds in spoken language) and knowledge about the relationship between written and spoken parts of speech, often referred to as grapheme–phoneme correspondence. Phonemes are the smallest units of sound which enable one to distinguish one word from another. They can consist of either individual or combinations of letters. Graphemes are the written forms of phonemes.

The emphasis upon phonological awareness has been fuelled by research findings (Bradley and Bryant 1983; Lundberg 1994) which indicated that young pre-readers who showed difficulties in perceiving rhyme and alliteration and segmenting words into their constituent sounds were more likely to demonstrate dyslexic profiles later in life. It is argued that the beginning reader needs to be able to perceive phonemes in syllables and words and then be able to manipulate these in order to be able to make a connection between speech and writing and to employ an alphabetic system to read and spell (Adams 1990). Other researchers (e.g. Fletcher *et al.* 1994) point out that while a major indicator of phonological weakness is an inability to segment spoken words phonemically, other related difficulties include imprecision in naming objects at speed (Katz and Shankweiler 1985) and limited short-term verbal memory (Brady 1991).

Interest in the role of phonological factors in reading has also been spurred by intervention studies such as that of Lundberg, Frost and Petersen (1988) which showed that pre-school children who receive phonological awareness training through listening and rhyming games make greater gains in reading and spelling than comparable control groups (for detailed discussion of the long-term outcomes of this study, see Lundberg (1994).

In order to assess phonological strengths and weaknesses, a group of educational psychologists has recently produced the Phonological Assessment Battery. This measure is claimed by its authors to have: 'considerable potential both for identifying poor readers with phonological difficulties and children with specific learning difficulties (dyslexia)' (Frederickson and Reason 1995: 203).

The PhAB contains subtests which assess Naming Speed, Fluency (e.g. name as many animals as you can), Rhyme Awareness, Alliteration (where each word has the same initial sound) and Spoonerisms (which involve the ability to switch initial sounds from one word to another). A number of studies are currently being conducted to ascertain the utility of this measure, some criticisms having been made about the value of the subtests (Whittaker, 1996). It has also been argued that it may be only those phonological skills which are used directly in reading which when taught explicitly will lead to gains in reading (Solity 1996).

Phonological deficit theory has now become the 'dominant cognitive theory for the underlying cause of dyslexia' (Nicolson and Fawcett 1995: 20). It is important to recognise, however, that while deficiencies in phonological awareness appear to be the most significant factors in studies of children with reading difficulties:

- we are a long way from being clear about which aspects of phonological processing are the most important for reading acquisition;
- it is unclear which groups of children, if any, should receive training in phonological skills (e.g. all preschool children, prereaders who appear to be encountering phonological difficulties, or older children who have been identified as failed readers);
- the nature and content of appropriate phonological training programmes

are yet to be determined. Furthermore, we do not know whether such training can be taught in isolation or, alternatively, whether it should be explicitly linked with the teaching of reading (Hatcher *et al.* 1994).

There is far more agreement about the statement that reading difficulties should not be considered as unitary. The nature of reading problems, their symptoms and their causes are likely to vary substantially from one child to the next. Thus, it would be unwise to employ phonological, or even language, difficulties as a global explanation for dyslexia (Nicolson and Fawcett 1995).

Despite the difficulties involved in agreeing upon an understanding of dyslexia, there is no shortage of assessment tools, many of which are marketed directly to teachers (who, it is suggested, will then refer suitable cases to an educational psychologist). Recent measures include the Dyslexia Early Screening Test and the Dyslexia Screening Test (both published by the Psychological Corporation) and a computerised program, the Cognitive Profiling System (produced by Chameleon Educational). While differing somewhat in the nature of their subtests, these measures involve assessments of those skills currently considered most important for a diagnosis of dyslexia such as memory, phonological awareness, auditory discrimination and verbal fluency.

The role of intelligence in the diagnosis of dyslexia

A cartoon recently published in a popular children's comic showed a young man fishing by a riverbank. His exaggerated facial features were drawn in a fashion suggestive of severe intellectual disability. A gamekeeper, pointing to a 'No fishing' sign was pictured shouting to him, 'Can't you read?' Because of the widely held association between illiteracy and intellectual impairment, the reader was invited to find this scenario humorous.

At the heart of the dyslexia debate lies the thorny issue of intelligence. In work with those with reading difficulties, the frequent parental comment, 'I know he can't read but he's not daft!' typically reflects the concern and frustration often felt by those who perceive the stigmatising impact of their child's difficulties in learning to read. In our society illiteracy is often perceived as shameful and, as demonstrated in the children's cartoon, indicative of limited intellectual functioning. It is no wonder then, that parents are often happy for their child to receive a quasi-medical diagnosis of dyslexia. In the minds of many, such a diagnosis helps to separate intellectual from literacy weakness and offers a picture of the dyslexic as someone who, while perfectly 'normal', has a particular difficulty which hinders their development in a highly specific area of functioning. In addition, as in medicine, it is hoped that a diagnosis will help to indicate an effective method of intervention.

For many, then, the dyslexic is typically frustrated and thwarted by being unable to read and write at a level commensurate with his or her intellectual functioning. Thus, it is unsurprising that perhaps the most widely used single criterion employed in diagnosis is whether there is a discrepancy between IQ and measured reading ability (Presland 1991). The most common method of ascertaining this is by predicting an individual's expected reading score on the basis of his or her IQ score. Where the difference between predicted and actual scores is great, the practitioner may suspect that a specific difficulty is present (McNab 1994).

Although the employment of IQ tests, such as the British Ability Scales (Elliott *et al.* 1983) or the Wechsler Intelligence Scales for Children (Wechsler 1992), is frequently a part of an assessment for dyslexia, there is a lack of consensus as to whether the practitioner should focus upon total IQ score or either the verbal or non-verbal subscales in isolation. Some commentators stress that an important diagnostic component is the particular performance of the individual on a specific group of subtests (which usually includes both verbal and non-verbal measures) considered to be particularly indicative of dyslexia. In the most widely employed IQ measure, the Wechsler Scales, key subtests are considered to be Arithmetic, Digit Span (a measure of short-term memory which requires the child to repeat increasingly lengthy strings of numbers spoken aloud by the examiner), Coding (where the child must match and draw symbols and shapes under time restriction) and Information (a test of general knowledge). Although such measures are widely employed in diagnosis (Dudley-Marling 1981), Pumfrey and Reason's (1991) detailed review of the field concluded that there were many difficulties in the adoption of subtest profile approaches, not least that such profiles did not translate into clear guidelines for intervention.

Increasingly, however, findings from research studies are resulting in recognition that dyslexia (or specific learning difficulties) are largely independent of intellectual functioning (e.g. Fletcher *et al.* 1994; Stanovich and Stanovich 1997). While poor readers with lower IQ scores may, by virtue of their more limited reasoning skills, be less able to use meaning, inference and syntactical knowledge to help them to make sense of text, they tend to experience no greater problems than their 'dyslexic' peers when they try to read individual words – the crucial area for dyslexia (Stanovich 1991). Such findings, then, seriously call into question the suggestion that dyslexics can be differentiated on the basis of discrepancies between intellectual functioning and reading ability.

Despite its questionable status, the IQ–reading ability discrepancy continues to be widely employed as an index of dyslexia by researchers and practitioners. In one survey of educational psychologists (Pumfrey and Reason 1991), 80 per cent of the sample indicated that discrepancies of one kind or another were sought when an assessment of an individual with suspected specific learning difficulties was being undertaken.

In one study, typical of those in this area, Ellis *et al.* (1996) sought to explore whether children identified as dyslexic differed from other groupings. One approach is to examine whether there are underlying differences between dyslexics and younger children whose reading skills are at a similar level.

> If dyslexics perform worse on a given task than children of the same age and IQ who are reading normally (chronological age controls) but similarly to younger normal readers (reading age controls), then it is possible that the dyslexic performance simply reflects the level they have attained in the development of reading. That is, their differences from chronological age controls could be a consequence of their failure to learn to read normally rather than reflecting some underlying cause of dyslexia. If, in contrast, the dyslexics perform worse than both the chronological age controls and the reading age controls on a given task, then that task might indeed be tapping some process whose deficient functioning lies close to the origin of dyslexia itself.
>
> (Ellis *et al.* 1996: 32)

In order to explore whether children identified as dyslexic did differ from other groupings, Ellis *et al.* (1996) identified and compared four groups of readers, all of whose reading age equivalents were in a similar range, 7.03 – 8.06 years. The groupings were as follows:

1   children categorised as dyslexic (mean age 10:03, mean IQ 118)
2   younger, normal readers (mean age 7:11, mean IQ 107)
3   ordinary poor readers (mean age 10:04, mean IQ 80)
4   precocious readers (mean age 6:02, mean IQ 126)

All the children were given a battery of tests including measures of phonological awareness, reading (letter matching, word recognition, non-word reading and reading passages of text), and visual processing, including visual matching and memory.

The findings indicated that the profiles of the dyslexic children were highly similar to those of the other groups. The authors concluded that: 'dyslexics are more like other children reading at the same level than they are unlike' (Ellis *et al.* 1996: 53).

As noted above, one reason why dyslexia is a sought-after diagnosis is that there is a very real danger that reading difficulty will be equated with limited academic ability. When this is the case, some children may encounter low teacher, peer and, possibly, parental expectations of their performance and intellectual challenge may be minimised. Because of the widespread perception that the dyslexic is often highly intelligent, it is often hoped that being assigned such a label will raise teacher expectations. In turn, it is hoped that this would result in the provision of a stimulating, demanding education which will stretch rather than demotivate the child. An example of the power of such labels is provided in the case study of Aidan, below.

Aidan, aged thirteen, was the younger of two brothers, both of whom had a long-standing history of reading difficulty. He attended a local comprehensive school, which, while enjoying a sound record of public examination success, employed a rigid system of streaming, based upon end of term examinations.

Assessment of Aidan's reading demonstrated a significant mismatch between his reading accuracy and reading comprehension (as measured by a standardised reading test). Aidan's reading accuracy was consistent with that of an average nine-year-old while his comprehension was superior by approximately two and a half years. Aidan's performance on a standardised spelling test was at an age equivalence of eight years and four months.

Intellectual assessment, using the Wechsler Intelligence Scales for Children (Revised), indicated that Aidan was functioning within the top 5 per cent of the population. He performed well on spatial tasks (such as recreating patterns using wooden blocks and ordering pictures to tell a story) and excelled on a number of verbal measures involving general knowledge, comprehension and reasoning. His only significant weakness involved a short-term memory task where he was required to repeat a string of numbers spoken aloud.

It was clear that Aidan could compensate for his poor decoding skills by employing his high intellect to assist him to make sense of text. In a manner similar to that when one is attempting to master a foreign language, he would use his understanding of the grammatical structures of language, and inferential skills, to guess words difficult to recognise and thus draw meaning from the text.

Reliance upon internal examinations for streaming decisions had resulted in Aidan being placed in the lowest stream. In discussion with him, it became clear that this was proving highly problematic. Aidan complained that his classmates often teased him for displaying enthusiasm in class and for the fact that his orientation to school life and peer relationships often seemed to mark him out as different. A further frustration stemmed from what was, for him, an unstimulating and unchallenging curriculum. Although Aidan experienced difficulty in achieving high grades in his examinations, this was largely a reflection of his underdeveloped literacy skills rather than an inability to understand the ideas and concepts which were presented to him. His teachers confirmed the fact that he was quick to grasp ideas and had a sound analytic ability yet, surprisingly, the possibility of inappropriate placement had not appeared to register with them.

In a series of meetings with school staff, the educational psychologist highlighted Aidan's superior intellectual ability, his frustration with the content of many of his lessons and his unhappiness in being placed within a class of somewhat disaffected, unmotivated youngsters. After prolonged debate, the teachers accepted the recommendation that Aidan should be placed in a higher stream. Furthermore, it was agreed that his written performance in end of term examinations should not be seen as adequately representing his learning. Aidan's teachers were asked to ensure that his schoolwork was intellectually challenging and not impeded by his difficulties in reading. This, of course, made significant demands upon his teachers who, in large part, were enthusiastic and diligent in tailoring aspects of their lesson delivery to meet his needs.

As notetaking was an important element of schoolwork, Aidan was subsequently encouraged to record notes using audiotapes. This necessitated the employment of a highly structured filing system in order to ensure ready access to these materials. Aidan's capacity for organisation, coupled with a high level of motivation and support from volunteer sixth formers, ensured that this proved highly effective. Direct intervention aimed at helping him to develop reading and spelling skills continued outside of classroom hours. Some months later his teachers reported that Aidan was far more cheerful and, despite ongoing difficulties with reading and spelling, was making excellent progress in his learning.

The key issue here is not that intelligence proved to be an important factor in diagnosing dyslexia. Nor can it be considered that by demonstrating his above-average intelligence, the appropriate 'treatment' was indicated. What intellectual assessment did help to highlight was that Aidan's ability to grasp and work with difficult ideas and concepts was being obscured by an inappropriate system of assessment placing too great a reliance upon written scripts. Confirmation of Aidan's abilities by the educational psychologist resulted in a changed classroom environment and higher teacher expectations, which, while not a 'cure' for his literacy difficulties, at least ensured that intellectual challenge was maintained.

The above case study serves as a good illustration of the benefits to an individual of a diagnosis of dyslexia. Not only did Aidan receive a more appropriate education, recognition of his intellectual abilities may have helped him to cope with the threats to his self-esteem caused by his placement and treatment by his peers. There is much evidence (e.g. Edwards 1994) that the dyslexic child may be treated harshly, feel humiliated, be discriminated against or undervalued, experience a range of highly negative emotions, and, as a result, develop a diminished sense of self. However, we should question whether such experiences are any less demeaning or harmful for those poor readers who are not labelled dyslexic. Indeed, does the case for sensitivity and special treatment for the dyslexic leave other poor readers to feel even more stigmatised as a result? It is possible that what may benefit some will prove costly to others. This is not to say that the unfortunate experiences of some dyslexics should be discounted, rather that schools need to provide sensitive and supportive environments for all children who encounter learning difficulties.

TO WHAT EXTENT DOES THE DYSLEXIC LABEL GUIDE THE EDUCATOR IN DEVISING APPROPRIATE FORMS OF INTERVENTION?

As has been noted, it has often proven difficult to differentiate between dyslexic and other poor readers. If causes and symptoms cannot be clearly identified for such a subgroup, does a diagnosis of dyslexia assist in formulating a clear intervention strategy?

It is generally considered that dyslexic children require teaching approaches which focus upon the ability to decode words using a knowledge of letter sounds, singly and in combination. Perhaps the associated teaching technique most associated with dyslexic children is multisensory learning. This highly structured approach involves the child learning the names, sounds and shapes of letters by accessing a number of sensory channels – hearing, touch, vision and movement. Such work is conducted individually or in small groups either in school or, typically, in a specialist centre for dyslexic children. A variety of multisensory programmes exists, some of the most common being based upon the Fernald Approach (Fernald 1943) and the Orton-Gillingham Method (Orton 1967). An outline description of these and other common approaches is provided by Pumfrey (1991: chapter 6).

Increasing realisation of the importance of phonological awareness has resulted in this receiving much greater emphasis in schools, particularly in work with the very young and those experiencing reading difficulties. Lessons typically involve the use of relatively straightforward, recognisable games designed to develop the child's ability to perceive and discriminate sounds in speech.

Much debate has focused upon whether the teaching of reading should focus upon the explicit instruction of decoding skills involving knowledge of letters and letter combinations or through 'whole-language' approaches in which phonic knowledge is acquired explicitly, or implicitly, through everyday reading and writing activities. It is important here to recognise that the naturalistic, whole-language (sometimes misleadingly called the 'real books') approach to instruction, undertaken in isolation, may be less suited to those children who experience complex reading difficulties: 'Wherever children who cannot discover the alphabetic principle independently are denied explicit instruction on the regularities and conventions of the letter strings, reading disability may well be the eventual consequence' (Adams and Bruck 1993: 131). Similarly, it would appear inappropriate to focus exclusively upon the processing of letter strings. Activities may soon become sterile, artificial and unattractive to children. The work of practitioners and researchers from the psycholinguistic, or 'whole-language', tradition has highlighted the importance of literacy as a means of communication, emphasised the importance of storytelling and stressed that interventions should reflect the fact that learning to read, like all learning, takes place in a social context. Clearly, teaching which draws upon approaches from these very diverse theoretical traditions would seem necessary for all children (Reason 1990).

Many practitioners and researchers cite the importance of early diagnosis and intervention (Miles and Miles 1984). It is argued that, if tackled early, with specialised and structured teaching, many children can be helped to progress to functioning within normal levels. The value of early, specialised intervention, however, is appropriate for all children with reading difficulties. The much vaunted Reading Recovery Programme (Clay 1985), for example, has demonstrated the effectiveness of daily, individual intervention with a wide spectrum of poor readers (Hurry 1996). It is, perhaps, somewhat disingenuous to state that, if dyslexia is not recognised and remediated swiftly, the problem will become greater – for such a statement is equally true for all children encountering reading difficulties.

As yet, there is insufficient evidence that there exists any particular teaching approach which is more appropriate for dyslexic children than for other poor readers (Stanovich 1991; Presland 1991). It appears likely that both groups benefit from a range of approaches which incorporate those traditionally associated with dyslexia – 'phonic, structured, sequential, cumulative and thorough' (Presland 1991: 218) – together with those which emphasise authentic tasks involving notions of contextualisation, communication, shared reading, relaxation, storytelling and parental support. This does not, of course, mean that one should no longer seek to provide an approach that is individually tailored to the needs of specific children, rather that one should not devise an intervention programme on the basis of a dyslexic/non-dyslexic categorisation.

There are many excellent texts which provide very practical guidance to teachers working with dyslexic children (see below for further details). In line with the arguments above, however, these would also appear to be valuable for any child experiencing reading difficulty.

TO WHAT EXTENT SHOULD THE DYSLEXIC LABEL RESULT IN THE CHILD RECEIVING ADDITIONAL SCHOOL/LEA RESOURCES AND/OR SPECIAL EXAMINATION ARRANGEMENTS WHICH WOULD NOT OTHERWISE BE MADE AVAILABLE?

Legislation and local educational authority provision

The 1996 Education Act and the 1994 Code of Practice on the Identification and Assessment of Special Educational Needs point out the requirement upon the school and the teacher to identify and assess children's special educational needs. Reflecting the views of many education professionals, rather than labelling children 'dyslexic', the Code prefers to speak of children with specific learning difficulties, whom it states:

> may have significant difficulties in reading, writing, spelling or manipulating numbers which are not typical of their general level of performance. They may gain some skills in some subjects quickly and demonstrate a high level of ability orally, yet may encounter sustained difficulty in gaining literacy or numeracy skills. Some children can become severely frustrated and may also have emotional and/or behavioural difficulties.
>
> (DfE 1994: 56)

In order to ascertain whether the child has 'specific learning difficulties', the Code states that assessors should examine whether:

• there are extreme discrepancies between performance (as measured by

levels of the National Curriculum) on maths, English and science or between the speaking and listening Attainment Target and those of reading and/or writing
- expectations of the child, based upon detailed observation and tests of intelligence and/or oral comprehension are significantly greater than performance on National Curriculum assessments and/or standardised tests of literacy or mathematics
- the child is clumsy, has difficulties in sequencing or in visual perception, has a memory deficiency or experiences a significant delay in language functioning
- there are severe signs of frustration, distress, and/or an inability to concentrate which appear to be associated with the child's learning difficulties; such difficulties may be manifested by withdrawn or disruptive behaviour

It is important to recognise that multi-agency assessment to establish whether there are grounds for the provision of extra resources from the local education authority (such as additional teacher or other adult helper time, computer hardware and software) should operate only if the child's difficulties match the criteria as set out within the Code of Practice. However, in the case of specific learning difficulties (SpLD) not only are the Code's criteria extremely wide-ranging, but it fails to indicate which criteria, singly or in combination, are necessary for an SpLD diagnosis. As local educational authorities are invited to make their own decisions on the criteria provided, there is little likelihood that consistent definitions will be adopted:

> The breadth and diversity of the criteria suggested, together with the lack of any clear conceptual coherence among them, make it difficult to think of adequate grounds on which LEAs could establish that a prima facie case for assessment did not exist.
>
> (Frederickson and Reason 1995: 197)

Frederickson and Reason suggest that despite all the research evidence to the contrary (noted above), there is a growing trend among educational psychologists to seek tight, measurable criteria, usually centring primarily on IQ–achievement discrepancies. Alternative discrepancy definitions which may be employed concern differences between reading and listening comprehension (Stanovich 1991) or between reading and other subjects of the curriculum (as suggested in the Code of Practice).

Bound up with these debates is the question of intervention and resourcing. Even if it proved possible to identify discrepancy variables which differentiated meaningfully between poor readers, what gains would follow? At present, discrepancy models make little impact upon intervention approaches; in reality, they are used to aid decision making about which children should receive additional support and other resources. Underlying this thinking is the issue of potential, that is, a belief that the child's underlying weaknesses inhibit the realisation of that which they could achieve.

Most commonly, we are presented with an image of an able child whose condition does not permit maximisation of his or her potential. Such children, it is often argued, would benefit more readily from the provision of additional resources (e.g. a word processor, part-time one-to-one adult support) than, say, a child whose poor reading stems from more global difficulties. At present, therefore, a child with reading difficulties and an IQ of 80 is far less likely to receive additional support than one with a similar reading profile but an IQ of 120. Such a situation hardly reflects growing research evidence that IQ has almost no value in predicting reading development in poor readers (Francis *et al.* 1996).

The case study of Aidan has indicated that it can be very valuable to recognise that reading difficulties may mask wider intellectual functioning. As a result of such a finding, teachers may address the content and mode of their educational delivery in order to ensure that the child is more appropriately challenged. Recognition of the need to assist the child in such a fashion, however, does not mean that his or her needs for additional resources are greater than those of less able poor readers. Indeed, it is arguable that ongoing adult support, guidance and regulation may be more necessary in the case of those with more global difficulties.

Special arrangements for public examinations

Another area of controversy surrounds special arrangements for public examinations taken by children with specific learning difficulties. Each year, the Joint Council for the GCSE outlines procedures for identifying those children who may require special examination arrangements. The 1997 criteria for specific learning difficulties are presented in Figure 11.1.

It is expected that those seeking special arrangements will set out full details about the nature and history of the child's difficulties (including an educational psychologist's report prepared within two years prior to the examination), how these disadvantage the candidate and an account of the arrangements which have been made by the school to assist the child.

The special arrangements permitted for GCSE examinations in 1998 most likely to be requested for children with specific learning difficulties (dyslexia) are listed below:

- an additional time allowance (up to 25 per cent)
- the reading aloud (or taping) of questions to candidates (where there is evidence of a significant discrepancy between reading ability and reasoning ability)
- access to a word processor where this is the candidate's usual method of communication (note: the use of spell checks is forbidden)
- the provision of a transcript of any section of the candidate's script which is difficult to decipher
- the use of an amanuensis

SPECIFIC LEARNING DIFFICULTIES
(INCLUDING NEUROLOGICAL DYSFUNCTION)

Identification of candidates for whom special arrangements may be requested.

Candidates are likely to have experienced difficulties in at least one of the areas given below.

Reading Accuracy   This would include candidates who are unlikely to be able to read the examination material with sufficient accuracy to avoid making mistakes which will affect the understanding of what they read.

Reading Speed   This will be a particular problem where the speed of reading is so slow that the candidate loses the sense of what he or she reads.

Spelling   This will include candidates with spelling difficulties which significantly slow their work rate and result in the use of alternative words which are easier to spell or who are unlikely to achieve any score in the marking of spelling.

Handwriting Speed   Candidates whose handwriting speed is so slow that it presents a particular problem should be trained to communicate the information required by questions as briefly as possible wherever this is appropriate. Where such a strategy is not sufficient, special arrangements may need to be sought.

Handwriting Legibility   This may relate to writing under time pressure and in such cases the previous section will apply. There are, however, candidates whose scripts are illegible despite their being allowed to write more slowly.

Other Difficulties   As well as the preceding areas of difficulty, some candidates have other specific problems, e.g. attention and concentration, clumsiness and disorganisation of such severity as to prevent a candidate from demonstrating attainment. Such difficulties as these and others are often found to be associated with neurological dysfunction.

Figure 11.1 SpLD criteria which may result in special examination arrangements for 1998
Source: Joint Forum for GCSE and GCE 1997: 29

Although it is noted in the Guidance that specific learning difficulties may be found in candidates throughout all of the GCSE grade range, special arrangements are not available for candidates defined as having moderate learning difficulties (usually identified by their significantly below-average intellectual functioning). In order to demonstrate specific learning difficulties, and thus benefit from those examination concessions noted above, it is usually expected that there should be a significant discrepancy between the candidate's cognitive (intelligence test) assessments and literacy skills. The use of a discrepancy criterion, of course, excludes large numbers of children for whom such arrangements might prove beneficial and, in practice, only a very small proportion of children with reading difficulties will receive such assistance. There is, however, no explicit guidance on exactly what levels of performance are appropriate and thus significant fluctuations exist. Sawyer *et al.* (1991), for example, found that psychologists' requests for additional time were based on candidates' reading accuracy age equivalencies ranging from seven to fourteen years regardless of the fact that the performance of many was of a standard which enabled them to read typical examination passages with little difficulty.

Such allowances, however, do not necessarily offer significant advantage to candidates. The use of additional time, for example, may prove counter-productive. In several cases it has been shown that rather than assisting the candidate to proof-read and edit their work (not always an attractive task for such individuals), the additional period has been inappropriately used to continue to write. This additional work may often prove to be inaccurate or betray a lack of understanding of the material which otherwise might have not been apparent (Hedderly 1996).

The reading aloud of questions is more likely to prove generally beneficial, as an inability to grasp exactly what is being asked is greatly disadvantageous to any candidate. Of course, such provision is likely to benefit all children with reading difficulties, not merely those who are eligible on the basis of their higher reasoning ability. It is arguable that any differences in ability or understanding of content would be demonstrated by the quality of the children's responses. In practice, however, to provide readers to all children who would profit from such a service would require time, personnel and organisation which would stretch the capacity of schools and examination boards. Thus, as with additional educational resourcing, those who are deemed to have most 'true ability' are provided with assistance less readily available to other poor readers.

OUTCOMES

Contrary to media accounts, a diagnosis of dyslexia and specialised intervention rarely results in immediate and rapid gains. Although improvements are to be anticipated, it is likely that difficulties, particularly those relating to phonological awareness, will persist into adulthood (Bruck 1990). Given this picture, it is hardly surprising that there is some (albeit limited) evidence that dyslexics tend to stop their education at an earlier age and have less success in employment (Spreen 1987). We are, however, familiar with accounts of many famous people such as Churchill and Leonardo da Vinci who, despite reading and spelling difficulties, achieved greatness. From such individuals, perhaps, we should recognise the fact that reading difficulties are not necessarily barriers to success. In addition to tackling reading difficulties directly, therefore, parents, teachers and others should ensure that assistance focuses upon the use of technological aids, the development of organisational strategies and, perhaps most importantly, the enhancement of the child's perceived competence and sense of self-esteem.

It is now possible to input text into computers using the spoken word rather than a keyboard and new programs offer the facility to provide input at a speed similar to that used in everyday communication. Such rapidly advancing technology, allied with the facility to scan text into word-processing packages and have this read aloud by a computerised voice, together with more traditional technological aids such as checks of spelling and grammar, will revolutionise the means by which many will handle the written word. One comprehensive package, 'Texthelp!', for example, provides a comprehensive range of facilities operating in several languages. These include, as one types, speech feedback at a number of levels, by letter, word, sentence or block of text. A speaking spellchecker and speaking thesaurus are supplemented by a word prediction facility which suggests suitable words. Automatic correction of frequently made phonetic spelling mistakes is particularly valuable for those who have difficulty with irregular words. All text, even that on Internet pages can be read aloud. To accommodate those with visual difficulties, text and background colours can be changed to suit individual preference. Such sophisticated programmes are still a long way from everyday use in schools, however, and reliance upon more traditional means of reading and recording is likely to continue for the foreseeable future.

CONCLUSIONS

It now seems likely that dyslexia is a specific condition with an underlying neurological basis and that advances in educational and medical research will eventually lead to meaningful discrimination between dyslexics and other poor readers. What is less clear is whether this will result in differential forms of intervention and treatment for dyslexics and non-dyslexics. As yet, a diagnosis of dyslexia, while often welcomed as a means of gaining resources or reducing the stigma attached to reading difficulty, offers little guidance to those whose task it is to provide appropriate learning experiences.

The literature is replete with a huge variety of intervention techniques, some which directly address specific visual- or language-based problems, some which are based upon techniques used for pre- and early readers, some which draw upon existing or new technologies to tackle or circumvent literacy difficulties, and others which merely reflect good practice in the teaching of reading (e.g. paired or shared reading). It seems likely that, despite the contradictions and inconsistencies of professional opinion (Bus 1989), decisions about the nature of intervention should continue to reflect children's individual needs rather than simple categorisation into one of two camps. Similarly, at the current time, there would appear to be insufficient moral or empirical grounds for allocating additional resources to those who are labelled dyslexic while leaving other poor readers – those, perhaps, deemed to have limited potential – to struggle unaided.

An alternative approach is to dispense with the search for differentiation on the basis of discrepancies between reading ability and other skills. Instead, reading impairment may simply be defined on the basis of low achievement. As Fletcher *et al.* (1994) point out, however, the likely numbers so designated could be substantial (up to 25 per cent of the population), and the financial implications of such a conceptualisation would be highly unattractive to policy makers and resource holders. It would seem, therefore, that resource considerations will ensure that poor readers will continue to be split into dyslexic/non-dyslexic groupings with differing access to resources and special consideration.

SOURCES OF FURTHER HELP

Local education authority support services

If there are concerns about a child's reading development, the local education authority's educational psychology service is often a valuable source of help in assessing the child's needs and in advising upon appropriate sources of support and assistance. Some LEAs also are staffed by support teachers with a particular expertise in reading difficulty.

Voluntary bodies

The British Dyslexia Association (BDA). 98 London Road, Reading, Berkshire RG1 5AU.

The Dyslexia Institute. 133 Gresham Road, Staines, Middlesex TW18 2AJ.

Literature

There are many useful texts which offer guidance on practical ways to support dyslexics and others with reading difficulties. Three good examples are:

J. Pollock and E. Waller (1994). *Day to Day Dyslexia in the Classroom* London: Routledge.

P. Ott (1997). *How to Detect and Manage Dyslexia* Oxford: Heinemann.

P. Heaton and P. Winterton (1996). *Dealing with Dyslexia*, 2nd edn. London: Whurr Publishers.

Public examinations

For further information about special arrangements for public examinations for children with special educational needs, contact:
Joint Forum for GCSE and GCE. Devas Street, Manchester M15 6EX.

REFERENCES

Adams, M.J. (1990). *Beginning to Read: Thinking and Learning about Print.* Cambridge, MA: MIT Press.

Adams, M.J. and Bruck, M. (1993). Word recognition: the interface of educational policies and scientific research. *Reading and Writing: An Interdisciplinary Journal* 5, 113–39.

Attwood, T. (1994). *Dyslexia in Schools: A Guide for Teachers.* Peterborough: First and Best Education Ltd.

Bishop, D.V. (1989). Unstable vergence control and dyslexia – a critique. *British Journal of Ophthalmology* 73, 223–45.

Brace, A. (1993). Experts hail cure for child dyslexia. *Mail on Sunday,* 27 June.

Bradley, L. and Bryant, P.E. (1983). Categorising sounds and learning to read: a causal connection. Nature, 301, 419–21.

Brady, S.A. (1991). The role of working memory in reading disability. In S.A. Brady and D. P. Shankweiler (eds) *Phonological Processes in Literacy: A Tribute to Isabelle Y. Liberman.* Hillsdale, NJ: Erlbaum.

Bruck, M. (1990). Word recognition skills of adults with childhood diagnoses of dyslexia. *Developmental Psychology* 26, 439–54.

Bus, A.G. (1989). How are recommendations concerning reading and spelling disabilities arrived at and why do experts disagree? *Psychology in the Schools* 26, 54–61.

Clay, M. (1985). *The Early Detection of Reading Difficulties.* Auckland: Heinemann.

Crisfield, J. (ed.) (1996). *The Dyslexia Handbook 1996.* Reading: British Dyslexia Association.

De Fries, J.C. (1991). Genetics and dyslexia: an overview. In M.J. Snowling and M. Thomson (eds) *Dyslexia: Integrating Theory and Practice.* London: Whurr Publishers.

Department for Education (1994). *Code of Practice on Identification and Assessment of Special Educational Needs.* London: HMSO.

Dudley-Marling, C. (1981). WISC and WISC(R) profiles of learning disabled children: a review. *Learning Disabilities Quarterly* 4, 307–19.

Edwards, J. (1994). *The Scars of Dyslexia.* London: Cassell.

Elliott, C.D., Murray, D.J. and Pearson, L. (1983). *British Ability Scales.* Windsor: N.F.E.R.-Nelson.

Ellis, A.W., McDougall, S.J. and Monk, A.F. (1996). Are dyslexics different? I. A comparison between dyslexics, reading age controls, poor readers and precocious readers. *Dyslexia* 2, 31–58.

Fernald, G. (1943). *Remedial Techniques in the Basic School Subjects.* New York: McGraw-Hill.

Fletcher, J.M., Shaywitz, S.E., Shankweiler, D., Katz, L., Liberman, I., Stuebing, K., Francis, D.J., Fowler, A. and Shaywitz, B.A. (1994). Cognitive profiles of reading disability: comparisons of discrepancy and low achievement definitions. *Journal of Educational Psychology* 86, 6–23.

Francis, D.J., Shaywitz, S.E., Stuebing, K., Shaywitz, B.A. and Fletcher, J.M. (1996). Developmental lag versus deficit models of reading disability: a longitudinal individual growth curves analysis. *Journal of Educational Psychology* 88, 3–17.

Frederickson, N. and Reason, R. (1995). Discrepancy definitions of specific learning difficulties. *Educational Psychology in Practice* 10(4), 195–205.

Hatcher, P., Hulme, C. and Ellis, A. W. (1994). Ameliorating early reading failure by integrating the teaching of reading and phonological skills: the phonological linkage hypothesis. *Child Development* 65(1), 41–57.

Heaton, P. and Winterton, P. (1996). *Dealing with Dyslexia.* (2nd edn). London: Whurr Publishers.

Hedderly, R. (1996). Assessing pupils with specific learning difficulties for examination special arrangements at GCSE, 'A' level and degree level. *Educational Psychology in Practice* 12(1), 36–44.

Hurry, J. (1996). What is so special about Reading Recovery? *The Curriculum Journal* 7(1), 93–108.

Irlen, H. (1983). Successful treatment of learning disabilities. Paper presented at the 91st Annual Convention of the American Psychological Association, Anaheim, CA.

Joint Forum for GCSE and GCE. (1997). *Candidates with Special Assessment Needs: Special Arrangements and Special Consideration, Regulations and Guidance.* Manchester: Joint Forum for GCSE and GCE.

Katz, R.B. and Shankweiler, D.P. (1985). Receptive naming and the detection of word retrieval deficits in the beginning reader. *Cortex* 21, 617–25.

Lundberg, I. (1994). Reading difficulties can be predicted and prevented: a Scandinavian perspective on phonological awareness and reading. In C. Hulme and M. Snowling (eds) *Reading Development and Dyslexia.* London: Whurr Publishers.

Lundberg, I., Frost, J. and Petersen, O.P. (1988). Effects of an extensive programme for stimulating phonological awareness in pre-school children. *Reading Research Quarterly* 33, 263–84.

Lyon, G.R. (1995). Towards a definition of dyslexia. *Annals of Dyslexia* 45, 3–27.

McNab, I. (1994). Specific learning difficulties: how severe is severe? *BAS Information Booklet.* Windsor: N.F.E.R.-Nelson.

Miles, T.R. and Miles, E. (1984). *Teaching Needs of Seven Year Old Dyslexic Pupils.* London: Department for Education and Science.

Miles, T.R. and Miles, E. (1990). *Dyslexia: A Hundred Years on.* Milton Keynes: Open University Press.

Nicolson, R.I. and Fawcett, A.J. (1995). Dyslexia is more than a phonological disability. *Dyslexia* 1, 19–36.

Orton, J.L. (1967). The Orton–Gillingham Approach. In J. Mooney (ed.) *The Disabled Reader.* Baltimore, MD: Johns Hopkins University Press.

Pavlidis, G. (1981). Do eye movements hold the key to dyslexia? *Neuropsychologia* 19, 57–64.

Pennington, B.F. (1995). Genetics of learning disabilities. *Journal of Child Neurology* 10, 69–77.

Presland, J. (1991). Explaining away dyslexia. *Educational Psychology in Practice* 6(4), 215–21.

Pumfrey, P. (1991). *Improving Children's Reading in the Junior School: Challenges and Responses.* London: Cassell.

Pumfrey, P. (1996). *Specific Developmental Dyslexia: Basics to Back?* Leicester: British Psychological Society.

Pumfrey, P. and Reason, R. (1991). *Specific Learning Difficulties (Dyslexia): Challenges and Responses.* London: Routledge.

Rayner, K. (1983). Eye movements, perceptual span and reading disability. *Annals of Dyslexia* 33, 163–73.

Rayner, K. (1993). Visual processes in reading: directions for research and theory. In D.M. Willows, R. Kruk and E. Corcos (eds) *Visual Processes in Reading and Reading Disabilities.* Hillsdale, NJ: Lawrence Erlbaum Associates.

Reason, R.E. (1990). Reconciling different approaches to intervention. In P. Pumfrey and C. Elliott (eds), *Children's Difficulties in Reading, Spelling and Writing.* London: Falmer.

Reeves, B. (1988). Reading through rose tinted spectacles. *Optician*, 29 January, 21–6.

Rutter, M. (1978). Prevalence and types of dyslexia. In A.L. Benton and D. Pearl (eds) *Dyslexia: An Appraisal of Current Knowledge.* New York: Oxford University Press.

Sawyer, C., Ferguson, L., Hayward, M. and Cunningham, L. (1991). On reading and the GCSE. *The Psychologist*, 4(5), 221–2.

Shute, R. (1991). Treating dyslexia with tinted lenses: a review of the evidence. *Research in Education* 46, 39–48.

Solity, J. (1996). Phonological awareness: learning disabilities revisited? *Educational and Child Psychology* 13(3), 103–13.

Spreen, O. (1987). *Learning Disabled Children Growing up: A Follow-up into Adulthood.* Lisse, Netherlands: Swets and Zeitlinger.

Stanovich, K.E. (1991). Discrepancy definitions of reading disability: has intelligence led us astray? *Reading Research Quarterly* 26, 7–29.

Stanovich, K.E. and Stanovich, P.J. (1997). Further thoughts on aptitude/achievement discrepancy. *Educational Psychology in Practice* 13(1), 3–8.

Stein, J.F. (1993). Visuospatial perception in disabled readers. In D.M. Willows, R. Kruk and E. Corcos (eds) *Visual Processes in Reading and Reading Disabilities.* Hillsdale, NJ: Lawrence Erlbaum Associates.

Stein, J.F. and Fowler, S. (1982). Ocular motor dyslexia. *Dyslexia Review* 5, 25–8.

Wechsler, D. (1992). *Wechsler Intelligence Scale for Children–Third Edition, UK* London: Psychological Corporation.

Whittaker, M. (1996). Phonological assessment of specific learning difficulties: a critique of the Phonological Assessment Battery. *Educational Psychology in Practice* 12(2), 67–73.

Wilsher, C.R. (1990). Treatments for dyslexia: proven or unproven? In G. Hales, M. Hales, T. Miles and A. Summerfield (eds) *Meeting Points in Dyslexia: Proceedings of the First International Conference of the British Dyslexia Association.* Reading: British Dyslexia Association.

Glossary

Affect is defined by the Oxford English Dictionary as a feeling or emotion, and so an affective disorder is an illness which results in disturbances to feelings and emotions. This can take two forms: the flattened and inert feelings of depression; or mania.

Agoraphobia is an abnormal fear of open and/or public spaces.

Anhedonia means that the young person has lost all enjoyment in life and now portrays a picture of gloom and despondency.

Antigens are substances which the human body sees as harmful and produces antibodies to neutralise their effect.

Beta blockers are drugs which block certain nerve receptors in the nervous system. This blocking prevents these nerves from working.

Bipolar illness is diagnosed in anyone who has had a manic episode which alternates with depressive disorder. It is not necessary for one illness to follow the other, though they sometimes do; the fact that both illnesses have occurred is sufficient to describe the problem as bipolar.

Conduct disorder is a specific diagnostic category which is used to describe the pattern of behaviour where there is repetitive and persistent misbehaviour (such as fighting, bullying, destroying property, and stealing) which is far more than would be expected for a child of that age.

Flashbacks are the re-experiencing of feelings, images or even physical sensations which are associated with a traumatic event of some kind, and cause distress when they are re-experienced.

Hallucinations are false perceptions and may involve any of the senses. The most well known is a hallucination involving hearing in which people believe they are hearing voices which are talking to them. This is often a feature of schizophrenic illness.

Hepatitis is an inflammation of the liver caused by infection, or the build up of toxic substances. If persistent it can lead to permanent failure of parts, or all, of the liver.

Hyperactivity is a label denoting that a child shows significant overactivity and an increased tempo of physical activity. The term is sometimes applied (wrongly) to describe all types of attention problem, though in fact this forms one element of one type of attention deficit disorder.

Intermittent reinforcement describes a schedule where reinforcement does not always follow the target behaviour. Intermittent reinforcement is more likely than continuous reinforcement to result in persistent behaviour which is resistant to extinction.

Kleinian therapy is a style of individual therapy that is often seen as particularly appropriate for children. It is based on a view that the beginnings of the super-ego can be identified within the first two years of life, and that any analysis should focus upon the infantile stages of development when anxiety and aggressive impulses are thought to have their origin. The other major element is the assumption that the most important drives that a person experiences are the aggressive ones.

Mania is an illness where the patient superficially appears very happy and energetic, with a greatly elated mood. They usually have very grandiose plans and ideas, but leap from subject to subject in a rapid fashion. The mood is quite unstable with aggression and violent outbursts often flaring up. This is classified as a psychotic illness

MAOIs, the monoamine oxidase inhibitors, form a class of drug most commonly used to treat depressive illness. They interfere with the destruction of the monoamines in the brain. These drugs do have to be used with great care because they react with many other drugs, such as cough mixtures, and certain foods, such as cheese and yeast extract products.

Neurosis is a mild form of psychiatric illness involving symptoms of anxiety and stress. Unlike the psychoses, there is no loss of external reality.

Oligoantigenic is a term which is used to describe something that is least likely to provoke an adverse reaction from the body's self-defence mechanisms because it contains no antigens.

Phobia is an intense, abnormal fear of a relatively harmless object or situation.

Phonological awareness concerns the ability to recognise different sounds in spoken language.

Psychosis is a severe mental illness, the hallmark of which is a loss of contact with external reality. It can be caused by medical problems such as infections or toxicity due to drugs but mostly is caused by major psychiatric illness. Usually these patients have hallucinations and delusions, the nature of which helps to distinguish the type of disorder. Problems to do with thinking and thought processes are usually seen in schizophrenia, whereas themes that are dominated by feelings and moods are seen in the affective disorders.

Secondary sexual characteristics are those sex-specific features of development which appear at puberty. These include the development of pubic hair, the deepening of the voice, and in boys the beginning of beard growth.

Short-term memory refers to that aspect of memory where a small number of chunks of information are held for a limited period of time (e.g. 'holding on' to a telephone number while searching for a pencil).

Unipolar illness is when the person only seems to suffer from a depressive element, and there is no suggestion that manic symptoms may surface later.

Index

222   *Index*